THE OXFORD HANDBOOK O
OF POLITICAL PHILOSOPHY

The Oxford Handbook of the History of Political Philosophy presents fifty original essays, each specially written by a leading figure in the field, spanning the entire subject of the history of political philosophy. They provide not only surveys of the state of research but substantial pieces that engage with, and move forward, current debates.

Part I addresses questions of method. Contributors discuss the contextual method, classically articulated by Quentin Skinner, along with important alternative methods associated with Leo Strauss and his followers, and contemporary post-modernism. This section also examines the value of the history of political philosophy and the history of the discipline itself.

Part II, Chronological Periods, works through the entire history of Western political philosophy. While most contributions address recognizable chronological periods, others are devoted to more specialized topics, including the influence of Roman Law, medieval Arabic political philosophy, Socialism, and Marxism.

Aspects of the history of political philosophy that transcend specific periods are the subject of Part III. Essays on topics such as democracy, the state, and imperialism trace theoretical developments over time.

The histories of major non-Western traditions — Muslim, Confucian, and Hindu — are discussed in the final Part, with special reference to their relationships to Western political thought.

THE OXFORD HANDBOOK OF

THE HISTORY OF POLITICAL PHILOSOPHY

Edited by

GEORGE KLOSKO

OXFORD

UNIVERSITY PRESS

OXFORD
UNIVERSITY PRESS

Great Clarendon Street, Oxford, OX2 6DP,
United Kingdom

Oxford University Press is a department of the University of Oxford.
It furthers the University's objective of excellence in research, scholarship,
and education by publishing worldwide. Oxford is a registered trade mark of
Oxford University Press in the UK and in certain other countries

Published in the United States of America by Oxford University Press
198 Madison Avenue, New York, NY 10016, United States of America

British Library Cataloguing in Publication Data
Data available

ISBN 978–0–19–967953–9

To the memory of
my mother, Minnette Klosko, and my father, Emanuel Klosko

CONTENTS

PART III THEMES

PART IV NON-WESTERN PERSPECTIVES

ACKNOWLEDGEMENTS

I am grateful to the distinguished authors of the essays presented here. Several contributions were made on relatively short notice, and others in spite of severe health problems. Several authors offered valuable suggestions concerning other possible contributions to this volume, including my own, and concerning possible authors. I wish to single out Stephen White and Terry Ball, who were especially helpful. I am grateful to Peter Momtchiloff, Philosophy Editor at Oxford University Press, for consistent guidance and ever helpful advice during the entire period in which this volume was conceived and brought to completion. The outside advisors for Oxford University Press made valuable suggestions, amongst them the need to include contributions on non-Western approaches. I am grateful to Sarah Parker and Catherine Berry for maintaining the volume's website, to Daniel Bourner and Ms. Parker for seeing the volume through the press, and to Hilary Walford for indefatigable copy editing. I am sad to report the death of one contributor, Perez Zagorin, who was not only an eminent historian but also a dear friend. His splendid essay on the development of religious toleration is the last thing he wrote. As ever, I am grateful to my wife, Meg, and daughters, Caroline, Susanna, and Deborah, for moral support.

List of Contributors

Shahrough Akhavi, Adjunct Professor of Political Science at Columbia University in New York.

Danielle Allen, Institute for Advanced Study, Princeton

Terence Ball, School of Government, Politics, and Global Studies, Arizona State University

Michael Baylor, Department of History, Lehigh University

Jonathan Beecher, Department of History, University of California, Santa Cruz

Richard Bellamy, Department of Political Science, University College London

Mark Bevir, Department of Political Science, University of California, Berkeley

Bernard R. Boxill, Department of Philosophy, University of North Carolina, Chapel Hill

Charles E. Butterworth, Department of Government and Political Science, University of Maryland

Terrell Carver, Department of Politics, University of Bristol

Janet Coleman, Department of Government, London School of Economics and Political Science

Jeffrey Collins, Department of History, Queen's University, Ontario

Richard Dagger, Department of Political Science, University of Richmond

Dennis Dalton, Department of Political Science, Barnard University

Daniel Devereux, Department of Philosophy, University of Virginia

Joshua Foa Dienstag, Department of Political Science, University of California, Los Angeles

Julian Franklin, Department of Political Science, Columbia University

Mark Goldie, Faculty of History, Cambridge University

John Gunnell, Department of Political Science, State University of New York, Albany, and Department of Political Science, University of California, Davis

Nancy J. Hirschmann, Political Science Department, University of Pennsylvania

Mikael Hörnqvist, Department of the History of Science and Ideas, Uppsala University

Jeremy Jennings, Department of Politics, Queen Mary University of London

Donald Kelley, Department of History, Rutgers University

George Klosko, Department of Politics, University of Virginia

Krishan Kumar, Department of Sociology, University of Virginia

Peter Lassman, Political Science and International Studies, University of Birmingham

Sophie Lunn-Rockliffe, Classics Department, King's College London

Neil McArthur, Department of Philosophy, University of Manitoba

Eric Mack, Murphy Institute, Tulane University

Phillip Mitsis, Department of Classics, New York University

Donald Moon, Department of Government, Wesleyan University

Christopher W. Morris, Department of Philosophy, University of Maryland

Terry Nardin, Department of Political Science, National University of Singapore

Anthony Pagden, Department of History, University of California, Los Angeles

Kenneth Pennington, Columbus School of Law and School of Canon Law, Catholic University of America

Daniel Philpott, Kroc Institute for International Peace Studies, University of Notre Dame

Raymond Plant, Law School, King's College London

Paul Redding, School of Philosophical and Historical Studies, University of Sydney

David Schmidtz, Arizona Center for Philosophy of Freedom, University of Arizona

Marshall Shatz, Davis Center for Russian and Eurasian Studies, Harvard University

Johann Sommerville, Department of History, University of Wisconsin, Madison

Mark E. Warren, Department of Political Science, University of British Columbia

David Weinstein, Department of Political Science, Wake Forest University

Richard Whatmore, Department of History, University of Sussex

Stephen K. White, Department of Politics, University of Virginia

Jonathan Wolff, Department of Philosophy, University College London

David Wong, Department of Philosophy, Duke University

Perez Zagorin, who died in 2009, was Joseph C. Wilson Professor of History at the University of Rochester

Catherine Zuckert, Department of Political Science, University of Notre Dame

INTRODUCTION

STUDY of the history of political philosophy has a long history. Along with political texts that date back to the ancient Greeks—and similarly far back in some non-Western cultures—came historical work in the field. An important extant example is Book II of the *Politics*, in which Aristotle examines some of his predecessors' views on ideal societies. Most notable, of course, is Plato, who is subjected to a harsh and largely inaccurate critique of aspects of the *Republic* and *Laws*. But, while Aristotle's account is generally recognized as bad history, it is still valuable as political philosophy. For instance, although Aristotle's attack on community of property in the *Republic* falls wide of the mark as criticism of Plato's actual proposals, Aristotle's main lines of argument have been recognized ever since as important criticisms of socialism.[1]

As this example illustrates—as is also evident in the field's name—the history of political philosophy spans two different disciplines, history and philosophy. In working in the area, it is essential to keep the two separate. As a branch of history, the field focuses on the great texts as historical objects. Although exactly what this entails is not without controversy—as is seen throughout Part I of this volume—there is now widespread agreement about how the historical meaning of texts is determined. Especially amongst philosophers, it is generally agreed that, in examining texts of past theorists, one should attempt to identify the actions they took, what they were *doing*, when they wrote them.[2] Although, once again, this approach is not without controversy, at root it encapsulates what many historians regard as common sense, and what they have always done. To determine what authors were doing, we should focus on the specific questions or problems they addressed, particular audiences they had in mind, results they wished to achieve, and similar concerns, although our ability to reconstruct the intentions of long dead authors will vary along with the clarity of

---

[1] For discussion, see Klosko (1993: ch. 4) and Stalley (1991).

[2] This is view associated especially with Quentin Skinner. See the list of Skinner's articles in the bibliography of Skinner (1978). Useful collections are Skinner (2002); as well as Tully (1989); see also the discussions by Bevir and Ball, Chapters 1 and 4, this volume.

particular intentions, the availability of evidence, and other factors. By this standard, Aristotle's account of Plato's communism—as with many of his other forays into the history of philosophy—comes up short.

But the history of political philosophy has other aims as well. In addition to being a historical figure, Aristotle was, of course, a great political philosopher. In his works, he called attention to specific aspects of the human condition and drew out their implications. In large part, it is the quality and depth of his insights that account for his works' classic status. Mill calls the great thinkers "one-eyed men" (Mill 2006 [1838]: 94). Although the views they developed capture only parts of reality, by focusing relentlessly on their chief concerns, they worked out timeless depictions of political life. To switch to another example, although the questions of political authority that Locke addressed differ significantly from our own, by studying the strengths and weaknesses of his approach, we prepare ourselves to address the related problems that directly concern us. More than this, because the works of the great theorists represent different approaches to questions of political association, their works provide an essential language, a set of references that can be employed by people working on related questions. Although Hobbes died more than three hundred years ago and the problems of authority he addressed differ in many respects from our own, all political philosophers understand what we basically mean by a "Hobbesian" approach, and should also recognize the value of developing such an approach with reference to specific contemporary concerns. For example, in the international arena, problems of nuclear proliferation and global warming are resistant to the blandishments of the UN—as, last century, the threat of war was not deflected by the League of Nations. Would an international body with Hobbesian authority be better able to deal with them? What are the advantages and disadvantages of such an arrangement?

In making this case, I am not saying anything new. Philosophers have long recognized that studying the history of philosophy is essential preparation in their field. In all or virtually all areas of philosophy, one comes to understand the ins and outs of a question by looking at how great figures in the past addressed related questions. For example, although the epistemological works of Descartes, Locke, Hume, and Kant do not address precisely the same questions, their concerns are sufficiently similar to one another and to contemporary epistemological questions to make studying their works not only relevant to but indispensable for sophisticated work on contemporary problems.

In addressing such issues, theorists do not rely on the authority of the historical Hume or Kant. To the extent they wish to develop positions similar to those of their great predecessors, they themselves take responsibility for defending the positions and the assumptions on which they rely. Because political philosophy is a part of philosophy, its history is relevant in much the same way. Because it is firmly rooted in two different fields, the history of philosophy, including the history of political philosophy, encounters special difficulties. Especially noteworthy, I believe, is failure to keep its two dimensions separate. Exactly how concerns of the two fields should relate to one another is a matter of considerable dispute. But, to my mind, a common problem is considering texts *too* philosophically. Scholars frequently distort a text's historical meaning—that is, the meaning intended by its author—by reading into it their own concerns, uncovering themes and arguments the author himself did not consider, or perhaps could not have conceived of. One measure of the greatness of any historical text is its relevance—that is, the extent to which it has interesting things to say about issues in other times and places, especially our own. And so, consciously or unconsciously, scholars are tempted to make texts appear more immediately relevant than they actually are—thereby, perhaps not incidentally, inflating the importance of their own research. It could almost be said that there is an institutional bias in favor of misinterpretation. A brief look at the literature on virtually any major figure in the history of political philosophy will confirm this tendency. Then again, philosophers may respond that, without significant application to contemporary issues, the history of political philosophy—as with the history of philosophy more generally—becomes pure antiquarianism—that is, studying historical artifacts simply for the sake of learning about them. But, as just noted, this criticism is wide of the mark. In studying great works of the past, we prepare ourselves to address issues that are of contemporary concern. In using the former to address the latter, it is imperative to recognize differences between an author's actual theory, expressed in his historical context, and a position *like* that one, based on assumptions similar to his or her own, but more useful for our present-day philosophical purposes. In other words, we should clearly distinguish between Locke's own theory and a "Lockean" theory. Although the latter is distinct from what Locke *said* and should not be passed off as a historically accurate account of his intentions, it may have significant philosophical value, along the lines discussed above.[3] However, once again, the history that is applied to contemporary problems should be accurate history, based on careful interpretation of the author's own meaning, as opposed to anachronistically reading into texts contemporary concerns. Although Hume may have addressed issues similar to those that interest contemporary philosophers, we should be careful not to distort his actual meanings in directly applying his views to problems of the present day.

Although this volume is a handbook of the history of political philosophy, dividing lines between that field and the closely related history of political theory and of political thought are not hard and fast. This volume is not confined to the history of political philosophy in a narrow sense. Many contributors are members of Politics or History departments and would probably identify themselves as political theorists or intellectual historians, rather than philosophers or historians of philosophy. To a large extent, these different fields overlap, and terms that designate them are often used interchangeably. But the terms also have "focal meanings." Political philosophy, strictly speaking, should be distinguished from political theory, and still more from political thought—although scholars will differ about criteria and precisely where to draw the lines.

---

[3] A work that clearly distinguishes between Locke's own theory and a Lockean theory is Simmons (1994).

Concerns of history and philosophy are related somewhat differently in each of the three fields. In the history of political theory and of political thought, the balance shifts in the direction of history. To my mind what distinguishes the three fields are levels of abstraction. Consider a basic political communication, such as an opinion piece or a letter to the editor of a newspaper. Such a composition probably expresses the author's views, in a form that is also largely devoid of overt philosophical content. In such a case, the author's intentions—what he or she was *doing* in writing the piece—are likely to be straightforward and so easy to make out. They may well be so clear that we do not consciously have to think about them. However, we could of course ask ourselves what questions the author was addressing, about their audience, about what they wished to accomplish, and so carefully bring their intentions to light.

Opinion pieces and letters to the editor are prototypical instances of political thought, at a fairly concrete and issue-specific level. As we move along a continuum of levels of abstraction, we eventually cross the dividing line between political thought and political theory, as the author's statements become more systematically worked out, drawing connections between multiple issues, perhaps supporting his or her political assertions with more abstract moral, religious, or psychological claims. If we accept this account, then many of the great works studied by political philosophers should actually be identified as political theory. Where we draw the line in regard to political philosophy is more difficult to say. To my mind, the key point concerns relationships between political views and other aspects of the author's philosophy, generally philosophical views that are more abstract and farther removed from politics—for example, metaphysical and epistemological views. Thus a work such as Hegel's *Philosophy of Right* would fit here, especially because Hegel viewed it as part of an overall philosophical system. One reason the work is so notoriously difficult is that it draws on methods of reasoning Hegel developed for other subjects of inquiry, which he assumes in *Philosophy of Right* and does not clearly explain (Hegel 1991 [1821]: 10). Although Hegel had definite political views that *Philosophy of Right* defends (as discussed in the essay by Paul Redding, Chapter 21, this volume), it is clearly less of a direct political intervention than Locke's *Second Treatise* and far less than a still more overt political tract, such as the *Vindiciae Contra Tyrannos* or another sixteenth-century resistance tract, George Buchanan's *The Powers of the Crown in Scotland*. While it seems odd to refer to *Philosophy of Right* as political thought, it is probably still odder to refer to the *Vindiciae Contra Tyrannos* or Buchanan's work as political philosophy. But, even in regard to works that differ relatively clearly from others, dividing lines in this entire area depend on considerations of degree and necessarily involve subjective judgments.

Because works in the history of political thought and of political theory have greater overt political content, specific features of their contexts aid in identifying their meaning. Because political texts were frequently intended to contribute to contentious political issues, their authors were often not alone in articulating their positions (see Skinner 1978: preface). Their contentions were frequently similar to those of other participants in contested political debates. Familiar examples of such positions are encountered in election campaigns, as is particularly evident in the "talking points" candidates and party operatives endlessly repeat. While this degree of echo may be exceptional, in many cases studying the contexts in which great political texts were written reveals multiple lines of argument common to partisans on different sides of the day's issues. These commonalities include overall patterns of argument, such as appeal to Chapter 13 of St Paul's *Epistle to the Romans* to support royal absolutism. In part, this reads: "Let every person be subject to the governing authorities. For there is no authority except from God, and those that exist have been instituted by God. Therefore, he who resists the authorities resists what God has appointed, and those who resist will incur judgment" (Oxford trans.).

In contrast, versions of social contract theory and appeals to the consent of the governed were commonly invoked in order to limit governmental authority. But more particular, developed lines of argument were also used, as can be seen in clear resemblances between Locke's arguments for resistance and those employed in other resistance tracts (Skinner 1978: ii. 239–40). Close commonalities between a proposed interpretation of a given text and arguments of other thinkers during that period may provide important support for a particular interpretation. Such resemblances are most likely to be effects of political conflicts and so are more common in the history of political thought than in political philosophy. It is presumably because Skinner places the great texts he studies in contexts of closely related expressions by other authors—and so tends to emphasize overt political content over abstract philosophical qualities—that he called his pioneering work *Foundations of Modern Political Thought*, rather than *Foundations of Modern Political Philosophy*. Although, once again, the essays in this volume generally range between the history of political philosophy and of political theory, there is relatively little attention to the history of political thought more narrowly construed, which provides relatively little philosophical reflection on political circumstances and events.

The history of political philosophy is a large field, with a long tradition of distinguished scholarship. Because it is not possible to encompass the entire subject within a single volume, this collection concentrates on four major areas, although not without some overlap between them. In addition to coverage of great theorists in their historical contexts, this *Handbook* addresses questions about how the subject matter should best be studied, along with important themes not identified with individual theorists, which transcend specific historical periods. Also, given increased attention to non-Western political theory in recent years, three major alternative traditions are discussed, especially in regard to their relationship to the history of Western political philosophy. Accordingly, the volume is comprised of four—unequal—parts.

Part I, "Approaches," covers questions of method. This section includes discussion of the contextual method, classically articulated by Quentin Skinner, which is widely regarded as the standard method for studying the history of ideas, including the history of political philosophy. Currently, the chief alternative methods are those associated with Leo Strauss and his followers and a less clearly defined postmodern approach.

These are examined, sympathetically, by scholars who subscribe to them. This section also inquires into the value of the history of political philosophy, as viewed by scholars working in numerous other fields, and includes an overview of the history of the discipline itself.

Part II, "Chronological Periods," provides an overview of the entire history of Western political philosophy. This part is comprised of twenty-three contributions. The authors of these pieces take a variety of approaches. Some provide discursive overviews of their periods, of course concentrating on what they view as most significant. Other essays are more focused, examining relatively narrow themes or aspects of the relevant periods. While most of these essays address recognizable chronological periods, as the title of the Part indicates, others are devoted to more thematic topics, including the influence of Roman law or medieval Arabic political philosophy, socialism, and Marxism.

Accordingly, dividing lines between Parts II and III are occasionally rough. Part III, "Themes," addresses aspects of the history of political philosophy that transcend specific periods and generally change and develop in interesting ways between periods. Discussion of these themes are frequently bound up with the contributions of individual great thinkers and so shed additional interesting light on material discussed in Part II. But these essays are concerned mainly with thematic material, as opposed to the thinkers themselves. Although the development of ideas discussed in this part is inextricably bound up with developments in political forms and institutions, this *Handbook* addresses the history of political philosophy, not the history of politics. Thus entries such as those on "democracy," "the state," and "imperialism" trace theoretical developments over time. Though these are, of course, heavily influenced by changes in democracy, the form of the state, and the politics of imperialism themselves, discussion focuses on theoretical dimensions of the relevant themes.

Part IV addresses three major non-Western traditions: Confucian, Muslim, and Hindu. In this section, scholars focus on different themes, including reflections on Western political philosophy from these other perspectives, contrast between Western and non-Western ideas, and the evolution of these different traditions of political philosophy.

References

HEGEL, G. W. F. (1991 [1821]). *Elements of the Philosophy of Right*, (ed.) A. W. Wood, trans. B. Nisbet. Cambridge: Cambridge University Press.

KLOSKO, G. (1993). *History of Political Theory: An Introduction*, vol. i: *Ancient and Medieval Political Theory*. Fort Worth, Texas: Harcourt Brace Jovanovich.

MILL, J. S. (2006 [1838]). "Bentham," in J. M. Robson (ed.), *The Collected Works of John Stuart Mill*, vol. x: *Essays on Ethics, Religion, and Society*. Indianapolis: Liberty Fund, 77–115.

SIMMONS, A. J. (1994). *The Lockean Theory of Rights*. Princeton: Princeton University Press.

SKINNER, Q. (1978). *The Foundations of Modern Political Thought*, 2 vols. Cambridge: Cambridge University Press.

SKINNER, Q. (2002). *Visions of Politics*, vol. 1: *Regarding Method*. Cambridge: Cambridge University Press).

STALLEY, R. F. (1991). "Aristotle's Criticism of Plato's Republic," in D. Keyt and F. D. Miller (eds), *A Companion to Aristotle's Politics*. Oxford: Blackwell, 182–99.

TULLY, J. (1989) (ed.). *Meaning and Context*. Princeton: Princeton University Press.

PART I

APPROACHES

CHAPTER 1

··

THE CONTEXTUAL
APPROACH

··

MARK BEVIR

THE contextual approach locates authors in their historical milieu. Contextualists argue that we typically get a better grasp of a text if we relate it to the influences and concerns of its author. This argument may intuitively appeal to intellectual historians, but it is notably more controversial when directed against less historical approaches to texts. Historical approaches to texts often stand in contrast to those literary and philosophical ones that treat texts respectively as idealized aesthetic objects and contributions to timeless debates.

There are several contextual, historical approaches to texts. They include much hermeneutics, reception theory, and the new historicism. Yet, in the history of political philosophy, the contextual approach is associated narrowly with J. G. A. Pocock, Quentin Skinner, and the Cambridge School they are often said to have inspired. In this chapter I will examine the rise of this contextualism, the theoretical arguments used to justify it, and its current standing and future prospects. I pursue several arguments. First, the label "Cambridge School" is highly misleading: Pocock and Skinner differ significantly from one another, while many of the other historians involved are suspicious of all theoretical statements and methodological precepts. Second, contextualism arose as a historical practice indebted to modernist empiricist modes of inquiry: contextualist theories arose only later, as Pocock and Skinner grabbed at philosophical vocabularies to defend that practice. Third, recent developments in contextualism involve a retreat from these vocabularies: in the absence of renewed theoretical debate, contextualism may lapse into naive empiricism or bland eclecticism.

MODERNISM AND METHOD

··

We will better understand contextualism if we locate it in the context of Whiggish and modernist traditions in Cambridge. Skinner has written that his early work "owed an obvious debt to the theoretical writings of Pocock and Dunn, and a still deeper debt to the approach embodied in Laslett's scholarship on the history of political thought" (Skinner 1988d: 233). Today Peter Laslett is the forgotten man of contextualism. Yet Pocock, as well as Skinner, has described his work as the inspiration for contextualism (Pocock 2006). After the Second World War, Laslett returned to Cambridge, where he had earlier got a double first in history, to take up a research fellowship at St John's College. He then edited a collection of Sir Robert Filmer's writings, took up a permanent fellowship at Trinity College, and began working on John Locke. Having discovered Locke's library, he used it to edit a critical edition of the *Two Treatises* (Laslett 1960).

In some respects Laslett's work fitted well in Cambridge traditions of political theory. At Cambridge, politics was studied as part of the History Tripos. Cambridge Fellows and students typically studied political theory with a more historical and less philosophical focus than their Oxford counterparts. In other respects, however, Laslett looks more novel even in a Cambridge setting. His approach overlaps with modernist empiricist modes of knowledge.[1] To be more precise, his work moves away from broad narratives of the development of ideas and institutions, and toward the systematic and rigorous use of bibliographies, unpublished manuscripts, and other evidence in order to establish particular facts and thus textual interpretations. In the nineteenth century, historians and political scientists typically wrote grand narratives about the triumph of the principles of nation, character, and liberty. By the middle of the twentieth century, many historians were writing detailed and even statistical accounts of industry, wages, political interests, and fluctuating birth and death rates. Modernist historians at Cambridge and elsewhere—historians such as Herbert Butterfield, Geoffrey Elton, Lewis Namier, and A. J. P. Taylor—believed that the rigorous application of empirical methods to historical and especially archival sources would generate secure facts on which to build an objective account of the past. They wanted to transform history from a Victorian romance into a professional discipline.

Laslett brought this modernist empiricism to the history of political thought. It is no accident that, soon after publishing his edition of the *Two Treatises*, he turned to more statistical studies of historical demography, eventually becoming co-founder and director of the Cambridge Group for the History of Population and Social Structure. Even more importantly, it is no accident that, while working on Locke, he began to edit a series of books, entitled *Philosophy, Politics, and Society*, which he introduced with a modernist manifesto (Laslett 1956). Here Laslett famously pronounced the death of

---

[1] I first introduced the concept of modernist empiricism in Bevir (2001). Elsewhere I use it to refer not only to an atomistic approach to facts and inquiry, but perhaps more significantly to the rise of formal and ahistorical modes of explanation. Clearly modernist historians were less likely than social scientists to reject historical explanations. Thus, modernist empiricism in the study of history appears primarily as the attempt to use empirical evidence to establish secure, atomized facts that then could conclusively determine the validity of broader historical theories and interpretations. For more recent studies of modernism in political science and British history, see respectively Adcock, Bevir and Stimson (2007) and Bentley (2005).

philosophical studies of ethical and political principles. He aligned himself with a lingering logical positivism that equated knowledge with empirical science and that limited philosophy to the rigorous analysis of language use as exemplified by the work of Gilbert Ryle and, in political philosophy, T. D. Weldon. For Laslett, this logical positivism implied that we should answer questions about politics less by philosophy than by empirical social science and a new history of ideas.[2] The new history of ideas would reflect logical positivism's transformation of the identity and role of philosophers. Philosophers appeared here less as people searching for a comprehensive metaphysics and more as people expressing normative views in much the same way as might other citizens and politicians.

In his edition of the *Two Treatises*, Laslett provided a triumphant example of such a history. Laslett approached the *Two Treatises* not as moral philosophy but using the sources and techniques of modernist historians. He drew heavily on archival and primary documents—Locke's library, lists of the books he owned, hand-corrected prints of the *Two Treatises*, his diary, and his personal correspondence. These sources provided facts on which to base historical reconstructions. For example, knowledge of the dates when Locke acquired and read books supported the claim that Locke wrote passages referring to those books only after those dates. Laslett thereby revolutionized our view of Locke. He showed that Locke had written most of the Second Treatise in 1679–80. Thus, he concluded, the *Two Treatises* could not possibly have been written as a defense of the Glorious Revolution; rather, it was "an Exclusion Tract" calling for a revolution (Laslett 1960: 61).

While Laslett brought modernist empiricism to the history of political thought, many Cambridge historians remained more committed to elder approaches to the subject. The nineteenth century was the great age of Whig history. Whig historians believed in the manly, decent, and practical character of the English. They thought that the unwritten constitution and the common law guaranteed practical liberties. They suggested that God (often a clearly Anglican God) was the scarcely hidden force behind Church, State, and history itself. Most importantly for us, they distrusted abstract statements of historical method, theological doctrine, or political principle. Even if the era after the First World War witnessed a broad shift from Whiggism to modernist empiricism, many historians retained a loose adherence to Whig themes. As an undergraduate, Skinner studied not only with Laslett but also with John Burrow and Duncan Forbes. Forbes, the elder of the two, taught a special subject on the Scottish Enlightenment that was a kind of capstone undergraduate experience for Skinner, John Dunn, and many other intellectual historians trained at Cambridge. Burrow and Forbes dismissed abstract methodological

---

[2] Laslett's claim that "political philosophy is dead" became notorious (Laslett 1956: p. vii). Less well known is his use of this claim to open the way to new, modernist ways of approaching political questions: "The intellectual light of the mid-twentieth century is clear, cold and hard. If it requires those who undertake to answer questions about politics to do so without being entitled to call themselves political philosophers, we must answer them nonetheless" (Laslett 1956: p. xiv). Modernist forms of social science provided the way to answer them.

debates and theoretical speculations. They wrote historical narratives recovering the ideas of the Whigs (Forbes 1952, 1975; Burrow 1966, 1981, 1988).

Recognition of the Whiggish and modernist traditions in Cambridge casts light on the complex contours of contextualism. When observers talk about a Cambridge School, they misleadingly associate all kinds of folk with the methodological positions of Pocock and Skinner. In fact many of the historians linked to the Cambridge School inherited a Whiggish distrust of abstract philosophical arguments and methodological precepts.

THEORETICAL JUSTIFICATIONS

Skinner has written in various places of how he set out to do "for Hobbes what Laslett had done for Locke" (Skinner 2002b: 42). He too explored archival sources, most notably Hobbes's private papers held by the Duke of Devonshire at Chatsworth. He even published "an unknown fragment" by Hobbes, arguing that it disproved deontological interpretations of his thought (Skinner 1965). Indeed, Skinner published at least six or seven papers on Hobbes before his first major article on methodology.[3] Clearly, as Skinner and Pocock have often acknowledged, their theoretical writings attempted to justify an existing historical practice. They defended the history of political theory against both reductionists who dismissed ideas as mere epiphenomena and canonical theorists who approached texts as timeless philosophical works. Their battle against reductionism has as much to do with history as with political philosophy: they were employed in history departments at a time when these were dominated by social and political historians who denounced the history of ideas as intellectually irrelevant and politically conservative. Their battle against the canonical theorists was that initiated by Laslett. They wanted to promote an approach that: (1) situated texts in their contexts, and (2) proved interpretations correct by establishing empirical facts using modernist methods. They wanted to undermine approaches that read authors as: (1) contributing to perennial debates; or (2) aiming at a coherent metaphysics.

Quentin Skinner

Skinner gave by far the most philosophically interesting defense of contextualism. He drew on the same new philosophy to which Laslett appealed in pronouncing the death of elder approaches to political philosophy. Like Laslett, he took Weldon to have shown

---

[3] Skinner has now published a three-volume collection of his papers, but the versions in this collection often differ in important respects from the originals, and some of the differences are accentuated by the choice of papers for inclusion (Skinner 2002a).

that much political argument was vacuous. Again like Laslett, he associated Weldon with the work of Ludwig Wittgenstein, who at the time was generally placed alongside Ryle and J. L. Austin and so was read as offering a kind of linguistic version of logical positivism. While Skinner rightly pointed to Collingwood as a background influence, it was these analytic philosophers who gave him his arguments.

We can begin to reconstruct Skinner's justification of contextualism by unpacking his theory of meaning. Skinner is often, and rightly, described as an intentionalist. But his intentionalism does not derive from his theory of meaning. To the contrary, far from identifying meaning with the beliefs or other intentional states of the author, he defines it squarely in terms of sense and reference. He thereby implies that texts have meanings in themselves based entirely on their semantic content. Indeed, he draws a sharp distinction between what a text means and what an author meant by it.

Skinner's move to intentionalism depends on his use of Austin's speech-act theory. He argues that, to understand an action, we have to grasp not only its meaning but also its intended illocutionary force. Skinner here treats meaning as transparent in a way that makes the main task of the historian, at least in theory, the recovery of illocutionary intentions. Consider one of Skinner's main examples: Defoe's tract *The Shortest Way with the Dissenters*. Defoe wrote that we should treat dissent as a capital offense, and the meaning of that is simply that we should treat dissent as a capital offense. However, to understand Defoe's tract, we have to grasp that its intended illocutionary force is parody: far from recommending that we hang dissenters, Defoe was ridiculing contemporary arguments against religious toleration.

We can now explore how Skinner uses these ideas to defend contextualism. He argues, most importantly, that to grasp illocutionary intentions we have to situate them in their historical contexts. He draws on Austin to argue that illocutionary intentions have to be recognizable as intentions to do a particular thing in a particular context. As he thus concludes, "to understand what any given writer may have been *doing in* using some particular concept or argument, we need first of all to grasp the nature and range of things that could recognizably have been done by using that particular concept, in the treatment of that particular theme, at that particular time" (Skinner 1988*b*: 77). In addition, Skinner constantly argues that contextualism is a modernist method in that it is a way of securing facts and thus textual interpretations. His methodological essays consistently claim that his particular contextualist method is a "necessary and perhaps even sufficient"—or, more colloquially, "essential"—requirement of understanding a historical text.[4] His argument here is that, because the expression and reception of illocutionary force requires shared conventions, historians must know the relevant conventions if they are to understand what an author was doing. His broader claim is that meticulous archival and primary research can enable historians to build up a body of factual knowledge that conclusively establishes what an author intended to do. As Skinner wrote, "if we succeed in identifying

---

[4] Skinner's use of philosophical argument to support modernist themes and proposals is even stronger in his earliest philosophical essay (Skinner 1966).

this context with sufficient accuracy, we can eventually hope to read off what the speaker or writer in whom we are interested was doing" (Skinner 1988*d*: 275).

The details of Skinner's justification of contextualism are less well known than his attack on canonical approaches (Skinner 1988*a*). Skinner challenges approaches that read past theorists as addressing perennial problems. He argues that authors cannot have intended to contribute to debates that were not around when they wrote: to understand a text, we must grasp the author's intention to address a particular question at a particular time. Skinner thus rejects the very idea of perennial problems in favor of an emphasis on the individual questions that a particular theorist intended to address at a particular time. He concludes that we should approach texts assuming that each is dealing with its own question, not that they all contribute to a common enterprise.

Skinner similarly challenges approaches that read authors as offering a coherent metaphysics. He argues that the mythology of coherence leads to "a history of thoughts which no one ever actually succeeded in thinking, at a level of coherence which no one ever actually attained" (Skinner 1988*a*: 40). In his view, authors intend to contribute to different fields of inquiry and to address different questions in the several texts they write over a number of years, and their intentions are thus too varied to constitute a coherent system.

J. G. A. Pocock

Pocock never exhibited the philosophical interests or sophistication of Skinner. He typically grabbed at more sociological vocabularies to provide a theoretical defense of contextualism. What is more, Pocock's sociological vocabularies lead to a contextualist theory very different from the one that Skinner built out of speech-act theory. Skinner presents language as a set of conventions that authors use in intentional acts. In contrast, Pocock has consistently adopted more structuralist vocabularies to suggest that language gives authors their very intentions. As Skinner recently expressed it: "he [Pocock] stresses the power of language to constrain our thoughts, whereas I tend to think of language at least as much as a resource to be deployed" (Skinner 2002*b*: 49). This difference appears not only in their theoretical justifications of contextualism but also in their historical studies. Skinner's historical works typically detail what an author was doing in the intellectual context of the time; he writes of how Machiavelli subverted the "advice to princes" genre, how Bolingbroke appealed to Whig principles to challenge the Whigs, and why Hobbes returned to the classical theory of eloquence. In contrast, Pocock pays more attention to languages that persist and develop over time: he traces the language of the ancient constitution across sixteenth- and seventeenth-century France and Britain, the language of civic humanism from renaissance Italy by way of Puritan Britain to America and its revolution, and the clash between languages of ancient virtue and modern commerce.

Unsurprisingly Pocock's theoretical justifications of contextualism focus on aggregate concepts such as paradigm, tradition, and language. These concepts capture the similarities and links between texts and authors that are so prominent in his historical studies. In many respects he seems less interested in providing a philosophical analysis of these concepts than in using them descriptively to give an account of his own historical practice. Nonetheless, like Skinner, he often tried not merely to describe a type of contextualism, but also to uphold it as a modernist method that alone could result in properly historical interpretations of texts.

Pocock suggests that paradigms (or languages) constitute the meanings of texts, since they give authors the intentions they can have (Pocock 1972, 1985). This suggestion leads directly to his emphasis on situating texts in their context. He argues that the historian must study paradigms precisely because they control political speech. The task of the historian is, in this view, "to identify the 'language' or 'vocabulary' with and within which the author operated, and to show how it functioned paradigmatically to prescribe what he might say and how he might say it" (Pocock 1972: 25). In addition, Pocock, like Skinner, implies that his variety of contextualism resembles a modernist method in that it is a way of securing facts and thus textual interpretations. Pocock allows that historians might be unable to prove that all their evidence is not a figment of their imagination, but, he adds sharply, neither can they prove they are not asleep and dreaming; for all practical purposes, contextualism secures the factual evidence that then secures interpretations. Thus, if historians do not adopt a contextualist method, they simply cannot reach an adequate understanding of a text: "it seems a prior necessity [of historical understanding] to establish the language or languages in which some passage of political discourse was being conducted" (Pocock 1985: 7).

Like Laslett and Skinner, Pocock contrasts a contextual approach with those that read theorists as contributing to perennial debates or seeking a coherent metaphysics. For Pocock, a focus on perennial problems falls foul of the emphasis of modernist empiricism on factual evidence. He argues that we cannot assume that political thought took place at the level of abstraction of some perennial problem. On the contrary, he continues, "the strictly historical task before us plainly is that of determining by investigation on what levels of abstraction thought did take place" (Pocock 1962: 186). Again, for Pocock, a focus on the coherence of an author's thought falls foul of recognition of the role played by paradigms and languages. He argues that languages are not unified but polyvalent structures that facilitate "the utterance of diverse and contrary propositions" (Pocock 1985: 9). Texts are, he continues, the products of these languages, inheriting their ability to say contrary things on many levels.

Debates and Revisions

Skinner and Pocock's theoretical justifications of contextualism aroused far more controversy than had contextualist histories. It was one thing to adopt a historical stance toward texts, and quite another to argue that a particular method was the sole route by which anyone, historian or not, could grasp the historical meaning of a text.

The mere adoption of a historical stance leaves open the choice of whether to adopt that stance, and the choice of how to study history if one does so. The justifications of contextualism subordinate such choices to the claims of a modernist method. They imply that historians can do good work only if they follow a particular set of method-ological precepts. Again, they imply that political theorists who adopt less historical approaches simply are not in the business of understanding texts: even if these other political theorists make interesting arguments, the arguments cannot be historical, so they may as well forgo discussions of past texts—as Skinner polemically pressed the point, "we must learn to do our own thinking for ourselves" (Skinner 1988a: 66).

Most criticisms of contextualism focus on the strong methodological claims of Skinner and Pocock. Even historians associated with the so-called Cambridge School would not uphold these strong claims. Many of them simply continue the long-standing Cambridge tradition of the historical study of political philosophy without committing themselves to a historicist philosophy let alone modernist method—I suspect Richard Tuck is one prominent example. Others follow Forbes, with his Whiggish proclivities, in that they conceive of history as a practical art that resists formulation in any philosophical language let alone a set of methodological precepts—I am pretty sure Stefan Collini is one example (Collini 2000).

Political theorists with weaker associations to Cambridge have been more vocal in criticizing Skinner and Pocock. Their complaints also focus on the contextualists' strong methodological claims. Critics complain that general prescriptions for historical study are unhelpful—but unfortunately they do not distinguish between philosophical and methodological prescriptions (e.g. Minogue 1981; Tarcov 1982). Similarly, critics bemoan the sterile antiquarianism of contextualism; they argue that our legitimate interests in historical texts go beyond the recovery of historical meanings to include reading them in relation to our problems (e.g. Leslie 1970; Tarlton 1973).

How have the contextualists responded to their critics, and perhaps more import-antly to the erosion of modernist ambitions in the human sciences? To some extent, the answer is that they have not responded; they have concentrated on writing histories. Pocock's theoretical writings always resembled descriptions of his practice more than a sustained philosophical justification of it. Increasingly, he has acknowl-edged as much. What he is after, it now seems clear, is just a vocabulary that conveys the type of historical objects he studies—"idioms, rhetorics, specialised vocabularies and grammars" all considered as "a single though multiplex community of discourse" (Pocock 1987: 22). Even Skinner, the most philosophically engaged of the early contextualists, has written very little since the 1970s on the philosophical justification of contextualism: he published a restatement of his views in 1988 in reply to early critics (Skinner 1988d), but the volume *Regarding Method* in his recent collected papers contains just two other essays written after 1979—a polemical attack on Elton and a retrospect relating his views to the history of concepts (Skinner 2002a).

While the early contextualists have done little to rework their theories, a pattern does emerge. First, contextualists are less committed to their modernist methods and the vocabularies with which they originally justified them. Sometimes they suggest that their approach rests less on particular analyses of speech-acts, paradigms, or *langue* than on a broad historicist sensibility. They distance themselves from their hegemonic claims for a particular method as a way of securing factual evidence and thus textual interpretations. Skinner has explicitly said, "I used to think far more in terms of correct interpretations, and to suppose that there is usually a fact of the matter to be discovered," whereas "I now feel that . . . the process of interpretation is a never-ending one" (Skinner 2002*b*: 50). Second, contextualists flirt with new theoretical vocabularies. In Skinner's case, the influence of meaning holism appears in his recasting discussions of sense and reference and illocutionary force in terms of the ascription of systems of belief, while the influence of anti-foundationalism appears in his recasting speech-acts as a concern with rhetoric and in his newfound hostility to facts. Finally, when the contextualists recast their theories in terms of a broad historicism or new vocabularies, they do perilously little to show how their later positions relate to their earlier ones. Do they still want to defend the strong methodological claims for which they are best known, and, if so, how would they now do so? Do they still believe in the analyses of speech-acts and paradigms that they once offered, and, if so, how would they reconcile those analyses with the very different vocabularies found in their more recent theoretical writings?

THE CONTEMPORARY SCENE

The contemporary standing of contextualism might seem paradoxical. Skinner and Pocock continue to write magisterial histories at an impressive rate. To some extent their battles have arguably been won. Certainly, historical studies of political theory are flourishing, and it is tempting to add that they are squeezing out studies that mine past texts for jewels of wisdom without bothering with either historical or philosophical defenses of the alleged jewels. Nonetheless, historical studies are flourishing in the absence of any sustained theoretical exploration of their nature, and long after the elder justifications for them have lost plausibility. Skinner and Pocock appear, quite rightly in my view, to have retreated from the strong methodological claims of their early work, but they have never explicitly repudiated these claims, nor provided anything like a clear statement of where their retreat leaves the philosophy of contextualism and historicism more generally.

Contemporary work on the theory of contextualism contains three main positions, which we might label "anti-methodological empiricism," "homogenizing eclecticism," and "post-analytic hermeneutics." Each position has its advocates. Skinner himself has made occasional comments that alternatively point toward and then pull away from each of them.

The retreat from strong methodological claims sometimes leads the contextualists to suggest that their approach is common sense or standard historical practice. This view is received enthusiastically by historians indebted to the more Whiggish strand in the so-called Cambridge School. For example, Bryan Young, who followed Burrow and Collini into the program in Intellectual History at the University of Sussex, restates the Whiggish view that philosophical concerns, let alone methodological ones, are a hindrance to the practice of history. Like Forbes, whom he credits as his inspiration, Young describes intellectual history as an art, a way of seeing, and an aesthetic (Young 2002). If Young is merely cautioning us claims about the sufficiency or necessity of any method, then his point is well taken. But there is no reason why a rejection of strong methodological claims should entail withdrawing from philosophical analysis. To the contrary, if invocations of "common sense" or "the art of history" are juxtaposed to philosophical reasoning, they are liable to lapse into naive empiricism; they are likely to imply that historians can engage in their empiricial studies without any need to reflect philosophically on the nature of what they do, whether it is justified, what forms of explanation they should adopt, or what kinds of justification they should offer for their conclusions.

As the contextualists retreated from their strong methodological claims, so there arose not only anti-methodological empiricism but also homogenizing eclecticism. This eclecticism appears as a tendency to equate contextualism with several other historical approaches to political philosophy: James Tully flattens the distinctions between contextualism and the critical post-structuralist legacy of Foucault (Tully 2002), and Melvin Richter and Kari Palonen flatten the distinctions between context-ualism and the history of concepts as developed by Reinhart Koselleck (Richter 1995; Palonen 2003). If such homogenizing is merely drawing our attention to a broad historicism in the human sciences today, then once again the point is well taken. But we should not mistake the identification of a broad historicism for a philosophical analysis of it. The contextualists, post-structuralists, and conceptual historians gener-ally offer different and even incompatible philosophical analyses of their historical practice. If we ignore these differences, we are in danger of promoting a bland eclecticism that elides important philosophical issues instead of confronting them.

Finally, the retreat from strong methodological claims has led contextualists to a broader historicism based on post-analytic hermeneutics. Skinner has long identified with the historicism of Collingwood, as well as drawing on arguments derived from analytic and post-analytic philosophers. In doing so, he and others raise the possibility, implicitly or explicitly, of moving from the vocabularies of speech-act theory and paradigms to meaning holism and, more specifically, analyses of the human sciences as exploring actions by attributing meanings and showing how these meanings fit into larger patterns of belief and rationality—analyses including the anti-naturalist empha-sis on interpretation of Charles Taylor and Peter Winch, and the more naturalist account of explanation offered by Donald Davidson. Skinner first wrote about these analyses in a 1972 article, "'Social Meaning' and the Explanation of Social Action," in which he drew on speech-act theory to provide a critical alternative to both the anti-naturalist account of interpretation and the naturalist commitment to explanation.[5]

---

[5] The only time Skinner returned to these philosophers, along with Davidson, Quine, and Taylor, was in a lengthy 1988 "Reply to Critics," in which he still staked out differences from them but with less emphasis on the ways in which his speech-act theory defined the key feature of understanding in terms opposed to the attribution of beliefs (Skinner 1988d).

Today, in sharp contrast, a rejection of his strong methodological claims may enable contextualists to rethink their theory and perhaps even their histories in terms of just such philosophical analyses.

CONCLUSION

When somebody offers you three alternatives before labeling one "naive" and another "bland," they are probably steering you toward the third. My own commitment is indeed to the use of post-analytic philosophy and especially meaning holism to rethink the nature of historicist approaches to political philosophy (Bevir 1999). What does this involve? Some commentators defend Skinner from critics by rereading him as a broad historicist rather than a proponent of a modernist method justified by speech-act theory (Palonen 2000; Stern 2002). Recently Skinner himself has even suggested— implausibly if not disingenuously—that his early methodological writings relied on the meaning holism of Davidson, W. V. O. Quine, and Wittgenstein, barely mentioning the speech-act theory that was actually so prominent in his writings.[6]

It is especially important, therefore, to say that a turn to post-analytic philosophy and meaning holism is not an easy option. We cannot just pretend that the contextualists have always been using these vocabularies. Nor can we pretend that these vocabularies are straightforwardly compatible with those they did in fact use— speech-act theory and paradigms. Nor, finally, can we blithely assume that these vocabularies are capable of supporting the main claims once made by the contextualists.

Quite the contrary: once we move from speech-act theory and paradigms to post-analytic philosophy and meaning holism, and once we move from strong methodological claims to a broad historicism, then we undermine, or at least strongly modify, all of the main positions associated with the early contextualists. Consider briefly the emphasis on linguistic contexts, the rejection of perennial problems, and the dismissal of concerns about coherence (Bevir 1994, 1997, 2000). First, if the study of linguistic contexts is not a necessary or sufficient method for understanding, there is no absolute requirement that historians pay attention to it. "Study the linguistic context" is just a useful heuristic, and, as such, it is no different from other maxims that sensible historians will follow, including "study the social and economic context" or "explore the biography of the author." Second, if we are not seeking the single correct

---

[6] That means that, when we find Skinner suggesting that he drew on "post-analytic philosophy" and "meaning holism" to analyze interpretation as the ascription of networks, systems, or webs of "belief" in accord with a presumption of rationality, we might suspect him of projecting later and largely unformulated arguments back onto his early published views (Skinner 2002a: 4–5). We search his work in vein for any sustained discussion of terms like "post-analytic" or "meaning holism." Moreover, we can but wonder how he now would reconcile the suggestion that interpretation is the ascription of beliefs and desires with his clear and oft-repeated belief that understanding consists in grasping the sense and reference of words and securing uptake of illocutionary force.

interpretation of a text, but ascribing beliefs to its author, then there seems no reason to suppose that we must do so at a particular level of abstraction. Yet, if we can couch past beliefs at a sufficient level of abstraction, we can often make them relevant to our concerns and even problems that have persisted more or less perennially throughout history. Finally, if interpretation involves the ascription of beliefs, we will be far more interested in their coherence than we would if interpretation were about identifying the particular speech-act being made. Indeed, if the ascription of beliefs depends on a presumption of rationality, then, far from a concern with coherence being a myth, it is an unavoidable aspect of every act of interpretation.

Of course, a post-analytic hermeneutics might sustain modified versions of the claims once made by Skinner and Pocock. We may argue that linguistic contexts are crucial to explanations of people's beliefs, that there is no cosmic agenda philosophers are bound to address, and that historians may conclude that people were not rational. Yet, these modified claims are not those for which the contextualists argued. There is, moreover, no sign that Skinner or Pocock themselves have much interest in deploying meaning holism to argue in defense of these modified claims, let alone to assess where a retreat to these modified claims would leave their earlier accounts of contextualism. In short, while historicist studies of political philosophy flourish, there is a woeful lack of philosophical analysis of their logic.

References

ADCOCK, R., BEVIR, M., and STIMSON, S. (2007) (eds). *Modern Political Science: Anglo-American Exchanges since 1880*. Princeton: Princeton University Press.

BENTLEY, M. (2005). *Modernizing England's Past: English Historiography in the Age of Modernism 1870–1970*. Cambridge: Cambridge University Press.

BEVIR, M. (1994). "Are There Perennial Problems in Political Theory?" *Political Studies*, 42: 662–75.

BEVIR, M. (1997). "Mind and Method in the History of Ideas," *History and Theory*, 36: 167–89.

BEVIR, M. (1999). *The Logic of the History of Ideas*. Cambridge: Cambridge University Press.

BEVIR, M. (2000). "The Role of Contexts in Understanding and Explanation," *Human Studies*, 23: 395–411.

BEVIR, M. (2001). "Prisoners of Professionalism: On the Construction and Responsibility of Political Studies," *Public Administration*, 79: 469–89.

BURROW, J. (1966). *Evolution and Society: A Study in Victorian Social Theory*. Cambridge: Cambridge University Press.

BURROW, J. (1981). *A Liberal Descent: Victorian Historians and the English Past*. Cambridge: Cambridge University Press.

BURROW, J. (1988). *Whigs and Liberals: Continuity and Change in English Political Thought*. Oxford: Clarendon Press.

COLLINI, S. (2000). "General Introduction," in S. Collini, R. Whatmore, and B. Young (eds), *History, Religion, and Culture: British Intellectual History 1750–1950*. Cambridge: Cambridge University Press.

FORBES, D. (1952). *The Liberal Anglican Idea of History*. Cambridge: Cambridge University Press.

FORBES, D. (1975). *Hume's Philosophical Politics*. Cambridge: Cambridge University Press.

LASLETT, P. (1956). "Introduction," in P. Laslett, *Philosophy, Politics and Society*. Oxford: Basil Blackwell.

LASLETT, P. (1960) (ed.). *John Locke's Two Treatises of Government: A Critical Edition with an Introduction and Apparatus Criticus*. Cambridge: Cambridge University Press.

LESLIE, M. (1970). "In Defense of Anachronism," *Political Studies*, 18: 433–47.

MINOGUE, K. (1981). "Method in Intellectual History: Quentin Skinner's Foundations," in J. Tully (ed.), *Meaning and Context: Quentin Skinner and his Critics*. Cambridge: Polity.

PALONEN, K. (2000). "Logic or Rhetoric in the History of Political Thought," *Rethinking History*, 4: 301–10.

PALONEN, K. (2003). *Quentin Skinner: History, Politics, Rhetoric*. Cambridge: Polity.

POCOCK, J. (1962). "The History of Political Thought: A Methodological Enquiry," in P. Laslett and W. Runciman (eds), *Philosophy, Politics, and Society*, 2nd ser. Oxford: Blackwell.

POCOCK, J. (1972). "Languages and their Implications: The Transformation of the Study of Political Thought," in J. Pockock, *Politics, Language, and Time*. London: Methuen.

POCOCK, J. (1985). "State of the Art," in J. Pocock, *Virtue, Commerce, and History*. Cambridge: Cambridge University Press.

POCOCK, J. (1987). "The Concept of a Language and the Métier d'Historien: Some Considerations on Practice," in A. Pagden (ed.), *The Languages of Political Theory in Early Modern Europe*. Cambridge: Cambridge University Press.

POCOCK, J. (2006). "Present at the Creation: With Laslett to the Lost Worlds," *International Journal of Public Affairs*, 2: 7–17.

RICHTER, M. (1995). *The History of Political and Social Concepts: A Critical Introduction*. New York: Oxford University Press.

Skinner, Q. (1965). "Hobbes on Sovereignty: An Unknown Discussion," *Political Studies*, 13: 213–18.

SKINNER, Q. (1966). "The Limits of Historical Explanations," *Philosophy*, 41: 199–215.

SKINNER, Q. (1988a). "Meaning and Understanding in the History of Ideas," in J. Tully (ed.), *Meaning and Context: Quentin Skinner and his Critics*. Cambridge: Polity.

SKINNER, Q. (1988b). "Motives, Intentions, and the Interpretation of Texts," in J. Tully (ed.), *Meaning and Context: Quentin Skinner and his Critics*. Cambridge: Polity.

SKINNER, Q. (1988c). "Social Meaning and the Explanation of Social Action," in J. Tully (ed.), *Meaning and Context: Quentin Skinner and his Critics*. Cambridge: Polity.

SKINNER, Q. (1988d). "A Reply to Critics," in J. Tully (ed.), *Meaning and Context: Quentin Skinner and his Critics*. Cambridge: Polity.

SKINNER, Q. (2002a). *Visions of Politics*. 3 vols. Cambridge: Cambridge University Press.

SKINNER, Q. (2002b). "Interview by Petri Koikkalainen and Sami Syrämäki," *Finnish Yearbook of Political Thought*, 6: 34–63.

STERN, B. (2002). "History, Meaning and Interpretation," *History of European Ideas*, 28: 1–12.

TARCOV, N. (1982). "Quentin Skinner's Method and Machiavelli's *Prince*," *Ethics*, 92: 692–710.

TARLTON, C. (1973). "Historicity, Meaning and Revisionism in the Study of Political Thought," *History and Theory*, 12: 307–28.

TULLY, J. (2002). "Political Philosophy as a Critical Activity," Political Theory, 30: 533–55.

YOUNG, B. (2002). "The Tyranny of the Definite Article: Some Thoughts on the Art of Intellectual History," *History of European Ideas*, 28: 101–17.

CHAPTER 2

....

THE STRAUSSIAN
APPROACH

....

CATHERINE ZUCKERT

THE "Straussian" approach to the history of political philosophy is articulated primarily in the writings of Leo Strauss. Strauss wrote extremely careful, detailed studies of canonical philosophical works along with essays explaining his approach (e.g. Strauss 1952, 1953, 1959, 1983, 1989a, b). The most controversial claim Strauss made was that philosophers in the past did not always present their thoughts openly and explicitly. They appeared to accept opinions dominant in their respective times and places in order to avoid persecution for their heterodox views and to preserve popular morality from the acidic effects of unrestrained questioning. They also used an "art of writing" to entice potential philosophers to begin a life of inquiry by following the hints the authors gave about their true thoughts and questions. The overriding purpose of Strauss's own studies was to prove that philosophy in its original Socratic form is still possible by showing the persistence of certain fundamental problems throughout the history of philosophy. The most pertinent of those problems, not merely to political philosophy but to human life as a whole, was the problem of justice.

As the attempt to replace opinions about political things with knowledge by subjecting those opinions to dialectical analysis, Strauss argued, "political philosophy is . . . fundamentally different from the history of political philosophy." No one would ask about "the nature of political things and the best, or the just, political order" without some historical knowledge of the variety of political institutions and convictions that have existed in different places at different times. However, no one would mistake the question about the best political order "for the question of how this or that philosopher or all philosophers had approached, discussed or answered" that philosophic question (Strauss 1959: 56). Nevertheless, Strauss insisted, study of the history of political philosophy has become a prerequisite for engaging in political philosophy in our time for two reasons. First, he pointed out, opinions we hold now are derivative from philosophical doctrines promulgated in the past. As we have acquired them, these opinions are often mere residues and abbreviations in the form of tacit presuppositions. "If we want to clarify the political ideas we have inherited, we must [make these presuppositions and their implications] ... explicit [as they were] in the past, and this can be done only by means of the history of political ideas" (Strauss 1959: 73). So understood, the history of political philosophy becomes fused with political philosophy. There is, however, a serious obstacle to undertaking such an investigation. One of *the dominant opinions* in our time is that all human thought is historically conditioned. If this "historicist" contention is true, political philosophy is impossible. The second and most pressing reason to study the history of political philosophy is, therefore, to investigate whether the "historicist" contention is correct.

Strauss concluded that it was not, and his refutation of the "historicist" contention has two parts: the literary and empirical or historical response to "historicism" he presents primarily in *Persecution and the Art of Writing* (1952); and the philosophical response to "radical historicism" he presents primarily in *Natural Right and History* (1953). Although much of the debate about Strauss's work and its effects has concentrated on his "novel" way of reading philosophical texts, Strauss himself insisted that "historicism" is based on a philosophical account of the character and limitations of human knowledge and that it can be refuted, therefore, only on the basis of a philosophical argument (Strauss 1953: 19). Both his literary and historical analyses of texts were explicitly intended to make the study of the history of political philosophy an introduction to philosophy instead of a mere report of the content and effects of the works of past authors.

Strauss's Rediscovery of a "Forgotten Way of Writing"

Recent historians of political thought have not recognized the "art of writing" that philosophers utilized in the past to escape persecution, Strauss argued, because these historians have shared the presuppositions of their liberal societies. Taking "for granted the essential harmony between thought and society or between intellectual progress and social progress," these historians did not understand the conflict philosophers in the past thought existed between philosophy and society, a conflict that led them to develop an indirect mode of communicating their most radical thoughts "between the lines." Insofar as contemporary "historical" accounts of the works of past authors proceed on the basis of modern liberal assumptions about the relation between thought and society, however, these accounts are obviously, if ironically "unhistorical." Liberal societies are relatively rare, recent developments. Most philosophers had not lived or written in societies that gave them complete freedom to say or publish what they thought. On the contrary, many past authors who openly disagreed with prevailing, officially endorsed opinions suffered penalties, ranging from social ostracism to torture and capital punishment.

The threat of persecution was only the first and most obvious reason, however, that past authors had not stated their true thoughts completely, openly, or explicitly. Because questioning accepted opinions creates doubt about the validity as well as the application of established moral norms, some pre-modern authors concluded, a completely public presentation of an unfettered philosophical search for truth is not compatible with the requirements of maintaining a stable political order. Attempting to act (or write) in a "socially responsible" manner, these authors sought to conceal their most radical questions and conclusions from all but their most careful readers.

There was a third reason, moreover, that some authors chose to communicate their thoughts incompletely and indirectly. Truly philosophical authors write not so much to propagate doctrines as to encourage younger readers to follow them in a life of inquiry. Such authors artfully attempt to arouse questions in the minds of their most attentive readers and then provide hints concerning the way those questions might be answered; but these authors leave their readers to think out the answers and the problems with these possible answers for themselves. Plato, who wrote only dialogues in which he presented conversations among others, was Strauss's model of such an author.

Strauss's ideas about concealed writing were controversial in his time, but they were historically rather commonplace. For instance, Strauss notes, up until the end of the nineteenth century, many philosophers and theologians thought that Thomas Hobbes and Baruch Spinoza were really atheists, even though they referred repeatedly to God, divine law, and the truth of Scripture in order to avoid the censors. There was an even more widespread consensus that some, if not all, ancient and medieval authors wrote esoterically. Strauss distinguished between heterodox modern philosophers who, looking forward to the abolition of persecution as such, "concealed their views only far enough to protect themselves as well as possible," and older authors who, "convinced that philosophy as such was suspect to, and hated by, the majority of men," concluded "that public communication of the philosophic or scientific truth was impossible or undesirable, not only for the time being but for all times" (Strauss 1952: 33–4).

Beginning in the nineteenth century, however, commentators had begun to insist that there was a fundamental continuity in the history of philosophy rather than a break, for example, between the ancients and the moderns. Historians argued that philosophers like Hobbes and Spinoza did not reject biblical teachings, but retained them, if in secularized form. Borrowing the notion of data collection from modern natural science, historians also began to insist that the way to know what any past author thought was to count up the times he repeated a claim or statement. Changes or variations were attributed to the "development" of the author's thought. Because philosophical works read in this manner reflected the dominant views of their times, and thus differed from each other according to the times and places in which they were written, "historicist" commentators concluded that the thought of the authors was not merely reflective of, but limited to, their respective times and places.

Strauss responded to the "historicists" by pointing out that the contemporaries of past authors did not read their works simply in terms of, or as expressions of, the context, in the way current historians did. Readers of philosophical works in the past tried to determine, first, what the author was arguing, and, second, whether it was true or not.

As a historian, Strauss observed, a scholar has to begin by trying to give an account of what was written "on the lines"—that is, what an author literally wrote. If a coherent and accurate account of the content of any given text can be given on the basis of the author's explicit statements, the analysis ends there. But Strauss cautioned: "The context in which a statement occurs, and the literary character of the whole work as well as its plan, must be perfectly understood before an interpretation of the statement can reasonably claim to be adequate or even correct." If an obviously intelligent and knowledgeable author makes "such blunders as would shame an intelligent high school boy, it is reasonable to assume that they are intentional, especially if the author discusses, however incidentally, the possibility of intentional blunders in writing." Emphasizing the importance of the literary form, Strauss added: "the views of the author of a drama or dialogue must not, without previous proof, be identified with the views expressed by one or more of his characters." Most important (and in the context of modern historical scholarship, most controversial), he concluded, "the real opinion of an author is not necessarily identical with that which he expresses in the largest number of passages" (Strauss 1952: 30).

In attempting to revive an understanding of the reasons for and an appreciation of "the art of writing," Strauss did not lay out a hermeneutical "method" to be applied to any or all texts.[1] In *Persecution* he first pointed out some of the kinds of indications or hints on the part of an author that should lead a careful reader to look for that author's true thoughts beneath the surface of the text. In analyzing specific works by four different authors Strauss then suggested a few general strategies for reading such texts. According to the classical teachers of forensic rhetoric, he noted, things placed in the middle are least exposed to superficial readers.[2] In explicating Farabi's treatment of Plato in *On the Purposes of Plato and of Aristotle*, Strauss thus observed that:

> at the beginning of the treatise *On the Attainment of Happiness* with which he prefaces his summaries of the philosophies of Plato and Aristotle, Farabi employs the distinction between "the happiness of this world in this life" and "the ultimate happiness in the other life"; [but] in the *Plato*, which is the second and therefore the least exposed part of a tripartite work, the distinction of the two kinds of happiness is completely dropped. (Strauss 1952: 13)

The observation that some topic or point comes in the middle of a list or text does not prove anything in itself, however. To account for the difference between what Farabi says at the beginning of his treatise and what he says in the middle, Strauss argued, a reader needs to observe that in what purports to be a summary of Plato's dialogues, including the *Gorgias*, *Phaedrus*, *Phaedo*, and *Republic*, there is no mention

---

[1] In his "Correspondence Concerning *Truth and Method*" (1978) Strauss denied that he had a general theory of interpretation like that Gadamer had put forth.

[2] Strauss (1952: 185) cites Cicero, *Orator* 15.50, *De oratore* 77.313.

of the immortality of the soul. Yet every reader of Plato would know that Socrates explicitly argues for the immortality of the soul in all four dialogues. It was the difference between what Plato said and what Farabi (with apparent incompetence or ignorance) failed to report (his silence, as it were) that persuaded Strauss that "Farabi avails himself of the specific immunity of the commentator . . . to speak his mind concerning grave matters in his 'historical' works, rather than in the works in which he speaks in his own name," where he "pronounces more or less orthodox views concerning the life after death" (Strauss 1952: 13–14).[3] Likewise, Strauss suggested, we often learn how an author writes by observing how he reads another text. Explicating "The Literary Character of the *Guide for the Perplexed*" Strauss pointed out "hints" provided by Maimonides' own reading of the Torah that help a careful reader decipher the "secrets" Maimonides stated he was communicating only in intentionally disordered "chapter headings."[4] Strauss began his essay on "How to Study Spinoza's *Theologico-Political Treatise*," however, with a long and complex analysis of the reasons we cannot and should not try to read Spinoza the way he read the Bible or Euclid.[5] Finally, although Halevi was the only author Strauss treated in *Persecution* who wrote a dialogue, Strauss did not conclude that Halevi used the form, like Plato, to defend philosophy. Following his own "rule" about taking account of the literary form and not identifying the author with the views of any particular character, Strauss argued that Halevi did not necessarily or in all cases subscribe to the arguments the scholar gave in order to persuade the pagan king to convert to Judaism. Nevertheless, Strauss concluded: "In defending Judaism, which, according to him, is the only true revealed religion, against the philosophers, [Halevi] was conscious of defending morality itself and therewith the cause, not only of Judaism, but of mankind at large" (Strauss 1952: 141). In sum, Strauss did not read the works of all four philosophers in the same way. In all cases, he did pay particular attention to the literary form and identified places where they contradicted themselves or the orthodox principles of their communities. Strauss admitted that no reading of a text in which an author has attempted to conceal his true thoughts can produce a certain conclusion. If one could prove without doubt the author did not believe what he said that he did, he would not be a master of "the art of writing."

---

[3] When Drury (1988: 117) accuses Strauss of using the same "specific immunity of the commentator" in attributing his own views to Machiavelli, she does not point out such a radical difference between the author and text commented upon and the view said to be found there.

[4] Strauss thus begins his essay on "How to Begin to Study *The Guide of the Perplexed*" (Strauss 1963: pp. xi–xiii) with an outline of the chapter headings that contrasts markedly with Maimonides' own explicit organization of the book.

[5] On the basis of his suggestion that an author often reveals the way he himself writes in the way he reads the works of others, many commentators have concluded that Strauss himself writes exoterically: e.g. Drury (1988); Pangle (2006); Smith (2006). As we see in the case of Spinoza, however, Strauss did not think that all authors should necessarily be read the same way they read others. Zuckert and Zuckert (2006: 115–54), argue that Strauss did not present a "secret teaching," although he did exercise "pedagogical reserve."

In reminding his readers of what he called "a forgotten way of writing" (Strauss 1959: 221–32), Strauss was attempting to show that neither the repetitions of nor the appeals to opinions that were dominant at the specific times and places in which various philosophers wrote proved that their thoughts were limited to those times and places. If readers found indications that an author held views or made arguments that contradicted the dominant opinions he announced, especially at the beginning and end of his books, readers should begin to suspect that the repetition of dominant opinions might serve to conceal that author's more heterodox views. In that case, readers had to go back, reread carefully, paying attention to the subject matter as well as the literary form of the work, trying to figure out the plan, in order finally to bring together the indications in a coherent account of an author's heterodox position. Moreover, by reminding his readers that philosophers had not always thought that unrestricted philosophical inquiry into the nature of all things is necessarily or completely compatible with the requirements of maintaining a decent society, Strauss was seeking to make his readers conscious of their liberal modern presuppositions and so to free his readers from the blinders imposed by those presuppositions.

Strauss's analysis of the works of Islamic and Jewish philosophers had a substantive as well as a methodological aim: to show that claims about the "continuity," if not the necessary direction and culmination, of the development of philosophy in the West as a "synthesis" of reason and (secularized) revelation were based on only part of the relevant evidence. In Islamic and Jewish communities, where revelation was understood as law, Strauss emphasized, the conflict between society and philosophy was evident, because philosophical investigations clearly raised questions about the truth and justice of the law. The dominant understanding of the history of philosophy had developed in Christian communities, where the conflict between society and philosophy was less clear, because in Christianity philosophy had been enlisted and subordinated to faith in theological defenses of a creed. Far from denying that different places and times were more or less conducive to the emergence of certain insights, Strauss explicitly raised "the obvious possibility . . . that the situation to which one particular doctrine is related, is particularly favorable to the discovery of *the* truth, whereas all other situations may be more or less unfavorable" (1959: 64). Finally, in order to raise the question concerning the truth of various claims, arguments, or doctrines, Strauss insisted, it is necessary not to assume that there has been progress—that is, that more recent thoughts or works are necessarily better or truer than older ones. Philosophical understanding is not the sort of thing one can accumulate like information.

Strauss's Philosophical Response to "Radical" Historicism

Strauss reiterated his fundamental objection to "historicism" at the beginning of *Natural Right and History*: The "historicist" proposition that all thought is historically conditioned or limited is self-contradictory, because the truth of that proposition is not restricted to its own time and place. This "historicist" thesis or "insight" cannot be proved or disproved by empirical or historical evidence of the kind he had offered in *Persecution and the Art of Writing*, because this thesis concerns the very possibility and grounds of human knowledge. The proposition that all thought is historically limited, but that this insight is available only to people living at this time, requires a philosophical justification. And, Strauss recognized, the "radical historicist" Martin Heidegger had offered such a justification.[6] To refute the historicist thesis, it was necessary to critique Heidegger's claims about the fundamentally historical character of human existence and the history of 'Being.' Strauss summarized "the thesis of radical historicism" as follows:

> All knowledge, however, limited and "scientific" presupposes a frame of reference ... [or] horizon ... within which understanding and knowing take place. Only such a comprehensive vision makes possible any ... observation ... [or] orientation. The comprehensive view of the whole cannot be validated by reasoning, since it is the basis of all reasoning. Accordingly, there is a variety of such comprehensive views, each as legitimate as any other ... Strictly speaking, we cannot choose among different views. A single comprehensive view is imposed on us by fate. (Strauss 1953: 26–7)

No one controls the time or place at which he or she is born. According to Heidegger, we are, nevertheless, "free either to choose in anguish the world view and standards imposed on us by fate or else to lose ourselves in illusory security or in despair" (Strauss 1953: 26–7).

Strauss agreed with "the radical historicist" that all understanding or knowledge presupposes a comprehensive view. It is not possible to understand any "object" or particular kind of being in isolation from all others. That is the reason earlier philosophers sought knowledge of the whole. Strauss also agreed with "the radical historicist" that modern natural science made it difficult, if not impossible, to achieve such a comprehensive view now. By reducing everything to homogeneous matter that can be measured quantitatively, Strauss (1959: 39) agreed with Heidegger, modern natural science makes it impossible to recognize anything distinctively human.

Strauss thus agreed with "the radical historicist" that we live in a time of crisis—philosophical as well as political. The historical explanation of the way in which human beings acquired their distinctive faculties was developed by philosophers attempting to make our understanding of human life consistent with a modern natural scientific view of the universe. This historical understanding of human life culminated, however, in showing that modern natural science is itself a human activity or product. But, because it does not allow for a distinction between human and other forms of being, modern natural science cannot give an account of its own origin or foundation. Indeed, neither

---

[6] Strauss did not name a particular proponent of the "radical historicist" thesis in *Natural Right and History*. But in his June 26, 1950 letter to Alexander Kojeve he wrote: "I have once again been dealing with Historicism, that is to say, with Heidegger, the only radical historicist" (Strauss 1991: 251).

history nor science can show why human beings should persist in a search for knowledge that does not result in knowledge, strictly speaking, because knowledge can only be knowledge of the whole. (Any claim to knowledge short of the whole is, as modern scientists often point out, subject to revision in light of further evidence.) In modern philosophy, the search for knowledge had been justified by promises of its beneficent effects on human life. But in the twentieth century the threat of nuclear war or other forms of environmental devastation and genetic engineering had made the beneficence of the effects of science increasingly questionable.

Heidegger's first response to the crisis posed by the development of modern tech-nology was political. On the basis of the analysis of human existence he gave in *Being and Time*, Heidegger proclaimed the need for a new kind of practical stance in the face of fundamental uncertainty—resolution. In his notorious 1933 address as rector, as well as in the lectures he gave in 1936 as an "introduction to metaphysics," Heidegger found that resolution embodied politically in German National Socialism. Confronted by the failure of the biologist Nazis to adopt his own historical understanding of the situation as well as by their failure to lead Germany to planetary rule, Heidegger later adopted a more passive "poetic" stance. He argued that the dangerous truth revealed by the potential of modern technology to transform everything was a necessary result of Western rationalism, and that Western rationalism was, in turn, a necessary outgrowth of Greek philosophy and its fundamental, if usually unrecognized, conception of Being as presence. Heidegger thought he could perceive the limits of the understanding of Being as presence that had first been announced in ancient Greece, because he lived at the time at which the possibilities of that understanding could be seen to have been fully worked out by previous thinkers.

Strauss (1979–80) thought that Heidegger's "destruktion" of the traditional under-standing of the history of philosophy had made it possible to re-examine the traditional understanding of that history in a way it had not been re-examined for centuries. By investigating the origins of that tradition in the works of Plato and Aristotle, on the one hand, and the Hebrew Bible, on the other, however, Strauss came to very different conclusions about the defining limitations or characteristics of human existence as well as the origins and history of Western philosophy.

According to the phenomenological analysis Heidegger presented in *Being and Time*, human beings ask what an object is—in itself—only when it stops working—that is, performing its function or being useful. In other words, Heidegger suggested, human beings initially and originally perceive "things" in the world in terms of their use; theory and thus the theoretical question concerning their essence or "being" are secondary and derivative. And, since it is derivative from practical experience, which is itself limited by time and space, "theory" or philosophy is defined and limited by its temporal origins in a way that had not been recognized hitherto.

Strauss argued, on the contrary, that the experience Heidegger claimed was funda-mental to human existence *per se* was, in fact, an experience peculiar to our time. As a result of the apparent success of modern natural science in providing people not merely with knowledge but with the ability to manipulate things, contemporary logical positivists had declared that anything that could not be studied with the techniques employed by modern natural scientists could not be known. Among the "things" that cannot be shown to be true by the collection and analysis of data are human judgments about good and bad, right and wrong. Told that their judgments about such fundamental matters were merely irrational expressions of feeling or arbitrary "values," people became uncertain about the rightness or wrongness, truth or falsity, of their judgments, and so anxious.

In *Natural Right and History* Strauss responded to Heidegger's claims about the history of philosophy by giving a different account of the origin, first of philosophy itself, and then of political philosophy—that is, of the human attempt to obtain knowledge about what is just, noble, and good. In pre-philosophical societies (like that described in the Hebrew Bible), human beings understand things in terms of their characteristic "ways." The most important of those "ways" are our own ways, the ways of our community. These ways, having been established, are said to be best because they are oldest. But to identify the good with the old, communities had to understand the origins of the old ways to be better than the current inhabitants—that is, to be gods or pupils of gods. Questions about the goodness of their own ways arose when people observed that there was a variety of ways or customs. To determine which ways were best, people had to distinguish what was said in each community, by tradition, from what human beings could observe for themselves—everywhere. At the same time, inquirers became aware of the distinction between that which was man-made and that which was not. Questions about the status (best or not) of the laws and the divine sources of the laws became joined with questions about the origins or causes: were they products of human action—that is, established by convention, or did they exist independently of human beings, by nature? "Philosophy... came into being when nature was discovered... by some Greek twenty-six hundred years ago or before" (Strauss 1953: 82). And he explained, "the philosophic quest for the first things presupposes not merely that there are first things but that the first things are always," because, according to a fundamental premise of reason, "no being emerges without a cause" (Strauss 1953: 89). In other words, the traditional equation of being itself with eternal, unchanging being was a requirement of reason or intelligibility itself. It was not, as Heidegger had maintained, the product of a faulty, because limited, understanding of being as presence, in implicit and, therefore, unrecognized contrast to the constant flow of things in time from past to future.

The Greek discovery of "nature" as a term of distinction denoting those things that did not come into being as products of human art or convention (in contrast to Heidegger's abstract "being," which referred merely to the totality or common denominator of all things) pointed toward, but did not itself constitute, the insight fundamental to political philosophy. Political philosophy arose after and out of philosophy, when Socrates raised the question about the best form of life for human beings. Socrates' famous turn to "the human things" did not mean that he turned away from any or all inquiries into nature. "Socrates was forced to raise the question as to what the human things as such are," by his observation that to be means to be something—that is, that "being" is essentially differentiated. (Cf. Strauss 1964: 19–21; 1989a: 126, 132–3.) And Strauss pointed out, "it is impossible to grasp the distinctive character of human things as such without grasping the essential difference between human things and the things which are not human, i.e., the divine or natural things. This, in turn, presupposes some understanding of the divine or natural things as such" (Strauss 1953: 122).

In asking whether human beings should choose to live justly, and thus what justice is, Strauss observed, in the *Republic* Plato shows that Socrates was forced to rise from discussions concerning merely human matters to questions concerning the structure and intelligibility of the whole.[7] Indeed, Strauss argued, the question raised in the *Republic* about the best way of life constitutes both the origin and the framework in which the character and limitations of the human search for knowledge become evident. He concluded his own very controversial reading of the *Republic* by stating:

> The teaching of the *Republic* regarding justice can be true although it is not complete, in so far as the nature of justice depends decisively on the nature of the city—for even the transpolitical cannot be understood as such except if the city is understood—and the city is completely intelligible because its limits can be made perfectly manifest: to see these limits, one need not have answered the question regarding the whole; it is sufficient for the purpose to have raised the question regarding the whole. (Strauss 1964: 138)

Like Heidegger, Strauss emphasized that human understanding requires a limited framework. We cannot come to know or define anything, much less orient or understand our relation to other things, if we are not able to determine the limits of the particular world in which we find ourselves. Unlike Heidegger, however, Strauss's rereading of Plato led him to conclude that this framework was provided not by "time," but by the "city."

> Socrates makes clear in the *Republic* of what character the city would have to be in order to satisfy the highest need of man. By letting us see that the city constructed in accordance with this requirement is not possible, he lets us see the essential limits, the nature, of the city. (Strauss 1964: 138)

Human beings come to understand the "transpolitical" only by seeing the limits of the political. Rather than concealing what lies beyond them, as Heidegger had argued time does by constituting the "horizon" of our vision, the limits of the city make us aware not merely of our desire to find and come into contact with something beyond those limits, but of our intimations that there is something "good in itself," even if we do not know and probably never will know exactly what that is (Strauss 1953: 31–2; 1959: 55).

---

[7] According to Strauss, Farabi and Maimonides copied Plato in presenting philosophy as a way of life in such an explicitly political framework.

Strauss argued that his contemporaries needed to undertake historical studies that would enable them "to understand classical philosophy exactly as it understood itself" (Strauss 1953: 33) for two reasons. First, an "original" understanding of the origins of philosophy shows that the phenomenological analysis upon which "radical historicism" is based is both incomplete and false. Second, understanding classical political philosophy as it is understood itself, in terms of an insoluble tension between philosophy and the city, leads to a new and different understanding of the history of philosophy that makes political philosophy still possible.

Rather than one continuous, inexorable, and necessary development, Strauss argued, the writings that constitute the history of Western philosophy reveal a series of fundamental dichotomies or tensions—between ancients and moderns, reason and revelation, poets and philosophers. The difference between "ancient" and "modern" philosophers might appear to be chronological, if not historical; but, Strauss insisted, it is not. Some authors writing in modern times can and have adopted an "ancient" stance (Strauss 1952: 182; 1989a: 63–71; 1989b: 269) The difference between ancients and moderns fundamentally concerns the relation between theory and practice. Whereas the "ancients" (who include medieval philosophers such as Maimonides and Farabi) thought that politics or "practice" should be understood and evaluated in terms of its goal, allowing some rare individuals to live the best life possible (philosophy), "modern" philosophers such as Machiavelli and Bacon insisted that "theory" ought to justify itself by producing beneficial practical effects. The judges of the goodness of these effects would not be the few philosophers, moreover, but the many subjects or citizens of the political associations human beings necessarily form in order to preserve themselves, both individually and as a race. Likewise, the difference between reason and revelation might appear to be the opposition between science and faith, but, Strauss argued, the enduring question signified by the contrast between "Jerusalem and Athens" concerns the best form of human existence, whether it is the life of reason or of morality (Strauss 1983: 147–73; 1989b: 249–310).[8] The difference between the poets and the philosophers also concerns the question of the best possible form of human existence: is there any way of life that is truly satisfying? That question found its "classical" expression in the differences between Aristophanes and Plato, but, Strauss pointed out, it was raised again by Friedrich Nietzsche at the "end" of philosophy (Strauss 1989a).

"Far from legitimizing the historicist inference," Strauss concluded, "history seems rather to prove that all human thought, and certainly all philosophic thought, is concerned with the same fundamental themes or . . . problems." And, "if the fundamental problems persist in all historical change, human thought is capable of transcending its historical limitation or of grasping something trans-historical" (Strauss 1953: 23–4). By showing that there are "fundamental problems" that "persist in all historical change, however much they may be obscured by the temporary denial of

---

[8] In contemporary terms that Strauss never used, the contention is that philosophical "consequentialist," as opposed to "deontological," morality is not truly moral or, therefore, right.

their relevance and however variable or provisional all human solutions to these problems may be," Strauss thought he had demonstrated how "the human mind liberates itself from its historical limitations." He did not think that anything more was "needed to legitimize philosophy in its original, Socratic sense" (Strauss 1953: 32).

REFERENCES

DRURY, S. (1988). *The Political Ideas of Leo Strauss*. New York: St Martin's Press.

PANGLE, T. (2006). *Leo Strauss: An Introduction to his Thought and Intellectual Legacy*. Baltimore: Johns Hopkins University Press.

SMITH, S. (2006). *Reading Leo Strauss*. Chicago: University of Chicago Press.

STRAUSS, L. (1952). *Persecution and the Art of Writing*. New York: Free Press.

STRAUSS, L. (1953). *Natural Right and History*. Chicago: University of Chicago Press.

STRAUSS, L. (1959). *What Is Political Philosophy? And Other Studies*. Glencoe, IL: Free Press.

STRAUSS, L. (1963). How to Begin to Study *The Guide of the Perplexed*: Introductory essay to *The Guide of the Perplexed*, trans. Shlomo Pines. Chicago: University of Chicago Press.

STRAUSS, L. (1964). *The City and Man*. Chicago: Rand McNally.

STRAUSS, L. (1978). "Correspondence concerning *Wahrheit und Methode*," *Independent Journal of Philosophy*, 2: 5–12.

STRAUSS, L. (1979–80 [1959]). "An Unspoken Prologue to a Public Lecture at St John's College in Honor of Jacob Klein," *Interpretation: A Journal of Political Philosophy*, 8: 1–3.

STRAUSS, L. (1983). *Studies in Platonic Political Philosophy*, (ed.) Thomas L. Pangle. Chicago: University of Chicago Press.

STRAUSS, L. (1989a). *The Rebirth of Classical Political Rationalism*, (ed.) Thomas L. Pangle. Chicago: University of Chicago Press.

STRAUSS, L. (1989b). *An Introduction to Political Philosophy*, (ed.) Hilail Gildin. Detroit: Wayne State University Press.

STRAUSS, L. (1991). *On Tyranny*, (ed.) Victor Gourevitch and Michael Roth. New York: Free Press.

ZUCKERT, C., and ZUCKERT, M. (2006). *The Truth about Leo Strauss*. Chicago: University of Chicago Press.

CHAPTER 3

....

POSTMODERN APPROACHES TO THE HISTORY OF POLITICAL THOUGHT

....

JOSHUA FOA DIENSTAG

UNLIKE the other traditions of inquiry discussed in this volume, the perspective on the history of political thought described here cannot be readily identified with a self-conscious school of practitioners. Rather, what I call the postmodern approach to the history of political thought has evolved through the practices of a variety of theorists in both Europe and the USA since the 1950s. Although I will maintain that Friedrich Nietzsche's philosophy is the originating point of this movement, neither he nor any of the other theorists described here left any canonical statements of methods to compare with the works of Quentin Skinner or Leo Strauss. Furthermore, those who employ this frame of analysis often see themselves not primarily as historians but as political theorists whose examination of the history of theory plays a limited, if important, role in their intellectual enterprise. Terms such as "deconstruction," "genealogy," and "radical herme-neutics" are often used to describe these methods, and it will be the purpose of this chapter to identify the origin of these styles of interpretation and, insofar as it is possible, their common sources. In attempting to characterize a diverse set of scholars I will necessarily have to operate inductively and make vast generalizations. So much for excuses.

NIETZSCHEAN ORIGINS

....

Language and Consciousness

At the broadest level, the postmodern approach displays an acute sensitivity to the role of language in politics, and in political theory itself, that originates in the work of

Friedrich Nietzsche. While every historian of political thought will, of course, acknowledge the importance of language in some way, it is important to understand how attention to language was especially intensified in the wake of Nietzsche's philosophy. His perspective has several distinctive contours, all deriving from the central claim that "the development of language and the development of consciousness... go hand in hand" (Nietzsche 1974 [1884]: 299).[1] The identity of language and conscious thinking means that language is not something that represents the "substance" of a theory or mediates between that substance and something else. Instead, there are no general grounds for distinguishing between a theorist's ideas and the language used in their expression. But further, since "consciousness is really only a net of communication between human beings," the theorist's words, whatever her intentions, are not objects under any individual's full control (Nietzsche 1974 [1884]: 298). The structure and origins of language are irreducibly social. This means, first of all, that language originates neither in nature nor in the internal workings of a single mind. Whatever it is that words and sentences signify, therefore, they cannot take that signification immediately from nature or from the individual that employs them. Textual interpretation cannot proceed simply by correlating words directly with their natural referents or with the intentions of their author but must contain an analysis of their social status and significance.[2]

What form that analysis might take is, of course, highly debatable, as will be discussed below. If these points were controversial in Nietzsche's time, they are now, in the wake of Saussure, Wittgenstein, and ordinary-language philosophy, considerably less so. Nietzsche used them to target both a Romantic interpretation of texts as a direct result of individual inspiration and, on the other hand, a utilitarian or Social Darwinist approach to philosophy that made it into a sort of technology with which to manipulate the natural world. These tendencies still exist, of course, but they are much less pronounced among historians of political thought. Now, one might deploy these points against a certain kind of Straussian who insists that philosophy proper can speak directly of "first things" or, alternatively, against a certain kind of Skinnerian who believes the meaning of a text can be fully derived from the intentions of the author. The generic term "postmodern" thus indicates here not a historical method but only the rejection of the attempt to make the history of political thought into a science or an analogue of a science, via the means of either the natural sciences or the historical sciences. More positively, it indicates a desire to place the nexus of society-language-consciousness at the focal point of interpretative practice.

[1] I cannot give here, what would otherwise be desirable—namely, a full account of the various antecedent sources of Nietzsche's views including Kant, Schopenhauer, and, more generally, nineteenth-century philology, Romanticism, and hermeneutics, to name the most important. In using Nietzsche as a focal point here (as, indeed, he became for later generations), I do not mean to imply that he invented this perspective out of whole cloth.

[2] Of course, this point does not mean that our words have no relation to the natural world or to authorial intentions but simply that the relationship cannot be a direct or unmediated one.

Language and its Limits

A second consequence of Nietzsche's perspective is perhaps more unusual. Connected to Nietzsche's claim that language and consciousness are co-constitutive is the idea that, in themselves, they represent only a small fraction of human experience and, even, human thought: "the thinking that rises to consciousness is only the smallest part" (Nietzsche 1974 [1884]: 299). Human beings, after all, existed in some way or other for generations without language. Furthermore, what is left out of our linguistic expressions may in fact be more important than what is within them: "the world of which we can become conscious is a surface- and sign-world, a world of generalizations and suppositions" (Nietzsche 1974 [1884]: 299; translation modified). Nietzsche here makes two closely related points that bear importantly on textual interpretation: first, human beings are deeper than their language is capable of reflecting. We have desires, interests, drives, and even thoughts that are only refracted, imperfectly reflected, or not reflected at all in our speaking, writing, and conscious thinking. Any attempt we make at understanding either the individual or politics must take this into account. Before Freud, Nietzsche was already using the term "the unconscious" to refer to this mental congeries, although it is important not to reduce Nietzsche's description of it to Freud's (see, e.g., Nietzsche 1967 [1887/1908]: 84–7).

Second, though, just as language is an imperfect representation of the writer or speaker who produced it, so it is an imperfect representation of the world it attempts to describe. Here the problem is not psychological but simply pragmatic: language must work by means of genera, but the world is infinitely individualized. That is, language is not designed to reflect the world, or the person, in its immeasurable particularization; rather, it is designed to effect communication between individuals about a common world they inhabit. In order for words to function, they must abstract from that world. No two trees are identical in every respect; the word "tree" does not capture the individual characteristics of any particular tree, but rather abstracts from many chosen examples to indicate a set of objects with some common properties. "Tree" means whatever we agree the most salient characteristics of this category are, an agreement that might easily be modified over time. When Nietzsche called truth "a mobile army of metaphors, metonyms, anthropomorphisms, in short, a sum of human relations," it is this generic and socially pragmatic property of language that he points to (Nietzsche 1989: 250). This much, perhaps, many students of language will find unobjectionable, though its implications for political philosophy are not always readily acknowledged. In order to understand any text, we must know not only what it refers to but the abstractions, assumptions, and metaphors embedded in its means of referral.

Language and Power

What Nietzsche insists on emphasizing about this process of abstraction is that it is always in the service of some social function. Every word, we might say, exists for some communicative *purpose*. There is no neutral method of generalization that could create a language equally suitable for all endeavors or all perspectives. Objects do not naturally differentiate themselves into sets that stand ready for conceptualization; they are grouped and demarcated by some particular set of people for some particular aims. Values are embedded in every word, expression, metaphor, and even our grammar and syntax. This process does not take place in a power vacuum; no part of it is exempt from the relations of power (including, at times, equality) that structure every social system—hence the metaphorical "army" of metaphors.

Therefore, of any particle of language, it is always legitimate to ask: what social purpose was served by this form of description of the world? And, in what way was the creation of language in this form an exercise of power? If one considers that these questions apply not just to words like "tree" but also to "person," "good," and "equal," then it is clear how radically skeptical this approach must make us of the truth-claims of many political theory texts, especially (but certainly not exclusively) those in the liberal tradition. Postmodernism points toward a form of textual analysis that will attempt to uncover or at least be sensitive to the past exercises of power that shape our contemporary vocabulary and the vocabulary of whatever text we examine. The remnants of power that remain legible in a text might be an expression of the author—but the author might also be the means by which a set of social arrangements or practices ventriloquizes. For an individual to be truly the master of the language he uses is, from this perspective, a relative matter and the exceptional case.

So language, at best, systematically distorts and, at worst, actively misrepresents both the speaker and the represented. The richness and diversity of thought and experience in a single individual are incapable of being expressed by even the most poetic of self-descriptions. And, insofar as the speaker attempts to depict a political system outside his or her own mind, he or she must make use of generalizations and expressions that were also distorted by the power-laden social process that produced them.

From the perspective of the historian of political thought, however, these "distortions" may themselves be as important or significant as what it is that they obscure. For we cannot determine in advance what will interest us more in any text that confronts us, the individual contribution of the author, insofar as we can determine it, or the other information that the text encodes about the circumstances of its production. Foucault's famous account of the daily regimen of a juvenile prison, for example, analyzes not a personal theory of a nineteenth-century author, but the encoding of a set of widely held beliefs about justice, development, and the relations of mind and body (Foucault 1979: 6 ff.). The point of the inquiry is not to uncover the motives of the author, to assess the truth of the claims encountered in the text, or even to understand what change he was attempting to enact—but rather to understand how the language invoked was symptomatic of a way of looking at the world that a set of contemporaries shared.

Nietzsche's Example

This account of the social status of language and its relation, on the one hand, to power and, on the other, to consciousness, leads to two related prongs of interpretation that I will refer to as "literary" and "skeptical." The literary element of interpretation insists that political theory texts be read with all the techniques that we routinely deploy on works of literature—for example, attention to metaphor, narrative, voice, as well as the social and personal prejudices embedded in grammar and vocabulary. The skeptical element requires us to research the (often hidden and often discontinuous) histories that underlie past and present terms of discourse. One element of the postmodern approach, that is, emphasizes the subtleties of the text before us; the other emphasizes the suppressions and absences that are necessary to enable what is before us to appear in the first place. Both are on display in the example that follows in which Nietzsche, in *Beyond Good and Evil*, analyzes one of the most famous lines in the history of philosophy, Descartes' famous *cogito*:

> when I analyze the event expressed in the sentence "I think", I acquire a series of rash assertions which are difficult, perhaps impossible, to prove— for example, that it is *I* who thinks, that it has to be something at all which thinks, that thinking is an activity and operation on the part of an entity thought of as a cause, that an "I" exists, finally that what is designated by "thinking" has already been determined—that I *know* what thinking is . . . it is a falsification of the facts to say: the subject "I" is the condition of the predicate "think." *Something* thinks: but that this "something" is precisely that famous old "I" is, to put it mildly, only an assumption, an assertion, above all not an "immediate certainty." For even with this "something thinks" one has already gone too far: this "something" already contains an *interpretation* of the event and does not belong to the event itself. The inference here is in accordance with the habit of grammar. (Nietzsche 1973 [1886]: 28–9; translation modified)

Here Nietzsche demonstrates how Descartes's statement, which is presented as self-validating, in fact relies on the "habit of grammar" to make a dubious experience into a sentence of certainty. Just to use the word "think" with regard to an experience we have is to characterize and generalize it. How do we know what "thinking" is, as opposed to "willing" or "feeling" unless we have already made a set of judgments? More importantly, how do we know that this experience that Descartes reports with the word "think" has anything in common our own experiences? And, most important of all, leaping from the experience labeled "thinking" to the sentence "I think" requires that we assert a causal relation between a postulated "I" and its effect. But, looked at this way, it is clear that it is the subject–object structure of Western languages that is doing all of Descartes's work for him. "Therefore I am" is superfluous; the conclusion was assumed outright by the language of the speaker. The point here is not (principally) to indict Descartes for faulty reasoning, but to reveal just how much our reasoning is shaped by abstractions and habits of grammar and syntax that are foundational elements of our languages. The mistake is not really Descartes's—or it is only his in mistaking the generic term "thinking" for something to be fully equated both with his complicated internal experience and with our own.

Our language, furthermore, embeds the supposition that ours is fully and only a world of causality. As Nietzsche would be the first to admit, this supposition is eminently practical. It has proved to be extraordinarily helpful in coordinating our social activity. It is only when we use it in ways it was not designed for—in this case, to conduct an inquiry into fundamental ontology—that it leads us particularly astray. Thus, the analysis of Descartes's "mistake" leads to a better understanding of the specific pragmatic characteristics of language, but not to a deeper grasp of thinking or identity, the nature of which our language presupposes and thus occludes. The interpretation thus only begins with the surface meaning of the words. It proceeds to make sense of the text both with reference to the unspoken thoughts and feelings that motivate it and with the power that it both expresses and hides.

However exemplary Nietzsche's analysis here may be, the history of political thought was a small, if integral, element in his overall philosophical project. But his example stimulated succeeding generations that I will describe here, very schematically, as belonging to three groups: hermeneutics; genealogy; and deconstruction. All these bear, in certain respects, the intermediate influences of Heidegger and Freud, whose contributions I cannot discuss here. I would argue, in any case, that, as far as interpretative method goes, both served more as a means of transmission and expansion for fundamentally Nietzschean insights than as originators of their own techniques, however influential their *particular* interpretations (say of Greek philosophy in Heidegger's case) or *particular* theories (say of the mind in Freud's case) may have been with these later generations.

HERMENEUTICS

The emphasis on language can lead, as I mentioned above, to a variety of modes of inquiry, each balancing the literary and skeptical tendencies in a slightly different way. The hermeneutical approach developed at first by Heidegger and, more completely, by Hans-Georg Gadamer is perhaps the least alien to traditional students of the history of political thought. Indeed, Gadamer's emphasis on grasping the "horizon" of an older text can seem not too distant from the contextual historian's demand to place a text within the conceptual frame of its contemporaries. This is not exactly a mistake; it is part of Gadamer's practice to understand textual meaning through historical inquiry. But Gadamer's call for a "fusing of horizons" is considerably more far-reaching in intent and outcome than the practice of the contextual historian (thus earning it the name "radical hermeneutics").

Gadamer's approach begins from what he refers to as "the universality of the hermeneutical problem." Following Nietzsche, he argues that, "in all our knowledge of ourselves and in all our knowledge of the world, we are already encompassed by the language that is our own" (Gadamer 1976a: 62). That is, the historian cannot examine language as he would any other artifact; language belongs both to the subject and to the object of study. It unites them, but in such a way that the objectivity that we could aspire to with regard to physical objects is impossible with regard to texts. Furthermore, again following Nietzsche, "speaking does not belong in the sphere of the 'I' but in the sphere of the 'We'" (Gadamer 1976a: 65). That is, the language of neither the subject nor the object is their individual possession or characteristic but rather something they share with a language community of some kind.

Having emphasized the social character of language, Gadamer adds to it the idea, drawn from traditional hermeneutics, that "the actuality of speaking consists in the dialogue" (Gadamer 1976a: 66). By "dialogue" Gadamer means that every spoken or written word can be ultimately understood as an answer to a question. In order to make sense of any utterance, whether in ordinary conversation or in an ancient or sacred text, we must understand the question to which it is an answer. This may motivate us, in part, to understand the contemporary context in which a text is created. But Gadamer emphasizes as well a different point: if understanding is dialogic, then the meaning of any text *for us* will depend as much on the questions that *we* pose to it as it does on the intentions of its original author and the questions he or she was consciously answering.

Thus Gadamer opposes the traditional hermeneutical dictum that the ideal interpreter is one who has purged his mind of prejudgments, or prejudices. Experience itself, he insists, in a twist on the Kantian *a prioris*, would be impossible *without* prejudices: "Prejudices are biases of our openness to the world. They are simply conditions whereby we experience something—whereby what we encounter says something to us" (Gadamer 1976a: 9). In saying this, Gadamer is scarcely trying to defend a casual or careless approach to history—rather, he makes the point that no text or object can speak to us *until we pose some kind of question toward it*. That question, whatever it is, will always be motivated, in some sense, by a real concern we have, a concern that will derive (however indirectly) from our own position, interests, values, and so on—in other words, from our prejudices. Whatever these are, if we are examining a historical text, they will very likely be quite different from those of the author or his contemporaries.

So, while Gadamer does not object to, and indeed encourages, an understanding of contemporary context, the pure project of recovering original intentions is to him both impossible and empty: impossible, because discarding all our prejudices would end inquiry itself; and empty, because meaning can be created and sustained only by what he famously refers to as "the fusing of horizons"—that is the *joining* of concerns between those who question and answer, even when they are separated by many centuries. Although a contemporary reader might well misunderstand a text because his own prejudices have led him astray, this criticism cannot be leveled from a perspective that insists that meaning lies there on a page, pre-existing an interpreter's attempt to grasp it, and therefore that an interpreter can be graded, so to speak, depending on how close to the mark he came—a tendency one might well ascribe to the Skinnerian approach. Rather, understanding derives first from finding the concerns that we share with our dialogue-partner and then accurately measuring our differences on the basis of those commonalities.

Thus, while recognizing the possibility for distortion in language, Gadamer ultimately emphasizes the capacity of language—and the process of understanding—to join us together and, indeed, to create "solidarity." His approach therefore emphasizes what I have called the literary tendency and minimizes, without eliminating, the skeptical. He always assumes that reader and text can be bound together in a community of meaning, whatever the initial distance between them. This approach is perhaps most clearly on display in his studies of ancient philosophy and of Hegel (e.g. Gadamer 1976b, 1986) where he attempts to recover what he believes we can and do share with the various forms of idealism they represent, even though we live in a skeptical age.

DECONSTRUCTION

The opposite tendency, within postmodern theory, is to emphasize that skepticism and discontinuity. Jacques Derrida used the term "deconstruction" as a label for his own approach, and, although he never intended for this term to denote a "method" (and certainly not a historical method) in any strict sense, we can at least set out what this approach entails for the history of political thought.

Though Derrida shares the sense with other postmodern theorists that we are always within language and that therefore "there is nothing outside the text" (Derrida 1974: 158), he opposes the hermeneutic practice of discovering or presuming continuities and instead sought to focus on their opposite. Deconstruction emphasizes discontinuities both within texts and between texts and their readers. Nietzsche's insistence that the text is only a surface beneath which an entire world lurks can be seen reflected in Derrida's claim that "it is not contradictory to think *together* the *erased* and the *traced* of the trace" (Derrida 1982: 66). Every text, that is, is premised as much on what it erases and suppresses as on what it records—and the recording is, in effect, a recording of that erasure as much as of the substance presented on the surface. Thus Derrida proposed that texts be read as much for what they hide or hold back as what they reveal. For example, Heidegger's seeming deconstruction of metaphysics, Derrida claimed, though purporting to reject all Western thought since the pre-Socratics, nonetheless both relied on and hid a continuing "metaphysics of presence" that is itself distinctly Western (Derrida 1982: 63–4).

Rather than a seamless dialogue of question-and-answer then, deconstruction produces a dissonant oscillation between speech and silence or between the explicit and the unspoken or unspeakable, which Derrida often refers to as a "supplement." This approach is on clear display in Derrida's famous analysis of Rousseau in *Of Grammatology*, which focuses on the latter's heretofore little-read *Essay on the Origin of Languages*. "Speech and the consciousness of speech . . . are the phenomenon of an auto-affection lived as suppression of difference... *The Essay*... opposes speech to writing as presence to absence and liberty to servitude" (Derrida 1982: 166–8). Rousseau, on this account, anticipates the general point that Derrida is trying to make that our freedom is found not in the explicit dialogue between two parties, as Gadamer would have it, but in the oscillation between spoken surface and unspoken depth. Writing, from this perspective, accelerates a process of the petrification of speech that is already visible in the history of language that Rousseau began to trace in the eighteenth century. Texts of political theory thus display the results of suppressions that may well be beyond the intentions of their authors and initially invisible to the community of interpreters.

Of more consequence to historians of political thought, perhaps, are the sort of conclusions Derrida draws in his influential essay "Declarations of Independence." Here he confronts the well-known circularity of the American founding document—it appears both to authorize and to be authorized by a political community that it brings into being, to be "the producer and guarantor of its own signature" (Derrida 1986: 10). To Derrida, this "indispensable confusion" is not a flaw but rather something "*required to produce the sought-after effect*" (Derrida 1986: 9). Neither is it something exceptional but rather, as his understanding of language demonstrates, "an everyday occurrence" (Derrida 1986: 10). In other words, the oscillation so visibly on display in this text is something that, with a little effort, we can see occurring in everything that bears a "signature" or a claim to identity. Where Gadamer wants to identify a solidarity produced by language, Derrida, by contrast, wants to show how identity always hides, and indeed is based on, a discontinuity. Our texts of political theory, no less than our founding documents, betray this unsteadiness.

Although often misunderstood, Derrida's interest in the instability and discontinuity of texts is born of a desire not to render them meaningless but, on the contrary, to find, in these phenomena, the real individuality that lurks (and can be trapped) beneath the surface appearance of language, much as Nietzsche did. If we fail to do so, on his account, our study of the history of political thought (or literature or anything) will only contribute to its mortifying hold on us.

GENEALOGY

If there is anything distinctive about what I will call the "genealogical" approach and associate with Michel Foucault, it is that it seeks a balance between the literary and the skeptical tendencies that I have been describing as elements of the postmodern approach. When Foucault writes as a historian of ideas, he seeks to understand both the living community of discourse from which a particular political practice arose as well as the suppressed or hidden sources of these practices. This technique is clearly in use in *Discipline & Punish*, which traces the origin of modern liberalism through both a sort of heterodox intellectual history and an institutional history that Foucault insists is the hidden foundation for ideas with which we are already familiar. Combining the two produces (in a Nietzschean phrase) "a genealogy of the present scientifico-legal complex," which takes as a methodological precept that "power and knowledge directly imply one another . . . there is no power relation without the correlative constitution of a field of knowledge, nor any knowledge that does not presuppose and constitute at the same time power relations" (Foucault 1979: 23, 27).

One implication of this view is the idea that the languages of law, criminology, pedagogy, and social psychology, for example, are inseparable from the modern institutions (prisons, schools, and, in the end, societies) that they simultaneously study and administer. Ultimately, however, there are no fields of knowledge that are exempt from this dynamic, and the book culminates in a exploration of "panopticism" through the work of Jeremy Bentham, whose model prison is explored in relation to both the social practices that inspired it as well as the liberal philosophy for which it functioned as an unacknowledged supplement. Bentham's prison design illustrates exactly how the political instantiation of philosophy and power are coterminous, how an outlook that appears to be based on objectivity, openness, and fairness can conceal an exercise of domination so automatic that, like the power embedded in language, it can operate invisibly and without the conscious intentions of any individual: "the perfection of power should tend to render its actual exercise unnecessary" (Foucault 1979: 201).

The term "genealogy" has been adopted by a wide range of historians and theorists, and it is often used to mean almost any kind of "discourse analysis" that considers itself "critical." To my mind, however, the distinctive element of this mode of inquiry is its attempted combination of hermeneutic efforts to grasp language paradigms from which we are at historical remove with a more material history that reveals the social practices that operate in tandem with these paradigms—a combination not too far distant from the sort of philology-cum-history that Nietzsche urged philosophers to practice. While it is difficult to identify here a simple method that one could readily impart to students, it would be hard to deny that our understanding of liberalism, for example, has been profoundly changed by the attention Foucault has focused on the institutional apparatus with which it has been interwoven—an interweaving that is practically invisible from the standpoint of other scholarly approaches.

CONCLUSION

While postmodernism is nothing if not a congeries of method, I have attempted to argue here that these diverse approaches have, if not a unity, than at least common sources and overlapping themes. The combination of moral skepticism and literary hermeneutics that these authors display, in varying combinations, results, I have maintained, from the attitude toward language that was given its first complete statement by Nietzsche. The denaturalization of language that Nietzsche was the first fully to perform yielded an approach to historical interpretation that, in various instantiations, has guided postmodern theorists ever since.

While this is not the place to expand on the political and moral implications of this attitude, it is worth noting that Nietzsche's main complaint as a philologist was that previous generations of historians—lacking a critical perspective on the intimate relations of language, consciousness, and power—had failed to do their jobs properly, at the expense of a human capacity for individuality that he was zealous to defend. While they agree on little else, it is a complaint his intellectual descendants collectively continue to voice.

REFERENCES

DERRIDA, JACQUES (1974). *Of Grammatology*, trans. Gayatri Chakravorty Spivak Baltimore: Johns Hopkins University Press.

DERRIDA, JACQUES (1982). *Margins of Philosophy*, trans. Alan Bass. Chicago: University of Chicago Press.

DERRIDA, JACQUES (1986). "Declarations of Independence," *New Political Science*, 15: 7–15.

FOUCAULT, MICHEL (1979). *Discipline & Punish*, trans. Alan Sheridan. New York: Vintage Books.

GADAMER, HANS-GEORG (1976a). *Philosophical Hermeneutics*, trans. Linge David E. Berkeley and Los Angeles: University of California Press.

GADAMER, HANS-GEORG (1976b). *Hegel's Dialectic*, trans. P. Christopher Smith. New Haven: Yale University Press.

GADAMER, HANS-GEORG (1986). *The Idea of the Good in Platonic-Aristotelian Philosophy*, trans. P. Christopher Smith. New Haven: Yale University Press.

NIETZSCHE, FRIEDRICH (1967 [1887/1908]). *On the Genealogy of Morals and Ecce Homo*, trans. Walter Kaufmann. New York: Vintage Books.

NIETZSCHE, FRIEDRICH (1969 [1872/1888]). *The Birth of Tragedy and The Case of Wagner*, trans. Walter Kaufmann. New York: Vintage Book.

NIETZSCHE, FRIEDRICH (1973 [1886]). *Beyond Good and Evil*, trans. R. J. Hollingdale New York: Penguin Books.

NIETZSCHE, FRIEDRICH (1974 [1884]). *The Gay Science*, trans. Walter Kaufmann. New York: Vintage Books.

NIETZSCHE, FRIEDRICH (1989). *Friedrich Nietzsche on Rhetoric and Language*, trans. Sander L. Gilman, Carole Blair, and David J. Parent. Oxford: Oxford University Press.

CHAPTER 4

....

THE VALUE OF THE
HISTORY OF POLITICAL
PHILOSOPHY

....

TERENCE BALL

To ask, "What is the value of *x*?" presupposes several possibilities. One is that *x* has no value at all. Another is that the value of *x* is in dispute, with some claiming that *x* is valuable for various reasons and others that it is valuable for other, competing, and perhaps even incompatible reasons. As we shall see, questions about the value of the history of political philosophy have been answered in both of the aforementioned ways. Some have held that political philosophy—and, by implication, its history—is "dead" and of no value whatever, while others have held that it has value, but disagree over what its value consists of.

And so to ask, "What is the worth or value of the history of political philosophy?" turns out to be a rather complicated question with many competing answers. The answer(s) one gives depends to a very large degree on the approach one takes or the "school" of interpretation to which one belongs.[1] Some answer that it is intellectually and perhaps spiritually edifying to study the thoughts of Great Thinkers who wrote the Great Books that constitute the canon of Western political philosophy from Plato onward. Others answer that there are "perennial questions" and "timeless truths" to be found in classic works of political philosophy that speak to us still. Some answer that the historical study of political ideas is valuable inasmuch as it reveals how philosopher-ideologues have legitimized and promoted the interests of the dominant social class. Others answer that such study reveals the roots or origins of present-day political movements such as communism and fascism. And others reply that the value of studying the history of political philosophy resides in discovering that there are no

---

[1] For a more personal (and perhaps partisan) take on several of the issues discussed here, see Ball (1995).

timeless truths or perennial questions, only changing conditions that give rise to different sorts of political-philosophical reflection. Such disparate views of the value of the history of political philosophy, in short, stem from widely differing views of how to approach and understand this history—and, not least, how to interpret the meaning and significance of classic works.

I propose to proceed in the following way. First I shall consider the possibility that the history of political philosophy and its scholarly study are without value. After dispatching this rather philistine view I then go on to show how various approaches to interpretation assign very different value to the study of the history of political philosophy. I try to show that, whilst each of these approaches has its strengths and weaknesses, some are stronger than others.

THE "VALUE" OF HISTORY

Let us begin with the worst case: that (the study of) the history of political philosophy is without value. That is not to say that the subject matter is without *some* sort of value—for example, entertainment value (some people find the oddest things entertaining). What is meant by this assertion is, rather, that the study of the history of political philosophy does not advance our knowledge of politics (or at least present-day politics) in any appreciable or measurable way. As one prominent political scientist complained at the onset of the "behavioural revolution" in political science, "Political theory today is interested primarily in the history of ideas" (Easton 1953: 236; compare Dahl 1956). And this, allegedly, is a bad thing, if one wishes to develop a *scientific* theory (or theories) of political behaviour.

An argument in defence of this view goes something like this: If political science is to be a science after the fashion of physics or any of the other natural sciences, then there is no legitimate place for the history of earlier theorising. After all, aspiring physicists study physics, not the history of physics. One can be a very fine physicist but be utterly ignorant of the theories propounded by Thales and the Ionian nature philosophers, or by Aristotle in his *Physics* or by Galileo or Kepler or Newton or any other major figure in the history of the natural sciences. While the study the history of science might be an interesting distraction it would be quite irrelevant to current research and theorising. And, as in physics, so in political science: one need not study the theories of Plato or Locke in order to be a good political scientist; indeed, the time and effort spent in studying such thinkers would detract from research into, and theorising about, present-day politics.

An answer to such an argument might run as follows. Historically, modern political science derives from political philosophy (just as the modern natural sciences derive from "natural philosophy"). And political philosophy is in important ways a backward-looking enterprise. A very considerable part of its subject matter is its own history, which consists of classic works from Plato to Rawls. In this respect political theory is quite unlike (say) physics. During the behavioural revolution of the late 1950s to the early 1970s theorists agreed with behaviouralists that one can be a very fine physicist without ever having studied the history of physics. But the same simply cannot be said of political philosophy. A student of political philosophy must have read, reread, and reflected upon the works of Plato, Aristotle, Machiavelli, Hobbes, Locke, Rousseau, Marx, Mill, and many others if he or she is to be competent in their chosen vocation. But—and here's the rub—there is more than one way to read, interpret, and understand the works that comprise the tradition of political philosophy. Thus Straussians contend with Marxists, Cambridge "new historians" with both, feminists with sexist-patriarchal constructions and readings of the canon, and so on, through a rather long list.

COMPETING "SCHOOLS" OF INTERPRETATION

I want now briefly to canvass several important and influential approaches to the history of political philosophy. These are the "perennial problems," the Marxian, "ideological origins," Freudian, feminist, Straussian, postmodernist, and the Cambridge School. Each answers our question about the value of the history of political philosophy in its own distinct and distinctive way. In delineating and describing these schools as I do here I have constructed a series of ideal types, though not (I hope) caricatures, in order to reveal and highlight their respective approaches to the study of the history of political thought and thence their differing views of the value(s) of that study.

Perennial Problems

Consider first the "perennial problems" or "recurring questions" approach to the history of political philosophy. According to this view there is a fairly fixed and finite set of questions raised by political philosophers from Plato to the present (Tinder 1979; Bevir 1994). And this is because there exist a number of recurring problems—problems posed by political life and activity—available to be addressed by political thinkers. As George H. Sabine, author of the once enormously influential *A History of Political Theory* put it: "Political problems and situations are more or less alike from time to time and from place to place" (Sabine 1939: 4). These include the problem of authority: who has (or ought to have) it, and how is that authority justified or legitimated? And the problem of political obligation: why am I (or is anyone) obligated to obey officials and laws of the state? Are there limits beyond which I am not required to obey and, if so, where are they? Is resistance (active or passive) sometimes justifiable and, if so, under what conditions?[2] And so on. All the great political philosophers of the past have addressed at least some if not all of these perennial problems. Thus Plato, speaking

---

[2] See Klosko's Chapter 44, this volume.

through Socrates in the *Crito*, answers in one way, Locke in the *Second Treatise of Government* in another, and Henry David Thoreau in *Civil Disobedience* in yet another.

From the "perennial problems" perspective, it is fairly easy to assay the value of the history of political thought, for that history purportedly constitutes a more or less coherent story about theorists addressing and answering essentially the same set of questions. The student of that history benefits by being exposed to and apprised of different ways of addressing and thinking about these persistent and recurring problems. We see, for example, that Plato conceived of one's obligation to obey the state and its laws in familial terms: Socrates says that the laws are like his parents: they have brought him into the civic world, made him who and what he is; and he can no more disobey them than he could jump out of his own skin or over his own shadow. Locke, by contrast, frames the question in contractual terms: we are each of us parties to a social contract that sets the terms and limits of our obligations; if any party oversteps those bounds, the contract is void and the contracting parties have no further obligations. And Thoreau thinks of the issue in romantic-individualist terms: if obeying any particular law undermines or compromises my most authentic innermost self, then I am under no obligation to obey it and perhaps even have a duty to disobey. To inquire into and reflect upon these different ways of framing and addressing the perennial problem of political obligation is both edifying and enlightening. And therein lies a major part of the value of studying the history of political philosophy.

Another source of value lies in using the "great books" of the past to cast light on the problems of the present. This is decidedly *not* a matter of asking (say) "What would Locke think about humanitarian intervention in an increasingly globalized world?" or some such, but, rather, asking what a "Lockean" perspective might reveal and illuminate. That is, such an approach would infer or distil more general principles and/or precepts from that historically situated thinker and attempt to apply them to present-day problems, as, for example, Simmons (1992) does in the case of contemporary human rights.

Marxian Interpretation

Karl Marx (Marx and Engels 1947: 39) contended that "the ideas of the ruling class are in every epoch the ruling ideas." By this he meant that the dominant or mainstream ideas of any era are those that serve the interests of the dominant class, largely by legitimating its members' wealth, power, and pre-eminent position in society. So it should come as no surprise, Marxists say, that in slave-owning societies slavery is portrayed by philosophers and other thinkers as normal and natural: Aristotle said so in fourth-century BC Greece, as did George Fitzhugh and other apologists for Southern slavery before the American Civil War. Similarly, in societies with capitalist economies, capitalism is widely portrayed as the most normal, natural, and efficient way to organize and run an economy. Other alternatives, such as socialism, are typically portrayed negatively, as aberrant, abnormal, unnatural, unjust, and inefficient. Ideas—including those to be found in works of political philosophy—combine to form a more or less consistent set or system of ideas that Marx calls an "ideology,' the point and purpose of which is to lend legitimacy to rule by the dominant class. Thus ideologies serve as smokescreens, hiding horrific reality from a credulous public, and presenting a rosy albeit false picture of a society that treats all its members fairly, that rewards the deserving and punishes the undeserving, and that distributes valued goods in a just and equitable manner.

A Marxian history of political philosophy aims to get behind appearances, to uncover the reality it obscures, and to expose what Marx (Marx and Engels 1947: 30) calls "the *illusion of that epoch.*" Such histories have value insofar as they perform the function of "ideology-critique"—that is, penetrate the veil of illusion and bring us closer to unveiling and exposing a heretofore hidden socio-economic reality.

By way of example I might mention C. B. Macpherson's *The Political Theory of Possessive Individualism* (1962). By "possessive individualism" Macpherson means the political theory that serves to support and legitimize those mainstays of modern capitalism—economic self-interest and the institution of private property. He focuses on Hobbes and Locke, in particular, as ideologists of and apologists for early capitalism. Both become, on Macpherson's Marxian reading, extraordinarily clever propagandists for the newly emerging capitalist order of the seventeenth century. A more *political* reading of Hobbes and Locke—for example, the former's role in the Interregnum and the Engagement Controversy (Skinner 2002: vol. iii) and the latter's in the Exclusion Crisis (Dunn 1969, 1984; Tully 1980, 1993)—gives way to a *socio-economic* interpretation of their achievement (note: not necessarily their intentions, since an ideologist need not consciously intend to legitimize existing economic and power relations).

From a Marxian perspective the value of studying the history of political philosophy is that it allows us to penetrate the veils of ideological illusion constructed by earlier political thinkers. With the wisdom of hindsight (and with the aid of Marxian theory) we can see clearly how this was done and how the consciousness of a credulous working class was distorted or obfuscated to disserve its class interests. And, as in the past, so too in the present: there are amongst us ideological obfuscators and apologists who need to be exposed and criticized. To paraphrase Marx, the present is also history.

Ideological Origins: Assigning Credit and Blame

In the twentieth century several totalitarian regimes and ideologies—communism and fascism foremost amongst them—came to power. One important and influential approach to the history of political philosophy views these ideologies as rooted in the thinking of earlier political theorists from Plato onward. These earlier theories, when adapted and put into modern political practice, allegedly produced Hitler and the Holocaust, and Stalin and the Gulag. John Maynard Keynes put the point vividly when he wrote:

> The ideas of economists and political philosophers, both when they are right and when they are wrong, are more powerful than is commonly understood. Indeed the world is ruled by little else. Practical men, who believe themselves to be quite exempt from any intellectual influences, are usually the slaves of some defunct economist. Madmen in authority, who hear voices in the air, are distilling their frenzy from some academic scribbler of a few years back. (Keynes 1936: 383)

It is therefore important to detect and expose the philosophical "origins" or "roots" of modern totalitarianism by rereading and reinterpreting the writings of earlier "academic scribblers" in light of the latter-day "fruits" of their theorizing. What is Plato's perfect republic, ruled by a philosopher-king who employs censorship and "noble lies," if not a blueprint for a Soviet-style communist utopia ruled by a Lenin or a Stalin, or perhaps for a Nazi regime ruled by an infallible *Führer*, backed by propaganda and the Big Lie? Much the same might be said about Machiavelli's ruthless prince, or Hobbes's all-powerful Sovereign, or Rousseau's *Social Contract* featuring an almost god-like Legislator, the General Will, the idea that people might be "forced to be free," and the state-worship implicit in his *religion civile* (Barker 1951; Talmon 1952; Crocker 1968).

From this perspective the value of the history of political philosophy is that it allegedly enables us to identify the culprits responsible for the ills of our time. And these ills are supposedly philosophical in their origins; that is, they are due to the ideas in men's (and women's) heads, ideas acquired from earlier thinkers either directly or through some sort of indeterminate intellectual osmosis.

It is worth noting that several prominent twentieth-century philosophers wrote histories of (political) philosophy which aimed to identify predecessors who bore at least partial responsibility for the Holocaust and other horrors of the age. Writing during the Second World War, Bertrand Russell remarked that "At the present time Hitler is an outcome of Rousseau; Roosevelt and Churchill, of Locke" (Russell 1945: 685). This, and the example of Sir Karl Popper's *The Open Society and its Enemies*, suggests that first-rate philosophers can be third-rate historians of philosophy—and of political philosophy in particular.

Yet it is difficult if not impossible to assign any precise meaning to the assertion that a modern political actor can be an "outcome" (Russell) or "slave" (Keynes) of an earlier thinker. Presumably what is meant is that a philosophical predecessor formulated ideas that became the foundation of an ideology which, when put into practice, resulted in human misery and mass murder. But how might one go about establishing the truth of such a claim? Neither Russell nor Popper is clear on this score. Neither goes so far as to claim that Hitler had read Rousseau, or that Roosevelt and Churchill had read Locke. But even if they did, that does not suffice to establish that they accepted their words and works as scripture, unless of course they tell us so. But one can peruse the two almost-unreadable volumes of *Mein Kampf* or the interviews in *Hitlers Tischgespräche* without coming upon something like, "In my youth I was particularly impressed by the writings of Rousseau, and his *Social Contract* in particular. I was thrilled by the General Will, the Legislator, and the civil religion, all of which I and my fellow Nazis incorporated into our ideology . . . " But of course one finds no such smoking gun—not even a popgun—in the speeches, writings, or table talk of Hitler or any other modern dictator.[3]

"Straussian" Histories

Followers of the late Leo Strauss (1899–1973) contend that a canon of works by Plato and a handful of other authors contains the Whole Truth about politics, a Truth which is eternal, unchanging, and accessible only to the fortunate few. In this respect their approach bears at least a superficial resemblance to the "perennial problems" school. But the "Straussian" approach is rather less accessible than that conventional view. And this is because, on their view, gaining access to the Truth requires that one take a somewhat circuitous route and adopt a special way of reading and of interpreting works in the history of political philosophy.[4] A "Straussian" approach to the history of political philosophy also appears, in one important respect, to resemble that of the "ideological origins" approach. Both wish to trace the roots of modern maladies to their philosophical sources.

Strauss's and the Straussians' historical inquiries and textual interpretations attempt to trace the origins and diagnose if not cure the multiple maladies of modern liberalism, moral relativism, historicism, and scientism that together contribute to "the crisis of our time" (Strauss 1972). The present being bankrupt, students of political philosophy must look to the past for guidance; they must be historians but not "historicists." Historicism is the relativist doctrine that different ages have different, if not indeed incommensurable, *mentalités*, and outlooks; accordingly, we moderns can hardly hope to understand, much less learn from, Plato and other earlier thinkers. If one subscribes to such an historicist view, the history of political philosophy becomes a large and crowded cemetery instead of what it can and should be—a source of genuine knowledge and a reliable guide for the perplexed (Strauss 1959).

To acquire such knowledge and guidance requires that we decipher the "real" meaning of the messages encoded by authors fearful of persecution and wishing to communicate with *cognoscenti* through the ages (Strauss 1952). For philosophy is dangerous; to espouse its truths in public is to risk ridicule and incomprehension, or even persecution, by the *hoi polloi* (*vide* the trial and execution of Socrates). Accordingly, most of the great political philosophers have written two versions of their philosophy—an "exoteric" one meant for consumption by the uninitiated, and a deeper "esoteric" doctrine to be decoded and understood by

---

[3] Revealingly, Hitler had printed on the back of every National Socialist membership card a list of required readings (*Bücher, die jeder Nationalsozialist kennen müss*). Books by Rousseau and all other major political philosophers are notably absent. A German translation of Henry Ford's *The International Jew: The World's Foremost Problem* features prominently on that list of forty-one books. See Ryback (2008: 57).

[4] For a more detailed and nuanced discussion of Strauss's contribution, see Catherine Zuckert, Chapter 2, this volume.

those initiated into the mysteries. A "Straussian" interpretation involves reading between the lines of the written text, so as to reveal its "real," albeit hidden, meaning.

The history of political philosophy therefore has value only insofar as its key texts are read aright. If the historian is aware of and attuned to the deeper esoteric doctrines of Plato and his progeny, then his or her history will have value and be valuable; but if not, not.

Psychoanalytic Interpretation

Historians of political philosophy have attempted to psychoanalyze Machiavelli (Pitkin 1984), Edmund Burke (Kramnick 1977), Martin Luther (Erikson 1958), Mahatma Gandhi (Erikson 1969), and John Stuart Mill (Mazlish 1975), among others. In each instance, the historian attempts to put a political philosopher on the psychoanalytic couch to see what subliminal or unconscious motivations were at work in his or her philosophy. The alleged value of such an approach is that we are thereby enabled to understand the subconscious sources of such works as Mill's *On Liberty* and to limn the limits of a more rationalist explanation. Thus we can view *On Liberty* less as a work of liberal political theory than as a *cri de cœur* and a son's declaration of personal independence from a stern but well-meaning father (James Mill). This is not what Mill consciously intended; but he was led by unconscious desires to declare himself independent of his father and, some twenty-three years after his father's death, to justify his own independence and autonomy (Mazlish 1975: ch. 15).

Psychoanalytic interpretations tend to use the text as a series of clues about its author's mental state(s). This can of course be of value if what we wish to understand is the latter instead of the former. But textual interpretation is not the same thing as limning un- or sub-conscious authorial motivation. Perhaps because of this and other shortcomings psychoanalytic interpretations have largely fallen out of favour among historians of political philosophy.

Feminist Histories

A feminist sensibility injects a strong strain of scepticism into the study of a "canon" of "classic" works.[5] For, as Susan Okin observes, "the great tradition of political philosophy consists, generally speaking, of writings by men, for men, and about men" (Okin 1979: 5). To study this tradition from a feminist perspective is to be struck by the extent to which the civic and legal status of women was long considered to be a subject of little or no philosophical interest and therefore outside the purview of historians of political philosophy, most of whom have until recently been male (Hannah Arendt and Judith Shklar being notable exceptions that prove the rule).

---

[5] For a fuller account of feminism, see Nancy Hirschmann, Chapter 46, this volume.

From a feminist or gender-centred perspective, the value of the history of political philosophy resides in its disclosure of subtle and not-so-subtle forms of sexism lurking in classic texts from Aristotle's *Politics* to the present. For the most part, male theorists have marginalized women by placing them outside the public or civic sphere in which men move and act politically (Elshtain 1981). In the name of protecting the weak, male philosophers have lumped women with children and idiots, and have therefore accorded them decidedly few or none of the rights and obligations of full-fledged citizens. And nowhere are these nefarious moves more evident than in the so-called classics of political thought. Feminist historians attempt to expose and criticize the misogyny lurking in the works of Plato, Aristotle, Machiavelli, Hobbes, Locke, Rousseau, Bentham, Mill, and Marx, amongst many others. The public/private dichotomy and the concept of consent in liberal theory is a sham, the social contract a "fraternal" construct, and the modern welfare state a covertly patriarchal institution (Pateman 1989). Not only are misogyny and patriarchy present in the history of political thought; they can be found in histories of political thought written by males whose interpretations of (say) Locke reproduce the latter's sexism by failing to detect or criticize its presence (Pateman 1989: ch. 5).

But feminist histories of political philosophy do not merely attempt to find and name villains. Some feminist historians have also sought heroines—and heroes—who have championed the cause of women's rights and related causes. Melissa Butler claims to find the "liberal roots" of feminism in Locke's "attack on patriarchalism" (Butler 1991). Jeremy Bentham has been honoured as "the father of feminism" (Boralevi 1984: ch. 2) and John Stuart Mill as its "patron saint" (Williford 1975). Others have disputed what they regard as misguided hero-worship (Okin 1979: ch. 9; Pateman 1988, 1989). The difference between outright misogynists such as Aristotle and Rousseau and their more enlightened liberal kinsmen were merely matters of degree, not of kind.

Some feminist historians have argued that although Aristotle (for example) is by modern lights a misogynist his *Politics*, suitably (re)interpreted, holds out the prospect of an active and engaged civic feminism, or "citizenship with a feminist face" (Dietz 1985). This prospect is precluded, or at least dimmed considerably, by inadequate interpretations of Aristotle and others from whom feminists might yet learn something of value about politics and citizenship. A "more generous reading" of Aristotle and other male theorists may yield political insight and civic lessons that angry attacks blind us to (Dietz 1985: 29). If feminists are to learn and apply these lessons, they must engage in more nuanced textual analysis and historical interpretation. And therein lies the challenge—and the value—of the history of political philosophy from a feminist perspective.

Postmodernism

Postmodernists tend to eschew "histories" of political philosophy, favouring instead "genealogies" in something like Niezsche's sense in *The Genealogy of Morals*. The postmodern sensibility is not a single, stable thing.[6] There are, to simplify somewhat, two main versions of postmodernism. One derives largely from Nietzsche and Michel Foucault; another, from Jacques Derrida. Because space is short I shall briefly say something about the former while bypassing the latter.

A Foucauldian approach to interpretation seeks to expose and criticize the myriad ways in which human beings are "normalized" or made into "subjects"—that is, willing participants in their own subjugation (Foucault 1980). Historians (or rather geneal-ogists) focus on the ways in which earlier thinkers—Rousseau or Bentham, for example—contributed ideas to the *mentalité* that paved the way for the creation and legitimation of the modern surveillance society. And conversely, postmodernist interpreters look for earlier thinkers who challenged or questioned or undermined these ideas. This Foucaul-dian approach is well represented by William Connolly's *Political Theory and Modernity* (1988). Connolly begins by suggesting that one view, earlier thinkers as collegial con-temporaries residing down the hall from one's office. To read their works is like dropping by for a friendly chat (Connolly 1988: p. vii). (This is perhaps the amiably unbuttoned postmodern-egalitarian equivalent to Machiavelli's "entering the ancient courts of ancient men," but without the Florentine's somewhat stringent dress code.) The reader's questions are posed, and criticisms made, from the perspective of the present—that is, of "modernity" and the constitution of the modern "subject."

In light of these concerns Connolly proposes to reread the history of political thought in a new and presumably more fruitful way. This permits us to see who has contributed to or dissented from the project of modernity and the construction the modern surveillance society. A postmodernist rereading relocates and realigns earlier thinkers along altogether different axes. A postmodernist reading of the history (or genealogy) of political thought not only exposes heretofore unsuspected villains; it also reveals heroes who have dared to resist the pressures and processes of "normalization." Amongst the former are Hobbes and Rousseau. That the historical Rousseau was exceedingly critical of the historical Hobbes does not matter for genealogical purposes. For we can now see them as co-conspirators, each having extended "the gaze" ever more deeply into the inner recesses of the human psyche, thereby further subjugating modern men and women. Amongst the latter, the Marquis de Sade and Friedrich Nietzsche are particularly prominent. "We can," Connolly contends, "treat Sade as a dissident thinker whose positive formulations are designed to crack the foundations upon which the theories of Hobbes and Rousseau rest" (Connolly 1988: 73). Whether this design was consciously formulated and put into play by the aristocratic French pornographer is doubtful at best; but like other genealogists Connolly eschews any concern with authorial intentions. Postmodernists are not at all concerned with what John Dunn (1968) has termed the "historical identity" of works of political theory; nor are they concerned with the differences that earlier thinkers saw amongst themselves. Rousseau hardly saw himself as Hobbes's soulmate—quite the contrary, on Rousseau's own telling—but this does not deter Connolly from lumping these thinkers

---

[6] For more on postmodernism, see Joshua Dienstag, Chapter 3, this volume; see further Dews (2003).

together as fellow labourers on and contributors to a common "project." What may be bad history might yet prove to be illuminating genealogy.

From a postmodernist perspective the value of a genealogy of political philosophy is that it allows us to illuminate the present by superimposing our own contemporary concerns upon the past, and detect (or perhaps construct) heretofore unnoticed affinities between disparate thinkers and texts, and the bearing they might (not) have on our own "postmodern condition" (Lyotard 1984).

The Cambridge School

The Cambridge School of "new historians" has, since the 1960s, advanced a distinctive programme of historical research and textual interpretation. Because Bevir has described its history and tenets elsewhere in the present volume, I shall not repeat these here, save to say that the Cambridge historians view works of political theory as forms of political action, grasping the point or meaning of which requires that one recover the intentions of the actor/author and the linguistic resources and conventions available to him or her (Skinner 1969; 2002: vol. i). A work of political philosophy is itself a political act or intervention consisting of a series of interconnected actions with words—"speech-acts" in J. L. Austin's sense—that are intended to produce certain effects in the reader: to warn; to persuade; to criticize; to frighten; to encourage; to console, and so on. Most political philosophers have not been armchair philosophers engaged in abstract thinking; they have been political actors engaged in high-level propaganda and persuasion on behalf of one or another political cause: the critique (or defence) of democracy; the critique (or defence) of royal absolutism; likewise for religious toleration, resistance, and regicide, the French (or other) revolutions, capitalism, the emancipation of slaves and/or women, and so on, through a rather long list of political causes and campaigns. Textual interpretation is largely a matter of restoring a text to the historical context in which it was composed and the question(s) to which it was offered as an answer.

The value of this approach is that it restores works of *political* philosophy to their *political* contexts—that is, the situations in which they performed political tasks. As Skinner puts it, "even the most abstract works of political theory are never above the battle; they are always part of the battle itself" (Skinner 2008: p. xvi). Studying these works helps us better to understand how political philosophy and political philosophers can intervene in, and perchance change, politics itself.

References

BALL, TERENCE (1995). *Reappraising Political Theory: Revisionist Studies in the History of Political Thought.* Oxford: Oxford University Press.

BARKER, ERNEST (1951). *Essays on Government*. Oxford: Oxford University Press.

BEVIR, MARK (1994). "Are There Perennial Problems in Political Theory?" *Political Studies*, 42: 662–75.

BORALEVI, LEA CAMPOS (1984). *Bentham and the Oppressed*. Berlin: de Gruyter.

BUTLER, MELISSA A. (1991). "Early Liberal Roots of Feminism: John Locke and the Attack on Patriarchy," in Mary Lyndon Shanley and Carole Pateman (eds), *Feminist Interpretations and Political Theory*. University Park: Pennsylvania State University Press.

CONNOLLY, WILLIAM E. (1988). *Political Theory and Modernity*. Oxford: Oxford University Press.

CROCKER, LESTER G. (1968). *Rousseau's Social Contract*. Cleveland: Case Western Reserve University Press.

DAHL, ROBERT A. (1956). "Political Theory: Truth and Consequences," *World Politics*, 11: 89–102.

DEWS, PETER (2003). "Postmodernism: Pathologies of Modernity from Nietzsche to Foucault," in Terence Ball and Richard Bellamy (eds), *The Cambridge History of Twentieth-Century Political Thought*. Cambridge: Cambridge University Press, ch. 16.

DIETZ, MARY G. (1985). "Citizenship with a Feminist Face: The Problem with Maternal Thinking," *Political Theory*, 13: 19–37.

DUNN, JOHN (1968). "The Identity of the History of Ideas," *Philosophy* (Apr.), 85–104.

DUNN, JOHN (1969). *The Political Thought of John Locke*. Cambridge: Cambridge University Press.

DUNN, JOHN (1984). *Locke*. Oxford: Oxford University Press.

EASTON, DAVID (1953). *The Political System*. New York: Knopf.

ELSHTAIN, JEAN BETHKE (1981). *Public Man, Private Woman*. Princeton: Princeton University Press.

ERIKSON, ERIK (1958). *Young Man Luther*. New York: Norton.

ERIKSON, ERIK (1969). *Gandhi's Truth*. New York: Norton.

FOUCAULT, MICHEL (1980). *Power/Knowledge*, (ed.) Colin Gordon. New York: Pantheon.

KEYNES, JOHN MAYNARD (1936). *The General Theory of Employment, Interest, and Money*. New York: Harcourt, Brace & World.

KRAMNICK, ISAAC (1977). *The Rage of Edmund Burke*. New York: Basic Books.

LYOTARD, JEAN-FRANÇOIS (1984). *The Postmodern Condition: A Report on Knowledge*, trans. Geoff Bennington and Brian Massumi. Minneapolis: University of Minnesota Press.

MACPHERSON, C. B. (1962). *The Political Theory of Possessive Individualism*. Oxford: Oxford University Press.

MARX, KARL, and ENGELS, FRIEDRICH (1947). *The German Ideology*. New York: International Publishers.

MAZLISH, BRUCE (1975). *James and John Stuart Mill: Father and Son in the Nineteenth Century*. New York: Basic Books.

OKIN, SUSAN M. (1979). *Women in Western Political Thought*. Princeton: Princeton University Press.

PATEMAN, CAROLE (1988). *The Sexual Contract*. Stanford: Stanford University Press.

PATEMAN, CAROLE (1989). *The Disorder of Women*. Stanford: Stanford University Press.

PITKIN, HANNA FENICHEL (1984). *Fortune is a Woman: Gender and Politics in the Thought of Niccolo Machiavelli*. Berkeley and Los Angeles: University of California Press.

POPPER, KARL R. (1962 [1945]). *The Open Society and its Enemies*. 4th edn. 2 vols. New York: Harper and Row.

RUSSELL, BERTRAND (1945). *A History of Western Philosophy*. New York: Simon and Schuster.

RYBACK, TIMOTHY W. (2008). *Hitler's Private Library: The Books that Shaped his Life*. New York: Knopf.

SABINE, GEORGE H. (1939). "What is a Political Theory?" *Journal of Politics*, 1/1 (Feb.), 1–16.

SIMMONS, A. JOHN (1992). *The Lockean Theory of Rights*. Princeton: Princeton University Press.

SKINNER, QUENTIN (1969). "Meaning and Understanding in the History of Ideas," *History and Theory*, 8: 3–53. [Reprinted with other methodological essays in Tully (1989).]

SKINNER, QUENTIN (2002). *Visions of Politics*. Cambridge: Cambridge University Press, 3 vols, vol. i.

SKINNER, QUENTIN (2008). *Hobbes and Republican Liberty*. Cambridge: Cambridge University Press.

STRAUSS, LEO (1952). *Persecution and the Art of Writing*. Glencoe: Free Press.

STRAUSS, LEO (1959). *What is Political Philosophy?* Glencoe: Free Press.

STRAUSS, LEO (1972). "Political Philosophy and the Crisis of our Time," in George J. Graham and George W. Carey (eds), *The Post-Behavioral Era*. New York: David McKay.

TALMON, J. L. (1952). *The Origins of Totalitarian Democracy*. London: Secker & Warburg.

TINDER, GLENN E. (1979). *Political Thinking: The Perennial Questions*. 3rd edn. Boston: Little, Brown.

TULLY, JAMES (1980). *A Discourse on Property: John Locke and his Adversaries*. Cambridge: Cambridge University Press.

TULLY, JAMES (1989) (ed.), *Meaning and Context: Quentin Skinner and his Critics*. Princeton: Princeton University Press.

TULLY, JAMES (1993). *An Approach to Political Philosophy: Locke in Contexts*. Cambridge: Cambridge University Press.

WILLIFORD, MIRIAM (1975). "Bentham on the Rights of Women," *Journal of the History of Ideas*, 36: 167–76.

CHAPTER 5

....

HISTORY OF POLITICAL PHILOSOPHY AS A DISCIPLINE

....

JOHN GUNNELL

WHETHER one speaks of the study of the history of political philosophy, the history of political theory, or the history of political thought, the reference is typically to one basic scholarly genre. Although this body of scholarship is now the province of a distinctly interdisciplinary academic practice, bridging, and including, fields such as philosophy, history, and literary criticism, it is professionally largely the product of a subdiscipline located primarily in departments of political science, politics, or government. There are, however, depending on national context, philosophical perspective, and methodological orientation, significant variations in the practices associated with the genre (Castiglione and Hampsher-Monk 2001). As Stefan Collini has noted, "there is no single enterprise or entity corresponding to what in English-speaking countries has most often been called 'the history of political thought,'" and, in order to understand this field, it is necessary to look at particular "*intellectual* and *academic* cultures." More specifically, he suggested that, "if one is interested in the historical development of the 'history of political thought,' one is interested in an aspect or episode of the intellectual and institutional history of academic disciplines" (Collini 2001: 281, 283). As a specific, self-ascribed, and institutionally differentiated "academic discipline," however, this practice, despite its European intellectual roots and infusions and its subsequent dispersion and developmental diversity, was largely a creation of nineteenth-century American political science. Its evolution during at least the first half of the twentieth century was also principally in the context of this discipline. For example, Robert Wokler (2001) has noted that, even in England, from where so much innovative work in this area has emanated and where the nineteenth-century idea of a science of politics gained significant impetus (Collini, Winch, and Burrow 1983), "the birth and rise of the study of political thought as a genuinely academic discipline" was largely a "twentieth century" development. Any systematic account of the descent of this enterprise and its contemporary character must focus on the United States and on the history of American political science (Gunnell 1993; Ball 2001; Farr 2006).

In the United States, the emerging social sciences, during the nineteenth century, were primarily the confluence of three closely related tributaries: elements of academic moral philosophy, often inspired by Scottish Enlightenment thinkers and, for example, as taught by John Witherspoon at Princeton, devoted to purposes such as civic education; individuals such as William Graham Sumner, who, in his case, left the clergy for Yale to teach a scientific understanding of society and elicit the secret of social progress; and movements such as those represented in the American Social Science Association, which invoked the cognitive authority of science as they pursued a variety of causes from abolition to civil service reform. As these intellectual pursuits coalesced and were institutionalized, during the last quarter of the nineteenth century, in the modern university and became the basis of increasingly differentiated disciplines and professions, from economics to sociology, there were problems of demarcation and of establishing the autonomy of these nascent enterprises. Given the social purposes that defined these early fields, there was also the problem of their practical as well as cognitive relationship to their subject matter. These problems contributed to the appearance of a rhetorical discourse that functioned at two levels. It addressed issues within the academy regarding the identity of these fields, but it was also concerned with justifying the role of social science to society and to the world of politics and public policy from which these fields had in part sprung—and about, and to, which they still intended to speak.

Although it would be a mistake to seek a one-dimensional explanation for the origins of the study of the history of political thought, the practice of recounting the history of political ideas most distinctly began and functioned as a rhetorical discourse devoted both to vouchsafing the identity and pedigree of the emerging discipline of political science and to urging its practical significance. It was in many respects more a "politics of history" than a history of politics. The work of authors such as Aristotle, Locke, and Rousseau were already central texts in the late-eighteenth- and early nineteenth-century American college curriculum in moral philosophy (Haddow 1939). This iconic literature, which eventually became the core of a classic canon, was presented not only as the progenitor of the ideas embodied in American institutions but as containing principles that should be inculcated in citizens and political leaders. Although political science, as a distinct discipline, was, as Bernard Crick (1959) so famously put it, an "American science of politics," the person most reasonably credited as its "founder" was the German émigré Francis Lieber, who grafted liberal German philosophical history, as represented by individuals such as Johann Bluntschli (*Allgemeine Staatslehre* (1851)), onto the indigenous political dimension of American moral philosophy and established the concept of the state as the domain of political science. From the point of his earliest writing on the study of politics (Lieber 1835*a*, *b*), he situated the classic authors, from Plato onward, as central actors in a neo-Kantian/ Hegelian drama of political history that was the story of the state and its search for freedom. Lieber designated these luminaries as the predecessors of the field of study that he was attempting to institutionalize, and the history of politics and political ideas was presented chronologically as moving toward culmination in American self-government (Lieber 1853). The emerging academic study of politics was, as a whole, devoted to justifying American institutions as the realization of popular government, and the history of political thought provided a provenance for both the discipline and its subject matter.

This embryonic study of the history of political ideas changed significantly after the late-nineteenth-century professionalization of social science. Lieber's basic vision of political science was adopted, adapted, and perpetuated by individuals such as Theodore Woolsey at Yale and Herbert Baxter Adams at Johns Hopkins, but it was Lieber's successor at Colombia, John W. Burgess, and the latter's colleagues and students, who most fully institutionalized the discipline of political science, including both the theory of the state and the attending study of the classic texts. For these early political theorists, history was conceived and advertised as a science, and the story they told was once again a democratic meta-narrative. The history of political theory was often explicitly presented as the history of political science, ranging at least from Plato to Bentham (e.g. Pollock 1890), and the School of Political Science at Columbia, which Burgess claimed was best described as a "School of Political Thought," emphasized the combination of the disciplines of history and political science.

Although Burgess was a dedicated Hegelian and viewed the course of American history and the history of political thought in these terms, those, such as the historian William A. Dunning, to whom Burgess allotted the task of teaching what became explicitly designated as the history of political theory were more broadly grounded. Dunning acknowledged prototypical predecessors such as Pollock but also Robert Blakey (1855), who had, maybe more than any previous writer, contributed to the idea of a progressive classic canon as well as presenting it as a history of the "great science" of politics. Dunning also noted French and German efforts such as those of Paul Janet (*Histoire de la philosophie morale et politique: Dans l'antiquité et les temps modernes* (1858)) and Bluntschli, but he sought to surpass these works and identify the study of the history of political theory as a distinct intellectual endeavor and subfield of political science. Dunning's three volumes on *A History of Political Theories*, written over a period of two decades (1903–20), established the history of political theory as an academic literature and a specific element of the university curriculum. Although Dunning depreciated the attempts of many of his colleagues to bring scholarship to bear on political life, or at least was wary of the efficacy and propriety of political advocacy, he continued to emphasize the unity of theory and practice by stressing and elaborating the assumption that political theory was *in* politics as well as an academic historical discourse *about* politics. And he maintained that the history of political theory was, on the whole, a story of the successive transformations that manifested the progress of democratic ideas and institutions as well as the concomitant evolution of political and social science.

Dunning's work was in many ways paralleled by that of Westal Woodbury Willoughby at Hopkins, who maybe more than anyone else insisted on the centrality of political theory in the discipline of political science. Willoughby also emphasized the importance of theory in political life and, even more than Dunning, the immanence of political ideas in the context of political practice (1903). He was one of the principals in founding the American Political Science Association and in designating political theory as a formally recognized subfield, but his work was also a significant catalyst in the ideological and methodological transformation in early twentieth-century political science. He sought to assimilate the study of the history of political thought to a growing image of political science as an empirical discipline. He claimed that the history of political theory was a repository of concepts for scientific political inquiry. He also maintained that, only by establishing a more scientific professional identity, and detaching the discipline from the kind of overt (and conservative) partisanship that he noted in the work of individuals such as Burgess, could political science become politically effective. But, like many of those trained at Hopkins, Willoughby defended a much more progressive political vision than the founders of the Columbia School. A perspective similar to that of Willoughby was, however, embraced, and elaborated, by Charles Merriam and many of those amongst the younger generation at Columbia such as Charles Beard. Despite his ideological and methodological break with Burgess and Dunning, after leaving Columbia and moving to the University of Chicago, Merriam had begun his career teaching and writing, from their perspective, about the history of political theory, in both Europe and the United States (Merriam 1900, 1903). He, and others such as his student Harold Lasswell, continued to believe that political science and political practice could be bridged by citizen education and by gaining the ear of political elites, but, like Willoughby, he argued that these goals could be accomplished only if political science achieved a more authentic scientific status. Merriam (1925) was the impresario of a new vision of political inquiry that emphasized emulating the methods of natural science, but the history of political theory continued to flourish as both the story of democracy and an account of the evolution of political science, which was intended to speak both to the academy and to the public.

For the first quarter of the twentieth century, political theory, as a distinct element of political science, continued, despite the new emphasis on empiricism, to be dominated by studies of the history of political thought that solidified and extended the classic canon (e.g. Carlyle and Carlyle 1903; Figgis 1907; Merriam and Barnes 1924). What had also taken place, however, by the mid-1920s was an Americanization, and Anglicanization, of the literature. This was in part a function of the turn away from German philosophy after the First World War, but there was also greater intercourse with England and the influence of scholars such as Ernest Barker and A. D. Lindsay, but also James Bryce and Harold Laski, who spent significant periods in the United States. The strictly Hegelian elements that had characterized the American adaptation faded away, but the essential characteristics of the form, such as the relativity of ideas leavened by an idealist image of progress, persisted.

Although the crisis of democratic theory in political science, during the 1920s, ended with the demise of the theory of the state as an account of popular sovereignty based on the existence of a homogeneous American "people," and was replaced by a theory of democratic pluralism (Gunnell 2004), the study of the history of political theory continued to function as a justification for American democracy and as the history of political science (e.g. Gettell 1924; Murray 1925). Many continued to build upon Dunning's work, and, apart from William Yandell Elliott's pointed criticisms of the new science of politics and pluralist theory (1928), there was little indication of tension between the study of the history of political theory and the new "scientific" direction in political science. The political polarization of the globe in the 1930s and a growing inferiority complex about the articulation of liberal democracy as an ideology provided incentives for an even stronger image of the great tradition as the past of both American politics and political science. Works such as C. H. McIlwain's *The Growth of Political Thought in the West* (1932) did much to endorse the assumption that the classic works were pivotal elements in an actual historical tradition that was the source of American liberalism. Even G. E. G. Catlin, who had been one of the most vocal contributors to, and defenders of, the new science (1927) advocated by Merriam and the Chicago School and who had been a critic of historical studies, eventually enthusiastically embraced the idea of the "Grand Tradition," and the Pantheon of classic authors, as an account of both the development of democracy and "a Science of Politics" (1939).

Among the proliferating number of texts, during the 1930s and 1940s, that served to underwrite liberal democracy, as well as often the discipline devoted to studying it (e.g. Cook 1936; Watkins 1948; Elliott and McDonald 1949), George H. Sabine's *A History of Political Theory* (first published in 1937) became, during the next two decades, the most paradigmatic and authoritative. Although Sabine claimed that political ideas were relative to their context, depreciated the assumption that past political theory yielded ultimate "truth," and stressed the danger of all transcendental perspectives from natural law to Marxism, he sustained the image of progress in both ideas and institutions. He claimed that the logic of the experimental method, which lay at the heart of both science and liberal democracy, ultimately ensured their survival and doomed the aberrational absolutist lapses of what was by then understood as totalitarianism. Sabine's work in many respects underwrote the methodological and democratic values of political science, but by the time that he believed it necessary to confront directly the question of "What is Political Theory?" (1939), a significant challenge to this vision was on the horizon.

It is often assumed that the behavioral revolution in American political science, and its renewed and vigorous commitment to an empirical science of politics, involved a rejection of the history of political theory in favor of what it characterized as scientific theory. It was, however, at least in part, a radical change in the literature associated with history of political theory that instigated and sustained the behavioral movement. Between the late 1930s and early 1940s, a significant number of, mostly German, émigré scholars arrived in the United States and gravitated toward the field of political theory, in which, by the mid-1950s, they had produced a fundamental sea change. This group included, most notably, Leo Strauss, Hannah Arendt, and Eric Voegelin, as well as members of the Marxist-oriented Frankfurt School such as Herbert Marcuse, Max

Horkheimer, and Theodor Adorno. They were, in several respects, a philosophically and ideologically diverse group, but, despite their differences, they embraced some common principles and assumptions that were inimical to the American account of liberal democracy, the American science of politics, and the vision of historical progress. There were, however, some partisans in the United States, such as John Hallowell (1950), who aided in the penetration of the genre, and others, such as Sheldon Wolin, who in many respects built upon their work. By the early 1960s, with the publication of what many saw as the principal successors to Sabine's book— Wolin's *Politics and Vision* (1960) and Strauss and Cropsey's *History of Political Philosophy* (1963)—a basic intellectual shift had occurred. The quite sudden behavioralist depreciation of the study of the history of political theory (e.g. Easton 1951) was in large measure a consequence of the contemporary literature increasingly becoming a rhetoric that was now devoted to undermining rather than defending mainstream political science and its scientific vision as well as the pluralist theory of democracy that had become emblematic of the discipline and had been so authoritatively re-elaborated by individuals such as David Truman (1951) and Robert Dahl (1956). Easton's reference to the "decline of political theory" into "historicism" may have sounded like the complaints of individuals such as Strauss, but his concern was with what he considered to be the lack of significance for political science of the work of individuals such as Sabine and Dunning, who, by focusing on the past, had failed to inspire new and relevant value theory as well as a much needed theoretical advance in empirical science. When Easton published *The Political System* (1953), the same year as Strauss's *Natural Right and History*, it was clear that the shadow of émigré thought informed his worries about the depreciation of the scientific spirit in political science.

Despite their embrace of United States as a political sanctuary, the émigrés were nearly all deeply suspicious of certain aspects of liberal democracy and its philosophical premises, and particularly of the pluralist version, which, on the basis of their perception of Weimar politics, they tended to view as a potential threshold of totalitarianism. Both because of their experience in the German educational system and because of their political and theoretical assumptions, they depreciated empirical science and perceived it as in opposition to philosophy and history and even as an adjunct to modern materialism and totalitarianism. Many were influenced by the work of individuals such as Martin Heidegger, Oswald Spengler, Stephan George, Carl Schmitt, and other representatives of anti-modernist persuasions that informed their images of the "crisis of the West" and the "decline" of politics and political thought. Since they all tended to view relativism in its various manifestations as a precursor of political nihilism, they reacted negatively to American pragmatism and the outlook of individuals such as Sabine and, instead, subscribed to some version of transcendental and foundational philosophy. In short, they could not, in most respects, have been more at odds with the substantive content and purpose of the field of political theory as it had evolved in the United States. The form of this intellectual vessel and the idea of the tradition were, however, both more congenial and more consonant with their intellectual background.

The account of the "great tradition" of political thought, as reconstructed by many of these individuals (e.g. Marcuse 1941; Voegelin 1952; Arendt 1958; Strauss 1959; Horkheimer and Adorno 1972 [1947]), became a much more dramatic and structured tale but now one detailing and explaining the decline of modern politics and political thought. Authors such as Machiavelli were cast as romantic or demonic protagonists in a world-historical plot containing distinct points of beginning, transformation, and, even, end. The history of political theory, as the discipline's built-in Whig history of itself, was fundamentally transformed. The new synoptic account of the tradition that took shape after the Second World War still often included the story of political science, but it was now a tragic tale of its flaws and irrelevance (Storing 1962). At the same time, however, the narrative singled out the enterprise that Wolin labeled as the "vocation" of political theory (1969), which, in the form of normative and historical academic political theory, was presented as surviving modernity, standing in opposition to the contemporary scientific and apolitical science of politics, and, in varying degrees, promising the recovery of lost remnants of truth about politics. For Wolin, liberalism and its "sublimation of politics" were at the heart of a modern crisis and the decline of political theory, which were abetted by contemporary political science.

Debates and worries in the 1960s about whether the whole history of normative political thought represented in the canon had been based on a logical mistake, and consequently whether traditional political theory was "dead" (e.g. Laslett 1956), were largely the product of philosophical controversies about positivism and its depreciation of the validity of value claims. Even this discussion, however, assumed the existence of the tradition as a piece of historical reality. Wolin's account of the "vocation," like the images propagated by the émigrés, had, by the late 1960s, become the basis of an identity for an emerging professional enclave that, while still professionally attached to political science, was becoming increasingly intellectually distant. This invocation of the great tradition, now as the past of contemporary academic political theory rather than mainstream political science, was also once again conceived as a way of bridging the gap between academic and public discourse, but it was also in many ways the last major manifestation of the history of political theory as a rhetorical discourse. The study of the history of political theory was, in many respects, becoming simply another element in a highly pluralized world of academic specialization. During the 1970s, with the winding-down of the debate between behavioral political science and the various partisans of what came to termed "traditional political theory," both sides of the controversy became the object of more reflective internal scrutiny. The philosophical grounds of mainstream political science's idea of natural science, and the methods that it had claimed to embrace, were severely challenged, and the past philosophical grounds of the study of the history of political theory, both pre- and post-mid-century, were also criticized.

By this point, the genre had become most vulnerable at the core of its self-ascribed identity—*history*. It was criticized on the grounds that it was a discourse about the past that was in various ways inadequately "historical" with respect to both method and substance. Several scholars, although hardly agreeing completely either about alternatives or about the criteria of historicity and interpretation, advanced extended critiques arguing that the story of the tradition had become a mythical pseudo-historical epic (e.g. Gunnell 1979). Beginning in the late 1960s and early 1970s, there was, in effect, an intellectual rebellion within the theory and practice of the study of the history of political thought that subsequently came to define a significant portion of work in the field. This insurgency was, initially, primarily located in England and drew on the idealist tradition represented by R. G. Collingwood as well as on post-positivist work in philosophy. Scholars such as Quentin Skinner (e.g. 1969; 1978), James Tully (1988), J. G. A. Pocock (e.g. 1962, 1971, 1975), and John Dunn (1968) rejected what they characterized as *post hoc* philosophical and ideological renditions of past political thought in favor of what they claimed was an authentic historical recovery of the meaning of texts. This was to be accomplished in part by a careful reconstruction of their political and linguistic context, and a recovery of the actual intentions of the authors. As much as the classic literature had been studied, it had, they claimed, been approached in terms of, and encased in, a priori frameworks that often obscured both the actual political character of these texts and their potential relevance for the present.

Despite the growing popularity of arguments such as those of H. G. Gadamer (1975) and various strains of post-structuralism and postmodernism, which emphasized the inevitably perspectival character of historical interpretation, the "new historicism" maintained that it was possible to transcend varieties of philosophical and "presentist" history. They claimed that, by the application of a method that yielded an objective account of the past, there could be an authentic understanding of the texts, authors, and the actual traditions to which they belonged. One of the problems of the new historicism, however, was that it was forged in the crucible of the old historicism, whose purpose was, in several senses, political. To suggest, for example, as Skinner did, that "real history" would in the end be relevant for such things as a better theoretical understanding of the connection between thought and action or that it was not possible to address classic texts philosophically unless they were first understood historically, that is, in terms of their real context and intention, was eminently reasonable. The basic subject matter, however, although much expanded beyond the iconic literature, was still largely defined by works, such as those of Machiavelli, Hobbes, and Locke, that had been part of the traditional genre and had been selected to serve its purposes. The question was why, exactly, this material was still being studied apart from the fact that it was there.

There is reason to suggest, however, that the new historicism was the outgrowth not simply of ideological and philosophical abstemiousness but rather in part of the idea, which had been so central to past assumptions about a science of politics, that it is possible to be most effectively political by being apolitical. It might not be surprising that, once the scholarly credentials of this approach had been established, the political motif tended to resurface (e.g. Skinner 1998), but at the same time, as in the case of social science as a whole, increased academization often means "being deprived of its political character" (Hampsher-Monk and Castiglione 2001: 8; see also Hampsher-Monk 2001: 159, 168). Skinner's early work, for example, reflected his antipathy for arguments as ideologically diverse as those of C. B. Macpherson (1962) and Strauss, and his concerns extended beyond methodological issues. Similarly, Pocock's *The Machiavellian Moment* (1975) represented a "political" agenda, even though it may not have extended much beyond the para-politics associated with issues such as those involved in the debate about whether the origins of the American founding were republican or liberal. The concern was hardly that those criticized were simply poor historians. Many embraced the new historicism and practiced it paradigmatically, but in a manner colored by various political inclinations. Whatever the commitments of its founders, the new historicism, like the old historicism, was, in the end and in many ways, an ideologically equal opportunity form of scholarship.

Although the study of the history of political thought has today achieved something of the order of a disciplinary status, pivotal programs such as that of the Cambridge School (Kuper 2002) are hardly secure from criticism any more than work that continues to reflect the basic forms of analysis advanced by individuals such as Strauss. Many have pointed to problems such as the gap between methodological promise and practice and a tendency to emphasize context over text (Gunnell 1998), but there can be little doubt that, if judged on the basis of generally accepted scholarly criteria, this literature, broadly construed in terms of the work of both its founders and many of those who have shared its goals, is, as a body of knowledge, more credible than much of the earlier scholarship. Claims about the meaning of texts presented in the context of summary claims about the character and meaning of a tradition extending from Plato to NATO are necessarily more representative of agony than argument. This is not to say that the new historicism as manifest in the work of organizations such as the Conference for the Study of Political Thought and journals such as the *History of Political Thought* have gained a hegemonic character, but it is to say that they have at least become a significant dimension of the genre, increased methodological self-consciousness, and made it difficult for anyone to engage in this enterprise without fully confronting the issue of what it means to interpret a text and make a historical argument.

One obvious benchmark for distinguishing between earlier and more recent work might be a comparison of the treatment of authors such as Machiavelli and Hobbes before and after 1960 (e.g. Strauss 1936; Skinner 1996). It would be difficult to deny that in the last quarter of the twentieth century there was a measurable increase in our understanding of both the contexts and the texts associated with what has been conventionally designated as the history of political theory. Both the initiators of the concern with more careful historical research and the second generation of scholars who might reasonably be understood as associated with it produced significant substantive work as well as methodological sophistication, and the attitude engendered spilled over into various other aspects of political history and historiography. Certainly work such as that of Michel Foucault, which also, by the late 1960s, had a significant impact on the general field of political theory, began to have an impact on the genre. His genealogical and archeological approach to studies of the conjunction of discourse and power situated in relatively incommensurable "epochs" and "epistemes" can, at least categorically, be considered as part of the study of the history of political thought, and his structural approach certainly challenged the emphasis on the intention of authors represented by the Cambridge School as well as the search for "truths" that individuals such as Strauss believed were buried as far back as pre-Platonic thought. There are, however, strong grounds for suggesting that this work is in many respects closer to the rhetorical histories of an earlier period than to any fundamental application of criteria of historicity. The emphasis on recovering textual meaning by placing texts in context and invoking authorial intention has more recently received a challenge from those embracing the application of new techniques of literary interpretation, including what are often labeled as deconstructive readings inspired by the work of individuals such as Jacques Derrida, which, in seeking to elicit meaning from discourse analysis, give much more detailed attention to textual intricacies and form than to social and political contexts. One might suggest that the continental impact on the genre, which was so fundamentally eclipsed between 1920 and 1950, has once again become a vital part of the dialogue.

There can be little doubt that, as a genre, the history of political thought will in many respects remain, and properly so, a vehicle of political commentary, and even a mode of apology, for a wide range of contemporary normative concerns, such as those, for example, associated with feminist political theory, post-colonialism, and varieties of democratic political philosophy. What makes a classic work classic (Condren 1985) may be in part a matter of historical evolutionary accident, but there is reason to suggest that many of the works comprising the canon are the product of some of the most creative minds that have engaged the subject of politics. And intellectual intercourse with such work inspires further creativity. At the same time, however, enhanced historiographical reflection suggests that claims that are arguable and based on defensible criteria of scholarship are more practically effective than mythical and rhetorical accounts that once dominated the study of the history of political thought.

REFERENCES

ARENDT, HANNAH (1958). *The Human Condition*. New York: Doubleday.

BALL, TERENCE (2001). "Discordant Voices: American Histories of Political Thought," in Dario Castiglione and Iain Hampsher-Monk (eds), *The History of Political Thought in National Context*. Cambridge: Cambridge University Press, 7–173.

BLAKEY, ROBERT (1855). *History of Political Literature from the Earliest Times*. London: Richard Bentley.

CARLYLE, R. W., and CARLYLE, A. J. (1903). *A History of Medieval Theory in the West*. New York: Putnam's.

CASTIGLIONE, DARIO, and HAMPSHER-MONK, IAIN (2001) (eds). *The History of Political Thought in National Context*. Cambridge: Cambridge University Press.

CATLIN, G. E. G. (1927). *The Science and Method of Politics*. New York: Knopf.

CATLIN, G. E. G. (1939). *The Story of the Political Philosophers*. New York: Mcgraw-Hill.

COLLINI, STEFAN (2001). "Postscript: Disciplines, Canons, and Publics: The History of 'the History of Political Thought,' in Comparative Perspective," in Dario Castiglione and Iain Hampsher-Monk (eds), *The History of Political Thought in National Context*. Cambridge: Cambridge University Press, 280–302.

COLLINI, STEFAN, WINCH, DONALD, and BURROW, JOHN (1983). *That Noble Science of Politics: A Study in Nineteenth Century Intellectual History*. Cambridge: Cambridge University Press.

CONDREN, CONAL (1985). *The Study and Appraisal of the Classic Texts: An Essay on Political Theory, its Inheritance, and the History of Ideas*. Princeton: Princeton University Press.

COOK, THOMAS (1936). *History of Political Philosophy from Plato to Burke*. New York: Prentice-Hall.

CRICK, BERNARD (1959). *The American Science of Politics: Its Origins and Conditions*. Berkeley and Los Angeles: University of California Press.

DAHL, ROBERT (1956). *Preface to Democratic Theory*. Chicago: University of Chicago Press.

DUNN, JOHN (1968). "The Identity of the History of Ideas," *Philosophy*, 48: 85–104.

DUNNING, WILLIAM A. (1902). *A History of Political Theories: Ancient and Medieval*. New York: Macmillan.

DUNNING, WILLIAM A. (1905). *A History of Political Theories, from Luther to Montesquieu*. New York: Macmillan.

DUNNING, WILLIAM A. (1920). *A History of Political Theories, From Rousseau to Spencer*. New York: Macmillan.

EASTON, DAVID (1951). "The Decline of Modern Political Theory," *Journal of Politics*, 13 (Feb.): 36–58.

EASTON, DAVID (1953). *The Political System: An Enquiry into the State of Political Science*. New York: Knopf.

ELLIOTT, WILLIAM YANDELL (1928). *The Pragmatic Revolt in Politics: Syndicalism, Fascism, and the Constitutional State*. New York: Macmillan.

ELLIOTT, WILLIAM Y., and McDONALD, NEIL A. (1949). *Western Political Heritage*. Englewood-Cliffs: Prentice Hall.

FARR, JAMES (2006). "The History of Political Thought, as Disciplinary Genre," in John Dryzek, Bonnie Honig, and Anne Philips (eds), *Oxford Handbook of Political Theory*. Olxford: Oxford University Press.

FIGGIS, JOHN NEVILLE (1907). *Political Thought from Gerson to Grotius*. Cambridge: Cambridge University Press.

GADAMER. H. -G. (1975). *Truth and Method*. New York: Seabury.

GETTELL, RAYMOND. G. (1924). *History of Poltical Thought*. New York: Century.

GUNNELL, JOHN G. (1979). *Political Theory: Tradition and Interpretation*. Cambridge: Winthrop.

GUNNELL, JOHN G. (1993). *The Descent of Political Theory: The Genealogy of an American Vocation*. Chicago: University of Chicago Press.

GUNNELL, JOHN G. (1998). *The Orders of Discourse: Philosophy, Social Science, and Politics*. Lapham: Rowman and Littlefield.

GUNNELL, JOHN G. (2004). *Imagining the American Polity: Political Science and the Discourse of Democracy*. University Park: Pennsylvania State University Press.

HADDOW, ANNA (1939). *Political Science in American Colleges and Universities, 1636–1900*. New York: D. Appleton-Century.

HALLOWELL, JOHN (1950). *Main Currents in Modern Political Thought*. New York: Holt, Rinehart and Winston.

HAMPSHER-MONK, IAIN (2001). "History of Political Thought and the Political History of Thought," in Dario Castiglione and Iain Hampsher-Monk (eds), *The History of Political Thought in National Context*. Cambridge: Cambridge University Press, 159–74.

HAMPSHER-MONK, IAIN, and CASTIGLIONE, DARIO (2001). "Introduction: The History of Political Thought and the National Discourses of Politics," in Dario Castiglione and Iain Hampsher-Monk (eds), *The History of Political Thought in National Context*. Cambridge: Cambridge University Press, 1–9.

HORKHEIMER, MAX, and ADORNO, THEODOR (1972 [1947]). *Dialectic of Enlightenment*. New York: Herder and Herder.

KUPER, ANDREW. (2002). "Political Philosophy: The View from Cambridge," *Journal of Political Philosophy*, 30: 1–19.

LASLETT, PETER (1956) (ed.). *Philosophy, Politics and Society*. 1st ser. New York: Macmillan.

LIEBER, FRANCIS (1835a). *Encyclopedia Americana*, vol. x. Philadelphia: Desilver.

LIEBER, FRANCIS (1835b). *Manual of Political Ethics*. Philadelphia: Lippincott.

LIEBER, FRANCIS (1853). *Civil Liberty and Self-Government*. Philadelphia: Lippincott.

MCILWAIN, CHARLES HOWARD (1932). *The Growth of Political Thought in the West*. New York: Macmillan.

MACPHERSON, C. B. (1962). *The Political Theory of Possessive Individualism: Hobbes to Locke*. Oxford: Oxford University Press.

MARCUSE, HERBERT (1941). *Reason and Revolution*. New York: Humanities Press.

MERRIAM, CHARLES (1900). *History of the Theory of Sovereignty since Rousseau*. New York: Columbia University Press.

MERRIAM, CHARLES (1903). *A History of American Political Theories*. New York: Macmillan.

MERRIAM, CHARLES EDWARD (1925). *New Aspects of Politics*. Chicago: University of Chicago Press.

MERRIAM, CHARLES EDWARD, and BARNES, HARRY ELMER (1924) (eds). *A History of Political Theories: Recent Times*. New York: Macmillan.

MURRAY, ROBERT H. (1925). *A History of Political Science from Plato to the Present*. New York: D. Appleton.

POCOCK, J. G. A. (1962). "The History of Political Thought: A Methodological Inquiry," in Peter Laslett and W. G. Runciman (eds), *Philosophy, Politics and Society*, 2nd ser. New York: Barnes and Noble.

POCOCK, J. G. A. (1971). *Politics, Language and Time*. New York: Atheneum.

POCOCK, J. G. A. (1975). *The Machiavellian Moment: Florentine Political Thought and the Atlantic Republican Tradition*. Princeton: Princeton University Press.

POLLOCK, FREDERICK (1890). *An Introduction to the History of the Science of Politics*. London: Macmillan.

SABINE, GEORGE H. (1937). *A History Political Theory*. New York: Holt, Rinehart and Winston.

SABINE, GEORGE H. (1939). "What is Political Theory?" *Journal of Politics*, 1: 1–16.

SKINNER, QUENTIN (1969). "Meaning and Understanding in the History of Ideas," *History and Theory*, 8: 3–53.

SKINNER, QUENTIN (1978). *The Foundations of Modern Political Thought*. New York: Cambridge University Press.

SKINNER, QUENTIN (1996). *Reason and Rhetoric in the Philosophy of Thomas Hobbes*. New York: Cambridge University Press.

SKINNER, QUENTIN (1998). *Liberty before Liberalism*. Cambridge. Cambridge University Press.

STORING, HERBERT J. (1962) (ed.). *Essays on the Scientific Study of Politics*. New York: Holt, Rinehart and Winston.

STRAUSS, LEO (1936). *The Political Philosopy of Hobbes: Its Basis and its Genesis*. Oxford: Clarendon Press.

STRAUSS, LEO (1952). *The Political Philosophy of Hobbes*. Chicago: University of Chicago Press.

STRAUSS, LEO (1953). *Natural Right and History*. Chicago: University of Chicago Press.

STRAUSS, LEO (1959). *What is Political Philosophy?* Glencoe: Free Press.

STRAUSS, LEO, and CROPSEY, JOSEPH (1963) (eds). *History of Political Philosophy*. Chicago: Rand, McNally.

TRUMAN, DAVID (1951). *The Governmental Process*. New York: Knopf.

TULLY, JAMES. (1988) (ed.). *Meaning and Context: Quentin Skinner and his Critics*. Princeton: Princeton University Press.

VOEGELIN, ERIC (1952). *The New Science of Politics*. Chicago: University of Chicago Press.

WATKINS, FREDERICK (1948). *The Political Tradition of the West: A Study of the Development of Modern Liberalism*. Cambridge: Harvard University Press.

WILLOUGHBY, W. W. (1903). *Political Theories of the Ancient World*. New York: Longmans, Green.

WOKLER, ROBERT (2001). "The Professiorate of Political Thought in England since 1914: A Tale of Two Chairs," in Dario Castiglione and Iain Hampsher-Monk (eds), *The History of Political Thought in National Context*. Cambridge: Cambridge University Press, 134–58.

WOLIN, SHELDON S. (1960). *Politics and Vision*. Boston: Little, Brown.

WOLIN, SHELDON S. (1969). "Political Theory as a Vocation," *American Political Science Review* 62: 6–82.

PART II

CHRONOLOGICAL PERIODS

CHAPTER 6

....

THE ORIGINS OF
POLITICAL PHILOSOPHY

....

DANIELLE ALLEN

POLITICAL PHILOSOPHY: THE ORIGINS
....

"POLITICAL philosophy" betrays by its name that its origins lie in Greece. Both words, "political," and "philosophy," derive from ancient Greek. "Philosophy" comes, of course, from *philia* or "love" and *sophia* or "wisdom," which, taken together, indicate the love of wisdom. "Political" derives from the adjective *politikos*, which means "belonging or pertaining to the *polis*." But what was a *polis*? Typically translated as city or city state, a *polis* was distinguished from other types of community by the presence of distinct activities, among them commercial exchange, judicial proceedings, and public deliberation.

Hellenic settlement began on the Aegean islands and the Greek mainland in the third millennium BCE. Fortified settlements, built around royal palaces and meant to fend off attacks of marauding pirates or competing communities, date to the middle of the second millennium BCE. The urban settlements that came to be called *poleis* date to some time around 1000 BCE; they were generally built around an *agora* or marketplace. The *agora* was indeed a place for exchanging the products of agriculture, craft, and trade, but not only this. *Agora* derives from the verb *ageirô*, which means "to gather," and itself generates the verb *agoreuô*, which means "to speak." In the marketplace, community leaders—tribal kings or princes, or priests, or elders renowned for their oratory and practical reason—gathered to dispense advice and adjudicate disputes. When they did their job well, achieving justice, they were said to "speak straightly." And when the community was faced with some threat to its survival or other challenge, community leaders assembled in this communal space to deliberate the question "What shall we do?" The *agora* was the place for the kinds of speech that characterized the shared life of the *polis*: judicial plaints; judgments; and deliberation.

Our earliest literary accounts of the judicial and deliberative activities of the market-place appear not in philosophical treatises but in poems: the Homeric epics, the *Iliad* and the *Odyssey*; and a didactic poem, the *Works and Days* by Hesiod. The *Iliad* and *Odyssey* are often attributed to an unidentified poet named Homer but are quite probably (particularly in the case of the *Iliad*) the final versions of poems that developed out of oral storytelling traditions. The *Iliad* is usually dated to the late eighth century BCE and the *Odyssey* to the early seventh century; they represent life in Mycenean Greece of the second millennium BCE, but commingle details from their own time. Hesiod lived in Boeotia in the late eighth century; he purports to describe his own time and place.

A famous passage from the *Iliad* captures the nature of the early *agora*. In Book 18 (lines 478–608), the god Hephaestus is charged with fashioning new armor for the great Greek warrior Achilles, who is about to return to the battlefield against the Trojans (of Asia Minor). The divine blacksmith fashions superlative armor, working onto the shield a glorious picture of the whole world, complete with a representation of two particularly fine human cities or *poleis*.

> And he forged on the shield two noble cities [*poleis*] filled with mortal men. With weddings and wedding feasts in one and under glowing torches they brought forth the brides . . . while choir on choir the wedding song rose high and the young men came dancing . . . And the people massed, streaming into the marketplace [*laoi d'ein agorê esan athrooi*] where a quarrel had broken out and two men struggled over the blood-price for a kinsman just murdered. One declaimed in public, vowing payment in full—the other spurned him, he would not take a thing—so both men pressed for a judge to cut the knot. The crowd cheered on both, they took both sides, but heralds held them back as the city elders sat on polished stone benches, forming the sacred circle, grasping in hand the staffs of the clear-voiced heralds, and each leapt to his feet to plead the case in turn. Two bars of solid gold shone on the ground before them, a prize for him who spoke straightest. But circling the other city camped a divided army gleaming in battle-gear, and two plans split their ranks: to plunder the city or share the riches with its people . . . But the people were not surrendering, not at all. They armed for a raid, hoping to break the siege . . . (*Iliad* 18.490–514)

Scholars have long debated the content of the legal procedures described in the first city, but the important point here is that a perfect (or at least divine) representation of a *polis* identified that community by reference to marriage, music, adjudication, war and self-defense, and deliberation over the distribution of material goods. These are the activities, then, that Hellenic culture at its origins identified as belonging to the *polis*—in short, as political.

But, if the origins of the concept "the political" lie in the *polis* itself, what about the concept "philosophy"? The noun *philosophos* for "philosopher" does not appear in writing prior to Plato's dialogues. As for *philosophia*, this word appears once in the corpus of the medical writer Hippocrates, before Plato establishes the term as a keyword in Greek literature, insisting that the name *philosophia* be applied very specifically to a new sort of activity invented by his teacher, Socrates. Does this mean that political philosophy did not exist before Socrates? This question is also much debated. The answer depends finally on what one means by "philosophy." The historian Herodotus gives us a hint. We find the first instance of the verb *philosopheô* in his text; he uses it to describe the activity of Solon (*c.*638–*c.*558), typically identified as one of the Seven Sages or wise men of antiquity and the founder of Athenian democracy. Indeed many thinkers, for whom politics was a prime concern, lived and wrote before Plato. In addition to Solon, they include Drako (*c.*621 BCE), the author of the earliest Athenian law code; Herodotus himself (*c.*485 to post 425), the father of history, who wrote an account of the Persian Wars, in which the Greek cities, led principally by Athens and Sparta, defeated an expansive Persian Empire; the Athenian dramatists, Aeschylus (525–456), Sophocles (496–406), Euripides (*c.*485–*c.*406), and Aristophanes (*c.*446–*c.*386); Thucydides (460/455–*c.*404), the author of *The Peloponnesian War*; sophists and teachers of rhetoric like Protagoras (*c.*485–?), Gorgias (*c.*480–375), Prodicus (*c.*470–post 400), and Hippias (mid-fifth century–?); politicians and rhetoricians like Pericles (495–429), Antiphon (480–411) and Lysias (*c.*445–*c.*380); and Presocratic philosophers such as Heraclitus (late sixth–early fifth centuries) and Democritus (*c.*460–380). Although this list of thinkers includes figures who wrote in verse (for instance, Solon and the dramatists) or aphorisms (Heraclitus), it also includes some who wrote in prose (for instance, Herodotus, Thucydides, Gorgias, and Lysias), and even some who wrote treatises such as "On Truth" and "On Concord" (Antiphon). Notably, these thinkers devoted significant intellectual energy to questions generated by Athens, which means to questions provoked by democracy.

Democractic politics does generate distinct intellectual problems. There is a sense in which democracy requires every citizen to be a political theorist, since democratic political life requires of citizens an intellectual capacity to master and trade in abstractions. The word "democracy," of course, means "rule by the people." The *dêmos*, or people, holds the power, or *kratos*. But who is this "people" that rules? Where is this "people"? We cannot point to any concrete object that actually is "the people." In contrast, in a monarchy one can point to the queen and say, "There she is, the queen who rules." In the latter situation, ruling itself is not an abstract idea. One can watch a queen give a command and see it followed by a soldier or minister and one thereby acquires the idea of rule. But how does one understand the activity of a "rule" carried out by an actor one cannot see, nor even summon to the mind's eye with an image of some kind? One can understand such rule only through abstractions. Among those needed to understand democracy are "rule of the people," "equality before the law," the principle that majority votes are decisive, and some concept like "rights." As we will see, such concepts emerged in the texts of the thinkers listed above, as did the capacity to analyze politics in abstract terms.

The origins of political philosophy lie simply in traditions of wisdom literature consisting substantially of advice to kings, but the pressure on wise advisors—Solon is an example—to counsel specifically democratic leaders and citizens forced the emergence of a more abstract vocabulary. We might, therefore, identify the origins of political philosophy as lying in the conversion of traditions of wisdom literature, under the pressure of the needs of democracy, into analytical accounts of politics that relied increasingly on an abstract and systematic conceptual vocabulary. And, if this seems a reasonable way to describe the origins of political philosophy, then we can pinpoint its birth in Herodotus' *Histories*.

HERODOTUS AND THE BIRTH OF
POLITICAL PHILOSOPHY

Justice, or *dikê* in Greek, is an old concept, dating to the earliest written texts, Homer and Hesiod. All cultures invent some concept like it. But it is not always the case that the concept of justice is then followed by the development of an abstract, conceptual vocabulary for discussing its content, the means of achieving it, or the evaluation of different efforts to define or pursue justice. Even Hesiod, in the early seventh century BCE, discusses justice not abstractly or analytically but through metaphor and figure. When justice is being abused, she is a woman being dragged through the marketplace (*Works* 213–24).

The first use of abstractions for political analysis occurs in Solon's poetry. His fragments date to approximately 590 BCE; roughly two hundred years later, in 399 BCE Lysias will write a courtroom defense speech with an abstraction in its title: "Apology on Charges of Subverting the Constitution or *Politeia*." Over the course of the two centuries between these men, the conceptual tools of political philosophy emerged. Solon, for instance, introduces the concept of *eunomia*, which means something like "well governed" or "well constituted." And Sophocles' *Antigone* (*c*.442 BCE) introduces the first instance of *autonomos*, from which we get the word "autonomy"; the chorus uses this apparently invented word to describe Antigone's behavior: she makes her own laws. Aeschylus in his trilogy the *Oresteia* (458 BCE)—about Agamemnon's return home from Troy, his murder at his wife's hands, and the efforts of his son Orestes to avenge that murder—provides our first example of an effort to make sense of voting as a procedure of decision-making. In the final play of the trilogy, the goddess Athena arrives to establish a new court to judge Orestes. He had killed his mother to avenge his father: was this a murder or a just punishment? The court splits its vote and Athena casts the tie-breaker, in favor of Orestes. Aeschylus seems to provide, here, an aetiology, or mythical legitimation, of the Athenian policy that the tied vote should go to the defendant. Why should a tied vote go to a defendant? For that matter, why should majority vote even be considered a reasonable mode of decision-making? These are hard philosophical questions provoked directly by democratic practice; and the *Oresteia* addresses them implicitly to legitimate majoritarian rule. In contrast, the orator and sophist Antiphon would make a case against majoritarianism in texts called *On Truth* (*c*.420s BCE) and *On Concord* (written sometime prior to 411 BCE). The Greek word for "concord" is *homonoia* or same-mindedness; it is close in concept to the words "unanimity" or "equanimity." If the title is original, Antiphon's text provides one of the first instances of this new abstraction, as does the final book of Thucydides' *History*, but the term will become very important in fourth-century Athenian life and thought. Both thinkers also paid significant attention to the philosophically important distinction between nature and culture or *physis* and *nomos*.

Herodotus' *Histories*, however, is the text that captures and marks the very birth of political philosophy. Scholars too often make the mistake of thinking of his history of the Persian Wars as a pleasure-seeking historical narrative or rattle-bag of good stories. It is both things but also has a rigorous analytical edge and displays a self-conscious interest in analytical political vocabulary. The *Histories* contains our first instances of four of political philosophy's foundational terms: not only the verb *philosopheô* or "philosophize" (Hdt. 1.30), but also the nouns *demokratia* or "democracy" (Hdt. 6.43), *isonomia* or "equality before the law" (Hdt. 3.80, 3.83), and *politeia* or "constitution" (Hdt. 9.34). It also provides our first example of an argument about which regime type is best—monarchy, oligarchy, or democracy—in the famous constitutional debate among a group of Persian noblemen, including Darius, who have just effected a coup and must decide what comes next. For Herodotus the questions of how regimes are founded, and with what consequences, are insistent theoretical concerns.

The correct translation of *Historiai*, the Greek title of Herodotus' book, would be not "Histories" but, say, *Researches* or *Investigations*. The word *historia* comes from the verb *historeô*, which means "to investigate." But what does Herodotus investigate (see Gagarin 2002: 13–14)? In the first paragraph of the book, he says that he wants to explain how the greatest people of his time came into conflict. He therefore investigates not merely how conflicts arise but also what constitutes a great people. This is a normative, not a descriptive, question, for it takes Herodotus onto the terrain of judging which are the better regimes. Take as an example his history of Sparta. He begins it:

> At an earlier date the Spartans had been the worst governed [*kakonomôtatoi*] people in Greece, both in their internal and external relations—for they would have no dealings of any kind with strangers. How the change to good government [*eunomia*] came about I will now relate. Lycurgus, a distinguished Spartan [brought good laws]. (Hdt. 1.65)

At the start of the *Researches*, as I will call the text, the Spartans are already a great people; the Athenians are not but will be by the book's end; and the Persians are great. They are Herodotus' main subject, and they provoke further questions, in particular about Cyrus, the first king of the Persians. Herodotus asks, "Who was this man who destroyed the empire of Croesus and how did the Persians win their predominant position in Asia?" (Hdt. 1.95). Herodotus, in short, investigates three questions that will preoccupy both Plato and Aristotle. Not only, "What makes a great people?" And "What makes a great regime?" But also, "What makes a great king?"

Herodotus' rattle-bag of kings and regimes is a precursor to Aristotle's great project of collecting constitutions from all over the Greek world. And Plato recognized Herodotus as having framed the necessary questions of political philosophy. Early in Book One of his

Researches, as part of explaining the growth of the Lydian empire, Herodotus relates the story of Gyges, the founder of a dynasty that leads to Croesus, great king of Lydia. Gyges was originally only a guardsman for King Candaules, but, in pride at his wife's beauty, Candaules asks Gyges to hide in her bedchamber so that he could see her undressing for bed and confirm her beauty for the king. The queen spots Gyges in a mirror and challenges him either to kill Candaules, marry her, and take the throne or to be killed himself. Will he kill or be killed? Will he do or suffer injustice? That is his choice. It is, of course, also the choice that defines Socratic ethics; Socrates will argue that it is always better to suffer than to do injustice. Gyges makes a different choice and kills the king, establishing his own dynasty. Plato's *Republic* also begins with Gyges. Glaucon introduces him to ask whether it is better to do or to suffer injustice, even if you can get away with it, and to ask about the relation between how one answers that question and the establishment not merely of any regime but of a beautiful one, a *kallipolis*.

Herodotus, then, more extensively records the birth of abstract political vocabulary than any prior writer, he records the first analytical discussions in comparative politics, and he pursues exactly those questions and modes of research that Plato and Aristotle will later prioritize in their own political philosophy. But his contribution goes beyond this. Even more important, his text explicitly attempts to convert the tradition of wisdom literature into a conceptual framework for analyzing politics. To see this, we will have to spend more time with the text itself.

Herodotus' *Researches* can be quite confusing, especially on a first read, because he does not tell his story in chronological order. Before we discuss his own ordering principle, it will be useful to have a sense of the basic chronology forming the backdrop to his analysis. It goes like this: at very early periods, two empires dominated the Near East, the Lydian and the Assyrian. The Assyrian empire eventually fragments, and that fragmentation is led by the Medes, who revolt from Assyrian rule. After the Assyrian empire has disintegrated, the Mede Deioces successfully consolidates the region and establishes stable rule, maintaining power for fifty-five years. He is the most successful, and therefore the most important, ruler in this first portion of the *Researches*. During the period of time that Assyria is disintegrating and Media is growing up in its place, Lydia remains stable, but its ruling family changes. Candaules mistakenly asks his guard Gyges to look at his wife, and Gyges' family ends up heading the regime; the most important member of this family is Croesus. Then three events happen in close proximity to each other. Cyrus, a Persian subject of the Median king, revolts and establishes a Persian empire. Then the king of Lydia, Croesus, who was brother-in-law to the overthrown Median king, attacks Cyrus, both for personal revenge and out of a desire to enlarge his own empire. But Cyrus wins, making Persia master of both Media and Lydia and from this point on the greatest power in the region. Eventually Cyrus is succeeded, first by his degenerate son Cambyses and then by an interloper Darius. Darius initiates the Persian Wars against Greece, and his own son Xerxes carries them on and loses them.

This, in chronological order, is the background to the Persian Wars between Persia and the unified Hellenic cities, led by Athens and Sparta. Herodotus starts, however, in *medias res* with Croesus, and the story of Croesus leads to the tale of Cyrus. They are the two characters in whom Herodotus is most interested. While Croesus is the first ruler we meet, Cyrus is the last one we see. The final paragraph of the *Researches* returns to the topic of Cyrus and praises him for having resisted the temptation to expand his empire. Among the rulers presented in the *Researches*, Croesus gets the first word and Cyrus the last. They are, furthermore, unified by a shared commitment to the Athenian legislator Solon, who, as one of the Seven Sages, is a prime exemplar of the tradition of wisdom literature (see Montiglio 2005). It is worth pausing on the account of how Croesus, king of Lydia, and Cyrus, king of Persia, meet and come to share a tradition of Solonian wisdom.

Confronted with the fact of growing Persian power, Croesus decides to attack Cyrus but loses decisively. Captured, Croesus is placed atop a funeral pyre to be burnt alive. What follows reveals the organizing principle of Herodotus' *Researches*.

> Croesus for all his misery as he stood on the pyre remembered with what divine truth Solon had declared that no man could be called happy until he was dead. Till then Croesus had not uttered a sound, but when he remembered, he sighed bitterly and three times, in anguish of spirit, pronounced Solon's name. Cyrus heard the name and told his interpreters to ask who Solon was; but for a while Croesus refused to answer the question and kept silent; at last, however, he was forced to speak. "He was a man" he said "who ought to have talked to every king in the world. I would give a fortune to have had it so." Not understanding what he meant, they renewed their questions and pressed him so urgently to explain, that he could no longer refuse. He then related how Solon the Athenian came to Sardis and made light of the splendor which he saw there, and how everything he said [namely, that any one can suffer a reversal of fortune] had proved true, and not only for him but for all men and especially for those who imagine themselves fortunate. (Hdt. 1.86)

This story affects Cyrus, and so he commands that the funeral pyre be extinguished; at the same time, Croesus prays to Apollo to be saved, and rain drenches the flames. Mortal and divine concur in the need to rescue Croesus and his knowledge of Solon from the pyre. From this point on, Cyrus and Croesus are fast friends, and Croesus consistently gives Cyrus good political advice—for instance, when he advises Cyrus how to deal with his unruly soldiers, how to set up an effective system of taxation, and how to deal with rebellious subject people. He becomes for Cyrus the sort of advisor that Solon had tried to be for him. Presumably, Solon's advice to Croesus is the basis for the Lydian's advice to Cyrus.

Who was Solon exactly? In 590 BCE the Athenian polis faced a crisis; socio-economic changes drove a rift between rich and poor. Excessive numbers of poor Athenians had fallen into bankruptcy and been sold into slavery. Unable to solve their problems, the Athenians nonetheless managed to install Solon as a mediator for the conflict. Solon served as *archon* or chief magistrate in the city and established a democratic constitution for the city. Among his reforms (see Ehrenberg 1990), he established the law that no Athenian could be sold into slavery and that all Athenian men, regardless of their wealth or income, might participate in the assembly; he thereby invented the idea of citizenship as a type of belonging that provides some set of inalienable rights. After completing his legislative program, he famously left Athens for ten years to travel the world, on the idea that only by leaving could he ensure that his reforms would remain separate from the partisan strife and so perhaps endure. Solon represents an important type of figure of Herodotus' day and even earlier. Greece, the Middle East, and Egypt all had ancient wisdom literature traditions in which traveling priests, sayers, and wise men advised princes. Their advice was largely practical. Think of the figure of Teiresias in Sophocles' plays *Oedipus the King* and *Antigone*. Oedipus asks Teiresias for advice on how to deal with the plague affecting his city and Teiresias advises him to track down the murderer of the previous king. Solon's poetry tells us that he left Athens, as does Herodotus' narrative and also a text called the *Constitution of Athens*, the only surviving document to have emerged from Aristotle's attempt to collect the constitutions of Greek cities. The *Constitution of Athens* describes Solon as having traveled to Egypt. Herodotus presents Solon, then, in the middle of these wanderings and purports to record the influence of this wise man on the major near Eastern kings Croesus and Cyrus.

There is, therefore, a paradox at the heart of Herodotus' *Histories*. The meeting between Croesus and Cyrus results in the epiphanic triple pronouncement of Solon's name, as the deep truth of a dying man's last words: "Solon, Solon, Solon." As advisor to Croesus, who became advisor to Cyrus, the Athenian Solon might be seen as the founder not only of democracy but also of durable monarchy. In thus foregrounding Solon in his histories of empires, Herodotus makes clear that he recounts tales not merely of royal dynasties but also of intellectual lineage. Nor does the intellectual lineage end with Cyrus, or even with Darius, who takes over the Persian empire only after winning a debate about whether democracy, oligarchy, or monarchy is best. Instead, Herodotus claims the Solonian lineage for himself. As Herodotus reports it, Solon's central lesson to Croesus was: "Call no man happy until he is dead" (Hdt. 1.30–2, 1.86–9). Even a rich and prosperous king might fall into disaster and end up as a beggar or burnt alive on a pyre. Conversely, a lowly guard (Gyges) or humble son of a herdsman (Cyrus) may rise to kingship but nonetheless one day end up again in ruin, in Cyrus' case with his head cut off and stuck in a sack of blood. Herodotus himself repeats versions of Solon's maxim throughout the *Histories* (Hdt. 1.5, 1.30–2, 1.86–9, 9.121). "Call no man happy" is the core principle organizing his analysis. Like Solon, Herodotus traveled all over the Greek world and through the Near East, including to Egypt; he too bases his authority on his extensive travels, as in the earlier tradition of wisdom literature (cf. Gagarin 2002 on sophists). Whereas Solon arrived in Lydia as a much-traveled advisor who could give counsel to a king, Herodotus appeared instead in Athens as a much-traveled advisor for the *dêmos*. His *Researches* was presented orally in Athens sometime prior to 430 BCE. With his text Herodotus effectively repatriates Solonian wisdom to Athens but only after having converted it from the rhymes and riddles of the traditional wise man into a conceptual framework for analyzing the merits of different types of regime.

It would be worth considering Solon's political reforms in light of the principle attributed to him to see what could be learned from each by setting them in relation to one another. But, for the time being, my focus is only on what Herodotus makes of Solon's central maxim, for "Call no man happy until he dies" is in fact a principle of radical egalitarianism: the future equalizes all people. No one can see the future; no one can, at the end of the day, control it. What John Rawls tried to do by constructing the veil of ignorance, Solon did by reflecting on the future. Human beings are equal, on Solon's reading, but not because they are all created by one God; nor are they equal by nature because of a law of nature, nor because of a Hobbesian view of everyone's ability to kill anyone else. They are equal because everyone is equally vulnerable before the future and the changes it can bring. While it makes sense that the founder of Athenian democracy would espouse a principle of radical egalitarianism, what are we to think about the fact that, as Herodotus describes him, he also taught such a radically egalitarian principle to monarchs?

Solon's famous "Call no man happy" principle implicitly has two prongs: (1) with respect to the future, all people are equal; we might call this a democratic fact of life; and (2) efforts to control the future are a central problem and project of politics; we might call this simply the fact of the future. The two facts of life about politics contained in Solon's maxim are both amplified by Herodotus' *Researches* into political regimes; Herodotus himself shows us how these principles are relevant to monarchies. To start, recognition of a democratic fact of life does not end at the discovery of a principle of equality. If one looks closely, one notices that every story that Herodotus tells about how someone rises to power includes details of how that future tyrant wins the support of the people. The centrality of democratic power to the construction of monarchy is clearest in the story of Deioces.

Deioces is the Mede who, after the disintegration of the Assyrian empire, rebuilds an empire for himself. He does this by undertaking, in a period of chaos and confusion, to be the most honest man in his village, and the villages around him. He offers to decide disputes and always decide them fairly, knowing full well that, if he does, everyone will come to depend on him. Indeed, he does become the most reliable dispenser of justice, and so everyone comes to trust him. When Deioces realizes how fully people depend on him to resolve disputes, he pretends he wants to give the job up. He ceases to do it, and the world of the Medes falls back into chaos and lawlessness until they beg Deioces to be king. The story of Deioces suggests the practical force of justice, that it can be an instrument in politics, and not only an aim, and that it exists in the middle of messy, human relations, not external to them. But it also underscores the role of popular consent and belief even in monarchy. Deioces is one of the longest ruling kings in Herodotus' *Histories*. Over and over again, Herodotus' stories about how rulers consolidate their rule (or fail to) make the point that even monarchies depend on democracy at some level; they too require the acquiescence of the people for stability. Herodotus' *Researches* thus amplify the first prong of Solon's principle by showing that all regime types must confront not one but two democratic facts of life—not only the fact of radical egalitarianism but also the fact that all regime types, except those that rely entirely on violence, have an element of democracy in them, because all regimes need popular consent.

Herodotus gives at least two examples of what monarchs can do with the Solonian insights that all people are equal before the future and that even monarchic power depends on democratic elements. The two most successful monarchs in Book One are Cyrus and Deioces. Each provides a different example of how to be a monarch given the fact of radical human equality. Cyrus regularly grants people pardon; he regularly forsakes revenge and turns enemies into friends. So he does with Croesus. So he does with Astyages, his grandfather who was the king who ordered that he be killed as a baby. He lets Astyages live in his court. So he also does, on Croesus' advice, with Pactyes when the Lydians revolt. He frees all the rebels and seeks to punish only Pactyes. Later Croesus will advise Cyrus' son Cambyses thus:

> My lord, do not always act on the passionate impulse of youth. Check and control yourself. There is wisdom in forethought, and a sensible man looks to the future. If you continue too long in your present course of killing your countrymen for no sufficient cause—and of killing children too—then beware lest the Persians rise in revolt. (Hdt. 3.36)

This is the sort of Solonian advice, dispensed via Croesus, that Cyrus followed at all points. In short, Cyrus regularly conceded the point of equality, that a reversal of fortune for him too was always possible, and so he tempered punishments with mercy. His approach to accepting the principle of radical equality in the monarchic context was to develop practices of equity.

Deioces, in contrast to Cyrus, always applied strict (*chalepos*) justice, with no lenience (Hdt. 1.100). We must presume that this means that he always applied the letter of the law and imposed the strictest penalties that the law allowed. But he, too, as we have seen, recognized the centrality of democratic political facts even to monarchy. His tactic was neither to concede the fact of equality nor to admit that he might suffer a reversal of fortune but to hide the fact of equality. Thus he built a palace with seven walls, painted them all different colors, and withdrew within them:

> Admission to the king's presence was forbidden, and all communication had to be through messengers. Nobody was allowed to see the king and it was an offence for anyone to laugh or spit in the royal presence. This solemn ceremonial was designed as a safeguard against his contemporaries, men as good as himself in birth and personal quality, with whom he had been brought up in earlier years. There was a risk that if they saw him habitually, it might lead to jealousy and resentment and plots would follow; but if nobody saw him, legend would grow that he was a being of a different order from mere men. (Hdt. 1.99)

In the face of the democratic facts of political life, Deioces opts not for equity but for a noble lie to shore up monarchical power.

Indeed, would-be leaders in Herodotus repeatedly find that one of the best ways to consolidate popular support for their rule is to manipulate the superstitions and/or religious convictions of their subjects, which is to say their subjects' resources for thinking about the future. This explains the centrality to the text of stories about omens, consultations with the Delphic oracle, and efforts to seek advice. Just as

Herodotus presents stories to amplify the content of the democratic fact of life identified by Solon, so too he uses his stories to amplify the significance of the future as a core political problem. One particularly memorable example of Herodotus' amplification of this problem is his description of the Persian method of deliberation:

> If an important decision is to be made, the Persians discuss the question when they are drunk, and the following day the master of the house where the discussion was held submits their decision for reconsideration when they are sober. If they still approve it, it is adopted; if not, it is abandoned. Conversely any decision they make when they are sober, is reconsidered afterwards when they are drunk. (Hdt. 1.133)

There is a profound insight implicit in this method of deliberation. When thinking about a momentous decision, one wants to know: "Will I feel the same way in the future?" One might also put the question thus: "Will this decision survive a major change in me?" Getting drunk is a way to test whether a decision will survive a serious change; drunkenness, by changing one's state dramatically, serves as a proxy for futurity. But is this really the best possible mode of deliberation, the best approach to the problem of the future?

Herodotus' most famous example of deliberation also occurs among Persians; it is the aforementioned Constitutional Debate in which the Persian noblemen, Darius, and his co-conspirators in the coup against Cyrus' son, the degenerate Cambyses, argue over whether democracy, oligarchy, or monarchy is best. The tendency among scholars is to look at the debate as the presentation of three conflicting opinions and as a report on the means (majority vote) by which decision is reached. But the text is actually more complicated. It is, after all, part of a narrative about how Persia became as powerful as it was when it attacked Greece. The narrative function of the debate is to explain how Darius came to power. The text does not simply present three coherent arguments side by side and weighted equally; instead it proceeds dialectically. The argument for democracy is incomplete; that incompletion motivates the case then made for oligarchy; but this argument, too, is incomplete and in turn motivates the argument for monarchy. Darius' argument wins partly because it comes last.

Let us go over the debate (Hdt. 3.80–2). First Otanes argues for democracy or, as he calls it here, rule by the many (*plêthos*); his argument makes explicit the democratic facts of life described above. Otanes assumes the attitude of truth-teller; he means to expose the secrets of politics: "all things lie in the many." In a world of primitive military technology, power comes from sheer numbers; people are always the ultimate source of power; and so democracy is the basic truth of politics. The pressing question for Otanes is how to respond responsibly to the democratic facts of life (of human equality in face of the future, of the presence of democratic power at the base of all regimes); regrettably, monarchs inevitably abuse their subjects and destabilize their regimes. The better solution, Otanes argues, is to give power to those who hold it in the first and last place anyway: the people. But Otanes has ignored the problem of the future. He has not explained how a democracy will handle deliberative uncertainty, so Megabyzus intervenes to advocate oligarchy.

Megabyzus begins by pointing out the people's ignorance and general irresponsibility. Megabyzus' solution to the problem of the future is to propose that several best men, judging together, will judge best. Oligarchy is the answer. But, just as Otanes had ignored the problem of the future, Megabyzus has ignored the democratic facts of life. He has ignored the fact that the securest source of power is the people as a whole. Oligarchic leaders fall into personal struggles for power, and inevitably divide the people into parties, as each vies to develop support for his own pre-eminence. By dividing the people, oligarchies weaken the regime as a whole and make it susceptible to outside takeover. Whereas Otanes articulated a means for maximizing the power of a regime but ignored the question of how regimes can develop intellectual capacities adequate to facing the future, Megazybus addresses the question of how a polity can acquire adequate deliberative resources, but ignores the question of how to maintain its powerbase in a united people. The stage is set for Darius' argument for monarchy as a resolution of this problem.

Darius argues:

> One ruler: it is impossible to improve upon that—provided he is the best. *His judgment will be in keeping with his character; his control of the people will be beyond reproach* . . . To sum up, where did we get our freedom from and who gave it to us? Is it the result of a democracy, or of oligarchy, or of monarchy? We were set free by one man and therefore I propose that we should preserve that form of government and, further, that we should refrain from changing ancient laws, which have served us well in the past. To do so would lead only to disaster. (Hdt. 3.82)

Darius' monarch must be committed to ancient laws; as such he must be committed to popular opinion and the force of custom. Darius' monarch will thus draw his power precisely from the people. But the monarch will be the best of men and so will be equipped to face the future. Monarchy is the only regime type, in this argument, that seems capable of dealing with the political problems of, on the one hand, power, and, on the other hand, forethought. Herodotus' arguments about regime types is thus constructed so that the argument for monarchy must win. This serves Herodotus' dramatic purposes, for Darius must somehow become king. But Darius' ascension to the throne is not the end of the story.

When Herodotus begins his story with Croesus, and so with Solon's lessons that no one can be called happy before his death, he introduces the central question of his text. It is this: how well can different regime types deal with: (1) the fact of human equality; (2) the inevitable presence of democracy in politics; and (3) the problem of the future? The great drama of the book, the overall conflict between Persia, Athens, and Sparta, offers an opportunity to judge the question of whether it is best to confront Solon's radically egalitarian lessons with democratic politics (Athens), with oligarchic politics (Sparta), with a monarchic politics of equity (Cyrus), or with a monarchic politics of illusion (Deioces, Darius, Xerxes). The drama of the history told in the *Researches* thus itself enacts the debate of Darius and his co-conspirators about which type of regime is best. It also anticipates Plato's own staging of a contest among types of regime in book IX of the *Republic*. Indeed, Herodotus' presentation of the argument about regime types, despite having a clear dramatic purpose, makes theoretical points, namely: (1) those who defend democracy must remember to explain how a democracy can develop knowledge and good judgment enough to face the uncertainty of the future; (2) those who wish to defend oligarchy must remember to explain how the oligarchs will be able to keep the people unified; and (3) those who wish to defend monarchy must explain how they will ensure that the best man will always be in office. To choose among regime types is really to select which problem to solve. And these analytical problems, neatly dissected by Herodotus, will be the basic stuff of Greek political philosophy for the following century.

SOLON, THUCYDIDES, GORGIAS, AND LYSIAS: ADVICE FOR DEMOCRATIC CITIZENS

In advance of the arrival of Socrates and Plato on the philosophical scene, a primary concern of Greek political thinkers was to answer the sorts of questions identified by Herodotus as specific to democracy—for instance, concerning human equality in face of the future and the problem of forethought. Political philosophy developed, in other words, through efforts to advise the *dêmos*. Advising the *dêmos* was no easy matter. As we have seen, Solon was chief magistrate (*archon*) in the city of Athens in 590 BCE and gave the city its first democratic institutions. But Plutarch reports that Solon first gained his great authority with the Athenians by giving them a piece of unpopular but ultimately successful advice. He was able to give this advice, though, only by pretending to be a madman spouting his advice in the agora in poetic form. Such efforts to advise the *dêmos* were made not only by Solon and Herodotus but also by thinkers like the politician Pericles (as represented by Thucydides), the sophist Gorgias, and the rhetorician Lysias.

Pericles (*c.*495–429 BCE) was Athens's leading general and politician during the middle of the fifth century BCE; he led the Athenians into and through the first phase of the Peloponnesian War, giving his famous funeral oration in 431 BCE, directly before being punished by the populace for his policy and dying during the plague in 429 BCE. Thucydides, like Pericles, was a general in Athens and from an aristocratic Athenian family. But in 424 BCE he failed in a military venture against the Spartans and was exiled from Athens for twenty years. Much of his *History of the Peloponnesian War* must have been written during this exile. He, too, was sensitive to the difficulties involved in advising the *dêmos*, a recurrent theme in his text, as with the case of Nicias in the Sicilian expedition. He provides a depiction of Pericles' funeral oration in his *History*; how accurately it captures Pericles' views we cannot be sure. But the speech must have been recognizable, at least, as the kind of thing the general would have said.

Gorgias was a different case. A teacher of rhetoric, he was from Sicily, the island off the southern tip of Italy, another part of the Greek world where democracy had taken hold. Gorgias first went to Athens in 427 BCE as a Sicilian ambassador to negotiate over a treaty. So impressed were the democrats with his speech-making that he stayed in Athens for some time to teach. Although he often subverted ordinary opinion, he was never threatened, as Socrates was, with execution. Why did the democrats think that Gorgias was worth listening to?

Lysias, like Gorgias, was a foreigner. His father, Cephalus, had settled in Athens and owned a shield-making factory, and Lysias and his brother Polemarchus inherited his status of resident alien. The conversation of Plato's *Republic* takes place in the house of Cephalus, which Lysias eventually inherits, and Polemarchus is present for the conversation. He was eventually executed during the reign of the thirty tyrants in 404/3 BCE, but Lysias survived and, after the restoration of the democracy, was briefly granted citizenship only to have it soon withdrawn. Athens had no professional lawyers, only hired speech-writers, and, despite being a resident alien, Lysias was one of these. He wrote speeches for citizens to use for prosecutions and defenses. The speech that we will consider here, "Apology against Charges of Subverting the Constitution," is a companion to Plato's *Republic*, both because it involves the same characters and because it reveals Cephalus' family, including Polemarchus and Lysias, to have been notable defenders of democracy. Delivered in 399 BCE, also the date of Socrates' *Apology*, it too is a defense against charges of upending the democratic constitution. In this speech, Lysias, the non-citizen, puts into a citizen's mouth words about what democratic citizens need to know in order to govern themselves well. A look at the advice given to the *dêmos* by Pericles (as represented by Thucydides), Gorgias, and Lysias will round out our consideration of the origins of political philosophy prior to Socrates and Plato and sharpen our understanding of how one key term in particular, *politeia* or constitution, emerged. Once again, the origins lie with Solon.

Solon's task as mediator was to resolve conflict between rich and poor, and, in his poems, he claims to have found a middle road between their divergent interests. He writes:

> I gave the common people as much privilege as they needed neither taking honor from them nor reaching out for more. But as for those who had power and were admired for their wealth, I arranged for them to have nothing unseemly. And I set up a strong shield around both parties, by not allowing either to defeat the other unjustly. (Poem 2)

But Solon's efforts to mediate inspired hatred from both sides. His poems are a response to his critics; they are an effort at civic education. He writes:

> As for the *dêmos*, if I may rebuke them openly: what they have now they would never have seen, even in their dreams. And the greater men, superior in might, may praise me and be friends. For if someone else had had my position, he would not have held back the *dêmos*, nor stopped before he'd stirred up the milk and taken off the fat. But I, I took my stand like a boundary stone in the ground between them. (Poem 5)

Each side needs to realize that it stands to profit from accepting some reduction of its hopes. The poor should recognize that greater liberty and peaceful coexistence with the rich will be better for them in the long run than policies that ruin the rich and make permanent enemies of their families and allies. Similarly, the rich should realize that they are better off living peacefully with the poor and reducing the reasons the poor might have to attack them. Both sides must recognize that peace requires a moderation of desire.

Solon's criticisms of the *dêmos* do not end here. Not only must citizens acquire virtues of moderation; they also need intellectual capacities that enable the selection of good leaders. Warning the Athenians about an aristocrat, Pisistratos, whom he rightly considers to be seeking a tyranny, Solon writes: "Each of you follows the footprints of this fox, and you all have empty minds, for you watch only the tongue of the man, his slippery speech, but you never look at what he actually does" (Poem 7). Democratic citizens need to learn how to judge the relationship between a leader's words and deeds. Finally, Solon insists that the new democratic citizens need to understand the value of lawfulness. He is emphatic but, again, vague: "Good government, or *eunomia*, makes everything fine and orderly and often puts those who are unjust in fetters; it makes rough things smooth, stops excess, weakens hubris, and withers the growing bloom of madness. It straightens crooked judgments, makes arrogant deeds turn gentle, puts a stop to divisive factions, brings to an end the misery of angry quarrels" (Poem 1). Solon establishes some abstract political ideals but leaves their content unspecified. In short, he marks out the territory of political philosophy but leaves it unoccupied, awaiting the future contributions of Pericles, Gorgias, and Lysias (among others).

Our access to Pericles' political thought comes almost entirely through Thucydides. The key text is the funeral oration of 431 BCE as Thucydides relates it. Each year an esteemed Athenian was elected to give a speech commemorating the accomplishments of that year's war dead. Pericles' oration is very rich, and here I comment only on his arguments about the kinds of intellectual capacities democratic citizens need to develop in order meet the future. Pericles agrees with Solon that democratic citizens should be particularly concerned for their capacities to select leaders and to maintain a strong commitment to legality. He praises his fellow Athenians because "we do not let our system of rotating public offices undermine our judgment of a candidate's virtue" and "we fear the laws" (Thuc. 2.37).

But, in contrast to Solon, he does not present politics as a process of managing class interests. The central object of analysis is no longer faction but the city itself and its well-being. Pericles focuses on how to make the city self-sufficient, arguing that every citizen must be self-sufficient. He argues: "In sum, I say that our city as a whole is a lesson for Greece, and that each of us presents himself as a self-sufficient individual disposed to the widest possible diversity of actions, with every grace and great versatility" (Thuc. 2.41). Every citizen has to be many things: a soldier; a politician; a speech-maker; a good judge of speeches. This is because "we Athenians alone think that a man who does not take part in public affairs is good for nothing while others only say he is 'minding his own business'" (Thuc. 2.40). Plato will disagree vehemently with this view, arguing instead that every citizen should become expert at the single activity for which he or she is best suited. And the Aristotelian *Constitution of Athens* describes the tyrant

Pisistratos as taking control of the city only to tell the Athenians that "they should go home and look after their private affairs—he would take care of the state" (*Const. Ath.* 15). Pericles' contrasting insistence that democratic citizens need to think of politics as everybody's business leads him to expand the range of virtues that are relevant to successful citizenship. He exhorts the Athenians to Solonian moderation but also to courage, forethought, manliness without harshness, wisdom without softness, friendliness, and openness.

Pericles offers two pieces of advice to the citizens for how they might train themselves to be people of this kind. First, he enjoins: "We citizens are the ones who develop policy, or at least decide what is to be done; for we believe that what spoils action [*ergon*] is not speeches [*logo*] but going into action without first being instructed through speeches" (Thuc. 2.40). The citizens must prioritize deliberative speech. Yet near the end of his own speech he adds the following conflicting advice. How are young Athenians to prepare themselves to meet the heights of valor achieved by those recently deceased? "Any long-winded orator could tell you how much good lies in resisting our enemies; but you already know this. Look at the power our city shows in action every day and so become lovers of Athens" (Thuc. 2.43). Somehow, if the citizens cultivate the right sort of affective bond to their city, they will develop the capacities and confidences that democratic citizens need (Wohl 2002). But cultivating the right sort of bond entails knowing when not to listen to speech-makers, as well as when to do so. The role of speech in politics is complicated.

In "Against Charges of Subverting the Democracy," Lysias, like Pericles, tries to tutor the emotions of the democratic people of Athens. Thus he offers judgments about how they might use their anger well or badly (e.g. Lys. 25.1). But he also, and more importantly, returns to the Solonian position that interest, not the common good or an ideal image of Athens, is the fundamental issue in politics. Early in the speech he offers this pronouncement:

> Now, first of all, you should reflect that no human being is naturally either an oligarch or a democrat: for whatever constitution a man finds advantageous to himself, he is eager to see that one established; so it is largely depends on you [Athenian citizens] whether the present system finds an abundance of supporters... There is thus no difficulty in concluding, gentlemen, that the questions dividing men are concerned not with types of constitution [*politeias*], but with personal advantage. (Lys. 25.8–10)

Democratic citizens must ascertain how best to satisfy the interests of as many people as possible in order to deepen and spread allegiance to their choice of regime. The best way to do this, Lysias argues, is by "allowing an equal enjoyment of civic rights, an equal share of the constitution [*metadidonai ex isou tês politeias*], to those who have done you no wrong" (Lys. 25.3).

But what does it mean to allow the equal enjoyment of civic rights or an equal share of the constitution, to those who have done the democracy no wrong? In the speech, Lysias repeatedly insists that the caliber of the city's judicial institutions is at stake. Do the citizens accurately judge between innocent and guilty? It is the democracy's ability to maintain satisfactory and fair legal institutions that gains it allegiance; citizens share in the constitution through access to just judicial procedures. With this important point, Lysias refines Solon's argument that *eunomia* can be the solution to managing the conflict of interest between rich and poor. Although rich and poor citizens have distinct material interests, they also, as individuals, desire the fair or just resolution to their disputes. Because rich and poor share an interest in just judicial proceedings, a city's capacity to sustain lawfulness can override, to some degree, the material concerns of partisans and generate allegiance across different factions. So Lysias cautions the jurors against condemning whole groups of people without considering individual cases (e.g. Lys. 25.35). And he cautions them against slander-mongers, those who abuse speech to undo the norms of trust and fairness that sustain the judicial system (e.g. Lys. 25.3, 25.27). Speeches, like Lysias' own, are necessary to sustain good governance, but they also bring danger.

An important thread in all these texts, then, is the importance to democracy of setting speech to work appropriately. And this brings us to Gorgias, who directly tackles the problem of language's contradictory resources. Those of his speeches that have come down to us are rhetorical set pieces, displays of technical prowess meant to win him students. Particularly interesting is a speech called "In Praise of Helen," which seeks to upend a standard Greek opinion—namely, that Helen of Troy was a bad woman. Gorgias defends her by arguing that she could have run off with Paris only for one of four possible reasons: because of the will of the gods; because she was seized by force; because of the power of love (which is either a god or a disease); or because she was persuaded by speech. The first three causes are obviously exculpating, so Gorgias' controversial argument is that the excuse of having been persuaded is equally exculpating. His claim is that, if Helen ran off because she had been persuaded by Paris, she was as innocent of her act as if she had been abducted. "Speech," argues Gorgias, "is a powerful tyrant [*dunastês megas*] and achieves the most divine feats with the smallest and least evident body." Persuasive rhetoric dominates us, the speech warns. But, if we accept Gorgias' warning about rhetoric—that is, if we are persuaded by his argument—does that then also mean that we have been dominated or mastered by him? How can we simultaneously prepare ourselves to resist rhetoric's dangers on Gorgias' advice and also be required to recognize ourselves, in the very moment when we choose resistance, as having been dominated by rhetoric? Gorgias' speeches catch readers in such conundrums; so "In Praise of Helen" suggests that we cannot use language to figure things out after all. This use of paradoxes to sow confusion is fundamentally anti-democratic. If language cannot effectively equip democratic citizens to meet the future, what hope is there?

Yet Gorgias was a popular teacher in democratic Athens. How could this has have been the case if his arguments were anti-democratic? In fact, his approach to speech-making highlights a type of knowledge for which democratic citizens do have a fundamental need. The standard method of the sophists was to teach their students to argue both sides of the question; they and their students produced what are called *dissoi logoi* or a pair of speeches, each arguing equally well for one of two opposed positions. In a teaching context, Gorgias' praise of Helen would be coupled, for instance, with a speech condemning her. And this is exactly how *The Constitution of Athens* describes the task that Solon took on as mediator:

> When the strife was severe, and the opposition of long standing, both sides agreed to give power to Solon as mediator, and entrusted the state to him; at that time he had written the poem which begins *Grief lies deep in my heart when I see the oldest of the Ionian states being murdered* . . . In this poem he champions both sides against the other [*pros hekaterous huper hekaterôn machetai*], and argues their position [*diamphisbêtei*], and then recommends an end to the prevailing rivalry. (*Const. Ath.* 5.2)

Solon was, it seems, the first known master of *dissoi logoi*. The ability to argue both sides of the matter might, therefore, be seen as the original democratic intellectual capacity. Gorgias' success in Athens suggests that the Athenians at least considered this to be the case.

One might worry that a cavalier relativism would be the likely result of such a teaching method, but instead it generates constitutionalism. Solon argued both sides but importantly did not take sides. Instead, he stood in the middle, a position that he describes with several striking metaphors. He "set up a strong shield around both parties, by not allowing either to defeat the other unjustly" (Poem 2); he "built strength from all sides, like a wolf wheeling about among many dogs" (Poem 4); and he "took [his] stand like a boundary stone in the no-man's-land between them" (Poem 5). Solon's compromises mark out the territory of a no-man's-land, a space aligned with no faction, no interest, no opinion. Of what use, though, is a no-man's-land, a position that accords with no one's interest, but that is opened up by the *dissoi logoi* of the first democratic citizen? Benedict Anderson has argued that, for the modern nation state to come into existence, citizens had to imagine themselves as part of a community with people in distant places whom they could not see. The ability of someone in Paris and another in Marseilles both to imagine themselves as part of some abstract entity called France made a French political community possible; newspapers helped create this imagined community. For sixth-century Athens, Solon's metaphors worked similarly to conjure into imaginable existence a new kind of communal space. He stands in a ground between two parties, claiming to be a partisan of each, and so he forces the two parties to ask themselves what unites them, what might be their common ground. We are seeing here the origins of the concept of *politeia* or constitution.

When Lysias says that the democrats need to provide civic rights to all, his Greek phrase more literally recommends that all citizens "have a share in the constitution" or *politeia*. As we have seen, the word *politeia* arises in Greek only after the origins of democracy, and the first instance of this word appears in Herodotus' *Researches*. The experience of listening to *dissoi logoi*, of seeing someone like Solon use such speeches to stand in a no-man's-land between factions, generates a space of mediation outside of faction shared by all citizens. This space comes to be called the constitution, and, in the form that Solon sets up the first Athenian institutions, the *politeia* is essentially a permanent structure for mediating conflict. The laws and institutions that Solon installs in the no-man's-land between the factions are to provide for ongoing mediation in place of his personal services, since he will shortly leave for Egypt. After his poems and his departure, the laws and institutions themselves will make the *politeia* imaginable. When Pericles tells the citizens to look at and to come to love Athens, he reveals that a shared space has indeed emerged out of the no-man's-land once occupied by Solon. That space can be preserved, then, only through maintenance of the constitution. And what gave substance to the constitution in people's daily lives, as Lysias argued, was above all the city's judicial institutions, the structure of mediation originally established by Solon. This structure of mediation is a good held in common; it may be the only one.

So what did democratic citizens need to know to face the future? As Lysias argues at the end of a developing tradition, the democrats needed to understand above all else how to maintain the constitution, understood as the institutions—primarily judicial but also deliberative—that had come to occupy the no-man's-land taken by Solon, and that gave citizens the opportunity to continue working through conflicts by means of opposed speeches or *dissoi logoi*. Gorgias' rhetorical teachings were valuable to the Athenians because they highlighted the basic process by which the idea of a constitution had come into existence. People could make directly opposed speeches, but achieve resolutions nonetheless. We are back to the image on Homer's shield with which we started. The *polis* was a place where two men each offered their case before a public audience and then groups of respected elders darted out to make judgments and offer straight speeches whose purpose was resolution; and the *politeia* was what those men and elders shared when they participated in those processes.

Conclusion

When Solon played his role in brokering a resolution to a major political and socio-economic crisis in Athens, he formalized institutionally the ideas about politics, law, and constitutions implied by earlier depictions of the activities that transpired in the agora. He made arguments about his actions and explained his political philosophy in poetry. It is Herodotus, however, who identified Solon as having had a political philosophy [*philosopheô*] (Hdt. 1.30). Herodotus himself drew on the Solonian political philosophy to investigate systematically how different regime types deal with the facts of radical human equality, the inevitability of democratic elements in human social life, and the uncertainty of the future, thus producing the first theoretical framework for analyzing political life. But other fifth-century thinkers—for instance, Pericles, Gorigas, and Lysias—also drew from the Solonian tradition, focusing on concepts like leadership, political judgment, the right training of the emotions, the value of aggressively competitive speech, the need for moderation and middle ways, and, most importantly, the idea of a constitution, to advise the *dêmos* how to live well. In so doing, these men advanced the development of political philosophy. When Plato came to write his *Politeia*, or the *Republic*, he would answer differently only those questions that political philosophy, as originally developed by Solon and Herodotus, and amplified by the other thinkers we have discussed, had already defined as central. The work of invention had already occurred.

References

Primary Sources

Aeschylus (1984). *The Oresteia: Agamemnon; The Libation Bearers; The Eumenides*, ed. W. G. Stanford, trans. Robert Fagles. Penguin Classics, Harmondsworth: Penguin.

Aristotle (1996). *Aristotle: The Politics and the Constitution of Athens*, trans. Stephen Everson. Cambridge: Cambridge University Press.

Gagarin, Michael, and MacDowell, Douglas M. (1998). *Antiphon and Andocides*. 1st edn. Austin, TX: University of Texas Press.

Gagarin, Michael, and Woodruff, Paul (1995). *Early Greek Political Thought from Homer to the Sophists*. Cambridge: Cambridge University Press.

Herodotus (2003). *The Histories*, ed. John M. Marincola, trans., Aubery de Selincourt. Penguin Classics. Harmondsworth: Penguin.

Hesiod and Theognis (1976). *Hesiod and Theognis: Theogony, Works and Days, and Elegies*. trans. Dorothea Wender. Penguin Classics. Harmondsworth: Penguin.

Homer (1998). *The Iliad*, ed. Bernard Knox, trans. Robert Fagles. Penguin Classics, Harmondsworth: Penguin.

Homer (2006). *The Odyssey*, ed. Bernard Knox, trans. Robert Fagles. Penguin Classics, Harmondsworth: Penguin.

Kirk, G. S., Raven, J. E., and Schofield, M. (1984). *The Presocratic Philosophers: A Critical History with a Selection of Texts*. 2nd edn. Cambridge: Cambridge University Press.

Lysias (2000). *Speeches*, trans. S. C. Todd. Austin, TX: University of Texas Press.

Sophocles (2000). *The Three Theban Plays*, ed. Bernard Knox, trans. Robert Fagles. 1st edn. Penguin Classics. Harmondsworth: Penguin.

Thucydides (1954). *The History of the Peloponnesian War: Revised Edition*, (ed.) M. I. Finley, trans. Rex Warner. Rev. edn. Penguin Classics. Harmondsworth: Penguin.

Secondary Sources

Balot, Ryan K. (2001). *Greed and Injustice in Classical Athens*. Princeton: Princeton University Press.

Balot, Ryan K. (2006). *Greek Political Thought*. Oxford: Wiley-Blackwell.

Bonner, Robert Johnson, and Smith, Gertrude (1930–8). *The Administration of Justice from Homer to Aristotle*. Chicago: University of Chicago Press.

Boyle, Brendan P. (2007). "The Athenian Courtroom: Politics, Rhetoric, Ethics," dissertation.

Cartledge, R. (1999). *Democritus: The Great Philosophers*. The Great Philosophers Series. 1st edn. London: Routledge.

Cogan, Marc (1981). *The Human Thing: The Speeches and Principles of Thucydides' History*. Chicago: University of Chicago Press.

Ehrenberg, V. (1990). *From Solon to Socrates: Greek History and Civilization during the 6th and 5th Centuries bc*. 2nd edn. London: Routledge.

EUBEN, PETER J. (1988). *Greek Tragedy and Political Theory*. Berkeley and Los Angeles: University of California Press.

FARENGA, VINCENT (2006). *Citizen and Self in Ancient Greece: Individuals Performing Justice and the Law*. Cambridge: Cambridge University Press.

FARRAR, CYNTHIA (1989). *The Origins of Democratic Thinking: The Invention of Politics in Classical Athens*. Cambridge: Cambridge University Press.

GAGARIN, MICHAEL (1989). *Early Greek Law*. Berkeley and Los Angeles: University of California Press.

GAGARIN, MICHAEL (2002). *Antiphon the Athenian: Oratory, Law, and Justice in the Age of the Sophists*. 1st edn. Austin, TX: University of Texas Press.

GAGARIN, MICHAEL, and COHEN DAVID (2005). *The Cambridge Companion to Ancient Greek Law*. Cambridge: Cambridge University Press.

GUTHRIE, W. K. C. (1977). *The Sophists*. Cambridge: Cambridge University Press.

GUTHRIE, W. K. C. (1991). *History of Greek Philosophy*. Cambridge: Cambridge University Press.

HARRISON, SIMON, LANE, MELISSA, ROWE, CHRISTOPHER, and SCHOFIELD, MALCOLM (2006). *The Cambridge History of Greek and Roman Political Thought*. Cambridge: Cambridge University Press.

HOURCADE, ANNIE (2001). *Antiphon d'Athènes: Une pensée de l'individu*. Brussels: Ousia Editions.

IRWIN, ELIZABETH (2008). *Solon and Early Greek Poetry: The Politics of Exhortation*. Cambridge: Cambridge University Press.

LEWIS, JOHN (2008). *Solon the Thinker: Political Thought in Archaic Athens*. London: Duckworth Publishers.

LORAUX, NICOLE (2006). *The Invention of Athens: The Funeral Oration in the Classical City*. New York: Zone Books.

McGLEW, JAMES F. (1996). *Tyranny and Political Culture in Ancient Greece*. Ithaca, NY: Cornell University Press.

MONTIGLIO, SILVIA (2005). *Wandering in Ancient Greek Culture*. Chicago: University Of Chicago Press.

OBER, JOSIAH (1998). *The Athenian Revolution*. Princeton: Princeton University Press, 1998.

OBER, JOSIAH (2001). *Political Dissent in Democratic Athens: Intellectual Critics of Popular Rule*. Princeton: Princeton University Press.

ROMILLY, JACQUELINE DE (1963). *Thucydides and Athenian Imperialism*, trans. Philip Thody. New York: Barnes and Noble.

SCHOFIELD, MALCOM (1999). *Saving the City: Philosopher-Kings and Other Classical Paradigms*. 1st edn. London: Routledge.

SLATKIN, LAURA (2003). "Measuring Authority; Authoritative Measures: Hesiod's *Works and Days*," in Lorraine Daston and Fernando Vidal (eds), *The Moral Authority of Nature*. 1st edn. Chicago: University of Chicago Press, 25–49.

SULLIVAN, JAMES JAN (2007). "Thucydides Politicus: The Political Dimension of Thucydides' History of the Peloponnesian War," dissertation.

VERNANT, JEAN-PIERRE (1984). *Origins of Greek Thought*. Ithaca, NY: Cornell University Press.

WOHL, VICTORIA (2002). *Love among the Ruins: The Erotics of Democracy in Classical Athens*. Princeton: Princeton University Press.

CHAPTER 7

···

CLASSICAL POLITICAL PHILOSOPHY: PLATO AND ARISTOTLE

···

DANIEL DEVEREUX

SYSTEMATIC political thought in ancient Greece begins with Plato, and quickly reaches its zenith in the rich and complex discussions in Aristotle's *Politics*. The political theories of both philosophers are closely tied to their ethical theories, and their interest is in questions concerning constitutions or forms of government: for example, what are the different kinds of constitutions, and what are the values characteristic of each type?; how should the different constitutions be ranked?; what is the ideal or best constitution, given realistic assumptions about human nature? Earlier thinkers had considered these questions; Herodotus, for example, sketches a fascinating debate by proponents of three forms of government: democracy, monarchy, and oligarchy (*Histories* 3.80–2); and in Euripides' *Suppliant Maidens* we find the following debate between Theseus, champion of Athenian democracy, and a messenger from Creon, ruler of Thebes.

> *Herald.* Who is tyrant of this city state? . . . To whom should I deliver this message?
> *Theseus.* First, you began your speech falsely, stranger, asking for a tyrant here. There is no rule of one man here: this is a free city. The people reign here, taking turns in annual succession. Even the poor man has a fair share, standing his ground against the rich.
> *Herald.* You give me a great advantage in this game—the city from which I come is ruled by one man rather than a mob. There is no one who puffs up my city with speeches and turns it this way and that for his private gain, no one who gives it immediate gratification and pleasure but harms it in the long run, then hides his mistakes with fresh slanders, thus slipping away from justice. How can the people set the city straight when they cannot even straighten out the speechmakers? . . . a poor man who works the soil, even if he's no fool, is still too busy to be able to look after public affairs; and it is distressing to the better sort when a good-for-nothing gains honor and power from the people through his speechmaking.

Theseus. Listen to me my clever herald . . . since you have turned this into a contest. There is no greater evil for a city than a tyrant! There will be no public laws, but one man will have control by owning the law and this will be unjust. When the laws are written down, both the rich and the poor have equal recourse to justice; if the wealthy are reviled they have no better standing than those of limited means, and a lesser man can overcome a great one if he has justice on his side. This is freedom—to ask "Who has a good proposal he wishes to introduce for public discussion?" And the one who responds gains fame while one who wishes not to is silent: what could be fairer than that in a city? (ll. 398–442; Gagarin and Woodruff 1995: 64–5)

Theseus praises democracy for its guarantees of freedom and equality before the law. But the Herald criticizes it for lack of good governance: the common people do not have time for careful consideration of political matters, and they inevitably come under the sway of demagogues; those who might provide better leadership—the "better sort"—are shunted aside. Theseus counters that democracy protects the rights of all citizens through written laws that guarantee equal treatment of rich and poor alike. As we shall see, these and other traditional arguments for and against different constitutions were the seedbed from which Plato and Aristotle developed their political theories.

There are a couple of historical factors that gave rise to such debates. First, in the centuries preceding Plato and Aristotle, Greek city states experimented with a great variety of constitutions and ways of organizing their political life. "Monarchy," "oligarchy," "democracy," "aristocracy," "tyranny" are all Greek words; and the forms they name—and combinations thereof—were to be found among the several hundred city states that made up ancient Greece. Given this variety, and the extensive intercourse between cities, it was inevitable that individuals (such as Theseus and the Herald) would be drawn into debates about the advantages and disadvantages of different systems. The second factor is colonization: during this period many city states established colonies along the coast of Asia Minor, as well as in Sicily and southern Italy. Distinguished individuals or committees were commissioned to draw up constitutions for these new city states. Individuals were thus invited to consider how best to organize a community, and what sorts of principles and values should guide such an effort. It was natural, then, for Greeks to view political constitutions as artifacts to be designed and modified, not as patterns received from on high nor as ineluctable expressions of a particular culture or society.

Among Plato's predecessors there was a tradition of political thought and debate, but he was the first Greek thinker to undertake a careful, systematic analysis of fundamental questions in political philosophy. His political views were shaped to a large extent by his conception of the "human good" and his view of the nature of knowledge. He believed that the purpose of a political community is to attain the best possible life for its inhabitants, and that the way to achieve this is to ensure that those who rule have an accurate understanding of human nature and of what makes a human life truly worthwhile. These starting points of Plato's political thought were the legacy of his mentor, Socrates. Socrates did not develop a theory of political constitutions or a model of an ideal state; his goal was to obtain knowledge of the human good—the values that determine how we ought to live our lives. He believed that such knowledge was indispensable to wise decision-making in the political sphere. It is thus appropriate that we begin this chapter with a discussion of Socrates' influence on Plato. We will then turn to Plato's masterpiece, the *Republic*, and consider his model of an ideal constitution. The *Republic* was written in mid-career, and in his later works Plato revised important elements of the theory of the *Republic*. After examining a few of these later developments, we will conclude with a discussion of Aristotle's complex and sophisticated analysis of political constitutions.

SOCRATES

Socrates was not a "theory-builder," nor did he write any philosophical works, and yet he was a pivotal figure in the history of ancient philosophy. He stimulated others through his questions: he was, as he says in the *Apology*, a "gadfly," stinging his followers and fellow citizens with his puzzling paradoxes and goading them to philosophical reflection (30e–31a). A few examples of his paradoxical claims are: "no harm can come to a good person"; "it is better to suffer than to do injustice"; "all wrongdoing is involuntary"; and "no one knowingly chooses to act badly." Since he left no writings, we know of Socrates' philosophical activities and ideas only through reports of others—chiefly through Plato's dialogues, in which he plays a dominant role. It is generally thought that the shorter Platonic dialogues (such as the *Protagoras, Laches, Charmides, Gorgias*) were written early in Plato's career, and were meant to give a fairly accurate portrait of Socrates' methods of inquiry and his philosophical concerns. Although Socrates claimed not to have knowledge of anything of importance, he had very strong convictions about what was valuable and worth striving for. He sets out these convictions in his *Apology*, his defense at his trial against the charges of impiety and corrupting the youth.

Socrates argues that virtue, wisdom, and truth are values of supreme importance; in comparison with these "goods of the soul," worldly goods like wealth, power, and fame are insignificant (29e–30a). The value of virtue and wisdom is at least partly derived from their effects on the quality of one's life, for Socrates claims that possession of these goods guarantees a happy, fulfilling life (36d). Socrates' confidence in the supreme value of the goods of the soul is the basis of his activity as a moral reformer. But he also claims not to have knowledge of these goods; for example, he denies that he knows the true nature of virtue. This is why he spends his days seeking such knowledge (38a).

Socrates' zeal to change his fellow citizens' values did not lead him to get involved in politics because he thought he could achieve more through personal interaction with individuals. But his value beliefs carried over to the political sphere: he thought the values that ought to determine how individuals live their lives should also shape the political life of the community (36cd). He contends that his fellow Athenians attach too much importance to wealth and power in their deliberations about public policies as well as in their day-to-day lives. And in the *Gorgias* he speaks scornfully of the wealth and power amassed by Athens during its brief empire, referring to its great public works projects as "trash."

> Disregarding justice and moderation, they [the leaders of the empire] filled the city with harbors, dockyards, walls, tribute payments, and such trash as that. And when that fit of sickness comes on, they [the people] will blame their advisers of the moment and sing the praises of Themistocles and Cimon and Pericles, the causes of their ills. (518e–519a)

This passage points to a fundamental Socratic principle: the policies and laws of a state should be based on an understanding of the nature of virtue and wisdom, and a recognition of their central importance to the civic life of the community.

The *Gorgias* also gives some idea of the sort of political reform that Socrates would recommend. He argues that what is needed is excellent political leadership, and that this depends on a special kind of knowledge, which he calls "the political art" (*politikê technê*). This art has two main parts: the art of legislation; and the art of "corrective justice," which are analogous to two arts concerned with the body: physical training and medicine (464b–466a). Just as medicine and physical training aim at producing and maintaining the good condition of the body, *health*, so legislation and corrective justice aim at producing the good condition of the soul, *virtue*. Socrates' conception of the political art is thus based on an analogy between health as the good condition of the body, on the one hand, and virtue as the good condition of the soul, on the other. And, as it turns out, Plato's account of justice and virtue in book IV of the *Republic* is an elaboration of this analogy.

The idea of a special kind of political expertise did not originate with Socrates; Protagoras and other so-called sophists set themselves up as teachers of the "political art" (*politikê technê* (*Protagoras* 319a)). Socrates' innovation was his particular conception of this expertise. The knowledge that Protagoras claimed to teach was a set of skills that guaranteed "success" as conventionally understood in the political arena— the kind of success enjoyed by Pericles and other admired leaders of Athens (*Protagoras* 318e–320a). For Socrates, on the other hand, the political art is primarily concerned with the moral improvement of the members of the city state. The goal of the expert statesman is to instill and maintain virtue (*aretê*) in the souls of his fellow citizens—"virtue" understood as a whole made up of such parts as justice, temperance, courage, and wisdom. The statesman uses the arts of legislation and corrective justice to accomplish this goal. Corrective justice operates like medicine: through rehabilitative punishment, it improves the condition of the soul by removing injustice and other vices (*Gorgias* 476a–479e). Legislation, on the other hand, is analogous to physical training: it fosters the development and maintenance of the virtues by instituting a program of education and training (464c–465c, 519cd).

In the *Gorgias*, Socrates also makes some of the same criticisms of Athenian democracy that the Herald makes in the passage from Euripides quoted earlier. He compares the Athenian assembly to a gathering of children who care only about what pleases them (521e–522c); and he charges them, as the Herald does, with being too much under the sway of demagogues—orators who ingratiate themselves with the people in order to serve their own private interest (502d–503a). This is his reason for calling the rhetoric taught by Gorgias a form of "flattery." We should be hesitant, however, to infer a general condemnation of democracy from Socrates' criticisms of Athenian democracy. He claims that Pericles and other admired Athenian leaders did not perform the proper function of a statesman. Rather than working to improve their fellow citizens, the Athenian leaders corrupted them by "catering to their appetites" (517bc). If they had done their job properly, these leaders would have had the opposite effect: they would have made their fellow citizens more just and temperate, less under the sway of their appetites; and, as a result, the people would have been better judges of what was in their, and the city's, best interest. A reformed democracy might meet with Socrates' approval. Although he did not attempt to describe the sort of constitution that would best accomplish the goal of the city state, he makes it clear that it must be one in which those who govern have a knowledge of the nature of virtue and how it is produced; and these leaders must exercise their governing powers for the sake of the well-being of their fellow citizens, not for their own private interest.

Although Socrates did not develop a theory of constitutions or a model of an ideal state, he set out several principles that would serve as foundations of subsequent political thought in the ancient period:

1. The aim of a political community is the happiness of its members; the laws and institutions of the community should be designed with this overarching aim in view.
2. Virtue is a necessary (and perhaps sufficient) condition of happiness; thus the inculcation of virtue must be a primary concern of the political community.
3. The inculcation of virtue requires that some individuals have an accurate understanding of the nature of virtue, and of how it is acquired through education and corrective justice; in other words, the community should be governed by leaders who possess the political art.

Socrates deserves credit for giving the impetus to what might be called the "virtue politics" of ancient political philosophy.[1]

---

[1] Another important political issue associated with Socrates is the basis of our obligation to obey the law, which is discussed in the *Crito*. Surprisingly, this issue is not taken up in any of Plato's later works or in Aristotle. For recent discussions of "Socratic politics," see Kraut (1984), Brickhouse and Smith (2000); Kamtekar (2006); and Klosko (2006).

Plato's Ideal State: The *Republic*

Socrates viewed himself as a political reformer *(Gorgias* 521de), but he did not propose any particular changes in the institutional framework of the city state; he focused on changing individuals and their values. Plato took the next step. He decided that the only way to achieve Socrates' political goals was to change the fundamental structure of the city—to develop and implement a blueprint of an ideally just and good city state. This blueprint or model is described in Plato's best-known work, the *Republic*. But the *Republic* contains much more than a description of an ideal city state; in fact, this description plays a subordinate role in an argument for the value of individual justice. Thus Plato's main concern in the *Republic* is ethical: through his mouthpiece, Socrates, he seeks to convince his audience that it always "pays" to be just and to avoid injustice.

In the first book of the *Republic*, Socrates' claim that justice "pays" is challenged by the hot-tempered Thrasymachus, a rhetorician and tyrannophile. He accuses Socrates of naivety and argues that one is better off being *un*just if one can get away with it. The debate between Socrates and Thrasymachus is inconclusive, and, at the beginning of book II, Thrasymachus' challenge is taken over by the two young brothers Glaucon and Adeimantus. They contend that, in order to make a convincing case for justice, Socrates must do three things: (1) give an account of the essential nature of justice and injustice; (2) show that justice is valuable for its own sake as well as for its consequences; and (3) show that the life of a just person is happier and more rewarding than the life of any unjust person. It is in connection with the first task that Socrates introduces a political dimension to the discussion. It is easier, he suggests, to discover what justice is in a city than in an individual: since the city is larger, its justice (and injustice) ought to be more apparent. He therefore proposes that they first determine what justice is in a city and then look to see what it is in the individual.

In the course of constructing the just city, Socrates distinguishes three main classes of citizens: the working class (consisting of farmers, artisans, shopkeepers, and so on); the armed forces (the so-called auxiliaries); and the ruling class (the "philosopher-kings"). Members of the latter two classes are selected at a young age on the basis of their natural abilities (374e–376c), and receive an education designed to instill the virtues of courage, moderation, and justice. Those who show unusual aptitude for intellectual pursuits are then given a "higher" education in mathematics and philosophy, and eventually become the rulers of the state. Those who do not receive the higher education become professional soldiers and educators, and are the helpers or "auxiliaries" of the rulers. This hierarchical structure of the ideal state is based on the assumption that there are natural inequalities among individuals in a community, inequalities in their abilities to achieve moral and intellectual virtues. In regard to these abilities, individuals fall into three groups: those who can achieve both moral excellence and philosophical wisdom; those who are able to achieve moral excellence and a lower level of intellectual excellence—not philosophical wisdom; and those who are naturally cut out for the life of a craftsman or service-provider, and who are able to achieve a more modest level of moral and intellectual excellence appropriate to such a life. This assumption of natural inequalities in regard to social or political roles is a fundamental principle underlying the design of Socrates' ideal city state, and it is surprising that he does not offer any supporting argument for it.

Another principle guiding the construction of the ideal city state comes to light in Socrates' response to an objection from his interlocutor, Adeimantus. After spelling out the "lower" educational program for the future rulers and auxiliaries, Socrates focuses on the economic aspects of their life. While the farmers and artisans own their own houses and enjoy a modest level of material prosperity, the rulers and the military class are not allowed to have private property or to own gold and silver; their standard of living is austere and spartan in comparison with that of the workforce. Adeimantus objects that this is unfair to the rulers and auxiliaries: Socrates is depriving them of a happy life, even though they make the greatest contribution to the city's welfare. Adeimantus is appealing to a principle of distributive justice: benefits derived from a cooperative enterprise should be proportional to one's contribution; since the contribution of the auxiliaries and rulers is the greatest, they should receive the greatest benefits. In his response (420bc), Socrates *seems* to reject Adeimantus' suggestion: while the proper aim in establishing a city is the happiness of its members, if the city is to be *just*, its aim cannot be to maximize the happiness of just one group of citizens—a just city is not one in which a particular group is "outstandingly happy, but rather one in which "the whole city is as happy as possible." Several interesting questions arise at this point. What is the justification for the claim that a *just* city is one in which "the city as a whole" is happy? What is it for a group or a city to be "happy"? What is it for a city "as a whole" to be happy?

The justification for Socrates' claim that a just city is one in which "the city as a whole" is happy seems to be an implicit appeal to a principle of distributive justice: if it is possible for all to achieve a certain level of happiness, it would not be fair to make one select group as happy as possible if that means depriving others of their happiness; fairness demands that no group within the city should be especially favored over others. Does this mean that all three groups should have an equal share of happiness, even if the result is that one or more of the groups will have less than it might otherwise have? Apparently not, for Socrates indicates later that the rulers, in spite of their Spartan lifestyle, have a happier life than members of the other two groups (cf. 420b with 518ab, 519c, 520e–521b). What determines the appropriate distribution to each group is the nature and "functions" of its members: for the members of each class there is a particular kind of life that allows them to flourish and reach their full potential, and in this life they will find happiness (421c). In the case of the productive class and the auxiliaries, the life assigned to them turns out to be the happiest they could possibly lead—if the city were designed to maximize the happiness of the workers or the auxiliaries, it would have exactly the same constitution (for the happiness of the auxiliaries, see 464d–466c). But Socrates suggests that, if it were designed to maximize the happiness of the ruling class, it might have a different structure;[2] thus the ruling class, which is the happiest, is the only one that ends up with less happiness than it might otherwise have had.

According to Socrates' argument, the members of each of the three classes will achieve happiness by working for the good of the community—that is, by making the contribution for which they are naturally best suited (421bc). This is what it is for "the city as a whole to be happy." It is also clear that Socrates holds that the happiness of the city, or of a class within the city, depends directly on the happiness of its members. And we should note that the distribution of happiness accords with Adeimantus' principle of distributive justice: the degree of happiness of each class is proportional to its contribution to the security, stability, and well-being of the community.

As noted above, it is the unusual economic aspects of the city that provoke Adeimantus' objection that the rulers and auxiliaries are not getting their fair share of happiness. The productive class has a moderate standard of living: they are neither rich nor poor, but have a relatively comfortable life. (Their standard of living is similar to that of the inhabitants of Socrates' "first city," described at 373ac.) The auxiliaries and rulers, on the other hand, have a more austere life; their basic needs are supplied by the productive class, but they are forbidden to own private property, and their living conditions are similar to those of a military encampment (415d–416e). In most city states of the time, there was a sharp division between rich and poor, and their constitutions were either oligarchies or democracies depending on which class had the upper hand at the time (cf. Aristotle, *Politics* 1296^{a}22–3). In Socrates' ideal city there is no division between rich and poor, because rich and poor do not exist. From the perspective of the producers, the rulers and auxiliaries are deprived of the comforts that make their *own* lives enjoyable. One could argue that, given their values and way of life, the producers would have little reason to envy the lifestyle of their superiors; on the contrary, they would naturally see their rulers and auxiliaries as enduring hardships in order to provide for the security and good governance of the state. The stated aim of prohibiting private property and productive activity in the ruling and auxiliary classes is to guarantee single-minded devotion to their tasks; but another important result is that the superior classes are dependent on the productive class for their most basic needs, and this is impressed upon them in the names used for the producers: they are to be called "payers of their wages" and "supporters" (463b). The economic structure of Socrates' city is a system of cooperation designed to strengthen ties of interdependence and eliminate traditional sources of envy and civil strife.

The economic arrangements, including the "communism" of the ruling and auxiliary classes, are written into the laws of the ideal city. Other parts of the legal code have to do with the selection and education of the guardians and rulers; the criminal justice

---

[2] A lottery system in which only a few of the philosophers would have to rule would allow most to avoid ruling, thus maximizing the aggregate happiness of the highest class. But if justice demands that each member "pay back" for benefits received (520bc), then all members of the ruling class must serve their tour of duty.

system and the special training of judges who will administer it (408c–410a); the conduct of war with Greeks and non-Greeks (466e–471c); restrictions on music and drama (377a–403c); and regulations concerning religious practices (427bc). To ensure that rulers support and adhere to the legal system, Socrates stipulates that they must acquire an understanding of the rationale behind the laws, the same understanding that guided the original lawgivers (497cd). The laws articulated in the *Republic* determine the most basic aspects of the political and social life of the state. These laws are referred to as "outlines" (*tupoi*), and Socrates leaves it to the future rulers to fill in details of the legal code (425ce). The rulers' understanding of the rationale and "spirit" of the laws will enable them to work out the details in accordance with the fundamental principles, and will also ensure that they will not make any significant changes in the legal system: the rulers of Socrates' ideal state are not "above the law" (445e; cf. 421a).

But, even if the rulers have a proper understanding of the rationale underlying the legal system, what is to prevent them from taking advantage of their position and illegally acquiring the luxuries and trappings that traditionally signify status and power—thus unleashing the vicious cycle of conflict between rich and poor? Socrates' response is that the rulers' education shapes their values in such a way that the usual temptations to abuse power have no appeal. In their education in "music and gymnastic" they are imbued with the Socratic doctrine that "wealth, power, and reputation" are of little significance in comparison with the "goods of the soul"—wisdom and virtue. But, more importantly, in their "higher" education in mathematics and philosophy they gain access to a transcendent world of purely intelligible objects—Platonic Forms—which makes them regard as petty the usual attractions of political power. Through their education in Forms, the philosopher-kings become passionate devotees of a life of study and meditation directed toward a realm of pure being. Socrates attempts to convey the transformative power of this experience through his famous Allegory of the Cave in book VII (514a–517c). Our life in this world is likened to the life of prisoners in a cave in which all that can be seen are dim shadows of reality. The education of the philosopher-rulers frees them from their bonds and guides them out of the cave into the sunlit world of reality. Once their intellectual "eyes" are accustomed to the bright light, they not only have a clear vision of the things imaged in the cave—they find the contemplation of these objects supremely satisfying and fulfilling (518ab, 519c, 580d–583a). When it is their turn to use their education for the benefit of the city—that is, to go back down into the cave and take up the task of ruling, they reluctantly agree to do so: they regard their sojourn in the cave as a burdensome distraction from the life and activity that they love above all else. They have no interest in the influence, prestige, and wealth that are the driving ambitions of most seekers of political power.

Socrates claims that philosophers will make better rulers not only because they will not be tempted to use their power for personal gain, but also because their knowledge of the essences of Goodness, Justice, and the other Forms will enable them to make better judgments regarding political matters in the cave. But there is room for skepticism about these claims, and since the time of Aristotle philosophers have pointed to glaring, and not so glaring, weaknesses in Socrates' theory. But, before considering its defects, let us point out some of the virtues of the ideal city of the *Republic*. First, there is the demand—astonishing for the time—that women be given equal treatment—that is, that they be given the same opportunities for education and careers as men. Socrates argues that, when it comes to ruling, or even military service, there is the same distribution of natural talents and capacities in females as in males. Thus, in the ideal state there will be men and women in each of the three classes, all pursuing their own special profession and achieving their appropriate level of happiness.

Since the institution of slavery was a common feature of Greek city states, the absence of slaves in Socrates' ideal state is also a striking break with tradition. In Aristotle's account of the origin of a city state, he includes slaves as natural and necessary parts of the community. By contrast, Socrates' account of the origin of the ideal state makes no mention of slaves; nor does he make any reference to the introduction of slavery in later stages of the development of the ideal state. The idea that some human beings are suited by nature to be the property of others seems to play no role in the political theory of the *Republic*.[3]

On the negative side, critics have pointed to the appalling lack of freedom and autonomy in Socrates' ideal state. There are strong reasons for doubting that a small ruling elite with no checks on its power will remain committed to an unselfish pursuit of the common good. But, even if the philosopher-kings were to measure up to Socrates' high standards and faithfully abide by the laws, it seems fair to say that the rest of the inhabitants are in the same position as slaves living under wise and benevolent—but extremely protective—masters. Unlike slaves, they cannot be bought or sold, and they can own their own land and dwellings; but, like slaves, they have little control over their lives. Even the music they can perform or listen to, and the books they can read, are severely restricted: Homer's great epic poems, the *Iliad* and *Odyssey*, and all of Greek tragedy are on the index of forbidden books. Socrates might counter that true freedom consists in the rule of reason over the passions and appetites: to be free, our reason must be liberated from its "enslavement" to the passions and appetites (589d–591a); only then can we see and pursue our true good (cf. *Meno* 86d: "since you do not try to rule yourself so that you might be free"). And, since the rule of philosopher-kings *is* the rule of reason, this "rational freedom" is achieved for all members of the ideal city (590ce). But, for those who have imbibed individualist, liberal ideals with mother's milk, the price of this "rational freedom" is too high: the subjects of Socrates' philosopher-kings have no more autonomy than slaves; they have no freedom to choose the goals they will pursue or to determine what sort of life they will lead. Lacking these essential goods, it is difficult to see how their lives could qualify as truly happy.

What about the risks involved in giving rulers unchecked, absolute power? Socrates seems quite confident that his ideal rulers, since they are intellectuals and philosophers,

---

[3] There is a reference to slaves at 433d, and there is a dispute as to whether this passage is clear evidence that the ideal state of the *Republic* includes slaves. For arguments in favor, see Vlastos (1968); for arguments against, see Calvert (1987).

will have no interest in the sorts of advantages and perquisites that generally accompany political power; and therefore they will not be tempted to abuse their power for personal gain. But, even if it is true that those devoted to the life of the intellect would be reluctant to take on the burden of governing a state, their attitude might change once they have tasted power and seen its attractions up close. Plato seems to recognize this danger in a striking passage in the *Laws*, a work of his old age. He argues that there must always be legal checks on the power of rulers, for, even if the ruler possessed the virtues and the "political art," his "mortal nature" would inevitably lead him to greed (*pleonexia*) and self-interested action (874e–875d). In his later years, Plato clearly thought it was much too risky to give unchecked power even to those who were experts in the "political art."

We should also consider an argument from Aristotle's *Politics* for allowing people from the lower classes to participate in decision-making. He contends that, even though "the many" individually may be inferior to a select few in regard to intelligence and virtue, when they meet and deliberate together in public assembly they often make better decisions than the elite—especially in matters in which their own interests are directly concerned (1281^b39–1282^b1). He also points out that, if "the many" are excluded from all political decision-making, they will be resentful and restive, thus undermining the stability of the constitution (1281^b28–30; cf. *Laws* 757de). Given Socrates' stress on the importance of unity and stability, it would seem reasonable to give members of the two lower classes some share in political power. Although Plato was open to such arguments in his later works, in the *Republic* he is deeply hostile to democratic ideals and institutions. He attacks democracy in two places in the *Republic*: in the "ship of state" parable in book VI, and in the account of defective, unjust constitutions in book VIII. As several recent scholars have pointed out, the critique of democracy in book VIII is not so much an attempt to describe how democratic constitutions actually work, but rather a caricature—a picture of what a democratic city would be like if its fundamental ideals were carried to their logical extremes (see Annas 1981: 299–302 and Scott 2000). The ship of state passage gives a more realistic picture of democracy, and also a clearer idea of why Plato is against giving the lower classes a share in political decision-making. Let us briefly consider the "lessons" of the parable.

The ship of state passage not only gives a description of how democracies of the time functioned, but also seems to have particular relevance to Athenian democracy. As we noted earlier, in the *Gorgias* Socrates sees Athens as a society corrupted by demagogues who used their rhetorical skills to ingratiate themselves with the people for the sake of private gain. In the ship of state parable, Socrates returns to the dynamic relationship between the people and its leaders in democratically governed city states (487e–489d). He asks us to imagine the people (the *demos*) as a shipmaster who is larger and stronger than his shipmates, but who does not see or hear well and whose knowledge of seamanship is similarly defective. The sailors, who represent the orators and politicians, do their utmost to persuade the master to turn over the helm to them so that they can consume the ship's stores. The sailors praise those who are most able to take command through persuasion or force as masters of the art of seamanship: they are unaware, says Socrates, that a true master of seamanship must attend to "the time of year, the seasons, the sky, the winds, the stars, and all that pertains to the art" (488d); the true master of seamanship corresponds, of course, to the philosopher-king, the expert in statecraft. The orators say only what the people want to hear, and they inevitably corrupt them by catering to their desires for praise, power, and wealth (492c–493a; cf. *Gorgias* 481de, 512e–513a). Neither the people nor the orators/politicians have what is needed to navigate the ship of state—the political art. The ship of state will be well governed only when experts in this art take command—that is, when philosophers become rulers. Just as navigational decisions should not be put to a vote but should be left to the expert navigator, so also political decisions should be the exclusive prerogative of the experts.

The ship of state passage indicates Plato's beliefs: (1) that there is a political art that gives one *expertise* in political decision-making, expertise comparable to that possessed by other practitioners of arts; and (2) that only a few people in a given community have the capacity to acquire the political art (493e–494a; cf. *Statesman* 300e). The first belief supports the claim that only those who have acquired the political art should have decision-making authority in the ideal state, and the second supports the view that only a few will be able to acquire this art—"the many" should have no share in decision-making, at least in the ideal state. However, as we have already noted, Plato's confidence that experts in statecraft can be trusted with unchecked power waned in his later years. He came to believe that, while education is of vital importance for good government, one must recognize that human beings are not gods and even the best should not be trusted with absolute power.

LATER DEVELOPMENTS IN THE STATESMAN AND LAWS

Plato's *Statesman* and *Laws* were written a number of years after the *Republic*. It is thus not surprising that these dialogues take up new questions and sometimes diverge from views in the earlier work. One major change, as we have noted, is Plato's attitude toward ideal rulers: he expresses doubts about whether expert knowledge of statesmanship is attainable, and, if attainable, whether its possession guarantees that one will use it for the common good (see *Statesman* 301de, 302e; *Laws* 874e–875d, 713c–714b). Corresponding to this difference is a greater interest in non-ideal constitutions and realistic possibilities for political reform. One "new" question that receives a good deal of attention in both the *Statesman* and *Laws* is the problematic nature of law and the proper role of a system of laws in the governance of a state. In order to give some idea of how Plato's political thought evolved in his later works, we will touch briefly on these two topics.

In the *Statesman* and *Laws*, Plato continues to hold that an ideal ruler is one who possesses the "political art." But there are differences in his understanding of what this art involves, and these differences relate to new insights into the problematic nature of law. In the *Republic*, the rulers of the ideal state must have an extensive training in mathematics and philosophy with the goal of acquiring knowledge of Forms, especially the "Form of the Good." They also need experience in the practical sphere, but this is mentioned only in passing (484d, 539e). In the *Statesman* and *Laws*, on the other hand, it is unclear whether the political art requires the sort of mathematical and philosophical knowledge considered to be essential in the *Republic*. What *is* stressed in these later works is a kind of knowledge that seems to be gained through experience—what Aristotle calls "knowledge of particulars" as distinguished from "knowledge of universals" (*Nic. Eth.* VI. 1141^{b}14–23, 1142^{a}11–16). Plato uses the example of medicine in the *Statesman* to bring out this point (294a–296a). Suppose that a physician gives a patient a set of rules to follow as part of his treatment. In light of changing circumstances, the physician may realize that some of the rules should be modified. The physician's expertise is shown in her recognition of occasions when what is prescribed by a rule does not fit the particular case; no collection of precepts set down in a book will be adequate for making the right sorts of judgments in particular cases—the book learning must be supplemented by years of experience. Plato suggests that laws in the political sphere are defective in the same way (294ac; cf. *Laws* 875d). As Aristotle would say, universal rules governing conduct inevitably have important exceptions, and one needs practical wisdom to recognize what is appropriate in the situation (*Nic. Eth.* II. 1103^{b}34–1104^{a}10). For Plato, it is the political art that enables one not only to legislate but to recognize exceptional cases where the law fails to achieve its end—the general good of the citizenry; in such cases the expert statesman will act against the letter, though not the spirit, of the law. For this reason, Plato argues in the *Statesman* that in the ideal situation ultimate political authority should belong to the expert statesman, not to the laws.

Some of Plato's comments suggest that an ideal statesman should rule autocratically, "without laws" (293cd, 293e–294a); however, in the passage referred to above (294ac) he says that "legislation belongs to" the political art; and in another place he says that the ideal statesman rules "in accordance with laws" (301ab; see also 297d, 300de, 305e). There seem to be two ways in which the ideal ruler of the *Statesman* is *not* bound by laws: (1) he is justified in not *adhering* to a standing law—even a law he has laid down—if his knowledge of the political art dictates a different course (300cd); and (2) he is justified in *changing* a law if that is called for by new and unforeseen circumstances (295c–296a). But he will govern "in accordance with the laws" in the sense that his decisions and commands will generally follow the letter of the law; and, in the exceptional cases in which they do not, they will be in accord with the "spirit" of the law.

Plato *seems* to hold that in non-ideal, "second-best" states laws should be immutable and strictly adhered to by both citizens and rulers (297de, 300e–301a). But the argument he gives in support of strict adherence implies that it is sometimes permissible to change the laws (300b). He points out that these laws inevitably involve errors, since they are not the product of the political art. But to violate them would be to commit a much greater error, because the laws have evolved over time through trial and error, and they were *improved* through experience and the careful deliberation of many people. Plato recognizes that legal codes often include procedures for changing laws (296a), and he seems to approve of changing (imperfect) laws in a careful and deliberate manner, relying on the advice and counsel of those with experience. Once these laws have been passed, they—and not the rulers—must be the ultimate authority in the state.

The *Statesman* is more pessimistic than the *Republic* about the possibility of achieving knowledge of the political art (301de, 302e), and it treats the concept of the ideal ruler, and the laws he produces, as models to be "imitated" by inferior constitutions. Plato distinguishes six types of inferior constitutions (in contrast with the four of the *Republic*), and classifies them according to two criteria: the number of rulers, and whether or not they govern according to law. Kingship (lawful) and tyranny (unlawful) are the two types of rule by one, aristocracy (lawful) and oligarchy (unlawful) the two types of rule by few, and there are two forms of democracy corresponding to lawful and unlawful rule by "the many." The lawful constitutions are "good imitations" of the ideal, the unlawful are bad imitations (300e–302e; "lawful" here seems to mean adhering to laws *conducive to the general good*: 297d). Of the good imitations, kingship is best, because power is more concentrated and the ruler is better able to achieve his goals. When power is dispersed, the ruling authority becomes less effective; thus aristocracy comes next after kingship, and lawful democracy is the least of the good imitations. For the same reason, tyranny is the worst of the bad imitations, and unlawful democracy the least bad (302e–303b).

There are several interesting differences between the classifications of "inferior" constitutions in the *Statesman* and *Republic*, the most striking being the different treatments of democracy. The *Republic* recognizes only an "unlawful" form of democracy (557e–558a), and it is ranked just above tyranny as the second worst constitution. In the *Statesman*, the unlawful form of democracy ranks third from the bottom, ahead of oligarchy and tyranny; and the lawful form is just below kingship and aristocracy, as the third best of the good imitations. Plato has clearly revised his earlier, extremely negative, assessment of democracy. Perhaps the main factor in this revised assessment is Plato's appreciation of the benefits of "lawfulness" in less than perfect constitutions and his recognition of a "lawful" form of democracy: a constitution in which the laws are aimed at the general good, and in which there are built-in safeguards to ensure that laws are obeyed and respected (298a–300c).

Given that "less than perfect" constitutions are the best one can realistically hope for, and that laws are of vital importance for these constitutions, it is surprising that there is no discussion of good and bad legislation in the *Statesman*. Perhaps when Plato wrote the *Statesman*, he had already decided (or had started) to write the *Laws*, a dialogue that focuses on the "second-best" constitution and gives a lengthy and detailed account of its system of laws.

In view of the *Statesman*'s ranking of constitutions, one might have expected the second-best constitution of the *Laws* to be a kingship. But in fact it is described as a mixture of monarchy and democracy (693de, 756e). The *Laws*, in contrast with the *Republic* and *Statesman*, ranks a mixed constitution above any of the unmixed forms, and develops for the first time a theory of mixed constitutions (here again anticipating Aristotle).

Athenians of the time would have recognized the constitution of the *Laws* as a revised form of their own constitution. There are the familiar *ecclesia* (public assembly) and *boulê* (council), and the office of *stratêgos* (general) with wide-ranging executive powers; many minor offices, methods of election and appointment, divisions of the population, and so on are modeled on Athenian precedents. In contrast with the ideal state of the *Republic*, most of the political institutions of the *Laws* would not have struck Plato's contemporaries as "revolutionary": the communism of the two upper classes of the *Republic* is gone; the gulf between ruling elite and the rest of the citizen body, as represented by the allegory of the cave, does not exist in the *Laws*; the *Republic*'s harsh restrictions on poetry and literature are relaxed. On the other hand, the equal treatment of women is carried over from the *Republic*, and, although private property is the rule, there are strict limits on the amount of property one may possess.

Given that all citizens in the "second-best" state of the *Laws* have the right (and obligation) to participate in the political life of the community, it might seem that Plato in his old age became an enlightened democrat. But, whereas in the *Republic* he used the term "citizen" (*politês*) loosely to designate members of all three classes, in the *Laws* he understands a "citizen" (as does Aristotle) as one who has the right to participate in political decision-making; and the class of citizens in the *Laws* corresponds (more or less) to the military and ruling classes of the *Republic*. The rest of the inhabitants—those who fill the role of the productive class in the *Republic*—are resident aliens and slaves with no political rights (919d–920a, 846d, 849bd). The *Laws* in effect combines the military and ruling classes of the *Republic*, thus expanding the group of political decision-makers; on the other hand, it introduces slavery and a large population of temporary "guest-workers" who cannot own land and are not considered members of the community.

Although Plato characterizes the constitution of the *Laws* as a mixture of monarchy and democracy, it might be more accurate to describe it as a mixture of oligarchy and democracy. There are four economic classes mandated by law, and the wealthiest class is four or five times better off than the lowest class. In the complex rules governing elections and appointments to high offices, there is a subtle bias in favor of the upper classes (cf. Aristotle, *Politics* 1266^{a}6–22). Public education is mandated for all citizens, but, since the better off have more resources and leisure, their children will be able to go further in their studies. Plato's intention was that the educational system would stress the importance of the virtues for the well-being of both individual and state. The strict limits on the accumulation of wealth and the educational system would thus serve as checks on the development of "oligarchic" values; in terms of its dominant values, the constitution of the *Laws* could be characterized as a mixture of aristocracy and democracy.

Two further innovations of the constitution of the *Laws* deserve our attention before we turn to Aristotle's *Politics*. We noticed earlier that the *Laws* warns against the corrupting influence of unchecked power (874e–875d, 713c–714b). The constitution of the *Laws* sets out an elaborate system of checks and balances designed to ensure that all officials adhere strictly to the laws (767e, 928b, 946d–947e; see Morrow 1960: 549–52). There is a special board charged with conducting reviews of officials' performance at the end of their terms (usually one or two years); if there is evidence of malfeasance, they have the power to indict. Through another mechanism, the examiners themselves undergo scrutiny at the end of their terms. Moreover, power is divided among several executive offices so as to balance each against the others, with the aim of preventing any one office from gaining excessive power. A second innovation has to do with the revision of the legal code. We noticed that in the *Statesman* Plato values stability in the laws but at the same time recognizes the need for revision in light of new circumstances. In the *Laws* he establishes a specific institution for revising laws when necessary or desirable. The "Nocturnal Council," a sort of think-tank made up of elder statesman and young interns, is charged with conducting research in moral, legal, and political theory, with special attention to the laws of the state (951de, 961a–969d). The council may send emissaries to other city states to investigate their laws, and may recommend changes in laws where that would be beneficial to the state. The Nocturnal Council is the closest thing in the *Laws* to the philosopher-rulers in the *Republic*, but— characteristic of the difference between the *Republic* and the *Laws*—it has no power to legislate or command; its function is strictly advisory.

ARISTOTLE'S *POLITICS*

Aristotle's *Politics* is devoted chiefly to the study of different constitutions or forms of government. He agrees with Plato that the goal of a political community is the general happiness of its members, and that a decisive factor in achieving this goal is the design of the constitution. On the other hand, his approach to political reform is much more practical and realistic than Plato's. He distinguishes four questions to be answered by the well-trained student of politics (1288^b10–35):

1. What is the ideally best constitution, that is, what would be the best constitution if one could determine conditions and circumstances—for example, location, size of population, general characteristics of inhabitants?
2. What is the best constitution for most existing city states—that is, assuming typical conditions and circumstances, which form of constitution would be best suited to attain the general happiness and not too difficult to implement?
3. What sort of constitution would be best for a particular city state, given its current constitution, its history and traditions, and the characteristics of its population?
4. What is the best way to preserve a given city state's constitution, even if very imperfect?

Of these questions, only the first was addressed by Plato in the *Republic* and *Laws*. Aristotle's three additional questions indicate a serious interest in improving the politics of actual city states of his time. The *Politics* is a handbook for future statesmen, but also for political *consultants*—experts who might travel to particular cities to study their institutions and recommend improvements.

Before turning to these questions about constitutions, Aristotle considers several prior questions. (1) What is a city state—how does it differ from other simpler types of communities? (2) What qualifies one as a citizen of a city state? (3) What is a constitution, and what are the most illuminating criteria for distinguishing and ranking different constitutions?

(1) In the opening chapters of the *Politics*, Aristotle argues that villages are naturally formed when several households join together, and city states arise from the joining-together of villages. City states are thus larger and more complex than villages or households (1252^{b}15–30; cf. 1291^{a}10–33). In each case, the "joining-together" is motivated by basic needs: provision of food, shelter, defense against aggressors. However, in the case of the city state, Aristotle says that it "comes into being for the sake of living, but continues in existence for the sake of living well" (1252^{b}29–30). In other words, city states were originally formed to provide basic necessities, but, once established, they reveal their true value by allowing for the development of our higher capacities—capacities that add immeasurably to the quality of human life. We see here an important difference between Aristotle and the Social Contract theorists of the seventeenth century: it is a mistake, he would claim, to think that one can determine the general purpose of civil society by considering the reasons that first led individuals to form such societies; and similarly to suppose that we gain the clearest view of our political or social nature by examining human beings in a pre-political "state of nature." Aristotle maintains that human beings are adapted by nature for life in complex, organized societies like city states.

(2) The opening chapters of book III are devoted to clarifying three basic concepts: "city state" (*polis*), "citizen" (*politês*), and "constitution" (*politeia*). The Greek terms are obviously closely related, and the concepts, as defined by Aristotle, are also interconnected. For instance, a "city state" is defined as a "community of citizens large enough for a self-sufficient life" (1275^{b}20–21); a "constitution" is defined as the "organization of the offices of a city state," especially the most important (1278^{b}8–10); and a "citizen" is defined in terms of the offices of a city state—"one who is eligible to participate in deliberative and judicial offices" (1275^{b}17–21). Aristotle's definition of a "citizen" thus presupposes a complex society with a constitution defining institutional arrangements for deliberation and judicial decision-making—that is, a "city state." Since the three concepts are definitionally intertwined, the concepts of "citizen" and "constitution" make their appearance only with the development of a city state.

Aristotle's definition of a "citizen" in terms of eligibility to hold offices is not meant to capture the ordinary usage of the term. In ordinary usage, "citizen" might loosely refer to a member of a political community. In the *Republic*, for instance, members of all three classes of the ideal state (rulers, auxiliaries, and producers) are called "citizens," even though the two lower classes are not "eligible to participate in deliberative and judicial" offices. In Aristotle's strict sense, only the rulers in the *Republic* qualify as citizens; similarly, in an aristocracy or oligarchy only a small number of individuals would qualify as citizens.

(3) One criterion by which constitutions are differentiated is the *number* of those holding political power (1279^a25-^b10; cf. Plato, *Statesman* 300e–302e). If power is restricted to a few, then the constitution is an aristocracy or oligarchy; if decision-making is open to "the many," then it is a democracy; and if there is just one person holding power, it is a monarchy or tyranny. A second criterion is the *aim* of the ruling powers—whether the aim is the common good of the community or the private good of those in power; in other words, the aim differentiates between exploitative and non-exploitative constitutions. Rule by one is either kingship (non-exploitative) or tyranny (exploitative); rule by a few is either aristocracy (non-exploitative) or oligarchy (exploitative). In the case of rule by "the many" who are relatively poor in comparison with "the few," it is democracy if exploitative, and is called a "polity" (*politeia*) if non-exploitative. (This constitution might also be called a "republic," if by this we mean a constitution in which the people are sovereign and laws are framed with a view to the common good.)

Five of the six constitutions thus distinguished are discussed in the remainder of book III (kingship) and in book IV (polity, democracy, oligarchy, and tyranny); aristocracy is treated only incidentally in III. 15–18; as we shall see, its full treatment is in book VII. Before beginning his formal discussion of kingship, Aristotle considers proponents' arguments for and against all of the different constitutions—arguments based on appeals to justice and quality of rule (III. 9–13). His verdict is that there are objections to all of them, and he argues, in the case of democracy, that, while it would not be just to give "the many" complete control, it would also be unjust to exclude them from all political offices (1281^a14-34). As for the quality of rule, he argues of "the many" that, even if individually they are inferior to the "few best" in character and intelligence, when they gather together and deliberate, their collective judgment is better—at least if they are not thoroughly corrupt (1281^a40-^b21; cf. Waldron 1995). On the other hand, since "the many" are individually inferior, it would be better to restrict eligibility for the highest offices. Aristotle's arguments in these chapters seem to endorse Solon's compromise between democracy and oligarchy: have "the many" elect the highest officials and conduct "audits" of their performance, but impose a property qualification for eligibility for those positions (1281^b31-38, 1282^a23-41, $1273^b35-1274^a3$).

The idea that one can compare the collective capacity for wise judgment of "the many" with that of the "few best" has an important, but not often noticed, role in Aristotle's discussion of kingship (and aristocracy) in Chapters 14–18 of book III. The main question considered in these chapters is whether kingship is the most "beneficial" constitution for city states, or whether it is beneficial for some but not for others.

Aristotle's summary answer is that, if there is one individual in a community whose virtue/wisdom is greater than the combined virtue and wisdom of the rest of the population, then it would be most beneficial *for this community* to be ruled by that individual (1288^{a}15–37). If, on the other hand, there is no individual in the community whose talents and abilities are greater than those of the rest when they meet together and deliberate, then kingship would not be most beneficial *for this community*.

In the earlier discussion of the "wisdom of the multitude," Aristotle argued that, unless the people are corrupt and degraded (cf. 1292^{a}4–30), their decisions on many issues will be better on the whole than those of a single outstanding individual or a small elite. This seems to imply that it is only when there is a deficiency in the people that kingship is to be preferred; if the people are up to the task of political deliberation and judgment, a different constitution—one that has democratic elements—will be preferable to kingship (or aristocracy). There is perhaps one other set of conditions in which kingship would be most beneficial. Aristotle mentions in several places that in their infancy city states were ruled by kings, and this was understandable, since it is more likely in a small community that one individual will stand out above the rest. As communities grew and became true cities, there were more individuals with intelligence and good judgment who were unwilling to put up with the rule of one (1286^{b}8–13, 1297^{b}16–28, 1313^{a}3–10). Thus the size of the population is a factor in determining whether kingship is an appropriate constitution: Aristotle apparently thinks that it is more likely that rule by one will be appropriate and beneficial in a relatively small, simple community than in a large one.

Aristotle's treatment seems to *marginalize* kingship. In the *Republic*, Plato refers to his ideal constitution as a kingship or aristocracy (445d), and in the *Statesman*, he argues that kingship is the best of the six constitutions he distinguishes (302e–303a). But for Aristotle, kingship is "beneficial" only in certain conditions: either in larger cities in which the people are not capable of effective deliberation, or in small, simple communities in which one individual stands head and shoulders above all the rest. In city states in which the people are up to the task of deliberation, a constitution that includes democratic elements is clearly preferable. And, according to Aristotle's arguments for the "wisdom of the people," the quality of government will be superior in such a mixed constitution. As we shall see in a moment, a "polity" or "republic" is a mixed constitution with strong democratic elements; the arguments we have considered so far seem to point to this constitution as superior to kingship—as we shall see, polity and aristocracy are the real contenders for the title "best constitution."

Aristotle characterizes polity as "the best constitution for most city states" (1295^a 25–34). While kingship is best for some city states, polity is "best for most," because it is a constitution suitable for the relatively large, developed city states that existed in Aristotle's time (1296^{a}7–13). As we noted earlier, polity is a mixed constitution combining democratic and oligarchic elements (1293^{b}32–34). It thus makes sense to discuss the different types of democratic and oligarchic constitutions (in IV. 4–6) before turning to polity (in IV. 8–12). One might wonder how a mixture of two *defective* constitutions could result in a "correct" constitution that aims at the common good. We should note that oligarchy and democracy are defined as rule by the rich and poor respectively (1279^b39–1280^a6). Aristotle describes polity as a "mean" between oligarchy and democracy in that it involves a compromise between the interests of the rich and poor; and by not favoring one group over the other, it manages to achieve the common good—at least in economic terms.

An example of how polity combines elements of oligarchy and democracy is by "taking legislation from both constitutions": choosing officials by lot is characteristic of democracy, while choice by election is characteristic of oligarchy; in a polity one might therefore establish a law that officials are elected, as in an oligarchy, but without any property qualification, as in democracy (1294^b6–13). A sign that a polity is "well mixed" is our ambivalence about how it should be described: one cannot decide whether it is democratic rather than oligarchic or oligarchic rather than democratic (1294^b14–40). And Aristotle contends that this kind of mixture is a guarantee of stability, for "none of the parts of the city state will wish for another constitution" (1297^a6–7, 1294^b38–40).

Aristotle mentions that most city states of his time were either democracies or oligarchies, and that a "well-mixed" polity was rare or non-existent (1296^a22–3, 1296^a36–8). And yet a polity should not be difficult to establish, since it is "the best constitution for most city states," and such a constitution is said to be "easier and more attainable by all" (1288^b38–9). Given that most city states are either democracies or oligarchies, and that polity is a mixture of these two constitutions, it is clear that most city states can become polities by making changes in the direction of the other—that is, by making a democracy more oligarchic and vice versa; and this is why Aristotle says that polity is "best for *most* city states." However, since there are different types of democracies and oligarchies, and each type can be analyzed into a particular organization of parts, one needs to know how the different kinds of parts fit together in different combinations (1290^b25–39, 1294^a30–5). Equipped with this sort of knowledge, the expert legislator will be able to design changes that will transform a given democracy or oligarchy into a polity.

Aristotle points out that a legislator can design laws that encourage the growth of a middle class (1296^b35–40, 1308^b28–31), and he regards a strong middle class as an essential element of a polity (1295^a25–$^b28$); just as the economic status of those who hold power is a defining criterion of democracy and oligarchy, so also in the case of polity—this is a constitution in which the middle class holds the balance of power (1295^b34–9). Aristotle claims that people of the middle class are not typically arrogant and high-handed, as the rich tend to be, nor are they as envious and prone to petty crime as the poor. They are, therefore, the best equipped both to rule and to *be ruled*, which is the mark of a good citizen (1295^b1–28, 1277^b7–16). These armchair "sociological" claims may strike us as dubious and dogmatic; on the other hand, it is commonly believed that a society with a strong middle class functions better and has greater stability than one divided between rich and poor—and Aristotle clearly shares this belief (1296^b34–1297^a7). The growth of a middle class provides greater opportunities for leisure and education, and thus the enhancement of the general level of political deliberation and the "wisdom of the people." It seems clear that Aristotle's lectures on ethics and politics were designed with this end in view (see *Nic. Eth.* 1102^{a}5–13, 1109^{b}30–35, 1152^{b}1–8, and especially 1180^{b}23–1181^{b}24).

After giving his account of the constitution that is "best for most" city states, Aristotle discusses, in books V and VI, which constitutions are best in particular circumstances and how different constitutions are preserved and destroyed. Finally, in books VII and VIII, he gives his account of the ideal constitution, discussing such topics as: size of population; geographical location; ownership of land; character of people; class divisions; and education. Given the detail and complexity of his discussions in the preceding books, Aristotle's account of the constitutional arrangements and institutions of the ideal state is surprisingly sketchy; since the discussion breaks off without reaching a conclusion in book VIII, it seems likely that a more detailed description of executive and judicial offices, methods of selection, and so on was planned but not completed, or has not survived.

Another surprising aspect of the description of the ideal constitution in books VII–VIII is the fact that Aristotle does not relate it to his earlier classification and discussion of constitutions in books III–IV—he does not, for example, tell us whether it is a kingship, an aristocracy, or a polity. In book IV, on the other hand, he says that "it is correct to call the constitution described in the earlier discussions an aristocracy," and goes on to say that this is the ideally best constitution (1293^{b}1–7, ^{b}18–21); this is puzzling since, prior to book IV, we find no thematic discussion of aristocracy. However, there is evidence that books VII–VIII were intended to follow book III: the last lines of book III announce that the next topic to be discussed is "the best constitution" (1288^{a}2–4). If books VII–VIII originally came before book IV, then Aristotle's comment that "it is correct to call the constitution described in the earlier discussions an aristocracy" would refer to the account of the ideal constitution in books VII–VIII.[4] Putting these pieces together, it seems likely that Aristotle would call his ideal constitution an aristocracy; it is clearly not a kingship, because there is a class of individuals who control the government; and it is not a polity, because participation in government is restricted to those who have virtue in the strict sense (1329^{a}2–17, 1293^{b}1–5, 1295^{a}25–31).

Aristotle divides up the population of his ideal state into three groups, which correspond roughly to the three classes in the *Republic*: at the bottom are the farmers and artisans; in the middle are those who make up the armed forces; and at the top are those who govern the state (1328^{b}2–23). In contrast with the constitution of the *Republic*, there is no difference in the natural capacities of soldiers and rulers; they receive the same education, and are separated only by age—the young serve in the military for a number of years, and then in middle age they begin their political careers (1329^{a}2–17, 1332^{b}32–1333^{a}2). Underlying this merging of the *Republic's* two upper

---

[4] According to this "original" plan, Aristotle first discusses kingship, aristocracy, and the ideal constitution, and then goes on to discuss the other "inferior" constitutions; and this is the plan Plato follows in the *Republic*.

classes is a different view of the kind of knowledge needed for political rule. Aristotle rejects the *Republic*'s view that metaphysical knowledge of transcendent Forms is necessary for good political rule; he develops a conception of a more accessible "practical wisdom" that encompasses a broad understanding of ethics and politics, combined with deliberative excellence based on years of experience (*Nic. Eth.*, bk VI). Aristotle apparently thought that the portion of the population corresponding to the two upper classes of the *Republic* would be able to attain practical wisdom, and thus be qualified to rule in the best state.

By combining the *Republic*'s class of rulers and auxiliaries, Aristotle makes his ideal constitution more inclusive, since political decision-making is not restricted to philosophers; but it is also, in a way, less inclusive, since women are excluded from the political life of the community. Moreover, the bulk of the population—the farmers, artisans, and so on—are excluded from the city state in ways that their counterparts in the *Republic* are not. Like the producers in the *Republic*, they are excluded from the political life of the community; but they are also, *unlike* their counterparts, excluded from owning land: only members of the military/political class are permitted to own land (1329^a17–26). And, while the artisans and farmers are necessary for the existence of the city state, they are not considered *parts* of it: they do not have a share in the city state, and are therefore not considered to be citizens (1329^a17–24, $^a34$–39). And, since they are not parts of the city state, their happiness is not considered as part of the overall happiness of the state—in fact, Aristotle apparently holds that they are not capable of leading happy lives, so there is obviously no need to take their happiness into account (1328^a37–40, 1328^b33–1329^a2, $^a19$–26). In the *Republic*, by contrast, the well-being and happiness of the productive class is no less important than that of the other two classes (419^a–421^c). A further repugnant aspect of Aristotle's ideal state (absent from the *Republic*) is its dependence on a large slave population (1330^a25–31); all in all, it is not a pretty picture.

Aristotle claims that his ideal state is "governed best" because those who govern possess unqualified virtue (1328^b33–1329^a2; cf. 1293^b1–7). But his earlier argument for the "wisdom of the many" seems to run counter to this claim: there he contended that the many may reach better decisions through deliberation than the few who are unqualifiedly virtuous and wise. Aristotle seems to present us with two conflicting criteria for determining the quality of government: (1) that government is best when those who govern are unqualifiedly virtuous, and this will be true of the ideal aristocracy described in books VII–VIII; and (2) that government is best that reaches the best decisions, and this will be a constitution in which the many, who are not unqualifiedly virtuous, will participate in decision-making. The polity or republic satisfies the second criterion, because all groups within the community, rich, poor, and middle class, have a significant role in decision-making; it also makes a gesture toward the first criterion by including restrictions to ensure that the best-qualified individuals occupy the most important offices. On the other hand, Aristotle might argue that, if those who possess unqualified virtue make up a sizeable portion of the population (though still a minority), and if they deliberate as a body, they will combine the assets of virtue and numbers.

And, as we have seen, those who take part in decision-making in his ideal state are more than just "a few."

Of the three "correct" constitutions, kingship is "best for some" but not most city states, polity is "best for most," and aristocracy is best without qualification. Aristotle considers polity and aristocracy to be superior to kingship, and aristocracy to be superior to polity. But his preference for aristocracy is tempered by his appreciation of the stability and greater inclusiveness of polity ($1296^b38–1297^a7$). In the subsequent history of political thought, it was the "well-mixed" polity that had the greater impact, not only in antiquity but also in the development of "republicanism" in the Renaissance.[5]

References

Primary Sources

Aristotle (1998). *Politics*, ed. and trans. C. D. C. Reeve. Indianapolis: Hackett.
Gagarin, Michael, and Woodruff, Paul (1995) eds. *Early Greek Political Thought from Homer to the Sophists*. Cambridge: Cambridge University Press.
Plato (1997). *Plato: Complete Works*, ed. John Cooper. Indianapolis: Hackett.

Secondary Sources

Annas, J. (1981). *An Introduction to Plato's* Republic. Oxford: Oxford University Press.
Barker, E. (1918). *The Political Thought of Plato and Aristotle*. London: Methuen.
Bobonich, C. (2008). "Plato's Politics," in G. Fine (ed.), *The Oxford Handbook of Plato*. New York: Oxford University Press, 311–35
Brickhouse, T. C., and Smith, N. D. (2000). *Plato's Socrates*. New York: Oxford University Press.
Brown, L. (1998). "How Totalitarian is Plato's *Republic*?" in E. N. Ostenfeld (ed.), *Essays on Plato's Republic*. Aarhus: Aarhus University Press, 13–27.
Calvert, B. (1987). "Slavery in Plato's *Republic*," *Classical Quarterly*, 37: 367–72.
Cooper, J. M. (2005). "Political Animals and Civic Friendship," in R. Kraut and S. Skultety (eds), *Aristotle's Politics: Critical Essays*. Lanham, MD: Rowman and Littlefield, 65–89.
Hansen, M. H. (1991). *The Athenian Democracy in the Age of Demosthenes*. Oxford: B. Blackwell.
Hansen, M. H. (1993). "The *Polis* as a Citizen-State," in M. H. Hansen (ed.), *The Ancient Greek City-State*. Copenhagen: Munksgaard, 7–29.
Hansen, M. H. (2006). *Polis: An Introduction to the Greek City-State*. Oxford: Oxford University Press.
Kamtekar, R. (2001). "Social Justice and Happiness in the *Republic*: Plato's Two Principles," *History of Political Thought*, 22: 189–220.

---

[5] See Skinner (1978: i, 49–65, 159). I am grateful to George Klosko and Kristin Inglis for helpful comments on an earlier version of this chapter.

KAMTEKAR, R. (2006). "The Politics of Plato's Socrates," in S. Ahbel-Rappe and R. Kamtekar (eds), *A Companion to Socrates*. Oxford: Blackwell, 214–27.

KEYT, D. (2006). "Aristotle's Political Philosophy," in M. L. Gill and P. Pellegrin (eds), *A Companion to Ancient Philosophy*. Oxford: Blackwell, 393–412.

KEYT, D., and MILLER, F. (1995) (eds). *A Companion to Aristotle's Politics*. Oxford: Blackwell.

KLOSKO, G. (1984). "Provisionality in Plato's Ideal State," *History of Political Thought*, 5: 171–93.

KLOSKO, G. (2006). *The Development of Plato's Political Philosophy*. Oxford: Oxford University Press.

KRAUT, R. (1984). *Socrates and the State*. Princeton: Princeton University Press.

KRAUT, R. (1997) (ed.). *Plato's Republic: Critical Essays*. Lanham, MD: Rowman and Littlefield.

KRAUT, R. (2002). *Aristotle: Political Philosophy*. New York: Oxford University Press.

KRAUT, R., and SKULTETY, S. (2005) (eds). *Aristotle's Politics: Critical Essays*. Lanham, MD: Rowman and Littlefield.

LAKS, A. (1990). "Legislation and Demiurgy: On the Relationship between Plato's *Republic* and *Laws*," *Classical Antiquity*, 9: 209–29.

LAKS, A. (2000). "The *Laws*," in C. J. Rowe and M. Schofield (eds), *The Cambridge History of Greek and Roman Political Thought*. Cambridge: Cambridge University Press, 258–92.

MILLER, F. (1995). *Nature, Justice and Rights in Aristotle's Politics*. Oxford: Clarendon Press.

MORROW, G. (1960). *Plato's Cretan City: A Historical Interpretation of the Laws*. Princeton: Princeton University Press.

OBER, J. (1998). *Political Dissent in Democratic Athens*. Princeton: Princeton University Press.

OSTENFELD, E. N. (1998) (ed.). *Essays on Plato's Republic*. Aarhus: Aarhus University Press.

ROWE, C. J. (2000). "The *Politicus* and other Dialogues," in C. J. Rowe and M. Schofield (eds), *The Cambridge History of Greek and Roman Political Thought*. Cambridge: Cambridge University Press, 233–57.

ROWE, C. J., and SCHOFIELD, M. (2000) (eds). *The Cambridge History of Greek and Roman Political Thought*. Cambridge: Cambridge University Press.

SANTAS, G. (2006). *The Blackwell Guide to Plato's Republic*. Oxford: Blackwell.

SCHOFIELD, M. (2006). *Plato: Political Philosophy*. New York: Oxford University Press.

SCOTT, D. (2000). "Plato's Critique of the Democratic Character," *Phronesis*, 45: 19–37.

SKINNER, Q. (1978). *The Foundations of Modern Political Thought*. Cambridge: Cambridge University Press.

TAYLOR, C. C. W. (1997). "Plato's Totalitarianism," in R. Kraut (ed.), *Plato's Republic: Critical Essays*. Lanham, MD: Rowman and Littlefield, 31–48.

VLASTOS, G. (1968). "Does Slavery Exist in the *Republic*?" *Classical Philology*, 68: 291–5.

WALDRON, J. (1995). "The Wisdom of the Multitude: Some Reflections on Book 3, Chapter 11 of Aristotle's *Politics*," *Political Theory*, 23: 563–84. Repr. in R. Kraut and S. Skultety (eds), *Aristotle's Politics: Critical Essays*. Lanham, MD: Rowman and Littlefield, 145–65.

CHAPTER 8

....

HELLENISTIC POLITICAL THEORY

....

PHILLIP MITSIS

THERE is an almost schizophrenic quality to much of the surviving evidence for political thought in the Hellenistic period. On the one hand, we sometimes are given glimpses of what may have been novel and detailed accounts of the origins and goals of political societies and the nature of political obligation. Similarly, we can be fairly confident that major thinkers offered sketches of idealized political arrangements that were probably meant to provide, among other things, normative critiques of contemporary familial, religious, socio-economic, and foreign relations. At the same time, there are indications that there were even attempts to provide analyses of successful political leadership and of the best means for effectively promoting political ideals. Yet, the philosophers usually taken to be most characteristic of the Hellenistic period and whose views were to prove by far the most influential for subsequent political thinkers—the Epicureans, Stoics, and sometimes, honorifically, because of their influence on the Stoics, the Cynics—all emphatically insist that individuals can achieve perfect happiness completely on their own and under any kinds of inhospitable political conditions—even, for instance, when being unjustly and arbitrarily imprisoned and tortured on the rack. For many, this deepest and most fundamental guiding principle of much of Hellenistic philosophical thought is sufficient in itself to undermine the notion that philosophers of the period could have hoped to formulate anything resembling plausible political philosophies. The worry here, I take it, is akin to Bernard Williams's complaint against Rawls that "political philosophy is not just applied moral philosophy" (see Williams 2005: 77). To the extent that, in all disputes about value, Hellenistic philosophers ostentatiously wave as a trump card such narrowly ethical notions as inner autonomy or hedonic contentment, we may reasonably wonder whether they are in any position at all to convincingly argue about politics and political theory. Again, to allude to Williams's claim, we might think that their exclusive insistence on the importance of an agent's inner states is just too "primitive" to be of any use for doing political philosophy. To be sure, such criteria might be enlisted, for instance, helpfully to structure disagreements about the kinds of reasons that can be brought to bear on particular ethical decisions; but they seem insufficient on their own to give us much traction on real questions of political disagreement, much less on such fundamental political decisions as the kinds of large-scale actions that should be undertaken by political authorities deploying institutional and state power. To the extent, then, that we think that political questions are not reducible to ethical ones, we may well be disappointed by the arguments of Hellenistic philosophers, even when, or perhaps especially when, they appear to be taking on most directly the kinds of questions commonly asked by political theorists.

So, for instance, to take a recent salient example that illustrates the problem. A. A. Long has marshaled an impressive array of evidence in an attempt to show that Stoicism pioneered two fundamental elements of liberal political and economic thought: first, that, by the mere fact of being human, every individual is the rightful owner of at least one thing—his own person; and, second, that human nature inclines individuals to acquire private property and to interact in political societies with one another as owners of property (see Long 1997). From such evidence we might be led to conclude, as Long does, that the Stoics attempted to offer an analysis of some key elements in what looks like a proto-Lockean account of the origins and nature of political societies. But such a conclusion becomes problematic once we remember that the Stoic, while watching a mob of anarchists loot and burn a shopkeeper's store, must cheerfully confirm that such actions are entirely in keeping with the providential rational order of the universe and, accordingly, are not only in the shopkeeper's own best interests, but also in those of his society generally and, indeed, the universe writ large. Consequently, whatever we may make of a moral attitude that allows Stoics to view property losses with utter indifference and to consider an agent's inner autonomy as the only thing of moral importance, we might reasonably conclude that such commitments inevitably limit the scope and interest, at least in a recognizably political sense, of any claims they might want to make about the nature of property and its meaning for members of a political community. Indeed, it would be hard to imagine a starker contrast between such a radically depoliticized, inward-looking moral perspective and the palpable political values and goals that structure, say, Locke's arguments about property.

In light of such worries, it is perhaps not surprising, then, that there has been a long tradition (see Sabine 1937; McIlwain 1940; Sinclair 1952), given famous expression by Hegel, that finds in Hellenistic philosophers' sometimes theatrical celebrations of individual autonomy and their ultimate disdain for the material conditions of life— that very Hegelian worry—an explanation not only for Hellenistic philosophers' failure adequately to address central questions of political philosophy, but also for their actually creating a gap in ancient thought between ethics and politics in the first place. So, for example, Isaiah Berlin writes, in an essay entitled "The Birth of Greek Individualism," that "once the seamless whole of the city state in which the public and the private are not distinguished is torn, nothing can make it whole again," with the result that public and individual values, "which had not been discriminate before, now

go in different directions (in the Hellenistic period) and, at times, clash violently"
(Berlin 2005: 319). This claim, as he realizes, is something of an exaggeration, since,
however large Plato and Aristotle—whom he takes as exemplifying the seamless whole
tradition—may loom in retrospect for the history of political thought, there certainly
were signs of such a split earlier among political thinkers, not to mention in the minds
of actual political actors, if one is to judge by the historical record. Yet, by the same
token, there was really nothing to compare with what quickly became so all-pervasive
and relentlessly systematic in the philosophy of the Hellenistic period. Moreover, it is
also true that, in the early modern period, the seminal arguments that political
philosophers made use of to think through the problems of reconciling private with
public interests were often those arising out of Hellenistic philosophy. Thus, as a
general characterization of the period, especially if one takes the long view from within
the traditions of political thought itself, Berlin's overall contrast can serve as a useful
starting point.

Of course, one can view this philosophical shift in focus from public to private as
ultimately having positive or negative effects depending on one's sympathies for
political argument rooted in either communitarian or individualist concerns. Once
our most central values no longer issue primarily from a particular political community, we are unlikely to view membership in it as having the same significance.
Accordingly, some theorists lament the loss of communal and social solidarity that
results from such a gap, and they are sharply critical, moreover, of the specific attempts
in the period to derive political and social arrangements from such decidedly individualistic values as Epicurean pleasure or the kind of rarely achieved individual moral
perfection touted by the Stoics. Among more vehement critics, such as Hegel and
MacIntyre, in addition to a kind of prelapsarian nostalgia for the solidarity and sense
of belonging offered by earlier political philosophy, one can discern a tone of scarcely
disguised indignation at the affront that the philosophers of this period present to
political theory itself, since Hellenistic philosophers no longer treat it as being capable
of dealing with questions that penetrate to the very essence of what makes us human.
Individual ethical aims are prior and more fundamental, and thus no longer merely
derivative from the larger goals and needs of states. As a consequence, it is as if, in
Berlin's words, "political philosophy had suddenly vanished away" (see Berlin 2005:
302) or at the very least, was left deeply humbled. Others, however, from Hobbes to
Berlin, have extolled in their own ways what they view as a new conception of the
individual, at last mentally liberated from the suffocating demands of the group and
from the need to make unthinking sacrifices of personal good for the public weal.
Instead of indulging in the naivety or bad faith that led Plato and Aristotle to arrange
individuals institutionally according to the needs of the polis through so-called natural
hierarchies, in their view Hellenistic philosophers, to their credit, at least set individuals mentally free to find their own personal happiness and individual salvation
according to rational moral principles. One perhaps might have to wait until the early
modern period for philosophers to harness these initial insights into anything resembling coherent political theories; but Hellenistic philosophers' inward turn, in the view

of such individualist theorists, crucially prepared the way for much of modern political theory as we know it.

Whichever side of this divide one lines up on, however, such a dramatic shift in perspective—from the defining feature of life being one's political group to the notion that one's own inner life provides the only genuine basis from which to view the world—is arguably responsible for ushering in a host of other enduring transformations that would deeply affect the subsequent course of political thought.

Berlin, who claims that Hellenistic philosophy is responsible for the first of three fundamental paradigm shifts in the history of political thought—the other two being Machiavelli's declaration of the incompatibility of values and German Romanticism's denial that questions of value are really genuine questions—offers a succinct and incisive catalogue of what traditionally has been taken to be the period's most salient shifts in theoretical perspective.

> Within twenty years or less we find, in place of hierarchy, equality; in place of emphasis on the superiority of specialists, the doctrine that any man can discover the truth himself and live the good life as well as any other man, at least in principle ... in place of loyalty, which holds small groups together, groups molded by tradition and memories, and the organic fitting-in of all their parts and functions, there is a world without national or city frontiers; in place of the outer life, the inner life; in place of political commitment, taken for granted by all the major thinkers of the previous age, sermons recommending total detachment. In place of the pursuit of grandeur, glory, immortal fame, nobility, public spirit, self-realization in harmonious social action, gentlemanly ideals, we now have a notion of individual self-sufficiency, praise of austerity, a puritanical emphasis on duty, above all constant stress on the fact that the highest of all values is peace of soul, individual salvation, obtained not by knowledge of an accumulating kind, not by gradual increase of scientific information (as Aristotle taught), nor by the use of sensible judgment in public affairs, but by sudden conversion—a shining of the inner light. Men are distinguished into the converted and the unconverted. There are no intermediate types; they are either saved or not saved, either wise or stupid. (Berlin 2005: 302–3)

It is worth quoting Berlin at such length because he is writing not only before the recent resurgence of scholarship on Hellenistic philosophy, but also before the even more recent renewal of scholarly interest in the political thought of the period.[1] For many contemporary scholars, no doubt, Berlin represents a traditional voice from the past that recent professional scholarship has made rather out of date. However, in what follows, I will consider a range of recent major reconstructions of Hellenistic political views by scholars who claim that the period did indeed engage in genuine political philosophy and that Berlin's traditional view needs to be displaced. In each case, I think, the arguments for these reconstructions fail to convince, at least on the basis

---

[1] "The Birth of Greek Individualism" is the first of the three Storrs Lectures that Berlin gave at Yale University in 1962.

of the surviving evidence. Moreover, even if we were to grant the plausibility of these reconstructions, when examined against the backdrop of Berlin's central distinctions and concerns, they would still fail to contradict his general conclusion that it is "as if political philosophy suddenly vanished in the Hellenistic period." This is not to argue, of course, that all of Berlin's characterizations are the last word about the period or that they necessarily extend beyond Epicureanism and Stoicism to include the writings of other Hellenistic philosophical schools of thought such as, for instance, peripatetic accounts of monarchy or constitutional change. But recent scholarship, I think, has given insufficient reason so far to replace the general paradigm given such powerful expression by Berlin. There is still too much truth in his overall argument; moreover, his sense of the basic criteria necessary for formulating a genuine philosophy of politics seems surer than that evinced by any of the proposed alternatives.

Before turning to these reconstructions, however, it is perhaps worth pausing a moment to address an argument that has often accompanied the traditional view and that continues to be a source of misunderstanding. For Hegel, the inward turn of Hellenistic philosophers occurred in tandem with the destruction of traditional Greek *polis* life and the loss of political autonomy that occurred at the hands of Alexander the Great. After Alexander's death in 323 BCE, the dissolution of the organic sense of community characteristic of the ancient *polis* and that had furnished the context for Plato's and Aristotle's political thinking continued apace throughout the various Hellenistic kingdoms Alexander's successors established and then ruled essentially as monarchies. A tradition of scholarship indebted to Hegel often postulated a direct link between this supposed destruction of the mentality of the ancient *polis* and the inward turn of Hellenistic philosophy: faced with an external world that had lost any sense of social cohesion and that precluded meaningful political activity, philosophers limited their theoretical aims to offering a kind of paregoric psychological therapy to help individuals cope with a new set of realities in which they no longer viewed themselves as having any meaningful political role to play. In many past scholarly accounts, the relations between these new political realities and the changing focus of philosophy were given either quasi-historicist or reductionist explanations of a not particularly sophisticated sort. By this, I mean that, although assuming something akin to the historicizing view that all philosophical questions must be settled strictly within the confines of the political, social, scientific, and cultural contexts in which they occur, they seldom, when making their arguments, moved beyond very general accounts of the historical conditions of the period to provide anything in the way of fine-grained examinations of, say, economic relations and social structures or of the actual details of political processes and forms of political organization in the period. Thus, a number of scholars have recently made what amounts to a two-pronged attack on the kind of overall theoretical view to which Berlin gives voice. They have pointed out, rightly, that the political, social, and economic conditions of the period are too complex to support any kind of simple contrasts. For example, many facets of traditional *polis* life continued to operate and to give shape and meaning to individual's lives; many premarket structures of economic exchange remained fairly static; and continuities in many forms of political and social relations clearly occurred. At the same time, we have evidence for the titles of works by individual philosophers, for instance, in the case of the Stoics, suggesting that they may have written fairly extensively on topics of traditional political theory, although nothing of the works themselves survives. We also have reason to believe that particular philosophers, at times, may have been engaged in various political activities or expressed particular political views (see Erskine 1990). Thus, a number of recent scholars, while decrying the historicism and reductionism associated with the traditional view, have come to the conclusion that we can reject the claim that Hellenistic philosophers turned radically inward because, in fact, the change in historical conditions was not as drastic as assumed on the Hegelian picture and we also seem to have evidence that philosophers themselves engaged in politics.

Such arguments, however, arguably fall prey to the very objection that they are leveling against earlier historicist and reductionist views, and, to a great extent, I think, tend to throw the baby out with the bath water. It hardly seems consistent to argue that we should avoid making straightforward causal claims between historical conditions and philosophical doctrine, and then to assume, because one has shown that the general historical picture of the earlier view can be discredited, that it means we can jettison in turn the theoretical claim that Hellenistic philosophy turns inward and away from political philosophy. Such an argument merely adopts the kind of straightforward causal inferences it finds objectionable, and it hardly shows that an inward turn among philosophers did not occur or could not have occurred within a differently described set of historical conditions. To take a parallel example, many social historians have offered divergent accounts of the historical conditions underlying the so-called linguistic turn in modern philosophy; but few would deny that such a fundamental change of philosophical perspective occurred, even if other forms of philosophical thought continued to thrive or if signs of such a turn have been discovered in earlier periods and in different social contexts.

By the same token, to argue that Hellenistic philosophers may have written works with titles suggesting a concern for political philosophy in any strong sense or that they personally engaged in politics is, on the one hand, to rely on an argument from silence and, on the other, to assume some easy continuity between philosophers' theoretical views and their lives. In the case of the former, we have no evidence that, say, Zeno's or Chrysippus' On Law or Chrysippus' On City and Law did anything more than just assert their strong ethical claims about individual moral autonomy and then go on to deduce fairly thin and idealized arrangements from them. Even in the case of Cleanthes, who further subdivided the usual Stoic division of philosophy—logic, physics, and ethics—and alone among the Stoics created a subcategory for politics under ethics, we have no idea how he may have treated what looks like more fine-grained political topics in such attested works as On Councils or On Law Courts; nor, more importantly, do we have any sense how such a discussion could coherently grow out of what we do have strong evidence for—his unwavering insistence on inner moral autonomy. Indeed, we have the evidence of one prominent ancient politician and political thinker in a position to know something of these works,

Cicero, who expresses the view that, although early Stoics were clever in argument, they did not deal with political institutions in a way useful to cities and nations (*De legibus* 3.14). Similarly, it can only be a matter of pure speculation how individual Stoics may have reconciled, if indeed they even attempted to reconcile, any of their engagement in politics with the claim attested for both Zeno and Chrysippus that the wise man participates in politics, just so long as nothing impedes him (DL 7.121). While it is certainly true that philosophers of this period were apt to view philosophy as a way of life in a manner mostly unthinkable for contemporary philosophers, it is still hardly clear that we are to understand this participation in a way that somehow undermines the claim that they turned their focus inward to their own moral condition. Apart from the restriction of political activity to the wise (something neither Zeno nor Chrysippus ever claimed to be), because only the wise, presumably, might perform virtuously or promote virtue in politics, this participation seems entirely in keeping with Berlin's overall claim. The wise man engages in politics just so long as he is not impeded by the necessity of engaging in any non-virtuous activity; but politics is no longer the central function of his life. Such a claim still signals a move to a perspective where moral autonomy and personal ethics are conceptually prior and that clearly differs from an earlier one in which agents' lives are viewed primarily within the context of a *polis*, with all of its attendant political commitments (cf. Annas 1995: 302 ff).

   It might be claimed, of course, that Socrates who so often provided a model for Stoicism mostly kept clear of politics because he too was devoted in the first instance to his pursuit of virtue. But Socrates regularly views his pursuit of virtue in the context of a particular close-knit *polis* in which he is goading his fellow citizens to virtue. Moreover, it would be hard to read the *Apology* and *Crito* without noticing the fundamental context that Athens provides for his thinking about his relation to the law and his own attempt to determine a properly moral course of action (Vasiliou 2008: 46–90). For the Stoics, the wise man engages in political activity just so long as nothing hinders him— that is, presumably something that might interfere with his moral perfection and his ability to follow the universal rational laws of nature; but he certainly does not need to do so in order to be happy or to fulfill his nature, nor does he view himself as being fundamentally a part of any particular conventional political community. And, in any case, we certainly hear far more from the Stoics about the potential hindrances that political life presents and the necessity of the wise man's detachment from external affairs. Moreover, the direction of the argument moves, in line with Berlin's claims, clearly from ethics to politics. Thus, while it may be true that the general argument that Hellenistic philosophy accomplished a fundamental shift in theoretical focus has often been accompanied in the past both by some dubious historical claims and by a series of dubious inferences from them, it seems to me that the force of Berlin's general contrasts still remains. Recent reconstructions of Hellenistic political views, rather than undermining them, on closer examination actually tend to bear them out, if one keeps philosophers' central ethical imperatives in proper focus when viewing the evidence.

I will be focusing almost entirely on the Stoics, since among Hellenistic philosophers their views have been singled out in the current scholarship as having the greatest claim to be considered important and influential in the history of political thought.[2] At the same time, they are almost alone in being invoked in contemporary political philosophical discussions. Somewhat surprisingly, perhaps, they have even been called on to speak to issues that figure in some of the most contentious of current political debates. To take one prominent example, Martha Nussbaum, in the course of arguing against Richard Rorty's call for Americans to give up the politics of indifference and to embrace both patriotism and a common feeling of national identity, argues that we would do much better to adopt "the very old idea of the cosmopolitan, the person whose allegiance is to the worldwide community of human beings" (Nussbaum 1996: 4). Appealing to a two-sentence summary of the main point of Zeno's *Republic* by Plutarch (CE 46–120) for the Stoic notion of a world citizen, she claims that it is "the source and ancestor of Kant's idea of the 'kingdom of ends', and has a similar function in inspiring and regulating moral and political conduct. One should always behave so as to treat with equal respect the dignity of reason and moral choice in every human being" (Nussbaum 1996: 8). Such a notion, she insists, can be appealed to in order to help ward off the many potential harms fostered by nationalism and partisan loyalties as well as such potentially morally blinding commitments as gender, class, ethnicity, and so on. At the same time, one of the strengths of the Stoics' political vision, in her view, is that it is able to combine a respect for universal moral laws and for each human qua human with a rich recognition of individuals' local affiliations. To arrive at this picture of cosmopolitanism with a communitarian face, she relies on an argument by the Stoic philosopher Hierocles (first–second century CE), who describes each of us as being surrounded by an extending series of concentric circles beginning with our innermost self, family, relatives, neighbors, and so on, and then ending with a final circle embracing humanity as a whole. On the basis of her interpretation of this text, she argues that the Stoics insist that we do not "need to give up our specific affections and identifications, whether ethnic or gender-based or religious. We need not think of them as superficial, and we may think of our identity as being partly constituted by them" (Nussbaum 1996: 9). With a few brief strokes, Nussbaum gives an incisive summary of the case that many contemporary scholars have tried to make for the reach and importance of Stoic political theory. She also touches on two of the main texts that have often featured most prominently in recent detailed reconstructions of

---

[2] It is a commonplace that the Epicureans reject politics and political involvement. The best recent account is Fowler (1989). This is not to claim that their idea of a social contract did not prove extremely fruitful for later political thinkers. But their view that happiness is an invulnerable inner state makes it hard to see why individuals would need to enter into a contract for the sake of their interests or participate in political institutions. The Epicurean ideal is one of mutual friendship between the wise with "no need of city-walls or laws and all the things we manufacture on account of one another" (Diogenes of Oenoanda new fr. 21.1.4–14 = LS 22S). Evidence for the antinomian Cynics is usefully collected in Dawson (1992).

Stoic political theory, and she offers interpretations of them that are, for the most part, in line with a wide consensus of current scholarly opinion.

Two things might initially strike the reader, however. The account we are given is based, in the first instance, on what can only be viewed as the slimmest and most problematic kind of evidence. In the case of the claim derived from Plutarch, for instance, as we shall see in more detail, we are confronted with an incredibly compressed report of the one main point of an entire work—and by someone who may never have read it. Imagine the task and the probable success of trying to divine the scope and goals of other major works of philosophy on the basis of such criteria. To this, we should probably add that the report is by a Platonizing author who is hostile to Stoicism and who elsewhere devotes volumes to picking out, often unfairly, what he takes to be contradictions in Stoic arguments. Second, Nussbaum's two-stepped argument depends on the possibility of extracting a coherent common argumentative goal from two texts with widely divergent aims that are written by different authors with deeply divergent intellectual affiliations; the passages occur, moreover, in different literary genres with very different conventions of argument. By the same token, we have no evidence that any ancient Stoic ever intended these two arguments to be put together in quite this way to form this particular argument. In other words, Nussbaum's reconstruction of the argument, in a deep sense, is a philosophical artifact for which we have no corresponding connected ancient argument. The particular link that she establishes between these two texts is thus the result of a modern reconstruction that itself depends on the monumental industry of scholars who have collected together every possible scrap of evidence for Stoic views, however hostile, indifferent, or careless. Here we might have at least hoped for some help from an ancient critic of the Stoics such as the voluminous and caustic Plutarch, for instance, to give us some indication that these two arguments were intended to form a connected whole. As one who has an eye peeled for surface contradictions in Stoic arguments, Plutarch might have been counted on for some entertaining comments on an overall Stoic argument that, on the one hand, claims that we should treat others in a way that rises above local group memberships as well as above such things as class, gender, and ethnicity to a proto-Kantian view of ourselves and others—that is, as cosmopolitans; at the same time, however, it enjoins us to think of our identities as being constituted by more local communitarian affinities, whether they are based on religion, gender, or ethnicity. Of course, it is clear that Nussbaum has a normative conception of such local affinities, and only the beneficial versions are supposed to go into defining our special humanity. But less scrupulous critics, such as Plutarch, might have made a good piece of work out of generating a series of unsympathetic contradictions between the two components of this argument that, at least at first blush, might seem both to eliminate and to embrace individuals' commitments to their local affinities. How am I supposed both to eliminate and to embrace, say, my gender and ethnicity in thinking about my moral obligations to others? Often, we can hope to rely on the Stoics' critics to help us divine the contours of arguments for which we have spotty evidence, even when they extend to some of the more arcane reaches of Stoic epistemology and logic. One might therefore have expected some ancient critical comment on an argument that supposedly resides at the very heart of Stoic political theory. The fact that on this score we are greeted with ancient silence may be indicative that we should approach it with caution.

It might be useful at this point to turn to these two key passages from Plutarch and Hierocles and look at them in more detail. This will give some sense of the kinds of evidence and inferences that typically go into any assertions about Hellenistic political theory, while also allowing us to assess the extent to which these arguments can hope to have a claim on the attention of political theorists.

The most famous and notorious passage about Stoic politics purports to give the key thesis of the most famous and notorious work of Stoic philosophy, the *Republic* of Zeno of Citium. By way of preliminaries, I offer my own translation and some observations about its overall context.

And, indeed, provoking much amazement, the *(R)epublic* (*politeia*) of Zeno, who founded the Stoic school of thought, strives to make this one main point, that we should not dwell in cities and communities each (of us) isolated by distinct legal ordinances (*dikaiois*), but that we should consider all human beings to be fellow community members and fellow citizens, and that there should be one form of life and organization (*kosmos*), just like a herd grazing together and brought up in a common pasture (or in a common custom or law).[3] Zeno, for his part, wrote this down, having imagined it to be unreal or as a mere image of the lawful orderliness (*eunomias*) of the philosopher and of the *politeia*, whereas Alexander provisioned talk with deeds (Plutarch, *De Alexandri magni fortuna aut virtute* i. 329a8–b7).

Plutarch is writing at a distance of some three hundred years from Zeno, and, in the particular biographical genre in which this comment occurs, he typically lets the overall context or goals of his argument control his selection and presentation of texts. He is neither claiming nor pretending to be holding up any philosophical doctrines for close analysis and scrutiny. This does not mean, of course, that we should dismiss any potential evidence that might be gleaned from what he says about Zeno,[4] but neither can we treat it as if it were a bit of straightforward reporting of a philosophical argument. Nothing of what he has to say about other philosophers in the context of this essay about the life and accomplishments of Alexander the Great has garnered even the slightest amount of attention, so it is not difficult for those skeptical about the worth of this report to suspect that it is the sheer lack of other evidence for Zeno's political thought that has mostly generated such intense scholarly interest in these particular remarks.

It is by no means certain that Plutarch had any first-hand familiarity with Zeno's work. In his *Life of Lycurgus* (31.1–18), for instance, he lumps Zeno and Diogenes

---

[3] There is a question of whether this should be *no-mos'* (pasture, habitation) or *no'-mos* (law, custom). Neither is impossible, since Plutarch is punning on both senses throughout the passage. The notion of sheep being reared in a common law is a bit strained, whereas the image of sheep grazing in a common pasture maintains the appropriate contrast with people living within distinct legal boundaries; hence I prefer Hembold's emendation *no-mos'*.

[4] The most detailed recent argument for Stoic cosmopolitanism, Vogt (2008) essentially rests its case on the validity of Plutarch's report and mostly takes it at face value.

together with his own preferred philosophical guide, Plato, as philosophers whose views are all in accord with Lycurgus' "main point" that the happiness both of a city and of an individual consists in virtue and in internal harmony or concord (31.5). Given what we know about stoic psychological theory, it is highly unlikely that in any of his writings Zeno subscribed to a view of happiness that identifies it with an individual's inner harmony or concord in this Platonic sense. Nor do we have any independent evidence for stoics ascribing happiness (*eudaimonia*) to a city taken as a whole or of their making Platonic analogies between the psychic states of an individual and the internal ordering of a polity. Plutarch's chief concern in this passage, however, is not to provide even the roughest account of philosophical differences, but to pin down a general contrast between philosophers, like Plato, Diogenes, and Zeno, who have left only a legacy of words, and Lycurgus, who established an actual city of individual and communal virtue and concord. Since he believes all recognized philosophers share the trait of being ineffectual, Plutarch seems perfectly happy to shoehorn all of them, even those he leaves unnamed, into the same vaguely Platonic framework.

By the same token, in our passage's comparison between Zeno and Alexander the Great, we see Plutarch making a correspondingly sharp contrast between a philosopher who has merely imagined something unreal and a man of action who has performed great deeds. The passage's concluding statement often has been taken, however, as evidence for the stronger claim that Zeno described an ideal, utopian political arrangement in his *Politeia* (Vander Waerdt 1994: 294–5). On its own, however, Plutarch's comment hardly licenses such a straightforward inference, since, in the general course of his discussion, he consigns all philosophers, including Aristotle, to the same boat. They all produce only words, not deeds. To ask whether those words recommend actual political arrangements or describe utopias is for Plutarch's purposes irrelevant, since both are equally ineffectual. Of course, this does not show that Zeno could not or did not conceive of a utopian city with correspondingly utopian political arrangements. But, given the overall context and Plutarch's preoccupation with contrasting words and deeds, we have no reasonable basis for drawing any conclusions about the actual content of Zeno's account of lawful orderliness (*eunomia*), if, indeed, he ever used this precise terminology.

Similarly, Plutarch's concluding claim about the orderliness of the philosopher and of the city seems of a piece with the kind of general Platonizing view also salient in his account of Lycurgus; hence, it too hardly inspires confidence. We might speculate that Zeno thought that there was some connection between the orderliness of the philosopher and that of the *politiea*, understood in a broader or more restricted sense; or we might wonder if only philosophers populated his *politiea*, since only the philosopher is mentioned here, even though this might seem directly to contradict his earlier claim about viewing all humans as fellow citizens; but all such inferences again would be based on mere speculation.

Plutarch, therefore, is keen in both of these contexts to contrast philosophers, who have left a legacy of nothing but words, with men of action such as Lycurgus and Alexander. In the larger context of his discussion of Alexander, however, he further insists that Alexander should qualify as a philosopher on the basis of his deeds. These deeds include bringing together men from everywhere and mixing together their way of life, characters, and marriages; bidding them all to consider the whole inhabited world as their fatherland; and enjoining them to regard good individuals as kinsmen (*suggeneis*) and those who are bad as foreigners (329c3–9 *passim*). It is worth keeping these particular accomplishments of Alexander in mind since they furnish the basic grounds for the overall contrast Plutarch is drawing between Alexander and the philosophers.

So far, I have managed to touch on only a few of the difficulties that scholars face in treating this kind of report and have done so mainly for illustrative purposes. At the risk of belaboring the point, it is perhaps helpful to remind ourselves, however, of what a tissue of suppositions such attempted reconstructions are made and how difficult it is to extract even the slightest bit of plausible information from reports that are embedded in these kinds of larger contexts.

In any case, according to Plutarch, Zeno's main point can be broken down as follows: (*a*) that we should not dwell in cities and communities each (of us) isolated by distinct legal ordinances (*dikaiois*); but (*b*) that we should consider all human beings to be fellow community members and fellow citizens; and (*c*) that there should be one form of life and organization (*kosmos*), just like a herd grazing together and brought up in a common pasture (or in a common custom or law).

The initial problem we face is that this text is systematically ambiguous between what from the point of view of moral and political philosophy is a rather bland and conventional claim and something potentially more exciting, as in Nussbaum's reading. On a deflationary reading of the passage, we might maintain that, in accordance with Plutarch's overall conclusion, what Alexander accomplished historically was to break down distinct legal ordinances and to make everyone members of the same community.[5] That Alexander was instrumental in joining communities together exactly in this way is one of Plutarch's most common refrains in the work and elsewhere he claims that, whereas only a few have read Plato's *Laws*, the myriads who previously were either living brutishly without laws or living under their own laws came to make common use of Alexander's laws (328e5–8). To follow out this deflationary line of argument, we have to suppose that Plutarch's primary concern is to illustrate these characteristic results of Alexander's actions and that he makes a reference to an ineffectual philosopher like Zeno on the basis of some rather tenuous and mostly irretrievable similarities, or in the same merely arbitrary way, for instance, as he does in the above reference to Plato's *Laws*.

For those defending the kind of cosmopolitan reading Nussbaum offers, on the other hand, there are a host of formidable obstacles. When taken out of its larger context, it is easy to see how (*b*), for instance, might conjure up moral and political attitudes such as a cosmopolitan respect for universal justice, equality, and the intrinsic mutual respect of all individuals by reason of their common humanity—especially when one is looking back through the lens of the later history of political theory. This is indeed heady stuff, of

---

[5] With the proviso that Plutarch claims that Alexander thought that only the good were kinsman and that the bad should be viewed as foreigners and hence no longer as fellow citizens.

course, but I doubt that a careful reading of the passage as a whole can actually support any of these claims. First, Plutarch can hardly be seriously concluding that what Alexander accomplished historically through his conquests[6] is such an earthly realization of the kingdom of ends. Moreover, it would severely undercut his own argument to show that Alexander only accomplished something that is a pale reflection of what Zeno was imagining. In fact, it is Zeno, he claims, who is capable of imagining only an image of what Alexander has achieved. The direction of explanation, then, goes from Alexander to Zeno, and those who support a high cosmopolitan reading leave Plutarch with the odd result of making Alexander's achievements rather second rate compared with Zeno's moral vision, which can hardly be Plutarch's point. By the same token, we have to be careful about how we read the modal claims in "we should not dwell in communities isolated by legal ordinances" and "we should consider all humans as fellow citizens." Proponents of cosmopolitanism typically interpret this as distinguishing two communities, "the local community of our birth, and the community of human agreement and aspiration . . . that is fundamentally the source of our moral obligations."[7] They then assume that Plutarch must be referring to the latter. But here Plutarch is surely making a different point that is in line with his central goal of favorably contrasting Alexander with philosophers. Philosophers say that people should live in a particular manner, but Alexander through his actions makes it the case that people actually live in that manner. Plutarch is not signaling a distinction between a natural and conventional community. Rather, he is claiming (no doubt tendentiously) that Zeno could at best urge people in words to live in a way that Alexander made possible in deeds.

By the same token, Nussbaum interprets (*a*) as a deep moral command enjoining that we should consider all human beings our fellow citizens with respect to such basic moral values as justice. What Plutarch actually says, however, is far less morally dramatic and, again, something readily achievable through territorial conquest rather than any deepened sense of moral recognition—that is, that people dwell together under the same legal ordinances.

Of course, it might be objected that there must be some basis of comparison with Zeno's views for Plutarch to be referring to him in this context. As we have seen, this is not necessarily the case, since Plutarch's comparisons are often merely arbitrary, but one possible candidate in this passage is the Stoic notion of the *koinos nomos*, or common natural law pervading all things. Plutarch shows an awareness of this central Stoic doctrine elsewhere and may be alluding to it here (see Vander Waerdt 1994: 272

---

[6] Vogt (2008), for instance, in giving her strong cosmopolitan reading of the passage, breaks off the final sentence before the concluding contrast with Alexander, presumably following Long and Sedley (67A). This leaves her in the odd position of offering an interpretation of the argument independently of its actual conclusion about Alexander.

[7] Nussbaum (1996: 7). Cf. Vogt (2008). In this context scholars typically allude to a claim by Seneca in his *De otio* that we all live in two such communities. This is an interesting later development in Stoicism, but the point of Plutarch's modal contrast here in relation to Zeno is different. For earlier Stoics, it seems fairly clear that only the wise and gods partake in a cosmic community of "human agreement and aspiration." (See Schofield 1991: 57–92.)

ff.). In Diogenes Laertius, we find a typical instance of this Stoic claim, for which there is much evidence:

> living in agreement with nature comes to be the end, which is in accordance with the nature of oneself and that of the whole, engaging in no activity forbidden by universal law (*ho nomos ho koinos*), which is right reason pervading everything and identical to Zeus, who is the director of the administration of existing things. And the virtue of the happy man and his good flow of life are just this: always doing everything on the basis of concordance of each man's guardian spirit with the will of the administrator of the whole. (DL7.88, trans. LS 63C)

The Stoics think that the universe is governed by a divine providential law and that one will be both virtuous and happy only if one follows it. But, even if we grant that (3) makes an allusion to the Stoic's claim that we should live by the divine commands of nature law, we still need to be careful about how we approach the claims in (1) and (2), and also about the political conclusions we draw from the passage. First, it is clear that, for Zeno, only the wise and the gods can live in accordance with the *koinos nomos*. Everyone else, of course, is still subject to the *koinos nomos* and thus *should not* dwell in isolated judicial districts (1) and *should* regard all humans as members of the same community and as fellow citizens (2). However, as we shall see, it is not at all clear that living according to divine law requires from the Stoic the kinds of generalized moral attitudes to others that characterize Kant's kingdom of ends, since, although everyone may have the potential to take part in this moral community, precious few actually do—only the wise and gods. Nor, as a consequence, does obedience to the *koinos nomos* necessarily require the kinds of political commitments Nussbaum links to a more generalized cosmopolitanism. Moreover, it should be remembered that Plutarch's main emphasis is on the difference between what Zeno could only imagine in words and what Alexander actually achieved through his conquests—bringing people to live together in common like a grazing herd. The actual image of grazing sheep, however, is most likely a Platonic one and is consonant with Plutarch's emphasis on how Alexander's conquests helped to bring peace and order to a chaotic world. In other contexts, moreover, such an image typically suggests a Platonic notion that sheep graze most harmoniously and safely under the eye of a benign and watchful shepherd/ruler. So we should be wary about the political message we can draw from this image and from the passage in general. The fact that someone is a fellow member of my community or a fellow citizen does not by itself guarantee that I view him as my equal, if my community is arranged in various social and political hierarchies. While it is true that, for the Stoics, we are all rational sparks of god and equal in that basic sense, this does not lead them to make any straightforward inferences to universal *political* equality. Indeed, just the opposite seems to be the case, and the surviving Stoic texts we have using the terminology of *isotês* or a*equalitas* all aim at capturing a notion of the impartial administration of law among individuals who are clearly assumed to belong to different levels of political and social hierarchies. Modern attempts to enlist Stoics in the ranks of cosmopolitan thinkers often merely assume that their cosmopolitanism entails a range of other political attitudes and ideals as well. The Stoics, however, typically argue that we may be given different social and political roles to play by fate, but it is a matter of moral indifference whether we play the role of, say, an Agamemnon or a Thersites (DL 7.160). No matter the role we play, we can still perfect our inner moral autonomy.

It is probably time to ask, however, what the upshot of this kind of philological detective work is for our understanding of the Stoics' political theory. At the risk of trying the patience of those not familiar with the field, I have tried to give a glimpse of the nature of the evidence that remains and the sorts of assumptions and arguments that surround it. I have argued that it is not very likely that this passage from Plutarch can carry the burden of even bland forms of political cosmopolitanism, much less anything that might contradict Berlin's view of the period. But, even if we granted a stronger cosmopolitan reading of the passage, we would still be left at best with a certain kind of thin moral regard for others that may be ethically commendable, but that leaves questions of political engagement and state institutional power untouched. Nothing in this passage, therefore, is incompatible with the traditional view that, in the Hellenistic period, philosophers turned inward and, giving up their interests in questions of political autonomy and participation, decided that the best thing for individuals to do from the point of politics was—perhaps to stretch the image—merely to graze together like contented and self-absorbed sheep. This is, no doubt, a deflationary view of the Stoic's political thought and perhaps much less interesting than what is on offer from several modern reconstructions. As is often the case, however, many philosophers become much more influential and turn out to be far more interesting for what they are thought to have said, as opposed to what they have actually said. Thus, this is not to claim that there cannot be considerable value in injecting such views of the Stoics into current debates for the sake of philosophical argument.

By a kind of nice irony, however, there are some other bits of stray evidence for Zeno's views that might put us a slight step closer to political thought, though of a darker and perhaps more sinister variety. Carl Schmitt, in trying to carve out a place for politics distinct from law (and from theories like cosmopolitanism based on moral laws), claimed that the fundamental concept of the political is defined by the criterion of friend and enemy. The Stoics, of course, do not share Schmitt's fascination with the kinds of ingrained violence that can be generated by conflicts between friends and enemies, but there is some tantalizing evidence that they may have expressed the realities of political difference in ways that sharply conflict with the idyllic vision of grazing sheep ascribed to them by Plutarch and those contemporary scholars who rely on him. There is a report in Diogenes Laertius that the associates of Cassius the Skeptic (again a hostile source) attacked Zeno for saying in his *Republic* that

> all who are not virtuous are foes, enemies, slaves, and estranged from one another, including parents and children, brothers and brothers, relations and relations . . . only virtuous people in the *Republic* (are) citizens, friends, relations, and free, so that for the Stoics, parents and children are enemies, since they are not wise. (DL 7.32 ff. = LS 67B modified)

In contrast to Plutarch, the skeptics mentioned in this passage actually purport to be quoting from Zeno's *Republic*, give detailed information that is plausible in light of what we generally know about Stoic ethical claims, and are obviously trying to engage in philosophical criticism, not write literary biography. On the basis of this evidence, which is arguably far more reliable, it becomes even harder to conclude that Zeno thinks that we are all members of a cosmopolitan community in any of the important political senses we have so far canvassed. Zeno thinks that only the wise are capable of being citizens, and that their wisdom alone is their ticket of admission to his *Republic*. It has been argued that we can perhaps reconcile this bleak view of the possibilities of our common humanity with Plutarch's account. When Plutarch says that Zeno's point was that we should consider all human beings as fellow citizens, it reflects a Stoic belief in a future ideal world in which all people would eventually become wise (Dawson 1992: 178). I doubt this is a plausible reading of Plutarch, for reasons that should be clear, but, in any case, such a brand of idealized, perfectionist cosmopolitanism is cold comfort for those, like Nussbaum, who are trying to defend the notion that Zeno believed that we all already live both in our conventional communities and in a universal moral community to which we have primary allegiance. Most likely, Zeno claimed that only the wise (and the gods) can evince the appropriate moral regard for each other, and it is never made clear in any of our evidence that the mass of mankind is similarly entitled to such regard. Indeed, he relegates the rest of mankind to relations of enmity and to living in political conditions that countenance all manner of unjust hierarchies. This may be a sad result for advocates of cosmopolitanism, but it would perhaps inch the Stoics' closer, in the minds of many, to a deeper acknowledgment of some of the harsher realities of actual political life.

Diogenes Laertius continues this report, however, by relating several other features that characterize life in Zeno's *Republic*. In essence, we are treated to a kind of antinomian laundry list of the traditional features of *polis* life that the new city of the wise will lack. It is a city that has been eviscerated of almost any positive recommendations whatsoever, much less institutions. Of course, it goes without saying that a Stoic sage might live in any kind of city and still be perfectly happy, since he has no fundamental commitments to any particular group of individuals, not even, perhaps, his fellow wise men.[8] If a group of wise Stoics did live together, however, their dwelling place according to Zeno would have no temples or statues of gods, no law courts, no gymnasia, no weapons, no money, and presumably no private property, for the wise do not need such things. General education would also be abolished. For one living according to the laws of reason, the political institutions based on irrational religious fears, worries about material goods and about status, or about defending one's self or one's own from others are unnecessary. At the same time, in his *Republic*, Chrysippus,

---

[8] "Nevertheless, though the sage may love his friends dearly, often comparing them with himself and putting them ahead of himself, yet all the good will be limited to his own being and he will speak the words which were spoken by the very Stilbo . . . after his country was captured, and his children and wife lost . . . in answer to the question whether he had lost anything. 'I have all my goods with me'" (Seneca, *Ep. Mor.* 9.18).

presumably following Zeno, advocates total sexual polymorphism, since sex is a matter of moral indifference, and it is nothing more than bits of flesh rubbing against each other. It might be the flesh of one's mother, daughter, sister, or anyone else male or female, it is all the same. In Plato's *Republic*, sexual communism is carefully controlled as a means of breeding the best citizens, and there is a built-in rider aimed at avoiding incest. For the Stoics, sex is an indifferent external consideration of the flesh that in no way touches inner moral autonomy. Such indifference to the flesh means, as well, that institutions surrounding the burial of the dead are also to be eliminated. Giving members of the community a proper burial was taken throughout the Greek tradition to be one of the most important and crucial political functions of the city state (cf. *Antigone*, Pericles' funeral oration at Thucydides 2.35 ff., etc.). Indeed, Herodotus (Hdt. 3.228) argues that what conventionally marks Greek culture off from Indian culture, for instance, is that the Greeks burn their dead while the Indians have the custom of eating them. The Stoics, taking to heart this kind of Herodotean lesson, argue that the treatment of the dead is a matter of pure convention. The dead are just flesh, so if you do not want to waste the meat, it is perfectly in keeping with nature to eat it.

On the basis of our passage in Plutarch, it has often been claimed that Zeno, like Alexander, was interested in a kind of world state. But, given these features of Zeno's *Republic*, it is difficult to see any operative conception of states and their political mechanisms in evidence at all. The regulation of public affairs is collapsed entirely into a vision of private morality—a private Stoic morality that makes political institutions unnecessary. Zeno's only positive recommendations involve the common use of wives and, perhaps, property, along with a revealing same-sex dress code. The last seems too frivolous to justify. Why should it matter to the wise how they and others dress, since it is merely a conventional covering of what is a matter of indifference? But the community of wives and property has led some to postulate a vision of a republic in which "communist institutions" bolster the "political virtue of its citizens" (see Schofield 1991: 22; Dawson 1992: 187). If one finds any whiff of communism in these two claims, however, it is one in which the state and its institutions have already withered away and we are left with an ethical ideal of wise citizens who are friends doing what friends proverbially do: sharing what they have in common. The Stoics do not recommend using property in common because they regard it, for instance, as an important good that has been monopolized by a particular powerful class and whose unfair distribution has led to injustice and various kinds of suffering that need to be eliminated. Nor do they think, as does Plato, that it is politically advantageous to separate state power and private property. All this is a matter of moral indifference to them. Thus, to speak of communist political "institutions" or Stoic "communism" in such a context seems rather feckless, at least given the political experience of the last hundred years.

Before turning to Hierocles, one final influential attempt to find a political dimension in Zeno's *Republic* needs to be mentioned. Malcolm Schofield offers a Platonizing version of the relations among Zeno's wise citizens based on Eros or erotic love. This might initially strike one as an odd claim, given the Stoics' concerted attempts to eliminate the passions from our lives, but Schofield argues that Zeno sought to guarantee civic harmony in the city of the wise by institutionalizing "radically sub-limated" erotic relations, primarily those associated with the traditional conventions of Greek pederasty (see Schofield 1991: 22–56). Zeno was spurred to incorporate such erotic relations and institutions because of his concern for the security of the city.

Schofield grounds his argument for what he calls Zeno's "city of love" on the following passage:

> Pontianus said that Zeno of Citium regarded Eros as god of friendship and freedom and the provider in addition of concord, but of nothing else. Hence in the *Republic* Zeno said: "Eros is the god which contributes to the city's security." (Athenaeus of Naucratis, *Deipnosophistai* 13.561 = LS 67D)

Questions about the reliability of this report are perhaps even more complex than those of our passage in Plutarch, and, of necessity, Schofield amasses in support of his argument a welter of other passages that present their own corresponding doxograph-ical difficulties. This is not the place to sort through them, so, at this point, my argument, unfortunately, will have to be nasty, brutish, and short. The Stoics are well known for reinterpreting the traditional gods and their attributes in light of their own theories. Even if we were to concede to Schofield the reliability of this passage, what it presents at best is a glimpse of a radical Stoic reinterpretation, not a Freudian sublimation, of the god Eros. Erotic love, which is traditionally linked to the creation of enmity, a loss of freedom, and is seen as being a chief source of social and political discord, is redescribed by Zeno as the god of "friendship and freedom and the provider in addition of concord (*homonoia*), *but nothing else*." Thus, rather than being a "city of love," Zeno's *Republic* is a city where love in any recognizable sense has been eliminated and given a self-consciously new, non-erotic, Stoic identity. By the same token, the Stoics straightforwardly replace erotic relations with relations of friendship (cf. DL 7.130) that are, presumably, compatible with one's freedom (*pace* Schofield 1991: 54) and *homonoia* (concord, like-mindedness). Schofield makes an heroic attempt to give Zeno's *Republic* political substance by contextualizing it in Plato's discussions of the political uses of *eros*, Spartan traditions of military pederasty, and the role that intense erotic relationships might play in cementing civil harmony and ensuring security. But this greatly underestimates the extent to which the Stoics are intent to effect a transvaluation of all values at every level, including those of standard ethical and political language. If we read this passage with Berlin's eyes, it becomes clear that Eros is being associated with three important Stoic ethical attributes, friendship, freedom, and like-mindedness (cf. Stob. *Ecl.* II. 108, 5 = SVF 3.630)[9] along with the city's *sôtêrian*, or safety. But the safety[10] of Zeno's

---

[9] It is interesting to compare Aristotle's use of this same vocabulary when he canvasses common views of friendship at *EN* 1155ª23–32. As he notes, these are the kinds of relations that eliminate worries about political justice.

[10] Schofield (2000) tries to make a parallel case for the Epicureans and attributes to them a corresponding worry about security. But, again, the inner invulnerability of the Epicurean wise man and his freedom from the fear of death are his only security, the inner security of *ataraxia*. Such a

Republic resides in just this—the virtues, like-mindedness, and inner moral freedom of its citizens, the wise. It is nothing over and above the kind of safety already enjoyed by individual wise men. It is not the kind of safety, that is, that depends on the ability of a state to protect material goods, lives, or other conventional goods that the Stoics view as morally indifferent (see Long 2007); moreover, since the bonds described here are merely the wise and friendly relations of the like-minded, no special sorts of just political or institutional arrangements are needed to preserve and protect it.

We can now leave Zeno's de-eroticized and depoliticized *Republic*, and turn to the claim that the Stoics formulated a communitarian vision of the world that somehow makes room for every other human being in a part of each of our identities. Here are some of the relevant excerpts from the passage in Hierocles (Stobaeus 4.671,7–673,11 = LS 57G) that have been used to support this claim:

> (1) Each of us is as it were entirely encompassed by many circles, some smaller, others larger, the latter enclosing the former on the basis of their different and unequal dispositions relative to each other. (2) The first and closest circle is the one which a person has drawn as though around a centre, his own mind. This circle encloses the body and anything taken for the sake of the body. For it is virtually the smallest circle, and almost touches the centre itself. (3) Next, the second one further removed from the centre but enclosing the first circle; this contains parents, siblings, wife, and children.

Hierocles proceeds to describe a set of expanding circles including near relatives, distant relatives, neighbors, fellow citizens, people from neighboring towns, and fellow countrymen. He concludes with the outermost and largest circle that encompasses all the rest, the whole human race. Then he offers this bit of advice.

> Once they have all been surveyed, it is the task of a well tempered man, in his proper treatment of each group, to draw the circles together somehow towards the centre, and to keep zealously transferring those from the enclosing circles into the enclosed ones . . . It is incumbent on us to respect people from the third circle as if they were those from the second, and again to respect our other relatives as if they were those from the third circle.

Hierocles has typically been taken to be offering an example of the Stoics' theory of social *oikeiosis* [11] and as such the account has gathered both praise and blame. We have touched on Nussbaum's praise (cf. Kristeva 1991: 56 ff.), but it is easy to see how less-communitarian-minded critics would find much to criticize in a view that appears to base moral regard on relations of distance to one's own personal desires and interests. It might be helpful, however, to begin with a few general observations about *oikeiosis*,

---

depoliticized view is poles apart from, say, Hobbes's worries in his contractual theory about self-preservation and political order.

[11] I leave this untranslated. Some suggestions include "appropriation" (Long and Sedley), "affinity" (Schofield), "familiarity" (Annas), "*conciliato*" (Cicero) followed by "conciliation" (Irwin), "domestic instinct" (Whewell), and "well-disposedness" (Pembroke).

since Hierocles apparently thought that there were three kinds: an egoistic sort that concerns oneself; a social one somehow analogous to family affection; and one aimed at external things (*Stoicheiosis*, col. 9). We are fairly well informed about Stoic accounts of an individual agent's *oikeiosis* to himself. The intent of these accounts is to explain how, starting with one's earliest natural impulses for self-preservation, one can come to view oneself as a self-conscious rational moral agent extended in time. Individual *oikeiosis* is a process of natural moral evolution by which agents come to recognize the value of reason in its own right and thus learn how to make proper moral judgments (see Inwood 1984). Our most secure evidence for social *oikeiosis* (e.g. Cicero, *de finibus* 3.62 and Plutarch, *On Stoic Self-Contradictions* 12) makes an analogy between parents' love for their children and our regard for others. In taking Hierocles' circles passage as an illustration of social *oikeiosis*, however, scholars have typically appropriated elements of the egoistic model of *oikeiosis* to the social version, and this has created difficulty. As a social mechanism, *oikeiosis* seems problematic if it involves merely projecting one's self-regard onto others or of identifying with others only to the extent that they answer to one's inner needs and self-concern. The worry is that such an account fails to give proper recognition to other individuals as being worthy of respect in their own right (see McCabe 2005). Moreover, it is hard to see how this tactic of viewing others from the perspective of one's own self-regard is supposed to foster the development of rational impartiality and the recognition that "one should always behave so as to treat with equal respect the dignity of reason and moral choice in every human being."

Complaints against such a view of social *oikeiosis* are arguably justified,[12] but they are aimed in this case, I would argue, at a phantom, since it is unlikely that Hierocles' parable of the circles is meant to illustrate social *oikeiosis*. In the first place, there is no mention of *oikeiosis* anywhere in the passage or of any related roots, nor does it correspond to Hierocles' own hints about the relation of family affection and social *oikeiosis* in the *Stoicheiosis*. Moreover, only a theory-driven reading of the Greek would lead one to conclude that Hierocles is claiming that every group in an outer circle should eventually be brought into the innermost circle of one's identity. Hierocles merely says that one should always try to treat those from an enclosing circle as we do those from the circle it encloses. This point is again made later in the passage when he claims that the "right point will be reached if, through our initiative, we reduce the distance of the relationship with each person. But we should do more, in the terms of address we use, calling cousins brothers, and uncles and aunts, fathers and mothers." It is clear that what Hierocles envisions in each case is trying to reduce the distance[13] by one circle, not eliminating distance entirely. He does not say, for instance, that we

---

[12] See the related objections of the Anonymous Commentator on Plato's *Theaetetus* 5.18–6.31 (LS 57H). I do not think that Hierocles and, therefore, Nussbaum are actually talking about the Stoic process of social *oikeiosis*, however. The fact that this passage from Hierocles is typically taken to be about *oikeiosis* may be mostly, as far as I can tell, an artifact of its juxtaposition in Long and Sedley with the Anon. Comm. passage (57H), even though that targets a different argument.

[13] It is perhaps worth pointing out that Hierocles' way of cataloguing relations in terms of distance does not map very neatly upon Nussbaum's categories of gender, religion, and ethnicity.

should call all men "brothers." Nor does Hierocles anywhere offer any theoretical psychological underpinning for this account or give the kind of developmental story typically ascribed to it. More importantly, this passage does not correspond to any of the known Stoic accounts that are actually identified as being about social *oikeiosis* and that cite parents' love for their children as the key bit of evidence from which to extrapolate to the claim that we have regard for others. Thus, I think that this passage is much better read as just a bit of homespun ethical advice of the sort we might expect to find in such a non-technical, rhetorical work that, frankly, has all the hallmarks of a popular self-help manual. Rather than propounding any deep claims about the nature of our social identity, Hierocles' image of the circles seems to be merely a vivid way of illustrating a commonplace bit of general, if not particularly taxing, practical moral advice. Thus, as in the case of our passage from Plutarch, modern reconstructions of this argument fail to persuade, and with them goes this key support for contemporary claims about the reach and importance of Stoic "political" thought.

My conclusions about the actual substance and scope of Hellenistic political thought have been almost entirely negative. But I would agree with Berlin's claim that, nonetheless, the radically depoliticized outlook of Hellenistic philosophers signaled one of the most revolutionary and crucial breaks in the history of Western political thought. Moreover, two of their central tenets—Stoic natural law and the Epicurean social contract—were to prove unexpectedly fruitful for later political thinkers, once their scope had been widened beyond the confines of Hellenistic philosophy's perfectionist vision of a group of wise men interacting among themselves and valuing above all their own inner perfection. This is, perhaps, an ironic result, given the nature of their own ethical vision and given that for them "political philosophy had suddenly vanished away"; but, however ironic, it is a result that perhaps serves as a useful historical reminder of the benefits of keeping track of individual ethical ideals when fashioning political institutions.[14]

References

Primary Sources

Arnim, H. von (1903–5). *Stoicorum veterum fragmenta*. Leipzig: Teubner.
Diogenes Laertius, (1964) ed. H. S. Long. Oxford: Oxford University Press.
Long, A. A., and Sedley, D. (1987). *The Hellenistic Philosophers*. Cambridge: Cambridge University Press.

---

[14] I am extremely grateful to Brad Inwood and the students of his graduate seminar and to Richard Sorabji and the graduate students in our joint seminar at NYU, both in the fall of 2008, for helpful discussion. I am also much indebted to Matt Evans, Paul Mitsis, David Robertson, and Iakovos Vasiliou for many, mostly unanswered, objections.

PLUTARCH, *De Alexandri Magni Fortuna aut Virtute=Mor.* 326D. Cambridge, MA: Cambridge University Press.

USENER, H. (1887). *Epicurea.* Leipzig: Teubner.

Secondary Sources

ANNAS, J. (1995). *The Morality of Happiness.* Oxford: Oxford University Press.

BERLIN, I. (2005). "The Birth of Greek Individualism," in *Liberty: Incorporating Four Essays on Liberty,* (ed.) H. Hardy. Oxford: Oxford University Press, 287–321.

DAWSON, D. (1992). *Cities of the Gods: Communist Utopias in Greek Thought.* Oxford: Oxford University Press.

ERSKINE, A. (1990). *The Hellenistic Stoa.* London: Duckworth.

FOWLER, D. (1989). "Lucretius and Politics," in M. Griffin and J. Barnes (eds), *Philosophia Togata: Essays on Philosophy and Roman Society.* Oxford: Oxford University Press, 120–50.

INWOOD, B. (1984). "Hierocles: Theory and Argument in the Second Century AD," *Oxford Studies in Ancient Philosophy,* 2: 151–83.

KRISTEVA, J. (1991). *Strangers to Ourselves.* New York: Columbia University Press.

LONG, A. A. (1997). "Stoic Philosophers on Persons, Property and Community," in R. Sorabji (ed.), *Aristotle and After, Bulletin of the Institute of Classical Studies,* suppl. 68. London: University of London, 13–32.

LONG, A. A. (2007). "Stoic Communitarianism and Normative Citizenship," in D. Keyt and F. D. Miller (eds), *Freedom, Reason, and the Polis: Essays in Ancient Greek Political Philosophy.* Cambridge: Cambridge University Press, 241–61.

McCABE, M. M. (2005). "Extend or Identify: Two Stoic Accounts of Altruism," in R. Salles (ed.), *Metaphysics, Soul and Ethics: Festschrift for Richard Sorabji.* Oxford: Oxford University Press, 413–43.

McILWAIN, C. (1940). *Constitutionalisms: Ancient and Modern.* Ithaca, NY: Cornell.

NUSSBAUM, M. (1996). *For Love of Country? A New Democracy Forum on the Limits of Patriotism.* Boston: Beacon.

SABINE, G. H. (1937). *A History of Political Theory.* Edinburgh: Harrup.

SCHOFIELD, M. (1991). *The Stoic Idea of the City.* Cambridge: Cambridge University Press.

SCHOFIELD, M. (2000). "Epicurean and Stoic Political Thought," in C. Rowe and M. Schofield (eds), *The Cambridge History of Greek and Roman Political Thought.* Cambridge: Cambridge University Press, 435–56.

SINCLAIR, T. A. (1952). *A History of Greek Political Thought.* London: Routledge & Kegan Paul.

VANDER WAERDT, P. (1994). "Zeno's *Republic* and the Origins of Natural Law," in P. Vander Waerdt (ed.), *The Socratic Movement.* Ithaca, NY: Cornell, 272–308.

VASILIOU, I. (2008). *Aiming at Virtue in Plato.* Cambridge: Cambridge University Press.

VOGT, K. (2008). *Law, Reason, and the Cosmic City: Political Philosophy in the Early Stoa.* Oxford: Oxford University Press.

WILLIAMS, B. (2005). *In the Beginning Was the Deed.* Princeton: Princeton University Press.

CHAPTER 9

....

EARLY CHRISTIAN
POLITICAL PHILOSOPHY

....

SOPHIE LUNN-ROCKLIFFE

EARLY Christian political philosophy is not a unified, theoretical, and coherent system, but is embedded in a range of Christian works of apology, theology, and exegesis. Literate (and therefore elite) Christians from the apologists to Augustine were subject to a range of political and social pressures, and their political thinking was often contingent and incidental (Dvornik 1966; Burns 1998). Furthermore, in this period the Church was not a single orthodox body but a collection of numerous sects, each self-confident in the belief that it was the true church and its rivals unorthodox upstarts, and supporting different canons of scripture, theologies, creeds, and ethics (Kelly 1958; Chadwick 2003). Different kinds of Christian political thinking were, like Christian theology, forged through a process of conflict and debate (Lim 1995).

Although there are many different early Christian political philosophies, they still share a common historical context. For the first three centuries Christians experienced sporadic persecution, initially on a relatively ad hoc local basis, but culminating in the more sustained and empire-wide persecutions of Decius in the mid-third century and Diocletian in the early fourth century (De Ste Croix 1963; Frend 1965). The Emperor Constantine supposedly converted to Christianity in a Damascene moment before battle in 312, and, although the authenticity of this conversion has been much debated, his subsequent promotion of the Church was undeniable and boosted its social prestige, wealth, and political importance (Barnes 1981; Lenski 2006). However, Constantine's conversion did not mark a definitive caesura in Christian political thinking, as many of the important questions raised during the persecutions continued to vex Christian thinkers in a new era of peace. What role do earthly rulers and kingdoms have in God's creation? How should the earthly Church be ruled and organized, and what criteria should determine membership? What is the ultimate goal of political life for Christians? What is the good life for Christians?

Between Constantine's reign and that of Theodosius at the close of the fourth century, emperors veered from the pious (Gratian, for whom Bishop Ambrose of Milan wrote a tract specifically *On the Faith*) to the 'heretical' (Constantius, an Arian), with a single pagan interruption. Julian, who reigned briefly in the 360s, was brought up as a Christian but reverted to paganism once in power and made a concerted effort to give to paganism the doctrinal and institutional structures that Christianity enjoyed (Bowersock 1978; Athanassiadi 1981). Over the course of the fourth century, the Church was bolstered by large if not necessarily steady or inexorable numbers of converts, and became increasingly wealthy and secular; entering the clergy now became a respectable alternative career path to entering imperial or local government (Lane Fox 1986; Brown 1992).

Besides the unifying experience of big political events, Christian writers of this era shared some fundamental cultural horizons. The Bible was the most important literary influence on Christians, whether high-flying intellectuals or more workmanlike readers and listeners. However, the contents of the Bible were not fixed in the Church's first centuries, and there were many theologically motivated disputes over which texts should be canonized to form scripture (Ehrman 2003). There were further difficulties of interpretation.

The belief that the Bible spoke with one voice was problematic since much of its contents were self-contradictory. Different hermeneutic methods—allegorical, typological, mystical, and literal—were thus developed to relate, explain, and reconcile the different books of the Old and New Testaments. Beyond this, Christians were exercised by the issues of how to expound what Scripture meant in theological terms (defining, for example, the nature of the Trinity and the relationship between its three persons), and in ethical terms (how were good Christians meant to live their lives?).

Literate Christians also crucially shared *paideia*: a training in classical culture that began with a school education in the pagan literary classics but encompassed a broader intellectual and moral formation (Jaeger 1962; Chadwick 1966; Averil Cameron 1991). An immersion in works by (among others) Homer, Cicero, and Virgil provided Christians with a common language and literary repertoire in which to communicate with non-Christians. However, the relationship between classical learning and Christianity was variously characterized by repudiation, tension, and accommodation. Many Christians saw the pursuit of eloquence and worldly learning as a vain distraction. Tertullian, writing in the third century, warned of the inadequacy of philosophy against Scripture in polemical terms: 'What has Athens to do with Jerusalem? What has the Academy to do with the Church?' (*On the Prescription of Heretics* 7). Jerome dreamed guiltily that God chastised him for being a Ciceronian, not a Christian (*Letter* 22). Augustine's demolition of much of Greco-Roman history and philosophy in the opening books of his *City of God* represents a wider hostility in Christian thought to philosophy's arrogant claims to truth and wisdom.

However, Augustine illustrates the paradox inherent in literate Christians' attitudes to classical learning; although many felt uneasy with the worldly taint of this culture, they were unable to escape its philosophical and literary influence. Augustine's conversion to Christianity was a culmination of years of philosophical study, and this apprenticeship is visible in his reformulation of Cicero's definition of the *res publica* (commonwealth) in book 19 of *City of God*. The attempt to convert pagan literature and ideas is found in many other Christian works: Constantine, in his *Oration to the Saints*, tried to save Virgil's *Eclogue* IV for a Christian audience by pointing out its messianic prophecy; and Ambrose wrote a treatise that was modelled on the title and structure of Cicero's *On Duties* (*De officiis*), but that transformed it from a text on secular duty to one on the duties of clerics. There were constant efforts to put philosophy to the service of theology. Clement of Alexandria founded a school of catechumens in which subjects taught ranged well beyond scripture and theology. He defended philosophy on the grounds that it was granted by God to the Greeks in the same way as the Law was given to the Jews, 'as a tutor escorting them to Christ' (*Stromateis* 1.5.28). It was a common rhetorical conceit for Christians to redefine philosophy *as* Christianity, and one that became more urgent during Julian's reign. He attempted to wrest Greek philosophy and culture from the Christians for his revived paganism, dubbed 'Hellenism', and even barred Christians from teaching in his school edict of 362 on the disingenuously scrupulous grounds that it was not right for them to teach 'pagan' material that conflicted with their faith (Downey 1957; Banchich 1993).

ATTITUDES TO EMPERORS AND EMPIRE

A wide range of attitudes to earthly rulers and polities can be found in early Christian literature. This can be explained partly by the changing circumstances of persecution and toleration to which writers responded, and partly by their writing for different audiences. Christians writing to their own communities described the diabolical animation of persecuting officials and emperors in apocalyptic tones borrowed from the Revelation of John, which in turn built on the Old Testament prophesies of Isaiah, Ezekiel, and Daniel. Lactantius' *On the Deaths of the Persecutors* is a grisly catalogue of the manner of death of persecuting emperors, and associates their activities closely with the diabolical; Domitian, for example, is described in Chapter 3 as 'instigated by evil demons to persecute the righteous people'. This association did not, however, lapse altogether with the conversion of Constantine. In the mid-fourth century the pro-Nicene bishops Hilary of Poitiers, Lucifer of Cagliari, and Athanasius of Alexandria were persecuted and banished for their theology by the Arian Emperor Constantius. They deployed dissenting diabolical language familiar from pre-Constantinian attacks on pagans to stigmatize a Christian but 'heretical' emperor as an Antichrist. Ambrosiaster, an anonymous Latin writer of the later fourth century, demonized all usurpers as imitating the archetypal tyrant, the Devil, for the mere fact of their usurping ambitions rather than for any perceived theological crimes (Lunn-Rockliffe 2007).

However, another attitude to earthly authority emerges from the apologies addressed by Christians to potentially persecuting pagan emperors and officials; these works, as their name suggests, were eloquent and impassioned justifications of Christians' existence. The apologists aimed to persuade the Roman authorities that Christians did not, as they were accused, harbour treacherous desires to overthrow earthly rule, and cast earthly rule in more conciliatory terms. Tertullian reassured Scapula, proconsul of Africa, that, since the Christian knows the emperor to be appointed by his own God, 'he must love, reverence, honour, and wish him well, together with the whole Roman Empire, as long as the world shall last' (*To Scapula* 2); he then declared that the emperor is next to God and inferior to him alone, exalting him above other men but shying short of the pagan divinization of emperors. Justin Martyr explained that Christians offered no challenge to earthly Roman rule in seeking a human kingdom, but fostered other-worldly ambitions for 'a kingdom which is with God' (*First Apology* 11). Origen went further than both, arguing in his *Against Celsus* (a tract refuting a pagan) that the coincidence of Jesus' birth with the reign of Augustus allowed the uniting of peoples in the empire, which in turn facilitated the spread of Christianity throughout the world. This bestowed a providential legitimacy on the rise of the Roman Empire.

Constantine's conversion to Christianity prompted Christian thinkers to provide a new account of the relationship between emperor and God (Barnes 1981). Eusebius, bishop of Caesarea, presented the emperor as friend of the *Logos* and appointed by God to rule over an empire whose unity and harmony mirrored God's heavenly kingdom (Hollerich 1990). In his oration *In Praise of Constantine* (1.6), Eusebius describes Constantine receiving 'as it were an image [*eikon*] of the Divine sovereignty' and 'directing in imitation [*kata mimêsin*] of God himself, the administration of this world's affairs'. God is thus the source of imperial power, and the archetype or model of the true king. Eusebius' theology of kingship also flows both ways: kings imitate the divine ruler, but God himself is figured in earthly terms as an absolute monarch over the cosmos. This taps into a reflexive kingship ideology developed by Hellenistic writers like Ecphantus and Diotogenes, whose language of *mimêsis* (imitation) he borrows and transforms (Baynes 1933–4; Chesnut 1978). The forging of a powerful connection between earthly and divine monarchy is not, however, confined to Greek Christianity. Lactantius, a Latin contemporary of Eusebius' and Constantine's, explains in his *Divine Institutes* (1.3) the existence of a single god by analogy with earthly monarchy; a king whose rule is shared with others is compromised in his power and perfection, and God, as necessarily perfect, must therefore be one.

Eusebius' idea of kingship is not merely a Christianization of Hellenistic philosophy, but builds on powerful scriptural language of God as king. It also stretches the range of typology to compare Constantine with biblical *exempla*, and blurs boundaries between royal and priestly office. Typology is a kind of scriptural exegesis that relates events and figures from the Old Testament ('types') to counterparts ('antitypes') in the New Testament, developing the idea that Christ's dispensation is foreshadowed in Jewish history. Eusebius extended his typological comparison beyond the Bible to contemporary history, relating Moses, a model of law-giving, prophetic, and military rulership, to Constantine (Rapp 1998*a*). Eusebius also aggrandized Constantine's role by attributing to him a kind of quasi-episcopal status. Constantine's interest in ecclesiastical affairs informed his convocation of bishops to discuss credal formulations at the Council of Nicaea in 325, and Eusebius reports in his *Life of Constantine* (4.24) that on another occasion the emperor informed a banquet of bishops: 'You are bishops of those within the church, but I am perhaps a bishop appointed by God over those outside' (see Rapp 1998*b*). Now, Constantine was not ordained and, in line with contemporary practice, was baptized only just before his death. Eusebius is, therefore, playing on the idea familiar from Roman religion that the emperor had a priestly function, enshrined in his title of *pontifex maximus* (high priest). Indeed, this pagan religious title was so ingrained that successive Christian emperors held it until Gratian finally renounced it in 375 (Alan Cameron 1968).

In contrast to Eusebius' assimilation of the roles of emperor and bishop, Ambrose, bishop of Milan in the later fourth century, famously sought to distinguish them (Bowersock 1986; McLynn 1994). Ambrose's relationships with the Emperors Valentinian II and Theodosius was not, as Eusebius to Constantine, propagandist. Instead, Ambrose stresses in various works that the emperor is subject to divine law, the precepts of which are communicated to him by God's priest. This subjection is shown to be necessary, because the world is 'slippery' (full of enticing opportunities to sin) and because the emperor is as fallible as, and yet exposed to greater temptations than, his subjects. Ambrose used the examples of Old Testament kings to show that emperors should both accept episcopal guidance and be ready to offer penance for sins they had committed. In 390, Ambrose threatened Theodosius with excommunication and forced him to do public penance for a punitive massacre the emperor had ordered at Thessalonica. In *Letter* 51 to Theodosius, Ambrose offered Saul as an example of a king who had sinned by killing the innocent, and requested that such examples inspire the emperor to 'remove this sin from your kingdom', with the direct command: 'You are a man, you have met temptation—conquer it.' Ambrose's *Apology of the Prophet David* proffered another pertinent biblical example in the powerful king David, who sinned but laudably repented when chastised by the prophet Nathan. Ambrose's levelling of the emperor to 'everyman', while modelled on biblical exemple, sometimes recalls the political vocabulary of the early imperial era. He reports in his *Funeral Oration on Theodosius* (34) how the emperor threw his royal attire on the ground, wept publicly, prayed for pardon, and was not embarrassed to do that which brings a blush to private citizens: to perform penance publicly. The suggestion that an emperor's proper behaviour as a pious Christian required him to humble himself as far as, perhaps further than, a *privatus* effectively Christianized the style of rule adopted by early emperors, who sought to avoid damaging charges of monarchy by casting the imperial position as merely that of a *princeps* (leading citizen) devoted to the maintenance of republican liberties (Wallace-Hadrill 1982). Such an appeal to civility may well have seemed rather far-fetched in Ambrose's day, given the increasingly formal nature of late antique court rituals of prostration and adoration that elevated the emperor far above ordinary mortals (MacCormack 1981).

Christians in the first four centuries argued variously that particular emperors were diabolically inspired, that the institution of empire itself was divinely ordained, and that emperors were men and sinners like any others. Another way of characterizing the origins of imperial power, and indeed all earthly political institutions, was that they were ordained by God to restrain sin. The third-century writer Irenaeus, in his *Against Heresies* (5.25), thus proposed that earthly rule 'has been appointed by God for the benefit of the nations (and not by the Devil, who is never at rest at all, indeed, who does not love to see even nations conducting themselves after a quiet manner), so that under fear of it men may not eat each other up like fishes...'

This kind of bleak assessment of the pragmatic necessity of political institutions was eventually developed by Augustine to accompany his articulation of the centrality of sin to man's post-fall political and social life. Augustine's idea of 'original sin' was not brand new (Leeming 1930). In his tract *Against Two Letters of the Pelagians*, he cited (and misattributed to Hilary) a crucial passage of Ambrosiaster's commentary on Romans 5:12: 'it is manifest that all sinned in Adam as in a lump [*massa*]: for he himself was corrupted through sin, and all those whom he begot were born under sin'. Augustine picked up on the phrase 'all sinned in Adam as in a lump' to describe mankind as a *massa peccati*, a 'lump of sin', whose guilt was therefore inherited and inescapable. His idea of 'original sin' was formulated in response to the work of Pelagius, eventually declared a heretic, who argued that man, through the free will with which God had provided him, and through God's law, could carry out God's commands as laid out in the New Testament, and thereby live a virtuous life. Pelagius denied that Adam's sin had vitiated human nature and that God's grace was indispensable to salvation, suggesting that it merely aided the good choices made by free will.

Augustine argued in his *City of God* that man's fallen nature was expressed through his unbridled *libido dominandi* (lust for domination), which resulted in chaos as man turned against man in the race to achieve unnatural power over others. Augustine cast slavery and political subjection alike as unnatural on the grounds that God created man to rule over the beasts, not over other men, and deployed God's command at Genesis 1:28 ('Let them have dominion over the fish of the sea, and over the birds of the air, and over every other creeping thing that creeps upon the earth') as evidence for the limited scope of man's pre-fall mastery. He then asserted that political rule was ordained by God after the fall to enable man to manage his fallen self (*City of God* 19.15). Other writers also argued against the existence of power relationships in creation. Gregory of Nyssa, in his *Fourth Homily on Ecclesiastes* 2.7, accused the slave-owner of condemning man to slavery 'when his nature is free and possesses free will'. He asserted that man's rule is confined to things without reason, using, like Augustine, God's command at Genesis 1:28 (Garnsey 1996).

ECCLESIOLOGY

Classical political philosophy was often concerned with the *polis* (city state). However, although early Christian thinkers were concerned with the state (now the Roman Empire, not the *poleis* of classical Greek antiquity) and its secular rulers, they extended the remit of political thinking to encompass the Church, an institution that had an other-worldly, spiritual rationale as Paul's body of Christ and an earthly political form in its clerical hierarchy. Christian writers frequently addressed themselves to the issue of the unity of the Church, which was perceived to be beset by numerous diabolically inspired heresies and schisms. Even before Constantine's conversion, church affairs had sometimes been adjudicated externally, and, under Constantine, firmer precedents were set for the imperial oversight of church discipline. Constantine seems to have perceived that there were ideological and practical advantages to unifying the empire through a single church and under a Christian monarch; in a letter to the quarrelling clerics Arius and Alexander of Alexandria, he explicitly juxtaposed the healing of a church riven by internal theological disputes with that of the body politic (Eusebius, *Life of Constantine* 2.64–5; Fowden 1993). This Christian adaptation of the *pax deorum*, the old Roman linkage between happy gods and a peaceful empire, was long-lived. Augustine tackled it in his *City of God* when pagans, disheartened by the sack of Rome in 410 by the Goths, complained that this was the just revenge of the pagan gods on the mortals who had, in their rash pursuit of another god, abandoned them. He responded by claiming that the attack had in fact been fairly tame, and that the Romans owed gratitude to Christ for the restraint shown them by the (*stereo*) typically cruel barbarians.

Two important aspects of ecclesiastical unity were how the Church should be ruled and organized, and what criteria, narrow and perfectionist or broad and laxist, should determine membership. Cyprian, third-century bishop of Carthage writing under persecution, articulated a powerful defence of a singular, united church in his treatise *On the Unity of the Church*. He cited several scriptural proof texts for Christ's intention to found a single united church, as well as developing a poetic range of organic metaphors for the Church's single and undivided source: a ray of sunlight; a tree; and a river. Cyprian explained how the Church's unity depended on monarchical bishops, successors to the apostles, in communion with each other and under the authority of Peter's successor at Rome. There is some debate over the extent to which Cyprian's articulation of apostolic origins for bishops privileged the place of Peter over all other bishops, as the key proto-primatial passage exists in two versions, possibly both authorial, with slightly different emphases. However, the description of the Church's reversion to a single *caput* (head) and *origo* (source), which Cyprian employed to describe the episcopal inheritance of the apostolic commission, developed both a linear idea of succession and a Pauline organological idea of the Church as the body of Christ, with Christ its head.

The targets of Cyprian's treatise were the Novatianist and Donatist sects, who had appointed their own rival bishops, thereby upsetting apostolic succession and dividing the church internally (Frend 1952; Merdinger 1997). Cyprian, like Eusebius after him, extended the range of typology; he cited the biblical example of Dathan, Chore, and Abiron (Numbers 16:1 ff.), unworthy usurpers of priestly office who came to sticky ends, to suggest the fates for upstart heretical anti-bishops of his own day (*On the Unity of the Church* 18). Cyprian's attack on these sects was not merely on grounds of discipline; he also took issue with the Donatists' perfectionist exclusion from the Church of Christians who had lapsed under persecution. Cyprian's argument for universality was to be developed by Optatus of Milevis, a bishop in North Africa in the middle of the fourth century who wrote a tract *Against the Donatists*. Optatus equated catholicity or universality with orthodoxy, arguing that a sect as small and geographically confined as the Donatists were in Africa could not claim the inheritance of the universal church spread by the apostles. Optatus' conception of the Church, building on Cyprian's, was much less exclusive than the Donatists'; he saw it accommodating saints and sinners rather than just the perfect (Merdinger 1997).

The struggle over if and how to accommodate lapsed Christians back into the Church raised a related problem; should, and could, lapsed clergy still exercise their priestly functions? Many of the struggles over episcopal succession in this period originated with claims that a particular bishop had been consecrated by a bishop whose own sacramental capabilities had been compromised by sin, be it heresy, schism, apostasy, or something else altogether. It became important for opponents of rigorists like the Donatists to affirm that a cleric's actions were unaffected by the quality of his life, but had universal efficacy from the fact of his ordination. Ambrosiaster develops this idea in his biblical exegesis. He repeatedly states that the high priest Caiaphas continued to prophesy even when he had sinned, as this gift was contingent on his office (*ordo*) not personal merit. Elsewhere, Ambrosiaster made the same distinction between office and person of kings. He explains that kings Saul and Nebuchadnezzar continued to prophesy and receive revelations even when they had proved themselves unworthy, as these gifts were granted to their rank (*ordo*). In pragmatic terms, he commanded that the king 'is to be honoured not for his own sake but on account of his rank [*ordo*]', even if he were a pagan (*Commentary on I Corinthians* 13.2.1). Ambrosiaster's plea for the Christian sufferance of pagan emperors was uncomfortably pertinent in the aftermath of Julian's reign, and somewhat at odds with the stance of the almost contemporary Ambrose, who chided emperors with such aplomb (Lunn-Rockliffe 2007). The coining of the idea of the 'king's two bodies', which was to flourish in later political thinking, demonstrates the interpenetration of theology and political thinking typical of the early Church (Kantorowicz 1957).

ESCHATOLOGY

Eschatology refers to *ta eschata* (Greek for 'the last things') and encompasses Christian expectations of the end of the world, resurrection, and universal judgment (Rowland 1982). The eschatological hope of the early Church explains the eagerness of some Christians for martyrdom and the indifference of others to the particulars of earthly politics. Cyprian, in his *On the Unity of the Church* (16), explicitly related the flourishing of heresies in his day with the approaching end of the world as prophesied in Scripture. This tendency to read contemporary persecution as heralding the apocalypse was widespread and was accompanied by a poetic insistence that Christians were like *peregrini*, pilgrims or travellers, on earth, separated from the true heavenly kingdom to which they belonged and to which they would ultimately return; the anonymous second-century letter to Diognetus describes how Christians show 'the wonderful and confessedly strange character of the constitution of their own citizenship. They dwell in their own fatherlands, but as if sojourners in them; they share all things as citizens, and suffer all things as strangers.' The discourse of Christians as *peregrini* alienated from earthly existence endured even when the second coming, initially expected with confidence, failed to materialize. It forms an important strand of Augustine's discourse of earthly and heavenly citizenship, as members of the earthly city are described as citizens who wholly belong to the fallen world compared to the citizens of the city of God, who are pilgrims on earth (*City of God* 15.1).

The idea that the truly important community is not this-worldly, but transcendent, was arguably a world view that owed much to Neoplatonism. Many of the educated Christians who expounded this idea were themselves steeped in this mystical philosophical brand of Platonism, and indebted to the language of ascent to the One found in its exponents' writings, such as Plotinus' *Enneads*. However, Christian eschatology also owed much to Scripture and theology. In his *City of God* Augustine developed Tyconius' division of mankind into two societies (Markus 1970; Babcock 1982; Van Oort 1991). Ironically, Tyconius was himself a Donatist, although one insufficiently hard line for the Donatists, who eventually ejected him. Augustine's two *civitates*, the city of God and the city of the Devil, were described in relation to the archetypal holy and impious societies of the Old Testament: Jerusalem and Babylon. He delineated how the city of God contained the good angels and predestined elect men, past, present, and future, who had responded to God's grace and whose object of love is God alone; and how the earthly city contained the fallen angels and the reprobate, all those whose passion is not for God but for themselves or other material objects. In characteristically Augustinian fashion, membership of either city is determined by the *object* of one's love. The cities are transcendent and invisible and their members scattered across space and time; neither is the city of God precisely coterminous with the Church, nor the earthly city with any earthly empire or state.

Augustine defended the earthly reality of a church containing both reprobate and good. His anti-Donatist predecessor Optatus, in turn developing Cyprian's ecclesiological inclusivity, had described how Christ's seeds and foreign seeds (the reprobate and the good) grow throughout the whole world in which there is one Church, and how after this 'common growth' there would be a 'harvest of souls' at Judgment (*Against the Donatists* 7.2). Augustine reimagined this natural metaphor in an image of good and bad fishes 'collected in the net of the Gospel', which in this world, as in a sea, swim together without separation. He justified this on eschatological grounds: 'both are, as it were, enclosed in the net until brought ashore. Then, however, the wicked will be separated from the good' (*City of God* 18.49). That is, the cities take shape only eschatologically, and man should not try to judge who is in which city. Augustine, like Optatus before him, was countering the Donatist belief that membership of the earthly church should be restricted to 'the pure'.

ASCETICISM

Augustine, like many Christians, deemed classical philosophers to have addressed the question 'what is the good life?' with an inappropriately earthly focus. He accused the philosophers of wishing, 'with wondrous vanity, to be happy here and now, and to achieve blessedness by their own efforts' and claimed that Christians sought a different, eschatological goal in salvation, 'our final happiness' (*City of God* 19.4). This characterization of pagan philosophy is highly simplistic, since much of, for instance, Stoic and Platonic thought deals with man's place in and relationship to the cosmos, and the transcendent realms of ideas and the divine. Christians who addressed the question of the 'good life' may well have been eschatologically focused, but they were still concerned to establish an ethical code for the here and now, and it is in this context that there arose urgent debate about the validity or even necessity of various forms of ascetic endeavour. Asceticism, from *askêsis* (exercise or training), referred to a range of practices of self-denial: flight from family and society, and restraint in or denial of food, drink, sex, and possessions. Asceticism was not a Christian invention; the idea of bringing the passions of the body under the kingly command of reason to achieve a state of *apatheia* was Stoic, and the pursuit of a solitary or mendicant life of self-denial was one valued by ancient philosophical sects such as the Cynics. Christian asceticism manifested itself in a variety of forms: Antony's solitary retreat from society into the wilderness; the formation of the first monastic communities; and a modest ascetic life in the city as pursued by Jerome's rich virgins and widows.

All these lifestyles entailed particular views of the body and society, which were regarded with suspicion by ecclesiastical and secular authorities alike (Brown 1988). Ascetics challenged an institutionalized, increasingly wealthy church by rejecting it as a vehicle for salvation, and monastic communities in particular threatened the bishop's authority by setting up their own communities with spiritual leaders (Chadwick 1993).

Their rejection of sex and property jeopardized the Roman valuation of marriage, childbearing, and inheritance (Curran 2000). Finally, the idea that the flesh was peculiarly vulnerable to diabolic temptation came close to a Manichean dualism (of a universe split evenly between good and bad, matter and spirit), which was marginalized and rejected by many Christians.

Christian treatises on the ascetic life were not just aimed at persuading fellow Christians that a life of holy detachment was preferable to a life of secular engagement. They also had pagan targets in their sights. John Chrysostom, a priest in Antioch in the second half of the fourth century, refashioned the classical Greek comparison between philosopher-king and tyrant in a treatise that compared instead the life and worth of a king and a monk. In his *Comparison between a King and a Monk*, John redefined philosophy as ascetic Christianity, thereby drawing the moral high ground away from the Emperor Julian, who had attempted to reclaim asceticism and Neoplatonism from the Christians for a resuscitated form of paganism. The treatise plays on the paradox that the apparently desirable wealth and power of a king is transitory and worthless, whereas the monk, despised by many, lives the best kind of life and will be rewarded with salvation and a life beyond in heaven.

References

Primary Sources

Ambrose (1977). *Apologie de David*, trans. P. Hadot and M. Cordier. *Sources Chrétiennes* 239. Paris: Éditions du Cerf.

Ambrose (2001). *De Officiis*, trans. I. J. Davidson. 2 vols. Oxford: Oxford University Press.

Ambrose (2005). *Ambrose of Milan: Political Letters and Speeches*, trans. J. H. W. G. Liebeschuetz. Liverpool: Liverpool University Press.

Ambrosiaster (1966–9). *Commentarius in xiii epistulas Paulinas*, ed. H. I. Vogels. CSEL 81. Vienna: Hoelder-Pichler-Tempsky.

Augustine (1971). *St Augustine: Anti-Pelagian Writings*, ed. P. Schaff. Nicene and Post-Nicene Fathers 5. Grand Rapids, MI: Eerdmans, 377–435.

Augustine (1998). *The City of God against the Pagans*, trans. R. W. Dyson. Cambridge: Cambridge University Press.

Clement of Alexandria (1991). *Stromateis books 1–3*, trans. J. Ferguson. Fathers of the Church 85. Washington: Catholic University of America Press.

Constantine (2003). *Constantine and Christendom: The Oration to the Saints, The Greek and Latin accounts of the Discovery of the Cross, and the Edict of Constantine to Pope Silvester*, trans. M. Edwards. Liverpool: Liverpool University Press.

Cyprian (1957). *The Lapsed; On the Unity of the Church*, trans. M. Bévenot. London: Longmans, Green.

Eusebius (1975). *In Praise of Constantine: A Historical Study and New Translation of Eusebius' Tricennial Orations*, trans. H. A. Drake. Berkeley and Los Angeles: University of California Press.

Eusebius (1999). *Life of Constantine*, trans. Averil Cameron and S. Hall. Oxford: Clarendon Press.

Hilary of Poitiers (1987). *Contre Constance*, trans. A. Rocher. Sources Chrétiennes 334. Paris: Éditions du Cerf.

Irenaeus (1992). *Against Heresies*, trans. D. J. Unger and J. J. Dillon. New York: Paulist Press.

Jerome (1933). *Letters*, trans. F. A. Wright. London: W. Heinemann.

John Chrysostom (1988). *A Comparison between a King and a Monk; Against the Opponents of the Monastic Life*, trans. D. Hunter. Lewiston: Edwin Mellen Press.

Justin Martyr (1948). *First Apology*, trans. T. B. Falls. Fathers of the Church 6. Washington: Catholic University of America Press.

Lactantius (1965). *On the Deaths of the Persecutors*, trans. M. F. McDonald. Fathers of the Church 54. Washington: Catholic University of America Press.

Lactantius (2003). *Divine Institutes*, trans. A. Bowen and P. Garnsey. Liverpool: Liverpool University Press.

Optatus of Milevis (1997). *Against the Donatists*, trans. M. Edwards. Liverpool: Liverpool University Press.

Origen (1953). *Contra Celsum*, trans. H. Chadwick. Cambridge: Cambridge University Press.

Tertullian (1914). *On the Testimony of the Soul; On the Prescription of Heretics*, trans. T. H. Bindley. London: SPCK; New York: E. S. Gorham.

Tertullian (1950). *To Scapula*, trans. F. A. Quain. Fathers of the Church 10. Washington: Catholic University of America Press.

Secondary Sources

Athanassiadi, P. (1981). *Julian and Hellenism: An Intellectual Biography*. Oxford: Clarendon Press.

Babcock, W. S. (1982). 'Augustine and Tyconius: A Study in the Latin Appropriation of Paul', *Studia Patristica*, 17: 1209–15.

Banchich, T. (1993). 'Julian's School Laws: Cod. Theod. 13.3.5 and Ep. 42', *Ancient World*, 24: 5–14.

Barnes, T. D. (1981). *Constantine and Eusebius*. Cambridge, MA, and London: Harvard University Press.

Baynes, N. H. (1933–4). 'Eusebius and the Christian Empire', *Annuaire de l'institut de philologie et d'histoire orientales*. Brussels: Mélanges Bidez, ii. 13–18.

Bowersock, G. W. (1978). *Julian the Apostate*. London: Duckworth.

Bowersock, G. W. (1986). 'From Emperor to Bishop; The Self-Conscious Transformation of Political Power in the Fourth Century', *Classical Philology*, 81: 298–307.

Brown, P. (1988). *The Body and Society: Men, Women, and Sexual Renunciation in Early Christianity*. New York: Columbia University Press.

Brown, P. (1992). *Power & Persuasion in Late Antiquity: Towards a Christian Empire*. Madison: University of Wisconsin Press.

Burns, J. H. (1998) (ed.). *The Cambridge History of Medieval Political Thought c.350–c.1450*. Cambridge: Cambridge University Press.

Cameron, Alan (1968). 'Gratian's Repudiation of the Pontifical Robe', *Journal of Roman Studies*, 58: 100–14.

Cameron, Averil (1991). *Christianity and the Rhetoric of Empire*. Berkeley and Los Angeles: University of California Press.

CHADWICK, H. (1966). *Early Christian Thought and the Classical Tradition*. Oxford: Clarendon Press.

CHADWICK, H. (1993). 'Bishops and Monks', *Studia Patristica*, 24: 45–61.

CHADWICK, H. (2003). *The Church in Ancient Society: From Galilee to Gregory the Great*. Oxford: Oxford University Press.

CHESNUT, G. F. (1978). 'The Ruler and Logos in Neopythagorean, Middle Platonic and Late Stoic Philosophy', in H. Temporini and W. Haase (eds), *Aufstieg und Niedergang der Römischen Welt*, 16/2 (Berlin and New York: De Gruyter), 1310–31.

CURRAN, J. (2000). *Pagan City and Christian Capital: Rome in the Fourth Century*. Oxford: Oxford University Press.

DE STE CROIX, G. (1963). 'Why Were the Early Christians Persecuted?', *Past and Present*, 26: 6–38.

DOWNEY, G. (1957). 'The Emperor Julian and the Schools', *Classical Journal*, 53: 97–103.

DVORNIK, F. (1966). *Early Christian and Byzantine Political Philosophy: Origin and Background*. 2 vols. Washington: Dumbarton Oaks Center for Byzantine Studies, trustees for Harvard University.

EHRMAN, B. (2003). *Lost Christianities. The Battles for Scripture and the Faiths We Never Knew*. Oxford: Oxford University Press.

FOWDEN, G. (1993). *Empire to Commonwealth: Consequences of Monotheism in Late Antiquity*. Princeton: Princeton University Press.

FREND, W. (1952). *The Donatist Church*. Oxford: Clarendon Press.

FREND, W. (1965). *Martyrdom and Persecution in the Early Church*. Oxford: Blackwell.

GARNSEY, P. (1996). *Ideas of Slavery from Aristotle to Augustine*. Cambridge: Cambridge University Press.

HALL, S. G. (1993). *Gregory of Nyssa: Homilies on Ecclesiastes: An English Version with Supporting Studies*. Berlin: W. de Gruyter.

HOLLERICH, M. J. (1990). 'Religion and Politics in the Writings of Eusebius: Reassessing the First Court Theologian', *Church History*, 59/3: 309–25.

JAEGER, W. (1962). *Early Christianity and Greek Paideia*. Cambridge, MA: Harvard University Press; London: Oxford University Press.

KANTOROWICZ, E. (1957). *The King's Two Bodies: A Study in Medieval Political Theology*. Princeton: Princeton University Press.

KELLY, J. N. D. (1958). *Early Christian Doctrines*. London: A. & C. Black.

LANE FOX, R. (1986). *Pagans and Christians*. Harmondsworth: Viking.

LEEMING, B. (1930). 'Augustine, Ambrosiaster and the massa perditionis', *Gregorianum*, 11: 58–91.

LENSKI, N. (2006) (ed.). *The Cambridge Companion to the Age of Constantine*. Cambridge: Cambridge University Press.

LIM, R. (1995). *Public Disputation, Power, and Social Order in Late Antiquity*. Berkeley and Los Angeles, and London: University of California Press.

LUNN-ROCKLIFFE, S. (2007). *Ambrosiaster's Political Theology*. Oxford: Oxford University Press.

MACCORMACK, S. (1981). *Art and Ceremony in Late Antiquity*. Berkeley and Los Angeles, and London: University of California Press.

MCLYNN, N. (1994). *Ambrose of Milan*. Berkeley and Los Angeles, and London: University of California Press.

MARKUS, R. A. (1970). *Saeculum: History and Society in the Theology of St Augustine.* Cambridge: Cambridge University Press.

MERDINGER, J. E. (1997). *Rome and the African Church in the Time of Augustine.* New Haven and London: Yale University Press.

RAPP, C. (1998*a*). 'Comparison, Paradigm and the Case of Moses in Panegyric and Hagiography', in M. Whitby (ed.), *The Propaganda of Power: The Role of Panegyric in Late Antiquity,* Mnemosyne supplementum 183. Leiden: Brill, 277–98.

RAPP, C. (1998*b*). 'Imperial Ideology in the Making: Eusebius of Caesarea on Constantine as "Bishop"', *Journal of Theological Studies,* NS 49: 685–95.

ROWLAND, C. (1982). *Open Heaven: a Study of Apocalyptic in Judaism and Early Christianity.* London: SPCK.

VAN OORT, J. (1991). *Jerusalem and Babylon: A Study into Augustine's* City of God *and the Sources of his Doctrine of the Two Cities.* Supplement to *Vigiliae Christianae,* 14. Leiden: Brill.

WALLACE-HADRILL, A. (1982). '*Civilis princeps*: Between Citizen and King', *Journal of Roman Studies,* 76: 32–48.

CHAPTER 10

··

THE INFLUENCE OF ROMAN LAW

··

DONALD KELLEY

"To jurisprudence the Romans gave the same definition as the Greeks gave to wisdom," wrote Giambattista Vico in *Diritto universale*, "the knowledge of things divine and human" (see further Kelley 1976, 1979a). But Greek wisdom (*sophia*) was largely theoretical, whereas the Roman counterpart (*sapientia*) was practical, following the inclination of Roman thought. Jurisprudence, as later scholars repeated, was "true philosophy" (*vera philosophia*). Moreover, "Roman law began, as it ended, with a code," declared Henry Sumner Maine, referring to the legendary law of the Twelve Tables, which Roman jurists supposedly took from the Athenians, and the Emperor Justinian's great sixth-century codification, that is, the *Corpus juris civilis*, which included the Code, the Digest, an anthology of classical jurisprudence, and the Novels, containing later legislation (Maine 1861: 1). The forms of Roman law were also imposed on the developing "law of nations" (*jus gentium*), embodying the customs of the "barbarians" conquered by the Romans. The philosophical inclinations of Roman jurists were also expressed in the concept of natural law (*jus naturale*), which came to serve as the ideal standard of Roman jurisprudence and was passed on to Christian doctrine and sometimes identified with the *jus gentium*.

Centuries of Roman jurisprudence were assembled in the great Byzantine collection, the Digest, by Tribonian and the other editors, and by then foreign—that is, Greek—alterations were already apparent. The pursuit of "Tribonianisms" was carried on by later scholars for centuries. Roman (civil) law was the basis for European common law, with many local variations, and it was tenuously preserved in the Justinian and Theodosian Codes, from which it passed into various national and especially municipal traditions (in a vast literature, see Koschaker 1947). Roman law became more formal when during the Renaissance of the twelfth century it came to be taught in the first universities, starting with Bologna and the teaching of Irnerius. The main channels of expansion were through the Glossators and post-Glossators, who commented on the main texts and on later legislation by the Holy Roman Emperors, which included "feudal law," but also by notaries and other proto-lawyers. Christian doctrine also became part of the "Roman" tradition, and canon and civil law (*utriusque juris*) were taught together in the universities as "civil science" (Berman 1983).

Over the centuries civil jurists devised rules and indeed the language of many spheres of human culture, among them property, labor, business, interest, trade, wealth, parental rights, family succession, crime, office, public law, and many subdivisions of these. The idea of contract was especially influential in the economic and political arenas, so was that of "liberty." Even more fundamental were the ideas of judgment, (judicial) truth and falsity, and prejudice. Underpinning all of this was the concept of "law" itself, whether individual enacted *lex* or more general *ius*, which came to mean both sovereign command and natural regularity. Originally *lex* was a command of the people passed by a magistrate, while *jus* was more general and included notions of equity and justice, *jurisprudentia*, or *juris scientia*, was defined as "the art of the good and the just" (*ars boni et aequi*) and was the result of the judicial work of the civilian jurists Kelley (1970). And, as Vico noted, Roman jurisprudence was represented both as the highest philosophy and as "true wisdom."

The political base of Roman law was adopted, or "received," by the national monarchies and the papacy. In other words, the ruler became the source of law: "the will of the prince is law," and he is not bound by the law (*princeps legibus solutus*). *Imperium* differed from *potestas* in that it applied to private as well as public authority. The *imperium merum*, the supreme magistrate's power, belonged to the emperor, and European kings claimed the same authority for themselves (*rex est imperator in regno suo*). The accumulation of royal privileges in the Middle Ages was gathered under this heading, and such was the basis of the idea of "sovereignty" as summarized by Jean Bodin and added to in published legislation. In his "Code of the French people" Napoleon posed as the new Justinian from whose will the whole law flowed and like him the modern emperor objected to "interpretation" of expressions of his will (Kelley 2002).

Roman law furnished the vocabulary and logic for much of the whole field of law. In the Middle Ages lists were made of vernacular translations and analogies, and these were accompanied by efforts of comparative law, such as medieval parliaments with the Roman Senate. But most European judges had been educated in the civil law, and their efforts of interpretation and later reform was based on the Latin language and the texts of Roman law. The "reason of the law" (*ratio legis*) was frequently contrasted with popular customs and with English Common Law. In the medieval universities scholastic jurists—Accursians and "Bartolists"—tried to eliminate the errors and inconsistencies of the law and rationalize it according to scholastic logic—and, despite their historical interests, so did many humanists as well as rationalist jurists following natural law, which was also an ideal to be found in the texts of classical law.

As an introductory law textbook, the Institutes of Justinian remained a model, and its form as well as much of its contents were taken over by derivative works over many later generations, especially in the age of print, down to the French Revolution and indeed to the present (Kelley 2002). Honoratus Draco even rendered it into Latin verse in 1551. What made the system of civil law complete and self-enclosed was that "truth" was defined as legal judgment (*res judicata*) and not as philosophical or linguistic correctness according to some extra-judicial standard. In this jurists were following the professional habits of theologians and philosophers in protecting their discipline from extra-disciplinary judgment, and students learned this from the very beginning.

Thus civil science had developed its own language and style of conceptualization. To begin with, according to the ancient Roman jurist Gaius, "all the law which we use pertains either to persons or to things or to actions," three categories that exhaust the external human condition—personality, reality, and action (Kelley 1979*b*). Persona refers to the notion of the free (and responsible) person, which meant the adult and property-owning male citizen, exercising his own free and responsible will. Minors were dependent, and so were women for the most part, not to speak of lunatics and "spendthrifts." Personhood could also apply to corporations, which were immortal apart from their individual members.

As Emerson put it,

> There are two law discrete
> Unreconciled—one for man, one for thing,

and this refers to the category of property, possession, and prescription. Thing (*res*) refers to legal and political as well as to economic and social "reality"—that is, to means of subsistence and "real estate" protected by the law. Lordship and *dominion* are separate categories but in feudal times overlapped with property.

The third and final member of this basic trinity was action, which meant the interactions of persons, especially in law (*legis actiones*), over the control of things. *Actio* represents the theoretical point where self-consciousness becomes social consciousness and where the defining faculty, in behavior and language, becomes the human will. It is the point where ethical, economic, and social norms, reinforced by religion, find communal sanction and institutional expression, and perhaps pass from oral to written form.

This trinity is analogous perhaps to language—subject, verb, and predicate— although in strictly legal terms. In the world of civilized humanity, one fundamental distinction is between the public and the private spheres—between the *respublica* and the *res privata*, or private property; a person, at least a male person, belonged to both spheres, both the family and the state, being the master in one and a citizen in the other. This corresponds also to the distinction between ethics and politics. A second fundamental distinction is that between war and peace, arms and good government, though its enduring nature has often been forgotten; and again this originally indicated a male monopoly.

The central social concept of Roman law was the willing and responsible person, and in the public sphere this meant the sovereign and his absolute power, which was to say that the emperor remained the sole source of the law and that he "was not bound by the laws" (*legibus solutus*). This concept of majesty (*maiestas*) was further developed by theorists, including Jean Bodin, on the concept of sovereignty. The European monarchs, in France, Spain, and even England, could not receive the "emperor's law," but they could and did emulate his power (*imperium*), and French lawyers repeated the medieval adage that "the king is emperor in his kingdom." Yet the idea of the imperial and even divine source of law in no way stood in the way of popular sovereignty—that is, the assumption that the people were the ultimate source of laws and in that sense the emperor was actually "bound to the law" not the rule of *legibus solutus*. The subsequent dialectic between absolutism and constitutionalism has informed the rest of Western history. Nevertheless, lawyers always maintained a "reverence for history," and the very first title of the Digest was an excerpt from Pomponius's work "on the origin of law" (Kelley 1970).

Custom (*consuetudo*), repeated patterns of social behavior, was also a fundamental category of the legal tradition, whether or not officially recognized as law (*jus consuetudinarium*) (Kelley 1990*b*). In Roman thought, custom is defined as "second nature" (*altera natura*). According to the jurist Bartolus, "Custom represents the will of the people," and ten of these (*decem facunt populum*) were sufficient for "proof" of a custom. For the Romans, custom was also a norm of the speech community as well as a form of law, and again the analogy with law was evident, especially through the rules of rhetoric. But, in the age of modern science, philosophy became more important than rhetoric, as natural law was extended into the human sciences. "Mankind is ruled by two things," Gratian declared in the *Decretum iuris canonis*, "natural law and custom." Natural law also had roots in ancient Roman law and jurisprudence, and from there it was absorbed into modern political and social as well as legal thought: such was the basis of justice.

The ruling principle was that "the Church lived by Roman law" (*Ecclesia vivit iure romano*), and this was the case for private as well as for public law. Canon law had theological and sacramental foundations but was given a legal and institutional framework with Gratian's work and the many subsequent glosses and commentaries and applications in canon law courts. In the universities scholars graduated "in both laws" (*utriusque iuris*) and served secular as well as ecclesiastical authorities. Canon law was divided between the "old" and the "new" law—that is, the old collections of canons and the post-Gratian decretals, and the commentaries followed the same order down to the *Code of Canon Law* of 1918. Unlike Roman law itself, which continued to insist on the banning of "interpretation," canon law was a system in a state of development.

The medieval revival of Latin learning made possible the recovery of civil law and the school of Bolognese Glossators on the Justinian text, whose work was increasingly adapted to the practice of the courts. Accursius summed up the opinions of the Glossators in his *Glossa ordinaria*, and he emphasized the natural character of laws and the state, arguing that the *Jus gentium* was the product of "natural reason." His work, the *Accursiana*, became authoritative in the courts. For the Glossators the civil law itself was "written reason" (*ratio scripta*), and their discussion of the texts was limited largely to grammar and rhetoric. Beginning in the thirteenth century the Post-Glossators, or Commentators, including the French School, focused on understanding the meaning of the laws and explaining the problems and contradictions of their predecessors. The most famous of the Post-Glossators were Bartolus and Baldus, and they contributed much to political thought, especially ideas of sovereignty, as well as to legal interpretation. The so-called *usus modernus pandectarum* became common law in Italy, and in the late fifteenth century Roman law enjoyed an official "Reception" and played a part in the reformation of the Holy Roman Empire (Wieacker 1967).

In the fourteenth century Lucas de Penna, who studied both civil and canon law (*utriusque juris*), commented on the Code, and his work became authoritative in Renaissance France for Bodin and others. For him the law was not only prudence but a natural "science," which meant it was based on reason and dependent on analysis in terms of cause and effect; and it was also a "sacred art" and a form of wisdom (*sapientia*), as Vico would later argue (Ullman 1946). Law was derived from justitia (*jus a justitia*), was in a way the "spirit of God"; and equity was an epiphenomen of justice. Human law was both the product of the prince's will, which is a function of God, and the "consent of the people"; but it must always be subordinate to divine law. Yet for Lucas the legislator should also take into account conditions of geographic location and time in a particular society as well as custom, which was "another nature," arguments that also placed limitations on the legislator's power and showed the extent of popular authority.

The influence affected many aspects of social thought and action. One was slavery, which violated natural law but was nevertheless within human law, although Christianity opposed its excesses, and so did canon law. The theory was worked out within the limits of civil and not natural law, and it relied on the authority of the state. Both civil and canon law struggled, and not always successfully, with the problem of the relationship between secular and ecclesiastical power, which included the authority of making appointments and rendering judgments.

In early modern times the texts of Roman law became the object of historical research as well as legal practice. The hunt not only for glossatorial corruptions and "Tribonianisms" but also for pre-Justianian sources of law, such as the Twelve Table, was pursued intensively, and in the sixteenth century Pomponius's *De Origine juris* became the inspiration for a long line of histories of Roman law, beginning especially with that of Aymar du Rivail in 1515, and later vernacular writings, such as those of Étienne Pasquier. The "conjunction of history and jurisprudence" was proclaimed by François Baudouin in 1561, and was pursued also by Jean Bodin in 1566; it marked both historical method and the question of historical sources (Kelley 1964). Historical interpretation was likewise applied to European customary and feudal law, and many histories of provincial French *coutumes* were written during and after the official movement to "reform customs," with the participation of the three estates.

Jurists had long been disturbed by the flaws in Roman law. The Bartolists tried to bring order to the texts through the dialectical method, and so did the humanists, whose historical approach did not prevent them from trying to "reduce law to an art." Law was supposed to be "true philosophy" (*vera philosophia*), and so it required not only formal structure but elevated moral and social goals. Amongst the leaders of those who attempted to "reform" jurisprudence were the French jurists Connan, Le Douaren,

Doneau, and Coras, according to a rational "method" and of course natural law. "The letter kills," Federicus Stephanus quoted from St Paul, "the spirit giveth life"; and from the seventeenth century the "spirit of the laws" indeed became the target of philosophical jurisprudence. More than two centuries before the time of Montesquieu many jurists had carried on the Romanoid effort of methodizing and of systematizing jurisprudence, and in 1689 Jean Domat published his *Civil Laws in their Natural Order*. As Leibniz (1667) noted: "Not content with the glory of being identified with the highest philosophy, jurisprudence is driven to occupy alone the throne of wisdom." And "rational jurisprudence" naturally figured as one of the forms of Vico's "new science," as did also the "history of eternal ideas" and a "system of universal law."

Meanwhile the profession of law proceeded along national lines, and practicing lawyers, like their academic colleagues and critics, moved to improve and to rationalize the complex and sometimes contradictory wisdom of their legacy, making use of course of their Romanist training. In France there was a long tradition of the "reformation" of law and attempts at unification, and the efforts were polarized between Romanist and customary parties, corresponding perhaps to the medieval and post-imperial distinction between the *pays de droit* and *pays de droit coutumier*. The unification movement culminated in the process preliminary to the Napoleonic codification. A reader of Roman law, Napoleon postured as a second Justinian in his great peacetime effort. "This code," wrote one admirer, "is founded principally on Roman law." Under Napoleon, too, Romanoid jurisprudence was extended to his empire, to other European states, and to many other parts of the world, including South Africa and Louisiana.

The eighteenth century was the age of codification movements in Europe. "We live under three codes," wrote Diderot, "the natural code, the civil code, and the religious code"; and all of these followed the forms and often the substance of Roman jurisprudence. Among others the Prussian Code was established at the end of the century, and so was that of Austria. Unlike philosophy, which was bound to reason, civil law was a "dogmatic" discipline, as Kant said, and it was tied to authority, which was largely textual. Yet Roman law, which had been an important part of general education throughout the history of higher learning, furnished materials not only for particular laws, especially those of possession, property, and citizenship, but also for judicial and therefore interpretation.

The "Roman foundations of modern law" have been detailed by H. F. Jolowicz (1957). Central is the distinction between private and public law—that is, law between individual persons and the law between government institutions (and sometimes persons). Individual rights include not only self-defense but also self-redress, at least in cases of necessity. There was also a distinction between actions *in rem* and actions *in personam*. From the time of Justinian rules of evidence were usually in written form, and "written law" became the target of much criticism. Law in many modern forms draws on the formulas devised by the Romans and the medieval commentators as well as by modern philosophers.

Natural law, which existed within civil law and yet was a source of legal ideals, led not only to abstractions but also to legal history. In the work of the Scottish School,

Montesquieu, Gustav Hugo, and others, the idea of legal evolution was worked out, and the culmination came with the German Historical School, especially with Friedrich von Savigny's history of Roman law in the Middle Ages, followed by his systematic work underlying the codification movement. The debate over codification was set off by A. W. Rehberg's study of the Code Napoleon in Germany and A. F. T. Thibaut's plea for a German code, and to the latter Savigny responded with a defense of the reception of modern Roman law (*usus modernorum Pandectarum*), in which Karl Marx was first trained before his rejection of this authoritarian tradition (Kelley 1978). The emphasis of the Historical School was on the practical development of "positive law," in opposition to the falsely "enlightened" views of purely rational jurisprudence and the tyrannical adaption by Napoleon. The Historical School also had branches in other disciplines, including philology, literature, political economy, political thought, sociology, anthropology, and indirectly religion and biblical criticism, all of them centered on the notion of a conscious subject–person.

In the nineteenth century the study of Roman law lost its ideological power and became part of philology and history, at least so concludes James Whitman (1990). Roman law was indeed important to history and related disciplines, being central to the works of such disparate scholars as Marx, Henry Sumner Maine, J. J. Bachofen, Theodore Mommsen, and Max Weber (see Kelley 1990a). In the modern human sciences the spirit of the tradition of Roman law continues—the words are different but the music is the same. Except in some corners of the world, Roman law has been absorbed, if not rejected, by history.

REFERENCES

BERMAN, HAROLD (1983). *Law and Revolution: The Formation of the Western Legal Tradition*. Cambridge, MA: Harvard University Press.

DOMAT, JEAN (1702). *Les Loix civiles dans leur ordre naturel*. New edn. Luxembourg.

JOLOWICZ, H. F. (1957). *Roman Foundations of Modern Law*. Oxford: Oxford University Press.

KELLEY, D. (1964). "Historia Integra: François Baudouin and his Conception of History," *Journal of the History of Ideas*, 35: 35–57.

KELLEY, D. (1970). "The Rise of Legal History in the Renaissance," *History and Theory*, 9: 174–94.

KELLEY, D. (1976). "Vico's Road: from Philology to Jurisprudence and Back," in G. Tagliacozzo and D. Verene (eds), *Gianbattista Vico's Science of Humanity*. Baltimore: Johns Hopkins University Press, 15–29.

KELLEY, D. (1978). "The Metaphysics of Law: An Essay on the Very Young Marx," *American Historical Review*, 83: 350–67.

KELLEY, D. (1979a). "Civil Science in the Renaissance," *Historical Journal*, 22: 777–94.

KELLEY, D. (1979b). "Gaius Noster: Substructures of Western Social Thought," *American Historical Review*, 84: 619–48.

KELLEY, D. (1990*a*). *The Human Measure: Social Thought in the Western Legal Tradition.* Cambridge, MA: Harvard University Press.

KELLEY, D. (1990*b*). "Second Nature: The Idea of Custom in European Law, Society, and Culture," in A. Grafton and A. Blair (eds), *The Transmission of Culture in Early Modern Europe.* Philadelphia: University of Pennsylvania Press, 131–72.

KELLEY, D. (2002). "What Pleases the Prince," *History of Political Thought*, 23: 288–302.

KOSCHAKER, PAUL (1947). *Europa und das römisches Recht.* Munich: C. H. Beck.

LEIBNIZ, GOTTFRIED (1667). *Novus methodus discendae docendaeque jusisprudendiae.* Frankfurt.

MAINE, HENRY SUMNER (1861). *Ancient Law.* New York: Henry Holt.

ULLMAN, WALTER (1946). *The Medieval Idea of Law as Represented by Lucas de Penna.* New York: Barnes and Noble.

VICO, GIAMBATTISTA (1974). *Opere giuridiche*, (ed.) P. Cristofolini. Florence: Sansoni.

WIEACKER, FRANZ (1967). *Privatrechtsgeschichte der Neuzeit.* Göttingen: Vanderhoeck & Ruprecht.

WHITMAN, JAMES Q. (1990). *The Legacy of Roman Law in the German Romantic Era.* Princeton: Princeton University Press.

CHAPTER 11

ARABIC CONTRIBUTIONS TO MEDIEVAL POLITICAL THEORY

CHARLES E. BUTTERWORTH

INTRODUCTION

THE title notwithstanding, the following exposition focuses primarily on political philosophy within the medieval Arabic–Islamic tradition of the Middle East. Political philosophy in general differs from political thought, on the one hand, and political theology, on the other, insofar as it seeks to replace opinion about political affairs by knowledge. Although it may adopt and adapt the speech and images that dominate in the political or religious sphere for sound rhetorical reasons, it remains as independent of religion as it does of any current political regime. Political philosophy in the medieval Arabic–Islamic tradition of the Middle East, in particular, differs from that in the medieval Arabic–Jewish or Arabic–Christian traditions in that it is beholden neither to political nor to theological currents, its occasional rhetorical bows to one or the other notwithstanding. Political thought, best exemplified by the genre known as "Mirrors for Princes," is always limited by the opinions that dominate the setting and time. Political theology or, for medieval Islam, jurisprudence focuses on how the beliefs and actions set forth in the religious tradition elucidate the conditions justifying warfare or the qualities an individual must have to be considered a suitable ruler.

Currently, a few scholars who explore political thinking within the medieval Arabic–Islamic tradition contest the proposition that anything resembling political philosophy so defined ever existed. For some, all philosophical endeavor is rooted in metaphysical presuppositions that must ultimately be traced back to a faith commitment or be explained in terms of a particular revelation. Others, persuaded there can be no political philosophy without detailed discussion of regimes, institutions, or constitutions, deny that anything prior to Ibn Khaldūn so qualifies. Momentary reflection on the way political philosophy was pursued by Plato and Aristotle reveals the insufficiency of both contentions. In the *Nicomachean Ethics*, Aristotle emphasizes that prudence or practical reason, the intellectual virtue guiding human conduct, is based on opinion—not knowledge. Characteristic of the best regime of the *Republic* is the attention given to the education of the ruling class, the guardians, rather than to formal structures or even to laws. Even the second-best regime set forth in the *Laws* accords as much attention to the character formation of the citizens as to the promulgation of laws.

Generally speaking, political philosophers in the medieval Arabic–Islamic tradition agree that Plato and Aristotle achieved the highest level of knowledge about the universe and its parts. That the revealed religions known through Moses, Jesus along with Paul, and Muhammad also claim to possess ultimate truth about these very things poses no conflict. As Alfarabi affirms, the meaning of philosopher, lawgiver, imam, and king is one (*Attainment*, sects 57–8). Their goals and activities are identical. Alfarabi's successors argue similarly, each in his own fashion. Averroes, holding Aristotle in the highest esteem even as he carries out his duties as judge and jurist, insists that truth cannot contradict truth. If a philosophic teaching appears to conflict with a scriptural one, interpretation of the latter will reveal the basic agreement between the two (*Decisive Treatise*, sect. 12 with sects 11 and 13).

Alfarabi and his successors rely mainly on Plato's *Republic* and *Laws*, plus Aristotle's *Nicomachean Ethics* and *Rhetoric*, in their expositions, but are conversant with Aristotle's works on logic, natural science, the soul, and being. They investigate law-giving so as to understand the political goal of prophecy. Indeed, Ibn Sina or Avicenna lauds Plato's *Laws* as the best explanation of prophetic law-giving (*Divisions*, 108). Particular differences notwithstanding, all insist upon what becomes clear to unaided human reason as the touchstone.

Prior to Alfarabi, philosophy within the Arabic–Islamic tradition is not properly political. It is focused more on divine science or metaphysics and on personal conduct—ethics. Alfarabi is the one who shows that inquiry into the highest matters depends on what one thinks about human things, especially about the ends human beings aim at and prize. He pays no attention to his immediate predecessors, Alkindi and Alrazi. Instead, he focuses on Plato and Aristotle, especially on what they have to teach about the way to return to philosophy when it has passed into oblivion or otherwise been overwhelmed.

Beholden as Avicenna is to Alfarabi, something he admits in passing, he nonetheless subjugates politics and political investigations to issues of personal conduct and to forays into mystical byways. Consequently, he draws the fire of religious traditionalists—something Alfarabi had studiously avoided. So, after Avicenna, a conversation among the philosophers begins—each taking note of his predecessors and explicitly agreeing or disagreeing with them. It continues unabated through Ibn Bajja, Ibn Tufayl, and Ibn Rushd or Averroes until Ibn Khaldūn. Then, after a hiatus during which renewed inquiry into the nature of the deity and subjects more closely associated with mysticism than with rationalism reigns (a vestige of sorts of what Avicenna first set into motion), philosophical inquiry starts again with al-Afghānī in the nineteenth century. There is also a spatial movement worth noting: after Avicenna, philosophic inquiry dies out in the east; for reasons that are not yet clear, it moves west to Andalusia, where it flourishes. Ibn Khaldūn, the last of the philosophers, brings philosophy back to Cairo as he writes and rewrites his famous *Introduction* (*Muqaddima*) to history. With his demise, philosophy disappears from the Arab and Islamic world—some might say never to return.

Here, the contributions of a few of these thinkers to political philosophy in the medieval Arabic and Islamic tradition are examined in order to show how one leads to another as well as to identify the major issues with which each was concerned. The exposition is necessarily selective and less than exhaustive. But every effort has been made to ensure that it is accurate and faithful to the authors being considered.

ALFARABI

Although there is doubt about Alfarabi's place of birth and the early years of his life, most scholars agree that he was born in about 870 beyond the Oxus River—either in Farab, Kazakhstan, or Faryab, Turkestan. In the course of his life, Abū Nasr Muhammad Ibn Muhammad Ibn Tarkhān Ibn Awzalagh al-Fārābī resided in Bukhara, Marv, Haran, Baghdad, Constantinople, Aleppo, Cairo, and Damascus. He studied Islamic jurisprudence and music in Bukhara, logic in Marv, and philosophy in Baghdad, where he also improved his grasp of Arabic. Around 905 or 910, Alfarabi went to Byzantium, maybe reaching Constantinople, to study Greek sciences and philosophy, and then returned to Baghdad to teach and write. In about 942, political upheavals forced him to Aleppo, then Egypt a few years later, and finally Damascus, where he died in 950.

Widely acclaimed as "the second teacher"—that is, second after Aristotle—Alfarabi is surely the most important philosopher within the Arabic–Islamic tradition. His writings, charming in their deceptive subtlety, are couched in simple language and straightforward sentences. Most often, he sets forth an apparently unobjectionable story about natural and conventional things. As the exposition unfolds, the reader discovers that Alfarabi has accounted for the natural order, prophecy, political leadership, moral virtue, civic organization, the order of the sciences, even the philosophic pursuits of Plato or Aristotle—in short, all the major subjects of interest to humans. He enumerates the reasons for which human beings associate, how civic life can best be organized to meet the highest human needs, the ways most actual regimes differ from this best order, and why philosophy and religion deem this order best.

These writings, extraordinary in their breadth and deep learning, extend through all the sciences and embrace every part of philosophy. Alfarabi qualifies as the founder of Arabic–Islamic political philosophy because he is the first to explore the challenge to traditional philosophy presented by revealed religion, especially in its claims that the Creator provides for human well-being by means of an inspired prophet–legislator. This is especially evident in his two accounts of the old political science in the last chapter of the explicitly popular *Enumeration of the Sciences*. Both presuppose the validity of the traditional separation between practical and theoretical science, but neither is adequate for the radically new situation created by the appearance of revealed religion. The two accounts explain in detail the actions and ways of life needed for sound political rule to flourish, but are silent about opinions—especially the kind of theoretical opinions set forth in religion—and thus unable to point to the kind of rulership needed now that religion holds sway. Nor can either speak about the opinions or actions addressed by the jurisprudence and theology of revealed religion. These tasks require a political science that combines theoretical and practical science along with prudence and that shows how they are to be ordered in the soul of the ruler.

In his *Book of Religion* and *Selected Aphorisms*, Alfarabi outlines this broader political science. It speaks of religious beliefs as opinions and of acts of worship as actions, noting that both are prescribed for a community by a supreme ruler or prophet. The new political science views religion as centered in a political community whose supreme ruler seems identical with the founder of a religion. Indeed, the goals and prescriptions of the supreme ruler are those of the prophet lawgiver. All that is said or done by this supreme ruler finds justification in philosophy, and religion thus depends on philosophy—theoretical as well as practical. Similarly, by presenting the art of jurisprudence as a means to identify particular details the supreme ruler failed to regulate before his death, Alfarabi makes it depend upon practical philosophy and thus part of this broader political science. In sum, his new political science offers a comprehensive view of the universe and identifies the practical acumen that permits the one possessing this understanding, either the supreme ruler or a successor endowed with his qualities, to rule wisely. Able to explain the various ranks of all the beings, this political science also stresses the importance of religion for uniting the citizens and for helping them attain the virtues that prolong decent political life. In the *Political Regime* and *Principles of the Opinions of the Inhabitants of the Virtuous City*, he further illustrates the new opinions. Their core is best stated in the *Attainment of Happiness*—the first part of his famous trilogy, the *Philosophy of Plato and Aristotle*—by his declaration that "the idea of the philosopher, supreme ruler, prince, legislator, and imam is but a single idea" (*Attainment*, sect. 58).

Alfarabi thus reaches to the core of revealed religion and presents it as consonant with the best understanding of the philosophy set forth by Plato and Aristotle. Politics is central to the proper human life because only in a well-ordered regime can people pursue their true end or purpose—ultimate happiness or perfection. Philosophers such as Plato and Aristotle are thus like lawgivers, religious leaders (imams), or kings in that they provide wisdom about that purpose and how it may be attained. Indeed, good rulers are to be distinguished from bad in terms of what they view as happiness, how they seek to bring it about, and whom they assist in enjoying it. By his allusions to different opinions and actions, Alfarabi constantly entices thoughtful readers to think more deeply about the goals of religion, philosophy, and politics—how they differ, as well as what they have in common.

AVICENNA

Abū ʿAlī al-Husayn Ibn Sīnā or Avicenna was born in Afshanah in 980; his family soon moved to nearby Bukhara, where he began his studies. Having proved himself in the study of the Quran and related works of literature by the age of 10, he turned to Indian mathematics and Islamic jurisprudence, then philosophy. Finding Aristotle's treatise on metaphysics nearly incomprehensible, he declared Alfarabi's *On the Goals of the "Metaphysics"* a most useful guide. Avicenna engaged in politics, first as an administrator for the local ruler whom his father served and then as a jurist for, and advisor to, different minor rulers. He also managed the affairs of the widows of rulers and served as physician to Shams al-Dawla, the Buyid prince of Hamadhan and Qirmisin—being named his chief minister or vizier on two occasions. He later joined the court of ʿAlā al-Dawla, whom he served as an intimate companion and learned advisor until his death in Hamadhan in 1035. Despite his engagement in politics, Avicenna composed no comprehensive treatise on the subject.

In the first chapter of the introductory volume to his famous *Healing*, Avicenna explains the general order of the whole work. After the part on logic is another part devoted to natural science. It is followed by a third part about mathematics, and the whole compendium concludes with Avicenna's explanation of the divisions and aspects of metaphysics. From this account of its scope, one might think Avicenna's *Healing* was devoted solely to theoretical philosophy or science, that it had nothing to say about practical philosophy or science. Indeed, it is not until the very end of his discussion of metaphysics or divine science that he speaks of the practical sciences or arts of ethics and politics. As he puts it, this "summary of the science of ethics and of politics" is placed there "until I compose a separate, comprehensive book about them"—a book he never wrote.

Avicenna's fuller teaching reveals, however, that ethical and political science belong after divine science intrinsically and not provisionally. The human manifestation of divine science and its practical proof, they testify to divine providence for humankind and thus to the truth of revelation more clearly than any of the other sciences investigated in the *Healing*. Because the correctness of what they teach can also be verified by Aristotelian or pagan reasoning processes, Avicenna elucidates the relationship he discerns between pagan philosophy and the revelation accorded the Prophet Muhammad.

His description of Plato's *Laws* as a treatise on prophetic law-giving indicates how interrelated he deems philosophy and revelation. Moreover, his focus on the political aspects of prophecy and divine law leads to reflection upon the most fundamental political questions: the nature of law, purpose of political community, need for sound moral life among the citizens, importance of providing for divorce as well as for marriage, conditions for just war, considerations that lay behind penal laws, and the purpose of human life. Although he does not address the origin of private property any more than he explains how future successors to the prophet–lawgiver might be raised so that they will have moral habits and character traits suitable to such a position, he provides the basic principles for readers to pursue these issues on their own. Differently stated, Avicenna's political teaching is propaedeutic rather than provisional: it provides an introduction to the fundamentals of political science and alerts readers to the need to think carefully about the strong affinity between the vision of political life set forth by the pagan Greek philosophers and that exceptional individual who surpasses philosophic virtue by acquiring prophetic qualities.

Whereas the opinions and actions Alfarabi sets forth help the citizens acquire the moral habits and dispositions that will allow them to live together harmoniously, and in such living to move towards ultimate happiness, Avicenna's prophet dwells more on beliefs that have no immediate political relevance. Some are anti-political or ascetic, as though the highest goal toward which thoughtful humans strive will weaken the ties between the soul and body so that they achieve separation from the body. Thus, Avicenna does not portray ultimate happiness as acquired through political association, but through turning away from political life and all other bodily concerns. This tension between the demands of political life and the demands of complete spiritual life derives from his subordination of philosophy and politics to religion, from his claim that the highest human achievement is pure intellectual or spiritual perception proper to a disembodied soul that has gone beyond the concerns of the practical intellect. Avicenna never explains what prompts the prophet to turn aside from this all-important goal of untrammeled spiritual perception to legislate for a political community.

Nor, despite his repeated insistence on the need to do away with or go beyond the practical intellect in order to develop fully the theoretical or spiritual intellect, does he ever make clear why the prophet's mastery of the practical moral virtues should constitute his superiority over the philosopher. Hence, Avicenna's several explanations of moral virtue and moral habits or ethics leave many questions still to be answered. The great turn toward political philosophy initiated by Alfarabi is ignored and even obscured by Avicenna.

IBN BĀJJA

After Avicenna, philosophy in general and political philosophy in particular move west to Andalusia. The first to come to light there is Abū Bakr Ibn al Ṣāʾigh or Ibn Bājja. He was born in Saragossa between 1085 and 1090, but political turmoil forced him to Granada and then to Seville. In both of these latter cities, he served as chief minister or vizier to local governors loyal to the Almoravid dynasty. He died in Fez in 1139, perhaps from a poisoned eggplant.

Ibn Tufayl speaks highly of Ibn Bājja's promise, but also blames him for being too involved with diversions and paying too little attention to his writing. The author of treatises on music, astronomy, logic, natural science, and metaphysics, Ibn Bājja also composed commentaries on several of Alfarabi's logical writings. Most important for our purposes here is his pursuit of the theme of the solitary, the individual whose intellectual and moral qualities put him at odds with the dominant opinions in imperfect regimes. Highlighted by Alfarabi in the *Political Regime*, Ibn Bājja develops it more in his *Governance of the Solitary*. Like Alfarabi, Ibn Bājja compares this exceptional individual to a weed insofar as he comes on his own to form correct opinions about the world and how to live as a human being that are in sharp contrast with the false, unsound opinions of his own city as well as of most other cities in existence at any time. He flourishes in spite of his surroundings, developing into a specimen distinct from those dominant in his own milieu.

Ibn Bājja reaches back to Plato and the *Republic* to establish the importance of the subject. He grounds his account in what Alfarabi has said about the tensions arising for those possessed of sound opinions and character as they interact with the dominant opinions and role models. Precisely because the best solution—bringing into being a perfect city that provides education suitable for all the citizens—is not likely, perhaps not even possible, Ibn Bājja focuses on the individual who manages to arrive at a proper understanding of the universe and the goal of human beings within it. That is, he indicates what that understanding should be and suggests, albeit obliquely, how it differs from the opinions and actions all too evident in actual regimes.

He sees the task as similar to that of a physician. In other words, he seeks to show how the solitary being might develop a healthy soul just as a physician seeks to show others how to attain healthy bodies. Moreover, he notes the importance of showing how to preserve that healthy soul and how that parallels the physician showing his patient how to preserve a healthy body. Such, at least, are the principles behind Ibn Bājja's exposition—the promises he makes about the exposition to follow. The actual exposition is not so successful. Instead of investigating natural and political science, upon whose elaboration he claims that an understanding of human perfection depends, Ibn Bājja engages in a rambling and inconclusive examination of the spiritual forms that constitute the universe and are somehow central to human well-being. Consequently, he never indicates how the solitary individual is to be formed or governed. The many suggestions he offers about the way the universe is to be intellectually apprehended and the soul of one who arrives at such an apprehension notwithstanding, his account remains all too imprecise and inconclusive to offer the guidance for which he so whetted readers' appetites.

In this respect, Ibn Bājja unwittingly contributes to the intellectual tension or quarrel introduced by Avicenna. Rooted as his enterprise is in the educational task of Plato's *Republic* and of Alfarabi's larger political teaching, Ibn Bājja's attention to the spiritual forms encourages those who would like to link philosophy—especially political philosophy—with religious and metaphysical themes. Indeed, Ibn Bājja so contributed to that non-rational perspective that his immediate successor, Ibn Tufayl, deems it necessary to restate the history of philosophy within Islam so as to redress the balance.

Ibn Tufayl

Muhammad Ibn ʿAbd al-Malik Abū Bakr Ibn Tufayl was born in Guadix, not far from Granada, in 1110. Reputed for his learning in philosophy, jurisprudence, theology, and logic, as well as natural science, he gained the favor of the Almohade ruler, Abu Ya'qūb Yūsuf, whom he served for many years as a political advisor and physician. Apart from his philosophical novel, *Hayy Ibn Yaqzān* (*Living the Son of Awakened*)—the only writing of his that has survived—Ibn Tufayl is known for the important role he played in presenting Averroes to Abu Ya'qūb as the person most capable of commenting on the works of Aristotle, this being a task Ibn Tufayl considered beyond his own reach. He died in Marrakesh in 1185.

Ibn Tufayl focused on the relationship between the rational acquisition of knowledge and the path to it pursued by those who favor mysticism or sufism in the philosophical introduction to *Hayy Ibn Yaqzān*. The work consists of three major parts. In the introduction, Ibn Tufayl explains his reasons for writing a book such as this and provides a general critique of philosophy, theology, and mysticism within the Arab world at his time. It is followed by the story of Hayy and by a formal conclusion in which Ibn Tufayl returns to the main theme of the work.

As he explains in the introduction, the tale of Hayy ibn Yaqzān comes as a response to a request from a friend that he unfold what he knows "of the secrets of the Oriental wisdom mentioned by the master, the chief, Abu ʿAlī Ibn Sīnā.'" The question, he says, moved him to a strange state and caused him to discern a world beyond the present; it also caused him to discern the difficulty of speaking intelligently and circumspectly about this state. To prove the latter point, Ibn Tufayl passes in review what mystics and philosophers have said about it. Desirous of avoiding their foolishness, he speaks about the state only to the extent necessary—all the while pointing out the errors of his predecessors. He insists it is to be reached by "theoretical knowledge" and "deliberative inquiry" and intimates that at least one philosopher—Ibn Bājja—reached that rank or perhaps even managed to go beyond it.

Ibn Bājja did not describe this state in a book; nor has any other philosopher—either because they had no awareness of it or because it is too difficult to explain in a book. Ibn Tufayl dismisses as useless for this task what has come down from Aristotle, Alfarabi, Avicenna, and all Andalusians prior to Ibn Bājja. Unfortunately, capable as he was of providing such an account, Ibn Bājja so busied himself with other less important pursuits that he failed to follow this one through to its end.

To meet his friend's request, Ibn Tufayl promises to expose the truth and knowledge he has learned from Alghazali and Avicenna (that is, from those who favor religious explanation or perhaps even mysticism more than rationalism), plus what he has gained from the philosophically inclined people of his time via study and reflection. Even so, he hesitates to give the results of what he has witnessed without also providing the principles, lest his interlocutor be content with a lower degree of insight. To arouse his interlocutor's longing and encourage him to move along the path, Ibn Tufayl offers the tale of Hayy ibn Yaqzān. In other words, though such as to leave us short of the end, it will indicate what the path is like.

Hayy is either self-generated from a lump of clay or comes into being as do all humans but is then put into the sea in a basket because his mother, the sister of a very proud monarch, has wedded beneath her status in secret and fears for the fruit of this union should her brother learn of Hayy's existence. However generated, Hayy grows up on a deserted island, nursed by a doe until he can fend for himself. During seven periods of seven years each, he discovers his natural surroundings and the way they interact, ascending by a series of basic inductive reasoning to an understanding of physics and its many divisions as well as mathematics and its parts. He also gains insight into the nature of the heavenly bodies and into the character of the creator as well as of his messenger and prophet, Muhammad. At no point does Ibn Tufayl draw attention to the inconsistency in this narrative of the way reasoning based on particular observations leads to general, even universal, principles and from them to particular religious doctrines. Yet he should have done so, for that is intimately related to the problem raised by the question that prompts this strange tale.

Hayy's education is all the more wondrous, for his enforced solitude deprives him of language. Only when he encounters Asāl, the inhabitant of a neighboring island who is discontent with the way his fellow citizens practice religion, does Hayy learn to speak. The two return to Asāl's island intent upon showing people the correct path, but fail miserably. Intelligent as each is, neither has any awareness of how to talk to human beings whose primary concerns are the securing of basic needs and then the enjoyment of pleasant respite. Only Salāmān, a friend of Asāl's who discerns that most people cannot appreciate the truths Hayy wishes them to grasp but is content to let them flounder, understands the limits of human reason. His complacent disinterest in the well-being of his fellow citizens not only baffles Hayy and Asāl but also deprives them of the possibility of learning about a lawgiver's and prophet's greatest skill: the ability to persuade others of his vision.

The tale ends with Hayy and Asāl deciding to return to their desert island to spend their remaining days meditating on divine matters. The people on the mainland are left with no solution to the problems that plague them, just as Ibn Tufayl's interlocutor is left with no clear answer to his quest. But a reader who has followed the narration through to the end and contrasted it with the critique of philosophy and mysticism presented in the introduction must note how important it is for those who know or are somehow inspired to be able to communicate their insights to others. Unless those who fully understand the way things are also have a sound grasp of rhetoric, they will never be able to help others elevate their thoughts and thus achieve a better political order. Ibn Tufayl succeeds, then, in reminding the reader through this delightful tale of Alfarabi's emphasis on the first ruler as prophet as well as lawgiver and philosopher.

AVERROES

Abū al-Walīd Muhammad Ibn Ahmad Ibn Muhammad Ibn Rushd, or Averroes, as he is more commonly known in the West, is renowned for his intellectual excellence and profound accomplishments in jurisprudence, medicine, poetry, philosophy, natural science, theology, and, above all, for his commentaries on Aristotle. He was born in Cordoba in 1126, the son and grandson of noted judges—his grandfather having served as the great judge of Cordoba and of Andalusia. The most important event in Averroes's life must be his presentation by Ibn Tufayl to Abu Ya'qūb as the person most qualified to undertake the task of commenting on Aristotle's works. Even while engaged in those commentaries, he continued to serve as a judge, became the personal physician to Abu Ya'qūb, and composed treatises on topics of more immediate concern to fellow Muslims, notably, the *Decisive Treatise*. Nonetheless, toward the end of his life, he was punished along with other prominent scholars on charges of being overly occupied with philosophy and "the sciences of the ancients" and banished to Lucena, a small town near Cordoba, for two years. Shortly after returning in favor to the court at Marrakesh in 1198, he died.

Averroes's political teaching is stated most directly in his commentaries, especially those on Aristotle's *Rhetoric* and Plato's *Republic*. In his more popular writings—the *Decisive Treatise* in particular—he seeks to nuance the broader themes set forth in the commentaries as he develops the question of the relationship between philosophy and divine law and, more pointedly, the important role of prophecy. Central to all of these questions is Averroes's discussion of the different kinds of political regimes and the best regime. Indeed, his discussion of that topic leads him to reflect more generally on other major political questions.

From Averroes's *Commentary on Plato's Republic* we learn, above all, that the simply best regime is one in which the natural order among the virtues and practical arts is respected. The practical arts and the moral virtues exist for the sake of the deliberative virtues, and—whatever the hierarchical relationship between the practical arts and the moral virtues—they exist for the sake of the theoretical virtues. Only when this natural order is reflected in the organization and administration of the regime can there be any assurance that all of the virtues and practical arts will function as they ought. In order to have sound practice, then, it is necessary to understand the principles on which such practice depends: the order and the interrelationship amongst the parts of the human soul. He reaches the same conclusion, albeit much more directly, by identifying the best regime in his *Middle Commentary on the Rhetoric* as the city whose opinions and actions are in accordance with what the theoretical sciences prescribe.

These principles permit Averroes to identify the flaws in the regimes he sees around him more clearly. They are faulted, either because they aim at the wrong kind of end or because they fail to respect any order among the human virtues. Thus he blames democracy for the emphasis it places on the private and for its inability to order the desires of the citizens. In his *Commentary on Plato's Republic*, he first emphasizes the need to foster greater concern for the public sphere and to diminish the appeal of the private then explains man's ultimate happiness in order to indicate how the desires should be properly ordered.

Some aspects of this teaching are problematic. However persuasive Averroes's arguments about the goodness of the best regime and the evils of the alternatives to it, one cannot fail to notice that he accepts without question the means advocated by Plato's Socrates for bringing it about and then preserving it once it has come into existence—means both immoral and unethical. With no hesitation, he recommends a lie to justify the class stratification fundamental to this regime. Moreover, he endorses deceptions concerning the equitable distribution of marriage partners, the way children will be accustomed to warfare, and the education of the wise. In addition, he approves of the proposition that older citizens who have allowed this regime to come into being will be expelled from it just as it is about to take shape. What Socrates proposed as preposterous suggestions and thus indications of just how impossible it would be ever to bring about the best regime, Averroes seems to accept as serious innovations.

Averroes accepts these lies, deceptions, and injustices because he contends that the plain truth is not always persuasive, that reason does not usually prevail. Most adults are like children in that they need to be trained to do what is right, and such training requires compulsion as well as deception. Unless the citizens can be induced to believe in a good that transcends their own immediate well-being, they will not make the sacrifices necessary for the establishment and functioning of the virtuous regime. Though a few may eventually come to understand why they must place the public good before their own private well-being and why they must subordinate their immediate desires to a more distant good, most will not. In other words, Averroes has a clear sense of the limits of reason and of the need to speak to people in language they understand—this being precisely what Hayy and Asāl lacked.

In the *Decisive Treatise*, Averroes points to this same problem by referring to a famous Quranic passage. Noting that most scholars agree upon the need to address people with different levels of learning in ways suitable to them, he urges that this is precisely what the Quran recommends. It is because religion, like politics, must take the whole citizen body into account that different kinds of speech and even different kinds of practices are justified. Moreover, those who would deny that the revealed law works in such a manner put the citizenry into danger. By explaining complicated matters of faith to those not able to follow the reasoning, these would-be teachers lead the less gifted into confusion and frequently into disbelief.

For Averroes, there is a major danger in using dialectic or demonstration to address those who can comprehend only preaching or rhetoric. On the grounds that the lawgiver, that is, the prophet, is similar to a physician—the lawgiver caring for souls and the physician for bodies—Averroes draws the practical consequences. First, such misguided teachers are doing little more than telling the populace not to heed the ministrations of the physician. Indeed, such teachers drive the people away from the one individual who can help them recover the health of their soul and preserve it from future sicknesses. The goal of the lawgiver or prophet is not to make the people physicians. That demands too much of them. Rather, his goal is to teach them the basic fundamentals with respect to the all-important health of their soul. For such an undertaking, there is no need to fret about the intricacies of the revealed book. The surface teaching suffices. That is what Averroes seeks to safeguard through his defense of rhetoric and the surface understanding of Scripture.

This is the core teaching of the *Decisive Treatise*, a writing for which Averroes apologizes but that he felt compelled to write in order to overcome the terrible strife between the proponents of religion and those of philosophy then prevalent. It is prompted by his own broad understanding of the complexity of the human soul tempered by a peculiar sense of what is needed for sound political life. In this manner, he brings together not only philosophy and religion but also the fundamentals of Plato's and Aristotle's approach to human nature and politics. And he thereby brings again to the fore the central focus on Alfarabi's political teaching.

IBN KHALDŪN

From the death of Averroes in 1198 to the advent of Ibn Khaldūn almost 200 years later, political philosophy gave way to mysticism and theosophy. It was also a period of great political upheaval. In the East were the Crusades plus the onslaught of the Mongols, who took Baghdad in 1258. And Andalusia became fragmented by internecine strife, even as Christian forces gained greater strength and strove to retake land seized centuries earlier. Whereas political philosophy flourished earlier amidst similar unrest, it now faltered and, upon Ibn Khaldūn's death, vanished forever. To be sure, faint echoes resonated here and there in Persian and Turkish "mirrors of Princes" literature with its particular advice to rulers and focus on remedies to help them preserve their reign. But not until almost 400 years later, when al-Afghānī burst upon the scene, was any serious kind of political writing to be found. That said, it is, nonetheless, necessary to speak of the last great instance of political philosophy preceding this great, lamentable drought.

ʿAbd al-Rahmān Ibn Khaldūn was born in Tunisia in 1332 and spent the first two-thirds of his life in North Africa and Muslim Spain. Then, in 1382, he fled from political turmoil in Tunisia to Egypt, where he remained until his death in 1406. Best known for the lengthy *Muqaddima* (Introduction) to his massive philosophical history of civilization, *Kitāb al-ʿIbar*, Ibn Khaldūn also deserves some attention for his numerous and varied political activities. Born and raised in Tunis, he read the Quran and studied the religious sciences as well as Arabic and poetry, then was educated in logic, mathematics, natural science, and metaphysics. He also received specialized training in court correspondence and administrative matters, subjects that allowed him to become a court secretary to the Marinid ruler Abu 'Inan in Fez at about the age of 22.

After some vicissitudes, including almost two years of prison, Ibn Khaldūn went to Grenada in 1362 to become an advisor and tutor to Muhammad V. That position lasted only about two years, no longer than his subsequent position as prime minister for Prince Abu ʿAbd Allah of Bougie. Following these forays into practical politics, Ibn Khaldūn endured several years of upheaval (1366–75), settled for about four years in Qal'at Ibn Salāma near Oran to begin work on his history, then moved to Tunis under the patronage of Abū al-ʿAbbās so as to have access to documents and libraries. That lasted only a few years before the desire to escape court intrigues determined him to seek tranquility in Egypt.

During the next quarter of a century he served the Mamluk Sultan Barqūq as judge and chief judge, was a professor at various universities (including the prestigious al-Azhar), and even once became a university president. A few years before his death in 1406, he met the famous Mongol chieftain Tamerlane. But the period in Egypt was, above all, a time for revising his massive history, *Kitāb al-ʿIbar* and working on its three-volume introduction.

The *Kitāb al-ʿIbar* is a multi-volume effort that, in Ibn Khaldūn's words, sets forth "the record of the beginning and the suite of the days of the Arabs, Persians, Berbers, and the most powerful of their contemporaries." Its introduction consists of six very long chapters that explore the character of human civilization in general and Bedouin civilization in particular, basic kinds of political associations, characteristics of sedentary civilization, arts and crafts by which humans gain their livelihoods, and, finally, different human sciences. Ibn Khaldūn starts by explaining the merit of history and how to go about writing it. Properly speaking, the reason to write history or, more precisely, the "inner meaning of history" is, by means of reflection, to get "at the truth, subtle explanation of the causes and origins of existing things, and deep knowledge of the how and why of events."

His enterprise is, therefore, "rooted in philosophy" and to be considered a branch of it. It begins by a thorough critique of history as it has come down through the ages. Many unqualified people have trammeled with the books of history written by competent Muslim historians: they have introduced tales of gossip imagined by themselves as well as false reports. Moreover, other historians have compiled partial reports of particular dynasties and events without looking to the way things have changed over time, without looking at natural conditions and human customs. Consequently, Ibn Khaldūn considers his task to be that of showing the merit of writing history, investigating the various ways it has been done, and showing the errors of previous historians. What needs to be known, and thus what he sets out to make known, are

> the principles of politics, the nature of existent things, and the differences among nations, places and periods with regard to ways of life, character, qualities, customs, sects, schools, and everything else ... plus a comprehensive knowledge of present conditions in all these respects ... complete knowledge of the reasons for every happening and ... [acquaintance] with the origin of every event. (*Muqaddima*, i. 43:11–18, my translation)

Such knowledge will, in turn, allow him to explain the nature of civilization and its accompanying accidents. His work promises to provide a comprehensive account of human social organization, its beginnings as well as its ends. As audacious as it is sweeping, the undertaking calls into question the transmitted or positive sciences central to the Islamic community as much as the practical sciences of politics and rhetoric.

As part of his attempt to redirect the focus of scholars and scholarship, Ibn Khaldūn criticizes the way political rule is understood in his day. Using the vocabulary of the political philosophers who preceded him, especially that of Alfarabi, he draws attention to the need humans have for political association and also to the way such associations develop over time, reach a point of greatness, and then degenerate. Central to his account of politics is an analysis of kingship and the tendency human beings have to introduce such rule in most circumstances. He notes the similarity between kingship and the caliphate prevalent among Muslims, but leaves the parallel without comment so that the thoughtful reader can draw out for himself the implicit criticism. At the same time, he introduces and applies the teachings of the political philosophers instead of those gathered from transmitted or positive sciences when analyzing issues most important to the Islamic community.

In this manner, Ibn Khaldūn grounds his new science fully in political philosophy. Deeming it "a deep root of wisdom" that provides an explanation of the "causes and reasons for the beginning of dynasties and civilization," he joins his undertaking to that of the historians and the philosophers who went before him. As he explains the way bedouins become sedentary and then develop new ways of life, ways that decline even as they have flourished, the constants in human social organization come to light: how people come together in social organization, strive to make a living, ascend from necessary tasks to finer ones discovered by means of discerning thought, and eventually seek for the cause of things. Clearly, the goal Ibn Khaldūn sets before himself in this work is not to provide an account of the best political regime, but to explain the nature of civilization and its accompanying accidents. To accomplish the latter, however, he must address the former and do so in a manner that will not shock the sensibility of his readers—above all those not willing to look beyond revealed texts and the lessons transmitted from them for wisdom about such questions. For this reason, Ibn Khaldūn criticizes the philosophical sciences even as he applies their teachings.

The distinction is not lost nor even very obscure for those who know how to read carefully, but Ibn Khaldūn had few such readers in his day and almost none subsequently. Among the Arabs, his book passed into obscurity as his successors focused on communing or achieving union with the divinity and reduced political inquiry to issues of personal morality or counsel to potentates. Fortunately, it found such favor among the Ottomans that numerous copies were made and preserved. When the seeds planted by al-Afghānī did bring forth a renaissance in learning among Arab peoples, Ibn Khaldūn's book came to the fore. By then, however, readers sufficiently familiar with the history of Arabic philosophy to discern the nuances in Ibn Khaldūn's exposition were not to be found.

CONCLUSION

The narrative must stop, but it is by no means at an end. Even now, in the absence of anything resembling philosophical inquiry, a struggle continues between those who pursue understanding rationally and those who insist that reason—especially unaided human reason—is too flimsy a stalk on which to lean. At times, it seems to be a quarrel between those who take their bearings from thinkers like Alfarabi and Averroes, and those who look to Avicenna and his followers. The former insist upon the possibility of a human solution to the all too human question of the best life, whereas the latter look to an extraneous, non-human source for clarity. As long as neither side brings the controversy to a halt by claiming infallibility for its position, such tension is well and good. Only through such debate is it possible to raise doubts about generally accepted opinions and about premises that have been accepted without question.

The challenge facing students of Arabic–Islamic thought today is to learn how to thwart attempts to shut off such debate by those who think they are defending religious purity or others who have been persuaded that ideas can be explained only in terms of their historical origins. In one respect, it is a greater challenge today precisely because there is no Alfarabi or Averroes to help refine the terms of the debate or to show how it fits into a larger problem. In another, it becomes easier to face precisely because we understand so much better just what these earlier thinkers were attempting to achieve and thus have a more comprehensive grasp of the relationship between philosophy and religion, as well as between philosophy and politics. From this perspective, it is patent that our task remains that of explaining what Alfarabi means when he claims that "the idea of the philosopher, supreme ruler, prince, legislator, and imam is but a single idea." Now, hopefully, the thoughtful reader sees that Alfarabi's understanding of reason is open both to philosophy and to religion, albeit with philosophy privileged.

REFERENCES

ALFARABI (2001a). *Alfarabi, The Political Writings: "Selected Aphorisms" and Other Texts*, ed. and trans., with an introduction, Charles E. Butterworth. Ithaca, NY: Cornell University Press.

ALFARABI (2001b). *Attainment of Happiness*, in *Alfarabi, Philosophy of Plato and Aristotle*, trans., with an introduction, Muhsin Mahdi.Ithaca, NY: Cornell University Press.

AVERROES (1974). *Averroes on Plato's "Republic,"* trans. Ralph Lerner. Ithaca, NY: Cornell University Press.

AVERROES (2001). *Averroës, The Book of the Decisive Treatise: Determining the Connection between the Law and Wisdom, and Epistle Dedicatory*, trans., with introduction and notes, Charles E. Butterworth. Provo, UT: Brigham Young University Press.

AVERROES (2002). *Averroès (Ibn Rušd). Commentaire moyen à la Rhétorique d'Aristote*, ed. and trans. Maroun Aouad. 3 vols. Paris: Vrin.

AVICENNA (1908). *Fī Aqsām al-ʿUlūm al-ʿʿAqliyya (On the Divisions of the Rational Sciences)*, in *Tis Rasāʾil* (Nine Epistles). Cairo, 104–18.

AVICENNA (1960). *Kitāb al-Shifāʾ, al-Ilāhiyyat (Book of the Healing: Divine Sciences)*, (eds) G. Anawati and S. Zayid. Cairo: al-Haiʾa al-ʿĀmma li-Shuʾūn al-Matābiʿ al-Amīriyya.

IBN KHALDŪN (1958). *The Muqaddimah, An Introduction to History*, trans. Franz Rosenthal. Bollingen Series XLIII. 3 vols. New York: Pantheon Books.

IBN KHALDŪN (1970). *Muqaddimat Ibn Khaldūn, Prolégomènes d'Ebn-Khaldoun, Texte Arabe, Publié, D'Après les Manuscrits de la Bibliothèque Impériale*, (ed.) M. Quatremère. Paris: Benjamin Duprat, 1858; repr. Beirut: Maktaba Lubnan. 3 vols.

IBN TUFAYL (1995). *Hayy ibn Yaqzan*, trans. Lenn Evan Goodman. New York: Gee Tee Bee.

CHAPTER 12

MEDIEVAL POLITICAL THEORY c.1000–1500

JANET COLEMAN

MEDIEVAL POLITICAL THEORY?

THIS chapter treats a selection of Christian political theorists who have been considered by scholars over many generations, indeed centuries, to have contributed to a variety of distinctive discourses about the relationships between individuals and authority. We are examining a period in which hierarchies were taken for granted, in which the universe itself was conceived as divinely ordered in terms of relationships between natural things and their originating source, each natural thing being subject to something higher than itself. Within this hierarchy each had its own purpose, role, and function, achieving its own good by being ordered to the good of what can be called a sovereign 'whole'. A hierarchy of 'rank' and status was not, however, an invention of medieval thinkers: they inherited it from ancient, especially imperial, Rome, a Rome that eventually came to be Christianized in the fourth century AD. There is a sense in which what political theorizing 'is' during the Middle Ages is a set of positions and justificatory explanations about 'sovereign power'. especially if and when such 'sovereignty' was known and experienced to be, institutionally, geographically, and culturally, 'fragmented' or 'parcelized' across Europe. The individual was conceptualized only as embedded within this holistic framework. He was considered to play his own role in the common and public welfare and where the coordinating direction of the whole was the remit of those with the power to make discretionary, but not arbitrary, decisions for the peace, security, and justice of the whole community. The coordinating power could be ascribed to one, few, or many—that is, to those who were authorized to give counsel to whoever represented the community as the 'head' of its governance. Who had the power to make law, and who to, impose it, were often seen as coordinate but separate capacities.

Here, however, we confront a problem: we are examining an intellectual and social matrix that is not modern. And what we mean today by political theorizing, indeed by words such as 'sovereignty', bears only some relationship to what medieval authors meant to elucidate. What that link is, and what the difference is, need to be examined briefly if we are, in the first instance, to try to grasp what they meant by writing in the ways they did.

Some scholars have argued that any examination of medieval reflections on authority and jurisdiction necessarily occurred in the absence of what we, today, would recognize as a clearly defined political sphere (Wood 2008: 200). This is either because one of our contemporary benchmarks for 'the political' is thought to be what *we* take to have been the ancient Greek *polis* and Greek philosophers' reflections on its nature and practices, or because our other benchmark is liberal, representative democracy with its institutions and practices. A good deal of what liberal, representative democracy came to mean was the consequence of certain nineteenth-century reassessments, not only of ancient Greek democracy but of conditions of living in society, post-American and post-French revolutions. The historical conditions that helped to bring about these revolutions showed that industry and commerce, serving world markets, rearranged the structures of different social status groups and with this came their members' respective 'liberation' through a kind of equality, individual rights, recognized in unified state law. This law redescribed 'community' as comprising independent individuals as asserters of their own wills; it thereby privileged individuality and enterprise through validating labour and private property as personal interests, but common to all. The 'political' therefore was reconfigured to suit this mode of living, a mode of living that was thought to come about through an *artificial* contract of instrumentally rational, self-interested individuals whose best calculations for creating the conditions of peace and security for the satisfaction of their individual desires and their own enterprises led them to construct the 'modern' state and its law. But to rely on what we take to have been ancient Greek and then nineteenth-century liberal reassessments of 'the political', from a *historian's* perspective of the *longue durée*, is a strangely modern, and perhaps Western, calculated deafness to other ways of speaking not only about socio-economic wholes but about the values, expressed or tacit, of participant members who were both ascribed roles and were simultaneously complicit in accepting roles. Whatever we might today think of Marx's historiography, in the *German Ideology*, he and Engels insisted, rightly in this author's view, on the following, which is often misinterpreted by those with a misconception of what their 'materialist' method implies:

> The way in which men produce their means of subsistence depends *first of all* on the nature of the actual means of subsistence *they find in existence* and *have to reproduce.* This mode of production must *not* be considered simply as being the production of the physical existence of the individuals. Rather it is a definite form of activity of these individuals, *a definite form of expressing their life, a definite mode of life on their part.* As individuals express their life, so they are. What they are, therefore, coincides with their production, both with what they produce and with how they produce. (Marx and Engels 1978: 42, emphasis added)

The nature of the actual means of subsistence that men found and reproduced during the Middle Ages will not be explicitly discussed here, not least because it is now the domain of economic historians. What will be discussed is some of the definite forms of activity, definite forms of their expressing their life, their *modes of life* that *followed on* from how they contrived their 'survival' and physical 'reproduction'. The 'mode of life' is the domain of ethical, socio-political, and religious discourses of the period and, hence, it is where we will find 'medieval political thought'. Perhaps surprising to some, it will reveal itself to be not some single 'ideology'. There is no doubt that, when people develop their material production and their material intercourse, their thinking and the products of their thinking alter. Language, as an expression of practical consciousness, arises from the necessity of intercourse with other men, the necessity of their being social creatures, and during our period 'material production' developed and the changes often served as the subject of intense debate: over property ownership; use; money; lending at interest/usury; obligations and obedience to authorities; the specification of reciprocal duties to others. We will discuss selected representative 'voices', which demonstrated how this necessity of intercourse came to be proliferated, especially among a diverse, and ever-expanding cadre of 'mental labourers'.

As populations increased and economies and trade expanded, as old Roman cities revived and new urban centres were established in newly settled lands, with crusades to the Holy Land taking in the sacking of Constantinople on the way, with universities being founded with the purpose of educating men who would serve ecclesiastical and secular administrations well beyond what earlier Cathedral schools had been able to provide, competitive discourses concerning the proper ordering of social and political life proliferated. They reveal perspectives as diverse as those of popes and princes, priests, monks, Dominican and Franciscan friars, merchants, civil lawyers, canon lawyers, laymen, a landed aristocracy that turned itself into urban mercantile elites engaged in banking and trade, all of whom 'engaged', often vituperatively, with one another, about how politics should be arranged and for what purpose. In short, we will be looking at a selection of political and philosophical ideas that were necessarily deeply embedded in the reproduction of the economic, social, and political worlds they experienced.

Medieval people were described by the writers we will examine as living together by means of reciprocal activities, where their mutual and hierarchically arranged duties were enshrined in law and backed by sanctions for the non-compliant. The political sphere *was* conceived by medieval contemporaries as clearly defined: but that different authors specified different boundaries to 'the political' is precisely what makes this period so interesting, not only in terms of the moments when different approaches to this question were articulated, but also for the future and later reinterpretations. Later political theorists in different contexts would be engaged in reusing, selectively, what they thought medieval authors had in mind, just as medieval authors reused, selectively, what they thought their own Roman and Greek predecessors had in mind. Medieval political theory developed from what they read and from how they applied what they read to how they lived.

What will not, however, be argued here is the view, held by some, that medieval jurists and medieval political thinkers are the sources of modern juristic and political theories and practices, and, in consequence, this is the reason that we should show an interest in them. The approach taken here is not to find the 'first modern', as political man or political theorist, during either the Middle Ages or the Renaissance. In the view of this author, he is not there to be found. Instead, what a student of this period needs to try to uncover are the questions *they* thought it important to answer. And, insofar as this is possible, we need to try to learn the languages they used with the meanings they wished to convey. Many such questions, answers, and meanings are neither those of Western, liberal democracies operating within capitalist economies, nor those provided by nineteenth-century liberal theorists or by German positivist legal scholars who took a unified view on state sovereignty and the state's legal personality. The latter in particular generated a debate as to whether or not 'the state' was a concept or reality during the long medieval period, and for the most part they answered 'no', with the consequence that whatever medievals 'had' it was not 'the political'. We shall observe that many medieval authors used the term *respublica*, commonwealth, to refer normatively simply to good governance under law, applicable both to monarchies and to mixed constitutions/republics as legitimate constitutional structural configurations of a *regnum* or a *civitas*. They could speak about plural *loci* of power within a frame of normative expectations, where the real danger was seen to be, *not* one constitutional structure or another, *not* monarchies versus republics, but the practices, anywhere, of arbitrary, tyrannical powers, and injustices.

Medieval writers who had something to say about politics were not engaged in an autonomous activity—that is, providing a univocal explanation of a strictly delineated and neutral sphere of individual (and equal) agency within 'the political space' and theorizing about it. Literate medieval men approached what we recognize as the socio-economic and political by having been trained in more comprehensive disciplines and discourses in which 'political action and thought' played only a part. Hence, what we might call 'political theorizing' about the state, the city, the collective, was part of a larger ontology, expressed in and through Christian theology. We shall discover, perhaps to the surprise of some today, that even this larger theological framework entailed numerous contemporary contested interpretations, with very different consequences for the practices of social and political life. And out of these contested interpretations several different ways of writing developed in order to treat: the nature of government, authority, law, the relationship of organized and institutional religion to society and *its* institutions, and what membership in collectivities of various kinds entailed (Reynolds 1984, 1997: 117–38).

No student of this period can expect to uncover the modern, Western, 'liberated', subjective individual, but what he or she can expect is to uncover a spectrum of normative languages used by medieval agents to describe the actions, projects, and purposes in which they believed themselves to be engaged (Coleman 1996a). The spectrum of languages is the consequence of literate men having been educated in a variety of disciplines, including theology, canon and civil law, and university arts faculty logic, rhetoric, natural science, and what they called practical moral philosophy. Practical moral philosophy was itself divided into three related but distinct subjects: what concerned the individual; what concerned the domestic and economic; and, lastly, what pertained to the political and civic. 'Political theory' as such was not a subject to be studied at the medieval university, but its elements could be, and were, picked up through studying in any of the various faculties (Coleman 2000: 5–80; Miethke 2000*a*). Some of the literature that will most interest us here is concerned with the ways in which a 'civil science' could be *separated* from what lawyers claimed as their own domain. Their authors used the characteristic genres of their respective disciplines as publicists for either Church or *regnum* or for other organized groups such as cities, craft guilds, or religious fraternities, each claiming legitimacy and power over their members. What emerges is a range of languages that may be called appropriate either to feudal relationships, or to corporate and customary relationships, or to theocratic visions of order and power, or to civil law prescriptions about rightful ownership of property with corollary expected services from those without such ownership but, nonetheless, with claims to 'use' by a natural law that was held to underpin whatever could be more locally established by civil or customary law.

The legacy of the languages and practices of imperial Roman law, of the insights and judgements of Roman Latin moralists and historians, of early Church law, of the guiding texts of Scripture and authoritative (and conflicting) commentaries of Church Fathers, of Latin translations of certain ancient Greek ethical and political texts, were each and all accessed by literate men during the Middle Ages for practical purposes. They adapted and departed from their ancient antecedents precisely because their own contexts differed from those of the past, and this was often realized and commented upon. To these numerous ancient documents they added their own reflections on contemporary and evolving practices, so that each of these diverse languages about authority and sovereign power could be shown to have its own defence of its origins, legitimacy, and authority. What the sources for this period reveal is that there were *competing* theoretical and practical justifications for differently conceived socio-economic and political collectivities, and, hence, they discussed what active participation, active citizenship, might mean within the larger consideration of who had legitimate authority to rule. Each had its own traditions of founding and maintenance, each dealt with what they respectively defined as those entities with legitimate authority and their 'just' relationship to individuals and groups arranged in hierarchies. It is in a selection of these medieval sources that we can locate what we should call medieval political theorizing (Maiolo 2007).

But even taking into consideration their diversities in method, in the chosen genres of discourse and the varied audiences they addressed, in their discrete reference to sources, all of which fuelled their substantive debates with one another, the 'frame' for all these theories was '*a definite form of expressing their life, a definite mode of life on their part*', and it is one that over the *longue durée* of European history penetrated beyond what is chronologically defined as the medieval centuries. It certainly reveals a continuity with the Reformation and Renaissance of the sixteenth century. What cannot be attempted here is a reassessment of the way we use terms like 'medieval', 'Renaissance'/'Reformation', or 'modern' (Coleman 2000; Monfasani 2006: 165–85; Fasolt 2007: 345–86, 2008: 364–80). Chronological periodization is a retrospective activity and imposes its own understandings of 'change', often implying a progressive evolutionism that actively looks for 'breaks' and antitheses to serve a vision of what is 'modern' and preferred, and what is 'pre-modern' and reviled. Chronology has been reconfigured both by 'confessional' (Protestant/Catholic) and by 'nationalist' narratives. But ruptures and reformations have been part of long-term social and intellectual processes everywhere, not least during the Middle Ages. We shall see how these helped to stimulate the kinds of political theories they left for posterity to read and discuss. And we shall, in addition, observe how a frame of social and status hierarchy could nonetheless encourage theories and practices that supported, rather than obliterated, the interests of the juridically unequal and presumed 'voiceless': the poor and propertyless.

INVESTITURE CONTEST AND THE GREGORIAN REFORM

From the Gospel of St Matthew (22:15–22) and recapitulated in St Paul's Letter to the Romans, Christians were held to a dual allegiance: giving what was due to Caesar and what was due to God. This was a perspective that advocated submission to human institutions in virtue of their moral, divine mission. Status hierarchies in the political world were to be reconciled with a more universal, spiritual claim that there were no distinctions between Greek and Christian, Jew and Gentile, slave and master, since Christ recognized no distinction of person. Baptism was the means to transcend all temporal frontiers of race, sex, nation, and social rank. Christian liberty, therefore, was an internal disposition, and, whatever local, positive civil law might conventionally establish as status liberties, Christian liberty could not be alienated or contravened.

As the Church, especially in the Latin West, came to develop its own, Roman-influenced, model of decision-making power and a hierarchical structure of institutions, recourse was had again to the Gospel of St Matthew (16:18–19). The authority of the bishop of Rome, founded in Christ's commission to St Peter to establish His church, entailed papal receipt of the keys to the kingdom of heaven. What he bound on earth would be bound in heaven; similarly with Christ's command to Peter (John 21:15–17) that he 'feed His sheep' came the justification for Christ's having passed on governance and care of all Christians to Peter and his successors. From here developed papal legal claims to jurisdiction over Christians, with each successive pope as the unworthy heir and vicar of Christ's commission. Already during the fourth century there had developed a view that clergy were superior to laity. By the mid-fifth century in the Latin West the Roman primacy over all other bishops was established, and the pope was called *principatus* of the Church. The Church was understood as an organically structured public corporation, a body (*corpus*) comprising a head (*caput*) and members. The head, the pope, was to be judged by no one; he was declared constitutional sovereign with a jurisdictional function as the final court of appeal in ecclesiastical cases. At the end of the fifth century an even more precise definition of the relationship between the Church and Caesar's Roman authority was attempted: Pope Gelasius argued that the world was governed in two ways, one priestly and the other secular. Both spiritual and temporal rulers derived their authority and function from Christ's 'decree' that these two powers exist in parallel and observe their respective limits; but, insofar as priests are in charge of religious matters, the Roman Emperor is the son of the Church. The lesser clergy recognize the primacy of the bishop of Rome, the pope. And only in secular affairs do they obey and use imperial laws. In a hierarchy of authoritative power, however, the clerical, with its heavier burden to render an account before God of the kings of men, was to supersede the temporal. From the sixth century the pope's power was seen to emanate from God as the principle of unity, God having transmitted the faculty of governing the Body of Christ to its head. As superior over a succession of grades and ranks, the pope transmits capacities to inferiors each with a specific task, each meant to be content with its status and differentiated role in the corporate, ecclesiastical hierarchy. What remained emphasized was this duality of power over men and the dual Christian allegiance, with an impossibility, at least in theory, of any Roman or successor king or emperor uniting in his person a combined headship of Church and state. But, where were the precise boundaries of ecclesiastical and temporal interests of men who were Christians but also Roman citizens? Centuries of skirmishes ensued.

The attempt to fix the boundary between sacred and temporal authority during the eleventh-century pontificate of Gregory VII is normally seen to have spawned *the* major and long-enduring debates in medieval political theory (and beyond) over the relation between temporal and spiritual powers. Gregory, an heir to the previous century's call for a reformation of the Church, freeing it from local feudal lords and their power to appoint their own candidates to Church offices, reinvigorated the debate with a call to a return to the Church's liberties. It had already been argued that spiritual benefices and positions of power with land could not be conferred by a layman. The *libertas ecclesiae* was an immunity, but not because of a grant or concession from secular governors. It came from Christ in the Petrine commission. Gregory thereafter set in motion what was to be the ongoing disputes that helped define in theory and practice the relative scopes of political and ecclesiological jurisdictions over men's lives. He had been engaged in a conflict with the Emperor Henry IV of Germany, and the pope pronounced that kings and emperors were no more than lay members of the Church, their primary duty being to aid the Church in its mission to secure the spiritual well-being of their subjects. The pope and his bishops were therefore the only ones in a position to judge the spiritual suitability of a king or emperor. An unsuitable lay governor could be excommunicated from the Church and his subjects released from their oaths of loyal obedience to him. Kings in the hierarchy of world governance were placed beneath the lowest of the orders of clergy. An appeal was made to what later came to be recognized as a ninth-century forged document: the Donation of Constantine. It purported to be a constitution of the fourth-century Christian Roman Emperor, Constantine, which said that he had donated the imperial palace, the crown, the very government of all of the Western Roman Empire to Pope Sylvester and his successors, in gratitude for his having been baptized and cured of leprosy. The papacy had been accorded imperial power. Gregory VII, in consequence, insisted that the pope alone had the rightful use of imperial insignia, and the Church itself was to be understood as autonomous and immune from all secular governance. Not only was the pope the final court of appeal, but through his will alone could new legislation be produced. In the twenty-seven propositions set out in his *Dictatus Papae* (Dictates of the Pope) and other letters, Gregory outlined a papal theocracy, curtailing powers of bishops, asserting Roman primacy, and insisting on the Roman Church's (not specifically the pope's) infallibility. Royal power, in consequence, was to be subjected to the priesthood not simply in religious matters but in all matters. The powers of binding and loosing committed to Peter by Christ, and hence to all popes in succession, included the power 'to remove from as well as to concede to anyone, according to his merits, earthly empires, kingdoms, principalities . . . and the possessions of all men'. Kings and emperors are, on this view, removable officials. (For an elaborate, vicious, and even amusing attack on this papal 'historiography', see the fourteenth-century Marsilius of Padua's *Defensor pacis*, Discourse 2 (Garnett 2006).)

The Lawyers

In establishing 'suitability' to rule as the test of lay kings, Gregory encouraged, in effect, a theory and practice of elective monarchy, where lesser lay princes were to select and propose a candidate for papal approval. Thereafter, Gregory encouraged a scholarly movement that investigated old archives, the decretals of former popes, earlier canons of Church councils and passages from early Church historians. This would lead to the establishing of a body of Church law, the canon law, which, from the twelfth century onwards, would show the Church to have been founded as the sovereign authority in the world, and by the means of its legal expertise, maintained as an autonomous, legislative, and governing institution. Church lawyers created their authoritative collection, brought together in one textbook by a monk Gratian and known as the *Concordance of Discordant Canons*, or simply as the *Decretum*. To this were added commentaries by jurists known as decretists and further compilations of papal letters (decretals), themselves commented upon by jurist 'decretalists'. Canon lawyers, examining earlier authorities and reading early Christian texts, which focused on community and collective organizations, the life of the early Church, and its councils, looked for reconciliations between conflicting authoritative statements, all in aid of papal sovereignty in its expanding role of making new law. It comes as no surprise that by the twelfth and thirteenth centuries many popes had trained as lawyers and some have argued that an observance of canon law when applied to matters of Church administration reveals the medieval Church to have operated as a proto-state. Those institutions that were destined to play important parts in later state formation, such as the impersonal, hierarchical, and specialized structure of offices, were first realized through canon law. Its legal instruments created centralized authority such as the power of a higher judge to summon cases, the right to lodge appeals, the very notion of office as separate from the personality of the incumbent, the concept of a juridical person, forms of collective decision-making and the majority principle. These came to be emulated by secular states (Padoa Schioppa 1997).

It was in the princely resistance to what has been called 'papal monarchy' that alternative theories of foundings and maintenance of legitimate temporal rule emerged. The civil Roman law, and notably the text of the Christian Roman Emperor Justinian's sixth-century collection, the *Corpus Iuris Civilis* (The Codex, Institutes, Digest, Novellae), were revived, studied especially in Bologna, and, with imperial support, sought to re-establish the emperor's rights in civil law to constitutional rule. Here, however, this late imperial compilation was found to provide authoritative statements to support not only monarchy but also constitutional government by the whole 'people'. Drawing on statements that affirmed divine *and* popular sources of rule, some commentators and theorists maintained that the source of all governing authority was indeed God, but it was granted separately and equally in cooperative spheres of power and jurisdiction to representatives of Church and 'regnum'. And the legislative capacities of a prince were to be balanced by an acknowledged role of the people in the creation of law, most notably by requiring their consent. Some explicitly discussed whether or not the *lex regia* was revocable by the people, and it was acknowledged that a ruler could not exercise unlimited power, even though they read the Roman law principle that 'what pleases the prince is law'.

The numerous ambiguities of Justinian's Roman law when applied to societies that were different from that of ancient imperial Rome allowed them to seek support for their own modes of living, reconstructing Roman law to suit their own needs. Hence, they found support for an individual's rights to private property against the claims of *imperium*; they found reference to an individual's power to dispose of what he owned by his own will; they found support for an individual's freedom to shape contracts; they adapted Roman law to recognize their own already constituted corporative associations, providing them with group legal status and an official representative who acted on the group's behalf. This representative's power was derivative, revocable, and could be modified and without recourse to 'state' concessions. The very nature of created law was at issue, and clarifications were sought as to who was entitled to create it. In *Deo auctore*, Justinian had asserted 'that we govern under the authority of God: our Empire is delivered to us by His Divine Majesty; and we rest all of our faith, not in arms, soldiers or our own skill but in our hopes in the providence of the supreme trinity and in Him alone'. Medievals asked: Should a sovereign ruler, whose office was to represent his subjects by bearing the personality of the public corporation, be declared a tyrant if he did not rule for the common good as determined by the consent of his subjects or at least that of his aristocratic counsellors? Could he be removed? Under what conditions is there a right of resistance, and does this right inhere in the community and its representatives or in an individual? Constantly selecting and interpreting Roman law with a view to their own particular circumstances, the commentators known as Glossators discussed whether custom could abrogate imperial laws, and they said that it could if custom were shown to be reasonable. In invoking the yardstick of *reason* and the requirement that men *explicitly* consent to what was reasonable, they highlighted that rational judgement, not simply authoritative will, justified obedience to the pronouncements and commands of civil, positive law (Kempshall 1999). Others would reverse the Gelasian and Gregorian hierarchy of Church over State altogether, insisting instead on an overlapping duality, but where the Church was a necessary but certainly subordinate, non-coercive, functional part of the state (Marsilius, *Defensor pacis*, Discourse 1).

Both canon and civil lawyers tackled many of the same questions to justify their respective understandings of the nature and source of sovereignty, meaning the power to legislate, judge, and command. Each tried to find a place for spirituality and the Church's administrative hierarchy in a society that saw its major conceptual and institutional debt to be Roman institutions and law, no matter how attenuated by local, regional, custom, a *ius commune*. On the agenda of their political theorizing was the discovery of a meaning for the Roman law dictum *maior et sanior pars* in order to clarify how the will of a corporate group was expressed. What was the meaning of *plena potestas*—on the part of the pope, of the corporate Church, of the prince? How to explain a theory of representation where a group was obliged by the acts of its representative agent with full power, even if that group had not previously consented to the representative's specific acts? What was the meaning of the Roman dictum: *quod omnes tangit ab omnibus approbetur* ('what touches all is to be approved by all'), a doctrine of consent that applied to corporate bodies and where the approval of the whole was required, and not that of each individual member? This doctrine came to support the notion that representative assemblies, acting on behalf of the whole who are touched by decisions taken, bind the whole; and what distinguished the right to govern one's own, *dominium*, from the right to administer what was not one's own, *jurisdictio*?

Medieval Political Theory as 'Civil Science'

Thus far, we have highlighted the emergence of legal experts in canon and civil law, to whom the name 'political theorists' should not seem anachronistic. They were engaged in discussing an inviolable, fundamental law framework in which sovereign rulers and legitimate communities operated, treating thereby the overriding right of a sovereign to rule and the overriding claim of a community to defend itself against the abuse of power. But it is to another, related enterprise that we need to turn in order to observe political theory being generated as a 'civil science' that consciously attempted to *separate* itself from the domain of lawyers.

Here we will see how certain thinkers came to understand the science of politics as a coordinating role of the prudent man, whose prudence is of the kind that is normally confined to the daily administration of public affairs, dealing with particular circumstances in practical and deliberative ways to secure the collective good of men. He will need to acquire the art of rhetorical persuasion to enable him, as governor, to motivate men to action with a view to the common good. Without the virtue of deliberative reasoning about particular circumstances and conduct, a virtue he can have learned only from experience and with a moral end in view—the good for man—he will not be able adequately to control, direct, and coordinate the whole to which he is responsible through good legislation.

This tradition of political theory as a civil science will emerge from a reading of Aristotle's *Rhetoric, Ethics,* and *Politics* as rediscovered and newly translated into Latin during the thirteenth century (Coleman 2000). New career options were being sketched for university arts faculty students who sought training to advise legislators or to take up judicial posts in Church or state/city hierarchies. For them, legal statements, being universal and therefore general, were insufficiently applicable to each and every case. Beyond the rule of law, men's actions, which should be judged leniently and in the circumstances, were cases for prudent judgement and equity, looking not to the letter of the law but to the intention of the legislator as well as to the intention of the agent. A dispute had arisen, and it would be one that would last for centuries, between *arts and theology faculty moralists*, on the one hand, and especially *civil and common lawyers*, on the other, concerning the right training for that most sovereign of practical sciences, *scientia politica*. Especially during the thirteenth century civil lawyers began to call themselves *politici*; but philosophers in the arts faculties who dealt with practical moral philosophy insisted that lawyers knew nothing of the moral virtues, because they read the wrong texts. It was in the arts faculty that a student would read the texts of the ancient philosophers and historians, along with the Church Fathers, and only from them could they extract appropriate ways to rule themselves, their families, and the city. Only if one had acquired what the arts faculty taught: how to read authoritative texts from the past, a knowledge of a theory of what language is, the logic of arguments, a familiarity with human psychology and the effects of persuasive speech, rhetoric, on men's motivation to act morally and for the collective good, was one thereafter in a position to influence legislators and princes. Lawyers were said to be trained in nothing more than massaging the letter of the law to suit their patrons, or the lining of their own pockets, influencing public policy through nothing more than flattery or through a dogmatic imposition of legal rules, without any understanding or interest in the moral principles behind the law.

The Natural and the Rational; Ius Naturale *and the Possession of all Things in Common*

Influenced by the numerous ancient texts they studied, literate men were content to describe society and community as *natural*, indeed organic. But what was natural increasingly came to be aligned with what was rational. What reason discovers was thought by some to reflect God's intention for men, so that they might live according to ordered reason where head and members of a Christian body public, the *corpus rei publica*, had distinct functions, ascribed duties, ordered to the common welfare, which could be known through human reason and implemented by human will. Especially in theological and pastoral texts, men and women were seen as morally responsible for their acts. A notion of human liberty is discussed in which an individual is held to have powers of agency prior to any historically specific political and contingent contraints that might be placed on his will to act or not on those powers. Justinian's *Institutes* (I.3.1–2) had referred to *libertas* as a man's natural power to do what he pleases so far as he is not prevented by force or law. Much discussion in our period was had over whether this *libertas* was to be applied to some natural instinct peculiar to man alone or to man and other animals, as some preregulated set of natural habits governed by a law of nature. From the classical jurists, Gaius and Ulpian, Justinian's *Institutes* had selected somewhat different understandings of natural law, *ius naturale*: from Ulpian: that the law of nature is that which nature teaches all animals and is not particular to the human race; and from Gaius: that the law that natural reason makes for all mankind is applied the same everywhere and is called the *ius gentium*. Medieval political theorists tried to determine if *ius naturale* should be fused with *ius gentium* or be applied also to non-human animals. Furthermore, Justinian had claimed not only that *ius naturale* was observed uniformly by all peoples but that it was sanctioned by divine providence and lasts for ever, being immune from change (*Inst.* I.2.11).

Canon lawyers had themselves defined a sphere of agency following on from what were taken to be natural, psychological capacities in men that enable them to assert, on behalf of all men, certain natural *iura*, 'rights' or capacities, that are independent of any civic order in which they may live.[1] This personal, inalienable, individual, moral autonomy was called a faculty or ability or power, the *ius naturale*, a power associated with reason and moral discernment. The *Decretum* described a notion of *ius naturale* as an instinct of nature that is common to all peoples. But Gratian also said that, through the gift of reason to the individual human soul *and* through the teachings of the Old and New Testaments, the *ius naturale* is God's supreme moral law. Gratian observed that the human race is ruled in two ways: by *ius naturale*; and by custom (C.16.9.3 dictum post c.15; Dist. 1, dictum ante c.1. and c.1). *Ius naturale* serves as a command: to do to another what one wants done to oneself and forbids doing to another what one does not want done to oneself. *Ius naturale* is an innate sense of right

---

[1] I have translated *ius/iura* as 'rights', because there is a debate in the scholarly literature about whether or not any of these authors was speaking of what we mean by 'subjective right(s)'.

and wrong. *Ius naturale* is the *ius* that is common to all nations, in that it is everywhere held by instinct of nature rather than by local, positive enactment. It is not a freedom to act as one desires or pleases on the moment; the freedom is in how one implements the will to follow the command: do unto others as thou would be done by. And Gratian's *Decretum* enumerates what substantively is known by *ius naturale* as an instinct of nature: the union of man and woman; the free generation and education of children; *the possession of all things in common*; *that there is one liberty for all, the acquisition of those things taken from air, land and sea*; the return of a thing deposited or money, entrusted; and the repulsion of force by force. Any customary or human, positive civil law that stipulates something contrary to this *ius naturale* is to be held null and void (Dist. 8 dictum post c.1).

Where positive law was held to be created by the sovereign, all sovereigns were to be conceived as bound by a prior *ius naturale* and, hence, by reasonableness. But most explosive is the assertion that by *ius naturale* all things are in common. How, then, does one justify private property? Is it mere convention and perhaps a custom that contravenes natural law? Indeed, can the *ius naturale* be invoked by anyone who voluntarily wishes not to own by civil law entitlement but only to use what is common?

Canonists' discussion of *ius* is always derived from *iustitia*. This was also the case for those in the mid-thirteenth century with Latin translations of Aristotle's *Ethics* and, less so, his *Politics*, on which they began to lecture and write commentaries. Insofar as *ius* is the plan for doing the just thing, directing conduct in relation to self and others, it is not a subjective 'right' but it is a subjective force or power. The individual agent is simply an example of a class of beings with normative capacities. Justice, when performed through acts, is an external balance between people that is discovered by reason and is a moral virtue. Twelfth-century theological and philosophical texts had already begun to emphasize a kind of ethical personalism by focusing on an individual's intentions behind acts. The *ius naturale* is a force or power of the soul, an instinctive moral orientation, a guiding of intentionality. A concern with human psychology, the functions and capacities of the soul, was integral to the university arts course education as it focused on practical moral philosophy. From this followed the specification concerning which laws *had* to be obeyed, and which powers or capacities, as *iura libertatis*, could never be lost, no matter how long a man may be held in bondage.

SOME THEMES AT THE HEART OF MEDIEVAL POLITICAL THEORY: PROPERTY AND POVERTY

The issue that came to highlight all of these themes: intentionality, *ius naturale*, reason guiding will, moral autonomy, natural hierarchies that are ordered to a common good, the scope and limitations of sovereign governance, legislation and judgement—was that over the *natural or conventional origins of property*? What follows is a selection of medieval political theories that confronted one another from the thirteenth into the fourteenth centuries and to which, equally selectively, later theorists would appeal.

Some expressed the view that private property is a social institution that engages our natural obligations to others. While property should be private, there was also a sense in which it should be common. While ownership and administration of property were the responsibility of individuals, worldly goods had to be shared with others in times of need. Some asserted a natural *ius* of the poor to the superfluities of the rich. They argued that the poor man who stole in times of necessity had a 'right' to what he had taken, even without the explicit consent of the owner. What the poor man takes is really his own *iure naturali*. Canonists came to insist that a person in need had a rightful power to do what was necessary to stay alive, and this was already stipulated in Gratian as by *ius naturale*. Civil judges may not recognize the poor man in need as having a rightful claim in law, but it was stated that 'many things are owed that cannot be sought by judicial procedure' and discretionary mercy must be invoked. Where a civil judge would not recognize a claim to equity, what is a man's due, beyond the strict letter of the law, then a bishop could use ecclesiastical courts' jurisdiction to compel a recognition of such a claim. A more universal, moral correction of positive law was required.

The Dominican Political Theory of Thomas Aquinas

Early in the thirteenth century, an attempt to adjust the religious life to the social and economic changes that had occurred during the previous centuries culminated in the papal establishment of the mendicant orders, Dominicans and Franciscans. Unlike monks, they set themselves up in cities, setting examples by living a simple, more apostolic life than that of the Church's ecclesiastical dignitaries. Dominicans early on recognized the universities as centres of recruitment to their own Order. Franciscans would soon follow. The intellectual efforts of Franciscans and Dominicans, lecturing in their own *studia* as well as in university theology faculties, contributed momentously to what is recognized as later medieval political theorizing. Thomas Aquinas is here taken as exemplary of those who were among the first generation to benefit from Latin translations of Aristotle's *Ethics* and *Politics*, and to integrate certain Aristotelian perspectives on politics into their Christian framework. It is important that we get a sense of what 'civil science' is for him.

Aquinas argues that there is a *natural object* of both the human intellect and the human will: it is the common good. There is one standard of truth or rightness for everyone, and it is equally known by everyone: all people realize that it is right and true to act according to reason and everyone is capable of doing this naturally and without supernatural revelation, without supernatural grace added to one's natural capacities. He discusses those stable principles of moral practice that underlie variant customs and civil laws that are specific to historical communities. There is a moral perception that to engage in certain behaviour is right or wrong, whatever the independent sanction in the civil or customary law. These primary practical principles are arrived at by induction and are naturally known ends, prior to the development of any virtue as means to them. Human moral discourse is constructed on a set of foundational principles, the *natural law*, which may be encapsulated as: the good is to be pursued and done and the evil avoided. Whatever practical reason thereafter naturally grasps to be particular human goods as means to the human end fall under the already known precept of the natural law as to what is to be done and what to be avoided. All those things to which a man has a natural inclination, his reason naturally grasps as 'goods' to be pursued and done. We share with other natural things inclinations to self-preservation, self-reproduction through sexual relations, and an inclination to care for our young. Alone among created beings we additionally have a natural inclination to live reciprocally in society. All of these inclinations are not matters of choice. The natural law is man's mode of living, his participation in the divinely created order of things, and through reason we shape our natural inclinations, through *lex* (law), to live in order to pursue the human good. Natural justice consists in a series of rational principles that follow upon the inclinations of our nature. Practical reason that is made positive in civil law regulates our natural inclinations to enable us to make the right choices for the achievement of our own good within the common good. Civil law must, therefore, be rational and conform to foundational principles of natural law.

According to Aquinas, imperfect things tend towards their own good, that of the individual. More perfect things tend towards the good of the species. The even more perfect tend towards the good of a genus. The most perfect, God, secures the good of all being and the good of the universe. By analogy, Aquinas argues that, since the good of the human community, that is, of the species, is the ultimate goal of human life, the *bonum humanum*, then not only is the common good more divine than any individual or less common good, but so too are those humans who are responsible for the *respublica*. The *ratio boni in communi* presupposes, for Aquinas, the participation, the natural subordination, of every individual's intellect and will in a hierarchy of goodness that culminates in God as an extrinsic principle of all that is. He takes this to be a conclusion of universal philosophical reason; it is not arrived at on the basis of religious revelation or faith. Every human can come to the conclusion that the whole community of the universe is governed by divine reason, that there is a rational guidance of created things, and this is called eternal law. Eternal law is conceived of as the plan of government in the supreme governor, God, so that all schemes of government of those who direct, as subordinates, must derive from this eternal law. All law in civil societies, so far as they accord with right reason, derive from this eternal law. Hence, the good of the just and well-organized community is one that, in being sought through good statecraft and good citizenship, establishes the necessary, if not sufficient, setting for the achievement of the individual's ultimate good. The best political society, on Aquinas's view, is one in which the moral underpinnings of civil law are taught by the Church, following divine positive law, notably the Ten Commandments. Citizens are virtuous not only through reasonable acts as encapsulated in civil positive law, thereby securing their external goal: the common good of the community. As Christians, and in seeking an internal goal, salvation, they follow the divine positive law as well. Rational creatures have their own natural goal in God, and this is secured through natural intellective cognition that is thereafter perfected by *caritas*, offered through the Church instructing in the precepts of divine law.

Law, *lex*, is therefore defined as ordinances of reason, intelligible to man, directed to the common good and promulgated by an authority. That authority may be a whole multitude, a group, or an individual acting on its behalf (*ST* 1a2ae q. 90, a. 4). Law is distinguished from mere command precisely because law has as its intelligible goal the common good. It is the intelligibility of law that makes subjection to its precepts rational and responsible behaviour. Hence, every prudent legislator intends to make his citizens just, *not simply obedient*. Free individuals, however, have the capacity to contravene both civil and natural law, since they are the only creatures capable of choosing to shape their natural inclinations in irrational, distorted ways. The doctrine of original sin allows for almost the total loss of natural law's precepts through sin and perversity, the consequences of persistent bad habits that can obscure the intelligibility of human ends. For Aquinas, after the Fall, we retain a rational ability to shape our moral dispositions, but our wills may not follow what is reasonable. His concern is to emphasize how rational capacities can, within our now fallen and natural limits, help men overcome 'lower nature' and perform a particular good. The *respublica*, be it *regnum* or *civitas*, is for Aquinas the most important thing constituted by human reason, politics being the most important science, since it treats of the most perfect things, the highest and perfect good in human affairs (Comment. On Aristotle's *Politics*; *ST* Ia2ae q. 90.3, ad 2). Its role is to enforce reason through law, which promotes right living, by compulsion if need be, where that compulsion legitimately belongs either to the community as a whole, or to its official representative, whose duty it is to regulate and, where necessary, inflict penalties.

Prudence, as an individual's exercise of right reason, enables him to judge and direct his actions, through which he will secure the goal of the common good. Following Aristotle, political prudence and legal justice aim to result in the common good, respectively ordering every action and every virtue in terms of those things that are capable of being ordered to the well-being of the *respublica*. Positive civil law as a dictate of reason aims to make men virtuous in their relations with others as exemplified in their exterior actions. But there is also the divine law, which concerns the relation of the individual in this life to God, who alone has knowledge of men's intentions behind their exterior acts. Aquinas thinks that the precepts of divine given law (*ST* Ia2ae q. 90, a. 4 concl.) can be known and understood by men: they are found in Scripture and taught by the Church. Divine law directs human life to man's final end, and its precepts enable him *without any doubt* to do what he should and avoid what he should. The perfection of virtue requires that man be upright, not only in his external acts, directed by just positive, civil law, but also in his intentions. Divine law allows men to regulate their *own* interior intentions. And, where legal justice cannot judge a man's intentions, divine law can and will mete out punishment in the afterlife. It is for this reason that men know that obedience is owed to all legitimate human authority, in *respublica* and Church, because it is based on the natural and divine order that is intelligible to them.

Aquinas had spoken of society as called 'public' when people communicate and deal with each other in constituting a *respublica*. All of the people in one *civitas* or *regnum* are associated in one *respublica*. Communication in the *civitas* or *respublica* is political speech that seeks to achieve concord in and for 'the common'. *Respublica* is, therefore, a generic type of political *communitas*, however, it may be constitutionally structured as *regnum* or *civitas*. Everyone knows by natural law that the good is to be pursued and done, the evil avoided, from which other conclusions may be deduced: do unto others as you would be done by; love thy neighbour as thyself, avoid ignorance and giving offence or harming others with whom one associates (*ST* Ia2ae 93.1).

Prudent deliberation about the historical, contingent, and particular leads to specific conclusions that are drawn from universally and equally known moral principles, whose standard of truth remains fixed. But, as history changes, secondary precepts, drawn from immutably known moral first principles, can change. On Aquinas's view, this does not mean that the natural law is altered over time but, rather, that it is added to. The additions are judged by practical reason in the circumstances. They are useful to social life. On this view, private and individual possession of material things is natural, in the sense of now useful to man in the circumstances. Hence, title to private property according to civil law is *permissible*, and is a secondary conclusion of natural law, emerging from the postlapsarian division of community into spheres of ownership and possession to further peace and commerce. It results from human agreement (not divine command) and is embodied in civil law. But, beyond the satisfaction of limited human needs and modest profit, the superabundance possessed by any individual is *owed* to the poor by *ius natural*, and it is to be used for the common welfare. It is now left to individuals to make provision for the poor from their own wealth, except in cases of urgent necessity, when a starving person may take what legally belongs to another without being considered a thief. God is the *dominus*, the absolute 'owner' and sovereign governor of the universe and, by natural law, known to all, He has commanded that we preserve ourselves by means of what is common (*ST* Ia2ae 94.5 resp. 2).

The Dominican Order came to refine these arguments during a period of its history in which conflict in the university, between popes, kings, and cities, was endemic. As a mendicant Order, Dominicans believed in common *dominium*, a corporate ownership according to which there would still be no 'mine and thine' but only 'ours'. Theft would be against natural law when it could be demonstrated that a member of the Order had appropriated to himself what is common to all. But Dominicans increasingly insisted that every individual is and has ever been a (natural) proprietor, and Adam in particular was a first proprietor, even before Eve. Our first parents were not simply users in common or singly; and, so, it came to be asserted that there could be no separation of use from ownership by natural law. Hence, Dominicans, like our first parents, were common owners, common proprietors, and not simply common users.

Franciscan Political Theory

The Franciscan voice on the numerous themes, discussed above, allows us to compare and differentiate medieval political theories into the fourteenth century. Their perspectives evolved, driven by the turbulent history of their Order, not least in crucial confrontations with Dominicans. They proposed to tackle our themes by focusing on the prelapsarian conditions of Adam and Eve; then, on what occurred after the Fall but before cities were established; and, third, on what politics is now for us in cities. The *Decretum* had already spoken of the natural community of goods by *ius naturae*, distinct from custom and constitutions. But, for Franciscans, and peculiar to their vow of poverty, the burning question was whether there is now a possibility to renounce property in the *civitas* and still not destroy the significance of politics for the here and now.

Thirteenth-century theologians had long engaged in polemics over mendicant, but specifically Franciscan, poverty. Arguments within the Franciscan Order itself continued the debate over apostolic poverty until the early 1320s (Lambertini 2000; Burr 2001; Nold 2003). To justify their Order's founding upon St Francis's concern to live a life of apostolic poverty, they proposed distinctive and evolving understandings of different kinds of *dominia*, meaning directing power over things and hence, with respect to exterior material goods, modes of proprietorship. Their focus on this word *dominium* is complex. In the state of innocence, some Franciscans observed that the *ius naturae* was a principle of *in*distinct dominion. But the distinctions of *dominia* familiar to us now are a consequence of the Fall and of positive, human law. On this view, natural law principles *precede* subsequent distinctions of *dominia*. This was a position that countered what had become the view of many Dominicans that after the Fall the law of nature was itself, and remained, the origin of the institution of distinct property, that property divisions were secondary precepts of the natural law, otherwise theft could not be against natural law and this implied that proprietorship, even of Adam as the first proprietor, was already presupposed *secundum ius naturalem*. Human positive law and property ownership on this view are derived as additional conclusions from natural law premises. Franciscans took issue with this.

For them, only the divine positive law, *the lex evangelica*, does not annul or contrast with the *lex naturae*. Human legislation, on the other hand, is simply approved by God but is not divinely instituted (following Augustine and the New Testament's recognition by Christ and the apostles of the law of Caesar). Hence, the most perfect mode of living is to 'have' only in common. The next best is to 'have' both in common and as one's own; and lastly *habere omnia propria*. However, the most supreme and perfect way to live, to 'have' nothing, neither as one's own nor in common, *nec in proprio nec in communi*, is lost to us after the Fall. 'Having' nothing either privately or in common is no longer for us a self-evident and immutable principle of non-dominating action in living communally. The only way it can be restored *in statu isto* is by living the Franciscan life, and this is a life not of 'having' but merely of 'using': but now it must be adopted *voluntarily*, and this is uniquely the Franciscan mission and vow.

The very distinct *dominia* after the Fall, not being by natural law, is by convention, politics, positive law, human contrivance, all of which were calculations to solve the postlapsarian problem of iniquity. According to the distinguished Franciscan theologian Duns Scotus, the natural law was *suspended* after the Fall, so that what was once a self-evident and immutable principle, *de iure naturae*, the communion of goods for common *use*, has been revoked. Humans, thereafter, established proprietorship of various kinds. *Meum* and *tuum*, as a consequence of iniquity, enlists sheer amoral utility calculations to keep the peace among fallen and quarrelsome men.

The well-known and evolving debates between Franciscans and their opponents were over what poverty actually meant in practice, in the sense of asking: what was the proper relation of human beings to material goods and to what is owed to others? Furthermore, poverty was as important to them as were humility and obedience. Poverty was part of a complex understanding of what harms the soul, and Franciscans argued that there was a duty to refuse to obey the orders even of a superior who required them to act in violation of their Rule since it was the Rule, as originally set out in Francis's Testament, which insisted on the responsibility of the individual to avoid sin. For Franciscans, having vowed an obligation to poverty, the question came to be couched in terms of how restricted the use of goods was meant, in their Rule, to be. What was meant by an obligation that bound them to their vow? Was it a vow to restricted use or merely to lack of ownership? To break a vow is a mortal sin, since oaths taken are to God. Had Franciscans, *could* Franciscans or anyone else, make vows to the kind of conduct that was indeterminate, so that poverty 'in act' was determined entirely by the individual in his own circumstance? Some, known as the Spiritual Franciscans, insisted that this was precisely Francis's intention: that each Franciscan vowed to embark on a certain path towards an envisaged goal of perfection, not a series of specified things but individual acts determined by present necessities and varied circumstances. Franciscans were not monks after all, and did not follow the monastic Rule of St Benedict. They were a mendicant Order and did not live in fixed places. Their Rule, and St Francis's intentions, were more perfect!

There came to be a shift in the understanding on the part of Franciscans, from their living only by bare necessities and drastically limited use, known as *usus pauper*, to simply being bound to a lack of possessions. But this did not obliterate what was an enduring principle: the Franciscan vow is to obligations to *use* not to own, *even consumables*, and this they took to be an evangelical vow from which even the pope cannot dispense. The rejection was of postlapsarian *dominia* in all their subsequent distinctions. But by whose authority does one interpret either Francis's intentions or that of Scripture as counsels to a perfect life voluntarily undertaken? Here we see numerous 'difficult' Franciscans continuing to engage questions about obedience to 'authoritative' commands that entailed sinning and that they took to imperil their own salvation. There remained the issue of *whose* discretionary power was at stake in the performance of any individual's acts. This was recognized to be one of *the* major issues in political theorizing and would remain so well beyond our period.

Francis's Testament and his Rule were in the most simple of terms statements of intention to obey superiors but not to compromise the purity of evangelical perfection. If this was a life that could be voluntarily chosen—it was that of Christ and the apostles and, as Francis had said and written, this is what he and his brothers sought to live—then not even the pope could absolve anyone from his evangelical vows. Scripture, on this view, provides intelligible counsels and examples to be imitated, without further gloss, for the New Testament consists in the testimonies of those most worthy of belief—Christ and his apostles. And *how* one lives these counsels depends on each individual's awareness of the historicity of original pronouncements and the authorial intentions behind them. Francis had been given the grace to be so inspired and to understand, having passed this on to his Order in his Rule in *his* times. This meant that the Franciscan Rule was identical in intention with the Gospel. It also implied that Christ and the apostolic community lived as though in the state of first innocence, where there was no distinct *dominium* but only *usus*, and this was by a 'right' neither to own things nor to use them, *ius nec in re nec in usus*. On this view, Christ and the apostles used goods only sufficient for daily survival, leaving, indeed offering, as much and as good for everyone else in need. They had *neither* objective *nor* subjective 'rights'. God originally was owner and sovereign *dominus*, and our first parents had use only of what was God's, granted to them and not by any 'right'. In Christ's coming, his kingship was explicitly not of this world. It was precisely the civil law and the purely human distinction of 'rights' to property that allowed Franciscans to renounce it, since they held private possession not to be by natural law, and natural law cannot be renounced.

After years of debate and turmoil, Pope John XXII finally affirmed that there simply was no possibility of an original separation of use from ownership by natural law, especially of consumables, before or, indeed, after the Fall: you ate it, you 'owned' it, it was 'yours'. Adam was, therefore, the first proprietor. John XXII was willing to accept that Franciscans could refuse a right to property ownership, individually and in common, but the Church wanted this conduct classified as a '*right*' of use. Franciscans insisted to the contrary. They were not criticizing property ownership since they were prepared to leave all such rights to the Church on their behalf. What they wanted to preserve for themselves was not a *right* of use. It was use *without* right.

Their clash with John XXII and those who advised him focused on a serious issue in political theorizing: what do obedience and obligation mean, not simply for Franciscans, or for members of all religious orders, but generally? John XXII said that obedience was *dominium* of the mind and soul in the performance of duties consequent on a vow. It was up to superiors to define how practices were to be measured in the circumstances, even to reverse the laws of their predecessors if the superior judges them harmful in the circumstances. He insisted that no religious Rule was identical with the Gospel. Franciscans, however, couched obedience and obligation in more circumscribed and limited terms: no one could be obliged, even by the pope, to violate an evangelical vow. This contravened evangelical liberty, an inalienable *ius* consequent on an obligation, granted by Christ to all individual Christians to survive, and help others in reciprocity to do the same, especially when anyone was in dire need. Where the papal position had insisted that the Holy Spirit leads the Church to an increasing knowledge but always under the guidance of the ecclesiastical hierarchy, Franciscans did not. Instead, for them, truth was not to be had by institutional authority; it was instinctive, self-evident, *per se nota* or known in experience by every individual. And in the Franciscan insistence to focus on the conventional institution of *distincta dominia* as human positive law, as an effect of human will alone, this will—even before the Flood—having been exhibited as a lapsed cupidity, *per iniquitatem*, we get the division of the earth from human will and not from the divine will. What God has done, after the Fall, is to attribute to human beings a power, a *ius*, and an authority of administration and regulation of the world. He does not tell us that this *need be* by property division. This is a purely human convention, and it is expedient in the circumstances. Politics, civic foundings, and maintenance are merely matters of utility.

The Oxford Franciscan William of Ockham eventually became embroiled in his Order's defence with Michael of Cesena, the General Minister of the Order. But well before Ockham's 'political moment' he was already using his university logic to support a reading of historical, authoritative, indeed Scriptural texts with a Franciscan sensitivity. He argued that an author's intentions in his text could be secured only by not thinking that every term had one single, timeless, and univocal meaning. It was the job of any reader to seek the author's intentions to determine what he meant by the words he used. He understood God as transcendent but that God had willed, *de potentia ordinata*, that we be given our own ways to find the truth as an object of natural human intelligence as it is 'now' (Coleman 2009).

When Ockham supported his Order's reading of the prelapsarian condition of Adam and Eve, he used the language of liberties and *ius/iura* as concessions by some higher authority: especially from God or nature. Neither princes nor popes could remove these powers or liberties. Hence, St Francis was correct in his interpretation of Scripture when he understood that Christ and the apostles did not own, but simply used the world. Human beings have a natural power of use, from God, before any subsequent human legal or positive rights of possession that men in communities thereafter established. Our capacity for right reason, *recta ratio*, does not imply that *dominium* was granted eternally to human beings, but it does allow us to know that we were granted *usus*. When Ockham recapitulates the prelapsarian conditions and powers of Adam and Eve, he says that they had perfect *non-proprietary* power over all things, ruling with right reason and not by coercion. Fallen nature, however, requires coercion; and *dominium* was established for utility and peace, and made 'concrete' in positive civil law. The idea of perfection before the Fall is *now* expressed by natural law that is in us, which lets us know, through our experiences and reasoning based on our experiences, that we have powers to use the world for survival without owning any part of it. Only God has rightful ownership/*dominium* of creation. Hence, after the Fall but before kings were established, men voluntarily divided up things, saying this is mine *a iure humano*. Possession and ownership of material things are logical conclusions of experience of our iniquity, now. The grounds for political legitimacy, then, are not sacred: they are conventional, utilitarian conclusions based on the historicity of acts of human will and reasoning in the circumstances.

For Ockham, reason is central to an exercise of our natural liberty. But what kind of reason is *recta ratio*? What is its relation to a good will if an action is to be morally right? He insisted, famously, that one's will is not necessarily determined by another created cause than the will itself, and he rejected the position that our will is determined by a judgement of reason as to the goodness of the willed act. He says we can will what is bad, even if willing what *recta ratio* suggests is essential to a good will. But, in our present postlapsarian state, we can and do will against the precepts of reason, and we know this from our very experience. Ockham's political understanding comes out of this, not least because what we owe to others, what we know or should know about our obligations to others, and even why and how we know what others are owed of a share in the common good, objectively, we do not infallibly and necessarily will to do or perform. Augustine plays a central role in shaping this argument. Ockham insists that intentions are central to all moral acts and they reveal an individual's habitual orientation to what is intrinsically valuable. There *are* directive divine commands in divine positive law, but these do *not* override each individual's need to be committed to his own moral judgements and acts that are independent of divine law precepts or commands. Here is where our natural right reason is engaged and where politics comes in again.

Ockham distinguished between a positive and non-positive moral science in his now much discussed *Quodlibets*. Positive moral science contains human and divine laws that oblige a person to pursue or avoid what is commanded or prohibited by a superior with the authority to legislate. But *non-positive moral science* is something *a priori* and prior to what jurists and legislators might discuss. Non-positive moral science is what directs human acts apart from any superior's precepts, be it a Church superior or a civil magistrate. The radically individualist thrust in the Franciscan position emerges here, in the moment of application of the precepts of a vow to individual circumstances. Non-positive moral science enables this through the way that principles are known to us, either *per se nota* or in experience, and thereby directs our acts. Ockham further announces that positive moral science, of divine or civil jurisprudence, is not demonstrative. But non-positive moral science is demonstrative in that it deduces conclusions (syllogistically) from principles known by every human individual, known *per se* or in experience. This is how we know natural law precepts—that is, what the will ought to conform itself to as *recta ratio*, and these consist in precepts like: avoid evil and sin. This non-positive moral science is certain, at least as certain as anything can be for us, since every individual has a greater experience of his own acts than of those of others or of other things. *Recta ratio* discerns right and wrong as well as the means to them. *Recta ratio* is a common knowledge and not an exclusive capacity of the learned or powerful. What is now 'natural' is simply what accords with natural reason, and the bottom line for Franciscans is that, even in our world, after the Fall, what is naturally reasonable is framed by the obligation to survive *and* to aid others, as God's individual creatures, in their survival (by begging and labour), each using the world for one's daily needs. That which is used is an individual decision of will and, in the Franciscan case, realizes natural equity. According to Ockham, the nominalist, the unity of the Franciscan Order is a *conceptual* collection of such individuals; but the *reality* is only *individuals* who vow individual poverty, and thus, being a community of individuals with a Rule, each applies it in his own circumstances.

Ockham grounds our moral powers in non-positive morality. Of course, politically and by the lawyers' positive moral science, we do have 'rights', accorded or ascribed, and *in foro externo*, to own and use, and we have commanded obligations to be fair and keep the peace among our neighbours. But can we speak of non-positive 'natural *rights*' of ownership and use? No. (Some modern commentators think we can; see McGrade 2006: 63–94.)

To conclude: Franciscans can voluntarily choose to live without positive *meum* and *tuum*: they can be *legally rightless*. What civil *meum* and *tuum* now do is to limit the postlapsarian and recognized common 'right' of *use*. But even this must be capable of being overridden in cases of extreme need. Since the Church now lives in times where property has been established, both in common and individually, non-positive morality still allows Franciscans to reject all forms of 'rights' to use and ownership, *voluntarily*, by taking a vow. To deny that this is an explosive medieval political theory would, at the very least, require that we forget or ignore its historical impact on future thinkers in future centuries, especially regarding the origins and justification of private property.

REFERENCES

Primary Sources

AQUINAS, THOMAS, *Pars Prima Summae Theologiae*, in *Sancti Thomae Aquinatis: Opera Omnia*, ed. Leonina, vol. iv, Rome, 1888.

AQUINAS, THOMAS, *Prima Secundae Summae Theologiae*, in *Sancti Thomae Aquinatis: Opera Omnia*, ed. Leonina, vol. vii, Rome, 1892.

AQUINAS, THOMAS, *In octo libros Politicorum Expositio*, ed. R. M. Spiazzi, Turin: Marietti, 1951.

AQUINAS, THOMAS, *In decem libros Ethicorum Aristotelis ad Nicomachum Expositio*, ed. R. M. Spiazzi, 3rd edn, Turin: Marietti, 1964.

AQUINAS, THOMAS, *Sententia libri politicorum* (*Super Politicam*), in *Sancti Thomae Aquinatis: Opera Omnia*, ed. Leonina, vol. xlviii, Rome, 1971.

GRATIAN, *Corpus Iuris Canonici*, ed. E. Friedberg, vol. i, *Decretum magistri Gratiani*, vol. ii, *Decretalium Collectione*, Leipzig 1879–1881; repr. Graz, 1956.

JUSTINIAN, *Corpus Iuris Civilis*, vol. I, *Institutes*, ed. P. Krueger, and *Digest*, ed. T. Mommsen; vol. ii, *Codex*, ed. P. Krueger; vol. iii, *Novellae*, ed. R. Schoell and W. Kroll, Berlin: Editio stereotypa, 1882, 1884, 1895.

MARSILIUS OF PADUA, *Defensor Pacis*, ed. R. Scholz, in *Monumenta Germaniae Historica: Fontes iuris germanici antique*, Hannover, 1933.

WILLIAM OF OCKHAM, *Opus nonaginta dierum*, in *Guillelmi de Ockham: Opera Politica*, vol. i, ed. J. G. Sikes and H. S. Offler, Manchester: Manchester University Press, 1940; rev. 2nd edn, 1974, 292–368; vol. ii, ed. J. G. Sikes and H. S Offler, Manchester: Manchester University Press, 1963, 307–509.

WILLIAM OF OCKHAM, *Summae logicae*, ed. G. Gal, New York: Franciscan Institute, St Bonaventure, 1974.

WILLIAM OF OCKHAM, *Breviloquium de principatu tyrannico*, in *Guillelmi de Ockham, Opera Politica*, vol. iv, ed. H. S. Offler, Oxford: Oxford University Press, 1997, 97–260.

WILLIAM OF OCKHAM, *De imperatorum et pontificum potestate*, in *Opera Politica*, vol. iv, ed. H. S. Offler, Oxford: Oxford University Press, 1997, 279–355.

WILLIAM OF OCKHAM, *Quodlibeta septem*, in *Venerabilis Inceptoris Guillelmi de Ockham: Opera Philosophica et Theologica*, ed. P. Boehner, G. Gal, S. F. Brown, et al., 17 vols, New York: Franciscan Institute, St Bonaventure; *Opera Philosophica*, 7 vols, 1974–1988; *Opera Theologica*, 10 vols, 1967–86; *Quodlibeta* in *Opera Theologica*, vol. ix.

Secondary Sources

BLACK, A. (1992). *Political Thought in Europe 1250–1450*. Cambridge: Cambridge University Press.

BURR, D. (2001). *The Spiritual Franciscans: From Protest to Persecution in the Century after St Francis*. University Park, PA: Pennsylvania State University Press.

CANNING, J. (1996). *A History of Medieval Political Thought 300–1450*. London: Routledge.

COLEMAN, J. (1983). 'Medieval Discussions of Property: *Ratio* and *Dominium* according to John of Paris and Marsilius of Padua', *History of Political Thought*, 4: 209–28.

COLEMAN, J. (1985). 'Medieval Discussions of Property: *Ratio* and *Dominium* in Thirteenth- and Fourteenth-Century Political Thought and its Seventeenth-Century Heirs', *Political Studies*, 33: 73–100.

COLEMAN, J. (1987). 'The Two Jurisdictions: Theological and Legal Justifications of Church Property in the Thirteenth Century', in W. Shiels and D. Wood (eds), *Studies in Church History, subsidia: The Church and Wealth*. Oxford: Blackwell, 75–100.

COLEMAN, J. (1988). 'Property and Poverty', in J. H. Burns (ed.), *The Cambridge History of Medieval Political Thought c.350–1450*. Cambridge: Cambridge University Press, 607–48.

COLEMAN, J. (1992). *Ancient and Medieval Memories: Studies in the Reconstruction of the Past*. Cambridge: Cambridge University Press.

COLEMAN, J. (1996*a*). 'The Individual and the Medieval State', in J. Coleman (ed.), *The Individual in Political Theory and Practice*. Oxford: Clarendon Press, 1–34.

COLEMAN, J. (1996*b*). 'The Science of Politics and Late Medieval Academic Debate', in R. Copeland (ed.), *Criticism and Dissent in the Middle Ages*. Cambridge: Cambridge University Press, 181–214.

COLEMAN, J. (2000). A *History of Political Thought from the Middle Ages to the Renaissance*. Oxford: Blackwell.

COLEMAN, J. (2006). 'Are There Any Individual Rights or Only Duties? On the Limits of Obedience in the Avoidance of Sin According to Late Medieval and Early Modern Scholars', in V. Makinen and P. Korkman (eds), *Transformations in Medieval and Early-Modern Rights Discourse*. Dordrecht: Springer, 3–36.

COLEMAN, J. (2007). 'Citizenship and the Language of Statecraft', in A. Molho and D. R. Curto (eds), *Finding Europe: Discourses on Margins, Communities, Images*. New York and Oxford: Berghahn.

COLEMAN, J. (2009). 'Using, Not Owning-Duties, Not Rights: The Consequences of Some Franciscan Perspectives on Politics', in Michael F. Cusato and G. Geltner (eds), *Defenders and Critics of Franciscan Life: Essays in Honor of John V. Fleming*. Leiden and Boston: Brill, 65–84.

FASOLT, C. (2007). 'Hegel's Ghost: Europe, the Reformation and the Middle Ages', *Viator*, 10: 345–86.

FASOLT, C. (2008). 'Religious Authority and Ecclesiastical Governance', in J. J. Martin (ed.), *The Renaissance World*. London: Routledge, 364–80.

GARNETT, G. (2006). *Marsilius of Padua and 'The Truth of History'*. Oxford: Oxford University Press.

HARDING, A. (2002). *Medieval Law and the Foundations of the State*. Oxford: Oxford University Press.

KEMPSHALL, M. (1999). *The Common Good in Late Medieval Political Thought*. Oxford: Oxford University Press.

KING, P. (1999). 'Ockham's Ethical Theory', in P. V. Spade (ed.), *The Cambridge Companion to Ockham*. Cambridge: Cambridge University Press, 227–44.

LAMBERT, M. (1999). *Franciscan Poverty: The Doctrine of the Absolute Poverty of Christ and the Apostles in the Franciscan Order 1210–1323*. 2nd edn. New York: St Bonaventure.

LAMBERTINI, R. (2000). *La poverta pensata: Evoluzione storica della definizione dell'identita minoritica da Bonaventura ad Ockham*. Modena: Mucchi.

McCORD ADAMS, M. (1987). 'William of Ockham: Voluntarist or Naturalist', in J. F. Wippel (ed.), *Studies in Medieval Philosophy*. Washington: Catholic University of America Press, 219–48.

McGRADE, A. S. (2006). 'Right(s) in Ockham: a reasonable vision of Politics', in V. Makinen and P. Korkman (eds), *Transformations in Medieval and Early-Modern Rights Discourse*. Dordrecht: Springer, 63–94.

MAIOLO, F. (2007). *Medieval Sovereignty: Marsilius of Padua and Bartolus of Saxoferrato*. Delft: Eburon.

MARX, K., and ENGELS, F. (1978). *The German Ideology*, (ed.) C. J. Arthur.London: Lawrence & Wishart.

MIETHKE, J. (2000*a*). 'Practical Intentions of Scholasticism: The Example of Political Theory', in W. Courtney and J. Miethke (eds), *Universities in Medieval Society*. Leiden: Brill, 211–28.

MIETHKE, J. (2000*b*). *De potestate papae: Die papstliche Amtskompetenz im Widerstreit der politischen Theorie von Thomas von Aquin bis Wilhelm von Ockham*. Tübingen: Mohrn Siebeck.

MONFASANI, J. (2006). 'The Renaissance as the Concluding Phase of the Middle Ages', *Bulletino dell'istituto storico italiano per il medio evo*, 108: 165–85.

MURRAY, A. (1978). *Reason and Society in the Middle Ages*. Oxford: Oxford University Press.

NEDERMAN, C. (1996). 'The Meaning of Aristotelianism in Medieval Moral and Political Thought', *Journal of the History of Ideas*, 57: 563–85.

NOLD, P. (2003). *Pope John XXII and his Franciscan Cardinal: Bertrand de la Tour and the Apostolic Poverty Controversy*. Oxford: Clarendon Press.

OAKLEY, F. (2005). *Natural Law, Laws of Nature, Natural Rights: Continuity and Discontinuity in the History of Ideas*. New York and London: Continuum.

PADOA SCHIOPPA, A. (1997). 'Hierarchy and Jurisdiction: Models in Medieval Canon Law', in A. Padoa Schioppa (ed.), *Legislation and Justice*. Oxford: Clarendon Press.

PENNINGTON, K. (1984). *Pope and Bishops: The Papal Monarchy in the Twelfth and Thirteenth Centuries*. University Park, PA: University of Pennsylvania Press.

PRODI, P. (2000). *Una storia della giustizia. Dal pluralismo dei fori al moderno dualismo tra coscienza e diritto*. Bologna.

QUAGLIONI, D. (2004). *La giustizia nel medioevo e nella prima eta moderna*. Bologna.

REYNOLDS, S. (1984). *Kingdoms and Communities in Western Europe 900–1300*. Oxford: Clarendon Press.

REYNOLDS, S. (1997). 'The Historiography of the Medieval State', in M. Bentley (ed.), *Companion to Historiography*. London: Routledge, 117–38.

SHOGIMEN, T. (2007). *Ockham and Political Discourse in the Late Middle Ages*. Cambridge: Cambridge University Press.

TIERNEY, B. (1982). *Religion, Law and the Growth of Constitutional Thought 1150–1650*. Cambridge: Cambridge University Press.

TIERNEY, B. (1997). *The Idea of Natural Rights: Studies on Natural Rights, Natural Law and Church Law 1150–1625*. Atlanta, GA: Scholars Press.

WOOD, E. M. (2008). *Citizens to Lords, A Social History of Western Political Thought from Antiquity to the Middle Ages*. London and New York: Verso.

CHAPTER 13

···

RENAISSANCE POLITICAL PHILOSOPHY

···

MIKAEL HÖRNQVIST

THE Renaissance stands before us both as a cultural golden age of titanic creativity, and as an era of transition struggling to contain and eventually succumbing to the historical forces that it unleashed. In the burgeoning age of unprecedented economic and demographic growth that followed on the breakdown of feudalism in Flanders and northern and central Italy in the twelfth and the thirteenth centuries, cities such as Bruges, Lyons, Genoa, Pisa, Florence, Siena, and Venice emerged as important commercial centers and nodes in an international network of trade, manufacturing, and banking. Within a few generations, a prosperous, self-conscious, and highly sophisticated urban culture had arisen, animated by the pragmatic and worldly attitude of the new merchant elites. Gradually, a political culture of participation, joint action, consultation, consent, and citizenship developed as a natural extension of the merchant and craft classes' commerical concerns. According to the emerging communal ethos, public magistrates should serve the common good of the city, setting aside their own private interest, decisions should be disciplined by laws that applied equally to all, and citizens were under obligation to contribute to the enhancement and greatness of their city. Although we are well advised not to exaggrerate the impact of this proto-republican ideology, which often served as little more than a blanket for underhand dealings, clientage, and perpetuated elite power, it cannot be denied that it played an important role in the shaping of the Renaissance merchant republic, its self-understanding and its collective identity.

As centers of administration, manufacturing, exchange, and consumption, held together by strong communal bonds but riveted by factions, the communes of central and northern Italy bore a close resemblance to the self-governing cities of antiquity. However, in one important regard their status differed radically from their ancient counterparts. While the Greek cities had developed their institutional culture and defined themselves politically in agonistic relation to their neighbors, and Rome had aspired to, and eventually acquired, the status of world ruler, the Italian city republics of the late Middle Ages had to carve out their political identities in a world dominated by Christian institutions and spirituality, and by the myth of Rome that lived on in the collective imagination and the precepts of Roman law. Although *de facto* self-ruling and sovereign, the Italian cities remained *de jure* subject to their medieval overlords, the Church and the Empire. Their subordination was not merely legal and spiritual, but had an important philosophical dimension as well. In the organicist understanding of the period, the city state related to the overlord like particular to universal, like part to the whole, and like member to the body in its entirety (Skinner 1978: i. 3–22; Pocock 2003: 31–48). The city's quest for independence and autonomy therefore involved more than preventing papal and imperial involvement in their internal affairs. On these premises, to achieve supreme authority, or sovereignty, meant either appropriating for themselves the status of the universal, to become a new Rome, or inventing a completely new way of conceptualizing politics. Since the idea of Rome and a united Christendom was the horizon within which Renaissance political thought developed, the alternatives to papal and imperial tutelage consisted in subverting the Roman–papal paradigm from within (Machiavelli's solution) or rejecting Rome altogether (the road taken by French *légistes* such as Hotman and Bodin).

This chapter will focus on the two most prominent, and arguably also most influential, political thinkers of the Renaissance period, Niccolò Machiavelli (1469–1527) and Thomas More (1478–1535). Although it is highly unlikely that either author knew of the existence of the other, let alone was familiar with his work, the fact that Machiavelli' *Prince* (1513) and *Discourses on Livy* (1514–18) and More's *Utopia* (1516) were written only a few years apart invites comparison. In an important sense, Machiavelli and More belong to the same historical moment. This was the quarter century between the discovery of the New World, figuring prominently in More's *Utopia* and referred to in the opening of Machiavelli's *Discourses*, and the Reformation. Within a few years after the appearance of the above-mentioned works, humanist experimentation and fascination for novelty and for things that were unheard of, were stifled and silenced by the general frenzy of confessional politics and loud calls for a return to order. Since these developments are competently treated elsewhere in this volume, I will in the following explore the alternatives that were muted or distorted by the political exigencies of post-Reformation Europe. In this context, Machiavelli and More stand out, in part because of the sheer quality and sophistication of their work, in part because of the relevance their probing approaches to politics continue to hold for us today.

While focusing on Machiavelli and More, we must, of course, not forget that there were many other Renaissance writers, humanists, philosophers, and others, who commented on politics and contributed to the overall development of political thought in the period. As a rule, their political ideas have to be extracted from official and private letters, historical chronicles, humanist dialogues, poetry, political pamphlets, and other, more occasional writings. But there are exceptions to this rule—as, for example, Leonardo Bruni's *Laudatio florentinae urbis* and Matteo Palmieri's *De vita civile*—that must be regarded as political treatises in their own right. However, the historical importance of these works does not primarily consist in the originality of their ideas, but in the ways in which they apply ancient republican ideals and Roman notions of *libertas, iustitia, virtus*, and the mixed republic to contemporary conditions. The Florentine republic that proudly emerges from these, and other civic humanist texts, is the self-designated heir of the ancient Roman republic, pursuing liberty at home and empire abroad (Hörnqvist 2000).

Niccolò Machiavelli is the heir and the crowning moment of this Florentine tradition. Having served the Florentine Republic as Secretary and diplomat from 1498, Machiavelli was dismissed from office in 1512, following the Medici family's return to power in Florence. He wrote his most famous works, *The Prince* and the *Discourses on Livy*, which also contain the core of his political teaching, during the subsequent period, when he was desperately seeking a way back into political life. In the limited space allotted here his theory will be presented with a degree of abstraction that is fundamentally foreign to Machiavelli's writings, which in Nietzsche's memorable formulation treat "the most serious matters," and develop "long, difficult, hard, dangerous thoughts" in the boisterous "tempo of the gallop" and in "the very best, most capricious humor" (Nietzsche 1989: 41).

The foundation of states is a recurrent and central theme in Machiavelli's work and a good place to start exploring his theory. Although classical authors treat the problems involved in the founding of states, it could be argued that none of them, with the possible exception of Plato, attaches the same importance to the subject that Machiavelli does. While his *Prince* is concerned with the founding of a new principality in Florence or central Italy, he deals in the *Discourses on Livy* with the founding of states in general and the founding of Rome in particular. The Florentine republic's lack of a proper foundation is discussed in the *Discourses* and is brought up again in the *Discursus Florentinarum rerum*, his proposal for a new Florentine constitution of 1520, presented to Giulio de' Medici. In *The Prince*, Machiavelli claims that "good laws [*buone legge*]," in combination with "good arms [*buone arme*]," are the foundation of all states. Priority seems to be given to arms, since there "cannot be good laws where there are no good arms, and where there are good arms there must be good laws" (*P.* 12).[1] The argument is resumed in Chapter 18, where Machiavelli claims that princes must know how to fight "with laws" as well as "with force" (*P.* 18). But force (or arms) and laws are not sufficient for a firm foundation. Laws are not persuasive in themselves, and a ruler who relies too heavily on military strength will not be able to gain popular support, without which every prince, and new princes in particular, must "fear everything and everyone" (*P.* 19). So what other factor could possibly be called upon to consolidate princely rule and power in general?

---

[1] References to Machiavelli's *Prince* are given in abbreviated form as *P.* followed by chapter number.

One possible answer is customs. In Chapter 2 of *The Prince*, it is true, Machiavelli claims that for hereditary princes to hold their states they need only observe the customary ways of their ancestors, but he then goes on to insinuate that such princes are inherently weak and vulnerable in the face of external aggression (see also *P.* 24). As Machiavelli's treatment of Roman history in the *Discourses* suggests, customs and mœurs might have a more reinvigorating and sustaining role to play in a republic, but, since customs need time to develop, they cannot be relied on at the founding moment of the state. Consequently, we have to look elsewhere for a third founding element capable of supporting arms and laws.

The nature of this third element is suggested by Machiavelli's discussion of Girolamo Savonarola, the Dominican friar who between 1494 and 1498 governed Florence informally from the pulpits of San Marco and the Cathedral. During his ascendency, Savonarola succeeded in persuading the Florentines that "he spoke with God" and that Florence, after the imminent fall of Rome, had been divinely elected to emerge as the new leader of Christendom (*D.* I.11).[2] But when religious enthusiasm waned and "the masses began to lose faith in him," Savonarola's "new orders" came to ruin, because the friar lacked the means that could keep "the support of those who had believed in him" and "made unbelievers believe" (*P.* 6). If Savonarola instead had been able to use armed force to protect his constitutional innovations, and had refrained from opposing the enactment of laws that he himself had promoted (*D.* I.45), he would have remained "powerful, secure, honored, and successful" (*P.* 6). Savonarola's example shows us two things. On the one hand, it demonstrates how religion, and Christian beliefs, can be exploited for political ends; on the other, it teaches that persuasion and religious manipulation, if unsupported by force and law, cannot serve as a viable and lasting foundation for states.

While there can be no doubt that Machiavelli personally considered the friar to be a fraud (in a private letter of 1498 commenting on his sermons, he speaks of his opportunism and his colorful "lies") (1997–2005: ii. 8), he was acutely aware of the broad support that Savonarola's teachings continued to enjoy among Florentines even after his death. That he thought of the Savonarolan legacy in connection to his long-term project for a foundation for Florence is suggested by a guarded remark in the *Discourses* concerning the friar's reputation: "I do not wish to judge whether it is true or not, because one should speak with reverence of such a man" (*D.* I.11). By advising against discussing whether the friar was a true prophet or not, Machiavelli seems to suggest to his young Florentine readers, the future leaders of the Machiavellian republic, that the Savonarolan legacy should be treated with the utmost respect, since it could be used as a tool and made to serve their purposes.

But, as we have already pointed out, religion and religious manipulation were only one element in Machiavelli's foundational project. It had to be reinforced by force and law. For a practical application of this theory, we may turn to Machiavelli's extensive

---

[2] References to Machiavelli's *Discourses* are given in abbreviated form as *D.* followed by book and chapter number.

writings on the new militia ordinance of 1506, the institution of which must be regarded as his main achievement during his time in the Florentine chancery (Hörnqvist 2002). In the preambles to the draft laws that he penned in connection to the project, the *Cagione dell'ordinanza* and the *Provisioni della ordinanza*, Machiavelli argues that, wherever power is exercised, the determining factors are "justice and arms," and that all republics that have maintained themselves and expanded have had as "their principal foundation two things, that is, justice and arms" (1997–2005: i. 26, 31). While Florence has already established the rule of law and efficient legal procedures, the city is said to be desperately lacking in arms and military organization. The proposed militia ordinance is designed to remedy this deficiency. To understand how it is possible for Machiavelli to regard the new militia and the recruitment of infantry conscripts in the *contado* as a founding, or refounding, of the Florentine state, we need to consider the role that policing and law enforcement played in the project. At the turn of the sixteenth century, the Florentine territorial state was badly shaken by a series of rebellions among the subject towns in its dominion, and Machiavelli's militia writings reflect these concerns. The militia reform was thus envisaged as a tool for disciplining and organizing the subjects of the unruly *contado*, and to bind them closer to the republic. Forced to serve as soldiers by public decree, the peasant conscripts were placed under the authority of commanders with the legal right to punish those who failed to respond to call-up notices or refused to follow orders. To exact obedience and create ties of loyalty, conscripts were requested to take an oath on the gospels, with words that "would most effectively bind them body and soul," as a catalog of the punishments to which they were liable was read out loud. In this example of applied principles, we see how arms, law, and religious persuasion are brought together and compounded to provide Florentine power with a firm foundation.

Before we proceed, it is important to clarify how radical Machiavelli's departure from medieval approaches actually was. First, he rejected the contention prevalent among medieval schoolmen and earlier Renaissance humanists that republics and principalities must be founded on justice. In Machiavelli's understanding, no necessary connection exists between good laws and justice. Laws are "good [*buone*]" when they compel obedience, preserve the liberty of the republic, and promote future expansion. Second, he choses to ignore the sharp distinction that had traditionally been drawn between legitimate and illegitimate use of force, and between just and tyrannical means of power in general. In fact, it could even be argued that Machiavelli in Chapters 17 and 18 of *The Prince* self-consciously assumes the role as a teacher in tyranny. Claiming that a ruler must know how to fight both as a man and as a beast, both with legal means and by using force, cruelty, and deceit, he exhorts his princely reader to imitate, or "use," the lion and the fox, two animals whom Cicero and Dante had famously portrayed as symbols of tyrannical and unlawful government (Hörnqvist 2004: 206). Third, Machiavelli's inclusion of religion among the foundational elements should not be mistaken for an attempt to impose religiously defined limits on secular authority, or to make secular rulers subject to religious authorities. To the contrary, it is the subversive potential of religion, and its natural tendency to evoke authorities and a realm above and beyond the secular ruler, that prompt Machiavelli to incorporate it in his tripartite foundation. A republic or a political order that fails to check religion and does not prevent it from developing outside its control, Machiavelli maintains, will make itself vulnerable to religious claims to supreme authority. By allowing a counter-power, however spectral and other-worldly, to hover above it, the state invites discord, dissension, and civil strife that it might not be able to contain. While militant Islam might here spring to mind, Machiavelli, of course, is thinking of Christianity (which he calls "our" religion, but treats as a religion among many). By constantly meddling in worldly affairs, the Papacy had used its spiritual power to keep Italy politically divided, without itself being strong enough, or committed enough, to impose its own political order on the peninsula. Perhaps we are here closing in on one of Machiavelli's chief aims in writing *The Prince*: to bring the Papacy under the control of a secular ruler, or, to be more exact, a new Italian, or Florentine, prince. To the extent that this holds true, the former Secretary was working in a tradition stretching back to Dante Alighieri and Marsilius of Padua, and pointing ahead to Napoleon Bonaparte's occupation of Rome.

The overriding lesson of this argument is that states cannot be founded on a single principle, but that all viable foundations contain at least three different principles: laws; arms; and religion (or religious persuasion). As Machiavelli's discussions of failed founders—Savonarola, Piero Soderini, Cesare Borgia, and so on—make clear, a founder who neglects one of these principles will not be able to give a strong and lasting foundation for his state.

The great importance Machiavelli attaches to laws, military strength, and the need to rein in religion at the foundation of states should be seen as an expression of his more general concern with the shape, or the form, of the republic. Machiavelli's constitutional theory, which receives its most elaborate treatment in the *Discourses*, takes its point of departure in a comparison of three of the most celebrated constitutions of the ancient world, the Athenian, the Spartan, and the Roman. He begins by offhandedly dismissing Solon's Athenian constitution as a misguided and short-lived experiment in democracy, which failed because it neglected to provide for the interest of the great, or the aristocratic few. Following Polybius' lead, Machiavelli instead concentrates on the Roman and the Spartan alternatives. In contrast to Solon, Lycurgus, the Spartan lawgiver, laid down a firm foundation for his state by combining monarchic and aristocratic elements, placing government in the hands of "a king and a narrow Senate" (*D.* I.6). However, since Lycurgus omitted giving representation to the people, or the many, his constitution could claim to be only partially mixed. In this regard, the Roman republic offers a more attractive solution. In great detail and with many asides, Machiavelli shows how the Roman constitution evolved as the result of a long and tumultuous historical process, fueled by the class struggle between the Senate and the plebs. Rome began as a monarchy, but Romulus, its founder, imposed from the very beginning, by reserving to himself alone the right to command the armies and to convoke the Senate, strict limits on the authority of the royal office. Romulus' orders proved so conformable to "a civil and free way of life [*uno vivere civile e libero*]" that, when the city later became a republic, the only innovation needed was the replacement of the king by two annually elected consuls (*D.* I.9). Later, the Tribunes of the plebs were introduced to check the power of the Senate and to safeguard the interest of the people, a function previously performed by the king. Having arrived at this stage, Machiavelli claims, Rome had developed a full-fledged and perfectly mixed republic, *una republica perfetta*, that provided for the one, the few, and the many (*D.* I.2). As a consequence of this processual constitutional approach, Rome had been able to increase its population, to arm its citizens, to expand its borders, and to conquer the world. On the basis of these observations, Machiavelli concludes that the Roman form of popular and imperial republicanism must be preferred to the Spartan policy of isolation, stability, and self-chosen weakness.

To understand the emphasis that Machiavelli places on each of the three constitutional elements, we need to turn to his view of the relationship between internal and external affairs, between *cose di dentro* and *cose di fuora*. Like most Florentine humanists and republican writers of the fifteenth century, Machiavelli refused to view liberty and empire as contradictory values or pursuits. Instead, as a representative of the Florentine Renaissance tradition, he subscribed to the idea that the republic has two ends—one internal, centered around the classical concept of liberty (*libertas*), and the other external, aspiring to acquisition of dominion (*imperium*), material goods, greatness, and glory. These two ends are distinct and based upon different sets of values, but, within the overarching framework of Roman republicanism, they are inextricably connected and, in a sense, complementary. Together they consitute the nerve center of the healthy republic, so that, when one of the categories is neglected, the other is bound to suffer as well, with corruption and tyranny as the result. On the basis of what has emerged here, it could be argued that liberty and empire are mutually constitutive in a way similar to how arms, law, and religion are tied together in Machiavelli's theory of the foundation of states.

In Machiavellian republicanism, an intimate link exists between the republic's dual pursuit of liberty and empire, on the one hand, and its mixed constitution and internal ordering, on the other. According to the Florentine thinker, there are, broadly speaking, two categories of men, or two humors (*umori*), those who desire not to be oppressed, but to live free, and those who want to command and dominate others. The former group Machiavelli calls the people (*popolo*) and the latter the great (*grandi*) (*P.* 9; *D.* I.4). In the constitutional context, they correspond to the the many and the few respectively. How can these contrasting desires, or appetites (*appetiti*) be satisfied or accomodated without endangering the other humor's demands and the republic as a whole? The answer offered by Florentine republicanism, but never explicitly stated, is to guarantee the liberty of the people, while opening up the road to empire and to glorious military undertakings for the great. This would result in a divided republic consisting of, on the one hand, inward-looking liberty-lovers, and, on the other, expansive and outward-looking glory-seekers. These two groups, or humors, are obviously opposite, and they correspond neatly to the republic's two ends as well as to the two ideological vocabularies, outlined above.

Since Machiavelli, as a true partisan of the mixed regime, refuses to side with either of the two categories, his republicanism cannot easily be characterized as either popular or elitist. On the one hand, throughout the *Discourses*, he describes the people, or the plebs, as gullible and easily deceived and the nobles as shrewd and cunning (cf. Mansfield 1996: 85, 94–5, 247). But, far from condemning the elite's manipulation of the populace's religious beliefs for political ends, Machiavelli praises it and even exhorts his contemporaries to revive it, as he puts it, by reinterpreting Christianity "according to virtue" (*D.* II.2). He contrasts the Roman Senate, which, according to him, "always judged things as they should be judged and always took the less bad policy for the better" (*D.* I.38), to the rash, undisciplined, and imprudent elites of modern Florence. But, on the other hand, it could be argued, Machiavelli endorses an aggressive and ferocious form of popular republicanism in which the general populace, acting as "the guardians of liberty," controls the elites by often harsh and brutal methods. According to Machiavelli, the nobility is in need of this check because of its inherent and unquenchable desire to dominate and its propensity for corruption, while the people are singularly suited for patrolling the nobility because of their love of liberty and their hatred of being dominated (*D.* I.3–5; McCormick 2001).

To solve this equation, we need to complicate Machiavelli's constitutional design further by adding a third category of men who, strictly speaking, can be assigned neither to the few nor to the many. Viewed from this third, additional or external, standpoint, the great and the people are remarkably similar. Exclusively focused on one, and only one, of the republic's two ends, they are both too self-absorbed to perceive anything beyond their own immediate concerns, and too fiercely partisan to care about the common good of the republic. Contemplated from this point of view, both parties reveal themselves as single-minded, self-interested, short-sighted, and one-dimensional. Their struggle for hegemony allows no compromises, and their inability to see the bigger picture causes them to define the republic exclusively in terms of liberty or empire respectively.

In Machiavelli's theory, the function of balancing these two potentially destabilizing forces and keeping them in check is assigned to a category of men whom the Florentine thinker alternately describes as prudent (*prudenti*) or wise (*savi*). As a rule, these rare individuals belong to the great, but they can also be found among the people. Refusing to view prudence as a class distinction, Machiavelli implies that the good and the prudent among the nobles should *use* the people—and their desire not to be dominated—against the bad nobles, the oligarchs whose desire to dominate poses a constant threat to the liberty of the republic.

Playing the one order against the other—the people against the nobles and vice versa—the prudent few, it could be argued, are the only part of the republic that act in the interest of the whole. While the task of the people is to safeguard the liberty of the republic, and that of the great to promote its expansion and growth, neither of these elements can be entrusted with the responsibility of the common good of the republic, since they are incapable of transcending their particular interests and their limited points of view. Nor can any of these orders be expected to act in the interest of justice, the cardinal virtue of classical republicanism, since justice can be reduced neither to liberty nor to empire. Justice, it could be argued, is a more complex quality than liberty and empire, and requires a dual or multidimensional perspective of which neither of these short-sighted and one-eyed parties is capable. If it is true, as I would like to suggest, that justice in the Machiavellian republic results from a proper balancing of the twin principles of empire and liberty, the interests of the great and the people, this balancing act is the unique competence of the prudent few. From an ill-defined position partly inside, and partly outside, the constitution, they oversee and administer the republic's precarious equilibrium so that the great and the people can continue to play their blinkered parts in its whole-hearted and uncompromising pursuit of the dual ends of empire and liberty.

Machiavelli's republican theory, of which we here have presented a generalized and far from exhaustive outline, was not only inspired by, but also intended to be applied to, Florentine political culture of the day. Within the Florentine context, Machiavelli's mixed constitution translated into a reinforcement of the executive power of the Gonfaloniere of Justice, the titular head of the republic, the introduction of a Senate, or a restricted council, consisting of 65 citizens elected for life, and the reopening of the Great Council, the ruling body of 3,000 citizens with control over finances, taxation, and elections, that had been instituted in 1494 under Savonarola's influence, but closed by the Medici upon their return to the city in 1512 (1997–2005: i. 733–45). The role Machiavelli envisages for his *prudenti* recalls that of the Florentine power elite, who convened in the so-called *consulte* and *pratiche*, to give their *parere*, or informed opinion, on matters of policy. The notion of *savi*, or wise men, he derives directly from Florentine political discourse, and, while he on more than one occasion speaks disparagingly of "the wise men of our city [*i savi della nostra città*]," and "the wise of our times [*savi de' nostri tempi*]," these comments should not be seen as a rejection of the function *per se*, but as a critique of how it was performed in contemporary Florence (Hörnqvist 2004: 108–10). It could also be argued that the role of the prudent man was one that Machiavelli himself played, or aspired to play, on his diplomatic missions, when he, in violation of protocol, ventured to offer the authorities back home direct, or indirect, advice on policy and intelligence matters.

Machiavelli's radically realistic view of politics in combination with his theory's close connection to contemporary Florentine conditions raises some important questions concerning his omissions and distortions. While it goes without saying that Machiavelli's work offers many sharp insights into the complex workings of Florentine Renaissance society, it should be equally clear that it simultaneously ignores or obfuscates certain aspects of it. Most importantly, Machiavelli's theoretical works (albeit not his chancery writings) seem next to oblivious to the ways in which economic factors structure society and contribute to social and political change. This is all the more surprising, since Florence at the beginning of the sixteenth century had for well over a century been a thriving proto-capitalist society, taking its income from banking, commerce, cloth-manufacturing, and other crafts. If there was a Florentine imperialism to speak of at the time, it was economic and cultural in character, not political or military. While Florentine artists and humanists spread their classicizing and vividly realistic styles across Italy and beyond, Florentine merchants were busy establishing important trading colonies in the major market cities of Europe, including Bruges and Lyons. The Florentine gold florin, which during the period served as an international monetary standard, carried the Florentine lily all over the Mediterranean and deep into the barbaric recesses of transalpine Europe. Florentine political discourse did not ignore these developments. The new, pragmatic mentality of this mercantile community is evident from the so-called *ricordi* of Florentine merchants and bankers (Bec 1967). Most Florentine humanists also embraced the ethics of the active life, centered on public service and the pursuit of worldly goods. They regarded commerce and private wealth as useful to the republic and supported a social order within which material prosperity was a prerequisite to family dignity, individual reputation, and office-holding (Baron 1988: ii, p. xxx; Jurdjevic 2001). In this regard, the civic humanists were more atuned with the socio-economic realities of Renaissance Florence than Machiavelli. The republic that they celebrated and he deplored was made up of merchants, bankers, and other guildsmen, focused on creating private wealth and business opportunities, and not of toga-clad Roman patricians and battle-scarred legionnaires, nursing dreams of ancient glory and greatness. As subsequent developments were to prove, Machiavelli's republican theory was ideally suited to organize and give cohesion to these economic impulses and expansionist aims. But, since the former Secretary, because of his Roman and classicizing bias, insisted on conceptualizing his republic in terms of honor, virtue, conquest, and glory, instead of free trade, enlightened self-interest, and accumulation of wealth, it could provide only a formal framework for this new politico-economic order, not its content.

If the economy in general, and the emergence of capitalist society in particular, are missing components in Machiavelli's political theory, Thomas More's *Utopia* forces these issues upon us with a vengeance. Begun in 1515, during More's stay in Bruges, as commissioned envoy for the Merchant Adventurers of London, shippers of cloth to Flanders, *Utopia* precociously comments on the effects of early capitalist exploitation in England. Wool trade had from the beginning of the High Middle Ages established strong economic ties between England, Flanders, and northern Italy. The luxurious pastures of the British Isles produced high-quality wool that was either shipped to Flanders or taken straight to Florence, where at the beginning of the fourteenth century some 30,000 workers were engaged in the manufacturing of colored cloths and fine woolen textiles. With wool trade and cloth-making followed divisions of labor, luxury markets, craft guild regulations, government-imposed quality controls and custom dues, staple ports, technical developments triggered by the prospect of increased profit, foreign competition, and the concentration of great wealth in the hands of a few—in short, capitalism.

The publication history and the circumanstances surrounding *Utopia* are highly complex and central to our understanding of the work. Even though this is not the place to give a full account of all these details, some background information is necessary for our subsequent discussion. Written in Latin and first published in 1516 in Louvain under Erasmus's editorial supervision, *Utopia* consists of two distinct books. Book I, often referred to as "the dialogue of counsel," relates a meeting in Antwerp between Thomas More (Morus), his friend Peter Giles, and a charismatic stranger, named Raphael Hythloday, who has traveled with Amerigo Vespucci to the New World, and recently returned from an extended stay at the imaginary island of Utopia. During their discussion, Raphael denounces the hierarchical and capitalist European society in general and the English enclosure movement—the process of fencing off and privatizing common land for sheep farming and the consequent eviction of tenant farmers from their homesteads—in particular. Book II contains Raphael's account of Utopian society and its social, political, and religious customs, based on common property and outward conformity with social norms. It ends with a brief exchange between him and Morus, in which the latter expresses qualified appreciation of the Utopians' communal way of living, while doubting its applicability to European conditions and deploring its lack of "nobility, magnificence, splendor, and majesty" (*U.* 84).[3]

It is generally believed that More wrote *Utopia* in two phases. While book II was composed during his mission to Flanders in May 1515, one assumes, based on a comment made by Erasmus in a letter of 1519, that book I was added later, probably after More's return to England (Sylvester 1977: 293). If this is so, Utopia originated as a free-standing monologue on Utopian society that was later, following the conventions of the humanist dialogue, placed within a narrative frame. Matters are further complicated by the fact that in the second authorized and revised edition of the work, printed by John Froben of Basle in 1518, More's text is accompanied by a collection of letters from humanist friends and personal acquaintances of More's, who, in commenting on the discovery of Utopia, sustain the fiction that we here are dealing with a real, and not an imaginary, people (Marius 1984: 241–2).

The scholarly literature on Utopia is sharply divided between those who identify Thomas More's own position on communism, private property, and political counsel with that of the fictitious Morus, his alter ego (Allen 1976; Sylvester 1977; Skinner 2002: ii. 213–44), and those who associate his deeper convictions with the views of the visionary Raphael (Hexter 1952; Greenblatt 1980; Wootton 2003). Any attempt at interpreting *Utopia* is forced to confront this issue. The aim of the following discussion is in part to contribute to this debate, in part to present a cross reading of More's *Utopia* and Machiavelli's theoretical works that will allow the two authors to comment on each other. This approach will enable us to expand on Morus's critique in *Utopia* of Raphael's utopian mode of thinking, and to expose the inherent limitations of Machiavellian realism. However, before we can open up this dialogue between Machiavelli and More, we need to establish some common ground.

---

[3] References to More's *Utopia* are given in abbreviated form as *U.* followed by page number.

There are some striking similarities and differences between the Machiavellian republic and the Utopian society that Hythloday portrays in *Utopia*. Perhaps the greatest contrast concerns their views of conflict. While Machiavelli regards conflict as constitutive, potentially devastating, but beneficial if managed correctly, the Utopians have gone to extreme lengths to abolish conflicts altogether. Their extremism in this regard reflects Raphael's own position in the exchange with Morus and Giles in book I. The Utopians' attempt to "root up the seeds of ambition and faction at home, along with most other vices," making themselves immune from internal strife (*U.* 84), is thus replicated in Raphael's declared desire to "destroy vices" (*U.* 16–17) and to "root out . . . the seeds of evil and corruption" (*U.* 20) in contemporary European rulers. As we will see, this relentless quest for social unity, harmony, and purity comes at a considerable price.

But there are also a number of intriguing similarities that unite Machiavelli's republic and the Utopians. The latter are thus a proud, sovereign, and autonomous people, who recognize no overlord and have a strong sense of their own superiority. With an unbroken tradition that goes back to the founding by King Utopus 1,760 years ago, they have known neither emperor nor pope. Their foundation can also be analyzed according to the principles laid down by Machiavelli. The Utopian authorities have a well-established monopoly of legitimate violence, and the state is militarily strong enough to withstand any attack from outside. Utopians are committed to the principle of rule of law, and their laws, which make no distinction between high and low, are, like those of Machiavelli, based on the assumption that men are wicked by nature and need to be restrained and castigated (cf. *U.* 36). Moreover, the Utopians have realized that religion needs to be placed under the control of the temporal authorities. Although their solution differs significantly from that of Machiavelli, the underlying principle is the same. While the Utopians show extreme tolerance toward religious beliefs as long as they express themselves in ways that do not challenge the civil authorities, incite to violence, contradict reason, or oppose Utopian customs and way of life (*U.* 74), they hold sacred the belief in divine providence and the immortality of the soul (*U.* 50, 74–5). Those who deny these doctrines are excommunicated and lose their status as citizens. The reason for this strong stance, we are told, is that the Utopians believe that someone who has "nothing to fear but the law, and no hope of life beyond the grave, will do anything he can to evade his country's laws by craft or break them by violence, in order to gratify his own private greed" (*U.* 75). The belief in the immortality of the soul is thus officially endorsed, not because it is held to be true beyond doubt, but because it is deemed politically and socially useful. Finally, it could be argued that in More's *Utopia* custom has acquired a foundational role similar to the one envisaged by Machiavelli's in his treatment of the Roman republic.

Perhaps, these similarities should not come as a surprise to us, since both Machiavelli and More, in typical humanist fashion, draw inspiration from ancient models, and the Roman republic in particular. While the Roman connection, of course, is openly acknowledged in Machiavelli, it is less evident in *Utopia*. However, it is clearly stated that, "some twelve hundred years ago," a group of shipwrecked Romans and Egyptians were hospitably received by the Utopians, who acquired from them, directly or indirectly, "every single useful art of the Roman civilization" (*U.* 30). These Roman visitors belonged to the imperial era, but the imprint they left on Utopian society seems to have had more to do with the austere mœurs and virtuous ideals of old Republican Rome, nostalgically remembered by Sallust, Livy, and other Roman writers of the late republic. The Utopian combined policy of amassing great public wealth and restricting private property could be interpreted as part of this legacy. Utopian warfare, which, like its Roman counterpart, is ostensibly defensive but effectively imperialist, leans heavily on Cicero's theory of the just war for its legitimacy. Although the Utopians, in traditional Roman fashion, speak of their allies as *socii* and *amici* (*U.* 64),[4] they show no more respect for their rights than for those of the other states. In this regard, they resemble not only the ancient Romans but the Machiavellian republic as well.

However, the correspondence between the Utopian polity and the Machiavellian republic that we have begun to establish seems to be called into question by the stance that Raphael in his critique of contemporary European society in book I takes on arms, laws, and religion. Objecting to the draconian English laws against theft and the imperialist designs of European kings, he evokes the principle of non-violence and God's holy law against killing. Denouncing positive laws, which, since they can be twisted and turned at the will of the ruler, are said to be worth little more than the paper on which they are written, he endorses the inflexible standards of justice. Condemning the craftiness of contemporary preachers and the willingness of the Church to accommodate Christ's teaching to the sinful ways of men, he embraces a rigorous form of Christianity that takes the sacred imperatives seriously and holds us to the uncompromising standard of Christ. A direct implication of this argument is to challenge the secular state's self-proclaimed right to use force, to define law, and to regulate religion according to its own interest and without being held accountable to a higher authority—be it God or natural law.

From what we have seen, Raphael's radical critique seems to implicate not only contemporary European rulers and their Machiavellian policies, but the Utopians as well. But this is not Raphael's intention at all. On the contrary, he holds up the Utopians for European princes to emulate, attributing to them his own radical views. The Utopians are accordingly described as peace-loving, committed to the principle of brotherhood of man, and opposed to the noxious maxims of power politics. The reason they have so little regard for treatises between states, we are told, is because they believe that "men are united more firmly by good will than by pacts, by their hearts than by their words" (*U.* 66). Raphael also emphasizes the fact that the Utopians have very few laws and that those they have are so clear and so simply worded that they can easily be understood and interpreted by each and everyone, even by the most simple-minded (*U.* 28; cf. *U.* 63–4). Utopian legal procedure does not involve contested evidence, but is only a matter of establishing plain truth (*U.* 63). The Utopians can maintain their straightforward relation to law and truth, because they have abolished private property

---

[4] "Hos Utopiani populos, quibus qui imperent ab ipsis petuntur, appellant *socios*, caeteros quos beneficijs auxerunt *amicos* uocant."

and, with it, the greed and the factions that are "the destruction of all justice" (*U.* 64). Because they live according to natural law, the distinction between positive law and justice has little meaning to the Utopians. Of course, they are not Christians, and, having never encountered Christian priests, the Utopians have not received the sacraments. Yet, they have from the very beginning been "well disposed" toward Christianity for the simple reason that it is "very like the religion already prevailing among them" (*U.* 73). In fact, not only is the Utopian manner of living compatible with Christian ideals; it also comes closer to fulfilling them than contemporary European ways. If people were not so blinded by pride, Raphael claims, but were alive to their own "true interest," and let themselves be led by the example, wisdom, and goodness of Christ, they would not hesitate to adopt Utopian laws (*U.* 84). If we are to believe Raphael, then, Utopian society is founded not on a monoply of arms, positive laws, and the subordination of religion to secular authorities, but on love of peace, the principle of justice, and true Christian values.

As George Logan (1989) has observed in a perceptive study, book I of *Utopia* is to an extraordinarily high degree centered on the traditional rhetorical topic of *honestas* and *utilitas*, the honorable and the expedient, the moral and the useful. In this debate, Raphael consistently contends that the honorable and the expedient are not only compatible or closely related, but basically identical. He thus condemns the English policy of authorizing capital punishment for theft as both unjust (against divine law), and inexpedient (contrary to public welfare) (*U.* 9, 13–14). He flatly rejects Morus's view that princes should be guided by indirect advice, partly because it involves lying, partly because it is impractical and would not work (*U.* 26–7). A king who keeps the people poor and suppressed, we are informed, is acting not only dishonorably but also against his own interest (*U.* 24). As Logan concludes: "The truly expedient policy in all these cases is one that is consistent with the dictates of morality and religion. We get the strong impression that Hythloday would say the same about any issue" (1989: 15–16). In a letter to his friend Erasmus of October 1516, More identifies this rigid, principle-based position with that of the academic philosopher: "You know how these philosophers regard their own decisions as immutable laws; I suppose from a love of consistency" (1961: 78). We re-encounter this view in *Utopia*, where Morus is made to object in similar terms to Raphael's radical and uncompromising dedication to principle: "This academic philosophy is quite agreeable in the private conversation of close friends, but in the councils of kings, where grave matters are being authoritatively decided, there is no place for it" (*U.* 25).

At a first glance, the Utopians seem indeed to confirm Raphael's contention that the honorable and the useful coincide. It could even be argued that this doctrine is the guiding principle of most, if not all, of their policies, laws, and customs. Thus, Utopians prefer to take their meals in common dining halls, not because it is forbidden to eat at home, but because it is thought both improper and inconvenient. They practice euthanasia for the incurably sick, we are told, in part because their priests consider it a holy and pious act, in part because the sick, who can no longer fulfill any of life's duties, have become "a burden to [themselves] and to others" (*U.* 60). The doctrine is restated in Raphael's praise for the Utopian institutions, which, he claims, are at one and the same time *prudentissima atque sanctissima*—most prudent *and* most holy (Logan 1989: 20). It is reiterated in his concluding claim that both our true interest and Christian goodness urge us to uproot pride, abolish private property, and adopt Utopian laws (*U.* 84).

But, if we turn to consider what the Utopians actually do, an altogether different picture emerges. In book I, Raphael had condemned the English class system for allowing "a great many noblemen" to "live idly like drones, off the labors of others" (*U.* 10), and for punishing by death the poor who steal for survival. This policy does not only set aside "God's laws against killing" (*U.* 15), but is also against equity, since there can be "no proportion or relation at all" between "killing a man and taking a coin from him" (*U.* 15). According to Raphael, the Utopians have found a more just way of distributing property and of punishing offenders. But, as we will see, this argument turns back on itself.

The Utopians have no need for capital punishment for theft, since they have banned private property. Instead they use forced labor as their favored method of punishing criminals. They call their convicts slaves, and treat them as their communal property, keeping them fettered and constantly at work (*U.* 59). The convict slave system and trading in slaves (*U.* 59) is an integrated part of Utopian society, and it could be argued that, without it, ordinary Utopians would not be able to maintain their privileged existence of leisure and material comfort. The presence of convict slaves in the midst of Utopian communal life, we are told, serves the purpose of imprinting the severity of the laws upon the minds of the Utopians. To ensure respect for the laws, recidivists are punished severely, as a rule by the death penalty (*U.* 62). Adulterers, for example, are punished with "the strictest form of slavery," and, if they repeat their offense, they are put to death (*U.* 62; cf. *U.* 45, 61). While the Utopians are consistent in their uncompromising approach to social unity, there exists a blatant, but in Raphael's account unacknowledged, discrepancy between their treatment of slaves and their professed humanitarianism. The institution of slavery, and the Utopians' use of slaves to perform brutalizing tasks—like hunting and the slaughtering of animals (which they believe "destroys the sense of compassion, which is the finest sentiment of which our human nature is capable" (*U.* 42)), fly in the face of their claim to care for their "fellow-creature's comfort and welfare," and to follow nature, which "cherishes alike all those living beings to whom she has granted the same form" (*U.* 51). It could be argued that, by treating their own, former citizens and captured prisoners of war like subhumans, the Utopians have deprived themselves of that very humanity of which they pride themselves, and which, on their own account, is "the virtue most proper to human beings" (*U.* 51). It may also be claimed that institutionalized slavery has a brutalizing effect upon Utopian society as a whole that makes mockery of their policy of assigning demeaning and dehumanizing tasks to their slaves (*U.* 42, 54). If slaves rebel against their condition, we are informed, they are tracked down and put instantly to death, "like savage beasts which neither bars nor chains can tame." Here, we may wonder who is the more human, the slaves who seek to regain their liberty, or the Utopians who, for the sake of social order and harmony, slay them like dogs.

A similar point could be made with regard to the Utopian practice of warfare. In book I, Raphael had proclaimed that "one never has war unless one chooses it," and that peace is "always more to be considered than war" (U. 12). In this connection, he objects to the use of hired mercenaries (U. 11) and condemns European princes for their desire to "acquire new kingdoms by hook or by crook," instead of concentrating on "governing well those they already have" (U. 8). He denounces the French for their "intricate strategies of war" (U. 21) and their disregard for peace treatises. He expresses disgust over the lawyer, who at Morton's argues that unoccupied soldiers should be particularly cherished for their boldness and nobility of spirit, which are necessary for the strength of the English army (U. 11).

For Raphael, the Utopians offer a healthy contrast to this warmongering. Devoting their lives to the pursuit of good and honest pleasures (U. 50), they "despise war as an activity fit only for beasts," and view military glory as utterly despicable (U. 66). They are also aware of the fact that "common people do not go to war of their own accord, but are driven to it by the madness of their rulers" (U. 68). Luckily, the Utopians have strong natural defenses (U. 31) that should enable them to live in peace unthreatened by their neighbors. However, as we have already seen, the Utopians are themselves guilty of exactly the same policies that Raphael in book I condemns in the French and other Europeans. Frequently, if not constantly, they engage in wars on behalf of their friends and allies that they could have avoided if they had so wanted. For, although Raphael claims that they never take up arms other than "for good reasons," it soon becomes clear that such reasons are not hard to come by. They include liberating their neighbors from tyranny and servitude, protecting them from danger, and avenging their prior injuries. The Utopians, we are told, do this "out of sympathy," but it is not far-fetched to assume that this neighborly concern also has something to do with the fact that these countries are in the habit of inviting the Utopians to rule over them (U. 64). Perhaps the fact that the Utopians themselves own, or occupy, huge amount of real estate in neighboring countries influences this policy as well. Be this as it may, it is certain that the Utopians' willingness to go to war does not end here. Their "good reasons" for taking up arms also include incidents involving merchants from neighboring countries, who have "been subjected to extortion in another country, either through laws unfair in themselves or through the perversion of good laws." On such spurious, not to say ridiculous, grounds, the Utopians recently stirred up a war that resulted in some "prosperous nations" being "ruined completely" (U. 66). The Utopians' resourcefulness in finding pretexts for military inventions brings to mind Erasmus's view that discussions of whether wars are just or not are pointless, since every state finds its own cause to be just, and there was never a lack of pretexts for going to war (Hale 1985: 36).

The Utopians also use the enormous wealth they have amassed from their wars to hire mercenaries, whom they pay lavishly and employ in order to avoid putting their own citizens at risk (U. 46). Their preferred recruits are the Zapoletes, a people whom they find so "disgusting and vicious" that mankind as a whole would be far better off if they were "exterminated from the face of the earth" (*U.* 69). Yet the Utopians have no qualms about using these subhuman beasts to exterminate and enslave those among their neighbors who dare to oppose them. Nor are the Utopians second to the French when it comes to devising clever strategies of war. Their conduct of war includes the stirring up of internal strife among the enemy, the assination of enemy leaders, the enslavement of *all* prisoners of war, the seizing of enemy land, the exacting of unforgiving vengeance on those who have wronged them (*U.* 67), and the refusal to distinguish between combatants and civilians, placing whole families in the line of battle, with the result that "the hand-to-hand fighting is apt to be long and bitter, ending only when everyone is dead" (*U.* 70). Convinced of the superiority of their own institutions and ways of life, the Utopians have set out to eliminate war by eliminating their enemies and dominating their neighbors so utterly that they cease posing a threat to them.

Slavery, war, and, more surprisingly, class are aspects of Utopian society that contradicts Raphael's rosy account of their communal way of life. In book I, Raphael describes contemporary English society as a conspiracy of the rich, dominated by "a handful of men," who "end up sharing the whole thing," while "the rest are left in poverty." The result is a divided society, in which "the rich are rapacious, wicked, and useless, while the poor are unassuming, modest men who work hard, more for the benefit of the public than of themselves" (*U.* 28). Raphael's egalitarian pathos notwithstanding, it could be argued that we in Utopia also encounter two categories of men, who are distinct enough to constitute two classes. On the one hand, there are the ordinary Utopians, who devote six hours a day to manual labor and enjoy long hours of closely supervised spare time. On the other hand, there is the Utopian elite, which Raphael passes over so briefly that a host of later scholars have been tempted to define Utopia as a classless society. But, as More in his own correspondence made abundantly clear, the Utopians are governed by a small and exclusive elite of very learned men. This ruling class is largely made up of persons who "from childhood have given evidence of unusual intelligence and devotion to learning" (*U.* 49) and, on "the recommendation of the priests and through a secret vote of the syphogrants [elected officals representing thirty families]," have been selected for a life of learning, completely freed from manual labor. From this scholarly caste, Raphael remarks in passing, are "chosen ambassadors, priests, tranibors, and the prince himself" (*U.* 39). The numbers of priest are kept low, in part to prevent their esteemed office from being "cheapened by numbers," in part because the Utopians—suddenly not so egalitarian—believe that it would be "hard to find many men qualified for a dignity to which merely ordinary virtues could never raise them" (*U.* 79). Although it is not altogether clear, we may also assume that it is from this intellectual elite that the Utopians choose their so-called Financial Factors, the officials who are sent out into the occupied territories to manage the vast estates that Utopia has procured there. These estate managers live "in great style and conduct themselves like great personages," while amassing a steady stream of rental income, which as a rule is brought directly into the public treasury (*U.* 72). Of course, this is in stark contrast to the moral doctrine of Utopian communism and modesty, according to which gold and silver are marks of disgrace. Indeed, at this point one may wonder whether this policy is not part of an overall strategy of institutionalized hypocrisy designed to "root up the seeds of ambition and faction at home" (*U*. 84). In any case, three different strategies for quenching or redirecting pride seem to be at work in Utopian society: one for the vicious and unruly (enslavement); one for ordinary citizens (communism and fear of shaming and enslavement); and one for the elite (esteem and hope of foreign posting). Perhaps we are allowed to glimpse the Utopian ruling class's secret design, when Raphael in book I, unwittingly, argues that a king who wishes to rule securely should "leave his subjects as little as possible, because his own safety depends on keeping them from growing insolent with wealth and freedom. For riches and liberty make men less patient to endure harsh and unjust commands, whereas meager poverty blunts their spirits, makes them patient, and grinds out of the oppressed the lofty spirit of rebellion" (*U*. 23–4).

Wealth, freedom, and insolence are indeed rare commodities in Utopia, while patience, injustice, and oppression there are aplenty.

A clearly distinguishable pattern is emerging here. It should now be clear that Raphael in book I, for whatever reason, is not merely levying criticism against contemporary rulers but also offering an elaborate and extremely studied point by point denunciation of Utopian practices. Of course, this is completely at odds with the fact that Raphael simultaneously holds up the Utopians, whom he later in book II extolls as an ideal that is supposed to remedy these tendencies. These observations allow us to return to our comparison of More and Machiavelli.

We have now unearthed three distinct positions on the relation between morality and politics. The first is that of Raphael, who subsumes the expedient under the honorable, arguing that the moral is also always the useful. Then, we have the reverse view that Rapheal indirectly attributes to the Utopian elites, which holds the useful and the expedient to be identical to the moral and the honorable. The Utopians' reluctance to recognize a moral good outside or independent of their own laws, political system, or way of life has the effect of short-circuiting any criticism that could be directed against them. Or, put differently, since *honestas* has been co-opted to Utopian *utilitas*, and been reduced to a mere wrapping of its self-interested actions and institutions, it cannot serve as a check on Utopian practices and policies. Here we are here faced with the intellectual cost of the unity and conformity pursued by Utopian society, the monstrous ideology that equates the honorable and the expedient, *honestas* and *utilitas*.

This second position has often been associated with Machiavellianism and with Machiavelli's own writings. But this is a vulgar and reductionist reading. For, in contrast to More's Raphael and the Utopians, who from opposite sides claim the identity of *honestas* and *utilitas*, Machiavelli's realism involves a tragic awareness of the fact that the two principles, though both valid, are irreducible, and, at a fundamental level, perhaps even irreconcilable. Often at odds with each other, they place conflicting demands on us that we cannot easily ignore and between which we must frequently negotiate. It is only the naive (Raphael) and the cynical (the Utopian elite) who fail to admit the irreconcilable nature of this conflict. This third, Machiavellian, position, which I also take to be that of Thomas More, the author of *Utopia*, holds that the expedient ignore the honorable at their own peril. Since a reputation for *honestas* and having a good and reliable character, or *ethos*, contribute to one's utility, it is in one's self-interest to maintain this reputation. The prudential Machiavellian reading shows that *utilitas*, unchecked and carried to its extreme, becomes self-defeating and not *utilitas* at all. True self-interest, self-interest well understood, to use Tocqueville's expression, requires that we use *honestas*, not to guide our actions and policies, but to moderate them. The Machiavellian prince is advised not to turn his back on morality, but to observe the virtues when possible and to "enter into evil" only when necessity requires that such a course be followed (*P.* 15). The moral standard—whether defined in terms of divine and natural law, or, more humanely, as the mœurs of the people and the ways of the land—continues to serve as the framework within which self-interested policies are pursued. Against this background, and as Machiavelli's treatment of the ancient Roman republic makes clear, it is of utmost importance to encourage, main-tain, and protect the moral standard of the citizenry. It also suggest that morality should not be viewed as an abstract principle, existing above or beyond society, but as an embodied opinion or customary practice embedded in society at large. This, I take it, is also acknowledged by Thomas More, when in the dialogue of counsel he has Morus, his alter ego, argue that perfectly good institutions are unattainable, since they require perfectly good men, and that instead one should "go through with the drama in hand as best one can, and not spoil it all simply because one happens to think another one would be better" (*U.* 26).

While Machiavelli's theory failed to accommodate and account for the changing economic realities, More was equally oblivious to the potential impact of scientific and technological developments. Utopian society is fundamentally archaic. There is no, or little, mention of scientific experiments and technological advances, which just a century later we encounter so prominently in Francis Bacon's *The New Atlantis* (1627). But, even though More's intention was not to portray an ideal commonwealth, as has all too often been claimed, he was to be outdone by his own fiction. By imagining that things could be radically different, economically and politically, and by suggesting that society could be rationally planned and socially engineered, *Utopia* opened up a new chapter in the history of political thought. Utopian thinking, which dares to think the "impossible," contains an implied, if not always intended, critique of Machiavellian realism and its obsession or fixation with the "probable" and the "possible." Since, from historical experience, we know that what was once deemed impossible has often proved very possible indeed, the utopian mode has an important role to play in a constantly evolving social reality. At the same time as it teaches us that Machiavellian realism needs to be complemented, it forces a new type of casuistry upon us. For from now on we have to distinguish not only between the possible and the impossible, but also between the ficticiously impossible, conditioned by historical circumstances, mental dispositions, and levels of economic, technological, and social developments, and the real impossibilities that are inscribed in human nature, natural law, and the overall working of reality. As the social and political experiments of the past century amply demonstrate, this is not a question of mere academic interest, but one that involves consideration of vital importance to the future of mankind.

REFERENCES

ALLEN, W. S. (1976). "The Tone of More's Farewell to Utopia: A Reply to J. H. Hexter," *Moreana*, 51: 108–18.

BARON, H. (1966). *The Crisis of the Early Italian Renaissance: Civic Humanism and Republican Liberty in an Age of Classicism and Tyranny*. Princeton: Princeton University Press.

BARON, H. (1988). *In Search of Florentine Civic Humanism: Essays on the Transition from Medieval to Modern Thought*. 2 vols. Princeton: Princeton University Press.

BEC, C. (1967). *Les Marchands écrivains, affaires et humanisme à Florence, 1375–1434*. Paris: Mouton.

GREENBLATT, S. (1980). *Renaissance Self-Fashioning*. Chicago: University of Chicago Press.

HALE, J. R. (1985). *War and Society in Renaissance Europe 1450–1620*. London: Fontana.

HANKINS, J. (2000) (ed.). *Renaissance Civic Humanism: Reappraisals and Reflections*. Cambridge: Cambridge University Press.

HEXTER, J. H. (1952). *More's* Utopia: *The Biography of an Idea*. Princeton: Princeton University Press.

HÖRNQVIST, M. (2000). "The Two Myths of Civic Humanism," in J. Hankins (ed.), *Renaissance Civic Humanism: Reappraisals and Reflections*. Cambridge: Cambridge University Press, 2000, 105–42.

HÖRNQVIST, M. (2002). "Perché non si usa allegare i Romani: Machiavelli and the Florentine Militia of 1506," *Renaissance Quarterly*, 55: 148–91.

HÖRNQVIST, M. (2004). *Machiavelli and Empire*. Cambridge: Cambridge University Press.

JURDJEVIC, M. (2001). "Virtue, Commerce, and the Enduring Florentine Republican Moment: Reintegrating Italy into the Atlantic Republican Tradition," *Journal of the History of Ideas*, 62: 721–43.

LOGAN, G. M. (1989). "The Argument of Utopia," in J. C. Olin (ed.), *Interpreting Thomas More's* Utopia. New York: Fordham University Press, 7–35.

McCORMICK, J. P. (2001). "Machiavellian Democracy: Controlling Elites with Ferocious Populism," *American Political Science Review*, 95: 297–313.

MACHIAVELLI, N. (1997–2005). *Opere*, (ed.) C. Vivanti. 3 vols. Turin: Einaudi.

MANSFIELD, H. C. (1996). *Machiavelli's Virtue*. Chicago: University of Chicago Press.

MARIUS, R. (1984). *Thomas More: A Biography*. New York: Knopf.

MORE, T. (1961). *Selected Letters*, (ed.) E. F. Rogers. New Haven: Yale University Press.

MORE, T. (1992). *Utopia: A Revised Translation, Backgrounds, Criticism*. New York: Norton.

NIETZSCHE, F. (1989). *Beyond Good and Evil: Prelude to a Philosophy of the Future* [1886], trans. W. Kaufmann. New York: Vintage.

POCOCK, J. G. A. (2003). *The Machiavellian Moment: Florentine Political Thought and the Atlantic Republican Tradition* [1975]. Princeton: Princeton University Press.

SKINNER, Q. (1978). *The Foundations of Modern Political Thought*. 2 vols. Cambridge: Cambridge University Press.

SKINNER, Q. (2002). *Visions of Politics*. 3 vols. Cambridge: Cambridge University Press.

SYLVESTER, R. S. (1977). "'Si Hythlodaeo Credimus': Vision and Revision in Thomas More's *Utopia*," in R. S. Sylvester and G. P. Marc'hadour (eds), *Essential Articles for the Study of Thomas More*. Hamden, CN: Archon Books.

WOOTTON, D. (2003). "Friendship Portrayed: A New Account of Utopia [1998]," in J. J. Martin (ed.), *The Renaissance: Italy and Abroad*. London: Routledge, 253–75.

CHAPTER 14

....

POLITICAL THOUGHT IN THE AGE OF THE REFORMATION

....

MICHAEL BAYLOR

THE REFORMATION CONTEXT

....

GEOFFREY Elton once suggested that significant political thinking occurs only when there are significant upheavals (Elton 1962: 458–9). The Reformation was certainly one such upheaval. A Latin Christian religious and ecclesiastical tradition that had endured for more than a thousand years shattered; in the space of a single generation (c.1520–50), evangelical reformers advanced a variety of new views about needed changes not only in the Christian Church but also in social and political life. This chapter makes no attempt to provide a comprehensive survey of what the reformers at the time termed secular or civil authority, what we would term the state. Rather, its focus is the political thought of the Protestant reformers, both those thinkers historians commonly refer to as moderate or "magisterial" reformers (especially Martin Luther, John Calvin, and Huldrych Zwingli) and those they refer to as "radical" reformers, a distinction that is discussed below.

Despite the many disagreements that divided the evangelical reformers, they were united in their absolute rejection of the authority of the traditional Roman Church. The reformers regarded the papacy as a perfidious if not diabolical institution and they repudiated not only the authority of the pope as head to the universal Church but also the canon law of the Church and the authority of the bishops and their episcopal courts. In this rejection, they broke with a basic assumption of medieval political theory: that God had established two institutional authorities to govern Christian life, the spiritual authority of the Roman Church and the temporal authority of the Roman

Empire. Medieval thinkers debated the issue of whether these two universal institutions were independent of one another, or, as papal theorists insisted, whether secular authority was inferior and subordinate to the higher authority of the Church. The Protestant reformers, however, broke decisively with this traditional view, and the result was a much more recognizably modern form of political theory. Although the political concerns of Protestantism remained profoundly religious, and most reformers retained in various guises the view that authority was bipartite, the political theory of the reformers was modern in its concentration on secular authority and the essential character, function, and scope of the state's power. In this sense, they made at least an indirect contribution to the modern idea of the state as an omnipotent power (Skinner 1978: ii. 352).

About civil authority there was much disagreement, even contradiction, among various Reformation thinkers. A fundamental cause for the reformers' diversity was the inherently ambiguous character of the state itself, as these Christian thinkers reflected on it. They were agreed, virtually without exception, that secular authority was divinely created; yet there was also something profoundly unchristian about it. The great symbol of temporal government was the sword. The sword represented the fearful power of violent physical coercion, at its extreme limit, the authority to execute. Disagreements arose over the issue of how Christians should relate to such an institution.

The diversity of Reformation political thought also emerged over the issue of whether secular authorities should play a positive, even a leading role in the renewal of Christianity to which Protestant reformers were committed. A number of leading reformers—Luther, Zwingli, Calvin, and their followers—took the view that, since the traditional church was corrupt and taught a false faith, temporal rulers, the magistrates, were the agents God had ordained to bring about religious reforms and a revitalization of Christian society. Without state direction and control, lawless disorder threatened. Hence, only those reforms should be instituted that the temporal authorities approved. Without their sanction, even pressing reforms must be postponed. Other reformers, those historians usually describe as radical—although in the emergent Reformation the categories magisterial and radical were fluid—had a less positive view of the state's role. The radicals took the view that secular authority, no less than ecclesiastical authority, was questionable and that the magistrates might well be part of the corruption and failure in Christendom that required reform. Hence, many radicals favored direct action from below: there should be no tarrying for the magistrate; devout individuals and local congregations should immediately institute needed Reformation, regardless of the will of their rulers. The conflict between magisterial reformers and radicals was an uneven one. Where the Protestant Reformation triumphed, moderate reformers enjoyed the support of the state and suppressed their radical opposition. But the dispute between the two produced the most important contrasts in the political thought of the Reformation.

The political environment in which the Reformation occurred obviously contributed to the divergence in the reformers' political thought. Some princes and some city councils opposed the reform movement and sought to repress it; others tolerated it but were cautious and hesitant about granting it their support; and still others came to support it enthusiastically for various reasons. In the mid-1520s, when there was still little official support, a massive popular insurrection, known as the German Peasants' War and partly inspired by the Reformation, produced a variety of challenging new political ideas. Its repression fundamentally altered the course of the Reformation and produced new divisions not only between magisterial and radical reformers but also amongst the surviving radicals.

THE MAGISTERIAL REFORMERS

Martin Luther, like Protestant reformers generally and like their medieval predecessors, regarded secular authority as instituted by God, despite its associations with coercion and repression. The key biblical passage he and others cited to support this view was the opening verses of the thirteenth chapter of St Paul's Letter to the Romans: "Let every soul be subject unto the higher powers. For there is no power but of God: the powers that be are ordained of God. Whosoever therefore resisteth the power, resisteth the ordinance of God: and they that resist shall receive to themselves damnation" (Rom. 13:1–2). This text the reformers commonly interpreted in both a general and a specific sense. Not only did God create the realm of secular authority in general and bind all to obedience to it; the actually existing rulers—the specific individuals currently holding office and exercising this authority—God had providentially ordained to fulfill the offices he had established. Another key text Protestant thinkers cited to support the divine foundation of the state was 1 Peter 2:13–14: "Be subject to every kind of human order, whether it be to the king as the foremost or governors as sent by him, as a vengeance on the wicked and a reward to the just." Both passages emphasized two things: the divinely ordained character of the state; and the supreme importance of obedience to it. John Calvin, for example, insisted that magistrates held a commission from God and were endowed with divine authority; in fact, they represented God and acted in his place (Höpfl 1991: 51).

For Luther, Calvin, and most Protestant thinkers, however, the view that God had established temporal government was qualified in an interesting and paradoxical way. In their view, the state was not part of God's original creation but resulted from Original Sin. Real Christians, all who truly believe in Christ and belong to God's kingdom, have no need of the secular sword and law. The notion that real Christians stand above politics led Luther to formulate an odd Christian utopianism: "And if all the world were true Christians, that is, if everyone truly believed, there would be neither need nor use for princes, kings, lords, the Sword or law ... Where all wrongs are endured willingly and what is right is done freely, there is no place for quarreling, disputes, courts, punishments, laws or the Sword" (Höpfl 1991: 9). In a truly Christian society, the state would indeed wither away. Luther realized, of course, the impossibility of this perfect world. But the other side of this utopianism was the conviction that God has established the state and its apparatus of coercion and repression because of unjust and wicked people. The state, in short, is bound up in a double negative: it is a punishment for human sin whose function it is to repress and punish further sin.

Luther developed this position by invoking his famous doctrine of the "two kingdoms," a modification of St Augustine's doctrine of the two cities. As he articulated this doctrine in his important 1523 tract, *On Secular Authority, how far does the Obedience owed to it extend?*:

> we must divide Adam's children, all mankind, into two parts: the first belong to the kingdom of God, the second to the kingdom of the world. All who truly believe in Christ belong to God's kingdom . . . Christ came in order to begin the kingdom of God and to establish it in the world.

Second, "all those who are not Christians belong to the kingdom of the world or are under the law. There are few who believe . . . and for the rest God has established another government outside the Christian estate and the kingdom of God and has cast them into subjection to the Sword" (Höpfl 1991: 8–10). The essential purpose of the secular state, then, is to restrain the evil impulses of humanity. Again following St Augustine, Luther compared the laws of the state to the chains that bind a savage, wild animal so that it cannot bite or tear, as its nature prompts it. Since the world as a whole is evil, and "scarcely one human being in a thousand is a true Christian," without the state and its coercive institutions, "people would devour each other and no one would be able to support his wife and children, feed himself and serve God. The world would become a desert." Given the sinfulness of humanity, it is only the state that prevents human life from collapsing into the anarchy of the jungle, where the strong do what they will and the weak suffer what they must, a condition later political thinkers, such as Hobbes, described as the state of nature.

The upshot, in the view of Luther—but also of Calvin and many other Protestant thinkers—is that "God has ordained two governments, the spiritual which fashions true Christians and just persons through the Holy Spirit under Christ, and the secular or worldly government which holds the unchristian and wicked in check and forces them to keep the peace outwardly and be still, like it or not." Calvin characteristically framed the issue with greater clarity: "there are two governments to which mankind is subject," one ruling over the soul and pertaining to eternal life, the other concerned with establishing "merely civil and external justice, a justice in conduct" (Höpfl 1991: 47). Protestants of every variety, of course, insisted that Christ headed the government pertaining to eternal life, not the pope.

Worldly government's essential purpose, then, is negative. Through the fear which its laws and coercive powers produce in the wicked and the unjust, some semblance of social peace and justice can be maintained, even if this is only a pale reflection of the true harmony and fellowship to be found in the kingdom of God. As Luther once put it, secular authorities are "God's jailors and hangmen," whom "divine wrath uses to punish the wicked and maintain outward peace." Well might Luther have agreed with Joseph de Maistre that the executioner is the cornerstone of society. An important consequence of this view of secular government's key purpose was that government need not be Christian to be effective or legitimate. Government's restraining function could be carried out effectively by a pagan or Muslim government.

Luther cautioned against the view that, because the society in which he lived, Christendom, was mostly peopled by nominal, baptized Christians, the law and the sword could be dispensed with. Real Christians are a tiny minority, and evil-doers, under the cover of their nominal Christianity, would simply take advantage of their freedom. The result of trying to rule the world according to the Gospel would be to unleash the beasts "and let them maul and tear everyone to pieces" while claiming to be Christians and subject to no secular laws. For Calvin, like Luther, the Gospel promises liberty only for the kingdom of God: "spiritual liberty and civil servitude can stand very well together." And Calvin, too, held that the desire to abolish the political order, regardless of its form, was the aim of "madmen and savages."

Calvin's political thought, far more than Luther's, took up the issue of the best form of government. Luther, a subject of the elector of Saxony, seems to have simply regarded hereditary monarchy as the given form of government and did not concern himself with the matter further, except to remark that no ruler should wage war against an overlord, be it a king, emperor, or any other liege-lord. Luther's conception of princely government was also patriarchal and paternal—the prince's power was modeled on that of the father of the household; the prince is the "father" of his territory; and, just as the male head of household was, in theory, the public face of the domestic sphere, so the authority of the prince should not transgress the domestic rights of the father in the family. Luther was aware, of course, that cities were ruled by elected councils but seems to have regarded these as naturally subservient to the monarchical authority of the prince or emperor who ruled over them. Calvin, more influenced by classical political theory, gave the question of the best form of government more attention, but began by taking a position against the utopian speculation of a thinker like Thomas More—it was not the business of private individuals to debate the "best state of a commonwealth"; they had no right to do this. But, having said this, he went on to assert that, in his view, an aristocracy was the best form, either a "pure" aristocracy or a "mixed" one, compounded with democratic elements—which Calvin referred to as a "polity" (see Höpfl 1991: 56–7). However, Calvin allowed that his opinion about the best government was due not to the form itself, but to the difficulty monarchs had controlling themselves. In fact, he admitted that, on the evidence of Scripture, God had especially commended the governmental form least palatable to mankind, "namely power exercised by one man" or monarchy. But, given the dangers of monarchy, rooted in the defects of human nature, Calvin thought it safer that several persons rule jointly. God had instituted among the Israelites an "aristocracy bordering on democracy" until the coming of King David, who was an image of Christ. This mixed aristocracy, for Calvin, was the best form for insuring a durable government and for reconciling civil liberty and magisterial restraint.

Regardless of its form, for mainstream Protestant theologians, secular government was an inherently ambivalent institution, one divinely instituted to maintain peace and order in the world, but one that served this purpose through fear and violence. This ambivalence confronted Protestant thinkers with questions to which various thinkers responded in different ways. Two issues loomed especially large. Could Christians participate in a government whose functions were so contrary to Christian moral values? Second, what kind of obedience did Christians owe a state that they themselves did not really need?

The magisterial reformers without exception, including Luther, Calvin, and Zwingli, but also such reputed radicals as Balthasar Hubmaier, argued that it was possible for Christians to participate in secular government and serve as magistrates. For them, nonetheless, scriptural passages such as Matthew 5:34 ff., in which Christ urged his followers not to go to law or to take up arms, presented an especially acute difficulty. This was because Protestants rejected the traditional medieval distinction between universally binding ethical injunctions, moral laws that all were to observe under pain of sin, and "counsels of perfection," moral teachings reserved only for the clergy, especially the monastic clergy pursuing a heroic life of Christian perfection. If the highest Christian ethical principles of non-violence and forgiveness applied to all, how could Christians participate in government, performing the functions required of a judge, a soldier, or an executioner?

Magisterial reformers solved this problem by resorting, again, to the distinction between the kingdom of God and the kingdom of the world, and by insisting on the value of Christian duty. Only the kingdom of God was a realm of love and forgiveness, without need of laws and force. The Christian belongs to this realm—but also lives in the world. While on earth, the Christian lives for and serves the neighbor, performing actions that are of no personal benefit but that the neighbor needs. In service to their neighbors, Christians may faithfully execute the duties of any office they hold. Most Protestant theologians, of course, found abundant biblical precedents for this position—not only the kings of the Old Testament but such New Testament figures as the Ethiopian eunuch (Acts 8:27 ff.), a captain whom the evangelist Philip converted, baptized, and then allowed to retain his office and return home. Two key conditions were important in the role of Christians as agents of the state. First, they had to have been properly installed in their office—either through election, hereditary descent, and coronation, or by being called to office by God in some other way. And, second, they must act as rulers or agents of the state with the right motivation or intention—that is, they must never act out of selfish personal motives, for example, from a desire for riches, power, or glory. They must impersonally fulfill the obligations of their office out of a desire to be of service to their neighbors. The general principle was that, since the secular state serves divine purposes, everything that government needs or does to fulfill its functions is also a service to God, including acting as lawyer, judge, or hangman.

In this way, according to Luther, Christians live a truly paradoxical life, both in the kingdom of God and in the secular world: "you both suffer evil and injustice and yet punish them; you do not resist evil and yet you resist it." The paradox here is analogous and directly related to Luther's famous paradox of Christian freedom, which he formulated in his widely read 1520 tract *The Freedom of a Christian*: "A Christian is a perfectly free lord of all, subject to none. A Christian is a perfectly dutiful servant of all, subject to all" (Luther 2002: xxx. 344). For Luther, freedom from the law and from being ruled by others was found in the realm of the spirit and the kingdom of God; on earth and in the kingdom of the world, servitude and duty prevailed. This restricted "spiritual" view of Christian freedom, espoused by Luther and Calvin, was one that, as we shall see, some Protestant thinkers came vigorously to contest.

For Calvin, the issue of a Christian's participation in government posed less of a problem. For him, the key principle to keep in mind was that, when magistrates inflict punishments, it was not their own act but only the carrying-out of God's judgment. In order to avenge the harm that evil-doers have done, God has given the sword to the secular authorities, his ministers, to carry out divine judgments. In Calvin's view, as long as this viewpoint was borne in mind, no scruple of conscience should arise for Christian magistrates in performing their duties. Insofar as the magisterial reformers made the "selfless" intention of Christian magistrates crucial to their ability to perform their function, they contributed not only to the omnipotent character of the modern state but also to its impersonal character.

The second key issue that the magisterial reformers had to take up was the extent of the obligation that Christians, as subjects or citizens, owed to obey the state. These reformers generally insisted that, even though Christians did not need secular government themselves, they were obliged to submit themselves to the government of the state that had legitimate authority over them. That is, for the sake of serving and supporting their neighbors and a state God had ordained to maintain the peace and order of the community, Christians were obliged to obey the state's laws, to pay its taxes, to honor those in authority, and so on. The Christian is subservient to secular authority, not because he needs its protection, but because others do. If Christians did not submit to civil authority, it would give a bad example to non-Christians, suggesting that they too need not obey the law. In order to fulfill the injunctions of Matt. 5:34 ff., for example, Luther insisted that Christians could not make use of the law courts in order to seek vengeance or their own private gain—rather, they were to suffer evil when it came to their own person or private interests. But they could go to law if it was done out of love and for the sake of their neighbors, a differentiating criterion that he also acknowledged as difficult to fulfill.

Calvin was especially insistent on the duty of all subjects to obey the commands of the magistrate. Subjects, he argued, were to revere magistrates as God's representatives and were to obey them not simply out of fear but because, in obeying them, they were obeying, in effect, God himself. The obverse was also the case: in resisting the magistrates whom God had ordained to rule, subjects were also resisting God. By way of an exception, Calvin granted that some subjects who are also office-holders, lesser magistrates whom a superior authority has commissioned to carry out supervisory functions, might have the right to resist or correct those above them. Calvin cited the Ephors of ancient Sparta and the Tribunes of the Roman republic as examples of such lesser magistrates (Höpfl 1991: 82–3). In general, no reformer was more insistent than Calvin on the absolute obligation to obey the voice of the magistrate as though it were the voice of God. However, Calvin's followers in France, the Netherlands, Britain, and elsewhere subsequently used his theory of the right of inferior magistrates to resist tyranny as the foundation for political theories that justified revolution against centralizing monarchies.

The magisterial reformers established one crucial exception to the obligation that Christians had to obey the laws of the secular state. This exception was when the state commanded something that transgressed its proper sphere of competence and violated divine law. Luther, for example, in his important tract *On Secular Authority*, set out the principle that the civil authorities had competence over all "external" affairs—that is, all that concerned the body, external behavior, property, public reputation, and other physical and public matters. The secular state had no authority when it came to spiritual matters, meaning those that pertain to people's souls and mind. Here, God alone has authority. Belief is a matter for the individual's conscience and cannot be compelled. In this way, Luther acknowledged the validity of the folk saying "thought is free" (*Die Gedanken sind frei*). Like Luther, Calvin asserted that, if those in authority commanded anything that violated God's will, such commands were to be set aside and ignored. Also like Luther, Calvin cited Peter in Acts 5:29 as a proof-text supporting the position that, when secular laws violated divine law, one was to obey God rather than man.

In general, however, Calvin, like Luther, insisted on the absolute duty of subjects or citizens to obey those whom God had placed in authority over them. Both these magisterial reformers took the view that, since God was responsible for placing magistrates in the offices they exercised, subjects had to suffer and passively endure even the actions of a ruthless, tyrannical government. The magisterial reformers took the view that God has ordained those who govern unjustly and intemperately for a specific purpose—to punish the iniquity of the people. Hence, subjects who suffer under a tyrannical government must endure the hardship as something that God has imposed on them for their sinfulness. As long as the actions of an unjust or arbitrary government inflicted harm that pertained to "external" matters, the Christian subject was obligated to obey, not resist. Luther and Calvin did take the position, however, that should secular rulers command something that violated divine law, Christians were not to comply with the command. But these leading Protestant reformers rejected any violent resistance to the state. At most, Christians were to disobey unlawful edicts— that is, to engage in passive resistance—and then accept willingly the consequences of their disobedience. The Sermon on the Mount, requiring Christians not to resist evil, entailed an acceptance, not of violations of divine law, but of the punishments that evil secular rulers inflicted on subjects for their disobedience.

What Luther and the other mainstream Protestant leaders were not willing to continence was violent resistance or rebellion. Physical opposition to God's ordained authorities was never justifiable. For Luther, deeply imbued with an Augustinian pessimism about human nature and the fragility of social peace, there was no imaginable crime worse than rebellion. He invariably saw political revolt as inspired by the devil and viewed those who engaged in "sedition" as worthy of capital punishment. In fact, in his famous 1525 tract condemning the rebellious German peasants, *Against the Robbing and Murdering Hordes of the Peasants*, he declared that rebels merited the death penalty three times over—for their blasphemy against God for engaging in rebellion against his ordained rulers, for their violent sedition in taking up arms against the secular authorities to whom they had sworn their obedience and in committing various crimes of robbery and murder, and, third, for cloaking their sins in the Gospel (Luther 2002: xlvi. 49–51). In Luther's view, "there is no evil deed on earth that compares with [rebellion]. Other wicked deeds are single acts; rebellion is a flood of all wickedness." Commoners who engage in rebellion "have become faithless, perjured, disobedient, rebellious murderers, robbers, and blasphemers, whom even a heathen ruler has the right and authority to punish" (Luther 2002: xlvi. 52). To embark on physical resistance against tyrannical rulers, for Luther, was to unleash social chaos and universal lawlessness. He went further—those who express sympathy for those suffering merciless punishments that rulers impose on rebels are also guilty of the rebellion and merit the same punishment.

Nevertheless, the political thought of Luther, like that of Calvin, came to contain an element that legitimized more than passive resistance or civil disobedience. In 1531, following the demand of Emperor Charles V and the Catholic estates of the Empire that the evangelical princes and cities return to the Roman faith, and the evangelicals' formation of the League of Schmalkalden to resist this demand, Luther modified his position on resistance. His tract *Dr Martin Luther's Warning to his Dear German People* offered no new scripturally based argument for opposing the emperor. But Luther now allowed that—speaking hypothetically—if war came, he would not reprove those who took to arms against the emperor and his allies; they were acting in self-defense (Luther 2002: xlvii. 19–20). Luther's notion was that defensive action to protect the Gospel was not insurrection. In this way, the political thought of Luther as well as Calvin contained elements that provided their followers, when threatened, with a justification for armed resistance against tyranny.

The magisterial reformers are defined not only by their hostility to active resistance against the state but also by their view that secular government is the institution to authorize and direct changes in public religious life. This view entailed that temporal rulers must play a positive as well as a negative role in the Reformation. That is, in addition to maintaining public order, which benefits the Church, secular government is the ordained agency for institutionalizing and protecting the transformation of Christendom that the reformers sought. On this subject, a wide measure of difference developed between Zwingli and Calvin, on the one hand, and Luther on the other. The difference may have been due, in large part, to the differing political environments in which they were active. The leading magisterial reformers in the Reformed tradition—Zwingli in Zurich and Calvin in Geneva—operated in small, independent urban centers that were republics in their constitutional form—that is, elected city councils ran public affairs. Luther, by contrast, was active in a large territorial principality ruled by a hereditary monarchy. The elector of Saxony's court was remote and the degree of his support for Luther's cause dependent on the piety of the individual who held office.

At the outset of the Reformation, in the early 1520s, Huldrych Zwingli, the leading reformer in the Swiss city of Zurich, developed a vision of Reformation that afforded the secular authorities a much more positive role than did Luther in Saxony. Already in Zwingli's *Sixty-Seven Theses* (1523), which he had formulated to defend the emergent Reformation in Zurich in a public debate with a representative of the bishop of Constance, Zwingli had set out a much more positive role for secular government in bringing about religious change than Luther was willing to allow in his tract *On Temporal Authority* of the same year. Zwingli's political thought began with the twin assertions (theses 34 and 35) that, although the pretensions of the spiritual authorities—that is, the Roman Church—had no basis in Christ's teachings, the authority and control of the secular power are based on the teaching and actions of Christ (Zwingli 1984: i. 243–8). This meant (thesis 36) that all the rights that the Church claimed in fact belonged to the secular authorities, provided they were Christian rulers. Zwingli, in short, made the Christian state the agency responsible for authorizing and overseeing changes in ecclesiastical affairs. The clergy might inform, even pressure, secular authorities about the specific changes that they needed to institute, but no alteration should be undertaken without the approval of the secular government. Zwingli also argued that all the laws of the state should be in accordance with God's will. According to Zwingli (thesis 42), if the temporal authorities were unfaithful and failed to rule according to divine law, transgressing the boundaries set by Christ, they could be deposed. Zwingli's position, which he summarized by asserting that the best state is ruled by God's will alone and the worst is ruled arbitrarily, had much influence among the radical reformers and the common people.

Calvin, like Zwingli, insisted that the purpose of the state is more than the establishment of justice in external matters, although this was the sphere to which he had limited it at the outset of his discussion. He defined the purpose of civil government in this way: "to foster and protect the external worship of God, to defend pure doctrine and the good condition of the church . . . to mold our conduct to civil justice, and to uphold and defend the common peace and tranquility" (Höpfl 1991: 49). Hence, Calvin gave the civil authority a dual function—to uphold "a public form of religion among Christians" and "humanity among men"—and, unlike Luther's more restricted and negative account of politics, Calvin maintained that an essential function of the state is to promote the Church. Calvin argued that not only scripture but also pagan writers held that no polity can be well constituted unless it made the duties owed to God its first priority. Hence, it would be an absurdity to have laws regarding only the well-being of men and not what is owed to God.

Luther, saddled with his doctrine of the two kingdoms, was inconsistent on the issue of the positive role of the state in religious reforms. On the one hand, he argued that its legitimate sphere of activity had nothing to do with spiritual affairs. On the other, from early on he opposed making changes of which the princes disapproved. Later, he came to the position that princes should care for the churches in their territories and institute needed reforms. In fact, Luther's position on this issue fluctuated depending on whether a specific ruler sympathized with or opposed the reforms he advocated. Hence, when Duke George of Saxony called on his subjects to hand over Luther's translation of the New Testament, Luther held that the prince had transgressed his sphere of competence and his subjects should ignore this edict because it violated divine law. But when Elector John of Saxony supported the Reformation, Luther claimed that the prince could institute changes by acting as an "emergency bishop." A few years later, he held that a prince's highest and most sacred duty was to reform the Church in his principality.

   The political thought of the magisterial reformers suffered, then, from a basic inconsistency, although this was less so for Zwingli than for Luther and Calvin. The latter two taught that secular government was properly limited to the realm of the physical and the public. Yet they also wanted secular authorities to support and institute the changes in religious life that they advocated. They held that the secular rulers, ordained by God, were the proper agents for institutionalizing Reformation and denied that subjects or private citizens had any right, either individually or collectively, not only to engage in active resistance but also to introduce religious reforms that the rulers disapproved.

The Radical Reformers

Already in the early 1520s, some evangelical leaders began to insist that autonomous Christian congregations and communities had the authority to institute the changes they saw fit, regardless of whether they had the approval of the secular authorities or not. The issue first arose in Luther's absence at Wittenberg, when Luther's university colleague Andreas Bodenstein of Karlstadt, and Luther's monastic brother Gabriel Zwilling, began to institute a sweeping series of changes—in the liturgy, vestments, communion elements, clerical celibacy, urban charity, and civic morality. The Saxon elector, Frederick the Wise, disapproved of the changes, some of which disregarded his explicit instructions. Luther quickly opposed this unauthorized form of Reformation— it was, he claimed, too fast for those of weak conscience and it transformed the freedom of the Gospel into a new law. Behind these objections was his wish not to contravene the will of his prince. Karlstadt, however, and other radical reformers as well, asserted that needed changes should be instituted immediately, without waiting for those who were not yet ready to accept them. Karlstadt saw Luther's concern for the consciences of the hesitant as a red herring, as was the claim that institutionalizing reform transformed Christian liberty into a new law. The real issue behind these disagreements concerned the role of the state as the authorizing agency of ecclesiastical reform. Those Reformation evangelicals that historians conventionally term "radical" reformers called for a locally based Reformation, one in which zealous individuals or small groups of the devout would bring about necessary reforms, without tarrying for the weak or the approval of the magistrates. Shortly after the Wittenberg disagreement, a similar division opened among evangelical reformers in Zurich. Some of Zwingli's followers from rural villages in territory belonging to Zurich stopped paying tithes. Zwingli supported the Zurich city council when it forbad tithe refusal and ordered that those who practiced it be punished.

Wittenberg and Zurich were not isolated cases. In the early 1520s, as the Reformation swept the German-speaking lands, Christian groups in various places began to institute changes regardless of whether those in authority approved or not. This broad and diverse revivalist movement quickly fused with social and economic grievances, often of long standing, and culminated in the German Peasants' War (1524–6), the most massive popular rebellion in European history prior to the French Revolution. Marked by a bitter anti-clericalism and a fervent apocalypticism, the grass-roots evangelical movement assumed, contrary to the magisterial reformers, that the Gospel contained principles for the collective life of Christians that included autonomy and freedom. Various local Christian groups adopted principles that Peter Blickle has termed a "communal Reformation" (Blickle 1992). Fundamental to this reform movement was the view that each community or congregation had the rights to select, install, and if necessary discharge its own pastor. Second, it had the right to take charge of its own economic life, to use its tithes to sustain its pastor, take care of its poor, and otherwise to determine its economic needs. Concealed within these principles was the view that each congregation had the right to determine Christian truth for itself. For the commoners, one fundamental truth was that all Christians were free and serfdom must be abolished. The peasants included these demands for personal freedom and community control in the Twelve Articles, the most widespread program of the popular insurrection (Baylor 1991: 231–8). In addition, if all were free, then all were also in this sense equal. There were occasions in the early 1520s when Luther appeared to support such principles. In 1523, he penned a tract entitled *That a Christian Assembly or Congregation has the Right and Power to Judge All Teaching and to Call, Appoint, and Dismiss Teachers, Established and Proven by Scripture* (Luther 2002: xxxix: 305–14). In his work of the same year, *On Secular Authority*, Luther also asserted that among Christians there should be no superiors, that "each is equally subject to all the rest." But by 1524–5 Luther backed away from these communal and egalitarian principles.

He rejected them, in part, because some reformers had come to call into question the legitimacy of the secular authorities. Thomas Müntzer—an erstwhile associate of Luther who became a rival and penetrating critic—reversed Luther's interpretation of Paul's Letter to the Romans, arguing that Paul's injunctions to obey worldly authority in Rom. 13:1–2 was contingent on their doing the duties laid out for them in verses 3–4. Müntzer was not alone in stressing the duties of rulers. Zwingli, too, insisted that magistrates must fulfill their duty to rule as Christians. Müntzer, however, took the contingent character of princely rule a step further. In his famous *Sermon to the Princes* he argued on the basis of Daniel 7 that, while the princes were the ordained means for defending good Christians from the godless, should they fail to perform this essential duty, the sword would be taken away from them. Here was a justification for revolution and an inchoate doctrine of popular sovereignty: God ordained secular government to serve the needs of the people; if those holding office failed in their duty, their power reverted to the people, who had the right to depose them. With the outbreak of the German Peasants' War, Müntzer identified himself with the rebellious commoners and argued that the rule of the existing temporal authorities had become so oppressive and contrary to Christian norms that the commoners had the right to take power from them and establish their own political order.

In his Confession, part of which was extorted under torture, Müntzer revealed that in the course of his travels to southwestern Germany in late 1524 and early 1525, he preached to the rebellious peasants and formulated "articles on how one should rule according to the gospel." It is unclear how these articles are related to a document later found in the papers of Balthasar Hubmaier in Waldshut, and known to us only in a summary version composed by an opponent. The document, commonly termed a Constitutional Draft (see Scott and Scribner 1991: 264–5), advised the commoners of each territory to come together and create a *Bund*—variously translated as a covenant, federation, union, or league. The Draft went on to insist that, because the rulers were oppressing and exploiting the common people, they needed to create their own political "order" according to the word of God. To do this, they should first invite the existing rulers to join their *Bund*. If the rulers refused, the commoners should take the sword from them and give it to new rulers, whom they would elect. The Draft also specified that, if the newly chosen rulers did not carry out the will of the people, they should be deposed and new elections take place. If those deposed sought revenge on their electors, the deposed ruler should suffer a "secular ban"—a worldly counterpart to ecclesiastical excommunication, the ban amounted to a boycott in which the affected person would be ostracized and cut off from all social and economic contact with the members of the Bund. The Draft, finally, asserted that, if the secular ban was ineffective in restraining a deposed leader, the *Bund* was to use military force to protect itself.

This Constitutional Draft, in short, laid out the framework for a new political order that adumbrated, in however vague and incomplete its formulation, a number of political ideas that anticipated modern constitutional notions. One was the doctrine of popular sovereignty, here expressed in a distinctively religious form—God has ordained secular government to serve the needs of the people; if it fails to fulfill its function, power reverts to the people, who have the right to choose new leaders. Second, the sovereignty of the people is expressed institutionally in the *Bund*, an assembly of insurgents that evidently would have to become representative (for example, through delegations from local communes, villages, and towns). Third, the Draft expressed an important elective principle, the notion that the common people had the right to determine their own leaders through elections. In particular, the Draft specified that the popular assembly should nominate twelve individuals and from them elect one as their ruler. Last, the Draft expressed the ideal of civic equality by explicitly asserting that political leaders should be nominated for election without regard to nobility or rank. In this way, the Constitutional Draft went beyond the magisterial reformers' denial that the clergy constituted a separate estate in society; it challenged the assumption that the nobles constituted a divinely ordained estate of secular rulers. The Draft frequently referred to Christian "brotherhood" or fraternity. This affective bond of unity was based on a notion of civic equality that transcended a conception of society based on social estates.

The political principles set out in the Constitutional Draft did not remain theoretical. During the course of the German Peasants' War, to take one example, rebels from the region around the imperial city of Memmingen formulated a Federal Constitution (*Bundesordnung*). It incorporated the essential principles of the Constitutional Draft in a document declaring the formation of a Christian union and association designed to increase brotherly love and to make sure that the spiritual and temporal authorities acted according to divine law. Leading Reformation theologians and preachers were named in the conclusion as competent to determine the substance of divine law. The federation defined itself as the representative of the territorial community (*Landschaft*) and called for peace and unity within its borders. The Federal Constitution did not call for a transformation in property relations or an end to a society of estates, but it did call for the nobility, who were not included in the union's membership, to submit themselves to the federation by agreeing not to use their castles as bases of opposition and by releasing their vassals from oaths. Vassals and servants should join the association and, if they refused to do so, they should leave the territory. The constitution treated cloisters in the same way as castles and called for all pastors and vicars to preach only the Gospel. Those who refused and who did not live moderately should be discharged. All agreements with the existing authorities should have the approval of "the common territorial community of this association." The union, as the representative assembly of the common people, claimed the right to veto any treaty or agreement the authorities might conclude.

When the rebelling peasants of the Black Forest sent this constitution or a similar document to the town of Villingen, near Freiburg im Breigau, and called for the town to enter their brotherhood or federation, they appended a set of articles specifying the punishment for refusing to join them. This Letter of Articles (*Artikelbrief*) detailed the terms of the "secular ban" the rebels would impose. The ban amounted to a total boycott; the peasants would have absolutely nothing to do with anyone who would not join the association—either associating with them or engaging in any economic activity with them. They immediately imposed this ban on all castles, cloisters, and ecclesiastical foundations and on anyone who supported the enemies of the association.

It is difficult to know to what extent the example of the Swiss influenced the political thought of the rebellious peasants and religious radicals of the German Peasants' War. There are reasons for thinking this influence was considerable. The revolt of 1524–6 was centered in southern Germany, especially the southwest and in close geographical proximity to the Swiss Confederation. The Swiss certainly presented the foremost example from the late Middle Ages of rural subjects who successfully resisted feudal lords by coming together and swearing an oath to become members of a regional association or federation. In 1499, the Habsburgs sought militarily to reassert their authority but were decisively defeated in the Swiss War. In the mid-1520s the aim of the commoners of the Black Forest, Swabia, and elsewhere was to "turn Swiss"—that is, to establish new regional political associations of commoners on the model of the Swiss (Brady 1985).

Perhaps the most important theoretical tract supporting the cause of the rebellious peasants explicitly invoked the Swiss example. This was the pamphlet *To the Assembly of the Common Peasantry*, published anonymously in Nuremberg in May 1525, and perhaps written by Christoph Schappeler, the Memmingen cleric who also helped compose the Twelve Articles (see Baylor 1991: 101–29). The pamphlet's title page featured the motto: "What increases the Swiss? The greed of the lords!" The work's political theory also showed the importance of the Swiss model. The tract argued that the unlimited, tyrannical power of the nobility and the authorities had produced the Swiss confederation and it advocated the superiority of republican, elective government over hereditary, monarchical rule, which was inherently inclined toward arbitrary and abusive tyranny. The work invoked the examples of both the ancient Jews and the Romans to show how a people prospered under a republic but declined with the coming of hereditary lordship.

The tract went on to develop a political theory that justified revolution. It asserted that the existing lords and rulers acted only to increase their own riches and power, and not to serve the true aims of Christian government, brotherhood, and the common good. The rulers' subjects have the right to depose them because they are ruling in a false and unlimited fashion. The subjects should replace the evil rulers with a communal or republican government, in which those who exercise power hold their offices through elections. Martin Luther's view that the Gospel is unrelated to temporal power was explicitly rejected, as was his claim that, because God had ordained the temporal authorities, their power may not be questioned. "On the peak of what monk's cowl is it written? Indeed, their [= the lords'] authority is from God, but so remotely that they have become the devil's soldiers and Satan is their captain." In a far-reaching break with traditional assumptions, the tract's author also called for an end to an estate-based conception of society and political authority: "If you now set up a tailor, shoemaker or peasant as your authority, to lead you faithfully in all brotherly loyalty and to maintain Christian brotherhood, that person should be regarded as a king or emperor and given all obedience."

The justification for revolution was a distinctively Christian one and based on the process by which the swift transformation in government should occur. The assumption was that an association of Christians should depose their rulers by simply disregarding the existing rulers' claim to authority; then, having elected their own replacements, the Christian brotherhood should prepare to fight a defensive war when the old rulers sought to regain the power they had lost. In this way, the enemies of the Christian union could not charge it with instigating violence. The violence it engaged in would be purely defensive. The treatise concluded by calling for the commoners, who had set aside their lords, to maintain solidarity with one another, their only hope of success. At its conclusion, the work again invoked the example of the Swiss, whose military success against their enemies the author ascribed to divine providence—but more immediately to their motivation: they triumphed when they fought for themselves, their country, their families, and to protect themselves from arrogant power.

It was among the thinkers of the Radical Reformation, then, that Reformation political thought broke decisively with several basic medieval and early modern assumptions about politics. Radicals like the authors of the Letter of Articles and the tract *To the Assembly of the Common Peasantry* rejected the assumption of a society based on social estates, each having its own privileges and immunities. In the name of Christian brotherhood, they envisioned a social order in which not only the special legal rights of the clergy would be eliminated—implied in Luther's theology but, in the last analysis, not fully realized—but also those of the nobility. The Letter went so far as to call on the nobility and the clergy to abandon their castles and cloisters and "live in normal houses like other pious people." These radical thinkers called for a society based on the notion that all Christians should enjoy the same rights and all should shoulder the same obligations to promote the common good. Given the early modern period's deeply engrained assumptions that the existing rulers were ordained by God and that, no matter how corrupt and wicked they were, subjects were passively to suffer their depredations and regard them as a just punishment imposed on society, the radicals' legitimation of revolution was remarkable.

Radical Reformers after
the Peasants' War

In the aftermath of the defeat of the commoners' rebellion of the German Peasants' War—decided militarily in a series of battles that crushed peasant bands in May 1525, but only stamped out finally in Alpine regions in 1526—the Reformation's radical evangelicals faced new challenges. No doubt, many insurgents abandoned their cause, accepting the defeat as evidence their cause lacked divine approval and had been inspired by the devil. Balthasar Hubmaier, for example, penned a treatment of secular politics, *On the Sword* (1527), that differed little from the view of Luther. Others attempted to come to terms with the defeat in ways that preserved the values and ideals of their communal Reformation. These thinkers developed the political thought of the Reformation in two new directions, both of which staked out positions even more radical than those taken by the programs of the rebellion. The two were not mutually exclusive. One was to call for a new kind of church that broke with a basic assumption of Christendom, the view that Church and society were essentially coterminous. The vehicle that these radicals used to articulate their innovative conception of the Church was the rejection of infant baptism. The baptism of infants, practiced since the age of the Emperor Constantine, was a ritual through which entry into the Church and birth into the society were conjoined. The radicals who rejected infant baptism and whom their enemies smeared as "Anabaptists" (re-baptizers) argued that the baptism of infants was non-scriptural and that this sacrament should be reserved for adults who had undergone a conversion experience and freely decided to join the Church. Anabaptists thus advocated a voluntaristic, "free church" that was distinct from the larger ecclesiastical and civil society. Rulers everywhere were quick to see those who practiced adult or believer's baptism as dissenters who threatened civic order and compliance with the laws of the state. And indeed Anabaptists did characteristically view the secular authorities, not as ordained by God but as inspired by the devil. They attempted to sever all connection to the state, rejecting loyalty oaths, going to court, the obligation to perform military service, and other demands of the cities and states in which they lived. Although the majority of those who advocated adult baptism were morally upright, practiced non-violence, and paid taxes, they represented a potential for subversion. An age that regarded uniformity of faith as the best guarantee of social peace was not willing to tolerate them, and so they suffered terrible persecution. The violence of the Anabaptists who seized control of the Westphalian city of Münster (1534–5) confirmed for most Catholic and Protestant rulers the need to persecute them ruthlessly. Thereafter, most Anabaptist groups rejected the sword altogether as a violation of Christian ethics and advocated non-violent resistance to state power. Small congregations of dissenting Anabaptists could hope to survive only by finding a noble patron and protector, someone willing to allow them to live in peace on his lands, or by dropping out of society, going underground, and surviving as a secret grouping, a separatist cell in the larger society.

The second direction that the radical political thought of the Reformation took in the aftermath of the Peasants' War was also foreshadowed by developments during the insurrection itself. This was a radicalization of the social gospel, with its egalitarian and communal values, toward ending private property. In his Confession, Thomas Müntzer asserted "*omnia sunt communia*"—all things should be in common—and distributed according to the needs of the people. It is unclear, however, whether he held this view or his captors imposed it on him. In any case, following the insurrection, some radical groups came both to advocate and to practice community of property. Foremost among the advocates was the author of a pamphlet *On the New Transformation of Christian Living* (1527), commonly ascribed to Hans Hergot, a Nuremberg printer and colporteur, who was executed for distributing the tract (see Baylor 1991: 210–25). The work both absolved the peasants of responsibility for the upheaval and called for a new society that would consist only of agricultural communities—cities would be done away with, as would the castles of the nobility and the cloisters of the clergy. God would unite all people in a single flock, ruled by "one shepherd," and "everything that grows on the land belongs to the church and the people who live there. Everything is bestowed for common use, so that people will eat from one pot, drink from one vessel, and obey one man insofar as it is necessary for the honor of God and the common good." The author's utopian vision was one in which social equality extended beyond the dissolution of a society of estates to economic equality—the ideal of modest sufficiency for all—achieved by redistributing property and ending both poverty and great wealth.

The leading practitioners of such communitarian ideals, those who developed Christian communism into a practical and pragmatic utopian society, were the Anabaptist followers of Jakob Hutter. The Hutterites first established themselves in Moravia in the late 1530s, under tolerant aristocrats, and led a collective life that shocked contemporaries by weakening the family in favor of communal property, work, worship, and meals. Young children, for example, were taken from their mothers at an early age and raised in large groups. The Hutterites' political structure was more oligarchic than democratic, with the group as a whole merely approving decisions made by a self-perpetuating leadership of elders and stewards. Nevertheless, the early Reformation's social radicalism lived on in the distinctive "brotherhood households" (*Bruderhöfe*) of the Hutterites, compared by their enemies to beehives or anthills.

Of all the Reformation's political thinkers, it was only the Anabaptists, including the Hutterites, who rejected the pervasive assumption that West European society as a whole was a Christian society. Most Protestant reformers of the sixteenth century shared the assumption that they could describe their society as a Christian commonwealth (*respublica Christiana*) or Christendom (*christianitas* or *Christenheit*). Just as the practice of pedobaptism was the ritual expression of this assumption, the reformers' reflections on politics were the ideological expression of how a Christian society should be governed and the obligations of Christians to their government. The irony, of course, is that, while Reformation thinkers continued to talk about Christendom in traditional ways, the Reformation itself fractured the unity of Latin Christianity and established a series of new churches and polities with differing creeds and rituals. In this way, the Reformation destroyed the unity that had provided the concept of Christendom with its foundation. By the middle of the seventeenth century—and chiefly as a result of a series of savage wars that were, in large part, religious civil wars—it no longer made sense for political thinkers to talk about Christendom.

References

Primary Sources

BAYLOR, M. (1991) ed. *The Radical Reformation*. Cambridge: Cambridge University Press.

CALVIN, J. (1960). *Institutes of the Christian Religion*. 2 vols. Philadelphia, PA: Westminster Press.

ESTEP, W. (1976). *Anabaptist Beginnings (1523–1533): A Sourcebook*. Nieuwkoop, Netherlands: B. de Graaf.

HÖPFL, H. (1991) ed. *Luther and Calvin on Secular Authority*. Cambridge: Cambridge University Press.

JOHNSTON, P., and SCRIBNER, B. (1993) eds. *The Reformation in Germany and Switzerland*. Cambridge: Cambridge University Press.

LUTHER, M. (2002). *Luther's* Works on CD ROM. 55 vols. St Louis, MO, and Philadelphia, PA: Concordia Publishing House and Fortress Press.

MATHESON, P., (1988) ed. *The Collected Works of Thomas Müntzer*. Edinburgh: T. & T. Clark.

SCOTT, T., and Scribner, B. (1991) eds. *The German Peasants' War*. Atlantic Highlands, NJ: Humanities Press.

WILLIAMS, G. H. (1957) ed. *Spiritual and Anabaptist Writers*. Philadelphia, PA: Westminster Press.

ZWINGLI, H. (1984). *Huldrych Zwingli: Writings*. 2 vols. Allison Park, PA: Pickwick Publications.

Secondary Sources

BLICKLE, P. (1981). *The Revolution of 1525*. Baltimore, MD: Johns Hopkins University Press.

BLICKLE, P. (1992). *Communal Reformation*. Atlantic Highlands, NJ: Humanities Press.

BLICKLE, P. (1997). *Obedient Germans? A Rebuttal*. Charlottesville, VA: University of Virginia Press.

BRADY, T. (1985). *Turning Swiss*. Cambridge: Cambridge University Press.

CARGILL-THOMPSON, W. (1984). *The Political Thought of Martin Luther*. New York: Barnes and Noble.

ELTON, G. (1962). "Constitutional Development and Political Thought in Western Europe," in G. Elton (ed.), *The New Cambridge Modern History*. Cambridge: Cambridge University Press, ii. 438–63.

HILLERBRAND, H. J. (1988) (ed.). *Radical Tendencies in the Reformation: Divergent Perspectives*. Kirksville, MO: Sixteenth Century Journal Publishers.

KEEN, R. (1997). *Divine and Human Authority in Reformation Thought: German Theologians and Political Order 1520–1555*. Nieuwkoop, Netherlands: B. de Graaf.

PACKULL, W. (1995). *Hutterite Beginnings*. Baltimore: Johns Hopkins University Press.

SKINNER, Q. (1978). *The Foundations of Modern Political Thought*, ii. *The Reformation*. Cambridge: Cambridge University Press.

STAYER, J. (1976). *Anabaptists and the Sword*. 2nd edn. Lawrence, KS: Coronado Press.

STAYER, J. (1991). *The German Peasants' War and Anabaptist Community of Goods*. Montreal and Kingston: McGill-Queens University Press.

CHAPTER 15

THE SCHOOL OF SALAMANCA

ANTHONY PAGDEN

THE members of the so-called School of Salamanca (or "Second Scholastic," as it is sometimes called) were, for the most part, the pupils, and the pupils of the pupils— from Domingo de Soto (1494–1560), and Melchor Cano (1509–60) to the great Jesuit metaphysicians Luís de Molina (1535–1600) and Francisco Suárez (1548–1600)—of Francisco de Vitoria, who held the Prime Chair of Theology at Salamanca between 1526 and his death in 1546. "Insofar as we are as we are learned, prudent and elegant," wrote Cano, "we are so because we follow this outstanding man, whose work is an admirable model for every one of those things, and emulate his precepts and his example" (1536: lib. XII, *Proemium*). Although they are often described vaguely as "theologians and jurists," they were all, in fact, theologians.[1] The discussion of the Roman law played a large role in their work, and their influence can be seen in particular in canon lawyers such as Diego Covarrubias y Leyva (1512–67), and in the civil lawyer Fernando Vázquez de Menchaca (1512–69) (Brett 1997: 245). But jurists were members of a distinct and, in the opinion of most theologians, inferior faculty. In the early modern world, theology, the "mother of sciences," because it dealt directly with first causes, was considered to be above all other modes of inquiry, and covered everything that belongs to what today is called jurisprudence, as well as most of moral and political philosophy, and what would later become the human sciences (Suárez 1971 [1612]: 2–8).

They were all university professors and all were in orders. But they also acted as informal and formal advisors to various groups from the Council of Castile to

---

[1] Anthony Anghie, for instance, describes Vitoria as "theologian and jurist" as did the great James Brown Scott, international lawyer who was responsible for the revival of interest in the School of Salamanca in the Anglophone world in the early twentieth century and for the re-edition of many of their works (Scott 1934; Anghie 2005: 13).

merchant guilds. Vitoria was asked about the justice of the Portuguese slave trade, the validity of clandestine marriages, and the legitimacy of increasing the price of corn during a poor harvest, to name but a few. Melchor Cano advised Philip II in his struggle with Pope Paul IV, and was even consulted as how best to defend the Canary Islands against attacks by French pirates. Francisco Suárez, whom Leibniz once called "the teacher of Europe," was questioned innumerable times on the Immaculate Conception, the election of the pope, on benefice, marriage contracts, and the preaching rights of the Dominicans. Some, Vitoria himself, Cano, and Domingo de Soto, were taken away for long periods from their lecture halls to become diplomats (Soto was a member of the Spanish delegation at the Council of Trent) and councilors or members of that select body of spiritual-cum-political advisors, the royal confessors (Beltrán de Heredia 1931; Suárez 1952 [1601–17]; Rau 1959; see also Sánchez 1993). They were, as we should say today, "public intellectuals." (See the comments of Janet Coleman, Chapter 12, this volume.).

As with all "schools," the Salamanca theologians rarely spoke with a single voice, and their concerns and their methods varied greatly. All, however, were broadly speaking Thomists—followers of St Thomas Aquinas (1225–74)—and, like Aquinas, neo-Aristotelians. They were all committed to the need to describe and explain the natural world, and mankind's place within it, in the same realistic terms Aquinas had used in his *Summa contra gentiles*. The truth of the Divine Law (the Decalogue and the Gospels), the primacy of the normative behavior of Christians, and the fitness of the political and social institutions of Europe had all to be maintained, without recourse to arguments from revelation, as the inescapable consequences of the rational mind drawing upon certain innate, and therefore self-evident, first principles. In pursuit of this objective, they lectured on topics that ranged from economics, to the laws of motion. In this chapter, however, I will focus on what they are best known for today: their discussion of the law of nature—the *ius naturae*—and of the law of nations (*ius gentium*), for which reason Vitoria has often been referred to (along with Hugo Grotius) as the "father of international law."

The law was divided into three broad categories. First, and embracing all the others, was the divine (or eternal) law. This was the creative *ratio* of God, and it was conceived by the Thomists as a set of norms (*regulae*) used by God at the creation in the same way, in Soto's comparison, as an architect uses a set of drawings. Next came the natural law, defined by Aquinas as "the participation in the Eternal Law by all rational creatures" (*ST* I–II. 91. 2 *in c*). This was believed to be innate. It consisted of a body of self-evident principles (*praeceptae*) implanted by God at the creation into the minds of all mankind, and accessible to reason. ("Props and buttresses," John Locke said of them, later, "leaning on borrowed or begg'd foundations" (*Essay on Human Understanding*, 1.IV.25).) These "innate ideas" or "innate senses" allowed human beings (but not animals) to see the world God had created as it really was, which meant that it allowed them to distinguish between good and evil, and to act accordingly, in precisely the same way that they all know that they must eat in order to survive and have sex in order to ensure the continuation of the species.

Last came the human (or positive or civil) law. This had ultimately to be derived from the natural law, or at least could not be in contradiction with it. But, since they relied upon human agency, all man-made laws could be abrogated and, in practice, varied widely from society to society. Occupying an uncertain middle ground between the natural and the human law was the "law of nations" (*ius gentium*), a body of laws that, in Vitoria's words, were deemed to have been enacted "by the whole world which is in a sense a commonwealth" (Vitoria 1991 [1528–39]): 40).[2] The question that troubled all the Salamanca theologians to differing degrees was how far this could be thought of as a part of the natural law. In Roman law—where the concept is first used— the law of nations was the law that governed the relationship between the Roman and non-Roman world (Donald Kelley, Chapter 10, this volume) It was, therefore, a civil law, and most of the Spanish Scholastics agreed with Soto that "the law of nations is distinct from the natural law and is included in the positive law" (Soto 1556: 367). However, the *ius gentium* had, in Suárez's words, "been introduced not by evidence but by the probable and common estimation of men" (1971 [1612]: iv. 130). It could, therefore, be deemed to have been enacted, if only *ex hypothesi*, by "the whole word which is in a sense a commonwealth," and this made it, if not part of the natural law, then certainly heavily dependent on it (Deckers 1991: 345–94). Later generations of writers on the law of nations, from Hugo Grotius to Giambattista Vico, would get around this problem by speaking of the *ius gentium* as a "secondary law of nature." (See comments by Donald Kelley, Chapter 10, this volume.)

For the School of Salamanca, this discussion over the nature and status of the law of nations had a direct bearing on one of the most pressing political questions of the sixteenth and seventeenth centuries. Did the Spanish and the Europeans in general, have the right to invade, and then occupy, the territories of non-Europeans, in particular in the Americas? Carl Schmitt's claim that during the "four hundred years from the sixteenth to the twentieth centuries" the entire course of European interna- tional law (*Völkerrecht*) had been "determined by a fundamental course of events; the conquest of a new world" may be an exaggeration (Schmitt 2003 [1950]: 69; translation slightly modified). But it is certainly the case that the debate over the legitimacy of the conquest of America marked a decisive turn in the development of what would later come to be called "international law."

In January 1539, Francisco de Vitoria delivered a *relectio* "On the Indies," or "On the American Indians." (A *relectio*, literally a "rereading," was a lecture given not, as were most lectures, on a particular text, but instead on a specific problem.) His intention, he told his audience, was to find an answer to the question: "by what right [*ius*] were the barbarians subjected to Spanish rule?" This question would remain a topic of often fierce debate both inside and outside the universities and the court until well into the

---

[2] The term used by all the Spanish Scholastics was, of course, *respublica*—literally the "common- thing." Since, however, the English term "republic" has come to denote a particular constitution, the now archaic term "commonwealth" seemed a more appropriate translation.

following century—by which time it would seem that, whatever the justice of the initial conquest, time, as the jurist Juan de Solórzano y Pereira (1575–1654) claimed, had transformed what might once have been a "tyranny... into a perfect and legitimate monarchy" (Solórzano y Pereira 1996 [1647]: i. 143–4).

In 1539, however, eighteen years after the destruction of the so-called Aztec Empire, and three years after the death of the last Inca ruler of Peru at the hands of Francisco Pizarro, what Vitoria referred as the "affair of the Indies" still had the power, as he told his colleague Miguel de Arcos, to "freeze the blood" in his veins (Vitoria 1991 [1528–39]): 331). The problem, as Vitoria pointed out, was that, as the American Indians "were previously unknown to our world," they obviously could not be "subjects by human law" (Vitoria 1991 [1528–39]): 233, 238). They could, therefore, be so only under the *ius gentium*. That, however, required that their subjugation be recognized as just by "all the world that is a commonwealth." The question, however, was: on what grounds?

The Castilian crown's own assertion of sovereignty in the Americas rested on two related, and highly contentious, claims. The first was the so-called Bulls of Donation. In 1493, Pope Alexander VI, acting on the supposition that the papacy exercised jurisdiction, in both spiritual and temporal affairs, over all humankind, had issued five papal bulls granting the Spanish monarchs, Ferdinand and Isabella, jurisdiction over the entire Western hemisphere. The second was the assumption that Charles V, as ruler of the oxymoronic "Holy Roman Empire of the German Nation" and, therefore, the legal heir of the Roman Emperors, was, as were they, "lord of all the world" (Pagden 1995: 29–62). Although the first of these claims continued to be upheld by royal officials well into the eighteenth century, neither, in the opinion of any of the members of the Salamanca School, had any validity.

To exercise universal *dominium*, the pope would, as Vitoria points out, have had to have acquired it though one of the three forms of law: divine; natural; or civil. Clearly, on the canon lawyers' own evidence, papal *dominium* could not derive from either civil or natural law. And, "as for divine law, no authority is forthcoming"; hence, "it is vain and willful to assert it." Furthermore, all the references to secular authority in the Bible would seem to indicate a clear distinction between the domain of Christ and that of Caesar. The pope's authority, as Innocent III had decreed in the twelfth century, was confined to spiritual rather than secular matters, except where strictly moral issues were involved (Tierney 1988: 127–38). Vitoria was prepared to concede that there were grounds for supposing that the pope might be in a position to act as an adjudicator between Christian rulers, and such rulers "are bound to accept his judgment to avoid causing all the manifold spiritual evils which must necessarily arise from any war between Christian princes" (Vitoria 1991 [1528–39]: 262). But papal "plenitude of power," however construed, could certainly not be extended to territories that had never fallen under any mode of papal or imperial jurisdiction. On these grounds at least, concluded Vitoria, "the Spaniards when they first sailed to the lands of the barbarians carried with them no right at all to occupy their territories" (Vitoria 1991 [1528–39]: 83–4, 260–4).

A similar argument could be applied to Charles V's presumption to be "Divine Maximilian or Eternally August Charles Lord of the World [*orbis dominus*]." As Soto pointed out, the Romans, despite their claims to universal sovereignty, had never, in fact, exercised jurisdiction over the entire world, for "many nations were not then subjugated as is attested by Roman historical writing itself; and this point is most obvious with regard to the other hemisphere and the lands across the sea recently discovered by our countrymen" (*De dominio*, quoted in Lupher 2003: 63; Soto 1556: 65). If that were the case, then it followed they could have no a priori jurisdiction over these places.

But, for Soto, there was a further, and in the long run far more compelling, reason why there could exist in the world no ruler of any kind with universal sovereignty. All the Spanish Scholastics were insistent that civil power could be transferred only by society acting as a single body. To create a truly *universal* empire, therefore, it would be necessary, said Soto, for "a general assembly to be called on which at least the major part consented to such an election." No one, however, could possibly imagine a general assembly of literally all the world. Even if, as the pre-history of civil society seemed to require, some such meeting had once been called, the new discoveries would have subsequently nullified its decisions, if only because, as Soto reiterated, "neither the name nor the fame of the Roman Caesars reached the Antipodes and the islands discovered by us" (Soto 1556: 304).

Soto was prepared to accept that "the imperial authority . . . surpasses all others, [and] it is the most excellent of all," but only because it involved the rule of more than one people (*natio*). It did not, however, he continued, "follow from this that it is the only one to dominate the world" (Soto 1556: 305).

Furthermore, and this was to become a crucial component of many later arguments against all extended empires, even if the emperor were able to *claim* universal sovereignty, he could not possibly exercise it in practice. For Soto, as for most of the Roman jurists (and later for Grotius), *dominium* was for use. "As power exists in order to be exercised [*potestas sit propter usum*], and its exercise is impossible over such extended territory, it would follow that such an institution is vain. But God and nature never do anything in vain [*nihil fecit frustra*]" (Soto 1556: 306).[3]

This implied, although Soto fails to spell it out, that any "universal monarchy," however constituted—including the Spanish—was necessarily illegitimate.

The demolition of any prior claim to universal sovereignty meant, in effect, that the sole grounds for legitimate occupation of Indian lands, and the assumption of jurisdiction over the Indians themselves, had to be based on the presumption that the wars waged against them had been just ones. The only kind of war anyone was prepared to consider just, however, was one that had been waged defensively, and in pursuit of compensation for some alleged act of aggression against either the perpetrators or their

---

[3] The phrase "nihil fecit frustra" derives from an oft-repeated Aristotelian axiom. See, e.g., *On the Generation of Animals* 741^{b}4.

allies (Russell 1975; Albert 1980). Yet, how could such a definition be made to apply to wars against a distant people who had manifestly caused no harm to any European prior to their arrival, and had then acted only in self-defence? The arguments used to justify non-defensive wars against most Muslims, that they occupied territories that had formerly been under Christian rule and were, therefore, usurpers, clearly did not apply to the Indians. Nor could the Indians be dispossessed simply because they were infidels, since for the Thomists all forms of political authority derived wholly from the natural law, and the *law* of nature did not change in accordance with a person's behaviour or beliefs. All legitimately constituted rulers—even Muslims—were, therefore, true *domini*. To claim otherwise was to fall into the heresy of Luther and Calvin that sovereignty (*dominium iurisdictionis*) depended upon God's grace, rather than God's laws (Skinner 1978: ii. 189–238). Furthermore, as Suárez observed, it was not man's task to vindicate God. If God wished to take revenge upon the pagans for their sins, he remarked acidly, "He is capable of doing so for himself" (Suárez 1954: 149–52).

What, however, if the Indians had not been in legitimate public and private possession of the territories they occupied *before* the arrival of the Europeans? If this were indeed the case, then their lands might be considered "empty," and their refusal to make way for the Spaniards might constitute grounds for a just war.

For this argument to apply, however, it had to be shown *either* that the Indians were in some sense less than fully human (or fully adult), in which case they could not be said to be true masters either of themselves or of their goods, *or* that, although both fully human and fully adult, they had somehow failed to fulfill the necessary conditions by which human beings were believed to acquire both political authority and owner-ship over land.[4]

In the first case, they would have to be either mad, or in some other way devoid of reason. It is under this heading that perhaps the most contentious attempt to deny the Indians their natural rights—Aristotle's theory of natural slavery—was introduced. A "natural" slave is one who, rather than being defined by his legal status, is defined by his psychological identity, since he is one, who contrary to the norm, possesses no independent autonomous self, and thus lacks the capacity for deliberation or moral choice (Fortenbaugh 1977; Williams 1993: 110–16). He is said to be capable of understanding but incapable of practical wisdom (*phronesis*), for "practical wisdom issues commands ... but understanding only judges" (*Nichomachean Ethics* 1143^{a}11). What this meant for Aristotle was that the slave was a kind of useful automaton, literally a "living but separate part of his master's frame" (*Politics* 1254^{a}8; see also Isaac 2004: 175–6)—"almost an animated instrument of service," as St Thomas Aquinas said

---

[4] The term *dominium* described, in Soto's definition, 'a faculty and right [*facultas et ius*] that [a person] has over anything, to use it for his own benefit by any means that are permitted by law' (Soto 1556: 280). The term "sovereignty," which I have used here rather loosely and which did not enter the language until later, translates *dominium iurisdictionis*—that is, the "faculty and right" that a sovereign has over jurisdiction or government. The analogous term, *imperium*, which is also frequently translated as "sovereignty," had a narrower range covering only the right to command.

later (Aquinas 1964 [*c*.1270]: 1447). For Aristotle, slaves were a feature of the natural world, and a necessary requirement for the proper functioning of the only true political form, the *polis*, since "a *polis* cannot be administered without them" (*Politics* 1283ª14–23). No *polis*, however, could be composed only of slaves—just as there could not be one made up solely of women and children.[5] If, therefore, the Indians could be shown to be slaves by nature, then they clearly could not be said to have "true *dominium* public and private" (Vitoria 1991 [1528–39]: 239).

The idea had considerable appeal, in particular amongst the settler populations in the Americas. But to most impartial observers, including every member of the School of Salamanca, it was not only ethnographically implausible—peoples such as the Aztecs and the Incas clearly constituted true civil societies (Pagden 1982: 68–79)—it also suggested that, if these Indians were such a race, they must be defective on a massive scale, which would imply that God himself had created some kind of semi-human aberration. For, said Vitoria, "our intellect is from God, and if it were to have a natural inclination towards error or falsehood then this would have to be attributed to God" (Vitoria 1932–52 [1526–46]: iii. 11).

Vitoria was prepared to accept that, *if* the Indians were, as so many claimed, "no more capable of governing themselves than madmen or indeed wild beasts," the Spanish monarch could claim a highly circumscribed right to take "them into his control." But, since this could be done only under the terms of the obligation we all have to our neighbors, such a right could be exercised only "for the benefit and the good of the barbarians and not merely for the profit of the Spanish" (Vitoria 1991 [1528–39]: 290–1). This point was pushed further, by Soto, generally more radical on most such issues than his predecessor, who argued that, not only could the Spanish crown not claim any degree of sovereignty over the Americas or their inhabitants; it could not even take possession of those things that the Indians did not themselves employ "without the consent of those who live there." This was an explicit reference to the precious metals that, in his view, the Spaniards had been mining illegally and that logically they should now restore to their rightful owners. The *ius gentium* applied equally to all peoples, and any exception made in favor of the Spanish claims in America would have also to apply in Europe; yet, Soto pointed out, "neither can the French enter into Spain for the same purpose, nor can we enter France without the permission of the French" (Soto 1556: 423).

It was also the case, as Melchor Cano had suggested in 1546, that, even if it were true that the Indians were some kind of children in need of civic education, the Christians would not be entitled to "take them into their care," if they had to conquer them in order to do so. For any act whose purpose is to secure the good of another is a precept of charity, and no act of charity can ever involve coercion. The position of the Castilian crown, Cano concluded, somewhat unflatteringly for his monarch, was like that of

---

[5] In *Politics* 1252ᵇ5, however, the *barbaroi* are said to be made up entirely of slaves. But then such peoples do not live in *poleis*, and are merely biding their time until they will be enslaved and thus put to their proper purpose.

a beggar to whom alms may be due, but who is not empowered to extract them (Cano 1546: 107).

Vitoria also introduced into the debate two more natural-law arguments in favor of the conquests, both of which were to have a lasting impact on all subsequent thinking about the legitimation of the intervention of one state in the affairs of another.

The first was what might be broadly described as the "humanitarian argument." It could be said, he wrote, that, "either on account of the personal tyranny of the barbarians" towards their subjects, or because of their tyrannical and oppressive laws, the Spanish have a right to intervene "in defense of the innocent." Furthermore, if, under pressure, the rulers of the "barbarians" refuse to abandon their crimes against their own people, then "their masters may be changed and new princes set up" (Vitoria 1991 [1528–39]: 287–8). Since such a norm clearly belongs to the *ius gentium*, any who actively resisted it, on the grounds that their own laws and customs compelled them to behave otherwise, provided cause for a just war. The Spanish are here merely acting on behalf, and by the authority, of a supposed international community.

Vitoria's conception of war "in defense of the innocent," in common with all attempts to justify armed intervention in the interests of "others," fails, of course, to specify very clearly what would count as "tyranny" and "oppressive laws." It was, too, an innovative move, since, in general, theories of the "just war" avoided claims made on behalf of third parties, unless these were specifically involved as "allies" (*socii*) (Barnes 1982).

In the case of the American Indians, the humanitarian argument for conquest, and the subsequent imposition of "new princes" and hence, in effect, the creation of new states—"regime change," as it is now called—was fairly circumscribed. In other, less specific, contexts, however, Vitoria substantially broadened the possible applications of the same argument. "It should be noted," he wrote, that "the prince has the authority not only over his own people, but also over foreigners to force them to abstain from harming others; this is his right by the law of nations and the authority of the whole world" (Vitoria 1991 [1528–39]: 305).

There were, in addition, further ways in which the Spanish Scholastics were prepared to extend the range of this injunction. One maintained that, if it was legitimate for a ruler to right a wrong on behalf "of the whole world," then it might also be legitimate for a prince to wage war in order to prevent any future, or further, deterioration in the *status quo*. This could even be extended so as to embrace the whole of humankind. Suárez, for instance, was prepared to argue that any way of life that involved such extreme violations of the natural law as human sacrifice and cannibalism posed a threat, not merely to the "innocent," but to the continuing existence of the entire "world-commonwealth." In which case, the Christian prince might go to war so as to restore what St Augustine had defined as the "tranquility of the order of all things" (*De civitate dei* XIX.13). In such circumstances, argued Suárez, "the natural power and jurisdiction of the human republic" could be mobilized as a "reason for universal conquest" (Suárez 1954: 158–61, 238).

What this implied, in effect, was that a European ruler could claim to make war upon an otherwise harmless adversary in order to establish what later generations of colonizers would call "civilization." Since, however, the purpose of such a war was only to remedy ills, the victor was only entitled to seize such movable goods as he deemed necessary to compensate for the losses he had incurred. He might also seize goods, and even persons, as punishment for wrongdoing. But what were termed "immovable goods"—that is territory, cities, and, crucially, what lay beneath the land—were another matter (Vitoria 1991 [1528–39]: 324). Once again, the Spanish Scholastics were faced with the uncomfortable truth that, while the behaviour of the Indians, prior to their "discovery," might have provided the Spanish crown justification for an invasion, it could not provide it with any grounds for subsequent conquest and occupation.

The second of Vitoria's arguments, and it was to have a long subsequent history, was based upon the, somewhat dubious, claim that the "division of things"—that is, the carving-up of the world into autonomous (and sovereignty-bearing) nations—had not obscured certain natural rights, which remained the common property of all human beings. Among these were what Vitoria called "the right of natural partnership and communication" (*ius naturalis societas et communicationis*) (Vitoria 1991 [1528–39]: 278). This was an allusion to the ancient obligation to offer hospitality to strangers, which Vitoria transformed from a Greek custom into a right under the law of nations. "Amongst all nations," he wrote, "it is considered inhuman to treat travelers badly without some special cause, humane and dutiful to behave hospitably to strangers."

> In the beginning of the world [he continued], when all things were held in common, everyone was allowed to visit and travel through any land he wished. This right was clearly not taken away by the division of property; it was never the intention of nations to prevent men's free mutual intercourse with one another by its division. (Vitoria 1991 [1528–39]: 278)

The right to hospitality and in particular to assistance in moments of danger is, of course, based upon a supposition of a common human identity. "Nature," said Vitoria, "has decreed a certain kinship a between men ... Man is not a 'wolf to his fellow men'—*homo homini lupus*—as Ovid says, but a fellow." All of this brings with it an obligation to friendship for "amity between men is part of the natural law" (Vitoria 1991 [1528–39]: 280).

It is also the case—and this Vitoria takes to be self-evidently a principle of the natural law—that "the Spaniards are the barbarians' neighbors, as is shown by the parable of the Samaritan (Luke 10:29–37); and the barbarians are obliged to love their neighbors as themselves," which meant that they could not "lawfully bar them [the Spaniards] from their homeland without due cause" (Vitoria 1991 [1528–39]: 279). Since the Indians clearly had attempted to bare the Spaniards from their homes by force, a just war might be waged against them.

Vitoria extended the same argument to commerce. By the terms of the law of nations, travelers (*peregrini*) may not be prevented from carrying on trade "so long as they do not harm the citizens." Therefore, "they [the Spaniards] may import the commodities which they [the Indians] lack and export the gold and silver and other things which they have in abundance." It was, Vitoria recognized, a two-way argument: if the "barbarians" could not interfere with the right of the Europeans to travel among and trade with them, then no European state could prevent another from doing the same thing. The French, for instance, could not lawfully "prevent the Spaniards from traveling to or even living in France and vice versa" (Vitoria 1991 [1528–39]: 279–80).

The problem with the argument, however, as Melchor Cano pointed out, was that, although Spaniards might have natural right as travelers, or even as ambassadors, they had gone to America as neither. "We would not," he concluded dryly, "be prepared to describe Alexander the Great as a 'traveler'" (Cano 1546: 142).

For Cano, the key issue was the power of the sovereign state. It was, Cano argued, clearly absurd to suggest that there might exist a law that would forbid a prince from controlling the passage of foreigners over his own territories. Such a law would, as Vitoria had recognized, prevent the Spanish king from forbidding the French from entering Spain if he so wished, which was contrary to actual practice and a violation of the civil laws of Castile. Did it mean, then, that the civil laws of Castile were contrary to natural law? If so, then the French would have as perfect a right to wage war against Charles V as he had to make war on the Indians. Implicitly at least it was clear that there simply could be no right that had somehow, mysteriously, survived the "division of things" that also implied that there could be no right under the law of nations that could overrule a promulgated civil law.

While these arguments were to have some considerable influence on subsequent thinking about empire, none of them could confer upon the Spanish crown what it most needed: grounds for true sovereignty over the Indians, much less undisputed rights over their property. In the end, most of the School of Salamanca could see that, if their arguments were to be taken to their proper conclusion, then, as Vitoria phrased it, "the whole Indian expedition and trade would cease." As Vitoria himself had pointed out, the only unassailable argument in favor of the retention of the Spanish colonies— other than the presumed goodwill of the Spanish monarchs—was the purely realist one: that more damage would be done by withdrawal, in particular since, in theory at least, most of the indigenous populations had now converted to Christianity, than by continued occupation. Otherwise there could be no moral, nor political, and even very little economic justification for remaining. "Look at the Portuguese," Vitoria concluded his *relectio*, "who carry a great and profitable trade with similar sorts of people without conquering them" (Vitoria 1991 [1528–39]: 291). Better emulate them than the Romans. As subsequent generations of natural-law theorists recognized, what the Spanish Scholastics had achieved was not only to have established the "law of nature and of nations" (*de iurae naturae et gentium*) as a staple component of international political philosophy until the nineteenth century. They had also offered a powerful set of arguments for the need for a recognized body of international civil law to regulate the predatory practices of the emergent European nation states.

References

Primary Sources

Aquinas, St Thomas (1964 [c.1270]). *In decem libros ad Nicomachum exposition*, ed. R. M. Spiazzi. Rome and Turin: Marietti.

Beltrán de Heredia, Vicente (1931). "Colección de dictámenes inéditos" [by Vitoria, 1526–46], *Ciencia tomista*, 43: 27–50, 169–80.

Cano, Melchor (1536). *De locis theologicis*. Salamanca.

Cano, Melchor (1546). *De Dominio indorum*, printed in Luciano Pereña, *Misión de España en América*. Madrid: Consejo Superior de Investigaciones Scientíficas, 1956, 90–146.

Rau, Virginia (1959). "Paresceres teológico-juridicos das universidades de Salamanca e da Alcalá en 1596," *Revista da facultade de letres* (Coimbra), 3/3: 11–27.

Schmitt, Carl (2003 [1950]). *The Nomos of the Earth in the International Law of the Jus Publicum Europaeum*, trans. and ed. G. L. Umen. New York: Telos Press.

Solórzano y Pereira, Juan de (1996 [1647]). *Politica Indiana, sacada en lengua castellana de los dos tomos del derecho i govierno municipal de las Indias occidentales*, ed. Francisco Tomás y Valiente and Ana María Barrero. 3 vols. Madrid: Biblioteca Castro.

Soto, Domingo de (1556). *De iustitia et iure*. Salamanca.

Suárez, Francisco (1952 [1601–17]). *Conselhos e paresceres* 2 vols. Coimbra: por ordem da universidade.

Suárez, Francisco (1954). *Disputatio xii. De Bello*, from *Opus de triplice virtute theologica, fide spe et charitate* [1621], printed in Luciano Pereña Vicente, *Teoria de la guerra en Francisco Suárez*. 2 vols. Madrid: Consejo Superior de Investigaciones Científicas.

Suárez, Francisco (1971 [1612]). *Tractatus de legibus ac Deo Legislatore*, ed. Luciano Pereña. 8 vols. Madrid: CSIC.

Vázquez de Menchaca, Fernando (1931–5 [1563]). *Controversiarum illustrium aliarumque usu frequentium, libri tres*, ed. Fidel Rodriguez Alcalde. 3 vols. Valladolid.

Vitoria, Francisco de (1932–52 [1526–46]). *Comentarios a la Secunda Secundae de Santo Tomás*, ed. Vicente Beltrán de Heredia. 6 vols. Salamanca: Universidad de Salamanca.

Vitoria, Francisco de (1991 [1528–39]), *Vitoria Political Writings*, ed. Anthony Pagden and Jeremy Lawrance. Cambridge: Cambridge University Press.

Secondary Sources

Albert, Sigrid (1980). *Bellum Iustum. Theorie des "gerechten Krieges" und ihre praktische Bedeutung fur die auswartigen Auseinandersetzungen Roms in republikanischer Zeit*. Frankfurter althistorische Studien 10. Kallmunz: Lassleben.

Anghie, Antony (2005). *Imperialism, Sovereignty and the Making of International Law*. Cambridge: Cambridge University Press.

Barnes, Jonathan (1982). "The Just War," in Norman Kretzmann, Anthony Kenny, and Jan Pinborg (eds), *Cambridge History of Later Medieval Philosophy*. Cambridge: Cambridge University Press.

Brett, Annabel (1997). *Liberty, Right and Nature*. Cambridge: Cambridge University Press.

Deckers, Daniel (1991). *Gerechtigkeit und Recht. Eine historisch-kritische Untersuchung der Gerechtigkeitslehre des Francisco de Vitoria (1483–1546)*. Freiburg: Universitätsverlag, Freiburg.

FORTENBAUGH, W. W. (1977). "Aristotle on Slaves and Women," in Jonathan Barnes, Malcolm Schofield, and Richard Sorabji (eds), *Articles on Aristotle*, ii. *Ethics and Politics*. New York: St Martin's Press, 135–9.

ISAAC, BENJAMIN (2004). *The Invention of Racism in Classical Antiquity*. Princeton: Princeton University Press.

LUPHER, DAVID A. (2003). *Romans in a New World: Classical Models in Sixteenth-Century Spanish America*. Ann Arbor: University of Michigan Press.

PAGDEN, ANTHONY (1982). *The Fall of Natural Man: The American Indian and the Origins of Comparative Ethnology*. Cambridge: Cambridge University Press.

PAGDEN, ANTHONY (1995). *Lords of all the World: Ideologies of Empire in Britain, France and Spain, 1400–1800*. New Haven and London: Yale University Press.

RUSSELL, FREDERICK H. (1975). *The Just War in the Middle Ages*. Cambridge: Cambridge University Press.

SÁNCHEZ, DOLORES (1993). *El deber de consejo en el estado moderno. Las juntas "ad hoc" en España (1471–1665)*. Madrid: Ediciones Polifemo.

SCOTT, JAMES BROWN (1934). *The Spanish Origin of International Law*. Oxford: Clarendon Press.

SKINNER, Q. (1978). *The Foundations of Modern Political Thought*. 2 vols. Cambridge: Cambridge University Press.

TIERNEY, BRIAN (1988). *The Crisis of Church and State 1050–1300*. Toronto: Toronto University Press.

WILLIAMS, BERNARD (1993). *Shame and Necessity*. Berkeley and Los Angeles, and Oxford: California University Press.

CHAPTER 16

....

THE EARLY MODERN FOUNDATIONS OF CLASSIC LIBERALISM

....

JEFFREY COLLINS

THE term 'liberalism' is of nineteenth-century vintage, but only the most pedantic historian would limit its use to that period. By then, Hume and the utilitarians had undermined traditional accounts of rights and contract, and 'liberalism' largely denoted a reforming mode of political economy. Nineteenth-century liberals were heirs more of Adam Smith than of Locke, and in this sense the term 'liberalism' post-dated the development of 'classic', natural-rights liberalism. The liberal revival of the Rawlsian era, however, presents itself as a rebuke to the utilitarians and, in part, a return to Lockean first principles (Rawls 2007: 103–58). Furthermore, current debates about liberalism tend to focus less on its political economy, and more on its moral and religious implications. The historical point of departure for such debates is the age of the scientific revolution and the religious wars, the era of Locke and Hobbes. For these reasons, this chapter will focus chronologically on the seventeenth century.

Two schemas have tended to structure historical interpretation of this period. 'Proto-liberalism' is presumed to be the victorious foe either of Christian political theology, or of antique republicanism. The present chapter will in some respects be guided by these two interpretative paradigms. It will, however, also critique the partialities and false coherences that these models at times entail. It is also important, in an essay of this kind, to avoid the self-congratulatory understanding of liberalism as a strictly emancipatory tradition, designed to protect individual rights from state power. In fact, early liberalism was largely derived from a seventeenth-century jus naturalism that was designed to buttress—rather than to hedge—the power of sovereignty.

This chapter will also avoid constitutional questions, and will instead foreground liberalism's theoretical fundaments. A partial list of these might include: a dedication to monopolistic sovereignty; belief in the artificiality of political order; an atomistic individualism; dedication to natural equality and popular sovereignty; deployment of the juridical language of rights and contract; a privileging of stability as the primary end of politics. Any historical sketch of 'early modern liberalism' is necessarily an interpretative exercise and thus historiographical, reflecting the dominant scholarly attempts to reconstruct liberalism's pre-history.

There is not space here to dig for the seeds of liberalism in the political thought of the sixteenth century. Leaving aside strained, Straussian efforts to trace liberalism back to Machiavelli (Strauss 1950: 161–87; Rahe 2008: 50–1), historians have more plausibly identified preconditions for liberalism in the intellectually fertile period of the religious wars. Particularly in France, those wars produced foundational works of resistance theory. These, both Catholic and Calvinist in orientation, construed sovereignty as an artificial construct of contracting individuals. They would also deploy an imagined state of nature, and typically contained a right of resistance. Such a constellation of ideas clearly anticipated liberalism in certain respects (Skinner 1978: 349–59). In others, however—particularly in their radical subordination of political to religious life—the illiberality of the resistance theorists could hardly be exaggerated. Liberalism's participation in the great turn to 'sovereignty', whereby the autonomy of political logic and the paramount importance of political stability were established, was more clearly foreshadowed by the main critics of the resistance theorists, *politique* thinkers such as Bodin. In some sense, later liberals would deploy the conceptual apparatus of the contractualists in the service of the *politique* project.

A further important development of the sixteenth century that here can be only passingly mentioned is the refinement, in scholastic thinking, of the idea of 'subjective individual rights'. Exactly when the classical and Thomistic definition of right as 'rightly ordered action' gave way to rights as zones of 'subjective' self-sovereignty is disputed (Brett 1997: 1–10). None denies, however, that the Jesuits of the second scholastic helped to advance this understanding of right as a 'free power'. This development was consequential for the later development of liberalism.

If certain building blocks of liberalism were set in place during the sixteenth century, that era's theocratic tendencies and hierarchic corporatism rendered the political theory of the period decidedly pre-modern. Subjective individual right, furthermore, continued to be hedged by natural-law obligations. For most historians, a plausible prehistory for liberalism begins only in the seventeenth century, when certain thinkers begin to weld together a contractual account of popular sovereignty, a *politique* understanding of political logic, and an account of right in which right as 'free power' begins to subsume (and not just complement) right as 'rightly ordered conduct'.

The result of these theoretical moves is known to moderns as the 'new natural law', and the thinker often privileged in its history is Hugo Grotius. Grotius was politically and intellectually active during the earliest decades of Dutch independence, producing works in far-flung contexts. The best known of these were *Mare liberum* (1609) and *De jure belli ac pacis* (1625). Broadly, Grotius's interest in natural law was a response to the problem of stabilizing politics during an era of moral disagreement and scepticism. He sought to justify state sovereignty along newly rationalized lines, freeing it from religious legitimization. This required locating the origins of political life in nature, and proceeding according to a scientific mode of analysis. Resulting were 'certain rules and laws of the most general nature' laying a 'foundation' for civil science (Tuck 1991: 505).

The originality of Grotius's political laws, and the extent to which they broke from scholastic thinking, have been debated (Brett 1997: 204–8; Tierney 1997: 326–35). There is little doubt, however, that he was a major contributor in reducing the complexities of traditional natural law to a spare natural right of self-preservation. For Grotius, self-preservation became the 'one and only universal right', justifying any action necessary for its own achievement. Grotius thus grounded much moral reasoning on self-interest. Not all actions were permitted by the right of self-preservation, but all moral, charitable actions needed to be justified according to this universal principle. Property and society, furthermore, emerged from the interactions of self-sovereign individuals asserting their natural right (Grotius 2004: 6). Property of a sort could be acquired naturally as part of self-protection. Humans, moreover, enjoyed a natural right to punish malefactors who transgressed the right of others (Tuck 1979: 62–3). The notes of sovereignty, particularly the right to execute justice, were thus present in the state of nature. States represented the accumulation of this right. Grotius thus developed the foundational 'idea that civil society is a construct by individuals wielding rights or bundles of property, and that governments possess no rights that those individuals did not possess . . . ' (Tuck 1987: 103).

Self-interest, and the rational account of the state emerging from it, became Grotius's bulwark against early modern scepticism. This entailed, not merely a minimization of natural law, but a scaling-back of the state's religious purposes. Unlike Locke or Pufendorf, Grotius denied that natural law would oblige only if it was construed as God's will. Rather, it was enough that the fundamental laws of nature (self-defence) were 'functionally' necessary for society. Famously, he asserted that natural law would oblige, even if it were to be theoretically granted that 'there is no God, or that he takes no Care of human Affairs'. This proposition had been entertained as a thought experiment by earlier scholastics, but Grotius went further than they had in suggesting that 'the dictates of reason could in themselves create obligation' to natural law (Zagorin 2009: 16–18).

Grotius's modern natural law thus diverged from scholastic jus naturalism, with its more complex theology and ethical reasoning (Tierney 1997: 323). Self-interest and self-possession, only lightly bound, grounded a contractual and rationalized account of sovereignty. That state would in turn protect subjects from the political projects of those religious believers whose faith in the old moral reasoning had survived the sceptical onslaught. The new natural law thus sought to empower the modern state to quell religious 'frenzy' and 'lack of restraint'.

Did it do so by moving in a recognizably 'liberal' direction? On this point the Grotian state was somewhat 'schizophrenic' (Tuck 1979: 63–4). Grotius's radical individualism—asserting not only a natural right to property but an unusual individual right to execute justice in the state of nature—did forecast Lockean thought.

Nevertheless, Grotius eventually developed a fairly absolutist account of the state. However extensive natural individual right was, it was radically surrendered to the purposes and right of sovereignty. Moved by fear of clerical power and its effects in the Dutch Republic, Grotius emphasized the total nature of the state's coercive power. This was chiefly targeted at power-hungry churches, but also minimized the individual right to resistance. Grotius cautiously defended the possibility that subjects might contract away their very freedom and become slaves. These points together constituted, effectively, a defence of absolutism (Tuck 1979: 78).

Grotius's legacy would be split between state absolutists and those who softened the draconian implications of his extreme contractualism. But, for both, Grotius was a critical figure breaking from scholastic accounts of justice, establishing that 'the law of nature was in effect the obligation men are under to preserve social peace, and that the principal condition for a peaceful community is respect for another's rights' (Tuck 1979: 67–73, 81).

THE GREAT DEBATE: HOBBES AND THE LIBERAL TRADITION

For historical debates over the origins of liberalism, the *locus classicus* is the career and thought of Thomas Hobbes. Hobbes was born into a high humanist culture rocked by religious war and neo-scepticism. He wrote during the tumults of the English Revolution and the formative years of the 'new natural law'. He died in the age of Locke. Straussians, communitarians, and anti-liberals such as Carl Schmitt have long used Hobbes as a way of associating liberalism with various malaises of modernity. Revival of interest in Hobbes's religious thought has also served to burnish his credentials as a 'proto-liberal', in that Hobbes arguably anticipated later liberalism most clearly in his account of religious power. Neo-republican thinkers have also found Hobbes an irresistible foil, an embarrassment for the modern liberal order. Such 'Hobbesian' accounts of liberalism have increasingly met with efforts to 'liberalize' Hobbes. Some have recast Hobbes as a religious tolerationist; others as a new-modelled 'virtue' theorist (Berkowitz 1999: ch. 1; Boonin-Vail 2002: *passim*; Zagorin 2009: 99–126). In short, very few any longer view Hobbes as liberalism's authoritarian opposite. Debate now orients itself around precisely specifying Hobbes's contribution to liberalism.

Hobbes's most clear-cut contribution to the liberal tradition is his crystallization of the new natural law. Hobbes offered accounts of natural law that included as many as nineteen laws, but he famously designated only two of these as 'foundational'. Natural law reduced to two 'precepts of reason': one, that 'every man ought to endeavour peace, as far as he has hope of obtaining it, and when he cannot obtain it, that he may seek and use all helps and advantages of war'; and, two, that, 'as far-forth as for peace and defence of himself he shall think it necessary, to lay down this right to all things, and be contented with so much liberty against other men, as he would allow other men against himself' (Hobbes 1994: 80).

The implications of Hobbes's use of traditional natural-law terminology have been much debated, but the most pressing observation about Hobbes's two 'fundamental natural laws' is the thoroughness with which the first conflates law with an imperially expansive natural right (justifying even war). No theorist has ever outdone this capacious account of subjective, individual right. History's most famed absolutist thinker thus built his political thought on a remarkably robust account of natural self-sovereignty. This interplay, between the monopolistic claims of artificial sover-eignty and the monopolistic rights of naturally self-sovereign individuals, is central to the later career of liberalism.

Hobbes's minimalist account of natural law as subjective right effectively reduced specific moral judgements to positive law. Until the formation of sovereignty, natural law was either not intended to oblige morally, or was incapable of doing so. Only force could create the conditions required for contracts to bind reliably. Virtue and vice were thereby rendered mere outcomes of sovereign arbitration. Here we glimpse the austere moral logic of utilitarian liberalism, which indeed helped to rehabilitate nineteenth-century interest in Hobbes.

Hobbes's memorable account of the state of nature—a 'war of all against all', 'solitary, poor, nasty, brutish, and short'—became his most distinctive doctrine (Hobbes 1994: 76–8). The misery of Hobbes's state of nature sprang from his deter-ministic account of humans as bestial and appetite-driven, perpetually prone to violence (though as much out of fear as wanton cruelty). The absolute authority of the Hobbesian sovereign was an inverse implication of the same account. The pressing motivation for creating sovereignty was the mere desire to preserve life, and the threat of returning to the state of nature through acts of political resistance was consequently grave (Hoekstra 2008: 109–22). Though notorious, Hobbes's state of nature was perhaps his least influential doctrine. Efforts to 'liberalize' Hobbes have typically dissented from it. Nevertheless, the use of a theoretical state of nature became a standard feature of classic liberalism, distinguishing it from naturalistic accounts of political authority, and undergirding universalizing accounts of human rights and political behaviour. Hobbes helped to entrench this liberal fascination with the pre-political.

Furthermore, Hobbes's account of the state of nature contained features that proved more durable within later liberalism. These include his assumption of an atomized individualism. For sixteenth-century thinkers, the 'people' were usually construed as a class. Hobbes fragmented the people. In their natural state, they were 'solitary', self-regarding, warring 'every man with every man'. Hobbes's popular sovereignty thus broke from medieval notions of authority 'ascending' from the collective 'people', and understood the people as an agglomeration of private interests and wills.

Additionally, Hobbes's account of the state of nature contributed to later, liberal egalitarianism. To be sure, Hobbes's equality principle was not particularly high-minded. It was, rather, an equality of raw animal ability. Differences of physical strength could be equalized through 'confederacy'. Before the origin of politics, language, and conventional science, 'faculties of the mind' were even more equally (meaning 'randomly') distributed in the state of nature. 'From this equality of ability ariseth equality of hope in the attaining of our ends' and thus the violent competition of the natural state (Hobbes 1994: 74–5). Hobbes portrayed the state of nature as a free-fire zone of rival wills and appetites. If some natural associations could mitigate this state of affairs, they did so only minimally and unreliably. Natural individuals might desire society for their own protection, but they were, in this state, unfit for stable society. On this foundation Hobbes built his egalitarian account of a subjective 'right of nature', defined as 'the liberty each man hath to use his own power, as he will himself, for the preservation of his own nature...' (Hobbes 1994: 79). Locke would defend human equality as a reflection of the image of God; Hobbes rendered equality an implication of animality.

To effect the transition from the realm of self-sovereignty to that of artificial, collective sovereignty, Hobbes deployed contractualism. Hobbes insisted on the real historical experience of original political covenants. To be sure, Hobbesian commonwealths were also legitimately founded by conquest: institution by a covenanting multitude was not a precondition of legitimacy (Hobbes 1994: 127–8). Hobbes's discussion of original covenants was more conceptually clarifying than historically descriptive, although Hobbes did live during times when such explicit social contracts were more imaginable than they are now. The Scottish National Covenant and the Leveller's *Agreement of the People*, both produced during the English Civil War, were efforts to 'institute' sovereignty in this way. But Hobbes was perfectly aware that most commonwealths did not enjoy such pristine origins, and 'consent' also operated to legitimate commonwealths founded by 'conquest'. Justifying this required Hobbes to deploy the category of implied consent. In this he established a polite fiction that has endured within natural-rights liberalism. Furthermore, though Hobbes was capable of writing that there was 'no obligation on any man which ariseth not from some act of his own' (Hobbes 1994: 141), he viewed all acts of consent as free, even if they were granted out of terror. He did not allow that consent could be illegitimately coerced.

Contractualism placed Hobbes, awkwardly, in an intellectual tradition tainted with the memory of religious war. Indeed, Calvinist resistance theory was vibrant during the English Revolution, fuelling the Scottish rebellion against Charles I. Hobbes distinguished his own version of contractualism in an effort to augment sovereign power and stigmatize resistance. Paradoxically, the theoretical moves he made in order to realize these authoritarian ends moved him closer to the liberal paradigm. First, he forbade political covenants with God (Hobbes 1994: 85). Earlier contractualists had bound kings to God through covenant, but had also made subjects (either directly, or mediately through the Church) parties to these covenants, and thus its guarantors. Political justice and godliness were in this way ensured. By decapitating the covenanting process, Hobbes both shed these religious ends and vitiated the logic of religious resistance. The 'mortal God' of sovereignty was no longer bound, in an enforceable way, to his divine superior.

Nor, indeed, was sovereignty bound by contract in temporal affairs. Hobbes did not construe sovereigns as parties to political covenants. Rather, natural individuals created the sovereign by covenanting among themselves. Sovereigns were created by covenants, but were not 'bound' to them as parties. If an abstract notion of sovereignty, indivisible at its source (although not necessarily in its exercise), is a precondition of modern liberalism, Thomas Hobbes commands an essential place. Bodin's important account of sovereignty influenced Hobbes, but the latter refined the notion of sovereignty as the 'artificial person of the state'. The Hobbesian state enjoys all coercive authority by virtue of its unity, but it also enjoys all 'right' by virtue of its implicitly contractual nature. It operates as a 'personator' of the polity's collected will (Hobbes 1994: 101–5; Skinner 2002: 177–208).

Each individual thus owns the acts of the state, and cannot distance him or herself from those acts by levelling accusations of injustice. Hobbes, however, did not always argue in this manner. At times he anticipated later liberal strategies by using the 'artificiality' of sovereignty as a way of distancing individuals from the state's actions. This was particularly true in his discussions of religious conscience. If a sovereign forbade Christianity, Hobbes wrote, 'such forbidding is of no effect; because belief and unbelief never follow men's commands . . . Profession with the tongue is but an external thing' (Hobbes 1994: 338). Here the sovereign is not presented as 'representational', and obedience is ensured by a rhetorical distancing of the sovereign's will from the subject's. Hobbes similarly required individual self-judgement to mediate political resistance. He preserved a right to resist when a subject's life—the original end of the social contract—was endangered. Hobbes presented this minimal right as a rare exigency. Nevertheless, adjudicating one's own safety in the Commonwealth remained a matter of self-determination. 'In this sense Hobbes may be seen as a proto-liberal,' Lucien Jaume has concluded, 'due to the capacity to judge that he allows the individual', even under the 'bond of submission' (Jaume 2008: 210; see also Martel 2007: *passim*).

Later liberalism would restrict the scope of Hobbesian absolutism, but did not challenge his definition of sovereignty as indivisible and self-justifying. Hobbes and the later liberal tradition share a strong suspicion of any independent, self-sufficient corporate authority. All corporate privileges descended from sovereign authority. Here is another very strict limitation on Hobbes's contractualism. What the sovereign granted or promised, the sovereign could legitimately revoke. Guilds, town corporations, aristocratic caste: all vestiges of corporatism were subsumed within Leviathan (Hobbes 1994: 146–55). Locke would adopt a less suspicious attitude towards corporate bodies within civil society, but later liberalism nevertheless denied all such lesser 'political' bodies any claim on independent authority.

Hobbes's greatest fear was the institutional power of the corporate church. A great deal of his writing was dedicated to theology and church polity. Hobbes deeply feared the potential for religious dogma to disrupt both stable political life and the strictly political reasoning necessary to its sustenance. Doctrines that 'dissolved' commonwealths included the claims that 'whatsoever a man does against his conscience is sin';

that 'faith and sanctity are not to be attained by study and reason, but by supernatural inspiration or infusion'; and that a commonwealth could divide religious and temporal authority, thus setting up 'a supremacy against the sovereignty, canons against laws, and a ghostly authority against the civil' (Hobbes 1994: 212–15). Hobbes subordinated all religious authority to the sovereign. Leviathan would fund and regulate churches, administer sacraments, formulate doctrine, and interpret scripture. This severely statist church targeted both zealous spiritual individualists and high-church 'clericalists'. The former threatened to unleash religious chaos, and the latter to maintain a rival 'state within a state'. Hobbes offered a notorious interpretation of Christian scripture and doctrine, foregrounding at every turn the political passivity of religion. Even under heathen power, Hobbes required that Christians conform, or accept martyrdom (Hobbes 1994: 340).

Facially, this authoritarian tendency in religious matters hardly looks 'liberal' at all. However, if theoretically coercive on religion, Hobbes could also counsel a considerable degree of religious toleration (Ryan 1983: *passim*). *Leviathan* spoke respectfully of individual religious conscience and of its resistance to coercion. The 'right' of conscience remained strictly internal, but Hobbes effectively advised sovereigns to adopt the principle of religious toleration and to grant some private license to dissent. Hobbesian toleration was a prudential measure. Nevertheless, *Leviathan*—written during a period of religious chaos—counselled a regulated settlement of quasi-voluntary church membership. This was justified because one could not reasonably 'require of a man endued with reason of his own, to follow the reason of any other man, or of the most voices of many other men' (Hobbes 1994: 482).

If Hobbes's occasional tolerationism has been fairly identified as an aspect of his proto-liberalism, it is equally true, if less comfortably so, that Hobbes's anti-clerical and statist impulses left their legacies to liberalism. Hobbes was a determined enemy of Augustinian or Thomistic dualism, whereby political power was surrendered to states, but moral and intellectual authority remained under the control of corporate religious power. He targeted the independence of clerics relentlessly, and this did not just extend to jurisdictional matters, but even to doctrinal and sacramental authority. He believed that the 'dispute for precedence between the spiritual and the civil power, had of late more then any other thing in the world been the cause of civil wars in all places of Christendom' (Malcolm 1994: 120). Hobbes wrote during the era of religious wars, and so his anti-clericalism was hardly gratuitous. Nevertheless, its lurid intensity remains astonishing.

Further, Hobbes's religious critique often targeted Christian orthodoxy itself. Hobbes feared the destabilizing effects of belief in an eternal afterlife (Strauss 1952: 19–21). His politics made bare life itself the highest common end of humanity. Many contemporaries, however, were willing to martyr themselves for religious truth (or for republican glory). Martyrs did not merely deny that life itself was the only shared good of humanity; they construed an exaggerated attachment to life as an obstacle or a temptation, and thereby cast doubt on its status as even a lesser human good. Rebutting such doctrines consumed a great deal of Hobbes's attention. Much of his voluble scriptural interpretation, for instance, was designed to further a project of ideological reform on behalf of the new-modelled state.

The anti-churchly and anti-Christian aspects of Hobbes's thinking cannot be dismissed as mere artefacts of a lost context. Hostility to corporate religion long remained a defining characteristic of classic liberalism. Liberalism sprang, in significant measure, out of efforts to craft tolerationist solutions to the problem of religious war. Hierarchical churches were understood as obstacles to those efforts. But it is also true that corporate religious practice, however pacified, did not easily accord with the individual autonomy that is an anthropological assumption of liberalism. Liberalism would thus privilege religion of a more interior and voluntarist kind. Hobbes anticipated this preference in both the positive and the negative senses. To celebrate his occasional toleration of individual conscience as 'liberal' and suggest that his intolerance of corporate religious practice was 'illiberal' is question-begging. Hobbes's illiberality, in this regard, is equally a part of the 'liberal' tradition (Collins 2005: 271–80).

By liberalism's friends and critics alike, Hobbes can thus be read as an extreme prefiguring of the liberal solution to moral disagreement (Manent 1987: ch. 3; Lilla 2007: ch. 2). Liberals foreground Hobbes's nascent tolerationism, and communitarians his coercion of religion, but they agree that Hobbes helped to move civil science past the political theology of Christendom.

An alternative account of Hobbes's proto-liberalism has been offered by neo-republican thinkers, who read him against the republican writers active during the English Revolution. Hobbes was regularly contemptuous of 'ancient' and 'democratical' texts. Some aspects of Hobbes's anti-republicanism are not particularly interesting theoretically, but a compelling 'liberal' reading of Hobbes's anti-republicanism has been offered by the historian Quentin Skinner. Skinner has highlighted the variant understandings of civil liberty circulating in the early modern period. Republicans of the era espoused a 'non-domination' understanding of civil liberty, whereby liberty was not merely freedom from active interference (negative liberty), nor did it entail a specific account of human flourishing (positive liberty). Instead, though it permitted subjects to set private ends, it demanded more than mere non-interference, and forbade the mere possibility of interference. The threat of arbitrary rule, rather than actual interference, constituted an unacceptable 'domination' (Pettit 1997: *passim*).

Hobbes, according to this reading, formulated what would become the liberal riposte to 'republican liberty'. A materialist, hostile to free will, Hobbes countered with a notoriously ungenerous definition of liberty as a mere absence of 'external impediments to motion'. Thus 'free men' were merely free from physical interference, as uncontained water was 'free' to flow. All action was necessitated by appetites and aversions, and a workable definition of civil liberty needed to reconcile liberty and necessity. Hobbes thus denied that anything but physical restraint—not even terror—could be considered a restraint upon civil liberty (Skinner 2008: 157).

Hobbes's understanding of liberty operated in diverse contexts, and whether Skinner is right to privilege his negative engagement with republicanism is an open question. Nevertheless, Hobbes's application of a narrow, 'non-interference' understanding of liberty to debates over the extent of *civil* liberty was a consequential intellectual move. It established the classic account of negative liberty, and it endorsed the view that civil liberties could be defined by the mere 'silence of the law'. To republicans, this was an apology for servile dependence and 'Enlightened' despotism. Modern neo-republicans identify the Hobbesian account of civil liberty as the original sin of the liberal tradition. There are limits to this point (Larmore 2001: 229–43), but it is true that utilitarian liberalism did follow Hobbes in construing liberty as non-interference. It may well be that this understanding of liberty is impoverished.

It becomes clear why Thomas Hobbes's bequest to liberalism has been such an inexhaustible subject. By deploying natural-rights contractualism and popular sovereignty in the service of an absolutist political programme, Hobbes revealed liberalism's proximity to robust accounts of sovereignty. He threw into high relief the tensions between natural-rights political thought and both Christianity and republicanism. Hobbes's narrow understanding of civil liberty; his attack on traditional accounts of *summum bonum*; his obsession with order over justice; his atomized account of individual interest: each of these prefigured features of the modern liberal order. To be sure, Hobbes contributed only to the theoretical foundations of liberalism. Constitutional liberalism (built on the separation of powers) and the liberal political economy of private property were both alien to him. Nor do modern liberals generally accept the asymmetry of Hobbes's balancing of self-sovereignty against state sovereignty. Nevertheless, these qualifiers cannot entirely efface the awkward status of Thomas Hobbes as a theoretical progenitor of liberalism.

THE BROADER IMPACT OF THE ENGLISH REVOLUTION

If liberalism is a theoretical tradition that developed largely in an Anglo-phone context, the English Revolutions of the Stuart era created the hothouse conditions that accelerated its growth. Among the parliamentarian factions of the Civil War era, the Levellers have commanded attention second only to that given Hobbes by students of liberalism. A disparate set of thinkers, the Levellers developed a radical account of popular sovereignty that targeted, in turn, the despotical tendencies of the Stuart monarchy, of the victorious parliament itself, and then of the usurping army under Oliver Cromwell. Their main theorists (John Lilburne, Richard Overton, and William Walwyn) were of modest station, and their writings proved ephemeral. Their influence was muted until their rediscovery in the twentieth century, but they evidence the surprisingly liberal forms that early modern political theory could assume.

The Levellers developed a radical political critique that was foundationally religious. Their early tracts attacked efforts to preserve a coercive national church. The Levellers were religious sectarians, and their pronounced individualism developed first as a spiritual mandate. Of religion Walwyn wrote, 'every man must examine for himself . . . or else he must be conscious to himself that he sees with other men's eyes and has taken up an opinion not because it consents with his understanding but for that it is the safest and least troublesome as the world goes . . .' (Sharpe 1998: 12). Free conscience was not merely internal, but informed a robust intellectual autonomy and a realm of free debate. Truth would advance by 'the efficacy and convincing power of sound reason and argument' (Sharpe 1998: 20). Such logic undermined not just priests, but the religious power of sovereignty itself. Early moderns most often cast religious toleration as a prudential virtue of statecraft, rather than a positive principle under-girding moral pluralism. But the Levellers' defence of free conscience generated a remarkably modern understanding of both individual autonomy and free civil society.

The egalitarian spirit of the Levellers informed a radical political programme. They did not engage in any Hobbesian finessing of the consent question. They understood equality as both a Christian inheritance and a 'birthright'. Wrote Overton: 'For by natural birth all men are equally and alike born to propriety, liberty, and freedom . . . even so are we to live, everyone equally and alike to enjoy his birthright and privilege; even all whereof God by nature has made him free.' The Levellers did not offer a detailed account of the state of nature, but they did espouse an original contractualism, with no man 'enslaved by his neighbour's might'. In order to 'preserve' themselves, individuals contact to create power, 'not immediately from God . . . but mediately from the hand of nature, as from the represented to the representers' (Sharpe 1998: 55).

Consent was an immediate concern for the Levellers. Their most famed production, the *Agreement of the People* (1647), reflected this. The *Agreement* constituted the 'first proposal in history for a written constitution based on inalienable natural rights' (Wootton 1991: 412). The document swept aside the traditional prerogatives of the king and parliament and gathered the explicit agreement of subjects for a new constitution. The *Agreement* thus sought, at once, the withdrawal of consent from a doomed regime and the granting of it to a new one. The latter would consist of a single, supreme assembly. If a king remained, he would be rendered a vestigial executor of assembly will. The plan contained elements that we might, without violence, charac-terize as 'liberal'. One such element was the requirement that the founding constitution be popularly ratified. Another was the demand that assembly representation be nu-merically rationalized. Thus did individuals and their interests become the atoms of politics, rather than localities, corporations, or castes (Sharpe 1998: 93–4). The Level-lers, furthermore, envisioned a dramatic expansion of the franchise to most males. In the words of Colonel Thomas Rainborough: 'really I think that the poorest he that is in England hath a life to live as the greatest he; and . . . every man that is to live under a government ought first by his own consent to put himself under that government' (Sharpe 1998: p. xv). Leveller democracy rejected all rights granted according to 'tenure, estate, charter, degree, birth, or place' (Sharpe 1998: 95).

Individualism, egalitarianism, and attachment to consent all marked the Levellers, but their social programme was perhaps still more 'liberal' in inclination. The

Agreement of the People struck a blow for the limited state by ensuring that government was primarily intended to 'secure the rights' of the governed, and that its powers were limited to those 'not expressly or impliedly reserved by the represented to themselves' (Sharpe 1998: 94). Leveller reforms, indeed, liberated individuals intellectually, religiously, and economically. The Levellers were surprisingly open to the accommodation of interest. They attacked corporate privileges and monopolies in all areas of life, and espoused the right of citizens freely to enter specific trades as vigorously as they did the right to free conscience. Private interests were in this sense not illegitimate unless they operated corruptly. The Levellers defended free trade and economic competition, and they were more interested in social mobility than in economic equality as such. These aspects of the Leveller's social and economic vision are perhaps more significant precursors of modern liberalism than Leveller constitutional theory proper (Houston 1991: 381–420).

Beyond the Levellers and Hobbes, most interpretative claims about the roots of liberalism in the English Revolution focus on the writings of the English republicans. English republican theory, produced primarily after 1649, was written to justify the ad hoc establishment of a kingless commonwealth. Republican writers, including Marchamont Nedham, John Milton, and James Harrington, subsequently wrote in coded opposition to the quasi-monarchical government of Oliver Cromwell. Traditionally, the republicans have been arrayed against the presumed proto-liberalism of jus naturalists such as Hobbes and Locke. They are cast as 'Commonwealthsmen', advocates of civic activism over individual passivity, of civil glory over mere stability, and of civic virtue over individual interest.

Increasingly, however, this polar model of liberalism and republicanism has been challenged. English republicans could be remarkably eclectic in their theoretical borrowings. Marchamont Nedham, for instance, married Machiavellianism and a hostility to kings with a jus naturalism borrowed from Grotius and Hobbes. Nedham deployed an interest-oriented contractualism in the service of protecting individual property rights. Breaking from Machiavelli, he privileged the establishment of legal stability over the glory of the imperial state (Worden 1994: *passim*; Sullivan 2004: ch. 3). Regular assembly elections were the surest way to 'regulate' ambitions and 'tumult'. Nedham even anticipated the doctrine of the separation of powers, warning that arbitrary power would result from leaving the 'legislative and executive powers' in the 'same hands'. Nedham's various writings demonstrate how English republicanism could, in certain moods, anticipate the conceptual and rhetorical strategies of Lockean liberalism: 'The end of all government', he wrote, 'is the good and ease of the people, in a secure enjoyment of their rights, without pressure and oppression' (Nedham 1767: 14–15; Rahe 2008: 236–8, 242).

The most famous republican of the age, James Harrington, was once widely taken as the very antithesis of liberalism. His influence was presumed to have distinguished an antique style of Commonwealth politics hostile to 'modern' contractualism. However, this interpretation has become increasingly contested. Harrington, to be sure, did not deploy the language of rights. His 'liberal republicanism' is assumed to have emerged from his theoretical use of 'interest', and from his highly procedural under-standing of justice. The careful bicameral arrangements of *Oceana*, according to which an upper assembly debated propositions while a lower, popular assembly merely voted between two proposals, were procedural devices intended to accommo-date (rather than suppress) interests (Harrington 1999: 21–5). Harrington's elaborate plans for rotation in office sought to check the kind of ambitious glory-seeking that Machiavelli happily accommodated (Cromartie 1998: *passim*; Harrington 1999: 118–24; Sullivan 2004: 161–3). His account of interest, his suspicion of rhetoric, his psychological theory, all be traced, in some measure, to the influence of Hobbes (Scott 1993; Remer 1995). It has become possible to speak of James Harrington as the 'subverter—rather than a transmitter—of the language of classical republicanism' (Davis 1998: 241).

There have been similar efforts to 'liberalize' Algernon Sidney, the Whig martyr whose writings exerted an enormous influence in the eighteenth century. Once cast as a leading member of a 'country' politics of virtue, Sidney is now often presented as a fundamentally Lockean thinker. Sidney did borrow from Machiavelli an assertive militarism and a willingness to tolerate healthy civil tumult, but he also deployed a fundamentally Hobbesian account of the state of nature and of the social contract. In the natural state, 'no one man or family is able to provide that which is requisite for their convenience or security, whilst everyone has an equal right to everything...' Humans enjoy a natural freedom and equality in the state of nature. Each will resign this equal right only 'in consideration of a greater good, which he proposes to himself'. Consent is thus fundamental to Sidney's account of sovereignty (Houston 1991: 128). And, if Sidney at times spoke of government as a reflection of virtue, he more often privileged the stable enjoyment of individual rights. He closely linked 'the safety of nations' with the preservation of 'the lives, lands, liberties, and goods of every one of their subjects' (Houston 1991: 109–11; Sullivan 2004: 220–3). The public interest was secured by policing the interactions of self-sovereign individuals. 'I may do what I please with [my house, land, or estate], if I bring no damage upon others. But I must not set fire to my house, by which my neighbour's house may be burnt' (Houston 1991: 199–200).

Finally, a liberal reading of Sidney emerges from his treatment of religious toleration. True religion, he wrote, lay in a 'rational and natural right of disputing what's uncertain, and of not receiving it till convinced that it's a certain truth'. Sidney rejected the civil religions favoured by other republicans, and instead defended an extensive individual autonomy and a strict separation of religious and political power (Houston 1991: 125). The English republicans, on the whole, only inconsistently anticipated this 'separationist' strategy, according to which religion was liberated but also privatized, but Sidney (like Milton) did prefigure this Lockean approach.

Placing the English republicans in any historical sketch of liberalism is impeded by their sheer eclecticism. Their persistent borrowings from the new discourses of rights and interests, however, undermine any effort to cast the English republicans as hostile interlocutors with an emerging liberalism. It might be most fruitful to consider republicanism primarily as a distinctive constitutional tradition. By co-opting the language of individual rights and interest into a political programme that was hostile to monarchy, they helped prepare the groundwork for the later emergence of liberal democracy as a constitutional cause. It is perhaps for this reason that revisionist historians have lately coined the neologism 'liberal republicanism' to characterize them. Their original contributions to the basic theoretical propositions of liberalism were unimpressive. But their use of those propositions to defend republican constitutional arrangements—such as Nedham's separation of powers or Harrington's bicameralism—provided an exit from the absolutist jus naturalism of Grotius and Hobbes.

LIBERALISM'S TWO PATHS: SPINOZA AND LOCKE

By the latter half of the seventeenth century, the foundation stones for classic liberalism were in place: a modern account of contracted sovereignty; a reformed natural law theory elevating rights; the rise of a discourse of interest; the decline of naturalistic accounts of hierarchical politics; a religious pluralism that undermined the political theology of Christianity. Some of these developments—consent and contract, egalitarianism, rights—were internal to Christian thinking; others—the valorization of interest, the revolt against traditional natural law, the move towards secularizing sovereignty—emerged from a more religiously sceptical intellectual culture.

The thinker who inherited these ideas and reformulated them for later liberalism was, of course, John Locke. If Hobbes divides later liberals, Locke figures as their common, celebrated ancestor. Before we consider Locke, however, and in an effort to capture some of the complexities of liberalism's emergence, a second transitional figure will be considered: Benedict Spinoza. Spinoza and Locke operated with a great many of the same political assumptions, but with divergent metaphysical and religious ones. Their political theories anticipated the fully matured liberal order. Their significant differences, however, betray the tensions that the early modern period would graft into the liberal tradition.

Locke and Spinoza were each born in 1632. They lived through tumultuous events: the English Civil Wars; the achievement of Dutch Independence; several Anglo-Dutch wars; the Orangist revolt against the de Witts; and (after Spinoza's death) the Orangist coup against England's James II. Both Locke and Spinoza were men of the new science. Both were accused, rather accurately, of religious heterodoxy. The political theory of each, indeed, significantly developed out of their views on religious toleration. It has been influentially argued that Spinoza was a much more radical figure than Locke. Certainly, Locke's religious and social views were the more conventional. Between their respective accounts of civil science, however, it was Locke who ran the greater risks. The extent of his direct participation in the various political plots against the brother kings Charles II and James II is debated, but it was sufficient to send him into exile in 1683. By justifying armed resistance to tyrannical monarchs, Locke risked his life.

Spinoza's political thought comes down to us in unfinished form. His *Political Treatise* was never completed. Politics is treated in both of Spinoza's major philosophical works, the *Theological-Political Treatise* (1670) and the *Ethics* (posthumously published in 1677). In both texts, however, it assumes a subordinate role to other theological and philosophical mandates. Indeed, the radical nature of Spinozist ontology helped determine the particular qualities of his political thinking. In metaphysics, Spinoza tried to preserve aspects of Cartesian dualism, and tended to present thought and matter as two separate realms. But this dualism was overlaid onto a Hobbesian materialism, and Spinoza somewhat awkwardly presented thought and matter as two attributes of the single substance that constituted the universe. Individual things were reduced to mere 'modes' of this substance (Bennett 1996: *passim*). These ontological fundaments—characterized by Hume as 'gloomy and obscure'—produced some striking results, including an understanding of nature as self-generating and self-sustaining, a naturalistic account of humans as determined matter embedded within the one substance, and a reductive (probably atheistic) account of God as nature. Spinoza preserved the mere husks of Cartesian dualism, and dispensed entirely with both the spiritual realm and human free will.

These philosophical propositions had profound political implications. Humans act as modes of the one matter, governed by its physical laws, striving only to preserve their own existence. The will is not free, but 'strives' in parallel with bodily effort. Reason itself is intrinsic to this process of striving, a kind of heightened perception of the mathematical relation of things (Spinoza 2002: 949). Why reason configured as an attribute of determined matter would prove truth-tracking is not particular clear, but Spinoza asserted that it did, at least for higher humans capable of the necessary perception. Such perceptions distinguished the wise few from the vulgar many, a distinction fundamental to Spinoza's political theory. Other politically consequential features of Spinoza's basic philosophy were his utter dismissal of incorporeal spirits, of miracles, and—except in his more rhetorical moments—of revelation.

Spinoza's philosophy could not be accommodated within Jewish or Christian orthodoxy. This was recognized early on, and resulted in his excommunication from his synagogue in 1656. By the 1660s he was notorious as the leader of an atheistically inclined circle. His writings were banned, burned, or suppressed before publication. Spinoza was well acquainted with the repressive apparatus of the confessional state. His political theory resulted from the marriage of his natural philosophy with this traumatic personal experience.

Spinoza inherited the new jus naturalism. He knew Hobbes's work well, certainly *De cive* and perhaps the Latin translation of *Leviathan*. If anything, he was more severe than Hobbes in construing 'natural law' as the mere binding force of natural necessity. Like Hobbes, Spinoza defined the 'supreme law of Nature' as the 'sovereign right' of each individual 'to do all that it can do' to secure its own existence. In the state of nature, the wise and the foolish are equally permitted to act in pursuit of this supreme interest (Spinoza 2002: 683). For the purposes of considering natural right, then, a rough equality of ignorance is assumed by Spinoza. Striving towards existence is no more than determined behaviour. The 'basis of the state' must be grounded on this 'right and established order of Nature', the natural rules that determine animal behaviour. Natural law in this sense 'forbids only those things that no one desires and no one can do'. Humans and their rights are but 'particles' within determined nature. Their right is their might, and they are motivated to deploy right for mere 'perseverance in existence'. In short, the 'natural right of every individual is coextensive with its power' (Spinoza 2002: 526–7, 683).

As with Hobbes, political life emerged, according to Spinoza, from a 'desire to live in safety free from fear, as far as is possible'. Life without 'mutual assistance' must be 'wretched', and thus natural humans come together to put their individual rights into 'common ownership'. The purpose of civil order is 'nothing other than the peace and security of life' (Spinoza 2002: 699). Perfectly rational humans would not require coercion to accomplish stable civil order; they would be naturally propelled towards it by enlightened self-interest. But fearful, irrational humans require an artificial mech-anism of enforcement. In the abstract, Spinoza's account of sovereignty was every bit as absolutist as that of Hobbes. As long as sovereignty endures, it is 'bound by no laws, and all must obey it in all matters; for this is what all must have covenanted tacitly or expressly when they transferred to it all their power of self-defence, that is, their right'. Natural humans reserved no right to themselves in the original covenant. Reason propels us, necessarily, towards this act of renunciation (we 'strive by nature for a civil order'), and 'it is our duty to carry out all the orders of sovereign power without exception, even if those orders are quite irrational' (Spinoza 2002: 529–30, 687, 701).

In important respects Spinoza would soften the Hobbesian system, but he did so by dissenting from Hobbes's account of prudent statecraft. He did not limit sover-eignty as a matter of right, and he understood the negation of individual right in the original contract to be absolute. Indeed, he argued this more firmly than Hobbes himself, preserving not even the right of self-defence. Like Hobbes, Spinoza grounded political life on individual interest, and he defined interest as animal appetite. Their shared materialist determinism strongly shaped their accounts of natural law, natural right, and 'reasonable' government. Like Hobbes, Spinoza surrendered to the sover-eign the convention-making power to define justice and injustice, virtue and vice (Spinoza 2002: 532–4, 555). With Spinoza, the new natural law reached its heretical apogee.

Spinoza claimed to have broken from Hobbes by preserving natural right 'in a State', where it could presumably be readily redeemed (Spinoza 2002: 892). But Hobbes also preserved a right to resistance and a significant scope for individual self-judgement when it came to adjudicating consent. In this sense individual natural right was, in fact, never abolished in Hobbes's system, and the state of nature itself persists as a possible condition (Spinoza 2002: 690). Where Spinoza really did differ from Hobbes is on questions of prudent statecraft. Whatever the rights of sovereignty, sovereignty was—like all things—bound by the limits of its power. Nature governs all. 'Nobody can so completely transfer to another all his right, and consequently all his power, as to cease to be a human being, nor will there ever be a sovereign power that can do all it pleases.' Laws requiring inhuman action would fail. The state could only govern to the extent that it could motivate obedience, by love or fear.

It will not do to exaggerate this divide between Spinoza and Hobbes. Hobbes himself knew that there were prudential limits to governance, and that utopian efforts at total control would fail. The two men merely differed on the kinds of policies that they espoused on prudential grounds. Where Hobbes favoured monarchy, chiefly for its inherent unity of interest and will, Spinoza favoured forms of democracy. Neither thinker de-legitimated any constitutional form as a matter of principle. Their differences on constitutional design were politically consequential, but theoretically superficial. Spinoza insisted on the legitimacy of existing monarchies, and even suggested that efforts to uproot long-established monarchies (such as the English) were wrongheaded. In this sense, Spinoza, like Hobbes, was deferential to established authority and stability (Spinoza 2002: 555–6).

Spinoza liberalized Hobbes's regime because he viewed wider freedom and participation as a more prudent way of channelling the natural passions of subjects, of domesticating their fearful irrationality. In this sense only was democracy more 'natural' in Spinoza's scheme. In this sense only was the 'welfare of the people' the highest law. When Spinoza argued that 'freedom' was the 'purpose of the state', he meant to suggest that granting individual liberty was the best way to reduce fear and induce the self-interested rationality that generated obedience. Rendering subjects mere 'beasts or puppets' was not unjust but impossible. In this way, Spinoza's liberalism was a strategic relaxing of sovereignty in the interests of augmenting effective power.

For Spinoza, politics was a method of channelling the passions, not suppressing them (Hirschmann 1977: 13–14, 22, 44–6). He rejected moralizing efforts to type appetites and emotions such as anger, envy, and pride as 'vices'. In this, though he spurned hedonism, he prefigured the thought of his student, Bernard Mandeville, and the amoral politics of individual consumption that accompanied liberal political economy. He also reflected a more immediate milieu, the Hobbesian republicanism of the Dutch brothers Johan and Pieter de la Court, who viewed republican democracy as a system with psychological and structural advantages in the great game of harnessing passions and interests. The human subject, for Spinoza, was an appetitive, glory-seeking being, striving always for the pre-eminence that would ensure enduring. Democratic government more closely approximated the lost condition of self-sovereignty than monarchy or aristocracy. But all constitutional forms achieved stability by establishing conditions in which the vulgar could vent their superstitions and satiate their appetites, and the wise could live a life of reflection and reasoned passivity (Spinoza 2002: 681–2). Freedom for the 'private citizen' could take either form, and either form would help ensure the state's highest end: stability. 'So the more a man is guided by reason—that is, the more he is free—the more steadfast he will be in preserving the laws of the state and in carrying out the commands of the sovereign whose subject he is' (Spinoza 2002: 691).

The paradoxes of Spinoza's 'liberalism' emerge nowhere more clearly than in his discussion of religious toleration. Spinoza enjoys a great reputation as an early modern tolerationist (Israel 2006: 155–62). But Spinoza's tolerationism was Hobbesian, a prudential measure designed to deprive the clergy of power and to pacify religiously plural subjects. Toleration prevailed where it could advance those ends, and gave way where it failed to do so. As with Hobbes, inner religious and moral reasoning was preserved as a free activity by its inaccessibility. Sovereignty could not restrain that inner realm (Spinoza 2002: 568–70). Outer acts, however, were subject to regulation. Even here, prudence would dictate that individual speech and debate be protected. Repressing them would generate unnecessary strife, and could be achieved only with 'great danger to the state'. Prudence could thus undergird toleration. But it could also require serious restrictions on the open practice of religion. External rites did not serve piety, in Spinoza's scheme, and could not serve a true knowledge of God (that is, of nature). It was thus unacceptable that 'the peace and tranquility of the state should be prejudiced on their account'. Private belief was free because it could not be stamped out. 'But the burden of propagating religion should be left to God or to the sovereign, on whom alone devolves the care of public affairs' (Spinoza 2002: 693). In his *Political Treatise*, Spinoza drew up strict limitations on the size, wealth, and splendour of minority religions. He also devised a national religious establishment dedicated to a 'very simple religion of a most universal nature', and governed by secular magistrates, who would act as the 'guardians and interpreters of the national religion' (Spinoza 2002: 740). Spinoza sought more a 'freedom from religion' than a 'freedom of religion'. The regulation necessary to hedge such a freedom entailed more coercion than we typically expect to find in a liberal, tolerationist doctrine. It is not unfair to suggest that such latent coercion underlay significant portions of Spinoza's political theory.

This may explain why modern liberals have preferred to trace their paternity through John Locke's line. There is a massive literature on Locke. Older scholarship tended to portray him as a paternal apologist for gentry capitalism, but the best revisionist work has recovered the full radicalism of Lockean thought, his commitment to equality, rights, and resistance. To be sure, Locke's political thought was built upon an ontology more traditional than Spinoza's. Locke's radically empiricist epistemology undermined the notion of innate ideas and any traditional philosophy reliant on that notion (Tully 1993: 183–90), but he eschewed reductive materialism. Locke maintained a kind of dualism between matter and the spiritual mind. He believed in the immortal soul and some version of free will (Marshall 1994: 334–5). He understood human reason as a reflection of the divine, and his commitment to equality was fundamentally theological (Waldron 2002: 64).

Locke kept his distance from Spinozism and tended implausibly to ignore Hobbes. Instead, he took the paternalist monarchism of Filmer as his main rhetorical foil (Harris 1994: 194–201). It is, however, more instructive to juxtapose Locke's civil science against those of Hobbes and Spinoza.

Locke's 'liberalizing' of the jus naturalist school was more theoretically thorough-going than Spinoza's. Most of Locke's departures from the Grotian–Hobbesian line can be located in his account of the state of nature and in his anthropological assumptions. Natural humans existed in a state of equality, without inherent 'subordination or subjection'. Locke envisioned them as interested individuals, able to 'order their Actions, and dispose of their Possessions and Persons, as they think fit, within the bounds of the Law of Nature . . .' That last phrase is significant. Unlike Hobbes and Spinoza, Locke did not reduce natural law to natural right. The 'state of liberty' was not a 'state of licence', and it was governed by rational natural law. Natural law included, but was not limited to, the duty to preserve oneself. Even where natural law directed itself towards preservation, it sought the common preservation of society, not mere self-preservation. Locke's natural law maintained a much fuller sense of the obligation of charity, and offered fairly traditional moral direction on matters such as the just use of property (Locke 1988: 269–71). Given his hostility to innatism, Locke struggled to identify purely rational grounds for natural law that did not reduce to self-interest, and he tended to rely on divine judgement to undergird virtue (Marshall 1994: 203). In the second of his *Two Treatises on Government* (1689), Locke declared it 'beside my present purpose to enter here into the particulars of the Law of Nature', but it was nevertheless politically significant that he did admit such wider particulars (Locke 1988: 275; Harris 1994: 268). A natural capacity for disinterested moral reasoning helped salvage Locke's state of nature from Hobbesian darkness.

Against Hobbes, Locke distinguished between the state of nature and the state of war. 'Want of a common judge with authority puts all men in a state of nature: force without right, upon a man's person, makes a state of war . . .' (Locke 1988: 25). This distinction at once preserved moral obligation in the state of nature, and the possibility of injustice in the sovereign state. Locke did not believe that natural humans, outside of political life, were incapable of sociable existence. He offered an elaborate stage theory of the state of nature. In the earliest stages of agrarian society, an informal communal-ism existed. Natural property rights were secured by the mixing of labour with land. This property possession was limited by the natural law against waste and by the requirement of plenty. Accumulation without waste required the invention of money by common consent, which permitted more abundant private possessions, a barter economy, and wage labour (Locke 1988: 288–96). Population growth followed, and with it contestation and the need for sovereign arbitration. Natural property gave way to property by 'settled agreement'.

The social contract was thus motivated not by mere fear for life but by the need for property protection. Society in many respects thus pre-dated sovereignty. These adjustments to the Hobbesian state of nature changed the motivations for the social contract, reserved greater right from the sovereign, and rendered a return to the state of nature less fearful. Throughout the seventeenth century, the jus naturalists had feared disorder more than tyranny; Locke reversed these phobias. He also expanded the acts of sovereignty that might trigger legitimate political resistance. Threat to equitable property right joined threat to life.

Locke also distinguished his account of the state of nature by insisting on an individual, natural right to execute justice according to the natural law (Locke 1988: 272–8). Executive power was thus not a mere creation of sovereignty but pre-dated it. This claim recalled medieval Europe's 'accusatory' system of criminal justice, but was nevertheless unusual and subversively populist in the seventeenth century (Tully 1993: 17–21, 25). It served to expand political resistance beyond the Hobbesian limits of self-defence.

Locke's social contract emerged when economic competition required a more vigorous assertion of positive law 'for the preservation of property'. An individual does not, according to Locke, surrender an expansive natural right to pursue his or her interests, but rather the 'power to punish offences against the law of nature, in prosecution of his own private judgement' (Locke 1988: 324–5). 'Political or civil society' was thus generated when 'executive' power was created, an authority to 'judge controversies' and establish law. Locke excluded absolute monarchy by arguing that such monarchs existed as in a state of nature, and thus could not resolve the 'inconveniences' of that state (Locke 1988: 326). Individuals would not agree to enslave themselves, 'nor think themselves in civil society, till the legislature was placed in collective bodies of men, call them senate, parliament, or what you please. By which means every single person became subject, equally with other the meanest men, to those laws which he himself, as part of the legislative, had established.' Individuals did not consent to obey mere sovereignty, but to obey 'the determination of the majority' (Locke 1988: 329–31). Locke thus married the natural-rights tradition with a requirement for representation reminiscent of Leveller and republican thought. Locke also offered a rudimentary separation of powers doctrine, whereby sovereignty was essentially equated with legislative power, and executive power was rendered secondary.

Locke's most radical doctrine was his right to resistance. He based it upon the transcendent quality of natural law, and the extensive ends of government beyond mere protection of life: namely, the preservation of self, 'liberty, and property', and the 'common good'. Theft, injustice, and self-destruction were not permitted to individuals under the law of nature, and they were, therefore, not rights that could be surrendered to sovereignty. Even legislative power was a 'subordinate' power given 'in trust' by the people (Locke 1988: 353, 357–8, 367). Locke had an extensive notion of consent, and, while he conceded the category of implied consent, he did not admit that conquest could viably generate free consent (Locke 1988: 386–8). Popular sovereignty survived in the political state, and Locke went well beyond the minimal right of resistance preserved by Hobbes. Resistance triggers included the failure to protect property or fairly to execute law, and even constitutional offences such as the suppression of the legislature by the executive (Locke 1988: 370). Certainly Locke did not wish to court tumult, and he argued that the critical mass of 'inconvenience' required to mobilize effective resistance would be only rarely established (Locke 1988: 380). Locke did not share Hobbes's minimal understanding of liberty as 'non-interference'. He feared the mere existence of arbitrary power (Locke 1988: 382–3). Although resistance was seemingly triggered only by 'inconvenience', which implied actual (not just theoretical) interference with rights, it must be remembered that Locke established representation and majority rule as 'rightful' aspects of the legitimate polity. Their mere absence was an inconvenience, no matter how enlightened the ensuing despotism.

The development of Locke's civil science was propelled by the development of his tolerationism. Early on, Locke espoused a statist, Hobbesian church, and opposed toleration of dissent. By the 1660s, with religious pluralism entrenched in England, he had adopted toleration as a cause, but had not yet presented religious freedom as a note of limited government (Harris 1994: 160–91). At this point he still hoped that royal prerogative might successfully establish toleration on *politique* grounds. Locke's position on toleration matured in the 1680s, when, in his classic *A Letter concerning Toleration* (1689), he went beyond 'toleration' and established free religious practice as a fundamental, inalienable right. This development was partly sustained with evidence from the Scriptures, emphasizing Christian passivity and interiority, and designating toleration as a 'mark of the true church'. More consequentially for later liberalism, Locke also defended toleration as part of his general theory of the commonwealth as a 'society of men constituted only for procuring, preserving, and advancing their own civil interests' (Locke 2005: 126). Religious belief, internal and self-adjudicated, was an inalienable right that could not be 'vested in the magistrate by the consent of the people' (Locke 2005: 130).

The Lockean state was thus secularized, shorn of its religious power but also of its religious obligations. This was partly a liberation of individual conscience, and partly a liberation of sovereignty to pursue its own ends without moral stricture. Churches became 'voluntary societies of free men', competing for adherents in a marketplace of worship. Free speech and free association were both fundamental rights implied by this vision (Locke 2005: 131–2). Locke characterized religion as a private matter, where 'every man may consider what suits his own conveniency' (Locke 2005: 139). And, though Locke was very willing to enforce morality when socially necessary, he pre-figured a vision of the state as 'morally neutral' when he wrote that 'the business of laws is not to provide for the truth of opinions, but for the safety and security of the commonwealth, and of every particular man's goods and person' (Locke 2005: 153).

Locke, in short, powerfully formulated the case for a 'separationist' liberalism, whereby secular and spiritual affairs were insulated from one another, and religious practice was rendered a private consideration (albeit one with a robust public presence in civil society). Two categories were excepted from this liberation: atheists, who were not reliable members of the social contract; and those who 'deliver themselves up to the protection and service of another prince' (Locke 2005: 157–8). This latter was aimed at Roman Catholics, and specifically at 'papalists'. It was a religious exclusion defended on political, rather than confessional, grounds, although Locke's antipathy to Catholic theology should not be underestimated. He maintained a strong, normative preference for individual, interior religion, and his sectarianism in this regard would be consequential in later liberalism.

Spinoza and Locke both cast long shadows over the Enlightenment and over modern political thought. The former arguably prefigured utilitarian liberalism, exerted influence over nineteenth-century materialism, and has been recently celebrated for anticipating the 'evolutionary' sociology currently hegemonic in some quarters (Israel 2006: 37). Furthermore, Spinoza's account of religious toleration, with its purgative and re-educational features, is reminiscent of some versions of perfectionist liberalism. Rawlsian liberalism, however, has been far more inclined to cast itself as a Lockean inheritance, a refinement of the 'theory of the social contract as found, say, in Locke, Rousseau, and Kant' (Rawls 1999: 10). Rawls's reconstruction of the liberal tradition has been pervasively influential, but the large role of Locke in liberal memory raises some interesting paradoxes. Locke's 'liberalization' of natural-rights contractualism was undoubtedly more complete than Spinoza's, and moved with more determination away from Hobbesian absolutism. We see in Locke, but not Spinoza, the broader slate of inalienable rights, the accommodation of resistance, and the 'first principles' defence of limited government that would mark later versions of classic liberalism. If in these ways, however, his 'liberalism' seems more durable and modern than Spinoza's, in other respects he was the more traditional thinker. His dualist ontology, his more elevated account of the human species, his belief in free will, his account of liberty, his attachment to natural law: these aspects of Locke were borrowed from the very republican, Christian, and scholastic traditions that are often cast as liberalism's historic foils. That the theoretical liberalism currently hegemonic in the West has returned to these springs is perhaps instructive of the profound influence that such early modern traditions continue to exert.

REFERENCES

Primary Sources

GROTIUS, H. (2004). *The Free Sea*, ed. David Armitage. Indianapolis: Liberty Fund. [First published 1609.]

HARRINGTON, J. (1999). *The Commonwealth of Oceana* and *A System of Politics*, ed. J. G. A. Pocock. Cambridge: Cambridge University Press. [First published 1656.]

HOBBES, T. (1994). *Leviathan: With Selected Variants from the Latin Edition of 1668*, ed. E. Curley. Indianapolis: Hackett. [First published 1651.]

LOCKE, J. (1988). *Two Treatises of Government*, ed. Peter Laslett. Cambridge: Cambridge University Press. [First published 1689.]

LOCKE, J. (2005). *The Selected Political Writings of John Locke*. New York: W. W. Norton.

NEDHAM, M. (1767). *The Excellencie of a Free-State* . . . London. [First published 1656.]

SHARPE, ANDREW (1998). *The English Levellers*. Cambridge: Cambridge University Press.

SPINOZA, B. (2002). *Complete Works*, trans. Samuel Shirley. Indianapolis: Hackett.

Secondary Sources

BENNETT, J. (1996). 'Spinzoa's Metaphysics', in Don Garrett (ed.), *The Cambridge Companion to Spinoza*. Cambridge: Cambridge University Press, 61–88.

BERKOWITZ, P. (1999). *Virtue and the Making of Modern Liberalism*. Princeton: Princeton University Press.

BOONIN-VAIL, D. (2002). *Thomas Hobbes and the Science of Moral Virtue*. Cambridge: Cambridge University Press.

BRETT, A. (1997). *Liberty, Right, and Nature: Individual Rights in Later Scholastic Thought*. Cambridge: Cambridge University Press.

COLLINS, J. (2005). *The Allegiance of Thomas Hobbes*. Oxford: Oxford University Press.

CROMARTIE, A. (1998). 'Harringtonian Virtue: Harrington, Machiavelli, and the Method of the *Moment*', *Historical Journal*, 41: 987–1009.

DAVIS, J. C. (1998). 'Equality in an Unequal Commonwealth: James Harrington's Republicanism and the Meaning of Equality', in Ian Gentles, John Morrill, and Blair Worden (eds), *Soldiers, Writers, and Statesmen of the English Revolution*. Cambridge: Cambridge University Press.

HARRIS, IAN (1994). *The Mind of John Locke: A Study of Political Theory in its Intellectual Setting*. Cambridge: Cambridge University Press.

HIRSCHMAN, A. O. (1977). *The Passions and the Interests: Political Arguments for Capitalism before its Triumph*. Princeton: Princeton University Press.

HOEKSTRA, K. (2008). 'Hobbes on the Natural Condition of Mankind', in Patricia Springborg (ed.), *Cambridge Companion to Hobbes's Leviathan*. Cambridge: Cambridge University Press.

HOUSTON, A. (1991). *Algernon Sidney and the Republican Heritage in England and America*. Princeton: Princeton University Press.

HOUSTON, A. (1993). 'The Levellers, Monopolies, and the Public Interest', *History of Political Thought*, 14: 381–420.

ISRAEL, J. (2006). *Enlightenment Contested: Philosophy, Modernity, and the Emancipation of Man, 1670–1752*. Oxford: Oxford University Press.

JAUME, L. (2008). 'Hobbes and the Philosophical Sources of Liberalism', in Patricia Springborg (ed.), *Cambridge Companion to Leviathan*. Cambridge: Cambridge University Press.

LARMORE, C. (2001). 'A Critique of Philip Pettit's Republicanism', *Noûs*, 35: 229–43.

LILLA, M. (2007). *The Stillborn God: Religion, Politics, and the Modern West*. New York: Knopf.

MALCOLM, N. (ed.) (1994). *The Correspondence of Thomas Hobbes*. 2 vols. Cambridge: Cambridge University Press.

MANENT, P. (1987). *An Intellectual History of Liberalism*, trans. Rebecca Balinski. Princeton: Princeton University Press.

MARSHALL, J. (1994). *John Locke: Resistance, Religion, and Responsibility*. Cambridge: Cambridge University Press.

MARTEL, J. (2007). *Subverting the Leviathan: Reading Thomas Hobbes as a Radical Democrat*. New York: Columbia University Press.

PETTIT, P. (1997). *Republicanism: A Theory of Freedom and Government*. Oxford: Oxford University Press.

RAHE, PAUL (2008). *Against Throne and Altar: Machiavelli and Political Theory under the English Republic*. Cambridge: Cambridge University Press.

RAWLS, J. (1999). *A Theory of Justice: Revised Edition*. Cambridge, MA: Harvard University Press.

RAWLS, J. (2007). *Lectures on the History of Political Philosophy*. Cambridge, MA: Harvard University Press.

REMER, G. (1995). 'James Harrington's New Deliberative Rhetoric: Reflection of an Anti-Classical Republicanism', *History of Political Thought*, 16: 532–57.

RYAN, A. (1983). 'Hobbes, Toleration and the Inner Life', in D. Miller and L. Siedentrop (eds), *The Nature of Political Theory*. Oxford: Oxford University Press.

SCOTT, J. (1993). 'The Rapture of Motion: James Harrington's Republicanism', in Nicholas Phillipson and Quentin Skinner (eds), *Political Discourse in Early Modern Britain*. Cambridge: Cambridge University Press, 139–63.

SKINNER, Q. (1978). *The Foundations of Modern Political Thought*, ii. *The Age of Reformation*. Cambridge: Cambridge University Press.

SKINNER, Q. (2002). 'Hobbes and the Purely Artificial Person of the State', in Q. Skinner, *Visions of Politics*, iii. *Hobbes and Civil Science*. Cambridge: Cambridge University Press.

SKINNER, Q. (2008). *Thomas Hobbes and Republican Liberty*. Cambridge: Cambridge University Press.

STRAUSS, L. (1950). *Natural Right and History*. Chicago: University of Chicago Press.

STRAUSS, L. (1952). *The Political Philosophy of Hobbes: Its Basis and its Genesis*, trans. Elsa Sinclair. Chicago: University of Chicago Press.

SULLIVAN, V. (2004). *Machiavelli, Hobbes, and the Formation of a Liberal Republicanism in England*. Cambridge: Cambridge University Press.

TIERNEY, B. (1997). *The Idea of Natural Rights*. Grand Rapids, MI: Eerdmans Publishing Company.

TUCK, R. (1979). *Natural Rights Theories: Their Origins and Development*. Cambridge: Cambridge University Press.

TUCK, R. (1987). 'The "Modern" Theory of Natural Law', in A. Pagden (ed.), *The Languages of Political Theory in Early-Modern Europe*. Cambridge: Cambridge University Press.

TUCK, R. (1991). 'Grotius and Selden', in J. H. Burns and M. Goldie (eds), *Cambridge History of Political Thought, 1450–1700*. Cambridge: Cambridge University Press, 499–529.

TULLY, J. (1993). *An Approach to Political Philosophy: Locke in Contexts*. Cambridge: Cambridge University Press.

WALDRON, J. (2002). *God, Locke, and Equality: Christian Foundations in Locke's Political Thought*. Cambridge: Cambridge University Press.

WOOTTON, D. (1991). 'Leveller Democracy and the Puritan Revolution', in J. H. Burns and M. Goldie (eds), *Cambridge History of Political Thought, 1450–1700*. Cambridge: Cambridge University Press.

WORDEN, B. (1994). 'Marchamont Nedham and the Beginnings of English Republicanism', in David Wootton (ed.), *Republicanism, Liberty, and Commerical Society: 1649–1776*. Palo Alto, CA: Stanford University Press, 139–93.

ZAGORIN, P. (2009). *Hobbes and the Law of Nature*. Princeton: Princeton University Press.

CHAPTER 17

···

ABSOLUTISM

···

MARK GOLDIE

ABSOLUTISM is a concept more readily deployed by political scientists than historians. The latter suspect a mismatch between an ideal type and the practical limitations of power in pre-modern states. Monarchs rarely achieved plenary authority over their peoples, being constrained by aristocracies, representative estates, customary jurisdictions, and fiscal, bureaucratic, and military weaknesses. Absolut*ism*, moreover, is a nineteenth-century term, which, in the liberal lexicon, too readily elides with despotism; rarely were monarchies systemically despotic. The term, however, retains value, to denote doctrines articulated by ideologists (chiefly but not only) of monarchy who aimed to redescribe the fissiparous polities inherited from the medieval world in terms that awarded rulers constitutional supremacy. Absolutism was designed precisely to address the mismatch between doctrine and power: the pen might achieve what the sword might not.

Absolutism is conventionally construed as an early modern phenomenon. This is both plausible and problematic. Renaissance monarchies sought to transcend medieval corporate governance: in German terminology, the fragmentation of power in 'estate states' (*ständestaat*) was subjected to royal correction (*königsmechanismus*). The French Estates General did not meet after 1615, until the Revolution, nor the Danish Estates after 1660. Reformation monarchies in turn sought to suppress papal jurisdiction, and Lutheran theology strengthened princely rule. Yet the intellectual resources of absolutism were far older than the Renaissance and Reformation. The conceptual career of absolutism might begin with Aristotle's distinction between *basileia* and *politeia*, a distinction that lay behind Sir John Fortescue's contrast between the (French) *dominium regale* and the (English) *dominium politicum et regale*: England was a 'political monarchy' and hence not absolute. Or it might begin with the Augustan revolution by which the Roman republic was transmuted into the imperial monarchy of the Caesars. Early modern monarchies constantly invoked Roman imperial language and symbolism: John Dryden, for example, acclaimed the restored Charles II as

Augustus Redivivus. Absolutism had a further lineage. In appropriating the language of divinity and in rendering earthly rulers godlike, it echoed Byzantine, Saxon, and even ancient Egyptian conceptions of sacerdotal kingship. Yet caution is needed. There lies deep in the modern sociological and anthropological imagination—one thinks of Max Weber and J. G. Frazer—a schematic bipolarity between traditional, religious, or charismatic modes of rule, and modern, secular, rational modes. Historically, this model is disastrously crude. It treats the 'divine right of kings' as a species of mysticism, progressively superseded by rational theories of civil society, and presumes a teleology that ignores the juridical rationalism, and innovativeness, of early modern monarchies. If this chapter confines itself to early modern absolutism, and emphasizes jurisprudence as much as 'divine right', it is partly in order to resist a naive reductionism concerning political theories that have often been deemed alien from rationalizing modernity.

Louis XIV, the monarch who created Versailles, had for his orator Bishop Bossuet, who best encapsulated absolutism. 'First, royal authority is sacred; secondly, it is paternal; thirdly, it is absolute; fourthly, it is subject to reason' (Bossuet 1990 [1709]: 57). We may take this as our prospectus, proceeding from absolute, to sacred, to paternal, to rational.

SOVEREIGNTY

The absolutism of *monarchs* was a contingent and temporary corollary of the principal juridical development of the early modern period: the emergence of the concept of sovereignty. Absolute monarchy was a free rider on a concept that would later unseat it. As Hobbes made clear, sovereignty could equally well inhere in a corporate body as in the single person of a monarch (*Leviathan*, ch. 19). Sovereignty betokened a monopoly of political authority within a specified territory. It was taken to be constitutive of statehood and it presupposed that any regime that lacked its attributes failed as a state. Sovereignty was inimical to the distributed and overlapping jurisdictions that characterize the medieval, and postmodern, worlds. It was centralizing and envisaged authority as unitary, indivisible, univocal; it resisted federal, devolved, or transnational sources of autonomous jurisdiction. 'Absolute' was an analytical expression: it meant categorical, unappealable, unmitigated. It was often termed 'mere' (*merum* = pure, unmixed). An entailment of sovereignty was that the sovereign was the sole source of legitimate coercive force: effectively, Weber's classic definition of the state. The preeminent theorist of sovereignty was Bodin who, in *Six Books of the Commonwealth* (1576), aspired to strengthen French monarchy in the wake of the Wars of Religion.

Theorists of sovereignty tended to resolve political authority into legislation. The sovereign was the legislator, the sole source of law. All jurisdictions subtended to the sovereign's, or they were *ultra vires*. Local law-making powers, of a city or region, were derivative, not autonomous. Likewise, authorities lying outside the state had no *legal* claim against the sovereign. Relations between states were thus inherently unstable, governed by voluntary agreements, or war, in the absence of any adjudicative authority. Treaties there may be, but international *law* was a misnomer, for where there was no sovereign there was no law. Arguably, seventeenth-century theories of sovereignty, notably in Grotius, Hobbes, and Pufendorf, were meditations on the avoidance within states of conditions subsisting between states: the sovereign state was the alter ego of international disorder.

A corollary of legislative power was judicial power, the final adjudication of disputes under law. The sovereign was the agent beyond whom no further appeal might be made; to assert a transcending appellate right was either to claim that another agent was in fact sovereign, or it was anarchic muddle-headedness. In Hobbes, the state of nature is a condition of clashing claims to adjudicate each on our own behalf: the sovereign is the person of the state to whom we cede our right of judgement.

It was remarked that monarchy was incidental to sovereignty. This claim carries exemplary force when the trajectory of English constitutional controversy is traced. The modern doctrine of parliamentary sovereignty inherited the conceptual apparatus of early modern monarchical absolutism: what was fashioned for Tudor and Stuart monarchs, against the Catholic Church and then against domestic opposition, finally underpinned the modern Westminster system. At the time of the Civil War, parliament's defenders, Henry Parker and William Prynne (the latter in *The Sovereign Power of Parliaments* (1643)), asserted, against royalists, that the state was indeed constituted by sovereignty, but that sovereignty lay in parliament, even, *in extremis*, parliament without the king. The Revolution of 1688 translated sovereignty from monarch to crown-in-parliament. The shibboleth of eighteenth-century textbooks was that, properly speaking, parliament, and not the monarch, was sovereign. Thus, Blackstone, in his *Commentaries* (1765), argued that parliament had that 'absolute . . . power, which must in all governments reside somewhere' (1979 [1765]: i. 49), a doctrine that culminated in nineteenth-century Austinian jurisprudence. Correspondingly, arguments for the sovereignty of the people took a similar conceptual form. Bodinian attributes of sovereignty came to be predicated of the people, and governors accounted fiduciary delegates or lessees of this sole and foundational source of authority. Absolute sovereignty became decoupled from monarchy.

REFORMATION

Absolutism's debt to the Reformation is paramount. There is a tendency to think of absolutism as functioning to suppress rival secular powers—nobilities and representative estates. Yet the theory of absolute sovereignty had a fundamental role in immunizing monarchies from ecclesiastical challenges, especially the papacy. Churches were held to have no final claim against sovereigns, for a church's authority was spiritual and moral, internal to the conscience, whereas all outward jurisdiction, affecting external action, was a delegation from secular authority. The English Act of Appeals (1533), terminating papal appellate jurisdiction, declared 'this realm of England is an empire, entire unto itself'. Here 'empire' denoted not terrain but *imperium*, sovereignty. Other statutes extended the existing offence of *praemunire*, the appeal to external authority. To defend the papacy was to assert *imperium in imperio*, an empire within the empire. Much of the rhetoric of 'divine right' kingship in James I and VI's *True Lawe of Free Monarchies* (1598) was directed to denying papal divine right, as also Calvinist (presbyterian) divine right, both of them sacerdotal challenges to his crown. (Lutheranism was kinder to monarchs than Calvinism.) Absolutism was an affirmation of national autonomy, personified in the monarch, in the face of the claims of Rome and Geneva. Absolutism was thus a child of antipopery and anti-Calvinism, and, when absolutists denounced domestic oppositions, Protestant sacerdotal as well as secular constitutionalist and populist, they called them all 'papist', because *any* claim to autonomous jurisdiction was a simulacrum of the pope's. 'Monarchy', wrote Sir Robert Filmer, 'has been crucified between two thieves, the pope and the people' (1991 [1680]: 132).

This pattern was not confined to Protestantism and occurred in Catholic traditions, notably the French Gallican, which separated religion from papal jurisdiction. Again, churchmen were said to have authority only *in foro interno* (in the internal conscience) by virtue of Christ's prescription, while the outward panoply of church courts, immunities, fiscal exactions, and the elevation of clergy to episcopal sees were all 'regalian', belonging to the civil power. Much French 'absolutism' amounted to anti-ecclesiastical regalism. Bossuet, the supreme theorist of French absolutism, drafted the Gallican decrees of 1682. In the eighteenth century, Gallican transplants infected Catholic Europe, in the 'jurisdictionalism' or 'Josephism' of the German, Italian, and Iberian lands. From Paulo Sarpi's Venice in 1606 to the Synod of Pistoia in 1787, Catholics assailed papal power as being inimical to sovereign integrity.

All these tendencies were loosely 'Erastian'. Much of the ideological accrual of authority by temporal princes was directed towards restraining priests. In this sense, absolutism was a secularizing phenomenon. By the eighteenth century, the critique of 'popery', or, within Catholicism, of 'Jesuitism', became generalized into a critique of 'priestcraft', the leitmotif of Enlightenment anti-clericalism. However, the enemies of stable monarchy were not only over-mighty priests but also incendiary religious dissidents. The ugly propensity of churches to persecute, and of religious sectarians to antinomian excess, rendered necessary absolute authority in secular sovereigns as a precondition of liberty and peace, indeed of tolerance. *Politique* absolutism was premised on the blessings of peace: sovereignty cured religious strife. There was an enduring connection between absolutism and religious toleration. Hobbesian sovereignty found pre-eminent enemies in the 'three knots' of 'praeterpolitical' ecclesiastical power: popery; prelacy; and presbytery (*Leviathan*, ch. 47). Religious dissenters desperate for relief from domineering churches often appealed to the 'Godly Prince'. Thus the Huguenot Pierre Bayle, radical theorist of toleration, kept faith with French absolutism, even when driven into exile. Similarly, eighteenth-century 'Enlightened despots' were lionized as more tolerant than their churches.

ROMAN LAW

Theorists of absolute sovereignty drew heavily on Roman law, and often invoked the idea of the *translatio imperii*, the inheritance by modern monarchies of Roman imperial authority. When Peter the Great of Russia adopted the title of emperor, he asserted descent from Byzantium, the Eastern Roman Empire. The emperor Justinian's law code, the *Digest*, offered precepts that became political commonplaces: *princeps legibus solutus est* ('the prince is the sole lawgiver'); *rex in regno suo est imperator* ('the king is emperor in his own realm'). Ulpian's third-century dictum, *quod principi placuit legis habet vigorem* ('what pleases the prince has the force of law'), became Antoine Loisel's sixteenth-century *qui veut le roi, si veut la loi*. It is true that, conversely, lessons hostile to rulers could be extracted from the *Digest*, notably the axiom that self-defence even against magistrates was permissible; nevertheless, absolutists construed the *Digest* as theorizing law as the emanation of the emperor's will. This jurisprudence had been put to forceful use by the medieval papacy, in asserting that it was *dominus mundi*, lord of the world, which enabled popes to claim a right to depose heretical or tyrannical monarchs, since all princes were subordinate to the sole papal *imperator*. Such claims culminated in Boniface VIII's *Unam sanctam* (1302), against which Dante and Marsilius of Padua directed their defence of earthly powers, and in whom the seeds of early modern sovereignty lay. Royal absolutism was the reverse image of what Catholic canonists had fashioned for the medieval papacy.

DIVINE RIGHT

The sovereignty of kings, seeking to trump the divine *imperium* of the papacy, masqueraded its jurisprudence as the divinity of kings. The 'divine right of kings' was a theological meditation on a juridical concept, not a species of mysticism, and rarely did absolutists endow monarchs with magical or sacerdotal attributes. It is true that there were echoes of the notion that, anciently, kings were priests: coronation rituals suggested this; French and English monarchs 'touched for the king's evil', curing sickness by the royal touch; Philip II of Spain projected an apocalyptic monarchism, aspiring to succeed the four 'universal' monarchies of the Book of Daniel; and English Royalists canonized 'King Charles the Martyr' for enduring Christ-like sacrifice in the face of republican regicide. Generally, however, sacerdotal cults of kingship were absent from treatises of political philosophy, not least because theologians, like lawyers, were juridically minded.

Theories of absolutism certainly deployed theological language. Kings were routinely described as God's 'vicegerents', authorized by God. There is a paradox here, since it is just as true to say that theology adopted a juridical idiom. God was said to govern the

universe as sovereign, sole legislator, arbiter, and dispenser of justice. Earthly government was the ectype of the divine archetype: kings governed as God governed. The
language of Christian divinity, after all, itself borrowed the Roman imperial lexicon:
Christ is 'king' and 'lord of lords', the Virgin is 'queen' of heaven. Theology depended
on secular jurisprudence as much as monarchy depended on divinity. Because
God's monarchy was the archetype of all rule, political language was ubiquitously
monarchical and need not necessarily betoken absolutism or even monarchy. Even
republics were bedizened with monarchic attributes. The republic of Genoa adopted
high royal symbolism, and *La Madonna della Città* was depicted holding crown and
sceptre, the mother of Christ crowned queen of the republic. Regality was the condition
of statehood, and divinity its language.

OBEDIENCE

Absolutism conspicuously appropriated religious form when expressed as a theory of
obedience. For subjects, the insistent duty consequent on the absolute authority of
sovereigns was absolute obedience, and its corollary, the utter illegitimacy of rebellion.
Non-resistance was a logical entailment of sovereignty. Since the sovereign was final
arbiter, to challenge sovereign decision contradicted the meaning of arbitration. This
juridical axiom was commonly couched in scriptural terms, and 'non-resistance and
passive obedience' was the theme of thousands of pulpit sermons. It was scripted into
the Elizabethan Homily on Obedience and explicated in catechisms, where the Fifth
Commandment, 'Honour thy Father...' was construed as enjoining obedience to
fathers of every type, natural, political, spiritual, and 'domestical'—blood fathers,
princes, priests, and masters. The Bible became an armoury for monarchy. 'By Me
kings reign and princes decree justice' (Proverbs 8:15); 'Fear God, honour the king,
meddle not with them that are given to change' (1 Peter 2:17). The most cited verses
were Romans 13:1-2, the 'Pauline Injunction': 'The powers that be are ordained of
God. Whosoever resisteth the power, resisteth the ordinance of God.' Expositors
pointed out that St Paul wrote under the Emperor Nero, so even a brutal tyrant must
not be resisted. Indeed, as the early Christian Fathers taught, tyranny was God's
condign punishment of sinful peoples, so that submission was all the more appropriate.
Theologians termed passive obedience the 'doctrine of the cross', since Christ's own
stance in the face of earthly powers had been stoic pacifism and willingness to suffer.
Across Europe, Lutheran divines invoked the Pauline Injunction; thus Olaus Petri in
Sweden in *Christian Exhortation* (1528), Andras Sckarosi in Hungary in *On Principality* (1540s), and Hans Wandel in Denmark in *Royal Law* (1663-72). As the most
categorical scriptural statement on civic duty, the Pauline Injunction caused considerable casuistical anxiety to anti-absolutists when they sought to legitimate the armed
overthrow of tyrants.

A prudential claim in absolutism was that besmirching sovereignty entailed anarchy. Absolutist theorizing was often provoked by civil breakdown, such as the French Wars of Religion, the Fronde, the English Civil Wars, or military defeats within the Scandinavian kingdoms. Without a monopoly of authority, Bossuet wrote, 'everything is in confusion and the state falls back into anarchy' (1990 [1709]: 83). Violence, rapine, and theft are the legacies of contempt for the fount of justice, and private violence is categorically worse than monarchical rule. There was an Augustinian strain here, entailing meditation on, and sovereign deliverance from, the unruliness of postlapsarian human passions. Filmer insisted that it is 'the greatest liberty in the world . . . for people to live under a monarch' (1991 [1680]: 2). Absolute authority lay in the sword of salutary discipline, symbolized most forcefully in that fundamental sovereign attribute, the right to take errant life, to execute criminals. The majesty of monarchy was nowhere more tangible than in the drama of the scaffold. He who may, in face of the commandment 'Thou Shalt not Kill', legitimately take life is indeed sovereign by divine right.

The doctrine of non-resistance had, however, a crucial caveat. It did not require that *any* sovereign command must be obeyed, since it remained a Christian's duty to refuse ungodly actions. Here, the duty was to disobey and accept the consequences, even death at the ruler's hands. Thus the subject offers 'active obedience' to godly commands and 'passive obedience' (in fact, passive resistance) to ungodly. In the face of barbarous persecution by pagan emperors, the early Christians had refused to deny their faith, but they raised no rebellion, and were martyred. In this respect, expositors of absolutism were scarcely flattering to princes; rather, they dwelt on the potential for despotism, and offered princes no more from subjects than indifference to earthly fates. Moreover, the caveat could license churches to exert spiritual authority against 'ungodly' rulers. James II of England was astounded that loyal bishops publicly refused his command to read a royal edict from their pulpits; in 1688, their godly refusal and trial for sedition unleashed a revolution. The recalcitrant bishops denied that they had resiled from the absolute monarchy they had avidly preached, since they offered no *physical* resistance, no declension from the sovereign monopoly of the temporal sword.

As in much else, Hobbes differed from the absolutist mainstream, because he detected a dangerous slippage in such renewals of sacerdotal hubris. Naaman the Israelite, he argued, was right to obey his master's command to worship the pagan god Rimmon (*Leviathan*, ch. 42). Any claim of conscience and 'true religion' against the monarch's judgement is the beginning of rebellion. Anglican theologians sometimes endorsed Hobbes's defence of civil authority against the 'anarchy of private conscience'. However, Hobbes, and his anti-clerical followers, travelled further than they towards scepticism, raising epistemic doubts about sacerdotal knowledge of 'true religion', and hermeneutic doubts about the perspicuity of Scripture. Churchmen wavered between invoking absolute authority against seditious 'conscience' and crypto-papistical appeals to spiritual authority against uncooperative monarchs. For Hobbes, such absolutism was incoherent and half-hearted.

ORIGINS

Absolutist theory offered an account of the origins of civil authority. It conceded that these origins could be various. Rule might begin in conquest or usurpation, and origins were not necessarily constitutive of legitimacy. Yet the special claim of *monarchy* to be the proper embodiment of earthly rule was enhanced by the patriarchalism that dominated much royalist writing. Prominent expositions were Filmer's *Patriarcha, or, the Natural Power of Kings* (c.1628, published 1680), and Bossuet's *Politics Drawn from the Very Words of Scripture* (1670s, published 1709), which asserted that all rule is paternal, and kingship a species of fatherhood; therefore, rebellion is parricide. The obligation of subjects to rulers was the same as the natural duty of children to parents, and wives to husbands. Patriarchalists were anxious to suppress misunderstanding about practices that may seem contractual: a woman may choose a husband, but does not thereby confer authority on him; a town may choose a mayor, but again does not confer authority. People designate, but they do not authorize.

Patriarchalism had two polemical advantages. First, it aligned rulership with the natural order. Monarchy, the rule of one, accorded with the hierarchies of divinely created nature. Beehives, ruled by a supreme bee, were paradigmatic of nature's monarchies. Hence Michael Hudson's title, *The Divine Right of Government... More Particularly of Monarchy, the only Legitimate and Natural Specie of Politique Government* (1647). Non-monarchical polities, such as aristocracies and democracies, were deviations from primordial nature, perversions invented by dysfunctional ancient Greeks. This style of argument often assumed Platonic form, drawing on the *Timaeus* in exploring the macrocosms and microcosms of the divine, angelic, animal, and human spheres.

Second, patriarchalism was scriptural, so that to deny it was blasphemous. Filmer's *Patriarcha* dwelt on the rights and powers of Adam, first husband, father, and king. Absolute sovereignty was Adamic and Abrahamic. The Book of Genesis was both descriptive and prescriptive of the civil order, and anti-patriarchalist theory was held guilty of heretical denial of the known history of the human race. For some authors, Adamic theory underwrote claims for primogenitive hereditary right in the royal succession, such as among French defenders of the Salic law, which debarred female inheritance, and among English Tories and Jacobites, who rejected parliamentary alteration of the succession.

Not all absolutists were patriarchalists; others were covenantal. They envisaged a natural condition of human equality, driven by imperatives of self-preservation, and destabilized by mutual threat and instability, such that it was rational to surrender private right to a common sovereign. The sovereign's powers were those that private individuals themselves exercised in the state of nature. Such a model could evade Genesis by predicating it as an atemporal thought experiment, the natural state denoting the condition we would be in, were government removed; or by reading into Scripture a post-patriarchal collapse of Adamic authority, in the anarchy of Babel or of lawless despots like Nimrod. Pufendorf adopted a hybrid model, a covenant among patriarchs, entered into by heads of families.

By premissing a natural right of self-defence, the covenantal model tended to leave open the possibility of a right of resistance *in extremis*, which is why royalist critics of Hobbes rejected it. Filmer's *Patriarcha* opens by objecting that many defenders of monarchy had begun with an erroneous hypothesis. Even if a covenant were deemed irrevocable, it was inescapable that civil authority was thereby predicated on the choices of the contracting parties. This was a house built on sand. Patriarchalists thought it no accident that defenders of papal power argued that, whereas papal authority was divine, secular states were contractual, mere human constructs. Cardinal Robert Bellarmine claimed thereby that papal authority was superior to secular. English Royalists and Tories accused their Parliamentarian and Whig enemies of borrowing their doctrine of the natural liberty of mankind from Catholic sources: once again, absolutism was a child of antipopery.

CONSTITUTIONS

A polemical achievement of absolutism's enemies was the elision of 'absolute' and 'arbitrary' power. In *Two Treatises of Government* (1988 [1689]) Locke repeatedly referred to 'absolute, arbitrary power', while Enlightenment authors invoked the notion of 'Oriental despotism' to denigrate European autocracies. Whig enemies of Stuart absolutism referred to the 'doctrine of the bow string', alluding to the Ottoman practice of strangling political enemies. If absolute monarchy were arbitrary, then it was fundamentally lawless; it reduced subjects, and law, to slavish dependency on whimsical wilfulness; on this view, absolute rule was no sort of civil rule, and was intrinsically illegitimate. Hume and Montesquieu expressed scepticism about these Whig commonplaces, insisting that European monarchies, even 'absolute', were not lawless despotisms. Yet Whig nostrums still persist in liberalism's caricatures of 'absolutism'. Bossuet complained that, 'in order to make the term absolute odious, many writers pretend to confuse absolute government and arbitrary government; but nothing is more distinct' (1990 [1709]: 81).

Most absolutists were constitutionalists. This fact either compromises their absolutism (and some scholars emphasize 'constitutional royalism') or is a paradox demanding resolution. Absolutists sought to redescribe, rather than abolish, constitutional forms. They did not challenge the making of laws in representative assemblies, but asserted that the prerogative of royal veto meant that law had no being without the monarch's will. Laws, strictly, were suppliants' petitions acceded by the Crown. English absolutists did not aim to abolish parliament, but argued a historical case that parliaments developed from the feudal monarchy's great council, and hence had no pristine pre-monarchic roots in the 'ancient constitution' of the Saxon past. In France, a historical quarrel between 'Romanists' and 'Germanists' persisted from the sixteenth to the eighteenth centuries, the former insisting that monarchy was heir to the Roman *imperium*, the latter to the modest tribal chieftains of Germanic, 'Gothic' antiquity, described in Tacitus' *Germania* (98 CE).

Anathema to the absolutists was the classical conception of the 'mixed' polity, a balanced and co-equal meld of monarchy, aristocracy, and democracy; a model, today loosely termed 'classical republican', that demoted the monarch from supremacy and rendered it but one element in a trinity. The idea of a 'mixed' polity was voiced from the Renaissance to the American Revolution as a retort to absolutism. For their part, absolutists regarded classical republicanism as a dangerously muddled neglect of the necessity of unequivocal sovereignty. In such a polity, there is no locus of adjudication when elements conflict. This objection corroded mixed monarchy claims made in Civil War England, and forced the king's enemies to the more dramatic assertion that sovereignty must lie in parliament or the people. For absolutists, there could be no concession to 'mixed monarchy'. When Charles I momentarily, but eloquently, conceded the mixed polity in his *Answer to the Nineteen Propositions* (1642), his absolutist allies repudiated it as a disastrous concession. Filmer entitled a tract *The Anarchy of . . . a Mixed Monarchy* (1648) and Hobbes wrote contemptuously of 'mixarchy'.

If absolutists rejected 'mixed' monarchy as incoherent, they nonetheless allowed 'limited' monarchy. The distinction was considerable. A virtuous monarch was self-limiting and, so long as his reserve powers were inviolate, a large fund of delegated powers remained. Magistracy ordinarily proceeded through regular channels, in assemblies of estates, courts of law, and local jurisdictions. Historically, the devolved authority of monarchs was embodied in customary law and deliberative institutions. It was even possible to create republics by royal fiat: town corporations and university colleges were self-governing republics, but existed by revocable royal charters. 'Monarchical republicanism' was not oxymoronic. But absolutists wanted it understood that self-government was not grounded in a prior, inherent right of the governed; rather, it existed by grace, condescension, concession: *concessio*. Medieval glossators had distinguished *concessio* from *alienatio*: sovereigns must not *alienate* their powers. There were no natural liberties, yet there were civil liberties, or franchises, ceded by authority. Lawyers distinguished the king's absolute and ordinary power, *potestas absoluta* and *potestas ordinata*. Absolute power was a reserve, immanent within ordinary courses. It was invoked in emergencies: who denied that rulers may order homes to be destroyed to prevent the spread of fire; or may mitigate the severity or incongruity of criminal jurisdiction through prerogative courts of equity?

Claims that monarchs were 'gracious' and 'condescending' became installed at the heart of republican objections to absolutism. Republicans asserted that, though we might have liberties under kings, such liberties were not worth the name if merely discretionary, for this makes us depend on the will of another: subjects; slaves even; and not citizens. The term 'condescension' passed from honorific to pejorative.

For Bodin, a distinguishing feature of European monarchies, howsoever absolute, was their obligation to respect private property, and hence to raise taxation only with the consent of estates, because private property subsisted in natural law. His contention was appropriated by opponents of monarchs, and his fiscal caveat arguably strains the plausibility of describing him as 'absolutist'. Yet no monarch, whatever his earthly powers, could trench on natural law. Charles Loyseau differentiated 'seigneurial' and 'sovereign' absolutism: in the former, the ruler treated his subjects' domains as personal property, but such was not the case with sovereign absolutism. Equally, royalists argued that, *in extremis*, sovereigns may raise taxes by their sole authority to defend the state from its enemies. Bodin's strictures notwithstanding, royal right to 'emergency' fiscal exaction proved a particular spur to absolutist theorizing. The natural right of property need not unduly abridge royal fiscal rights. If natural law was one potential constraint on absolute rule, other restrictions could be regarded as requirements of the principal of non-contradiction: a sovereign cannot act to abridge his own sovereignty and cannot bind his successors.

The doctrine of *concessio* was married to the language of counsel. Virtuous monarchs were counselled monarchs and wise governance depended on the deliberations of courtiers, churchmen, and assemblies. This was no theory of 'checks and balances'; rather, it was a branch of ethics. Just as the proper conduct of the self depended on reason informing the will, so royal will was enhanced and perfected, rather than compromised, by acting in accordance with right reason through counsel. Human reasoning was fallible and counsel repaired the defects of a single intellect. For Bodin, it was not command, but rightful command (*droit commandement*), in accordance with divine and natural law, that properly constituted law (*Six Books*, i. 8). Even apparently adulatory genres of 'divine right', such as the Court masques of Caroline England, contained counsel and criticism as well as compliment. Charles de Grasaille, in *Royal Rights of France* (1538), while styling kings God's vicegerents, insisted that counsel was 'part of the prince's person', the 'soul' of the prince (Lloyd, Burgess, and Hodson 2007: 465).

As noted earlier, absolutists had a constant eye to the theology of God's governance, because earthly rule should replicate divine. God himself ordinarily limits his rule to the regular channels of the natural order, and binds himself to promises he has made. His omnipotence is not arbitrary, since his will is perfectly counselled by his reason. While absolutist theory leaned towards a voluntaristic jurisprudence of the omnipotence of sovereign will, it was constantly countervailed by a moral philosophy of the princely cultivation of reason through counsel.

Absolutists were accordingly emphatic that absolute rule was distinct from tyrannical. A vast corpus of homiletic literature adjured monarchs to conduct themselves with temperance, mercy, charity, justice, the Christian and Stoic virtues, and reprobated the hideous deformities of tyranny, for which there were innumerable classical and biblical exemplars. Tyranny was a condition (to which any polity was prone) in which rulers served private passion rather than public good. Consequently, absolutists had much to say about the character, habits, and formation of princes. The genres of the 'mirror for princes' and the 'education of a Christian prince' long persisted, recurring, for example, in Fénelon's *Telemachus* (1699). James VI and I lectured his son Henry, in *Basilikon*

Doron (1598), on kingly virtues, and subtitled his *True Law* 'the reciprocal and mutual duty betwixt a free king and his natural subjects'.

Virtue elided with practical skills, the *virtù* or prudence of princes. Machiavellian arts of kingship could be tamed within conventional discourses of virtue: prudence joined with piety. Justus Lipsius's *Politicorum* (1589) advocated moderation, self-control, prudence. The term 'reason of state' was popularized by Jean Botero's eponymous treatise of 1589, to denote those arts that equip a ruler to serve the happiness and prosperity of its people. In the eighteenth century, the misnamed 'Enlightened despots' described themselves as the first servants of public well-being.

Monarchs were said to be elevated only in relation to their fellow mortals, but their equals in subordination to divine and natural law. No sovereign could authorize murder, adultery, or bestiality. Such a position depended, however, on the unproblematic transparency of divine law, or on the authority of churches as interpreters of divine law, priests teaching kings. What disturbed Hobbes's fellow royalists was his scepticism about such certitude and his anti-clerical rejection of church authority as undermining civil. The civil power must, for Hobbes, be arbiter of divine precept; anything else was *lèse majesté*. To its critics, Hobbism was hyper-voluntarism, collapsing reason and virtue into mere will, the position of Plato's Thrasymachus, for whom justice was the fiat of the strongest. There was a *risqué* strand in English Restoration stage plays, in which Hobbesian sovereigns self-authorized the seduction of virgins, on the claim that law, and even morality, are only what sovereigns stipulate. Some theorists akin to Hobbes, if more Byzantinist than jurisprudential, steered close to sacerdotal kingship, for whom monarchs were supreme pastors in interpreting God's word. In Hungary, Janos Pataki's *Mirror of Kings* (1626) urged that kings 'reach the laws of God for the people to hear' (Lloyd, Burgess, and Hodson 2007: 195). But, in the main, the 'divine right of kings' remained a two-edged sword: it exalted rulers as *dei vicaria*, vicars of God on earth, while constraining them within bounds of divine law known to *all* who were adequately informed. Such was the unresolved paradox of absolutism.

REFERENCES

Primary Sources

BAYLE, PIERRE (2000 [1697]). *Political Writings*, ed. S. L. Jenkinson. Cambridge: Cambridge University Press.

BLACKSTONE, SIR WILLIAM (1979 [1765]). *Commentaries on the Laws of England*. 4 vols. Oxford: Oxford University Press.

BODIN, JEAN (1992 [1576]). *On Sovereignty* [extracts from *Six Books of the Commonwealth*], ed. J. H. Franklin. Cambridge: Cambridge University Press.

BOSSUET, JACQUES-BÉNIGNE (1990 [written from 1670s, publ. 1709]). *Politics Drawn from the Very Words of Scripture*, ed. P. Riley. Cambridge: Cambridge University Press.

FÉNELON, FRANÇOIS (1994 [1699]). *Telemachus*, ed. P. Riley. Cambridge: Cambridge University Press.

FILMER, SIR ROBERT (1991 [written c.1628, publ. 1680]). *Patriarcha and Other Writings*, ed. J. P. Sommerville. Cambridge: Cambridge University Press.

HOBBES, THOMAS (1991 [1651]). *Leviathan*, ed. R. Tuck. Cambridge: Cambridge University Press.

JAMES VI and I (1994 [1598–1610]). *Political Writings*, ed. J. P. Sommerville. Cambridge: Cambridge University Press.

LEIBNIZ, GOTTFRIED (1972 [1677–1714]). *Political Writings*, ed. P. Riley. Cambridge: Cambridge University Press.

LOCKE, JOHN (1988 [1689]). *Two Treatises of Government*, ed. Peter Laslett. Cambridge: Cambridge University Press.

LOYSEAU, CHARLES (1994 [1610]). *A Treatise of Orders and Plain Dignities*, ed. H. Lloyd. Cambridge: Cambridge University Press.

PUFENDORF, SAMUEL (1991 [1682]). *On the Duty of Man and Citizen According to Natural Law*, ed. J. Tully and M. Silverthorne. Cambridge: Cambridge University Press.

WOOTTON, D. (1986 [1570–1714]) ed. *Divine Right and Democracy*. Harmondsworth: Penguin.

Secondary Sources

BRETT, A., and TULLY, J. (2006) (eds). *Rethinking the Foundations of Modern Political Thought*. Cambridge: Cambridge University Press.

BURNS, J. H. (1996). *The True Law of Kingship: Concepts of Monarchy in Early-Modern Scotland*. Oxford: Oxford University Press.

BURNS, J. H., and GOLDIE, M. (1991) (eds). *The Cambridge History of Political Thought, 1450–1700*. Cambridge: Cambridge University Press.

DALY, J. (1978). 'The Idea of Absolute Monarchy in Seventeenth-Century England, *Historical Journal*, 21: 227–50.

DALY, J. (1979). *Sir Robert Filmer and English Political Thought*. Toronto: Toronto University Press.

FIGGIS, J. N. (1896). *The Divine Right of Kings*. Cambridge: Cambridge University Press.

FRANKLIN, J. H. (1973). *Jean Bodin and the Rise of Absolutist Theory*. Cambridge: Cambridge University Press.

GOLDIE, M. (2011). *Politics, Religion, and Ideas in Restoration England*. Woodbridge: Boydell.

GOLDIE, M., and WOKLER, R. (2006) (eds). *The Cambridge History of Eighteenth-Century Political Thought*. Cambridge: Cambridge University Press.

HENSHALL, N. (1992). *The Myth of Absolutism*. Harlow: Longman.

KEOHANE, N. (1980). *Philosophy and the State in France*. Princeton: Princeton University Press.

JACKSON, C. (2003). *Restoration Scotland, 1660–1690: Royalist Politics, Religion, and Ideas*. Woodbridge: Boydell.

LLOYD, H. A., BURGESS, G., and HODSON, S. (2007). *European Political Thought, 1450–1700*. New Haven: Yale University Press.

MCDIARMID, J. F. (2007) (ed.). *The Monarchical Republic of Early Modern England*. Aldershot: Ashgate.

MEINECKE, F. (1957). *Machiavellism: The Doctrine of Raison d'État and its Place in Modern History*. London: Routledge, Kegan, Paul.

MILLER, J. (1990) (ed.). *Absolutism in Seventeenth-Century Europe*. Basingstoke: Macmillan.

MOUSNIER, R. (1973). *The Assassination of Henry IV: The Tyrannicide Problem and the Consolidation of French Absolute Monarchy in the Early Seventeenth Century*. London: Faber.

OAKLEY, F. (1998). 'The Absolute and Ordained Power of God and King in the Sixteenth and Seventeenth Centuries', *Journal of the History of Ideas*, 59: 669–90.

ORESKO, R., GIBBS, G. C., and SCOTT, H. M. (1997). *Royal and Republican Sovereignty in Early Modern Europe*. Cambridge: Cambridge University Press.

PHILLIPSON, N., and SKINNER, Q. (1993) (eds). *Political Discourse in Early Modern Britain*. Cambridge: Cambridge University Press.

POCOCK, J. G. A. (1987). *The Ancient Constitution and the Feudal Law*. Cambridge: Cambridge University Press.

SCHOCHET, G. (1975). *Patriarchalism in Political Thought*. Oxford: Blackwell.

SKINNER, Q. (1978). *The Foundations of Modern Political Thought*. 2 vols. Cambridge: Cambridge University Press.

SKINNER, Q. (1998). *Liberty before Liberalism*. Cambridge: Cambridge University Press.

SOMMERVILLE, J. (1986). *Politics and Ideology in England, 1603–1640*. London: Longman.

TUCK, R. (1979). *Natural Rights Theories: Their Origin and Development*. Cambridge: Cambridge University Press.

TUCK, R. (1993). *Philosophy and Government, 1572–1651*. Cambridge: Cambridge University Press.

CHAPTER 18

ENLIGHTENMENT POLITICAL PHILOSOPHY

RICHARD WHATMORE

ENLIGHTENMENT AND ENLIGHTENMENTS

TOLERATION, secularization, and an associated critique of confessional religion might have served previous generations as organizing themes for an account of Enlightenment Political Philosophy. Today we are unsure whether there was an Enlightenment, a plurality of Enlightenments marked by particular historical circumstances and specific political and religious commitments, or competing 'rival enlightenments' seeking to remove alternatives from European intellectual life (Hunter 2001). Historians are divided about the origins of enlightenment and its course across Europe, employing terms such as 'the radical enlightenment' and 'the conservative enlightenment', or, more interestingly, focusing on the differences between denominational enlightenments, such as the Anglican, Lutheran, Catholic, Calvinist, Orthodox, or Jewish enlightenments.

The relationship between eighteenth-century political philosophy and that of previous centuries is equally subject to ardent controversy, pitting those who continue to perceive classical philosophies to be the mainstay of political argument throughout the early modern period against those who argue that Hugo Grotius, or alternatively Thomas Hobbes, transformed political thought through their natural jurisprudence, and inaugurated a long eighteenth century synonymous with enlightenment, stretching from the publication of Grotius's *On the Laws of War and Peace* (1625), or Hobbes's *Leviathan* (1651) to the French Revolution (1789–99), or the Vienna Settlement (1815). In short, we are unsure whether there was an Enlightenment or several enlightenments, how they interacted and which survived, what it or they amounted to if there was one or several, when it or they began, or when it or they ended.

Two prominent attempts have been made in recent years to bring clarity to the political philosophies of the enlightenment era. The first is Jonathan Israel's assertion of a radical enlightenment critical of state and clerical authority, and of social hierarchies, which he traces from rebellions such as the Fronde in France (1648–53), the Masaniello revolt in Naples (1647), and the civil wars in England, Scotland, and Ireland between 1638 and 1660, up to their culmination in the French Revolution (1789–99) (Israel 2001). Israel's contention is that an intellectual revolution occurred from the mid-seventeenth century that enabled the great upheaval in politics of the end of the eighteenth century to occur:

> A revolution of fact which demolishes a monarchical courtly world embedded in tradition, faith, and a social order which had over many centuries the distribution of land, wealth, office, and status seems impossible, or exceedingly implausible, without a prior revolution in ideas—a revolution of the mind—that had matured and seeped its way through large sections of society over a long period before the onset of the revolution in actuality. (Israel 2001: 714)

The radical enlightenment that signified this revolution developed in the midst of related enlightenment philosophies associated with such luminaries as René Descartes, Isaac Newton and John Locke, and Gottfried Leibniz, but the extreme character of the radical enlightenment was due to its author, Baruch Spinoza (1632–77). Spinoza rejected the mind–body dualism in favour of a perception of nature as a single substance, and this led him to reject the immateriality of the soul, to view religions as solace for weak and misguided minds, and to see churches and governments as being established for the service of human populations rather than for the maintenance of order. Israel has traced the influence of Spinoza's diverse and challenging writings throughout the eighteenth century, and particularly among *philosophes* such as John Toland and Dennis Diderot, and their disciples among the rebels and revolutionaries who challenged clerical, aristocratic, and monarchical hierarchies across Europe in the decades before 1789. Modern and democratic republicanism is portrayed as a central theme of enlightenment political philosophy, and one whose lineage tied radical religious beliefs to revolutionary politics during the eighteenth century, developing from a trickle to a flood in the process.

Sense of the contrasting scholarly perception of enlightenment political philosophy is evident by comparing Israel's views with those of John Robertson's *The Case for the Enlightenment: Scotland and Naples 1680–1760* (2005). For Robertson, the key to the reform projects that defined the Enlightenment was the discipline of political economy, derived from a form of Epicureanism associated with Augustinianism. Since the early seventeenth century numerous writers had argued that Epicurean natural philosophy, in the guise of the other-regarding *honnête homme*, was compatible with Christianity. In a parallel development, Augustinians such as Blaise Pascal and Pierre Nicole were arguing that human flourishing and contentedness depended on the individual pursuit of self-interest. In the subsequent generation, such figures as Pierre Bayle in Holland and then Giambattista Vico at Naples, Bernard Mandeville in

England, and later David Hume in Scotland, developed the argument that sociability derives from the passions and was not founded upon either religion or morals.

A controversy ensued about the relationship between economic development and the positive passions or virtues and the negative passions or vices. The central idea of the Enlightenment was that the wealth and interconnectedness generated by commerce was the key to human progress and at a more mundane level both societal survival and national security. This generated debates about the role of inequality in commercial society, the role of agriculture and different forms of private property in the genesis of trade, the extent of necessary reliance upon luxury goods and international markets, the moral content of the fully commercial society, and the likely role of religion within it. Such were the issues that obsessed the generations of Jean-Jacques Rousseau (1712–78) and Adam Smith (1723–90), and that shaped diverse reform projects from physiocracy to freemasonry in the second half of the eighteenth century. Robertson's enlightenment is radical, in the sense of studying and envisaging huge changes within human society, but there is no connection between radical religious beliefs and revolutionary politics. For Robertson, there is a far stronger emphasis upon the limits of human capacity, and of the need gradually to shape or indirectly to influence the passions, rather than seeking to set in train an immediate and unreflective transformation of one form of society into another.

In terms of describing enlightenment political philosophy, both Israel's and Robertson's stories are wanting. In Israel's case, while a radical enlightenment indebted to Spinoza can be charted across the eighteenth century, and came to full bloom in the 1790s, the main focus of political enquiry was elsewhere. Increasing numbers of scholars are recognizing that eighteenth-century thought was distinctive, not because of the gradual growth of forms of democratic politics that went on to define the modern world, but because of the impact upon political thinking of the war for international supremacy between Britain and France (Hont 2005). From a French perspective, the eighteenth century ought to have been the story of their dominion across Europe and of the entrenchment of their global empire (Sonenscher 2008). Yet, in practice, the French became fascinated by Britain in the eighteenth century, being the state that had stolen their thunder (Sonenscher 2007). The fundamental reason was British supremacy in the arts of war, as Samuel Johnson was held to have reminded his audience:

> It being observed to him that a rage for everything English prevailed much in France after Lord Chatham's glorious war [the Seven Years War], he said he did not wonder at it, for we had drubbed those fellows into a proper reverence for us, and their national petulance required periodic chastisement. (Boswell 1830 [1791]: 193)

While the generations of Richlieu, Mazarin, and Colbert considered England to be a minor state relative to the larger empires of Spain and Habsburg Austria, from the first decades of the eighteenth century it is difficult to find a Frenchman who did not proffer an opinion with regard to the rising power and prospects of his island neighbour. Voltaire's *Lettres sur l'Angleterre* of 1733, a book that was reprinted fifteen times before 1778, was representative of an era of obsessive interest in things British, signified by the coining of the noun *anglomanie* in the aftermath of the Seven Years War (Fougeret de Montbron 1757). Speculation about the consequences of British military success, and its political, economic, and possibly religious foundations, became a dominant trope in political philosophy across Europe.

This general context becomes clear by considering a passage first published in 1751 by the French writer Laurent Angliviel de la Beaumelle from *Mes Pensées ou le Qu'en dira-t-on?* The passage explains the transformation of political thought that was taking place because of the commercial revolution that had made trading states more powerful than their rivals. This, in turn, meant that all students of politics had to look to Britain for an evaluation of their likely future, because Britain was the foremost trading power. Decisive contrasts and continuities were revealed with the old world of amoral reason-of-state politics associated with France:

> The French are at present less hated, because they are less feared, but are they less formidable? . . . The French and English have divided Europe between them, which of the two have acted the most conspicuous part? The last century was the age of France, the present is the age of England. Louis XIVth was arrived at universal monarchy, that is, to such a degree of power as enabled him alone to make head against all. The English will acquire it in their turn. This will be the case, when under the shadow of the jealousies they shall raise against France, as she herself had raised against the house of Austria, they shall have so far improved their marine and trade, as to engross to themselves all the riches of Europe. The universal monarchy of England will be more durable, because it will be more solid; and it will be more solid because it will be more slow. In some respects it will be more equitable, because a nation of kings is generous. In others more weighty, because this nation of kings will be at the same time a nation of merchants. And in other respects more humbling, for nothing is so haughty as the empire of the sea. Louis XIVth did not come to that short instant of universal monarchy, but by oppressing his subjects during the whole course of his reign. England will come to it by enriching her people; the one took the direct high road of despotism, the other will pass through the untrodden paths of liberty . . . The blindness of some states is beyond conception. They take umbrage at the ambitious pretensions of an empire which must be exhausted of men and money, for the conquest of a province; and they are not alarmed at the progress of a people, who every ten years acquire, without any struggle, the revenues of a rich province. Is he not the true monarch of the world, who carries on its trade? (La Beaumelle 1753: 85–7)

Does this mean that Robertson, whose work focuses on England and France as the essential backdrop to developments in Scotland and Naples, takes the laurel? While Robertson does far more than Israel in terms of describing what was going on in enlightenment political philosophy, he too neglects the German *Aufklärung* and those areas of northern and eastern Europe where reform was constrained by the practical fact that the British and French models could not be adopted because of the gap between the circumstances of each society (Tribe 1988; Haakonssen and Whatmore 2008; Hunter 2008). In many of the smaller states of Europe, including states across Germany and in Scotland, reform was tied to the redirection of Stoicism, the development of eclecticism or common sense philosophy, and was often taken forward by the bureaucrats who served central government, by envisaged reforms of the law, and by the schemes of public and private education developed within major universities (Haakonssen 1996).

The fundamental fact is that eighteenth-century ideas were endlessly speculative, generating a politics that was ever uncertain about strategies for maintaining peace and security, engaged with and seeking to influence the unpredictable flux of markets, concerned about public credit, and likely to end in war: only the 1720s were peaceful. In consequence, the majority of political philosophizing was concerned with the maintenance of states, the avoidance of decline, and the means of extending national strength and of guaranteeing national independence. One of the most important facts to recall when studying eighteenth-century political thought is that it was very different from what we understand by political philosophy today. Few thinkers had any sense of a general science of politics. Those who did, such as David Hume, were, like their contemporaries who were critical of aspirations of universal philosophizing, mostly interested in particular facts and the unique blend of circumstances that explained the formation of states and their national standing, and the resulting conditional rules that might be derived from them. This meant that political philosophy was intertwined with history. It was also inseparable from political economy and from religion, because these forces played a dominant role in evaluation of the contemporary health of individual states. Some contemporary political philosophers might not recognize discussions of trade and empire, or sovereignty and security, as themes central to the history of political philosophy. This would be a mistake in studying the eighteenth century.

One of the most interesting effects of the extreme instability of the system of international relations during the enlightenment era was that it became commonplace to predict a reduction in the numbers of states across Europe. Modern history was expected to follow its ancient counterpart because the rise of a new Carthage or Rome (Britain and France) always caused petty sovereignties, and sometimes the greatest states, to decline and fall. The prediction was made that 'in less than a century there will not be above seven or eight sovereignties in all Europe where formerly there were above a thousand' (Lloyd 1771: 60–1). There was uncertainty as to how many European states were compatible with peace, global markets, and empire, and also what form of state would survive the contemporary international turbulence. Political philosophy was seen to be the surest means of working out what the future of Europe would be, and how the seemingly insurmountable problems of the present would alter the political contours of the continent.

This chapter is organized around the political philosophy of the four major forms of state to be found in eighteenth-century Europe. Such an approach is necessarily selective. It seeks to give a sense of some of the dominant themes and ideologies in political argument. Equally valid narratives could be constructed focusing on ideas about the state of nature, rights, duties, contract, laws (natural, positive, and conventional), liberties, property, perfectibility, public happiness, conscience, and toleration, and the relationship between church and state. All of these topics were widely discussed in eighteenth-century political philosophy. The intention behind this chapter is to give voice to the prominent feelings of intellectual innovation and crisis, and this necessarily precludes discussion of many of the themes listed above. In consequence, the following section deals with the absolute monarchy of France, because eighteenth-century politicians and philosophers of every stripe anticipated a renaissance of French power, and because French politics were illustrative of the ideologies of governance that were common to monarchies of the time. This necessitates an overview of the political philosophies that informed British political culture, on the grounds that it was the rise of this mixed and composite monarchy that caused intellectual turbulence elsewhere. The eighteenth century saw the last gasps, and on occasion the last hurrahs, of hundreds of petty sovereignties that existed across Europe. Political philosophy in the small states—republics, monarchies, and principalities—are the subject of the third section.

The chapter ends by considering one of the most important developments in political philosophy, paralleling an increased usage of the words 'despot' and 'despotism' in political argument. The terms were used to castigate the empires of the east, called by contemporaries 'oriental despotisms', and were more and more frequently applied to other forms of state. This development signified concerns about the future but also a willingness to contemplate innovation in politics. Many commentators believed that oriental despotism would become the dominant form of state once the warring civilizations of the West had burned themselves out, laying the foundations for a new dark age of barbarism, and possibly of religion (Pocock 1999a, b, 2003a, 2005). Arguments about despotism were equally prevalent in considering the immediate impact of the French Revolution. The Revolution was deemed by many observers to be a new challenge to enlightenment philosophy, having created democratic forms of despotism and barbarism that were much more deadly than anything to be found in the states of the East.

POLITICAL PHILOSOPHY IN FRANCE AND BRITAIN

When most observers of the enlightenment era speculated about politics, they thought about the respective merits of the political and economic systems of Britain and France, the legacy of the attempts by Louis XIV of France to create a universal monarchy on mainland Europe, the remarkable British experiment in tying mixed government to a growing national debt, and the likely futures of each state: whether they managed to restore peace, defeated each other by war, or fell exhausted before a larger power such as Russia or China. Throughout the enlightenment period, the anticipated revival of French power was an obsessive issue for commentators, necessarily tied to the question of the prospects for Britain, with uncertainty lying in the extent of British debt, the ability of the mixed government and the Anglican Church to maintain civil peace, and the consequences of the seventeenth-century republican legacy for this composite polity in the longer term. If commerce was vital for national strength, and if public credit essential as a national resource for war, there were question marks over the greed and corruption that appeared to follow trade, the risk of a monarch reneging on any debt and ruining his creditors, and the fear that the power associated with commerce was a sham, subject to inevitable decline by war, or economic competition from poor countries enjoying lower costs and paying lower wages. In consequence, this was the great age of the comparative analysis of political systems and of study of the distinctive political philosophies that were held to characterize particular states. Comparative analysis usually began with France, which was the dominant state at the beginning of the eighteenth century.

In the third and final part of Bishop Jacques-Bénigne Bossuet's monumental *Discours sur l'histoire universelle* (1681), he considered 'the particular causes of the revolutions of empires which princes ought to study'. By far the most important case, he quickly made clear, was Rome. This was not solely because it had 'encompassed all the empires of the universe', and in Bossuet's opinion had been the source of law and forms of civility (*politesse*) that continued to be envied by the moderns. It was also because France was establishing an empire that would ultimately be greater than that of Rome. French statesmen were expected to learn from the example of their antique forebears. The key figure in Bossuet's story of the rise of France to greatness was the modern Jupiter, Louis XIV, of whom Cardinal Guillaume Dubois said 'with a furrow of his brow he frightens the universe'. Following the 'wisdom, piety and justice' of his ancestor Charlemagne, Louis was 'astonishing the world with [his] exploits'. He alone, Bossuet predicted, would set a limit to his conquests (Bossuet 1966 [1679]: 401–29). Seven hundred years after Rome's ruin in the West, the expectation of many contemporaries was that Louis would re-create a similarly expansive empire.

The major benefit of such a political edifice, Louis's supporters agreed, was its capacity to establish peace after one of the bloodiest centuries in European history. As the King united the people behind him and headed the largest standing army seen in modern Europe, the feats of arms undertaken in his name were continuously and publicly celebrated. The King marshalled the latest military technology in his cause and gave *savants* opportunities to shape ministerial policy. Once the enemies of France had been vanquished, a universal monarch would reign, dispensing justice and maintaining a balance of power between the diverse elements of society. Peace and order would be accompanied by prosperity, especially for Paris, the metropolis at the centre of the empire.

The question of France's capacity to create a universal monarchy was naturally more problematic. Such a state had to be large enough to defeat its rivals and be blessed with extensive natural resources. It also had to have a population capable of filling and sustaining the massed ranks of the army and the marine. Alternatively, it had to have enough wealth, or access to the wealth of financiers, to be able to buy mercenaries or slaves who would then fight on behalf of the 'free' subjects. These factors alone were not deemed by the French to be sufficient to create a state that might aspire to universal monarchy. The additional need and the most significant, one that Bossuet underscored, was for the empire to be governed by an absolute monarch.

The French believed themselves to be fortunate in having a king whom God had chosen to command them. He alone was responsible for the laws of the state, their execution, and the dispensation of justice. Sovereign power resided in his person and legislative power belonged to him alone. As successive Bourbon monarchs put it, they ruled 'without dependence or division'. In the eyes of such princes, the people existed as one only through them; the rights and interests of the nation were necessarily identical to the King's. Public order was believed to emanate from the person of their sovereign. He was the representative of the nation in the sense that he alone determined what the public good was and what acts had to be undertaken for the safety of the people. No private person or corporation had any public existence or status except in accordance with the will of, and in deference to the authority of, the prince.

The benefits associated with this perspective on sovereignty were evident in the history of *le grand siècle*. Kings from Henri IV had supplied the nation with unchallenged and enlightened leadership. They had the authority and the will to maintain the state. The greatest philosophers and scientists of the day had been their advisers. With the safety and happiness of the people as their inspiration and glory their reward, absolute monarchy was for good reason perceived to be the most effective model of state organization for modern empires. Its efficiency, speed of action, and patronage of the sciences and fine arts affirmed this. As the great jurist Jean Bodin put it in his *Six Books of the Commonwealth* (1576), the ship of state was best piloted by one person, just as a family was naturally governed as a monarchy. Sovereign kings alone had the power to prevent the recurrence of religious wars. A monarch such as Louis XIV, the founder of academies of music and science, was held to be enlightened. He was also a mystical figure to be venerated as a God by the people. Master of the *arcana imperii*, he had thaumaturgical powers that ensured the ignorant were as obedient as the wise.

The major question for enlightenment political philosophy was whether such a form of government, however successful it had been in the past, could adapt itself to modern commercial society. Issues of succession, the transition of power from one monarch to another, remained prominent in European political philosophy. Commercial society posed new challenges. One popular argument was that the discipline associated with absolute government alone could cope with the problems generated by trade, and could police a society characterized by diversity and potential antagonism to social hierarchy. Another common claim was that where self-interest reigned only absolute monarchs could educate and guide individuals to equate their passionate impulses with the public good. In such argument alternative forms of state were presented as the fount of anarchy, having governments characterized by the division of parties, no agreement upon policy, and in consequence little capacity for the necessary government of the passions. Contemporary evidence at the beginning of the eighteenth century supported this view. The logic of international power appeared to dictate French supremacy, which had been bolstered by the erection of Jean-Baptiste Colbert's mercantile system for the development and control of trade. After Charles II had died childless in 1702,

Spain, France's only rival in terms of size, appeared to be moving inexorably towards Bourbon dominion. Yet within a few decades universal monarchy had become so inconceivable that it attained the status of national myth. In the 1730s Montesquieu disputed whether anyone could have taken seriously a French attempt at world empire. The reason for such a change in perspective on the dominant form of state in political philosophy lay with the rise of Britain.

The 'Glorious Revolution' of 1688–9 saw the Dutch stadtholder William of Orange-Nassau crowned, alongside his wife Mary Stuart, as King William III of England, following James II's forced renunciation of the throne and departure for France. Sovereignty was henceforth shared between monarch and parliament. A Protestant succession was guaranteed, and parliamentary agreement became necessary for war and peace, royal patronage, legislation, and taxation. In addition to the passing of an Act of Toleration (1689), which favoured Protestant non-conformists, the Revolution inaugurated an era of growing international prominence for the English state. The Revolution was immediately significant in European politics, as it added England to the grand alliance of Holland, Spain, Savoy, and the Holy Roman Empire, which was fighting to limit Louis XIV's ambitions during the Nine Years War (1688–97). With the creation of Britain by the union of England and Scotland in 1707, a mixed and composite monarchy, founded on the sovereignty of monarch in parliament, increasingly asserted itself in European politics. This was further encouraged when Prince George of Hanover ascended the throne in 1714 as George I. He was the eldest son of Ernest August, Elector of Hanover and Sophia of Bohemia, and the great-grandson of James I. On occasion, and not without malice, this German connection was referred to as the 'Hanover-rudder'.

The first decades of the new state were especially troubled. Partly this was due to the challenge to the succession presented by the growing Jacobite cause in England and Scotland. It was equally due to the War of the Spanish Succession (1701–14), which ultimately saw remarkable British victories by Marlborough over Louis XIV's forces and a peace favourable to the allies signed at Utrecht in 1714. Moreover, British political thinking was bedeviled by uncertainty about the long-term capacity of Britain to survive as a composite state. Since it was founded on commerce and public credit, a common belief held that Britain's power was unnatural, resting on illegal, amoral, and therefore unstable foundations. Britain's strength violated accepted political and economic logic, because British stability relied upon superiority over France, a state at the summit of its power, which could not long be replaced in prominence by a nation that was inferior in size, population, and natural resources. Many English writers were pessimistic about the workings and future of their constitution and were convinced of the superiority of French civilization. The history of the previous four hundred years confirmed the supremacy of absolute monarchy. The Renaissance republics had exemplified the dangers of bellicosity, corruption, division, and permanent political crisis. England's republican experiment had given way to monarchy. The alternative form of government to absolute monarchy, mixed monarchy, was also in decline.

Mixed monarchies in which powerful aristocracies enjoyed extensive political powers, such as those of Sweden or Poland, had rapidly diminished.

From a British perspective, politics was characterized by a divide between those who believed France would sooner or later defeat their state in war, causing an upheaval that might see a return to absolute modes of governance, and those who believed that the remarkable successes of the composite polity could be maintained in the longer term. Pessimists were generally more prominent than the optimists. As the essayist and divine John Brown put it, in his famous *Estimate of Manners*, in France the national spirit of union was stronger because 'the *compelling* power of the *Prince* directs and draws every thing to one point, and therefore, in all common situations, effectually supplies their place' (Brown 1757: 103). Such views echoed across the century, even after the great victories over France of the Seven Years War (Young 1769: 416–30, 440–2). Those who expected France to win out were not advocating that Britain return to an absolute monarchy aspired to by the Stuarts. Rather, they tended to oppose war, the mercantile system that was held to have made trade a tool for the growth of empire, and the perceived growing power of the Crown against the independence of the House of Lords and House of Commons (Massie 1761; Price 1772: 39).

War with the North American colonies in alliance with France raised fear of immanent French dominion to new heights. Richard Price's *Fast Sermon* of February 1781 was typical in expressing the view that France *had* regained international supremacy (Price 1991: 114). An added obsession was the rise of militant Catholicism. John Brown was equally prominent here, summarizing the concerns of many Protestants when he wrote that 'Enthusiastic religion leads to conquest; rational religion leads to rational defence; but the modern spirit of irreligion leads to rascally and abandoned cowardice' (Brown 1757: 90). Brown's fundamental worry was that Catholicism was more suited to a degenerate age, being a religion of passion and fury rather than reason. When France defeated Britain at war, Catholicism would equally overwhelm Anglicanism.

These jeremiad philosophies were challenged by writers who continually extolled the success of Britain as a model mixed or limited monarchy. Advocates of the capacity of Britain to maintain itself in its present form often looked to long-standing examples of mixed states, such as Denmark, or the constitution of the German Empire (Anon. 1731; Anon. 1745; Haakonssen and Horstbøll 2007). More often, however, they appealed to the history of England, drawing on the tradition of Sir John Fortescue (1397–1479), whose *The Difference between an Absolute and Limited Monarchy; As it More Particularly Regards the English Constitution* was republished in 1714, 1719, and 1724. One of the key arenas for political-philosophical argument became historical writing. Debate about the Saxon origins of limited government, and its derivation from the freedoms enjoyed by members of the ancient German tribes, became central to the defence of mixed government in the eighteenth century (Squire 1745; Stuart 1770). History was useful because of the implied continuity of mixed government, and also because it gave confidence to those who claimed Britain could remain in its present constitutional form despite the global conflicts it faced. Furthermore, links with ancient liberties could be contrasted with the continuity of absolute monarchy lauded in French historiography by Jean-Baptiste Dubos (*Histoire critique de l'établissement de la monarchie françoise dans les Gaules* (1734)) and others. Focus upon a national history revealing the antiquity and continuity of a parliament-limited monarchy was equally prominent in the more analytical defences of mixed government of Sir William Blackstone (*Commentaries on the Laws of England* (1764–9)) and Jean-Louis Delolme (*Constitution d'Angleterre ou État du gouvernement anglais comparé avec la forme républicaine et avec les autres monarchies de l'Europe* (1771)).

Evidence of the success of the defences of mixed government could be found in the increasing reluctance of radicals to call themselves republicans, or to contemplate the abandonment of monarchy. Even those who believed that the seventeenth-century republican tradition had a role to play in late-eighteenth-century politics, such as Catherine Macaulay, took pains to emphasize that they supported a mixed rather than a republican form of government for late-eighteenth-century Britain. Preference for mixed government was determined by the necessity of social order. In addition, an established system of hierarchical ranks was required to prevent the rule of the ignorant or the rise to power of a corrupt demagogue. Macaulay was explicit on this point. The 'whole art of true and just policy' was 'to preserve the natural subordination established by God himself' (Macaulay 1769–72: iv. 332). Richard Price used similar arguments to defend himself against the charge of republicanism in *The Evidence for a Future Period of Improvement in the State of Mankind* (1787); Britain simply had 'too many high and low' to countenance such a transformation (Price 1991: 164–5).

British defences of mixed government saw their parallel in French circles early in the eighteenth century (Carcassone 1927: 24–41). Absolute monarchy had always seen its sovereignty challenged by claimants for the rights of *parlements*, the Estates General, the national custom of Salic Law, and, less frequently, the people as a whole (Puaux 1917; Rothkrug 1965). Advocates of monarchical sovereignty had accepted that it was compatible, in the French case, with various bridles on the King, identified most famously by Claude de Seyssel in *La Monarchie de France* (1519) as religion, justice, and polity. Jean Bodin, for whom sharing sovereignty with an aristocracy or the people was 'altogether impossible and incompatible', nevertheless believed French kings to be constrained by the fundamental laws of the kingdom and the requirement, imposed by God, to rule in the interests of their subjects as a whole. In the reign of Louis XIV, the Burgundy circle refined and reiterated many such claims. The Duc de Saint Simon and Henri de Boulanvilliers, both members of this circle, defended what they called 'feudal' or 'mixed' government (Ellis 1988).

It is significant that, in France as in Britain, solutions to political problems that entailed the transformation of the state were opposed before the French Revolution. An illustrative example is that of Louis XIV's most severe critic the Archbishop of Cambrai, François de Salignac de la Mothe-Fénelon. Fénelon's *Telemachus* (1699) was among the most published books of the century. Fénelon argued that reigns similar to Louis XIV's would result only in further wars, the retardation of the domestic economy, and the loss of life and liberty for French subjects. He sketched an alternative development path for France in accordance with ideals of agrarianism, pacifism, and justice. Fénelon wanted France to turns its back upon the race for trade and also to abandon offensive strategies for war. Corrupt commerce was to be countered by having an isolated commercial port at the edge of a self-contained economy in which the urban populace had been forcibly returned to the land, and with an armaments industry that made 'Salentum' (France) militarily more powerful than any other European power (Hont 2006). This new state was to be created by absolute means, once an enlightened king realized the true interests of the state and the dangers presented by commerce and the lust for empire.

Critics of *Telemachus* were wary of reliance upon arbitrary power for the implementation of the projected reform programme, and were also fearful of a France that allowed Britain to dominate world trade. The Abbé de Saint-Pierre's *Projet de paix perpetuelle* (1712–), Jean-François Melon's *Essai politique sur le commerce* (1734), Montesquieu's *Considérations sur les causes de la grandeur des Romains et de leur décadence* (1734), and Voltaire's and Frederick the Great's *Anti-Machiavel* (1740) each preferred to rely upon a balance of economic power as the surest means to European peace, and the political philosophies they developed were means to such an end. Saint-Pierre envisaged a 'European Union' comprising a free market and political union into a confederation of states, with the intention of cutting the link between commerce and war, making trade become a force for peace and social stability. Montesquieu's main aim, in his *Considérations* and *Réflexions sur la monarchie universelle en Europe* (1724), was to prevent a repeat of the neo-Roman experiments of Louis XIV, by warning that the combination of republican militarism and external economic growth would create a state that could not cope with luxury. While decline was inevitable because of the capacity of poor countries to undercut the wages paid by richer states, he argued that peace was possible in Europe through the creation of monarchies that fostered international commerce, creating de facto a global and pacfic commercial republic. Melon's widely commented-upon *Essai* responded most interestingly to Montesquieu. Against the latter, Melon had no faith in the establishment of an economic balance of power in the Europe of his day, because competing states would always find reasons to go to war to increase their power. Melon argued that a policy of defeating Britain by economic policy rather than by war was the superior strategy for France, which would destroy the 'great monopolist' and lay the foundations of a genuine economic balance.

The greatest work of political philosophy of the enlightenment era, Montesquieu's *De l'esprit des loix* (1748), pursued a related line of argument in refusing to contemplate French adoption of British political practices. Indeed, Montesquieu warned against experiments in British-style constitution building or planned transformations of national character. Although full of praise for 'the people in the world who have best known how to take advantage of each of these three great things at the same time: religion, commerce, and liberty', Montesquieu was one of the most pessimistic writers of the century concerning Britain's prospects for survival as a major European power. He was as certain as the ageing Hume that the delicate balance between the executive and legislative powers in Britain would ultimately be destroyed by the corrupting influence of public credit. Furthermore, the political upheavals of the seventeenth century had undermined the nobility, a process that was being completed by the progress of commerce. Montesquieu believed that a state that began the century as 'a republic hiding under the form of a monarchy' would end it as 'a popular state or else a despotic state' (Montesquieu 1748: xx. 7). This opinion developed from Montesquieu's assertion that the most stable and successful states separated sovereignty and government, and established intermediate, subordinate, and dependent powers across political institutions to prevent despots or demagogues from arising. Montesquieu and many of his followers accepted that Britain might return to a republican form of government because of domestic turbulence. Few authors, however, conceived of republicanism or democracy in a state like France, where absolute monarchy remained entrenched. It is ironic that Britain, the state that proved the most stable, was for contemporaries deemed the most likely to change its form.

POLITICAL PHILOSOPHY IN EUROPE'S SMALL STATES

By the 1720s the belief was near-universal that small states, and small republics in particular, could no longer stand against large commercial monarchies in war. Commerce made republican government increasingly problematic because of the incapacity of such states to defend themselves against larger rivals resourced by public credit and mercantile power, with extensive agricultural and commercial sectors sustaining them. Dreams of republican empire inspired by Machiavelli, or renascent classical republics founded on envisaged modern counterparts of the ancient slave economies, were impractical because of reduced means of self-defence, and in consequence had ceased to be direct models for statesmen and projectors (Pocock 2003b). With less and less frequency, and mainly through the republication of historic authors, the Machiavellian view was expressed that small republics could defend themselves in war because of their civic valour, which was a product of their liberty. Small republics could not, it was argued, cope with luxury, could not defend themselves against larger states, and had been in terminal decline for two centuries through their corruption and divisions. Like other small states, they would fall to predatory enterprises, as appeared to be happening across Europe by the 1760s. The marquis de Chastellux in De la Félicité publique (1772) clearly had contemporary experience in mind when he wrote that 'nothing can be more deplorable, and at the same time more contemptible, than republics in their decline. Their ancient customs seem to be new sources of vice and ignominy' (Chastellux 1774 [1772]: ii. 217–18).

The sense of a crisis for republics was usefully captured by Adam Ferguson, the Professor of Moral Philosophy in the University of Edinburgh, in An Essay on the History of Civil Society (1767), where he explained that small republics were no longer masters of their own destiny. Vocally refusing to give up their precarious liberty, they pretended to be independent at the same time as their prospects were ever more uncertain, while their capacity for self-defence was minimal. They found themselves in the unenviable position of having little influence over their own future while for ever fighting against the slavery that had become their actual condition (Ferguson 1767: 91). Ferguson saw modern Europe as being infested by 'a contagion of monarchical manners'. Accordingly, the republics and free cities would have to adapt themselves to the modern lust for trade and empire, and work out means of avoiding collapse in circumstances where Britain or France might seek to conquer them, or see competitors in the east of Europe do likewise, in the manner of the dismemberment of Poland.

The examples of declining 'sister' states were ceaselessly commented upon as potential futures for the small states of Europe. Poland obsessed Europeans as the great republican monarchy in decline, having too independent a standing army, monarchs with interests at odds with the public good, and an uncertain division of powers between church and state. The situation of the small communities within the Russian empire was also instructive, because Russia contained so many different forms of state within an absolute monarchy that appeared to function as a federal empire. At the end of the century William Tooke was fascinated by what he called the 'mixed republican monarchy' of 'the Kalmuks and Kirghises'; but the most singular component of the Russian polity he held to be its Sparta: 'the military democracy of the Kozaks, the essence and aim of which is war, and even of which we have been witnesses of a corruption, in its denying the other half of the human race all civil and domestic community'. Tooke also considered the relationship between religious belief and politics to be significant in Russia, having seen 'the most monstrous polytheism' and 'total unacquaintance with any idea of a supreme intelligence' (Tooke 1799). Existence with an absolute monarchical confederation was another possible future for the small republics, but one that none of them recommended or welcomed. Closer to the centre of Europe, France and Britain appeared to be perpetually acquiring new territories, with the republic of Genoa ceding Corsica to France an apt example, and the British acquisition of Gibraltar another.

Much of the history of small states in Europe was concerned with alliances or treaties of peace, either to increase the combined strength of smaller states against larger neighbours, or to shelter within the shadow of an allied empire that was sufficiently powerful not to be overwhelmed by others. The great means to self-preservation by keeping a general peace was deemed to be the balance of power. From this perspective large states were often described as levers within a greater political balance that would ensure peace by pitting states of equal weight against one another. The policy David Hume advised to maintain the balance of power was alliance with weaker states against the stronger, following the rule pursued by the Athenians, in the war between Thebes and Sparta, who 'threw themselves into the lighter scale, and endeavoured to preserve the balance' (Hume 1994 [1741]: 154). Yet, as Hume was writing, the relative disparity of power between large states meant that the option of treating small states as bulwarks against invasion, or protectorates marking spheres of influence, had come to be questioned. Partly this was due to the nature of war—namely, the capacity of able generals to overrun extensive territories with greater speed than in the past. Furthermore, the complicated balance of power established by the Treaty of Westphalia (1648) rested on a series of renewable alliances, the breaking of which would have been a direct challenge to the entire system. Some contemporaries noted that a successful balance of power necessitated exactly the breaking of alliances, as it was vital to move from one party to another if any balance was to be maintained. The Dutch republican Pieter de la Court concluded that, for small and relatively weak states like Holland, alliances made no sense. Supporting 'great potentates', such as France, England, or Spain, would simply make them 'greater and mightier'. All written alliances 'are interpreted in favour of the greatest [state]'. Most ominously, alliances led small states to be drawn into war, and they ended up fighting on behalf of the larger states whose dominion over them thereby intensified. Small states had to stand alone and rely on their own capacity for arms:

> They that eat cherries with great men, must pay for them themselves; and besides, suffer them to choose the fairest, and expect at last to be pelted with the stones, instead of thanks for the favour received . . . And if anyone doubts of the truth of these inferences, viz. That all superior powers, especially the monarchs and princes of Europe, play with their allies as children do with nine-pins, which they set up, and immediately beat down again as they please; and that he that first performs is ever the loser, and suffers shame, let him read the Histories of Francisco Guicciardino, and Philip de Commines. (Court 1712 [1662]: 30–5)

Europe had moved from a system of international relations founded on a balance of powers to one based on spheres of influence, with each great state obsessed with marking its territory and in defending its boundaries, which went well beyond the confines of national territories as traditionally conceived.

The tragedy was that the traditional means of small states to challenge monarchical aggrandizement was also being questioned. The convention by which small states united to form a larger association for defence explained the prosperity of the ancient Greek states, the successful barbarian resistance to Rome between the Rhine and the Danube, and the constancy of republican government in Germany, Holland, and Switzerland. Unions of states traditionally followed ancient models, and particularly the union of the tribes that created Israel, and established civil government among the Hebrews. For much of European history, however, such unions were deemed impractical or failed to be long-standing, the classic case being the union of Calmar between Norway, Sweden, and Denmark (1397). The difficulty was of envisioning a union that was capable of standing against Britain and France, or of adapting itself to a world in which they were the dominant powers. One of the most significant peculiarities of the eighteenth century was the aversion to national unions as opposed to large state aggrandizement. The Anglo-Scottish union was the great exception, although it was not seen to be a successful model to be imitated by other states until Jacobite challenges had been thwarted. Furthermore, it was seen by its opponents to be another case of a large state extending its empire at the expense of the small state of Scotland. The message the Anglo-Scottish experiment sent to advocates of union was that uniting small states with larger states, rather than creating conglomerations of small states, alone might save the weaker sovereignties of Europe, although in doing so they risked the loss of their identity and independence.

Unions of small republics were no longer taken seriously by political commentators, because of the difficulty of establishing and of maintaining confederations. In the longer term, patriotic and nationalist movements seeking to create more powerful and prominent unitary states, based on shared geographical, cultural, or ethnic identities, sought to challenge the dominion of their larger neighbours, with singular consequences for modern European history. Making small states into large states or into larger unions of states has, of course, been the preferred solution to the problem of small state weakness in recent times, or at least from the North American founding. Eighteenth-century thought was distinctive because schemes for European or Atlantic unions were generally described as utopian rather than visionary. With the larger powers seeking to increase national resources in order to undertake global wars against competitor empires, and with a vast number of small and weak sovereignties across Europe, many of which were well known as commercial centres, the temptation for large states to use union as an excuse for the development of empire was too great. National unions involving larger states could rarely be trusted to benefit smaller partners.

Many commentators were concerned that small states in general, and republics in particular, were about to disappear as political forms, being unsuited to commercial development and political improvement. Detailed strategies for reform, such as that developed by the Scots anti-unionist Andrew Fletcher, who envisaged a completely closed agricultural economy within a Europe of federated republican governments of equal size, failed to provide a mechanism for the transition from the fallen politics of the present to the utopian republican confederation. In such circumstances, the end point of republican argument appeared to be monarchical Britain, following John Adams's point in *A Defence of the Constitutions of Government of the United States of America* (1787) that the distinction between monarchy and republic no longer mattered.

PHILOSOPHIES OF DESPOTISM

In a century of near-constant war, contemporaries became obsessed by the question of whether the modern world would follow its ancient counterpart and replay the old cycle of decline and fall. The reason was not straightforwardly a recurrence of the luxury and inequality that was commonly viewed as having brought down Rome, raising the 'social question' of how to resolve antagonism between rich and poor. Rather, perceptions of imminent crisis and widespread uncertainty about the future were traceable to the financial instruments available to modern states, and particularly to the evolution of public credit, which was deemed to be a Janus-faced force for good or for evil. Many eighteenth-century observers focused upon the likely negative effects of national debts. The standing armies funded by credit were expected to lead to the tyrannical rule of new Caesars. Bankruptcy caused by excessive credit was associated with popular rebellion headed by a latter-day Spartacus. Perhaps the most feared possibility was voluntary bankruptcy, whereby a monarch expanded credit to strengthen the military capacities of his or her state, then sacrificed the creditors in the name of national survival or imperial glory, creating a potentially all-powerful polity inimical to liberty and addicted to war. The deadly consequences of unintended national bankruptcy, or monarch-inspired planned bankruptcy, for the 'princes and states fighting and quarrelling amidst their debts, funds and public mortgages' were likened by David Hume to a cudgeling match in a china shop in his essay 'Of Public Credit' (Hume 1753 [1741]: iv. 119). As the century wore on, and the global war for international supremacy between Britain and France intensified, the concomitant rise in national debts was held by many to presage Armageddon.

However unrealistic such nightmare scenarios might appear with the benefit of hindsight, every speculator about eighteenth-century politics accepted that adding a debt to a state had important consequences both for the relationship between state and citizen, and for relationships between competing states. In an era of experiment with representative government and more general constitutionalism, one danger commonly identified was that the imperative of paying the national debt would lead wealthy creditors to control politicians and statesmen. Alternatively, high taxes would beggar the populace, or at the very least reduce commercial competitiveness, making rich states prey to their poorer neighbours. If the existence of certain institutional hierarchies kept creditors content, public debts could pay lip service to constitutionalism and create an authoritarian fiscal–military state on the foundations of representative government. Numerous commentators believed that exactly this happened during the revolutionary government of the Year II of the First French Republic and during Bonaparte's First Empire.

The great irony was that, as commerce escalated, governments became overburdened by debt because of the growing costs of war. The consequence was clear to Montesquieu: 'We are poor, with the riches and commerce of the whole world; and soon, by thus augmenting our troops, we shall all be soldiers, and be reduced to the very same situation as the Tartars' (Montesquieu 1748: bk XIII, ch. 17). Reference to Europeans becoming tartars signified an increasingly widespread prophecy of the fall of Europe's effeminate and exhausted monarchies before vast marauding slave-based armies from the East. Rousseau anticipated exactly this in his *Social Contract*:

> The Russian Empire will try to subjugate Europe, and will itself be subjugated. The Tartars, its subjects or neighbours, will become its masters and ours: This revolution seems to me inevitable. All the Kings of Europe are working in concert to hasten it. (Rousseau 1997: 73)

An even more lurid description of this process was provided in *Émile*, where Rousseau foresaw a 'century of revolutions' by which 'the great become small, the rich become poor, and monarchs become subjects' (Rousseau 1762: ii, bk III, 59–60). The transition mechanism was anticipated to be states newly termed 'oriental despotisms' (Boulanger 1764 [1761]). Following Montesquieu's description of despotic states in *De l'esprit des loix*, oriental despotisms were deemed to be governed by fear and lacking any formal notion of law. Montesquieu believed that a descent into despotism was likely for European states in which government was too popular or too monarchical. The only preventative was to firm up and maintain the noble-based system of ranks that ensured moderate government, by establishing intermediate powers between the populace and the Crown.

Many Europeans became obsessed by China in the eighteenth century as the most stable state in history with respect to government. The sometimes brutal but immediate and efficient rule of the emperors was admired particularly by the physiocrats in France, led by François Quesnay. In the second half of the eighteenth century they promoted the idea of 'legal despotism', which envisaged monarchs not having to act as legislators because of the self-evidence of rational laws. Analyses of eastern states were necessarily comparative, and were conducted with reference to western and eastern history. The key question was how to explain the seemingly unique development of the towns and cities of western Europe by comparison with other parts of the world. For the physiocrats, the danger of genuine despotism lay in the growth of a mercantile system that controlled trade for national aggrandizement at the expense of agricultural production. The exemplar of the mercantile system was British economic policy, and the physiocrats described as unnatural a Europe in which such a state could thrive, while oppressing the trade of competitor states such as Ireland. The physiocrats recommended the complete freedom of trade, imposed by a legal despot, believing that this would ensure a rapid rise of agricultural prices, leading to the development of agriculture at the expense of the towns. Only such a radical policy would address the decline in population that was believed to characterize modern Europe, and prevent the slow fall into war and anarchy that was the corollary of Britain's trading supremacy.

Adam Smith's remarkable response to this perspective on the evolution of contemporary European polities was formulated in his *Wealth of Nations*, and more particularly in the third book, 'Of the natural progress of opulence'. Smith described the physiocrats as the unwitting advocates of despotism, as their counsel entailed both war and revolution. In the most composed, moderate, and phlegmatic political philosophy of the enlightenment era, Smith preferred to secure abundance by changing the terms of trade between manufactured and subsistence goods, ensuring a long-term and permanent rise in agricultural prices. Smith accepted that Europe's historical development had been 'unnatural' by comparison with other parts of the world because it commenced with long-distance trade and only latterly created a productive agricultural system. Against the physiocrats he argued that such a growth path could not be reversed by ambitious statesmen. Against Montesquieu's history of European liberty, founded on the Germanic feudal polities in which the nobility existed as an intermediate power between sovereign and people, Smith argued that there was no active political agency that had established modern liberty, which was rather a product of the unintended consequences of commerce, after the Gothic tribes destroyed Roman agriculture, but had left both cities and international commerce intact (Hont 2005).

The language of despotism was equally employed to explain the last and most unexpected development in European politics during the enlightenment era: the French Revolution. Edmond Burke famously argued, when France became a republic in 1792, that popular sovereignty and aggressive patriotism had created a new form of state. Burke called it 'the Republick of Regicide', whose innovations included the capacity to thrive despite bankruptcy and whose unparalleled national unity 'conquered the finest parts of Europe, distressed, disunited, deranged, and broke to pieces all the rest' (Burke 1991–98, 108, 119). Such an outcome had not been intended by the fathers of the revolution in France. At the same time they were seeking to transform both politics and society. This is clear from the abbé Emmanuel-Joseph Sieyes's three pamphlets, *Vues of the Executive Means Available to the Representatives of France in 1789, An Essay on Privileges*, And *What is the Third Estate?*, published between November 1788 and May 1789, which convinced members of the Estates General to embrace the new doctrine of 'national sovereignty'. Sieyes defined national sovereignty as a union of productive labourers within a specified territory. He was convinced that founding a political system upon such an idea would rapidly transform the international authority of the state. This view of national sovereignty, or what Sieyes called 'the constituting power of a state', was incompatible with aristocracy as traditional conceived. It was equally incompatible with an independent role for the church in politics separately from the state. National sovereignty entailed an end to absolute monarchical sovereignty, and could not be squared with the sovereignty of a monarch in parliament.

Defining the nation as the locus of sovereignty further required the affirmation of 'Frenchness' against regional diversity. The Revolution in France was accordingly defined by the transformation of monarchy, aristocracy, church, and national identity. Every subsequent observer acknowledged that Sieyes's ideas were among the most radical to be canvassed at Paris when measured against any during the following decade of revolutionary enquiry. For their author, however, they formed part of a still broader system of integrated reform proposals by means of which Sieyes expected to create happy citizens by restoring France to greatness and by thoroughly modernizing the state. Sieyes wanted to establish a French 'third way', entailing neither mixed government nor forms of economic or political despotism. It began with the replacement of Montesquieu's noble-based system of ranks with intermediate powers founded on social groups generated by industry and by civic distinction. Sieyes overwhelmed his contemporaries by stating that he could couple a stable political system supported by public credit with thriving commerce. He signalled that he could do this in answering the question posed in the title of his most famous work, *What is the Third Estate?*, by responding, 'everything'. Making a third estate of productive labourers 'everything' entailed a system of representative government that mirrored the representative system of commercial society. Representation signified anyone acting on behalf of another, from street cleaner to king. A properly functioning system of representation was the product of the free operation of the division of labour, unhindered by political or mercantile manipulation. In politics, it necessitated the separation of powers between executive, legislative, and judicial functions, because an over-mighty state would present barriers to the natural extension of the division of labour. It also required an elected system of office-holders for each branch of public administration.

Sieyes followed Jean-Jacques Rousseau's *Considérations sur le gouvernement de Pologne et sur sa réformation projetée* (1770–1) in arguing that the rule of the wise, able, and popular would be secured only by a graduated electoral system. Those who sought election to the higher offices of state had to have served at the base of the political pyramid and to have worked their way up, something that could ultimately result in an elected head of state (from a very small number of eligible candidates) at the apex of the executive branch. At the same time, citizens would elect from among the existing civil and military office-holders those willing to serve in a non-political office. Sieyes had the idea of distinguished individuals acting as a moral counterweight to political office-holders, and this was the basis of what became the French Legion of Honour in 1802. The Legion was expected to combat socially generated inequality and the resulting pre-eminence of the propertied. Ultimately, a service-based hierarchy would coexist alongside a property-based hierarchy, establishing a dual bulwark against oligarchy or plutocracy (Sonenscher 2007).

Sieyes labelled his combination of unitary sovereign, limited government, and graduated elections a 'monarchical republic'. He opposed it to 'republican monarchy', advocated by Voltaire, which relied upon disinterested or virtuous kingship. It was also different from Thomas Paine's republican 'polyarchy', in which a sovereign people elected a committee of executive statesmen to provide enlightened leadership. Sieyes believed all these alternate forms of government to be flawed because they relied upon the virtue of politicians, rulers, or statesmen. His system alone set virtue aside. The stability and quality of rule supplied by a monarchical republic meant that public debts would cease to be dangerous, and could be used, as they needed to be, for both welfare and warfare. Sieyes perceived that Montesquieu's reformed French monarchy would have evolved into Britain, as the noble class became commercial and subservient to the Crown. By contrast, his own system was designed to prevent the corruption that corroded commerce in other forms of state. By precluding the emergence of sinister interests, commerce in a monarchical republic would tend to create moderate wealth for an increasing number of families, while the division of labour fostered mass production, allowing productive citizens to work less and enjoy higher standards of living.

The tragedy was that, early in the course of the Revolution, and certainly by September 1789, Sieyes had recognized that the revolutionaries were not following his script for constitutional change and a national refounding. Rather, Sieyes's notion of the nation was hijacked by the Jacobins, with their populist rhetoric promising more powerful forms of community, and social bonds capable of guaranteeing national security to a greater extent. Sieyes coined the term *ré-totale* to describe what was happening in France, and more especially the dreadful consequences of the Jacobin social state based on consensus. Sieyes contrasted *ré-totale* with his own version of a legitimate polity, which he called a *ré-publique*, meaning a union based on minimal agreement. The *ré-totale* of the Jacobins soon became what Istvan Hont in *Jealousy of Trade* (2005) has called the 'ethnocultural state', capable of overcoming rivals by the sheer force of popular identity with the national community of citizens. For having laid the foundations of such a philosophy, many contemporaries of the 1790s held Sieyes accountable for having caused the Terror. Yet Sieyes was outflanked in 1793 by the Jacobins. In 1799, when as a consul he once again attempted to put his ideas into practice, he was outmanœuvred by Napoleon. At the fall of the First Empire, Britain was seen to have won the ideological battle as well as the military, when Louis XVIII signed the *Charte constitutionnelle*, institutionalizing mixed government in France. Many former republicans, such as Germaine de Staël and Benjamin Constant, appeared to become anglophiles in politics, and interest in Britain's history and government reached a peak during the Bourbon Restoration.

The majority of eighteenth-century reformers were convinced that, if politics was a science, it was a science of particular cases. Differences between small and large or Catholic and Protestant states, rich and poor or agrarian and commercial polities, and between monarchies and republics, indicated that the passions and the interests were shaped by local factors, by geography, and by history. What worked in France would not necessarily work in Britain, and was certain not to function similarly in North America, because of the gulf in circumstances, experiences, and difficulties. Many French writers in the 1790s felt by contrast that human nature could be reformed according to universal principles, and principles of general applicability. Sieyes at times presented his views in such a fashion, and promised global reform via a science of politics that would overcome now second-order factors, such as climate or size, which had made the study of politics so different for Montesquieu's generation. The lesson of the Revolution was seen by many to be that a more powerful state could be created by a homogeneous citizen body acting as a political agent, with homogeneity best expressed in ethnic terms. This was a political vision with universal application. Accordingly, it signalled the end of enlightenment political philosophy.

References

Primary Sources

Anon. (1731). *Lex regia: or the Royal Law of Denmark. Writ in the Danish Language by Order of Frederick III . . . Subscribed by his Majesty on the 4th Day of November 1665. Translated into English by a Lover of the British Constitution.* London.

Anon. (1745). *The Constitution and Government of the Germanic Body. Shewing how this State has Subsisted for Three Hundred Years Past, under the Emperors of the House of Austria . . . Compiled from the Fundamental Laws of Germany; The Histories of the Empire, and the Best Authorities. Translated from the Original.* London: J. Nourse.

Bossuet, J. B. (1966 [1679]). *Discours sur l'histoire universelle à Monseigneur Le Dauphin. Pour expliquer la suite de la Religion, & des changemens des Empires.* Paris.

Boswell, J. (1830 [1791]). *The Life of Samuel Johnson, LLD: Comprehending an Account of his Studies, and Numerous Works, in Chronological Order; a Series of his Epistolary Correspondence and Conversations with Many Eminent Persons; and Various Original Pieces of his Composition.* London.

Boulanger, N. A. (1764 [1761]). *The Origin and Progress of Despotism: In the Oriental, and Other Empires of Africa, Europe, and America.* Amsterdam.

Brown, J. (1757). An Estimate of the Manners and Principles of the Times. 2nd edn. London: Davis and Reymer.

Burke, E. (1991–). *First Letter on a Regicide Peace* [1795], *The Writings and Speeches of Edmund Burke.* 10 vols. Oxford: Oxford University Press.

Chastellux, F.-J. De (1774 [1772]). *An Essay on Public Happiness.* 2 vols. London.

Court, P. de la (1712 [1662]). *The Interest of Holland as to their Alliances with France, Spain, England, &c.* London.

Ferguson, A. (1767). *An Essay on the History of Civil Society.* Edinburgh.

Fougeret de Montbron, L. -C. (1757). *Préservatif contre l'anglomanie.* Minorca.

Hume, D. (1753 [1741]). *Essays and Treatises on Several Subjects.* 2nd edn. Edinburgh.

Hume, D. (1994 [1741]). *Political Essays*, ed., K. Haakonssen. Cambridge: Cambridge University Press.

La Beaumelle, L. A. (1753). *Reflections of *****Being a Series of Politcal Maxims, Illustrated by General History, as well as by Variety of Authentic Anecdotes (Never Published Before) of Lewis XIV . . . Fleury, and of Most of the Eminent Personages, in the Last and Present Century.* London.

Lloyd, H. (1771). *An Essay on the Theory of Money.* London.

Macaulay, C. (1769–72). *The History of England from the Accession of James I to the Elevation of the House of Hanover.* 5 vols. London: Edward and Charles Dilly.

Massie, J. (1761). *The Rotten and Tottering State of the Popular Part of the British Constitution Demonstrated—By J. Massie.* London.

Montesquieu, C. L. de Secondat, Baron de (1748). *De l'esprit des loix ou du rapport que les loix doivent avoir avec la constitution de chaque gouvernement.* Geneva: Barrillot et fils, Geneva.

Price, R. (1772). *An Appeal to the Public on the Subject of the National Debt.* London: T. Cadell.

Price, R. (1991). *Political Writings*, ed. D. O. Thomas. Cambridge: Cambridge University Press.

Rousseau, J.-J. (1762). *Émile; ou, De l'éducation.* 2 vols. Frankfurt.

Rousseau, J.-J. (1997). *The Social Contract and Other Later Political Writings*, ed. and trans. V. Gourevitch. Cambridge: Cambridge University Press.

Squire, S. (1745). *An Enquiry into the Foundation of the English Constitution; Or, an Historical Essay upon the Anglo-Saxon Government both in Germany and England.* London: W. Bowyer.

Stuart, G. (1770). *An Historical Dissertation concerning the Antiquity of the English Constitution.* 2nd edn. London: T. Cadell.

Tooke, W. (1799). *View of the Russian Empire during the Reign of Catharine the Second, and to the Close of the Present Century.* 3 vols. London.

Young, A. (1769). *Letters concerning the Present State of the French Nation . . . With a Complete Comparison between France and Great Britain*. London: W. Nicoll.

Secondary Sources

Carcassone, E. (1927). *Montesquieu et le problème de la constitution française au xviiie. siècle*. Paris: J. Dedieu, Paris.

Ellis, H. A. (1988). *Boulainvilliers and the French Monarchy*. Ithaca, NY: Cornell University Press.

Haakonssen, K. (1996). *Natural Law and Moral Philosophy: From Grotius to the Scottish Enlightenment*. Cambridge: Cambridge University Press.

Haakonssen, K., and Horstbøll, H. (2007). *Northern Antiquities and National Identities*. Copenhagen: The Royal Danish Academy of Sciences and Letters.

Haakonssen, K., and Whatmore, R. (2008). 'Commerce and Enlightenment', *Intellectual History Review*, 18/2: 283–306.

Hont, I. (2005). *Jealousy of Trade: International Competition and the Nation-State in Historical Perspective*. Cambridge, MA: Harvard University Press.

Hont, I. (2006). 'The Luxury Debate in the Early Enlightenment', in M. Goldie and R. Wokler (eds), *The Cambridge History of Eighteenth-Century Political Thought*. Cambridge: Cambridge University Press.

Hunter, I. (2001). *Rival Enlightenments: Civil and Metaphysical Philosophy in Early Modern Germany*. Cambridge: Cambridge University Press.

Hunter, I. (2008). *The Secularisation of the Confessional State: The Political Thought of Christian Thomasius*. Cambridge: Cambridge University Press.

Israel, J. (2001). *Radical Enlightenment: Philosophy and the Making of Modernity 1650–1750*. Oxford: Oxford University Press.

Pocock, J. (1999a). *Barbarism and Religion*, i. *The Enlightenments of Edward Gibbon, 1737–1764*. Cambridge: Cambridge University Press.

Pocock, J. (1999b). *Barbarism and Religion*, ii. *Narratives of Civil Government*. Cambridge: Cambridge University Press.

Pocock, J. (2003a). *Barbarism and Religion*, iii. *The First Decline and Fall*. Cambridge: Cambridge University Press.

Pocock, J. (2003b), *The Machiavellian Moment: Florentine Political Thought and the Atlantic Republican Tradition*. Princeton: Princeton University Press.

Pocock, J. (2005). *Barbarism and Religion*, iv. *Barbarians, Savages and Empires*. Cambridge: Cambridge University Press.

Puaux, F. (1917). *Defenseurs de la souveraineté du peuple sous le régime de Louis XI*. Paris: Fischbacher, Paris.

Robertson, J. (2005). *The Case for the Enlightenment. Scotland and Naples 1680–1760*. Cambridge: Cambridge University Press.

Rothkrug, L. (1965). *Opposition to Louis XIV*. Princeton: Princeton University Press.

Sonenscher, M. (2007). *Before the Deluge: Public Debt, Inequality, & the Intellectual Origins of the French Revolution*. Princeton: Princeton University Press.

Sonenscher, M. (2008). *Sans-Culottes: An Eighteenth-Century Emblem in the French Revolution*. Princeton: Princeton University Press.

Tribe, K. (1988). *Governing Economy:, The Reformation of German Economic Discourse 1750–1840*. Cambridge: Cambridge University Press.

CHAPTER 19

THE SCOTTISH ENLIGHTENMENT

NEIL McARTHUR

SCOTLAND during the eighteenth century was a country with a small, impoverished population (the first comprehensive census, in 1801, lists a population of 1.6 million), yet its citizens made a contribution to the intellectual and artistic life of Enlightenment Europe well out of proportion to their numbers. In philosophy, the Scottish Enlightenment can be seen as beginning in 1725 with the publication of a series of treatises by Francis Hutcheson (who was actually born in Ulster, though he moved to Glasgow in 1729). David Hume published the first volumes of his *Treatise of Human Nature* in 1739, and achieved fame over the following three decades through the publication of several volumes of essays and his monumental *History of England*. Adam Ferguson's *Essay on the History of Civil Society* appeared in 1769. Adam Smith published his *Theory of Moral Sentiments* in 1759, and his *Inquiry into the Wealth of Nations* in 1776. These extraordinary masterpieces are only the most enduring testaments to the vitality of an intellectual community that also included Henry Home (Lord Kames), William Robertson, Sir James Steuart, Thomas Reid, John Millar, and numerous other less-remembered figures. Though their writings cover aesthetics, theology, metaphysics, and the philosophy of mind, among numerous other topics, the members of this community were deeply engaged with the politics of the time, and the problems of political philosophy were of central concern to them.

JUSTICE, ALLEGIANCE, AND THE MORAL SENTIMENTS

Francis Hutcheson became influential in Britain and ultimately in Europe and America by developing a moral theory that grounds our judgments of right and wrong in our innate moral sentiments. He intends this theory to provide a refutation of philosophical egoism, which was associated with Hobbes and Mandeville, as well as (in a less extreme form) Locke. Philosophical egoism accounts for our allegiance to law and government as the result of our self-interested desire for peace and security, given people's natural competitiveness and aggressiveness toward one another. The existence of a moral sense supposedly establishes that, alongside our natural desire to pursue our own happiness, we equally have a natural interest in the happiness of others. Hutcheson criticizes Hobbes and Locke for taking an unduly pessimistic view of the state of nature, which he calls a condition of "peace and good-will, of innocence and beneficence," and he argues that the moral sense helps explain the existence of the rules of justice (Hutcheson 2007: 127). These rules are at least partly the product of our innate feelings of benevolence operating on the problems of personal security and the protection of property (cf. Hume 1932: ii. 47; Hutcheson 2007: 136).

Hutcheson acknowledges the evident fact that people do not always act in order to promote the general good. In his account of human motivation, self-interest is perpetually competing with benevolence to determine our actions—and as a result he concedes a coercive role for law and government to enforce these rules in a reliable and uniform way. However, he believes that the moral sense gives all citizens a desire for the public good, even if this desire does not always dictate their behavior, and thus that the state can legitimately act not just to protect us but to coordinate our actions better to promote this common good (cf. Hutcheson 1755: ii. 223; Hutcheson 2007: 236). Where it does so, this gives us added grounds for allegiance beyond the purely self-interested ones posited by the egoist. But this doctrine is two-sided. It equally gives us reasons for rejecting the legitimacy of the state if it is not successful in promoting the common good. Dismissing Hobbesian fears about the dangers of rebellion, Hutcheson says men should not be hindered "when opportunities offer, and there is any hope of success, to attempt, even by such violence as may occasion some temporary anarchy, to obtain such amendments of any foolish concerted plans of polity as . . . may procure greater good than what overbalances these temporary inconveniencies in the violent change" (Hutcheson 1755: ii. 220). His reputation as a political radical was well deserved.

Hume acknowledges the existence of natural moral sentiments, tracing their operation to what he calls "sympathy"—an involuntary, physiological reaction to the joys and sufferings of others. But, while sympathy is a powerful mechanism, it is also a partial and unreliable one. It easily gives way to self-interest or to other, more capricious emotions. He argues that our sense of justice, which explains our adherence to the laws, therefore cannot be the product of any innate disposition we have. It must be instead what he calls an "artificial" virtue. His use of this term is easily misunderstood, as it was by many contemporary readers (Hutcheson included). Hume readily concedes that the rules of justice exist to defend universal and permanent human interests, specifically the interest we all have in protecting and freely disposing of our property—and are in this sense certainly grounded in human nature. But they are social conventions, which evolve through time and persist because we all realize that we have a selfish interest in their operation (Hume 2000: 3.2.2.24, p. 320).[1] Sympathy does not disappear entirely from his account. It acts to transform this self-interested motive to accept the rules of justice into a properly moral one. But it is not on its own sufficient to establish or support these rules.

In arguing for justice as an artificial virtue, Hume also challenges the contract theory of government (to which Hutcheson subscribes). According to the versions of this theory current at the time, we owe allegiance to government because we or our ancestors have consented, either explicitly or tacitly, to its authority. Hume argues that the notion of explicit consent has no grounding in the history of society. From what we can tell, government evolved gradually, with the "chieftains" who act as the first magistrates acquiring their authority not by the choice of the people but "during the continuance of war." Experience instructed people in the evident utility of state authority during peacetime, and thus they came to accept it as legitimate. Hume also rejects Locke's notion of tacit consent, on the grounds that it depends on a person's freedom to leave her home country if she does not like its government, and on another nation being willing to accept her—conditions that rarely obtain. But Hume wants to do more than just refute the arguments made in support of the contract theory. He also seeks to convince his readers of his alternative account based on the ongoing utility of social institutions. We owe our government allegiance, not because of any prior commitments, real or imagined, but because we have an interest in its continuance to keep our property secure.

Shortly after the publication of the *Treatise*, an anonymous reviewer (possibly Hutcheson) wrote that "here . . . is the system of Hobbes dressed up in a new taste" (quoted in Mossner 1982: 139). The accusation is not unfounded, though neither is it quite fair. Hume rejects the egoistic account of human nature, which denies the very existence of non-selfish motives, but he nevertheless admits that self-interest is the only adequate explanation for the evolution, and ultimately the legitimacy, of civil society (Hume 2000: 3.2.8.5, p. 348). He concedes a right to resist tyrannical regimes, although he insists that this right should be invoked only "in cases of grievous tyranny and oppression" (Hume 2000: 3.2.10.1, p. 354). Like Hutcheson, Hume encourages magistrates to undertake various schemes for promoting the public interest (Hume 2000: 3.2.7.8, p. 345). But, unlike his predecessor, he does not think political authorities depend for their legitimacy on their willingness or ability to do so.

---

[1] All references to Hume's *Treatise* (Hume 2000), his *Enquiry* (Hume 1998), and Smith's *Wealth of Nations* (Smith 1976) include references (where applicable) to the book, chapter, section, and paragraph from which the relevant quotation is taken. This system of internal numbering can be found in any standard edition of these works.

LIBERTY, EQUALITY, AND FORMS
OF GOVERNMENT

The major Scottish Enlightenment figures were all tied to the Whig party in Scotland—although, given the personal and amorphous nature of political parties at the time, this tells us little about their philosophical ideas. However, it can be said that they were all sympathetic to the basic Whig principles of freedom of conscience, limitations on royal power, and a commitment to the rule of law—and all supportive of the 1689 Settlement that enshrined (however imperfectly) these ideals. Hutcheson makes freedom of conscience an important theme in his writing, and he allied himself with reform movements within the Church of Scotland. Hume makes it a key task in his essays and *History* to advocate for the Whig ideal of government by "laws, not men," and one of the important unifying motifs of his *History* is the slow but steady process by which "king and people were finally taught to know their proper boundaries" (Hume 1983: vi. 476). He argues that the ideal state must balance liberty and authority, and he thinks it does so through laws that are public, uniform in their execution, and applicable to the magistrates themselves as well as to citizens (Hume 1985: 12). Both Hutcheson and Hume see political liberty as a means to such more fundamental ends rather than a good in itself, though both agree that, as Hume puts it, "the Republican Form of Government is by far the best" (Hume 1932: ii. 306). They conceive of a republic not as a democracy, however, but as a government where power is shared among different branches of government. Both men's ideal is a mixed government not dissimilar to that of Britain, though both think that an ideal state should have more equal representation in the lower house than there currently was in the British Parliament—though a property qualification for voting should be retained—as well as an upper house without hereditary peers. Smith has little to say about such constitutional questions. He was a supporter of both freedom of conscience and the rule of law, but his emphasis is above all on economic liberty: the freedom to pursue our private interests through market transactions. (See below.)

Though not democrats in a modern sense, Hutcheson, Hume, and Smith were all in some sense egalitarians, and many people see this as a key aspect of their legacy. One historian has, controversially, even tried to maintain that Hutcheson was the chief influence on Thomas Jefferson in crafting the American Declaration of Independence (Wills 1978). While few scholars have supported this view, it is certainly true that Hutcheson's moral sense theory contributed to a growing conviction among Enlightenment intellectuals that there exist no innate differences between human beings. This theory implies that people are born with equal moral capacities—that it is these capacities rather than their rational abilities that are the most important to their status as persons, and that our innate dispositions, when properly attended to, incline us to take all people as equal subjects of moral consideration. Hume also contributed to this egalitarian trend with his "science of man," which takes as its premiss that human nature is universal, and he agrees with Hutcheson that the very "notion of morals" implies a sentiment "so universal and comprehensive as to extend to all mankind" (Hume 1998: 9.1.5, p. 147). For his part, Smith insists that "the difference between the most dissimilar characters, between a philosopher and a common street porter, for example, seems to arise not so much from nature, as from habit, custom, and education" (Smith 1976: 1.2.4, i. 28–9). All three men opposed slavery, and Hutcheson wrote in support of greater equality for women.

Despite their commitment to notions of inherent equality, however, Hutcheson, Hume, and Smith all believe that the impact of "habit, custom, and education" creates differences in character and ability that cannot be ignored. They further hold that attitudes of subordination and deference are necessary supports to the social order. None goes as far as Lord Kames, who says explicitly that the moral sense is simply weaker in some people than others (Kames 1788: iv. 17). But they all express, within the context of an admittedly imperfect society, a suspicion of the common people, and more specifically of their ability to contribute directly to political decision-making. Hume and Smith emphasize the desirability of changes in the social and economic structure to improve the condition of the poor. But they do not call for broad political equalization, and they insist that social changes must happen slowly, through the development of commerce, rather than as a deliberate result of demands of justice by the lower classes. It was left to Smith's pupil, John Millar, to explore the full egalitarian potential of Scottish Enlightenment ideas. His *Origin of the Distinction of Ranks* (Millar 2006) explores at length the hope that the growth of commerce will improve the position of women and the working classes, and he publicly supported the French Revolution.

THE DEVELOPMENT OF POLITICAL ECONOMY

Hume and Smith made major methodological advances in the study of economics. Underlying their interest in economic issues, however, is a broader philosophical agenda: to defend the pursuit of private interest through market transactions as a means not only to personal happiness, but to positive social development more broadly. Hume never wrote a complete treatise on political economy. His ideas are contained instead in a small number of essays on economic topics. The essays are written as sharp assaults on what their author sees as the misguided ideas and practices of his day, and his *History of England* contains numerous equally stinging critiques of the policies of past regimes. Here Smith follows his example. He described *The Wealth of Nations* as a "very violent attack . . . upon the whole commercial system of Great Britain" (Smith 1987: 251). Smith's ambition is to present general principles that can guide the practice of political economy, but his work is not written as a systematic textbook. It is structured instead as a series of interventions, often highly passionate and polemical, in contemporary debates.

In most cases, Hume and Smith are provoked in their attacks by governments doing too much rather than too little. Hume dismantles arguments that trade protection is in the national interest. His discussion of the Tudor period in the *History of England* features an intermittent but sustained polemic against monopolies and exclusive companies, which he thinks are the chief forms of destructive state intervention in the market. (The former prohibited competition within England, and the latter monopolized foreign trade in a particular commodity.) Smith takes up the cause of free trade and the attack on monopolies, but he also broadens his critique to include guilds and their systems of mandatory apprenticeships, the restrictions on the free movement of labor, and the laws that limit the use and transfer of people's property— for instance, those mandating primogeniture and allowing for entailments (which enable landowners to restrict the freedom of their heirs)—among a wide array of other topics.

Smith concludes that we should bear a standing presumption against government action in the economy. "Little else is required," he says, "to carry a state to the highest degree of affluence from the lowest barbarism but peace, easy taxes, and a tolerable administration of justice; all the rest being brought about by the natural course of things" (Smith 1980: 322). He argues against state interference with individual economic actors on the dual grounds that it is inherently unjust and also self-defeating. "No human wisdom" is sufficient to dictate the decisions of individuals because no central authority could ever acquire or process the necessary information (Smith 1976: 4.9.51, ii. 687). Further, the task of regulating the economy, in opposition to people's natural inclinations, forces the government to assume tyrannical powers, which inevitably has destructive consequences in other spheres.

To the consternation of many later advocates for a free market, however, Smith allows for significant exceptions to this general laissez-faire doctrine. He shares with Hume a belief in the possibility of beneficent state intervention in the life of society. Smith identifies numerous specific areas where direct government action can benefit the people. These include "Public Works and Institutions which are necessary for facilitating the Commerce of Society," a system of public education, and various kinds of regulations to protect the public (Smith 1976: i. 6). We must conclude that both Hume and Smith take a pragmatic, consequentialist approach to the role of the state, one very distant from the more dogmatic libertarianism adopted by many later free-market advocates (see Viner 1927). For these two thinkers, the presumption against state action is a defeasible one that must be tested against available evidence and reasonable predictions about what will promote the general happiness—even when people's "natural liberties" are at stake (see Smith 1976: 2.2.94, i. 324; Hume 1998: 3.1.8, p. 85). While it is easy to be frustrated by the apparently ad hoc nature of their recommendations for state action, these should be seen as part of their broader commitment to a cautious, empirically based approach to the study and governance of society, an approach that is self-consciously reflective of the methods of the "new science" developed over the previous centuries.

In arguing for government policies promoting the development of commerce, both men challenge the anti-capitalist arguments of the Christian moralist and "civic republican" writers. Hume and Smith insist that people need not be ashamed in finding fulfillment in their private market transactions, and in the rewards that result. This implies, against the civic republicans, that political and military achievement is in no sense a necessary prerequisite to true happiness. Hume is willing to go so far as to argue that capitalism actually improves people morally. He told Horace Walpole: "I beg you . . . to consider the great difference in point of morals between uncultivated and civilized ages" (Hume 1932: ii. 111). Comparing an inhabitant of feudal England to a modern resident of commercial society, he says that the latter is "a better man and a better citizen" than the former and that his life is a "more laudable" one (Hume 1983: iii. 76–7). Hume's moral defense of capitalism is based on his belief that commercial societies inevitably become more "civilized," meaning that their inhabitants are more benevolent and humane. The material rewards made available by commerce act as an incentive to stimulate what Hume calls people's "industry," or in other words their desire to labor and improve their condition. This increase in industry in turn stimulates the sciences and the arts, as well as connecting people together in bonds of sociability via the interactions that commercial relations bring. All these act to develop people's sympathy for their fellow humans and to strengthen their desire to act benevolently toward them. More widespread selflessness is therefore the paradoxical result of the pursuit of self-interest. By binding foreign nations together economically, capitalism also makes for a more peaceful world.

We should not imagine that this moral defense of capitalism reflects the consensus view of Scottish Enlightenment thinkers. On the contrary, civic republican ideas in particular retained a strong hold on many in the period. These ideas play a prominent role in Hutcheson's writings, though perhaps the most cogent advocate for them is Adam Ferguson. In his *Essay on the History of Civil Society*, Ferguson acknowledges many of the benefits of commerce but also expresses numerous reservations about its impact. For Ferguson, self-interest alone is simply inadequate to ensure that a nation possesses the necessary cohesion and strength to protect itself against dissolution or invasion. He also points to the damage done by the division of labor on the character of the workers, whose mental faculties are dulled by repetitive toil. A society dominated by commerce cannot, he believes, provide the venue for full human flourishing and the development of virtue. Smith acknowledges this concern, and his proposals for public education are designed to address it, by ensuring that workers have access to a full range of intellectual stimulation (Smith 1976: 5.1.f.50–7, ii. 781–6). And both he and Hume are willing to admit that the pursuit of luxury may become excessive, and thus have a negative impact on people's moral character. Despite these reservations, however, they remain among the most compelling early advocates for a distinctively liberal vision of commercial society, in which the operation of the free market provides people with the freedom and resources to realize their individual conceptions of the good.

Skepticism, Conservatism, and Reform

David Hume is sometimes referred to as a founder of modern conservative philosophy. This is largely in virtue of his philosophical skepticism, which calls into question the validity of any principles that are supposedly timeless or rooted in the nature of things. According to his epistemological precepts, we are so constituted as to be denied any direct insight into ultimate reality, including the truth about human nature, and so we can make no valid claims about the essence of humanity or society beyond what we can establish through concrete observation. However, the implications of this skepticism for politics remain a matter of dispute. Many commentators have agreed with Leslie Stephen, who says that Hume "inclines to the side of authority as the most favourable to that stagnation which is the natural ideal of a sceptic" (Stephen 1876: ii. 185). Hume certainly insists that we should approach the prospect of constitutional change or rebellion with extreme trepidation, insisting that "a blind submission is commonly due to magistracy" (Hume 2000: 3.2.10.2, p. 354). But he argues for this caution on consequentialist, rather than specifically skeptical, grounds. "We ought always," he says, "to weigh the advantages which we reap from authority, against the disadvantages" (Hume 2000: 3.2.10.1, p. 354). He thinks that, in this balancing of costs and benefits, the risks of radical change or rebellion almost always outweigh the benefits, since we may provoke civil conflict or even destroy civil society altogether—an outcome that is bound to be worse than life under even the most ineffective or tyrannical regime. Such a conclusion draws on no specifically skeptical premiss, and Hume makes no explicit attempt to apply his skeptical principles to his discussions of political and social questions. In fact, he offers normative judgments about different laws and policies and different forms of government, ones that seem at odds with any thoroughgoing skepticism about the existence of any normative criteria in political theory (see McArthur 2007).

Smith follows Hume in his wariness concerning political change. His *Wealth of Nations* can hardly be seen as a conservative text—it calls for drastic changes to a vast array of contemporary policies—but he insists that the reforms he calls for should be pursued in such a way as not to undermine existing political authorities. In a biographical treatment written after Adam Smith's death, his pupil and friend, Dugald Stewart, says that Smith was one of several authors of "celebrated works" on political topics who "aimed at the improvement of society—not by delineating plans of new constitutions, but by enlightening the policy of actual legislators." Stewart says that such speculations "have no tendency to unhinge established institutions, or to inflame the passions of the multitude" (Smith 1980: 311). Rather than seeing Hume as committed to an unquestioning acceptance of established regimes, we should rather view him and Smith as both engaged in the project Stewart outlines, one that motivates numerous Enlightenment political writers: that of determining how to direct and reform existing regimes in order to protect our basic liberties and promote commercial and cultural development, without threatening the constitutional framework of these regimes and risking social upheaval (see Hume 1983: iv. 354).

It is, of course, possible to assert that Hume's skeptical philosophy has implications for political philosophy that he does not himself draw. Specifically, one might argue that the aims of many modern radicals and egalitarian liberals depend on metaphysical convictions that cannot survive Hume's critique of epistemological certainty (see Livingston 1984). It is certainly true that an acceptance of Humean skepticism prevents us from basing schemes for reform or revolution on any criteria that cannot be rooted in empirically observable facts about our experience. However, it may be difficult to find many modern political philosophers, either liberal or radical, who consider their theories entirely divorced from such facts. John Rawls, who is often cited as a proto-typical "foundationalist liberal," is in fact at pains to point out that his theory of justice is intended to make sense of the conflicting and competing claims of liberty and equality already deeply imbedded in the Western democratic tradition, and he explicitly calls his method "nonfoundationalist" (Rawls 2001: 31).

PHILOSOPHICAL HISTORY

Scotland was divided internally between the more prosperous, urbanized lowland areas and the poorer and more "feudal" Highlands. The revolts of 1715 and 1745 dramatically illustrated the scope of this divide, as armies of Highlanders descended with the Pretender on the lowland cities. It is within this context that we can understand one of the distinctive features of the Scottish Enlightenment: its enduring interest in the distinction between "barbarous" and "civilized" societies, and in the conditions of progress from one to the other. In order to make sense of this process, the Scottish philosophers looked to the data of history, which they set themselves to gather. "I believe this is the historical Age," David Hume told his friend William Strahan, "and this the historical Nation" (Hume 1932: ii. 230). He himself set the trend with his six-volume *History of England*, which initiated a new style of history writing: detached from partisan disputes, yet sharply analytical in its assessments of the individuals and policies of past eras.

The historical investigations of the Scottish Enlightenment reveal the considerable influence of Montesquieu, but they also develop the Frenchman's project in important new directions. Montesquieu's work provided a model for the comparative study of different societies—and more specifically the relationship between their systems of law and government, and the manners and character of their people. However, he did not attempt to theorize how societies change through time, content instead to appeal to climate and physical geography to explain differences between nations. The Scottish writers, as they pursued their historical investigations, sought to explain the varying ways in which, and varying rates at which, different societies evolve and change, and more specifically to explain how and why some become more "civilized" than others. Not content to reduce this process to any single variable, they instead looked to the complex interactions between the societies' political, legal, social, and material elements.

The methodological foundation for philosophical history may be traced to Hume. As we have seen, in the *Treatise* he argues that the institutions of law and government evolve gradually, without any deliberate act of design, and are supported by people's continuing interest in their existence. His *History* can be seen as an extended case study in how society and its institutions develop through the unintended consequences of people's attempts to solve the immediate challenges of living together and bettering their condition. This approach was adopted by other Scottish philosophical historians. Ferguson captures it eloquently when he says: "Mankind in following the present state of their minds, in striving to remove inconveniences, or to gain apparent and contiguous advantages, arrive at ends which even their imagination cannot anticipate . . . Every step and every movement of the multitude, even in what are called enlightened ages, are made with equal blindness to the future, nations stumble upon establishments, which are indeed the result of human action but not the execution of human design" (Ferguson 1996: 119).

The ongoing historical inquiries undertaken by the Scottish philosophers represent a significant reconception of the boundaries of political philosophy. These inquiries are arguably closer than those of nearly any of their predecessors to what we would now recognize as political science. These philosophers attempt to apply empirical methods systematically to the study of social institutions, and to assess impartially the impacts of various state policies and the behavior of rulers and officials on the overall well-being of the people. (It is worth noting here that they see religion as a piece of data to be analyzed alongside other beliefs and institutions.) However, we should not imagine that, in trying to develop a scientific method suited to the study of society, the Scottish writers thereby abandoned any normative purpose. As we have seen, Hume openly equates increased levels of "civilization" with more widespread virtue among the people. Lord Kames, William Robertson, and John Millar all follow him in this view, and Smith largely seems to as well—though (as we have seen) he shares some of Ferguson's reservations. And, though the facts of history taught them that unintended consequences have tended to determine the direction of history, the Scottish writers did not believe that philosophers and policy-makers must surrender hopes of affecting the direction of change. On the contrary, they were convinced that critical reflection on historical data could help reveal principles that "enlightened legislators" could follow in order to create a more liberal, commercial—and as they saw it, more civilized—society. Whether they were right in their confidence that such a society is invariably attended with greater levels of moral development and human fulfillment, of course, remains a matter for dispute.

REFERENCES

Primary Sources

FERGUSON, A. (1996). *An Essay on the History of Civil Society* [1769], ed. F. Oz-Salzberger. Cambridge: Cambridge University Press.

HUME, D. (1932). *The Letters of David Hume*, ed. J. Y. T. Greig. 2 vols. Oxford: Clarendon Press.

HUME, D. (1983). *The History of England* [1754–61], ed. W. B. Todd. 6 vols. Indianapolis: Liberty Fund.

HUME, D. (1985). *Essays: Moral, Political and Literary* [1758], ed. E. F. Miller. Indianapolis: Liberty Fund.

HUME, D. (1998). *An Enquiry Concerning the Principles of Morals* [1751], ed. Tom L. Beauchamp. Oxford: Oxford University Press.

HUME, D. (2000). *A Treatise of Human Nature* [1739–40], ed. D. F. Norton and M. J. Norton. Oxford: Oxford University Press.

HUTCHESON, F. (1755). *A System of Moral Philosophy*. 2 vols. in 1. Glasgow: R. and A. Foulis; repr. New York: Augustus M. Kelley, 1968.

HUTCHESON, F. (2007). *Philosophiae moralis institutio compendiaria with a Short Introduction to Moral Philosophy* [1742 and 1747], ed. Luigi Turco. Indianapolis: Liberty Fund.

KAMES, LORD (H. HOME) (1788). *Sketches of the History of Man*. 3rd edn. 4 vols. Edinburgh: William Creech.

MILLAR, J. (2006). *The Origin of the Distinction of Ranks; or, An Inquiry into the Circumstances which Give Rise to Influence and Authority in the Different Members of Society* [1771], ed. Aaron Garrett. Indianapolis: Liberty Fund.

SMITH, A. (1976). *An Inquiry into the Nature and Causes of the Wealth of Nations* [1776], ed. R. H. Campbell and A. S. Skinner. Oxford: Oxford University Press.

SMITH, A. (1980). *Essays on Philosophical Subjects* [1795], ed. W. P. D. Wightman and J. C. Bryce. Oxford: Oxford University Press.

SMITH, A. (1987), *Correspondence*, ed. E. C. Mossner and I. S. Ross. Oxford: Oxford University Press.

Secondary Sources

FLEISCHACKER, S. (2004). *On Adam Smith's Wealth of Nations: A Philosophical Companion*. Princeton: Princeton University Press.

FORBES, D. (1975). *Hume's Philosophical Politics*. Cambridge: Cambridge University Press.

HAAKONSSEN, K. (1989). *The Science of a Legislator: The Natural Jurisprudence of David Hume and Adam Smith*. Cambridge: Cambridge University Press.

HONT, I., and IGNATIEFF, M. (1986) (eds). *Wealth and Virtue: The Shaping of Political Economy in the Scottish Enlightenment*. Cambridge: Cambridge University Press.

LIVINGSTON, D. W. (1984). *Hume's Philosophy of Common Life*. Chicago: University of Chicago Press.

MCARTHUR, N. (2007). *David Hume's Political Theory*. Toronto: University of Toronto Press.

MOSSNER, E. C. (1982). *The Life of David Hume*. Oxford: Oxford University Press.

RAWLS, J. (2001). *Justice as Fairness: A Restatement*. (Cambridge, MA: Harvard University Press.

ROBERTSON, J. (2005). *The Case for the Enlightenment. Scotland and Naples 1680–1760.* Cambridge: Cambridge University Press.

STEPHEN, L. (1876). *History of English Thought in the Eighteenth Century.* 2 vols. London: Smith, Elder and Co.

VINER, J. (1927). "Adam Smith and Laissez-faire," *Journal of Political Economy,* 35: 198–232.

WILLS, GARRY (1978). *Inventing America: Jefferson's Declaration of Independence.* Garden City, NY: Doubleday.

CHAPTER 20

EARLY NINETEENTH-CENTURY LIBERALISM

JEREMY JENNINGS

The broad outline of liberal doctrine across Europe in the first half of the nineteenth century can be easily delineated (see Smith 2002): liberals shared a fundamental commitment to individual liberty; to religious toleration; to limited government and the rule of law. They believed that the legitimacy of government derived from the consent of its citizens but, for the most part, doubted that this entailed a commitment to universal suffrage (see Mill 1992: 1–42; Guizot 2002). They also believed in the superior efficiency of a market economy based upon free trade and private property. They agreed less about the philosophical foundations of their beliefs—being split, roughly speaking, between supporters of Lockean natural law, Kantianism, and Benthamite utilitarianism—and, as time went on, even less about the practical implications of their principles. The criticisms directed against liberalism can likewise be listed without difficulty. Liberalism ignored the social constitution of humankind and was scornful of the common good. It sacrificed the public to the private and belittled political participation. It neglected the pursuit of virtue and prized only economic man, reducing individuals to pleasure-seeking machines. It disparaged authority (especially of a religious kind) and displayed an excessive faith in reason. It accepted, and even welcomed, inequality. This much is well known and does not require further investigation here.

Another important trait of liberalism—certainly from John Locke onwards—was the analysis of the arbitrary power of the state. Indeed, Locke went so far as to distinguish between despotism, usurpation, and tyranny, as well as the illegitimate power that derived from conquest (Locke 1992: 380–405). What I would like to do in this chapter is use the discussion of forms of arbitrary power as a thread that will allow the highlighting of certain key themes in liberal thought up to the mid-nineteenth century. At the outset the focus will fall upon liberalism in France, but the chapter will conclude with a discussion of liberalism in Britain, specifically with an analysis of the writings of

John Stuart Mill. By way of background, I will begin by analysing the account of despotism as rule by fear provided by Montesquieu in the mid-eighteenth century, and then show how Alexis de Tocqueville was able to formulate a new concept of the oppression most likely to occur in modern societies. I will do this by suggesting that we might take the concept of usurpation, formulated by the third of the great liberal thinkers of France, Benjamin Constant, as a point of transition.

Montesquieu was not the first in France to use the term 'despotism'. It had been widely used in France by aristocratic as well as Protestant opponents of Louis XIV. It had been given wide currency by Pierre Bayle and others such as Fénelon and Boulainvilliers, to the point that, even before Montesquieu was to place the concept of despotism at the heart of *The Spirit of the Laws*, there existed a broad understanding of despotism as a form of arbitrary rule by a single sovereign power limited neither by law nor by secondary powers (see Boesche 1990; Krause 2001). Despotism was further associated with other key features of the Sun King's reign: the centralization of power; religious intolerance; the pursuit of military glory; and financial corruption and mismanagement. To this Montesquieu was to add several other features, the most important of which was the description of despotism as rule by fear.

'The nature of despotic government', Montesquieu wrote, 'is that one alone governs according to his wills and caprices' (Montesquieu 1989: 21). The despot, then, had no rules by which he was bound and was strong because he was free to take life away as he chose. The despot's subjects obeyed him because he could destroy them, and for no other reason. In short, fear was used to 'beat down everyone's courage and extinguish even the slightest feeling of ambition' (Montesquieu 1989: 28–9). The people were to be made 'timid' and 'ignorant' while education was reduced 'to putting fear in the heart and teaching the spirit a few very simple religious principles'. As there was no virtue, men acted only with the comforts of life in view and therefore expected to be rewarded for everything they did. 'In despotic states', Montesquieu observed, 'the usage is that one does not approach a superior, or even a king, without giving him a present'. In return, all were paid for their services. As Montesquieu commented: 'the worst Roman Emperors were those who gave the most' (Montesquieu 1989: 67–8).

The goal of despotic government, for all its reliance upon caprice and fear, was nothing other than order and tranquillity, where all showed 'passive obedience' and everyone 'blindly submits to the absolute will of the sovereign'. The fate of each was to be reduced to 'instinct, obedience, and chastisement'. Under despotism, as in republics, everybody was equal, but under despotism this was because everyone counted for nothing.

Montesquieu summarized this deplorable state of human existence in one observation. 'When the savages of Louisiana want fruit', he wrote, 'they cut down the tree and gather the fruit. There you have despotic government' (Montesquieu 1989: 59). In other words, despotic government was government driven by instinctive actions and irrational appetites. It destroyed the very thing that sustained its life. It was government where power was not counterbalanced and that lacked the all-important ingredient of moderation. In institutional terms, power was not divided between the executive, legislative, and judicial branches. 'Amongst the Turks', Montesquieu wrote, 'where these three powers are placed upon the head of the Sultan, there exists a terrible despotism'. 'Political liberty', he concluded, 'is only to be found under moderate governments'. This, in turn, begged the question of what was meant by political liberty. For Montesquieu it was defined in terms of the absence of fear and, its corollary, an individual's sense of personal 'security' guaranteed by law. 'In a society where there are laws', Montesquieu stated, 'liberty can consist only in having the power to do what one should want to do and in no way being constrained to do what one should not want to do . . . Liberty is the right to do everything that the laws permit' (Montesquieu 1989: 155–9).

There were various antidotes to despotism, of which one of the most important was commerce. By commerce was meant not merely the exchange of goods but also the creation of new patterns of social intercourse. 'Where there is commerce', Montesquieu observed, 'there are mild customs' (Montesquieu 1989: 378). In particular, 'the natural effect of commerce is to lead us towards peace'. In the right circumstances, he believed, 'the spirit of commerce brings with it the spirit of frugality, economy, moderation, work, wisdom, tranquillity, order and rule' (Montesquieu 1989: 48).

Still, Montesquieu acknowledged, commerce could be subverted in the cause of despotism. Writing of the financier John Law and his infamous 'System', for example, he remarked that he 'was one of the greatest promoters of despotism that had until then been seen in Europe' (Montesquieu 1989: 19). Was there not then the danger that, in a commercial society, material interests would so dominate that citizens would place the satisfaction of physical comforts before the claims of liberty, thus opening up the possibility of a new form of despotism?

Certainly this has been the view of one influential commentator on Montesquieu. According to Roger Boesche, Montesquieu's writings contain a second theory of despotism, one grounded upon the isolation, frivolity, and self-interest of citizens in a commercial society (Boesche 1990). Here we need to recognize that Montesquieu made an important distinction between commerce 'ordinarily founded on luxury' and commerce 'more often founded on economy'. If the latter rested on 'the practices of gaining little . . . and of being compensated only by gaining continually', the former sought 'to procure for the nation engaging in it all that serves its arrogance, its delights, its fancies'(Montesquieu 1989: 340). Moreover, if Montesquieu associated 'economical commerce' with 'government by the many', he associated commerce of luxury with 'government by one alone'. As in all things for Montesquieu, what mattered was that the spirit of moderation should be observed and thus that in modern 'commercial' republics excessive inequalities were to be avoided.

Ultimately, however, this proved not to be the case. Commerce, whether for good or for ill, would brush aside such restrictions, in the process reconfiguring the 'the general spirit' of society. Once this had been perceived to have occurred, those who came increasingly to regard themselves as liberals had the task of forging a new doctrine that would graft the fundamental insights of Montesquieu concerning the nature of liberty and its preservation upon a society dominated by new social classes, new political institutions, and new commercial activities. This was no easy task. Moreover, in those circumstances new forms of despotism, only half suspected by Montesquieu, were to appear.

Participants in the French Revolution did not hesitate from citing Montesquieu. He was read consistently as a fierce critic of all forms of despotism. It was also the case that the tripartite division of governmental functions outlined by Montesquieu acted as a consistent point of reference in the constitutional debates that took place after 1789. However, as the Revolution turned away from the goal of constructing a balanced constitution towards that of using the state as a moral agent, Montesquieu faded from view. Most importantly, the idea that figured at the very heart of Montesquieu's thought—namely, 'power must check power by the arrangement of things'—was consistently ignored. By the side of demands for unity of political action, the moderation associated with the system of balances and manufactured equilibrium had little attraction. France slid slowly into Terror and then into the despotism of Bonapartist rule. It was upon this experience that Benjamin Constant was to reflect.

'We have finally reached', Constant announced at the beginning of his text *Of the Spirit of Conquest and Usurpation* (1814), 'the age of commerce, an age which necessarily replaces that of war' (Constant 1988: 53). This increasingly familiar argument led him next to suggest that, for modern nations, war had lost both its attraction and its utility. From this it followed that 'any government that wished to drive a European people to war and conquest would therefore commit a gross and disastrous anachronism' (Constant 1988: 54). Constant's conclusion was that a nation that, like France under Bonaparte, pursued conquest on this scale would become 'the object of universal horror' and also that the success of the conqueror would come to an 'inevitable end'. The system of conquest would be 'banished from the earth and branded by this last experience with eternal reprobation' (Constant 1988: 83).

Constant reached the same conclusion about usurpation: it is impossible, he announced, for usurpation to endure, so removed was it from the spirit of the modern age. Nevertheless, Constant was aware that he was describing something that was also new. It was not the same as despotism. It was not to be confused with monarchy. Rather, it was a novel form of government displaying its own distinctive and destructive pathologies. To make the point, Constant provided a sustained comparison between monarchy and usurpation, both forms of government in which power was in the hands of one man, but both very different from each other, despite the 'deceptive resemblance' (Constant 1988: 87–94).

The example of monarchy to which Constant referred was that of England. There, he wrote, we see that

> the rights of all citizens are safe from attack; that popular elections keep the body politic alive, despite certain abuses which are more apparent than real; that freedom of the press is respected; that talent is assured of its triumph; and that, in individuals of all classes, there is the proud, calm security of the man embraced by the law of his country. (Constant 1988: 87)

Here, by contrast, is Constant's vivid account of France under the regime of a usurper.

> We see there [he wrote] usurpation triumphant, armed with every frightful memory, the heir of all criminal theories, believing itself justified by all that has been done before it, strong through all the outrages, all the errors of the past, displaying its contempt for mankind, its disdain for reason. Around it are grouped all ignoble desires, every clever calculation, all refined degradations. (Constant 1988: 143)

Treachery, violence, and perjury were routinely required. Principles were invoked, only to be trampled upon. Greed was awakened. Injustice emboldened. For want of legitimacy, the usurper surrounded himself with guards, engaged in 'incessant warfare' and was forced to 'abase' and 'insult' all those around him in order that 'they may not become his rivals'.

Constant ended his description by drawing attention to what, in his opinion, was the most decisive innovation introduced by usurpation, an innovation that served to differentiate it from earlier forms of despotism, and that made the latter preferable to the former. Usurpation parodied and counterfeited liberty. It demanded the assent and approbation of its subjects. Through persecution it exacted signs of consent. Despotism, he wrote, 'rules by means of silence, and leaves man with the right to be silent; usurpation condemns him to speak; it pursues him to the intimate sanctuary of his thoughts and, forcing him to lie to his own conscience, denies him the last consolation of the oppressed' (Constant 1988: 95–7).

How had it been possible for this descent into a new, and more extensive, form of arbitrary government to occur? It arose, Constant stated unequivocally, as a consequence of a revolution that had fundamentally misunderstood the nature of liberty in modern, commercial society. This is how at this point Constant phrased the argument for which he was later to be best known. 'The liberty which was offered to men at the end of the last century', he wrote, 'was borrowed from the ancient republics'. That conception of liberty, Constant continued, consisted 'in active participation in the collective power rather than in the peaceful enjoyment of individual independence'. The ancients, in short, gained their greatest enjoyment from public life and little pleasure from their private existence; consequently they 'sacrificed individual liberty to political liberty'. By contrast, 'almost all the pleasures of the moderns lie in their private life'. Individuals wished to be left in 'perfect independence in all that concerns their occupations, their undertakings, their sphere of activity, their fantasies'. This was a form of 'civil liberty' virtually unknown to the ancients (Constant 1988: 102–5).

The next move was to sketch out a form of government that would be legitimate and that could not be counterfeited. This Constant attempted most systematically in his *Principles of Politics* (1815). At the heart of his answer was the conviction that the task would be accomplished not by attacking the holders of power but rather by attacking power itself, by placing guaranteed restrictions upon the possible abuse of power, by limiting not a particular form of sovereignty but sovereignty itself. No ruler, Constant wrote, even if his claim to legitimacy derived from 'the assent of the people', possessed 'a power without limits'. Similarly, the sovereignty of the people was not unlimited and should be 'circumscribed within the limits traced by justice and by the rights of individuals' (Constant 1988: 263–78). More precisely, and in line with the argument previously advanced by Montesquieu, the limitation of sovereignty could be made into a reality 'through the distribution and balance of powers'. As with Montesquieu, the model referred to was the English constitution.

Constant perceived several distinct advantages to this system of government, all of which, he believed, aided the preservation of liberty. The first was a 'vivid sentiment of public life' (Constant 1988: 239). The second derived from the independence of the judiciary. The third was freedom of the press. Next, Constant believed that constitutional monarchy provided the means of reducing the role of the army to that of its proper function: repelling foreign invaders. The final guarantee of liberty sprang from the independence of municipal and local authorities. In this we touch upon one of the central themes of French liberalism in the nineteenth century: namely, the preservation of local independence as a means of restricting the power of despotic, central government (see Dijn 2008). French liberals became obsessed by what they saw as the systematic destruction of all intermediary powers and the consequent subjection of an undifferentiated and amorphous population at the hands of a highly organized, centralized bureaucratic power. Constant spoke of 'individuals, lost in an unnatural isolation, strangers to the place of their birth, cut off from all contact with the past, forced to live only in a hurried present, scattered like atoms over an immense flat plain'. While Alexis de Tocqueville is the best-known exponent of this argument, it is important to realize that he was by no means the first to diagnose the nature of this new threat to liberty.

Constant quickly adapted the fundamentals of his thought to the new circumstances of the restored monarchy. Between 1822 and 1824 he published his *Commentaire sur l'ouvrage de Filangieri* (Constant 2004), a work that restated many of his by-now standard arguments linking the age of commerce with the need for constitutional government. When offered legislative improvement by government, he argued, the people should demand 'constitutional institutions'. In this text was also to be found Constant's clearest endorsement of the principles of economic liberalism. He argued in favour of competition and against state intervention and protectionism in the economy. He likewise called for reduced and fair taxation, commenting that all arbitrary taxation was a form of robbery. He argued that inheritance laws should leave people free to dispose of their wealth as they saw fit. The right of emigration should never be restricted, as it was wrong to treat man as a 'passive agent in the hands of authority'. He also declared that the abundance that would follow as a consequence of free trade would not promote luxury but overcome poverty. In conclusion he affirmed that 'the functions of government are negative: it should oppress evil and leave good to operate by itself'. The general motto of all governments should be 'laissez passer et laissez faire' (Constant 2004: 316–32).

In making these arguments Constant disclosed the influence of Adam Smith upon his thought. So too his ideas were broadly in line with those of Jean-Baptiste Say and Destutt de Tracy on the principles of political economy (Destutt de Tracy 1817; Say

2001). Both writers had disputed the theory of production associated with the earlier physiocratic school. This entailed, first, a rejection of the physiocratic notion that agriculture was the primary source of wealth and, second, a repudiation of the attachment of the physiocrats to the centralized state as a vehicle of economic progress. This had the radical implication of challenging the central physiocratic assumption that the 'sterile' class was largely composed of those not engaged in agricultural activities. This new vision saw the productive class as those engaged in industry and the sterile class as largely composed of agrarian *rentiers*. This position was to become economic orthodoxy amongst nineteenth-century French liberals, and was no better expressed than by the brilliant pamphleteer Frédéric Bastiat in his merciless assaults upon the 'economic sophisms' associated with socialism and protectionism (Bastiat 2001).

In the years remaining to him Constant continued to restate these principles. He did so, for example, in a long review of Charles Dunoyer's *L'Industrie et la morale considérées dans leur rapport avec la liberté* (Constant 1826). What is intriguing about the latter text is that it allows us to catch a glimpse of what Constant imagined might be a second new form of despotism. Constant, like Montesquieu, was broadly optimistic about the effects of commerce upon society. In this article he reaffirmed this but (in a distinct echo of the theme to be found in the final paragraphs of his famous lecture on the liberty of the ancients when compared to that of the moderns) (Constant 1988: 307–28) recognized that the pursuit of individual enjoyment and physical pleasure ran the risk of diminishing our nobler, more civic-minded sentiments.

Yet Constant suggested that this tendency should not be over-exaggerated. Rather, in a postscript to the review he turned his fire against what he termed 'un papisme industriel' and which he clearly associated with the new doctrine of Saint-Simonianism. In contrast to the *individualisme* developed by Dunoyer, this 'new sect' saw all diversity of thought and activity as an expression of anarchy. Terrified that not all people thought the same (or the same as their leaders), the Saint-Simonians invoked a spiritual power designed to reconstitute a broken unity. Under the guise of coordinating our thoughts and actions, they sought, in Constant's opinion, 'to organize tyranny'. Constant's response could not have been clearer: this supposed 'moral anarchy' was nothing other than 'the natural, desirable, happy state of a society in which each person, according to his own understanding, tastes, intellectual disposition, believes or examines, preserves or improves, in a word, makes a free and independent use of his faculties'. Nevertheless, in these few remarks on Saint-Simonianism, Constant had identified what would become a growing threat to liberty and the breeding ground for a new type of despotism.

Only six years later Tocqueville was to provide a very different analysis of the goal towards which society was moving, but here too the threat of despotism was ever present. The first point we might make is that in his analysis of Bonapartism or 'Caesarism', Tocqueville added little to the meticulous dissection provided by Constant (Tocqueville: 2001: 185–7, 247–8: see Richter 2004). Moreover, the very qualities of the despotism he came to diagnose in America have their roots firmly within this and the earlier analysis of despotism provided by Montesquieu. As Tocqueville's text is well known, I will limit myself to the briefest outline of his argument. In America, men were more equal in wealth and in intelligence than anywhere else in the world. The aristocratic element has been destroyed to the point of extinction and thus it could be said that 'the people govern in the United States'. By dint of circumstances, this has produced moderate government, founded upon 'the enlightened will of the people' and the responsible behaviour of individual citizens. Yet, although the form of government was representative, it was obvious that opinions, prejudices, interests, and even the passions of the people could find no lasting obstacles that prevented them from making themselves felt in daily life.

Herein lay the potential for a problem of enormous magnitude: the tyranny of the majority. In America this could take a variety of forms. 'It is of the very essence of democratic governments', Tocqueville wrote, 'that the empire of the majority is absolute'. The interests of the many were to be preferred to the interests of the few, and the people had the right to do anything they wished.

The dangerous consequences of this—each with distinct echoes of arguments previously advanced by Montesquieu and Constant—were as follows. It increased legislative instability, because the majority insisted that its desires be indulged 'rapidly and irresistibly'. It favoured the arbitrariness of the magistrate, because the 'majority, being an absolute master in making the law and in overseeing its execution, having equal control over those who govern and over those who governed, regard public officials as its passive agents'. Most importantly, the tyranny of the majority existed as a moral force exercised over opinion. 'I know of no other country', Tocqueville famously observed, 'in which there is such little independence of mind and real freedom of discussion as in America'. The majority drew 'a formidable circle around thought'. More than this, it was a tyranny that left the body alone but enslaved the soul. No despotism of the old order, Tocqueville opined, had had the possibility of such untrammelled power.

If, then, liberty was ever to be lost in America, the fault would lie with the omnipotence of the majority. Yet, to date, Tocqueville argued, the tyranny of the majority had had little effect upon political society, the distressing consequences being limited to its impact upon 'the national character of the Americans'. The American 'is enclosed strictly within himself and tries to judge the world from there'. Isolated from each other, Americans acted from their passions, preferring equality to liberty. They were a prey to individualism, 'the reflective and peaceable sentiment that disposes each citizen to isolate himself from the mass of those like him' (Tocqueville 2002: 482).

However, the threat of democratic despotism was curtailed by a set of constitutional limitations upon majoritarian power. First there was the federal constitution itself. Next, Tocqueville admired the two-chamber legislative system, because it provided balanced and moderate government. Unknown to the republics of antiquity, this principle was to be seen as an axiom of the political science of the modern world. Third, Tocqueville admired the American system of decentralized administration, witnessed first hand in the townships of New England. Municipal institutions,

Tocqueville believed, constituted the strength of free nations. To this he added freedom of the press and the legal profession, which even in America preserved an aristocratic spirit and thus acted against any potential tyranny of the majority. Above all, crude self-interest and materialism, two of the greatest dangers posed to liberty by an age of equality, could be combated by free institutions embodying the principle of association. The art of association was the mother science of democracy, and what struck Tocqueville was that Americans everywhere came together to form associations with a view to securing common aims and objectives. In short, Tocqueville believed that the political and social institutions of America had been so constructed as to strengthen what we might term the habits of freedom.

To read *Democracy in America*, as with so much else by Tocqueville, is to be constantly enriched and enlightened. Yet, the nature of the tyranny he was describing (and for which he sought an expression that exactly reproduced the idea) was one composed of elements long familiar to his fellow French liberals. This is not to suggest that Tocqueville was not the great thinker that he is rightfully taken to be, for his genius is to have transposed this description of tyranny to a new setting, America, and to have projected it into all of our futures.

Where, then, are the differences between Montesquieu, Constant, and Tocqueville to be found? At its simplest, despotism for Montesquieu derived from one ruler and was imposed upon the people; usurpation, according to Constant, was government by one ruler in the name of the sovereignty of the people; while, for Tocqueville, tyranny was exercised by the democratic majority over and against the minority. Beyond this, it was Tocqueville himself who marked out the originality of the new form of despotism. The following is a long quotation but is one that takes us to the heart of the issue.

> In past centuries, one never saw a sovereign so absolute and so powerful that it undertook to administer all the parts of a great empire by itself without the assistance of secondary powers; there was none who attempted to subjugate all its subjects without distinction to the details of a uniform rule, nor one that descended to the side of each of them to lord it over him and lead him. The idea of such an undertaking had never presented itself to the human mind, and if any man had happened to conceive of it, the insufficiency of enlightenment, the imperfection of administrative proceedings, and above all the natural obstacles that inequality of conditions gave rise to would soon have stopped him in the execution of such a vast design. (Tocqueville 2002: 661)

Despotism in the past, then, 'was violent but its extent was limited'. Even under the greatest power of the Caesars, the different peoples of the Roman Empire preserved their diverse customs and were administered separately, the details of individual and social existence ordinarily escaping the emperor's control.

It is clear that Tocqueville was of the opinion that the Empire of Napoleon Bonaparte was the first to overcome these obstacles to despotism. 'Napoleon', he told his fellow members of the *Académie Française* in 1842,

> possessed the knowledge of the nineteenth century and he acted upon a nation that was almost deprived of laws, customs and sound principles . . . This allowed him to

build a despotism that was more rational and well-constructed than anyone would have dared attempt before him. After having promulgated in the unitary spirit all the laws destined to regulate the countless interactions between all citizens and with the State, he was able simultaneously to create all the powers charged with executing these laws and to structure them in such a way as, taken together, to form a vast but simple machine of government, of which he alone was the motor.

It was 'the most perfect despotism' yet created (Tocqueville 1989: 264–5).

The new ingredient made evident in the democratic social state was that, if government now possessed these extensive instruments of administrative control, it would operate in a society characterized by near equality. Therefore, as Tocqueville wrote in *Democracy in America*, 'if despotism came to be established in the democratic nations of our day . . . it would be more extensive and milder, and would degrade men without tormenting them' (Tocqueville 2002: 662). This would be a power that 'does not tyrannize, it hinders, compromises, enervates, extinguishes, dazes, and finally reduces each nation to being nothing more than a herd of timid and industrious animals of which the government is the shepherd' (Tocqueville 2002: 663). Our leaders will not be tyrants but rather schoolmasters and we will console ourselves with the thought that we have at least chosen them ourselves.

It was at this very late stage of his argument that Tocqueville identified a further source and cause of despotism and one that was largely, if not entirely, unfamiliar to both Montesquieu and Constant (see Boesche 2006: 59–84, 189–210). Moreover, it was a source of despotism that Tocqueville himself had arguably overlooked in volume i of *Democracy in America*. The main thrust of Tocqueville's argument was that it was the equality of conditions that favoured the centralization of power. Yet, this was not the whole picture. 'In the modern nations of Europe', Tocqueville now observed, 'there is one great cause that . . . contributes constantly to extending the action of the sovereign or increasing its prerogatives . . . This cause is the development of industry, which is favoured by the progress of equality' (Tocqueville 2002: 655–6). By bringing a multitude of people together in the same place, new relations were created: 'The industrial class needs to be regulated, overseen, and contained more than other classes, and it is natural that the prerogatives of government grow with it.' To that extent, the industrial class, in Tocqueville's words, 'carries despotism within itself and that despotism naturally spreads as it develops' (Tocqueville 2002: 657). More than this, as nations industrialized, they felt the need for roads, canals, ports, and 'other semi-public works'. The more democratic a nation, the harder it was for these to be provided by individuals and the easier it was for the state to step in. In such circumstances, not only was government the 'greatest industrialist', but it tended also to become the master of all the others. Thus, governments came to appropriate the greater part of the produce of industry. It was this phenomenon, one that was entirely new and that was simply unknown to Montesquieu and only glimpsed by Constant (for both of whom commerce was, above all, a source of freedom and emancipation), that powerfully contributed to a novel form of despotism in which state control became ever more intrusive and minute and where all initiative was taken away from the private individual and handed over to a government that constantly extended its reach.

This was Tocqueville's chilling description of the new features of despotism.

> I see [he wrote] an innumerable crowd of like and equal men who revolve on themselves without repose, procuring the small and vulgar pleasures with which they fill their souls. Each of them, withdrawn and apart, is like a stranger to the destiny of all the others... Above these an immense tutelary power is elevated, which alone takes charge of assuring their enjoyments and watching their fates... It willingly works for their happiness; but it wants to be the unique agent and sole arbiter of that; it provides for their security, foresees and secures their needs, facilitates their pleasures, conducts their principal affairs, directs their industry, regulates their estates, divides their inheritances. (Tocqueville 2002: 663)

It could be argued that this has proved to be the most pervasive despotism of the modern age, and so much so that we have largely ceased to see it as a form of despotism. Be that as it may, the overall point is that Tocqueville, like Montesquieu and Constant before him, provided two accounts of despotism, with distinct causes and distinct pathologies.

Let us conclude this part of the chapter with two thoughts from Tocqueville. The first is his comment that, for all the faults of the system of soft despotism, it was still 'infinitely preferable to one which, having concentrated all powers, would deposit them in the hands of one irresponsible man or body' (Tocqueville 2002: 664). The worst of all tyrannies was that described by Montesquieu: arbitrary and indiscriminate rule by fear. Constant concurred. Second, 'in the democratic centuries that are going to open up individual independence and local liberties will always be the product of art' (Tocqueville 2002: 645). Montesquieu, Constant, and Tocqueville all agreed that liberty was a fragile construction and that it would always need protection.

Liberals in early nineteenth-century Britain were largely immune from the political and cultural pessimism that was to overcome Tocqueville in his later years. Their experience was one of political reform and of economic growth through the gradual extension of free trade, such that they saw the Industrial Revolution as both inevitable and without need of correction by state intervention. This mood was clearly expressed by Richard Cobden, John Bright, and the supporters of the Manchester School. Their political triumph was the repeal of the Corn Laws in 1846. It received more eloquent articulation from the pen of T. B. Macaulay. In his review of Southey's *Colloquies* (Macaulay 1972: 34–78), Macaulay defended the manufacturing system and denied that it was a 'system of actual servitude'. The people lived longer, were better clothed, and were more populous than ever before. He denounced Southey's 'exaggerated' notion of the wisdom of governments, arguing that there was no reason for believing that 'a government is more likely to lead the people the right way than the people to fall into the right way of themselves' (Macaulay 1972: 59). Nothing, he went on, is so galling 'to a people not broken in since birth' as 'paternal' or 'meddling' government. This was not to say that the 'lower orders' did not suffer hardships, but, he concluded:

'Our rulers will best promote the improvement of the people by strictly confining themselves to their own legitimate duties . . . Let the Government do this—the People will assuredly do the rest' (Macaulay 1972: 78).

At first glance this might also appear to have been the opinion of John Stuart Mill, the most important and influential nineteenth-century British liberal political thinker. Mill's psychologically painful disengagement from Benthamite utilitarianism— Bentham, he wrote, was 'a systematic and accurately logical half-man' (Mill 1963: 95)—left him convinced not only that a philosophy that could teach only 'the merely business part of social arrangements' was inadequate but also that what was needed was an ethical creed that focused upon 'the internal culture of the individual' and 'the cultivation of the feelings' (Mill 1969: 80–110). There were to be many dimensions to this philosophical reworking of utilitarianism, but several of the important themes were first disclosed in Mill's detailed commentary on Tocqueville's *Democracy in America* (Mill 1969: 173–267).

Seeing the comparison between Montesquieu and Tocqueville, Mill echoed the latter's concern that democracy produced hasty and short-sighted government, and that it confused the interests of the majority with the interests of all. However, Mill went on: 'The tyrant which we fear, and which M. de Tocqueville dreads, is of another kind—a tyranny not over the body but over the mind.' The individual, on this view, would simply be ground down by weight of numbers: 'all being nearly equal in circumstances, and all nearly alike in intelligence and knowledge, the only authority which commands an involuntary deference is that of numbers' (Mill 1963: 240–2). The challenge, therefore, was 'to make head against the tendency of democracy towards bearing down individuality and circumscribing the exercise of the human faculties within narrow limits'. The corollary was that it was function of government 'to sustain the higher pursuits of philosophy and art; to vindicate and protect the unfettered exercise of reason, and the moral freedom of the individual' (Mill 1963: 254). However, Mill subtly changed the force of Tocqueville's argument by claiming that the threat came not from the rise of democratic man but from the likely prevalence of the 'commercial class' and 'the unbalanced influence of the commercial spirit'. Its 'complete predominance', Mill contended, not only would forge a 'homogenous community' but also 'would commence an era either of stationariness or of decline' (Mill 1963: 363–4). What was now required, therefore, was 'a great social support for opinions and sentiments different from those of the mass'. According to Mill, given the happy absence of the military spirit, the elements that should compose this support were 'an agricultural class, a leisured class and a learned class' (Mill 1963: 264). If Mill felt it necessary to spell out the counterbalancing element in the agricultural class—they should, Mill wrote, 'represent the type opposite to the commercial—that of moderate wishes, tranquil tastes, cultivation of the excitements and enjoyments near at hand, and compatible with their existing position' (Mill 1963: 265)—he felt that the countervailing capabilities of a leisured class and a learned class were 'at once apparent'. 'It is', Mill opined, 'one of the greatest advantages of this country over America that it possesses both these classes' (Mill 1963: 266). The prospects for the future greatly depended upon their preservation.

Mill's conclusion was unequivocal. The dominance of the commercial class in modern society was inevitable. This ought not necessarily to be regarded as an evil, but the most powerful class must not become all-powerful. 'Now, as ever', he wrote, 'the great problem in government is to prevent the strongest from becoming the only power; and repress the natural tendency of the instincts and passions of the ruling body to sweep away all barriers which are capable of resisting, even for a moment, their own tendencies' (Mill 1963: 267).

This question continued to preoccupy Mill for the remainder of his life. For example, it is central to the argument advanced in *Considerations on Representative Government* (1861). Here Mill began by disputing the claim that there could be any such thing as a good despotism—'Evil for evil', he argued, 'a good despotism, in a country at all advanced in civilisation, is more noxious than a bad one; for it is more relaxing and enervating to the thoughts, feelings, and energies of the people'—in order to explain that there 'is no difficulty in showing that the ideally best form of government is that in which the sovereignty, or supreme controlling power in the last resort, is vested in the entire aggregate of the community' (Mill 1968: 207). Given that 'in a community exceeding a single small town' all could not participate personally, it followed that 'a perfect government must be representative'. Nevertheless, the representative system contained two '*positive* evils': 'general ignorance and incapacity . . . in the controlling body' and 'the danger of its being under the influence of interests not identical with the general welfare of the community' (Mill 1968: 243). The greatest danger, then, was one long familiar to liberal writers: 'the sinister interest of the holders of power'. The task was equally familiar: 'to provide efficacious securities against this evil' (Mill 1968: 254). In this instance, Mill recommended a system of proportional representation and plural voting designed to secure the selection of 'the very *élite* of the country' and the protection of minorities.

Much better known has been Mill's attempt to defend the individual from the tyranny of the majority via what he misleadingly termed his 'one very simple principle': namely, that the state can rightfully limit the liberty of action of a person only 'to prevent harm to others'. The only liberty worthy of the name, Mill contended in *On Liberty* (1859), was that of 'pursuing our own good in our own way'. Against the 'tyranny of prevailing opinion', therefore, Mill posited the advantages for 'the permanent interests of a man as a progressive being' of liberty of conscience, of discussion, of tastes and pursuits. Yet, Mill's sphere of non-intervention proved surprisingly porous. In the final chapter of *On Liberty* entitled 'Applications', Mill wrote the following:

> it is the proper office of public authority to guard against accidents. If either a public officer or any one else saw a person attempting to cross a bridge which had been ascertained to be unsafe, and there was no time to warn him of the danger, they might seize him and turn him back, without any real infringement of his liberty; for liberty consists in doing what one desires, and he does not desire to fall into the river. (Mill 1968: 151–2)

With this one example, Mill gave ground to all those who would later argue in favour of collectivist legislation designed to protect individuals from either their own ignorance or their folly.

Similar themes were addressed by Mill in his *Principles of Political Economy* (1848), and there again, as each new revised edition revealed, the principle of non-interference was subject to a progressive dilution. The general principles underlying Mill's argument might be summarized as follows: industrial progress generates 'increase of capital, increase of population, and improvements in production'. However, there were two negative aspects to this optimistic scenario. First, Mill believed that, despite the progressive state of wealth, 'the great class at the base of the whole might increase in numbers only, and not in comfort nor in cultivation' (Mill 1970: 60). Second, he identified 'the tendency of profits to fall as society advances' (Mill 1970: 88). The technical details of the latter argument can be passed over: Mill's conclusion cannot. In a country such as England, he argued, it would be but a short time before 'all further accumulation of capital would for the present cease'.

This in turn led Mill to imagine that we would soon attain a 'stationary state' where industrial progress would stop. Moreover, Mill announced that he did not 'regard the stationary state of capital and wealth with the unaffected aversion so generally manifested towards it by political economists of the old school'. Indeed, he went on to say that 'I confess I am not charmed with the ideal of life held out by those who think that the normal state of human beings is that of struggling to get on; that the trampling crushing, elbowing, and treading on each other's heals . . . are the most desirable lot of human kind' (Mill 1970: 113). Fortunately, as far as Mill could see, the stationary state of capital did not entail a stationary state of human improvement.

Next, Mill was led to consider 'the probable future of the labouring classes' in such circumstances. In brief, Mill imagined that the workers would steadily move towards a position of 'self-dependence' and that they would no longer be satisfied with 'the patriarchal or paternal system of government'. Cooperation and partnership would become the norm. The prospects for the future, therefore, depended upon the extent to which the labouring classes could 'be made rational beings'. Reassuringly from Mill's perspective, it was quite consistent with this that 'they should feel respect for superiority of intellect and knowledge' (Mill 1970: 125).

The central question that had to be addressed, however, was that of the proper functions of government with regard to the economy. 'No subject', Mill contended, 'has been more keenly contested in the modern age' (Mill 1970: 304). Mill's starting point was almost identical to the position he was later to take in *On Liberty*.

> There is [Mill wrote] a circle around every individual human being, which no government, be it that of one, of a few, or of the many, ought to be permitted to overstep . . . the point to be determined is, where the limit should be placed, how large a province of human life this reserved territory should be. (Mill 1970: 306)

In answering this question at great length, Mill gave full voice to the arguments against state intervention. It necessitated high taxation and 'onerous restrictions'. It led to an increase in the authority and influence of government. Government action tended to be inefficient. 'Most things are ill-done; much not done at all', Mill wrote. Importantly, individuals were deprived of the 'practical education' that arose from spontaneous action in pursuit of collective goals. 'Such a system', Mill wrote, 'more completely than any other, embodies the idea of despotism, by arming with intellectual superiority as an additional weapon, those who already have legal power' (Mill 1970: 313). Echoing Tocqueville, he wrote that it would be 'the government of sheep by their shepherd'. So, at first glance, Mill's conclusion was definite. 'Laisser-faire', he wrote, 'should be the general practice; every departure from it, unless required by some common good, is a certain evil' (Mill 1970: 314).

What common good, if any, allowed such a departure? To answer that question Mill made a distinction between the necessary and the optional functions of government, and immediately conceded that the former were 'more multifarious than most people are at first aware of' (Mill 1970: 145–52). Next, he considered an extensive series of cases where the individual as consumer could not be regarded as a 'competent' judge of his or her own interests. Here, Mill avowed, 'the foundation of the *laisser-faire* principle breaks down entirely'. Then came cases where the interference of the law was required 'not to overrule the judgement of individuals . . . but to give effect to that judgement' (Mill 1970: 329). Examples included factory act legislation and the provision of a minimum subsistence for those out of work or in poverty. Then came cases where 'there is no individual specially interested in performing them, nor would any adequate remuneration naturally or spontaneously attend their performance' (Mill 1970: 342). These ranged from the building of lighthouses to the maintenance of a learned class and the establishment of colonies. To what conclusion did these 'exceptions' lead? 'The intervention of government', Mill wrote, 'cannot always practically stop short at the limit which defines the cases intrinsically suitable for it. In the particular circumstances of a given age or nation, there is scarcely anything really important to the general interest, which it may be desirable, or even necessary, that the government should take upon itself, not because private individuals cannot effectively perform it, but because they will not' (Mill 1970: 345). Whether or not he fully appreciated it, Mill thereby opened up the possibility of a significant extension of collectivist activity on the part of the state. The new, welfare liberalism later associated with writers such as L. T. Hobhouse and T. H. Green was on the horizon, and the liberals, in the words of Herbert Spencer, were about to become advocates of 'legislative aggression'.

Across the Channel, events had likewise taken a worryingly illiberal turn, but for different reasons. The Revolution of 1848 had brought into existence a 'social' republic committed to a recognition of the right to work. With its collapse came the Second Empire of Napoleon III and the suppression of political freedoms. In these circumstances, when the French had again fallen for the seductive charms of Caesarism, Alexis de Tocqueville was led to enquire into the causes of the failure of liberty to establish itself upon a secure foundation. His answer, most famously articulated in *The Old Regime and the Revolution* (1856), was that the roots of despotism lay deep in French history and had yet to be eradicated. The revolutionaries of 1789 had sought not to destroy the instruments of despotism but to use them to serve their own ends. Faced with such a disturbing conclusion, Tocqueville did not hesitate to restate the core doctrine of early nineteenth-century liberalism: liberty, he wrote, consists 'in the pleasure of being able to speak, act, and breathe without constraint, under the government of God and the laws alone. Whoever seeks for anything from freedom but itself is made for slavery' (Tocqueville 1998: 217).

REFERENCES

BASTIAT, F. (2001). *Selected Essays on Political Economy*, (ed.) G. B de Huszar. New York: Foundation for Economic Education.

BOESCHE, R. (1990). 'Fearing Monarchs and Merchants: Montesquieu's Two Theories of Despotism', *Western Political Quarterly*, 43: 741–61.

BOESCHE, R. (2006). *Tocqueville's Road Map*. Lanham MD: Lexington Books.

CONSTANT, B. (1826). *Revue encyclopédique*, xxix. 416–35.

CONSTANT, B. (1988). *Political Writings*, (ed.) B. Fontana. Cambridge: Cambridge University Press.

CONSTANT, B. (2004). *Commentaire sur l'ouvrage de Filangieri* (1822–4). Paris: Belles Lettres.

DESTUTT DE TRACY. A. L. C. (1817). *A Treatise on Political Economy*. Georgetown: Joseph Milligan.

DIJN, A. DE. (2008). *French Political Thought from Montesquieu to Tocqueville: Liberty in a Levelled Society?* Cambridge: Cambridge University Press.

GUIZOT, F. (2002). *The History of the Origins of Representative Government in Europe* (1820–2). Indianapolis: Liberty Fund.

KALYVAS, A., and KATZNELSON, I. (2008). *Liberal Beginnings: Making a Republic for the Moderns*. Cambridge: Cambridge University Press.

KRAUSE, S. (2001). 'Despotism in the Spirit of the Laws', in D. Carrithers, M. A. Mosher, and P. Rahe (eds), *Montesquieu's Science of Politics: Essays on the Spirit of the Laws*. Rowman & Littlefield, 231–72.

LOCKE, J. (1992). *Two Treatises of Government* [1690], (ed.) P. Laslett. Cambridge: Cambridge University Press.

MACAULAY, T. B. (1972). *Thomas Babington Macaulay: Selected Writings*, (1830), (eds.) J. Clive and T. Pinney. Chicago: University of Chicago Press.

MILL, J. (1992). *Political Writings*, (ed.) T. Ball. Cambridge: Cambridge University Press.

MILL, J. S. (1963). *John Stuart Mill: Essays on Politics and Culture*, (ed.) G. Himmelfarb. New York: Anchor Books.

MILL, J. S. (1968). *Utilitarianism, Liberty, Representative Government*, (ed.) A. D. Lindsay. London: Dent.

MILL, J. S. (1969). *Autobiography* [1873], (ed.) J. Stillinger. Oxford: Oxford University Press.

MILL, J. S. (1970). *Principles of Political Economy* (1848), (ed.) D. Winch. Harmondsworth: Penguin.

MONTESQUIEU, C. L. (1989). *The Spirit of the Laws* [1748], (ed.) A. M. Cohler, B. C. Miller, and H. S. Stone. Cambridge: Cambridge University Press.

RICHTER, M. (2004). 'Tocqueville and French Nineteenth-Century Conceptualizations of the Two Bonapartes and their Empires', in P. Baehr and M. Richter (eds), *Dictatorship in History and Theory: Bonapartism, Caesarism and Totalitarianism*. Cambridge: Cambridge University Press, 83–102.

ROSENBLATT, H. (2008). *Liberal Values: Benjamin Constant and the Politics of Religion*. Cambridge: Cambridge University Press.

ROSENBLATT, H. (2009) (ed.). *The Cambridge Companion to Constant*. Cambridge: Cambridge University Press.

SAY, J. B. (2001). *A Treatise on Political Economy* [1803]. New Brunswick: Transaction Books.

SMITH, G. W. (2002). *Liberalism: Critical Concepts in Political Theory*. London: Routledge.

SULLIVAN, R. E. (2009). *Macaulay: The Tragedy of Power*. Cambridge, MA: Belknap Press.

SWEDBERG, R. (2009). *Tocqueville's Political Economy*. Princeton: Princeton University Press.

TOCQUEVILLE, A. DE (1989). 'Discours de M. de Tocqueville prononcé dans la séance publique du 21 avril 1842', *Œuvres complètes*, xvi. Paris: Gallimard.

TOCQUEVILLE, A. DE (1998). *The Old Regime and the Revolution*, i [1856], (ed.) F. Furet and F. Mélonio. Chicago: University of Chicago Press: Chicago.

TOCQUEVILLE, A. DE (2001). *The Old Regime and the Revolution*, ii. *Notes on the French Revolution and Napoleon*, (ed.) F. Furet and F. Mélonio. Chicago: Chicago: University Press.

TOCQUEVILLE, A. DE (2002). *Democracy in America* [1835, 1840], (ed.) H. C. Mansfield and D. Winthrop. Chicago: Chicago University Press.

WELCH, C. B. (2006) (ed). *The Cambridge Companion to Tocqueville*. Cambridge: Cambridge University Press.

CHAPTER 21

GERMAN IDEALISM

PAUL REDDING

For over a hundred years, idealist philosophy has been often dismissed as a nineteenth-century aberration—a purportedly backward-looking philosophy that seeks consolation in religion in the face of a rapidly secularizing world. But from such an assessment it is difficult to see what could possibly have led the philosopher–literary theorist, Friedrich Schlegel, at the end of the eighteenth century to link the idealist philosophy of his contemporary, J. G. Fichte, to the French Revolution, on the one hand, and Goethe's revolutionary novel *Wilhelm Meister*, on the other, as 'the greatest tendencies of the age' (Schlegel 1991: 46). Politically, idealism would eventually be replaced by 'materialism' in Marx's transformation of Hegel's 'absolute idealism', while philosophically idealism was replaced by various anti-idealist doctrines in the twentieth century. But idealism still has its advocates, one recent supporter, in claiming 'idealism as modernism' (Pippin 1997), essentially reinstating Schlegel's assessment. For such a view, idealist philosophy, like the French Revolution and modern literature, is grounded in the characteristically modern idea of human freedom. In this chapter, I present an account of some of the implications for political thought to be found in three leading idealists from the late eighteenth and early nineteenth centuries: Immanuel Kant, J. G. Fichte, and G. W. F. Hegel.

KANT'S 'IDEALIST' PHILOSOPHY AND ITS CONSEQUENCES FOR POLITICAL THEORY

Immanuel Kant (1724–), perhaps the most recognized philosophical representative of the 'German Enlightenment', is known for his system of 'transcendental idealism', elaborated throughout the 1780s in his three great 'critiques': *Critique of Pure Reason* (1781, 2nd edn 1787); *Critique of Practical Reason* (1788); and *Critique of Judgment*

(1790). Clearly transcendental idealism represents an approach that is in many ways at odds with the more naturalistic and empiricist strands of philosophy prominent within the Anglophone tradition, and to appreciate its relevance for political philosophy some common misunderstandings need correcting. Perhaps the most common here is the assumption that links the *Idealismus* of Kant and the German idealists with the type of 'immaterialist' theocentric metaphysics of the eighteenth-century Bishop of Cloyne, George Berkeley.

Kant sometimes glossed the qualifier 'transcendental' with 'formal', contrasting an idealist approach to the *form* of the world as experienced and known with Berkeley's idealism concerning its 'matter' (e.g. Kant 1999: 445). This underlying 'form–matter' distinction, coming ultimately from Aristotle, in fact plays a crucial role in the German idealist tradition and separates it from the empiricist–naturalist tradition more common in British philosophy. To be an idealist about 'form' is basically to construe the various aspects of the experienced world that *traditional metaphysics* had taken to reflect features of the world 'in itself' as somehow relative to the knowing subject's own cognitive capacities. Kant, trying to link transcendental idealism to the modern 'scientific' point of view, famously used the analogy of Copernicus. While for experience it *seems* that the sun moves about the earth, in truth it is *our movement* that explains the sun's *apparent* motion (Kant 1998: B113 n). Analogously, what naively appear to be features of the world itself are actually features that result from our own ways of understanding it. Thus, rather than, like Berkeley, attempting to reduce 'matter' to a reality that is fundamentally mind-like, Kant's idealism leaves the material world intact and sees its *formal properties* as relative to the rational subject who knows and acts within that world.

In *Critique of Pure Reason* Kant distinguishes two such subject-related 'forms' that organize our experience and knowledge of the world. First, he interprets the *tridimensionality* of space and the *unidirectionality* of time as resulting from the way we represent to ourselves objects in their spatio-temporal relations. That is, these are formal or structural features of our 'pure intuitions' of space and time, not objective properties of space and time themselves. But objects as experienced and known also have a morphologically distinct *conceptual* form that is reflected in the logical structure of the *predicative judgements* we make about them. Thus, besides the pure intuitions of space and time, our experience and knowledge are also organized by a universal set of 'pure' a priori concepts or 'categories'. With his idealism about space and time, Kant was continuing Leibniz's 'relationalist' critique of Newton's substantivist interpretation of space and time (Leibniz and Clarke 2000). But, with his thesis of *two* distinct representational forms—intuition and concept—Kant was also critical of Leibniz for not having distinguished them.

Kant's appeal to the distinction between 'matter' and 'form' signals an implicit acceptance of features of Aristotle's 'hylomorphic' conception of objects that had been largely rejected by the empiricist–naturalist tradition. Aristotle had effectively reinterpreted Plato's doctrine of the 'ideas' or 'forms' such that they imparted an organization to the (otherwise formless) 'matter' of the world. That the matter making up a cat, say, had a distinctly *feline* formal organization, was responsible for it being what it was: a *cat*. In the early modern period, the Aristotelianism prevalent in later medieval philosophy came to be challenged by a more *nominalist* outlook that had accompanied early modern science. This nominalism, however, had generally been resisted within continental Europe by the approach of Leibniz and his followers—the tradition from which later *idealist* thought was to emerge. Instead of abandoning Aristotelian thought, Leibniz had attempted to *reconcile* a version of Aristotle's hylomorphic conception of individual substances with modern mechanistic science (Mercer 2001; Redding 2009).

Kant's own appeal to the philosophy of ancient Greece is clearly apparent in his references to Plato in the *Critique of Pure Reason* (Kant 1998: A313/B370–A320/B377), where he attributes a fundamentally *practical* status to Plato's 'ideas' or 'forms', which he interprets as types of *non-empirical* concepts. Ideas should not be understood as rationally graspable *prototypes* of empirical things, or even, as in Aristotle, as *actually* incorporated in the *matter* of those things 'in themselves'. Rather, the relevance of 'ideas' is primarily for *the will*—that is, for the structure that they can give to the practical intentions upon which we act. It is to the extent that the human will can be directed by rational ideas—for Kant, ideas generated by the subject itself—that humans can be *free*. For Kant it was significant that Plato had, in the dialogue *Republic*, used his doctrine of ideas as the basis for the constitution of an ideal polis. That the organization of a just state could *in some sense* be 'deduced' from rational 'ideas' would remain the distinguishing characteristic of all *idealist* approaches to politics, but, in his work of the 1780s, Kant was to concentrate more on *moral* rather than *political* issues.

In the *Critique of Pure Reason*, Kant gives 'ideas' a subsidiary role within theoretical philosophy, where they are thought of as guiding or 'regulating' all attempts to unify empirical knowledge in its scientific extension. But in contrast, in the case of *morality*, ideas are conceived of as 'constitutive' and not just regulative—that is, they are capable of determining the content of volitions. Thus, rejecting all attempts to ground morality in empirical features of human existence such as prudential reasoning or moral sentiment, Kant believed that morality had an entirely *rational* foundation (Kant 1997*a*, *b*). In particular, as beings capable of conceptually articulated reason, we are able to determine our wills according to a universally applicable moral law—a law that we ultimately give ourselves. Of course, as finite embodied actors we are *also* subject to the empirical determinations of our natural inclinations, so the moral law must have the form of a command or 'imperative' that we issue to ourselves. As necessary and universal, it cannot be conditional upon any contingent circumstances, such as in-clinations. It cannot, then, be a 'hypothetical' imperative. It must have the form of a *categorical* imperative.

The broad framework of Kant's transcendental idealism had unfolded over the decade that was to end in the explosive political events set off in France in mid-1789 when, at the convened Estates General, the 'third estate' transformed itself into a 'National Assembly' claiming to represent the 'will of the people'. With its radical and innovative conception of the autonomous self-legislating will, Kant's revolutionary philosophy seemed to be at one with its time. Indeed, like many of the revolutionaries themselves, Kant himself had been inspired by the philosophy of Jean-Jacques Rousseau (1712–78), and many have seen in Kant's conception of the individual 'self-legislating' and universalistic *moral* will a parallel with Rousseau's political doctrine of the *general will*. The course of the revolution throughout the 1790s, with its descent first into the Terror and ultimately into a military dictatorship, prompted concerns among those otherwise sympathetic to the Rousseauian principles of Kant's approach. Such concerns would ultimately be reflected in the direction taken by Hegel. But these years were *also* the years during which Kant's own approach to politics took its definitive shape, and similar concerns are reflected in the development of his own philosophy.

Kant's Transformation of the Natural Law and Social Contract Traditions

In very broad terms, we might think of the development of modern political theory during the Enlightenment as facing the problem of gradually extracting its conception of the norms governing political life from the enframing metaphysico-theological assumptions of medieval and early modern thought. Two intersecting approaches can be discerned here, one involving a secularization of the notion of *natural law*, the other seeking to ground the legitimacy of political arrangements on the consent of the subjects in a *social contract*. Kant's formal idealism drew upon, and was to have implications for, both of these conceptions.

The idea of a 'natural law' regulating human existence can be traced back to the ancient philosophy of the Stoics, but the idea of natural law that was inherited from the medieval period conceived it as issuing from God's command and derived largely from the work of Thomas Aquinas. In the early modern period, the notion became transformed by the likes of Hugo Grotius (1583–1645), Samuel Pufendorf (1632–94), and Christian Thomasius (1655–1728). For the most part, these thinkers still saw natural law as deriving from God, although in Grotius was the suggestion that it would have validity from reason alone even were there no God. One possible path for the 'detheologization' of natural law was to go generally in the direction of treating 'natural law' from an empirical point of view, reducing it to a type of prudential means–ends rationality in the style suggested by Hobbes. Kant was to open another path, however.

Kant's conception of the moral law has clear links to this earlier natural-law tradition. It has been argued that one finds in the German natural lawyers ideas developed by Kant such as that of the compatibility of freedom with obligation (with a concomitant distinction between obligation and *coercion*) that obligation *itself* has motivational force independent of a subject's empirical desiring, and that the law has a necessarily *imperative* form (Schneewind 1993; 1998: 518–22). Moreover, the idea that the rightness of the moral law follows from its *universality* clearly links up to Rousseau's idea of the *volonté générale* and, before that, to seventeenth-century theological discussions of the 'general' nature of God's willing (Riley 1986). But Kant also *diverged* from this tradition, perhaps most strikingly in detaching the moral law from the will of God, and it was his *formal* idealism that allowed him to do this with the idea of the moral law as somehow legislated by the human mind itself.

In contrast to the idea of submission to a natural law of divine origin, Thomas Hobbes (1588–1679) saw the grounds of an individual's obligation to positive law as resting in that individual's own voluntary *consent* to the law. This was the notion at the heart of his conception of the 'social contract' developed in the work *Leviathan* of 1651 (Hobbes 1994). Moreover, in his decidedly anti-Aristotelian account, Hobbes sought the explanation of such social behaviour in the type of explanation found in the new sciences. No Aristotelian teleology was needed as the movements of any of the isolated parts—the egoistic individuals—could be described in terms of the basic attributes of those parts. Thus, Hobbes introduces appetite and aversion as quasi-mechanically acting affective states, causally brought about by perceptual interaction with the world and manifesting themselves in particular actions. With this, Hobbes contributed to a generally *naturalistic* and *empiricist* approach to a modern natural-law tradition, but this was seen by some to have internal problems.

As has often been pointed out, Hobbes's contractarian account faces the problem of capturing why grounding political law in the consent of subjects *counts as* justification, since the normative role played by the free willing of subjects appears to be at variance with his naturalistic account of the will (Riley 1982: 58; Schneewind 1998: 91). But, if this aspect of Hobbes's account of the social contract was not to be particularly relevant to Kant's normative project, *Rousseau*'s version certainly was. Rousseau's conception of the social contract involved a conception of the will that was far removed from Hobbes's individualistic and psychologistic one and allowed for the *formation* of a 'general will' that could not be reduced to an aggregate 'will of all' (Rousseau 1997: 60).

While in the 1780s Kant had published a number of essays with broadly political themes, his writings most directed towards unravelling the *political* consequences of his approach to the freedom of the will appeared throughout the 1790s. In fact, the ideas broached in essays such as 'On the Common Saying: "That may be true in theory, but does not apply in practice"' of 1793 and 'Perpetual Peace' of 1795 (Kant 1991), were not systematically developed until his *Metaphysics of Morals* of 1798 (Kant 1996). The events in France, of course, had given particular urgency to questions facing Kant and his followers. Kant had been positively disposed towards the revolutionary events, despite the fact that he excluded from his list of basic political rights: the right of revolution.

Kant appeals to the notion of social contract to underpin the legitimacy of the state, but the social contract can in no way be conceived as any historical fact (Kant 1996: 111–12). Combining his transformation of Plato's approach with the modern appeal to the social contract, Kant treats the contract as a *regulative idea* against which the legitimacy of *actual* forms of sovereignty can be assessed. With this, Kant underpins

Rousseau's distinction between the general will and the empirical 'will of all'. Such a treatment of the social contract as *idea* allows Kant to extend the notion beyond the constitution of nation states to envisage a 'league of nations' as a telos of historical development (Kant 1996: 114–20). A cosmopolitan condition ensuring 'perpetual peace' may never be achievable, but it can serve as the idea of an end to which humans may strive and in their striving come ever closer to approximating.

For Kant's followers, a crucial question was whether transcendental idealism had furnished a specifically *moral* basis for political philosophy, or whether politics had its own distinct normative basis. The answer to this was not easily deduced from Kant's critical works of the 1780s, and his followers in the 1790s were divided. Even from the point of view of the later *Metaphysics of Morals*, Kant's answer seemed ambiguous. The two parts of that work examine the metaphysical principles of the doctrines of political 'right' and moral 'virtue' respectively, and demarcate the *external actions* to which the principles of political right apply and the *inner intentions or ends* relevant to morality. But this separation was, nevertheless, generally thought to be *internal* to a unified account that suggested an overarching 'moral' framework (Pippin 2006). The first unambiguous attempt to justify political arrangements by recourse to a *non-moral* but otherwise *Kantian* conception of the free will was that of J. G. Fichte.

FICHTE'S APPLICATION OF THE 'WISSENSCHAFTSLEHRE' TO POLITICAL PHILOSOPHY

Johann Gottlieb Fichte (1762–1814) had first attracted attention in 1792 with a controversial work, *An Attempt at a Critique of All Revelation*, claiming to draw the consequences of transcendental philosophy for *religion*, and in 1794 he was appointed to a chair of 'Critical Philosophy' at the University of Jena, a position he held until his dismissal in 1799 on the grounds of alleged atheism (La Vopa 2001). During the Jena years and after, Fichte worked at building a *system* of idealist philosophy, named the *Wissenschaftslehre* ('doctrine of science'), that was meant to unify the distinct theoretical and practical parts of Kant's critical philosophy. Its first version appeared in 1794–5 (Fichte 1982) and in *Foundations of Natural Right according to the Principles of the Wissenschaftslehre*, published in 1795–6 (Fichte 2000), he applied this approach to a theory of rights. Here Fichte introduced the notion of intersubjective 'recognition' (*Anerkennung*) that would later be a crucial concept for Hegel.

Politically, Fichte was a supporter of the French Revolution and was generally regarded within Jena as having strong 'Jacobin' sympathies that persisted though the period of the Terror, a time when the original enthusiasm of many early sympathizers had waned. Early in the decade a *link* between the austere purism of Kant's moral philosophy and the slide of the Revolution into terror had been suggested by Fichte's contemporary at Jena, Friedrich Schiller (1759–1805). In *On Grace and Dignity* (1793) Schiller had been critical of what he took to be the antagonistic relation within Kant's moral philosophy between rational duty, on the one hand, and sentiment and inclination, on the other, suggesting that such a polarization amounted to an 'oppression' of man's sensuous nature. In 1794–5, this idea was further developed in *On the Aesthetic Education of Man* (Schiller 1967), in which, appealing to individual and collective *life*, and with clear reference to the type of revolutionary puritanism unleashed in France, Schiller warned of the dangers of the external *imposition* of rational form on a natural living body (Schiller 1967: Second Letter). Schiller advocated a way around this by appealing to ideas from Kant's account of *aesthetic* judgement in the *Critique of Judgment* of 1790, thus playing up the role of aesthetic culture in the state as a way of mediating the opposing terms of Kant's dichotomous thought (Beiser 2005). Schiller was to influence the ideas of the so-called early romantics (Beiser 1996, 2003) as well as Hegel, but relations between Schiller and Fichte were strained, and Schiller seems to have identified Fichte as part of the Kantian problem. However, Fichte's *own* separation of political right from Kantian morality might be seen as *his* way of addressing the problem that Schiller had diagnosed in Kantian moral purism.

In an earlier work trying to apply the principles of Kant's idealism to the French Revolution, Fichte had actually attempted morally to ground universal human rights in the Categorical Imperative (La Vopa 2001: chs 2–3). This effectively made the purpose of the state the moral *perfection* of its citizens. In the 'Introduction' to the *Foundations of Natural Right*, however, he states that, while the rule of right *also* belongs to the moral conscience, 'this is not part of the philosophical doctrine of right, which ought to be a separate science standing on its own' (Fichte 2000: 10–11). Thus 'in the doctrine of right there is no talk of moral obligation; each is bound only by the free, arbitrary decision to live in community with others'.

As the full title of his text states, Fichte attempts to arrive at the rational foundations of right 'according to the principles of the *Wissenschaftslehre*'. The key to this idealist mode of philosophizing, in which all content is meant to be 'deduced' out of an initial formula stating 'I = I', is to see the 'I' in question as a version of what Kant, in the *Critique of Pure Reason*, called the 'transcendental unity of apperception', and to see the 'deduction' as akin to Kant's associated 'transcendental deduction' of the forms of experience and knowledge. Briefly, for Kant the condition of *unifying* my empirical beliefs *as* beliefs about entities belonging to a single world is to regard them as beliefs belonging to a single *unified* rational subject. This ideal *universal* subject he calls the 'transcendental unity of apperception'. In the revised 'Transcendental Deduction' of the second edition of the *Critique of Pure Reason*, written to counter the charge of immaterialism, Kant attempts to 'deduce' from this principle of the unity of the transcendental I and its representations, the categories and other formal preconditions of rational experience (Henrich 1982*a*).

In *Foundations of the Entire Science of Knowledge* [*Wissenschaftslehre*] of 1794 (Fichte 1982), Fichte describes the need to discover the 'primordial, absolutely unconditioned first principle of all human knowledge', a first principle 'intended to express that *Act* which does not and cannot appear among the empirical states of consciousness, but rather lies at the basis of all consciousness and alone makes it possible' (Fichte 1982: 93). Starting from the 'laws of common logic', including the law of identity, Fichte moves to the principle that 'I = I', the 'Principle of Identity'. In an apparent analogy with Descartes's famous 'cogito' argument, Fichte asserts that from the knowledge of 'I am I' can be deduced 'I am': '*The self begins by an absolute positing of its own existence*' (Fichte 1982: 99). But the analogy with Descartes is, in fact, misleading. Fichte can think of the 'I' as 'self-positing' because he is explicitly *critical* of the idea that the 'I' is the name of any type of 'thing' or substance, including Descartes's *non-physical* 'mental' substance. The 'I' has the fundamental mode of existence of an *activity*, and an activity that cannot be thought of as the activity *of* an underlying substance that *acts*. Thus Fichte famously describes the 'I' with the neologism *Tathandlung*—a type of 'fact-act'—in contrast to a *Tatsache* or 'fact-thing'. In the *Foundations of Natural Right* it becomes clear that, in contrast to Descartes, Fichte in fact has a strongly *embodied* conception of what it is to be an 'I' (Nuzzo 2006).

The *Wissenschaftslehre* thus proceeds in such a way, but, whereas Kant's 'transcendental deduction' had aspired to deduce the 'formal' conditions of experience (the categories and the forms of intuition, and the principles according to which these different forms were related), Fichte's aspirations—as more consistent with the implicit 'hylomorphic' dimensions of Kant's thought and prefiguring the direction taken by Schelling and Hegel—seem to extend equally to a deduction of the *material* conditions of rational self-consciousness. Thus, German idealism after Kant has been described as a continuing 'struggle against subjectivism' (Beiser 2002). In the *Foundations of Natural Right* this more material deduction thus extends to the condition of the thinker being the bearer of *rights* (*Rechte*) living within a *just state* (*Rechtsstadt*).

FICHTE AND INTERSUBJECTIVE RECOGNITION

In *Foundations of Natural Right* Fichte departs from any standardly *theoretical* understanding of self-consciousness by making *intentional willing* a condition of self-consciousness or 'self-positing', the first theorem stating that 'a finite rational being cannot posit itself without ascribing a free efficacy to itself' (Fichte 2000: §1). But a subject can ascribe such free efficacy (*freie Wirksamkeit*) to itself only in virtue of its being aware of its capacity to make a difference within the external world, and so it must thereby also posit and determine 'a sensible world outside of itself' (§2). This raises a problem, however, since the subject 'cannot ascribe an efficacy to itself without having posited an object upon which such efficacy is supposed to be exercised' (§3 (1)), and here a type of infinite regress threatens, as 'the explanation of the possibility of consciousness already presupposes consciousness as real'.

Fichte's proffered solution here was to set idealist conceptions of the subject, especially that of Hegel, on a new and innovative path. It is a condition of *being* a rational subject that one belongs to a community of mutually recognizing rational subjects: '*the finite rational being cannot ascribe to itself a free efficacy in the sensible world without also ascribing such efficacy to others, and thus without also presupposing the existence of other finite rational beings outside of itself*' (Fichte 2000: §3). We must be able to think of that which determines the subject's action (its 'exercise of efficacy') not as the action of some pre-existing *object*, as this leads to the regress: we must think of it as the action of the *subject itself*. The subject must be determined '*to be self-determining*'. Here Fichte reinterprets the idea about freedom under the constraint of rational law noted in earlier treatments of natural law: a subject is determined to be self-determining when it is determined by a speech-act *issuing from another*. But in Fichte this is not the *command* of a superior, but 'a summons [or solicitation, *Aufforderung*] to the subject' from another *equal*, who calls upon it 'to resolve to exercise its efficacy' (Fichte 2000: §3, III). With this idea of *inter-subjective existence* as a requirement for rationality as such, Fichte seems to anticipate recent appeals to 'social pragmatics' (Brandom 1994, 2002) or the 'second-person standpoint' (Darwall 2006) in discussions of rationality. Fichte's second theorem, which states that the finite rational being cannot 'ascribe to itself a free efficacy in the sensible world' without 'presupposing the existence of other finite rational beings outside of itself', in turn leads to a third, specifying the *nature* of the relation within which one must stand to such other rational beings as a 'relation of right'.

With his theory of intersubjective recognition, Fichte was not simply appealing to the ancient idea that human existence is necessarily *social* (Brinkmann 2002). Rather, Fichte tries to capture the idea that the activity of the subject has *dual* conditioning. It is conditioned by factors that the subject posits as both internal and external to itself. 'The subject has now posited itself as containing within itself the ultimate ground of something that exists *within it* . . . but it has likewise posited a being outside itself as the ultimate ground of this something that exists within it' (Fichte 2000: §4, 1). That which is 'within it' is its own efficacious capacity; that which is 'without it' is another subject 'summonsing' it to efficacious free activity. 'The ground of the subject's efficacy lies simultaneously *within itself* and in the being *outside itself*. If the external being had not exercised its efficacy and thus had not summoned the subject to exercise its efficacy, then the subject itself would not have exercised its efficacy.' But Fichte analyses this complex arrangement with respect to both 'form' and 'content'. When he glosses 'with regard to form', 'with regard to the fact that there is activity at all', we hear the echoes of Aristotle's (radically non-Cartesian) idea of the soul as the 'form of the body' and as the explanatory principle of the body's movement. But, whereas for Aristotle such form, as the form of a self-subsistent *substance*, was not dependent on anything *outside itself*, for Fichte 'with regard to form . . . the ground of the subject's efficacy lies simultaneously *within itself* and in the being *outside itself*'. Nevertheless, just as in Aristotle, form is always embodied in matter, Fichte immediately points out that the subject's activity 'is also conditioned with regard to its content [or matter, *Materie*]', and this *too* is subject to conditioning from without, as 'a particular sphere is allotted to the subject as the sphere of its possible activity' (Fichte 2000: §4, 1).

The sphere of the subject's activity—the range of objects upon which it can act—conditions the *content* of that activity in that it limits the range of possible actions 'the subject has chosen from among the possibilities contained in the sphere: the subject constitutes its freedom and independence out of these possibilities' (Fichte 2000: §4, 1). But, while this 'sphere of possibilities' is in one sense simply conditioned by the material environment within which the subject is located, the availability of objects to be worked upon is *also* subject to the actions of other finite rational beings in as much as they limit their *own* actions, allowing the first subject free access to the material sphere that it can regard as *its own*.

We can regard this as part of Fichte's innovatory way of addressing the question that is as crucial for political philosophy as it is perplexing: the nature of the property relation itself. For Fichte, the relation that I stand to my property cannot be understood in abstraction from my relation to other agents in the world who *recognize* or *acknowledge* my exclusive access to what is mine by refraining from acting on those things. Thus, as an *idealist*, Fichte does not attempt to ground this relation in anything *deeper* than the activity of mutual recognition itself. His theory of property thus stands in contrast to that of Locke, for example, who had made ownership of created objects a consequence of the creator's natural 'ownership' of his own activity (Locke 1988: bk 2, ch. 5). For Fichte, 'labouring upon' the world is still centrally connected with property rights, but the capacity to labour upon a part of the world—the 'sphere of my activity'—is itself a *consequence* of my access to that part of the world recognized *as mine*.

Fichte's account of intersubjective recognition has important consequences for the content of his political theorizing. Fichte ascribes not only the right to subsistence as a basic human right; he extends the right to *work* to the right of unimpeded access to a range of objects upon which one's wilful activity can be exercised (Fichte 2000: §19 (D). Thus Fichte's orientation has been seen as anticipating aspects of later nineteenth-century *socialist* thought. Moreover, his more interventionist approach to the state that coheres with the demand for the preservation of this right goes along with a stress on the *coercive* powers of the state that also mark his thought off from that typical of liberalism. Indeed, critics have linked these aspects to fundamental tensions within his underlying theory of recognition, the idea of the 'summons', for example, sitting uneasily with the reciprocal dimension of the recognitive relation of right (Williams 1992, 2002; Brinkmann 2002). It is now common to see *Hegel* as the idealist critic who addresses these sorts of problems from within his own transformative appropriation of Fichte's 'recognition-theoretic' approach (Siep 1979; Williams 1992, 2002).

Hegel and the Logical Foundations of Political Philosophy

··

Georg Wilhelm Friedrich Hegel (1770–1831) was born and schooled in Stuttgart and attended a seminary in nearby Tübingen, where any plans for a pastoral life seem to have been undercut by an interest in philosophy shared with fellow seminarians Friedrich Schelling and Friedrich Hölderlin. The period of Hegel's stay at the seminary, between October 1788 and July 1793, makes it easy to appreciate his intense interest in contemporary political events. An enthusiastic supporter of the revolution, Hegel, nevertheless, had sympathies that were more in line with the federalist intentions of the Girondists than the centralism of the Jacobins (Pinkard 2000).

By the late 1790s, Schelling had been appointed to the University of Jena, where he was joined by Hegel in 1801. Hegel's years at Jena, which would be terminated with the closure of the university in 1807 following the occupation by Napoleon's troops after the Battle of Jena, saw him experimenting with various ways of conceiving the structure of his idealistic system, and completing in that year his first great work, the *Phenomenology of Spirit*. His academic career was interrupted for about a decade, but Hegel nevertheless ended up as occupant of the chair of philosophy at the recently opened University of Berlin, first occupied by Fichte after his expulsion from Jena. Hegel's best-known work of political philosophy, *Outline of a Philosophy of Right* (1821), is often described as involving an abandonment of his earlier revolutionary sympathies, but this is exaggerated. The conception of the state in that work is broadly compatible with the type of constitutional monarchy that had been the goal of most of the revolutionaries in the revolution's early stages. At one time it was even common to represent Hegel as the precursor of twentieth-century totalitarianism (e.g. Popper 2003), but this view is now rejected by many interpreters (e.g. Avineri 1972; Honneth 2000; Neuhouser 2000; Pippin 2008). The more favourable interpretations of Hegel have been bound up with a reinterpretation of Hegel's central and difficult notion of *Sittlichkeit* or 'ethical life'. Thus, while this was earlier often taken to indicate a radically anti-individualist ontology, with individuals somehow absorbed within an 'organic' social whole, recent interpreters have approached it in the light of Hegel's development of Fichte's account of intersubjective recognition.

In the tradition stemming from Kant and Fichte, the normative foundations for political thought were associated with the idea of a 'will' that was able, in some way, to transcend the particularity and 'arbitrariness' of its 'immediate' starting point, and thereby attain freedom. This conception of the 'elevation' of the individual will to something more general and representing the interest of the community was in contrast to the type of empiricist–naturalist starting point found in Hobbes, where the individual's will was simply identified with their natural appetites. Opposing such an atomistic starting point, Hegel would indeed appeal to what in the first instance looks like Aristotelian organicist holism, and consistent with this employs a form of

Aristotelian logic in his 'deductions' within the *Outline for a Philosophy of Right*. Undoubtedly it is the 'holism' and 'organicism' of such an approach that has led to the concern of liberals about the eclipse of the status of the *individual* within his philosophy, but, for Hegel, such holism has to be reconciled with the 'recognitive' framework taken from Fichte in which the individual subject of 'abstract right' plays a central role.

In the 'Preface' to the *Philosophy of Right*, Hegel says that the 'speculative' logic on which the organization of that work is based is meant to overcome the inadequacies of the 'forms and rules of the older logic'—that is, of Aristotelian logic. Nevertheless he is dismissive of the modern reactions that simply 'cast aside' the logical approach 'to make way for the arbitrary pronouncements of the heart, of fantasy, and of contingent intuition' (Hegel 1991a: 10). The subject matter to be treated is 'concrete', but from the point of view of science (*Wissenschaft*), 'the content [*Inhalt*] is essentially inseparable from the *form*'. As with Fichte, Hegel starts from something apparently simple and given—the individual's subjective will—and progressively unpacks those organized contexts that can be seen as the conditions for the existence of that apparent 'given'.

As we have seen, Kant had already alluded to the idea of a type of 'transcendental deduction' of the features of a just state in his references to Plato's *Republic* in the *Critique of Pure Reason*, and in the essay 'Perpetual Peace' he was to appeal to a *logical* basis for the constitutional doctrine of the separation of powers. The difference between well-formed republican states and formless despotic ones hangs on the relationship that exists between the legislative and executive functions in each. A republican constitution is one that *subordinates* the actions of a particular executive to a representative legislature giving expression to the public will—essentially, the Rousseauian *volonté générale*. In contrast, despotism exists where the executive *itself* legislates such that 'the public will is administered by the ruler as his own will'. But, 'the legislator can unite in one and the same person his function as legislative and as executor of his will just as little as the universal of the major premiss in a syllogism can also be the subsumption of the particular under the universal in the minor' (Kant 1963: 96).

Kant's device of appealing to a 'syllogism', providing a non-instrumental justification for Montesquieu's separation of powers (Ripstein 2009: 174–5), is much more systematically employed by Hegel in the *Philosophy of Right* to capture the form of the state that best promotes freedom. However, Hegel builds on ideas that are still ultimately Kantian.

THE WILL AND ITS RIGHT

In 'Part One' of the *Philosophy of Right*, 'Abstract Right', Hegel discusses property relations in a way clearly influenced by Fichte's *recognitive* treatment in the *Foundations of Natural Right*. But, equally clearly, Hegel's treatment is meant to overcome the limitations of Fichte's approach.

To be *recognized*, the will must be *expressed*, and the first such expression considered is that of desire expressed in action. As in Fichte, there must be some empirical object at which my action is directed, allowing my desire to be recognized: 'My inner act of will which says that something is mine must also become recognizable [*erkennen werden*] by others. If I make a thing mine, I give it this predicate which must appear in it in an external form, and must not simply remain in my inner will' (Hegel 1991a: §51, add.). We can recognize the will of others in actions such as 'taking possession', 'using', 'alienating', and, most complexly, in the exchange of property encoded in a commercial contract (Hegel 1991a: pt 1, sects 1 and 2). Crucially, the contract 'presupposes that the contracting parties *recognize* [*anerkennen*] each other as persons and owners of property; and since it is a relationship of objective spirit, the moment of recognition [*Anerkennung*] is already contained and presupposed within it' (Hegel 1991a: §71). The necessity of recognition here is clearly bound up with the most explicit mode of 'taking possession'—that of giving others a sign (*Zeichen*) 'in order to exclude them and to show that I have placed my will in the thing' (Hegel 1991a: §58, add.).

In earlier work from his Jena period, involving a critical appropriation of Fichte's recognitive theory, Hegel had suggested that the recognitive relation was the core of *all* forms of human ('spiritual') life, not just those mediated by property rights (Williams 1992, 1997). This broadening of the notion of recognition now forms the basis of his *non-Fichtean* account of the state. The 'recognition' involved in the contract is, as Adam Smith had observed, based on self-interest, and so here the individual subject will see the 'recognitive' dimension as secondary to its status as instrument for satisfying its desire. This is why contracts must rely on the coercion of the state for their enforcement. But Hegel contrasts such a form of social relation with those which typically do *not* need to be externally coerced—the bonds of love between family members, for example. So, while up to the treatment of contract Hegel's 'deduction' has proceeded in a broadly Fichtean way, in 'Part 3: Ethical Life', the necessarily coerced legal relations central to Fichte's account of the state become contextualized within more inclusive conceptions of 'ethical life' that nevertheless remain essentially *recognitive* (Pippin 2008: ch 7).

ETHICAL LIFE AND THE STRUCTURE OF THE MODERN STATE

Like Aristotle (1998: bk. 1), Hegel treats the state in the first instance as made up of families or households. The state is the whole and the family its basic part. But the modern state differs from the ancient polis in terms of the development of what Hegel calls 'civil society' (*burgerliche Gesellschaft*), which is a peculiarly modern form of unity holding among households effectively based upon the commercial economy. Within civil society, individual representatives of families (for Hegel, only males) relate to each other, but, because of the recognitive relations structuring civil society, these otherwise family members gain a different 'form' of determinate recognition. To become a participant within civil society, the individual who was otherwise a 'moment' within a family 'bound together' by mutual affections must be 'released from the concept to self-sufficient reality' (Hegel 1991a: §181).

Hegel uses his own development of the Aristotelian syllogistic to represent this situation. The state is to be thought of as the universal, and the family, its part, as a particular, but here 'universality' must not be conceived as the more abstract term, but rather the *more concrete*. From this point of view, the universal 'Athenianness', say, is not to be thought of as an abstract determination shared by every particular Athenian: rather, it is that *unified form of life* in which each Athenian citizen participates and which is responsible for their identity *as* an Athenian. It is this holism that has led many to interpret Hegel's 'ethical life' (*Sittlichkeit*) as radically anti-individualistic, with the individual having little more than an epiphenomenal reality. Were Hegel to think of the Greek polis as some a-historical norm, this would indeed be justified, as Hegel thinks of the ancient polis as effectively having no resources for the recognition of individuals in terms other than provided by their given social roles. In this sense, relations within the ancient polis resemble relations within a family. But the development of civil society has provided a context in which the individual can be recognized as a bare bearer of rights. Thus Hegel's description of the 'moments' of families as being 'released from the concept' on entering into and participating in civil society is particularly significant. A little of the background of Hegel's logic is necessary to appreciate this point.

In Aristotelian logic there is a strict distinction between 'particularity' and 'singularity'. For Aristotle, a *particular* is an individual represented *as* the subject of a *particular* judgement, and so represented by some common name or 'kind term'—'this *Athenian*', for example. Such judgements are logically different from *singular* judgements in which an individual is referred to *without reference* to any kind term but by a proper name (a singular term)—'Socrates', for example. In the traditional syllogism there had been no genuine place for singular judgements, and, as it turns out, Hegel thinks that, in the ancient polis, neither had there been a genuine context for the 'singular' individual to be recognized *as such*: there one is always recognized as the bearer of some *particular* social role. But modernity has given rise to a context—the commercial economy centred around the production and exchange of need-satisfying goods—that allows the particular family member to acquire a new conception of himself as a '*self-sufficient particular*' as well as that of family member. This context is civil society, and the form of recognition involved there is as an 'abstract' bearer of legal rights—a legal 'person'. Whereas qua family member, an individual gains a self-conception *as* bound to particular others (as brother of..., father of..., cousin to..., and so on), in civil society that individual can be recognized in terms of an apparently abstractly 'self-sufficient' generalization (Redding 1996: ch. 9). In this realm, an individual is abstracted from their concrete identity, such that a '*human being counts as such because he is a human being*, not because he is a Jew, Catholic, Protestant, German, Italian, etc.' (Hegel 1991a: §209, remark).

Stripped of their determinate identities in this way, each 'person' is akin to those 'natural' humans from which Hobbes or Adam Smith start *their* thinking about human association, and they are able to *think of themselves* in that way. Of course Hegel does not accept this *as* a starting point—such individuals are products of a definite form of social life and dependent on it—but, while he insists on the primacy of the 'whole' from which the self-subsistent atom determined as a natural organism is released, he nevertheless follows Smith as seeing 'universality' as reconstituted in a novel way on the basis of the effects of this 'release' into self-sufficiency. This form of recognition, and the changes in theoretical and practical relations that flow from it, leads to the social accumulation of goods in ways not found in traditional societies (Hegel 1991a: § 189). But it also leads to social and psychological pathologies because of the stripping of the concrete identities involved. Thus, in a way that anticipates Marx and Engels, Hegel describes the social mechanisms that generate an economic and cultural underclass unable to benefit from the accumulation of social goods (Hegel 1991a: §§185, 200).

So, although Hegel had adopted much of the general form of traditional syllogistic logic, his interpretation of it was far from being standardly Aristotelian. As with Aristotle, for Hegel the simplest categorical form taken by the world is hylomorphic. Initially, at least, individuals are to be thought of as instances of hierarchically organized kinds—this individual is first a 'Jones', say, and then an 'Englishman', and so on. But, *unlike* the case in Aristotle, the individual *can* be recognized as stripped of any particular conceptual form and determined as a 'singular' (or 'self-sufficient') particular, and still exist *within* society. This can look like a move to a more *nominalist* approach to social existence, and yet for Hegel it is nevertheless misleading to think of such an existence as having escaped from conceptual determination as such, as nominalism has it. Along with the categories of *universality* and *particularity*, that of *singularity* is itself to be understood functionally in terms of the role it plays in the forms of recognition that mediate social life. But the role *it* plays is that of construing the individual *as* the bearer of an 'abstract' universal. Hegel thus reinterprets Aristotle's way of taxonomizing the various syllogistic 'figures' in terms of which of the categories of universality, particularity, or singularity plays the dominant role. As Dieter Henrich puts it, Hegel's syllogisms are 'integrated conceptualizations of something that is itself already an intrinsic determination of form' but that 'the kind of union conceptualized here is always grounded in a differentiated unity and in the differentiation of the singular moments involved' (Henrich 2004: 244).

Because they have different, in fact *opposed*, principles of unification, the family and civil society, qua two contrasting forms of social organization within modern life, embody different 'syllogisms'. What Hegel says about the relations of individuals within the family coheres with his description of 'the categorical syllogism' in his *Science of Logic* (Hegel 1969: 696–8), as there the mediating or 'middle term' binding the extremes of universality and singularity is the *particular* (it is *as a family* member that the singular biological organism becomes socialized, integrated into 'the universal'). In contrast, it is the 'hypothetical syllogism' that captures the relations in civil society, as there 'singularity' (here, the natural biological being with its desires and capacities in which the 'self-sufficient particular' is instantiated) is the *middle term* uniting particular families into a 'negative unity' in the state (Hegel 1969: 700). Like Fichte, Hegel sees the unity of *civil* society as only ensured by coercively enforced laws regulating the interactions of all such self-sufficient *singulars* (*Einzelner*) (Hegel 1991a: §157) in their competitive interactions. And, while 'many modern exponents of constitutional law have been unable to offer any view of the state but this' (Hegel 1991a: §182, add.), this system of institutions making up civil society is just 'the *external state, the state of necessity and of the understanding*' (Hegel 1991a: §183), it is not the state as *philosophically* understood, that is, understood by 'reason'.

Hegel's critique of the 'external state' is often taken as evidence for his support for a state with the form of unity seen in the classical polis, but this is not the case. The 'syllogism' capturing the rational state (structurally akin to the 'disjunctive syllogism' (Hegel 1969: 701–4)), is meant to integrate the syllogisms instantiated in the family and civil society, 'mediating', not *absorbing*, them. A simple 'organic' model of the state in which parts, like organs in an organism, are *never* released from the identity-conferring functional roles within the whole, cannot capture this. Hegel's syllogistically 'organicist' theory of the state thus cannot be equated with other naturalistic or 'organological' models (Wolff 2004: 292) with which it is often confused. The difference lies in his attempt to integrate the subject as 'abstract bearer of rights' into the greater whole.

Hegel's attempts at 'deducing' the state are, from a contemporary point of view, complex, ambiguous, and unclear, but the nature of the underlying political view expressed in them is not. Hegel is attempting to incorporate much of the individualistic rights-based approach of modern liberalism, while at the same time rejecting the naturalistic and empiricist assumptions on which it typically relies. He is also trying to diagnose the problems of modern civil society, such as the systematic production of extremes of wealth and poverty, and the subjective effects of the dissolution of concrete identities, and to point to remedies that do not sacrifice the increase in freedom that the rights-based relations of modernity have produced. Rather than a precursor of twentieth-century totalitarianism (Popper 2003), Hegel was closer to the moderates of the early phase of the French Revolution, favouring a 'republican' monarchy something like that codified in the constitution of 1791 (Furet and Halévi 1996). In fact, he has been seen by some as the greatest theorist of constitutional monarchy (e.g. Yack 1980).

HEGEL'S *REPUBLICAN* MONARCH

Hegel political solution of constitutional monarchy might have few supporters today, but it is important to separate it from any royalist reaction to the revolutionary politics of 1789 (Ritter 1982). For Hegel, the constitutional monarch is part of the recognitive arrangement to reconstitute a cohesive social unity out of the freed and atomistic modern 'singular' subjects that are the bearers of abstract rights. Moreover, Hegel's motivations are fundamentally republican, as he sees the constitutional monarchy as part of the process of giving necessary *form* to popular sovereignty. Thus he contests the view of popular sovereignty that simply opposes it to the monarchical state and leaves 'the people' as an unarticulated 'formless mass' (Hegel 1991a: §279 remark), a worry clearly exemplified for him in the excesses of the French Revolution, deriving from its excessively 'abstract' assertion of universal rights.

In terms of constitutional structure, Hegel's idea of representation is both like and unlike the conventional liberal view. Within the context of civil society, the *Stände* (estates) are those 'masses' into which the economic realm of production, consumption, and exchange is differentiated. But Hegel also makes the estates the *channels of political representation*. Individuals are not directly represented *as such* in the legislature, but rather as members of some corporation or estate. We might say that it is the objective interests that are primarily represented and that individuals are represented in virtue of having those interests. It is thus that the legislature is composed of two houses, one representing the 'substantial' agricultural estate being the house of an hereditary nobility, the other being composed of deputies representing the corporations (Hegel 1991a: §§308, 311). The participation of the third 'universal estate' is secured via its role in the executive. That the individual is not immediately represented in the legislature contrasts with the conventional liberal approach and highlights the distinctness of Hegel's own concept of representation. Hegel shares Rousseau's scepticism concerning an individual's spontaneous or untutored ability to understand his or her own interests. Representation by estates thus provides a mechanism for a more 'objective' representation of any individual's material interests via their participatory role in the economy.

For Hegel, neither an individual's immediate view of what is in his or her own interest, nor that of any concrete 'circle' to which he or she belongs, could be in any way foundational. Thus representatives must not be considered as 'commissioned or mandated agents' (Hegel 1991a: §309); that is, they are not simply channels for the transmission of their constituents' interests as immediately understood by them. Rather, this first-person 'subjective' view must be brought into dialogue with other similarly particular views, on the one hand, and a more 'universal' view represented by state functionaries on the other. Thus the play of interests as represented in the legislature is not like a system of forces that mechanically resolve into some single force within which the components are expressed as vectors. It is meant to involve a self-correcting attempt of the deputies to *think* from the viewpoint of all.

It is not surprising that Montesquieu's doctrine of the (conveniently tripartite) separation of powers finds a role in Hegel's constitution articulated with this logic. When reconceived in this syllogistic way, the tripartity of the distinction will be thought in terms of the relation of singular, particular, and universal *within* the political self-legislating will. Of these, the legislative function of the formulation of *universally applying laws* will occupy the position of the universal, while the executive in its function of *carrying out* the laws in the realm of particularity will stand in the place of the particular. But Hegel replaces Montesquieu's judiciary as third power with the *monarch* who instantiates the category of singularity (Hegel 1991a: §§272–3).

Like many of the French revolutionaries prior to the fall of Louis XVI, Hegel wants to give the monarch a constitutional role constrained by the more substantive roles of *creating* and *executing* laws that are given over to the other two powers (Hegel 1991*a*: §§ 279–80). The monarch merely has to add his *name* to that which had been decided upon and advised by his officers, but 'this *name* is important: it is the ultimate instance and *non plus ultra*' (Hegel 1991*a*: §279, remark). He has to add the words 'I will it' and supply that element of singular subjectivity that 'the will' needs in its full development. Without it, that which is willed will come to be seen as only a mechanical or natural result of the interested reasonings of the legislative representatives. It will not be grasped as consciously *posited*. The king's 'I will', therefore, constitutes a form of address within which citizens can each recognize themselves in terms of the singular determination they receive in civil society. Without such possible recognition to bind them back into an identification with the whole, they would remain alienated from a common life that they would perceive as external and foreign.

Hegel's concrete suggestions concerning how to advance by constitutional means the universalization of freedom in the modern world did not survive him. Rather than trying to *mediate* the effects of the emerging capitalist economy, the post-Hegelian *left* eventually argued for the elimination of the 'external state' and the property rights that the external state aimed to protect. In contrast, the Hegelian right regressed back into a nostalgic and religious commitment to the pre-modern 'organological' state in which the individual was not represented as such. Today, Hegel's *solutions* may not be extant, but, sympathetically read, Hegel can be still seen as having developed a credible *idealist* approach to politics that attempted to diagnose and address problems that are all too obviously still very much with us.

REFERENCES

Primary Sources

ARISTOTLE (1998). *Politics*, trans. H. Rackham. Cambridge, MA: Harvard University Press.

FICHTE, J. G. (1982). 'Foundations of the Entire Science of Knowledge', in *The Science of Knowledge*, ed. and trans. P. Heath and J. Lachs.Cambridge: Cambridge University Press. [First published 1794–5.]

FICHTE, J. G. (1988). *Early Philosophical Writings*, trans. and ed. D. Breazeale. Ithaca, NY: Cornell University Press.

FICHTE, J. G. (2000). *Foundations of Natural Right*, ed. F. Neuhouser. Cambridge: Cambridge University Press. [First published 1795–6.]

HEGEL, G. W. F. (1969). *Science of Logic*, trans. A. V. Miller. London: Allen and Unwin. [First published 1812–16.]

HEGEL, G. W. F. (1977). *Phenomenology of Spirit*, trans. A. V. Miller. Oxford: Oxford University Press. [First published 1807.]

HEGEL, G. W. F. (1991a). *Elements of the Philosophy of Right*, ed. A. W. Wood, trans. H. B. Nisbet. Cambridge: Cambridge University Press. [First published 1820.]

HEGEL, G. W. F. (1991b). *Political Writings*, ed. L. Dickey and H. B. Nisbet. Cambridge: Cambridge University Press.

HOBBES, T. (1994). *Leviathan, with Selected Variants from the Latin Edition of 1668*, ed. E. Curley. Indianapolis: Hackett. [First published 1651.]

KANT, I. (1963). 'Perpetual Peace', in *On History*, ed. L. W. Beck. Indianapolis: Bobbs Merrill. [First published 1795.]

KANT, I. (1987). *Critique of Judgment*, trans. W. S. Pluhar. Indianapolis: Hackett, 1987. [First Published 1790.]

KANT, I. (1991), *Political Writings*, 2nd enlarged edition, ed. H. S. Reiss, trans. H. B. Nisbet. Cambridge: Cambridge University Press.

KANT, I. (1996). *The Metaphysics of Morals*, trans. M.Gregor. Cambridge: Cambridge University Press. [First published 1798.]

KANT, I. (1997a). *Groundwork of the Metaphysics of Morals*, ed. M. Gregor, intro. C. M. Korsgaard. Cambridge: Cambridge University Press. [First published 1785.]

KANT, I. (1997b). *Critique of Practical Reason*, ed. and trans. M. Gregor. Cambridge: Cambridge University Press. [First published 1788.]

KANT, I. (1998). *Critique of Pure Reason*, ed. and trans. P. Guyer and A. W. Wood. Cambridge: Cambridge University Press. [First published 1781, second edition 1787.]

KANT, I. (1999). *Correspondence*, ed. and trans. A Zweig. Cambridge: Cambridge University Press.

LEIBNIZ, G. W., and CLARKE, S. (2000). *Correspondence*, ed. and intro. R. Ariew. Indianapolis: Hackett. [First published 1717.]

LOCKE, J. (1988). *Two Treatises of Government*, ed. P. Laslett. Cambridge: Cambridge University Press. [First published 1689.]

ROUSSEAU, J.-J. (1997). *The Social Contract*, ed. V. Gourevitch. Cambridge: Cambridge University Press. [First published 1762.]

SCHILLER, F. (1967). *On the Aesthetic Education of Man: In a Series of Letters*, ed. and trans. E. M. Wilkinson and L. A. Willoughby. Oxford: Clarendon Press. [First published 1794–5.]

SCHLEGEL, F. (1991). *Philosophical Fragments*, trans. P. Firchow, foreword R. Gasché. Minneapolis: University of Minnesota Press.

Secondary Sources

AVINERI, S. (1972). *Hegel's Theory of the Modern State*. Cambridge: Cambridge University Press.

BEISER, F. C. (1996) (ed.). *The Early Political Writings of the German Romantics*.Cambridge: Cambridge University Press.

BEISER, F. C. (2002). *German Idealism: The Struggle against Subjectivism, 1781–1801*. Cambridge, MA: Harvard University Press.

BEISER, F. C. (2003). *The Romantic Imperative: The Concept of Early German Romanticism*. Cambridge, MA: Harvard University Press.

BEISER, F. C. (2005). *Schiller as Philosopher: A Re-Examination*. Oxford: Oxford University Press.

BRANDOM, R. B. (1994). *Making It Explicit*. Cambridge, MA: Harvard University Press.

BRANDOM, R. B. (2002). *Tales of the Mighty Dead: Historical Essays in the Metaphysics of Intentionality*. Cambridge, MA: Harvard University Press.

BRINKMANN, K. (2002). 'The Deduction of Intersubjectivity in Fichte's *Grundlage des Naturrechts*', in D. Breazeale and T. Rockmore (eds), *New Essays on Fichte's Later Jena Wissenschaftslehre*. Evanston, IL: Northwestern University Press.

DARWALL, S. (2006). *The Second-Person Standpoint: Morality, Respect, and Accountability*. Cambridge, MA: Harvard University Press.

FURET, F. and HALÉVI, R. (1996). *La Monarchie republicaine: La Constitution de 1791*. Paris: Fayard.

HENRICH, D. (1982*a*). 'The Proof-Structure of Kant's Transcendental Deduction', in R. Walker (ed.), *Kant on Pure Reason*. Oxford: Oxford University Press.

HENRICH, D. (1982*b*). 'Fichte's Original Insight', trans. D. R. Lachterman, in D. E. Christensen et al. (eds), *Contemporary German Philosophy*, i. University Park, PA: Pennsylvania State University Press.

HENRICH, D. (2004). 'Logical Form and Real Totality: The Authentic Conceptual From of Hegel's Concept of the State', in R. B. Pippinand O. Höffe (eds), *Hegel on Ethics and Politics*. Cambridge: Cambridge University Press.

HONNETH, A. (1995). *The Struggle for Recognition: The Moral Grammar of Social Conflicts*, trans. J. Anderson. Cambridge: Polity Press.

HONNETH, A. (2000). *Suffering From Indeterminacy: An Attempt at a Reactivation of Hegel's Philosophy of Right*, trans. J. Ben-Levi. Assen: Van Gorcum.

LA VOPA, A. J. (2001). *Fichte: The Self and the Calling of Philosophy, 1762–1799*. Cambridge: Cambridge University Press.

MERCER, C. (2001). *Leibniz's Metaphysics: Its Origins and Development*. Cambridge: Cambridge University Press.

NEUHOUSER, F. (2000). *Foundations of Hegel's Social Theory: Actualizing Freedom*. Cambridge, MA: Harvard University Press.

NUZZO, A. (2006). 'The Role of the Human Body in Fichte's *Grundlage des Naturrechts* (1796–97)', in T. Rockmore and D. Breazeale (eds), *Rights, Bodies, and Recognition: New Essays on Fichte's* Foundations of Natural Right. Aldershot: Ashgate.

PINKARD, T. (2000). *Hegel: A Biography*. Cambridge: Cambridge University Press.

PIPPIN, R. B. (1997). *Idealism as Modernism: Hegelian Variations*. Cambridge: Cambridge University Press.

PIPPIN, R. B. (2006). 'Mine and Thine? The Kantian State', in P. Guyer (ed.), *The Cambridge Companion to Kant and Modern Philosophy*. Cambridge: Cambridge University Press.

PIPPIN, R. B. (2008). *Hegel's Practical Philosophy: Rational Agency as Ethical Life*. Cambridge: Cambridge University Press.

POPPER, K. (2003). *The Open Society and its Enemies*, ii. *The High Tide of Prophecy: Hegel, Marx, and the Aftermath*. London: Routledge.

REDDING, P. (1996). *Hegel's Hermeneutics*. Ithaca, NY: Cornell University Press.

REDDING, P. (2009). *Continental Idealism: Leibniz to Nietzsche*. London: Routledge.

RILEY, P. (1982). *Will and Political Legitimacy: A Critical Exposition of Social Contract Theory in Hobbes, Locke, Rousseau, Kant, and Hegel*. Cambridge, MA: Harvard University Press.

RILEY, P. (1986). *The General Will before Rousseau: The Transformation of the Divine into the Civic*. Princeton: Princeton University Press.

RIPSTEIN, A. (2009). *Force and Freedom: Kant's Legal and Political Philosophy*. Cambridge, MA: Harvard University Press.

RITTER, J. (1982). *Hegel and the French Revolution: Essays on* The Philosophy of Right, trans. R. D. Winfield. Cambridge, MA: MIT Press.

SCHNEEWIND, J. B. (1993). 'Kant and Natural Law Ethics', *Ethics*, 104/1: 53–74.

SCHNEEWIND, J. B. (1998). *The Invention of Autonomy: A History of Modern Moral Philosophy*. Cambridge: Cambridge University Press.

SIEP, L. (1979). *Anerkennung als Prinzip der praktischen Philosophie: Untersuchungen zu Hegels Jenaer Philosophie des Geistes*. Freiburg: Alber Verlag.

STERN, R. (2009). *Hegelian Metaphysics*. Oxford: Oxford University Press.

WILLIAMS, R. R. (1992). *Recognition: Fichte and Hegel on the Other*. New York: State University of New York Press.

WILLIAMS, R. R. (1997). *Hegel's Ethics of Recognition*. Berkeley and Los Angeles: University of California Press.

WILLIAMS, R. R. (2002). 'The Displacement of Recognition by Coercion in Fichte's *Grundlage des Naturrechts*', in D. Breazeale and T. Rockmore (eds), *New Essays on Fichte's Later Jena Wissenschaftslehre*. Evanston, IL: Northwestern University Press.

WOLFF, M. (2004). 'Hegel's Organicist Theory of the State: On the Concept and Method of Hegel's "Science of the State"', in R. B. Pippin and O. Höffe (eds), *Hegel on Ethics and Politics*. Cambridge: Cambridge University Press.

YACK, B. (1980). 'The Rationality of Hegel's Concept of Monarchy', *American Political Science Review*, 74/3 (1980), 709–20.

CHAPTER 22

··

EARLY EUROPEAN
SOCIALISM

··

JONATHAN BEECHER

WHAT is socialism and when did it become a significant ideology in the Western world? Some historians have attempted to trace its history back to the earliest antiquity—to the lament for a lost Golden Age, to myths of the Age of Kronos when goods were held in common and harmony reigned. Others have sought the origins of socialism in a more recent antiquity—in the Athens of Solon and the Croton of Pythagoras, or in the ascetic Jewish sect of the Essenes near the Dead Sea (see Lakoff 1973). Still others have found elements of socialism in the egalitarian strivings that seem to have marked human history since the earliest societies. As a self-conscious movement and ideology, however, socialism came into being in France and in the Romantic period.[1]

The first self-proclaimed socialists were contemporaries of Hugo, Delacroix, and George Sand; and the word *socialisme* itself was first used in the early 1830s. One of the earliest uses of the term was in an article by Pierre Leroux published in 1834 in the *Revue encyclopédique*. "I am the first to have made use of the word SOCIALISM," wrote Leroux later. "It was a neologism then, a necessary neologism. I invented the word as a contrast to 'individualism,' which was beginning to be widely used" (Leroux 1863: i. 255). Although others had already used the term, Leroux was right to claim that he gave it currency and right also that at its beginnings socialism was explicitly contrasted

---

[1] In England the word "socialist" seems first to have appeared in print in 1827 in the *Co-operative Magazine* published by the followers of Robert Owen (Beer 1953: 185–8). "Socialism" in English apparently dates from 1837, and Gregory Claeys has shown that "something like an identifiably socialist outlook existed in economic questions...by 1840" (Claeys 1987: 164). Still the terms "socialist" and "socialism" seem to have come into general use more quickly in France and Germany than in England (Williams 1976: 238–43), and it has been argued that "socialism began to exert a definite and continuous influence on British political thought...only in the last two decades of the nineteenth century, with the growth of permanent political organization" (Pelling 1954: 6).

to egoism and individualism. This contrast was to be a fundamental feature of early socialism.[2]

It was only during, or just prior to, the revolution of 1848 that the word *socialisme* came into common usage in France. As Marie d'Agoult wrote later: "Until [1848] the radical écoles and sects were only considered in isolation under the names 'Babouvism,' 'Saint-Simonism,' 'Fourierism,' etc., without referring them to the common principle that has made it possible to designate them all under the general term of 'socialism'" (Stern 1862: 33 n.). What was or is that common principle? If pressed for a modern definition, we might say that the term *socialism* has generally been understood to refer to a movement or theory of social organization advocating the collective ownership and democratic management of the means for the production and distribution of goods. We might add that socialists have generally emphasized the importance of cooperation, planning, and public ownership as opposed to the competition and profit-seeking of individual entrepreneurs under capitalism. But this definition is hardly adequate to the first socialists, who were writing out of a broader sense of social and moral disintegration. They were looking for order and authority in a world torn apart by revolution, and their ideas were presented as a remedy for the collapse of community rather than for any specific economic problem.

General definitions and descriptions are often useful. Nonetheless, when we consider socialism as a historical phenomenon, developing and changing over time, neat definitions dissolve and we are confronted by a set of widely varied aspirations. Some socialists are committed to the extensive use of state power; others want to eliminate the state altogether. Some are revolutionary; others parliamentary. Some preach class struggle; others class collaboration. Some call for the abolition of private property; others seek to combine public management with the extension of private ownership in at least some spheres. So varied and apparently contradictory are the views of self-proclaimed socialists that thoughtful observers have argued that the word "socialism" is itself meaningless. "First, it is meaningless intrinsically," writes Martin Malia, "because its economic programs do not, and cannot, realize its moral ideal in a manner that compels recognition as true socialism. Second, it is meaningless, historically, because it has been claimed by so many mutually incompatible social formations that it loses all concrete focus" (Malia 1994: 24).

---

[2] Leroux's article "De l'individualisme et du socialisme," *Revue encyclopédique*, 60 (October 1833), 94–117, was actually published only in mid-1834. In reprinting this text in 1845, Leroux noted that he had initially distanced himself from socialism and that he had "always opposed absolute socialism." During the early 1840s, he added, the term had taken on a broader sense than he could identify himself with: "For a few years now people have gotten used to calling 'socialist' all thinkers interested in social reforms, all those who criticize and reject individualism, all those who speak under different terms of social providence, of the solidarity that joins together not only the members of a state but the whole human race" (*La Revue sociale*, 1/2 (Nov.), 19–22. Amongst those who used the term *socialiste* prior to Pierre Leroux was the Fourierist Charles Pellarin in *La Réforme industrielle*, 15 (Apr. 12, 1833), 174 (see Gans 1957).

An added problem confronting anyone who seeks to make historical sense of socialism is that the history of socialism was long written on the basis of two assumptions: (1) that it was only with the work of Marx and Engels that socialism became established on a precise and scientific footing; and (2) that working-class movements were, or would become, the bearers of socialism. These views are no longer tenable. Now we can see a series of discrete socialisms, beginning with the romantic or "utopian" socialism of the 1830s and 1840s and culminating with today's feminist and ecologically minded socialisms.

What I propose to do in this chapter is to focus on the early history of socialism, beginning with the work of the romantic or "utopian" socialists and concluding with a consideration of four new forms of socialism that emerged during the pivotal years following the European revolutions of 1848 and continued to have resonance well into the twentieth century. Marxism was, of course, one of these new forms of socialism, and I will say something about its early history. Since the present volume includes a separate essay on Marxism, I will limit myself mainly to a discussion of Marx's writings on 1848, and I will touch on the challenges posed to Marxism by anarchist socialism and Russian agrarian socialism during the 1860s. But I want to begin by considering the problem of utopian socialism.

The Problem of Utopian Socialism

The term "utopian socialism" was first given currency by Friedrich Engels in his pamphlet "Socialism: Utopian and Scientific" (1880). For Engels the term referred to a group of early nineteenth-century social theories and movements that criticized nascent capitalism and contrasted to it visions of an ideal society of plenty and social harmony. The three principal utopian socialists were the Frenchmen Henri Saint-Simon (1760–1825), Charles Fourier (1772–1837), and the British factory-owner Robert Owen (1771–1858). Although these thinkers differed in significant ways— only Fourier was in any strict sense a utopian—all three attempted to find some solution for the social, economic, and cultural dislocations caused by the French and industrial revolutions. All three began to write around 1800, published major works a decade later, and attracted followers who created Owenite, Saint-Simonian, and Fourierist movements in the 1820s and 1830s.

"Socialism: Utopian and Scientific" offers a shrewd, well-informed and sympathetic interpretation of the work of the utopian socialists. But this essay (originally part of a polemic against the economist Eugen Duhring) was never intended to provide a comprehensive assessment of utopian socialism. Instead Engels emphasized aspects of utopian socialism that anticipated the Marxist critique of capitalism and dismissed much of the rest as "fantasy" unavoidable at a time when capitalist production was "still very incompletely developed." Engels praised Fourier as a brilliant satirist of bourgeois society, Robert Owen as an articulate spokesman of the demands of the working class, and Saint-Simon as the inspired prophet of a post-capitalist industrial order. At the same time, however, Engels criticized the utopian socialists for ignoring the importance of class conflict and failing to think seriously about the problem of how the ideal society might be brought into being. What the utopian socialists had failed to grasp, in Engels's view, was the fact that the development of capitalism and the growth of the factory system were themselves creating the material conditions both of proletarian revolution and of humanity's ultimate regeneration (Engels 1880).

Despite its polemical origins, "Socialism: Utopian and Scientific" provided a paradigm within which historians worked for almost a century. In histories of socialism from G. D. H. Cole to George Lichtheim, the utopian socialists were seen as "precursors" whose theories were flawed by their faulty understanding of history and class conflict. The problem with this perspective is that it is both teleological and reductionist: teleological because it assumes that socialism reached its final "scientific" form in the writings of Marx, and that the work of the utopians was valuable only insofar as it anticipated that of Marx; reductionist because it treats the development of socialism largely as a reflection of the rise of the working-class movement. Given the ideological baggage associated with the term "utopian socialism," and given also the fact that most of the so-called utopian socialists were not in any strict sense utopian thinkers, I will speak of them and their followers as romantic socialists.

FEATURES OF ROMANTIC SOCIALISM

Recently, some historians have called for a reassessment of romantic socialism that would grasp its inner logic and place it in its historical context. Viewed in this perspective, romantic socialism would seem to have four main features.

(1) It can be seen in economic terms as a reaction to the rise of commercial capitalism, and as a rejection of the prevailing economic theory that the best and most natural economic system is one where the individual is free to pursue private interests. Coming at an early point in the development of capitalism, the romantic socialists had a first-hand view of the results of unregulated economic growth. They shared a sense of outrage at the suffering and waste produced by early capitalism, and they all called for at least some measure of social control of the new productive forces unleashed by capitalism.

(2) However, the critique and the remedies proposed by the romantic socialists were not merely economic. Competition for them was as much a moral as an economic phenomenon, and its effects could be seen just as clearly in the home as in the marketplace. Thus the romantic socialist critique of bourgeois society resembled that of conservatives like Thomas Carlyle and socially conscious novelists such as Balzac and Dickens. They believed that the French and

Industrial revolutions had produced a breakdown of traditional associations and group ties, that individuals were becoming increasingly detached from any kind of corporate structure, and that society as a whole was becoming increasingly fragmented and individualistic. Egoism was the great problem: the Saint-Simonians called it "the deepest wound of modern society" (Bouglé and Halévy 1924: 148–9). And the romantic socialists' vision of a better world was clearly the result of a search for some substitute for the old forms of community that egoism and individualism were destroying.

(3) The romantic socialists all disliked violence and believed in the possibility of the peaceful transformation of society. Fourier and Saint-Simon had lived through the French Revolution and had been imprisoned during the Terror; they had no desire to see their ideas imposed by force or violent revolution. In any case they believed that this would not be necessary. Like Robert Owen, Fourier, and Saint-Simon expected to get support for their ideas from members of the privileged classes. In that sense they were social optimists, and their optimism was rooted in their belief in the existence of a common good. Like the Enlightenment philosophes, they were convinced that there was no fundamental or unbridgeable conflict of interests between the rich and the poor, the propertied and the property-less.

(4) Finally, there is an important point to be made about the form in which the romantic socialists presented their ideas. Each described himself as the founder of an exact science—a science of social organization—which would make it possible for mankind to turn away from sterile philosophical controversy and from the destructive arena of politics and to resolve, in scientific fashion, the problem of social harmony. But one of the striking features of the thought of the romantic socialists is that, while they consistently presented their theories as rooted in the discovery of the true laws of human nature and society, they also spoke in the tones of religious prophets. Each of them saw himself as writing in a cultural and religious vacuum—at a time when the traditional Christian Churches had lost their authority and when the great task confronting thinkers was to reach an understanding of the world that not only would be scientifically compelling but would also serve as a replacement for a now moribund Christianity.[3] For them the laws of nature were the laws of God, and the new science was the true religion. This blending of science and religion, and prophecy and sociology, was one of the hallmarks of the thinking of the romantic socialists in the period prior to 1848.

[3] On the question of the origins of socialism in the search for a replacement for the Christian religion, see the forthcoming work of Gareth Stedman Jones, *Before God Died: The Rise and Fall of the Socialist Utopia.*

ROMANTIC SOCIALIST THINKERS
AND MOVEMENTS

The movements created by the followers of Saint-Simon, Owen, and Fourier flourished in the period 1830–48. First on the scene were the Saint-Simonians, a group of brilliant young people, many of them graduates of the École Polytechnique, the most prestigious school of engineering and applied science in France. Gathering around Saint-Simon in his last years, they were intrigued by his insights concerning the ways in which the powers and resources of the emerging industrial societies might be harnessed so as best to promote human welfare. They were particularly fascinated by his final work, *Le Nouveau Christianisme*, in which he argued that the industrial society of the future would require a new religion to bring people together and to give a moral basis to society. Saint-Simon died in 1825. But his followers regarded him as the prophet of a new world in which science and love would work together to bring about the material and moral regeneration of humanity. After his death in 1825, they founded journals and organized lecture tours designed to elaborate and spread his ideas. By 1830 they had created what they themselves described as a "faith"—a new religion that aimed simultaneously at harnessing the productive forces of the emerging industrial society, at bettering the condition of "the poorest and most numerous class," and at filling what they perceived as the moral and religious vacuum of the age. Eventually the movement was torn apart by a series of painful schisms, in the course of which the charismatic Prosper Enfantin (1796–1864) made himself "supreme father," excommunicated various "heretics," and issued a call for the "rehabilitation of the flesh." After a brief period of communal living, a spectacular trial, and a general exodus to Egypt in search of the "Female Messiah," the Saint-Simonian movement broke up. But in their sober years of maturity many of the former Saint-Simonians went on to play important roles in French public life, promoting the colonization of North Africa, the development of railroads, and the industrialization of France during the Second Empire (Manuel 1956; Carlisle 1987; Picon 2002).

The Owenites and the Fourierists were less spectacularly eccentric than the Saint-Simonians. But each group attracted many followers during the 1830s and 1840s. The main appeal of Robert Owen's theory was its simplicity. Owen, a wealthy British factory-owner, believed that education and environment were the keys to the creation of a healthy, productive, and cooperative workforce. At his textile mill in New Lanark, Scotland, Owen provided good housing and good education as well as pensions, sick funds, and communal stores. New Lanark thrived, and Owen went on to invest the profits in a series of bolder experiments in worker management and communal ownership. Initially he had hoped to convince his fellow capitalists of the merit of his ideas; but by the early 1830s he and his followers were deeply involved in labor organization and the effort to create a great national federation of trade unions. This effort peaked in 1833–4, but for another decade the principal Owenite journal, *The New Moral World*, continued to attract a substantial working-class readership. Most of the energy of the Owenites, however, went into a series of attempts to create working-class communities in which property was held in common and social and economic activity was organized on a cooperative basis. Inspired to some degree by the successful model factory that Owen himself had created at New Lanark in Scotland, seven such communities were created in Britain between 1825 and 1847 and another in America at New Harmony, Indiana. None of them lasted very long. But the cooperative trading stores and societies created by working-class followers of Owen were more successful. By 1830 there were already hundreds of them in Britain, selling goods to their members at close to cost price; and the history of the modern cooperative movement is generally traced from the founding of an Owenite store at Rochdale in 1844 (Thompson 1966: 779–806; Harrison 1969; Claeys 1987).

The followers of Charles Fourier also attempted to create experimental communities or "Phalanxes" based on his ideas. Fourier's ideas took the form of a grand theory that included an elaborate map of the human psyche and an even more elaborate description of the good society, as well as a cosmology, a theory of history, and alluring accounts (fully published only in the twentieth century) of the "new amorous world" that he foresaw. Fourier's theory was nothing if not detailed. But central to his thinking was the belief that in a rightly ordered world there would be no disparity between our desires and our ability to satisfy them. Fourier insisted that the basic human drives— "the passions" as he called them—were meant to be expressed, and that "civilization" (always a pejorative term for Fourier) produced poverty, conflict, and unhappiness because it was based on the repression of the passions. Fourier's utopia was an attempt to describe the kind of society that would have to exist to make possible the economic, social, psychic, and sexual liberation of humanity. The key institution was the Phalanx, a community of 1620 men and women of varied tastes, inclinations, ages, and social backgrounds. Within this community, work and play would be organized in small groups (and "series" of groups); children would be raised collectively; and all activities would be organized according to the "dictates" of the passions (Beecher 1986).

In trying to give substance to Fourier's ideas, his followers necessarily watered them down, practicing what one of them called a "useful weeding-out" of the bolder sexual and cosmological speculations, and shifting the emphasis from instinctual liberation to the organization of work. Only one practical application of Fourier's ideas had much success in France. This was the "Familistère," a factory producing cast-iron stoves created by Jean-Baptiste Godin at Guise, which survived into the twentieth century. In America, however, some twenty-five Fourierist Phalanxes were established in the 1840s and a few more later. The most famous, Brook Farm, attracted numerous writers and intellectuals, one of whom, Nathaniel Hawthorne, left a wry portrait of the community in his *Blithedale Romance* (Guarneri 1991).

Some of the French followers of Fourier attempted to draw on his ideas in the creation of producers' and consumers' cooperatives. Particularly notable was the effort of the silk merchant Michel Derrion to create a network of consumer cooperatives at Lyons. This attracted a considerable following among the *canuts* or silk-weavers of Lyons in the 1830s (Gaumont 1935). A decade later, however, French Fourierists turned away from both community-building and the organization of cooperatives and drew closer to the democratic and republican critics of the July Monarchy of King Louis Philippe. Under the leadership of the Polytechnicien Victor Considerant (1808–93), Fourierism became a political movement for "peaceful democracy" that was to play a brief but significant role in 1848 (Beecher 2001).

The 1840s in France were also marked by the rise of a new generation of romantic socialists who emerged to create sects and ideologies of their own. Étienne Cabet (1788–1856), a former conspiratorial revolutionary who had been influenced by Robert Owen while in exile in England, attracted a substantial working-class following with the austere and authoritarian communist utopia described in his novel *Voyage en Icarie* (1839). Convinced that inequality was the root of all evil, Cabet stipulated that all goods should be held in common and that every citizen would eat the same food, wear the same clothes, and live in the same kind of dwelling (Johnson 1974). The former Saint-Simonian Pierre Leroux (1797–1871) propounded a mystical humanitarian socialism, arguing that social reform should be guided by a new religion of humanity. The Christian socialist Philippe Buchez (1796–1865) helped found a working-class journal, *L'Atelier*, and inspired groups of artisans to form producers' cooperatives. There was also an important group of feminist socialists, many of whom had passed through Saint-Simonianism or Fourierism, who began to find a voice in the 1840s. Flora Tristan (1803–44), Pauline Roland (1805–52), and Désirée Véret (1810–91?) all pursued and deepened Charles Fourier's insight that the emancipation of women is the key to all social progress. And Tristan's proposal for a workers' union *in L'Union ouvrière* (1843) can now be seen as a kind of early syndicalist utopia (Grogan 1998: esp. 97–114).

As they spread and multiplied, the ideologies of romantic socialism became part of a broad current of democratic and humanitarian thought in which the boundary lines between socialism and democratic republicanism became blurred. By 1848 romantic socialism had merged with other ideologies of the democratic Left to form a single movement that was broadly democratic and socialist. The shared beliefs that held this movement together included a faith in the right to work and in universal (male) suffrage, a belief that the differences between classes and nations were not irreconcilable, and a program of "peaceful democracy" that assumed that, if politicians would only appeal to the higher impulses of "the people," a new era of class harmony and social peace would begin.

THE REVOLUTIONS OF 1848 AND THEIR CONSEQUENCES

In 1848, with the fall of the July Monarchy in France and of repressive police states in much of the rest of Europe, European liberals and radicals at last had their chance at power. On February 24 a democratic republic was proclaimed in France, and a provisional government (including the socialist Louis Blanc) was empowered to set up a program of National Workshops that would guarantee all citizens the right to work. By the end of March, liberal constitutional governments had been proclaimed in Vienna, Berlin, Milan, Budapest, and Prague. Within the great sprawling Habsburg Empire Hungary and Bohemia were the centers of nationalist revolutions; and there were also stirrings of nationalist revolt in Moravia, Lombardy, Galicia, and present-day Romania. Elections were organized all over Europe, and for a few months in the spring of 1848 it seemed that a "democratic and social republic" in France might be in a position to give reality to the visions of the early socialists.

But universal suffrage proved to be no panacea for the Left. When national elections were held within the framework of the old social order and amongst populations that were still largely illiterate, the result was generally to return traditional elites. Furthermore, liberals and radicals had no experience in the exercise of power. In Germany the liberal majority in the Frankfurt Parliament frittered away their opportunities, taking almost a year to draw up a constitution and then offering the office of emperor to Friedrich Wilhelm of Prussia, who promptly refused to accept a crown touched by "the smell of revolution." In France the democratically elected National Assembly turned out to contain a majority of conservative royalists, and its fierce repression of the working-class insurrection of June 1848 shattered the dream of the utopian socialists that a "democratic and social republic" might usher in a new age of class harmony. Thereafter the program of "peaceful democracy" ceased to have any political meaning. The result of the failure of the 1848 revolutions, then, was to crush the idealistic and humanitarian aspirations of the second generation of romantic socialists and to destroy the vision of class collaboration that had been central to their thought.

Traditional accounts of the history of socialist thought pass quickly over the two decades following the defeats of 1848–9. The 1850s and 1860s were a time of relative prosperity and rapid economic growth, and many of those who had believed before 1848 that capitalism and the factory system would not, and should not, survive reconciled themselves to its permanence. This was also a time of repressive police regimes that left little opportunity either for open agitation or for free discussion of socialist ideas (Cole 1961: ii. 1; Lindemann 1983: 100). Nevertheless, socialism lived on in London, Brussels, Geneva, and other places of exile. And, if idealistic, humanitarian, and romantic socialism died on the barricades in 1848, it can still be said that in some respects the years 1848–51 constituted a crucible from which several new varieties of post-romantic socialism emerged. As William Sewell has written: "It was between 1848 and 1851 that socialism first took shape as a mass movement, and French labor and socialist movements of subsequent years continued to bear the marks of their origins" (Sewell 1980: 275). These comments can be applied not only to France but also to the rest of Europe. Indeed, it seems that four new forms of socialism emerged in this period.

DEMOCRATIC STATE SOCIALISM

The first of these was democratic state socialism, which was represented in France by Louis Blanc (1811–82) and in Germany by Ferdinand Lassalle (1825–64). Louis Blanc was a talented journalist who had acquired considerable influence in the 1840s as a critic of the July Monarchy and as the author of a widely read work, *Organisation du travail*, in which he attempted to merge socialism and democratic republicanism. Describing in dramatic terms the corrosive effects of the system of free competition that prevailed in the contemporary industrial societies of France and England— starvation wages, unemployment, high mortality, the break-up of the family—Louis Blanc focused particular attention on the young. He argued that child labor, venereal disease, alcoholism, and miserable or non-existent schools were all features of a "homicidal system" that brutalized children and produced the "decrepit, stunted, blighted, rotten generation" that would inherit the earth (Blanc 1845: 83).

What was to be done? Louis Blanc insisted that reform would have to come from government; and what that meant was that political reform would have to precede social reform. Only a democratically elected republican government was up to the challenge. Its task would be to organize work first by guaranteeing the right to work, and second by providing credit to workers so that they could form producers' associations (or "social workshops") within their trades. As a member of the provisional government in February 1848, Louis Blanc persuaded his colleagues to issue the proclamation committing the Second Republic to "guaranteeing work to all citizens." The next day the provisional government decreed the immediate establishment of a program of National Workshops to provide jobs for the unemployed; and shortly thereafter Louis Blanc was appointed chairman of a labor commission charged with investigating and reporting on the problem of work.

It quickly became apparent that the labor commission was powerless—a "ministry of pious wishes" as Marx called it (Marx 1964: 42)—and that the National Workshops were a stop-gap measure that had nothing in common with Louis Blanc's "social workshops" except for the name. After four months the government decided to shut down the National Workshops on the ground that they were costly and unproductive and concentrated too many unemployed workers in Paris. It was this dissolution of the National Workshops, which was announced on June 22, that prompted much of the working-class population of Paris to rise up in revolt against the newly elected National Assembly. As has already been pointed out, the crushing of this revolt killed the high hopes that the February revolution had inspired among many radicals.

Facing charges for his role in events leading up to the June insurrection, Louis Blanc fled to London in August 1848 to begin an exile that was to last more than two decades. On his return to France in 1870, after the fall of the Second Empire, he was elected to the National Assembly of the newly created Third Republic. Refusing to take part in the Paris Commune but critical of the repression that followed its defeat, he ended his days as a moderate democratic socialist, hostile to doctrines of revolution and class struggle and favorable to a socialism resting on public ownership and combined with workers' control in industry and a democratic parliamentary system in politics.

If Louis Blanc can now be seen as an ancestor of modern, reformist democratic socialism, his thought had a more immediate and contemporary link with that of the German socialist Ferdinand Lassalle. Fourteen years younger than Blanc, Lassalle took upon himself the task of creating a working-class political movement in Germany after the debacle of 1848. What Blanc and Lassalle shared was the belief that socialism required state intervention, not merely to regulate industrial activity but actually to organize the conduct of industry through the creation of associations of workers. In the 1860s Lassalle took over this notion and applied it to the conditions of Bismarck's Prussia, calling on the Prussian state to provide capital for the development of self-governing producers' cooperatives. Like Louis Blanc, Lassalle also had confidence in universal manhood suffrage as a means of transforming the state into an expression of popular will. Once universal suffrage was established, Lassalle argued, the state would cease to be an enemy of the people and would instead become the instrument of their emancipation (Cole 1961: v. 299–300).

ANARCHIST SOCIALISM

This view of the state as an instrument of the workers' emancipation was anathema to the thinkers representing the second type of socialism to emerge in the aftermath of the 1848 revolutions. This is the anarchist socialism of Pierre-Joseph Proudhon (1809–65)[4] and Mikhail Bakunin (1814–76). Proudhon was a provincial autodidact of working-class origin who had won notoriety in 1840 with the publication of *Qu'est-ce que la propriété?* with its provocative (and misleading) declaration that "Property is theft" (Castleton 2009). In the mid-1840s he was in regular contact with the silk-weavers or *canuts* of Lyons, who had been at the forefront of the French workers' movement since the early 1830s, and he seems to have been influenced by their program of mutual aid or *mutualisme*. At about the same time Proudhon was also in contact with a group of foreign exiles in Paris, which included several young German Left Hegelians and "four or five Russian boyars." One of the Russians was Mikhail Bakunin, and among the Germans was an unknown radical exile, the 26-year-old Karl Marx. Long afterwards Marx recalled all-night conversations during the course of which he had "infected"

---

[4] Proudhon resists classification. He was a fiercely contrarian thinker who introduced the term anarchism into the political vocabulary of his time and strongly criticized many contemporary socialists. Yet he called himself a socialist and actually coined the term "scientific socialism." His influence on nineteenth-century European socialism was second only to that of Marx. Thus, although no collectivist, he belongs as much to the history of socialism as to the history of anarchism. Castleton (2009) is a particularly rich and nuanced account of his early development.

Proudhon with Hegel's philosophy. In the immediate aftermath of their initial meet-ings Marx effusively praised Proudhon as a trenchant social critic, whose work "pres-ents for the first time the possibility of making political economy a true science." So impressed was Marx by Proudhon that in May 1846 he invited the Frenchman to serve as Paris correspondent of an international committee designed to establish links between socialists and communists in Germany, France, and England. Proudhon responded cautiously, warning against the dogmatism of the Left ("Let us not set ourselves up as the apostles of a new religion...") and questioning whether significant social change could be brought about by a revolutionary seizure of power. This exchange between Proudhon and Marx foreshadowed their lifelong differences (Proudhon 1929: 432–7; see also Billington 1980: 287–305; Haubtmann 1982: 622–31; Vincent 1984: 91–5).

Whatever Proudhon's doubts about revolution in general, the February revolution in France drew him into a new life. It made him a public figure—an elected "representa-tive of the people"—and a highly influential journalist. He was one of the very few French intellectuals vigorously to protest against the massacres of the June Days; and between 1848 and 1851 he became both the scapegoat of the Right—the prime target of the attacks of the Party of Order—and the spokesman for "the people" betrayed by the democratic republic that they had helped to create. At the same time Proudhon began to produce a series of works in which he argued that the working class must emancipate itself without the help of the government and elaborated a vision of a new social order based on mutual aid and small-scale cooperation rather than on national units and parliamentary politics.

Proudhon wrote two major works attempting to explain the failure of the democratic and socialist Left in 1848. His central point was that the revolutionaries had failed because of their inability to get beyond the old Jacobin faith in a providential state. In his view, all efforts to impose social reform by decree were doomed to failure; and thus he was particularly critical of the role played in 1848 by Louis Blanc during his brief tenure as a member of the provisional government. It was essential, Proudhon argued, to return control of the productive process to the workers themselves and to create conditions in which individuals, acting freely on their own initiative, could organize their own collective life. In the "industrial democracy" that was Proudhon's ideal, productive units would be the property of all those employed in them, and the whole of society would be organized around an economic federalism of democratically self-governing trades.

During the 1850s and 1860s Proudhon's followers played an important role in the agitation and organizational activity that led up to the creation at London in 1864 of the First Workers' International. Three of them—Henri-Louis Tolain, Charles Limou-sin, and E. E. Fribourg—were amongst the first French correspondents of the Interna-tional; and their aims echoed Proudhon's. The society to which they aspired was one in which every man would own property and receive the full fruit of his labor, either individually or as a member of a cooperative producers' group; and these groups were to be organized on a voluntary mutualist basis rather than under state auspices. But the ascendancy of Proudhon's followers within the International was short lived. By 1868 they were supplanted by the Bakuninists. Still it is clear that Proudhon's opposition to authority, his vision of industrial democracy, and his insistence on the dignity of work had a continuing appeal to workers in France and beyond (Hoffman 1972: 327–39, Vincent 1984: 220–1, 232).

Mikhail Bakunin was a Russian nobleman and a lifelong revolutionary and political exile. A participant alongside Richard Wagner in the Dresden revolution of 1849, Bakunin was more uninhibited in advocating violence and more unequivocally collectivist than Proudhon. Bakunin met Proudhon in Paris in the 1840s and never ceased to regard him as "the master of us all"—the most profound of all the socialist thinkers. Bakunin shared with Proudhon the belief that all systems of government were bad and that the state could never be the instrument of human emancipation. Like Proudhon, Bakunin also looked forward to a society composed of mutually supporting groups of producers federating into larger associations for larger purposes. Bakunin also rejected just as emphatically as did Proudhon Marx's desire to capture the state machine rather than destroy it. Not surprisingly, then, Bakunin took Proudhon's place as Marx's leading opponent.

Still Bakunin and Proudhon disagreed on a number of important issues. Proudhon favored peaceful change, and Bakunin was a lifelong proponent of violent revolution. Proudhon admired, and Bakunin detested, the traditional patriarchal family. Proudhon opposed, and Bakunin favored, the collectivist tendency within the cooperatist movement. These and other differences between the two thinkers can be traced, I think, to their radically different conceptions of human nature. Proudhon was a pessimistic moralist with a deep awareness of the aggressive and antisocial impulses at work in all human beings. One of the reasons for his unwavering belief in the importance of paternal authority was precisely that he regarded a father's authority as essential to control such antisocial impulses. Thus, despite his hostility to the exercise of political authority, Proudhon knew very well the damage people could do to one another if all authority were rejected. As Albert Lindemann (1983: 161) has written about Proudhon): "The rule of the father represented a kind of basic minimum if social cohesion were to be preserved."

Bakunin's view of human nature was vastly more optimistic, and he was therefore open to the idea of an essentially non-repressive society. He believed that human beings are naturally sociable—that social solidarity is in fact a deep-rooted instinct. Thus, while Proudhon feared the possible outcome of violent revolution, Bakunin believed that the destruction of the bonds of law and traditional custom would lead not to chaos but rather to a richer, fuller life for all. For this reason Bakunin insisted that the creation of a new and better society would not require the re-education of the masses or the transformation of human nature, but only the release of "the pent-up natural instincts and [social] energies" of a repressed people (Bakunin 1990: p. xxxiii; see also Lindemann 1983: 161). Bakunin empathized with bandits and brigands, with the poor and the downtrodden. These people were, he insisted, the least corrupted by state worship and bourgeois values. Thus he celebrated "the profound and passionate desperation" of peasant rebels such as Stenka Razin and Emilian Pugachev, who had led great popular insurrections in seventeenth- and eighteenth-century Russia. "In all these purely popular movements, insurrections, and revolts," he wrote, "we find the same hatred of the state, the same desire to create a peasant world of free communes" (Bakunin 1990: 40; see also pp. 7, 203, 211).[5]

If Bakunin's enthusiasm for violent revolution set him apart from Proudhon, he also obviously differed from Marx in his thinking about the most likely agents of revolution. Bakunin had little confidence in the urban proletariat: in his view this class was, at least in its upper strata, "riddled with bourgeois principles, aspirations and vanity." Instead he looked to landless peasants, the urban *lumpenproletariat*, displaced artisans, vagrants, outlaws, and finally what he described as the "intellectual proletariat" consisting of educated but often unemployed intellectuals who had "turned their backs on the class that begot them" (Bakunin 1990: 6, 212). Bakunin believed that, while the coming social revolution would be "multi-national, multi-racial [and] world-wide" (Bakunin 1990: 45), it would have its origin in relatively backward parts of Europe—in countries like Italy, Spain, and Russia, which had not yet industrialized, where the peasantry remained large and impoverished, and where workers were unskilled and unorganized.

Bakunin won some of his most zealous and determined followers in just these countries. In Italy, where he found a second home for a few years in the 1860s, he conspired and organized with such success that the creation of a vigorous anarchist movement there was, to a large extent, his personal achievement. His influence in Spain, which was exercised largely through disciples, was in some respects even greater. By the early 1870s large numbers of artisans and workers from Catalonia, and rural laborers from Andalusia had adopted Bakunin's ideas. Thus, in describing Bakunin as "the creator of the peasant anarchism of Southern and Eastern Europe," Gerald Brenan could add: "This is especially true of Spain, the only country where his ideas took root in a mass movement . . . everything of importance in Spanish anarchism goes back to him" (Brenan 1960: 132; see also Hobsbawm 1979: 176).

---

[5] Bakunin's attitude toward the peasant commune was more critical than that of any of the thinkers considered below in our discussion of Russian agrarian socialism. He believed that there were three positive features to the commune: (1) the belief that all land belongs to the people; (2) the communal ownership of land; and (3) the combination of self-government and hostility to the state. But these positive features were linked, according to Bakunin, to three negative features that "clouded" the minds of the peasants: "(1) patriarchalism, (2) the swallowing up of the individual by the commune, and (3) faith in the tsar" (Bakunin 1990: 205–6, 210–11). To Bakunin's mind the commune was not an institution around which a movement or an ideology could be built. As he wrote to Herzen in 1866: "The *obshchina* has been deprived of any real internal development and today is much what it was five hundred years ago. It has had no freedom, and without freedom any social movement is unthinkable" (Venturi 1960: 431).

Russian Agrarian Socialism

The third form of socialism that emerged out of the failure of the European Left in 1848–51 was what could be described as Russian agrarian socialism. Here the inspiration came from the Russian émigré intellectual Alexander Herzen (1812–70). But others who helped shape this form of Russian socialism include the radical journalist Nikolai Chernyshevsky (1828–89), and the Russian populists Peter Lavrov (1823–1900), and Nikolai Mikhailovsky (1842–1904). What all these individuals had in common was the belief that the Russian peasant commune, the *mir* or *obshchina*, could serve as the basis for an indigenous Russian socialism.[6]

Alexander Herzen, the illegitimate son of a wealthy Moscow nobleman, left Russia for the West in 1847. By that time he had already made his mark as a leading member of Russia's radical "Westernizing" intelligentsia. Having read widely in Saint-Simon, Fourier, and the German Young Hegelians, Herzen claimed that, correctly understood, the Hegelian dialectic was an "algebra of revolution." He welcomed the revolutions of 1848, and in a series of essays and philosophical dialogues published between 1848 and 1852 he described his initial hopes and attempted to explain why, all over Europe, the revolutionary movement had proved to be such a grotesque failure. In these works he argued that European, and especially French, civilization was a deeply bourgeois civilization, obsessed by money, property, and profit, and that Western democrats and socialists would never be able to emancipate themselves completely from the acquisitive and individualistic traditions of bourgeois Europe. By 1849 Herzen had come to see Europe as the reincarnation of Rome in its decline, and he began to look to Russia and to the Slavic peoples as the bearers of a new socialist ideology that would sweep away the market system and political economy, which was all that the European bourgeoisie had to offer. Herzen soon came to believe that the Russian peasant commune, with its unique traditions of self-management, might serve as the basis for an authentically Russian socialism (Malia 1961).

There were two key elements in Herzen's Russian socialism. The first was a critique of capitalism that focused more on the mores and the consumption patterns of late capitalism than on the economic hardships of the period of primitive accumulation. Herzen was opposed to capitalism not only because it produced poverty and exploitation in its early stages but also because he believed it degraded people with its crass material values and its mass culture. Much of Herzen's social criticism was in fact an attempt to characterize the culture of capitalism and the links between the dominant values, tastes, and mores of bourgeois society and an economic system founded on the free market and on respect for the rights of property-owners to do whatever they

---

[6] The terms *mir* and *obshchina* are sometimes used interchangeably, but there is an important difference: *mir* refers to the Russian peasant commune as a self-governing community, while *obshchina* refers to the commune as an economic or geographical unit.

wished with goods or land or resources in their possession—no matter how fragile or limited these resources might be. Herzen also stressed what we might describe as the hegemonic character of the new bourgeois culture—the way in which its values and virtues of moderation and punctuality, thrift and decorum, were accepted by those members of the working class who wished to rise within bourgeois society, a society in which, as Herzen remarked sarcastically, "the bright image of the shopkeeper hovers as the ideal before the eyes of the casual laborer" (Herzen 1968: iv. 1688).

The second central element in Herzen's Russian socialism was the idea that the peasant commune contained in itself the basis of a new and higher social form. Here Herzen stressed the fact that there were traditions of self-government (or at least self-management) associated with the commune, and also the fact that within the commune land was periodically redistributed among families so that the whole notion of property ownership had a different meaning in the Russian context than in that of Western Europe. Thus the members of the commune identified themselves not with a particular piece of land but rather with the commune as a whole. Land belonged to the whole community, and each member had an equal right to its use, but never to absolute ownership of it in the Roman and Western sense. And the individual's sense of identification with the whole community—rather than with a particular piece of land—was reinforced by traditions of self-management that also existed within the village commune. These traditions included: (1) the decision by consensus of most agricultural questions concerning planting, harvest, and redistribution; (2) the election of peasant judges to handle the community's affairs; and (3) what Herzen saw as the general shared psychological traits of the peasants—distrust of the state, of bureaucracy, and in general of all authority.

In his later years Herzen came under attack from the younger generation of Russian radicals who came to constitute a new "mixed-class" or non-gentry intelligentsia. These people, the "nihilists" of the early 1860s and the "populists" of later years, differed in their plebian style of life and in many of their beliefs from Herzen and his aristocratic contemporaries. But in one important respect Herzen had something to say that was vital in shaping the views of later Russian radicals. He drew their attention to the possibilities latent in the Russian peasant commune. Both Herzen's detestation of capitalism and his hopes concerning the commune were shared by the radical journalist Nikolai Chernyshevsky, and by the Russian populists (*narodniki*) who created a revolutionary movement in Russia in the 1860s and 1870s.

Chernyshevsky, who enjoyed immense moral authority among Russian radicals in the decade prior to his exile to Siberia in 1864, believed that the commune might, under favorable circumstances, be transformed into a socialist community in post-revolutionary Russia. Though the commune had its faults, Chernyshevsky argued, it contained in embryo the elements of a just and rational social organization. Chernyshevsky did not share the Slavophile view of the peasant commune as a uniquely Russian institution. He thought of it as a type of social organization common to all agricultural societies prior to the spread of private land ownership. He attributed its survival in Russia to the fact that the Russian masses had not yet been seized by the desire for private property. Thus Chernyshevsky shared Herzen's belief that the very backwardness of Russia's economy might facilitate Russia's development of socialist forms of life and production (Venturi 1960: 150–2; Woehrlin 1971: 208–15; Shanin 1983: 182–90).

Russian populism went through several phases. With the "going to the people" movement of 1873 and 1874, it was a grass-roots movement of young people seeking to educate the peasants, but also on a more fundamental level seeking simply to make contact with the peasantry. After 1878, however, a split took place within the populist movement, and a militantly revolutionary party emerged. This was the People's Will party, an underground terrorist organization seeking to bring change through the assassination of high officials, notably the Tsar. For these revolutionary populists, the continued existence of the peasant commune was proof of the collectivist mentality of the Russian peasantry. They also considered the commune an asset in their struggle against the Tsarist regime and a model for the future organization of local government. In their official program, drafted in 1880, they specified that in the future socialist society labor would be carried "not individually, but socially, through communes [obshchinas], cooperatives [and] associations," and that in the future Russian politics would be "based on a federative alliance of all obshchinas" (Shanin 1983: 11–13, 231–2). Thus the peasant commune remained central to the thinking of Russian radicals down until the rise of Russian Marxism.[7]

Here it is worth noting a great irony. While most Russian Marxists eventually followed Plekhanov and Lenin in arguing that, with the development of capitalism in Russia, the peasant commune was undergoing disintegration, Marx himself was open to a wider range of possibilities. Early in 1881 he was contacted by Vera Zasulich, writing on behalf of the People's Will organization. She wanted to know Marx's opinion concerning the assertion, often made by his followers, that the commune was an "archaic form" condemned to disappear. If the commune was fated to perish, she wrote, then so also was the contemporary Russian socialist movement, whose members would have no alternative but to devote themselves to "more or less ill-founded calculations as to . . . how many centuries it will take for capitalism in Russia to reach something like the level of development already attained in Western Europe" (Shanin 1983: 98–9).

Marx, who had learned Russian and had been studying Russian agrarian history for more than a decade, gave a great deal of thought to this request. His reply went through four drafts, but the letter he actually sent on March 8, 1881 was succinct. He wrote that the argument in the first volume of *Capital* concerning the transition from feudalism to capitalism was "expressly restricted to the countries of Western Europe" and thus provided "no reasons either for or against the vitality of the Russian commune." But, he added, "the special study I have made of it, including a search for original

---

[7] In addition to Shanin's fascinating study, three other works that offer extensive and illuminating comment on the role of the peasant commune in the thought of the Russian populists are Venturi (1960), Wortman (1967), and Walicki (1989).

source-material, has convinced me that the commune is the fulcrum for social regeneration in Russia"—provided "the harmful influences assailing it on all sides" were first eliminated (Shanin 1983: 123–4). The final qualification of course adds an element of uncertainty. Nevertheless, this exchange is fascinating because it shows that, at the end of his life, Marx was far less dogmatically committed to the idea of a single historical path than were many of his followers.[8] Indeed, it has been argued cogently by Gareth Stedman Jones that "the recurrent points of emphasis in Marx's later writings were that the pre-history of man had been that of primitive communities, that capitalism was an unnatural and ephemeral episode in the history of mankind, and that man's future lay in a return to a higher form of a primordial communal existence" (Stedman Jones 2007: 198–9).

Marxism

This brings us to the fourth and final current of socialist thought to emerge in the wake of the revolutions of 1848: Marxism. If we consider Marx's thought in relation to 1848, I think three points can be made. First, Marx's ideas took shape in the 1840s—in the heyday of social romanticism. Second, his revolutionary hopes were seriously challenged by the failure of the revolutions of 1848. Third, he subsequently saw himself as speaking to a disillusioned and disabused age—an age that no longer had much hope for "peaceful democracy" and no longer saw universal male suffrage as a vehicle of radical social change.

---

[8] Marx's thinking about Russia's future development underwent considerable change in the years between the publication of the first volume of *Capital* (1867) and his death in 1883. In *Capital* he had written that "the country that is more developed industrially only shows, to the less developed, the image of its own future" (Marx 1961: 8–9). He had also derided Herzen's enthusiasm for the Russian peasant commune. He left no doubt that Russia, like Germany, would have to go through a process of capitalist development and industrialization similar to that of England. After 1872, with the success of the Russian translation of *Capital* and the opening of a heated debate within the Russian intelligentsia as to the prospects of capitalist development in Russia, Marx began to change his mind. He learned Russian and tried to keep abreast of the controversy over capitalism in Russia. In the preface to the 1882 Russian edition of *The Communist Manifesto* Marx and Engels wrote: "Now the question is: can the Russian *obshchina*, though greatly undermined, yet a form of the primeval common ownership of land, pass directly to the higher form of communist common ownership? Or on the contrary must it first pass through the same process of dissolution as constitutes the historical evolution of the West? The only answer to that possible today is this: If the Russian Revolution becomes the signal for a proletarian revolution in the West, so that both complement each other, the present Russian common ownership of land may serve as the starting point for a communist development" (Marx and Engels 2002: 196). In one of the unsent drafts of his letter to Vera Zasulich, however, Marx went farther, suggesting that a "transition from village commune to advanced communism might be possible without a proletarian revolution in the West." Gareth Stedman Jones discusses this issue succinctly in a long note to his edition of *The Communist Manifesto* (Marx and Engels 2002: 260–1) and more fully in his fascinating recent essay on the late Marx (Stedman Jones 2007). See also Walicki (1989: 179–94).

The Communist Manifesto appeared at Brussels in January 1848, just a few weeks before the outbreak of revolution in Paris. Published as the platform of the Communist League, a small workers' association composed largely of German émigrés, the Manifesto reached a tiny audience and then dropped out of sight. It was not to be reprinted in significant numbers until 1872. Still it constituted a milestone in Marx's intellectual biography, marking the culmination of a remarkable process of intellectual growth that had entered its decisive phase in November 1843 when Marx settled at Paris as a political exile from Germany. During his sixteen months in Paris, Marx established his lifelong partnership with Friedrich Engels, discovered the proletariat, and worked through a process of critical reflection on the ideas of Hegel and Feuerbach to his own understanding of the social nature of human productivity. Becoming aware, as he later put it, that "the anatomy of civil society is to be sought in political economy," he reached the conclusion that political and legal relations could be understood neither "from themselves nor from the so-called general development of the human mind, but rather have their roots in the material conditions of life" (Marx 1978: 4).

Expelled from Paris in February 1845, Marx moved to Brussels, where, over the following year, he collaborated with Engels on the writing of The German Ideology. Although this work remained unpublished until 1932, it enabled Marx and Engels to work out the essentials of a new view of history in which class struggle was seen as the driving force of history and shown to be the expression of conflict between the development of human productive forces and prevailing forms of ownership and organization. The call to revolution in The Communist Manifesto was based on this view of history. By the beginning of 1848 Marx had come to believe that the bourgeoisie, which had "accomplished wonders far surpassing Egyptian pyramids, Roman aqueducts, and Gothic cathedrals" (Marx and Engels 2002: 222), was rapidly creating the conditions of its own downfall and that the establishment of communism would be achieved by an armed rising of the working class.

Like Proudhon and Herzen, Marx sought to make sense of the failure of the Left in 1848. In attempting to do so, he wrote two brilliant essays: "The Class Struggles in France, 1848–1850," which first appeared as a series of four articles in the Neue Rheinische Zeitung in 1850, and "The Eighteenth Brumaire of Louis Bonaparte," published in America in a small German-language weekly journal, Die Revolution, in 1852. In these works Marx's nominal purpose was to draw lessons for the German working class from the defeats of the French proletariat between 1848 and 1851. He did so by systematically contrasting the world of historical reality—the class struggle—and the realm of shadow and illusion in which historical actors imagine that their speeches and posturing and parliamentary maneuvers make a difference. He explained brilliantly how the provisional government mirrored the conflicts of the classes that had created it, how the two major bourgeois factions and the two competing royalist houses could all agree in supporting Louis Napoleon Bonaparte, and how Louis Napoleon could have appeared as a savior to the impoverished small peasant. What is most striking about these essays is their extraordinary rhetorical power—the literary skill with which Marx evokes the ghosts and shadows, the dreams and riddles and masquerades that constitute the realm of ideology and illusion and blind the participants to the real meaning of their action. Marx's essays on 1848–51 give substance to his theories of ideology and false consciousness, and they do so in a way that fuses the spell-binding power of the imagery and the spell-banishing power of the historian.

One other striking feature of the first of these essays, and of Marx's correspondence for the years 1848–50, is that they show how reluctant Marx was to give up his revolutionary hopes. He begins *The Class Struggles in France* with the statement that "every important part of the annals of the revolution from 1848 to 1849 carries the heading: Defeat of the revolution!" (1964: 33). But he goes on to insist that the defeats—and especially the crushing of the June insurrection—have prepared the way for future victories: "Only through the defeat of June," he writes, "were all the conditions created under which France can seize the initiative of the European revolution" (1964: 59). And the third part of this work concludes with the claim that the victory of three radical candidates in Parisian by-elections on March 10, 1850 constitute "the revocation of June 1848" and mean that "the moral influence of capital is broken" (1964: 128–9). Likewise, in Marx's correspondence, one finds him writing on June 7, 1849 that "a colossal eruption of the revolutionary volcano has never been more imminent than it is in Paris today" (Marx and Engels 1982: 199). Six days later an insurrection of sorts did occur, but it was hardly colossal, and its principal result was the imprisonment or exile of dozens of radical leaders. Nonetheless Marx could write to Engels optimistically two months later (August 17, 1849) that the increasingly reactionary nature of the French government gave hope for an immediate revolutionary insurrection (Marx and Engels 1982: 211).

By 1850 such hopes had become impossible to sustain. In an article on the current economic situation written in October 1850 Marx declared that the return of industrial prosperity in England, France, and Germany had put an end to the period of revolutionary unrest initiated in 1848. The revolutionary events of 1848 had been provoked by the economic crisis of the late 1840s, and a new wave of revolutions was not possible, Marx believed, until the next cyclical trade crisis.

> While this general prosperity lasts, enabling the productive forces of bourgeois society to develop to the full extent possible within the bourgeois system, there can be no question of a real revolution. Such a revolution is only possible at a time when two factors come into conflict: the modern productive forces and the bourgeois forms [relations] of production . . . A new revolution is only possible as a result of a new crisis; but it will come, just as surely as the crisis itself. (Marx 1993: 131)

Marx still looked forward to a proletarian revolution. But now he believed that it might be decades away.

When Marx wrote this article, he had already been a resident of London for more than a year. At the outset he was active in the affairs of the large and querulous community of German political exiles in the British capital. But in June of 1850 he obtained a pass to the reading room of the British Museum, which was to be a second home to him for the next three decades. During these decades there were periods in which his revolutionary hopes returned. He was much involved in the founding of the First Workers' International in 1864, and the Paris Commune of 1871 inspired fresh hopes. But for much of the last three decades of his life Marx was absorbed in the task of working through his critical analysis of the capitalist mode of production. Significantly, his emphasis in this work was not on proletarian revolution but rather on the inevitability of the breakdown of capitalism.

EPILOGUE

Each of the movements just discussed was to have resonance well into the twentieth century. One of the distinctive features of European political life in the half century preceding the First World War was, as Geoff Eley has pointed out (2002: 109), the central role played by national social democratic parties in tandem with nationally federated unions. Socialist parties were formed all across Europe between the 1870s and 1890s, and during the course of the twentieth-century socialist governments in Britain, France, Germany, Austria, and Scandinavia continued to build on the tradition of interventionist state socialism initiated by Louis Blanc and Ferdinand Lassalle.

The great nineteenth-century anarchists Proudhon and Bakunin both played a shaping role in the development of twentieth-century syndicalism and anarcho-syndicalism in Italy, Spain, and France. As Paul Avrich has noted (1967: 73), the followers of Proudhon and Bakunin in the First International were already proposing the formation of workers' councils designed both as weapons in the class struggle and as the structural basis of the future libertarian society. On the other hand, the tradition of Russian agrarian socialism described here lost its most essential element as a result of the weakening of the peasant commune with the reforms initiated in 1906 by Peter Stolypin and then with the forced collectivization of agriculture under Stalin. In 1917 the leaders of the Socialist Revolutionary party still saw themselves as the heirs of Herzen, Chernyshevsky, and the Populists, but within a few years they were liquidated or driven into exile.

Finally Marx, who began to acquire a significant following only after the founding of the First International in 1864, did not live long enough to see his ideas become the official doctrine of the German Social Democratic Party. But Engels, who outlived Marx by a dozen years, devoted himself unceasingly to the spread and popularization of Marx's ideas; and, at the time of Engels's death in 1895, Marxist parties and movements were an important feature of the political life of every European country.

In 1917 with the Bolshevik Revolution Marx's ideas (or Lenin's adaptation of them) became the central element of the ruling ideology of the Soviet Socialist Republic. It can be, and often has been, argued that the socialist idea was irremediably compromised by the sorry history of the USSR. But to make this claim is, I believe, to ignore the richness of the socialist tradition, the early history of which I have tried to describe here.

REFERENCES

Primary Sources

BAKUNIN, MICHAEL (1990). *Statism and Anarchy* [1873], ed. and trans. Marshall Shatz. Cambridge: Cambridge University Press.

BLANC, LOUIS (1845). *Organisation du travail* [1840]. 4th edn. Brussels: Société Belge de Librairie.

BOUGLÉ, CÉLESTIN, and HALÉVY, ELIE (1924) eds. *Doctrine de Saint-Simon. Exposition. Première année, 1829*. Paris: Rivière.

ENGELS, FRIEDRICH (1880). "Socialism: Utopian and Scientific," repr. In *The Marx–Engels Reader*, ed. Robert Tucker. 2nd edn. New York: Norton, 1978, 683–717.

HERZEN, ALEXANDER (1968). *My Past and Thoughts*, 4 vols. [1855–1868]. New York: Knopf.

LEROUX, PIERRE (1863). *La Grève de Samarez*. Paris: Dentu.

MARX, KARL (1961). *Capital. A Critical Analysis of Capitalist Production*, vol. i [1867]. Moscow. Foreign Languages Publishing House.

MARX, KARL (1964). *Class Struggles in France, 1848–1850* [1850]. New York: International Publishers.

MARX, KARL (1978). Preface to *A Contribution to the Critique of Political Economy* [1859]. In *The Marx–Engels Reader*, ed. Robert C. Tucker. 2nd edn. New York: Norton, 3–6.

MARX, KARL (1993). *Surveys from Exile* [1849–1852], ed. David Fernbach and trans. Paul Jackson. London: Penguin.

MARX, KARL, and ENGELS, FREDERICK (1982). *Collected Works*, xxxviii. *Letters 1844–1851*. New York: International Publishers.

MARX, KARL, and ENGELS, FREDERICK (2002). *The Communist Manifesto* [1848], intro. and notes Gareth Stedman Jones. London: Penguin.

PROUDHON, PIERRE-JOSEPH (1929). *Les Confessions d'un révolutionnaire* [1850], ed. Daniel Halévy. Paris: Rivière.

STERN, DANIEL [MARIE D'AGOULT] (1862). *Histoire de la Révolution de 1848* [1853]. 2nd edn. 2 vols. Paris: Charpentier.

Secondary Sources

AVRICH, PAUL (1967). *The Russian Anarchists*. Princeton: Princeton University Press.

BEECHER, JONATHAN (1986). *Charles Fourier: The Visionary and his World*. Berkeley and Los Angeles: University of California Press.

BEECHER, JONATHAN (2001). *Victor Considerant and the Rise and Fall of French Romantic Socialism*. Berkeley and Los Angeles: University of California Press.

BEER, M. (1953). *A History of British Socialism*. 2 vols. London: George Allen and Unwin.

BILLINGTON, JAMES (1980). *Fire in the Minds of Men: Origins of the Revolutionary Faith*. New York: Basic Books.

BRENAN, GERALD (1960). *Spanish Labyrinth*. Cambridge: Cambridge University Press.

CARLISLE, ROBERT (1987). *The Proferred Crown. Saint-Simonianism and the Doctrine of Hope*. Baltimore: Johns Hopkins University Press.

CASTLETON, EDWARD (2009). "Comment la propriété est devenue le vol, ou l'éducation de Pierre-Joseph Proudhon," in Pierre-Joseph Proudhon, *Qu'est-ce que la propriété?* Edition présenté par Robert Damien, introduite et annotée par Edward Castleton. Paris: Le Livre de Poche, 43–108.

CLAEYS, GREGORY (1987). *Machinery, Money and the Millenium. From Moral Economy to Socialism, 1815–1860*. Princeton: Princeton University Press.

COLE, G. D. H. (1961). *A History of Socialist Thought*. 7 vols. London: Macmillan.

ELEY, GEOFF (2002). *Forging Democracy: The History of the Left in Europe, 1850–2000*. Oxford: Oxford University Press.

GANS, JACQUES (1957). "L'Origine du mot 'socialiste' et ses emplois les plus anciens," *Revue d'histoire économique et sociale*, 30: 79–83.

GAUMONT, JEAN (1935). *Le Commerce véridique et social et son fondateur Michel Derrion* Amiens: Imprimerie nouvelle.

GROGAN, SUSAN (1998). *Flora Tristan: Life Stories*. London: Routledge.

GUARNERI, CARL (1991). *The Utopian Alternative: Fourierism in Nineteenth-Century America*. Ithaca, NY: Cornell University Press.

HARRISON, J. F. C. (1969). *Quest for the New Moral World. Robert Owen and the Owenites in Britain and America*. New York: Scribner's.

HAUBTMANN, PIERRE (1982). *Pierre-Joseph Proudhon: Sa Vie et sa pensée (1809–1849)*. Paris: Beauchesne.

HOBSBAWM, E. J. (1979). *The Age of Capital, 1848–1875*. New York: Mentor.

HOFFMAN, ROBERT (1972). *Revolutionary Justice: The Social and Political Theory of P.-J. Proudhon*. Urbana, IL: University of Illinois Press.

JOHNSON, CHRISTOPHER (1974). *Utopian Communism in France. Cabet and the Icarians, 1839–1851*. Ithaca, NY: Cornell University Press.

LAKOFF, SANFORD (1973). "Socialism from Antiquity to Marx," *Dictionary of the History of Ideas*. 4 vols. New York: Scribner's, iv. 284-94.

LINDEMANN, ALBERT (1983). *A History of European Socialism*. New Haven: Yale University Press.

MALIA, MARTIN (1961). *Alexander Herzen and the Birth of Russian Socialism, 1812–1855*. Cambridge, MA: Harvard University Press.

MALIA, MARTIN (1994). *The Soviet Tragedy. A History of Socialism in Russia, 1917–1991*. New York: Free Press.

MANUEL, FRANK (1956). *The New World of Henri Saint-Simon*. Cambridge, MA: Harvard University Press.

PELLING, HENRY (1954) (ed.). *The Challenge of Socialism*. London: Adam and Charles Black.

PICON, ANTOINE (2002). *Les Saint-Simoniens. Raison, imaginaire et utopie*. Paris: Belin.

SEWELL, WILLIAM, JR. (1980). *Work and Revolution in France. The Language of Labour from the Old Regime to 1848*. Cambridge: Cambridge University Press.

SHANIN, TEODOR (1983) (ed.). *Late Marx and the Russian Road. Marx and "the Peripheries of Capitalism."* New York: Monthly Review Press.

STEDMAN JONES, GARETH (2007). "Radicalism and the Extra-European World: The Case of Karl Marx," in Duncan Bell (ed.), *Victorian Visions of Global Order*. Cambridge: Cambridge University Press, 186–214.

THOMPSON, EDWARD (1966). *The Making of the English Working Class*. New York: Vintage.

VENTURI, FRANCO (1960). *Roots of Revolution: A History of Populist and Socialist Movements in Nineteenth-Century Russia*. New York: Knopf.

VINCENT, K. STEVEN (1984). *Pierre-Joseph Proudhon and the Rise of French Republican Socialism*. New York: Oxford University Press.

WALICKI, ANDRZEJ (1989). *The Controversy over Capitalism. Studies in the Social Philosophy of the Russian Populists*. Notre Dame, IN: University of Notre Dame Press.

WILLIAMS, RAYMOND (1976). *Keywords. A Vocabulary of Culture and Society*. London: Fontana/Croom Helm.

WOEHRLIN, WILLIAM (1971). *Chernyshevsky: The Man and the Journalist*. Cambridge, MA: Harvard University Press.

WORTMAN, RICHARD (1967). *The Crisis of Populism*. Cambridge: Cambridge University Press.

CHAPTER 23

THE MARXIAN TRADITION

TERRELL CARVER

Karl Marx (1818–83) and his sometime collaborator and long-term friend, Friedrich Engels (1820–95), are rightly regarded as the founders of a highly significant tradition in the history of political philosophy. However, this was never their aim at the time of writing. Their relationship to politics as activists, and their broad political orientations as socialists, were both clear from the early stages of their careers. Indeed, this was true even before they began to collaborate extensively together in late 1844. But throughout their careers their relationship to philosophy was much more problematic, and so requires careful elucidation.

The Marxian tradition, established as such in Marx's later lifetime, was certainly one of political thought and action, but the reception of these ideas and selected texts into the mainstream and canon of the Anglophone history of political philosophy was largely a post-Second World War development. The portmanteau term Marxism, while having a history of its own and still very much in common use, occludes a number of contextually crucial distinctions that bear on philosophical and other interpretative issues connected with the Marxian tradition. These include the variety of doctrinal formulations coming from political and academic sources, the relative importance of some ideas and texts as opposed to others, and questions of overt and putative authorship and authority in relation to Engels and Marx themselves.

In general terms, the Marxian tradition contributes to the history of political philosophy by highlighting economic activity, social class, exploitation, the state, ideology, historical progress, revolutionary change, and a 'good society' that is socialist or communist in character. It is generally acknowledged that the tradition is weakest on questions of morality, ethics, justice, rights, gender, representation, institutions, constitutions, obligation, authority, leadership, rulership, citizenship, religion, and the like, though there have been notable debates on all these subjects. However, it is possible to argue that all the concerns of the history of political philosophy today must be seen in the light of the Marxian tradition of ideology critique—that is, an understanding of political ideas that situates them in an economic context of class politics.

MARX: EARLY ACTIVITIES AND WRITINGS

Marx was born in Trier in the Prussian Rhineland into a family of Jews emancipated during the era of Napoleonic occupation (1806–13). His father converted to Lutheranism (in a Catholic area) in 1824 in order to continue to practise as a lawyer under the Prussian monarchy, but it is clear that father and son held a 'free-thinking' attitude to religious belief. Their intellectual and political outlook was based instead on the critical rationalism and overt anti-clericalism that flowered during the French Revolution and revolutionary wars of liberation. The young Karl had a classical education, albeit with considerable religious instruction in Christianity, as was required at the time. The Kingdom of Prussia was overtly Christian, of course, drawing its authority from the various religious establishments, discouraging criticism and 'free thought' as subversive, and celebrating citizen obedience to hereditary monarchical government. This was a form of political authority directly opposed to popular sovereignty, elected representation, and constitutional checks on the power of the state.

In these regimes of the 1820s and 1830s, popular participation in politics, even in the press or public discussion, was discouraged and repressed, through formal as well as informal means. Rulers, courtiers, and bureaucrats of the time viewed these practices as a threat to public order and governmental security. Moreover, these regimes were not as progressive in economic terms as many middle-class, commercially minded people would have liked. Popular interventions in politics were thus cross-cut with middle-class commercial interests in liberal ideas and policy proposals relating to legal reforms and free trade. The battle for popular sovereignty was limited to a potential political class that was propertied and literate, as only very radical revolutionaries were prepared to consider working-class (and occasionally female) participation in political life and decision-making. Because pre-modern legal, monetary, taxation, and property systems lingered in Germany, the political ferment was not confined to procedural and constitutional issues of speech and representation. Economic and political liberalization, as opposed to dynastic and religious conservatism, was already a battle line well known to Karl as he grew up. However, these struggles were seldom overt, even in terms of speech, association, and publicity (for which there were no constitutional rights), never mind public agitation of any kind (which was never licensed).

Marx was sent to the University of Bonn to study law, and then, after some student scrapes, to the University of Berlin, in order to qualify in that profession. During these years he associated with 'free thinkers' and rationalists, who were highly critical of the current philosophies that—in their view—supported the overtly anti-liberal and sometimes reactionary monarchical regimes. While he took a doctorate (by post) from the University of Jena in 1841, with a dissertation on Greek philosophy, he can by that stage not have had any realistic hopes of an academic position. This was because of the radical reputation of his associates and their exclusion from academic careers in Germany for political reasons.

Marx began to work for a liberal paper in Cologne, *Die Rheinische Zeitung* ('The Rhenish Gazette'), during a brief period of 'tolerated' but still censored press 'freedom' in Prussia. These works addressed the politics of economic hardship as experienced by local agricultural workers. The monarchical state took no real responsibility for these conditions, viewing poverty as in some sense inevitable. These early articles, dating from 1842, effectively set up a Marxian outlook on current political structures and proposed liberal reforms that relates broadly to socialism (Marx and Engels 1975a: 224–63, 332–58). This was a view that posed a 'social question'—namely, that of poverty—and a 'social solution', namely, that of collective or cooperative actions that would transform political and social relations such that poverty would no longer exist. While Marx could not declare himself a socialist, or indeed a radical, in any overt way, without compromising the newspaper's permission to publish, the tenor of the argument in his small output of locally engaged articles is clear enough.

ENGELS: EARLY ACTIVITIES AND WRITINGS

Engels was born in Barmen in modern Wuppertal, Germany, in the Berg district of Prussia not far from Düsseldorf and no great distance from the industrializing towns of the Ruhr. This was a Protestant family that had had commercial and manufacturing interests for some generations in the area, and lately had moved into transnational trading as well, with offices in Bremen and factories in Manchester, England. His parents were strict Pietists, a fundamentalist sect, rooted in Bible study and suspicious of free-thinking rationalism, regarding it as a road to loss of faith and the ultimate sin of atheism. His education was thus unremarkable, and he left school at 16 with no question of university enrolment, but rather a planned and predictable career in the family firms. He used his opportunities away from home to read freely and write scandalously—and therefore anonymously—about his native environment. These 'Letters from Wuppertal' were published in the Hamburg press in 1839, when the author was 18, presenting a grim picture of industrial pollution, moralizing hypocrisy, and poverty-stricken workers. Engels fixed the blame firmly on the propertied classes and governmental complicity (Marx and Engels 1975b: 7–25).

Politically Engels aligned himself with the wider cultural movements in Germany through which popular nationalisms were mobilized in defiance of the dynastic and aristocratic orders. He was thus a spare-time liberal journalist and literary commentator, necessarily writing under pseudonyms. Doing compulsory national service in Berlin, he again used his spare time autodidactically, attending lectures at the university there, though without matriculation for a degree. He contributed press reports on the academic controversies in the Prussian capital through which liberalizers gained some public purchase, and against which conservatives felt obliged to stage refutations. By late 1842 Engels was a highly practised journalist, well acquainted with the commercial and manufacturing scene in Germany and England, and a self-educated radical, with an unusual line in eye-witness observation of working-class poverty and working conditions.

POLITICAL COLLABORATION AND THE REVOLUTIONS OF 1848

Engels visited the editorial offices of the *Rheinische Zeitung* in Cologne in 1842, meeting Marx very briefly, and, rather more importantly, Moses Hess (1812–75), another associate, and self-declared socialist or communist (the terms were used interchangeably then). Hess advocated a classless society where poverty and exploitation would be resolved, deriving this vision largely from French sources. From the German perspective this was highly advanced, and indeed rather over the horizon, as constitutional and representative structures had not yet been established there, as they had been in France after 1789. In periods of empire and monarchical restoration in France these institutions had survived, even if in attenuated form, and the liberal ideals of popular sovereignty, republican secularism, and the 'rights of man' were an established—if never unthreatened—part of the political culture. The associates of the *Rheinische Zeitung* were thus cast as students and adapters of the French ideals, balancing enthusiasms for ultimate futures with the practicalities of promoting popular sovereignty in politically repressive circumstances. When he visited the Rhineland, Engels was on his way to Manchester to work for associates in his family's manufacturing enterprises, and Marx and other editors later accepted his reports from England on politics, culture, and technological change. Engels chronicled the Chartist movement for large-scale (male) enfranchisement and free trade for the German press, which was in itself highly provocative, and he also reported in reverse on continental radicalism for the English press. Representative institutions and some measure of popular suffrage (somewhat broadened in 1832) were already well established in Britain, as was the comparative freedom to organize and agitate politically (relative to the situation in France and Germany).

After the *Rheinische Zeitung* had been closed down by the government in the spring of 1843, Engels submitted a long article, 'Outlines of a Critique of Political Economy', to Marx and various remaining and newly acquired editorial associates (Marx and Engels 1975c: 418–43). This group was then working in emigration in Paris, where German-language political materials, unacceptable to the authorities in Germany, could be printed and clandestinely circulated. Marx welcomed this tightly argued work by Engels, which drew on English-language sources in political economy that he was not yet able to study. He immediately drafted a 'Summary' that set out the critique of these economic categories and doctrines as a project. This became his life's work and *magnum opus*, published in part many years later as the various volumes of *Capital* (Marx and Engels 1975c: 375–6). Previously his route into these matters of 'material'—that is, economic interest had been through the appropriation of French and particularly British political economy that G. W. F. Hegel (1770–1831) had undertaken in his very well-known and widely circulated *Philosophy of Right* (1821). Marx was also starting to read some French political economists, and British ones in French translation.

Owing to the character of political, cultural, and intellectual life in Germany during the 1830s and 1840s, Hegel and his posthumous philosophical legacy were themselves political issues. Dynastic conservatives, on the one hand, and liberalizing radicals, on the other, sought to capture his thought—which was self-consciously encyclopedic in scope—for their own. Given that such issues could not be openly debated, even in academic settings, it is unsurprising that coded conflicts were the usual medium for airing differences. Hegel's work, on any reading, was well suited to this, because he had historicized and politicized philosophy, in opposition to the timeless and abstract character of Kantian epistemological critique. Moreover, the centrality of 'becoming', rather than fixity, in all his philosophizing licensed modes of thought that were present centred and future oriented. Writing with deliberate ambiguity, and probably changing his political views somewhat over time, Hegel had produced an œuvre on a very large scale. However, some decades later this could be interpreted in terms that were relevant to politics, culture, society, and religion—but in multiple, and even oppositional, ways.

By education and university training, Marx was the more suited to engaging seriously with this discourse, whereas Engels's role in this respect was more that of reporter and popularizer. However, the engagement with both 'Young' and 'Old' Hegelians (radical liberalizers and dynastic conservatives, respectively), and therefore an engagement (in Marx's case) with Hegel's texts themselves, followed from their political alignment with German radicals. This joint political project did not follow from any prior vocational commitment to philosophy in itself or to philosophizing as an activity.

When Engels returned from England to the Continent in late 1844, he met Marx again in Paris. The two agreed to collaborate on a joint work, developing their political position. This was, of course, in practical alignment with any number of middle-class liberals, who were opposed to dynastic rule, religious conformity, intellectual repression, and anti-commercial restrictions. But as communists the two were keen to raise the 'social question' of industrial poverty, even if such economic 'development' was not yet widely advanced. Moreover, they both excoriated the tendency of those trained for philosophical debate to make political problems sound as if they were soluble through philosophical means alone, merely by arriving at correct ideas and principles. Given that this Hegelian discourse was itself idealist—that is, ascribing ultimate reality to ideas and consciousness, in some sense, rather than to a world of material things and activities—it was not difficult for Marx and Engels to get the philosophers of the time in their political sights. They agreed to collaborate on a joint critique, as a way of radicalizing liberal and radical politics, thus forcing pen-pushing philosophers into more effective forms of activism—or relegating them to the sidelines.

Engels departed to write up his notes, taken from observation in and around Manchester and from published sources in English, resulting in the remarkable volume

The Condition of the Working Class in England, published in 1845 (Marx and Engels 1975*d*: 296–583). Marx wrote most of the (separately signed) chapters in a joint satirical work, *The Holy Family*, by Engels and Marx (in that order), published the same year in Frankfurt am Main (Marx and Engels 1975*d*: 5–211). As an empirical and shocking study, the former was widely noticed and reviewed. As a sarcastic and overblown attack on academic Young Hegelians, the latter attracted only slight attention in wider circles. Following these efforts Engels abandoned the family business and joined forces with Marx and others in Brussels, to which the editorial associates had moved after receiving expulsion orders from France, owing to their radical activities. The two embarked on further critiques of the overly philosophical and cripplingly idealist German schools of thought, and also on critical reviews summarizing foreign varieties of socialist and communist thought. Very little of this material found its way into print at the time.

Choosing a high-profile target promised to be a more successful political strategy, and in very late 1846 and early 1847 Marx drafted a critical attack on the influential French socialist Pierre-Joseph Proudhon (1809–65). This was a response to the latter's *System of Economic Contradictions, or the Philosophy of Poverty* (1846), an appropriation of Hegel purporting to answer the 'social question'. Marx responded with *The Poverty of Philosophy*, written in French and published in Paris and Brussels in 1847, his first work to attract any very widespread notice in the European press and in radical circles on the Continent (Marx and Engels 1976*a*: 105–212). Besides a political association with the Brussels Correspondence Committee, a middle-class group encouraging representative government and commercial reform throughout Europe, the two joined the rather more radical Communist League, again a loosely organized propaganda group with an international membership. Through some manœuvring, they secured a commission to write a party manifesto for the group, and Engels produced two drafts that have survived. The jointly written final manuscript does not, and the text was last in Marx's hands before it went to the printer in London in early 1848.

In this *Manifesto of the Communist Party*, the historical sweep of the main narrative and its emphasis on productive technologies are more like Engels's early journalism than either Marx's local newspaper articles or his erudite polemics against Hegelian philosophers (Marx and Engels 1976*a*: 477–519). However, the biting sarcasm and reductive vision of conflict and resolution are perhaps more like Marx's prior idiom. Of course, the document was written to satisfy other radicals on the organizing committee. Nonetheless, there is every indication that it represents an agreed position and outlook from which, according to the historical record, Marx and Engels never significantly departed.

The *Manifesto* was not written as a philosophical work, though it qualifies as political philosophy in terms of its content. Most works in the traditional canon of political philosophy were written as political interventions, rather than as rigorous works of philosophical enquiry and logical reasoning, though there are some exemplars that are effectively both. The *Manifesto* is focused on politics, and how to understand it in historical and contemporary terms. But this discussion is not pursued in overt engagement with philosophers (other than with Proudhon) or even with philosophical ideas as such, though there are perhaps a few vague and passing allusions.

Insofar as the history of political philosophy presumes some knowledge of, and views on, the origins and history of modern civilization, and insofar as it also requires some views on the current and optimum future structures of society and politics, the *Manifesto* eminently qualifies as a classic work. The authors attempt an ambitious recasting of history into a wholly secular and indeed atheistic form, declaring it to be a history of class struggles, and conceptualizing these in a variety of categories, mingling economic and social advantage and disadvantage, domination and subordination. They then periodize, not by reign or religion or empire or some similar scheme of 'rise and fall', or divine intervention or providence of any kind. Rather they view the history of civilization as a developmental process of class formation and dissolution deriving from practical activities and corresponding forms of social organization.

The principal focus in the *Manifesto* is on the 'modern bourgeoisie' or commercial classes, and their relationship to feudal structures and classes, on the one hand, and to the 'modern industrial proletariat' or working classes, on the other. The most novel aspects of the discussion are the emphasis on the enormous increase in productive capacity afforded by modern manufacturing industries, the globalizing of markets that destroy traditional activities and cultures, and the concomitant crises of capital—that is, monetary wealth productively invested—that the modern bourgeoisie cannot control. Proletarians, so the authors argue, have the incentives to organize a superior system of productive and distributional relationships. They would also necessarily create a different social order and popular culture purged of bourgeois religion, family values, selfish individualism, and other hypocrisies, which the *Manifesto* triumphantly lists.

The text offers a number of important theses in political philosophy: 'The history of all hitherto existing society is the history of class struggles . . . But every class struggle is a political struggle' (Marx and Engels 1976a: 482, 493). And 'one fact is common to all past ages, viz., the exploitation of one part of society by the other' (Marx and Engels 1976a: 504). Further, 'intellectual production changes in character in proportion as material production is changed', and 'the ruling ideas of each age have ever been the ideas of its ruling class' (Marx and Engels 1976a: 503). Similarly, 'the executive of the modern State is but a committee for managing the common affairs of the whole bourgeoisie' (Marx and Engels 1976a: 486). It also contains a list of typical communist demands, a critical review of other forms of socialism, and some guidance on local tactics in various countries.

The unsigned *Manifesto* was smuggled into Germany and achieved some circulation there, though it is not thought to have played any role in the revolutionary events of 1848 that swept across continental Europe. These swiftly overtook the activities of the nascent Communist Party and its international committee. Marx and at times Engels returned to radical journalism in Cologne, publishing a *Neue Rheinische Zeitung* ('New Rhenish Gazette'), and, in Engels's case, seeing some slight element of active service as an armed partisan in the retreat of the revolutionary forces through south-west

Germany (Marx and Engels 1977*a*: 15–529; 1977*b*: 3–480). Both made their way to England, with Marx residing in London, and Engels in Manchester, where the latter returned to work for the family businesses, supporting himself and the Marx family through very hard times. For the duration of this exile Marx divided his energies between political activities of interest largely within the émigré '48er community, pamphlet-style political interventions aimed more widely, and researches for his large-scale critique of political economy. This was a projected multi-volume, German-language work giving a critical account of the theory and practice of global capitalism. Only the initial volume was ever fully finished and published in successive editions under authorial supervision. This was *Capital*, vol. 1 (1867, 1872, 1872–5 (French trans.), 1883) (Marx and Engels 1996).

THE MARXIAN TRADITION

The founding moment for the Marxian tradition was the republication of the *Manifesto of the Communist Party* as the *Communist Manifesto*. This appeared in Leipzig in 1872 with an introduction signed by Marx and Engels, self-consciously marking it as a historical document, rather than an updated political programme in any direct sense. Its publication as a popular pamphlet was prompted by the editors of *Der Volksstaat* ('The People's State'), among them Wilhelm Liebknecht (1826–1900), another '48er exile and long-time London associate of Marx and Engels.

After the German amnesty of 1862, Liebknecht, unlike Marx or Engels, returned home permanently and pursued socialist political activities within the framework of organized workers' associations. As the monarchical orders in Germany became more unified under Prussian rule, and more constitutional in stages, Liebknecht became co-founder, eventually, of the Sozialdemokratische Arbeiterpartei Deutschlands (SDAP) in 1869, one of the ancestors of the successful mass party Sozialistische Arbeiterpartei Deutschlands (SAPD). This was founded at a unity congress in 1875, and later renamed Sozialistische Partei Deutschlands (SPD) in 1890. Liebknecht, and his political partner August Bebel (1840–1913), were effectively 'the Marx party' in Germany, codifying, publicizing, and adapting his ideas—as they understood them through correspondence with the originators—within the framework of mass political participation.

While socialist political activity was still taking place within practices of overt and covert state repression, the conjunction of mass organizations and political agitation with electoral campaigns in the 1870s was profoundly different from the circumstances of the 1840s. The resurrection of the *Manifesto* was thus an educative device for a new generation, evoking the prior struggles of the 1840s, and promoting Marx and Engels to pride of place in the history of socialist thought in Germany. The reissue of their pamphlet in 1872 was a move to intellectualize current socialist thinking and policy production in Germany. Indeed, looking at what was available from former times, the choice made sense.

The *Manifesto* is presciently focused on technological transformation and class politics in modernizing industrial societies. Politically it looks forward to an era in which socialist politics can be pursued within a liberal framework, but always pushing hard on crucial economic issues and developing a fundamental analysis of capitalism and its crises. It also speaks to the imperialist projects of the time, where non-Western and non-capitalist economies were brutally incorporated into the world market.

However, as the SDAP battled its rival, the Allgemeiner Deutscher Arbeiterverein (ADAV), for political influence and mass membership, the move to acquire intellectual superiority was an important one, given the personality cult still surrounding the ADAV's colourful and charismatic leader, Ferdinand Lassalle (1825–64). While the two parties merged as equals in 1875, the eventual victory of 'the Marx party' was celebrated with the adoption of the overtly Marxist Erfurt Programme in 1891, accompanied by an intellectual commentary from Karl Kautsky (1854–1938), the leading new-generation theoretician of 'the Marx party'.

At the time the Marxian tradition was inaugurated there was very little work by Marx or Engels in print and readily available, limited in fact to *Capital*, vol. 1, and scattered articles and pamphlets, if they could be found at all, or (in many cases) correctly identified. For that reason the canon had yet to be constructed. This occurred through a gradual process of republication, which in turn required framing the works with explanatory prefaces and introductions. Only a very few of these were penned by Marx himself. After Marx's death in 1883, Engels embarked on a career in this respect, writing approximately two dozen such works, or about two a year, to introduce republished items (including some of his own). Crucial in this process were the terms—if not actually the printed text— of a book review that Engels had written, at Marx's behest, advertising the first published instalment of his critique of political economy. Engels published his 'Karl Marx: A Contribution to the Critique of Political Economy' in mid-1859, and in it he composed the biographical account that he later updated and revised—many times—through which he explained to the reading public who Marx was, what exactly was important and unique about his thought, and why that thought constituted scientific knowledge (rather than mere political opinion or philosophical conjecture) (Marx and Engels 1980: 465–77).

Given that Liebknecht and Bebel were 'the Marx party' in Germany, and given that their association with Engels continued unbroken from around 1850 until the latter's death in 1895, it is easy to see that the establishment of a Marxian tradition was not in the first instance a scholarly project, but a political one. It was also one that drew heavily on direct lines of long-term association and intimate friendship that were always alluded to. The 1872 edition of the *Communist Manifesto* was not merely an insertion of an admittedly dated political document into a contemporary situation, where it might have some effect. For instance, this was the case with the republication in 1869—during the run-up to the Franco-Prussian War—of Marx's 1852 tract *The Eighteenth Brumaire of Louis Bonaparte* (Marx and Engels 1979: 99–197). While Liebknecht could not have known the eventual outcome of these tradition-building activities, his strategy certainly looked over and beyond any particular current contro-versy, much as the *Manifesto* itself framed political issues within epochs. Ironically the original publication was unsigned by Marx and Engels, whereas the new edition went forth to a public who were invited to make the authors iconic.

Icons need memorials, and Engels provided very suitable ones for Marx after the latter's death eleven years later. Engels's English-language 'Speech at the Graveside of Karl Marx' was very widely circulated in French and German (Marx and Engels 1989: 467–71), and a third edition of the now familiar—and now Marx-identified—*Communist Manifesto* was prepared, this time with an introduction by Engels alone. In it he summarized the 'basic thought' in the text, and said that it belonged 'solely and exclusively to Marx' (Marx and Engels 1990a: 118).

These two works thus built on the tradition-making activities, begun on a mass scale in 1872, but not in a completely consistent way. The graveside speech compared Marx, as a man of science, to Charles Darwin (1809–82), the latter having—according to Engels—'discovered the law of development of organic nature upon our planet'. Marx's fundamental law was one of human historical movement and development in general, and he had additionally formulated a special instance, explaining the creation, structure, and ultimate demise of modern society as a class-divided entity crucially split between capitalists and wage-labourers. Science, for Marx (and rather unlike Darwin), was thus—in Engels's view—a 'grand historical lever' of revolution, and Marx therefore a 'Revolutionist'. These laws, Engels related, were in themselves 'simple and self-evident', and so not at all reasonably denied. Moreover, they were the 'undisputed creed of universal socialism', which was hardly the case then or later. This was an aspirational claim, linked by Engels to a 'fraternal bond of union of the working men of all civilised countries of Europe and America' (Marx and Engels 1989: 463–4).

Engels's summary of the *Manifesto*, in his Preface to the 1883 edition (dated 28 June, after Marx's death), was rather more succinct. It was limited to the class struggle perspective outlined in the text itself, and—as was also true in the text—innocent of any overt framing as science, founded on an apparatus of laws (Marx and Engels 1990a: 118–19). Both texts are equally innocent of any framing of Marx as a philosopher, necessarily engaged with other philosophers. There is thus a tension within the Marxian tradition between the scientific Marx—who could be seen to transcend unscientific modes of thought, such as philosophizing—and a Marx who arrived at his version of science precisely through an encounter with philosophy that could only have involved the great philosophers of the age. An engagement with these questions about the Marxian tradition requires an examination of Engels's texts rather than Marx's, as it is through Engels's efforts at republication (with consequent framing narratives) that Marx's texts, from 1883 onwards, were recovered for mass circulation. This was first by Engels himself, and then by succeeding editors to whom the task and papers ultimately descended.

ENGELS AND THE FORMATION OF THE
MARXIAN CANON

Engels introduced and effectively recovered the following texts by Marx (date of original publication in parentheses) in approximately this order: *Communist Manifesto* (1848), *Wage-labour and Capital* (1847), *The Poverty of Philosophy* (1847), *Speech on Free Trade* (1847), *The Eighteenth Brumaire of Louis Bonaparte* (1852), *Karl Marx before the Cologne Jury* (1853), *Theses on Feuerbach* (unpub. 1845), *Critique of the Gotha Programme* (unpub. 1875), and *The Civil War in France* (1871). These represent very substantially the contents of the single-volume 'selections' that have appeared in most of the world's languages since the 1930s. He also published a short biography of Marx ('Marx, Heinrich Karl') in 1892, which was widely republished the following year, the anniversary of the latter's death, and many times afterwards (Marx and Engels 1990b: 332–43). While this work follows the outline of Marx's autobiographical sketch in his Preface to *A Contribution to the Critique of Political Economy* (1859) (Marx and Engels 1987a: 261–5), the narrative and additional detail are very strikingly the origin of the biography and bibliography that established the contextual terms of the Marxian tradition in the history of political philosophy—rather more so than his earlier short biography of 1878 'Karl Marx' (Marx and Engels 1989: 183–95).

Engels's prefaces and introductions were influential in explaining that Marx had discovered—as Engels had already stated in his published and widely publicized piece 'Karl Marx's Funeral'—'the simple fact, hitherto concealed by an overgrowth of ideology, that mankind must first of all eat, drink, have shelter and clothing, before it can pursue politics, science, art, religion etc.'. Continuing his paraphrase of both the *Communist Manifesto* and Marx's (essentially unavailable) Preface to *A Contribution to the Critique of Political Economy*, he continued:

> therefore the production of the immediate material means of subsistence and consequently the degree of economic development attained by a given people or during a given epoch form the foundation upon which the state institutions, the legal conceptions, art, and even the ideas on religion, of the people concerned have been evolved, and in the light of which they must, therefore, be explained, instead of *vice versa*, as had hitherto been the case. (Marx and Engels 1989: 467–8)

Engels had publicly attributed these ideas to Marx—though in works signed by himself—since 1859, notably achieving wider circulation in the later, more open political climate than Marx had achieved in the 1840s. Most famously these were *Herr Eugen Dühring's Revolution in Science* (generally known as *Anti-Dühring*) (1878), which went through three editions in the author's lifetime and was widely reprinted and read thereafter (Marx and Engels 1987b: 5–309), and a French-language pamphlet version derived from this text distilling the doctrines of 'the Marx party'. This was *Socialism: Utopian and Scientific* (1880), which then appeared in German in 1891 and English in 1892 (Marx and Engels 1989: 281–325). This popular work was avowedly written to gain political ground through widespread dissemination of a distinctive intellectual outlook—distinctive, that is, from that of rival socialisms and socialist thinkers. In these writings Engels took more freedom to present Marx as the author of a distinctive method, from which the substantive propositions of 'the materialist interpretation of history' (termed 'laws' by Engels) had resulted.

These synthetic accounts were derived, ultimately, from Engels's 1859 review and biography of Marx, in which he had quoted Marx's own brief intellectual autobiography, 'guiding principle', and 'general conclusion' from the Preface to *A Contribution to the Critique of Political Economy* (Marx and Engels 1980: 465–77). Engels framed his explanatory gloss in terms through which his later works proceeded, and which thus established the tradition through which Marx was popularly understood. These terms were philosophical in character: materialism; metaphysics; dialectic; interaction; contradiction; and reflection. The conjunction of Marx and Hegel was established in this context by Engels, though in a way that differed somewhat from Marx's autobiographical account, which mentioned neither method nor dialectic. There Marx himself had linked his own interest in the *Philosophy of Right* with his historical investigation into legal and political relations, and with Hegel's concept of civil society (borrowed from French sources). Marx's conclusion that the anatomy of civil society was to be sought in political economy indicated that he viewed Hegel's work on social relations as preliminary but rather ancillary to his own project.

From 1859 onwards Engels portrayed Marx's encounter with Hegel, by contrast, as one in which Marx had bested the greatest philosopher of the age at his own game—namely, the dialectic. This had the later effect of magnifying any comment on Hegel or dialectic by Marx to a remark of great significance. In 1878 Engels's first Preface to *Anti-Dühring* mentioned neither Marx nor Hegel nor dialectic, whereas his Preface to the second edition, written in 1885 after Marx's death, was rather different. Engels framed Marx's work as a philosophical operation, and his account of this process as the authorized one:

> I must note in passing that inasmuch as the mode of outlook expounded in this book was founded and developed in far greater measure by Marx, and only to an insignificant degree by myself, it was self-understood between us that this exposition of mine should not be issued without his knowledge . . . Marx and I were pretty well the only people to rescue conscious dialectics from German idealist philosophy and apply it in the materialist conception of nature and history. (Marx and Engels: 1987*b*: 9, 11)

Succeeding Editors of the Marx Canon

After Engels died in 1895, the process of producing a canon was continued by Eleanor Marx-Aveling (1855–98), Marx's daughter, who produced the English-language *Value,*

Price and Profit in 1898 from notes that Marx had made in 1865 (Marx and Engels: 1985: 101–49). Kautsky, who had access to many more papers, published various manuscripts as *Theories of Surplus Value* in three parts (a 'fourth volume' of the *Capital* sequence) over the period 1905–10. More notably, Kautsky was also responsible for a second edition in 1897 of Marx's *A Contribution to the Critique of Political Economy*. This made the original text of Marx's Preface, and thus the 'general conclusion' and 'guiding principle', a mass-circulation item, easily read and reproduced. Eduard Bernstein (1850–1932), a contemporary of Kautsky in 'the Marx party', was also responsible for publishing shorter pieces of recovered material, and after that the mantle descended to Franz Mehring (1846–1919), Marx's first scholarly biographer, and then to Gustav Mayer (1871–1948), who did the same for Engels.

The 1920s produced the highly charged conjunction of the ruling Bolsheviks in the Russian Soviet Republic and the Kommunistische Partei Deutschlands (KPD) in Germany, who formed and financed a Marx-Engels Institute, operating jointly between Moscow, Berlin, and Frankfurt. This enterprise was dedicated to a broad historical archiving and commemorating of the workers' movement internationally, and to the more specific task of recovering and transcribing all the works of Marx and Engels, published and unpublished, and also to numerous large-scale translation projects, particularly into Russian. Their editorial teams initiated the *Marx-Engels Gesamtausgabe* (now referred to as MEGA[1]), the first volume of which appeared in 1927, and forty-two were planned. While the Second World War put an end to the project (of which only twelve volumes were published in thirteen books), and indeed the Stalinist purges had taken a toll on the editors beforehand (including Ryazanov), the project was revived in the 1950s in an institute operated between Moscow and East Berlin, and run by the two respective communist parties. Its first project was a large-scale German-language series of scholarly but easily consulted volumes that mirrored a Russian edition. This was overtaken in the 1970s with a fully rethought and heavily funded projected edition of all works by Marx and Engels, reproduced in their original languages, and executed in accordance with the scientific principles of modern textual scholarship (now referred to as MEGA[2]).

As originally conceived, MEGA[2] incorporated vast amounts of contextual detail on the origin and reception of each individual work, and included prefaces with editorial introductions framing the texts with a theoretical and political 'line' consistent with Marxism as construed by the political parties involved. Since the fall of the Deutsche Demokratische Republik (DDR or East Germany), and the subsequent collapse of the USSR or Soviet regime in Russia, the project has been reorganized with less emphasis on political editorializing, and considerably reduced resourcing. The Marxian tradition—as principally established by Engels—is thus ongoing through textual recovery, book production, and contextual framing.

Perhaps the last great popularly political work by a revolutionist and theorist to set the Marxian tradition in place was V. I. Lenin's (1870–1924) short work 'Karl Marx: A Brief Biographical Sketch with an Exposition of Marxism' (1918) (Lenin 1964: 43–91), which often functions as a kind of foreword to editions of the Marx-Engels selected works. Lenin wrote that in his work Marx combined German philosophy, English political economy, and French socialism and revolutionary doctrines, and that Marxism—as a faithful reflection of this body of theory—could be traced to, and expounded from, his critical encounter with these three traditions. Thus, by the 1930s, works that were anti-Marxist, as well as those that reproduced what had become a standard—if hotly debated—Marxist account, engaged with Marx in a way that had been framed in terms of a necessary intellectual history to be mastered. This intellectual history entailed a pair of icons analogous to Marx (Darwin and Hegel), a twin set of discoveries (a general and special law of social development), a method (scientific because dialectical and 'materialist'), and a canon of selectively assembled and readily available works in numerous translations.

THE MAINSTREAM ANGLOPHONE RECEPTION OF THE MARX CANON

In the history of political philosophy, two Anglophone scholarly works from this period stand out as particularly influential and widely read, right through the later 1950s and well beyond. These were Sidney Hook's (1902–89) *From Hegel to Marx: Studies in the Intellectual Development of Karl Marx* (1936) and Isaiah Berlin's (1909–97) popular biography *Karl Marx: His Life and Environment* (1939). Until the very late 1960s these were the most readily available and highly regarded mainstream works of non-Marxist commentary.

Hook was a young American Marxist and supporter of Soviet Communism who broke with the Stalinist regime and communist movement in 1933, moving eventually to an anti-Marxist and ultimately conservative political position. His book on Marx was the first in English to frame the man and his work as a philosopher whose thought could be examined independently of communist and Marxist politics, and indeed in principle independently of mainstream Marxism as doctrinally expounded. He was also the first to make use of the scholarly MEGA[1] edition, in which early manuscript materials were published for the first time. These included works from 1843–7, in which Marx was engaged, as noted above, with Hegel's works and ideas, and with young Hegelians whose criticisms of the master he deemed insufficiently thorough and whose politics was, therefore in his view, insufficiently radical.

Hook's work thus marked a major shift in the Marxian tradition as it became available for transmission to and through the history of political philosophy. In his hands Marx was an object of research, particularly in philosophy, rather than a transmitter of political doctrines into a revolutionary project. While to a large extent Hook approached Marx within the established tradition of interpretation, Hook's highly critical (though not completely hostile) position established a new kind of dialogue with his subject and with his audience, one in which academic standards of judgement (rather than immediately political ones) would come into play. In that way Marx was neither icon nor demon, and the expected outcome of study was intellectual understanding, rather than political solidarity.

While MEGA[1], as a party-political production, was intended to add manuscripts and other materials to the standard canon, that in itself was a somewhat non-canonical activity for two reasons. Because of the scholarly apparatus, bulky format and limited print-runs, MEGA[1] was not a very readable mode of presentation for popular audiences. Moreover, its inclusion of unpublished materials was guaranteed to disturb the already interpreted stock of texts—authoritatively approved by Marx and/or Engels—which had been made widely available, and then framed with Engels's prefaces and introductions.

Unpublished materials combine the twin dramas of mystery and discovery with a chance to find a 'Marx' who does not yet exist within the framework of interpretation already set by Engels and other commentators of 'the Marx party'. Moreover, the character of many of these unpublished early materials made it easy to reframe Marx altogether as a philosopher, and indeed a political philosopher, engaged in a familiar activity—philosophical criticism—albeit on somewhat unfamiliar territory and in a somewhat unfamiliar way.

In the Anglophone philosophical tradition of the time, Hegel's works were not widely known, studied, and admired, so part of Hook's project was to present them as significant objects for engagement, and thus to promote philosophical interest in Marx's encounter. For Hook, Marx's criticism of Hegel was intriguing, not because it was politicized, but rather because it reconceptualized history in terms of technological and industrial progress, and because it recast the relationship between politics and ideas, on the one hand, and practical, even commercial activity, on the other. Put very simply, whether Marx was right or wrong about history and ideas became a philosophical question in the first instance (and whether it had any particular political import, a secondary matter).

Berlin's biography of Marx was a somewhat similar exercise, though rather more comprehensively planned as a survey of Marx's thought and activities throughout his life, and rather more written from standard canonical sources than from newly published manuscript ones. As a non-Marxist (and indeed as someone who had virtually no knowledge of Marx or Marxism before writing the book), the young Berlin duly noted the Marxist framing of Marx and his work, but then proceeded to reread canonical works in his own way, failing—perhaps deliberately—to engage at length with any differences or discrepancies this might throw up between his evocation of Marx and the doctrinal Marx readily available elsewhere.

Berlin's Marx was a much more polymathic figure than Hook's, though the two books share an appreciation of the continental philosophical tradition, of which Hegel was then the last major figure, and an urge to make this mode of philosophizing more respectably mainstream in the Anglophone intellectual world. Berlin's Marx was a revolutionary liberal of the '48er mould in central European history, and rather more a romantic than a scientist. He was also presented as an intellectually driven but humanly flawed and tragic personality. Perhaps inadvertently Berlin showed readers a way of engaging with Marx that simply involved reading his texts on something like their own terms, contextualized in a general historical sense involving all kinds of ideas and movements, but not already inserted into the framing generated by Engels and subsequent Marxists. Berlin simply left Marxists (and anti-Marxists) to fight other battles on other grounds, and rather effectively made Marx a 'thinker', not just a philosopher, with a wide popular appeal and an interdisciplinary academic profile.

In the post-war period after 1945, scholars in the history of political philosophy have accepted Marx as a canonical thinker, and a small selection of his vast output has become standard reading and a familiar point of reference. In the Anglophone world the availability of works by Marx and Engels in English translation greatly increased through the mid-1960s with the publication of numerous selections and collections, both those derived from communist party sources and those produced through commercial presses. The fifty-volume *Collected Works* began to appear in 1975 and was completed in 2004, though many of the major translations reproduce nineteenth-century texts. The traditional canon, largely set by Engels, still circulates widely in popular and student editions. Marx (without much Engels) can also be found in new translations in two volumes of *Political Writings* in the series 'Cambridge Texts in the History of Political Thought'.

SHIFTING VIEWS WITHIN THE CANON

The new canon, however, is not quite the same as the pre-Second World War list, though this is not simply a matter of inclusion and emphasis. Rather the status of unpublished works has risen relative to works published in the authors' lifetimes, for reasons mentioned above: to capitalize on mystery and discovery, as well as to generate what appears to be a more philosophical kind of content and discussion. The persistent devaluation of Marx's *magnum opus*, *Capital*, vol. 1, continues, a direct consequence of the promotion of Marx as a philosopher. Commentators in the history of political philosophy have been largely engaged with works and ideas in an idiom more familiar to philosophers and historians than the 'economics' thought to inhere in Marx's later works, but not in his earlier manuscripts. Engels, despite his (now controversial) editing of Marx's 'economic' manuscripts as *Capital*, vols 2 and 3, was also far happier on this philosophical ground. However, arguably there is more 'economic' material in the early writings than commentators have been wont to see, and more philosophical material of interest to historians of political philosophy in *Capital*, vol. 1, than they have generally recognized.

Interest in the Marx canon on the part of political philosophers in the post-Second World War period shifted dramatically to two rather self-contained areas: the previously unpublished and quite extensive manuscripts of 1843–6, framed as Marx's crucial philosophical engagement with Hegel and the Young Hegelians; and, by contrast, a few published paragraphs in the Preface to *A Contribution to the Critique of Political Economy*, where Marx outlined his 'general conclusion' and 'guiding principle'. This text was republished in 1897, as noted above, but prior to the 1950s it was rather peripheral to the canon, especially in relation to Engels's late works, where 'dialectics' was expounded.

The recovery of the 'early manuscripts' 1843–6 effectively established a canon of the 'young Marx', alternative to the traditional canon, where the list of notable works had effectively begun with those published in 1847. Comments from the few of 'the Marx party' who had ever seen this early manuscript material, such as Engels and Mehring, had generally been dismissive. This alternative was established in Shlomo Avineri's (1933–) influential *The Social and Political Thought of Karl Marx* (1968), and in the successive works (beginning in 1969) of David McLellan (1940–), culminating in *Karl Marx: His Life and Thought* (1973) and further studies. These accounts of the 'early works' were framed as philosophical confrontations and debates, beginning with Hegel and his 'transformative' critic Ludwig Feuerbach (1804–72), and they brought previously unknown or little-read works by Marx into view, such as: *Critique of Hegel's Philosophy of Right* (unpub. 1843); the published 'Introduction' to that work (1844); *Economic and Philosophical Manuscripts* (unpub. 1844); and 'On the Jewish Question' (1844).

Works by Avineri and McLellan, which followed the reception and debate of these early Marx materials in French circles (from the late 1930s onwards), effectively popularized a new philosophical concept—'alienation'—in Anglophone philosophical circles. Their commentary and investigation proceeded in an obviously non-Marxist way, largely shorn of the traditional substantive concerns with contemporary working-class politics and the Marxist methodological apparatus of science and dialectics. Arguably, though, this enthusiasm for a new political philosophy of 'man and society', derived from a 'Marx before Marxism', was more in tune with the diverse intellectual and political currents of the 1960s than were the terms of traditional Marxist philosophy, or indeed the politics of international communism, where a quite different canon prevailed, commencing with Kautsky and Bernstein, on the one hand, and Lenin and Mao Zedong (1893–1976), for example, on the other.

This reception of Marx's work generated a new problem in the history of political philosophy—namely, the relation between the 'young' and the 'old' Marx. This was framed as a relationship between a form of social thought that was Hegelian and therefore philosophical, as opposed to a social science that was said to be empirical, even material and deterministic. Various intellectual and chronological points of transition were offered to periodize and solve this problem. Alternatively, there have been counter-arguments that a resolution of this apparent discrepancy can be found only by carefully analysing the political thrust of Marx's texts and aligning this with a developmental account of his growing expertise with the object of his critique, political economy.

In a contrasting development, the Preface to *A Contribution to the Critique of Political Economy* was recovered as a lens through which to read the rest of Marx in terms of 'the materialist interpretation of history' (Engels's phrase of 1859 covering Marx's 'general conclusion' and 'guiding principle'). Marx's generalizations were interpreted both as a synchronic theory of 'economic structure' and 'legal and political superstructure' and as a diachronic theory of 'social revolution', 'transformation', and 'progress' (Marx and Engels 1987a: 263). This post-Second World War treatment of Marx contrasted with traditional Marxist approaches, where the truth of these propositions was simply assumed, or was related philosophically, as Engels had done, to a materialism derived 'scientifically' from Hegel's dialectic.

G. A. Cohen (1941–2009) and a number of allied 'analytical Marxists' in a self-styled though quite loosely organized Anglophone philosophical school promoted this appropriation of Marx. Theirs was a method-driven approach, in that the rigour and clarity associated with post-Popperian 'analytical philosophy' implied, for adherents to the school, a thoroughgoing rejection of Hegelian dialectical logic and a contrary validation of empirical testing and defensible certainties. Cohen's Marxist background had familiarized him with 'the materialist interpretation of history', and, following on from the politicized anti-Marxist critiques of the 1950s, he proposed to reformulate Marx's 'general conclusion' and 'guiding principle' in a rigorous and testable way. To do this he drew on the historical or empirical researches undertaken by others, some of them colleagues in the 'analytical Marxism' school. Cohen's project proceeded from the later 1960s onwards up to and beyond the book-length publication of *Karl Marx's Theory of History: A Defence* in 1978, which represents the major published exegesis (on very particular philosophical terms) of this hitherto minor text.

Marx had himself been notably unconcerned to publish extensively on questions of method. Engels had relied more directly on the *Communist Manifesto* for an account of 'class struggle' and on his own methodological excursions in later works into a dialectical version of materialism. Cohen's conclusion was that he himself had reformulated Marx's theory in the most rigorous and convincing way possible, and that on those terms it was testable, but that in the end empirical evidence had not supported the strict truth of its propositions. However, arguably Cohen's dichotomy between a rigorous and clear method admitting only empirically testable propositions, and its supposed sole counterpart in a Marxist dialectics that has no defensible philosophical foundation, is something of a false one. Critics of Cohen, and further interpreters of Marx, have argued that there are other options, and that Marx himself was not attempting either of these in any case.

THE MARXIAN TRADITION IN THE HISTORY
OF POLITICAL PHILOSOPHY

The most enduring presence of the Marxian tradition in the history of political philosophy is ideology critique, which exists as a method and body of thought in ways that are largely independent of the 'positions' and controversies within and around the Marx-Engels-Marxist framework of agreement and disputation. The ideas, and the term itself, arise simply enough in the enduringly canonical *Communist Manifesto*:

> The charges against Communism made from a religious, a philosophical, and, generally, from an ideological standpoint, are not deserving of serious examination.
>
> Does it require deep intuition to comprehend that man's ideas, views and conceptions, in one word, man's consciousness, changes with every change in the conditions of his material existence, in his social relations and in his social life?
>
> What else does the history of ideas prove, than that intellectual production changes its character in proportion as material production is changed? (Marx and Engels 1976*a*: 503)

The remainder of the passage explains that ideological outlooks rest on a notion of 'eternal truths such as Freedom, Justice, etc.' thought to be common to 'all states of society'—that is, the contrary of the thesis just stated rhetorically above. The 'Communist revolution' is then presented as 'the most radical rupture with traditional property relations', resulting in the 'total disappearance of class antagonisms' and so the 'most radical rupture with traditional ideas' (Marx and Engels 1976*a*: 503–4). This evidently includes the entire framework through which morality, religion, and politics had hitherto been conceived. But precisely what this would be like in terms of ideas and practices was left, perhaps necessarily, unspecified.

While the word ideology dates back to the 1790s, and while it had a complex developmental history up to canonical republication of the *Communist Manifesto* in 1872, the reception of the term into the history of political philosophy has been most significantly from and through the Marxian tradition. In his later canonical works *Anti-Dühring* and *Ludwig Feuerbach and the End of Classical German Philosophy* (1888), Engels devoted considerable space to defining and using the concept of ideology to develop and support quite specific historical and methodological claims. Overall this fitted the way that Marx's work was increasingly being received as that of a philosopher, requiring philosophical commentary and critical engagement.

These two things—'the materialist interpretation of history' and ideology critique—came together when manuscripts of 1845–6, loosely termed *The German Ideology* by Mehring in 1905, were later 'discovered' to be of great significance in 1923. This was announced by the chief editor of MEGA[1], David Ryazanov (1870–1938), who claimed that in them scholars could trace the precise philosophical moves through which the 'materialist interpretation of history', and the eponymous concept of ideology, were authoritatively formulated by Marx. Notwithstanding the fact that Engels and Mehring had both earlier dismissed these manuscripts as uninteresting in precisely these respects, publication of the jointly written texts proceeded to completion in 1932 as a single volume in the scholarly MEGA[1]. Partial Russian and English translations preceded this, and fuller translations followed afterwards. This work thus became canonical in the later 1930s, and the concept of ideology, and ideology critique as a historical and political mode of analysis, became methodologically mainstream.

There has been considerable debate since that time as to the truth of the general assertion—that ideas are always to be understood and evaluated in relation to their social conditions of production. There are also allegations of self-contradiction, in that the thesis that there are no defensible timeless truths must itself be an ideological assertion, which must in turn be understood and evaluated in relation to its own social conditions of production. However, as opposed to a philosophical search for timeless truths to which social conditions ought to correspond, or must necessarily correspond, the acceptance in principle of a relation between systems of thought and changing social conditions has become powerful and widely accepted in political philosophy. Political philosophy has supported the study of systems of ideas as ideologies or '-isms' (for example, liberalism, Marxism, ecologism, Fascism, feminism, and so on), which are then analysed in relation to their social conditions of production, those from which they arise and those changed ones relevant to their decline. Systems of thought may also, of course, be judged against timeless moral or religious ideals as a matter of non-Marxian philosophizing, but that exercise would follow, if it is undertaken at all, from the construction of an '-ism' in the first place.

CHALLENGES: WHO IS MARX? AND WHAT IS PHILOSOPHY?

The Marxian tradition in the history of political philosophy has developed in an increasingly philosophical framing, and the canon of texts has shifted over time in terms of content, prioritization, and occlusion. Contextualizing accounts that tell us who Marx was, and what sorts of projects he was engaged in, have also metamorphosed, such that his reception as a mainstream philosopher has become possible. One of the most quoted of the newly prioritized canonical works is Marx's 'Theses on Feuerbach', where he writes in a recognizably philosophical idiom against an opponent well known as a philosopher. This short text of three pages arrived in print as an annex to Engels's philosophically oriented *Ludwig Feuerbach and the End of Classical German Philosophy*, which was little read by Anglophone political philosophers. While not strictly part of *The German Ideology* manuscripts, the 'Theses' are generally included in the editions of that work published since the 1930s, and also in major Marx-Engels collections. Anglophone interest in unpublished early manuscripts has been intense, not least in *The German Ideology*, where it is assumed that Marx's confrontation with Feuerbach and Hegel significantly continued, albeit in the highly problematic textual fragments that constitute Part One of the book. The two works together have thus been made to constitute a philosophical Marx who did not exist until the twentieth century.

From Marx's perspective in the 1840s, fame as a philosopher was the last thing he wanted for himself, as he made clear in published and unpublished works. He wrote as an activist, a communist allied with liberal revolutionists, in a situation where—as it happened—political agitation in print or by speech was necessarily (owing to state repression) conducted in highly coded and supposedly neutered terms as philosophical debate. Of course, much of this work now reads like philosophy, and indeed philosophical reflection of the highest and most original order. Marx takes on many of the standard topics on which the history of political philosophy offers reflection, and he engages with some of the standard authors and texts with which historians of political philosophy are familiar.

However, in Marx's scathing critiques of philosophical dilettantism, where philosophers were—in his view—dabbling in politics, there is the germ of a conception that philosophy as traditionally practised cannot be a world-changing activity, rhetoric to that effect notwithstanding. Quite how he expected his own activities to be characterized, and indeed how he felt after they had—during his lifetime—so little changed the world, remains open to speculation. Nonetheless his aphoristic eleventh thesis on Feuerbach presents a pertinent challenge: 'The philosophers have only *interpreted* the world in various ways; the point is to *change* it' (Marx and Engels 1976b: 5; emphasis in original).

REFERENCES

AVINERI, S. (1968). *The Social and Political Thought of Karl Marx*. Cambridge: Cambridge University Press.

BERLIN, I. (1939). *Karl Marx: His Life and Environment*. London: T. Butterworth.

COHEN, G. A. (1978). *Karl Marx's Theory of History: A Defence*. Oxford: Clarendon Press.

HOOK, S. (1936). *From Hegel to Marx: Studies in the Intellectual Development of Karl Marx*. New York: Reynal & Hitchcock.

LENIN, V. I. (1964). *Collected Works*. 4th edn, vol. 21. Moscow: Foreign Languages Publishing House.

McLELLAN, D. (1973). *Karl Marx: His Life and Thought*. Basingstoke: Macmillan.

MARX, K., and ENGELS, F. (1975a). *Collected Works*, vol. 1. London: Lawrence & Wishart.

MARX, K., and ENGELS, F. (1975b). *Collected Works*, vol. 2. London: Lawrence & Wishart.

MARX, K., and ENGELS, F. (1975c). *Collected Works*, vol. 3. London: Lawrence & Wishart.

MARX, K., and ENGELS, F. (1975d). *Collected Works*, vol. 4. London: Lawrence & Wishart.

MARX, K., and ENGELS, F. (1976a). *Collected Works*, vol. 6. London: Lawrence & Wishart.

MARX, K., and ENGELS, F. (1976b). *Collected Works*, vol. 5. London: Lawrence & Wishart.

MARX, K., and ENGELS, F. (1977a). *Collected Works*, vol. 7. London: Lawrence & Wishart.

MARX, K., and ENGELS, F. (1977b). *Collected Works*, vol. 8. London: Lawrence & Wishart.

MARX, K., and ENGELS, F. (1979). *Collected Works*, vol. 11. London: Lawrence & Wishart.

MARX, K., and ENGELS, F. (1980). *Collected Works*, vol. 16. London: Lawrence & Wishart

MARX, K., and ENGELS, F. (1985). *Collected Works*, vol. 20. London: Lawrence & Wishart.

MARX, K., and ENGELS, F. (1987a). *Collected Works*, vol. 29. London: Lawrence & Wishart.

MARX, K., and ENGELS, F. (1987b). *Collected Works*, vol. 25. London: Lawrence & Wishart.

MARX, K., and ENGELS, F. (1989). *Collected Works*, vol. 24. London: Lawrence & Wishart.

MARX, K., and ENGELS, F. (1990a). *Collected Works*, vol. 26. London: Lawrence & Wishart.

MARX, K., and ENGELS, F. (1990b). *Collected Works*, vol. 27. London: Lawrence & Wishart.

MARX, K., and ENGELS, F. (1996). *Collected Works*, vol. 35. London: Lawrence & Wishart.

CHAPTER 24

....

NINETEENTH- AND TWENTIETH-CENTURY LIBERALISM

....

DAVID WEINSTEIN

INTRODUCTION

....

HISTORIES of the liberal tradition are easy to write as long as one knows how to tell a mundane story. Short stories, like this one, are easier still because nuance is an impossible luxury. Nevertheless, I will forgo as best I can writing just another dreary short story, focusing instead on trying to draw some contrasts that will hopefully capture something non-trivial about liberalism. My narrative proceeds unconventionally. It appropriates Philip Pettit's distinction between "value-centered" and "contract-centered" theorizing and asks us to consider nineteenth- and twentieth century English-speaking liberalism as a quest for inviolable universal moral principles. It also suggests that interpreting the liberal tradition accordingly encourages us to pay far more attention than we have to nineteenth-century utilitarianism and to the new liberalism.

Elsewhere, I have argued that Anglo-American political theory, especially contemporary analytical liberalism, has become too self-referential and consequently insufficiently attentive to its own variegated past. It has compressed its past according to its current conceptual and logical preoccupations, whether metaphysical, merely political, or otherwise (see Weinstein 2004). Some analytical liberals fret about whether the good or the right should have priority, while others agonize about whether liberalism is compatible with value pluralism and with multiculturalism. Some worry about liberalism's compatibility with distributive justice at home and globally. Still others anxiously debate the ontological status of the self presupposed by liberalism and whether liberalism therefore devalues community and eviscerates identity.

Whatever their conceptual anxieties, analytical liberals, implicitly if not explicitly, filter the liberal tradition through the lens of these worries. This is hardly surprising and surely unavoidable to some extent. But, while we cannot avoid compressing the liberal tradition through our present philosophical preoccupations, while we cannot escape fusing past and present philosophical horizons, we can certainly navigate between them with more or less awareness of what we are actually doing. We can go to sea philosophically with lesser or greater self-understanding of how we endlessly navigate these intersecting horizons and continually renarrate the liberal tradition.

As I have also argued, inspired partly by Michael Freeden's similar thinking, too many contemporary analytical liberals see liberalism as beginning with Hobbes and Locke, as next reformulated classically by Mill, and then as receding into the wilderness of mere history of political thought thanks to the linguistic turn and the vogue of emotivism before being resurrected so magnificently by Rawls. This truncated narrative is congenial to liberalism's contemporary concerns. For instance, seventeenth-century contractualism fits neatly into *a* liberal tradition seen retrospectively through the conceptual and justificatory concerns of Rawls and his legacy.

I will call this the Rawlsian liberal tradition. Now this liberal tradition marginalizes much, however innocently. More than likely, it is unaware that it is a very peculiar liberal tradition or a very peculiar rational reconstruction. For instance, it severely marginalizes new liberals and idealists such as T. H. Green, Bernard Bosanquet, L. T. Hobhouse, D. G. Ritchie, and J. A. Hobson. From the overpowering perspective of Rawlsian liberalism, these liberals seem little more than an eclectic hodgepodge, wrong-headedly mixing metaphysics and too much moral philosophizing with their political theorizing. But new liberals and idealists alike wrote highly original political philosophy, parts of which contemporary liberals have repeated inadvertently with false novelty. Communitarian liberals in particular, such as Joseph Raz, Thomas Hurka, David Miller, and Harry Frankfurt, have followed unawares new liberals and idealists by combining socially constructed conceptions of individuality, self-realization as a moral ideal, and stringent moral rights. Likewise, contemporary liberal utilitarians such as Jonathan Riley, who quite explicitly take inspiration from Mill, replay much from the new liberals unknowingly. Insofar as new liberals saw themselves improving Mill more than anyone else, we should not be surprised that such contemporary attempts to build on Mill retravel so much new liberalism.

New liberals, then, were consequentialists, even Green. Of course, calling them consequentialist as *we* now understand the term is controversial. That is, they were consequentialists in *our* sense and not in *their* sense. In fact, there was no *their* sense, because contemporary consequentialism had not yet been invented. Calling the new liberals consequentialists is therefore admittedly anachronistic. But we must not forget that their moral theory emerged when classical utilitarianism dominated nineteenth-century English moral philosophizing. And though Green criticized Mill more than Hobhouse, Ritchie, or Hobson, he nevertheless agreed with Mill extensively. Idealists like Bradley also agreed with Mill quite extensively or, at least, we should concede that Bradley agreed with Mill much more than later critics of idealism have recognized. In other words, too, there is more continuity or similarity between utilitarianism and idealism than most now appreciate, just as there is more similarity between utilitarianism and the new liberalism than most recognize. This should not be surprising, given that the new liberalism was also part idealism.

By far, the Rawlsian liberal tradition's disinterest in Sidgwick is most curious of all. Rawls wrote *A Theory of Justice* with Sidgwick in mind more than anyone else. The Preface makes this clear and therefore ought to be read with greater attentiveness. Rawls writes that until recently we have been "forced to choose between utilitarianism and intuitionism," both of which are deeply flawed (Rawls 1999b: p. xvii). Whereas intuitionism is capricious and unsystematic, utilitarianism is too tyrannically systematic, sacrificing individual integrity to fanatical aggregating maximization.

Rawls, at least as early as 1971, saw himself as crafting an alternative to what he regarded as moral philosophy's two primary rivals—namely, intuitionism, on the one hand, and classical utilitarianism best represented by Sidgwick, on the other. Whereas classical utilitarians, like Sidgwick and J. S. Mill, viewed intuitionism as their primary and most dangerous adversary, Rawls, in turn, deemed both intuitionism and utilitarianism inadequate and unsavory. Classical utilitarians rightly rejected intuitionism for being unsystematic and whimsical. But, according to Rawls, classical utilitarians avoided both by destroying the moral integrity of persons. Classical utilitarians certainly systematized practical reasoning, substituting rationality for caprice, but at the unnerving cost of transforming individuals into mere channels of utility maximization. For Rawls, then, classical utilitarianism escaped the folly of intuitionism only by substituting its own alternative folly. Classical utilitarianism aggressively systematized liberalism but only by unacceptably rearranging its conceptual furniture in a way that made it no longer identifiably liberal.

So, in Rawls's view, classical utilitarianism improved intuitionism by systematizing it but by sacrificing its liberal credentials. It disfigured liberalism beyond the pale of anything worthy of the name. *A Theory of Justice* attempted to rescue liberalism from utilitarianism's systematizing excesses all the while salvaging some of its theoretical coherence. *A Theory of Justice* is an inventive attempt to order, justify, and refine our deepest liberal intuitions. It mimics Sidgwick's ambitions without forgoing liberalism's ethical appeal. It "best approximates our considered judgments of justice and constitutes the most appropriate moral basis for a [liberal] democratic society" (Rawls 1999b: p. xviii). Moreover, Rawls continues, following Sidgwick: "I believe that an important test of a theory of justice is how well it introduces order and system into our considered judgments over a wide range of questions" (Rawls 1999b: p. xix).[1] The liberal tradition has never been quite the same ever since.

---

[1] It should come as no surprise, then, that Rawls wrote an approving Foreword to the Hackett 1981 reissue of the 1907 seventh edition of Sidgwick's *Methods of Ethics*. For instance, Rawls says there that Sidgwick's "originality consists in his conception of moral philosophy and of the way in which a reasoned and satisfactory justification of any particular moral conception must proceed from a full knowledge and systematic comparison of the more significant moral conceptions in the philosophical

Rawlsian liberals have continued ignoring Sidgwick despite Sidgwick's importance for Rawls. That they have ignored new liberals just as much is less puzzling, for, after all, the advent of twentieth-century analytical philosophy made short work of British idealism, which stigmatized new liberals, including Green especially. Green and the new liberals were thrown out with the metaphysical bath water of idealism. Perhaps Sidgwick's criticisms of Green had something to do with this, though Sidgwick seems always to have regarded Green as a worthy opponent (see Weinstein 2007: 54–5).

INTERPRETING LIBERALISM

James Fishkin has suggested that we live in a moral culture of "absolutist expectations" where these expectations for "rationally unquestionable, inviolable, and complete principles" invariably come to grief with the reality of incompatible and indeterminate values. Consequently, liberalism now faces a crisis of legitimacy (Fishkin 1997: 157). For Fishkin, presumably, Rawls's endeavor to rescue liberalism from utilitarianism constitutes one form of absolutism unsuccessfully replacing another.

Notwithstanding whether Rawls's rescue efforts have succeeded and whether or not they are symptomatic of our culture's failed quest for absolute moral principles, his liberalism is surely absolutist, like Sidgwick's, at least in the sense of trying to systematize *our* moral intuitions about justice. And this goes for much contemporary analytical liberalism that remains his legacy. So Rawlsian liberalism, like the utilitarian versions of liberalism that Rawls saw himself supplanting, remains systemically ambitious. Whether one prioritizes right over good or vice versa, one is an absolutist either way.

Absolutist political philosophizing, including contemporary liberal varieties, invariably produces what Bernard Williams refers to as "funny" intellectual history (Williams 1980: 118). Its humor stems, in part, from its being a narrative quest for the systematic accommodation of principles now dear to us. It invites us to read historical philosophical texts naively as anticipations of what we are these days committed to resolving. We consequently ignore these texts' very different historical contexts, assuming that all we need to do is read them ever-so fastidiously the way we read our own contemporaries.

But earlier generation liberals often had concerns other than ours. At least, we should not assume that their concerns were exactly ours. We should, therefore, read them, as Pettit suggests we read any historical event, conspiratorially:

> All of this is to say that there is a conspiratorial aspect to the reconstructive style of intentional [historical] explanation. We get on side with the agents under investigation; we get to breathe with them, in the etymological sense of "con-spire." We

tradition" (Sidgwick 1981: p. vi). Rawlsian liberals have ignored Sidgwick's legacy for Rawls. American political theorizing, in particular, knows next to nothing about Sidgwick and very little more about utilitarianism. Mill, of course, is revered as canonical, but it is mostly the Mill of *On Liberty* and not the Mill of *Utilitarianism*, which was published just two years later in 1861.

adopt the concepts in terms of which the contents of their observations and beliefs are defined; we countenance the presumptions of evidence in virtue of which those contents seem like plausible things to espouse, we give our seal of approval, or at least of rational understanding, to the habits of inference by which accepting the propositions involved rationally leads to the beliefs and actions under explanation . . . (Pettit 1996: 235)

And while conspiratorial interpretations of the liberal tradition may uncover absolutist preoccupations like our own, we should nevertheless be open to the prospect that it will not. Getting "in tune" with our liberal past may often comfort us, because this past proves so familiar after all. But it may not be, provoking us to think analytically in novel ways.

Much like Pettit, Isaiah Berlin insists that "no true history of ideas" can possibly be written unless you "enter imaginatively into the mental world of the philosophers you are discussing" by seeing their problems from the "inside." As for Pettit, *Einfühlung* (empathy) is indispensable, though for Berlin certain core philosophical problems and ideas have always remained "transhistorical." The central "great ideas which have occupied minds in the Western world" have always had "a certain life of their own . . ." (Jahanbegloo 1992: 24, 26, 28).

Now Berlin, as much as Pettit, seems to be invoking Skinner's method of textual interpretation, which Pettit, for his part, concedes (see Pettit 1996: 239). Unless we imaginatively re-enact past philosophical texts' meaning by understanding them from within, we will just end up re-enacting ourselves through them. As liberals, we will merely rediscover ourselves, digging up our own particular absolutist ambitions and concerns, or anti-absolutist ones, wherever we happen to cast our spade.

VALUE-CENTERED VERSUS CONTRACT-CENTERED LIBERALISM

As noted, Pettit distinguishes between two kinds of liberal political theorizing, namely "value-centered" and "contract-centered" thinking. Whereas the former assesses political institutions for their systematizing "categorical properties" such as their justice or utility, the latter judges them for whether or not they are the product of a historical contract, or at least compatible with a hypothetical one. For Pettit, value-centered liberal theorizing is either deontological or consequentialist.

Value-Centered Deontological Liberalism

Contemporary deontological liberals, such as Robert Nozick and Ronald Dworkin, hold that certain rights are indefeasible, trumping all competing values. But Nozick's natural-rights liberalism is ungrounded intuitionism.

Dworkin's liberalism is more nuanced though ultimately absolutist and intuitionist. For him, equality, specified as equality of resources, is *prima facie* sovereign, leading David Miller to characterize his liberalism as egalitarian in the "simple sense." More recently, in *Sovereign Virtue*, Dworkin justifies equality of resources by appealing to the "challenge model" of non-consequentialist value. According to the "challenge model," lives lived in critical self-reflection from the *inside* exhibit "ethical integrity," whereas habit-driven lives or lives devoted to promoting external states of affairs typical of consequentialist thinking are lived mechanically from the *outside*. Moreover, according to the "challenge model," living from the "inside" requires having sufficient basic resources. Resources egalitarianism "flows from" the "challenge model." If all of us are to have a real chance at meeting the challenges we set for ourselves, then we need equal basic resources and therefore have basic rights to them (see Dworkin 2000*b*: esp. ch. 6). Elsewhere, Dworkin says that equal resources "flow from" equal concern and respect in the sense of being "consistent with" them (see Dworkin 2000*a*: 15–16). Here, equal concern and respect seem to ground our rights to equal resources. But "flow[ing] from" and "being consistent with" are ambiguous, exposing Dworkin to the charge that his justification of rights is intuitionist.

Harry Frankfurt, likewise a neo-Kantian, has accused Dworkin of confusing equality with sufficiency. For Frankfurt, "what is important from the point of view of morality *is* not that everyone should have *the same* but that each should have *enough*" to satisfy their urgent needs. And urgency "has to do with what is *important*" (see Frankfurt 1997: 261, 270). Whatever is important has to do with what people actually care about and gives them satisfaction. Concern for equality in itself is alienating, much the way that single-minded concern for maximizing happiness is alienating. So, for Frankfurt, Dworkin's egalitarianism is overly and unnecessarily demanding when all that justice requires are equal opportunities to live meaningful lives, which, as we shall see, is what new liberals earlier prescribed.

By contrast, Iris Marion Young has criticized liberal egalitarians like Dworkin for not being demanding enough by ignoring the institutional context, such as the language and symbols that mediate social interaction, decision-making procedures as well as family and gender biases, of the distribution of income and wealth. No less than income and wealth, these condition "people's ability to participate in determining their actions and their ability to develop and exercise their capacities." Young calls her theory a "modified Millian" account of justice (see Young 1990: 21, 250).[2]

Notwithstanding Frankfurt's and Young's criticisms of egalitarians like Dworkin, ungrounded intuitions, whether in the form of natural rights or equality, are capricious as Bentham long ago insisted. Or, as R. M. Hare has more recently insisted, "intuitions prove nothing" and have often been used to support "outrageous" claims. "We want arguments," which intuitionists too often fail to provide (see Hare 1997: 223–4). Hare continues:

---

[2] See also Okin (1989) for how liberal egalitarian theories ignore private sphere oppression.

> Rights are the offspring of *prima facie*, intuitive principles, and I have nothing against them; but the question is, What *prima facie* principles ought we to adopt? What intuitions ought we to have? On these questions the rhetoric of rights sheds no light whatever, any more than do appeals to intuition (i.e. to prejudice, i.e. to the *prima facie* principles, good or bad, which our upbringings happen to have implanted in us.) The worth of intuitions is to be known by their fruits; as in the case of the principles to be followed by judges in administering the law, the best principles are those with the highest acceptance-utility, i.e. those whose general acceptance maximize the furtherance of the interests, in sum, of all the affected parties, treating all those interests as of equal weight, i.e. impartially, i.e. with formal justice. (Hare 1997: 224)

For Bentham, too, of course, utilitarian consequentialism was intuitionism's only compelling alternative. For Rawls, while utilitarianism had indeed been intuitionism's sole credible rival thus far, it was no less problematic in turn, causing Rawls to propose justice as fairness as a superior alternative.

Value-Centered Consequentialist Liberalism

Rawls notwithstanding, utilitarian consequentialism remains powerfully influential among moral philosophers if not among political theorists, especially political theorists in the United States. For contemporary utilitarians like Hare, Jonathan Riley, and Brad Hooker, basic moral rules and/or moral rights serve as direct "decision procedures" for guiding individual actions, whereas the principle of utility functions *indirectly* as a background "criterion" for assessing rules or rights themselves. For indirect utilitarians, respecting basic moral rules and fundamental rights best maximizes general utility in the long term, though perhaps not in some short term, individual circumstances.

Indirect utlilitarians, especially those like Riley who stress combining basic liberal rights, rather than moral rules, with the principle of utility, tend also to follow Mill in championing individual flourishing. For these *liberal* utilitarians, happiness is maximized whenever individuality thrives, and individuality thrives best wherever fundamental moral rights are respected.

Liberal utilitarianism, then, combines the systematizing force of maximization with the liberal attractiveness of basic rights and the cultivation of individuality. It strives to make utilitarianism ethically appealing as an authentic liberalism without forgoing its value-centered absolutism—namely, maximizing happiness.

Contemporary critics of liberal utilitarianism, including especially those who once argued otherwise, such as David Lyons and John Gray, deny that rights with genuine moral force can be coherently combined with maximizing utility (see Lyons 1982; Gray 1989). According to them, either maximizing utility always trumps rights, depriving them of their moral force, or rights always trump maximizing utility, in which case utilitarianism vanishes. Only one value can be absolute in the end. Value monism excludes competing values with independent normative force. We can be either liberals or utilitarians, but not both. And naturally, if combining rights with utility is futile, then all attempts to combine stringent moral rules with utility are likewise just as futile, rending rule utilitarianism no less incoherent than liberal utilitarianism.

Now, according to Amartya Sen, absolutist theories of justice typically and correctly "separate out some basic issues as being inescapably relevant, but they cannot plausibly end up...with an exclusive choice of some highly delineated formula of relative weights as being the unique blueprint" of justice (Sen 1999: 286–7). And this goes for utilitarian theories of justice, however they twist and turn to accommodate fundamental moral rights, but not necessarily for consequentialist theories. Indeed, to "ignore consequences in general...can hardly be an adequate basis for an acceptable evaluative system" (Sen 1999: 66). Happily, for Sen, whether or not utilitarianism can successfully accommodate rights with independent moral force and whether or not liberal utilitarianism is therefore incoherent does not hold for other varieties of consequentialism. By artificially restricting the domain of evaluation to happiness or pleasure, utilitarians reduce rights to merely instrumental value, effectively stripping them of independent normative force. In other words, utilitarianism cannot take rights seriously. Liberal utilitarianism may be hopelessly problematic but not liberal consequentialism:

> There is no particular reason to insist on an impoverished account of a state of affairs in evaluating it...In the context of decision theory and rational choice, I have argued for the importance of paying particular attention to "comprehensive outcomes" (including actions undertaken, processes involved, and the like *along with* the final outcomes), instead of confining attention to only the "culmination outcome" (what happens at the very end). (Sen 2000: 491–2)

Whereas "culmination" outcome consequentialism excludes "process" rights from the state of affairs assessed, "comprehensive" outcome consequentialism includes them. "Culmination" outcome consequentialism, including especially its *utilitarian* varieties, therefore cannot take rights seriously, rendering liberal utilitarianism deeply problematic. Liberal utilitarianism may well be incoherent but not necessarily liberal consequentialism.[3] Sen elsewhere refers to "comprehensive" outcome consequentialism as "consequence-based" consequentialism or as "deontic-value inclusive" consequentialism (Sen 1982, 2001).

Whether the classical utilitarians were indeed "culmination" outcome consequentialists may be beside the point, since our analytical distinctions were not available to them. Rawls was correct in insisting in his 1955 "Two Concepts of Rules" that classical utilitarians were practical reformers whose utilitarianism was "not simply an ethical theory" and therefore hardly an "attempt at philosophical analysis in the modern sense" (Rawls 1955: 33 n. 21). In short, we should avoid reading our analytical distinctions and preoccupations into their theorizing, which was generated by different

---

[3] For an account of how Sen's "comprehensive" outcome consequentialism accommodates rights in terms of "capabilities" to "function," see Weinstein (2004: 4–18).

historical circumstances. Rawls nevertheless denied that the classical utilitarians advocated straightforward maximization but instead argued for maximizing happiness "subject to the constraint that no one's rights may be violated" (see Rawls 1955: 26). Furthermore, and contrary to what he would later claim in *A Theory of Justice*, classical utilitarianism's liberal credentials could be sustained by stating it "in a way which accounts for the distinction between the justification of an institution [including presumably moral rules and rights] and the justification of a particular action under it" (Rawls 1955: 26).

But, whatever classical utilitarians like Bentham, Mill, and Sidgwick were and however they may now seem to us, they were not "straightforward" maximizers, as Rawls once perceptively acknowledged but, by *A Theory of Justice*, seemed to forget. Classical utilitarians tried to "take seriously the distinction between persons." Bentham never advocated crude maximization, as J. P. Kelly and Frederick Rosen have forcefully argued (Kelly 1990; Rosen 1990). And, as considerable recent scholarship on Mill has shown, Mill never tired of insisting that considerable self-regarding freedom of action was essential for maximizing happiness. Wherever individual rights to security and freedom are zealously protected, experiments in living thrive, maximizing general happiness in turn. Moreover, insofar as individual flourishing includes moral flourishing, greater respect for moral rights increases (see especially Gray 1983; Riley 1988).

Sidgwick, who has informed Rawls's thinking more than most realize as I have suggested, was a liberal utilitarian too but certainly of a more conservative kind, in part because he combined the principle of utility with moral rules instead of moral rights. For Sidgwick, utility was best promoted *indirectly* by the "middle axioms" of common-sense morality, though these moral rules warranted refinement whenever doing so clearly and significantly improved maximizing general utility. Sidgwick, then, was what we would call a rule utilitarian, though not of the rule-worshipping kind.

By the end of the nineteenth century in England, idealism and the new liberalism began challenging classical utilitarianism. Idealists like F. H. Bradley and Bernard Bosanquet argued that, because individuals are socially constituted, individual flourishing required everyone flourishing. Hence, justice entailed everyone having the equal opportunity to flourish or self-realize. In Bradley's case, particularly in his 1876 and much-revised *Ethical Studies*, this meant citizens fulfilling the conventional duties of their "station" though one's duties changed as society changed, requiring that duties not be taken uncritically.

Bosanquet's 1899 *Philosophical Theory of the State* articulates politically Bradley's earlier moral theory. For Bosanquet, equal opportunity societies empowered citizens with "positive" as well as "negative" liberty. Both ensured real "extensive choice to self-determination" through a system of strong though not indefeasible rights as the "condition and guarantee of our becoming the best that we have it in us to be." Such a system, by hindering "hindrances of the good life," promotes self-realization indirectly in much the same way that Mill's system of strong rights encouraged self-development without counter-productively seeking to impose it (Bosanquet 2001: 21, 139, 147).

Now new liberals like Green, Hobhouse, Ritchie, and Hobson followed idealists by combining communitarian social ontology with positive freedom. And they likewise followed Mill, as noted previously, especially where they combined stringent moral rights with consequentialist practical reasoning. For them much as for Mill, fundamental moral rights best promoted everyone's self-realization indirectly and ultimately general happiness. In Green's words, rights realize our moral capacity but negatively by "securing the treatment of one man by another as equally free with himself, but they do not realize it positively, because their possession does not imply that . . . the individual makes a common good his own" (see Green 1997*b*: sect. 25). Moreover, being fully free in realizing oneself morally was being both "outward[ly]" and "inward[ly]" free, which meant having the enabling "positive power or capacity of doing . . . something worth doing" *and actually* "doing . . . something worth doing" (see Green 1997*a*: 371). Or, as Hobhouse put it, full freedom was being "moral[ly]" as well as "social[ly]" free (see Hobhouse 1949: 57).

For new liberals as for Bosanquet, moral rights indirectly promoted everyone's self-realization by ensuring each equal opportunities to flourish. But, compared to Bosanquet, equalizing opportunities required more robust redistribution of wealth, transforming the new liberalism into what Hobhouse called "liberal socialism" and what we would identify as liberal egalitarianism. For new liberals, then, equal opportunity was a chimera unless our options were fortified by vigorously empowering positive freedom and positive rights.

The new liberalism's socialism is commonplace. But, as I suggested earlier, new liberals, especially Ritchie and Hobson, were *considerably* more indebted to classical utilitarianism then the received view acknowledges. Indeed, as I have insisted, new liberals, including even Green, were fundamentally what *we* call consequentialists if not outright utilitarians. Again, the new liberalism cut its teeth when utilitarianism dominated Victorian political philosophizing.[4] The new liberalism, then, was an eclectic assortment of utilitarianism, communitarianism, and neo-Kantian perfectionism. No doubt the authority of contemporary value-centered liberalism, whether in its simple deontological or consequentialist varieties, has sharply hindered contemporary analytical liberals from taking the new liberalism seriously. From the former's perspective, the latter has seemed confused, idiosyncratic, and therefore forgettable. And this may be why contemporary value-centered liberals have also ignored liberal utilitarianism as, in their judgment, a misbegotten and jumbled conceptual exercise. As we shall soon see, contemporary contract liberals have diminished our regard for the new liberalism and even liberal utilitarianism just as much and probably more.

---

[4] For a far more nuanced account of new liberalism's debts to classical utilitarianism, see Weinstein (2007). For a criticism of my interpretation of Green on this score, see Simhony (1995). See also Simhony and Weinstein (2001).

Contract-Centered Liberalism

David Gauthier writes that just societies are neutral regarding substantive conceptions of good, aiming at nothing beyond the preferences of their members. A just society is "a co-operative venture for mutual advantage" that "enables each to promote what she holds good." It is anti-utilitarian in that it does not "introduce a social good as a function of individual goods." It is "concerned only to enable each person to realize the greatest amount of her own good, on terms acceptable to all" (Gauthier 1986: 341).

Gauthier's moral contractualism is Hobbesian. For Gauthier, morality is prudential and strategic. We construct it to advance our self-interest by taming our selfishness. And what we construct are permanent, if not quite absolute, practical truths. Morality is not arbitrary even though contingent. Gauthier nevertheless wonders, acknowledging Rorty's influence, whether he is simply "contributing to the history of ideas of a particular society, in which peculiar circumstances have fostered an ideology of individuality and interaction that coheres with morals by agreement" (Gauthier 1986: 20).

Neo-Kantian versions of contractualism such as those of Rawls, Barry, Larmore, and Scanlon are more absolutist, as I have been using this term, than Gauthier's. That is, they aspire to justify permanent principles of justice on the basis of one or very few more general, underlying moral principles. Not unlike egalitarian liberals such as Dworkin, they feature strong rights. Of course, by the time of *Political Liberalism*, Rawls had abandoned discovering once-and-for-all justice principles, being content to articulate and refine principles congenial to his cultural contemporaries. Rawls never left Sidgwick entirely behind.[5]

Brian Barry's contractualism is informed, implicitly at least, by Sidgwick too. For Barry, justice as impartiality systematizes *our* considered conceptions of justice. It focuses our thinking about justice by encouraging us to think "for ourselves in a more structured way" (Barry 1998: 195). Justice as impartiality, moreover, takes seriously our deeply pluralistic and often conflicting conceptions of good while simultaneously seeking to adjudicate between them. Much like Scanlon's contractualism, it allows vetoing principles of justice that nobody could reasonably accept. Whatever principles survive reasonable rejectability are necessarily impartial. Reasonable rejectability also favors the worst off, just as it does for Scanlon. And it precludes utilitarian reasoning, since most would reject it as overly demanding. Most would reject it because it unreasonably favors extreme impartiality that only saints are capable of.

Barry's contractualism, then, embraces pluralism. But pluralism does not preclude discovering shared principles of justice. Barry, in other words, does not follow Berlin to where David Miller and William Galston have gone, causing Galston to comment that Barry was once "more than willing to acknowledge the existence of plural and

---

[5] Charles Larmore tries to "occupy a point between" Gauthier and Rawls. Though he follows later Rawls in not grounding liberalism in a "comprehensive moral ideal," he insists that his political liberalism is not merely an object of consensus but a "correct moral conception" (see Larmore 1990: 354).

conflicting" principles and goods. However, he now "resembles Ronald Dworkin in his confidence that sound principles plus strenuous reasoning are equal to the Herculean task of finding singular right answers to most of life's problems" (Galston 2005: 181).

PLURALISTIC LIBERALISM

Pluralistic liberalism is the revenge of twentieth-century Romanticism, which is not to say that nineteenth-century liberalism was unequivocally and thoroughly rationalistic. As I have suggested, new liberals eclectically combined what many contemporary liberals regard as irreconcilable normative principles. But their systematizing ingenuity makes them sufficiently rationalistic and absolutist all-the-same.

With Berlin, we encounter robust pluralism for which fundamental values are irreconcilable, making all attempts at systematizing them futile and even dangerous.[6] Though multiple and impossible to systematize, our core values are nevertheless objective. Herder was half correct. Irreconcilability does not entail subjectivism. Our multiple, conflicting values are not "arbitrary creations of men's subjective fancies" (Berlin 2000: 12). Otherwise, empathy and mutual understanding between often very different cultures would never exist. Communication "is possible between individuals, groups, cultures, because the values of men are not infinitely many; they belong to a common horizon—the objective, often incompatible, values of mankind—between which it is necessary often painfully to choose" (Jahanbegloo 1992: 108). Those who think otherwise, those still intoxicated by our moral culture's "absolutist expectations," are disguised intuitionists: "But I am quite clear that I do not have the faculty which detects absolute moral rules. Somebody like Leo Strauss believes in them because he believes in a faculty which some call 'reason'... I envy him" (Jahanbegloo 1992: 109).

Moreover, for Berlin, because values are irreconcilable and yet objective, pluralism favors negative freedom because negative freedom facilitates unavoidable choosing between these incommensurate values. Berlin, however, sometimes reformulates negative freedom as robust positive freedom (see especially Weinstein 2004: 418–19). And he has even conceded that positive liberty is no less valid than negative liberty, though "pseudo-positive" liberty has done more damage historically than "pseudo-negative" liberty (Jahanbegloo 1992: 41).

David Miller's liberalism is pluralistic and non-absolutist too, though, unlike Berlin's, it is not objective. And it is certainly more egalitarian than Berlin's. Miller follows Walzer, insisting that egalitarian societies recognize multiple goods distributing them according to desert, need, or equality. Miller insists that a "society whose distributive practices are radically pluralistic—recognizing many irreducibly different kinds of social goods, each having its own criterion of just distribution—may achieve an

---

[6] Early on, Berlin criticized utilitarianism for being absolutist by promising too much (see Berlin 1937).

overarching equality of status among its members" (see Miller 1995: 199). As long as no distribution of basic goods dominates, complex equality, providing all the opportunity to flourish, is achievable. Miller also follows Walzer insisting that the "enemy of equality is *dominance*, which occurs when holders of one good are able to capitalize on their position in order to obtain other goods for which they do not fulfil the relevant criteria" (Miller 1995: 203). But he adds that we need to worry about pre-eminence where "one sphere of distribution may become so pre-eminent that people can be ranked socially simply on the basis of how they perform in that sphere" (Miller 1995: 212). Complex equality neutralizes pre-eminence no less than dominance.

Notwithstanding Miller's notion of complex equality, his strong egalitarianism combined with his concern for promoting self-development is refurbished new liberalism though it is unclear how familiar he is with the new liberals. Miller's strong egalitarianism also draws from Sidgwick by way of Rawls's reflective equilibrium. We discover principles of justice most suitable for us by philosophically refining and systematizing as best we can our intuitive notions about justice (see Miller 1999: 58). But Miller seems no more interested in Sidgwick than he is in the new liberals.

With William Galston, we also get straightforward pluralistic liberalism that is objectivist like Berlin's and unlike Miller's. For Galston, "while the distinction between good and bad is objective, there are multiple goods that differ qualitatively from one another and that cannot be ranked-ordered" (see Galston 2005: 2). Not only is rank ordering pointless but, because it is so pointless, it often generates "dangerous moral tunnel vision." We should, therefore, eschew vigorously trying "to gratify our understandable desire for moral harmony by obliterating our awareness of unavoidable moral costs" (Galston 2005: 112). Following Berlin, Galston also holds that value pluralism produces a strong presumption in favor of liberty. Moreover, value pluralism privileges "political liberalism"—namely, the importance of "an understanding social life that comprises multiple sources of authority—individuals, parents, civil associations, faith-based institutions, and the state, among others—no one of which is dominant in all spheres, for all purposes, on all occasions" (see Galston 2005: 1–2). Pluralists, including Berlin, are typically insensitive to how value pluralism entails political pluralism according to Galston. And because, for Galston, moral costs are unavoidable, liberal pluralists should stick to using government to promote "basic decency"—namely, guaranteeing universal human rights and basic needs (Galston 2005: 3). Galston refers to the requirements of "basic decency" as "minimal universalism," which suggests that he thinks that satisfying basic moral requirements is not necessarily morally costly. His "minimal universalism" also evokes Karl Popper's insistence that liberal governments concentrate on the negatively utilitarian goal of minimizing life's worst evils (see Popper 1989: 337).

Now Galston's value pluralism is intriguing for the way in which it *explicitly* invokes Rossian intuitionism:

> Nonetheless, because critics have raised questions about the relationship between
> positions I espouse and some central questions of modern moral philosophy, it may

clarify matters to state that value pluralism as I understand it commits me to what Brad Hooker labels "Rossian generalism" and John Rawls calls "intuitionism" rather than to the full-blown thesis of moral particularism. There are certain considerations whose moral valence is invariant—that always count as reasons for or against a course of action—but there are no fully general rules for weighting or rank-ordering the multiple considerations that bear on the choice-worthiness of that option. My position is Rossian in the additional sense that some considerations establish strong presumptions in favor of particular choices (Ross calls them *prima facie* duties). (Galston 2005: 7)

Galston's liberalism thus highlights how pluralism and intuitionism are mutually reinforcing. Neither tends to suffer as much from the "absolutist-expectations" afflicting value-centered and contract-centered liberalism.

George Crowder and Joseph Raz have combined liberal pluralism with strong perfectionism, which Berlin surely would have found unacceptable. For Crowder, value pluralism implies perfectionism because, "on the pluralist view, there are many legitimate conceptions of the good" and the "best of these have liberal components, namely the virtues required for pluralist choice." In short, pluralism "commends the promotion of liberal . . . ways of life." Hence, liberal states may actively promote liberal forms of good "not just domestically but globally" (Crowder 2002: 470–1).

Raz has championed liberal perfectionism most doggedly. Raz privileges autonomy understood as giving shape to one's life. However, the ways in which we can shape our lives are multiple and often incommensurable, entailing pluralism. For Raz, then, it is not so much that pluralism entails perfectionism as with Crowder, but that perfectionism entails pluralism. In any case, like Crowder, Raz argues that governments should encourage citizens to make themselves better and virtuous by providing them with wide-ranging opportunities, though governments must avoid trying to *make* citizens morally better and virtuous. Perfectionist "goals need not be pursued by the use of coercion." That is, a "government that subsidizes certain activities, rewards their pursuit, and advertises their availability encourages those activities without using coercion" (Raz 1986: 417).

Raz's perfectionist liberal pluralism, like so many other contemporary versions of liberal egalitarianism, replays the new liberalism especially for the way in which rights indirectly promote autonomy by equalizing opportunities meaningfully.[7] For Raz, as for new liberals, government cannot make citizens virtuous, but it should certainly provide them with genuine opportunities to make *themselves* virtuous. The former harms citizens while the latter empowers them. And for Raz, as for Green and Hobhouse in particular, living autonomously means, in part, "identify[ing]" with and remaining "loyal" to higher-order desires. Perhaps contemporary perfectionist

---

[7] For another sophisticated defense of perfectionist liberalism that retravels the new liberalism, see Hurka (1993). See also Wall (1998), which likewise argues that committing to autonomy is fully compatible with perfectionism. See also Weinstein (2007: ch. IV) for an extended discussion of Raz, Hurka, and the new liberals.

liberalism would seem to us much less out of step and idiosyncratic were we more familiar with Green at least.

Liberal pluralism abandons not just "absolutist expectations" but objectivism too with Richard Rorty. Much like Berlin and other value pluralists, he denies the existence of "algorithms for resolving moral dilemmas" we find most vexing. Those who think otherwise remain theologians and metaphysicians at heart (Rorty 1989b: xv). Rorty, then, agrees with Berlin that we need to forgo the "jigsaw puzzle approach to vocabularies, practices and values," which futilely tries to systematize them. But he further denies that values are objective, as Berlin stubbornly insists (Rorty 1989a: 45). Berlin, therefore, remains a metaphysician. For him, to reiterate, values are plural yet objective. For Rorty, they are neither. But being neither is no reason to give up on liberalism, leading Rorty to call himself a liberal "ironist." For Rorty, this means forsaking in particular the quest for a "transhistorical 'absolutely valid' set of concepts which would serve as 'philosophical foundations' of liberalism" (Rorty 1989a: 57). It means committing to liberalism, despite discarding Enlightenment rationalism.

Rorty views not only Dewey as a non-foundational liberal but Oakeshott and Rawls as well, though presumably he has in mind later Rawls. Rorty sees Habermas as a reluctant non-foundational liberal who wants to "updat[e]" and salvage Enlightenment rationalism with "communicative reason." But Habermas's "substitution of 'communicative reason' for 'subjective-centered reason'" is little more than a "misleading way of making the same point I have been urging: A liberal society is one that is content to call 'true' (or 'right' or 'just') whatever the outcome of undistorted communication happens to be, whatever view wins in a free and open encounter." Rorty's "residual difference" with Habermas "is that his universalism makes him substitute such convergence for ahistorical grounding, whereas my insistence on the contingency of language make me suspicious of the very ideas of 'universal validity' which such convergence is supposed to underwrite" (Rorty 1989a: 67).

Rorty, then, welcomes Judith Shklar's notion of a liberal as someone who condemns cruelty and the fear it causes as the worst forms of behavior (Rorty 1989b: xv).[8] And he appeals to Mill probably thinking of her as well: "J. S. Mill's suggestion that governments devote themselves to optimizing the balance between leaving people's private lives alone and preventing suffering seems to me pretty much the last word" (Rorty 1989a: 63).

But Rorty's non-foundational liberalism more than looks to Mill through the dystopic lens of Shklar. As we have seen with so many other contemporary liberals, it reiterates, mostly unawares, the new liberals too: "The social glue holding together

---

[8] For Seyla Benhabib, Shklar is an "antimetaphysical" liberal whose rejection of metaphysical theorizing derives from a distinctive "antifoundationalism." Rorty, then, not surprisingly summons her (see Benhabib 1996: 56). See also Shklar (1989: 31), where she says that liberalism "must restrict itself" to restraining "abusers of power in order to lift the burden of fear and favor" from citizens so that they can live their "lives in accordance with their own beliefs and preferences, as long as they do not prevent others from doing so as well."

the ideal liberal society . . . consists in little more than a consensus that the point of social organization is to let everybody have a chance at self-creation to the best of his or her abilities, and that that goal requires besides peace and wealth, the standard 'bourgeois freedoms'." Discussion in such an ideal society will focus on, among other things, "how to equalize opportunities for self-creation and then leave people alone to use, or neglect, their opportunities" (Rorty 1989c: 84–5). Rorty's non-foundational liberalism, then, replicates fundamental new liberal concerns effectively, making it non-foundational new liberalism. We should be less than surprised. Rorty, after all, was much influenced by John Dewey, who was, in turn, greatly influenced by Green. Alan Ryan has called Dewey a "midwestern T. H. Green" (see Ryan 1995: 12).

LIBERALISM, MULTICULTURALISM, AND COSMOPOLITANISM

Non-foundational versions of liberalism such as Rorty's and Miller's typically eschew cosmopolitanism. In Rorty's case, liberal solidarity is only possible with those we see "as 'one of us,' where 'us' means something smaller and more local than the human race" (Rorty 1989d: 191). Human solidarity with humanity as such is an impossible "philosopher's invention, an awkward attempt to secularize the idea of becoming one with God" (Rorty 1989d: 198). And, because solidarity with all of humanity is impossible, moral ambiguity between cultures is inevitable.

Similarly with Miller, "loyalty to the human race as a whole is meaningless." Loyalty means favoring members of some group or community. Contrary to cosmopolitans, nationality is not morally irrelevant. For Miller, nations are the "only possible form in which overall community can be realized in modern societies." Hence, national loyalty is the only feasible overall loyalty. And, if national loyalty is the only feasible comprehensive kind, then social justice is incompatible with cosmopolitanism because social justice requires comprehensive loyalty. Only national communities can achieve meaningful social justice. Only these communities can "satisfy socialist ideals" (see Miller 1992: 88, 93)

Will Kymlicka agrees with Rorty that liberals must see themselves as "local" members, as citizens of national groups smaller than the entire human race, if the values they favor, including especially equal respect for persons, can thrive. But, for Kymlicka, if equal respect requires equal citizenship rights, especially "equal access to a common 'field of opportunity,' then some minority cultures are endangered" (Kymlicka 1989: 152).[9] In other words, equal respect requires respect as members of cultural communities *and* as citizens. Membership in the former is no less crucial than membership in the latter. Minority rights are often no less essential than individual rights.

---

[9] See also Kymlicka (1995) for his attempt to reconcile minority rights with liberal equal opportunity.

Now Charles Taylor, Chandran Kukathas, and others have dismissed Kymlicka's multicultural citizenship as theoretically misconceived and unworkable. On Taylor's account, many cultural groups want to be recognized not for the sameness with non-members but for their difference. Liberalism cannot be fully accommodated with multiculturalism much less with cosmopolitanism. The more we opt for liberalism, the less we can indulge in multiculturalism (see Taylor 1994). Kukathas deems multi-culturalism's incompatibility with liberalism as unproblematic because committing to liberalism permits tolerating illiberal subcultures as long as their members can exit them freely (Kukathas 2003). Even Barry, despite his sustained and much harsher criticism that multiculturalism is incompatible with liberalism, makes opting out a condition for allowing groups to engage in illiberal practices (see Barry 2001). Susan Okin, though, demurs, because opting out is often not realistic for many women (Okin 1999).

Liberalism nevertheless entails cosmopolitanism for many. Martha Nussbaum has recently defended robust liberal cosmopolitanism. For her, nationality is just as "mor-ally irrelevant" as ethnicity, class, and gender, making humans everywhere our "first allegiance." Cosmopolitans may favor local spheres of concern, such as nation and family, but only insofar as favoring them is "justifiable in universalistic terms" (Nuss-baum 1996a: 13). That is, the "primary reason a cosmopolitan should" indulge local allegiances is not because the "local is better per se, but rather that this is the only sensible way to do good" (Nussbaum 1996b: 135–6). However, this reason for indulg-ing local attachments generates what Samuel Scheffler calls "Nussbaum's dilemma": "Either we must argue that devoting special attention to the people we are attached to is an effective way of doing good for humanity at large, or we must suppose that those people are simply worth more than others." That is, we must either attach purely instrumental value to our personal relationships, which is "pathological," or we must "deny the equal worth of persons" (Scheffler 2001b: 118, 121). For Scheffler, then, cosmopolitans must accept "some sorts of 'agent-centered restrictions'" (see Scheffler 2001a: 110). But conceding that these restrictions "are seen as presumptively decisive is not to say that they can never . . . be outweighed by other [cosmopolitan] consider-ations" (Scheffler 2001b: 121). Of course, the ambiguity of determining when cosmo-politan considerations override these restrictions is where Scheffler's moderate cosmopolitanism "comes up short," just like where Brad Hooker confesses moderated rule consequentialism does (Hooker 2000: 136). And it is just where Nussbaum's robust cosmopolitanism also "comes up short," since she says that coercive humani-tarian intervention against cultures practicing gender inequality should be avoided *unless* "genocide, mass rape and torture" are at stake (Nussbaum 2004: 165). But how bad do these evils have to be for cosmopolitan "considerations" to kick in overriding considerations of national sovereignty? Liberalizing cosmopolitanism is much like trying to liberalize consequentialism.

Peter Singer defends cosmopolitanism just as fearlessly as Nussbaum but on utilitar-ian grounds. He famously argues that international social justice is both feasible and demanding. Singer insists that, if "it is in our power to prevent something bad from happening without thereby sacrificing anything of *comparable* moral importance, we ought, morally, to do it" (emphasis added). Hence, it follows that "we ought, morally, to be working full time to relieve great suffering of the sort that occurs as a result of famine or other disasters" (Singer 2000*a*: 107, 113; see also Singer 2000*b*). Our cosmopolitan obligations, then, require that we in the first world sacrifice drastically to improve the great suffering of billions of others. At the very least, we at least "should prevent bad occurrences unless, to do so, we had to sacrifice something morally *significant*" (emphasis added), which would require us to forgo our lavish ways but less drastically (Singer 2000*a*: 115). Though strict morality requires reducing ourselves to levels of marginal utility, we could still go far in making the world a much better place short of causing something "significantly bad to happen" to us. We can still do enormous good without going all the way in sacrificing to the limit of "comparable" importance.

For Neo-Kantian cosmopolitans, like Onora O'Neill, international justice requires that we simply do our best to "secure at least minimal entitlements to the necessities of life for all." We should, therefore, protect poor states from damaging, exploitative transactions by regulating and policing international markets more effectively (O'Neill 2000: 140–1). Charles Beitz thinks more is required. Beitz trades on Rawls, arguing that state representatives negotiating behind a veil of ignorance would choose and enforce a global difference principle aimed at alleviating the plight of the poorest states (see Beitz 1979). Rawls, of course, balked at deploying the difference principle internationally, calling Beitz's approach "cosmopolitan" in contrast to his own (Rawls 1999*a*: ch. 16).

Cosmopolitanism is just more of the liberalism of "absolutist expectations." Like some versions of the latter, it tries to square the impersonal standpoint for universal impartiality with the personal standpoint. We ought not to ignore Thomas Nagel's conclusion that "the problem of designing institutions that do justice to the equal importance of all persons, without making unacceptable demands on individuals, has not been solved—and that this is partly so because for our world the problem of the right relation between the personal and impersonal standpoints within each individual has not been solved" (Nagel 1997: 251). Nagel's problem, then, is no less than Sidgwick's dualism of practical reasoning. And it is Rorty's confession that our lives are torn between public and private sides: "The existence of these two sides . . . generates dilemmas. Such dilemmas we shall always have with us, but they are never going to be resolved by appeal to some further, higher set of obligations which a philosophical tribunal might discover and apply" (Rorty 1989*d*: 197).

CONCLUSION

I have tried to write this chapter as something of a companion piece to my earlier "English Political Theory in the Nineteenth and Twentieth Centuries." That essay told a story of nineteenth- and twentieth-century political theory in England. This essay both expands that narrative to nineteenth- and twentieth *English-speaking* political thought and confines it to *liberal* political thought. It also narrates this story differently. In my earlier essay, I identified several substantive strands of English political theorizing, focusing primarily on liberal utilitarianism, liberal egalitarianism, socialism, and feminism. I concentrated on the first two especially and described the evolution of each chronologically. I also argued that American political *theorists* in particular have undervalued liberal utilitarianism's salience in the liberal tradition, which is due in part, I argued, to the declining role that the history of political thought has played in contemporary American political theory compared to its English counterpart.

I continue to hold this view more strongly than ever, but I now also believe that American political theorizing's comparative disinterest in moral philosophy has contributed to marginalizing liberal utilitarianism. I also believe that this same disinterest is responsible for why American political theory has always been indifferent to the new liberals, Dewey's early appreciation of Green aside. Utilitarians, past and present, and new liberals have always seen themselves as doing moral philosophy as much as political theory. This essay tries to recapture these dual concerns by narrating the liberal tradition in the twentieth century especially, as well as the nineteenth century, by paying greater attention to moral theory. How regrettable and ironic that Rawlsian liberals have abandoned so much moral philosophizing when Rawls never did. We at least should read Mill's *Utilitarianism* with the same reverence that we read his *On Liberty*. Mill was a utilitarian first and foremost. We would do equally well to read Sidgwick's incomparable *Methods of Ethics* no less reverently. And we ought to take up just as diligently the new liberals, too, including especially Green's *Prolegomena to Ethics*.

Whereas my earlier narrative was traditionally thematic and chronological, this newer effort instead combines Fishkin's claim that we live in a philosophical culture of "absolutist expectations," with Pettit's distinction between "value-centered" versus "contract-centered" liberal theorizing to create a template for narrating the history of liberal political thought. Other templates exist and might be equally fruitful. We can use them to draw different, overlapping pictures of the liberal tradition. We can narrate it this way or that. But it seems to me particularly useful, or "fertile" in Popper's sense, to recount this tradition in the nineteenth and twentieth centuries as primarily a "value-centered" absolutist quest that gave way in the 1950s to less ambitious "contract-centered" excursions. Many quickly found these wanting in turn, leading them to retreat to the even more modest and yet more entangling snarls of value pluralistic liberalism.

Writing just another history of liberal political thought in the nineteenth and twentieth centuries is, to repeat, often all too easy. But, thankfully and notwithstanding the result, that has hardly been the case here.

REFERENCES

BARRY, B. (1998). "Something in the Disputation not Unpleasant," in P. Kelly (ed.), *Impartiality, Neutrality and Justice*. Edinburgh: Edinburgh University Press, 186–257.

BARRY, B. (2001). *Culture and Equality*. Cambridge: Polity.

BEITZ, C. (1979). *Political Theory and International Relations*. Princeton: Princeton University Press.

BENHABIB, S. (1996). "Judith Shklar's Dystopic Liberalism," in B. Yack (ed.), *Liberalism without Illusions*. Chicago: University of Chicago Press, 55–63.

BERLIN, I. (1937). "Utilitarianism," Isaiah Berlin Virtual Library, Isaiah Berlin Literary Trust, Wolfson College, Oxford, http://berlin.wolf.ox.ac.uk

BERLIN, I. (2000). *The Power of Ideas*. Princeton: Princeton University Press.

BOSANQUET, B. (2001). *The Philosophical Theory of the State* [1899]. South Bend, IN: St Augustine's.

BRADLEY, F. H. (1927). *Ethical Studies*. Oxford: Oxford University Press.

CROWDER, G. (2002). "Two Value-Pluralist Arguments for Liberalism," *Australian Journal of Political Science*, 37: 457–73.

DWORKIN, R. (2000a). "Equality—An Exchange," *Times Literary Supplement*, 1 Dec.: 15–16.

DWORKIN, R. (2000b). *Sovereign Virtue*. Cambridge, MA: Harvard University Press.

FISHKIN, J. F. (1997). "Liberty versus Equal Opportunity," in L. P. Pojman and R. Westmoreland (eds), *Equality*. Oxford: Oxford University Press, 148–58.

FRANKFURT, H. (1997). "Equality as a Moral Ideal," in L. P. Pojman and R. Westmoreland (eds), *Equality*. Oxford: Oxford University Press, 261–73.

GALSTON, W. A. (2005). *The Practice of Liberal Pluralism*. Cambridge: Cambridge University Press).

GAUTHIER, D. (1986). *Morals by Agreement*. Oxford: Oxford University Press.

GRAY, J. (1983). *Mill On Liberty: A Defence*. London: Routledge.

GRAY, J. (1989). "Mill's and Other Liberalism's," in J. Gray (ed.), *Liberalisms: Essays in Political Philosophy*. London: Routledge, 217–38.

GREEN, T. H. (1997a). "Lecture on 'Liberal Legislation and Freedom of Contract'," in Peter P. Nicholson (ed.), *Collected Works of T. H. Green* [1881]. Bristol: Thoemmes Press, iii.

GREEN, T. H. (1997b). *Lectures on the Principles of Political Obligation*, in Peter P. Nicholson (ed.), *Collected Works of T. H. Green* [1886]. Bristol: Thoemmes Press), ii.

HARE, R. M. (1997). "Justice and Equality," in L. P. Pojman and R. Westermoreland (eds), *Equality*. Oxford: Oxford University Press, 218–28.

HOBHOUSE, L. T. (1949). *The Elements of Social Justice* [1922]. London: Allen and Unwin.

HOOKER, B. (2000). *Ideal Code, Real World*. Oxford: Oxford University Press.

HURKA, T. (1993). *Perfectionism*. Oxford: Oxford University Press.

JAHANBEGLOO, R. (1992) (ed.). *Conversations with Isaiah Berlin*. London: Phoenix Press.

KELLY, J. P. (1990). *Utilitarianism and Distributive Justice*. Oxford: Oxford University Press.

KUKATHAS, C. (2003). *The Liberal Archipelago: A Theory of Diversity and Freedom*. Oxford: Oxford University Press.

KYMLICKA, W. (1989). *Liberalism, Community and Culture*. Oxford: Oxford University Press.

KYMLICKA, W. (1995). *Multicultural Citizenship*. Oxford: Oxford University Press.

LARMORE, C. (1990). "Political Liberalism," *Political Theory*, 18: 339–60.

LYONS, D. (1982). "Utility and Rights," in J. W. Chapman and J. R. Pennock (eds), *Ethics, Economics and the Law*. NewYork: New York University Press, 107–38.

Miller, D. (1992). "Community and Citizenship," in S. Avineri and A. DeShalit (eds), *Communitarianism and Individualism*. Oxford: Oxford University Press, 85–100.

Miller, D. (1995). "Complex Equality," in D. Miller and M. Walzer (eds), *Pluralism, Justice and Equality*. Oxford: Oxford University Press, 197–225.

Miller, D. (1999). *Principles of Social Justice*. Cambridge, MA: Harvard University Press.

Nagel, T. (1997). "Equality and Partiality," in L. P. Pojman and R. Westermoreland (eds), *Equality*. Oxford: Oxford University Press, 250–61.

Nussbaum, M. (1996a). "Patriotism and Cosmopolitanism," in M. Nussbaum (ed.), *For Love of Country?* Boston: Beacon, 3–17.

Nussbaum, M. (1996b). "Reply," in M. Nussbaum (ed.), *For Love of Country?* Boston: Beacon, 132–44.

Nussbaum, M. (2004). "Women and Theories of Global Justice," in D. K. Chatterjee (ed.), *The Ethics of Assistance*. Cambridge: Cambridge University Press, 147–76.

Okin, S. (1989). *Justice, Gender and the Family*. New York: Harper Collins.

Okin, S. (1999). "Is Multiculturalism Bad For Women?" in J. Cohen, M. Howard, and M. Nussbaum (eds), *is Multiculturalism Bad For Women?* Princetown: Princetown University Press, 7–26.

O'Neill, O. (2000). "Transnational Economic Justice," in O. O'Neill, *Bounds of Justice*. Cambridge: Cambridge University Press, 115–42.

Pettit, P. (1996). *The Common Mind*. Oxford: Oxford University Press.

Popper, K. (1989). "Prediction and Prophecy in the Social Sciences," in K. Popper, *Conjectures and Refutations*. London: Routledge, 33–65.

Rawls, J. (1955). "Two Concepts of Rules," in J. Rawls, *Collected Papers*, (ed.) S. Freeman. Cambridge, MA: Harvard University Press, 20–46.

Rawls, J. (1999a). *The Law of Peoples*. Cambridge, MA: Harvard University Press.

Rawls, J. (1999b). *A Theory of Justice*. Cambridge, MA: Harvard University Press.

Raz, J. (1986). *The Morality of Freedom*. Oxford: Oxford University Press.

Riley, J. (1988). *Liberal Utilitarianism*. Cambridge: Cambridge University Press.

Rorty, R. (1989a). "The Contingency of a Liberal Community," in R. Rorty, *Contingency, Irony and Solidarity*. Cambridge: Cambridge University Press, 44–69.

Rorty, R. (1989b). "Introduction," in R. Rorty, *Contingency, Irony and Solidarity*. Cambridge: Cambridge University Press, pp. xiii–xvi.

Rorty, R. (1989c). "Private Irony and Liberal Hope," in R. Rorty, *Contingency, Irony and Solidarity*. Cambridge: Cambridge University Press, 73–95.

Rorty, R. (1989d). "Solidarity," in R. Rorty, *Contingency, Irony and Solidarity*. Cambridge: Cambridge University Press, 189–98.

Rosen, F. (1990). "The Origin of Liberal Utilitarianism," in R. Bellamy (ed.), *Victorian Liberalism*. London: Routledge, 58–70.

Ryan, A. (1995). *John Dewey*. New York: W. W. Norton.

Scheffler, S. (2001a). "Relationships and Responsibilities," in S. Scheffler, *Boundaries and Allegiances*. Oxford: Oxford University Press, 97–110.

Scheffler, S. (2001b). "Conceptions of Cosmopolitanism," in S. Scheffler, *Boundaries and Allegiances*. Oxford: Oxford University Press, 111–30.

Sen, A. (1982). "Rights and Agency," in *Philosophy of Public Affairs*, 76: 3–39.

Sen, A. (1999). *Development as Freedom*. New York: Anchor Books.

Sen, A. (2000). "Consequentialist Evaluation and Practical Reason," *Journal of Philosophy*, 9: 477–502.

SEN, A. (2001). "Reply," *Economics and Philosophy*, 17: 51–66.

SHKLAR, J. (1989). "The Liberalism of Fear," in N. Rosenblum (ed.), *Liberalism and the Moral Life*. Cambridge, MA: Harvard University Press, 21–38.

SIDGWICK, H. (1981). *The Methods of Ethics* [1907]. Indianapolis: Hackett.

SIMHONY, A. (1995). "Was T. H. Green a Utilitarian"? *Utilitas*, 7: 121–44.

SIMHONY, A., and Weinstein, D. (2001) (eds). *The New Liberalism*. Cambridge: Cambridge University Press.

SINGER, P. (2000a). "Famine, Affluence, and Morality," in P. Singer, *Writings on an Ethical Life*. New York: Ecco Press, 105–17.

SINGER, P. (2000b). "The Singer Solution to World Poverty," in P. Singer, *Writings on an Ethical Life*. New York: Ecco Press, 118–24.

TAYLOR, C. (1994). "The Politics of Recognition," in A. Gutmann (ed.), *Multiculturalism: Examining the Politics of Recognition*. Princeton: Princeton University Press, 25–74.

WALL, S. (1998). *Liberalism, Perfectionism and Restraint*. Cambridge: Cambridge University Press.

WEINSTEIN, D. (2004). "English Political Theory in the Nineteenth and Twentieth Centuries," in G. F. Gaus and C. Kukathas (eds), *Handbook of Political Theory* Sage. London: Publications, 410–26.

WEINSTEIN, D. (2007). *Utilitarianism and the New Liberalism*. Cambridge: Cambridge University Press.

WILLIAMS, B. (1980). "Political Philosophy and the Analytical Tradition," in M. Richter (ed.), *Political Theory and Political Education*. Princeton: Princeton University Press, 57–75.

YOUNG, I. M. (1990). *Justice and the Politics of Difference*. Princeton: Princeton University Press.

....

CHAPTER 25

POLITICAL PHILOSOPHY AND THE IDEA OF A SOCIAL SCIENCE

....

PETER LASSMAN

THE idea of a 'social science' or of a 'the moral and political science' seems to have first come into use in France from around the 1760s. It appears that the first recognizably modern understanding of the term 'social science' was developed during the French Revolution (Wokler 1998: 35–76). From its origins the search for a science of politics modelled upon the perceived success of the natural sciences has been shaped at least as much by political objectives as by pure intellectual curiosity. From their first appearance, the concepts of a social science or of moral or political science were used interchangeably. It was generally understood that, despite important differences of emphasis between its various proponents, the point of such a science would be to provide an intellectual grounding for the 'art of government'. In the aftermath of the French Revolution social science would provide the principles for an alternative to what was felt to be the superficial attempts made so far by legislators and statesmen to effect social and political reform.

There can be no doubt that the emergence of the social sciences has had a transformative effect upon the language and style of modern political philosophy. Modern political philosophers generally express themselves and reflect upon the limits of their theories in ways that have been profoundly influenced by the theory and practice of the social sciences. The problem is to discern precisely what that effect has been. For example, there is a highly influential argument that sees the advent of social science as an attempt to undermine or replace the practice of political philosophy as it had generally been understood. The worry is that a genuine science of society would leave no room for the freedom of political conduct and judgement that characterizes an understanding of the practice of politics that is generally valued by political agents and political philosophers. That the intention to create a social science was in the first place often guided by political motives and is best understood in the context of political argument makes the question even more complex. Furthermore, if a social science were possible, then it would appear that politics in its normal sense would become unnecessary. The implication is that political questions would be thought of as administrative problems that could be solved under the guidance of scientific expertise. In addition, if we consider that pervasive argument and disagreement about public affairs are constitutive of political life, then it would seem that the existence of politics in this sense stands as an insuperable barrier against what might otherwise be considered to be the commendable idea of constructing a social science. On the other hand, it is probably an anachronistic error to see the contrast between social scientists and political philosophers in such stark terms. As projects for a social science from Auguste Comte to Karl Popper have been inseparably bound up with political ideals, it could be argued that the language of social science from the mid-nineteenth to the mid-twentieth century was often, in reality, a form of political philosophy carried on by other means.

From its origins in ancient Greece, political philosophy has sought the foundations of political order. Political philosophers have often looked for a way of supporting their arguments that rises above the immediate concerns of partisan politics. In the modern context it has been impossible for political philosophers to ignore the claims that have been made on behalf of scientific knowledge as the only respectable ground for doing so. In addition there has also been a persistent belief that, if we are unable to provide our sciences with a firm foundation, then we will not be able to provide one for our politics either. A clear example is provided by Hobbes when he argued that if

> the moral Philosophers had done their job with equal success, I do not know what greater contribution human industry could have made to human happiness. For if the patterns of human action were known with the same certainty as the relations of magnitude in figures, ambition and greed, whose power rests on the false opinions of the common people about right and wrong [*jus et iniura*], would be disarmed, and the human race enjoy such secure peace that (apart from conflicts over space as the population grew) it seems unlikely that it would ever have to fight again. (Hobbes 1998: 5)

Of course, the idea of a political science has a long history. Various figures such as Aristotle, Hobbes, Machiavelli, and Hume are often mentioned in this respect. This is a plausible view if all that is meant by this is that knowledge of politics, both philosophical and prudential, ought to be put on a more systematic footing than was usually to be expected. However, at least from the late eighteenth century and certainly during the nineteenth century, the idea of a social and political science modelled in one way or another upon the successes of the natural sciences became firmly established.

One of the defining characteristics shared by most political thinkers during the nineteenth and early twentieth centuries was the unavoidability of reflection upon their work in terms of its relationship, or lack of one, with the claims made on behalf of the new forms of social and political science. As the idea and nature of a social or political science became a common topic of debate, the absence of agreement about the form, character, and purpose that a political science ought to possess became readily apparent. According to John Stuart Mill, for example, all 'speculations concerning forms of government bear the impress, more or less exclusive, of two conflicting theories respecting political institutions; or, to speak more properly, conflicting conceptions of what political institutions are'. Political institutions, Mill argued, according to one view are conceived 'as wholly an affair of invention and contrivance'. As political institutions are 'made by man, it is assumed that man has the choice either to make them or not, and how or on what pattern they shall be made. Government, according to this conception, is a problem, to be worked like any other question of business.' In addition, those who adopt this view of political philosophy 'look upon a constitution in the same light . . . as they would upon a steam plough, or a threshing machine'.

There is another kind of political philosopher, in Mill's view, who, instead of holding to this mechanical image of politics and society, regards 'it as a sort of spontaneous product, and the science of government as a branch (so to speak) of natural history'. According to this view, political institutions cannot be chosen and designed. The political institutions of a society are regarded as 'a sort of organic growth' from the life of that society. The political philosopher can attempt to understand the 'natural properties' of those institutions, and he must take them as he finds them. These two doctrines represent a 'deep-seated difference between two modes of thought'. Neither is completely false, but it would be a mistake to rely exclusively upon one of them at the expense of the other (Mill 1972: 188–90).

Questions concerning the nature of political science were uppermost in the minds of the leading political thinkers of the modern age. A clear and representative example is provided by James Bryce in his presidential address to a joint meeting of the American Political Science Association and to the American Historical Association held in 1909. Acknowledging that the term 'Political Science seems now generally accepted', Bryce, nevertheless, felt impelled to ask: 'What sort of science is it?' In answering his own question, Bryce was certain that political science could not be anything like an exact or physical science. Nor could political science be anything like a less exact science such as meteorology. Clearly the 'data of politics are the acts of men', and by 'calling Politics a Science we mean no more than this, that there is a constancy and uniformity in the tendencies of human nature which enable us to regard the acts of men at one time as due to the same causes which have governed their acts at previous times'. Perhaps more to the point was the question of the relationship of political science to the study of history. The basic subject matter of political science is 'the acts of men', and these are recorded in history. Political science, Bryce concluded, is no more a science than is history, 'because its certainty is no greater than the certainty of history' (Bryce 1909: 1–19).

Political science, in Bryce's formulation, 'stands midway between history and politics'. It draws its materials from history and applies them to politics. If political science exists, conceived in more or less naturalistic terms, we have to ask what purpose it serves. This question takes on a particularly pressing quality in a democracy. The point of political science must be that its findings and conclusions are made use of in the education of citizens and statesmen. In Bryce's account this gives rise to a basic tension within political science. Is it a science that discovers fundamental truths about the nature of politics or is it a discipline whose purpose is to produce knowledge that serves to promote progressive policies? Put another way, can a political science steer clear of political controversy? And, if it cannot, what kind of science is that?

It is an indication of the popularity of the idea of a social science that Bernard Bosanquet, in his 'The Philosophical Theory of the State' published in 1899, had no doubt that he had to address the problem of the 'probable permanence of the difference' between the aims of sociology, the name given to the new science of society, and those of social philosophy. Although he argues that it is possible to see several origins for the idea of a science of society, it is upon Auguste Comte whom Bosanquet confers the honour of having established a specifically modern version of this idea. The central claim of Comte's doctrine of positivism was that a new science of 'social physics' or 'sociology' was both possible and desirable. Its 'essence was the inclusion of human society among the objects of natural science; its watchwords were law and cause . . . and scientific prediction' (Bosanquet 2001: 58). The difference between Comte's version of sociology and the existing tradition of social philosophy was that the 'modern enquirer—the sociologist as such' who uses the language of physical science—looks for the laws and causes that determine collective human life. The essential difference between sociology and political philosophy is missed if we concentrate too much on what they superficially seem to have in common. Despite the fact that they both desire to comprehend the interdependence of all parts of the polis, Bosanquet pointed out that the central question of social or political philosophy was to ask 'what is the completest and most real life of the human soul?' (Bosanquet 2001: 59).

Modern idealist philosophy, to which Bosanquet was a notable contributor, had, since the work of Rousseau and Hegel, revived this ancient tradition of political enquiry. However, this revival was confronted by the existence of a flourishing tradition of research that had taken root especially in France and America, where it found a home in the new university departments of political science and sociology. In Bosanquet's view, the parallel existence of two independent streams of thought was one of the remarkable cultural phenomena of nineteenth-century culture. Despite his scepticism about most of the intellectual claims made on its behalf, it was clear to Bosanquet that philosophy could not afford to ignore the existence of the social sciences. The two traditions now existed side by side, and in his opinion they ought to be thought of as complementary in their contribution to our political understanding. Summarizing this conclusion, he affirmed that 'philosophy gives a significance to sociology; sociology vitalises philosophy' (Bosanquet 2001: 83).

There is a significant body of thought that disagrees with this diagnosis. Rather than observing their complementary existence, it sees the Western tradition of political philosophy that begins with Plato as undermined by and even coming to an end at the same time as the new social sciences emerge. Accounts of the simultaneous rise of social science and the decline of political philosophy have been influential and popular.

This is especially so for those political philosophers working in the mid-twentieth century who felt themselves to be on the list of endangered species. The story as told, for example, by Hannah Arendt has been responsible for much of the way in which the distinction between political philosophy and social science is understood in these terms. The appeal of this particular view of the predicament of political philosophy often rests upon the way in which it is bound up with a theory of cultural decline that focuses upon 'the loss of the political' in the modern world. For Arendt, 'the unconscious substitution of the social for the political betrays the extent to which the original Greek understanding of politics has been lost' (Arendt 1958: 23). Similarly, Sheldon Wolin made it clear that the basic point of his survey of Western political thought was to counter the 'marked hostility' and 'even contempt' for political philosophy that had become de rigueur among the new breed of political scientists (Wolin 2004: p. xxiii). Although influenced by Arendt, the diagnosis advanced by Wolin had a different emphasis. For Wolin it was not simply 'the animus against politics and the political that is characteristic of our time'. Instead, the emergence of the modern social sciences was, in part, a symptom of something much deeper. Certainly for Wolin 'modern social science appears plausible and useful for the same reason that modern political philosophy appears anachronistic and sterile: each is symptomatic of a condition where the sense of the political has been lost' (Wolin 2004: 259). However, the trouble with the new social and political sciences is that they find politics in too many places. This 'sublimation of the political' has the counter-intuitive effect of seeing politics in areas of social life that have previously been thought of as being outside the political domain. If we see politics in too many places, we lose sight of the specific character of 'the political'. If we cease to appreciate the nature and value of politics as an autonomous domain, then it is not too surprising to find that it can be subsumed under a general concept of 'society'—that is, in turn, amenable to scientific investigation (Wolin 2004: 315–89) .

Although these general observations do indicate some fundamental conceptual shifts in the history of political thought, it is also important not to be too carried away by overdramatic accounts of the death of political philosophy at the hands of social science. Historians of political thought are often keen to point to the danger of being misled by the presuppositions of a 'teleological and anachronistic' disciplinary history (Collini, Winch and Burrow 1983: 10–11). On close inspection it appears that histories of this kind are prone to present a misleadingly simple picture of the 'discovery of essentially self-regulating or historicist models of "economy" and "society"' that undercut the idea of an autonomous political realm. As an antidote to this 'epic' way of writing the history of political philosophy it has been pointed out, for example, that in nineteenth-century Britain many of the political thinkers who are portrayed in such backward looking disciplinary histories as feeling threatened by the emergence of social science were, in fact, more likely to think of themselves as building on the foundations for a genuine political science that had been laid by their predecessors in the eighteenth century. Figures such as Montesquieu and Condorcet, as well as the cast of Scottish moral philosophers and historians that includes Adam Smith, David Hume, Adam

Ferguson, and John Millar among their number were all interested in producing a more scientific account of politics. Nevertheless, as a mild counter to these claims it still must be admitted that all attempts to construct a systematic study of 'things political' during the nineteenth and twentieth century still had to confront the emerging 'cultural hegemony of the philosophy of history' and 'the science of society' (Collini, Winch, and Burrow 1983: 11).

Such broad generalizations must also be tempered with a recognition of the distinct national differences that existed in the ways in which political philosophy and the social sciences developed and responded to each other. For example, in the nineteenth and early twentieth centuries it is mainly in Britain and France that the social sciences sought to establish themselves as academic disciplines by self-consciously modelling themselves on the natural sciences, or, more accurately, on a particular understanding of the natural sciences. In Germany the story is more complicated. Here the idea of a natural science of society found it very hard to establish itself against very powerful intellectual and political opposition. Nevertheless, this is not to say that the idea of a social science had no influence on political thinking. For example, it would be foolish to ignore the way in which the dream of a social science grew increasingly influential in Germany when transmitted through the spread of Marxian and Darwinian theory. At the same time, national traditions in political philosophy ought not to be thought of as closed systems. Ideas have never been constrained by national boundaries.

Although the spectre of science has come to haunt political thought throughout the modern period, it has to be recognized that conceptions of science have themselves been open to considerable dispute. There are several strands in the philosophy of science and most have, in varying degrees, influenced political theorists. The major and most influential philosophy of science was, and to a large extent still is, positivism in its various formulations. The origins of this philosophy are associated primarily with Comte and, in England with some qualification, John Stuart Mill. In essence, the central idea of positivism is the unity of method between the sciences, both natural and human. However, this unity takes the natural sciences as the ideal form against which all other versions of scientific endeavour are to be evaluated. Scientific explanation must, according to this account, be causal explanation understood in terms of the subsumption of individual cases under general laws. As far as the plan for a science of man is concerned, the basic difficulty is that positivism in all its varieties cannot accept, or at least has great difficulty in accepting, explanations couched in terms of human intentions, motives, or purposes. Of course, the idea of constructing a natural science of society met with opposition as soon as it was first propounded. Opposition to a science of society based on naturalistic principles existed in all European societies, but the debate was most marked in Germany. Here the distinction between the competing goals of naturalistic explanation and interpretative understanding became a central topic for all discussions of the appropriate methods for the study of politics and society.

The clearly stated political aim of Comte's positive science was the moral and political renewal of European society. As with all attempts to create a science of society, it is the perceived contrast between the advanced state of our understanding of nature and our primitive understanding of man as a social and political being that is considered to be the major drawback to progress. As far as Comte was concerned, the profound economic and social transformation of European society signified a new era in which the new positive sciences would replace metaphysics as the foundation for our understanding of the world. This, in turn, would make it possible for the new breed of scientists to apply their knowledge of sociological laws that would enable them to explain, predict, and control the forces that create change and order in society.

In reality, the only law that Comte could claim to have discovered was 'the law of the three stages'. Of course, this is not a scientific law in the strict sense but is more of a generalized description of the supposed progress of the human race. The progression from the theological and metaphysical stages of social development culminates, perhaps unsurprisingly, with Comte's own positive system. Of course, the idea of humanity progressing through three stages was not new even when Comte proposed it. Turgot, Quesnay, Condorcet, and Saint-Simon had all advanced similar ideas. The significant point, however, is that Comte's whole system was aimed at providing a supposedly scientific basis for social and political reform. As John Stuart Mill pointed out, this idea of inevitable progressive development provided Comte with the ammunition to dismiss all the contending political doctrines of the time. He was able to deride all those with whom he disagreed on the grounds of their theories being hopelessly 'metaphysical' (Mill 1961: 73).

John Stuart Mill was an enthusiastic supporter of the Comtean claim to have set 'the moral sciences' on the right path. Mill, however, was also an important representative of another stream of scientific thought. If Comte and, possibly, Marx belong to an 'organic-evolutionary' tradition characterized by a holistic view of society that is explained in functional and historicist terms then Mill can be regarded as offering an alternative. Mill belongs to a more analytical tradition that is individualistic in its methods and seeks to be rigorously deductive. It does not offer a view of societies as organic wholes governed by their own laws of development. According to the Millian view of social science, 'the laws of the phenomena of society are, and can be, nothing but the laws of the actions and passions of human beings united together in the social state' (Mill 1961: 59). These two competing ideas still dominate our conceptions of the nature of social science (Skorupski 1989: 276).

Bosanquet's view of peaceful coexistence between social science and political philosophy turned out to be too sanguine. Writing half a century later in a now much quoted statement, Peter Laslett claimed that, 'for the moment, anyway, political philosophy is dead' (Laslett 1956: p. vii). Laslett observed that the 300-year-old tradition of philosophical writing in English on politics from Hobbes to Bosanquet seemed to be at an end. Laslett offered the thought that one reason for this might be that the sheer horror of political events in the twentieth century had made politics too serious to be left to philosophers. This, he admitted, tends to contradict the idea that it is often the perception of crisis that provides the reason why 'the great thinkers of the past addressed themselves to political philosophy'. However, if political philosophy is 'for the moment' dead, the question of responsibility remains.

Political philosophy, Laslett argued, had been killed off by two related developments. Sociology, especially in its Marxist form, and analytical philosophy, especially under the influence of logical positivism, had both made political philosophy seem, at best, an outmoded and, at worst, nonsensical enterprise. Of course, when Laslett made his controversial claim, he was aware of the work of many political thinkers who stand as a counter to the extreme claim of the death of political philosophy. He mentions H. L. A. Hart, Karl Popper, and Michael Oakeshott and could have continued with, for example, Hannah Arendt, Isaiah Berlin, Leo Strauss, John Plamenatz, and Friedrich von Hayek. Nevertheless, it is undeniable that none of them produced or attempted to produce a philosophical work that could, for example, be recognized as a twentieth-century equivalent of Hobbes's *Leviathan*. We ought not, however, to assume that the achievements of political science were universally recognized. Many would agree with the claim that 'what is called political science . . . is a device, invented by university teachers, for avoiding the dangerous subject politics, without achieving science' (Cobban 1953: 335). Nevertheless, there is a grain of truth in Laslett's claim about the death of political philosophy. Political philosophers had since at least the end of the eighteenth century and certainly throughout the nineteenth and twentieth centuries found themselves faced with the prospect of coming to terms with the implications not only of the idea but also of the practice of social science. Of course, the very idea of a social science could be dismissed out of hand on philosophical grounds (Winch 1958; Oakeshott 1991: 5–42).

A more moderate and typical response to the claims of the social sciences that is indicative of the way in which the intellectual environment of political philosophy has been altered can be illustrated by the example of John Rawls. A marked feature of his *A Theory of Justice*, the book that is most often mentioned as heralding the rebirth of political philosophy in the twentieth century, and of his later work is the use of the theories and concepts of modern social science and, in particular, of economics and 'common sense political sociology' (Rawls 1999, 2001). It now appears that modern political philosophy cannot proceed in either ignorance or denial of the contributions to our understanding made by the theories and findings of social and political scientists. It can be objected that there is nothing radically new here. Clearly most of the important political philosophers who make up the traditional canon were deeply interested and involved in the intellectual and scientific debates of their time. Although this is undeniably true, what is new is the emergence of a distinct idea of science that has become attached to our investigation of the social world. This, in turn, is linked to academic specialization in universities and the continuing dispute and uncertainty about the precise nature of the relationship between political science and political philosophy. Thus, for example, in a typical expression of this state of affairs George Catlin could remark that 'politics, like Gaul, is divided into three parts. From the *practice* of politics at least in theory, we distinguish the *theory*. But the theory itself is divided into political science and political philosophy' (Catlin 1957: 2). The problem was and remains how the three parts are to be related to each other (Stears 2005: 325–50).

Laslett's remarks about the death of political philosophy were also oddly anachronistic. They appear to presume the existence of a set of distinct practices in the past called 'political philosophy' and 'political or social science'. The aim of constructing a political or social science in fact took many forms, and it was, of course, driven as much by political as by philosophical arguments. Nevertheless, it is not an exaggeration to say that political thinking during the nineteenth and twentieth centuries was influenced by the decisive new intellectual development of a strong belief in the unity of science. According to this view, a true social science is both possible and necessary. It is hard to find any major political thinker during this period who was not touched, either positively or negatively, by this development. Of course, it must not be forgotten that the desire to create a social or political science that would inform, modify, or even replace what was felt to be an older and outmoded tradition of political philosophy was itself often driven by political concerns.

There are two other factors that give the modern development of social science and political philosophy their peculiar character. The first is that positivism in its various forms was the dominant philosophy of science until at least the middle of the twentieth century. All other philosophies of science were, to a large degree, defined in terms of their opposition to positivism. Of course, it is possible to point to earlier appeals to the authority of science made by political philosophers. However, what is distinctive in the modern period is the dominance of one particular idea or set of ideas of a social science and its subject matter. This development can be considered to be at least as important as the emergence of the distinct political ideologies that pervade, if not modern politics, then at least most modern textbooks of political science. Modern political thought and social and political science still exists in the shadow of the ideas of science most associated with positivism.

Philosophers and political thinkers as diverse as Auguste Comte, Karl Marx, Emile Durkheim, Herbert Spencer, and J. S. Mill were all agreed that 'the study of society could be advanced if its practitioners succeeded in assimilating the spirit and general methods employed in the more "exact" sciences. By means of observation, classification of data, and testing, social phenomena could be made to yield "laws" predicting the future course of events' (Wolin 2004: 320). This idea of a social science was influential and popular with political thinkers across the ideological spectrum. Nevertheless, although the idea of a social science permeated the intellectual landscape, it found it very difficult to find a secure place in the academic world. It ought not to be forgotten that in Europe sociology, the 'queen of the sciences' in Comte's description, enjoyed a precarious existence well into the second half of the twentieth century whenever attempts were made to organize it as a distinct academic discipline. If sociology and social science in general can be described as a kind of 'third culture' situated between the natural sciences and the humanities, then it was a battlefield where Enlightenment and counter-Enlightenment traditions fought over its true nature and purpose (Lepenies 1988: 7). The idea of a science of politics thought of either as a subdivision of the general science of society, sociology, or as a related but distinct mode of enquiry is an additional complication in the relationship between political philosophy and social science. In institutional terms, that political science and sociology were conceived as distinct academic disciplines was essentially an American achievement. Nevertheless, this development took place to a large degree within an intellectual context strongly influenced by European ideas and preoccupations.

The existence of a general social science presupposes a concept of social reality that defines its distinct properties. If society is to be thought of as a suitable object for scientific investigation based on the model of natural science, then it must be thought of as possessing a unified and law-governed structure. Of course, if this logic is followed, then the question of the place of politics within the general framework of society becomes an even more difficult problem. Even if we agree that the historical evidence produces a more nuanced view of the development of modern political thought than that offered by theorists such as Wolin and Arendt, it is also undeniable that their analyses cannot be dismissed completely. They are right to point out that modern political philosophy has come to recognize that it operates with a vocabulary that is shaped to a large degree by the unavoidable influence of the language of the social sciences.

The emergence of a concept of 'society' in distinction from the concept of 'the state' or of government is one of the most significant developments in the intellectual history of modern political philosophy. The concept of 'society' indicates a distinct site in which human development takes place and, as such, it creates the condition for the possibility of a scientific investigation of its nature and structure. This clearly gives credence to the idea of a science of society that can either supplant or radically transform the practice of political philosophy. It has been argued that in the early nineteenth century the 'three great schools of political thought—the liberals, the sociologues, and the socialists'—all agreed that society, as opposed to the state and political institutions, is 'the locus of the irreversible and irresistible movement of history. In this sense, the sociological viewpoint penetrates and dominates all modern political thought' (Manent 1998: 52).

The modern concept of society has a complex history. In genealogical terms there are several distinct ways in which the idea of the existence of society as a reality distinct from government and the state emerged. It is possible to chart the transformation of the older term 'civil society' from around the end of the eighteenth century. The idea of an inclusive political community, a polis, or civil society inherited from the ancient Greeks and Romans was radically transformed into a dualism consisting of civil society as a separate entity existing in opposition to the state. This new understanding of the relationship between these separate entities, in effect, made the idea of a social science that subsumed or replaced the older tradition of political or civil philosophy plausible. Both conceptions of civil society, the ancient and the modern, coexist in Kant's political writings (Ritter 1982). However, a more striking example of the radical separation between civil society and the state is to be found in Hegel's political philosophy. In his *Elements of the Philosophy of Right* under the general heading of 'ethical life' Hegel's central organizing principle is the clear distinction that he makes between civil society (*bürgerliche Gesellschaft*), the family, and the state (Hegel 1991). In addition, the attempt to understand the French Revolution played an important role in the genesis of the modern idea of 'society'. In the wake of the Revolution it appears that 'the men of the nineteenth century no longer lived merely in civil society or the state, they lived in a third element that received various names, usually "society" or "history"' (Manent 1998: 81).

Consideration of Hegel's distinction between the state and civil society played a central role in the development of Karl Marx's idea of society. From his early critique of Hegel's theory of the state Marx developed a distinct and influential view that, nonetheless, in the interests of constructing a theory that would serve both to understand and to overthrow the capitalist mode of production, constructed a concept of society that aimed to transcend the classical idea of politics. Marx advanced a radical critique of the classical idea of politics while at the same time putting forward an analysis of the alienating effects of the modern capitalist mode of production from the standpoint of a reconstructed Hegelian concept of society. For Marx the state and politics in pre-communist society are forms of human alienation. As such they must be overcome if humanity is to emancipate itself. It is clear that for Marx 'political emancipation is at the same time the dissolution of the old society on which rests the sovereign power, the essence of the state alienated from the people' (Marx 1977: 55). The implication is that, in emancipating itself through abolishing the state, mankind at the same time abolishes politics and the state.

The problem here is that the proposal for a general science of society seems to create a conceptual structure that leaves no room either for politics understood as an autonomous activity or for political philosophy as it had been traditionally understood. The later development of the idea of a separate political science that is distinct in its subject matter from other social sciences and in particular from sociology, the 'Queen of the Sciences' according to Comte, raises even more difficulties and confusions. It is quite clear that, for Auguste Comte, the man who gave us the terms 'positivism' and 'sociology', the point of having a science of society was that it would supplant the earlier tradition of political philosophy and provide practical politics with a more secure foundation. As a result, the achievement of genuine social scientific knowledge would replace the need for politics with all its uncertainties, contingency, and unpredictability. But the paradoxical nature of these intellectual developments lies in the fact that, despite their supposed methodological advances and theoretical refinements, they could not escape the fate of remaining in essence practical or political sciences. In other words, they cannot escape the fact that they are in reality a form of political philosophy but expressed in the language of social science. However, if the social sciences are, essentially, political sciences, they are sciences of a new kind that take as their immediate subject matter a new set of questions and problems. It is not too surprising to find that many of the political thinkers of the nineteenth and early twentieth centuries were keen to argue that a new kind of political science was necessary in order to understand the new kind of society that was being created in both Europe and in North America.

The two most significant figures who have come to dominate the contemporary understanding of the history and structure of modern social science are Émile Durkheim and Max Weber. This is a curious development, as neither would approve of most of what goes on in the modern social sciences. In fact, they represent two contrasting and opposed conceptions of the nature of social science and its relationship to politics. Their work also exhibits two distinctly different ways of responding to the predicament of the social and political theorist who is obliged to work in the radically new intellectual context in which the claims of science occupy centre stage. While Durkheim's work provides an example of the criticism that social science has an inherent tendency to avoid or downplay reflection on political topics, this is certainly not the case for Max Weber. In fact, consideration of Weber's thought points in an opposite direction to that indicated by Durkheim and his followers. It is clearly an error to think of social theory or social science as possessing a unified view of politics. While it is true that there is a clear tendency within much of the social theory of the nineteenth and twentieth centuries to avoid explicit discussion of political topics, there is also an, at least, equally powerful sense of the tragic dimension of modern politics that can lead, as in the case of Karl Mannheim, for example, to an overwhelming vision of 'disillusioned realism'. Karl Marx (discussed elsewhere in this volume), who is often named as part of the trinity of founders of social modern science, presents a special case. Marx's use of causal language ought not to be allowed to hide the fact that his style of thinking remained essentially Hegelian (Von Wright 1971: 7–8).

Émile Durkheim offers an interesting example of the central claims and limitations of the modern idea of a social science. In particular, it is in its relationship with philosophical reflection upon politics that these difficulties become evident. While a science of society was possible in Durkheim's view only if it steered clear of partisan politics, it, nevertheless, found itself to be unavoidably engaged in political argument. In fact, the origins of Durkheim's thought are to be found in the analysis of philosophical and political questions. This is an observation that has often been made, and it is a point that Durkheim makes repeatedly himself.

Durkheim stated explicitly that he began with philosophy and that he was always drawn back to it by the nature of the problems that he faced. Despite his claims to be constructing a new science, Durkheim's major works are engaged in an analysis of central themes drawn from the canon of classical political philosophy. This is clearly evident in his early work *The Division of Labor in Society* (Durkheim 1933). The title page contains an important quotation from Aristotle's *The Politics*: 'a state is not made up only of so many men, but of different kinds; for similars do not constitute a state' ($1261^a23–5$). Durkheim's contrast between two types of social solidarity, organic and mechanical, which are the central concepts in this study, is clearly modelled on Aristotle's criticism of Plato's ideal polis as set out in the *Republic*. In his thesis of 1892 (written in Latin) on 'Montesquieu's Contribution to the Establishment of Political Science' Durkheim discusses *scientia politica* and the study of *res politicae*. His intention was to replace this older terminology with the concepts of social science (Durkheim 1997).

Durkheim claims that political science originated in France in the work of the philosophes. In particular, it is in Montesquieu's *The Spirit of the Laws* that he found the foundations for this new discipline. Despite the possibly confusing terminology, Durkheim considers the newer form of social science to be an advance over the kinds of political philosophy that had been practised in the past. For example, he argues that Montesquieu departed from the familiar Aristotelian classification of the six forms of polis that had become an established feature of European political thought. In doing so Montesquieu did not base his classification upon 'an abstract idea of the state' or upon 'some a priori principle' but on 'the things themselves' (Durkheim 1997: 32). Montesquieu's achievement, in Durkheim's opinion, was to have understood that 'political things' are capable of being the objects of science. However, one of Montesquieu's basic errors, in Durkheim's view, was to have thought that the form of government determines the form of society when, in reality, the real relationship is the reverse. The basic barrier that has to be overcome in order to establish a genuine science of politics is the entrenched idea that there are special properties of political life that make it 'so changeable, so diverse and multiform as not to seem reducible to fixed and definite laws. Nor . . . do men willingly believe that they are bound by the same necessity as other things in nature' (Durkheim 1997: 73).

Durkheim recognized that a general science of 'social facts', sociology, had to face up to the problem of defining its subject matter. The 'very facts which are ascribed as its subject matter are already studied by a whole host of specific disciplines', which includes political philosophy (Durkheim 1982: 175). Durkheim's response was to argue that 'sociology is and can only be the system, the *corpus* of the social sciences'. In other words, in order to avoid the dangers of producing either an empty formalism or a grand encyclopaedism, sociology must become the transformative method for all the sciences of man.

Durkheim, although not a positivist in a straightforward sense, owed much, despite his observations to the contrary, to the basic proposals of the founder of that movement, Auguste Comte. The aim of both Comte's and Durkheim's versions of sociology was to find an objective and scientific account of the totality of social existence. In order to achieve this aim, the new science of sociology must free itself from all preconceptions. This is particularly difficult for this new science, because 'sentiment so often intervenes. We enthuse over our political and religious beliefs and moral practices very differently from the way we do over the objects of the physical world' (Durkheim 1982: 73). The presumption is that a truly scientific sociology would provide the sound and secure platform from which we would be able to discard our previously held political commitments. Despite his wide knowledge of the history of political philosophy, Durkheim failed to notice, or at least failed to admit, that this is a point of view that is itself bound to be politically controversial.

Critical discussions of Durkheim's thought often point to the contradiction between his ideal of scientific detachment and his conviction that the point of the acquisition of social scientific knowledge was to enable practitioners to become experts whose task is to enlighten and guide society about its true needs (Lukes 1982: 19). For Durkheim the advance of sociology would create a state of affairs in which the 'duty of the statesman is no longer to propel societies violently towards an ideal which appears attractive to him. His role is rather that of a doctor: he forestalls the outbreak of sickness by maintaining good hygiene, or when it does break out, seeks to cure it' (Durkheim 1982: 104). This means that the scientific sociologist is drawn inevitably into political debate. This is unavoidable if those misleading moral and political preconceptions that stand in the way of progress are to be avoided. A clear illustration of this is provided by his discussion of socialism. Durkheim sees it as a rival, but mistaken, social theory. Socialism is dismissed as 'not a science, a sociology in miniature—it is a cry of grief, sometimes of anger, uttered by men who feel most keenly our collective *malaise*. Socialism is to the facts which produce it what the groans of a sick man are to the illness with which he is afflicted, to the needs that torment him' (Durkheim 1962: 41). Durkheim and his followers failed to see any contradiction between their claims to be constructing a detached and objective social science and the way in which this overtly supported the institutions and secularism of the Third Republic.

Of course, despite its aim to achieve the status of science, Durkheim's sociology could not be anything other than an 'inherently political' enterprise in its formulation of problems, in its proposed explanations, and in its conception of what is to be explained. Clearly a social science of this kind presents a certain way of constructing its own subject matter and, therefore, has a definite point of view about what the nature of politics and, in particular, of what constitutes feasible political conduct (Lukes 1982: 20). This is not a state of affairs that is peculiar to the Durkheimian enterprise. It has been the fate, one could argue, of all attempts by social and political scientists to distance themselves from the world of politics.

Although political questions, both philosophical and practical, do occupy a central place in the formation of Durkheim's thought, he did not consider the possession and struggle over the distribution of power to be important. When he did discuss relations of power, he saw them as aspects of a more general structural ordering produced, most importantly, by the development of the division of labour (Poggi 2000: 124). This stands in direct contrast with the work of Max Weber. The fact that, despite being contemporaries, they seem to have been unaware of each other ought not to be as surprising as it is often supposed. Despite the fact that they are often placed together as founders of modern sociology, they were, in fact, working with completely different intellectual projects (Colliot-Thélène 2007). Weber has become assimilated into the canon of modern social science in a gradual and uneven way. As far as the Anglo-American world is concerned, the initial impact of Weber's thought owes much to the arguments of Talcott Parsons (1937). In his attempt to justify the academic legitimacy of sociology as a social science with its own distinct subject matter, Parsons sought to demonstrate the basic convergence of ideas in the theories of both Weber and Durkheim. The aim of this attempt at theoretical synthesis was to provide a foundation for social science. The end product was an image of society as a social system composed of functioning subsystems of which the political system was one. Of course, following on from this formulation, it is not too surprising that Parsons and those political scientists influenced by him did not pay much attention to the more controversial problem of Weber's political thought. Unfortunately, as Weber's contemporaries knew, this was a deeply misleading picture. It was only with the intellectual migration from Weimar Germany that the record began to be put right. Weber, on the other hand, had made it clear throughout his life that politics was and remained his 'first love'.

Weber's idea of a social science is complex. His appreciation of the uniqueness of historical events made him deeply sceptical of the generalizing claims made by most contemporary social scientists. In contrast with Comte, J. S. Mill, and Durkheim, there is no acceptance of the necessity nor even of the possibility of finding natural laws of society. Indeed, Weber argued that, even if we possessed knowledge of such laws, they would be irrelevant for our understanding of the unique features of social and cultural reality in which we are interested. The more general the law, the more it would be devoid of content. Furthermore, in an even stronger contrast with Durkheim and most other contemporary social scientists, Weber did not see the need for a concept of 'society' at all. He pointed out that the concept of the 'social' when used without further substantive elaboration was too vague and ambiguous to be of any real use (Weber 1949: 68). His nominalist account of concept formation was designed to make us aware of the misleading and, even, possibly dangerous nature of the uncritical use of all collective concepts .

Weber is reported as saying that anyone who wanted to make sense of the modern age had to recognize that we live in 'a world substantially shaped by Marx and Nietzsche' (Hennis 1988: 146). It has been argued that Weber is best understood not as a sociologist in the modern sense but as a political thinker who can be placed in a line of predecessors who include Machiavelli, Rousseau, and Tocqueville. Even if we accept this interpretation, it is also evident that Weber's political thought was also 'post-Marxian' in the sense that, in common with most modern social scientists, he had ceased to think of the state as the most important arena for human development. This is reflected in a recurring tension in his social and political thought. While working with a modern distinction between the state and society that is consistent with much of Marx's criticism of Hegel's *Philosophy of Right*, Weber was also deeply aware of the autonomous and distinct nature of political questions. In debunking some of the more extreme contemporary metaphysical theories of society and the state, he was clear that the state ought to be regarded as no more than one institution among others. The modern state in Weber's famous formulation is, in fact, described 'sociologically' in an anti-Aristotelian manner 'in terms of a specific means' that is peculiar to it and not in terms of its purposes. The modern state is 'that human community which (successfully) lays claim to the *monopoly of legitimate physical violence* within a certain territory' (Weber 1994: 310–11).

In a strong contrast to Durkheim and most of those who called themselves sociologists or even political scientists in France, Britain, and America in the early twentieth century, Weber saw politics in terms of the relentless struggle for power and the unavoidable 'rule of man over man'. The modern state is a 'relationship of *rule* [*Herrschaft*] by human beings over human beings, and one that rests on the legitimate use of violence (that is, violence that is held to be legitimate)'. Those who are engaged in politics are 'striving for power, either as a means to attain other goals (which may be ideal or selfish), or power "for its own sake", which is to say, in order to enjoy the feeling of prestige given by power' (Weber 1994: 311). The state is characterized metaphorically as a 'machine' or as an 'enterprise'. As such it is not to be thought of as being anything more than one institution among many. In addition, leadership is a central aspect of the politics of the modern state. All forms of leadership require justification. Weber refers to this as the need for legitimacy. However, he does not seek a philosophical grounding of rule but, instead, describes the three 'ideal types' of 'inner justification' for claims to legitimacy. The concepts of tradition, charisma, and legality as forms of the legitimation of political rule serve to provide what he considered to be a more realistic alternative to the classical triad of monarchy, aristocracy, and democracy. Weber's political and social thought is remarkable for its relentless and thorough destruction of all political illusions. His account of the modern 'iron cage' ('steel casing' is more accurate) of the modern world is also a contributing to the 'disenchantment' of politics.

When Laslett sought to ascribe responsibility for the death of political philosophy, the Marxists and the academic sociologists were prominent among those he blamed. According to Laslett, the Marxists dismiss all political philosophy as socially determined ideology. The Marxists are 'quite simply not interested in the perennial debates which exercised the political philosophers in the past'. The academic sociologists have inherited the same prejudices. However, in keeping with the implicit tensions within this body of ideas 'they seem to alternate between an attitude which proclaims that political philosophy is impossible and an urgent pleading for a new political philosophy which will give them guidance and make sense of their conclusions' (Laslett 1956: p. viii). This attitude is seen at its most extreme, in Laslett's view, in the work of Karl Mannheim.

Karl Mannheim's early work provides a clear example of the deep disenchantment and 'disillusioning realism' that is frequently the outcome of this kind of sociological analysis of politics. Karl Mannheim expressed the problem of a science of politics most directly in his essay of 1929 'The Prospects of Scientific Politics: The Relationship between Social Theory and Political Practice' (in Mannheim 1960). The question that Mannheim attempted to answer was 'Why is there no science of politics?' He recognized two basic difficulties that stand in the way of the creation of a science of politics. One is the inherent unpredictability and novelty of political events. The other is the unavoidable fact that the political thinker is a participant observer whose own style of thinking and ideological standpoint cannot attain complete detachment from the political world. Mannheim could not provide a convincing answer to his question apart from appealing to the new stratum of 'free-floating intellectuals', as the possible providers of an answer never gained much support even from Mannheim himself. Of course, Mannheim's account of the idea of a science of politics reveals a view of politics as a field of human activity that seems to be 'irrational' or outside the boundaries of rational organization. A science of politics is necessary in order to provide a counterweight to the irrationality and contingency of politics. As such it would provide the foundation for a rational politics.

Mannheim's account of the possibility of a science of politics is bound up with his theory of ideology. This is the central component of his 'sociology of knowledge'. The main concern of Mannheim's 'sociology of knowledge', despite its seeming claim to generality, is focused essentially upon political thought. In an early essay on 'Conservative Thought' (in Mannheim 1971) Mannheim introduced the idea of a 'morphology' of 'styles of thought'. Political ideologies, such as conservatism, could be studied as distinct 'styles of thought' in a way that is analogous to 'styles of art'. In addition, Mannheim argued that each style of thought has distinct social roots. The problem that arises is that the principle of the social determination of thought undermines any idea of a strict separation between politics and philosophy. If we 'penetrate deeply enough', we will find that 'certain philosophical assumptions lie at the basis of all political thought, and similarly, in any kind of philosophy a certain pattern of action and a definite approach to the world is implied'. All philosophy is in some fundamental sense an expression of ways of making sense of society and this takes its most tangible form in 'the political struggle' (Mannheim 1971: 142).

Although it is true that Mannheim did not accept the possibility of a social science constructed on naturalistic or positivist principles, the difficulties that he found himself facing are a clear and revealing example of the problems that emerge when politics is made an object of social scientific enquiry. Mannheim was quite clear that political argument ought not to be confused with academic discussion. Political argument 'seeks not only to be in the right but also to demolish the basis of its opponent's social and intellectual existence' (Mannheim 1960: 34). The origins of the sociology of knowledge are, in fact, to be found in the practice of democratic politics. It is in the nature of political conflict and especially in democracies that 'the unmasking of the unconscious motives' that bind a social group together is made apparent. For Mannheim this means that, as long as 'modern politics fought its battles with theoretical weapons, the process of unmasking penetrated to the social roots of theory' (Mannheim 1960: 35). The main implication of this way of looking at political thought is that it tends to produce a sense of 'disillusioning realism'. The Marxist weapon of using the concept of ideology as a means for demonstrating what it sees as the illusions of liberalism can be turned back upon the critic: 'nothing was to prevent the opponents of Marxism from availing themselves of the weapon and applying it to Marxism itself' (Mannheim 1960: 67). Although the potentially corrosive effects of this mode of investigation were easy to recognize, formulating a convincing response that did not descend into the restatement of dogma was not always so easy.

The 'disillusioning realism' of Mannheim's reduction of all political philosophy to the status of ideology has self-destructive implications for any faith in the possibility of political philosophy and of rational political debate. Despite his attempts to find an escape route from the threat of relativism, Mannheim realized that the logic of his argument must apply to his own ideas too. Nevertheless, the question remained. How can there be a genuine science of politics if politics itself is characterized as a relentless struggle for power? There are two obvious ways of avoiding this problem. One is to deny the centrality of the struggle for power as the defining feature of all politics. The other is to argue that the concept of science deployed by Mannheim and most other thinkers who have similar political ideas is hopelessly misguided.

This is, essentially, the response made by Karl Popper. Popper's work in social and political philosophy takes up the familiar problem, some one hundred years after Comte, of 'the somewhat unsatisfactory state of some of the social sciences and especially of social philosophy'. His interest in this problem was, he tells us, 'greatly stimulated by the rise of totalitarianism and by the failure of the various social sciences and social philosophies to make sense of it' (Popper 1957: 2). Popper's account of the nature of social scientific knowledge is set out as a response to what he considered to be the confusions that have contributed to the disasters of twentieth-century politics. Although not a positivist in the strict sense, Popper agreed with Comte and J. S. Mill in their defence of the unity of method between the natural and social sciences. The problem was that their understanding of science was deficient. Repeating a familiar pattern, Popper argued that a social science free from the errors of historicism inherited from Marx, Comte, and Mill was necessary for political reasons. A science of society that had overcome the errors of the past would provide the necessary intellectual support for the 'open society' (Popper 1945).

The idea of a political science has always been guided as much by political reasons as by intellectual curiosity. From Comte's dream of a 'positive polity' to Karl Popper's argument for the 'open society', it is impossible to separate the project of a science of politics from the world of political argument. Even if the strong claims made for a social science constructed on naturalistic foundations are generally ignored or merely paid lip service by most practitioners of social science, the general intellectual environment in which political philosophy has been conducted over the last century has been irreversibly transformed. Most modern political philosophers accept that understanding of the limitations of the scope of politics that has been taken for granted by political scientists and sociologists. That is to say, rather than seeing their task in terms of an understanding of the polis as a unity, they accept the description of a particular sector of social life as 'politics' (Lefort 1998). In this sense, the claim that there has been a retreat from a genuine engagement with 'the political' does make sense. On the other hand, the social scientific study of politics, whatever the status of its claims to possess genuine scientificity, has had the effect of forcing political philosophers to consider seriously the feasibility of their normative aspirations. While stubborn social facts might prove to be obstacles to the ambitions of political theory, the question of the significance of those supposed facts is itself a philosophical question (Nagel 1991: 21–32).

REFERENCES

ARENDT, H. (1958). *The Human Condition*. Chicago: University of Chicago Press.

ARISTOTLE (1988). *The Politics*, (ed.) S. Everson. Cambridge: Cambridge University Press.

BOSANQUET, B. (2001). 'The Philosophical Theory of the State' (and related essays) [1899], (ed.) G. F. Gaus and W. Sweet. South Bend, IN: St Augustine's Press.

BRYCE, J. (1909). 'The Relation of Political Science to History and to Practice', *American Political Science Review*, 3: 1–19.

CATLIN, G. (1957). 'Political Theory. What is it?' *Political Science Quarterly*, 72: 1–29.

COBBAN, A. (1953). 'The Decline of Political Theory', *Political Science Quarterly*, 68: 321–37.

COLLINI, S., WINCH, D., and BURROW, J. (1983). *That Noble Science of Politics*. Cambridge: Cambridge University Press.

COLLIOT-THÉLÈNE, C. (2007). 'Speaking Past One Another: Durkheim, Weber, and Varying Modes of Sociological Explanation', in *Max Weber's 'Objectivity' Reconsidered*, (ed.) L. McFalls. Toronto: University of Toronto Press.

DURKHEIM, E. (1933). *The Division of Labor in Society* [1893]. New York: MacMillan.

DURKHEIM, E. (1962). *Socialism* [1928], (ed.) A. W. Gouldner. New York: Collier Books.

DURKHEIM, E. (1982). *The Rules of Sociological Method* [1895], (ed.) S. Lukes. London: Macmillan.

DURKHEIM, E. (1997). *Montesquieu's Contribution to the Establishment of Political Science* [1892], ed. and trans. W. Watts Miller and E. Griffiths. Oxford: Durkheim Press.

HEGEL, G. W. F. (1991). *Elements of the Philosophy of Right* [1821]. Cambridge: Cambridge University Press.

HENNIS, W. (1988). *Max Weber. Essays in Reconstruction*. London: Allen and Unwin.

HOBBES, T. (1998). *On the Citizen* [1642], (ed.) R. Tuck and M. Silverthorne. Cambridge: Cambridge University Press.

LASLETT, P. (1956) (ed.), *Philosophy, Politics, and Society*. 1st ser. Oxford: Basil Blackwell.

LEFORT, C. (1998). *Democracy and Political Theory*. Cambridge: Polity Press.

LEPENIES, W. (1988). *Between Literature and Science: The Rise of Sociology*. Cambridge: Cambridge University Press.

LUKES, S. (1982). 'Introduction', in E. Durkheim, *The Rules of Sociological Method* [1895], (ed.) S. Lukes. London: Macmillan.

MANENT, P. (1998). *The City of Man*. Princeton: Princeton University Press.

MANNHEIM, K. (1960). *Ideology and Utopia* [1936]. London: Routledge.

MANNHEIM, K. (1971). *Conservative Thought* [1927], in *From Karl Mannheim*, (ed.) K. H. Wolff. New York: Oxford University Press.

MARX, K. (1977). *On the Jewish Question* [1843], in *Selected Writings*, (ed.) D. McLellan. Oxford: Oxford University Press.

MILL, J. S. (1961). *Auguste Comte and Positivism* [1865]. Ann Arbor, MI: University of Michigan Press.

MILL, J. S. (1972). *Representative Government* [1861], in *Utilitarianism, On Liberty, and Considerations on Representative Government*, (ed.) H. B. Acton. London: Dent.

NAGEL, T. (1991). *Equality and Partiality*. New York: Oxford University Press.

OAKESHOTT, M. (1991). *Rationalism in Politics and Other Essays*. Indianapolis: Liberty Press.

PARSONS, T. (1937). *The Structure of Social Action*. New York: Free Press.

POGGI, G. (2000). *Durkheim*. Oxford: Oxford University Press.

POPPER, K. (1945). *The Open Society and its Enemies*. London: Routledge and Kegan Paul.

POPPER, K. (1957). *The Poverty of Historicism*. London: Routledge and Kegan Paul.

RAWLS, J. (1999). *A Theory of Justice*. Rev. edn [1971]. Cambridge, MA: Harvard University Press.

RAWLS, J. (2001). *Justice as Fairness*. Cambridge, MA: Harvard University Press.

RITTER, J. (1982). *Hegel and the French Revolution*. Cambridge, MA: MIT Press.

SKORUPSKI, J. (1989). *John Stuart Mill*. London: Routledge.

STEARS, M. (2005). 'The Vocation of Political Theory', *European Journal of Political Theory*, 4: 325–50.

VON WRIGHT, G. H. (1971). *Explanation and Understanding*. London. Routledge and Kegan Paul.

WEBER, M. (1949). '"Objectivity" in Social Science and Social Policy' [1904], in Weber, *The Methodology of the Social Sciences*, (ed.) E. Shils and H. A. Finch. New York: Free Press.

WEBER, M. (1994). *Political Writings*, (ed.) P. Lassman and R. Speirs. Cambridge: Cambridge University Press.

WINCH, P. (1958). *The Idea of a Social Science*. London: Routledge and Kegan Paul.

WOKLER, R. (1998). 'The Enlightenment and the French Revolutionary Birth Pangs of Modernity', in *The Rise of the Social Sciences and the Formation of Modernity. Conceptual Change in Context, 1750–1850*, (ed.) J. Heilbron, L. Magnusson, and B. Wittrock. Dordrecht: Kluwer.

WOLIN, S. (2004). *Politics and Vision*. Expanded edn. Princeton: Princeton University Press.

CHAPTER 26

CONTEMPORARY ANGLO-AMERICAN POLITICAL PHILOSOPHY

GEORGE KLOSKO

THE DEATH OF POLITICAL PHILOSOPHY

ACCORDING to a now familiar narrative, in the middle of the twentieth century, political philosophy was "dead," but it has since been resurrected in a new form. Credit for the death certificate is given to Peter Laslett. In the Introduction to a volume of essays published in 1955, Laslett bemoans the absence of major philosophers writing in English, like the tradition of thinkers "from Hobbes to Bosanquet" that he cites (1956: p. vii).

The absence of great theorists writing in English is surprising, as the early decades of the twentieth century were rich in political theory. Across Europe a host of thinkers composed major works. Renowned figures include Max Weber, Émile Durkheim, Georges Sorel, and a group of thinkers, commonly referred to as the "Machiavellians," which included Gaetano Mosca, Vilfredo Pareto, and Roberto Michels. Both before and after 1917, the Marxian tradition was enormously important in practical politics and was at the center of raging theoretical debate. Major theorists in this tradition include Lenin, Eduard Bernstein, his "revisionist" opponent, Leon Trotsky, Rosa Luxembourg, Antonio Gramsci, and Georg Lukacs. Marxism's implications for sociology and other academic fields were explored by members of the "Frankfurt School," notably Max Horkheimer, Theodor Adorno, and Herbert Marcuse. In *Ideology and Utopia* (1936 [1929]), Karl Mannheim developed the sociology of knowledge. In addition to founding psychoanalysis, Sigmund Freud turned his doctrine to concerns of political theory in *Civilization and its Discontents* (1936 [1929]) and other works. This list of thinkers can be extended, but about its impressiveness, there is little doubt.

Impressive as the list is, it contains few works that should be described as "political philosophy"—according to what we now mean by the term. For the most part, works are better described as "social theory." Dividing lines between these fields are, of course, rough, but, as a general rule, these works are deeply rooted in empirical investigations of society. Many present grand claims about society's overall development or evolution. While political philosophy should not, of course, be conducted in isolation from social and political conditions, in works of Weber and Durkheim, Mosca, Pareto, and many Marxian theorists, there is deep intermixture of normative and empirical concerns, with the former proceeding directly from the latter. The same is clearly true of Freud, though his own empirical grounding is of course in psychology.

L. T. Hobhouse, whose *Liberalism* (1911) is one of few works written in English that merits a place on the list, was also a sociologist, at least by academic affiliation. He occupied the first chair of sociology in Great Britain (at the London School of Economics). But to some extent, Hobhouse stands apart from the other authors noted. In justifying the movement from classical liberalism to a new socialistic liberal theory, Hobhouse developed arguments that are more overtly normative than many in the other works noted, although, in his case too, normative claims were bound up with grand theses concerning the evolution of liberal societies. One major figure who belongs on the list is John Dewey, perhaps the only social or political theorist in the United States at that time about whom this could be said. Dewey stands apart from these thinkers in, among other respects, being an academic philosopher, much of whose work should be described as political philosophy.

If at mid-century political philosophy was largely moribund in English-speaking countries, we should ask why this was so. Laslett mentions the possible futility of writing political philosophy in the aftermath of such horrors of the Second World War as the Holocaust and Hiroshima. However, the great struggle of the cold war was in large part a war of ideas. This took center stage in the works of major political philosophers writing in English, including Isaiah Berlin, Karl Popper, and Hannah Arendt. The same is true of Jacob Talmon's *The Origins of Totalitarian Democracy* (1955). But, although Laslett's lament was doubtless exaggerated, the enterprise of political philosophy was stiffly challenged by philosophical views worked out earlier in the century, especially "logical positivism," developed in the 1920s by the so-called Vienna Circle. Holding a stringent conception of meaning, these thinkers were dismissive of ethical pronouncement, which they viewed as expressions of emotion. To say that murder is wrong is to express one's revulsion at the practice—to say something along the lines of "Boo murder"—rather than something akin to factual or scientific statements. In *Language, Truth, and Logic* (1946), A. J. Ayer packaged logical positivism for the English-speaking world. In his words:

> Thus if I say to someone, "You acted wrongly in stealing that money" . . . It is as if I
> had said, "You stole that money," in a peculiar tone of horror, or written it with the

addition of some special exclamation marks. The tone, or the exclamation marks, adds nothing to the literal meaning of the sentence. It merely serves to show that the expression of it is attended by certain feelings in the speaker. (1946: 107)

For many decades, attitudes along these lines influenced beliefs about how political society should be studied. Along similar lines, as the study of politics in the USA became political science, political scientists were suspicious of normative pronouncements—and of practitioners of normative political theory. In the words of David Easton (1953), a widely respected political theorist:

> The assumption, generally adopted today in the social sciences, holds that values can ultimately be reduced to emotional response conditioned by the individual's total life experiences . . . The moral aspect of a proposition . . . expresses only the emotional response of an individual to a state of real or presumed facts. (1953: 221)

The influence of logical positivism is apparent here, while similar views were held by many political theorists, to say nothing of political scientists, at that time. During this period, political philosophers largely confined themselves to studying the history of political philosophy and to linguistic analysis. Thus, in a well-known work, T. D. Weldon confined attention to analyzing the language of politics, as opposed to normative assessments of political and social institutions and affairs (Weldon 1953).

THE RAWLSIAN RESURRECTION

After mid-century, circumstances changed dramatically. According to many theorists, responsibility for the revival of political philosophy belongs to John Rawls. Especially in his monumental *A Theory of Justice* (1971), Rawls provided a compelling model of how political philosophy could be done on a grand scale. Attributing the revival of political theory to Rawls alone is, of course, overly simple. Within a few years of Laslett's pronouncement, well before *Theory* appeared, several notable works were published. These include H. L. A. Hart's *The Concept of Law* (1961) and Brian Barry's *Political Argument* (1965). Berlin's highly influential analysis of different forms of freedom, "Two Concepts of Liberty," was delivered in 1957. Still, Rawls's work made a substantial difference. In 1962, in an article titled "Does Political Theory Still Exist?" Berlin claimed that "no commanding work of political philosophy has appeared in the twentieth century" (Berlin 1962: 1). According to many people, this situation changed in 1971, with the appearance of Rawls's "Olympian" work (Laslett and Fishkin 1979: 1).

The impact of *Theory* should be attributed to contributions both methodological and substantive. Viewing justice as the "first virtue of social institutions" (1971: 3), Rawls attempts to provide an account of justice more convincing than that of then dominant utilitarianism. Rawls is impressed with utilitarianism's rigor. Still, its implications are not always correct, as these can entail sacrificing the interests of individuals for the sake of overall public good.

The striking methodological device Rawls introduces in *Theory* is a revised version of the social contract, familiar from works of Locke, Rousseau, and Kant. According to these theorists, preferred forms of government are chosen by individuals in a condition without government, a "state of nature" (see Sommerville, Chapter 33, this volume). Rawls alters traditional accounts of the contract by having his individuals choose principles of justice rather than forms of government. These principles are to apply to society's "basic structure," the social, political, and economic institutions that distribute "fundamental rights and duties and determine the division of advantages from social cooperation," thereby strongly affecting people's prospects (Rawls 1971: 7). While in many works in the contract tradition there is some ambiguity as to whether the state of nature is intended to be an actual historical situation or a hypothetical construct, Rawls is clear that the choice in question is entirely hypothetical. The most original feature of Rawls's simulacrum of the state of nature—his "original position"— is a "veil of ignorance" behind which choosers are situated. The hypothetical choosers are given knowledge of "the general facts about human society," including theories in economics, politics, and other fields (1971: 137–8). But, to prevent them from selecting principles of justice that benefit themselves unduly, they are deprived of knowledge of their particular characteristics—for example, age, race, religion, social position, even the generation and country to which they belong (1971: 137). As a result, the original position represents a fair situation in which to choose principles of justice, and Rawls calls his conception "justice as fairness."

Rawls's contract argument is too complex to be discussed adequately here. The problem of selecting principles is complicated by the veil of ignorance. The representative individuals, who choose the principles, are supposed to choose those that are most beneficial to themselves. But behind the veil, how can they advance their interests, if they do not know what their interests are? To address this question, Rawls introduces "primary goods," "things that any rational man can be presumed to want," because they are necessary for whatever plan of life one pursues (1971: 62). Among primary goods, Rawls includes liberties, income and wealth, opportunities, and the social bases of self-respect. Since he assumes that more primary goods are preferable to less, the process of choice becomes selecting principles that provide the largest possible package of primary goods.

Rawls argues that, under conditions of uncertainty resulting from the veil of ignorance, rational choosers will pursue a conservative strategy. Concerned that, after principles have been chosen and the veil lifted, they may find themselves in unfavorable positions in society, they will pursue a maximin strategy, so occupants of the lowest positions are disadvantaged as little as possible. They will choose two principles. The first provides equal and maximum liberty for all members of society. The second is in two parts. The first part guarantees equal opportunity; the second addresses economic distribution. Even though there is a presumption in favor of economic equality, because incentives promote economic growth and so an increased standard of living for everyone, inequalities are accepted, if they benefit the least advantaged members of society. This is Rawls's famous "difference principle." Rawls contends that justice as fairness is superior to utilitarianism, because the two principles, and not utilitarian principles, would be chosen in his original position. Along with this particular argument is a general claim that his position is again superior to utilitarianism, because applying the principles would lead to what we view as a more just society than what would result from utilitarianism.

REFLECTIVE EQUILIBRIUM

Rawls's reason for employing a social-contract device are made clear in his article "Justice as Fairness" (1958), which presents the first version of what was to become the full-blown theory of *Theory*. His ideal is a society in which the moral principles that govern basic institutions can be justified to all members of society. In such a society, people "can face one another openly and support their respective positions, should they appear questionable, by reference to principles which it is reasonable to expect each to accept" (1958: 178). This is a far cry from many societies in which inequalities are not justified at all, or, if they are, are attributed to forces beyond human control. Thus what Rawls means by "fairness" is closely akin to hypothetical consent; the principles that we believe would be chosen in a hypothetical, fair situation are principles we should accept. "It is this notion of the possibility of mutual acknowledgment of principle by free persons who have no authority over one another which makes the concept of fairness fundamental to justice" (1958: 179). Rawls's position could just as easily be called "justice as mutual acknowledgment."

However, this ideal requires more than that particular principles would be chosen by hypothetical individuals behind a veil of ignorance. In order for any choice in a hypothetical state of nature to have justificatory force, not only must it be the appropriate option, but the conditions under which it is chosen must be plausible. Although Rawls's reformulated social contract attracted enormous attention, it is actually subordinate to another and different methodological strategy, the method of "reflective equilibrium," which is one of Rawls's most important contributions.

Rawls's interest in questions of method in ethics can be traced back to his doctoral dissertation. In his first published article, "Outline of a Decision Procedure for Ethics" (1951), drawn from his dissertation, Rawls attempts to identify a secure perspective from which to make moral judgments. The proper judge must possess certain attributes. She should be sane, as opposed to suffering from mental illness, intelligent, well informed, not have a strong personal interest in the case at hand, have adequate time to deliberate, and so on. Judgments made from this perspective are likely to be more reliable than others that lack these qualities. In *Theory*, Rawls calls such judgments "considered judgments." Moral beliefs in which we have greatest confidence should serve as "provisional fixed points" around which to construct overall moral theories. Examples Rawls provides in *Theory* are that racial discrimination and religious intolerance are wrong. An account of justice inconsistent with these convictions is likely to be incorrect (1971: 19–20).

Reflective equilibrium is a method of justification based on establishing coherence within one's moral beliefs. Rawls sets aside controversial meta-ethical issues such as the nature of ethical judgments and whether moral truth is possible or accessible. Similarly, he sets aside the possibility of deducing a conception of justice from self-evident first principles. Rather, "its justification is a matter of the mutual support of many considerations, of everything fitting together into one coherent view" (1971: 21). Reflective equilibrium aspires to create an integrated structure of moral beliefs and principles. General principles should imply results that are intuitively sound, while one's understanding of particular cases should be consistent with intuitively sound principles. In order to achieve consistency, one must work back and forth between principles and particular cases, revising one's understanding of each to achieve overall coherence. Thus Rawls describes moral theory as "Socratic" (1971: 49).

This method overlays the contract argument of *Theory*. In order to generate the most plausible theory of justice possible, one's accounts of both the original position and the principles of justice that are chosen should make intuitive sense. The features of the original position should be reasonable and non-controversial, but this position should also be shaped so its inhabitants will choose the most plausible possible principles, resulting in an optimum balance between position and principles. In such a case, there results an equilibrium between the contract argument and our overall intuitive judgments. The equilibrium is "reflective" because, in order to attain it, we must subject our views of all components of the argument to critical examination, revising them as appropriate.

Theory of Justice generated a flood of critical commentary. Most discussions focus on the contract argument and principles that result. But, in this context, I wish to emphasize the work's methodological accomplishments. As an approach to ethical and political problems, reflective equilibrium is not precisely defined. Adherents of the method disagree about specific features, and not all claim to follow in Rawls's theoretical footsteps. Still, however much subsequent theorists were directly influenced by Rawls, since the publication of his work, a great many theorists have engaged in a similar style of political philosophy—generally referred to as "analytical," "liberal," or "Rawlsian" theory (for good brief discussions, see Miller and Dagger 2003). Influenced by linguistic philosophy, adherents of this style of argument pursue rigor and clarity. They carefully explain terms they use and, like Rawls, generally set aside questions of moral foundations. They base their arguments on considered convictions they believe to be shared by their readers, employing carefully crafted examples to sharpen intuitions. Like Rawls himself, practitioners of this style of argument address practical issues, and one of Rawls's great accomplishments was to move past the logical positivists' skepticism about moral judgments and demonstrate how practical normative issues could be approached.

To a large extent Rawls's influence has lain in his demonstration of what his method could accomplish. In his well-known work *The Structure of Scientific Revolutions*, Thomas Kuhn discusses the process through which scientific disciplines are established (Kuhn 1962). Central is a pioneering accomplishment, the achievement of a Copernicus or Galileo. Impressed by such accomplishments, other practitioners imitate them. Their methods and standards for assessing their own success or failure are derived from those of the great pioneer. Kuhn refers to such pioneering works as "paradigms." They are not only generally accepted as providing methods and standards for further research, but they become institutionalized when used as models in the education of future practitioners. In contemporary political philosophy, *Theory of Justice* plays such a role. It is known by all practitioners, and provides a common point of reference and, more indirectly, an accepted example of the methods and standards appropriate for first-class work in the field.

The reflective equilibrium method is subject to criticism. A common objection is that the intuitions from which practitioners proceed are socially constructed. The method does not approach moral truth; all it does is put in order intuitions that result from indoctrination by the subject's society. In "Outline of a Decision Procedure," anticipating such an objection, Rawls responds that people who expect moral truth expect too much. The questions he asks must be addressed if people are to live together harmoniously. Clearly, the most likely way to approach such questions is on the basis of moral ideas in which we have greatest confidence. Rawls notes how foolish it would be to proceed from other ideas, in which we have less faith (Rawls 1951: 196). Thus the moral beliefs from which we proceed are not "arbitrary commitments or sentiments that we happen now to share," to use one critic's words (Lyons 1975: 146), but, again, those we hold most securely. What is more, these are moral beliefs that critics themselves most likely share. Justification under reflective equilibrium is *ad hominem*, directed at the critic. To use Joel Feinberg's words, if a given argument is successful, it demonstrates "to the person addressed that the judgment it supports coheres more smoothly than its rivals with the network of convictions he already possesses, so that if he rejects it, then he will have to abandon other judgments that he would be loath to relinquish" (Feinberg 1984: 18).

A related criticism is perhaps more cutting. Rawls may well exaggerate the extent to which inhabitants of modern societies hold similar beliefs. In *Theory*, he does "not even ask" if one person's sense of justice is the same as those of other people (Rawls 1971: 50). As we will see below, in the years following publication of *Theory*, Rawls came to take the fact of disagreement more seriously and attempted to modify his justificatory strategy. But, to the extent that the people Rawls addresses share his basic moral intuitions, reflective equilibrium can be an effective means to practical consensus.

RESPONSE TO RAWLS

....

For a difficult, almost 600-page work of moral and political philosophy, *Theory of Justice* was a phenomenon. As of this writing, some forty years after its publication, the work has sold around 400,000 copies in English and been translated into at least 28 languages. Bibliography on Rawls includes several thousand items (Pogge 2006: 3). However, along with acclaim, much scholarly commentary on *Theory* is highly critical, while much of this criticism was accepted by Rawls himself. Within a few years after completing *Theory*, he began to move justice as fairness in a new direction.

One apparent reason for the enormous impact of Rawls's work is that it was right for the times. His powerful defense of individual liberty and justification for providing all members of society adequate resources to pursue their plans of life helped move equality to the center of political philosophy and dovetailed with demands of rising social movements, for racial equality, women's rights, and equal treatment of other minority groups. Rawls's account of equality was criticized from a variety of different directions (Wolff, Chapter 36, this volume). Ronald Dworkin argued that his view did not sufficiently address the distinction between deserved and undeserved equality, a defect Dworkin attempted to remedy with a brilliant alternative proposal (Dworkin 1981*a*, *b*). While Dworkin, like Rawls, placed distribution of resources at the center of equality, Amartya Sen argued that the focus of justice should be the use to which resources are put, equal ability to develop capabilities, for which different people require different resources (Sen 1980). G. A. Cohen criticized Rawls's focus on basic structures, arguing that the proper focus of a just society should be just individuals rather than the justice of institutions (Cohen 1989, 1997). Taking things in a more radical direction, Iris Marion Young attempted to move beyond "the distributive paradigm," arguing for a conception of justice based on demands of social movements (Young 1990: ch. 1). Perhaps the most influential response was Robert Nozick's development of an alternative, "historical" theory of distributive justice—discussed below.

Other criticisms directly influenced Rawls's evolution. H. L. A. Hart raised important objections to Rawls's treatment of liberty (Hart 1975). Rawls's claim that liberty cannot be traded off for other values faces obvious problems. For one, liberty is regularly traded off against other values—for example, property, in any system of private property. Moreover, liberties themselves can conflict. Rawls fails to provide an index of liberties, which ones take precedence over others, to guide us in trade-offs.

A widespread criticism addressed Rawls's contention that the difference principle would be chosen behind the veil of ignorance. If people do not know their particular situations, standard probabilistic reasoning dictates that they choose to maximize average shares. Rawls rejects this conclusion as overly risky. But theorists responded with a mixed principle. Rather than the difference principle, the result should be a principle that combines an adequate minimum level (poverty line) below which people cannot sink and which maximizes average share above that level (Barry 1973: ch. 8; 1989: ch. 6; Fishkin 1975; Harsanyi 1975). It is interesting to note that participants in simulated choice experiments behind a veil of ignorance, conducted in the United States, Canada, and Poland, consistently and overwhelmingly selected a mixed option, 77.8 percent of the time. A principle similar to the difference principle was chosen only 1.2 percent of the time (Frohlich and Oppenheimer 1992: 60).

According to Rawls himself, an especially severe difficulty concerned the "stability" of justice as fairness. Rawls was concerned that a principle of justice be able to generate its own support, which, in his terms, means it is "stable." In what Rawls calls a "well-ordered society," people come to accept the principles of justice and to behave in accordance with them. This ideal is threatened by the pluralism of liberal societies. Inhabitants of these societies belong to widely different cultural and religious traditions and hold different overall philosophical views, what Rawls calls "comprehensive" views. Pluralism conflicts with general acceptance of the principles of justice. As developed in *Theory*, the principles are defended from a particular perspective and so are in effect grounded in a particular comprehensive view. In order to develop principles that could be accepted by proponents of other comprehensive views, Rawls was eventually led to present a radically revised account of justice as fairness.

ANARCHY, STATE, AND UTOPIA

Three years after publication of *Theory*, Rawls's Harvard colleague Robert Nozick published *Anarchy, State, and Utopia* (Nozick 1974), which is, after *Theory*, probably the most celebrated and widely discussed work in political philosophy in recent decades. In contrast to Rawls's defense of the social welfare state, Nozick's conclusions are libertarian. His main purposes in the work are reflected in its title. He attempts to refute the anarchist contention that a legitimate state is not possible by demonstrating how a state could come into existence without violating anyone's rights. This "minimal" state is charged only with protecting rights, including a strong conception of property rights, and enforcing contracts. Anything more than this is illegitimate, and Nozick mounts a full-scale assault upon conceptions of distributive justice that require more. The result is not only sustained criticism of Rawls's theory but Nozick's development of a powerful alternative view.

Although individual rights are central to Nozick's project, his justification of them is only cursory—as he was well aware (1974: p. xiv). To establish the possibility of a legitimate state, Nozick presents an "invisible hand" argument. As in the famous argument of Adam Smith, Nozick attempts to show how a result that is not directly anticipated by political actors, in this case, the emergence of a state, is brought about through their actions in pursuit of other goals. Nozick posits a state of nature based on Locke's. Without a common power to keep order, people, feeling threatened, have strong incentives to band together in protective associations. Because of the distinctive nature of protection, individuals not only want to be in *a* protective association, but in the strongest one possible, which is able to provide protection from other associations and their members. Thus the logic of protection causes individuals to leave their own associations and join the one that is strongest. This process strengthens that association further, giving other individuals incentives to join it, a process that continues until it emerges as the "dominant protective association" or "ultra-minimal state," which wields de facto authority in the relevant territory. Even people who do not join voluntarily are legitimately absorbed by this entity. Because of dangers that could result from their using force to defend themselves, the dominant protective agency may prevent them from doing so. But it must compensate them for this loss by protecting them. With everyone subject to this association's protection, the "minimal" state is achieved.

To counter claims that the state should do more than protect rights, Nozick presents a "historical" theory of distributive justice. This is comprised of three principles: just acquisition; just transfer; and rectification. Possessions are held legitimately, if they are acquired justly or result from just transfers, and so distribution of property should be based on historical events: "Whatever arises from a just situation by just steps is itself just" (Nozick 1974, 151). The principle of rectification, about which Nozick says little, is necessary to remedy distributions that came about unjustly. Nozick contrasts his historical view and what he refers to as "patterned" or "end-state" theories, according to which legitimate distribution must correspond to a "structural" principle of distribution such as Rawls's difference principle or a principle of utility.

Nozick's position amounts to support of the free market. His main objection to end-state principles is that they impinge upon the liberty of property-holders. For example, if people wish to pay extra to see Wilt Chamberlain play basketball, and he will play only if he receives an especially high salary, this will not be allowed, if it contravenes the required principle. Patterns prevent "capitalist acts between consenting adults" (1974: 163). Every time a transaction departs from the mandatory end-state distribution, the state must intervene.

Distributions that result from market transactions may be unacceptably inegalitarian if assessed against Rawls's principles. But Nozick believes Rawls's overall strategy based on the veil of ignorance is misconceived. The veil of ignorance misconstrues the nature of property. Property is not something that one finds already in existence, to be distributed according to whatever principle one prefers. According to Nozick's historical theory, property comes into the world attached to the people who produce it. Nozick contends that Rawls's method of developing principles of justice behind a veil of ignorance is unfairly biased toward egalitarian principles. If property exists in the form of ready-made stuff—manna from heaven—to be distributed to all alike, and each person has an interest in getting the largest possible share, a principle of equal distribution must result. But is this how property should be construed? (Nozick 1974: 198). Along similar lines, if students in a class are placed behind a veil of ignorance and asked to distribute grades on a chemistry test, the resulting distribution will be equal, which is obviously unfair to the students with greater ability in chemistry or who studied harder. In separating people from what they have produced, the veil of ignorance undermines the concept of desert, while this in turn entails an insupportable conception of the person.

Nozick contends that Rawls's principles violate the Kantian injunction to treat people always as ends in themselves, never merely as means. Behind the veil of ignorance, people's special talents and abilities become resources to be used to promote the interests of all alike. As Rawls writes: "the difference principle represents, in effect, an agreement to regard the distribution of natural talents as a common asset" (Rawls 1971: 101). Does this mean that gifted people are used as means to the advancement of others? One could respond that this is treating people's *talents* as means, rather than the people themselves. But Nozick answers that this response is convincing only "if one presses *very* hard on the distinction between men and their talents, assets, abilities, and special traits," and he questions the defensibility of the conception of the person that results from pressing on this distinction (Nozick 1974: 228; emphasis in original).

Nozick's arguments did not, of course, go unanswered. For instance, his account of rights was criticized for being not only inadequately defended but overly strong, especially in regard to an absolutist view of property rights. Supporters of economic redistribution criticized the Wilt Chamberlain example. In focusing on particular voluntary transaction, the example presupposes the fairness of background institutions and does not recognize that a long series of voluntary transactions could have highly undesirable overall results, which would not have been accepted voluntarily by many community members. Nozick's criticism of the veil of ignorance neglects representative individuals' knowledge of how society works and their concern with long-term effects of the principles they choose. For example, if places in medical school were assigned arbitrarily, as Nozick apparently thinks the veil implies they would be, the eventual result would be incompetent doctors, which would adversely affect future members of society. Concern with a society that works well requires that many scarce opportunities be assigned to people best able to make use of them—in other words, to people who deserve them.

Communitarianism

As advanced by a series of thinkers during the 1980s and 1990s, communitarianism attracted enormous attention. Important figures include Alasdair MacIntyre, Charles Taylor, Michael Walzer, and Michael Sandel. Communitarians criticize the universalist pretensions of liberal theory and the kind of abstract moral theorizing to which it gives rise. Not only are moral standards rooted in the norms of particular communities, but the same is true of standards of inquiry. According to Macintyre: "standards of rational justification themselves emerge from and are part of a history in which they are vindicated" within a specific tradition (Macintyre 1988: 7). Along similar lines, Walzer argues that social criticism must be conducted within frameworks of beliefs and traditions of specific societies (Walzer 1987). As a set of philosophical claims, commu-nitarianism is far more detailed and defensible in its criticisms of liberalism than in any full-blown alternative. This is especially clear in communitarianism's most celebrated work, Sandel's *Liberalism and the Limits of Justice* (1982), which is largely a detailed criticism of *A Theory of Justice*.

In this work, Sandel presents alternative views of individual identity and standards of distributive justice, both of which he roots in the community. He criticizes Rawls's account of the liberal "self," "the conception of the moral subject" that Rawls posits (Sandel 1982: 49). Arguing backward from the original position to the conception of the person it presupposes, Sandel identifies an "unencumbered self," devoid of the particular attributes that make us who we are. Rather than viewing these as essential to the subject, Sandel claims, liberalism is committed to an abstract self that *chooses* its identity, as it chooses the moral principles to which it subscribes. This view of the self is insupportable: "we cannot coherently regard ourselves as the kind of beings" a Raw-lsian ethic requires that we be (Sandel 1982: 14).

According to Sandel's alternative view, the individual is not an abstraction inhabit-ing a ghostly original position. Rather, an individual is who she is because she lives in a particular time and belongs to a particular community. Factors such as her national-ity and religion are responsible for central aspects of her personality, while her moral life is built around relationships with other community members. Particular difficulties Sandel raises include the impossibility of grounding an acceptable conception of the person on the liberal unencumbered self. Like Nozick, he also criticizes Rawls for violating the Kantian injunction, by allowing the community to regard the attributes of individuals as means to promote the interests of other people.

Communitarianism should be credited with raising important questions concerning the nature of the liberal self. To some extent, the movement's popularity was connected with great interest in questions of identity that accompanied the rise of identity politics in the last half of the twentieth century. But, in spite of the power of some critical arguments, communitarianism has not worn well. There are clear reasons for this. To begin with, as Rawls argues, Sandel misunderstands the original position. The individuals posited there do not reflect Rawls's conception of human nature, but are hypothetical constructs, composed of the characteristics that we believe make for the most appropriate hypothetical choosers of our moral principles (Rawls 1985: 239 n. 21). Moreover, Will Kymlicka appears to have provided an account of the liberal self that defuses Sandel's objections. Liberalism does not posit a self devoid of particular attributes, an abstract, pre-existing entity that chooses its identity. Rather central to liberalism is the idea that people have the ability to maintain critical distance from their particular attributes, which they are able to revise if they wish to do so. A person is free to change her profession, to move from the USA to the UK, to switch religions, even surgically to change her sex. In this sense but only in this sense does liberalism recognize a gap between the self and its attributes and priority of the former to the latter (Kymlicka 1988; accepted by Rawls 1993: 27 n. 29). In *Political Liberalism*, Rawls presents the related idea of the "political conception of the person." In liberal society, one can change attributes—hair color, political party, and, again, even sex—without affecting one's rights or standing in society (Rawls 1993: 30). There is no substance to the claim that liberal theorists do not recognize the importance of particular attributes of the self. As Kymlicka argues, it is because people are concerned with these and wish to get them right that they may wish to change them.

Finally, in spite of its critical edge, communitarianism is hard put to provide positive moral recommendations. An injunction to act in accordance with the norms of our society and our identities may be well and good in a society that is extremely homogeneous, but, in modern liberal societies, norms often conflict. How do we decide which ones to follow? To address questions along these lines, one has no alternative but to engage in the kind of abstract moral reasoning communitarians decry. Moreover, extremely homogeneous societies are historically oppressive against minorities and anyone who does not conform to the dominant type. Faced with the possibility that at least some social norms are unjust, the communitarian, again, must engage in the process of ethical reflection to which communitarianism presents itself as an alternative.

THE EVOLUTION OF RAWLS'S THOUGHT

To address the problems noted above, Rawls recast justice as fairness as a "political" liberalism, moving his position in a communitarian direction by rooting it in the particular culture of liberal society. In his pioneering article "Justice as Fairness: Political not Metaphysical" (1985), Rawls reformulates justice as fairness as expressly intended to serve the practical function of allowing inhabitants of pluralistic societies to live together cooperatively. As Rawls uses the term, a "political" conception, as opposed to a comprehensive view, addresses a narrow range of practical issues. Although Rawls believes that profound disagreement is the normal result of the free use of reason, a society can be well ordered if people generally agree on a set of essential moral principles—a "political" conception of justice—which each person understands from the perspective of his or her own comprehensive view. The result is what Rawls calls an "overlapping consensus." Justice as fairness is one set of principles that can fulfill this function.

Rawls claims that a liberal theory of justice will be accepted only in *liberal* societies. Such societies have undergone an often painful process of historical development, especially since the Protestant Reformation and ensuing centuries of religious warfare, which has caused their inhabitants to recognize the need to cooperate on some basis other than shared religious or other comprehensive views. As the idea of tolerance has been accepted in regard to questions of religion, it must be extended to philosophical differences as well. Rather than being based on philosophical agreement, justice as fairness is now developed from generally recognized "intuitive ideas" present in the public culture of liberal societies. The main intuitive ideas are conceptions of the person as free and equal, and of society as a cooperative enterprise for mutual advantage. Rawls believes liberal societies have developed a particular conception of the person, as having two "moral powers," the ability to choose a conception of the good and to pursue it in a plan of life, and the ability to live cooperatively with others. The process of choosing principles of justice behind the veil of ignorance in Rawls's revised original position is to promote the development of these moral powers. The primary goods are reconceived as goods that are necessary for the development of the moral powers, and so principles according to which people receive the largest possible share of these goods that should promote maximum development of the powers.

Because of the pluralism of liberal societies, Rawls argues that choice of principles of justice should be "freestanding," not based on particular comprehensive views. If the choice is made on the basis of the intuitive ideas, the results should be acceptable to adherents of different comprehensive views, thereby achieving an overlapping consensus. This reconceived argument also responds to the criticism of Hart. As Hart recommended, Rawls replaces concern with maximizing "liberty" with maximizing a particular list of liberties. These include freedom of thought, liberty of conscience, political liberties, and the like (Rawls 1993: 291). Rawls's conception of the person with interests in furthering the growth of the moral powers provides a way to index different liberties. Because freedom of speech, of conscience, or of religion are more necessary for development of the moral powers than, for example, economic rights, they take precedence.

Rawls retains his belief that justice as fairness will be the result of the choice procedure. He believes that his first principle of justice, the equal liberty principle, will clearly be chosen. But he has less confidence in the difference principle. While he continues to believe that the difference principle is the preferred principle of economic distribution, he recognizes that there is no knockdown argument for it over other plausible principles and that the balance of considerations in its favor could strike other people as less weighty (1993: 156–7; 1996: pp. xlviii–xlix; 2002: sects 36 ff.) In his later works, Rawls describes a liberal doctrine as comprised of three elements: a set of basic rights and liberties; assignment of special weight or priority to these, so that they are not outweighed by considerations of overall social utility; measures ensuring adequate resources to enable citizens to make use of their rights (Rawls 1997: 774). The third component distinguishes the liberalism of the social welfare state from earlier forms of liberalism (see Moon, Chapter 40, this volume) and from libertarian views such as Nozick's. Recognizing a variety of ways in which this requirement can be met, Rawls is content to have established justice as fairness as one of a set of acceptable liberal views.

An important component of political liberalism is Rawls's doctrine of public reason, which is also made necessary by the pluralism of liberal societies. In addition to agreed-upon principles of justice, liberal legitimacy requires agreement on standards of argument to be employed in addressing political issues. Rawls describes the latter too as arising from the original position. In addition to deciding on principles of justice, the representative individuals must generate "a companion agreement" on epistemological principles, which will define "the guidelines for public inquiry," and so the "principles of reasoning" and "rules of evidence," for public discussion (Rawls 2002: 89).

Liberal legitimacy requires that forms of argument be acceptable to the entire range of reasonable citizens. Thus public reason must also be "freestanding." When "constitutional essentials" and matters of basic justice are at issue, arguments used must be independent of particular comprehensive views. In terms of substantive content, this implies reliance on "presently accepted general beliefs and forms of reasoning found in common sense, and the methods and conclusions of science, when these are not controversial" (Rawls 1993: 224; 1997: 773–80).

Much of the criticism directed at *Political Liberalism* has focused on Rawls's view of public reason. A prominent line of attack is launched by proponents of religious comprehensive views, who claim public reason is unfair to religious citizens. To begin with, it unfairly limits their freedom, in forcing them to set aside essential parts of their identities when engaging in public debate, which is a burden non-religious citizens do not bear (Wolterstorff 1997: 94; Eberle 2002: 232; Stout 2004: 68, 75–7). Along similar lines, while professing fairness, public reason is biased toward secular world views, as its results seem invariably to align with such views. Rawls's religious critics argue that what justice actually requires is allowing citizens to support their views with the arguments they believe to be most forceful, regardless of whether or not they draw on specific comprehensive views. Proponents of this position believe that Rawls is not correct about the public culture of liberal societies. These societies, it is argued, present a different conception of the free and equal citizen, as one who is free to argue from his or her comprehensive view, while all citizens are equal in possessing this right (McConnell 2000). So construed, freedom is participatory, closer to Benjamin Constant's "freedom of the ancients" than "of the moderns" (Constant 1983 [1819]) Along similar lines, critics offer an alternative construal of respect. In the words of William Galston: "we show others respect when we offer them, as explanation, what we take to be our true and best reasons for acting as we do" (Galston 1992: 109).

Proponents of public reason have a response to this line of argument. The implications of such open advocacy could lead to tyranny of the majority, endangering the rights to minorities. But critics of public reason prefer to rely on substantive elements of the political system. As Christopher Eberle argues, liberal citizens have learned from past horrors and have taken steps—for example, the Bill of Rights—to make sure they will not happen again (Eberle 2002: 161).

In a society as religious as the United States, it is unlikely that public culture will support positions as liberal as those Rawls advocates (Klosko 2000). Rawls was probably aware of this problem, as indicated by his interest in the utopian role of political theory in his last works. In *Justice as Fairness: A Restatement*, he writes: "We view political philosophy as realistically utopian: that is, as probing the limits of practical political possibility" (Rawls 2002: 4). Debate over public reason is currently ongoing. Whether liberal public culture will catch up with Rawls's vision remains to be seen.

FEMINISM AND LIBERALISM

In the second half of the twentieth century, concerns of equality that were prominent in Anglo-American political philosophy were obviously influenced by currents in society—for example, struggles for civil rights and women's rights and on behalf of other oppressed groups. A central demand on the part of all these groups was to be treated with "equal concern and respect" (Dworkin 2000). Major contributions to political philosophy were made in conjunction with these movements. I will briefly discuss questions concerning treatment of women and cultural minorities.

For much of Western history, women enjoyed markedly inferior status. In many societies, they had little or no public identity and few if any civil rights. According to J. S. Mill in *The Subjection of Women* (1939 [1869]), such treatment of women was a residue of earlier forms of tyranny. Liberal societies had abolished slavery and authoritarian government. Mill was confident this last form of subordination would also pass away.

Many feminist theorists argue that traditional liberal political theory pays insufficient attention to concerns of women, in particular to childrearing (see Hirschmann, Chapter 46, this volume). Criticisms are developed from a variety of perspectives. Radical feminist theorists resist "male" models of reasoning and posit alternative feminist epistemology. More moderate views address disadvantages women confront from a philosophical framework that is essentially liberal. My concern in this section is the latter perspective, especially in a well-known work by Susan Okin. More radical perspectives cannot be discussed here.

A particular target of feminist critics is the private/public distinction that is a basic feature of liberal political philosophy. As traditionally viewed, the distinction was between the private realm of the family and home and the public sphere, which encompassed the worlds of politics, business, and wider society. According to traditional views, the home and family were off limits to government interference. An unfortunate implication of this position was that fathers and husbands, generally physically stronger than their wives and children, were able to violate their rights with impunity. For instance, until fairly recently, most states did not recognize marital rape. Husbands were held to have the right to have sex with their wives whenever they pleased, while this subject was viewed as a private matter, closed to government. Interpreted along these lines, the private/public distinction could serve to oppress women.

Achievement of equality for women required reformulation of the distinction. This concern is central to Okin's *Justice, Gender, and the Family* (1989), in which she extends criticism of the private/public distinction to address issues concerned with unpaid work in the home. Okin makes a powerful case that the way unpaid work is distributed in existing societies oppresses women—although at present (2010), perhaps somewhat less than twenty years ago, when her book was published.

Okin's analysis turns on economic circumstances. The labor market rewards people according to their skills and experience. Unpaid domestic work—taking care of the home and caring for children—is not only burdensome in itself, but takes up time and energy that could otherwise be used to improve one's skills and marketability. Because the bulk of such work is done by women, the division of domestic labor places women in disadvantageous positions. To some extent, women find themselves in this position because of gender expectations. Many women do not prepare adequately for the labor market, intending to be wives and mothers. Because their earning capacity is generally lower than that of their husbands, they are in weaker bargaining positions within the marriage. For similar reasons, they are less able to leave their marriages through divorce, which generally means a drastic fall in their standard of living, as opposed to that of husbands, who, with more marketable skills, tended to raise their standard of living after divorce. Lacking marketable skills and effectively unable to divorce, many women find it difficult to resist unfair distribution of domestic work: "gender structured marriage involves women in a cycle of socially caused and distinctly asymmetric vulnerability" (Okin 1989: 138; emphasis removed).

Besides being inherently unfair to women, this situation has unfortunate social implications. Oppressive homes are ill suited to produce democratic citizens. Because the family is a "school of justice" (Okin 1989: 17–24), equality for women not only means improvement in their own lives but should also help the next generation fulfill their role as citizens of democracies.

In order to remedy this situation, Okin argues, the dividing line between private and public must be rethought. Just as laws have been passed to protect women from marital rape and other forms of domestic violence, so other policies can promote equality in the home. The existence of affordable, high-quality day care and more flexible work schedules could increase many women's opportunities to work outside the home. Since women have been victimized by no-fault divorce, alimony and child-support payments should be increased, with payment enforced. Similarly, the general belief that a post-divorce husband's earnings belong entirely to him should be countered. If the wife made sacrifices to help him acquire marketable skills, some percentage of his future earnings should be awarded to her. Not only would such reforms directly contribute to women's economic well-being, but, by improving women's prospects outside their marriages, it would increase their ability to exit and so also strengthen their bargaining positions within marriage.

In *Justice, Gender, and the Family*, Rawls is one of Okin's targets. She contends that Rawls largely overlooked injustice to women. Unaccountably, sex is not mentioned as one of the characteristics knowledge of which is shielded by the veil of ignorance. In *Theory*, Rawls says almost nothing about the family, although it is one of society's basic institutions, as Rawls defines them (Okin 1989: 92–3), and so should be a central concern. In "The Idea of Public Reason Revisited" (1997), Rawls responds, accepting Okin's criticisms but saying that his shortcomings on this subject are his fault, rather than a fault of his theory itself (1997: 787 n. 58). However, he raises additional issues of gender equality that liberal political philosophy has difficulty addressing. Many women voluntarily subordinate themselves to their husbands—and raise their daughters to do so as well—in accordance with religious beliefs. Liberal theory is deeply concerned with preserving rights, including, of course, religious liberty, which falls within the private sphere. Liberal theory demands that women have the opportunity to live equally in society, if they choose to do so. But, if they do not, forcible intervention in family life to counter unfavorable gender identities will oftentimes cross the boundaries of permissible state activities (Rawls 1997: 764–5).

MULTICULTURALISM

Problems of multiculturalism result from the pluralism of modern societies, as different cultural groups demand recognition of their identities and special accommodations for their cultural practices. According to Kymlicka, the standard liberal position on these issues is the assimilation model of the melting pot. As long as people are not discriminated against, they can achieve equality and blend into the larger culture. This position too rests heavily on the private/public distinction. Individuals are to be able to practice their cultures in their private lives, as long as their practices do no harm, while they are protected from oppression by the right to exit their cultural groups. On this model, the state is to be neutral between cultures. But, Kymlicka argues, public culture cannot possibly be neutral. For instance, the state must privilege a particular language or languages, while something similar holds for recognition of particular holidays, which favor specific groups.

Kymlicka's positon is a liberal multiculturalism. He upholds the crucial liberal value of autonomy and makes his case on liberal grounds. He contends that culture is necessary to provide a framework of values within which people can make autonomous choices; understanding one's culture "is a precondition of making intelligent judgments about how to lead our lives" (Kymlicka 1995: 83). It not only provides options, it also provides "the spectacles though which we identify experiences as valuable" (1995: 83; quoting Ronald Dworkin).

Kymlicka argues that, in certain cases, cultures are justified in receiving protection against the larger society. This does not hold for what he calls "ethnic groups," members of which came to their new country voluntarily, as immigrants. In doing so, they in effect agreed to accept the existing public culture. They are, of course, free to practice their cultural traditions in their private lives and voluntarily to associate with other members of their groups, but they do not have legitimate complaints if their language or customs are not officially recognized. National minorities, in contrast, are "previously self-governing, territorially concentrated cultures" that were incorporated into larger states (1995: 10). Members of these groups did not come to a new country voluntarily but were forcibly included in the new country through war or annexation. Examples are American Indians and inhabitants of Quebec, which became a province of Canada after the Seven Years War. Because members of these groups did not consent to the existing national culture, Kymlicka defends various special rights for them that enable them to preserve their culture whilst experiencing minority status. These include rights of self-government, special representation, and what he calls "polyethnic rights." The last category includes rights to public funding of cultural practices and exemptions from various laws and requirements that interfere with practice of their culture. An important example is restrictions on the use of English in Quebec, to preserve its Francophone culture. Similarly, among Pueblo Indians in the American Southwest, the tribal religion is given special authority, which, according to Kymlicka, amounts to a theocratic government that discriminates against members who do not accept the tribal religion (Kymlicka 1995: 40).

As liberal societies become more pluralistic, the kinds of issues that Kymlicka raises have become increasingly prominent. Issues are especially problematic in regard to illiberal groups in liberal societies. From the liberal point of view, practices of these groups, such as denying women education or forcing them to marry in their early teens, are illegitimate. Under these practices, women are denied basic rights, and that is more or less all there is to it. But, from the point of view of illiberal groups, the larger society is denying them the right to practice their culture or religion. In a multicultural society, only they are denied this opportunity.

A vigorous liberal response is presented by Brian Barry, in *Culture and Equality* (2002). Barry defends basic liberal values and believes that, with scant exceptions, they should apply throughout society. He has an especially forceful response to complaints on behalf of illiberal groups. He contends that the protests are generally made by men, especially older men in positions of authority, while the people suffering are generally female and young. To assess the legitimacy of some oppressive practice, one should ask the people who actually bear the weight of it.

GLOBAL JUSTICE

In recent years, theorists have begun to address problems of global distributive justice. Proceedings from basic assumptions concerning the equality of all human beings and the injustice of arbitrary inequalities leads to unsettling conclusions. Because the country in which one is born is obviously a matter of chance, global inequalities cry out for redress. These concerns are intensified by the existence of enormous differences in wealth between countries. To be born in a rich country makes it likely that one will live in material comfort and relative ease, while birth in a poor country could well have opposite consequences. However, strong redistributive duties on the part of inhabitants of rich countries toward inhabitants of poor countries run counter to common moral intuitions, according to which people have special obligations toward their fellows. Duties toward impoverished people in other countries are widely recognized. But these are generally viewed as requirements to meet pressing needs, to insure physical survival, as in the case of famine victims, or victims of natural disasters. These duties require far less than the demands of equality at the heart of justice. In their approaches to questions of global justice, theorists generally fall into two camps. "Cosmopolitans" support strong duties of global justice, and so argue for extensive redistribution. "Statists" uphold special distributive requirements toward compatriots. In order for the latter to make their case, they must establish strong, morally relevant differences between relationships to one's compatriots and to people in other countries.

As in many other areas, at the present time, the most prominent author on global justice is Rawls, whose *Law of Peoples* (1999) upholds a non-cosmopolitan perspective. Viewing society as a cooperative venture for mutual advantage, Rawls (1971: 4) argues that justice centers on fair distribution of the advantages and disadvantages that result from social cooperation, and so contrasts duties of justice, which are owed only to people with whom one stands in cooperative relationships, with weaker duties, owed to people generally. Once again, the latter require only assistance to those in dire need, as opposed to requirements to redress distributive inequalities.

Ever since the appearance of *Theory of Justice*, Rawls's approach has been criticized for moral arbitrariness. If the veil of ignorance eliminates knowledge of one's country, the process of reasoning behind the veil of ignorance that Rawls describes should result in a global difference principle. Concerned that they may end up being members of impoverished countries, the representative individuals will argue for strong redistributive duties (Barry 1973: ch. 12; Beitz 1979). In *Law of Peoples*, Rawls argues against a global original position as invading the autonomy of non-Western countries (Rawls 1999: 82–3, 60). He argues against redistributive duties stronger than duties to rescue those in need. Because a country's public culture determines its economic fortunes, Rawls argues that the most effective way to help what he calls "burdened societies" is to help them develop just or decent basic institutions (1999: 105–13).

Cosmopolitan theorists have developed strong arguments for global distributive justice. Rawls's claim that concerns of cooperation make justice a domestic matter has been criticized. As argued especially by Charles Beitz (1979), cooperative relationships similar to those within countries are also present in the international realm. Examples include communications, travel, and multinational corporations, while a network of global institutions has arisen, including the World Bank and World Trade Organization. The economies of many countries are bound up with these factors, which, it is argued, amount to a global basic structure.

Arguments for global distributive justice have also been made on other grounds. Thomas Pogge makes his case on the basis of injustices rich countries have perpetrated against poor (Pogge 2002). These go back to colonial times, but include unfair trade agreements, and, strikingly, standard features of international law, which disadvantage people in poor countries. These include resource and borrowing privileges, which are enjoyed by countries' rulers. Because of these provisions, rulers of poor countries, ruling essentially by force and lacking any usual claim to legitimacy, are able to plunder their countries' natural wealth and also to borrow in their countries' names, in order to advance their own interests rather than those of their countries. Their misbegotten riches are used for personal luxuries and, especially, the purchase of arms, which keep them in power. Other theorists, take different tacks—for example, arguing from strong conceptions of human rights, including economic rights, which transcend national borders (Shue 1996; Buchanan 2003; Caney 2005).

The most prominent defense of special requirements toward compatriots proceeds from distinctive qualities of domestic institutions, which are not present in the international sphere. In an important article, Michael Blake attributes the need for justice to the existence of coercive institutions within states (Blake 2001). Beginning with liberalism's concern to promote autonomy, Blake argues that the coercive measures that exist in liberal societies are incompatible with autonomy and therefore require justification. They could be legitimized if subjects consented to them or would consent under appropriate circumstances. Distributive justice—for example, implementation of Rawls's difference principle, comes in to meet this need, as people would consent, once they realized "that no alternative principle could have made them any better off" (Blake 2001: 283).

A similar argument is presented by Thomas Nagel, who also proceeds from society's coercive institutions (Nagel 2005). The state, unlike other forms of association, is nonvoluntary. Ordinarily, we do not have a choice whether to join it, while an "institution that one has no choice about joining must offer terms of membership" that meet high standards (2005: 133)—higher than those provided by weaker moral requirements owed people in other countries. Nagel focuses on the peculiar nature of coercion in democratic societies, that individuals are not only subject to it, but, through representative institutions, are also its authors. According to Nagel, it is this double-sided nature of state coercion that triggers requirements of justice, "that creates the special presumption against arbitrary inequalities in our treatment by the system" (2005: 128–9).

At the present time, the subject of global justice has moved to the center of philosophical debate. As with overall focus on the subject of equality, this development can in large part be attributed to changing social and political circumstances. As the world has become increasingly globalized, concerns of people in other countries have leapt to the fore, and moral dimensions of increased international interaction have been subject to increased scrutiny.

Concluding Remarks

A central theme in the above account is the political nature of contemporary political philosophy. In reviewing major currents in the field, I have repeatedly noted relationships between developments in society and philosophical responses. In modern democratic societies, political issues are battled on the plane of ideas. Contemporary political philosophy is largely a practical discipline, devoted to developing and criticizing the philosophical perspectives that undergird social policies.

Recent years have witnessed explosive growth in the field. There has been a proliferation of new journals, including *Philosophy and Public Affairs*, *Political Theory*, and

Journal of Political Philosophy. Production of new books and monographs has become a floodtide. One problem with this output, as Kymlicka notes in his valuable overview of the subject, is that it has become too great for any scholar adequately to keep up with (Kymlicka 2002: viii). In his 500-page survey, Kymlicka concentrates almost exclusively on questions of equality, which he views as at the heart of contemporary political philosophy. The above account largely supports this assessment, although theorists have not neglected other subjects. In recent years, there have been important studies of rights, democracy, political obligation, tolerance, and many other topics discussed in this volume.

The main theorists and theories discussed in this chapter are vigorously attacked. Within the Anglo-American tradition, philosophical justification of the welfare state has called forth libertarian responses, especially works of Friedrich Hayek, James Buchanan, and other important thinkers, in addition to Nozick (see Eric Mack, Chapter 41, this volume) The tradition itself has been criticized from alternative perspectives, including multiculturalism, feminist theory, critical race theory, and the point of view of traditional religions. Debates on innumerable subjects are ongoing. As Rawls says, the free use of human reason leads inevitably to disagreement. But this is in welcome contrast to the field's moribund condition a half century ago.

REFERENCES

Ayer, A. J. (1946). *Language, Truth, and Logic.* London: V. Gollancz.

Barry, B. (1965). *Political Argument.* London: Routledge.

Barry, B. (1973). *The Liberal Theory of Justice.* Oxford: Oxford University Press.

Barry, B. (1989). *Theories of Justice: A Treatise on Social Justice*, vol. i. Berkeley and Los Angeles: University of California Press.

Barry, B. (2002). *Culture and Equality: An Egalitarian Critique of Multiculturalism.* Cambridge, MA: Harvard University Press.

Beitz, C. (1979). *Political Theory and International Relations.* Princeton: Princeton University Press.

Berlin, I. (1962). "Does Political Theory Still Exist?" in P. Laslett and W. G. Runciman (eds), *Philosophy, Politics, and Society.* 2nd ser. Oxford: Basil Blackwell.

Berlin, I. (1969 [1957]). "Two Concepts of Liberty," in *Four Essays on Liberty.* Oxford: Oxford University Press.

Blake, M. (2001). "Distributive Justice, State Coercion, and Autonomy," *Philosophy and Public Affairs*, 30: 257–96.

Buchanan, A. (2003). *Justice, Legitimacy, and Self-Determination: Moral Foundations for International Law.* Oxford: Oxford University Press.

Caney, S. (2005). *Justice beyond Borders.* Oxford: Oxford University Press.

Cohen, G. A. (1989). "On the Currency of Egalitarian Justice," *Ethics*, 99: 906–44.

Cohen, G. A. (1997). "Where the Action Is: On the Site of Distributive Justice," *Philosophy and Public Affairs*, 26: 3–30.

CONSTANT, B. (1988 [1819]). "The Liberty of the Ancients and the Liberty of the Moderns," in *Constant: Political Writings*, ed. and trans. B. Fontana. Cambridge: Cambridge University Press.

DWORKIN R. (1981*a*) "What is Equality? Part 1: Equality of Welfare," *Philosophy & Public Affairs*, 10: 228–40.

DWORKIN R. (1981*b*). "What is Equality? Part 2: Equality of Resources," *Philosophy & Public Affairs*, 10: 283–345.

DWORKIN R. (2000). *Sovereign Virtue: The Theory and Practice of Equality* (Cambridge, MA: Harvard University Press.

EASTON, D. (1953). *The Political System*. New York: Knopf.

EBERLE, C. (2002). *Religious Conviction in Liberal Politics*. Cambridge, MA.: Cambridge University Press.

FEINBERG, J. (1984). *Harm to Others*. New York: Oxford University Press.

FISHKIN, J. (1975). "Justice and Rationality: Some Objections to the Central Argument in Rawls's Theory," *American Political Science Review*, 69: 615–29.

FREUD, S. (1936 [1929]). *Civilization and its Discontents*, trans. J. Riviere. London: Hogarth.

FROHLICH, N., and OPPENHEIMER, J. (1992). *Choosing Justice: An Experimental Approach to Ethical Theory*. Berkeley and Los Angeles: University of California Press.

GALSTON, W. (1992). *Liberal Purposes*. Cambridge: Cambridge University Press.

HARSANYI, J. (1975). "Can the Maximin Principle Serve as a Basis for Morality?" *American Political Science Review*, 69: 594–606.

HART, H. L. A. (1961). *The Concept of Law*. Oxford: Oxford University Press.

HART, H. L. A. (1975). "Rawls on Liberty and its Priority," in N. Daniels (ed.), *Reading Rawls*. New York: Basic Books, 230–52.

HOBHOUSE, L. (1911). *Liberalism*. London: Williams and Norgate.

KLOSKO, G. (2000). *Democratic Procedures and Liberal Consensus*. Oxford: Oxford University Press.

KUHN, T. (1962). *The Structure of Scientific Revolutions*. Chicago: University of Chicago Press.

KYMLICKA, W. (1988). "Liberalism and Communitarianism," *Canadian Journal of Philosophy*, 18: 181–203.

KYMLICKA, W. (1995). *Multicultural Citizenship*. Oxford: Oxford University Press.

KYMLICKA, W. (2002). *Contemporary Political Philosophy: An Introduction*. 2nd edn. Oxford: Oxford University Press.

LASLETT, P. (1956). "Introduction," in P. Laslett (ed.), *Philosophy, Politics, and Society*. Oxford: Basil Blackwell.

LASLETT, P., and FISHKIN, J. (1979). "Introduction," in P. Laslett and J. Fishkin (eds), *Philosophy, Politics, and Society*. 5th ser. New Haven: Yale University Press.

LYONS, D. (1975). "Nature and Soundness of the Contract and Coherence Arguments," in N. Daniels (ed.), *Reading Rawls*. New York: Basic Books, 141–67.

McCONNELL, M. (2000). "Believers as Equal Citizens," in N. Rosenblum (ed.), *Obligations of Citizenship and Demands of Faith*. Princeton: Princeton University Press, 90–110.

MACINTYRE, A. (1988). *Whose Justice? Which Rationality?* Notre Dame, IN: University of Notre Dame Press.

MANNHEIM, K. (1936 [1929]). *Ideology and Utopia*, trans. E. Shils and L. Wirth. London: Paul, Trench, Trubner.

MILL, J. S. (1989 [1869]). *The Subjection of Women*, in S. Collini (ed.), *J. S. Mill: On Liberty and Other Writings*. Cambridge: Cambridge University Press.

MILLER, D., and DAGGER, R. (2003). "Utilitarianism and Beyond: Contemporary Analytical Political Theory," in T. Ball and R. Bellamy (eds). *The Cambridge History of Twentieth-Century Political Thought*. Cambridge: Cambridge University Press, 446–69.

NAGEL, T. (2005). "The Problem of Global Justice," *Philosophy and Public Affairs*, 33: 113–47.

NOZICK, R. (1974). *Anarchy, State, and Utopia*. New York: Basic Books.

OKIN, S. M. (1989). *Justice, Gender, and the Family*. New York: Basic Books.

POGGE, T. (2002). *World Poverty and Human Rights*. Cambridge: Polity.

POGGE, T. (2006). *John Rawls*, trans. M. Kosch. Oxford: Oxford University Press.

RAWLS, J. (1951). "Outline of a Decision Procedure for Ethics," *Philosophical Review*, 60: 177–97.

RAWLS, J. (1958). "Justice as Fairness," *Philosophical Review*, 67: 164–94.

RAWLS, J. (1971). *A Theory of Justice*. Cambridge, MA: Harvard University Press.

RAWLS, J. (1985). "Justice as Fairness: Political not Metaphysical," *Philosophy and Public Affairs*, 14: 223–51.

RAWLS, J. (1993). *Political Liberalism*. New York: Columbia University Press.

RAWLS, J. (1996). *Political Liberalism*. Rev. paperback edn. New York: Columbia University Press.

RAWLS, J. (1997). "The Idea of Public Reason Revisited," *University of Chicago Law Review*, 64: 765–807.

RAWLS, J. (1999). *The Law of Peoples*. Cambridge, MA: Harvard University Press.

RAWLS, J. (2002). *Justice as Fairness: A Restatement*. Cambridge, MA: Harvard University Press.

SANDEL, M. (1982). *Liberalism and the Limits of Justice*. Cambridge: Cambridge University Press.

SEN, A. (1980). "Equality of What?" in S. M. McMurrin (ed.), *The Tanner Lectures on Human Values*. Cambridge: Cambridge University Press, 195–220.

SHUE, H. (1996). *Basic Rights: Subsistence, Affluence, and US Foreign Policy*. 2nd edn. Princeton: Princeton University Press.

STOUT, J. (2004). *Democracy and Tradition*. Princeton: Princeton University Press.

TALMON, J. L. (1955). *The Origins of Totalitarian Democracy*. London: Secker & Warburg.

WALZER, M. (1987). *Interpretation and Social Criticism*. Cambridge, MA: Harvard University Press.

WELDON, T. D. (1953). *The Vocabulary of Politics*. London: Penguin Books.

WOLTERSTORFF, N. (1997). "The Role of Religion in Decision and Discussion of Political Issues," in R. Audi and Wolterstorff, *Religion in the Public Square*. Savage, MD: Rowman and Littlefield.

YOUNG, I. M. (1990). *Justice and the Politics of Difference*. Princeton: Princeton University Press.

....

CHAPTER 27

CONTEMPORARY CONTINENTAL POLITICAL THOUGHT

....

STEPHEN K. WHITE

"CONTINENTAL Philosophy" is generally understood as a contrast term for "Anglo-American, Analytic Philosophy." On its face, we seem to have a distinction rooted in geography, the continent in question being Europe. But the geographic distinction has always been a very rough one, and the implied travel restrictions have often been violated. Thus a recent volume was playfully entitled *American Continental Philosophy* (Brogan and Risser 2000). In fact, some of the best Continental philosophers today are American, Canadian, and British. But does this rough geographical distinction sit atop a serious philosophical one? A good case can be made that the answer is "yes," at least when we are speaking of Continental *Political* Philosophy In what follows, I will make this case and argue that, because the distinction between the two philosophical orientations is important, it should be cultivated rather than either suppressed or *Aufgehoben*—a term Hegel used to explain how one perspective is dialectically negated by another, meaning that the first is partially overcome and yet also partially preserved in a new, more adequate synthesis of the two.

CONTINENTAL PHILOSOPHY AND CONTINENTAL POLITICAL THOUGHT

....

What is the relation of Continental Philosophy to Continental *Political* Philosophy—more frequently called Continental Political Thought? It is acceptable to think of the latter as at least partially a subcategory of the former. Clearly, the term "Continental

Philosophy" emerged first. Nevertheless, as I will show in a moment, the field of Continental political thought took shape as a response to a somewhat independent problem and thus has an at least somewhat independent profile.

It is generally agreed that "Continental philosophy" is a term that emerged in the 1950s, to help differentiate the kind of philosophy done in the United Kingdom from that done on the Continent (Passmore 1957: 11, 459–60; Glendinning 1999: 3–19; Cutrofello 2005: p. iv). The former focused on ordinary language and conceptual analysis, with a premium placed on clarity and rigor. This approach was contrasted with phenomenology and existentialism especially, views that some British philosophers denigrated as too "preoccupied with God, with dread, with consciousness, with personal belief, with deconstruction, or with politico-economic class struggle." These preoccupations were judged to condemn philosophy to remaining "a form of poetic monologue or obscurantist mystery-mongering" (L. J. Cohen, cited in Glendinning 1999: 12). Such characterizations leave little doubt that the distinction between Continental Philosophy and Anglo-American, Analytic Philosophy contained a more or less explicit desire that the European approach should be suppressed on English-speaking soil.

This animus has waxed and waned but never entirely disappeared. Nevertheless, over the last decades of the twentieth century, the Continental side increasingly found its footing in both the UK and the USA. Evidence for this is easy to find: there is now a dictionary of Continental philosophy; at least one "Guide"; two encyclopedias dedicated just to Continental philosophy; and a continual flow of articles and books by English-language publishers (Glendinning 1999; Solomon 2003; Protevi 2005; Leiter and Rosen 2007). Organizationally, there is a flourishing Society for Phenomenology and Existential Philosophy (founded in 1962); and there was a substantial movement in the American Philosophical Association in the 1980s seeking that group's authorization of a more "pluralistic" view of the discipline of philosophy.

Definitions of Continental Philosophy can be distinguished as strong or weak. By "weak," I mean efforts that try to avoid contentious philosophical claims and merely offer a diplomatically sensitive sorting in terms of time and place. Thus, Leiter and Rosen speak of Continental Philosophy as "(primarily) philosophy after Kant in Germany and France in the nineteenth and twentieth century" (Leiter and Roset 2007: 1). A stronger definition, on the other hand, would be one like Simon Critchley's, which not only refers us to different philosophical routes after Kant, but also associates those routes with differing positions on topics such as "nihilism" and "emancipation" (Critchley 2001: pp. iii–iv, 22).

My attempt at a useful definition of Continental *Political* Thought (hereafter CPT) will be of the strong sort and thus contentious from the start. This definition rests on a particular narrative. I see the tradition of CPT coming into focus not as a result of the appearance of a philosophical problem—how to philosophize after Kant—but rather as a result of a problem in public life: how to engage the political and cultural ferment that began in the Western democracies in the 1960s. During this period, just about every form of authority associated with the modern West's conception of itself was critically assaulted to one degree or another. A bumper sticker popular at the time summed up this attitude: "Question Authority."

Any strong definition will systematically exclude certain thinkers who might be included on weaker criteria. Thus, on my view, Continental political thought does not include Raymond Aron or Benjamin Constant. For some, this might appear patently outrageous. They would challenge my exclusion of important thinkers who were educated in Europe or lived most of their professional lives on that continent. What other strange patterns of exclusion might emerge from my definition? Would I be perverse enough to imagine a future twenty years from now in which almost all contemporary "Continental" political theorists were English or American? Although I doubt this will happen, I do have to accept that possibility. But perhaps, after a moment's reflection, this would not be so outrageous. After all, in the USA, we seem to get along perfectly well at breakfast time ordering and eating something named "English muffins." The fact that no such muffin actually exists in England causes no great outrage, except perhaps for the hungry but ignorant American tourist having breakfast in a London bed and breakfast who persists in demanding an English muffin, after the waiter has reacted cluelessly to this diner's initial order.

My definition revolves around a radical questioning of authority. Now this sort of questioning was traditionally associated with the Enlightenment in the eighteenth century. Kant summed up this attitude in his famous definition of Enlightenment as: "Man's release from self-incurred tutelage" (Kant 1991: 54; my translation). This release depended on a coordinated rational assault upon those institutions (religious, educational, political) that had claimed to provide authoritative guidance for centuries. The ferment of the 1960s gave the Enlightenment motto an ironic twist, for the questioning was now directed precisely against the hegemonic authority of "enlightened" values themselves, especially the core conceptions of the individual, reason, and freedom.

This radical questioning of authority beginning in the 1960s and continuing to the present emerged in the context of various cultural and political opposition movements in the USA and Europe against racism, war, colonialism, sexism, environmental degradation, capitalism, and the sclerotic institutions of the modern welfare state. Radically new social and political perspectives appeared, such as Herbert Marcuse's *One-Dimensional Man* in 1964, which in turn, excited further retrospective interest in the philosophical currents and ideas upon which these thinkers drew, such as the Frankfurt School of Critical Theory, Hegel—an accessible English edition of *The Phenomenology of Mind* (most now translate this as "Spirit") appeared in 1967—and a more humanistic version of Marx, whose *Economic-Philosophical Manuscripts* first appeared in a widely available English translation in 1961 (Fromm 1961; Marcuse 1964; Hegel 1967; Wiggershaus 1994). Another focus of growing critical reflection was Friedrich Nietzsche. In the immediate post-Second World War period, he was often associated with Nazism. The determined work of scholars like Walter Kaufmann who, as editors and translators, began, in the 1960s, to change this, created the basis for the appreciation of new perspectives on Nietzsche and his possible implications for political theory (on Kaufmann, see Strong 1975; also http://philosophy.princeton.

edu/walter_kaufmann.html (accessed 8 Nov. 2010)). In sum, it was a retroactive, constitutive glance, cast in the context of the 1960s, that brought to life the tradition of CPT.

In Europe, the political upheavals of the 1960s were crucial in the intellectual formation of a new generation of philosophers. This was especially true in France, where the crisis of authority crystallized in the May 1968 rebellion. This event had a deep influence on thinkers such as Michel Foucault, Jacques Derrida, François Lyotard, and Gilles Deleuze—who brought new, post-Marxist perspectives to bear, such as post-structuralism, deconstruction, and postmodernism (for overviews, see White 1991; Patton 2000; Bennett 2004).

My proposal that we associate CPT with a radical challenge to Enlightenment values is hardly novel. But I want to specify this suggestion further in a fashion that may be more contentious. What is common to the radicalism of Continental political thinkers is twofold. First, there is the common postulation that modern Western social life, despite its many achievements, carries within it a certain "malignancy." And, second, this postulation stands in a relationship of mutual incitement with a distinctive style of philosophical inquiry. Let me refer to these two commonalities as the "primary" characteristics of CPT. Later, I will introduce several "secondary" characteristics as well. No individual, secondary characteristic is required to place some thinker among the Continentals. To be included, one must exhibit only some subset of secondary characteristics in company with the two primary ones.

PRIMARY CHARACTERISTICS

Regarding the first characteristic, I choose the term "malignancy" carefully. Its broad range of meaning can be easily lost, because we tend today to collapse it into a very specific medical sense; that is, into the idea of a cancerous growth that cannot be arrested. Now I do want to draw upon some of the connotations associated with this current usage, such as the fact that a malignancy of this sort is systematically invasive, not directly willed by anyone, and may be lethal to its host. But it is also important to recognize that "malignancy" does not refer exclusively to the realm of medicine. In *The Oxford English Dictionary* the first meaning listed does not concern pathology, but rather challenging authority, both political and spiritual. Thus, when I say that CPT postulates a malignancy in modern social life, I mean partially that it identifies some logic embedded in that life that undermines, in a deep and systematic way, the authoritative values or institutions that prevail there.

My argument then is that the major figures in the tradition of CPT affirm the existence of some malignancy in one or more of the foregoing senses. For Marx, it takes the form of the systematic "alienation" of labor and the extraction of "surplus value" from the worker in the expansion of capitalism (Marx 1988: 69; see also Marx 1978b). In Rousseau, it appears as the "self-love" (*amour propre*) that gives rise to those deleterious forms of modern, "enlightened" thought and behavior that systematically undermine the possibility of a society whose members exhibit "civic virtue" (Rousseau 1964). Another, more contemporary example is found in the work of Michel Foucault, who sees modern institutions largely in terms of the expansion of "disciplinary" power and/or "bio-power" into areas of social life where the prevailing interpretations envision only an expansion of freedom and humaneness (Foucault 1977, 1991; Agamben 1998).

From my point of view, it is crucial only that thinkers conceive the existence of such a malignancy and thus a deeply rooted threat to the ongoing achievements of the modern West. Beyond that, they can differ in the way they understand the causes of that phenomenon, who is responsible for it, and what might cure it. When Marx spoke of "surplus value," he made it clear that this sort of exploitation was caused by the specific form that class domination took under capitalism. Eliminate the "bourgeoisie" through socialist revolution, and you eliminate expropriation. For Foucault, however, disciplinary power is more deeply embedded in the very texture of modern life. There is no collective "subject" who is responsible finally for its spread. Rather, he says, disciplinary power is ultimately caused by "an attentive malevolence that turns everything to account" (Foucault 1977: 139). No large-scale revolution can change this; only perhaps small-scale initiatives or "insurrections" that create spaces somewhat resistant to the "normalizing" imperatives of large institutions, both public and private (Foucault 1977: 177–94; 1980: 81–5). Rousseau is closer to Foucault than Marx in how deeply invasive his malignancy is in the body of Western modernity. The idea of a real cure is so difficult for him to conceive that he has recourse to the classical Greek idea of the (almost mythical) foreign "legislator" who is completely immune from the disease and can thus create radically new laws and institutions, the operation of which may bring relief (Rousseau 1987: bk II, ch. 7).

The three figures I have used to illustrate my malignancy criterion might make one wonder whether it picks out only thinkers on the Left. But that is certainly not correct. One can point, for example, to Leo Strauss or Martin Heidegger. Malignancy for Strauss is constituted by the growing influence of historicism and the systematic elimination of the standards of natural *Right* in the wake of the modern vogue for thinking only of individual *rights* (Strauss 1953). For Heidegger, the malignancy is constituted by the growing prevalence of that modern ontological mode of engagement with the world he calls *Gestell* or "enframing," by which he means that our primary stance toward others and the world around us is one of a grasping aimed at ever-expanding control (Heidegger 1977).

The second common feature of CPT is a certain "style" of philosophical analysis. In using this term, I do not mean anything systematic enough to warrant designation as a "methodology." Rather, I simply mean a way of starting the analysis of topics, questions, and concepts. CPT tends to problematize beginnings more than Anglo-American, Analytic Philosophy. It is suspicious of conventional or common sense starting points, typically arguing that they surreptitiously reflect, and thus leave unchallenged, whatever it is that is being identified as the malignancy of modern society. Nietzsche's "genealogy of morals" operates so as to take the common self-understanding of Western morality and trace its origins back to motivations of rancor and resentment present in Judaism's and early Christianity's attitudes to their Roman masters (Nietzsche 1994). The writings of Nietzsche have been deeply drawn upon by CPT over the last several decades.

Given Nietzsche's prominence, it is important here to note that his hostility to religion (this also applies to Marx) does not automatically translate into anti-theism being a necessary characteristic of CPT. In fact, beginning in the 1990s, a rather more open attitude toward religion began to emerge. This is not primarily a matter of the mass conversion of Continental philosophers to a given religion; rather it involves a growing awareness that the radical questioning of the foundations of Western thought has too often imagined that it could launch its critique without assuming any basic commitments on its own part. More recently, Continental thinkers have begun to understand that a non-foundationalist position will have its own ontological commitments that need to be placed in question along with those of believers in religious foundations (White 2000; Derrida 2002b).

Such reflections on philosophical beginnings can have a leavening influence on matters that many philosophers had taken as settled. Especially significant here is the familiar Enlightenment narrative of secularization, in which God is scripted as just fading away slowly in our rear-view mirror. Recently, Charles Taylor has taken up this question in a sustained fashion. What is distinctive about Taylor is not the simple fact that he is a Christian, but rather that his work re-examines the history of religious disputes in the West, since the late fifteenth century, and carefully teases apart a much richer and complex set of "spiritual" options for us today than are available in the conventional secularization story. For Taylor, the malignancy in Western modernity is found in this imperial narrative, as well as in the idea of the "disengaged self" who is the protagonist of that tale (Taylor 2007; see also 1989).

Another critical take on the reductivist logic of the secularization story occurs in William Connolly's work. Unlike Taylor, he is not a theist, but rather an "immanent naturalist"; yet he also wishes to pry open our spiritual alternatives so that they extend beyond the familiar—but false—dichotomy of theist–atheist (Connolly 2002: 85–7). A similar, more open attitude to the realm of spirituality in CPT is evident in Judith Butler's recent work. She is, of course, known initially for her *Gender Trouble* (1999), a work that falls squarely in the Continental category on the basis of its interrogation of our seemingly self-evident onto-logic of male and female. But more recently, in seeking a mode of thought and commitment that can sustain her insights, she has affirmed a "possible Jewish ethic of non-violence" (Butler 2006: 131).

Butler's underlying style of analysis has a quality that I see in much contemporary CPT. By her own admission, she is in the business of persistently "making trouble" for what is normal, rational, and authoritative in Western modernity. But this is, ultimately, not trouble for trouble's sake, but rather trouble in the name of drawing us away from more one-dimensional, celebratory accounts of modern society and toward ones that seek to comprehend it more as a complex and "ambiguous achievement" (Connolly 1993: 241–2).

CONTRAST WITH ANGLO-AMERICAN, ANALYTIC POLITICAL THOUGHT

A useful way to provide further clarification to the meaning and implications of my sketch of CPT is to fill out the contrasting picture of Anglo-American, Analytic Political Thought. The first characteristic of CPT is, as I indicated above, the postulation of some malignant logic in modern Western life. This malignancy can be conceived in quite different ways; but, however it is understood, its existence means that one can neither survey modern society as an unproblematic vista of the progress of reason and freedom, nor look to the future with an easy sense of confidence.

Anglo-American, Analytic Political Thought, on the other hand, typically starts from a more fundamental affirmation, often only implicit, of the mainstream, progressive understanding of the modern West and its basic values. For CPT, this, in effect, betrays a failure of critical intelligence from the very start. Fundamental problems may be missed, because they remain below the line of philosophical vision. It is not that analytic thought is uncritical. On the contrary, it works on all sorts of problems that arise in modern life. The failure, from the viewpoint of CPT, involves rather the level at which problems are identified. In analytic thought, they are typically constituted at the level of "normal" consciousness and conventional opinion. Now, at first sight, this might appear to be an unfair criticism. John Rawls, for example, develops a theory of justice that raises some deep questions about the degree of inequality capitalism permits; moreover, Rawls claims that his theory of justice might even be appropriate for a socialist society (1971: 280). But this sort of defense does not really answer the critical force of CPT's concern. This is so, because there is, in Rawls, no systematic critique of the logic of capitalism, as there is in Marx; or of gender, as there is in Butler; or of race, as there is in Franz Fanon (1963). Looking just at capitalism, it is useful to contrast Rawls with a contemporary representative of CPT—namely, Jürgen Habermas. Although one can find some interesting parallels between Habermas's "discourse ethics" and Rawls's theory of justice, the former's contribution remains linked with a postulation of the malignancy of strategic reason and "systems rationality" in modern economies and polities. The harm Habermas identifies resides ultimately in the way, in capitalism, these modes of reason increasingly threaten to marginalize or "colonize" social and political practices that, when healthy, are guided by a "more comprehensive" form of reason that is implicit in our linguistic interaction and alone constitutes the medium within which the normative legitimacy of practices can be sustained and transmitted over time (Habermas 1984: 10–23; 1987: 283–373).

At this point, defenders of analytic thought would probably respond that my way of characterizing that perspective is too one-sided. They might protest that CPT's way of constituting problems in a self-proclaimed radical fashion is fatally flawed. Continental thinkers' continual second-guessing of conventional, everyday political consciousness amounts to a blatant disregard of the opinions of ordinary citizens. In effect, CPT displays a disregard for democracy. Additionally, the emphasis of analytic theory on clarity, and its preference for tackling discrete problems—as opposed to more profound but also more amorphous ones—is based on understanding political theory's most basic obligation to be one of trying to resolve conceptual problems so as to facilitate better coordination of actors in a democratic society. Felicitous political theory, for the analytic philosopher, helps interaction avoid blockages that stem from conceptual confusion and misunderstanding.

Given this basic self-understanding, it should come as no surprise that much of recent Analytic Political Thought has organized its self-understanding around a single paradigm or research program. Beginning in the mid-1970s, Rawls's theory of justice came to provide the broad framework and key questions for research for many Anglo-American theorists. Rawlsian criteria have provided the metric in terms of which progress in political theory is to be gauged. As one might expect, Continental political theorists have actively contested this paradigm, arguing, for example, that its assumptions about modern Western political life still allow in too much inequality, are too dismissive of religion, or are too hostile toward those who prefer a society pursuing a vision of its own collective good, a goal that might in particular cases trump aspects of the individual liberty that Rawls makes relatively sacrosanct. And such criticisms would be defended in the name of the mandate of upsetting normal expectations and the concepts upon which they are based.

One might offer a summary characterization of the two approaches in terms of a simple contrast. Analytic thought looks for closure both in what is taken to be at issue at the start of an investigation and in the achievement of a clear-cut resolution of the problem being investigated. CPT, on the other hand, seeks to problematize starting points and may be satisfied at the conclusion of an investigation, even if no resolution of the initial problem has been reached, as long as the theorist has achieved a deeper or broader understanding of a constellation of issues that inform the matter being investigated. In sum, analytic political theory offers us lucidly moderate reflection upon moral–political life that promises better to coordinate our interactions, whereas CPT offers us systematically radical reflection that promises to open up the possibility of reimagining ourselves and our political life.

Secondary Characteristics

The following characteristics are secondary in the sense that no one necessarily appears in the work of every Continental political theorist. Any particular theorist will display rather some subset of these qualities. In sum, I am arguing that to be designated as a Continental political theorist one's work must possess the two primary characteristics I elucidated earlier, as well as some subset of these other, secondary characteristics.

The latter can be gathered under two broad headings. The first heading involves the *philosophical tools* needed to diagnose the malignancy the theorist postulates and orient our reaction to it. The second heading involves the *kind of transformation* the theorist imagines is needed to combat or overcome that malignancy or that may arise out of that overcoming.

Philosophical Tools

1. A crucial feature of many variants of CPT is a critique of science or modern reason in a broad sense. Such critique is aimed squarely at the Enlightenment and its legacy. The first to use this tool was Rousseau in his "Discourse on the Sciences and Arts" in 1751. This essay was his entry in a contest to provide the best answer to the following question: "Has the restoration of the sciences and arts tended to purify morals?" (Rousseau 1964) For any good Enlightenment *philosophe*, the answer was, of course, "yes." He was certain that the progress of sciences and arts would bring with it an enhancement of morality and justice. For Rousseau, however, the relationship is inverse: the former sort of progress brings with it a regress of the latter. Here Rousseau establishes himself as the first great critic of the Enlightenment and, on my definition, the first Continental political theorist. He thinks that the emphasis on science and technology, with their promise of economic progress, creates a citizenry devoid of any virtues that relate to public life. Modern citizens are concerned only with "me," never "we."

A number of prominent nineteenth-century Continental theorists did not follow Rousseau in his emphatic critique of Enlightenment reason, science, and technology. For example, Hegel's view of Enlightenment reason is mixed. In *The Phenomenology of Spirit* (1807), he attacks the Enlightenment for what he says is the corrosiveness of its logic of abstract individual freedom—leading inevitably to the Terror of the French Revolution; but he never divorces himself from the broad legacy of the Enlightenment (see Hegel 1967). A similar ambivalence is displayed by Marx. Although he thinks that the economic science of his day is "bourgeois ideology," he also contrasts that mode of knowledge with his own true science of society. That science lets him understand that capitalism cannot operate on any other basis than individual, instrumental reason. When capitalism undergoes revolution, this basis will be overcome. In the highest stage of communism, practical reason will bound up with the real "species-being" (*Gattungswesen*) of humans—that is, with our character as freely productive creatures. Only then will practical reason bond with a "we" that will come to displace "me" in the individual's mind, when she is faced with evaluating some social policy. Practical reason in this sense will find the operative criterion of distributive justice to be "from each according to his abilities, to each according to his needs" (Marx 1978*a*: 531).

In the mid-twentieth century, a new sort of full-scale attack on science and instrumental practical reason appeared. The late 1940s saw the publication of both Heidegger's "The Question Concerning Technology," and Max Horkheimer and Theodor Adorno's *The Dialectic of Enlightenment* (Heidegger 1977; Horkheimer and Adorno 2002). Heidegger repeatedly emphasizes that his concern is not with technology *per se*, but rather with the ontological stance within which scientific reason and technological progress are pursued. Late-modern society increasingly knows only one constitutive attitude for engaging the world, *Gestell* or "enframing." He means by this that the world is always already experienced as stuff to be grasped, ordered, and thus potentially controlled. This growing malignancy projects humans into the role of masters of the world. Heidegger contrasts this with a radically different stance for engaging the world—both natural and social—that he calls *Gelassenheit* or "letting be" (Heidegger 1966: 59–63). Heidegger's work is notoriously difficult to understand, but it is not difficult to see ways in which his distinction between types of ontological stance has opened avenues of critical social reflection. For example, a Heideggerian perspective can inform a radical environmentalist position (Thiele 1995). Further, one might be led to reflect upon ways in which the implicit ideal of ever-increasing mastery demotes the fact of our mortality to the role of an inconvenient irritant rather than a central constituent of our self-conception. This sort of reflection might in turn induce us to think more carefully about the spiritual options we envision today. Similarly, it might draw us toward a more radical opposition to certain sorts of policies. Consider here the policy of the US government regarding the war in Iraq that it launched in 2003. Americans are officially prohibited from showing images of the coffins of dead US soldiers. Although the government claims that it is only protecting the privacy of the soldiers' families, it seems that the operative imperative is rather one involving control of the American population's understanding of the true horrors of war. Thus deaths are rendered as abstract "costs" within what is portrayed as a soon-to-be-successful war. The reality of war is thus masked for the average citizen. (This policy was eliminated by President Obama in 2009.)

Horkheimer and Adorno's critique (2002) of Enlightenment reason is every bit as radical as Heidegger's. Also, like Heidegger, they trace the source of the modern malignancy to before the golden era of classical Greece; back, that is, to the Homeric world. Odysseus is the figure that demonstrates their point. His whole journey back to Greece is an engagement with the world in which he debunks myths, outwits gods and magical creatures, and rationally manages the labor of his crew, as he systematically strategizes his way home (2002). The point Adorno and Horkheimer wish to make is that, although each step may be rational in itself, the implicit framework that shadows the whole project is one that affirms the world as only material to be ordered and controlled. By the twentieth century, they argue, this framework has come to dominate modern society. Thus, the will to control and master has become its own end and is repeated compulsively and endlessly by the engines of the infinite expansion of capitalism. Thus enlightenment itself, initially defined in opposition to myth, "relapse[s] into mythology" (Horkheimer and Adorno 2002: pp. xvi, 20).

Despite the fact that in the 1980s Foucault's work was often seen as antithetical to that of the Frankfurt School, there is a real similarity when it comes to the sort of critique of theoretical and practical reason I have been elucidating. For Foucault, the very act of conceptualizing a domain of possible knowledge also constitutes a field of potential power in the sense of disciplinary control. Two of his most well-known works deal with this theme. In one he shows that medical science in the field of psychiatry operates through the binary of the sane/insane, in turn generating a field of power that polices individuals in terms of who falls on the wrong side of the norm of saneness (Foucault 2001). In perhaps his most famous work, *Discipline and Punish*, he shows how the field of criminology, operating through the binary of normal/abnormal, positions us a similar way (Foucault 1977).

In his very early work in the 1960s, Habermas followed his mentors, Adorno and Horkheimer, and developed a critique of science that understands itself in a positivist fashion; that is, in a way that essentially reduces reason to an instrument through which we enhance control of the world. But, as mainstream philosophy of science advanced to more sophisticated self-portraits, Habermas refined his critique, so that the malignancy no longer resides in science itself, but rather in a metastasizing of strategic and systems rationality. What is at risk in late-modern, capitalist societies with large welfare states is what Habermas (in the 1970s and 1980s) begins to call "communicative" reason. By this, he means something like our implicit modern democratic sense of the rightness or fairness of the normative structures in a society. This sense is sustained and reproduced over time in everyday "communicative action" (Habermas 1970: 115–48). In short, we all carry with us some level of conviction regarding the legitimacy of the existing normative structures around us and of the new ones we continually propose and contest in our linguistic interaction.

It is only from the perspective of communicative reason that we can adequately grasp the malignancy within late-modern society. Communicative reason stands as the most basic form of practical reason, because it alone gives us a viewpoint adequate to understanding how the meaning and legitimacy of normative reality is created, preserved, and passed on. Neither strategic nor systems rationality has that capacity; rather the place of each of these forms in a given social order must finally depend on a communicatively rationalized agreement. This comprehensive conception of reason allows Habermas to have a unique perspective on capitalism and the state. He does not claim that capitalism is, in itself, irrational in the fashion of traditional Marxism, but rather that its micro-level strategic rationality and macro-level systems rationality present themselves as unquestionable imperatives. This is the source of an ongoing crisis today in which these modes of rationality continually force themselves into spheres of action that previously were ordered by convictions rooted in tradition or communicative reason. Habermas refers here to a "colonization of the lifeworld" (Habermas 1984, 1987). By this, he means things like: at the micro-level, the emergence of markets for babies and body parts; and at the macro-level, the way in which the systemic necessities of capitalism are increasingly presented as neutral imperatives that we are assured are no more matters of legitimate political contestation than the recommendation of a plumber that my clogged drain can only be fixed by removing whatever is blocking it.

2. A second tool frequently used by CPT is skepticism of Enlightenment universalism in relation to ethical and political life. The underlying concern here is that the claims of universalism have often been entangled with and masked the interests of power. Marx is the most obvious example of a classical Continental thinker who satisfies this criterion. His notion of ideology revolves around the way in which a dominant economic class makes its own interests appear to represent justice for all. Although the Frankfurt School rejects the full Marxist framework that underlies such claims, it has always been heavily invested in analyzing various ways in which dominant interests in capitalist societies consistently present themselves as universally valid (for a recent example, see Honneth 2008). The best description of this analytical presumption is provided by Paul Ricoeur, who speaks of critical theory as a "hermeneutics of suspicion" (Ricoeur 1970: 27).

Despite the critical stance on Enlightenment universalism that Continental theorists of this ilk display, they have never intended to throw universalism totally overboard. The critique has been intended to clear the ground for a non-deceptive universalism. This characteristic runs from Marx to Habermas, although there are exceptions, especially Adorno. His hermeneutics of suspicion was so unqualified that his universalism ultimately retreated to an otherworldly "standpoint of redemption" (Adorno 2005: 247).

Another kind of challenge to universalism emerged with Nietzsche and has been pursued further in recent decades by thinkers identified with such labels as "postmodern" or "post-structural" (White 1991; Bennett 2004). Nietzsche's challenge took the form of revealing the questionable moral character of the enlightened universalism that emerged from the roots of early Christianity. Nietzsche's *Genealogy of Morals* of 1887, as I indicated above, reveals the moral core of Christianity—values like humility and equality—to be systematically entangled with more questionable motivations. Oppressed early Christians, he argues, cleverly transformed the lowly qualities of their timid "herd" into the highest universal virtues of humankind (Nietzsche 1994). Foucault famously borrows Nietzsche's genealogical method to raise similar questions about, for example, the birth of the modern prison. Although it appears to emerge as a vehicle of universally valid, enlightened morality and humane rehabilitation, replacing the horrors of torture under monarchical rule, Foucault exposes it as simultaneously the archetypical instrument of effective disciplinary control.

The assault on universalism is also evident in the work of Jacques Derrida. The moral-political import of his method of "deconstruction" is to highlight how something or someone is always excluded whenever the net of a universal framework is cast upon any problem or population, and how this gesture is followed by a deceptive claim to have fully resolved or characterized the situation (Derrida 2002*a*). For Derrida, any claim of identity—of a problem, person, group—is *constitutively* related to what is different and excluded. The positing of an identity—say, citizen of the USA—is always given conceptual life by contrasts with "others" who are symbolically external to that identity. Moreover, the need to feel secure in my identity creates a continual pool of hostility and resentment toward those external others who seem to threaten that identity, such as "unworthy" asylum seekers or illegal immigrants.

This kind of insight about identity is often tied to an ontological claim about the "agonistic" or conflictual character of the world. Unlike the predominant legacy of the Enlightenment, this view does not see human affairs as moving, however slowly, toward a single ideal of the good society in which most political conflict will dissolve. Some Continental thinkers attend primarily to the task of elucidating the necessity of this agonistic counter-perspective, but others not only advocate that view, they also attempt to articulate a political ideal that incorporates that ontological portrait of the world. I will say more about the character of this transformed political ideal in a moment.

A final current of skepticism toward Enlightenment universalism runs from J. G. Herder in the late eighteenth century to Charles Taylor (1985) today. Herder is in some ways the first strong pluralist, in the sense of proposing that the good of humankind is not singular but rather plural. For Herder, our conception of the good is embodied in the collective entity of the "people" (Herder 1968). Peoples are defined by common language, traditions, and institutions. Within this view, the health and survival of these entities becomes crucial. Cultures are not simply instruments for enhancing the good of individuals, as Enlightenment individualism would tell us. It is important to note here that this pluralism does not necessarily translate into a full affirmation of agonism. Although, for both Taylor and Herder, there may in fact be a lot of agonism in the world, one nevertheless has a theistically imbued obligation to proceed carefully, always looking for signs and grounds of possible moral reconciliation.

3. A third important tool in CPT's repertoire emerges from a certain type of account of meaning and language. This tradition goes back to Herder and forward to twentieth-century philosophers like Hans-Georg Gadamer (2004). The argument I just elucidated in regard to a pluralism of peoples or cultures is typically part of a broader notion that understanding meaning in general is possible only through one's being in a particular social and cultural context. There is no standpoint of "nowhere in particular," and thus no context-free, royal road to the meaning of things. Today, this position is not restricted to Continental philosophers; it has also become increasingly accepted by analytic philosophers as well. High-profile evidence of this comes from Rawls himself. In his initial theory in 1971, he understood his conceptualization of justice to be staking an unmediated claim to be categorically illuminating *the* truth about justice. In his second book, *Political Liberalism* (Rawls 1993), however, he shifted his stance to one of claiming that his reflections only emerge from, and are valid within, the context of a "modern democratic society" in which there is "a pluralism of incompatible yet reasonable comprehensive conceptions of the good" (1993: p. xvi).

This attention to the plurality of perspectives on the good has been given an additional turn recently by some Continental theorists who seek to unsettle the hegemonic perspective of the West in a novel fashion: by opening up a new field of reflection that is called "comparative political theory." A skeptic here might immediately retort that the use of comparative methods is hardly an activity invented by CPT. This is true in a sense, but the skeptic misses the fact, stressed by those who are pioneering this field, such as Fred Dallmayr, that the perspective at the heart of comparative political theory is a deeply hermeneutical one that owes more to philosophers like Gadamer than to quantitatively trained political scientists who are experts in the comparative analysis of things like political parties or trade policies (Dallmayr 1999).

This broad approach to meaning is accompanied in many Continental theorists by a particular way of comprehending language. They find the malignancy of modern society to be connected to a propensity to comprehend language as, in essence, an instrument that, when properly wielded, enhances the efficiency with which we can pursue our projects. No Continental theorist would contest the idea that language functions instrumentally much of the time, and that this is a good thing. Rather, the concern is that, when this function is identified as the essence of language, we thereby occlude or deny the significance of another way that language operates. We might phrase this distinction as one between language as instrumental or "action-coordinating" versus "world disclosing" or "world opening" (White 1991: x; Kompridis 2006: 30 ff.). When essentialized, the former fits smoothly into a self-image of modern man as disengaged, calculating, and on the way to ever-greater sovereignty and control of his world, both natural and social. Heidegger is perhaps the philosopher who draws out most vividly the dangers of this sort of essentialism and who works the hardest to elucidate world disclosure, and why it is so significant. It is easy to see how, for Heidegger, the instrumental view of language is interwoven with the ontological stance of *Gestell* that I discussed earlier. A structurally similar argument is Derrida's idea of the always operative feature of language called *différence*, which holds that, when we try to make meaning clearly and fully present in language, we nevertheless always also generate unintended meanings that *differ* in the sense of contrast and that are *deferred* in time (Derrida 1982: 1–28). The underlying commonality of such emphases on the "world disclosing" character of language involves both the claim that our modern self-image of ourselves as masters of language is a delusion, and that our limits here need to be better acknowledged. A self-image tied more to the idea of world disclosure simultaneously draws us toward the fundamental importance of a kind of humility, as well as an enhanced sense of why human creativity should be understood not as demiurgic, but rather as a capacity always having to cooperate with the never fully manageable context of language.

Transformation

Given CPT's postulation of some sort of malignancy in modern Western society, it is hardly surprising that there is usually also sustained attention given to the possibility of some transformation that will overcome or at least combat more effectively the danger or harm that malignancy carries with it. This transformation may be imagined as unfolding at a collective or an individual level, or both. Nietzsche attends primarily to radical change at the individual level. He pins his hopes on those relatively few individuals who might undergo a self-recreating process that frees them from much of the West's heritage of moral and political thinking. Heidegger, at least after his relatively brief association with fascism, also pretty much reduces his message to one aimed at drawing the individual into the ontological stance of *Gelassenheit*.

Carl Schmitt, on the other hand, looks primarily to a transformation of the political order in which the "natural" human dynamic of friend and enemy will be given free rein (Schmitt 1996). And Rousseau, in the *Social Contract*, imagines a revolutionary transformation in both spheres, as do Marx, Sartre, and Franz Fanon (for Sartre, see McBride 1991). If we portray Rousseau and Marx as representing the most vivid dreams of revolutionary transformation in CPT, we also have to tell a story of the Continental tradition's progressive abandonment of those dreams. Or perhaps one should say that by the late twentieth century the dreams may have still been vivid, but that the notion of operationalizing them in grand programs fusing self and social transformation had atrophied. In the ferment of the 1960s, one still had some major thinkers who were wedded to notions that were at least vaguely revolutionary in a Marxist sense, such as Sartre and Marcuse. Today, even the vague revolutionary appeals are few and far between.

In place of totalizing conceptions of revolution, there is now a range of mostly more modest attempts to think about how the malignancy within Western modernity can be effectively resisted or blunted. We might here differentiate three kinds of oppositional perspectives on transformation.

1. For Continental thinkers who focus their critique on the dangers of individualism, as both a distorting conceptual lens for understanding social life and a deleterious ideal, the changes required to overcome them are both methodological and political. Hegel was the first to think along these lines. For him, political theory cannot comprehend the social world as composed simply of individuals and the state, but rather must acknowledge the role played in modern society by all sorts of mediating institutions and traditions, within which the "I's" identity and conception of the good are given their meaning (Hegel 1991). This general direction has been picked up in recent decades by a variety of thinkers often referred to as "communitarians." Prominent here are Alisdair MacIntyre (2007), Taylor (1994), and Gadamer (see Ingram 1995 for a good sense of Gadamer's position). They emphasize the importance of traditional institutions, such as religious ones, as well as defend policies that may place restrictions upon some individual freedoms in the name of preserving the cultural integrity of endangered forms of life. In this vein, Taylor has defended language laws in Quebec that discourage the use of English and promote the French-speaking culture there in several ways that a more liberal, laissez-faire cultural policy would reject.

2. A second oppositional perspective grows out of critiques of the homogenizing universalism of the modern West, within which presumptions of agreement or consensus are too confidently projected onto other cultures, language groups, races, religions, and so on. As I indicated above, proponents of this view typically espouse an agonistic ontology. This view implies that we should, as a matter of fact, expect our universalist projections to be frequently upset. Although no normative maxims regarding how we ought to change ourselves follow logically from an agonistic ontology, thinkers of this persuasion often—either explicitly or implicitly—recommend a transformation that is attuned to this ontological insight. The central aim here is to elucidate the shape of a transformed political order that can accommodate—even welcome—some level of ineliminable contestation among the identities and interests of different constituencies. Not surprisingly, this ideal can take many forms. For thinkers who have taken up the agonistic banner since Nietzsche, we might imagine a spectrum between "unrelenting" and "tempered agonism" (White 2009). Schmitt (1996), with his notion of politics as a perpetual struggle of "friend" against "enemy," might be seen as anchoring the "unrelenting" end of that spectrum, on the one hand, and Connolly with his "ethos" of "critical responsiveness" to the other within "agonistic democracy" might be seen as anchoring the "tempered" end, on the other (Connolly 1995: 178–88; 2002: p. x). Some of the thinkers who fall in between are Arendt (1958), Foucault (1991), Bonnie Honig (1993), and Chantal Mouffe (1999, 2000). What characterizes the "tempered" position is some attempt to weave the insight about agonism together with certain modest or sobered Enlightenment ideals.

3. A third approach to transformation emerges out of the failures of Marxism. It frequently overlaps to some degree with the second sort of approach, but it is worthwhile to keep the two analytically distinct. This third perspective wants to retain the populist, democratic element of Marx and the socialist tradition, but simultaneously distance itself from a central ontological figure that classically accompanied it: the collective revolutionary subject of capitalism—namely, the industrial "proletariat." For Marx, the struggle for class-consciousness was about workers coming to imagine themselves into the role of the first class in human history whose interests will be equivalent to those of all humanity. Its victory will, in effect, bring history to an end. For Continental thinkers like Habermas (1996) and Ernesto Laclau (2005), any idea of a collective subject representing all legitimate views is a dangerous illusion. Its presence in Marxism constitutes the primary way in which this current of thought remained tethered to commitments of the Enlightenment. The delusion at issue is simply one more manifestation of imagining some historical particular to be the universal embodiment of all legitimate values.

This insight can be followed by somewhat different strategies for thinking about what is to take the place of the discredited universalization gesture. In Habermas, this discrediting does not eliminate all possibility of affirming alternative, universalist approaches. He sees his own work as articulating a universalism no longer tied, as it is in Marx, to a metaphysics of history, but rather to "communicative reason" with whose criteria every actor is always already entangled. These criteria have to do with our intuitions regarding the procedural requirements that would have to be fulfilled, if we were going to feel confident that any given contested norm was fair or legitimate. The requirements would include such things as that all parties who might be affected by a contested norm have the opportunity to participate in its evaluation.

For Habermas, the criteria of a communicative, practical reason provide a rough normative guidance for a universalist ideal of deliberative democracy (Habermas 1996). The key question for such an ideal is whether political life embodies a variety of deliberative practices robust enough to sustain the legitimacy of the prevailing political order. The answer to this question for any given late-modern, Western society will be a complex one. There is no simple repository of rightness, be it the proletariat or any other group, to which we might point.

A variety of other Continental thinkers similarly distance themselves from the metaphysics of the proletariat, but they are skeptical as well of Habermas's procedural universalism. Laclau rejects any such basis for political life, arguing instead that the repository for radical hopes lies in the attainment of "hegemony" by what he calls a "popular ensemble" or, more simply, the "people" (Laclau 2005: 238, 250). A somewhat similar approach, although now drawn from an analysis of capitalism as a global "Empire," is presented by Michael Hardt and Antonio Negri (2000). They look to the emancipatory potential of a "new proletariat" (2000: 53). Its character is no longer to be tied to a philosophy of history that assigns capitalism a necessary trajectory, but rather to the global "bio-power" of Empire, "bio-power" here referring to a totalizing management of human populations (2000: 23–7; on "bio-power," see also Foucault 1991 and Agamben 1998). The new proletariat or "multitude," as they call it, is composed of that vast group of everyone who labors under the domination of capital. This new, rather diffuse subject and its emergent, unorthodox potential to organize itself must be conceived on the model of "a distributed network" like the Internet (Hardt and Negri 2004: p. xv). As it organizes itself, the multitude has the capacity to embody both the full recognition of the concrete singularity of all its component groups, as well as the collective achievement of democratic commonality or universality. The goal finally is to achieve, for the first time, real democracy: "the rule of everyone by everyone, a democracy without qualifiers, without ifs and buts" (2004: pp. xv, 237).

CONCLUSION

These enthusiastic claims about a radically new democratic form of power return us abruptly to the battle lines between CPT and Anglo-American, Analytic Political thought that I laid out at the beginning of this chapter. Adherents of the latter tradition would probably, and with good reasons, throw up their hands in exasperation when confronted with Hardt and Negri's grandly amorphous portrait of democracy.

Proponents of CPT, on the other hand, might look past the rhetorical overkill and, with their own good reasons, admire the sheer audacity of imagination displayed in a work like *Empire*. Whatever the book's failings, the reader may nevertheless come away from it with a deeper sense of how our largely state-centered tradition of Western political thought will be challenged in the "globalizing" century ahead of us.

Who is ultimately right in this argument? My preference would be to push this issue of a final judgment down near the bottom of the list of significant questions facing political theory. I opt rather for a pluralistic discipline in which both types of reaction are given breathing space and allowed to pursue their different trajectories. Adherents of CPT and analytic political thought should cultivate both the self-confidence and the generosity of mind needed to allow the tension between them to persist. My wager is that the world of political ideas will be richer for it. In saying this, I do not mean to discourage those who try to work synthetically across both traditions. That should be much admired. The only caveat I would emphasize is that we should not blend away too quickly and confidently the distinctive sources of CPT.

Almost a half-century ago, Sheldon Wolin famously remarked that great political theory is typically a response to some major political crisis (2004). Deep political problems, wars, and the disorder of traditional institutions sometimes call forth innovative leaps in political imagination. Looking back over the period since the Second World War, it seems reasonable to script Rawls into the role of a new addition to the canon of great political thinkers. His theory of justice is an effort to clarify the liberal ideals he carried into his service in the Second World War, as well as to express his opposition to the inequalities that existed in the USA in the 1960s (Geuss 2005: 29; Pogge 2007: 19). Can one say anything comparable about CPT? I believe so, but it requires a broadening of our understanding of Wolin's framework. When thinking in terms of possible signal moments in political theory, it is easiest to pick out the work of individual philosophers as what gets engendered by political crises. The amendment I would make to this framework is simply that one should see political crises as sometimes calling forth not only individual *works*, but also novel *traditions* of thought. This is what occurred with CPT. For those in the 1960s who felt that something was deeply amiss in the authoritative ideas and institutions of modern Western life, there was a need for conceptual perspectives that offered radical analyses and answers. It was in relation to this need that a new tradition was constituted.[1]

[1] I would like to thank Jane Bennett and Andrew Norris for careful readings and comments on an earlier version of this chapter, and Regev Ben Jacob for research assistance.

References

ADORNO, T. (2005). *Minima Moralia: Reflections on a Damaged Life* [1951]. London: Verso.

AGAMBEN, GIORGIO (1998). *Homo Sacer*. Stanford, CA: Stanford University Press.

ARENDT, H. (1958). *The Human Condition*. Chicago: University of Chicago Press.

BENNETT, J. (2004). "Postmodern Approaches to Political Theory," in G. Gaus and C. Kukathas (eds), *The Handbook of Political Theory*. London: Sage.

BROGAN, W., and RISSER, J. (2000) (eds). *American Continental Philosophy: A Reader*. Bloomington, IN: Indiana University Press.

BUTLER, J. (1999). *Gender Trouble: Feminism and the Subversion of Identity* [1990]. New York: Routledge.

BUTLER, J. (2006). *Precarious Life: The Powers of Mourning and Violence*. New York: Verso.

CONNOLLY, W. (1993). *The Terms of Political Discourse* [1974]. Princeton: Princeton University Press.

CONNOLLY, W. (1995). *The Ethos of Pluralization*. Minneapolis: University of Minnesota Press.

CONNOLLY, W. (2002). *Neuropolitics*. Minneapolis: University of Minnesota Press.

CRITCHLEY, S. (2001). *Continental Philosophy: A Very Short Introduction*. Oxford: Oxford University Press.

CUTROFELLO, A. (2005). *Continental Philosophy: A Contemporary Introduction*. New York: Routledge.

DALLMAYR, F. (1999). *Border Crossings*. Lanham, MD: Lexington Books.

DERRIDA, J. (1982). "Différance," in *Margins of Philosophy* [1968]. Chicago: University of Chicago Press.

DERRIDA, J. (2002a). "The Force of Law," in *Acts of Religion*, (ed.) G. Anidjar [1990]. London: Routledge.

DERRIDA, J. (2002b). "Faith and Knowledge," in *Acts of Religion*, (ed.) G. Anidjar [1996]. London: Routledge.

FANON, F. (1963). *The Wretched of the Earth*. New York: Grove Press.

FOUCAULT, M. (1977). *Discipline & Punish: The Birth of the Prison* [1975]. New York: Vintage Books.

FOUCAULT, M. (1980). "Two Lectures," in C. Gordon (ed.), *Power/Knowledge* [1977]. New York: Pantheon Books.

FOUCAULT, M. (1982). "The Subject and Power," in H. Dreyfus and P. Rabinow (eds), *Michel Foucault: Beyond Structuralism and Hermeneutics*. Chicago: University of Chicago Press, 208–28.

FOUCAULT, M. (1991). "Governmentality", in G. Burchell, C. Gordon, and P. Miller (eds), *The Foucault Effect: Studies in Governmentality*. Chicago: University of Chicago Press, 87–104.

FOUCAULT, M. (2001). *Madness and Civilization: A History of Insanity in the Age of Reason* [1961]. New York: Routledge.

FROMM, E. (1961). *Marx's Concept of Man*. New York: Frederick Ungar Publishing Co.

GADAMER, H.-G. (2004). *Truth and Method* [1963]. New York: Continuum Publishing Group.

GEUSS, R. (2005). *Outside Ethics*. Princeton: Princeton University Press.

GLENDINNING, S. (1999). *The Edinburgh Encyclopedia of Continental Philosophy*. Edinburgh: Edinburgh University Press.

HABERMAS, J. (1970). "Toward a Theory of Communicative Action," in H. P. Dreitzel (ed.), *Patterns of Communicative Behavior*. New York: Macmillan Company.

HABERMAS, J. (1984). *The Theory of Communicative Action*, i. Boston: Beacon Press.

HABERMAS, J. (1987). *The Theory of Communicative Action*, ii. Boston: Beacon Press.

HABERMAS, J. (1996). *Between Facts and Norms: Contributions to a Discourse Theory of Law and Democracy*. Cambridge, MA: MIT Press.

HARDT, M., and NEGRI, A. (2000). *Empire*. Cambridge, MA: Harvard University Press.

HARDT, M., and NEGRI, A. (2004). *Multitude: War and Democracy in the Age of Empire*. New York: Penguin.

HEGEL, G. W. F. (1967). *The Phenomenology of Mind* [1807]. New York: Harper and Row.

HEGEL, G. W. F. (1991). *Elements of the Philosophy of Right* [1821]. Cambridge: Cambridge University Press.

HEIDEGGER, M. (1966). "Conversation on a Country Path about Thinking," in *Discourse on Thinking* [1959]. New York: Harper and Row.

HEIDEGGER, M. (1977). *The Question Concerning Technology and Other Essays* [1954]. New York: Harper Perennial.

HERDER, J. G. (1968). *Reflections on the Philosophy of the History of Mankind* [1784–91]. Chicago: University of Chicago Press.

HONIG, B. (1993). *Political Theory and the Displacement of Politics*. Ithaca, NY: Cornell University Press.

HONNETH, A. (2008). *Reification*. Berkeley and Los Angeles: University of California Press.

HORKHEIMER, M., and ADORNO, T. (2002). *Dialectic of Enlightenment: Philosophical Fragments* [1947]. Stanford, CA: Stanford University Press.

INGRAM, D. (1995). *Reason, History, and Politics*. Albany, NY: State University of New York.

KANT, I. (1991). "An Answer to the Question: What is Enlightenment" [1784], in *Kant: Political Writings*, (ed.) H. Reiss. Cambridge: Cambridge University Press.

KOMPRIDIS, N. (2006). *Critique and Disclosure*. Cambridge, MA: MIT Press.

LACLAU, E. (2005). *On Populist Reason*. London: Verso.

LEITER, B., and ROSEN, M. (2007) (eds). *The Oxford Handbook of Continental Philosophy*. Oxford: Oxford University Press.

LYOTARD, J. (1984). *The Postmodern Condition*. Minneapolis: University of Minnesota Press.

LYOTARD, J. (1988). *The Differend: Phrases in Dispute*. Minneapolis: University of Minnesota Press.

MCBRIDE, W. (1991). *Sartre's Political Theory*. Bloomington, IN: Indiana University Press.

MACINTYRE, A. (2007). *After Virtue* [1981]. Notre Dame, IN: University of Notre Dame Press.

MARCUSE, H. (1964). *One Dimensional Man*. Boston: Beacon Press.

MARX, K. (1978a). "Critique of the Gotha Program," in *The Marx-Engels Reader*, (ed.) R. C. Tucker. New York: W. W. Norton, 525–41.

MARX, K. (1978b). "Capital Volume One," in *The Marx-Engels Reader*, (ed.) R. C. Tucker. New York: W. W. Norton, 294–438.

MARX, K. (1988). *Economic and Philosophic Manuscripts of 1844* [1844]. New York: Prometheus Books.

MOUFFE, C. (1999). "Introduction," in C. Mouffe (ed.), *The Challenge of Carl Schmitt*. London: Verso.

MOUFFE, C. (2000). *The Democratic Paradox*. New York: Verso.

NIETZSCHE, F. (1994). *On the Genealogy of Morals* [1887]. Cambridge: Cambridge University Press.

PASSMORE, J. (1957). *A Hundred Years of Philosophy*. London: Penguin.

PATTON, P. (2000). *Deleuze and the Political*. New York: Routledge.

POGGE, T. (2007). *Rawls: His Life and Theory of Justice*. Oxford: Oxford University Press.

PROTEVI, J. (2005). *The Edinburgh Dictionary of Continental Philosophy*. Edinburgh: Edinburgh University Press.

RAWLS, J. (1971). *A Theory of Justice*. Cambridge, MA: Belknap Press of Harvard University Press.

RAWLS, J. (1993). *Political Liberalism*. New York: Columbia University Press.

RICOEUR, P. (1970). *Freud and Philosophy: An Essay on Interpretation*. New Haven: Yale University Press.

ROUSSEAU, J. (1964). *First and Second Discourses* [1751, 1753]. New York: St Martin's Press.

ROUSSEAU, J. (1987). *Basic Political Writings*. Indianapolis: Hackett.

SCHMITT, C. (1996). *The Concept of the Political* [1932]. Chicago: University of Chicago Press.

SOLOMON, R. (2003). *The Blackwell Guide to Continental Philosophy*. Oxford: Blackwell Publishing.

STRAUSS, L. (1953). *Natural Right and History*. Chicago: University of Chicago Press.

STRONG, T. (1975). *Friedrich Nietzsche and the Politics of Transfiguration*. Berkeley and Los Angeles: University of California Press.

TAYLOR, C. (1985). *Philosophy and the Human Sciences*. Cambridge: Cambridge University Press.

TAYLOR, C. (1989). *Sources of the Self*. Cambridge, MA: Harvard University Press.

TAYLOR, C. (1994). "The Politics of Recognition," in A. Gutmann (ed.), *Multiculturalism*. Princeton: Princeton University Press.

TAYLOR, C. (2007). *A Secular Age*. Cambridge, MA: Belknap Press of Harvard University.

THIELE, L. (1995). *Timely Meditations*. Princeton: Princeton University Press.

WHITE, S. (1991). *Political Theory and Postmodernism*. New York: Cambridge University Press.

WHITE, S. (2000). *Sustaining Affirmation: The Strengths of Weak Ontology in Political Theory*. Princeton: Princeton University Press.

WHITE, S. (2009). *The Ethos of a Late-Modern Citizen*. Cambridge, MA: Harvard University Press.

WIGGERSHAUS, R. (1994). *The Frankfurt School*. Cambridge, MA: MIT Press.

WOLIN, S. (2004). *Politics and Vision*. Princeton: Princeton University Press.

CHAPTER 28

....

POLITICAL PHILOSOPHY IN
A GLOBALIZING WORLD

....

TERRY NARDIN

POLITICAL philosophy in a globalizing world is not confined to thinking about global-ization. But neither can the topic be avoided. "Global" is one of those words, like "modern" or "postmodern," that people seize upon to define the present moment. The defect of such "now-terms," as they have been called (Megill 2005: 180), is that their popular appeal depends on their imprecision. Because they are imprecise—vaguely evocative as well as ambiguous—they are terms that require analysis, not analytical terms. "Globalization" is identified with economic trends such as the internationaliza-tion of commerce and finance, cultural trends such as the spread of English, and political trends such as the erosion of state sovereignty and the emergence of transna-tional policy networks (Scholte 2005: 54). At a deeper level, it is identified with a technologically enabled compression of space and time in which transactions are increasingly independent of distance and instantaneous (Scheuerman 2004). These trends are in turn connected with worries about climate change, resource depletion, and financial stability that are globally significant and appear to require more than local solutions.

But perhaps these efforts to define globalization are too specific and contemporary. The word "global" means, at its most elementary, spherical. The idea that the earth is round, not flat, we owe not to Columbus but to the ancients (Garwood 2007). And, if the earth is round, it is also necessarily finite and bounded, which means that earthly events are at least potentially interconnected. This interconnection has long been a theme of philosophers. Kant writes that, "since the earth is a globe," human beings "cannot disperse over an infinite area, but must necessarily tolerate one another's company." As a result of European exploration and settlement, a universal community "has developed to the point where a violation of rights in *one* part of the world is felt *everywhere*" (Kant 1991 [1795]: 106–8). Marx converts Kant's moral point into an economic one when he observes that the need for expanding markets "chases the bourgeoisie over the whole surface of the globe," giving "a cosmopolitan character to production and consumption in every country" (Marx and Engels 1978 [1848]: 476–7). Lenin, writing in 1917, thought that the resulting competition for opportunities to invest surplus capital must lead to imperial rivalry and the collapse of capitalism. Twentieth-century geopolitics was premised on the idea that the world had become a "closed system" in which "every shock, every disaster or superfluity, is now felt even to the antipodes" (Mackinder 1962 [1919]: 29). Claims like these, and their implicit teleology, foreshadow current ideas about globalization.

If globalization means increasing interdependence—moral, economic, and ecological—it invites reflection on how this interdependence is affecting the study of political philosophy. Judging from the contents of this handbook, political philosophy remains a largely "Western" enterprise. But, if globalization has not yet produced a noticeably more inclusive community of political philosophers or historians of political thought, it has arguably generated new topics. Some are substantive, such as international inequality, cultural diversity, and transnational democracy: topics that transcend the politics of the modern state and are coming to be seen as part of a distinctly "global" politics. Others are methodological: how to resolve the tension between universal and local perspectives, understand traditions of political thought beyond the West, enable dialogue between traditions, or do "comparative" political philosophy. These methodological concerns raise questions about the character of political philosophy as well as its content.

Global Politics

Political philosophy in the modern period has focused on the European territorial state understood as a legally constituted order. And it has given particular attention to three characteristics of the state understood in this way: a recognized office of authority within the territory; an apparatus of governing attached to this office; and an association of human beings to be authoritatively governed (Oakeshott 2008 [1975]: 204). Each has attracted controversy and generated a tradition of political discourse. The first is a tradition of justificatory argument concerned with the constitution of a state and the authority of its government. The second is a tradition of instrumental reflection concerned with the acquisition and exercise of power. The third is a tradition concerned with determining the character of the state as an association and, related to this, the responsibilities of its government. This last is a concern with the proper aims and activities of a government, not how the authority to govern should be constituted or legitimized or how the power to govern can be effectively used.

What happens when we transfer these concerns to the global level? In the absence of a world state, we are left with two possibilities. The first is to discuss the relations between separate states in the absence of centralized institutions for making and applying law. This is the traditional discourse of international politics, which is sometimes about authority (as in debates about sovereign rights, non-intervention, and the criteria of just war), sometimes about power (as in debates about the skills of the diplomat, the importance of sea power, or the efficacy of nuclear deterrence), and sometimes about the character of international society (as in debates about whether the society of states should be regarded as a framework for coexistence among states or a cooperative venture to promote individual rights, democracy, economic development, or other values). In recent years, these concerns have generated a branch of political philosophy called "international ethics" or "international political theory" (Brown 2004; Nardin 2008). Besides conceptual inquiries and political arguments, the field has also experienced a renewed interest in the history of international thought (Pangle and Ahrensdorf 1999; Tuck 1999).

The second possibility is a discourse on the authority, power, and responsibilities of existing, emerging, or potential international institutions. There is an international legal order and, possibly, an emerging global one, but no world state. This has not stopped philosophers since Kant from speculating about whether the authority to govern should be relocated from sovereign states to a supranational authority and about what constitutional form that authority should have. For Kant, the best possible supranational order would be an expanding and potentially universal federation of republican states. Each would have to be republican, for only a state governed by the rule of law internally could be counted on to respect the rule of law internationally. And each republic would retain its independence, partly because it has a right to it and partly because to establish a single world state would be imprudently to put all the world's eggs in one basket. The attention paid to Kant's ideas about global government by Habermas, Rawls, and other philosophers is evidence of his continued importance (Bohman and Lutz-Bachmann 1997; Höffe 2006).

Subsequent debates over the role of great powers, the threat or advantages of empire, the role of the United Nations, and the lessons of the European Union have continued the line of inquiry begun by Kant. With globalization, however, debate has moved away from confederation to focus on the idea of constitutionalism without the state. According to some, a new global legal order can be discerned in the growth of human rights law and the practice of applying foreign, transnational, international, and supranational law in national courts, or in the proliferation of specialized international tribunals to handle war crimes or settle disputes within the legal regimes regulating trade, fisheries, and other transnational activities (Joerges, Sand, and Teubner 2004). Taken together, these developments signal the emergence of a global legal system that is more institutionalized than traditional international law, even though it falls short of being a state. Skeptics respond that the word "constitution" implies a degree of coherence that these disparate practices fail to achieve. Unlike international law, which is ultimately a system of general rules regulating relations between states, this alleged "global law" is fragmented into separate functional regimes with specialized tribunals to settle disputes within the jurisdiction of each regime but without principles or procedures to reconcile differences between them. The result is that "traditional international law is pushed aside by a mosaic of particular rules and institutions, each following its embedded preferences" (Koskenniemi 2007: 9).

Besides discussion of the constitutional form of a global legal order, there is discussion of the authority of international institutions, in particular the UN system and what some see as a system of informal institutions ("networks") for global governance. Debates over the legal powers—the authority—of UN organs like the Security Council or the International Court of Justice are a staple of international legal discourse, but the question for political deliberation is not the legal question of what authority these institutions have but the broader question of what authority they ought to have and how that authority can be justified. Strictly speaking, existing institutions are without proper authority to make global policy because their powers rest on treaties that can prescribe obligations only for those states that are party to them. Critics argue that international institutions are being driven by policy imperatives to ignore international law and even their own procedures, while informal governance networks improperly confuse public and private decision-making. The likely outcome, they think, is not a cosmopolitan democratic global order but "empire" (Hardt and Negri 2000; Cohen 2004). Just as Kant worried that a world state might be despotic, theorists of global order today worry that policy-oriented "governance" is undermining the international rule of law.

One of the central claims about global governance is that it works in a normative regime shaped by private as well as public acts and through what has come to be called, without irony, "private authority" (Hall and Biersteker 2002). Private authority—the shift of public responsibilities to corporations, interest groups, religious organizations, security agencies, mercenaries, and mafias—does not strengthen public authority but undermines it by placing important functions beyond public oversight, by replacing non-instrumental rules regulating conduct with instrumental rules aimed at promoting policy goals, and by multiplying independent regulatory regimes that fail to compose a coherent legal order. In early modern Europe the problem of multiple, competing, and contested authorities spanning the public and private realms led to the invention of the idea of a single, identifiable "sovereign" authority in a state. The same problem may now need to be solved at the global level.

Much of the global governance debate is instrumental: it is concerned with the effective power of international institutions, not with claims to legal authority or moral legitimacy. A recurring theme is that public–private governance networks can be more effective than formal institutions in advancing desirable policies (Slaughter 2004), though after the 2008 global financial crisis celebration of "networks" was tempered by talk of clearing away the "cobwebs" of antiquated regulatory regimes. That discussion begs the question, however, of the propriety of "governance," a term with distinctly administrative and anti-democratic connotations. Political philosophers are just beginning to consider that question (Held 2004; Kuper 2004).

The question of propriety cannot be answered without defining the character and purpose of government or governance at the global level. At issue here is not the

constitutional form, authority, or power of international institutions—whether formal
or informal, centralized or dispersed—but rather their proper task or responsibility. Is
it to regulate the interactions of states and of private entities engaging in transactions
that cross national boundaries? Or is their responsibility to pursue substantive policies
affecting global welfare? There is a long tradition of dispute about the character and
purpose of the modern state: whether it should be understood as a framework of non-
instrumental laws within which persons can freely pursue their own self-chosen ends,
or as an enterprise for advancing collective religious or economic ends through laws
and policies conducive to that enterprise. A similar dispute is now emerging at the
global level (Hurrell 2007; Cohen 2008). The stronger global institutions become, the
more attention will be paid to the question of what such institutions should be doing—
what purposes they should pursue and what conceptions of the global community are
implied by different views of the proper purpose of global governance.

The contest between these alternative conceptions of the state is evident in the
debate over "global justice." For some, a just global order is an international order in
which states respect each other's independence, accept the legitimacy of religious and
other cultural differences, and settle their disputes peacefully. For others, it is an order
in which states cooperate and international institutions act to reduce economic inequality. In political philosophy this conception is defended by those who think that
what Rawls called "the difference principle"—which prescribes that goods should be
distributed equally within a society unless their unequal distribution benefits its worst-
off members (Rawls 1971: 75–80)—applies globally (Beitz 1979). Others base redistributive arguments on utility or human rights (Pogge 2002; Singer 2002). Few,
however, challenge the premise that a purpose of political institutions is to provide
economic benefits and lessen economic inequality.

For Rawls, distributive justice meant allocating goods in a society understood as a
collective enterprise—in his words, a "cooperative venture for mutual advantage"
(Rawls 1971: 4). But he did not regard international society as either actually or ideally
a venture of this kind, and his remarks on reducing global economic inequality treat it
as a matter of beneficence, not distributive justice. States—and, by extension, international institutions—have an obligation to assist societies burdened by poverty to
establish just and effective orders. The obligation to relieve poverty may be "imperfect"
in the sense that "no man can say how much another should give to the poor, or when a
man has given too little to save his soul," but as Samuel Johnson joins Kant in
affirming, it is an obligation nevertheless (Boswell 1952 [1791]: 218). But, Rawls
argues, the principles of distributive justice that hold in a liberal egalitarian state do
not hold outside that context because those principles belong to a comprehensive
doctrine, liberal egalitarianism, that cannot be enforced globally if legitimate cultural
differences are to be respected (Rawls 1999: 105–20). The principles that guide our
response to economic inequality must be principles that could be acknowledged by all.
They are, in other words, "thin" or universal principles, not the "thick," community-
based principles of liberal egalitarianism (Young 2006: 34–5). This does not mean that

dealing with poverty is only a matter of charity, however, for it is possible on the Kantian grounds that Rawls implicitly adopts to argue that there are enforceable duties to prevent economic harms arising from violence and exploitation. For Rawls, as for Kant, a global federation would rest on the principle that freedom must be respected and violence suppressed, not on the principle of beneficence—in Kantian terms, on Right, not Virtue. It would provide a legal framework for coexistence: a civil order, not a corporate enterprise.

What would politics in a global civil order entail? The word "politics" is often used so broadly as to drain it of meaning. In the context of civil order, it implies more than a struggle for power or the distribution of substantive goods. It implies a structure of laws and institutions within which public decisions are made. Revolutionary movements that would do away with law are anti-political, as are ideologies of instrumental governance that blur the boundaries between public and private, government and business, state and civil society. Politics proper involves deliberation eventuating in legislative decisions: decisions regarding the common rules of a non-voluntary association understood to be an association of "citizens," not a community of believers or an enterprise of stakeholders. Politics means deliberating on the common rules of a state— rules that prescribe binding obligations that are properly enforceable as law on subjects who cannot easily avoid the obligations they prescribe. On this definition of politics, global politics is the politics of an actual, emerging, or potential global state.

That state will be a legal association of a certain limited sort: a "liberal" or "rule-of-law" association. But its aim will not be to *advance* liberal values or the rule of law. Its aim will be to regulate a community *premised* on individual liberty and regulated by laws that are compatible with that premise: non-instrumental laws whose character is captured, perhaps imperfectly, in the expression "rule of law." The politics of such an association will lie in deliberating on the terms of association: debating and deciding what the laws should prescribe and whether those laws and the policies they permit or require are reasonable for such an association to have in the contingent circumstances in which it finds itself (Nardin 2009).

"Global politics," then, is deliberation focused on the desirability of laws for a global association. It does not exclude deliberation on international law because states will continue to be important if global association takes shape along confederal lines. Global politics at the present moment means deliberating about the terms of an implicit global legal order—one that may or may not be emerging. What sorts of considerations should be taken into account in this deliberation? What would be the desirable shape of a more explicit global constitution? On what would its authority rest? How can the community it constitutes be effectively governed? And what are the proper aims and responsibilities of its governing institutions? These are questions that future debates on global politics will have to address. Politics, so understood, is not confined to arguments about policy: political debate goes deeper than policy debate to focus on laws and, ultimately, constitutional principles.

GLOBAL PHILOSOPHY

If we ask whether globalization has altered political philosophy, one answer might be that, although it has given philosophers new issues to think about, the terms in which these issues are discussed—equality, rights, democracy, justice, utility, responsibility—are familiar ones. If it is argued that, as a result of globalization, differences between states are being replaced by differences between civilizations, one might reply that the clash of civilizations is an ancient theme in political literature (Pagden 2008). And, if it is said that globalization demands a cosmopolitan ethic that prescribes, at a minimum, respect for different ways of life, this theme too has long been part of political thought. To know how globalization has changed political philosophy we need to know how philosophers are handling these themes in the context of globalization.

The tension between universal and local claims became prominent in a series of debates among political philosophers in the 1980s, starting with the attack on Rawls's "deontological liberalism" from the perspectives of "communitarianism" (Sandel 1982) and "interpretation" (Walzer 1987). This led Rawls to advance the idea of "public reason" as a way of transcending the "comprehensive doctrines" of different communities, including the community of liberal egalitarians (Rawls 1993). Others have appealed to human rights, individual autonomy, or freedom of association (Kymlicka 1995; Kukathas 2003) to reconcile claims of cultural particularity and liberal equality. But is the principle that cultural differences should be respected a universal principle or a local one? Debate has moved on from asserting local culture against liberalism to recognizing that at least some versions of liberalism are better conceived as local than as universal and, conversely, that traditions often coded as local, such as Islam or Buddhism, can be seen as universal. So another way to understand the tension between universal morality and communal *mores* is that it is a contest not between universalists and defenders of the local but between universalisms.

In its most recent phase, the debate has moved up to the international level to focus on the moral significance of national boundaries. But the universalists in this debate are more concerned to make the point, against defenders of nationalism and political realism, that boundaries are not morally significant than to clarify the understanding of morality on which that universalism is based. This may reflect a style in analytical philosophy of valuing "good arguments" without worrying too much about how they fit together. It is, therefore, sometimes hard to see what system of moral principles is being advanced as "cosmopolitan"—by Barry (1998) or Moellendorf (2002), for example—or what concept of justice is being advanced as "global" by theorists—such as Caney (2005)—who write about justice beyond the state. But, even if the principles are unclear or contested, the claim that they are universal at least connects current debates with a discourse running back to antiquity whose resources are available to be exploited (Nussbaum 2002; Appiah 2006). Against an Epicurean ethic of self-care, Stoic cosmopolitanism asserted the idea of morality as a set of precepts prescribing duties for all rational beings by virtue of their rationality. This rational ("natural") morality ("law") can be found in the moral beliefs and practices of different peoples, but its authority rests on reason, not convention. There is, then, a long tradition in the West of distinguishing a common morality consisting of rationally grounded moral principles that stand above conventional beliefs and practices from one that rests on agreement between different traditions—a modern *ius gentium* or law common to different peoples. Slavery was permitted under the law of nations but not by natural law.

An appeal to natural law does not, however, settle all questions of content, method, or foundation. Divergent views of "reason" have led philosophers to find the universal in basic goods (Aquinas), prudential rationality (Hobbes), generalized egoism (Hume and Bentham), human freedom (Kant), and even—returning full circle to local experience—tradition or custom (Burke and Hegel), and these differences persist. Disagreement over what authority the universal and the local should have in relation to each other is sharply evident in discussions of humanitarian intervention (Nardin and Williams 2006). Should universal principles be coercively imposed? If governments are required to respect basic human rights—and especially if countries in which those rights are grossly violated lose their immunity to intervention and their leaders become liable to criminal prosecution—we are led towards a Kantian view of justice as morally permissible coercion.

Many remain suspicious that a universal ethic can be found in the traditions of the West. A truly universal ethic would have to take account of the moral experience and ideas of other civilizations. Central to the project of developing a cross-cultural global ethic is an appeal to "dialogue" as a means of bridging cultural differences. The point of dialogue, on this view of it, is "to identify and broaden areas of possible consensus" and "to consider ways of accommodating enduring differences" (Kymlicka 2007: 1). But such aims are practical, not philosophical, as their origin in inter-faith dialogue and ecumenical theology testifies. The dialogue model also encourages the fallacy that the participating traditions are univocal. But traditions are plural, not homogenous. A tradition is defined as much by its questions as by its answers or doctrines: questions generate disagreement as well as agreement. When we distinguish "Western" political thought from various non-Western traditions, the differences that define it—Greek versus Roman, ancient versus modern, democratic versus authoritarian, conservative versus liberal, patriarchal versus feminist, modernist versus postmodernist—are subordinated to generalizations of the sort that cross-cultural comparison seems to invite. The category "non-Western," being a residual, is even more misleading. The arguments of those who claim, in dialogue, to speak for a tradition must always be regarded skeptically.

The ideal of an agreed global ethic motivates at least some of those who advocate for "comparative political philosophy." The point of comparative inquiry, on this view of its character and purpose, is to construct a foundation of common ideas for an emerging global community, "a new world order of human solidarity," as Gadamer put it in a late interview (Pantham 1992: 133). All cultures must contribute to this enterprise to guarantee solidarity and legitimacy. "In terms of long-range political vision, comparative political theorizing supports global democratic cooperation over oligarchic or imperial control and dialogical interaction over hegemonic unilateralism and monologue" (Dallmayr 2004: 254). Political inquiry must be dialogical because only then can cultural imperialism be avoided. One wonders, though, whether cross-cultural dialogue might itself be one of those Western ideas, along with comparative inquiry, that non-Westerners are being asked to buy into (Jenco 2007: 742–5). The goal of de-parochializing political philosophy is distinct from that of developing common principles for a culturally diverse world.

A more modest goal of comparative political inquiry is to enlarge the canon of texts that define the field of political philosophy (Shogimen and Nederman 2008). Canon revision is ongoing, as the recent promotion of Nietzsche (who did not write on "politics" as usually conceived) and Kant (whose political writings had long been regarded not only as minor but as evidencing dementia) illustrates. One can expect that this canon will eventually include non-Western texts, as philosophers pay attention to a wider range of political experience and thinking. Responding to the growing prestige and influence of India and China, support for scholarship on these and other non-Western societies will make the political thought of peoples outside Christian Europe and America more widely accessible, bringing it within the reach of those who study and teach the texts and themes that have in the past defined the field. Islamic political thought has been particularly fortunate in the attention paid to it in recent years (Lewis 1988; Black 2001; Crone 2004). Jewish political thought is also receiving attention (Walzer, Lorberbaum, and Zohar 2000) and there is increasing attention to the political thought of ancient and modern China. This *Handbook* has essays on Confucian, Hindu, and Islamic political thought.

A less parochial discipline would be one that studied the texts and traditions of different peoples without deforming that study by making it the instrument of a project for global solidarity. Historians, anthropologists, and translators know the dangers of anachronism and incomprehension that arise when scholars read their own assumptions into the experience they are trying to understand, and they have developed methods to insulate inquiry against those dangers. Even if we think of comparative inquiry in practical rather than philosophical terms, its primary value lies in comprehending ways of thinking that, in being different from our own, invite us to reconsider ideas we take for granted. The lesson of hermeneutics would seem to be the anti-foundational one that we should study the political thought of past or distant peoples not to affirm or deny but rather to understand and explain. Anti-foundationalism invites genuine comparative inquiry in a way that inquiry premised on a dialogic quest for solidarity does not.

The soundest reason for investigating political thinking beyond the West is to learn—for the sake of literature, history, and philosophy—about modes of thought that might add something to the ideas of the Greeks, Romans, medieval Christians, and modern Europeans on which contemporary political philosophy rests. Scholarship on Jewish, Muslim, and Chinese political thought is the preserve of specialists, and a Western philosopher interested in it would until recently have been regarded, by those who think that political philosophy belongs to analytical philosophy or liberal egalitarian politics, as having wandered outside the field. The problem of understanding non-Western political thought is compounded by the fact that non-Western scholars are often trained in Western universities and examine the politics of their own societies though the lens of Western scholarship. And, because contemporary non-Western thought has been shaped by decades, and even centuries, of contact with the West, to study it is often to study the ideas of reformers who have relied on Western practices and texts to make their case.

A methodological question that especially needs to be considered is how much non-Western political thought, ancient or modern, is truly philosophical in the sense that it aims at explanation rather than at political change. The political writers of ancient China and India consider ideas about virtue, military strategy, legal order, and leadership that have analogues in the West, but the most philosophical—the most abstract, critical, and systematic—Western inquiries, like those of Aristotle, Aquinas, Hobbes, Spinoza, Hegel, or Rawls, appear to have few Eastern parallels. Could it be that, like physics or economics, political philosophy has been a Western discipline—invented in the West even if, today, practiced around the world?

Those who defend the existence of non-Western political philosophy argue for a broader definition of philosophy. And, of course, the broader the definition the easier it is to find parallels. Forms of government, the justification of political authority, techniques of political rule, the character of good government, and the responsibilities of rulers are important practical concerns in many societies. But to discuss them is not necessarily to engage in "philosophy" understood as an inquiry aimed at defining abstract ideas, making distinctions, uncovering presuppositions, and constructing systematic theories. Political philosophy is a subset of political thought, not coextensive with it. It does not follow that, because we find political thought in many societies, we will find it everywhere—arguably, politics itself, like many human practices, is an invention, and there may have been times and places without it, just as there are times and places in which political philosophy has been unknown or has not flourished. Nor does it follow that wherever we find politics and thought about politics we necessarily find political philosophy, any more than it follows that wherever we find economic activity we find the science of economics.

"Global political philosophy" is not a synonym for "global politics." To earn its name, political philosophy must involve more than practical engagement with political questions—if it were only this, the distinction between political philosophy and politics would disappear. Political philosophy demands thinking *about* politics and requires a certain distance from its subject matter. Its aims are primarily interpretative, analytical, and explanatory, not immediately practical. To philosophize is to examine political ideas and the presuppositions of political arguments. And, because this examination can proceed at a high level of abstraction, it is less tied than practical political thinking to the contingencies of the moment. It may wander into politics by making political assumptions or having political implications, but as a distinct kind of inquiry its aims are different. Contra Marx, the point of philosophy is to understand the world, not to change it. Political philosophy in this sense is only one part of "political thought," most of which in any society is politics itself under another name.

REFERENCES

APPIAH, A. (2006). *Cosmopolitanism: Ethics in a World of Strangers.* New York: W. W. Norton & Company.

BARRY, B. (1998). "International Society from a Cosmopolitan Perspective," in D. Mapel and T. Nardin (eds), *International Society: Diverse Ethical Perspectives.* Princeton: Princeton University Press, 144–63.

BEITZ, C. (1979). *Political Theory and International Relations.* Princeton: Princeton University Press.

BLACK, A. (2001). *The History of Islamic Political Thought: From the Prophet to the Present.* London: Routledge.

BOHMAN, J., and LUTZ-BACHMANN, M. (1997) (eds). *Perpetual Peace: Essays on Kant's Cosmopolitan Ideal.* Cambridge, MA: MIT Press.

BOSWELL, J. (1952 [1791]). *The Life of Samuel Johnson.* New York: Modern Library.

BROWN, C. (2004). "Political Theory and International Relations," in G. Gaus and C. Kukathas (eds), *Handbook of Political Theory.* London: Sage, 289–300.

CANEY, S. (2005). *Justice beyond Borders: A Global Political Theory.* Oxford: Oxford University Press.

COHEN, J. (2004). "Whose Sovereignty? Empire versus International Law," in *Ethics and International Affairs*, 18/3: 1–24.

COHEN, J. (2008). "Rethinking Human Rights, Democracy, and Sovereignty in the Age of Globalization," *Political Theory*, 36/4: 578–606.

CRONE, P. (2004). *God's Rule: Government and Islam.* New York: Columbia University Press.

DALLMAYR, F. (2004). "Beyond Monologue: For a Comparative Political Theory," *Perspectives on Politics*, 2/2: 249–57.

GARWOOD, C. (2007). *Flat Earth: The History of an Infamous Idea.* Basingstoke: Macmillan.

HALL, R., and BIERSTEKER, T. (2002). *The Emergence of Private Authority in Global Governance.* Cambridge: Cambridge University Press.

HARDT, M., and NEGRI, A. (2000). *Empire.* Cambridge, MA: Harvard University Press.

HELD, D. (2004). *Global Covenant: The Social Democratic Alternative to the Washington Consensus.* Cambridge: Polity.

HÖFFE, O. (2006). *Kant's Cosmopolitan Theory of Law and Peace.* Cambridge: Cambridge University Press.

HURRELL, A. (2007). *On Global Order: Power, Values, and the Constitution of International Society.* Oxford: Oxford University Press.

JENCO, L. (2007). "'What Does Heaven Ever Say?' A Methods-Centered Approach to Cross-Cultural Engagement," *American Political Science Review*, 101/1: 741–56.

JOERGES, C., SAND, I., and TEUBNER, G. (2004) (eds). *Transnational Governance and Constitutionalism.* Oxford: Hart Publishing Co.

KANT, I. (1991 [1795]). *Political Writings*, (ed.) H. Reiss. Cambridge: Cambridge University Press.

KOSKENNIEMI, M. (2007). "The Fate of Public International Law: Between Technique and Politics," *Modern Law Review*, 70/1: 1–30.

KUKATHAS, C. (2003). *The Liberal Archipelago: A Theory of Diversity and Freedom.* Oxford: Oxford University Press.

Kuper, A. (2004). *Democracy beyond Borders: Justice and Representation in Global Institutions*. Oxford: Oxford University Press.

Kymlicka, W. (1995). *Multicultural Citizenship: A Liberal Theory of Minority Rights*. Oxford: Oxford University Press.

Kymlicka, W. (2007). "Introduction: The Globalization of Ethics," in W. Sullivan and W. Kymlicka (eds), *The Globalization of Ethics: Religious and Secular Perspectives*. Cambridge: Cambridge University Press, 1–16.

Lewis, B. (1988). *The Political Language of Islam*. Chicago: University of Chicago Press.

Mackinder, H. (1962 [1919]). *Democratic Ideals and Reality*, (ed.) A. Pearce. New York: W. W. Norton & Co.

Marx, K., and Engels, F. (1978 [1848]). "Manifesto of the Communist Party," in *The Marx–Engels Reader*, (ed.) R. Tucker. New York: W. W. Norton, 469–500.

Megill, A. (2005). "Globalization and the History of Ideas," *Journal of the History of Ideas*, 66/2: 179–87.

Moellendorf, D. (2002). *Cosmopolitan Justice*. Boulder, CO: Westview Press.

Nardin, T. (2008). "International Ethics," in C. Reus-Smit and D. Snidal (eds), *The Oxford Handbook of International Relations*. Oxford: Oxford University Press, 594–611.

Nardin, T. (2009). "Globalization and the Public Realm," in B. Arditti and N. O'Sullivan (eds), *The Concept of the Public Realm*. London: Routledge.

Nardin, T., and Williams, M. (2006) (eds). *Humanitarian Intervention*. New York: New York University Press.

Nussbaum, M. (2002). "Patriotism and Cosmopolitanism," in J. Cohen (ed.), *For Love of Country?* Boston: Beacon Press, 3–20.

Oakeshott, M. (2008 [1975]). "The Vocabulary of a Modern European State," in L. O'Sullivan (ed.), *The Vocabulary of a Modern European State: Essays and Reviews 1952–88*. Exeter: Imprint Academic, 203–43.

Pagden, A. (2008). *Worlds at War: The 2,500-Year Struggle between East and West*. New York: Random House.

Pangle, T., and Ahrensdorf, P. (1999). *Justice among Nations: On the Moral Basis of Power and Peace*. Lawrence, KA: University Press of Kansas.

Pantham, T. (1992). "Some Dimensions of the Universality of Philosophical Hermeneutics: A Conversation with Hans-Georg Gadamer," *Journal of Indian Council of Philosophical Research*, 9/2: 130–42.

Pogge, T. (2002). *World Poverty and Human Rights: Cosmopolitan Responsibilities and Reforms*. Cambridge: Polity.

Rawls, J. (1971). *A Theory of Justice*. Cambridge, MA: Harvard University Press.

Rawls, J. (1993). *Political Liberalism*. New York: Columbia University Press.

Rawls, J. (1999). *The Law of Peoples*. Cambridge, MA: Harvard University Press.

Sandel, M. (1982). *Liberalism and the Limits of Justice*. Cambridge: Cambridge University Press.

Scheuerman, W. (2004). *Liberal Democracy and the Social Acceleration of Time*. Baltimore: Johns Hopkins University Press.

Scholte, J. (2005). *Globalization: A Critical Introduction*. Basingstoke: Palgrave Macmillan.

Shogimen, T., and Nederman, C. (2008). *Western Political Thought in Dialogue with Asia*. Lanham, MD: Lexington Books.

Singer, P. (2002). *One World: The Ethics of Globalization*. New Haven: Yale University Press.

Slaughter, A. (2004). *A New World Order*. Princeton: Princeton University Press.

Tuck, R. (1999). *The Rights of War and Peace: Political Thought and the International Order from Grotius to Kant*. Oxford: Oxford University Press.

Walzer, M. (1987). *Interpretation and Social Criticism*. Cambride, MA: Harvard University Press.

Walzer, M., Lorberbaum, M., and Zohar, N. (2000). *The Jewish Political Tradition*, i. *Authority*. New Haven: Yale University Press.

Young, I. (2006). *Global Challenges: War, Self-Determination, and Responsibility for Justice*. Cambridge: Cambridge University Press.

PART III

THEMES

CHAPTER 29

....

DEMOCRACY

....

MARK E. WARREN

THE ideal of democracy today is hegemonic owing to its successes. When compared to various forms of autocracy, monarchy, theocracy, oligarchy, and dictatorship, democracies are better at solving, routinizing, and institutionalizing basic problems of common social life and collective action. These successes of democracy, however, are relatively recent and far from perfected (Tilly 2007). Although theories of democracy date back 2,400 years to Thucydides and Aristotle, for most of recorded history democratic institutions and practices have been highly exceptional: political systems incorporating key elements of democratic systems appeared in Athens and Rome, and there were certain local assembly practices among the Vikings and other places in Northern Europe during the Middle Ages; among the Iroquois Nation in North America; and in some Italian city states in the late Middle Ages and Renaissance. Institutions now associated with democratic systems as parts of territorially extensive and complex societies did not begin to appear until the Glorious Revolution in England (1688), which established the sovereignty of an elected parliament. But if we understand "democracy" as requiring competitive elections for leadership and a universal adult franchise, then it is a very recent system. By this measure, there were no electoral democracies in 1900, 22 of 154 countries were democracies in 1950, and 119 of 193 countries today, with 89 of those ranking highly enough in protecting basic rights and practicing a rule of law to count as liberal democracies (Puddington 2009: 2).

My focus here is on the historical origins of ideas that articulate and justify contemporary democratic theory and practice. My method is straightforward: I shall survey the conceptual questions embedded in the concept of democracy inherited from the Greek, *demokratia*—literally, the power (*kratos*) of the people (*demos*) (Ober 2008), though commonly translated as *rule of the people*. Embedded in this concept of democracy we find at least four basic classes of questions:

- Questions having to do with the definition and constitution of "the people" as an agency capable of rule. Who are "the people"?

- Questions having to do with the objects of rule, including self, community, society, and state. At what level of organization is "self-government" directed?
- Questions having to do with the means and mechanisms of rule, including devices such as voting, checks and balances, and deliberation. How is the rule of the people translated into collective decisions and actions?
- Questions having to do with the purposes and justifications of rule. Why is democracy good?

The answers to these questions form, as it were, the history of democratic theory from the perspective of what historical democratic ideas and practices might contribute to the present and future of democracy. This approach should not be confused, of course, with the histories of particular texts, institutions, or practices, which would require attention to contingencies and contexts that I cannot offer here (cf. Tully 1988; Tilly 2007).

WHO ARE THE PEOPLE? DEMOCRACY AND CONSTITUENCY

Historically, the question as to what constitutes the people who self-govern has been neither the first nor the most obvious question to ask, in large part because "the people" pre-existed the question of self-rule, in the forms of tribes, ethnic communities, or nations. And yet, even in the Athenian case, we can see that "the people" required construction. The constitutions from Solon through Pericles' reforms incorporated numerous boundary rules that constructed a *demos*, most of which recur in the history of democracy.

We can think of these boundaries as comprising distinct principles of inclusion and exclusion. Some appeared "natural," based on family, communal, and ethnic membership. Others reflected earned entitlement, based on contributions to the collective, such as military training, service, and financial contributions, all of which were important to Athenian conquest. Still others were based on capacities inferred from property qualifications, status (especially free versus slave), sex, and age (Finley 1983; Hornblower 2002: ch. 12). In the Athenian case, these contribution- and capacity-based boundaries operated in conjunction with tribal constituencies that were, primarily, based on location, and thus on the basic assumption that territorial membership is fundamental.

These kinds of constitutive boundaries were carried over into the modern rebirth of democracy in the eighteenth and nineteenth centuries, while being overwritten by two others. The first followed from the fact that the modern democratic project was reborn, and thus encapsulated, within nation states—the large, terrfitorial, administratively capable political units that, in much of Europe at least, had been consolidated under absolutist monarchs. Thus, problems of democratic inclusion were primarily conceived as overcoming distinctions of wealth, sex, race, ethnicity, and religion in favour of the principle of residence (Rehfeld 2005).

The triumph of residential constituency over more parochial identities was pushed along by a second modern force: a universalizing ethic that had its origins in Christianity (Held 2006: 30). The ethic was expressed in the modern natural-rights tradition from Hobbes through Jefferson, in Kant's ethics, as well as in Bentham's utilitarian insistence that the pains and pleasures of each individual are intrinsically and equally worthy. In themselves, these universalizing ethics were not sufficient to motivate democratic empowerments such as the franchise. Democracy, as Dahl (1998: chs 6–7) has noted, depends not only upon the (universal) ethic of intrinsic moral worth, but also on a belief in equal capacities for self-government. Thus, many judgments about who were, effectively, part of the self-governing people excluded those deemed lacking in capacities for self-government by virtue of intrinsic irrationality (Locke: infants, lunatics, and colonized people), lack of independence (Kant: women, servants, and others without property), or moral defects as indicated by a lack of property (Madison).

It is important to the logic of conceptual evolution, however, that, in contrast to the earlier (but still operative) tribal, communalistic, and national conceptions of "peoples," these new justifications for exclusion paid indirect tribute to the modern universalizing impulse within much Western political theory. Capabilities-based exclusions have for the most part been eroded by the broadly accepted view that the burden of proof is upon those who would exclude, with the result that the franchise and accompanying rights and empowerments of citizenship are now mostly universal in principle within the established democracies, if not always in practice.

We also find within the history of ideas, however, three other conceptions that treat the constitution of "the people" as itself a "political" act—that is, as a consequence of institutions or discursive processes rather than as something "given" by a dominant community or nation, or in the form of classes that assign political entitlements to themselves. The first of these "political" understandings of the people can be found in the Roman concept of *res publica*—the affairs of the public. As rediscovered in the early modern period and incorporated into republican thought (Pocock 2003), the concept suggested that the unit of self-rule was a *public*, which constituted itself through its political and discursive activities oriented toward common affairs. It is thus the *public*, rather than merely "people," from which a government is to take its direction (Urbinati 2006). On this conception, peoples are, in part, reflexively constituted through public discourse (Habermas 1989 [1962]).

Second, Locke's contract theory includes a distinct but related conception. Individuals form a society through contracted association, prior to entrusting their affairs to a government (Locke 1963 [1689]). While Locke's conception implausibly suggested the existence of pre-social individuals, it had the (democratic) advantage of understanding "peoples" as a chosen commitment, itself a "political" act that carried with it common obligations. So, in contract theory, the boundaries of the "people" are explicitly normative, and require (in principle) continuing justification with references to the interests of individuals and the purposes of collective action—a concept incorporated into contract theory from Kant (1996 [1797]) through Rawls (2005).

This normatively constructivist way of thinking about "peoples" is importantly connected to representation as a constitutive device (Pitkin 1967; Urbinati 2005). Beginning with Rousseau's conception of the General Will, the "people" becomes an explicitly normative construction, reflecting the ideal of a consensus on any given issue (1978 [1762]). The concept of the General Will over-idealized consensus. But the notion that the people may generate a normatively justifiable will on any given issue that is not discoverable prior to political processes becomes the core ideal of deliberative conceptions of democracy (Habermas 1996; Rawls 2005; Held 2006). And, in a similarly productive way, Tocqueville (1969 [1835]) conceived of peoples as constituted through associations: that is, through serial, overlapping, purpose-driven collectivities that are closely responsive to common problems as they emerge.

A third important reflexive conception of "the people" is embedded in the notion of "mixed government," theorized by Aristotle (1981 [c.335–323 BC]) and Montesquieu (1989 [1748]), practiced by the Romans, and developed as a system of separated powers in the 1789 American constitution (Hamilton, Madison, and Jay 1987 [1788]). According to the logic of separated powers, boundaries of inclusion and exclusion are, in part, an effect of the design of political institutions. The concept of separated powers implies that governments should represent multiple, overlapping versions of the people, constituted in different ways through distinct and competing devices of representation. The notion that distinct mechanisms of representation might combine different constituencies into an effective government challenged the ideas—found in Hobbes and Rousseau—that the concept of unified sovereignty must be expressed in unified institutions.

These reflexive strains have yet to be gathered for what is one of the most challenging contemporary issues of democratic theory within the context of globalization—namely, figuring out how the means, mechanisms, and spaces of collective action might match those who are affected by collective decisions, without which the rule of the people cannot exist (Young 2000; Bohman 2007; Goodin 2007).

OVER WHAT DO THE PEOPLE RULE? DEMOCRACY AND SCOPE

The question of boundaries of the people leads quite naturally to the question of scope. Over what do the people rule? What is the extent of their rule? Historically, the answers have been: (1) rule over the *self*, as in the notions of liberty and self-governance; (2) rule over the *state*, which involves popular control over the apparatus that maintains a territorial monopoly over the means of violence; (3) rule together with others though social units such as associations and communities, or *society*; and (4) rule over the conditions and limits of *market* organization.

Questions of scope gain their meaning from societies that are differentiated into domains with their own principles of order and replication—particularly the domains of self, society, market, and state. Such questions had precursors in ancient conceptions of tyranny as the arbitrary, non-bounded use of power, in Christian views of the limits of worldly power, in liberal distinctions between public and private spheres, and in republican conceptions of non-domination. But questions of scope have become more pressing in late modern societies owing to high levels of domain differentiation as well as increasing global interdependencies—trends that multiply the potential sites of collective action.

Assembly democracy in Athens was constructed in large part for reasons of protection against tyranny and to realize liberty. The example remains relevant today because, in its origins, democracy was conceived as the political system that enables rule over the self. Indeed, it is precisely the capacity for self-rule that distinguishes, in the Greek view, humans both from animals and from those deemed incapable of self-rule by condition or necessity, such as slaves and women (Thucydides 1952: II.40; Arendt 1958; Aristotle 1981 [c.335–323 BC]: bk IV, pt IV). This close conceptual link between self-rule and collective rule is central to early republican thought, such as that of Marsilius of Padua. It was theorized by Rousseau as the solution to the problem of freedom within society, which found its way into Marx's radically democratic understanding of communism, and which remains an important part of the developmental strains of liberal democracy from J. S. Mill and John Dewey as well as from more contemporary participatory theories of democracy (Pateman 1976; Macpherson 1977; Barber 1984).

Because the Greek conception of democracy as self-rule developed within the context of relatively undifferentiated societies, however, questions of scope were blurred, so much so that majority tyranny over individuals and minorities could be justified as essential to self-rule. This danger was exemplified by the trial of Socrates, and was certainly at the root of Plato's view that democracy was a bad form of government. In the modern period, the archetypical example is Robespierre's abuse of Rousseau's ideal of the General Will, which enabled a political vanguard to claim representation of "the people" against opponents, on behalf of their common (or general) self (Arendt 1997). Likewise, Marx's de-differentiated conception of democracy as decision-making by "the associated producers" (1993 [1867]: ch. 48) failed to anticipate the accumulations of power by modern administrative states, and thus (inadvertently) justified the claims of vanguard party states to represent an undifferentiated "people," with tyrannical results.

In contrast, the early liberal opposition to absolutist states produced unambiguous, rights-based differentiations between the domains of the private and social life, and that of the state. Thus, when liberal polities democratized, the justifications were primarily "protective" (Macpherson 1977). As James Mill argued, the vote should be more broadly distributed to empower people against abuses of state power (Mill 1992 [1820]).

A cost of early liberal democracy was, however, that rule over self, society, and increasingly autonomous market structures lost its political meaning and location, thus reducing the potential scope of democratic rule. Marx pointed to this alienation of citizenship in *On the Jewish Question* by noting that equal political rights free "private property, education, occupation, to *act* in *their* way—i.e., as private property, as education, as occupation, and to exert the influence of their *special* nature"—producing new relations of domination and exploitation within society and markets (1978 [1843]: 33).

What Marx did not notice is that liberal-rights regimes also enabled the self-organization of civil society—and thus a pluralization of the sites and scope of democratic rule. The key theorist of this development was Tocqueville, who made the democratic case for rights and liberties by noting that they both enable and encourage sites of collective action organized through the levels and means appropriate to the task (1969 [1835]: bk II, sect. 2, ch. 5).

More generally, attentiveness to questions of the proper scope and locus of rule run deeply within the republican tradition, of which Tocqueville is an exemplar, with its emphasis on non-domination, boundary maintenance according to the distinctive qualities of social organization and their goods (Walzer 1984; Pettit 2000). Resources can also be found in neo-Kantian strains of thought, according to which "despotism" means a violation of the autonomy of individuals, which can issue in more extensive questions about what kinds of participation and protection individuals require of various domains to flourish (Cohen and Arato 1994; Habermas 1996; Held 2006: ch. 10). And, finally, those strains of thought that understand power deeply (Dewey 1993 [1935]; Young 2000) also understand potentials for self-determination and self-development as embedded in every social relation of vulnerability, suggesting that democratic mechanisms of rule should be matched to the power relations to which individuals are subject.

How Do the People Rule? Democratic Means and Mechanisms

In contrast to the questions of constituency and scope, the question of *how* the people rule—means and mechanisms such as deliberation, voting, and majority rule—is more familiar. Democratic institutions should effect inclusions by distributing power in the form of votes and political rights to all potentially affected by decisions. Then these powers should be re-aggregated into processes that produce decisions that could be justified to those affected.

This is a tall order, made taller by features of modern societies. The institutions of assembly democracy, practiced by the Athenians, imagined by Rousseau, and practiced briefly in the Paris Commune, have inherent limits. Exigencies of population size, large territories, time, and complexities of governing limit the reach of assembly democracy, although specific mechanisms—deliberative assembly, choice of representatives by lot, and rotation of office—though forgotten for millennia, are finding renewed relevance today (Ober 2008). The representative forms of democracy that began to emerge in the late eighteenth century, however, enable democracy to expand in scope, capacity, and relevance. Since people need not be present for their interests and perspectives to be included in decision-making, representation mechanisms can expand democratic control over large, dispersed populations. At the same time, representative mechanisms enable decision-making bodies small enough to engage in considered deliberation, producing, in effect, a division of labour such that the limitations of citizens' time and attention are mitigated by a political elite whose profession it is to make decisions about complex matters.

At least this is the functional story. The historical story is framed primarily by the fact that modern representative institutions did not have democratic origins but evolved out of negotiations between nobles and monarchs, and were progressively extended to ascendant classes (Manin 1997; Urbinati 2005). Indeed, the Greeks viewed election (as opposed to lottery) as oligarchic rather than democratic. These origins frame the key political problem: can institutions be designed in such a way that representatives are accountable to the peoples and publics they should serve? As civic republicans from Rousseau through Tocqueville feared, when labour is divided between citizens and a political elite, the resulting passive citizenry may be incapable of holding elites to account, who for their part may become detached, self-serving, corrupt, tyrannical, or simply ineffective.

From the perspective of democratic theory, then, we should understand the evolution of modern democratic institutions as responses to the problems of accountability introduced by representation. Among the earliest were checks and balances among branches of government, introduced by Locke (1963 [1689]) and theorized by Madison. By separating powers and constituencies, Madison sought to design institutions that would supply the motives for the elites in one branch of government to oversee and limit the elites of another (Hamilton, Madison, and Jay 1987 [1788]: no. 51).

The separation of powers has a lesser noted positive relationship to democracy as well. Democratic accountability requires, in part, that citizens know what decisions their representatives are making, and the reasoning that justifies them. As Habermas (1996: ch. 4; see also Kant 1991 [1793]; Bentham 1999 [1816]) has pointed out, the separation of powers serves to protect the deliberative, talk-based political judgment within legislatures and judiciaries from executive powers of coercion and economic inducement. Separating powers enables deliberative judgment to take up residence with the coercive domain of the state, which is in turn a necessary condition for citizens to direct, monitor, and judge their representatives (see Rosanvallon 2008).

These institutional potentials for voice and deliberation function "democratically," however, only when combined with empowerments of the people. The most basic of these empowerments is, of course, the vote, which, in the archetypal Western cases, was typically extended after constitutional regimes were established (Macpherson 1977).

The extent to which the vote functions democratically, however, is contingent upon several other basic conditions. The first of these is constituency definition, discussed above. Much attention within the history of democracy has been paid to the universality of the franchise. It is just as important to ask, however, whether those who are potentially affected by collective decisions can use their votes to affect these decisions— either directly or by voting for representatives. "Universality" should be understood as relative to those affected by issues, though there is little within the history of democratic theory that addresses this question (cf. Young 2000; Goodin 2007).

Second, the power of the vote is only as good as the design of the electoral system that aggregates votes into decisions and decision-making bodies. The key cleavage among systems is between plurality and proportional systems (J. S. Mill 1951 [1861]: ch. 10; Duverger 1972: 23–32). The mechanics of single-member district mechanics are majoritarian: they reflect and consolidate a will of the majority, while excluding minorities. The multi-member district mechanics of proportional systems leads to representative bodies that are more inclusive and often more deliberative, but also more prone to gridlock, just because they include more interests. Majoritarian systems are strong in forming *agents* of the people, but risk tyranny of the majority. Proportional systems are more *representative* of the people, but risk undermining democracy by dispersing accountability, and magnifying the veto powers of small minorities.

Finally, the effectiveness of the vote as a means for holding representatives accountable depends upon other political rights, particularly the rights to speak, petition, and associate, which enable individuals to understand their interests, to relate their interests to institutions and policies, and to organize their votes into effective blocs (Dahl 1998). Although rights have Roman origins, they are primarily a modern device with medieval roots, most famously in the Magna Carta, which by the time of the English Civil War was a broadly recognized symbol of freedom. Their political effects went further, however, as they protected and enabled civil societies and public spheres, both necessary to give direction to representative government and to hold it to account (Tocqueville 1969 [1835]; Habermas 1996).

An important consequence of the expansion of the franchise was that it reignited interest in citizens' capacities. For Kant (1991 [1793]); Jefferson (1998 [1787]), and others, the economic and social independence of citizens was a justification for limiting the franchise. Rousseau, Tocqueville, J. S. Mill, Dewey, and others reversed this logic, arguing that inclusion required economic conditions (broad distributions of property), social conditions (a robust associational life), and policies (public education) that underwrite citizen independence and capacities (Macpherson 1977: ch. 3).

Yet, while representative institutions at one time enabled democracy to expand in space and complexity, modern social developments are renewing the relevance of direct forms of democracy. They are doing so not—as Rousseau and Marx imagined— generating the social conditions for societies to be governed as communities. Rather, they are as a means of governing society as a whole, but rather by pluralizing the sites of collective action both within and beyond the state (Cohen and Arato 1994; Warren 2002, 2003). It is in part for this reason that older, citizen-oriented ideals in ancient and civic republican thought have reappeared in associative theories of democracy that emphasize associative alternatives to state organization and collective action (Cole 1920; Hirst 1994), in participatory theories of democracy (Pateman 1976; Macpherson 1977; Barber 1984), and—more recently—in deliberative theories that emphasize the multiple locations of deliberative judgment within complex societies (Cohen and Arato 1994; Habermas 1996; Young 2000), as well as in democracy beyond borders (Bohman 2007). These theories have been enabled by the successes of constitutional regimes in pluralizing the site and opportunities for collective action, which in turn multiplies the opportunities for active citizenship (Warren 2002).

JUSTIFICATIONS OF DEMOCRACY: WHAT IS DEMOCRACY FOR?

From a normative perspective, a *democracy* is any system of institutions, social structures, and practices that maximizes *self-determination* and *self-development* relative to other possible alternatives, given (*a*) the social interdependencies of human life, and (*b*) an ethic that views each human life as intrinsically and equally worthy (Dahl 1998: pt 2; Young 2000: ch. 1). That is, the meaning of "democracy" resides in its goods for individual self-rule, given that self-rule is dependent upon contributions of others, distributed among others, and vulnerable precisely because of these dependencies and distributions.

These ideas encompass virtually all of the justifications of democracy that can be found in the history of political thought. Their shared sense is that democratic institutions, social structures, practices, and cultures perform the dual functions of mitigating the risks of these interdependencies while maximizing and distributing their potentials. The risks of social interdependencies are such that each serves as an occasion for the exercise of power—over the security of body, over the necessities of life and livelihood, or over identity and the meaning of existence. Various pernicious forms of power—coercion, oppression, and domination—work on these need-based vulnerabilities. *Self-determination* involves mitigating these risks for individuals. This is why the "rule" in "rule of the people" has, historically, been associated with liberties and protections, from the Athenian concern to avoid tyranny through the devices of lottery and rotating offices, to development of the rule of law, which provides knowable and secure domains of action. From a modern perspective, a key democratic function of social differentiation is that it tends to assure that no political decision is likely to be so far-reaching that it totalizes damages to livelihoods—thus leaving deliberation, negotiation, and voting as the best and least costly options for responding to political conflict. This is also why, from a normative perspective, it makes little sense to polarize the conceptions of liberty, freedoms, and protections, on the one hand, and democracy, on the other, as has so often been the case in democratic theory. Without liberty and

freedom, "democracy" loses its connection to self-determination and becomes normatively vacuous (see, e.g., Habermas 1996).

The norm of self-development is no less connected with the concept of democracy
than that of self-determination. The logic is straightforward: self-rule, whether exercised over the self directly or through common decisions, is a capacity requiring
development. Capacities include abilities to speak, reason, learn, deliberate, justify
preferences to others, as well as certain civic capacities, including attentiveness to
common affairs, and capacities for recognition and reciprocity. These expectations
were prominent in Pericles' funeral oration, and can be extracted from Aristotle's view
that speech and common self-rule are definitive of humans and human capacity
(Arendt 1958). The same strains can be found in neo-Kantian strains of liberal political
thought: human capacities for autonomy—that is, reflective self-direction—are intimately related to capacities for political rule (Habermas 1996; Held 2006: ch. 10).
Similar normative goods are prominent, for example, in Jefferson, Tocqueville, Mill,
Cole, and Dewey. In each case, democracy is conceived as more than an *instrumental*
good for registering preferences and enabling protections. It is an intrinsic good insofar
as it is a form of self-determination and self-development, which are in turn justified in
terms of some encompassing conception of human purpose.

The institutions associated with "democracy" such as majority rule, voting, separation of powers, and political rights serve these normative goods when they *transform
the media through which collective decisions are made from coercion, authoritarian
imposition, tradition, drift, or default into talk and voting*. The normative importance
of this transformation cannot be overstated. Decisions made in the former ways
will, typically, violate the capacities of individuals for self-determination and self-
development. In addition to violating these norms, they have a host of associated
defects: they tend to be poor on information, ineffective, and unresponsive. Decisions
are often defensive or reactive—focused on keeping power-holders in power. Typically,
they will fail to motivate, because they are not aligned with the wills of the people. And,
often, they fail in their legitimacy, particularly in pluralized, post-conventional societies
no longer united by common national identities, religions, or ethnic identities.

In contrast, the democratic media of talk and voting are intrinsically linked to good
societies. Talk and its various subcategories—deliberation, rhetoric, argument, debate,
discussion, and the like—is the medium through which individuals develop their
preferences and link their preferences to their wills. It is the medium through which
individuals can understand and emphasize the interior lives of others, and can come to
understand the world from the perspectives of others. It is talk that enables common
reasons and wills to form, and that can generate the allegiance, energy, creativity, and
enthusiasm of individuals. Talk maximizes the flow of information and arguments, and
dramatically increases the chances that they will be tested. Epistemically speaking, talk-
based decisions are likely to be better than those made without the benefit of talk-based
testing, as noted as early as Aristotle and developed by J. S. Mill. Finally, these same
processes allow issues to be resolved over time, with the results sedimented into
trustworthy institutions. As long as this progressive institutionalization of consensus

does not become petrified, it can function to direct costly democratic resources—the time and attention of citizens—to their best uses, focused on areas in which decisions must be made in the face of conflict (Warren 1999).

CONCLUSION

We can understand the history of democratic ideas, then, as the identification of means of organizing collective decisions and actions that are successively more legitimate, effective, and normatively robust. That said, democratic theory now faces challenges not anticipated within most of its history, framed as it was by the existence of communities, city states, and states, and threatened primarily by concentrated state powers, size, scale, and complexity. These issues remain, but they are now cross-cut by the challenges of globalizing issues and constituencies, pluralizing venues of collective action, extensive marketization of distribution, and new forms of identity politics. The history of democratic thought, however, provides deep resources, if only we understand that it is not fundamentally about particular institutional designs, but rather about maximizing self-determination and self-development under conditions of power and conflict.

REFERENCES

Primary Sources

ARENDT, H. (1958). *The Human Condition*. Chicago: University of Chicago Press.

ARENDT, H. (1997). *On Revolution*. London: Penguin.

ARISTOTLE (1981 [c.335–323 BC]). *Politics*, ed. Trevor Saunders. London: Penguin.

BARBER, B. (1984). *Strong Democracy: Participatory Politics for a New Age*. Berkeley and Los Angeles: University of California Press.

BENTHAM, J. (1999 [1816]). *Political Tactics*, ed. Michael James, Cyprian Blamires, and Catherine Pease-Watkin. Oxford: Clarendon Press.

BOHMAN, J. (2007). *Democracy across Borders: From Dêmos to Dêmoi*. Cambridge, MA: MIT Press.

COLE, G. D. H. (1920). *Social Theory*. New York: Frederick A. Stokes.

DAHL, R. (1998). *On Democracy*. New Haven: Yale University Press.

DEWEY, J. (1993 [1935]). "Liberty and Social Control," in *The Political Writing*, ed. Ian Shapiro and Debra Morris. Indianapolis: Hackett.

DUVERGER, M. (1972). *Party Politics and Pressure Groups*. New York: Thomas Y. Crowell.

HABERMAS, J. (1989 [1962]). *The Structural Transformation of the Public Sphere*, trans. T. Berger. Cambridge, MA: MIT Press.

HABERMAS, J. (1996). *Between Facts and Norms: Contributions to a Discourse Theory of Law and Democracy*, trans. William Rehg. Cambridge, MA: MIT Press.

HAMILTON, A., MADISON, J., and JAY, J. (1987 [1788]). *The Federalist Papers*. London: Penguin Classics.

HIRST, P. (1994). *Associative Democracy: New Forms of Economic and Social Governance*. Amherst, MA: University of Massachusetts Press.

JEFFERSON, T. (1998 [1787]). *Notes on the State of Virginia*, ed. Frank Shiffelton. London: Penguin Classics.

KANT, I. (1991 [1793]). "On the Common Saying: 'This may be True in Theory, but it does not Apply in Practice'," in *Political Writings*, ed. H. H. Reiss. Cambridge: Cambridge University Press, 237–49.

KANT, I. (1996 [1797]). *The Metaphysics of Morals*, ed. Mary Gregor. Cambridge: Cambridge University Press.

LOCKE, J. (1963 [1689]). *Two Treatises on Government*. Cambridge: Cambridge University Press.

MACPHERSON, C. B. (1977). *The Life and Times of Liberal Democracy*. Oxford: Oxford University Press.

MARX, K. (1978 [1843]). "On the Jewish Question," in *The Marx–Engels Reader*, ed. Robert Tucker. 2nd edn. New York: W. W. Norton.

MARX, K. (1993 [1867]). *Capital: A Critique of Political Economy*, iii. London: Penguin Classics.

MILL, J. (1992 [1820]). "Government," in *Political Writings*, ed. Terence Ball. Cambridge: Cambridge University Press, 1–42.

MILL, J. S. (1951 [1861]). "Considerations on Representative Government," in *Utilitarianism, Liberty, and Representative Government*, ed. H. B. Action. London: Dent.

MONTESQUIEU, C. DE (1989 [1748]). *The Spirit of the Laws*. Cambridge: Cambridge University Press.

PATEMAN, C. (1976). *Participation and Democratic Theory*. Cambridge: Cambridge University Press.

RAWLS, J. (2005). *Political Liberalism: Expanded Edition*. New York: Columbia University Press.

ROUSSEAU, J.-J. (1978 [1762]). *The Social Contract*, trans. J. Masters and R. MASTERS. New York: St Martin's Press.

THUCYDIDES (1952). *History of the Peloponnesian War*, ed. M. I. Finley. London: Penguin Classics.

TOCQUEVILLE, A. DE (1969 [1835]). *Democracy in America*, trans. George Lawrence. Garden City, NY: Doubleday.

WALZER, M. (1984). *Spheres of Justice: A Defense of Pluralism and Equality*. New York: Basic Books.

YOUNG, I. (2000). *Inclusion and Democracy*. Oxford: Oxford University Press.

Secondary Sources

COHEN, J. and ARATO, A. (1994). *Civil Society and Political Theory*. Cambridge, MA: MIT Press.

DUVERGER, M. (1972). *Party Politics and Pressure Groups*. New York: Thomas Y. Crowell.

FINLEY, M. I. (1983). *Politics in the Ancient World*. Cambridge: Cambridge University Press.

GOODIN, R. E. (2007). "Enfranchising All Affected Interests, and its Alternatives," *Philosophy and Public Affairs*, 35/1: 40–68.

HELD, D. (2006). *Models of Democracy*. 2nd edn. Stanford, CA: Stanford University Press.

HORNBLOWER, S. (2002). *The Greek World 479–323 BC*. London: Routledge.

MANIN, B. (1997). *The Principles of Representative Government*. Cambridge: Cambridge University Press.

OBER, J. (2008). "What The Ancient Greeks can Tell us about Democracy," *Annual Review of Political Science*, 11: 67–91.

PETTIT, P. (2000). *Republicanism: A Theory of Freedom and Government*. Oxford: Oxford University Press.

PITKIN, H. (1967). *The Concept of Representation*. Berkeley and Los Angeles: University of California Press.

POCOCK, J. G. A. (2003). *The Machiavellian Moment: Florentine Political Thought and the Atlantic Republican Tradition*. Rev. edn. Cambridge: Cambridge University Press.

PUDDINGTON, ARCH. (2009). *Freedom in the World 2009: Setbacks and Resilience*. Arlington, VA: Freedom House.

REHFELD, ANDREW (2005). *The Concept of Constituency*. Cambridge: Cambridge University Press.

ROSANVALLON, P. (2008). *Counter-Democracy: Politics in an Age of Distrust*. Cambridge: Cambridge University Press.

TILLY, C. (2007). *Democracy*. Cambridge: Cambridge University Press.

TULLY, J. (1988). *Meaning and Context: Quentin Skinner and his Critics*. Princeton: Princeton University Press.

URBINATI, N. (2005). "Continuity and Rupture: The Power of Judgment in Democratic Representation," *Constellations*, 12/2: 194–222.

URBINATI, N. (2006). *Representative Democracy: Principles and Genealogy*. Chicago: University of Chicago Press.

WARREN, M. E. (1999). "Democratic Theory and Trust," in Mark E. Warren (ed.), *Democracy and Trust*. Cambridge: Cambridge University Press, 310–45.

WARREN, M. E. (2002). "What can Democratic Participation Mean Today?" *Political Theory*, 30: 678–702.

WARREN, M. E. (2003). "A Second Transformation of Democracy?" in Bruce Cain, Russell Dalton, and Susan Scarrow (eds), *New Forms of Democracy? The Reform and Transformation of Democratic Institutions*. Oxford: Oxford University Press.

CHAPTER 30

···

RIGHTS

···

KENNETH PENNINGTON

EVERY human society has possessed a rudimentary notion of rights that protected individuals in law and sometimes from the law. One of the most notable characteristics of Western societies has been the development of individual and group rights in legal, theological, and philosophical thought of the first two millennia. It has often been noted that thinkers in Non-Western societies have not had the same preoccupation with rights. One of the contemporary consequences of this divergence has been the accusation that Western democracies have wished to impose their norms on unwilling and unreceptive societies, especially through treaties of the United Nations.

The very concept of rights is laden with numerous problems. Universality is the most basic and difficult. Thomas Jefferson claimed in the American Declaration of Independence (1776) that individual human beings have rights that are not dependent upon any human system of law:

> We hold these truths to be self-evident, that all men are created equal; that they are endowed by their Creator with certain inalienable rights; that among these, are life, liberty, and the pursuit of happiness; that to secure these rights, governments are instituted among men, deriving their just powers from the consent of the governed; that whenever any form of government becomes destructive of these ends, it is the right of the people to alter or abolish it.

The main rights that Jefferson listed were equality, liberty—today he would most likely have written "freedom"—and the right of consent and of resistance. All these rights have, as we will see, long histories in the Western tradition. However, some modern thinkers have rejected Jefferson's claim that all human beings have "inherent and inalienable rights." Not all of Jefferson's contemporaries were taken with his rhetoric. Jeremy Bentham's trenchant rejection of natural rights in his *Anarchical Fallacies* was an anticipation of the thought of legal positivists who dominated rights thinking in the twentieth century. Rights, they asserted, are based on positive law. In anticipation of their thought, Bentham argued: "That which has no existence cannot be destroyed—

that which cannot be destroyed cannot require anything to preserve it from destruction. *Natural rights* is simple nonsense: natural and imprescriptible rights, rhetorical nonsense,—nonsense upon stilts" (Bentham 1843: 501). Those who have found Bentham's arguments compelling have observed that all pre-modern and modern systems of rights have been the product and the expression of the beliefs and morals of individual societies, religions, and cultures. They also have pointed out, quite rightly, that human societies have either not recognized the same rights as others or have embraced conflicting rights. As Brian Tierney has noted: "All civilized societies have cherished ideals of justice and right order, but they have not normally expressed those ideals in terms of individual natural rights—it would be hard, for instance, to imagine a Confucian Hobbes or Locke" (Tierney 1997: 1–2). Consequently, if human rights are only a product of Western ideas of justice, they cannot have universality. In an age that is dominated by conceptions of law embracing some form of legal positivism, many scholars recognize only individual rights that have been established by the constitutional jurisprudence of individual countries or their legal systems. This is particularly true of the legal culture in the United States. One of the consequences of legal positivism's jurisprudence of rights is that American citizens have a greater claim to these rights than non-citizens. Another more general consequence is that, since the nation state has become the repository and defender of rights, it has granted itself the power to strip them from citizens and non-citizens alike.

The discussion of rights in the modern world has focused on several questions that I will ignore in this chapter focusing on the history of rights. Perhaps the most important that I will omit is how rights are currently defined and categorized. Modern thinkers have distinguished two broad categories of rights: subjective rights or natural rights (which Jefferson called inalienable), and rights bestowed upon persons by the legal system. However, the analysis has not stopped there. Wesley Newcomb Hohfeld (1923) created a complex and sophisticated categorization of rights that has sharpened our understanding about exactly how we may define a particular "right," but his analysis of "rights," which he placed into categories of claims, liberties, privileges, powers, and immunities, has almost no historical roots—although they have been applied to the thought of historical figures (Thomson 1990; Reid 1991; Tierney 2006).

In the English-speaking scholarship, rights have also been captive to an impoverished vernacular that has complicated scholarly study and analysis. This lack of suppleness of the English language has led to the Balkanization or compartmentalization of thinking about law and rights in English and American jurisprudential thought. This Balkanization recapitulates and confirms the categories of "law" and "right" in our language as completely separate ideas. A passage from Hobbes's *Leviathan* illustrates this point:

> The RIGHT OF NATURE, which Writers commonly call *Jus Naturale*, is the Liberty each man hath, to use his own power, as he will himselfe, for preservation of his own Nature . . . A LAW OF NATURE, (*Lex Naturalis*), is a Precept, or generall Rule, found out by Reason, by which a man is forbidden to do, that, which is destructive

of his life, or taketh away the means of preserving the same, and to omit, that, by which he thinketh it may be best preserved. For though they that speak of this subject, use to confound *Jus* and *Lex, Right* and *Law*; yet they ought to be distinguished; because RIGHT consisteth in liberty to do, or to forbear; Whereas LAW determineth and bindeth to one of them: so that Law and Right differ as much as Obligation and Liberty, which in one and the same matter are inconsistent. (Hobbes 1968: 189; cf. Oakley 2005: 87–9)

Hobbes certainly knew that *ius* had more meanings than "right." By Hobbes's time *ius naturale* was commonly translated as a natural right but was also commonly translated as natural law. To distinguish between natural right and natural law Hobbes was forced to use *lex naturalis* to describe a binding law of nature. If he had been writing in any other European language, he could have used the same term to define both meanings— for example, *droit naturel* or *diritto naturale*. This fact would have made his neat distinction between a "right" and a "law" far more difficult to make. Earlier writers were always aware that when they wrote "ius naturale" to mean natural law, they did not and could not divorce it from the penumbras of norms, rights, and duties that natural right (*ius naturale*) contained in its DNA (Pennington 2008: 589–91).

For the history of "rights thinking," it is important to understand the difference between *ius* and *lex*. Unlike the words "right" and "law" in English, the word for law and right in Latin and in most European languages, even in the Germanic and Slavic languages, is equivocal. Depending on the context, *ius, diritto, droit, derecho, Recht,* and *prawo* mean law, the legal system, and right. English is the exception. In English, the concepts of law and rights are separate categories, each word having its own cluster of meanings. A reader in French, German, Italian, Spanish, and Polish is constantly reminded that the word "law" means more than just "the principles and regulations established by government and applicable to a people";[1] it also connotes the power of persons to exercise or vindicate rights. Consequently, when French, Italian, German, and other legal systems distinguish between the "law" and the "rights" created by law, they must differentiate between "law" and "subjective laws," terminology that makes no sense in English (for example, droit objectif et les droits subjectifs), but is easily understandable and precise in other languages. English and American law dictionaries currently used in law schools ignore rights entirely in their definitions of law.[2] In order to excavate "rights" from the word law, we must turn to older, pre-John Austin, English dictionaries, where we find definitions of law that encompass the "rights and obligations of states, of individuals, and of artificial persons and local communities among themselves and to each other."[3]

---

[1] *The Random House Dictionary of the English Language: The Unabridged Edition* (New York: Random House, 1967), 812.

[2] e.g. *Black's Law Dictionary with Pronunciations*, (ed.) Joseph R. Nolan and Jacqueline M. Nolan-Haley (6th edn; Kansas City: St Paul, 1990), 864–5, gives a purely positivistic and institutional series of definitions and never mentions rights of individuals or groups.

[3] *Bouvier's Law Dictionary and Concise Encyclopedia*, (ed.) Francis Rawle (3rd edn; Kansas City: St Paul, 1914), ii. 1876.

Thinking about rights can be shaped by our language but also by our historical perceptions about how and where rights emerged in Western jurisprudential thought. If we presume that rights are a creation of the democratic, constitutional nation state, invented to protect its citizens, and graciously bestowed on the citizens of the nation state by a benevolent Leviathan, we might assume that rights are not universal but unexpected byproducts of the transition from the *Ancien Régime* to the modern world. In this construct, citizens do have a greater claim to these rights than non-citizens. The nation state alone becomes the repository and defender of the rights of its citizens. On the other hand, if one understands rights as being a web of norms that transcends the present, as having deep roots in the past, and as having a universal validity and applicability extending far beyond the treaties, constitutions, and declarations, rights become powerful principles that could serve as antidotes to the excesses of the modern state whose jurisprudence is permeated with the doctrine of legal positivism (Pennington 2003). It is to this past that we now turn.

Historically, the emergence of rights in European jurisprudence is intimately connected with the terms *ius naturale* and *lex naturalis* in Western jurisprudence and theological thought. Although Hobbes did not know it, his use of *lex naturalis* had a history that stretched back to late antiquity. The Christian theological tradition had long connected the Golden Rule contained in Matthew 7:12 and Luke 6:31 ("Do unto others as you would have others do unto you") with a principle of natural law. Theologians did not, however, adopt the terminology of Roman law, *ius naturale*, but consistently called the Golden Rule a principle of *lex naturalis*. The first person who seems to have connected the Golden Rule with natural law was a disciple of Jerome in a letter he wrote at his teacher's death. Prosper of Aquitaine († *c*.465) linked the Golden Rule to natural law in his commentary on the Psalms. Haimo of Halberstadt († 853) declared in two sermons and his biblical commentaries that natural law consisted of two precepts: "Do onto others . . ." and "What you do not want done to yourself, you should not do to others (cf. Tobias 4.16). Whatever the law and the prophets will ordain can be comprehended within these two precepts." Remigius of Auxerre († 980) rehearsed the tradition in his commentary on Genesis. In the late eleventh and early twelfth centuries Rupert of Deutz († 1129–30) declared that natural law is written on the hearts of men, and its expression was the Golden Rule. Hugh of St Victor († 1141) and Honorius Augustodunensis († 1156) repeated the tradition. In the Christian theological tradition, the Golden Rule was a precept and command of Hobbes's *lex naturalis*. It may have been a binding *lex* in Hobbes's definition, but the maxim was much more of a *ius than a lex*. (For the Latin texts and citations of all the authors cited in this paragraph, see Pennington 2008: 575–6.)

Later medieval theologians still continued to use the term *lex naturalis*, especially Thomas Aquinas, but in jurisprudence *ius naturale* triumphed in the early twelfth century.[4] The origins of *ius naturale* lie in the thought of the philosophers and jurists of

---

[4] Thomas Aquinas had much less influence on the development of "rights thinking" than one finds in standard textbook accounts.

the ancient world. They thought that there were rules for human behavior based upon objective, eternal norms and conceived of these norms as having been established by nature and reason. The Romans were the first to coin the term *ius naturale*. The Roman orator Cicero († 43 BCE) summed up an important strand of ancient thought when he argued in his *De republica* 3.22 that "true law was right reason that was congruent with nature." He concluded that "there was one eternal, immutable, and unchangeable law." In the third century CE the jurist Ulpian defined natural law as what "nature teaches all animals," including human beings. He distinguished natural law from the *ius gentium* that was common only to human beings and established by their customary usages. Ulpian cited the union of men and women ("what we call marriage") and the procreation of children as examples of natural law (*ius naturale*). Most significantly, the Roman jurist Paul defined *ius naturale* as what was equitable and good. It was not just a command or an obligation that demanded obedience. *Ius naturale* required humans to make moral and ethical choices. Ulpian's and Paul's definitions were later included in the Emperor Justinian's comprehensive codification (*c*.533–6) of Roman law (Pennington 2008). Justinian's codification also included an introductory textbook for the study of law called the *Institutes*. The definition of natural law in the *Institutes* moved the source of natural law from the behavior of creatures to God: "Natural laws [*naturalia iura*] are established by divine providence and always remain firm and immutable" (*Institutes* 1.2.11). A little later the authors of the *Institutes* asserted that the *ius gentium* is identical with natural law (*Institutes* 2.1.11). In every European law school from the eleventh to the seventeenth century, professors and students studied and pondered Paul's, Ulpian's, and the *Institutes'* definitions—and their contradictions. The Roman jurists were not inclined to interpret *naturalia iura* as natural rights. Rather they discussed the passage in positivistic terms. They were "natural laws" (Weigand 1967: 8–64; see also Reid 1991: 52–5 for a valuable discussion of *ius* in Roman law and a discussion of the interpretative literature).

When Isidore of Seville composed (*c*.620) his encyclopedic *Etymologies* (5.4), he combined the two traditions that had circulated in the ancient world and produced the most important definition of *ius naturale* in the European legal tradition (Pennington 2008: 581).

> Natural law [*ius naturale*] is common to all nations. It has its origins in nature not in any constitution. Examples of natural law [*ius naturale*] are the union of men and women, the procreation and raising of children, the common possessions of all persons, the equal liberty of all persons, the acquisition of things that are taken from the heavens, earth, or sea, the return of property or money that has been deposited or entrusted. This also includes the right to repel violence with force. These things and similar are never unjust but are natural and equitable.

There are several points about Isidore's definition that should be noted. His first two items, union of men and women and the procreation of children, were probably taken from the jurists. The common possession of all persons was a concept found in ancient philosophical and in early Christian thought (Tierney 1959: 27–35; 1997: 70–3). If the first two might be considered both rights and duties, the common possession of all persons is simply a description of the primitive state of humanity. It was neither a *ius* nor a *lex*. The phrase would have, as we shall see, a very important role in the development of ideas about rights. Isidore's phrase, *omium una libertas*, the equal liberty of all persons, is particular puzzling and intriguing. No one has traced the source of the idea in Roman law or in Christian theology. However, in spite of the radical implications of the phrase for the illegitimacy of slavery, jurists found ways to obviate its subversive message. Isidore's last three examples of *ius naturale* move his definition of *ius naturale* out of the realm of commands and mandates of a legal system and into the realm of rights. Isidore enumerated three examples that can only be rights: the right to acquire a *res nullius*; the right to receive property deposited as well as the obligation to return property to its owner; and the right of self-defense. Isidore's use of the word *acquisitio* ("acquisition") clearly focuses on a person's right to acquire property when it is a *res nullius*. One might argue that it is a mandate or a law of the *ius naturale* that the air, the sea, and wild animals are the property of no one, but that mandate would not necessarily establish a person's right to acquire a *res nullius*. The same point can be made about the gratuitous contract of deposit. The right of self-defense, perhaps the most universal of all rights, is undoubtedly a *ius* that is not a *lex*. The main point is that Isidore, unlike the Roman jurists, was clearly thinking of *ius* as a right in these last three examples of *ius naturale* in his list. If he had to translate *ius naturale* into English when he contemplated the norm of self-defense, he would have rendered the phrase not as "natural law" but as "natural right."

From Isidore to the jurist Gratian in the twelfth century there was virtually no discussion of natural law as a norm for human society among the jurists. As part of his plan to bring order to the chaotic state of church law, Gratian (*c*.1120–40) compiled a legal collection of ecclesiastical norms. At the beginning of his canonical collection, called the *Decretum*, he discussed the various types of laws that regulated and guided the behavior of human beings. In the opening sentence of his collection Gratian brought natural law to the forefront of all future discussions about the structure of all human law: "The human race is ruled by two things, namely, natural law and customary usages. Natural law is what is contained in the Law (i.e. Old Testament) and Gospels." Gratian concluded that natural law dictated that "each person is commanded to do to others what he wants done to himself," connecting natural law with the biblical injunction to do unto others what you would have them do unto you (Matthew 7:12). By defining natural law as the duty to treat other human beings with care and dignity, Gratian stimulated jurists to reflect upon the central values of natural law: the rendering of justice and the administering of equity in the legal system. To define the contents of natural law, he placed Isidore's definition of natural law on the first page of his *Decretum* (D.1 c.7). Gratian's excavation of Isidore's text is quite remarkable, because it had not been part of the canonical or Roman law tradition. Together with the texts of Roman law discussing *ius naturale* in Justinian's compilation, Gratian's *Decretum* became one of the standard introductory texts for the study of law (the *ius commune*) in European law schools, and Isidore's definition became one of the most important starting points for all medieval discussions of natural law (Weigand 1967: 121–96).

Gratian clearly thought that Isidore did not think of *ius naturale* as a set of laws (*leges*) but as a set of principles. The core principle could be summed up by the Golden Rule. The most influential canonist of the twelfth century, Huguccio (*c.*1190), underlined Gratian's interpretation:

> The return of property or money that has been deposited or entrusted: This by right [*ius*] or evangelical command, in which anyone is ordered to do unto others what he wishes to be done to him, and anyone is prohibited from doing unto others what she would not wish to be done to her. Reason and the judgment of reason approve the restitution of those things deposited with me or entrusted to me. (Pennington 2008: 584)

Huguccio had much more to say about *ius naturale*. He located the origin of natural law in human beings. Natural law is reason, and that reason is a natural power of the soul (*naturalis vis animi*) that permits them to distinguish good from evil. This reason is called *ius* because it commands and "law" (*lex*) because it binds. Huguccio also summed up twelfth-century juristic opinion on the force of natural law in human affairs. Natural law, he observed, consists of three levels of authority: commands; prohibitions; and indications or declarations (*demonstrationes*). An example of a command is the precept to "love your Lord God." A prohibition of natural law may be taken from the Ten Commandments, "Thou shalt not steal." The third level of natural law leads human beings to choose what is licit and good over what is bad and evil. For example, in Gratian's excerpt from Isidore of Seville, liberty is a state that should be granted to all human beings. Huguccio noted, however, that all men are not free. Natural law leads men to liberty but does not command it. He explained that, although liberty has its roots in natural law, God introduced slavery into the world because of human sins. Although medieval thinkers had to confront Isidore's elegant and stirring maxim that expressed the basic norm of human freedom (*una libertas omnium*) constantly, they could not overturn the institution of slavery that was endemic in their world or undermine the rights of slave-owners.

Huguccio and the canonists also introduced the idea of permissive natural law. As Tierney has pointed out, permissive natural law was often seen as natural rights. Already in the late twelfth century, jurists formulated definitions of *ius naturale* that emphasized the rights of human beings to exercise their free choice (Tierney 1997: 66–9). Huguccio, for example, used the concept of permissive natural law to analyze private property rights. If natural law dictated that private property was not a right (Isidore's "the common possessions of all persons" seems to indicate that it was not), then how can the right to private property be justified? His answer was a permissive natural law (Tierney 1997: 142; 2002: 400–1):

> By the law of nature something is mine and something is yours, but this is by permission not by precept, for divine law never commanded that all things be common or that some things be private, but it permitted that all things be common

or some private. Consequently by natural law something is common and something is private.

This right to private property that was protected by natural permissive law rested primarily on Gratian's first principle of *ius naturale*. Later jurists understood the connection. As the great lawyer pope of the thirteenth century, Pope Innocent IV wrote that the property rights of the first occupant of property was protected by the command to "do unto others as you would wish others would do unto you" (Tierney 2002: 401)

The early jurists did not think that all rights were natural rights. Gratian began his *Decretum* by dividing all law into two categories, natural law, and long-standing and accepted customs (*mores*). Consequently, the canonists who used the *Decretum* in their classrooms for the next four centuries were forced to consider the equivocal meanings of *ius naturale*. Like his Roman predecessors, Gratian lived in a thought world in which *ius* was understood primarily as an objective law; however, by the second half of the twelfth century, canonists were commonly using *ius* to mean "right."

The canonist Rufinus (*c*.1160) was an important figure in developing the language of natural rights. While commenting on Gratian's *ius naturale*, he observed: "Natural 'ius' is a certain force instilled in every human creature by nature to do good and avoid the opposite." This definition of ius naturale became commonplace (Tierney 1997: 62).

By the year 1300, the jurists of the *Ius commune* had developed a sturdy language of rights and created a number of rights derived from natural law. During the period from 1150 to 1300, they defined the rights of property, self-defense, non-Christians, marriage, and procedural rights—especially the rights of defendants—as being rooted in natural, not positive, law. By placing these rights squarely within the framework of natural law, the jurists could and did argue that these rights could not be taken away by the human prince. The prince had no jurisdiction over rights based on natural law; consequently these rights were inalienable (Pennington 1993; Reid 2004).

The jurists' analysis of the rights of the poor represented another strand in rights thinking, what modern scholars have called passive rights (Reid 1991: 58–9). Gratian's *Decretum* included a number of texts that contained trenchant admonitions to provide for the poor. Perhaps the most poignant of these passages was one taken from the writing of Rufinus of Aquileia (*c*.344–*c*.410) that masqueraded as the words of Ambrose in Gratian (Weigand 1967: 308): "No one may call his own what is common, of which if he takes more than he needs, it is taken with violence." Rufinus' words echo across the centuries and were paraphrased by Proudhon's "Property is Theft."

Rufinus' words do not directly lead to the idea that the poor have a right to subsistence, but the twelfth-century jurists had the vocabulary and the inclination to do so. Huguccio was, again, a key figure. He declared that by natural law we should keep what is necessary and distribute what is left to the needy. This is particularly true in times of famine and great need. Later jurists expanded Huguccio's thought and formulated a "right" of the poor to steal or to take food in times of need. As the foremost jurist of the thirteenth century, Hostiensis, put it: "One who suffers the need of hunger seems to use his right rather than to plan a theft." The natural rights of the poor to subsistence became a commonplace of medieval and early modern thought. At the end of the seventeenth century, John Locke could rehearse this idea that was by then five centuries old: "He has given his Brother a Right to the Surplusage of his Goods; so that it cannot justly be denied him when his pressing Want calls for it." But Locke could also write that "Charity gives every man a Title to so much out of another's plenty, as will keep him from extream want" (texts cited in Tierney 1997: 71–6). The jurists decided that the theft of foodstuff and clothing in times of great need was not a criminal act or even a sin. This right was rejected by the Common Law systems but is still to be found in most Civil Law systems.

The historical significance of this jurisprudential development is that scholars who have discovered the language of natural rights only in the philosophical writings of fourteenth- and fifteenth-century philosophers, most frequently in the work of William Ockham or Jean Gerson, have overlooked the importance of twelfth-century jurisprudence in shaping Western thought. Tierney's arguments that the twelfth- and thirteenth-century jurists shaped the language of rights and prepared the way for rights thinking among theologians and jurists have generated a broad range of responses. The reactions of scholars are far too complex to be summarized here. Some have agreed with Tierney that the twelfth- and thirteenth-century jurists produced a jurisprudence preparatory for natural rights. Others have argued that natural rights or what are today called subjective rights or human rights never existed in the minds of the medieval theologians and jurists. They have maintained that the jurists and theologians thought only in terms of rights granted by natural law (as today's legal positivists would claim that all rights are derived from positive law) and did not think of them as subjective rights inhering in individual human beings. They think that the mandates and commands of natural law vitiated any possibility that natural subjective rights could exist (see the trenchant comments and analysis of Wolterstorff 2008: 30–43).

One example may illustrate the problem of interpreting the thought of the jurists when they invoked *ius naturale*. During the late Middle Ages the jurists created an absolute right of a defendant to a public trial, what today we call due process. Included in this right was the right to be cited, to have a trial in a public court, to hear the evidence and its source, to present witnesses, and to have a sentence rendered publicly. When the jurists discussed these absolute rights of due process, they always asserted that this right was based on *ius naturale*. Consequently, even the pope or the emperor could not take away these rights. When Johannes Monachus (*c.*1300) wrote that "a summons is 'de iure naturali' and that even the pope may not bring suit against a defendant without a summons" was he thinking "natural right" or "natural law?" Or both? (This texts and others are in Pennington 1993: 160–4.) We will never know. We can, however, concur with Tierney that such language and thought prepared the way for natural rights. Others have argued that for the most part medieval jurists thought of natural rights as "were based upon a purportedly objective assessment of the teachings of natural law and the Christian religion. That is obviously much less true of the natural human rights found in modern law" (Helmholz 2003: 324–5).

Other scholars have argued that only much later, when thinkers like Hobbes rejected the idea of natural law as a set of commands and embraced the idea of natural rights, could the idea of modern rights emerge; rights are a modern invention and represent a break with the past (e.g., illustrating these differing and conflicting conclusions, Villey 1975, Tuck 1979, Fortin 1996, Finnis 1998, Helmholz 2003; see the fine summary of the literature in Tierney 1997: 1–9, with further reflections in Tierney 2002, Oakley 2005: 87–109, Wolterstorff 2008: 1–64). The complexity of modern opinion is daunting. Consequently, even a brief sketch of the range of scholarly interpretations of medieval conceptions of *ius naturale* would severely tax the allotted scope of this chapter. Even more difficult would be a sure statement about when we can first see a definition of *ius* that is exactly what we mean by rights today. At this point one can only wait for a *communis opinio* to emerge after the debate has run its course.

Before Tierney's work there was already a growing conviction, if not a consensus, among some scholars that the origins of rights thinking began in the later Middle Ages. According to this line of thought, the bridge to the modern world of rights extends from the theologians William Ockham and Jean Gerson in the fourteenth and fifteenth centuries to the great jurist, Hugo Grotius, in the seventeenth, with a collection of Spanish jurists and theologians, the "Second Scholastics," in between. William Ockham is undoubtedly the most important but the most difficult thinker in this list. Ockham dealt with *ius naturale* in a series of polemical works that he wrote during the great dispute with Pope John XXII (1316–34). His language and his interpretation of *ius naturale* rested primarily on the writings of the jurists (in contrast to Thomas Aquinas). As part of his attack on papal authority, Ockham developed a clear recognition that the people had rights that limited ecclesiastical and secular authority. Although he hedged his generalization with the admission that Ockham's rights were not the same as those of modern rights theorists, Tierney put forward the possibility that Ockham "created, perhaps for the first time, an ecclesiology and political theory founded on the concept of natural rights" (Tierney 1997: 170–94).

The last historical context that was crucial for the development of a tradition of "rights thinking" in the European tradition was the discovery of the New World and new peoples in the sixteenth century. If a number of Spanish thinkers had not been confronted by this new set of problems, "rights" could have withered on the vine. Certainly the sixteenth and seventeenth centuries were not great ages for human freedom in other areas. The doctrine of absolutism became acceptable coin of political discourse, religious toleration reached abysmal depths never before seen, censorship became a tool of European secular and religious regimes to control thought, witches were discovered in every crack and crevice, Puritanism became the first and most important virtue that was added to the other seven: this list could be extended almost endlessly. Yet the discovery of lands populated with pagan peoples sparked a debate about their rights. Some of the best minds of the sixteenth century asked hard questions. Could native peoples have a just title to their lands? Could their lands be taken from them? Could they be enslaved? American courts have only begun to grapple with these issues since the 1980s, and the general public has only just begun to recognize the great injustice done to the rights of native Americans.

Francisco de Vitoria († 1546) studied at Paris and established a school at Salamanca during the first half of the fifteenth century. While Spanish conquistadors plundered the New World, Vitoria explored the moral and legal ramifications of their conquests. The key issue was *dominium* or lordship, but which could also mean "right." Could the American natives justly possess property and rightfully rule over their lands? The legal tradition was mixed. In the thirteenth century, two jurists took opposing sides. Pope Innocent IV, who wrote a massive commentary on canon law (*c.*1240), concluded that infidels did possess just *dominium*, and their lands could not be taken from them without cause. Their rights could be taken away only if they sinned against natural or divine law. The greatest canonist of the century, Hostiensis, concurred with Innocent in his early work but around 1270 changed his mind. Perhaps swept away by the crusading enthusiasm of Pope Gregory X, he concluded that, since the birth of Christ, just *dominium* existed only within the confines of the Christian Church. No one outside the Church could exercise *dominium* legitimately. During the fourteenth and fifteenth centuries, jurists embraced either Innocent's or Hostiensis's opinion but without, one feels, great passion, for the problem had no real immediacy.

Vitoria was a bloodless academic who dissected the meanings of rights in his laboratory. Bartolomé de Las Casas labored among the Indians in the New World for twenty years. He saw the atrocities committed by the Spanish. He preached the brotherhood of man and the natural rights of all humans, and argued vehemently that the Indians had a natural right to liberty, could exercise *dominium*, and must consent to any claim of Europeans to rule over them. Francisco Suárez († 1614) developed the vocabulary of *ius* and *ius naturale* as "right" and "natural right" even further in his great work *De legibus* (Tierney 1997: 301–15).[5]

Manuel González Téllez († 1649) wrote one of the last extended canonistic discussions of *ius naturale* that was framed by the medieval jurisprudential tradition in the preface to his commentary on the Decretals of Gregory IX. Téllez used and cited Thomas Aquinas extensively. What is particularly striking is that Téllez wrote about natural law primarily in terms of "*praecepta* (precepts or maxims)" not in terms of *leges*. The most fundamental of these norms, wrote Téllez, was that human beings should and can distinguish between good and evil. For the remainder of these norms he turned to the jurisprudential tradition. Human beings should live honestly and should not injure their neighbors. Lastly, everyone should give each person his *ius* in contracts, restitutions, and payments of debts, whose rendering may be assigned to reason and natural equity. All of these norms, Téllez concluded by turning back to Gratian's dictum at the beginning of the *Decretum*, can be found in the divine wisdom of Christ's admonition found in Matthew 7: "Do unto others as you would have others do unto you." Téllez recognized that *ius naturale* could be a set of divine *leges* and

---

[5] For more detail on the rights thinking of the Spanish Scholastics, see Anthony Pagden, Chapter 15, this volume.

commands but emphasized the principles that helped human beings to recognize rights (Pennington 2008: 588–9).

The main conduit though which the concept of natural rights flowed into modern political thought was the Dutch Protestant jurist, Hugo Grotius († 1645). In *De jure belli*, Grotius grappled with the meanings of right (*ius*) in all of its multifarious meanings. The major theme of his book on the law of war was to prove that "just wars were fought to defend or assert rights or to punish violations of them." He explored all the meanings of *ius* and defined it as "a moral quality of a person, enabling him to have or to do something justly" (Tierney 1997: 316–42 at 325). Grotius borrowed his definitions of right from the sixteenth-century Spanish theologians, but, because of his Protestantism and that of his readers, he hid his sources in a thicket of classical quotations. Grotius has often been called the "Father of International Law." He also might be called the "Modern Father of Natural Rights," for Grotius influenced "all the major rights theorists of the next century, Selden, Hobbes and Locke in England, Pufendorf, Leibniz and Thomasius in Germany, Domat and Pothier in France" (Tierney 1997: 340).

When medieval and early modern jurists and theologians thought of rights, they thought of *ius naturale*. Their analysis of that phrase over centuries is the origin of our rights thinking today. They recognized *ius naturale* as *leges naturalia* but also as a set of precepts, rights, and duties encapsulated in the other meanings attributed to *ius* from the ancient Roman jurists to Grotius. When they define natural law and natural rights today, many thinkers have embraced positivistic sets of rules, prohibitions, and norms, shaped and fashioned according to each of their belief systems, that are and always have been the defining feature of *lex*. Human beings may never agree on universal rules of a *lex naturalis*, but they might agree on universal precepts that shape the penumbra of rights surrounding *ius naturale*.

References

BENTHAM, JEREMY (1843). "Anarchical Fallacies: Being an Examination of the Declarations of Rights Issued during the French Revolution," in *The Works of Jeremy Bentham*, (ed.) John Bowring. Edinburgh: William Tait, ii. 489–534.

BRETT, ANNABEL S. (1997). *Liberty, Right and Nature: Individual Rights in Later Scholastic Thought*. Cambridge: Cambridge University Press.

FINNIS, JOHN (1979). *Natural Law and Natural Rights*. Oxford: Clarendon Press.

FINNIS, JOHN (1998). *Aquinas: Moral, Political, and Legal Theory*. Oxford: Oxford University Press.

FORTIN, ERNEST (1996). "On the Presumed Medieval Origin of Individual Rights," in *Collected Essays*, ii: *Classical Christianity and the Political Order*, (ed.) J. Brian Benstead. Lanham, MD: Rowman and Littlefield, 243–64.

HELMHOLZ, RICHARD H. (2003). "Natural Human Rights: The Perspective of the *Ius commune*," *Catholic University Law Review*, 52: 301–25.

HELMHOLZ, RICHARD H. (2005). "Natural Law and Human Rights in English Law: From Bracton to Blackstone," *Ave Maria Law Review*, 3: 1–22.

HOBBES, THOMAS (1968). *Leviathan*. London and New York: Penguin.

HOHFELD, WESLEY NEWCOMB (1923). *Fundamental Legal Conceptions as Applied in Judicial Reasoning and Other Legal Essays*, (ed.) Walter Wheeler Cook. New Haven: Yale University Press.

OAKLEY, FRANCIS (2005). *Natural Law, Laws of Nature, Natural Rights: Continuity and Discontinuity in the History of Ideas*. New York and London: Continuum.

PENNINGTON, KENNETH (1993). *The Prince and the Law, 1200–1600: Sovereignty and Rights in the Western Legal Tradition*. Berkeley and Los Angeles, and London: University of California Press.

PENNINGTON, KENNETH (2003). "Sovereignty and Rights in Medieval and Early Modern Jurisprudence: Law and Norms without a State," *Rethinking the State in the Age of Globalisation: Catholic Thought and Contemporary Political Theory*, (ed.) Heinz-Gerhard Justenhoven and James Turner. Politik: Forschung und Wissenschaft, 10; Münster. LIT Verlag, 117–41.

PENNINGTON, KENNETH (2004). "Natural Law," in *Dictionary of the Middle Ages: Supplement 1*. New York: Charles Scribner's Sons and Thompson-Gale, 417–20.

PENNINGTON, KENNETH (2008). "Lex naturalis and Ius naturale," *Jurist*, 68: 569–91.

REID, CHARLES J. JR, (1991). "The Canonistic Contribution to the Western Rights Tradition: An Historical Inquiry," *Boston College Law Review*, 33: 37–92.

REID, CHARLES J. JR, (2004). *Power over the Body, Equality in the Family: Rights and Domestic Relations in Medieval Canon Law*. Emory University Studies in Law and Religion. Grand Rapids, MI, and Cambridge: William B. Eerdmans Publishing.

STRAUSS, LEO (1950). *Natural Right and History*. Chicago: University of Chicago Press.

THOMSON, JUDITH JARVIS (1990). *The Realm of Rights* (Cambridge, MA: Harvard University Press, 49–50.

TIERNEY, BRAIN (1959). *Medieval Poor Law: A Sketch of Canonical Theory and its Application in England*. Berkeley and Los Angeles: University of California Press.

TIERNEY, BRIAN (1997). *The Idea of Natural Rights: Studies on Natural Rights, Natural Law and Church Law 1150–1625*. Emory University Studies in Law and Religion; Atlanta, GA: Scholars Press.

TIERNEY, BRIAN (2002). "Natural Law and Natural Rights: Old Problems and Recent Approaches," *Review of Politics*, 64: 389–420.

TIERNEY, BRIAN (2005). "Historical Roots of Modern Rights: Before Locke and After," *Ave Maria Law Review*, 3: 23–43.

TIERNEY, BRIAN (2006). "Hohfeld on Ockham: A Canonistic Text in the Opus nonaginta dierum," *Medieval Church Law and the Origins of the Western Legal Tradition: A Tribute to Kenneth Pennington*. Washington: Catholic University Press of America, 365–74.

TIERNEY, BRIAN (2008). "Natural Law and Natural Rights," in John Witte Jr. and Frank S. Alexander (eds), *Christianity and Law: An Introduction*. Cambridge: Cambridge University Press, 89–103.

TUCK, RICHARD (1979). *Natural Rights Theories: Their Origins and Development*. Cambridge: Cambridge University Press.

VILLEY, MICHEL (1975). *La Formation de la pensée juridique moderne: Cours d'histoire de la philosophie du droit*. 4th edn. Paris: Éditions Montchrestien.

WEIGAND, RUDOLF (1967). *Die Naturrechtslehre der Legisten und Dekretisten von Irnerius bis Accursius und von Gratian bis Johannes Teutonicus.* Münchener theologische Studien, 3: Kanonistische Abteilung, 26. Munich: Max Hueber Verlag.

WOLTERSTORFF, NICHOLAS (2008). *Justice: Rights and Wrongs.* Princeton: Princeton University Press.

CHAPTER 31

THE STATE

CHRISTOPHER W. MORRIS

IT is often said that the subject matter of political philosophy is the nature and justification of the state. Given the presence of the state in our lives, this is not surprising. For many political thinkers the state assumes center stage. Hegel thinks that political science is "nothing other than an attempt to comprehend and portray the state as an inherently rational entity" (Hegel 1991: 21; emphasis omitted). In our time philosophers often take the state for granted. John Rawls famously understands "the primary subject of justice [to be] the basic structure of society," restricting his attentions to a society "conceived for the time being as a closed system isolated from other societies," and assuming that "the boundaries of these schemes are given by the notion of a self-contained national community" (Rawls 1971: 7, 8, 457). Contemporary political philosophers often follow suit, disagreeing about what states should do, and simply assuming that they are the proper agents of justice or reform.

Our concept of the state seems to be largely modern. The very term "the state" does not seem to pre-date modern times (Skinner 1989: 90–131). The history of philosophy and the development of political concepts seem to be central to understanding the state.

STATES

We should start by getting clear about the phenomena. What are we talking about when we refer to the state? Let us first note some facts about our world. Today virtually the entire land mass of the globe is the territory of one state or another. The exceptions to this generalization are surprisingly few (for example, Antarctica). Some territories are contested still today (for example, Kashmir, much or all of the land occupied by Israel), but they are also surprisingly few in number. Compare a political geographer's map of the world today, the kind that represents countries with different colors, with globes of the world three or four centuries ago, and next with maps of medieval Europe.

By contrast to earlier times, it is immediately evident that states now control virtually every piece of land. There are virtually no stateless people today. There are still nomadic peoples, but they all now find themselves on the territory of a state (for example, Mongolia).

Today, the principal political entity or form of political organization is the state. Politically, the globe is a system of states, governed by a complex variety of forces and institutions (large states, the remnants of empires and spheres of influence, international law, international institutions). It was not always thus. The state that we now take for granted is in large part a modern creation—or, to put the point less controversially, there are significant differences between modern states and earlier forms of political organization.

How then to understand our states? There is considerable lack of clarity about the concept, and it is important to start by disambiguating the term. In American English, "state" is often used interchangeably with "government." In many contexts, of course, "state" is used by Americans to designate the sub-units of the US Federal systems, the founding thirteen colonies having been states or "commonwealths" (see the Articles of Confederation of 1781). In the USA, "the state" is often used to refer to the central or federal government. By contrast, in Europe the distinction between state and government is much clearer. In parliamentary systems, the heads of state and of government are clearly distinct; governments may fall or even be overthrown without imperiling the state. Government and state cannot be identified for a number of reasons. States consist of much more than central governments; the institutions that comprise the state include, in addition, the judiciary, state bureaucracies, standing armies and militia, the police, and often the schools and universities, and agencies charged with controlling information and mass media.

The state is a cluster of institutions, in addition to those we label as "the government." But it is more than this too. The state is also a particular *form of political organization*. This is how Karl Marx put it:

> Through the emancipation of private property from the community, the State has become a separate entity, beside and outside civil society; but it is nothing more than the form of organization which the bourgeois necessarily adopts both for internal and external purposes, for the mutual guarantee of their property and interests. (Marx and Engels 1978*b*: 187)

Joseph Raz also thinks of states as forms of political organization and usefully distinguishes between states, governments, and the law: "the state, which is the political organization of a society, its government, the agent through which it acts, and the law, the vehicle through which much of its power is exercised" (Raz 1986: 70). The idea of the state as a distinctive form of political organization of a society will help to sharpen the contrasts between our modern political societies and earlier forms of political organization. The state in this particular sense is often referred to by the term "nation state," but it may be best to save this one for another concept (see below).

Contemporary Anglo-American philosophers tend to think of the state quite broadly. Compelled to offer a definition, they invariably cite Max Weber's oft-quoted characterization: "a state is a human community that (successfully) claims the monopoly of the legitimate use of physical force within a given territory." In the same address, Weber goes on to note that "the right to use physical force is ascribed to other institutions or to individuals only to the extent to which the state permits it. The state is considered the sole source of the 'right' to use violence" (Weber 1946: 78). This characterization overemphasizes the state's coercive powers while underplaying its claim to authority (see the discussion of sovereignty below), and it is incomplete in a number of ways. But it is worth noting that it too simple for a thinker as astute as Weber; elsewhere he gives a much more complete and helpful characterization:

> Since the concept of the state has only in modern times reached its full development, it is best to define it in terms appropriate to the modern type of state, but at the same time, in terms which abstract from the values of the present day, since these are particularly subject to change. The primary formal characteristics of the modern state are as follows: It possesses an administrative and legal order subject to change by legislation, to which the organized corporate activity of the administrative staff, which is also regulated by legislation, is oriented. This system of order claims binding authority, not only over the members of the state, the citizens . . . but also to a very large extent, over all actions taking place in the area of its jurisdiction. It is thus a compulsory association with a territorial basis. Furthermore, today, the use of force is regarded as legitimate only so far as it is either permitted by the state or prescribed by it. (Weber 1947: 156)

The original, oft-quoted characterization from Weber's address, "Politics as a Vocation," is a good example of what we might call a broad definition of the state. Most broadly still, we may think of the state as a particular form of political organization of a society, one where power is highly concentrated and where government is intolerant of rivals to its rule. This conception of states is useful to anthropologists who study the emergence of chiefdoms, with rulers who possess a right to command and to tribute, and is distinguished from earlier, decentralized anarchic communities (for example, tribes without rulers). But to appreciate both the kinds of political societies we live in and the contributions made by modern political philosophy, a narrower characterization is needed, something like that expressed in the second citation from Weber above or one that I develop elsewhere.

Modern states are distinctive territorial forms of political organization, ones that claim sovereignty over their realms and independence from other states. These states are a particular form of political organization that constitutes a unitary public order distinct from and superior to both ruled and rulers, one capable of agency. The institutions that are associated with them—in particular, the government, the judiciary, the bureaucracy, standing armies—do not themselves constitute the state; they are its agents. The institutions through which the state acts are differentiated from other political organizations and associations; they are formally coordinated one with another and relatively centralized. Relations of authority are hierarchical. Rule is direct and territorial; it is relatively pervasive and penetrates society legally and administratively. The state claims sovereignty; that is, it claims to be the ultimate source of political authority in its territory. And it claims a monopoly on the use of legitimate force within its territory—or, more exactly, it claims the sole right to determine who may coerce others. The jurisdiction of its institutions extends directly to all persons present on the territory, be they members or mere residents or visitors. The state expects and receives the loyalty of its members and of the permanent inhabitants of its territory. The loyalty that it typically expects and receives assumes precedence over that loyalty formerly owed to family, clan, commune, lord, bishop, pope, or emperor. Members of a state are the primary subjects of its laws and have a general obligation to obey by virtue of their membership. In its relations to other public orders, the state is autonomous (see Morris 1998: 45–6).

States in this narrow, modern sense are often called "nation states." This term is misleading for it collapses the distinction between two importantly different kinds of states—namely, multinational states (for example, Belgium, Switzerland, the United Kingdom, Canada, the United States) and states with a single nation or states that privilege one national people (for example, Japan, Germany, Israel). The term "nation state" might usefully be restricted to the latter. Sometimes "nation" is used to refer to countries (see, for example, the United Nations... The Wealth of Nations). But the term also has an established use to refer to national groups, especially to those the members of which are moved by nationalist sentiments. Nations in this sense are large social groups, the members of which share certain properties (for example, language, history, customs, ethnicity, religion) and are relatively conscious of this shared condition. Many national groups or peoples aspire to have a nation state of their own, and many states aspire or pretend to be "nation states"—that is, the state of a single national group. Interestingly, states that emerge from earlier empires—for example, China, Russia, the United States (in the nineteenth century)—are multinational, many of the residing nationalities the result of former imperial expansions and conquests.

The distinction between nations and states is of contemporary importance for many reasons. One is the existence of multiple projects of "nation building," popular during the early post-colonial periods of the twentieth century and more recently (Iraq, Afghanistan). These projects might be better understood as "state building" endeavors or attempts. The existence of such projects reminds us that, although virtually all of the land mass of the globe is the territory of a state, some of these are "failed" or "quasi-states" (Jackson 1993).

MODERN STATES AND MODERN POLITICAL PHILOSOPHY

Clearer about the subject of our chapter, we look now to some of the contributions of political philosophers. Given our suggestion that a narrow and modern characterization of states helps put the phenomena in perspective, our history will not be chronological. We shall start with modern philosophy and then only later turn to medieval and Graeco-Roman contributions. The standard potted histories of the theory of the state start with classical Athens, say a few words about Rome and a bit less about medieval Europe, and then leap to early modern philosophy, as if Hobbes and others just picked up the discussion where it had left off.

We noted above that the term "state" and its cognates are modern. The concept emerges in early modern times with the distinction between the persons of the rulers, and the office and institutions they occupy. But this is not all. There also emerges the concept of the polity, that is, the state, as an order distinct from its agents and institutions, something reflected in the distinctions discussed earlier between "state" and "government." The modern use of "state" to refer to a public order distinct from both ruled and ruler, with highly centralized institutions wielding power over inhabit-ants of a defined territory, seems to date back no earlier than the sixteenth century (see Skinner 1978: 352 ff.; 1989; for additional references, see Morris 1998: ch. 2). The word derives from the Latin *stare*, to stand, and *status*, standing or position. *Status* also connotes stability or permanence, which is carried over into "estate," the immediate ancestor of "state." (The English "state" is derived from "estate"; the French *l . . . État* was originally *l . . . estat*. The Spanish for state, *el estado*, preserves the etymology.) But the modern use of the word is new:

> Before the sixteenth century, the term *status* was only used by political writers to refer to one of two things: either the state or condition in which a ruler finds himself (the *status principis*); or else the general "state of the nation" or condition of the realm as a whole (the *status regni*). What was lacking in these usages was the distinctively modern idea of the State as a form of public power separate from both the ruler and the ruled, and constituting the supreme political authority within a certain defined territory. (Skinner 1978: 353)

The development of a new vocabulary signals a new conception of the polity, that of an order that is separate from ruler and ruled (or citizen), separate from other polities like it, and operating in a distinct territory. The term originates with a description of the status of the monarch or the estates of the realm and develops into the term for a kind of political order.

The (modern) state develops gradually. Boundaries become well-defined borders. The state's territory ceases to be conceived as the ruler's property. Jurisdiction becomes largely territorial. Politics and the economy are increasingly centralized and "nationa-lized" (that is, extensive with the domain of the state). Standing armies and "police" become commonplace; armies eventually become very large by historical standards. And state appropriation of resources, facilitated by the growth of different bureau-cracies and of "statistics" (originally data about the state), grew enormously. In early modern Europe these changes were not easily discernible. By the nineteenth century they were. Today they are taken for granted and treated as unremarkable.

Thomas Hobbes (1588–1679) is perhaps the greatest philosophical theorist of the state. We treat him today as one of the founders of modern political thought and appreciate his individualism and modernism better than his contemporaries. But we may not always recognize his extraordinary prescience regarding the emerging form of the state. As is well known, Hobbes was concerned about civil strife and the ways in which significant divisions in British society and elsewhere in Europe led to war. He took very seriously the threat posed by religion disagreement. Much of his thinking is a response to this. But he was also a brilliant and insightful thinker, and developed a general analysis of the modern state that is useful to this day.

The state for most moderns is an artificial entity, *contra* classical conceptions of the *polis*. For Aristotle, not only is a human being "by nature a political animal," so the *polis* "is among the things that exist by nature" (Aristotle, *Pol.* 1253ª2–4). Hobbes's view of political society is different. "For by Art is created that great Leviathan called a Common-wealth, or State, (in latine Civitas) which is but an Artificiall Man..." (Hobbes 1991: introduction). At the center of his account lies the Sovereign: "the *Soveraignty* is an Artificiall Soul, as giving life and motion to the whole body." Like Jean Bodin (1529/30–96) before him (Bodin 1992), Hobbes makes the sovereign and, more importantly, the concept of sovereignty central to the new emerging political order. This order is created by agreement ("the *Pacts* and *Covenants*, by which the parts of this Body Politique were at first made, set together, and united"). Its sovereign is the creator of laws. These laws are the only genuine ones, unless we consider the so-called laws of nature to issue from the Deity. He accords primary importance to law, understood as "the word of him, that by right hath command over others" (Hobbes 1991: ch. 15).

Hobbes's account of law bears some resemblance to influential nineteenth-century positivist accounts of law, especially those of Jeremy Bentham (1748–1832) and John Austin (1790–1859). But it is importantly different from theirs. The first thing to note in the citation above are the words "*by right* hath command" (emphasis added). Hobbes's is a command theory, but for him mere might does not make right or even law; the sovereign commands by right. Equally important is his understanding of the relation between law and reason. He notes in the introduction that "*Equity* and *Lawes* [are] an artificiall *Reason* and *Will*..." Contemporary readers will recognize here an early statement of what we now call conceptions of "public reason." He distinguishes command and counsel: "Law in generall, is not Counsell, but Command; nor a Command of any man to any man; but only of him, whose Command is addressed to one formerly obliged to obey him" (Hobbes 1991: ch. 26). The commands of the sovereign are those of someone with normative power over its subjects—political authority, we would say. Command, on Hobbes's view, is importantly different from counsel or any other hypothetical imperative: "Command is where a man saith, *Doe this*, or *Doe not this*, without expecting other reason than the Will of him that sayes it." A command of the sovereign is a reason for action. In particular, it is a reason for action that is meant to settle the question of what subjects are to do. This aspect of Hobbes's account is often insufficiently appreciated (but see Hart 1982: 244, 253).

Part of the importance of Hobbes's account of the sovereign, both for our understanding of the state and for the development of influential conceptions of it, lie in the details of his understanding of sovereignty. States claim sovereignty; if legitimate, they presumably have this power. (This inference is controversial, and I challenge it in a number of places; see Morris 1998 and 2008.) The power they claim is that to create law over people who find themselves in their territory, law that obligates them to act as required and that is supposed to be a reason for action for them, one that takes precedence over other considerations. The authority of the sovereign allows no rival. In Hobbes's time the competing authorities of religious officials and sources were important rivals to the authority of the Crown or the emerging state; in our time the claims of clan and nation may be added to the list. The sovereign possesses sovereignty and is thus the ultimate source of authority in the realm; he brooks no rivals.

Hobbes's account famously understands sovereignty to be absolute; it is unconstrained normatively. There is no other source of authority for subjects of the realm, except the Deity and His law. (It is not clear that it makes that much difference if we interpret Hobbes's theory theistically. He gives the sovereign the power to determine the "Attributes . . . in the Worship of God, for Signs of Honour . . ." (Hobbes 1991: ch. 31). Neither the Deity nor His servants have much of a role to play in political affairs when Hobbes is through with them.) The sovereign is not itself subject to civil law, the law it creates. Hobbes's account and ones similar to his make constitutional constraint seemingly impossible. In addition, the sovereign's power is indivisible. Hobbes thought that divided powers lead to strife and the destruction of the polity. We can call this the classical conception of sovereignty. (In addition, classical sovereignty is inalienable. It cannot be represented or transferred without being destroyed.) Hobbes's defense of it was too populist and individualist for many of his fellow royalists. For us, partisans of limited constitutional government, it is implausible or unacceptable. Hobbes, of course, had many arguments in support of his view, and they are not all easy to defeat. But the most important claims for us may be two. The first is that modern states claim, at least initially, something like classical sovereignty. The second is that, even if this is wrong and we can give an account that understands the state's authority to be limited, it remains the case that the state is the ultimate determinant of what the law is and how it is to be understood. The state ascertains the limits to its power (see Raz 1979, 1986; Green 1988). It is hard to have states, of the kind we have, without their claiming something like this power.

Hobbes thought, as was customary, that there were only three possible kinds of commonwealths or states: monarchy; aristocracy; and democracy. The difference turns on "the difference of the Soveraign, or the Person representative of all and every one of the Multitude": the representative can be one man (monarchy); an assembly of all (democracy or popular commonwealth); or of some (aristocracy). His favorite was clearly monarchy; multitudes, he thought, always suffer from problems of division and conflict. It was for Jean-Jacques Rousseau (1712–78) to adapt the classical account of sovereignty to the modern republican state. His concerns were not Hobbes's, worrying less about the disorder and strife affecting the stateless natural condition of humankind and more about human freedom and men's self-estrangement. He adapted Bodin's and Hobbes's notion of sovereignty to republican states. His is an account of popular sovereignty: the sovereign is and can only be the people ("We the People").

Rousseau also thinks of sovereign power as indivisible, inalienable, and absolute. But the fact that it is popular and that its will must be the general will means that the sovereign state cannot act against the members will. The general will is the will of all members, or, rather, includes the will of every member of society. Its formal defining conditions are generality of source (all interests are included) and generality of object (the absence of partiality) (Rousseau 1964: bk II, sects 1–2). These features of the general will mitigate many of the worrisome aspects of the unconstrained nature of classical sovereignty. Like the rational will of Immanuel Kant's ethics, Rousseau's general will is intrinsically self-constraining. But it is not clear that the general will of the people could not decide to exploit another group who happen not to be citizens of their state. The internal constraints of sovereignty, unlike those of Kantian ethics, do not rule that out. The general will is always in the public interest, and it is always right (Rousseau 1964: bk II, sect. 3). But that is compatible with its acting against the interests of outsiders. Rousseau can invoke an account of natural law, as he sometimes does in other writings. But this risks undermining the conception of sovereignty. We need not resolve these questions about Rousseau's theory. Our purpose is only to highlight the ways in which he adapted classical sovereignty to popular republican states.

The natural-law tradition is generally antagonistic to classical sovereignty. There are ways of trying to reconcile the two. Bodin, after all, thought that sovereigns were constrained by (genuine) natural laws. But the thought that the ultimate source of authority in a realm resides with the sovereign does not easily coexist with that of the existence of genuine laws that are prior to and independent of the state, and accessible to private individuals. The Church was hostile to the developing doctrine of state sovereignty in early modern Europe, and the concept plays little role in Catholic political thought (see Maritain 1951). On the classical view, if the state requires me to do something, I must do it, even if the act in question is wrong by standards of justice that bind me as well as the state.

It is interesting to note that John Locke's (1632–1704) political thought makes no use of the classical concept of sovereignty for his analysis of political society (Locke 1988). His endorsement of natural-law theory make it impossible for him to accept Hobbes's analysis of the state. Given that humans are free by right in a state of nature, prior to the establishment of political society, the latter could not be legitimate unless founded on consent. Locke—correctly, for a natural-rights theorist—requires consent to be actual rather than hypothetical, and as such states are both difficult to legitimate and certain to be limited in their powers (As there is so much confusion on the point, we should note that explicit and implicit [or tacit] consent are species of actual consent. Hypothetical consent, by contrast, is not a dated event or an act of someone's will; it cannot bind for Locke. Explicit consent is required for full citizenship; implicit or tacit consent yields fewer civil rights and obligations; see Simmons 1993.) This feature of his account makes it difficult for large states to achieve the legitimacy they claim; few people in our states have accorded them the kind of broad, free, informed consent that Locke's account seems to require. (This conclusion is controversial; its most able defender is John Simmons 1992, 1993; see also Nozick 1974: pt I.)

Locke has more followers than Hobbes today, given that he favored constrained or limited government. His work contributed toward the development of the theory of limited government, as well as to the constitutions of particular states (for example, the United Kingdom, the United States). His account is more appealing to us. Hobbes's claim that divided government is self-destructive does not seem to be true in light of the longevity of many constitutional regimes. Still, there are reasons to worry about the capacity of constitutional means to constrain our leviathans; most states today exercise more powers than envisaged at the time of their establishment.

State power can obviously be an instrument of exploitation. Locke and many other theorists appreciated how the powers claimed by states could be oppressive. Karl Marx's class analysis of the state in "bourgeois" society is interesting in this regard. He thought of state power as an instrument of the dominant class. In the *Communist Manisfesto* he and Friedrich Engels say that "the executive of the modern state is but a committee for managing the common affairs of the whole bourgeoisie" (Marx and Engels 1978a: 337). (See Elster 1985: ch. 7 for a discussion of Marx's other, more subtle characterizations of states.) On one reading the movement to communism is anarchist. As Engels famously argued in *Anti-Dühring*:

> The state was the official representative of society as a whole, its concentration in a visible corporation. But it was this only insofar as it was the state of that class which itself represented, for its own time, society as a whole: in ancient times, the state of slave-owning citizens; in the Middle Ages, of the feudal nobility; in our own time, of the bourgeoisie. When at last it becomes the real representative of the whole of society, it renders itself unnecessary. As soon as there is no longer any social class to be held in subjection, as soon as class rule, and the individual struggle for existence based upon the present anarchy in production, with the collisions and excesses arising from this struggle, are removed, nothing more remains to be held in subjection—nothing necessitating a special coercive force, a state. The first act by which the state really comes forward as the representative of the whole of society—the taking possession of the means of production in the name of society—is also its last independent act as a state. State interference in social relations becomes, in one domain after another, superfluous, and then dies down of itself. The government of persons is replaced by the administration of things, and by the conduct of processes of production. The state is not "abolished." It withers away. (Engels 1969: 333)

This view of states emphasizes, as do many, the coercive nature of states. Without this coercion, the state ceases to be, becoming a means of "administering things." Insofar as states are more than instruments of coercion, the expression of anarchist hope is premature.

Pre-Modern Europe

There is not space adequately to review all of the major contributions of classical and medieval philosophy and jurisprudence to the modern state, and other chapters in this volume touch on these topics. The influence of Roman law and republican government, and the rediscovery of Aristotle in the twelfth and thirteenth centuries, are obvious important influences. It is most of all important to understand the context for the emergence of the modern state.

The modern state emerged first in Western Europe in early modern times. There the victory of kings and other political actors over their rivals—the Church and the Holy Roman Empire on the one side, the nobility and the independent towns on the other— led to the development of institutions and practices that give us our states. The political organization of medieval Europe was quite different from that of our world. Simplifying a thousand years of European history, medieval Europe consisted of complex, cross-cutting jurisdictions of towns, lords, kings, emperors, popes, and bishops, without clear hierarchies of political authority or unitary systems of law. Governance tended to be indirect or mediated. No single person or agency had power to control most persons outside of a small area. In fact, no agency even knew how many people there were in a realm, much less where exactly the borders were. Without reliable maps, "statistics," and large competent bureaucracies, rulers could not do very much. Equally important, political rule was characteristically personal, consisting in relations between individual kings, princes, lords, vassals, and others. There was no clear distinction between a ruler's realm and his property. Rule over subjects and land could be acquired by purchase, conquest, marriage, or inheritance. People's rights and obligations depended on their place in complex relations with others, and not on their location in a particular territory.

Medieval Europe, of course, bore traces of the political institutions of classical Greece and of Rome. But it is primarily the contrasting features of political life in the Middle Ages that need to be recalled; I note five general features that highlight the contrasts with the modern state. First, most people were governed by rulers whose practices and institutions were not likely to survive their deaths or those of their sons. The realms governed by these rulers would not have precise boundaries, and the lands in their possession often would not be contiguous. The general contours of their realms would change quite frequently, often with marriage or death. Second, their rule was largely personal; the allegiance of their subjects was owed to their person, not to them qua holder of an office. Thus, with their demise, some of their subjects might have to take new oaths to a new ruler. Some of these rulers might have attendants who assisted them in the little activity of governance that they performed, but their departure would leave behind no officials or institutions to speak of. The Church and some of the self-governing towns were exceptions here. Third, in addition to being personal, rule was largely indirect or mediated. A lord might have specific obligations of allegiance to a king—for instance, to provide a specific number of knights in the event of a conflict with a neighboring monarch or prince—which might be fulfilled by parties unknown to the king. And a king's rule over peasants would be mediated by several classes of individuals. Rule for the most part would be light, compared to our time, even if the burdens of the peasantry were usually heavy.

Fourth, people might find themselves the subject of several different rulers or systems of rule. The authority of kings competed with that of lords and princes, independent towns, popes and bishops, and emperor. And one could not easily make the distinction familiar in our world between the "internal" and "external affairs" of a realm or rule. Lastly, a person's allegiance or loyalty to a ruler would not exclude similar allegiance to others. And there might be no settled view as to whose word would take precedence in a conflict. These are some of the most important distinguishing features of the world from which the modern state emerged. By contrast, as we have seen, governance in the modern state is relatively centralized, unified, uniform, hierarchical, direct, impersonal, and territorial. The state is distinct from the government, and the former becomes a corporate agent, distinct from the rulers, with a legally recognized personality. The modern state, it must be emphasized, is a relatively new and complex form of political organization.

The classical Green *poleis* were either cities or cities with empires, and Rome was an empire. For such polities the unity of political society is something inherently problematic. Similarly, for much of medieval history, the unity of political society that we typically take for granted is unknown. With the weakening of the political powers of Christendom and the rise in the power of secular rulers, especially powerful monarchs, late medieval and early modern Europe was more hospitable to the emergence of the forms of political organization we have been studying. I have mentioned in passing the influences of Roman law. *Quod principi placuit legis habet vigorem* ("What pleases the ruler has the force of law"), and *Princeps legibus solutus est* ("The ruler is not bound by the laws"), well-known principles from Ulpian (*c.*170–228), are obvious influences on the early modern state.

The rediscovery of Aristotle, mentioned above, was an important event in the theoretical development of the early modern state. Aristotle's notion of *autarkeia* (self-sufficiency) is especially important for the conceptualization of the state. Walter Ullmann exaggerates perhaps when he argues that our concept of the state, "understood as an independent, self-sufficient, autonomous body of citizens which lived, so to speak, on its own substance and on its own laws ... came about in the thirteenth century as a result of the influence of the Greek philosopher Aristotle" (Ullmann 1965: 17; see also Aristotle, *Pol.* I.2.1252^{b}27–30). But this notion of a self-sufficient political community played an important role in the development of the modern state.

THE STATE SYSTEM

As we noted earlier, the global political order is a system of states, one governed by a complex variety of forces and institutions. These are large states, the remnants of empires and spheres of influence, international law, and a variety of increasingly important international institutions (for example, UN, WTO). The state system has evolved considerably over the last several centuries, and it is hard to characterize it in ways that are not controversial. What interests us here is principally the relation between the character of states and external constraints such as international law or juridical bodies.

The classical conception of sovereignty characterized earlier, especially as understood by Hobbes (and Rousseau), would imply that sovereign states were unconstrained. Specifically, there could be no "international" law that was genuine law. For Hobbes this was a simple implication of his account, given that there is no international sovereign or lawgiver. This implication is developed in the nineteenth century by legal philosophers influenced by Hobbes, especially John Austin. His account is developed in his published law lectures of 1832, *The Province of Jurisprudence Determined* (Austin 1995). He strips Hobbes's account of all normative elements, identifying laws with commands backed by force. A law is essentially a command, with a threatened penalty for disobedience, made by "a sovereign person." The latter is understood to be the superior to which "the bulk of the given society are in a habit of obedience or submission . . ." and this superior is not in a habit of obeying anyone else. Austin is well known as one of the first "legal positivists" ("The existence of law is one thing; its merit or demerit is another"). His interest for us is the role he played in developing the view that there can be no genuine international law (Austin 1995: lectures I, V–VI).

The influential legal philosopher H. L. A. Hart (1907–92) challenged Austin's account of law, in ways that left room for the possibility of international law (Hart 1994: ch. x). Noting the many differences between municipal and international law, Hart argues that the rules of the latter bear many similarities to those of the former: they are spoken of as obligatory, there is general pressure for conformity, and violations are grounds for legal consequences (Hart 1994: 220). Since Hart penned these words half a century ago, there has been tremendous growth of international law. Just as it seems obvious that states can be constitutionally limited—that is, *constituted* as limited—so it seems obvious that they can be normatively constrained by international law. So the classical conception of sovereignty seems mistaken, and it is rejected by most theorists today.

This argument may, however, be too quick. Even if these classical theorists of the state are wrong about the illimitable nature of sovereign authority, they were on to something about the state. States are not illimitable; there are too many limited states for this claim to be credible. But it is important to appreciate, as was noted above, that limited states claim to be limited only by constraints they recognize. When they are limited by external norms, it is because they acknowledge or incorporate these. There are limits to the authority of states but only those recognized by the state (Rousseau 1964: II, ch. 4, p. 373). That states are limited only by constraints they *recognize* or *acknowledge* does not necessarily mean that these constraints are *created* by them. The claim that states determine, recognize, or judge their own limits, interpreted to allow for an independent fact of the matter and for error, is not at all implausible. There is something about a state or the legal system of a state that makes it hard to see how states could not make this claim. (For further discussion, see Morris 1998: 195–8, 204–13.) There is more to be said here, and the questions raised are of the utmost importance for understanding the ways in which the state system may be transformed.

We should consider, if only briefly, some of the pressures on states and the state system. Many observers have thought that the state or the "nation state" is being transformed, and we ought to note how this is said to be taking place. Many of the features of the changing world order are often thought to threaten the dominance of states as we have characterized them. Many features of modern states are striking: their great power; their territoriality; and the large number of tasks and functions they take on. But increasingly these are under significant pressure. The tasks and functions of states are in many ways being scaled down. Since the end of the Second World War, states everywhere have shed public corporations, nowhere so strikingly as in the formerly communist world. Many of the welfare state services provided by government, especially after the Second World War, have been scaled back, in no small part because of expense and shrinking budgets. In many states the military and police are supplemented by private services, paid for by the state or by private parties. A variety of non-state judicial services are increasingly used by businesses. Especially in countries like the USA, private educational institutions are important, and an increasing part of the budget of American institutions of higher education is coming from non-state sources. Compared with a century or two ago, our states are very active; compared to the post-war period, they have cut back to a considerable extent, even if their budgets are still very large.

In the middle of the previous century most mid-size or large states could set their own economic policies, regulate their currencies, and impose a good many controls on trade with other countries. Those powers have largely been diminished, even for the strongest states. A variety of organizations, many non-governmental, now besiege all states, pressuring them to reduce some activity or increase others (for example, imprisonment or execution of political dissidents, environmental protection, restructuring of institutions, free trade). Some private organizations or individuals, wealthier than many countries, can initiate development or aid programs that few governments would think of undertaking. A variety of new players, neither states nor agents of states, are increasingly challenging the traditional competencies of governments. They are also threatening the state's dominance.

In one respect these non-state entities are like states: they are corporate beings, with lives that extend beyond those of their members or employees. In other respects they are quite different: unlike territorial states, these agencies are not linked to territories and usually have no jurisdiction and make no law. They pressure and facilitate, and they sustain larger movements of individual people. They are often more nimble and effective than state agents. Especially noteworthy here are those organizations that are able to support and organize guerrilla wars and terrorist attacks on major states.

Add to these developments increasing bodies of international law, still in its infancy, and myriad treaties and multinational and international organizations such as the EU, NATO, the World Bank, the IMF, and the world of states is undergoing important transformations. Economic interdependence and, in some respects, integration are causes of surprising kinds of political cooperation and integration (the EU is one obvious kind of example; for others see Slaughter 2004). But it is hard for philosophers and political theorists to predict the shape of things to come—"the Owl of Minerva begins its flight with the onset of dusk" (Hegel 1991: 23). It does seem that the state system is being transformed. War has built the state ("War is the health of the state," Randolph Bourne), and the conflicts of the beginning of the twenty-first century may reinforce the state, especially the large ones. But, in the long term, it seems that the dominant form of political organization of our time, created in early modern Europe, may be transformed quite radically. What may replace it? In light of our emphasis on the multiple forms of political organization that preceded the modern state, it is appropriate to quote Hedley Bull. He speculates that it is "conceivable that sovereign states might disappear and be replaced not by world government but by a modern and secular equivalent of the kind of universal political organization that existed in Western Christendom in the Middle Ages" (Bull 1977: 254).

THE FUNCTIONS OF GOVERNMENT

I have focused on abstract questions about the nature of the state, on the ways in which the modern state differs from other forms of political organization. Something needs to be said about what we want states for, or, more specifically, governments.

Many classical thinkers thought that the principal end of political society was the good of its members. ("Anyone who intends to investigate the best constitution in the proper way must first determine which life is most choiceworthy . . ." (Aristotle, *Pol.* VII.1.1323^{b}14–15).) And, unlike many modern theories, these classical views do not understand someone's good "subjectively," as consisting in the satisfaction of his or her desires or something of the kind. Many important modern thinkers by contrast understand the state as an instrument serving the needs and wants of its subjects or citizens. Hobbes has a view of this kind. One thing that is notable about it is his minimal account of the tasks of the sovereign. The Artificial Man described in the Introduction to the *Leviathan* finds its strength in "The *Wealth* and *Riches* of all of the particular members" and "its *Businesse*" the "*Salus Populi* (the *peoples safety*)". If one looks carefully at the tasks he expects sovereigns to take on, they are by our standards remarkably minimal. Even if the Sovereign may do whatever it thinks is necessary for the "protection and defence" of Natural Men, its principal task is maintaining order and defending the realm, and for this it need not do all that much (see Morris 1986, 1988).

One might expect to find a similar view in the work of that great Scottish philosopher who is one of the founders of political economy or what we now call economics. Adam Smith (1723–90) is often cited as a great defender of *laissez-faire* policies and the "minimal state." This caricature is not entirely mistaken; he did think the "system of natural liberty" preferable to all others. Unlike Hobbes, Smith clearly appreciated the extraordinary productive activities made possible by the protections that states could offer the person and property of its members. By securing order, government would not only make life less brutish and short; it would make possible extraordinary wealth. If we think of Hobbes's minimal understanding of the important tasks of government as "protective," then Smith also assigned governments a more "productive role," that of encouraging the production of important "public goods" to use our technical term for non-rivalrous and non-excludable goods (for example, good roads, bridges, canals, harbors). In *The Wealth of Nations*, Smith explains what he thinks are the three central duties of sovereigns:

> According to the system of natural liberty, the sovereign has only three duties to attend to; three duties of great importance, indeed, but plain and intelligible to common understandings: first, the duty of protecting the society from violence and invasion of other independent societies; secondly, the duty of protecting, as far as possible, every member of the society from the injustice or oppression of every other member of it, or the duty of establishing an exact administration of justice; and, thirdly, the duty of erecting and maintaining certain public works and certain public institutions which it can never be for the interest of any individual, or small number of individuals, to erect and maintain; because the profit could never repay the expence to any individual or small number of individuals, though it may frequently do much more than repay it to a great society. (Smith 1976: bk IV, ch. 9, para. 51)

Governments secure order (their protective function) and facilitate the production of important public goods (their productive function) (the labels "protective" and "productive" are borrowed from Buchanan 1975). There is now considerable agreement about these tasks of government. What many later thinkers would have us add to this list is a concern with the *distribution* of goods and assets. Government have for some time been called upon to alter the distribution of wealth by effecting transfers from some to others. Certainly, governments and other instruments of power have been used to take from the many and give to the few. But for the last century or so many important thinkers have thought that a major task of government is assistance to the poor and disadvantaged, and the transfer of resources from the well off to the less well off. We might think of this as a "redistributive" task of government. The Utilitarian tradition has played an important role in emphasizing this task of government. While many have argued since the beginning of political thought that the status quo distribution of wealth is *unjust*, utilitarians do not put much importance on the virtue of justice and instead focus on the aggregate well-being or welfare of all (indeed, all sentient beings). The early Utilitarians—the "Philosophical Radicals"—were partisans of what we now call *laissez-faire* or "pro-market" policies. But the greatest happiness principle easily licenses redistributive programs if these significantly increase aggregate well-being. Twentieth-century utilitarians and their economic siblings have long defended such policies. The redistributive functions of government remain more controversial, I suppose it is fair to say, than the protective and productive ones.

REFERENCES

Primary Sources

ARISTOTLE (1998). *Politics*, trans. C. Reeve. Indianapolis: Hackett.

AUSTIN, J. (1995). *The Province of Jurisprudence Determined* [1832], ed. W. Rumble. Cambridge: Cambridge University Press.

BODIN, J. (1992). *On Sovereignty: Four Chapters from Six Books of the Commonwealth* [*Les Six Livres de la République*] [1593], ed. J. Franklin. Cambridge: Cambridge University Press.

ENGELS, F. (1969). *Anti Dühring* [1894]. 3rd German edn. Moscow: Progress Publishers.

HEGEL, G. (1991). *Elements of the Philosophy of Right* [1820], ed. A. Wood, trans. H. Nisbet. Cambridge: Cambridge University Press.

HOBBES, T. (1991). *Leviathan* [1651], ed. R. Tuck. Cambridge: Cambridge University Press.

LOCKE, J. (1988). *Two Treatises of Government* [1689], ed. P. Laslett. Cambridge: Cambridge University Press.

MARX, K., and ENGELS, F. (1978*a*). *The Communist Manifesto* [1848], in *The Marx–Engels Reader*, ed. R. Tucker. 2nd edn. New York and London: W. W. Norton, 331–62.

MARX, K., and ENGELS, F. (1978*b*). *The German Ideology* [1932], in The Marx–Engels Reader, ed. R. Tucker. 2nd edn. New York and London: W. W. Norton, 110–64.

ROUSSEAU, JEAN-JACQUES (1964). *Du Contrat social* [1762], in *Œuvres complètes*, B. Gagnebin and M. Raymond eds. Paris: Pléiade, Gallimard.

SMITH, A. (1976). *An Inquiry into the Nature and Causes of the Wealth of Nations* [1776], eds, R. Campbell and A. Skinner. Indianapolis: Liberty Classics.

WEBER, M. (1946). "Politics as a Vocation" [1919], in *From Max Weber: Essays in Sociology*, trans. and eds, H. Gerth and C. Wright Mills. New York: Oxford University Press, 77–128.

WEBER, M. (1947). *The Theory of Social and Economic Organization* (pt I of *Wirtschaft und Gesellschaft*), trans. A Henderson and T. PARSONS. New York: Oxford University Press.

Secondary Sources

BUCHANAN, J. (1975). *The Limits of Liberty*. Chicago: University of Chicago Press.

BULL, H. (1977). *The Anarchical Society: A Study of Order in World Politics*. New York: Columbia University Press.

ELSTER, J. (1985). *Making Sense of Marx*. Cambridge: Cambridge University Press.

GREEN, L. (1988). *The Authority of the State*. Oxford: Clarendon Press.

HART, H. (1982). "Commands and Authoritative Legal Reasons," in *Essays on Bentham*. Oxford: Clarendon Press, 243–68.

HART, H. (1994), *The Concept of Law* [1961]. 2nd edn. Oxford: Clarendon Press.

JACKSON, R. (1993). *Quasi-States: Sovereignty, International Relations and the Third World*. Cambridge: Cambridge University Press.

MARITAIN, J. (1951). *Man and the State*. Chicago: University of Chicago Press.

MORRIS, C. (1986). "Leviathan and the Minimal State: Hobbes' Theory of Government," in G. Moyal and S. Tweyman (eds), *Early Modern Philosophy: Epistemology, Metaphysics, and Politics: Essays in Honour of Robert F. McRae*. Delmar, NY: Caravan Books, 373–95.

MORRIS, C. (1988). "A Hobbesian Welfare State?" *Dialogue*, 27/4: 653–73.

MORRIS, C. (1998). *An Essay on the Modern State*. Cambridge: Cambridge University Press.

MORRIS, C. (2008). "State Legitimacy and Social Order," in J. Kühnelt (ed.), *Political Legitimization without Morality*. Heidelberg: Springer, 15–32.

NOZICK, R. (1974). *Anarchy, State, and Utopia*. New York: Basic Books.

RAWLS, J. (1971). *A Theory of Justice*. Cambridge, MA.: Harvard University Press.

RAZ, J. (1979). *The Authority of Law*. Oxford: Clarendon Press.

RAZ, J. (1986). *The Morality of Freedom*. Oxford: Clarendon Press.

SIMMONS, J. (1992). *The Lockean Theory of Rights*. Princeton: Princeton University Press.

SIMMONS, J. (1993). *On The Edge of Anarchy: Locke, Consent, and the Limits of Society*. Princeton: Princeton University Press.

SKINNER, Q. (1978). *The Foundations of Modern Political Thought*. 2 vols. Cambridge: Cambridge University Press.

SKINNER, Q. (1989). "The State," in T. Ball, J. Farr, and R. Hanson (eds), *Political Innovation and Conceptual Change*. Cambridge: Cambridge University Press, 90–131.

SLAUGHTER, A. M. (2004). *A New World Order*. Princeton: Princeton University Press.

ULLMANN, W. (1965). *Medieval Political Thought*. Harmondsworth: Penguin.

CHAPTER 32

SOVEREIGNTY

DANIEL PHILPOTT

THE CONCEPT OF SOVEREIGNTY

SOVEREIGNTY ought to be scuttled, more than one scholar of international affairs has suggested. It has borne too many conflicting meanings over the centuries to be defined stably, some skeptics say (Oppenheim 1905; Carr 1964; Falk 1993; Bartelson 1995). It is morally odious, others such as philosopher Jacques Maritain say (Maritain 1951).

But there arguably exists a definition of sovereignty that is flexible enough to accommodate much of the concept's historical diversity yet concrete enough to be meaningful: supreme authority within a territory. To pose such a definition is not to offer a moral defense of it but rather to specify a concept that continues to serve as the chief organizing principle of the international states system, for better or for worse.

Each term in the definition expresses an important dimension of the concept. Authority—"the right to command and correlatively, the right to be obeyed," in Robert Paul Wolff's definition (Wolff 1990)—implies that sovereignty is a matter of right or legitimacy, not one of mere power. Legitimacy here does not mean intrinsic moral validity, a different issue, but rather some sort of consensually conferred authoritative sanction, whether this be natural law, a divine mandate, a constitution, or international law. Virtually everywhere in the world today, sovereignty is buttressed by law. The United Nations Charter enshrines the principle, whilst a vast majority of the world's states have a constitution that specifies who the holder of sovereignty is.

But if sovereignty's authority is a matter of legitimacy, not mere power, it must also correspond to actual practice. A colony or independence-seeking nation, for instance, can assert a right to sovereignty or even call itself a sovereign, but until it actually exercises authority over its own affairs vis-à-vis outsiders and its own people, it cannot meaningfully be said to hold sovereignty. Sovereignty for it is only an aspiration.

But authority alone does not specify sovereignty; plenty of holders of authority exist who do not have sovereignty. Another ingredient is crucial: supremacy. The holder of sovereignty's authority is highest and may not be questioned or opposed. Supremacy was stressed by sovereignty's first modern articulators, sixteenth-century French philosopher Jean Bodin and seventeenth-century English philosopher Thomas Hobbes, and has been reflected widely by users of the concept ever since.

A final ingredient is territoriality. This is the principle that defines the set of people who live under the holder of sovereignty, or the supreme authority. People are members of a political community, it proposes, by virtue of their residence within a set of geographic borders. Like supremacy, territoriality is a feature of modernity. In Europe by the seventeenth century, it had become the continent-wide *de facto* organizing principle for politics. Some international-relations scholars have noted the parallel between sovereignty and private property, also a modern principle based on territoriality (Kratochwil 1986; Ruggie 1993). In the thought of Thomas Hobbes, the two principles run in parallel. To be sure, territoriality has existed in other times and places, but never so pervasively. Elsewhere, principles of membership such as kinship, tribe, religion, and feudal ties have enjoyed great prominence as well. In medieval times, people were members of Christendom by virtue of their religious affiliation, one that followed them wherever they traveled. Most sharply opposite from territoriality is the wandering tribe, whose membership principle is connected only remotely, if at all, to a particular land. As self-determination and irredentist movements make clear, territoriality often does not succeed in defining membership so as to correspond with the identity of a "people" or "nation." Yet, it is still the organizing principle to which separatist peoples aspire, underlying its ubiquity. Even supranational and international institutions like the European Union and the United Nations do not supersede territoriality, for they are composed of states that are themselves based on the principle of territorial membership.

To reassemble these ingredients, then, sovereignty is supreme authority within a territory. Within this general definition, an astonishingly diverse array of claims has been put forth over the centuries as to who is entitled to hold supreme authority within a territory. It is often particular claims about who the holder of sovereignty is or ought to be around which political philosophers and constructers of ideology have built their thought. Monarchs have claimed sovereignty according to the divine right of kings; Rousseau bequeathed sovereignty to the general will; colonists have claimed sovereignty over and against empires; nationalists claimed it for nations based on liberal republican principles in the wake of the French Revolution; communists, fascists and theocrats have claimed it, too. Today, the Vatican, Iran, Lesotho, and the United States are all sovereign states. Such diversity is testimony to the adaptability and survivability of the principle. Despite its remarkable breadth, though, the diversity can be organized somewhat through three dimensions along which forms of sovereignty vary: the holders of sovereignty, the absolute or non-absolute character of sovereignty; and the configuration of the internal and external dimensions of sovereignty.

As the above examples illustrate, sovereignty can be held by diverse authorities and actors. Bodin and Hobbes thought that the sovereign was above other sources of positive law, though Bodin, and arguably Hobbes, too, considered the sovereign bound by the divine and natural law. Both preferred monarchs (Hobbes 1968 [1651]; Bodin 1992 [1576]). Over time, new concepts of sovereignty's holders would arise. Democratic theorists would speak of popular sovereignty. Most modern liberal democracies today conceive of sovereignty as exercised by the people ruling through a constitution.

Perhaps surprisingly, sovereignty can also be absolute or non-absolute. This is surprising, because it might seem that supremacy implies absoluteness. But, whilst supremacy is always an attribute of sovereignty, it is possible that a holder of authority might be sovereign—or supreme—in some affairs whilst it is not sovereign in others. Absoluteness is a matter of the scope of authority: Is the holder of authority sovereign in all affairs or only some? Throughout much of the era of the modern states system, states considered sovereignty absolute. But, in certain instances, sovereignty has been non-absolute. To the extent that the UN may legitimately authorize or undertake intervention in states where genocide or other massive human rights are taking place, these states' sovereignty is non-absolute. In the matter of human rights, its authority is subject to outside oversight and interference. European federation, originating in the European Coal and Steel Community in 1951, has also yielded non-absolute sovereignty as member states have "pooled" their sovereignty regarding certain matters into international institutions (Keohane and Hoffmann 1991). Over decades, the range of these matters has only widened. The European Union, established in the 1992 Maastricht Treaty, for instance, created a common currency among eleven of the member states and even set goals for increased collaboration in foreign and defense policy. Along with the common market established in the 1950s, these matters are ones where sovereignty is, or is destined to be, non-absolute. Other, less sweeping, developments in international law and organization have also curtailed the absolute sovereignty of the state. The boundaries of absolute and non-absolute sovereignty are ever shifting and evolving.

A third distinction—that between internal and external sovereignty—describes not so much different kinds of sovereignty, but different aspects of sovereignty wherever it exists. A holder of sovereignty wields authority within a territory but also, at the same time, vis-à-vis outside states and organizations, from whom it may legitimately expect non-interference. This right to non-interference from the outside in a state's own basic prerogatives of authority is external sovereignty. It corresponds to what international legal scholar Alan James (1986) calls constitutional independence. In the modern states system, it is the state that enjoys external sovereignty vis-à-vis other states. Indeed, by the seventeenth century non-intervention in the affairs of other states had become a basic norm of the European states system. In the twentieth century, the United Nations Charter established it for the entire world through its clauses affirming "territorial integrity" and "political independence." Yet, just as the boundaries of absolute and non-absolute sovereignty evolve, so, too, the area in which states are externally—and simultaneously internally—sovereign shift, too.

What has been described here is the principle of sovereignty, one that has formed the foundation of the international states system since roughly the Peace of Westphalia in

1648. But to describe the principle is not to assert the sanctity of its practice. In his important work *Sovereignty: Organized Hypocrisy* (1999), political scientist Stephen D. Krasner catalogues states' frequent violations of sovereignty over the history of the states system, whether through contracts, conventions, coercion, or imposition. States have intervened regularly in other states; the Federal Republic of Germany was subject to Allied supervision during the cold war; through the European Court of Human Rights, European states commit themselves to the arbitration of human rights disputes. But, in making his case for the many instances in which sovereignty is violated as a "regulative" norm of the international system, Krasner overlooks another, deeper role for rules—their constitutive role (Rawls 1955). Sovereignty is the principle that constitutes states and the rules by which they are to interact in the first place. It is violated, to be sure, but it also defines the very rules that are subject to violation. In this constitutive sense, sovereignty has enjoyed profound success over the centuries. It is the only principle of political organization and membership in human history to cover virtually the entire land surface of the globe (this critique draws from Philpott 2001*b*).

SOVEREIGNTY ASCENDANT

The history of sovereignty can be told as a double movement. The first vector is a trajectory of centuries, first toward a European sovereign states system, triumphing around the time of the Peace of Westphalia, then toward a globalization of the sovereign states system, culminating in the wave of colonial independence in the 1960s and 1970s. The second movement, beginning well before the first culminated, is the curtailment of absolute sovereign prerogatives, most dramatically in the second half of the twentieth century, especially in the launching and development of European federation and in the rise of internationally sanctioned intervention following the end of the cold war. Running in the opposite direction from the development of a sovereign states system around the time of Westphalia, this second movement involves the development of international norms that consensually circumscribe sovereignty. Both of these historical movements were attended by corresponding movements in the history of ideas.

The movement toward a sovereign states system in Europe appears most vividly in relief against Europe during a period in which little sovereignty existed at all: the High Middle Ages, roughly between the eleventh and the thirteenth centuries. Then, both the pope and the Holy Roman Emperor exercised authority over affairs within the territories of kings and nobles, but so, too, kings and nobles exerted checks on the authority of the pope and the emperor. Vassals often paid fealty not only to their lord but to other authorities living outside their lord's territory. The pope and other bishops exercised authority that was by any modern definition temporal, leading crusades, adjudicating political disputes, levying taxes, holding and governing large tracts of land, and serving as advisors to princes, whilst temporal authorities exerted important prerogatives over the Church, exercising a hand in its appointment of bishops, and, most of all, at times coercively enforcing religious adherence. The *Respublica Christiana* was held together by a common religion, that of the Catholic Church. Contrasting this configuration with the modern states system, international relations theorist John Gerard Ruggie calls it "heteronomy" (Ruggie 1986).

Gradually, over the next three-and-a half centuries, Europe shedded this heteronomy piece by piece, eventually arriving at a uniform replication of one particular form, the sovereign state. Around 1300, Britain and France began to look like sovereign states, historian J. R. Strayer (1970) has argued; Spain and Sweden followed in their wake. But Europe remained distant from a sovereign states system as late as the early sixteenth century. It was then that King Charles V united Spain, exerted rule over the Netherlands, and became Holy Roman Emperor, gaining rights over lands in Central Europe and becoming the armed enforcer of the Catholic Church's temporal rights as well as religious orthodoxy inside the Holy Roman Empire. But he was not sovereign within the Empire, either. A stride toward a sovereign states system was the 1555 Peace of Augsburg, which allowed German rulers to enforce their faith, Catholic or Protestant, within their own territories according to the formula *cuius region, eius religio*. The settlement remained highly contested, though, leading ultimately to the Thirty Years War, which did not end until the Peace of Westphalia in 1648. Significantly, one of the chief dissolving agents of medieval unity was the Protestant Reformation, for it was religion that had held together the heteronomous authority structure of medieval Europe (Philpott 2001*a*). Scholarly dispute now exists over whether Westphalia is properly viewed as the origin of modern international relations (Krasner 1993; Osiander 2001; Philpott 2001*a*; Teschke 2003; Straumann 2007; Nexon 2009). It is hard to deny, though, that roughly in the middle of the seventeenth century the long transmogrification of the European continent from medieval heteronomy to a modern states system was consolidated. This new authority structure, which might be called the Westphalian Synthesis, consisted of five historical strands. Each strand expresses a dimension of the sovereignty that emerged; importantly, each also represents a diminishment of the temporal powers and unifying effect of the medieval Catholic Church.

The emergence of the sovereign state as virtually the sole form of *de facto* constitutional authority on the continent and the accompanying decline of the transnational authority of the Holy Roman Empire at and in the wake of the Peace of Westphalia represent the first strand. The second strand was a general diminishment of international intervention, proscription of which was to become a defining norm of the international system in the eighteenth century. Since the primary occasion for armed intervention after the Reformation began in 1517 was the enforcement of religious uniformity (or defense of religious diversity), reaching a climax in the Thirty Years War, the fading of intervention indicated the fading of religion's political role. A corresponding third strand was a general, continent-wide "Erastianism" by which churches became subordinated to the authority of states. Throughout Germany, as well as in Sweden, England, and Scotland, Protestant churches had generally placed their governance under the authority of monarchs. Reformation historian Euan Cameron

(1991) writes of the Lutheran churches that they "became very largely departments of state in their respective territories." In Catholic France, too, the king asserted increasingly strong control over the Church during this period. Still rare in Europe, either in practice or in political thought, was a principled endorsement of individual religious freedom. The fourth strand complements the third: a sharp decrease in the temporal powers of religious authorities. Less and less did Catholic prelates hold office, raise revenue, or rule large tracts of land. True, the Papal States and ecclesiastical temporal prerogatives persisted, but these prerogatives were becoming more and more rare—just as the Protestant reformers had hoped. The fifth strand was the rise of nationalism as an identity and source of loyalty. Challenging a previous wave of scholarship that located the origins of nationalism in nineteenth-century European industrialization (Anderson 1983; Gellner 1983; Hobsbawm 1992), a more recent wave of scholarship dates these origins instead in sixteenth- and seventeenth-century Britain, France, Spain, Germany, and Sweden and identifies religion as one of nationalism's key formative sources (Colley 1992; Hastings 1997; Marx 2003; Smith 2003). Redirecting loyalties toward the state, nationalism reinforced further the Westphalian authority structure.

Over the next three-and-a-half centuries, the sovereign states system expanded over the face of the globe through a sequence of colonization and eventual dissolution of colonial empires into replicated political forms: first in Latin America, then in South Asia, then in Africa and elsewhere. Today, the world consists of 195 states.

As Europe underwent its long transformation from the Middle Ages to Westphalia, certain contemporary philosophers came to embrace and espouse the idea of sovereignty. Reflecting the role of religion in the transformation and construction of authority, most of them sought not only to elevate the state but to diminish the powers of prelates, especially those of the Catholic Church.

Bodin and Hobbes were early modern Europe's two most prominent articulators of sovereignty. Bodin was the first European philosopher to write about the concept systematically, as he did in *The Six Books of the Commonwealth* (1992 [1576]). Writing in the midst of a generation-long civil war between Calvinist Huguenots and the Catholic monarchy that tore France apart, he reasoned that only in a unified political body whose authority was above and indeed the source of other human law could order and peace be restored. The medieval notion of segmented and dispersed authority would have to be laid to rest. The authority that he described was sovereignty.

The holder of sovereignty, Bodin thought, was obliged to obey natural and divine law. He also forbade the sovereign from confiscating property and breaking agreements with other sovereigns. But these obligations he regarded as moral ones, not ones that were subject to the appeal or judgment of any other human authority. In this sense, sovereignty for Bodin was absolute. Finally, Bodin thought that a government with sovereign powers could take the form of a monarchy, aristocracy, or democracy—Aristotle's three categories of regimes. Monarchy, though, was the form that he favored.

Hobbes also wrote amidst civil war and came to see sovereignty as the only hope for solution. Sovereign authority, he thought, was erected by people inhabiting a precarious state of nature, one that they escaped by means of a contract through which they alienated their natural right to protect themselves to a Leviathan. The Leviathan, a mortal god, held supremacy, standing above the law and remaining free of any obligations to other authorities. Law was in fact the Leviathan's own command; others were absolutely obliged to obey it. Religious authorities were to be shorn of temporal prerogatives; the sovereign would be head of the Church. Only the Leviathan could tame the chaos that religion brought to the realm.

Two other early modern thinkers are notable for this discussion, neither of whom explicitly discusses sovereignty but both of whom call for something very much like it and envision a stripped down Catholic Church. The first is Italian Renaissance philosopher, Niccolò Machiavelli. Concerned with establishing a well-ordered, prosperous state during a time of destructive conflict between Italy's city states, Machiavelli sought to describe what the behavior of a prince ought to look like. He did not want the prince to be constrained by natural law, the laws of the Church, or any norm that manifested the obligations of Christendom, but rather to be prepared "not to be good" and to do what was necessary for the unity of the state. Unbound by the laws of the Church or even by natural law, the prince would, in effect, be supreme within his territory, a singular, united body.

The second is Martin Luther, whose theology advocated just the denuding of the Catholic Church's temporal prerogatives that would take place over the next century-and-a-half in Germany and elsewhere. He envisioned two forms of governance, what he called "the realm of the spirit," which pertained to the soul of the believer, and "the realm of the world," the order of secular society where governmental institutions were run by magistrates through law and coercion. Both realms realized certain goods, but goods that separate authorities ought to provide, with church leaders enacting spiritual duties, and princes and other secular rulers performing temporal duties. This meant that ecclesiasts would stop raising taxes and armies, and holding temporal offices. Taking up these dislodged powers were territorial princes, who, indeed, would now monopolize temporal authority: Erastianism, sovereignty. "By the destruction of the independence of the Church and its hold on extra-territorial opinion, the last obstacle to unity within the state was removed," wrote political philosopher, J. N. Figgis. He continues: "The unity and universality and essential rightness of the sovereign territorial State, and the denial of every extra-territorial or independent communal form of life, are Luther's lasting contributions to politics" (Figgis 1916 [1907]).

Philosophers continued to take up the concept of sovereignty over the course of the Westphalian era in international politics. Proponents of international law like the eighteenth-century philosopher, Emerich de Vattel, adopted roughly the Westphalian notion of sovereignty, coupling it with his stress on the equality of states in the international system. Rousseau built upon but also revised the work of Bodin and Hobbes by endorsing sovereignty but placing it in the collective will of the people within a state. Popular sovereignty would inform the French Revolution and its legacy of liberal republicanism.

In the twentieth century, a vivid defense of sovereignty reminiscent of Hobbes and Bodin was propounded by German philosopher, Carl Schmitt, in his *Political Theology*, originally published in 1922 (Schmitt 1985 [1922]). "Sovereign is he who decides on the exception," reads the first line of that book. That is, the sovereign is one who can and ought to place himself above the law, especially in times of emergency when the sovereign must act to save the nation. Schmitt decried liberal nationalism, which he thought naive and insufficiently cognizant of the role of power in politics. Having set forth these ideas during the crisis of Weimar Germany, Schmitt became an ardent supporter of the National Socialist regime during the 1930s—a regime whose use of emergency powers embodied his conception of sovereignty.

SOVEREIGNTY CHALLENGED

Against the vast historical trajectory of sovereignty's rise and spread runs a vector toward the curtailment of sovereignty, at least absolute sovereignty. It can be found in minority treaties imposed on East European states by Western powers in the late nineteenth and early twentieth centuries, in the growth of human rights conventions after the Second World War, in the development of European federalism during the same period, in the rise of internationally sanctioned intervention after the cold war, in the establishment of international criminal tribunals and then the permanent International Criminal Court in the 1990s, in the dispute-resolution mechanisms of the World Trade Organization, and in scores of makeshift arrangements, exceptions, and adaptations to practical reality, the sort that Krasner catalogues so well. In the rise of major conventions and institutions that curtailed sovereignty, the Holocaust was a pivotal historical moment, yielding the Universal Declaration of Human Rights and the origins of European federalism amongst its other upshots.

The Universal Declaration of Human Rights of 1948 left sovereignty intact in a formal sense. A statement of principles, it was not legally binding on states. But its proclamation of over thirty rights of individuals was a first step toward creating an international consensus on states' obligations to the people within their borders. In the 1960s, two international legal covenants—the Covenant on Civil and Political Rights and the Covenant on Economic, Social, and Cultural Rights—created formal, legal obligations amongst states, though a provision of stipulating that these obligations do not interfere with sovereignty again left sovereignty intact. Over the course of the cold war, an international consensus—at least a formal, declaratory one—formed around the idea of human rights through these and other covenants: the Genocide Convention of 1948; the European Convention for the Protection of Human Rights and Fundamental Freedoms of 1950; the Helsinki Accords of 1975; the United Nations Convention Against Torture of 1987; and many others. In the legal obligations of states, however weak their enforcement and implementation remained, sovereignty became limited.

Challenging sovereignty—and indeed its long-standing attendant norm of non-intervention—more directly has been the growth of internationally sanctioned intervention after the cold war. Occurring in Iraq in the 1990s, the former Yugoslavia, Bosnia, Kosovo, Somalia, Haiti, Cambodia, Liberia, and elsewhere, this intervention involves the UN or another international organization sanctioning measures, usually involving military operations aimed at remedying some large-scale injustice like genocide or massive starvation, which member states of the UN would have widely considered illegitimate interference in internal affairs prior to the end of the cold war. Crucially, in contrast to peacekeeping operations during the cold war, many of these operations lacked the consent of the target state's government or of the conflicting parties in a civil war. A close cousin of internationally sanctioned intervention—and often conducted hand in hand with it—has been UN peace-building operations, efforts to reconstruct societies that often involve international actors temporarily assuming the duties of sovereign states, including conducting elections and providing protection for citizens. Between 1989 and 1999, the UN sent out thirty-three peace operations, more than double the fifteen missions that it had conducted during the previous four decades (Paris 2004). A steep growth in UN peace-building operations as well as in military operations approved by the Security Council between 1987 and 1994 together constitute what has been called a "UN Revolution." One of the central ideals of this revolution is the circumscription of sovereignty.

The consensus and stability of this ideal ought not to be overstated. US military operations in Iraq in 1999 and 2003 failed to elicit the prior approval of the United Nations Security Council, as did NATO's intervention in Kosovo in 1999. China, a powerful permanent member of the Security Council, remains highly wary of any measure that would interfere in a country's internal affairs. Notable failures to intervene exist, too, most famously in the case of Rwanda in 1994.

Still, the idea of internationally sanctioned intervention continues to enjoy widespread support within international organizations, member states, and non-governmental organizations. Garnering wide international attention today is *The Responsibility to Protect*, a document produced by the International Commission on Intervention and State Sovereignty (2001), a group convened by the Government of Canada in response to a challenge by UN Secretary General Kofi Annan. Arguing for an international obligation to intervene in countries where genocide and other large-scale sufferings are taking place (subject to a "reasonable chance of success"), the document centers upon a sharp revision of the classical conception of sovereignty. Rather than an absolute notion that frees states from obligations to their own citizens as well as from the oversight of outsiders, sovereignty entails a "responsibility to protect" that may be taken up by outsiders when individual states fail to uphold it toward their own citizens. For a non-absolute and conditional notion of sovereignty, *The Responsibility to Protect* serves as a manifesto in the way that Hobbes's and Bodin's thought stands as classical statements of absolute sovereignty.

European integration, described above as a source of non-absolute sovereignty in the case of states, competes in significance with internationally sanctioned intervention as a contemporary circumscription of sovereignty. It is fitting that, mirroring the early modern theorists of sovereignty's rejection of the temporal powers of the medieval Catholic Church, the most committed supporters of European integration have been Catholic Christian Democratic parties, motivated precisely by a rejection of absolute sovereignty and a desire to recover a civilization based on universal values, values that now include human rights and democracy. Creating a complex conglomerate of prerogatives in which different member states have integrated their affairs in different respects and to different degrees, the contemporary European Union begins to imitate medieval Europe's heteronomy.

As with absolute sovereignty, the idea that sovereignty would be limited and conditioned by international law, institutions, and obligations also enjoys a long pedigree. During the centuries when Bodin, Hobbes, and Machiavelli wrote, so, too, did Christian philosophers such as Francisco Suarez, Alberico Gentili, and Hugo Grotius, who acknowledged the emerging sovereign state as a legitimate institution, but in a presumptive and limited, not an absolute, sense. Each of them recognized the legitimacy of something very much like internationally sanctioned intervention in the case of a cruel prince, justified by values held in common by humankind.

Bertrand de Jouvenel, in his *Sovereignty: An Inquiry into the Political Good* (1957), does not advocate discarding the idea of sovereignty, which is needed for internal order and external defense. But he sharply criticizes what he views as the modern notion of sovereignty, one reflective of Hobbes, in whose "horrific conception everything comes back to means of constraint, which enable the sovereign to issue rights and dictate laws in any way he pleases. But these means of constraint are themselves but a fraction of the social forces concentrated in the hands of the sovereign" (1957: 197). He believes that philosophers writing in the wake of Hobbes, such as Locke, Pufendorf, and Rousseau, "were to feel the lure of this mechanically perfect construction," whatever differences they may have had over the locus of sovereignty and the form of the regime that practiced it (Jouvenel, 1957: 198).

Jouvenel's solution is to constrain the sovereign authority so that it only wills what is legitimate. Crucially, morality has a validity independent from what the sovereign wills. "There are . . . wills which are just and wills which are unjust," he argues, appealing to the perspective of "Christian thinkers" (1957: 201). "Authority" indeed "carries with it the obligation to command the thing that should be commanded" (1957: 201). But what is capable of constraining the sovereign will? Doubting that the right constitution or design of judicial institutions can be adequate, Jouvenel looks to the shared moral concepts of the citizenry for a check.

Jacques Maritain goes further, unqualifiedly excoriating sovereignty in Chapter 2 of *Man and the State* (1951). "It is my contention," he writes there, "that political philosophy must get rid of the word, as well as the concept, of Sovereignty." This is true, not because it is outdated or ambiguous, but because it is "intrinsically wrong and bound to mislead us if we keep on using it . . ." (1951: 29–30). To Maritain, Hobbes's and Bodin's notion of sovereignty was idolatry. Their conception rendered the sovereign into an entity transcendent over and unacceptable to the people and the common good. In fact, the legitimate authority of government is rooted in its relationship to natural law and cannot be transferred to some part of the body politic, whether it be a monarch, the people, or the institutions of the state. Sovereignty undermines the prospect of international law or a federated state, encourages centralized power, and destroys democratic accountability—ideals in which Maritain strongly believes.

If Schmitt and the National Socialists of Germany represented the apotheosis of absolute sovereignty, unaccountable to its own people, outside states and institutions, and least of all a transcendent moral order, thinkers like Maritain, Jouvenel, and the authors of *The Responsibility to Protect*, along with the architects of European federation and advocates of internationally sanctioned intervention, represent an effort to recover the idea espoused by Suarez, Gentili, and Grotius that sovereign authority, like all authority, is accountable to something larger than itself.[1]

References

Primary Sources

BODIN, JEAN (1992 [1576]). *On Sovereignty: Four Chapters from Six Books of the Commonwealth*. Cambridge: Cambridge University Press.

GROTIUS, HUGO (1901 [1625]). *The Rights of War and Peace*. London: M. Walter Dunne.

HOBBES, THOMAS (1968 [1651]). *Leviathan*. Harmondsworth: Penguin.

JOUVENEL, BERTRAND DE (1957). *Sovereignty: An Inquiry into the Political Good*. Chicago: University of Chicago Press.

MARITAIN, JACQUES (1951). *Man and the State*. Chicago: University of Chicago Press.

OPPENHEIM, L. (1905). International Law. London: Longmans, Green, and Co.

SCHMITT, CARL (1985 [1922]). *Political Theology: Four Chapters on the Concept of Sovereignty*, trans. G. Schwab. Chicago: University of Chicago Press.

Secondary Sources

ANDERSON, BENEDICT (1983). *Imagined Communites*. London Verso.

BARTELSON, JENS (1995). *A Genealogy of Sovereignty*. Cambridge: Cambridge University Press.

CAMERON, EUAN (1991). *The European Reformation*. Oxford: Oxford University Press.

CARR, E. H. (1964). *The Twenty Years' Crisis, 1919–1939*. New York: Harper & Row.

COLLEY, LINDA (1992). *Britons: Forging the Nation*. New Haven: Yale University Press.

FALK, RICHARD (1993). *Sovereignty*. Oxford: Oxford University Press.

FIGGIS, J. N. (1916 [1907]). *From Gerson to Grotius 1414–1625*. 2nd edn. Cambridge: Cambridge University Press.

GELLNER, ERNEST (1983). *Nations and Nationalism*. Ithaca, NY: Cornell University Press.

---

[1] The present chapter draws on Philpott (2001*a*) and Daniel Philpott, "Sovereignty," in Edward N. Zalta (ed.), *The Stanford Encyclopedia of Philosophy*, http://plato.stanford.edu/entries/sovereignty

HASTINGS, ADRIAN (1997). *The Construction of Nationhood: Ethnicity, Religion and Nationalism*. Cambridge: Cambridge University Press.

HINSLEY, F. H. (1986). *Sovereignty*. 2nd edn. Cambridge: Cambridge University Press.

HOBSBAWM, E. J. (1992). *Nations and Nationalism since 1780: Programme, Myth, Reality*. Cambridge: Cambridge University Press.

International Commission on Intervention and State Sovereignty (2001). *The Responsibility to Protect*. Report. Ottawa: International Development Research Centre.

JAMES, ALAN (1986). *Sovereign Statehood*. London: Allen & Unwin.

KEOHANE, ROBERT O., and HOFFMANN, STANLEY (1991). "Institutional Change in Europe in the 1980s," in R. O. Keohane and S. Hoffmann (eds), *The New European Community: Decisionmaking and Institutional Change*. Boulder, CO: Westview Press.

KRASNER, STEPHEN D. (1993). "Westphalia and All That," in J. Goldstein and R. O. Keohane (eds), *Ideas and Foreign Policy: Beliefs, Institutions, and Political Change*. Ithaca, NY: Cornell University Press.

KRASNER, STEPHEN D. (1999). *Sovereignty: Organized Hypocrisy*. Princeton: Princeton University Press.

KRATOCHWIL, FRIEDRICH (1986). "Of Systems, Boundaries, and Territoriality: An Inquiry into the Formation of the States-System," *World Politics*, 39: 27–52.

MARX, ANTHONY W. (2003). *Faith in Nation: Exclusionary Origins of Nationalism*. New York: Oxford University Press.

NEXON, DANIEL (2009). *The Struggle for Power in Early Modern Europe: Religious Conflict, Dynastic Empires, and International Change*. Princeton: Princeton University Press.

OSIANDER, ANDREAS (2001). "Sovereignty, International Relations, and the Westphalian Myth," *International Organization*, 55/2: 251–87.

PARIS, ROLAND (2004). *At War's End: Building Peace after Civil Conflict*. Cambridge: Cambridge University Press.

PHILPOTT, DANIEL (2001a). *Revolutions in Sovereignty: How Ideas Shaped Modern International Relations*. Princeton: Princeton University Press.

PHILPOTT, DANIEL (2001b). "Usurping the Sovereignty of Sovereignty?" *World Politics*, 53/2: 297–324.

POGGE, THOMAS (1992). "Cosmopolitanism and Sovereignty," *Ethics*, 103: 48–75.

RAWLS, JOHN (1955). "Two Concepts of Rules," *Philosophical Review*, 64: 3–32.

RUGGIE, JOHN GERARD (1986). *Continuity and Transformation in the World Polity: Toward a Neorealist Synthesis*, (ed.) R. O. Keohane. New York: Columbia University Press.

RUGGIE, JOHN GERARD (1993). "Territoriality and beyond: Problematizing Modernity in International Relations," *International Organization*, 47/1 (Winter), 139–74.

SMITH, ANTHONY D. (2003). *Chosen Peoples: Sacred Sources of National Identity, Sacred Sources of National Identity*. Oxford and New York: Oxford University Press.

SPRUYT, HENDRIK (1994). *The Sovereign State and its Competitors*. Princeton: Princeton University Press.

STRAUMANN, BENJAMIN (2007). "The Peace of Westphalia (1648) as a Secular Constitution," IILJ Working Paper No. 2007/07. New York.

STRAYER, J. R. (1970). *The Medieval Origins of the Modern State*. Princeton: Princeton University Press.

TESCHKE, BENNO (2003). *The Myth of 1648: Class, Geopolitics and the Making of Modern International Relations*. London: Verso.

WOLFF, R. P. (1990). *The Conflict between Authority and Autonomy*. Oxford: Basil Blackwell.

CHAPTER 33

....

THE SOCIAL CONTRACT (CONTRACT OF GOVERNMENT)

....

JOHANN SOMMERVILLE

SOCIAL-contract theories flourished in Europe in the sixteenth, seventeenth, and eighteenth centuries, had roots extending far further back, and continue to be influential today. John Rawls revived one type of contract theory in the mid-twentieth century, while another featured in the work of Robert Nozick. There is no single social-contract theory, though all writers in the contractarian (or contractualist) tradition make some appeal to contract as a key ingredient in explaining the origins of society or government, and the obligation of individuals to obey those who hold political authority over them. One kind of theory centers on a real or hypothetical contract between individuals to establish a political society—a contract of society (*pactum associationis, Gesellschaftsvertrag, pacte d'association*). Another focuses on a contract between the society or people, on the one hand, and the ruler or government, on the other—a contract of government (*pactum subjectionis, Herrschaftsvertrag, pacte de gouvernement*). Some thinkers developed theories that had a place for both varieties of contract. Others added further levels of complexity—for instance, positing a contract between the people, their king, and God, which committed the two former to uphold the true religion as established by the latter, or adding to the contracts of society and government a third contract that instituted a constitution (*Verfassungsvertrag*).

In the heyday of theorizing about the social contract, it was the contract of government that received most attention. Commonly, writers who argued that rulers derive their powers from a contract with the people went on to claim that those powers are limited by the contract, and that, if rulers ignore its terms, the community can call them to account. Such ideas played an important part in Dutch arguments for independence from Spain in 1581, and in the American case for throwing off subjection to Britain in

1776. Often, contractualist thinkers adopted an approach to contract that was at once theoretical or philosophical, and historical. They contended that people were at first born politically free and equal, asserting that by nature no one has political authority over anyone else. When people joined together to form political societies, they proceeded, authority must at first have been in the hands of the whole community, since no one had any greater right to exercise it than anyone else. It followed that all states were at first self-governing democracies. However, the sovereign people could elect to transfer its authority to one or a few governors. It could do this by means of a contract that laid down the conditions on which the new ruler was to exercise power. The exact nature of these conditions in any particular country could be discovered not by theorizing, but only by examining historical evidence of contracts between the people and its governors. Some contractualists have taken a much more purely philosophical approach, using the social contract to cast light on what must always and everywhere be true about states. They include Hobbes, Rousseau, Kant, and Rawls. Hobbes is also a fine example of a thinker who developed a theory of contract that vindicated not limited but absolute government.

ANCIENT GREECE AND ROME

Although ancient writings contain no full-blown theory of social contract, it is arguable that some key contractualist ideas are to be found in the works of Plato and others. In *Crito* (50a–54d), Socrates refuses to flee from Athens, although he has been unjustly condemned to death. He explains that by enjoying the protection and benefits of Athenian laws he has acquired an obligation to obey them, and to accept judgments made in accordance with them, unless he can persuade the state to change them. To escape death by leaving Athens would be to break his contractual obligations, and to undermine the laws and the state. According to Socrates, the very fact that he had lived quietly under Athenian law for seventy years, when he could have emigrated voluntarily to some other city if he had preferred its laws, gave him an obligation to stay and obey. It is possible to see in this discussion the kernel of the claims that political obligation arises from consent and that this consent can be expressed tacitly.

In the *Republic* (358e–359b), Glaucon put forward an account of justice as a contract between self-interested people who calculate that they will benefit more from an arrangement in which they agree to avoid harming each other than from one in which everyone is free to try to inflict injury on others. This agreement, said Glaucon, marked the beginning of legislating and covenanting among humans. Like Glaucon, Epicurus grounded justice on mutual agreements between people to refrain from acting aggressively against each other (*Key Doctrines* 31–8). The Stoics, on the other hand, viewed justice as natural and rational. So too did Cicero (*De legibus* 1.18–23), and he attacked contractual theories of justice that based it upon self-interest. Later writers in the social-contract tradition usually founded justice on natural reason

and not on contract, though Hobbes is a partial exception. Hobbes and other contrac-
tarians endorsed the Roman law principle that by nature people are born free and
equal, though Hobbes differed drastically from most of them in the conclusions he
drew from this claim. Another Roman legal idea that influenced later thinking on the
social contract was that of the *lex regia* or royal law, by which the Roman people
supposedly transferred power to Augustus and later emperors. Like Roman law, the
ancient texts of the Christian Bible provided material for contractualists, especially in
Old Testament discussions of God's covenants with the children of Israel. Of course, it
was also possible to discover in Scripture such non-contractarian theories as the divine
right of kings.

THE MIDDLE AGES

Feudal thought stressed the mutual obligations between lords and vassals. In return for
protection, vassals were held to owe their lords obedience. Such ideas were still alive in
the seventeenth century. After the defeat of Charles I in the English Civil War, some
thinkers (including Hobbes) argued that people no longer owed obedience to the king
or (on his death) to his son Charles, but to the victorious parliamentarians, since the
latter were now protecting them. In 856, the term *pactum* (pact; contract) was used to
describe an agreement between Charles the Bald (King of the West Franks) and his
leading subordinates. The agreement specified that they were empowered to bring him
back to reason if he reneged on the deal. The feudal relationship between the king and
his barons was a personal one; the barons took an oath to the king personally, and
not as head of state, or representative of the people. But it was an easy step for the
barons to add the claim that they were acting for the people, and in 858 rebels in the
West Frankish kingdom did just that. Mid-ninth-century Frankish ideas on kingship, it
has been said, came "close to contract theory and a right of resistance" (Nelson 1988:
228–9).

Aristotelian and Thomist thinking stressed that political society is natural to man.
This did not entail that human will, or agreements between people, are irrelevant to the
establishment of particular societies. Aristotle (*Politics* 1253^{a}29–30) declared that
nature impels us toward society, but nonetheless argued that whoever first constructed
a political association was the greatest of benefactors. Like Aristotle, medieval natural-
law thinkers held that people can achieve the goals appropriate to human nature only
within political society. It was, they contended, natural for people to establish political
societies, and set up kings or other rulers to govern them. They commonly claimed that
the powers of kings and other governors are derived from the people. This opened the
possibility that when the people first set up governors it placed contractual conditions
upon them. The Augustinian canon Manegold of Lautenbach, who wrote around 1085,
is sometimes seen as an early proponent of social contract theory, since he said that, if a
ruler breached the pact (*pactum*) by virtue of which he had been instituted, his subjects

were freed from their obligation of obedience to him (e.g. Stead 1914: 11). But more recent scholarship convincingly claims that the term *pactum* here alludes not to a legal contract between king and people but rather to the royal virtues that kings should possess, and that distinguish true monarchs from tyrants (Fuhrmann 1975; Nelson 1988: 246–7).

A clearer reference to a contract between king and people occurs in the *De regno ad regem Cypri* (*On Kingship, to the King of Cyprus, c.*1267), often attributed to St Thomas Aquinas. This work asserted that, if a community has the right to elect its king, it can depose him should he fall into tyranny. This would be true even if it had subjected itself to him permanently, for by acting tyrannically he deserved that "the pact made with him by his subjects" should not be kept. However, the book made clear that not all political societies were of this kind, arguing that if the right of appointing the king belonged to some superior (the pope or emperor are obvious examples), the people should appeal to that person. He also admitted that in some cases the only recourse against tyranny was to pray to God (Aquinas 1959: 30–2).

In the late 1200s, Jean de Meung's poem the *Roman de la Rose* depicted a peasant community that appointed a head whose rulership was a trust, revocable at will. The notion of social contract as trust also featured in the more cautious work of his younger contemporary, the Franciscan philosopher Johannes Duns Scotus (Dunbabin 1988: 516–17). In the early fourteenth century, the heterodox but influential thinker Marsiglio of Padua contended that in every political society legislative power is held by the "people or association of citizens or its weightier part" (Black 1992: 65), which has the authority to elect rulers (1992: 66) and which can judge and depose them (1992: 67). The idea that the weightier part of the people might count as the whole long remained commonplace, licensing a small male social elite to act for the entire society. Marsiglio's contemporary, William of Ockham, held that "all rulers derive their power from 'their people'" (Black 1992: 73) and allowed the community to depose its king in extraordinary circumstances. In England in 1327 and 1399, aristocratic opponents of the monarch arranged his deposition, and on both occasions they tried to show that their actions were backed by the people's authority (Dunbabin 1988: 517). In the late 1300s and early 1400s, conciliarists such as Jean Gerson affirmed that in ecclesiastical matters a General Council of the Church, as the representative body of the faithful, is superior to the pope, and can discipline him if he falls into error. Gerson put forward a similar analysis of secular society, arguing that kings derive their powers from the people, and that the whole community remains superior to its ruler (Skinner 1978: ii. 116–17.) On his account, the king's authority depends on the continuing consent of the people, but such consent could be expressed tacitly, by mere acquiescence. Gerson argued that the French monarchy was hereditary by custom, and that custom betokened the consent of the people (Dunbabin 1988: 517–18). Nicholas of Cusa (a conciliarist who eventually changed sides) declared that, since by nature people are free and equal, only "election and consent" can establish the "authority of one common ruler," but he acknowledged that consent could be tacit, expressed through custom (Nicholas of Cusa 1991: 98, 101).

Later conciliarists included Jacques Almain and John Mair. The latter taught George Buchanan, an influential sixteenth-century contractualist who is discussed below. The former argued that in every commonwealth the ruler derives political power from the community by means of a positive law, that the community retains power superior to that of the ruler, and that it can use this to depose a king who "rules not to the edification but to the destruction of the polity" (Almain 1997: 136–7). This account contains many of the elements that later featured in full-blown contractualist thinking, though Almain derived the king's power from a law rather than a contract. There is also in Almain's thought, and was to remain in later thinking on the social contract, something of a tension between contractualist ideas and the notion that the community continues to be superior to its ruler. From the contractualist perspective, the force of the contract is to limit the king's power, and show when he can be resisted. But, if the community is his superior, and can discipline him whenever it finds that his rule is destructive, there is little need for a contract setting out the terms on which he holds authority. There were many contractual agreements between kings and their subjects in the Middle Ages, including the English Magna Carta of 1215, but these were rarely seen as relics of an original contract by which the people transferred power to the king. The fifteenth-century judge, Sir John Fortescue, approached this position when he traced England's form of government to an agreement—"Fortescue's social contract" (Dunbabin 1988: 515)—between (the mythical) Brutus (great-grandson of Aeneas) and his followers when they first invaded the land (Fortescue 1997: 86).

PROTESTANT AND CATHOLIC RESISTANCE THEORISTS

The idea of the social contract began to feature in political writings when it became polemically useful in the course of the civil wars about political and religious issues in France, Scotland, and the Netherlands during the later sixteenth century. In 1572, thousands of Protestants were massacred in France. A number of Protestant thinkers abandoned the policy of negotiating with the Catholic authorities for toleration, and instead began to advocate armed resistance. Theodore Beza claimed that royal power is derived from a grant by the people, and is made not absolutely but on certain conditions. If the king breaks the conditions, power reverts to the people. He surveyed the forms of governments of a number of European countries, arguing that in each the authority of the king was limited by conditions imposed by the people. If the king failed to abide by the limitations, he could be brought to his senses by special officials such as the ancient Spartan ephors, or by "inferior magistrates" (provincial governors and aristocrats) and local representative institutions. Conditions that unjustly oppressed the people (for example, because they had been extracted by force, if the first king was a conqueror) were automatically invalid (Beza 1965: 47, 50, 54–63, 67–8). The author of the *Vindiciae contra tyrannos* (probably Philippe Duplessis-Mornay) argued for two original contracts. The first was between the people, the king, and God, in which the monarch and his subjects agreed to promote true religion. In the second contract, the king promised to "rule justly and according to the laws" and the people agreed to obey him "so long as he commanded justly" (Brutus 1994: 54, 130–1). In successive monarchies, the book said, kings inherit only those powers that their ancestors had possessed, and remain accountable to the people, an immortal corporation. The people chose not only the king, but also inferior magistrates who helped him govern, and who, like the ephors in Sparta, could call him to account if he misruled (Brutus 1994: 46, 80, 90, 92.) Just as the conciliarists had shown that a general council of the Church is superior to the pope, the book remarked, so the officers of the kingdom, representing the people as a whole, were superior to the monarch, though he was above his individual subjects.

The Scottish reformer John Knox argued in 1558 that every Christian country was as much bound to God by "league and covenant" as Old Testament Israel had been (Knox 1994: 103). Another Scot, George Buchanan, sounded a more secular note in his *De jure regni apud Scotos* (*On the Law of the Kingdom amongst the Scots* (1579)), written to justify the deposition of Mary Queen of Scots in 1567. Buchanan's theory was similar to those of Beza and the *Vindiciae*, but he paid more attention to the pre-social condition of humans. It has been suggested that Buchanan, and a little later the Catholic who wrote under the name Rossaeus (probably William Rainolds), inaugurated a strand of contractualism that was to include John Locke. Like Locke, the argument goes, Buchanan and Rossaeus accepted the idea of a pre-social state of nature, held that individuals in the state of nature had been empowered to enforce natural law, and argued that popular sovereignty was inalienable—while other resistance theorists thought it could be permanently delegated to inferior magistrates or others (Salmon 1987.) The principle that the people is permanently sovereign in every state was stressed by the German resistance theorist, Johannes Althusius, in his *Politica methodice digesta* (*Politics Arranged Methodically* (published in 1603 and in enlarged editions in 1610 and 1614)). According to Althusius, political societies or commonwealths are themselves composed of smaller associations such as cities and provinces, each of which is founded on the consent of its members. The commonwealth, in turn, was the product of a contract between its constituent cities and provinces. This contract laid down fundamental laws defining the powers of the government (Althusius 1979: 169). The ruler was inferior to the commonwealth as a whole, and could be resisted if he subverted the law (1979: 152, 395). The appropriate magistrates to lead resistance were the ephors (1979: 143 –6). Just who they were varied from place to place, but in Germany they were the seven electors, and in England the parliament (1979: 144–5, 155).

Resistance theories circulated among Protestants in France after the massacres in 1572, but they turned into something of an embarrassment for them when in 1584 the Protestant Henri of Navarre became heir to the French throne. From the mid-1580s supporters of the Catholic League adopted arguments based on contract, and sometimes taken directly from the Protestant theorists, to claim that resistance was justified against heretical or tyrannical rulers, and that in France non-Catholics could not inherit the monarchy. Royal power, said Jean Boucher, is derived from a mutual contract between the king and the people. If the king broke it, the Estates—representing the people—could depose him (Boucher 1595: 40, 55). He argued that people are by nature free, that royal power stems from a grant from the community, and that the community as a whole possesses the same power over the king as he holds over individuals. Both king and people, he said, are bound by a pact with God (Boucher 1529: 12b, 13b, 20a, 20b). Rossaeus noted that royal power varied widely in different countries and argued that this was because the people had originally granted their kings varying measures of authority. Contract theorists in general claimed that natural law required that people establish governments, but did not prescribe any particular form of government. Rossaeus was typical in remarking that what form was best varied with circumstance, and in leaving it up to the original people to institute the one they preferred. He contended, however, that in all Christian countries a necessary part of the contract between king and people was the provision that they both maintain the true religion—namely, Catholicism. Since Henri of Navarre was not (yet) a Catholic, he was therefore not qualified to be king (Rossaeus 1592: 9, 10, 44).

Henri did convert to Catholicism, and won the French throne. French Catholics toned down or abandoned resistance theory. But a Catholic fanatic murdered Henri in 1610, and many people believed there was a link between this act and resistance theory, especially as presented by the Jesuit Juan de Mariana, who like Buchanan and Rossaeus went into some detail on the state of nature, and who allowed a private individual to assassinate a tyrant if the latter prevented the representative assembly of the people from meeting and from passing judgment on his misrule (Mariana 1599: 16–20, 76, 79). The Parlement of Paris ordered the burning of the book. Thereafter, Catholics were increasingly careful about French political sensitivities. Francisco Suárez in *Defensio fidei catholicae* (*Defense of the Catholic Faith* (1613)) argued that when the people grants power to a king it fully subjects itself to him, and he drew an analogy between this case and that of individuals who give or sell themselves into slavery. So earlier contract theorists were wrong to claim that the people is permanently superior to its ruler. However, Suárez continued to argue that the extent of the king's power depends on the original contract between ruler and people, and he allowed resistance in certain circumstances. He held that ancient records and immemorial custom provided guides to the contents of the contract (Suárez III.3.2; 1856–78: xxiv. 213). The Elizabethan Protestant, Richard Hooker—much quoted by Locke—similarly maintained that monarchs were bound not only by the original "articles of compact" but also by subsequent agreements made by express consent, or tacitly in "custom reaching beyond the memory of man." Hooker was virtually silent on rights of resistance (Hooker 1989: 145). Another common view was that royal coronation oaths were repetitions of the original contract.

Later Catholics usually had still less than Suárez to say about resistance, at least in hereditary monarchies. In the elective monarchy of Poland, kings were obliged to agree to a formal contract from 1573, and nobles asserted a right of resistance. Similar rules applied in Hungary until 1687. Elsewhere, theories grounding *all* government in contract and claiming rights of resistance in *every* state found their most vigorous expression in times of political conflict or civil war. In the English Civil Wars of the 1640s, parliamentarians commonly used contractualist ideas to justify fighting the king's supporters. Sometimes contractualist thinking was combined in radical ways with arguments based on appeals to England's ancient constitution (e.g. Greenberg 2001: 214–15, 218–19). The claims—already present in Fortescue—that the English people had ancient customary rights to consent to legislation and taxation, fitted neatly with the contention that these rights were based on contract and that the king could be resisted if he infringed them. Henry Parker's highly influential political pamphlets put forward the arguments that kings get their power from the people and may be resisted if they fail to adhere to the conditions on which it was granted to them. Parker contended that the people was equivalent to parliament. Outside parliament, it was a headless multitude, incapable of expressing any united will; in parliament it could speak clearly through the voice of the majority (the standard account of Parker's views is Mendle 1995). This view had affinities with the medieval notion that the weightier part of the people really was the people. It was not an attitude that commended itself to the parliamentarian army, or to the Levellers, a quasi-democratic political party that sprang up in the 1640s. Army propaganda asserted that parliament is accountable to the people as a whole, and the Levellers took the same line, calling for frequent parliaments and a wide franchise. In their writings, the "people" came to mean something like "all the people"—or, at least, all adult males who were not domestic servants or in receipt of charity. The 1640s and 1650s in England also saw the spread of the idea that executive and legislative power should be separated, in the sense that no person or assembly should hold a monopoly of both. The distinction between executive and legislative power was clearly made by the parliamentarian theorist, Philip Hunton, in 1643, but rarely occurs earlier (Hunton 1643: 5, 26).

GROTIUS, HOBBES, PUFENDORF, AND LOCKE

From the 1560s, the Dutch engaged in a long and ultimately successful revolt against Spain. Some Dutch theorists adopted contractualist ideas of resistance to justify the revolt (e.g. Van Gelderen 1992: 101, 149, 162). Once the Dutch rebels had established their own authority, justifying revolt became less of a priority. The best known of early modern Dutch theorists, Hugo Grotius, adopted contract theory, but limited rights of popular resistance. He rejected the idea that the people holds perpetual sovereignty and that it can discipline its king whenever he abuses power, arguing that this principle had caused great mischief in the world. Just as one individual could give himself into slavery, he said, so a people could fully subject itself to a ruler (Grotius I.3.8.1; 2005: 260–1). He denied that inferior magistrates have any power to resist the king, arguing that their authority is wholly subordinate to that of the monarch (I.4.6; 2005: 354). But he did admit that, if the king had received power on the specific condition that he would forfeit it by performing some specified act, then he would forfeit it by doing that act, and he argued that in extreme cases all peoples, and even individuals, could defend themselves by force (I.4.12; 2005: 376; I.4.7; 2005: 356–8).

Rousseau saw Grotius as an advocate of absolute monarchy, and grouped him with Hobbes as a theorist who inclined toward the view that it is fine for a small number of rulers to exploit large numbers of subjects, as if the "human race belongs to a hundred men" (Rousseau 1973: 167). Hobbes was in fact a far more trenchant absolutist than Grotius. He is sometimes seen as the founder of the social-contract tradition, or at least as a major early proponent of it. But in many ways his theory was calculated to subvert conclusions that the tradition had long been invoked to support. Earlier social-contract theorists commonly used the idea of contract to show that governments hold limited power, though the limits dwindled in thinkers such as Grotius. Hobbes employed the concepts of contract and of the state of nature to remove the limitations almost altogether. He portrayed the state of nature as a condition of war of all against all, and argued that life there would be so bad that reason would prompt people to make a contract with each other to hand over their rights to an absolute sovereign. In *Leviathan* (1651) he argued that individuals institute a commonwealth by agreeing to authorize the acts of such a sovereign (Hobbes 1991: 120). In this account, the agreement is a contract of society, between individuals. There is no contract of government, and the sovereign remains in the state of nature, free from any contractual obligations. Since everyone has authorized the sovereign's acts, no one can justifiably complain about them. However, individuals in Hobbes's theory retain the right of self-defense against direct attack. Some critics at the time contended that it is difficult to draw any satisfactory distinction between this supposedly narrow right of self-defense and the apparently much wider rights recognized by resistance theorists, and the argument has been revived since (Hampton 1986: 197–207).

The influential German thinker Samuel Pufendorf disagreed with Hobbes on how unpleasant the state of nature was, and argued that the ruler's power is derived from a contract with the people (Pufendorf 2.2.4, 5, 9; 1934: 163, 166, 172.) Indeed, he held that political society stems from two separate contracts plus a decree. The first contract sets up the political society, which then deliberates on what its form of government should be, a point that is decided by majority vote. The society then issues a decree introducing the desired constitutional arrangements, and finally makes a second contract with the rulers it appoints to govern (7.2.7–8; 1934: 974–7). He downplayed rights of resisting established rulers, arguing that it was normally the ruler's job to define what duties subjects should perform and not vice versa, but recognizing rights of resistance in extreme circumstances (7.2.10; 1934: 979; 7.8.6; 1934: 1110). John Locke's theory contrasts strongly with Pufendorf's. Locke made do with a single contract or compact, by which individuals established a self-governing political society. The people remained supreme, but entrusted legislative power to one person or assembly (Locke, *Second Treatise*, paras 97, 135, 149.) In well-ordered commonwealths, legislative and executive power would be held by different persons or assemblies (paras 143–4.) The legislative power was superior to the executive, but inferior to the supreme power of the people (para. 149.) Most earlier contract theorists denied that by nature individuals held the power of executing the law of nature (as opposed to the power of self-defense). Locke specifically asserted "this strange doctrine": "That in the state of Nature every one has the executive power of the law of Nature" (para. 13). An implication was that in some circumstances power might revert not only to the people as a whole, but even to individuals (para. 168).

Transformation, Decline, and Revival: Hume, Rousseau, Kant, Rawls, and Nozick

Locke's political ideas remained influential through the eighteenth century and beyond, not least in America during the Revolutionary period. But in philosophical circles the old contractualist ideas came under attack. An important text in this connection is David Hume's essay "Of the Original Contract" (1748). Hume claimed that almost all governments "have been founded originally, either in usurpation or conquest" (Hume 1987: 471). So the original contract was a fiction. Locke and his predecessors portrayed the contract as at once philosophically and historically based. Theory showed that governments must derive their power from the community, and history provided evidence of actual agreements in custom, oaths, and contracts. Locke's successors often stressed the philosophical rather than the historical aspect of contractualism. In his *Social Contract* (1762) Rousseau argued that a properly constructed society would be based on an agreement between individuals to subordinate their private wills to the general will, which expressed the true interests of the community. The sovereign was the people as a whole. It appointed magistrates, but did not enter into any kind of binding contract with them (Rousseau 1973: 242–3). This was a depiction of Rousseau's ideal democratic society rather than a theory of much use in criticizing or reforming existing arrangements in eighteenth-century Europe. Nevertheless, the French Revolution was frequently linked to Rousseau's ideas. Rousseau's social contract was never implemented. In Prussia, Immanuel Kant argued that there was no historical basis for thinking that any original contract had actually been made. But he argued that as "an *idea* of reason" the concept was useful, and could provide an important test of proposed legislation, for "if the law is such that a whole people could not *possibly* agree to it . . . it is unjust." The examples he gave show that he particularly had in mind legislation that unfairly discriminated for or against particular groups (Kant 1991: 79). There is a reasonably straight line from this position to John Rawls's Kantianly contractualist social and political principles, set out in *A Theory of Justice*. And the more individualistic and libertarian contractualism of Robert Nozick's *Anarchy, State, and Utopia* clearly owes a substantial debt to Locke.

Social-contract theory remains central to modern discussions of political obligation and the nature of justice, though in the past couple of centuries it has somewhat fallen out of favor, not only at the level of high philosophy but also more generally. Suggested reasons for this include its associations with the French Revolution, which led to a reaction against it in European monarchies; suspected links between contractualism and the arguments of the Confederates in the American Civil War; and the modern stress on the politics of interest groups, which arguably de-emphasizes the relationship between the people as a whole and its government. These reasons may be evidenced by history, but that does not mean they are good. Social-contract theory may still have important insights to offer.

REFERENCES

Primary Sources

ALMAIN, JACQUES (1997). *A Book concerning the Authority of the Church*, in J. H. Burns and Thomas M. Izbicki, eds, *Conciliarism and Papalism*, Cambridge: Cambridge University Press, 134–200. First published in 1512.

ALTHUSIUS, JOHANNES (1979). *Politica methodice digesta of Johannes Althusius (Althaus) with an Introduction by Carl Joachim Friedrich*. New York: Arno Press. This is a reduced facsimile of a book published by Harvard University Press, Cambridge, MA, in 1932; the text is from the 1614 edition. The book was first published, in a shorter version, in 1603.

AQUINAS, THOMAS (1959). *Selected Political Writings*, ed. A. P. d'Entrèves, with a translation by J. G. Dawson, Oxford: Basil Blackwell. The work here cited, *De Regno ad regem Cypri (On Kingship, to the King of Cyprus)*, was first published *c*.1267.

ARISTOTLE, *Politics*. First published *c*.330 BC.

BEZA, THEODORE (1965). *De Iure Magistratuum*, ed. Klaus Sturm. Neukirchen-Vluyn: Neukirchner Verlag des Erziehungsvereins. First published in 1576. (A version in French appeared in 1574.)

BOUCHER, JEAN (1529). *De Ivsta Henrici Tertii Abdicatione*. Paris: Nicolaus Niuellius (1529 is a misprint for 1589). First published in 1589.

BOUCHER, JEAN (1595). *Apologie pour Iehan Chastel*. First publication.

BRUTUS, STEPHANUS JUNIUS (1994). *Vindiciae contra Tyrannos, or, concerning the Legitimate Power of a Prince over the People, and of the People over a Prince*, ed. and trans. George Garnett. Cambridge: Cambridge University Press. First published in 1579. Probably written by Philippe Duplessis-Mornay.

BUCHANAN, GEORGE (1579). *De iure regni apud Scotos*. Edinburgh, John Ross. First publication. A modern critical edition is *A Dialogue on the Law of Kingship among the Scots*, ed. Roger A. Mason and Martin S. Smith. Aldershot: Ashgate, 2004.

CICERO, *De legibus*. Begun around 52 BCE; not completed; first printed in 1498.

EPICURUS, *Key Doctrines*. First published in Diogenes Laertius, *Lives of Eminent Philosophers*, *c*.220.

FORTESCUE, SIR JOHN (1997). *On the Laws and Governance of England*, ed. Shelley Lockwood. Cambridge, Cambridge University Press. The *Governance of England*, cited here, was first published *c.*1471.

GROTIUS, HUGO (2005). *The Rights of War and Peace Book I*, ed. Richard Tuck. Indianapolis: Liberty Fund. First published (in Latin as *De jure belli ac pacis*) in 1625.

HOBBES, THOMAS (1991). *Leviathan*, ed. Richard Tuck. Cambridge: Cambridge University Press. First published in 1651.

HOOKER, RICHARD (1989). *Of the Laws of Ecclesiastical Polity: Preface, Book I, Book VIII*, ed. Arthur Stephen McGrade. Cambridge: Cambridge University Press. Book VIII, here cited, was first published in 1648; Hooker died in 1600.

HUME, DAVID (1987). *Essays Moral, Political, and Literary*, ed. Eugene F. Miller. Rev. edn. Indianapolis: Liberty Fund. The essay here cited, "Of the Original Contract," was first published in 1748.

HUNTON, PHILIP (1643). *A Treatise of Monarchie*. London: John Bellamy and Ralph Smith. First publication.

JEAN DE MEUNG, *Roman de la Rose*. First published *c.*1280.

KANT, IMMANUEL (1991). *Political Writings*, ed. Hans Reiss, trans. H. B. Nisbet. 2nd edn. Cambridge: Cambridge University Press. The work cited here, "On the Common Saying: 'This May be True in Theory, but it does not Apply in Practice,'" was first published in 1793.

KNOX, JOHN (1994). *On Rebellion*, ed. Roger A. Mason. Cambridge: Cambridge University Press. *The Appellation of John Knox*, cited here, was first published in 1558.

LOCKE, JOHN, *Two Treatises of Government*. First published in 1689.

MANEGOLD OF LAUTENBACH, *Liber ad Gebehardum*. First published *c.*1085.

MARIANA, JUAN DE (1599). *De rege et regis institutione*. Toledo: Pedro Rodríguez.

MARSIGLIO OF PADUA, *Defensor pacis* (*The Defender of the Peace.*) First published in 1324.

NICHOLAS OF CUSA (1991). *The Catholic Concordance*, ed. Paul Sigmund. Cambridge: Cambridge University Press. First published in 1433.

NOZICK, ROBERT (1974). *Anarchy, State, and Utopia*. New York: Basic Books. First publication.

PLATO, *Crito*. First published *c.*390 BCE

PLATO, *The Republic*. First published *c.*380 BCE.

PUFENDORF, SAMUEL (1934). *De jure naturae et gentium*, vol. 2, trans. C. H. Oldfather and W. A. Oldfather. Oxford: Clarendon Press. First published in 1672.

RAWLS, JOHN (1971). *A Theory of Justice*. Cambridge, MA: Belknap Press of Harvard University Press. First publication.

ROSSAEUS, GUILELMUS (1592). *De Ivsta reipub. christianae in reges impios et haereticos authoritate*. Antwerp: Ioannes Keerbergius. First published in 1590.

ROUSSEAU, JEAN-JACQUES (1973). *The Social Contract and Discourses*, ed. G. D. H. Cole, J. H. Brumfitt, and JOHN C. HALL. London: J. M. Dent & Sons. *The Social Contract*, cited here, was first published in 1762.

SUÁREZ, FRANCISCO (1856–78). *Defensio fidei catholicae*, in *Opera omnia*, xxiv. Paris: Juan Luis Vives. First published in 1613.

Secondary Sources

BLACK, ANTONY (1992). *Political Thought in Europe 1250–1450*. Cambridge: Cambridge University Press.

DUNBABIN, JEAN (1988). "Government," in H. Burns (ed.), *The Cambridge History of Medieval Political Thought c.350–c.1450.* Cambridge: Cambridge University Press, 477–519.

FUHRMANN, HORST (1975). "'Volkssouveränität' und 'Herrschaftsvertrag' bei Manegold von Lautenbach," in Sten Gagnér, Hans Schlosser, and Wolfgang Wiegand (eds), *Festschrift für Hermann Krause.* Cologne and Vienna: Böhlau Verlag, 21–42.

GREENBERG, JANELLE (2001). *The Radical Face of the English Constitution.* Cambridge: Cambridge University Press.

HAMPTON, JEAN (1986). *Hobbes and the Social Contract Tradition.* Cambridge: Cambridge University Press.

MENDLE, MICHAEL (1995). *Henry Parker and the English Civil War: The Political Thought of the Public's "Privado."* Cambridge: Cambridge University Press.

NELSON, JANET (1988). "Kingship and Empire," in J. H. Burns (ed.), *The Cambridge History of Medieval Political Thought c.350–c.1450.* Cambridge, Cambridge University Press, 211–51.

SALMON, J. H. M. (1987). "An Alternative Theory of Popular Resistance: Buchanan, Rossaeus, and Locke," in J. H. M. Salmon, *Renaissance and Revolt: Essays in the Intellectual and Social History of Early Modern France.* Cambridge: Cambridge University Press, 136–54.

SKINNER, QUENTIN (1978). *The Foundations of Modern Political Thought.* 2 vols. Cambridge: Cambridge University Press.

STEAD, M. T. (1914). "Manegold of Lautenbach," *English Historical Review,* 29: 1–15.

VAN GELDEREN, MARTIN (1992). *The Political Thought of the Dutch Revolt 1555–1590.* Cambridge: Cambridge University Press.

CHAPTER 34

CITIZENSHIP

RICHARD BELLAMY

NORMATIVE theorizing about citizenship has been dominated by three different models—the republican, the legal, and the liberal democratic—reflecting respectively the civic experiences of city republics, empires, and nation states (Bellamy 2008a: ch. 2). The first two originated in ancient Greece and Rome. As Pocock (1995) and Walzer (1989) have observed, these provided the classical models of citizenship not only by belonging to the 'classical' period of history but also in setting the terms of much later debate. However, from the seventeenth century onwards, these two models were gradually adapted and, to some degree, combined, to form a third model suited to the new socio-political reality of commercial and industrial nation states. The key contemporary debate surrounds whether we are witnessing the emergence of a fourth, cosmopolitan, model of citizenship appropriate to a global age, and how far it departs from these earlier three.

REPUBLICAN CITIZENSHIP

Republican citizenship developed in the context of the ancient city states of Greece and Rome, with later republican writers tailoring these ideas to the commercial civic republics of the Renaissance and the republican states that emerged following the English, American, and French revolutions. Republican writers see liberty as a civic achievement that results from all citizens having an equal say in ruling the polity. However, they differ greatly over why and how such participation might be brought about and what the resulting liberty consists in.

Aristotle's *Politics* (335–323 BC) provides the canonical text of the Greek version of republican citizenship, with ancient Athens the model. Aristotle regarded human beings as 'political animals' because it is in our nature to live in political communities—indeed, he contended only within a *polis* or city state could human potential be fully realized.

However, he believed people played the roles appropriate to their natural station in life, with only some qualifying as *politai* or citizens. Though neither the qualifications Aristotle deemed appropriate for membership of this select group nor the duties he expected of them are regarded as entirely suitable today, they have cast a long shadow over the history of citizenship and their inner rationale still underlies much contemporary thinking.

To be a citizen of Athens it was necessary to be a male aged 20 or over, of known genealogy as being born to an Athenian citizen family, and to be a patriarch of a household, a warrior—possessing the arms and ability to fight, and a master of the labour of others—notably slaves.[1] So gender, race, and class defined citizenship, and many of the main later debates have turned on how far they continue to do so. As a result, large numbers were excluded: women, though married Athenian women were citizens for genealogical purposes; children; immigrants or 'metics'—including those whose families had been settled in Athens for several generations, although they were legally free, liable to taxation, and had military duties; and above all slaves. It is reckoned that the number of citizens in Athens fluctuated between 30,000 and 50,000, while the number of slaves was of the order of 80,000–100,000. Therefore, citizenship was enjoyed by a minority, though a substantial one. Yet, this was inevitable, given the high expectations of citizens. For their capacity to perform their not inconsiderable citizenly duties rested on their everyday needs being looked after by the majority of the population, particularly women and slaves.

Aristotle described as citizens those who 'rule and are ruled by turns' (Aristotle, *Pol.* 1259^{b}1). Though the duties involved differed between polities and even different categories of citizen within the same polity, at some level citizenship involved 'the power to take part in the deliberative or judicial administration' (Aristotle *Pol.* 1275^{b}1). In Athens this meant at a minimum participating in the assembly, which met at least 40 times a year and required a quorum of 6,000 citizens for plenary sessions, and, for citizens aged over 30, doing jury service—again, a frequent responsibility given that juries required 201 or more members and on some occasions over 501. Though jury service was paid, jurors were chosen by lot from among those who presented themselves, to discourage both its becoming a regular income and jury packing. In addition, there were some 140 local territorial units of government, or *demes*, with their own *agorai* or assembly points for public discussion of local affairs and passing local decrees.

Meanwhile, many citizens could not avoid holding public office at some point. Apart from generals, who were elected by the assembly and could serve multiple terms if successful, public officers were chosen by lot, served for one or two years maximum, with key roles often rotated between office-holders. These devices aimed to increase the likelihood that all had an equal chance of exercising political power, with the short

---

[1] For details of Athenian and Roman politics, see Finley (1983).

terms of office and the checks operated by the different bodies on each other ensuring this power was severely circumscribed. Yet, though there were no career politicians, citizenship itself, if one adds military service and participation in local affairs, was a fairly full occupation.

Athens was unusual among Greek city states in being so democratic. Indeed, Aristotle, who periodically resided in Athens but was not born there and so not an Athenian citizen, expressed a personal preference for systems that mixed democracy with aristocratic and monarchical elements. However, even in those systems that did so, citizenship remained fairly onerous. Like Plato, Aristotle esteemed the austere citizenship code of Sparta. By contrast to Athens, where the arts, philosophy, and leisure were much admired, Sparta emphasized military service above all else. Children were separated from their families aged 7, subjected to a rigorous training, and thereafter attached to a 'mess'. Given they still had to attend the Assembly, Spartan citizens became even more permanent public servants than their Athenian counter-parts. In fact, it was precisely their limited opportunities to develop private interests that Plato in particular so admired.

Aristotle acknowledged that such forms of citizenship were possible only in small states. That was important not just so everyone could have a turn at ruling and to keep the tasks of government sufficiently simple as to be manageable without a professional bureaucracy or political class, but also because it was only in smaller settings that the requisite civic virtues were likely to be fostered. Although the Athenians probably invented the idea of taking a vote to settle disagreements, unanimity was the ideal and most issues were settled by consensus—if need be following extended debate. Aristotle surmised that such concord or *homonoia* depended on a form of civic friendship among citizens that was likely only in tightly knit communities. Citizens must know each other, share values, and have common interests. Only then will they be able to agree on what qualities are best for given offices and select the right people for them, harmoniously resolve disputed rights, and adopt collective policies unanimously. Even so, agreement rested on citizens possessing a sense of justice, being temperate by exercising self-control and avoiding extremes, having a capacity for prudent judge-ment, being motivated by patriotism, so they put the public good above private advantage, and being courageous before danger, especially military threats. In sum, a citizen must belong not 'just to himself' but also to 'the *polis*'.

Though the Greek model of citizenship was the privilege of a minority, it provided a considerable degree of popular control over government. True, the Assembly and Council tended to be dominated by the high born and wealthy, while Aristotle's ideal of concord was often far from the reality, at least in Athens. There were persistent tensions between different classes and factions, with disagreements often bitter and personal, ending with the physical removal of opponents through ostracism and even their execution on trumped-up charges of treason. Nonetheless, in a very real sense those people who qualified as citizens did rule, thereby giving us the word democracy from the Greek *dêmokratia* or people (*dêmos*) rule (*kratos*). Unsurprisingly, Greek citizenship has appeared to many later thinkers as the epitome of a true condition of political equality, in which citizens have equal political powers and so must treat each other with equal concern and respect. They have viewed the trend towards delegating political tasks to a professional class of politicians and public administrators with foreboding, as presaging a loss of political freedom and equality, and lamented the— in their opinion—short-sighted tendency for ever more citizens to desert public service to pursue personal concerns. By contrast, critics of this model of citizenship argue that it was not so much an ideal as hopelessly idealized. In reality, it was doubly oppressive. On the one hand, it rested on the oppression of slaves, women, and other non-citizens. On the other hand, it was oppressive of citizens in demanding they sacrifice their private interests to service of the state. As we saw, the two forms of oppression were linked: citizens could dedicate themselves to public life only because their private lives were serviced by others.

Liberal thinkers have condemned these last features of Greek republican citizenship as potentially despotic (Constant 1819; Berlin 1969). They criticize not just the way non-citizens got treated as less than fully human, but also the demand for the total identification of citizens with the state, with all dissent seen as indicative of self-interest rather than an alternative point of view or valid concern. They castigate such regimes as both repressive and corrupt—not least in diverting all talent away from the private sphere of the economy on which the wealth of a society rests. Ironically, making the public sphere the main avenue of personal advancement did not prevent, but promoted, the abuse of power for private gain. They trace these problems to a flawed view of liberty that falsely links freedom with civic participation. Aristotle's defence of this linkage rested on a perfectionist account of human flourishing, with civic involvement a means to human self-realization, whereby individual and collective autonomy can be reconciled by subsuming private interests under the public interest. Many liberals reject such 'positive' conceptions of liberty as suggesting that human freedom lies in the pursuit of particular ends rather than in being free from interference to pursue one's personal good in one's own way. They claim freedom of this latter sort merely requires a just constitutional regime that limits the power of government to maximizing freedom from mutual interference and has no intrinsic link with democracy.

Both republican and imperial Rome offer important contrasts in these respects. The Roman republican model of citizenship is sometimes collapsed into the Greek model. But, while there are some similarities, there are also striking differences. Though classes existed in Greek society, including among those who qualified as citizens, the ideal of citizenship became classless with the aspiration to 'concord' a product of putting class and other private interests to one side. By contrast, the Roman republic was born of class discord and the struggle of the plebeians to obtain rights against the patricians. For the theorists of the Roman model—Cicero (44 BC), the historians of the Roman republic and, drawing on them, Machiavelli (1513–17)—this ongoing class conflict gave politics and citizenship a much more instrumental character than the Greek model theorized by Aristotle. Roman citizens never possessed anything like the political influence of their Athenian counterparts. Despite the creation of Tribunes of the People, elected by a Plebeian Council, true power rested with the Senate. While entry to the Senate ceased to depend on rank around 400 BC, since it was composed instead of the popularly elected magistrates, it was dominated by the patricians— especially among the higher magistracy, particularly the Consuls who formed the executive. The slogan *Senatus Populusque Romanus* ('The Senate and the Roman People', frequently abbreviated to SPQR) suggested a partnership between the Senate and the people within the popular assemblies. In reality, Senate and people were always in tension, with the influence of the plebeians waxing and waning depending on their importance as support for different factions among the patricians.

Applying these ideas to Renaissance Florence, Machiavelli argued the Roman experience showed how the selfish interests of the aristocracy and the people could be restrained only if each could counter the other. The republic institutionalized such mutual restraint by ensuring no person or institution could exercise power except in combination with at least one other person or institution, so both could check and balance each other. The need to divide power in this way was elaborated by later republican theorists. It was a key feature of the city states of Renaissance Italy, especially Florence and Venice, which inspired Machiavelli's writings on the subject, and informed the constitutional debates of the English Civil War of the seventeenth century and the political arrangements of the Dutch republic into the eighteenth century. In the work of the American *Federalists*, especially Madison, the division of powers became a central element of the US Constitution (Hamilton, Madison, and Jay 1787–8).

Underlying this account was a distinctively realist view of citizenship, which would be more easily adaptable to modern democratic politics than the Greek view. Instead of viewing the private interest and the public interest as diametrically opposed, so that all elements of the first had to be removed from politics, the public interest emerged from the clash and balancing of private interests. Consequently, citizens had self-interested reasons to participate because they could ensure only that their concerns figured in any collective decisions so long as they took part and were counted. Philip Pettit (1997) and Quentin Skinner (1998) have argued that the neo-Roman version of republicanism rejects the 'positive', Aristotelian view of liberty as self-mastery for a 'negative' account of freedom as the absence of domination or mastery by another. Citizens need not identify their will with that of the polity; merely seek to ensure that government and the laws address the interests of all in an equitable manner through being obliged to 'hear the other side'. This argument also differs from the liberal notion of liberty as freedom from interference in suggesting both that it is the capacity for arbitrary interference rather than interference *per se* that limits freedom, and in stressing that freedom is a civic rather than a natural condition. Liberty results from a political system where none is the master of others because all have an equal influence over how public policies are framed and implemented.

LEGAL CITIZENSHIP

As the Roman Republic became overlaid by the Empire, the link between citizenship and private interests underwent a dramatic change. Eligibility for Roman citizenship was at first similar to the criteria for Greek citizenship—citizens had to be native free men who were the legitimate sons of other native free men. As Rome expanded— initially within Italy, then over the rest of Europe and finally into Africa and Asia—two important innovations came about. First, the populations of conquered territories were given a version of Roman citizenship while being allowed to retain their own forms of government, including whatever citizenship status they offered. Second, the version of Roman citizenship given was of a legal rather than a political kind—*civitas sine suffragio* or 'citizenship without the vote'. So, the Empire allowed dual citizenship, though it reduced Roman citizenship to a legal status. As a result, the legal and political communities pulled apart. The scope of law went beyond political borders and did not need to be co-extensive with a given territorial unit. To cite the famous case of St Paul— on arrest in Palestine, he proudly declared himself 'a Jew of Tarsus, a city in Cilicia, a citizen of no mean city'. But, not being in Tarsus, it was his additional status as a Roman citizen that allowed him to claim rights against arbitrary punishment, thereby escaping a whipping, and to ask for trial in Rome.

According to the Aristotelian ideal, political citizenship had depended on being freed from the burdens of economic and social life—in order both to participate and to ensure that public rather than private interests were the object of concern. By contrast, legal citizenship has private interests and their protection at its heart. Within Roman law, legal status belonged to the owners of property and, by extension, their possessions. Since these included slaves, a free person was one who owned himself. So conceived, as in many respects it remains to this day, law was about how we could use ourselves and our things and those of others, and the use they may make of us and our things. As the example of St Paul shows, the resulting privileges and immunities, including the right to sue and be sued in given courts, were far from trivial. However, that the rule of law can be detached from the rule of persons, in that those subject to it do not have to be involved in either its making or its administration, creates disadvantages as well as advantages. The advantage is that the legal community can, as we saw, encompass a number of political communities and hold their rulers and officers to account, thereby limiting their discretion to act against the law. Law can be universal in scope and extent, enabling millions of dispersed individuals to pursue their private interests by engaging and exchanging with each other across space and, through such legal acts as bequests, through time, without any direct contact. The disadvantage lies in these same citizens becoming the imperial subjects of the law's empire, who are ruled by it rather than ruling themselves. Yet the rule of law is only ever rule through law by some person or persons. Law can have many sources and enforcers, and different laws and legal systems will apply to different groups of persons and have differing costs and benefits for each of them. If law's empire depends on an emperor, then the danger is that law becomes a means for imperial rule rather than rule of and for the public.

Of course, a tradition quickly emerged that identified the source of law beyond the will of any human agent or agency, seeking it instead in nature, God's will, or reason. These arguments offer different intellectual constructions of what they claim to be the fundamental law of all human associations. Such law supposedly operates as a superior or higher law, which binds all political rulers—whether an absolute monarch or the people themselves—and trumps whatever laws they may pass. These depictions of fundamental law proved tremendously influential in international law, especially human rights law, and fed into cosmopolitan conceptions of citizenship, as we shall see. A natural affinity also exists between this account and the liberal view of liberty as non-interference and its deployment in defence of market institutions. These liberal versions developed out of attempts to square the circle by bringing together the rule of law and the rule of citizens within the ideal of a social contract. Emerging in the seventeenth and eighteenth centuries as an account of the justification and limits of the powers of the monarch within a state, it takes as its starting point the equal status of human beings as proprietors of themselves and co-possessors of the world. The underlying intuition is that a just political and legal sovereign power would be one that free and equal individuals could be expected unanimously to consent to. Such consent, the theory goes, would only be given to a power that offers fair and equitable mechanisms, and rules for securing their common interest to be able to pursue their own good in their own way, freeing them from the uncertainties of mutual harm without itself becoming a source of harm to them. In other words, it tries to unite the political ideal of the equality of virtuous citizens, who rule and are ruled in turn so as to uphold the public interest, with the legal ideal of individuals as rights bearers, who pursue their private interests protected by the rule of law. This argument does not necessarily rest on any actual consent by citizens to generate their obligation to obey a just sovereign. For many theorists in this tradition, it is sufficient that the political and legal system is so organized that we could imagine all citizens *ought* hypothetically to consent to it—or, at least, have no compelling reason not to do so. The idea of a contract is simply a device for thinking about which political and legal arrangements and principles treat people equitably and justly.

As with theories of God-given or natural law, the terms of the contract are likely to be viewed differently by different theorists, according to the moral and empirical presuppositions they bring to bear in their characterizations of human nature and the causal structure of social relations. For example, the social-contract theories of the seventeenth-century English philosophers Thomas Hobbes (1651) and John Locke (1690) portray quite different accounts of human nature and social relations, producing divergent views of what we would consent to. For Hobbes, human beings were apt to pursue their self-interest aggressively and distrust others. Consequently, they were inclined to consent to any sovereign power capable of offering them security against the risks individuals posed to each other. By contrast, Locke had a much more benign view of human nature and thought Hobbes underestimated the degree to which state power might be an even greater danger to individual liberty than other individuals. He hypothesized that people need consent only to a limited form of government. Such differences as those between Hobbes and Locke indicate that there are liable to be as many views of 'higher law' as there are theorists of it. The disagreements among theorists mirror those between citizens and return us once more to the dilemma that the source of the rule of law will always lie within the rule of persons: what the rule of law is thought to mean and how that law is interpreted and applied always lies with people. For Jean-Jacques Rousseau (1762), in what many see as an elegy for republican citizenship, this circumstance meant a social contract had to be permanently enacted among the citizens of a *polis*. Yet, like his ancient Roman and Greek predecessors, Rousseau found it hard to conceive how such a system could be possible outside a *polis* and, here closer to the Greek than the Roman view, a renunciation of private interests unlikely in commercial societies.

Liberal Democratic Citizenship: Uniting Republican and Legal Citizenship?

The problem of creating a modern republic confronted the two great revolutions that inaugurated the modern democratic era—the American Revolution of 1776 and the French Revolution of 1789. Both attempted to resolve it by seeing their constitutional settlements as instances of an actual contract between citizens. So, the putative authors of the American Constitution are 'We the People of the United States', while the French Declaration of the Rights of Man and the Citizen declares 'the source of all sovereignty lies essentially in the Nation'. However, these formulas preserve a dualism between the 'public' political citizen, who acts as a collective agent—the 'people' or the 'nation'— and the private, 'legal' citizen, who is the subject of the law and the possessor of 'natural' rights to liberty, property, and the pursuit of happiness. Civic virtue gets assigned to a single constitutional moment and enshrined in the institutions that popular act creates, leaving selfish citizens to pursue their personal interests under the law. Meanwhile, a tension between the two models remains. It is doubtful that even the most well-designed institutions and laws can economize too much on the virtues of citizens, or that citizens feel they are 'theirs', if—the founding moment apart—they cannot actively participate in shaping them.

  The liberal democratic regimes that emerged during the nineteenth and twentieth centuries struggled with this tension, mixing in their different ways elements of both the republican and the legal forms of citizenship. Lying midway between a city state and an empire, the nation state emerged as their most viable alternative—able to combine certain key advantages while avoiding their disadvantages. If the *polis* was too small to survive the military encroachments of empires, the empire was too large to allow for meaningful political participation. The nation state had sufficient size to sustain both a complex economic infrastructure and an army, while being not so large to make a credible—if less participatory—form of democracy impossible. As a result, it became subject to pressures to create a form of citizenship that could successfully integrate popular and legal rule by linking political participation and rights with membership of a national democratic political community.

The sociologists T. H. Marshall (1950) and Stein Rokkan (1974) established what has become the standard narrative of the evolution of modern democratic citizenship. They saw citizenship as the product of the interrelated processes of state building, the emergence of commercial and industrial society, and the construction of a national consciousness, with all three driven forward in various ways by class struggle and war. The net effect of these three processes was to create a 'people', who were entitled to be treated as equals before the law and possessed equal rights to buy and sell goods, services, and labour; whose interests were overseen by a sovereign political authority; and who shared a national identity that shaped their allegiance to each other and to their state. In a brilliant essay, Marshall argued there had been three periods in the historical evolution of citizenship as a given group fought to attain equal status as a full member of the community. The first period, from the seventeenth to the mid-nineteenth centuries, saw the consolidation of the civil rights needed to engage in a range of social and economic activities, from the freedoms to own property and exchange goods, to liberty of thought and conscience. The second period, from the end of the eighteenth century to the start of the twentieth, coincided with the gaining of political rights to vote and stand for election. The third period, from the end of the nineteenth century to the mid-twentieth, involved the creation of social rights that gave citizens 'the right to share to the full in the social heritage and to live the life of a civilised being according to the standards prevailing in society'.

Though modelled on Britain, Marshall's account reflects not just the new liberal and social-democratic consensus behind a welfare state fashioned by such British thinkers as T. H. Green, L. T. Hobhouse, and W. H. Beveridge, but also similar intellectual and political movements elsewhere, like the Solidarists in France and progressives in the United States (Kloppenberg 1986; Bellamy 1992). Nevertheless, his argument has attracted considerable criticism. He is said to overlook the role external pressures played in promoting rights (Mann 1987), while the three sets of rights neither arose in quite the order or periods that he mentions, nor proved quite as complementary as he assumed. Thus, social rights emerged in most countries before rather than after political rights—often being offered by the politically dominant class in the hope of damping down demands for political rights. Social and civil rights can also clash, as with the right to property (Bellamy, Castiglione, and Santoro 2004). However, these corrections to the details of his argument are perfectly compatible with its underlying logic, whereby the development of legal rights stems from a subordinate group employing formal and informal political strategies to win concessions from those with power in their fight to be treated with equal concern and respect.

Writing in the 1950s, when the economies of West European countries were in the ascendant and welfare spending expanding, it was natural for Marshall to view social rights as the culmination of the struggle for an ever more inclusive and egalitarian form of citizenship. Needless to say, subsequent events have tended to challenge that optimistic conclusion. It is not just that many aspects of the post-war welfare settlements Marshall celebrated got eroded during the economic downturn and restructuring of the 1970s, 1980s, and 1990s. Many of the economic and social assumptions on which this settlement rested have also been criticized by those seeking further to expand rather than to curtail citizenship (King and Waldron 1988). Environmentalists have attacked the emphasis on increasing economic production (Dobson 2003), feminists its continued overlooking of the subordinate role of women in the labour market (Lister 2003), multiculturalists the failure even to mention issues of ethnicity (Kymlicka 1995), cosmopolitans its focus on the nation state (Benhabib 2004), and so on. Again, these observations do not necessarily contradict the main thrust of his argument. They merely indicate how each attempt to realize a form of equal citizenship generates its own unanticipated shortcomings and problems—producing new struggles over the way the political community, rights, and participation are defined.

COSMOPOLITAN CITIZENSHIP?

In different ways, the proliferation of new forms of citizenship—Green, feminist, multicultural—reflect the various challenges confronting nation states at the start of the twenty-first century. On the one hand, globalization has weakened the capacity of states to provide citizens with the basic goods of economic well-being and security from a range of military, health, environmental, and other threats. It has also heightened inter-state mobility, creating unprecedented levels of migration, and intensified the sense of responsibility for the impacts states have on each other—particularly of the rich on the poor. On the other hand, within states the discriminatory character of the standard criteria for citizenship have been criticized not just by feminists, the disabled, and ethnic minorities, but also by minority nations, indigenous peoples, and religious and cultural minorities seeking various forms of group rights and self-government.

The first challenge has led to calls for cosmopolitan citizenship. According to a doctrine going back to the ancient world and associated particularly with the Roman stoics, a cosmopolitan is literally a 'citizen of the world' or *kosmopolitês*. The Greek derivation of this term suggests that world citizenship implies a world polity. However, few cosmopolitans believe such a concentration of power would be desirable. Instead, following Kant (1795), they see cosmopolitan norms as operating in the context of a federation of free states. They advocate a form of legal citizenship governed by international rights norms, as have developed since the Second World War. Yet, theorists differ greatly as to whether such norms are relatively 'thin', enjoining humanitarian assistance to asylum seekers and aid in the event of natural disasters, the prosecution of crimes against humanity, such as genocide, and respect for each state's right to self-determination, but no significant transfers of resources between states, let alone between individuals across the globe (Miller 2000), or are 'thick', involving treating all borders as morally arbitrary and justifying a weakening and even transcendence of national citizenship so that peoples may move freely and wealth may be redistributed on a global scale (Nussbaum 1996). These disagreements reveal how even a 'thin' legal cosmopolitan citizenship confronts the dilemma of how such laws are to be framed and implemented, and their administrators held accountable without a similarly extensive political power, raising the republican worry that the empire of cosmopolitan law will be but a cover for the imperial rule of certain persons.

Some advocate a federal scheme of global democracy to meet this difficulty (Held 1995). However, these proposals fly in the face of the second challenge. As the European Union—the most developed supranational legal and political system—illustrates, creating a workable public sphere on such a scale faces formidable problems. Linguistic and cultural diversity means that the European peoples have little sense of forming a demos, while the size of the Union means that their votes count for less and provoke complaints that its decision-makers are remote and unaccountable (Bellamy, Castiglione, and Shaw 2006). Indeed, most of the member states confront increasing claims to devolve power to cultural and national minorities. Rather than seeing cosmopolitanism as involving supra- or post-national citizenship and institutions, therefore, it might be better to see it as a means whereby states offer reciprocal rights of recognition to each other and their citizens, collaborate to tackle global problems, and foster the global extension of liberal democratic citizenship rather than making us global citizens. Indeed, in many respects this offers the most appropriate characterization of European citizenship within the EU, which has cemented democratization in Spain, Portugal, Greece, and the former Soviet bloc, and allowed the free movement of citizens between the member states (Bellamy 2008b; Kymlicka 2008). In this way, states remain the context for our exercising republican citizenship and accessing legal citizenship, but we do so in ways that are compatible with the similar exercise of such rights by others across the world (Bellamy 2008a: ch. 4).

REFERENCES

Primary Sources

ARISTOTLE (1988 [335–323 BC]). *The Politics*, ed. S. Everson. Cambridge: Cambridge University Press.

CICERO (1991 [44 BC]). *On Duties*, eds. M. T. Griffin and E. M. Atkins. Cambridge: Cambridge University Press.

CONSTANT, B. (1988 [1819]). 'The Liberty of the Ancients Compared with that of the Moderns', in *Political Writings*, ed. B. Fontana. Cambridge: Cambridge University Press, 308–28.

HAMILTON, A., MADISON, J., and JAY, J. (2003 [1787–8]). *The Federalist*, ed. T. Ball. Cambridge: Cambridge University Press.

HOBBES, T. (1991 [1651]). *Leviathan*, ed. R. Tuck. Cambridge: Cambridge University Press.

KANT, I. (1970 [1795]). 'Perpetual Peace', in *Political Writings*, ed. H. Reiss. Cambridge: Cambridge University Press, 93–130.

LOCKE, J. (1988 [1690]). *Two Treatises of Government*, ed. P. Laslett. Cambridge: Cambridge University Press.

MACHIAVELLI, N. (1970 [1513–17]). *The Discourses*, ed. B Crick. Harmondsworth: Penguin.

MARSHALL, T. H. (1950). *Citizenship and Social Class*. Cambridge: Cambridge University Press.

ROKKAN, S. (1974). 'Dimensions of State Formation and Nation Building', in C. Tilly (ed.), *The Formation of National States in Western Europe*. Princeton: Princeton University Press, 562–600.

ROUSSEAU, J.-J. (1968 [1762]). *The Social Contract*, ed. M. Cranston. Harmondsworth: Penguin.

Secondary Sources

BELLAMY, R. (1992). *Liberalism and Modern Society*. Cambridge: Polity.

BELLAMY, R. (2008*a*). *Citizenship: A Very Short Introduction*. Oxford: Oxford University Press.

BELLAMY, R. (2008*b*). 'Evaluating Union Citizenship: Belonging, Rights and Participation within the EU', *Citizenship Studies*, 12: 597–61.

BELLAMY, R., CASTIGLIONE, D., and SANTORO, E. (2004) (eds). *Lineages of European Citizenship: Rights, Belonging and Citizenship in Eleven Nation-States*. Basingstoke: Palgrave.

BELLAMY, R., CASTIGLIONE, D., and SHAW, J. (2006) (eds). *Making European Citizens: Civic Inclusion in a Transnational Context*. Basingstoke: Palgrave.

BENHABIB, S. (2004). *The Rights of Others: Aliens, Residents and Citizens*. Cambridge: Cambridge University Press.

BERLIN, I. (1969). *Four Essays on Liberty*. Oxford: Oxford University Press.

DOBSON, A. (2003). *Citizenship and the Environment*. Oxford: Oxford University Press.

FINLEY, M. (1983). *Politics in the Ancient World*. Cambridge: Cambridge University Press.

HELD, D. (1995). *Democracy and the Global Order*. Cambridge: Polity.

KING, D., and WALDRON, J. (1988). 'Citizenship, Social Citizenship and the Defence of Welfare Provision', *British Journal of Political Science*, 18: 415–43.

KLOPPENBERG, J. T. (1986). *Uncertain Victory: Social Democracy and Progressivism in European and American Thought 1870–1920*. Oxford: Oxford University Press.

KYMLICKA, W. (1995). *Multicultural Citizenship*. Oxford: Clarendon Press.

KYMLICKA, W. (2008). 'Liberal Nationalism and Cosmopolitan Justice', in S. Benhabib, *Another Cosmopolitanism*, (ed.) R Post. Oxford: Oxford University Press, 128–44.

LISTER, R. (2003). *Citizenship: Feminist Perspectives*, 2nd edn. Basingstoke: Palgrave.

MANN, M. (1987). 'Ruling Strategies and Citizenship', *Sociology*, 21: 339–54.

MILLER, D. (2000). *Citizenship and National Identity*. Cambridge: Polity.

Nussbaum, M. (1996). 'Patriotism and Cosmopolitanism', in J. Cohen (ed.), *For Love of Country*. Boston: Beacon Press, 3–17.

Pettit, P. (1997). *Republicanism: A Theory of Freedom and Government*. Oxford: Clarendon Press.

Pocock, J. G. A. (1995). 'The Ideal of Citizenship since Classical Times', in R. Beiner (ed.), *Theorizing Citizenship*. New York: SUNY, 29–52.

Skinner, Q. (1998). *Liberty before Liberalism*. Cambridge: Cambridge University Press.

Walzer, M. (1989). 'Citizenship', in T. Ball, J. Farr, and R. L. Hanson, *Political Innovation and Conceptual Change*. Cambridge: Cambridge University Press, 211–19.

CHAPTER 35

PROPERTY

DAVID SCHMIDTZ

THE RIGHT TO EXCLUDE

WORKING within a Lockean tradition, William Blackstone (1765) characterized property as the "sole and despotic dominion which one man claims and exercises over the external things of the world, in total exclusion of the right of any other individual in the universe" (1979: 2). In practice, though, property rights in the Anglo-American tradition have always been hedged with restrictions. The dominion to which Blackstone refers is limited by easements, covenants, nuisance laws, zoning laws, regulatory statutes, and more generally by the public interest.

Wesley Hohfeld (1913) distinguished between rights and liberties. I am at liberty to use P just in case my using P is not prohibited. I have a right to P just in case my using P is not prohibited, plus I have the additional liberty of being able to prohibit others from using P. That is to say, the difference between a mere liberty and a full-blooded property right is that, with the latter, there is an owner who holds a right to exclude other would-be users.

Today, the term "property rights" generally is understood to refer to a bundle of rights that could include rights to sell, lend, bequeath, use as collateral, or even destroy. (John Lewis is generally regarded as the first person to use the "bundle of sticks" metaphor, in 1888.) The fact remains, though, that at the heart of any property right is a right to say no: a right to exclude non-owners. In other words, a right to exclude is not just one stick in a bundle. Rather, property is a tree. Other sticks are branches; the right to exclude is the trunk.

This is not merely a stipulation, because, unless an owner has a right to say no, the other sticks are reduced to mere liberties rather than genuine rights. Thus, I could be the owner of a bicycle in some meaningful sense, even if for some reason I have no right to lend it to my friend. By contrast, if I have no right to forbid you to lend it to your friend, then I am not the bicycle's owner in any normal sense. The tree would be missing its trunk, not just one of its branches.

This does not settle what, if anything, can *justify* our claiming a right to exclude, but it does clarify the topic. When we ask about *owning* a bicycle as distinct from merely being at liberty to use it, we are asking first and foremost about a right to exclude.

THE POINT OF PROPERTY

When are we justified in claiming a right to exclude? There are legal questions, of course, but there are also moral questions about what the law *ought* to be. Claims about natural rights and natural law concern what legal rights ought to be, not what legal rights happen to be.

Dutch thinker, Hugo Grotius (1625) secularized the idea of natural law. In his hands, natural-law theory became a naturalistic inquiry into the question of what social arrangements were most conducive to the betterment of humankind, given fundamental facts about human nature. Grotius argued that there would be laws of nature, dictated by requirements of human nature, even if (perish the thought) there were no deity. Human societies almost invariably create property as a legal category, so property rights are indeed artifacts in that sense, yet the very fact that humans create (and generally respect) property is part of our natures. Moreover, as Carol Rose puts it, "property is designed to *do* something, and what it is supposed to do is to tap individual energies in order to make us all more prosperous" (Rose 1994: 2). People create property rights for a purpose, and in a given time and place there will always be a fact of the matter about whether they work.

John Locke (1690), following Grotius, argued that God gave the world to humankind in common for the betterment of humankind, and therefore intended that people have the right to do what they need to do to put the earth to work. Individual persons own their own selves. To be sure, persons are God's property, but, as against other humans, no one but the individual alone holds the right to say yes or no regarding how his or her body is to be put to work. The premise of self-ownership is controversial, but no alternative is less controversial. (It may be controversial to say a person has a right to say no to a proposal to use her body in a certain way, but it is more controversial to say she does not.)

This right to choose how to put our bodies to work would be useless in that original state, and God would be leaving us to starve, unless we were at liberty to make a living by laboring upon otherwise unowned objects in the world. We normally are not at liberty to seize what already belongs to someone else—seizing what belongs to someone else normally does not contribute to the betterment of humankind—but when a resource is unowned, we can come to own it by mixing our labor with it in such a way as to make it more useful. Thus, we acquire a crop by virtue of being the ones who planted and harvested it, and we acquire the land underneath the crop by virtue of being the ones who made that land ten, a hundred, or a thousand times more productive than it had been in its unappropriated wild condition.

Locke was not envisioning a world where little or no wild land remained for latecomers, but implicitly he argued that latecomers could *afford* to respect the claims of those who had arrived first. Indeed, what Locke would have seen today is how much *better* it is to arrive late, after all the appropriating is done. We latecomers benefit from generations of people already having done the hard work of making the land and the overall economy hundreds of times more productive than it was during the age of first appropriation, more than doubling life expectancy in the process (Schmidtz 2008).

John Locke thus extended the idea of self-ownership to include the external resources that people could make part of themselves, in effect, by mixing their labor with them. The extension is controversial, but the subtle essence of it is not. The subtle idea is that there is a question about who has the least obstructed claim to a resource. So, if we look at a piece of land that Bob alone worked on and improved (cleared, planted, and so on), then here is a fact that matters to anyone who cares about persons: only Bob can reap the fruits of the land that Bob improved without having to seize the fruits of another person's labor.

The point is not that Bob has some metaphysically extraordinary connection to that piece of land. The idea is that Bob has a *bit* of a connection, and no one else can establish a comparable connection without at the same time disregarding Bob's prior claim. The first labor-mixing thus raises the bar on what it takes to justify subsequent acts of taking possession. (Inevitably, there will be a subsequent owner, but legitimizing transfer and subsequent ownership usually involves getting consent from the previous owner. The sort of labor-mixing that would help to justify *first* appropriation would be beside the point.)

Traffic Management

To Carol Rose (1994), a fence is a *statement*—announcing to the world that you will defend what is inside, and asking people to curb themselves so you will not need to, thereby saving everyone a lot of trouble.

The whole point of a fence is to *get in the way*, which sounds hard to justify. But here is another way to conceive of property: property rights are like traffic lights. Traffic lghts move traffic not so much by turning green as by turning red. Without traffic lights, we all in effect have a green light, and the result is gridlock. By contrast, a system where we face in turn red and green lights is a system that keeps us moving. It forces us to stop from time to time, but we all gain in terms of our ability to get where we want to go, because we develop mutual expectations that enable us to get where we want to go, uneventfully. Red lights can frustrate, but the game they create for us is positive-sum. We all get where we are going more quickly, more safely, and more predictably, in virtue of knowing what to expect from each other. (As Locke might have argued, even "pedestrians" are better off in an effective system of *commercial* traffic, because the trucking and bartering that constitutes commercial traffic is what enables 20-year-old have-nots eventually to become 40-year-old haves.)

We do not want *lots* of rights for the same reason that we would not want to face red lights every fifty feet. Getting our traffic management system right is a matter of getting the most compact set of lights that does the job of enabling motorists to know what to expect from each other, and thereby get from point A to point B with minimal delay.

Traffic lights hardly do anything. They sit there, blinking (as Jason Brennan puts it in Schmidtz and Brennan 2010). Yet, without them, we are not as good at knowing what to expect, and consequently not as good at getting where we need to go while staying out of each other's way. The same could be said of property conventions.

How to Respect the Right to Exclude

Calabresi and Melamed (1972) distinguish three ways of respecting property. In normal cases, property is protected by a *property rule*, meaning no one may use it without the owner's permission. In other circumstances, P is protected by a *liability rule*, meaning no one may use it without compensating the owner. In a third case, P is protected by an *inalienability rule*, meaning no one may use P even with the owner's permission.

The fundamental rationale for liability rules is that sometimes it costs too much, or is impossible, to get consent, and sometimes the contemplated use is compellingly important. Further, every time we pull out of a driveway, there is some risk that our plans will go awry and we will end up accidentally damaging someone's property. Where a property rule would require us to get advance permission from every property owner against whom we run the risk of accidental trespass, a liability rule requires instead that we compensate owners after the fact if we should accidentally damage their property.

The analogous rationale for an inalienability rule is that there are forms of property so fundamental that we would cease fully to be persons if we were, for example, to sell them. We may, say, regard my kidney or my vote as my property, and yet deny that this gives me any right to sell such things. In this respect, we would then be treating my right as inalienable.

The takings clause of the Fifth Amendment of the US Constitution specifies that public property may not be taken for public use unless just compensation is paid. The clause does not explicitly affirm the public's right to seize private property for public use, although that is the implication. We can see the takings clause, then, as affirming that, even when a compelling public interest precludes treating a private property right as protected by a property rule, the public must still respect the right to the extent of treating it as protected by a liability rule.

As a rule, the protection that liability rules afford is not good enough. Here is the problem. Suppose someone steals your car, then brings it back undamaged with the gas tank full. Lack of damages notwithstanding, the fact remains that your rights were violated in a serious way. For property rights to do what they are supposed to do, the right to exclude needs to have "teeth," which is to say it needs to be protected by property rules, not liability rules, and the penalty for *intentional* trespass must be real, not nominal. Thus, in 1997, Judge Bablitch of the Supreme Court of Wisconsin, in the case of *Jacque* v. *Steenberg Homes Inc.*, reaffirmed the centrality of property rule protection to a properly functioning system of property. In that case, Steenberg intentionally crossed Jacque's property to deliver a motor home to Jacque's neighbor, despite Jacque having denied Steenberg's request for permission. A lower court had awarded Jacque $1 in compensatory damages (because there had not been any significant damage) and denied any punitive damages on the ground that merely nominal damages could not sustain substantial punitive damages. Judge Bablitch ruled that this would have been the correct ruling in a case of *accidental* trespass, but in a case of *intentional* trespass, punitive damages themselves must be substantial enough to deter.

Common Law

Philosophy is part of what drives the evolution of Anglo-American conceptions of property, but the history of property is not only a history of ideas. Philosopher David Hume (in his *History of England* (1778)) wrote that, so long as the property system was as precarious as it was in the Middle Ages, there could be little industry. To Hume, the so-called Dark Ages were as dark as they were because people were not free. In particular, they were not free to choose how to make a living. Moreover, they lacked secure title to the products of their labor.

What changed? Hume treats as of singular importance the rediscovery of Justinian's Pandects in Amalfi, Italy, in 1130 (Hume 1983: bk II, 520). The Pandects were a digest of state of the art Roman civil law, commissioned by Emperor Justinian, and produced by the day's leading legal scholars (c.530). Within ten years, lectures on this newly discovered civil law were being given at Oxford. As law and legal thinking evolved, there emerged a class of independent jurists whose job was to apply known and settled laws. This is *common* law—that is, evolving judge-made law. English King Henry II in the late 1100s extended this evolving body of judicial precedent, making its scope national rather than local. Much of the history of property law's evolution in the Anglo-American world is thus a history of judge-made legal precedent. *Jacque* v. *Steenberg Homes* is an example.

The remainder of this chapter discusses several other legal cases illustrating the sorts of principles that drive the evolution of the common law of property.

EXTERNALITIES

....

Any given transaction has costs and benefits. I sell you a widget for $1.50. The benefit of the transaction to me is $1.50, minus what it cost me to bring that widget to market. Presumably we are both better off, because we traded by consent. I manufactured the widget for, let us say, 79 cents, so I am better off. You use your new widget to manufacture a gizmo that you can sell for a profit of $3.14, so you too are better off.

What can go wrong? Suppose you use your new widget at 4 a.m. in a way that makes an ear-splitting noise, and your neighbors lose sleep. Thus, a transaction can have costs or benefits to parties other than the buyer and seller. An *external* cost is a cost imposed on bystanders. An external benefit is a benefit that falls on bystanders.

When you make that horrible noise with the widget I sold you, neighbors are worse off. You and I are better off, but bystanders are worse off, which makes it unclear whether society as a whole is gaining or losing.

But now consider a different case. Suppose you do not make any noise with the widget, but you do make lots of gizmos, and offer them for sale at $1.99 rather than what had been their going rate of $3.14. As a result, people who had been selling gizmos for $3.14 are worse off. Both cases are cases in which innocent bystanders are made worse off, but the second case is legitimate somehow. Being awoken in the middle of the night by an ear-splitting widget noise is arguably a form of trespass, but in the second case, my customers are not my property, and your "stealing" a customer from me is not stealing so much as simply outperforming me and thus taking business from me that never was mine by right. From a social perspective, when a transaction affects the supply and demand for gizmos, and the price of gizmos changes in response, this is a good thing for the neighborhood, not a bad thing. Falling gizmo prices reflect the fact that supply increased relative to demand, and therefore from the community's perspective there is less reason for any particular manufacturer to be making gizmos. So, falling price induces the appropriate response. Externalities that affect people's welfare only by affecting prices are called *pecuniary* externalities, and from a social perspective they are beneficial, because changing prices induce buyers and sellers to adjust their behavior in ways that benefit customers.

In 1707, the case of *Keeble* v. *Hickeringill* came before the Queen's Bench of England. Keeble was a farmer who had set up a system of decoys to lure waterfowl into traps. He would then sell the captured birds. His neighbor, Hickeringill, began to fire guns into the air so as to frighten the birds away and interfere with Keeble's business. Keeble filed suit. Judge Holt ruled in favor of Keeble. Holt reasoned that Keeble was minding his own legitimate business and Hickeringill had no right to interfere. Holt refers to another case where a defendant interfered with a neighbor's school *by starting a better school*. The defendant won in that case, because the students were not the plaintiff's property. The plaintiff had no right to be protected against the defendant "stealing" the students by offering the students a better alternative. Holt next considered a hypothetical situation where a defendant interferes with a neighbor's school by firing guns into the air and frightening the students away. That would be an intentional trespass, because the defendant would be aiming to sabotage the plaintiff's product, not to enhance the defendant's product. Judge Holt drew a distinction between genuine and merely pecuniary externalities (centuries before the technical terms were coined), refining the property system so as to limit genuine externalities while leaving intact the liberty to compete in the marketplace, thereby making it easier for neighbors to live, and make a living, together.

Sometimes externalities are not worth eliminating. When people live miles apart, we do not bother to develop laws regulating shooting of guns into air. As population density rises, a cost becomes worth internalizing at some point. Likewise, there is an external cost to driving, but we do not want people to stop driving. We just want to limit the cost to reasonable levels. *Eliminating* external costs is not the aim. It will always be part of the idea of being a good neighbor that it is worth living among neighbors despite minor irritations, and good neighbors take reasonable steps to tread lightly on their neighbors' normal sensibilities. There is no perfect substitute for being considerate. No system of law will enable us to be good neighbors just by obeying the law.

POSSESSION

In the case of *Armory* v. *Delamirie* (1722), a chimney sweep discovers a ring, pockets it, then takes it to an appraiser. The appraiser pockets the jewel that had been in the ring. The chimney sweep sues the appraiser for the return of the ring. The court rules that the question is not who is the true rightful owner, but whether there has been a wrongful transfer from the plaintiff to the defendant. The court determines that there has indeed been a wrongful transfer and rules that it must be undone. This was among the first cases to establish possession as marking presumptive ownership. The chimney sweep was not the ring's rightful owner, but his simply possessing the ring conferred a right to maintain possession against those who would take it without consent.

A person has to feel safe in going to the market and engaging the services of others in mutually beneficial commerce. If a jeweler has a right to take your stuff, then you will not feel comfortable taking your stuff to a jeweler. One of the main purposes of law in general and property law in particular is to make people feel safe in going to market to truck and barter. If property rights are sufficiently secure, then one need not conceal one's valuables; on the contrary, one can *flaunt* their value, openly advertising what one has for sale, thereby making it easier for the whole community to do business.

POSITIVE-SUM GAMES

In 1880, in the case of *Ghen* v. *Rich*, the court learns that Ghen fired a bomb lance into a fin-back whale. The dead whale sank, then washed up on the coast of Massachusetts, where it was found by Ellis. Ellis sold the carcass to Rich, who extracted oil from the blubber. Hearing of this, Ghen filed a claim for the value of the oil extracted. Ghen's case rested on the custom in the whaling community of treating the person who first harpooned a whale as establishing possession and thus ownership. In 1881, Judge Nelson of the Massachusetts District Court ruled in favor of Ghen, crediting whalers for developing norms that facilitate the whaling trade. Whaling ports were concentrated, close-knit communities. Norms were propagated there: simple, transparent norms that invested property rights in whalers who were good at producing what the larger community needed whalers to produce.

Judge Nelson acknowledged that whether an act counts as establishing possession and thus presumptive ownership is a matter of convention. In some whaling communities, the "iron holds the whale," meaning that fatally harpooning a whale is enough to establish possession. In whaling communities where the most commercially valuable whales are too dangerous or too difficult to attach to one's boat, this is all that reasonably can be asked. (This was the rule applying to the fin-back, which is why the first possessor was Ghen, not Ellis.) In other whaling communities, though, where the prized whales are slow and docile, the mark of first possession is more stringent. In those communities, the rule is "fast fish, loose fish," meaning one has not established possession until the whale is fastened to the boat (see Ellickson 1991).

Carol Rose identifies two overarching principles for defining rules of possession. First, establishing possession should involve doing something unambiguous, something that notifies the world of what one is claiming. Second, establishing possession by the rules should involve useful labor, something that adds to the value of what one is claiming.

TRANSACTION COSTS

In *Hinman* v. *Pacific Air Transport* (1936), a landowner sues an airline for trespass, asserting a right to stop airlines from crossing over his property. The court's predicament: on the one hand, a right to say no is the backbone of a system of property that in turn is the backbone of cooperation among self-owners. On the other hand, much of property's point is to facilitate commercial traffic. Ruling that landowners in effect can veto the air traffic industry is the kind of red light that would gridlock traffic, not facilitate it. The Hinman verdict is explainable in terms of *transaction costs* (costs incurred in concluding a transaction—commissions, time, and money spent on transportation to and from the market, equipment and space rentals, time waiting in line, and so on). The cost of airlines transacting with every landowner for permission to pass over the owner's land would render air traffic out of the question. The ruling was that the right to say no does not extend to the heavens but only so high as a landowner's actual use. Navigation easements subsequently were recognized as allowing federal governments to allocate airspace above 500 feet for transportation purposes.

Justice

Common-law judges need to formulate simple rules, in the spirit of equality before the law, that enable litigants to get on with their lives, knowing how to avoid or minimize future conflict. In *Hinman*, a property system had come to be inadequately specified relative to newly emerging forms of commercial traffic. In a targeted, not overly clever way, Judge Haney made the system a better solution to the particular problem confronting his court. Judge Haney's verdict left us with a system of rights that we could *afford* to take seriously.

The right to say no is an institutional structure that facilitates community by facilitating commerce in the broadest sense. The right to say no safeguards a right to come to the market and contribute to the community, thereby promoting trade, and thereby promoting progress. When people have a right to say no, and to withdraw, then they can afford *not to withdraw*. They can afford to trust each other. That is, they can afford to live in close proximity and to produce, trade, and prosper, without fear.

By the same token, the right to say no is not a weapon of mass destruction. It is a device whose purpose is to facilitate commerce, not prevent commerce, so it must not put people in a position to gridlock the system. The right to say no is meant to be a right to decline to be involved in a transaction, not a right to forbid people in general to transact. In *Hinman*, the plaintiff's interpretation of his right to say no implied a right to gridlock airlines, so the edges of the right to say no had to be clarified.

That is to say, property's purpose as a means of production (how the law has to evolve in order to continue to serve its purpose) has to condition the contours of justice, not the other way around. Therefore, taking justice seriously has to involve treating justice as something that comes second, not first, because taking justice seriously has to involve treating justice as something a society can afford to take seriously. In the *Hinman* case, for example, whether justice recognized a right to say no that extends to heaven had everything to do with whether such extension was a viable way of managing the commercial traffic of a peaceful and productive community of sovereign, individual equals (see Schmidtz 2010).

Zoning

The case for zoning begins with a problem of internalizing externalities, combined with a conjecture that a given externality problem cannot be solved because the cost of transacting is too high. Neighborhood associations create covenants forbidding industrial development. Sometimes, though, there are holdouts whose interests lie in a different direction, and who want to retain the option of selling their land to industrial concerns. Thus, neighborhoods often seek to reserve to themselves a right—as neighborhoods—to say no to such sales. *Euclid* v. *Ambler Realty* (1926) is the basis of all subsequent zoning in the United States. In 1922, the village of Euclid, a suburb of Cleveland, adopted a comprehensive zoning plan. In the middle of this village, though, was a large tract of land owned by Ambler Realty. Ambler sued Euclid, alleging that the zoning plan robbed Ambler of the greatest value of its land, because the parcel was in the immediate vicinity of a railroad that made it better suited for industrial than residential use.

A district judge found the zoning ordinance unconstitutional. The Fourteenth Amendment says, in part, that "no State shall make or enforce any law which shall abridge the privileges or immunities of citizens of the United States; nor shall any State deprive any person of life, liberty, or property, without due process of law; nor deny to any person within its jurisdiction the equal protection of the laws." The US Supreme Court overturned this ruling. There was a concern that zoning had been used to create neighborhoods barring minorities, immigrants, and people with criminal records. Everyone knew that one of zoning's uses was to protect residents from renters and low-income groups by creating single-family residential zones, minimum acreage lot requirements, and so on. Still, the court saw no such concerns in play in *Euclid*. So, the court decided (with three dissenting votes) that their job was to rule on the merits of the case rather than on the general principle, acknowledging that zoning *could* be used as a tool of oppression but holding that it was not being abused in the case in hand. If and when neighborhoods abused the option of zoning, they could and would be sued, and future courts would then define and refine zoning's legitimate limits.

EQUALITY BEFORE THE LAW

In 1911, thirty of the thirty-nine property owners in a St Louis neighborhood signed a covenant barring the sale of their parcels to non-whites. In 1945, the owner of one such parcel sold to Shelley, an African-American family. Neighbors sued to prevent Shelley from taking possession. Dodging the moral issue, the trial court dismissed the suit on technical grounds, ruling that the covenant was valid only on condition that all the neighborhood owners sign, and not all had. The Supreme Court of Missouri reversed this decision, arguing that the people who signed the agreement had a right to do so, and their exercising such right violated no provision of the Constitution. Shelley, by now occupying the property, counter-sued, saying the covenant did indeed violate the US Constitution's Fourteenth Amendment, which guarantees to each citizen "equal protection of the laws." The case went to the US Supreme Court, which ruled that private racist covenants are constitutional, but *public enforcement* of such covenants is not. Private covenants do not involve or implicate the state, but public enforcement of private covenants does.

Shelley terminated half a century of effort to segregate via covenant. The idea of covenants is neutral in the abstract, but in practice was used overwhelmingly to exclude African-Americans. *Shelley* signaled that courts would scrutinize actual patterns of discrimination, not merely formalities. The lawyer arguing Shelley's case was Thurgood Marshall, an African-American and future justice of the US Supreme Court, who would go on to argue, in *Brown* v. *Board of Education* (1954), that "separate but equal" is unconstitutional, because there was precious little equality in segregation's results, as put into practice since *Plessy v. Ferguson* (1896).

What we are left with today is a right to enter covenants, exchange easements, and so on, so long as those changes aim at making the community a better place. One can enter into private agreements, but one cannot bind future generations by creating racist covenants that *run with the land*. Being a racist is one thing; binding future owners to participate in a racist covenant is another. Once a covenant is designed to run with land, the covenant is not just a contract issue anymore. It has become a property issue. In property law, there are *limiting doctrines* that prevent idiosyncratic wishes of previous owners from running with the land. Idiosyncratic contractors can agree to whatever idiosyncratic deal they want, but their agreement does not bind future buyers of their property. Restrictions on property that run with land have to be justified, when challenged, by argument that such restrictions are reasonably expected to be of value to subsequent owners. Which raises a question: could racially restrictive covenants reasonably be expected to be of value to subsequent white owners? Perhaps, but here is the crux. For a court to acknowledge that whites have a legitimate interest in excluding blacks would be for the state to acknowledge racism as legitimate. And *that* is what the Fourteenth Amendment's "equal-protection" clause forbids.[1]

[1] I thank Christopher Freiman, Daniel Silvermint, and Cathleen Johnson for helpful comments. I also thank Dean Don Weidner and all the wonderful faculty at Florida State College of Law for hiring me as a visiting professor for the fall semester of 2007, where I taught property and did much of the research for this chapter. I could not have written this chapter without their excellent advice and warm encouragement.

References

BLACKSTONE, WILLIAM (1979). *Commentaries on the Laws of England* [1765]. Chicago: University of Chicago Press.

CALABRESI, GUIDO, and MELAMED, A. DOUGLAS (1972). "Property Rules, Liability Rules and Inalienability: One View of the Cathedral," *Harvard Law Review*, 85: 1089–1128.

DEMSETZ, HAROLD (1967). "Toward a Theory of Property Rights," *American Economic Review* (Papers & Proceedings), 57: 347–59.

ELLICKSON, ROBERT C. (1991). *Order without Law: How Neighbors Settle Disputes.* Cambridge, MA: Harvard University Press.

ELLICKSON. ROBERT C. (1993). "Property in Land," *Yale Law Journal*, 102: 1315–1400.

GROTIUS, HUGO (2005). *Rights of War and Peace* [1625]. London: Elibron.

HARDIN, GARRETT (1968). "The Tragedy of the Commons," *Science*, 162: 1243–48.

HOHFELD, W. (1964). *Fundamental Legal Conceptions* [1913, 1917]. New Haven: Yale University Press.

HUME, DAVID (1983). *History of England* [1778]. Indianapolis: Liberty Fund Press.

LEWIS, JOHN (1888). *Law of Eminent Domain.* Chicago: Callaghan and Co.

LOCKE, JOHN (1960). *Second Treatise of Government* [1690] (ed.) P. Laslett Cambridge: Cambridge University Press.

ROSE, CAROL (1985). "Possession as the Origin of Property," *University of Chicago Law Review*, 52: 73–88.

ROSE, CAROL (1986). "The Comedy of the Commons: Custom, Commerce, and Inherently Public Property," *University of Chicago Law Review*, 53: 711–87.

ROSE, CAROL (1994). *Property and Persuasion.* Boulder, CO: Westview.

SCHMIDTZ, DAVID (2008). *Person, Polis, Planet: Essays in Applied Philosophy.* New York: Oxford University Press.

SCHMIDTZ, DAVID (2010). "Property and Justice," *Social Philosophy and Policy*, 27: 79–100.

SCHMIDTZ, DAVID, and Brennan, Jason (2010). *A Brief History of Liberty.* Oxford: Blackwell.

CHAPTER 36

EQUALITY

JONATHAN WOLFF

EQUALITY IN THE HISTORY OF POLITICAL PHILOSOPHY

MORE than one thinker has seen the development of civilization as the increasing penetration of ideas of equality into ever more spheres of life. John Stuart Mill, for example, seems to have such an idea in mind when he writes:

> The entire history of social improvement has been a series of transitions by which one custom or institution after another, from being a supposed primary necessity of social existence, has passed into the rank of an universally stigmatized injustice and tyranny. So it has been with the distinctions of slaves and freemen, nobles and serfs, patricians and plebeians; and so it will be, and in part already is, with the aristocracies of colour, race, and sex. (Mill 1962 [1863]: 320)

To trace the history of the concept of equality in political philosophy is to explore the answers that have been given to the questions of what equality demands, and whether it is a desirable goal. Yet, as we see from Mill's observations, it is a topic that threatens to transform itself into many others. Considerations of unjust inequality appear in numerous different spheres, such as citizenship, sexual equality, racial equality, and even equality between human beings and members of other species, each of which is represented elsewhere in this volume. I will not, therefore, attempt to break down the discussion of equality and inequality into different subsections, but rather will focus on one central question: of equality as an issue of distributive justice, or, to put it more broadly, of equality of fortune.

In all spheres, including the economic, the progress mentioned by Mill took a good deal of time to build up much momentum, both in theory, and, even more so, in practice (for similar observations concerning the broader concept of distributive justice, see

Fleischacke 2004). Ancient Greek political philosophy, despite Aristotle's famous conceptual analysis of equality (Aristotle (1995*b*), is generally hostile towards the idea of social and economic equality. Plato's account of the best and most just form of the state in the *Republic* is a society of very clear social, political, and economic hierarchy (Plato (1955). Aristotle saw no objection to the restriction of citizenship to a narrow class of those who resided within the political community, and, notoriously, argued in defence of slavery (Aristotle (1995*a*). By contrast, Stoic thought, especially in the hands of the Cicero—who regarded himself as an 'outsider'—was more sympathetic to the idea of equality, and Roman law contains the idea that everyone is by nature free and equal, at least in theory. Christian writers, of course, saw human equality as stemming from the premise that we are all created equal in the eyes of god (Hoekstra 2008). However, such views were not translated into demands for political and economic equality, even by major Christian philosophers such as Aquinas or Augustine.

It is with Hobbes that the idea of equality is put to work, albeit in an unusual style and context. In his argument for the absolute sovereign, Hobbes first conceives of human beings existing in a state of nature, where each is free from political, legal, and, arguably, moral constraint. Such a situation, Hobbes argues, would be one of mutual fear, precisely because of natural equality. By this Hobbes appears to mean both the normative claim that no one is naturally subservient to another, but also the factual thesis that no one is so pre-eminent in strength or ability to be invulnerable to others. Equality, therefore, amounts to each person's ability to kill each other person, with co-conspirators if necessary. Such limited adherence to factual equality is also compatible with assuming a great deal of natural inequality in strength, prudence, and intelligence, which Hobbes also stresses throughout his works (Hobbes 1996 [1651]; Hoekstra 2008).

Whether Hobbes's egalitarian starting point leaves any trace on his subsequent account of the organization of the state is less clear. There is, clearly, one highly significant inequality in the Hobbesian state; that between the sovereign and the citizens. Of distribution of wealth between the citizens, though, Hobbes says little, although when enumerating the laws of nature he argues that equity requires equality, and the sharing in common of those things that cannot be divided equally. However, whether Hobbes felt that these laws of natures had implications for the laws of property is less clear. It is likely that Hobbes's denial of natural inequality, and advocacy of natural equality, was intended to provide a background to the thesis that social and material inequality in civil society exists on the licence of the sovereign, and not that such inequality violates natural law (Hobbes 1996 [1651]).

Equality is more obviously part of Locke's explicit project. At pains to refute the feudal conception of the divine right of kings, Locke argues, on the grounds of both biblical interpretation and natural reason, that human beings are born 'free and equal', with natural rights to life, liberty, and estate. The right to estate, however, in itself has few distributive implications. Locke, famously, provided a 'labour-mixing' argument for the justification of private property, in which the first person to mix his or her labour with land or any other natural resource, previously held in common, becomes entitled to that land, subject, first, to the 'non-spoilage' proviso that what is taken must not be allowed to spoil, and, second, the 'sufficiency' proviso, which asserts that one person's appropriation is justified only on the proviso that 'enough and as good' is left for others. Although there is some interpretative controversy, the standard interpretation is that Locke intends this latter proviso to set out a necessary condition for justified property acquisition, and hence those appropriating property must, at a minimum, leave those without property in no worse state than they would have been had there been no individual ownership (Locke 1988 [1690]; for discussion, see Waldron 1980). This provides an assurance of some sort of social minimum, at least for those able to work. A further passage, from Locke's *First Treatise* (sect. 42), states that 'God has given no one of his children such a property . . . but that he has given his needy brother a right to the surplusage of his goods . . . when his pressing wants call for it' (Locke 1988 [1690]: 170). This is often regarded as also providing some sort of social minimum, but, like the reasoning based on the sufficiency proviso, falls far short of any concern for significant material equality. Like Hobbes, Locke seeks to undermine the case for any form of natural social or economic hierarchy, but such opposition is quite consistent with accepting inequality based on human convention.

With Jean-Jacques Rousseau, a concern for material and social equality becomes much more embedded into an overall view of the nature of a desirable political community. In the *Discourse on Inequality*, Rousseau, in somewhat exaggerated style, attributes many of the problems of civilization to the institution of property and subsequent inequality. 'The first man who, having enclosed a piece of land, thought of saying, *This is mine*, and found people simple enough to believe him, was the true founder of civil society. How many crimes, wars, murders, miseries, and horrors might mankind have been spared, if someone had pulled up the stakes or filled in the ditch, and shouted to his fellow-men: "Beware of listening to this imposter; you are ruined if you forget that the fruits of the earth are everyone's and that the soil itself is no one's"' (Rousseau 1958a [1754]: 84).

In *The Social Contract* Rousseau connects economic equality to the conditions of political stability, arguing that, for a society to be governed by the general will, no citizen should be rich enough to buy another, and no citizen so poor as to be obliged to sell himself. It is tempting, therefore, to assume that Rousseau's opposition to material inequality was largely instrumental, in that material inequality would undermine political equality. While this instrumental defence is certainly part of his view, Rousseau appears also to oppose material inequality itself, as an unattractive aspect of contemporary society (Rousseau 1958b [1762]).

It would be wrong, though, to present the philosophical tradition as becoming increasingly favourable to ideas of equality in any linear fashion. Hume, in *his Enquiry concerning the Principles of Morals*, argued that equality is, 'extremely PERNICIOUS to human society'. Hume argues:

> Render possessions ever so equal, men's different degrees of art, care, and industry will immediately break that equality. Or if you check these virtues, you reduce society to the most extreme indigence; and instead of preventing want and beggary

in a few, render it unavoidable to the whole community. The most rigorous inquisition too is requisite to watch every inequality on its first appearance; and the most severe jurisdiction, to punish and redress it. (Hume 1975 [1751]: 194)

In this single passage Hume makes three trenchant arguments against equality: first, it is unsustainable; second, it leads to extreme economic inefficiency; and, third, it requires tyranny if it is to be enforced. Such arguments remain of great importance in the contemporary debate, and anticipate some of the arguments of Robert Nozick (1974), as we shall see later in this chapter.

Hume's opposition to equality did not settle the debate, but it may have encouraged a more complex analysis. John Stuart Mill, for example, expressed a type of double-mindedness about equality. On the one hand, he believed that a 'levelling' of property—sharing it equally among all—would be a disaster for society, leading to a loss of initiative, incentives, and productivity, to the disadvantage of all, including those who at present hold no property. So concerned was he about this prospect that, in *On Representative Government*, he notoriously proposed that democratic voting proced-ures should be skewed to give the propertied or the educated 'plural votes' to avoid the prospect that the poor, who were the numerical majority, would gain power and attempt to introduce levelling schemes (Mill 1993). On the other hand, in *Principles of Political Economy and Chapters on Socialism*, he seemed to regard it as inevitable that, as long as human beings continued to progress, eventually the division between capitalist and worker would be overcome, and production would be undertaken by associations of workers, collectively owning the capital they used for production (Mill 2008).

Hence, despite their differences, there is a certain common ground between the hopes for the future of Mill and Karl Marx. Both were inspired by French Socialism to look forward to a society in which 'the free development of each is the condition for the free development of all' (Marx 2000; Marx and Engels 2000 [1848]; Mill 2008), and that class-based society and exploitation would be transcended. Of course, their analysis of how such a society might be achieved, and their understanding of their own role in that process, differed considerably. Unlike Marx, Mill did not advocate revolution, or see himself as the intellectual collaborator with a mass movement. Neither thinker, however, offered much in detail about how such a society would be organized, as both viewed future society not as the realization of an idea, as Marx puts it, but the result of a historical process, which could not be anticipated in its full form. Another way of putting this point is that, while the 'Utopian Socialists' such as Owen, Saint-Simon, and Fourier, put forward detailed ideas of a just society, to which reality must be made to conform (see Kolakowski 1981), Marx and Mill gave priority to the process of history, which, they both predicted, would generate some form of socialist organization. Equality, for both, was not so much a matter of equal division of some resources (although many existing inequalities would be reduced) but rather the ending of social classes based on differential ownership of the means of production and exploitation. Indeed, Marx argued that taking the idea of equality literally is self-defeating, for, he claimed, rendering different individuals equal in one respect will make them unequal in some other respect. Marx's own view of a society of equals was one in which each contributed according to ability, and received according to need (Marx 2000).

EQUALITY IN CONTEMPORARY POLITICAL PHILOSOPHY

The central point of reference for the debate about equality in contemporary political philosophy is, of course, John Rawls's *A Theory of Justice*, first published in 1971, and somewhat revised in 1999, with important further contributions from Ronald Dworkin (1981*a*, *b*, 2000), and Amartya Sen (1980, 1992, 1997).[1] Rawls offers a complex theory, which he summarizes in the following terms:

1. Each person is to have an equal right to the most extensive total system of equal basic liberties compatible with a similar system of liberty for all.
2. Social and economic inequalities are to be arranged so that they are:
   (*a*) to the greatest benefit of the least advantaged . . . and
   (*b*) attached to offices and positions open to all under conditions of fair equality of opportunity. (Rawls 1971: 302; 1999: 266)

For present purposes we should concentrate on only the first half of Rawls's second principle, known as the Difference Principle, as it is this that is the primary focus for the topic of economic distribution. Criticisms of Rawls's Difference Principle come from many directions. Shortly after the publication of a *Theory of Justice*, Robert Nozick published *Anarchy, State, and Utopia*, offering a strikingly different 'libertarian' approach to political philosophy, in which the government is restricted to the role of a 'minimal state' to protect person and property, and has no right to engage in redistribution from one person to another, except to rectify theft or fraud. The attempt to achieve equality is, on this view, a violation of property rights, and also an infringement of individual liberty (Nozick 1974).

Rawls was also criticized by thinkers more sympathetic to the idea of equality, such as Dworkin, who can be read as raising two central challenges (Dworkin 1981*b*; see also Kymlicka 2002). The first develops Nozick's objections, and can be put like this: Rawls's Difference Principle seems to be indifferent to the question of why it might be that someone is among the worst off. Some people may be badly off because they are unable to work, or unable to find work. But others may unemployed simply through choice. Are they equally deserving or entitled to benefit from the work of others? Can it be fair to tax those who work in order to benefit others who have the same opportunities, but

---

[1] Much of the material in this section draws on Wolff (2007).

from their own free will choose not to make use of them? The Difference Principle, however, does not require answers to these questions, apparently redistributing goods to the worst off, whatever the reason for their ill fortune. In Dworkin's view this is contrary to equality. Equality should, other things being equal, allow those who work hard to reap the rewards, while those who chose to do less should bear the consequences of their choices, if they are freely made.

Dworkin's second objection, also made by Sen, raises a new difficulty. The Difference Principle distributes material resources, identifying the worst off as those who have the least income and wealth. However, some people have much more expensive needs than others. In particular, people who are severely disabled, or have expensive medical requirements, may find themselves unable to pay the expenses needed to achieve a reasonable level of well-being, even if their income does not put them among the worst off.

The natural response to the problem of expensive needs, such as those of disabled people, would be to move to a more subjective index of well-being, such as happiness or preference satisfaction. However, Dworkin argues that this would be a mistake. First he unleashes a battery of objections against the coherence of a welfare measure—essentially the difficulty of determining when two different people are at the same level, which, of course, is central to any theory of equality. But the argument that is most distinctive and has had the greatest impact is the problem of expensive tastes. Imagine two people who have the same ordinary tastes, talents, and resources, and the same ability to convert resources into welfare. Now one of them—Louis—decides that he wants to change his tastes, and manages to develop a taste for pre-phylloxera claret and plovers' eggs, and is consequently unsatisfied with beer and hens' eggs, therefore needing more money to achieve a comparable level of welfare to others. According to Dworkin, the theory of equality of welfare would require a transfer of resources from the person with ordinary tastes to the person with newly developed expensive tastes, in order to equalize their welfare. This, he plausibly argues, is deeply counter-intuitive (Dworkin 1981a).

Dworkin argues that the difficulties with expensive tastes can be avoided by his theory of equality of resources, rather than equality of welfare. What matters, on such a view, is the share of resources people have, rather than how happy or satisfied those resources make them. And the distinct problem of subsidizing those who choose not to work can be avoided by incorporating a notion of responsibility within the theory of equality. It is possible to make people responsible for matters within some domains, but not within others. Dworkin, therefore, makes a distinction between one's ambitions—including the realm of the voluntary choices one makes—and endowments, which we can think of as including in-born talents, genetic predispositions, and so on. Dworkin's theory is that, while equality requires compensation for the bad 'brute luck' of being born with poor endowments, or unforeseeable poor luck in other aspects of life, it does not require compensation for poor 'option luck', which typically includes the results of freely made choices.

There remains, however, the question of how to determine the appropriate level of compensation or subsidy. Dworkin makes the brilliant observation that insurance is a device for converting brute luck into option luck. It may be a matter of pure chance whether lightning strikes my house. But, if an easily available insurance policy would protect me from loss, chance is now reduced to choice. Dworkin's argument is that, if, against a background of equality, insurance is available against a hazard, and a person decides not to insure, then the appropriate level of compensation can be settled through insurance, and there is no case in justice for subsidizing the uninsured by taxing others who beforehand were no better off.

However, it is not possible to obtain insurance against all bad brute luck, for we are affected from the moment we are born. Some people are born with low talents, or, as already discussed, with disabilities. But insurance against bad brute luck that has already happened is not available. Nevertheless, as Dworkin argues, it is possible to imagine what insurance one would take out, hypothetically, behind a veil of ignorance in which you knew the prevalence of, and disadvantage caused by, different types of disability, but did not know whether or not you personally were affected. Knowing this information should allow one to decide whether to insure, and if so at what level. Averaging the decisions gives a standard hypothetical premium and payout, and these can be used to model a just tax and transfer scheme. A similar move is available to model appropriate welfare payments for those of low talent. Dworkin thus provides a theory of equality that has many attractive features (Dworkin 1981b). However, not all contemporary theorists of equality see the issues in the same terms.

Unconditional Basic Income

Before looking at direct responses to Dworkin, it is worth looking at a group of theories, according to which, contrary to Dworkin, each person is entitled to a payment from the state in addition to anything (or nothing) he or she may earn from other sources. This is the theory of 'unconditional basic income', which has been defended in various ways. For example, it has been argued that, if some prefer to work and some prefer not to, then neutrality between conceptions of the good requires us not to punish those who decide not to work (Van Parijs 1995; Levine 1998). It can also be argued that unconditional basic income would have various consequential advantages, such as ending discrimination against part-time workers, and requiring work with poor conditions to be paid a decent wage (Van Parijs and van der Veen 1986).

An alternative defence starts from the assumption that all human beings are joint owners of the earth and its resources. To simplify, we can imagine each of us as the owner of one share in 'Earth PLC'. Those using any of the world's resources must pay a rent, which is returned to the shareholders as a dividend. Accordingly, anyone who uses more than a per capita share of the world's resources owes more rent than he or she will get back in dividend; those who use less will get more dividend than they must pay in rent. This, of course, yields a payment for everyone, however they act, although, of course, some will pay more in rent than they receive back in dividend (Steiner 1994). The theory of basic income, however defended, is, of course, highly controversial, at least in part because it (deliberately) has a limited place for individual responsibility.

Equality of Welfare Reassessed

Dworkin, as we saw, considers and rejects equality of welfare as a possible response to the problem presented by the fact that disabled people may need more resources than others to achieve an acceptable standard of living. His argument is based on the example of Louis's expensive tastes. Richard Arneson, however, suggests that this argument is ineffective. Louis deliberately cultivated his expensive tastes. He could have achieved the same level of welfare as other people by remaining content with hens' eggs and beer, but he chose otherwise. Arneson points out that Dworkin's distinction between theories of resources and theories of welfare cross-cuts with another, between what we could call 'outcome' and 'opportunity' theories. It is true, Arneson, accepts, that equality of welfare outcomes would require subsidizing Louis's deliberately cultivated expensive tastes. However, Louis does have equality of *opportunity* for welfare, but he squanders it by deliberately cultivating expensive tastes. If he was born with expensive tastes, then the case for subsidy is more compelling, for he would then lack equality of opportunity for welfare. Hence, Arneson argues, Dworkin has drawn the wrong conclusion from his example. In effect, Arneson suggests, Dworkin has compared equality of welfare *outcomes* with equality of *opportunity* for resources. The expensive-tastes argument shows that equality of welfare outcomes is unacceptable, but this is a reason for moving to an opportunity conception, not a resources conception (Arneson 1989).

G. A. Cohen argues in a similar way, although, unlike Arneson, he claims that an adequate theory of equality must use what he called the 'currency' of 'advantage' that incorporates both welfare and resources. Cohen endorses one of Dworkin's arguments against pure welfarism; that it would have the bizarre consequence that it would require transfers from the very cheerful poor—such as Dickens's Tiny Tim—to the wealthy but miserable—such as Scrooge. But equally, Cohen argues, it would be wrong to follow Dworkin and endorse a pure resource-based metric in which people were not compensated for pain and suffering (Cohen 1989). These issues continue to be debated (see the papers in Burley 2004).

Equality, Priority, and Sufficiency

A different line of criticism of the theory of equality focuses on the question of whether equality is of value in itself. A traditional argument against equality is that it requires levelling down: that, if there is a choice between equality at a lower level and inequality at a higher level, then equality is required, even if it makes literally every individual worse off. Although familiar, few egalitarians took this argument seriously, brushing it aside one way or another, until Rawls presented the difference principle, in which inequalities are tolerated when they are to the advantage of the worst off (Rawls 1971, rev. 1999). This is intended to prevent levelling down.

It is not always clear, however, whether Rawls should be treated as a defender or critic of equality, as his theory does permit inequality (Daniels 1975; Nagel 1979). The situation, however, has been clarified by work by Harry Frankfurt and by Derek Parfit, which generates distinctions between a range of theories of different strength and commitment. First, Frankfurt argues that egalitarians are not, or at least should not, be concerned with equality as such, but with whether individuals are leading sufficiently good lives, where 'sufficiency' is to be understood non-comparatively. What matters, argues Frankfurt, is whether people have enough to live a good life. Comparisons with others are alienating, and deflect oneself from the value of one's own life (Frankfurt 1987). Whatever we think of the claims of the alienating nature of comparisons, it cannot be denied that there is a certain attraction to such a sufficiency view, as distinct from equality.

However, there are further options. Parfit describes a Rawlsian-style view as one of 'priority to the worst off', which again is distinct from equality. Indeed, this view comes in various strengths. Rawls's own view is one of absolute priority, where the claims of the worst off must always be given priority. Parfit's view is one of a form of 'weighted priority', in which the claims of the worst off have greater weight than then claims of others, but can, at least in theory, be outweighed. On this view there is such a thing as 'asking too much', even if you are the worst off in society (Parfit 1998).

Sen and Capability Theory

In parallel to Dworkin, Amartya Sen also developed an alternative to Rawls. Sen was particularly exercised by Rawls's index of well-being in terms of primary goods, and by the fact that this ignored the plight of people with unusual or extensive needs. Sen's suggestion is that evaluation of how well an individual's life is going, from the point of view of whether he should be offered state support, should measure neither the resources someone has, nor the welfare he is able to derive, but his 'capability to function'. A functioning is what a person can 'do or be': achieve nourishment, health, a decent life span, self-respect, and so on. A person's 'capability set' is the alternative sets of functionings he is able to achieve with his resources and opportunities, and a capability, therefore, is the freedom to achieve a functioning.

This pluralist view of well-being is often regarded as a more realistic account than any theory of welfare or resources. It also contains within it a particular theory of responsibility. If one has the capability to achieve functionings, but neglects to do so, then one is responsible for one's own situation and does not have a claim in justice against others for help. This notion of freedom and responsibility, within a theory of equality, has made the theory attractive to many.

Sen's theory has become extremely important in development economics, influencing policy within organizations such as United Nations, encouraging a move away from income measures of poverty, to 'lack of basic functioning' (United Nations 2005). This has been among the contributions that won him the Nobel Prize in Economics in 1998. However, political philosophy has found it harder to incorporate Sen's theory, for two main reasons. First, Sen has always refrained from setting out a definitive list of human functionings. Second, on a pluralist view, it is very hard to understand what equality means. Equality seems to require a way of measuring functionings against each other, but the essence of a pluralist view is that this is not, in general, possible. Solving the first problem, as Martha Nussbaum has attempted to do in laying out an account of essential human functionings, simply brings out the difficulty of the second (Sen 1980, 1992, 1997; Nussbaum 2000).

Nevertheless, the contributions of Frankfurt and Parfit have allowed political philosophers to make better use of Sen's approach, in that a 'sufficiency view' of capabilities has appeared a more promising approach (Anderson 1999; Nussbaum 2006), in which the goal of social policy is to bring each person to a threshold level of sufficiency in each capability. There are, however, severe difficulties when resource constraints make this impossible. The theory will need to be supplemented in some way to deal with priority setting between competing claims, and many of the initial difficulties reassert themselves. However, the position may not be completely hopeless, and it has been argued that it is possible to combine a prioritarian position with a (modified) capability view (Wolff and de-Shalit 2007).

'A Society of Equals' and the Critique of Luck Egalitarianism

The distinctive innovation of the theories of Dworkin, Cohen, and Arneson is to combine individual responsibility with a concern for equality, by making a distinction between those aspects of one's life and fortune for which one is responsible and those for which one is not. Together, in a phrase coined by Anderson (1999), those theories are collectively referred to as 'luck egalitarianism', as their goal is to 'neutralize' the effects of luck on individual lives.

It may be, however, that attempting to make this distinction appears to have a number of unfortunate effects. For example, it will have to split claimants into those who are responsible for their plight and those who are not, which in some circumstances can be humiliating even for those who are entitled to help, who, for example, might have to argue that they are untalented in order to qualify for state support (Wolff 1998). Furthermore, many of the policies strictly entailed by the theory seem deeply inhumane. For example, those who have become disabled through 'bad option luck' are responsible for their own disability, on the luck egalitarian view, and strictly should not be entitled to any state help. In response, Anderson suggests that the 'negative aim' of egalitarianism should not be to eliminate the effects of bad luck, but to end oppression, domination, and exploitation. An equal society is not one that has eliminated the effects of luck, but one that has achieved relations of equality between individuals (Anderson 1999). Such a view has also been defended in recent writing by Samuel Scheffler (2003).

This move towards 'relational' or 'social' equality picks up a concern running from an older tradition in thinking of equality, exemplified in the works of such thinkers as R. H. Tawney (1931), and carried forward by Bernard Williams (1962), Michael Walzer (1983), Richard Norman (1998), and David Miller (1999). The central idea is that a society of equals has to create conditions of mutual respect and self-respect and thereby overcome hierarchical divisions. This type of view has strong affinities with the feminist theorists Iris Marion Young (1990) and Nancy Fraser (Fraser and Honneth 1998). There are numerous variation on this theme, but the core idea in an equal society is one in which people relate to each other in certain ways, rather than one that distributes resources, well-being, or capabilities equally. Of course, distribution will also be important, but its importance is secondary or derivative, on such a view.

Equality in Practice

In recent years there has been increasing attention to the topic of the relation between theory and practice. Much work in political philosophy is based on 'ideal theory' or 'full compliance'. That is, its aim is to set out a theory for the just society, without raising questions of how, historically, such a society could be achieved, and assuming that all citizens will follow the rules. However, there is a lurking question about the application of such theories to the real world. It may be impossible to implement a theory for many reasons: that it makes unreasonable demands of human beings; that it is not fully coherent; that there is no political will; that there is no route from where we are to where we would be, and so on. For this reason some theorists are beginning to think that philosophers should pay greater attention to the question of how to improve the actual world, rather than try to design principles for a world we may never see (Barry 2005; Wolff and de-Shalit 2007).

References

ANDERSON, ELIZABETH (1999). 'What is the Point of Equality?' *Ethics*, 109: 287–337.
ARISTOTLE (1995a [written 350 BCE]). *Politics Books I and II*, (ed.) T. Saunders. Oxford: Clarendon Press.

ARISTOTLE (1995*b* [written 350 BCE]). *Politics Books III and IV*, (ed.) R. Robinson. Oxford: Clarendon Press.

ARNESON, R. (1989). 'Equality and Equal Opportunity for Welfare', *Philosophical Studies*, 56: 77–93.

BARRY, BRIAN (2005). *Why Social Justice Matters*. Cambridge: Polity.

Burley, Justice (2004) (ed.). *Dworkin and his Critics*. Oxford: Blackwell.

COHEN, G. A. (1989). 'On the Currency of Egalitarian Justice', *Ethics*, 99: 906–44.

DANIELS, NORMAN (1975). 'Equal Liberty and Unequal Worth of Liberty', in N. Daniels (ed.), *Reading Rawls*. New York: Basic Books.

DWORKIN RONALD (1981*a*). 'What is Equality? Part 1: Equality of Welfare', *Philosophy & Public Affairs*, 10: 228–40.

DWORKIN, RONALD (1981*b*). 'What is Equality? Part 2: Equality of Resources', *Philosophy & Public Affairs*, 10: 283–345.

DWORKIN, RONALD (2000). *Sovereign Virtue*. Cambridge, MA: Harvard University Press.

FLEISCHACKER, SAMUEL (2004). *A Short History of Distributive Justice*. Cambridge, MA: Harvard University Press.

FRANKFURT, H. G. (1987). 'Equality as a Moral Ideal', *Ethics*, 98: 21–43.

FRASER, NANCY, and HONNETH, AXEL (1998). *Recognition or Redistribution?* London: Verso.

HOBBES, THOMAS (1996 [1651]). *Leviathan*. Cambridge: Cambridge University Press.

HOEKSTRA, KINCH (2008). 'Hobbes on Equality'. http://fsi.stanford.edu/events/hobbes_on_equality

HUME, DAVID (1975 [1751]). *An Enquiry into the Principles of Morals*, in David Hume, *Enquiries*, (ed.) P. Nidditch. Oxford: Clarendon Press.

KOLAKOWSKI, L. (1981). *Main Currents of Marxism*, i. Oxford: Oxford University Press.

KYMLICKA, WILL (2002). *Contemporary Political Philosophy: An Introduction*. 2nd edn. Oxford: Oxford University Press.

LEVINE, ANDREW (1998). *Rethinking Liberal Equality*. Ithaca, NY: Cornell University Press.

LOCKE, JOHN (1988 [1690]). *Two Treatises of Government*, (ed.) P. Laslett. Cambridge: Cambridge University Press.

MARX, KARL (2000 [written 1875, first published 1891]). *Critique of the Gotha Programme*, in *Karl Marx: Selected Writings*, (ed.) David McLellan. 2nd edn. Oxford: Oxford University Press.

MARX, KARL, and ENGELS, FREDERICK (2000 [1848]). *The Communist Manifesto*, in *Karl Marx: Selected Writings*, (ed.) David McLellan. 2nd edn. Oxford: Oxford University Press.

MILL, JOHN STUART (1962 [1863]). *Utilitarianism*, (ed.) Mary Warnock. Glasgow: Collins.

MILL, JOHN STUART (1993 [1863]). *Considerations on Representative Government*, in *Utilitarianism and Other Writings*. London: Everyman.

MILL, JOHN STUART (2008 [written 1848 and 1873, first published 1879]). *Principles of Political Economy and Chapters on Socialism*. Oxford: Oxford University Press.

MILLER, DAVID (1999). *Principles of Social Justice*. Cambridge, MA: Harvard University Press.

NAGEL, THOMAS (1979). 'Equality', in his *Mortal Questions*. Cambridge: Cambridge University Press.

NORMAN, RICHARD (1998). 'The Social Basis of Equality', in A. Mason (ed.), *Ideals of Equality*. Oxford: Basil Blackwell.

NOZICK, ROBERT (1974) *Anarchy, State, and Utopia*. Oxford: Basil Blackwell.

NUSSBAUM, MARTHA (2000). *Women and Human Development*. Cambridge: Cambridge University Press.

NUSSBAUM, MARTHA (2006). *Frontiers of Justice*. Cambridge, MA: Harvard University Press.

PARFIT, DEREK (1998). 'Equality and Priority', in *Ideals of Equality*, (ed.) Andrew Mason. Oxford: Blackwell.

PLATO (1955 [written 360 BCE]). *The Republic*, (ed.) H. D. P. Lee. London: Penguin.

RAWLS, JOHN (1971, rev. 1999). *A Theory of Justice*. Oxford: Oxford University Press.

ROUSSEAU, JEAN-JACQUES (1958a [1754]). *Discourse on Inequality*, in Jean-Jacques Rousseau, *The Social Contract and Discourses*, (ed.) G. D. H. Cole. London: Everyman.

ROUSSEAU, JEAN-JACQUES (1958b [1762]). *The Social Contract*, in Jean-Jacques Rousseau *The Social Contract and Discourses*, (ed.) G. D. H. Cole. London: Everyman.

SCHEFFLER, SAMUEL (2003). 'What Is Egalitarianism?', *Philosophy and Public Affairs*, 31: 5–39.

SEN, AMARTYA (1980). 'Equality of What?', in S. M. McMurrin (ed.), *The Tanner Lectures on Human Values*. Cambridge: Cambridge University Press, 195–220.

SEN, AMARTYA (1992). *Inequality Re-examined*. Cambridge, MA: Harvard University Press.

SEN, AMARTYA (1997). *On Economic Equality*. Expanded edn. Oxford: Clarendon Press.

STEINER, HILLEL (1994). *An Essay on Rights*. Oxford: Blackwell.

TAWNEY, R. H. (1931). *Equality*. London: George Allen and Unwin.

UNITED NATIONS (2005). *Human Development Report*. http://hdr.undp.org

VAN PARIJS, PHILIPPE (1995). *Real Freedom for All*. Oxford: Oxford University Press.

VAN PARIJS, PHILIPPE, and VAN DER VEEN, ROBERT (1986). 'A Capitalist Road to Communism', *Theory and Society*, 15: 635–55.

WALDRON, JEREMY (1980). *The Right to Private Property*. Oxford: Oxford University Press.

WALZER, MICHAEL (1983). *Spheres of Justice*. Oxford: Blackwell.

WILLIAMS, BERNARD (1962). 'The Idea of Equality', in Peter Laslett and W. G. Runciman (eds), *Philosophy, Politics and Society*. 2nd ser. Oxford: Blackwell.

WOLFF, JONATHAN (1998). 'Fairness, Respect and the Egalitarian Ethos', *Philosophy and Public Affairs*, 27: 97–122.

WOLFF, JONATHAN (2007). 'Equality: The Recent History of an Idea', *Journal of Moral Philosophy*, 4: 125–36.

WOLFF, JONATHAN, and DE-SHALIT, AVNER (2007). *Disadvantage*. Oxford: Oxford University Press.

YOUNG, IRIS MARION (1990). *Justice and the Politics of Difference*. Princeton: Princeton University Press.

CHAPTER 37

....

FREEDOM

....

RAYMOND PLANT

FREEDOM or liberty—the terms will be used interchangeably in this account—is obviously of fundamental importance to politics. The ideal of a free society is one that animates a range of political positions, and its pursuit has been a galvanizing force in both national and international politics. It is, however, a difficult concept to analyse, and indeed some of the complexities about liberty reflect an intrinsic connexion between liberty and wider ranges of political ideas in which it may be differently embedded and understood. In their turn, such ideas will be linked to ways of life and political cultures of which they were or are a part.

Ideas about freedom have varied through Western history. One of the major variations is to be found in the contrast between positive and negative liberty. So, for example, for the member of the Athenian city state in the fourth century BC, freedom essentially meant participation as a citizen in the governance of the city and maintaining its autonomy and independence against encroachments—a perspective illustrated, for instance, in the funeral speech of Pericles at the beginning of the Peloponnesian War (Thucydides 1954: 117). On this view, liberty was associated with particular types of civic virtue, and a free man (and it was men only) could be free only by living such a life oriented to the discharge of civic obligations. Freedom was directed at a collective good, and virtue was living a life that would facilitate the achievement of this good or this type of human flourishing and fulfilment (Aristotle 1947) This also meant that the law could not be seen as the opposite of freedom, since the law required the performance of such duties (Herodotus 1998: 440). Freedom was not seen as being about preserving an area of private life free from the encroachment of the law. Indeed, the law in this period in Greek city states controlled private life to a very high degree. As Demaratus said to Xerxes in explaining the fighting prowess of the Spartans: 'their master is the law' (Herodotus 1998: 440). But the important point was that citizens were actively involved in law-making, and so the law was not to be seen as an alien power. This kind of approach is usually seen as embodying a positive conception of liberty: freedom is not just or even freedom from coercion and interference but, rather, is realized in living a particular way of life in accordance with a conception of virtue. Positive liberty in this sense is goal directed and implies that to be free involves living in accordance with certain moral values. This has been an enduring theme in Western thinking about liberty and was important in Roman and in what Quentin Skinner has called 'neo-Roman' conceptions of liberty (Skinner 1998). It can also be found as a central theme in Christian thought in the idea that the service of God and living in accordance with the will of God is 'perfect freedom', as the Book of Common Prayer says. This echoes St John's Gospel, 8:32, when Jesus says: 'And ye shall know the truth and the truth shall make you free.' It is also important in the theories of those philosophers—perhaps most notably a thinker like Spinoza—who believed that there are wholly rational metaphysically based goals of human action and that these are not matters of choice. Freedom means living in accordance with such rationally given goals (Hampshire 1960; Berlin 1997). So the moral values that give positive freedom its content may be community based, as in the Greek and Roman case; they may be religiously based, as in the Christian example; or they may be founded on some metaphysically posited assumptions about the nature of reason and humanity, as in the case of Spinoza.

However, a liberal account of freedom will differ in fundamental respects from those advanced by both ancient and modern defenders of virtue-oriented views of positive freedom. Central to the liberal idea is that freedom is the absence of coercion: A is free when B does not prevent him or her from doing what he or she desires to or does not require him or her to do what he or she would not choose to do. Given such a conception of liberty, the liberal ideal of a free society becomes 'a situation in which as many individuals as possible can realise as many of their ends as possible, without assessment of the value of these ends as such, save in so far as they may frustrate the purposes of others' (Berlin 1969: 153 n.). This is also a view that Berlin ascribes to John Stuart Mill and Benjamin Constant, whom he calls 'the fathers of liberalism' (Berlin 1969: 161). It is also central to John Rawls's *A Theory of Justice*—the most considerable statement of liberal political thought in the second half of the twentieth century (Rawls 1972: 235–43). The emphasis, therefore, is upon the freedom of individual choice and not the value of what is then chosen in contrast to the positive approach to freedom (Berlin 1969). On the negative view, the only basis for the assessment of the choices made by free—that is, uncoerced—individuals is where those choices prevent others choosing to pursue their own goals and purposes whatever they may be. Thus freedom can be limited only for the sake of freedom.

In a sense this position may seem to be uncontroversial to the modern mind, because such a conception of freedom seems to make few controversial moral demands. On the positive view of freedom, it seems as though we have to have some kind of agreed set of moral goals such that virtue is acting in the furtherance of such goals, whereas it might be argued that we now live in much more diverse and pluralistic moral communities and we cannot expect agreement on what the ends of human life actually are. Nor can we accept any longer religious or metaphysical arguments that seek to set out in a rationally authoritative way the ends and goals of human life. The growth of moral diversity and the decline in both religious belief and scepticism about metaphysical claims mean that freedom has to be detached from the pursuit of particular goals and purposes and from community-based, religious, or metaphysically grounded claims about the ends of human life. In these circumstances of modernity we need to see freedom as being focused on individual choice and the framework of rules that will prevent the choices of one person infringing the choices of another. A framework of law securing mutual non-coercion is the liberal ideal in contrast to the positive liberty view of law as embodying some sort of morally authoritative set of substantial moral purposes.

There may be different ways in which this account can be made more specific and less abstract, but, as a starting point, it might be thought to be uncontroversial and acceptable, whatever one's own political point of view. So perhaps the point made earlier that the specification of the concept of liberty involves the engagement of other political ideas and the ideological positions within which they are embedded might seem rather far-fetched, since the idea of freedom as freedom from coercion seems to be morally uncontroversial, empirical, and objective. It is empirical and objective because, if freedom is the absence of coercion, we can give an objective and empirical account of what constitutes coercion and thus of liberty, which is the absence of coercion so defined. This view assumes that the idea of coercion is itself free from controversy.

This is, however, far from being the case. In one sense it can be regarded as uncontroversial, but that position is bought at the cost of a very narrow view of the nature of freedom and one that hardly fits our ordinary understanding of it. The uncontroversial idea of coercion is when A makes it *impossible* for B to do X or impossible for B not to do Y. Impossibility looks to be a wholly uncontroversial type of restraint. I make it impossible for you to go to the cinema, which is what you want to do, by locking you in the house. This is a wholly empirical and objective situation. It does not involve any morally controversial issues and nor do we need to link the idea of coercion as impossibility with other concepts. It is a brute matter of fact as to whether A has made it impossible for B to do Y. This is the view that, for example, Thomas Hobbes articulated in Chapter 14 of *Leviathan* (Hobbes 1955 [1651]: 84): 'By Liberty, is understood, according to the proper signification of the word, the absence of external impediments...' The factual and objective nature of this claim is very important in that, if the sense of coercion is intrinsically *subjective*, then freedom, as the absence of coercion, will itself become a subjective state. There would be no distinction to be drawn between *being* free (objective state of affairs) and *feeling* free (subjective perception). For many thinkers the maintenance of this distinction is of vital importance and in that context the claim that the absence of coercion is a wholly objective position and has to do with impossibility is of vital importance. The idea of impossibility is also linked to that of prevention. If A prevents B from doing Y, then, on this understanding of prevention, A has made it impossible for B to do X—by locking him or her in the house, for example.

However, it is not clear that things are as simple as this. It is, of course, true that A making it impossible for B to do X is a form of coercion. There are, however, two deep difficulties with this as a full account of the nature of coercion.

The first is that it does not cover all the sorts of cases that we would normally regard as cases of coercion. This is particularly true of the case of threats. Threats are usually seen as forms of coercion, and, indeed, the coerciveness of the law depends upon the threats contained in it: if A does X, then he or she will go to prison. A threat does not make it impossible for A to do X; rather it imposes the threat of a sanction if he or she does X. A threat is not a form of rendering something impossible; it is an attempt to change behaviour by imposing or attaching higher costs to the behaviour than existed before the threat was issued. So, A can make it impossible for B to do X by locking B in the house or A can attach a threat to B's desire to do X such as, if B does X, he or she will lose his or her job. Now this does not make it impossible for B to do X. It does, however, make it a very costly choice, and people may well respond to that choice in different ways: B may say: 'I won't do X because of the threat'; C may decide to do X under the same threat because he or she knows that another job will be easy to secure. This, however, is the rub. Impossibility is a situation that affects both B and C in the same way, or so it might be thought so far in the analysis. Threat, on the other hand, has to be linked far more to the scale of values and the preference schedules of the person who is threatened as to whether the person believes him or herself to be coerced by the threat. In an simple case, B may see a threat as coercive: I cannot park there because the notice says there will be a fine of £50 payable; C may see the same threat as an opportunity and the fine almost as an equivalent of a parking fee, or even as an offer (if C is rich)—I can park here for only £50! The point here is that a threat is a much more subjective matter than prevention or impossibility. This matters because, if freedom is the absence of coercion and coercion has a subjective element to it, then freedom becomes subjective. This has an effect on the idea of equal freedom. How could we know that citizens enjoy equal freedom if threats are part of coercion and the perception of the threat as coercive depends upon the scale of values and preferences of the person so threatened (Steiner 1974).

This moves us quite a long way from the seemingly objective and factual basis of impossibility. However, before leaving this point it is worth examining the view that impossibility itself is subjective. The argument here reflects the same point as was made about threats. It may be that character and temperament make a difference to impossibility. The point here is this that the factual nature of coercion as impossibility has to be bought at the cost of a wholly physicalist account of A making it impossible for B to do X. That is to say that A makes it physically impossible for B to act in this way by means of physical restraint, and anything beyond that, however strong the condition that A lays on B, will be a threat rather than coercion from this physicalist point of view just because how severe the threat is will depend on subjective judgement. If A issues a threat say to a politician B: 'Do X and I will assassinate you', this does not make it impossible for B to do X. It leaves B with a choice and a choice that will reflect his scale of values and preferences (Hayek 1960: 138). Undoubtedly some people would be deterred from doing X, but others of strong mind and character may persist in doing it. On the physicalist view of coercion, the threat of assassination is not coercive: it is a threat and does not make it impossible for B to do X. There is, however, a question mark over this. If impossibility has to be reduced to purely physical incapacitation to be a form of coercion and the threat of death is not therefore a form of impossibility just because it engages the subjective point of view of the person threatened, then it seems that coercion can apply only to a very small number of cases and that the threat of murder is not an infringement of liberty because it is not coercive in the impossibilist sense of coercion. There may be a consistent line here, but it is bought at the cost of being a very implausible account of coercion and thereby of freedom as a political ideal.

If we admit threats to the scope of coercion, does this not make the idea of freedom as the absence of coercion inextricably subjective? This is possible, but there is potentially a way out of this difficulty. The subjectivist problem is that a threat and even whether it is perceived as a threat has to involve the scale of values of the person threatened, and that makes it subjective. However, it is possible to argue that there are certain types of human goods that may be regarded as generic or universal, so that a threat against those sorts of goods can always be regarded as coercive. On the face of it this might look like a return to full-blown positive ideas of freedom outlined earlier, requiring a community to have either a unified sense of a flourishing human life or some religious or metaphysical basis for such a conception. However, there is a difference from older forms of positive freedom and what they require to underpin them. The idea here is that there are universal values and universal norms of human flourishing in terms of which freedom has to be understood in that a threat to those values will always be a form of coercion and freedom is the absence of coercion. So, for example, it might be argued that a good such as life itself, a good such as autonomy, and the fulfilment of basic needs can be regarded as universal or generic goods—if not for all human beings then at least within a particular society with a particular culture. What gives them this generic status is that they are necessary conditions for the pursuit of any other good, whatever it may turn out to be. In this sense, while it is a positive conception of freedom, it is so in a rather different way from those mentioned earlier (Gewirth 1978). Those conceptions of positive freedom diminished or even eliminated the scope of individual choice: freedom is living in accordance with metaphysically, religiously, or socially given values and does not focus on choice. The current idea, however, retains the centrality of choice and the fact that what is chosen is not subject to moral evaluation other than when it infringes the choices of others but at the same time argues that there are in fact certain types of goods that are essential preconditions of choice. Such goods are generic goods or primary goods (Rawls 1972; Gewirth 1978; Plant, Lesser, and Taylor-Gooby 1981). A threat to these goods is in fact a threat to the possibility of choice and is thus inherently coercive. This would certainly make the idea of coercion normative in that a threat would be coercive if it was a threat against a generic good but not necessarily at the cost of subjectivism, if we can agree on a set of generic goods that would then be central to the idea of coercion and thus to the idea of freedom. However, the issue of whether there can be a coherent account of generic or necessary goods is itself a large issue in political theory. It is revealing that the revival of this idea in political theory has been called 'neo-Aristotelian' (Nussbaum 1990, 1993). The point at this stage of the analysis, however, is that without such an account it might well seem that freedom would become radically subjectivist. Nevertheless, it is argued by critics of this approach that ideas about basic needs and other sorts of generic goods are subject to quite a lot of interpretation and dispute, and that the escape from subjectivism may be more apparent than real. Also, as Amartya Sen has argued, the ideas of basic needs and primary goods may be inadequate do the work suggested by theorists who support the universal goods approach. This argument turns upon the point that people will have different capacities and abilities in terms of transforming basic or primary goods into instruments for achieving their self chosen ends. So, if we are to secure equal or even fair allocations of freedom we have to look at the types and sources of differential capacities to make use of primary or generic goods. This again is going to involve moral controversy (Sen 1999).

This leads on to two further interrelated points: the relationship between freedom and a range of choice and the link between that question and determining whether a society is free or unfree. Does our view of freedom link up intrinsically with the idea that to be free a person has to have a range of significant choice open to him or her? There is nothing in the idea of freedom as being just the absence of coercion that would require this. A defender of this view of what is normally called negative liberty would say that the question of the identification of liberty is one thing and what someone is able to do with it, and the choices that are open to that person, is quite another. Liberty is negative; it is about the absence of coercion; the alternative view is a positive account that requires that there should be a range of morally significant choices open to a person before we can count the person as being free. On the negative view of liberty, the range of choices open to a person has nothing to do with freedom and again is a way of subjectivizing liberty (Hayek 1960). What is a morally significant range of choice? How is it to be decided what it is? How would it fit with the idea of equal freedom? We can make sense of the idea of equal freedom if we are all to be equally free from the same forms of coercion, but what about if freedom were to be understood as having a particular range of choices? How would such a moralized concept of positive freedom fit with the fact that we live in pluralistic and morally divergent societies, and therefore agreement about a morally significant range of choice is difficult if not impossible to attain?

One way of trying to fix more clearly the issues at stake here would be to ask the question of how we could know that one society is freer than another. If freedom is to be a useful idea in politics, then we need to know how to answer this question. From the standpoint of a defender of a strictly negative view of freedom, this poses a difficult if not fatal objection to the positive theorist who links freedom with a range of significant choice. Any account of such a range is going to be highly controversial and yet would be central to the judgement that society A is a freer society than society B, because A reflects this range of choice, which might include, for example: the ability to choose a government, to emigrate, to be able to criticize the government, to own property, and so on. One has only to start considering what might fall within the range to see that it is controversial. From the negative liberty point of view in which there is a desire to avoid morally controversial assumptions, the answer to the question as to whether society A is freer than society B has to be *quantitative*. If freedom is the absence of coercion, then the central question at stake here is that of how many rules there are preventing action in society A as opposed to society B, not what morally significant range of choice is available in society A as opposed to society B. We avoid that qualitative question by a focus on the quantitative one about the number of coercive rules operative in each society. This reduces the issue to a quantitative and empirical one, not a highly moralized one, as it would be for the defender of positive freedom. Leaving aside the fact that, as we have seen, the issue of coercion may not be as uncontroversial as this argument assumes, there are in its own terms defects in it. As Charles Taylor has pointed out, this purely quantitative approach is likely to lead to highly counter-intuitive results, because it is almost inevitably going to be the case that an underdeveloped society is going to have fewer coercive rules, since there are fewer differentiated areas of life to which such rules would apply (Taylor 1985). So, to take Taylor's own example of Albania under communist rule, it may well be that there were in fact fewer coercive rules there than say in the UK at the same period, because there was very little needed in the way of traffic regulation, very little in the way of financial rules, very little if anything in the way of rules to do with property and contract, and so forth. So, on a purely quantitative and empirical view of it, we would arrive at the highly counter-intuitive result that Albania was a freer country than the UK at the same time. Surely the answer is, the defender of positive liberty will say, that whatever the number of rules there are certain important things that one is able to do in the UK that you were unable to do in Albania, and it is this contrast between being able to realize certain valuable human abilities and not the bare number of rules that makes one society freer than another. In a sense this brings us back to the issue of necessary or generic goods mentioned earlier and what is the link between freedom and ability to realize such basic or generic goods.

This also extends the range of such basic goods to include ideas about independence and non-domination as well as a set of basic or primary goods to meet basic physical needs. If we regard autonomy as crucial to an account of human goods, then such goods as independence and non-domination are also necessary goods for the achievement of freedom (Skinner 1998). Along with other primary goods, such features are essential to those abilities that are conditions of agency and action.

The defender of negative liberty may well seek to deny any link between liberty and ability. On this view there is a categorical distinction between A being free to do X and A being able to do X. Whether someone is able to do what he or she is free to do has nothing to do with the nature of freedom. This position relies on the following claim: there must be a categorical difference between freedom and ability because when I am free I am not coerced; within that sphere of freedom as the absence of coercion there is an indefinitely large number of things that I am free to do in the sense that I am not prevented from doing. However capable, clever, and rich I am, I am able to do only a small number of that indefinitely large number of things. Hence freedom and ability are not extensionally equivalent. This attempt to draw a distinction between freedom and ability is centrally important in the theory of freedom and is also politically relevant. Hayek, for example, argues in *The Constitution of Liberty* (Hayek 1960: 17) that, if freedom is identified with ability or power, then the liberal ideal of a free society in which there is equal freedom from coercion becomes transformed into a socialist order, because freedom means ability, and the state as the guarantor of equal freedom would have to go as far as it could to equalize abilities, and this would mean radical redistribution of all sorts of resources to improve the abilities of the least able in the interests of arriving at a free society. This is apart from the question about how we should identify, fix, and rank the abilities that bear most on the exercise of liberty. This again is a normative exercise about which we should not expect agreement. It also raises a more metaphysical question in the view of the defender of negative liberty—namely, that positive freedom that links freedom, ability, and the realization of a set of valued human goods has to presuppose quite a complex and detailed account of human nature and human agency, which is absent from the position of negative liberty—so it is said. Such a conception of human nature and human agency is going to be highly disputable and does nothing to help fix the idea of liberty in a clear and operational way.

So we need to look in more detail at the issue of agency and ability. It can certainly be argued that the defender of negative liberty is wrong in thinking that he or she can produce a full account of negative liberty that does not raise similar questions. I have already pointed out that the concept of coercion, which is central to negative freedom, either has to be restricted to impossibility, which is implausible, or is in fact going to engage some quite large-scale account of those goods, a threat to which will always be regarded as coercive (Hayek 1960: 138), and any defence of such a set of goods is going to have to draw upon ideas of human nature, agency, and ability. The only alternative is to take the view that coercion is always subjectively perceived, and that therefore there is no distinction between feeling free and being free. This is an even worse position—radical subjectivism about freedom and coercion—than the alternative view, which has to include an account of agency and ability.

However, there is a more constructive way of looking at the matter than this. In order to see why we do need a conception of agency in order to have a fully developed concept of freedom, we might consider what conditions have to be satisfied to make it intelligible to ascribe freedom to an individual. After all, a stone is an individual thing, and, while it may roll down a hill and be moved, we would find it unintelligible to ascribe freedom to it (unless, of course, as in children's stories, human characteristics were given to the stone). The ascription of freedom applies only to agents who are capable of reasoned choice. This is a necessary condition of the concept of freedom being intelligible to us. So, if agency is a necessary condition of the ascription of freedom, it is difficult for the defender of negative liberty to rule out of court the concept of agency and its specification. In terms of its specification, it might be thought to require both basic needs being met and generic human capacities and capabilities being recognized as central to the ascription of freedom to such an agent. This point can be made a bit more concrete in a simple example. As we have seen, there is an argument to say that freedom and ability are two separate things, but this can be doubted. It makes no sense to ask whether someone is free to do something that no one is able to do. It is not intelligible to ask whether someone is free to jump from Oxford to New York, because it is not a human capability. No one was free to run a hedge fund in 1066, since no one was capable of doing so, and there was no institutional setting to make it possible. From these examples we might want to say that a *generalized ability* to do X is a necessary condition of determining whether A is free or unfree to do X. If a generalized ability is a necessary condition for the ascription of freedom or unfreedom, then it cannot be the case that there is a categorical difference between freedom and ability. So, on this account we have to set the range of freedom within the range of human capabilities, and we cannot do that without knowing what they are, which are the most important, and which enable human beings to flourish the most. The answers to these questions will be disputable, but they cannot be bypassed. Hence, it is very difficult to argue that freedom and ability are separate things and that an account of freedom can be given without engaging with some view of capabilities.

Defenders of negative liberty have wanted to resist the link between freedom and ability for another reason too. That is that they have wanted to say that freedom as the absence of coercion is clear and definite; the ability to make use of freedom thus defined is best seen in terms of a set of conditions for freedom. Thus, while each person may be free to dine at the Ritz Hotel in the sense of not being prevented from doing so, nevertheless the resources that one needs to dine at the Ritz should be seen as conditions without the fulfilment of which one would not be able to do so. The conditions for dining at the Ritz are, however, different from the objective definition of the freedom to dine at the Ritz. The question of whether an individual has the resources to do so or not is quite a different matter. On this view, there is no logical connection between the conditions and the freedom. This, however, may be doubted if one takes into account the agency-focused view of freedom set out as an alternative above. There is in addition an argument that involves no departure from negative accounts of liberty but that shows that conditions are not just contingent features of freedom (Swift 2001). If a country has a law that bans a particular group of people from using the trains, then we would normally regard that as a coercive law (putting on one side some of the issues about coercion cited earlier). At the same time, a railway company—or for that matter the state, if the railway is nationalized—may say that no one is free to travel on the train without a valid ticket. The ticket costs money, which A does not have. Hence he or she is not free to travel on the train. That is to say the condition of not having the money enters into the specification of the freedom in question and therefore is not merely a contingent factor or condition of freedom but part of what makes the individual free to travel on the train. On this view, therefore, questions about conditions and abilities cannot be separated from the basic nature of freedom.

I want now to go back to the issue of the individual's own consciousness of freedom and take up a different theme, although it is linked to the idea of the perception of coercion or prevention. What are we to make of the idea that someone may be prevented from doing something, not by some form of external coercion but by something about their own character or their own nature. An obsessive compulsive disorder gets in the way of A doing X and indeed may require him or her to do Y (to follow the dictates of the compulsion and wash his or her hands every few minutes, let us say), which otherwise A would not do. The question for this account is does this situation have any political significance? Or is it just a matter of personal pathology? Some have argued that there is a link between mental disorder and a political order, such that personal pathologies cannot be separated from the social context in which someone finds him or herself and that this social situation may well have some strong political salience. On this view, a pathology that prevented someone from doing something has political significance and might be thought of as a form of coercion that arises at least indirectly from society at large. Certainly R. D. Laing (1967), Herbert Marcuse (1964), and Eric Fromm (1963) have argued in this sort of way, and this idea of freedom as liberation not just from the coercive power of the state but also from aspects of one's own self that inhibit the capacity for action was a powerful one in the 1960s (Berlin 1997). It has a resonance in the argument deployed in this chapter too in the following way. In the discussion about coercion and impossibility, I pointed out that circumstances that might lead one person to regard a course of action as impossible for him or her might for another person be seen as a challenge but one that could be overcome. That is to say that the perception of coercion is related to features of an individual's mental state. If this state is pathological, then so too is likely to be the perception of the potentially coercive set of circumstances. Again this would reinforce two points made earlier. The first is that, once we move beyond physicalist types of impossibility, then the perception of coercion has a strong psychological element and that this will lapse into subjectivism without some idea of the basic goods of agency. In the pathological state, the basic goods approach becomes even more important in the sense that, if such goods constitute some kind of generic or universal feature of agency, then a failure to recognize these goods may be part of the threshold for the judgement that this failure of perception is indeed pathological as opposed to being only an alternative perception. This idea is consistent with one of the criticisms of positive freedom that it is intrinsically paternalistic. If being free involves pursuing and recognizing a set of basic goods, does this sanction interference with an individual to ensure that he or she is pursuing these goods, even if that is not what he or she desires or has a conscious interest in. This would be a modern version of Rousseau's dictum about 'forcing someone to be free'. In the view of critics of positive freedom, this is an intrinsic feature of positive freedom.

I now want to turn to the idea of rights and the link between rights and freedom. It is frequently argued that there are two ways of grounding ideas of basic moral rights and they are liberty and interests. In this chapter on liberty I shall concentrate on rights and liberty. Again, the distinction between negative and positive liberty is important here. On the negative view of rights, a right is a protection against forbidden forms of coercion: the right to life is a right not to be killed; a right to property is a right not to have the property sequestrated; a right to bodily integrity is a right not to be raped, assaulted, and so forth. These are essentially rights to negative freedoms. The duties imposed on others by such rights claims are also negative. They are fundamentally to do with forbearance. I respect your right to life by abstaining from killing you, your right to property by abstaining from seizing it, and your rights in your body by not abusing your body in proscribed ways. These forbearances are also duties in respect of negative liberty. Negative liberty is compromised by coercion, so respecting another person's negative liberty implies that I will not coerce them. On this view, there is an intrinsic link between negative liberty and essentially negative rights, along with the recognition of mutual forbearance in the common interest of securing negative freedom.

If, however, freedom is seen in a positive way as involving the satisfaction of needs and the development of powers and abilities, then the connection with rights become very different. On the negative view, rights are respected by forbearance and not by positive action, whereas, if rights are positive in terms of the protection of positive freedom, then in turn this requires positive action to protect rights. However, there is a difference, it is argued, in that, in the case of negative rights, the corresponding negative duties lie on both individuals and the state, since these are negative duties that can always be performed whether by the individual or by the state. In each case all that is required is that the individual refrains from coercion. This is not the case with positive rights, which are typically going to be social, economic, and welfare rights. In order for these rights to be protected, the absence of coercion is not enough. There is a positive duty to provide the resources necessary for meeting the right in question. No longer is the right to life, for example, to be seen as a negative right not to be killed—that is a defence of negative freedom—but as a right to the means to life as a positive right in defence of positive freedom. The problem, as critics see it, is that such rights, unlike negative rights, run up against the issue of scarcity. Positive duties involve costs, whereas duties of forbearance are costless. This leads to the point that positive rights typically cannot be held against all others—fellow citizens and the state—since fellow citizens as individuals do not have the resources to meet these positive claims. So, if positive rights protect positive freedoms, it is argued by critics that this implies a fundamental difference between what it means to respect liberty in the negative sense and what it means in the positive sense, and in the latter case it means that the state has to take responsibility for the duty, which can be held equally in terms of negative rights against both the state and the individual. So the difference between negative and positive liberty means that there are differences between the duties in respect of these two sorts of liberties and differences in the role of the state and one's fellow citizens in terms of protecting each type of liberty (Plant 2009).

The issue of freedom and coercion enters in another way too, and that is in the context of the market economy. It is central to the ideas of economic liberals and libertarians that the outcomes of free markets are legitimate, whatever may be the degree of inequality that attends those outcomes (Hayek 1960; Nozick 1974). The point is that, if each act of exchange in a market is uncoerced, then it is legitimate. The aggregate effect of the innumerable acts of uncoerced exchange that occur in a market is to produce at any one time a 'pattern' of income and wealth. That pattern, however, is not intended by anyone and is legitimate because it has arisen out of free exchange.

In a sense, uncoerced exchange gives a kind of procedural legitimacy to the outcome. We have, however, seen that the issue of coercion is a complex and disputable one, and yet it lies at the heart of free-market defences. On the impossibility understanding of coercion, an exchange is coercive only if someone is physically forced into it— otherwise it is an act of free exchange. This is somewhat implausible as a full account of coercion and yet, if we move to the idea of threat, this is quite complex in economic contexts. As we saw, a threat may well depend upon the perception of the person threatened, and in the economic context this is likely to be heavily influenced by that person's economic position and the resources that he or she has. So what would be a coerced or for that matter uncoerced contract in economic terms is likely to depend on the relative bargaining powers and resources of the parties to the contract. Two points are worth making about this. The first is that, on the pure theory of negative liberty, resources do not bear upon the issue of freedom, but yet they are bound to do so in the context of coercion or lack of it in respect of economic contracts. What constitutes a contract that you cannot refuse will depend very much on the resources of the individual who is party to the contract (Green 1888; Hayek 1960). So, if coercion is partly a matter of perception, this is problematic, since it lies at the heart of the economic liberal view of the legitimacy of market outcomes. Obviously a positive theory of liberty would regard any transaction that threatened basic or generic goods as potentially coercive, and a free market would have to be modified in its operation to protect those goods or to have an extra-market set of arrangements like the welfare state to protect the goods.

So we can see that the issue of liberty is crucial to modern politics as one of the central values of the modern world, but it is much easier to invoke than to analyse.

REFERENCES

Primary Sources

ARISTOTLE (1947). *Rhetoric*, trans. J. H. Freese. Loeb Classical Library. London: Heinemann.
GREEN, T. H. (1888). 'Liberal Legislation and Freedom of Contract', in *The Works of T. H. Green*, iii, ed. L. Nettleship. London: Longmans and Green.
HERODOTUS (1998). *Histories*, trans. R. Waterfield. Oxford: Oxford University Press.
HOBBES, T. (1955) [1651]. *Leviathan*, ed. M. Oakeshott. Oxford: Basil Blackwell.
THUCYDIDES (1954). *The Peloponnesian War*, trans. R. Warner. London: Penguin.

Secondary Sources

BERLIN, I. (1969). *Four Essays on Liberty*. Oxford: Oxford University Press.
BERLIN, I. (1997). 'From Hope and Fear Set Free' (1964), in *The Proper Study of Mankind*, (eds) H. Hardy and R. Hausheer. London: Chatto and Windus.
FROMM, E. (1963). *The Sane Society*. London: Routledge.

Gewirth, A. (1978). *Reason and Morality*. Chicago: University of Chicago Press.

Hampshire, S. N. (1960). 'Spinoza and the Idea of Freedom', *Proceedings of the British Academy*, 46: 195–215.

Hayek, F. von (1960). *The Constitution of Liberty*. London: Routledge.

Laing, R. D. (1967). *The Politics of Experience and the Bird of Paradise*. London: Penguin.

Marcuse, H. (1964). *One Dimensional Man*. London: Routledge.

Nozick, R. (1974). *Anarchy, State, and Utopia*. Oxford: Blackwell.

Nussbaum, M. (1990). 'Aristotelian Social Democracy', in R. N. Douglass et al. (eds), *Liberalism and the Good*. London: Routledge.

Nussbaum, M. (1993). 'Non-Relative Virtues: An Aristotelian Approach', in M. Nussbaum and A. K. Sen (eds), *The Quality of Life*. Oxford: Clarendon Press.

Plant, R. (2009). *The Neo-Liberal State*. Oxford: Oxford University Press.

Plant, R. Lesser, H., and Taylor-Gooby, P. (1981). *Political Philosophy and Social Welfare*. London: Routledge. [2nd edn, 2009.]

Rawls, J. (1972). *A Theory of Justice*. Oxford: Oxford University Press.

Sen, A. K. (1999). *Development as Freedom*. Oxford: Oxford University Press.

Skinner, Q. (1998). *Liberty before Liberalism*. Cambridge: Cambridge University Press.

Steiner, H. (1974). 'Individual Liberty', *Proceedings of the Aristotelian Society*, 74: 43.

Swift, A. (2001). *Political Philosophy*. Cambridge: Polity.

Taylor, C. (1985). 'What's Wrong with Negative Liberty?' in *Philosophical Papers*, ii. Cambridge: Cambridge University Press.

CHAPTER 38

DOMINATION
AND SLAVERY

BERNARD R. BOXILL

In North Carolina in the mid-nineteenth century, John Mann, who had hired Lydia, a slave, from her master Eli Jones, shot and wounded her when she tried to run away to avoid being punished. A lower court found Mann guilty of battery, and fined him $5, but North Carolina's Supreme Court overturned the conviction. Supporting its action, the Chief Justice Thomas Ruffin stated that it is "inherent in the relation of master to slave" that the "power of the master had to be absolute, to render the submission of the slave perfect" (see Finkelman 2003: 129–32). Although a later case, *State* v. *Hoover Ruffin*, denied that the master's power had to be so absolute as to include a right to kill his slaves, this still left the master with a right to inflict practically any physical brutality on his slaves short of murdering them in order to obtain their perfect submission.

By insisting that the master must have the perfect submission of his slaves, and the right to abuse his slaves almost without limit, in order to obtain that submission, Ruffin implied that the slaves of the American South were not the pliant individuals Aristotle described as natural slaves (see Aristotle 1996: 15–19). Apparently these black women and men were determined to be free, presumably because they firmly believed that they would be better off free. But some of Ruffin's contemporaries—for example, pro-slavery writer George Fitzhugh—persisted in justifying their enslavement with the Aristotelian argument that they were better off enslaved than free; and some champions of the working class did complain that slaves were well off and indeed better off than many Northern workers (see Fitzhugh 1988: 18–19).

Abolitionists indignantly dismissed the complaint, but there was something to it. Frederick Douglass reported that some slave masters fed their slaves well, never overworked them, never whipped them except for misconduct, and, in general, ruled mildly with "some sense of justice" and "some feelings of humanity" (see Douglass 1987: 158). By comparison many free workers could seem badly off. Of course, they had greater freedom of movement than the slaves, but some slaves enjoyed considerable freedom of movement. Douglass himself when he was the slave of Hugh Auld in Baltimore found his own employment, had his own lodging, and could come and go more or less as he pleased (as long as he remained in the general area and did not try to escape north), although Auld saw him once a week to take most of his earnings (Douglass 1987: 193).

In what way, then, and by how much was the working man better off than the slave? Douglass allowed that the difference might not be great. The slaveholders, he claimed, had succeeded in making the laboring white man "almost" as much a slave as the "black slave himself" (Douglass 1987: 188) But some contemporary philosophical discussions go much further, suggesting that essentially the laboring white man and the black slave were both enslaved. For example, this is the clear implication of Philip Pettit's discussion of domination, freedom, and slavery in his book *Republicanism* (Pettit 1997: 31–5). According to Pettit, a person is dominated when someone has the capacity to interfere in her choices "without reference" to her "interests," or "opinions," and to choose to do so "at their pleasure" (Pettit 1997: 52). She is free if she is not dominated. Pettit calls her freedom "republican freedom," marking it off from the two conceptions of liberty, negative and positive, that Isaiah Berlin had distinguished and made famous in his 1958 essay "Two Concepts of Liberty" (Pettit 1997: 17–28) As Berlin had explained, positive freedom is associated with participation in a democratically self-governing community and is the liberty of the ancients; and negative freedom is the absence of interference and is the liberty of the moderns. According to Pettit, republican liberty—freedom as non-domination—is the liberty of Cicero, the ancient Romans, and the American Founders (Pettit 1997: 19, 44).

Pettit claims next that, in the republican tradition, domination is slavery, implying that, since the American Founders had adopted or inherited that tradition, and believed that they were dominated by the British Parliament, they therefore spoke appropriately when they claimed to be slaves (Pettit 1997: 31–2). Domination may be slavery in the republican tradition; and many American revolutionaries did protest that they were slaves. But many well-informed people on both sides of the Atlantic dismissed these protestations as at best rhetoric and at worse hypocrisy. They were outraged that the revolutionaries complained so loudly of being enslaved while themselves holding black people in a condition that was on all accounts far worse than the "slavery" that they claimed to be in and were making war to abolish. Pettit makes no mention of this fact, although it raises awkward questions for his suggestion that the American revolutionaries claimed appropriately to be enslaved. For example, if many of their contemporaries judged these claims to be outlandish, then domination could not have been widely thought to be slavery, for it was patently the case that the British Parliament dominated the Americans. Of course, republicans might have held domination to be slavery, although few others agreed with them, but in that case it is odd that the American revolutionaries used a vocabulary so out of step with that of their contemporaries, especially when they had claimed in their Declaration of Independence to be anxious to explain their actions to the world. Had they adopted the republican philosophy in order to be able to call themselves slaves, using this self-appellation to arouse their righteous indignation at British domination? If so, they should have been aware that their protestations of enslavement would seem like self-serving bombast to those outside the republican tradition and would win them the evil reputation of being liars and hypocrites, rather than the fame they sought (see Adair 1974: 3–36).

I will argue that domination is not slavery. It may have been slavery in ancient Rome, but it was not slavery in eighteenth-century America and Europe. According to the republican definition of domination, practically everyone was dominated, white as well as black, English as well as Americans, the rich as well as the poor. But everyone saw the radical and patent difference between the condition of whites and that of the black men and women held in bondage in the Americas, and most (who did not have an axe to grind) had the moral decency not to try to obscure it by using the same term "slavery" to refer to both conditions.

DOMINATION AND FEAR

As if to confirm that the republican tradition was right to equate domination and slavery, Pettit describes them as both characteristically condemning their victims to lives of fear, deference, flattery, and slyness. Thus he writes that dominated persons live "in a position where fear and deference will be the normal order of the day" (Pettit 1997: 64); he cites the authors of *Cato's Letters* warning that "a life of Slavery" is "a continual State of Uncertainty and Wretchedness, often an Apprehension of Violence, of the lingering Dread of a violent Death" (Pettit 1997: 33); Algernon Sidney's claim that slavery produces "meanness of spirit and its worst effect, flattery"; and Mary Wollstonecraft's claim that the domination of wives by husbands drives wives to "sly tricks" and "cunning," noting that Wollstonecraft describes the condition of those women as one of "slavery" (Pettit 1997: 61).

Presumably Pettit gives fear a prominent place among the characteristics of the life of dominated and enslaved people because he is anxious to prove the wickedness of dominating people. But he undoes this proof by citing the American revolutionaries as dominated and enslaved, for, with the possible exception of Jefferson fleeing on horseback when the British approached Monticello, the revolutionaries seemed defiant rather than fearful. "Give me liberty or give me death" is not the lament of a man living in "fear and deference." Pettit's emphasis on fear as characteristic of dominated people is especially significant, since he insists that the dominator need never actually interfere arbitrarily in the choices of the dominated. It is "important to see," he writes, "that domination goes with the accessibility of arbitrary interference to another, and that the improbability" of interference does not make for its "inaccessibility" (Pettit 1997: 64). In that case, if Pettit believes that the dominated do nevertheless typically live in fear, he must assume that people live in fear even of dangers they know to be very distant. But we do not normally live in fear of such dangers. If we did, we would always live in fear, because *necessarily* we always live with distant dangers; living with them is a part of the human condition, an essential aspect of our mortality and vulnerability, and we all (excepting infants and the demented) know it.

Some dominated people live with only distant dangers, because their dominators are kindly, but many have themselves taken steps to *make* their dangers distant. Consider the wives Mary Wollstonecraft describes as resorting to "sly tricks" and "cunning" in response to the domination of their husbands, the slaves Algernon Sydney describes as resorting to "flattery" to soften the rigors of their domination, and to their number let us add Sambo, the sly and cunning slave trickster of the American South, and Quashie, the similarly sly and cunning slave trickster of the Caribbean. These individuals behaved as they did *from* fear. They foresaw a possible future evil, and fear of that evil disposed them to devise their strategies of slyness and flattery to avoid it. But there is no reason to believe that they continued to live in fear, *after* devising and implementing their strategies, and after seeing that these strategies worked. To insist that they did is to fall back on the already refuted claim that people live in fear of distant dangers. Neither is it plausible to argue that, even if the strategies of Sambo and the sly wives were successful, they still lived in fear, because only fear could *keep* them using the strategies. We are all constantly doing things, like taking medicine, eating (and breathing!) to avoid death, but we do not live in constant fear of death. If the objector insists that we do live in fear, I give him the word "fear," but insist on the essential point that on his account living in fear does not mean living miserably.

Consider finally Hobbes's argument that we institute the sovereign from fear of the "continual fear and danger of violent death," which are "the worst of all" miseries of the state of war (Hobbes 1994: 76). If we remained in continual fear even after establishing a sovereign, he would have to admit that instituting the sovereign was a colossal failure. Locke objected that it was because he said it substituted the danger of pole cats and foxes for the danger of a lion, since no one of his subjects can resist him (Locke 1988: 328). But polecats and foxes do not frighten us the way that other human beings do in the state of nature. And we are not frightened by distant dangers and the sovereign poses only a distant danger to any one of his subjects; he can kill any one of them if he chooses to, but it is very unlikely that he will choose to kill any particular one of them, at least if they are numerous. (And if they are not numerous, he may not certainly be able to kill any one of them.)

In sum, there is no reason to suppose that sly wives who are confident of their slyness will live in fear of their husbands. Indeed, sometimes it is the husbands who come to fear them, even while continuing to dominate them. Masters, too, sometimes fear certain of their slaves—even while continuing to dominate them. As Douglass recounts, Aunt Katy had a "strong hold" over "old master," who was her master (Douglass 1962: 34).

Nothing I have said implies that the enslaved and the dominated live happy lives. Normally many do not. But fear is not the only thing that makes us unhappy, and focusing on it as characteristic of the dominated ignores the well-established human capacity to invent strategies to make dangers distant and consequently to live without fear—even if unhappily. As we shall see, ignoring that capacity helps to obscure the difference between domination and slavery.

DOMINATION AND IMAGINATION

In the exchange between Hobbes and Locke just mentioned, Locke would have argued more cogently had he contended that the subjects of a Hobbesian sovereign are likely to be unhappy and dissatisfied even if they do not live in fear. But he would still not have caught Hobbes unprepared. Hobbes was well aware of the tendency of normal human beings to become unhappy and dissatisfied once they believe that their dangers are distant. Thus, while he allowed that individuals could cooperate with each other and make their dangers distant without the help of a sovereign, he warned that the peace and security they thus gained would always be short lived, because, as soon as human beings make their dangers distant, they at once become quarrelsome. In his memorable words, "man is . . . most troublesome when he is most at ease" (Hobbes 1994: 109). Hobbes therefore understood that even the sovereign's confirmed readiness to use his overwhelming power to punish rebellion or disobedience will not be sufficient to guarantee peace. His power may cow his subjects into good behavior, but, as soon as their good behavior makes the danger of punishment distant, they begin to feel at ease, and they become troublesome. In other words, Hobbes understood that threatening disobedience with severe punishment is often self-defeating, since, if it makes people obedient, it makes their dangers distant, and consequently puts them at ease, which then makes them "troublesome."

According to Hobbes, the most important cause of the somewhat self-destructive tendency of human beings to become troublesome when they are at ease is that "art of words" by which "some men can represent to others, that which is good, in the likeness of evil, and evil, in the likeness of good; and augment, or diminish the apparent greatness of good and evil." This art is one of the consequences of the "compounded" imagination, which enables us to put together different parts of the images of things we have perceived by sense to make images of things that we have not have perceived by sense, as, for example, "when from the sight of a man at one time, and of a horse at another, we conceive in our mind a Centaur" (Hobbes 1994: 9). To guarantee peace, the sovereign must, therefore, do more than to threaten disobedience with punishment; he must find means to control the imaginations of his subjects after his threats have made them obedient and put them at ease. To this end Hobbes was especially insistent that the sovereign control the works of art that he allowed into the commonwealth. Probably he worried that, because art is an especially moving product of the compounded imagination, it would dangerously stimulate the already naturally restless imaginations of the subjects. Hobbes gives a typically insightful and cynical example of the power of art to do this. He writes: "when a man compoundeth the image of his own person with the image of the actions of another man, as when a man imagines himself a Hercules or an Alexander, which happeneth often to them that are much taken with romances, it is a compound imagination..." (Hobbes 1994: 9). The danger to the commonwealth was that the images of himself that a man dreams up when he reads romances need not remain mere pleasant fantasies, but can lead the dreamer to become disruptive and dangerous. Thus Hobbes argues that one of the "most frequent causes" of rebellion and discord is the reading of "histories of the ancient Greeks and Romans," from which young men "receiving a strong and delightful impression of the great exploits of war" have sometimes "undertaken to kill their kings, because the Greek and Latin Writers, in their books, and discourses of policy, make it lawful, and laudable, for any man to do so; provided before he do it, he call him tyrant." Accordingly, Hobbes gave the sovereign advice on how to curb the imaginations of his subjects. He should suppress such books. "I cannot imagine," he writes, "how any thing can be more prejudicial to a monarchy, than the allowing of such books to be publicly read" (Hobbes 1994: 214–15).

Douglass's experience confirmed Hobbes's primary insight that, though people may live without fear when their dangers are distant, this very absence of fear, which puts them at ease, also frees their imagination and makes them troublesome and unhappy with their condition. When Douglass was hired out to the kindly Freeland, who treated him well, his dangers were distant and he was at ease. But then, precisely as Hobbes would have predicted, once he was at ease his imagination insistently painted him beautiful dreams of freedom and he became "restless and discontented." Summing up the process, Douglass wrote that, if you treat a slave well, "work him moderately— surround him with physical comfort—dreams of freedom intrude. Give him a bad master, and he aspires to a good master; give him a good master, and he wishes to be his own master" (Douglass 1987: 161–2).

Douglass's experience also confirmed that the slave masters had grasped Hobbes's second insight that, in order to prevent people from becoming troublesome, once threats have cowed them into obedience, one must control their imaginations. Thus he recounted how the slaveholders supplemented their policy of punishing misbehavior with other strategies designed to paralyze the slaves' imaginations even when they had *not* misbehaved. As Douglass put it, if the "bad slave had to be whipped to be *made* good," it was also the case that the "good slave must be whipped to be *kept* good" (Douglass 1987: 159). One especially effective strategy was to fill the slave with the fear of unexpected torture made *independently* of misbehavior. The system of one Rigby Hopkins, Douglass reports, was to whip his slaves "in advance" of their "deserving it" (Douglass 1987: 159). But it was Covey who perfected this system. Douglass's reflections on the effects of Covey's strategy confirm its effectiveness. Being preoccupied with thoughts of being whipped, he reports, drove troublesome dreams of freedom from his mind. "When I was looking for the blow about to be inflicted upon my head, I was not thinking of my liberty; it was my life" (Douglass 1950: 157). And he summarized the strategy as follows: "Beat and cuff your slave, keep him hungry and spiritless, and he will follow the chain of his master like a dog" (Douglass 1987: 161). A second strategy was to use a carefully controlled religion that encouraged the idea that the world was a vale of tears anyway and that justice would come in the afterlife; another was to make some products of the compounded imagination so dreadfully wrong as to be unthinkable (Jefferson 1984: 269). Yet another was conditioning—for example, according to Douglass, encouraging slaves to get drunk on holidays in order to make them compound freedom with nausea and in this way make freedom unattractive. A fourth was to punish slaves for even thinking of a different way of doing something; and a fifth was to prevent slaves from learning to read, from exchanging ideas, from listening to what their masters say among themselves, and in general from becoming aware of any worlds dangerously different from the world of slaves and masters that they beheld. The consequences of failures to enforce these restrictions underline their necessity. Mrs Auld, the slave-holder's wife, taught Douglass to read; the book *The Columbian Orator* fell into his hands; and both events had evil consequences for slavery (Douglass 1987: 92, 99). Summing up the various strategies and their purpose, Douglass wrote: "To make a contented slave, you have to make a thoughtless one. It is necessary to darken his moral and mental vision, and as far as possible to annihilate his power of reason. He must be able to detect no inconsistency in slavery . . ." (Douglass 1987: 194).

Presumably these strategies could eventually become unnecessary if the slave became convinced that escape was impossible. As this conviction sank in, her imagination producing delightful visions of freedom that she knows will never come true and that emphasize the dreariness of her life could become a source of torment to her. In that case, she may herself stifle her imagination and deliberately force it into harmless directions or to stick to the humdrum and the dull routine of slave life. As a result, hope may fade, as it is constituted in part by the imagination's delightful visions of freedom, and give way to despair and compliance. But the disposition to dream of freedom tends to reassert itself if there is the smallest respite, especially if the slave gets even the briefest glimpse of beauty. Douglass's experience provides an example. He reports that when he was a slave of Covey he lived close to the Chesapeake Bay and on summer Sabbaths, the only days that Covey did not beat him, he often gazed at its "broad bosom" that was "ever white with sails from every quarter of the habitable globe." Even when prospects of freedom seemed most remote, the beauty of the scene stimulated his imagination. Those "beautiful vessels," he wrote, "robed in purest white, so delightful to the eye of freemen, were to me so many shrouded ghosts, to terrify and torment me with thoughts of my wretched condition." Sometimes the ships moved his imagination in another way and he would think of them as "freedom's swift-winged angels, that fly around the world," and would be moved to "pour out his soul's complaint" to them, "O, that I were free! O, that I were on one of your gallant decks, and under your protecting wing! Could I but swim. If I could fly!" (Douglass 1987: 136).

So, even Covey's method was not foolproof. Indeed, sometimes it backfired dramatically. The constant torture could drive the slave to conclude that death was better than his life filled with torture. When that happened, the slave lost his fear of death and became very dangerous to his master. Thus Covey's torture drove Douglass actually to fight him. Normally slaves shrank from such a desperate measure, since it was inflexibly punished with death, but, as Douglass reports, he had reached "the point at which

I was not afraid to die" (Douglass 1987: 152). His comments on the consequences of the incident, for luckily for him Covey did not have him killed, is that he had become "a freeman in fact," while he remained "a slave in form" (Douglass 1987: 152). Covey's torture had freed him from the fear of death, and by fighting Covey he had served notice that he was prepared to be killed to avoid being tortured and consequently also lived free of the fear of torture. Living without these fears put him at ease and freed his imagination. Though he remained a slave "in form," for he would be shot if he attempted simply to walk off the plantation, by claiming to be a "freeman in fact," Douglass was therefore celebrating the supreme importance of the freedom of the imagination. And, of course, as a result he became troublesome.

The lesson that Douglass learned from that incident is worth reflecting on. It tells us that some, if not all, human beings are capable not only of making their dangers distant and as a result living at ease and without fear, but also of living without fear of even immediate dangers. The American revolutionaries performed the feat and, as I mentioned earlier, were mostly fearless, although they lived in grave and sometimes immediate danger. How misleading then it is to make fear and deference characteristic of the dominated!

CONCLUSION

Dominated people are not typically fearful and deferential, as Pettit suggests they are. Remember that most of us are dominated, and many of us at least are not fearful and deferential. Making fear characteristic of the dominated ignores the capacity of human beings to make their immediate dangers distant and to live without fear of the dangers they have thus made distant; indeed, some human beings manage to live without fear even of immediate dangers that they cannot make distant. When dominated people live without fear despite their dangers either distant or immediate, their imaginations are free to roam at will, and consequently they become troublesome. Many dominators do not mind such troublesomeness as long as it does not go beyond certain limits. They find it a small price to pay for the liveliness of mind that it usually brings with it. John Adams dominated Abigail Adams, as a glance at their letters to each other show, but, as these letters also show, he did not try to prevent her from being well read in literature, philosophy, and politics and abreast of avant-garde ideas. The freedom he allowed her, and it was only a negative freedom, made her somewhat troublesome, but he obviously delighted in the liveliness of her mind that came with it. Other dominators allow those they dominate to be troublesome, because the liveliness of mind that comes with it makes their domination economically profitable. People cannot operate complicated machinery when they are distracted by fear. And some dominators are prevented by law from crippling the imaginations of those they dominate. Jailors normally may not prevent convicts from reading what they like, writing and receiving letters, and exchanging ideas with others. Such convicts may be behind bars, but their souls may be free, as the poet assures us is possible.

As Orlando Patterson points out, slaves are not always held as sources of economic profit. Indeed, in some societies slaves are economic liabilities to their masters. Their masters nevertheless hold them as slaves in order to display their power and greatness. It is important that such slaves show no sign of thinking or acting independently of their masters, as this would suggest some limit on their masters' power. In other words, they must be completely submissive to their masters. Masters who have slaves partly for economic profit also display their power by making their slaves completely submissive to them. Accordingly, while slave masters are, of course, also dominators, they are not like the ordinary dominators considered above who for various reasons want the people they dominate to retain some independence of mind. Slave masters want and are permitted and able to use almost any strategy to control the imaginations of their slaves and consequently to compel their submissiveness. Ordinary dominators allow those they dominate to think, to exchange ideas, and to imagine. Douglass, responding to claims that the Irish were slaves as usual, got the distinction between domination and slavery right. The Irish, he wrote, "can speak and write"; they have their "Conciliation Hall . . . their reform Clubs, and their newspapers." But "how is it with the American slave? Where may he assemble? Where is his Conciliation Hall? Where are his newspapers?" (Douglass 1982: 258–9).

Since the most important and reliable of the strategies to deaden the slaves' imagination is to compel them to live in constant fear, there would be no difference between slavery and mere domination if domination *per se* made people fearful. In that case, the mere dominator would also be a slave master. But, as I have insisted, domination does not normally make people fearful, or at least not for long. Almost invariably dominated people devise strategies to make their dangers distant and to avoid living in fear. It is this stubborn human disposition to imagine, a tribute to both our reason and our will, that drives the masters of slaves to the extremes of cruelty, manipulation, and conditioning that we associate with slavery, but not with mere domination.

One consequence of my analysis is that it enables us firmly to reject the complaints of the American revolutionaries that they were slaves of the British Parliament. Whether or not domination is slavery in the republican tradition, these complaints ignored the important difference between slavery and mere domination. The imaginations of slaves are cribbed, confined, and paralyzed, or in constant and immediate danger of being so. The merely dominated are guaranteed the freedom of their imaginations. Thus the revolutionaries may have been dominated, but they were not enslaved. Their minds were among the freest in history. The learning and intellectual sophistication of the Founding Fathers that astounds modern readers attests to this fact. As one commentator has put it, they had free access to, and fully availed themselves of, the veritable "treasure trove" of Europe's most radical and advanced philosophy. Probably the revolutionaries knew that they were not really slaves and used their complaints of enslavement to help foment a righteous indignation against British domination. The lie may have been necessary or helpful to that end, but it detracted from the fame that they sought and forever tainted their reputations. Republicanism should be praised for reminding us of the evils of domination, but blamed for obscuring its difference from slavery. All domination is bad, but only domination of the imagination is slavery. As a result, the slave who has by luck or courage or guile managed to avoid the exercise of that domination against him is the most dangerous of all slaves.

References

Adair, D. (1974). *Fame and the Founding Fathers: Essays by Douglass Adair*. [1967], (ed.) Trevor Colbourn. Indianapolis: Liberty Fund.

Aristotle (1996). *The Politics* and *The Constitution of Athens*, (ed.) Stephen Everson. Cambridge: Cambridge University Press.

Douglass, F. (1950). *The Life and Writings of Frederick Douglass*, I [1846], (ed.) Philip S. Foner. New York, International Publishers.

Douglass, F. (1962). *The Life and Times of Frederick Douglass* [1892]. New York, Collier Books.

Douglass, F. (1982). *The Frederick Douglass Papers* [1850], II, (ed.) John W. Blassingame. New Haven: Yale University Press.

Douglass, F. (1987). *My Bondage and My Freedom* [1855], (ed.) William L. Andrews. Chicago, University of Chicago Press.

Finkelman, P. (2003). *Defending Slavery: Proslavery Thought in the Old South, A Brief History with Documents* [1829], (ed.) Paul Finkelman. Boston: Bedford St Martin's.

Fitzhugh, G. (1988). *Cannibals All* [1856], (ed.) C. Vann Woodward. Cambridge, MA: Harvard University Press.

Hobbes, T. (1991). *Man and Citizen* [1642], (ed.) Bernard Gert. Indianapolis: Hackett.

Hobbes, T. (1994). *Leviathan* [1651], (ed.) Edwin Curley. Indianapolis: Hackett.

Jefferson, T. (1984). *Jefferson, Autobiography, Notes on the State of Virginia, Public and Private Papers, Addresses, Letters* [1787], (ed.) Merrill D. Peterson. New York: Library of America.

Locke, J. (1988). *Two Treatises of Government* [1690], (ed.) Peter Laslett. New York: Cambridge University Press.

Pettit, P. (1997). *Republicanism: A Theory of Freedom and Government*. Oxford: Clarendon Press.

CHAPTER 39

···

IMPERIALISM

···

KRISHAN KUMAR

EMPIRE AND IMPERIALISM

···

THERE have been empires aplenty in the past—indeed much of recorded history is a history of empires. But imperialism, as an idea and a doctrine, is of relatively recent vintage. In its common understanding, it was first established not much earlier than the middle of the nineteenth century. This both simplifies and complicates our task. It simplifies it because we have to deal only with the most recent period of empire. It complicates it because this temporal constriction involves a severe narrowing of the field. It can lead us to ignore the varieties of empire that are to be found throughout history, in all parts of the globe. It also has the tendency to play down the legacies of past empires, the ways in which they influenced both the thinking and the practices of modern empires. There is a traceable imperial tradition, certainly in the West, that can be occluded or ignored by too strong an emphasis on those empires, and that historical period, that gave rise to systematic theorizing about empire and imperialism.

Imperialism relates to the theory and practice of the European empires of the nineteenth and twentieth centuries. There were European empires before that, of course, many of which had a continuous history from those earlier times well into the twentieth century. These include some of the best known: the Ottoman; Portuguese; Spanish; Austrian; Russian; Dutch; British; and French empires, all of which had their origins in the fifteenth and sixteenth centuries (Aldrich 2007). Running alongside these was the even longer-lasting though sometimes ineffectual Holy Roman Empire, whose important role in keeping the imperial idea alive in the Middle Ages and beyond has unfairly been slighted owing to the popularity of Voltaire's quip that it was 'neither Holy, nor Roman, nor an Empire' (Muldoon 1999).

Most important of all, perhaps, are the memory and legacy of the Roman Empire (and behind that, the empire of Alexander the Great) (Koebner 1961: 18). No modern empire could forget Rome; all aspired in some way or the other to imitate it. Themes from the Roman Empire—the idea of universality, of the civilizing mission, of the inevitable decline and fall of empires—haunted modern empires. From the end of the Roman Empire in the West also came the concept of *translatio imperii*, the transmission and handing-over of the imperial mission from one culture and civilization to another. The Holy Roman Empire of Charlemagne first established the idea. It was challenged by the Byzantine Empire, which, as the Roman Empire in the East, with uninterrupted existence right up to 1453, saw itself as the legitimate successor to Rome. Later the Spanish, with their Christianizing mission in the New World, laid claim to the title—a claim disputed later by the French, British, and other modern empires (Pagden 1995). Even the Ottomans in the early years, newly installed in the Byzantine capital of Constantinople, saw themselves as the heirs of Rome.

Thus one can see the artificiality of cutting off one period of history and designating it the period of imperialism. The cross-cutting ties and influences, across space and time, are too great (one should remember the enormous impact of Alexander on Middle Eastern and Asian concepts of empire). Empire is a multifarious and many-stranded project, making easy definition treacherous. Noting that 'the imperial historian . . . is very much at the mercy of his own particular concept of empire', two of the best-known scholars of empire observed that, 'since imperial historians are writing about different empires . . . it is hardly surprising that these historians sometimes contradict each other' (Gallagher and Robinson 1953: 1). No doubt there are 'family resemblances' between all instances of empire, else we would not use the same word to describe them. The fact that there is a tradition of empire also indicates similarities and continuities of meaning and purpose. Nevertheless, it would be well to be warned in advance that one cannot, for any useful purpose, expect to find a sufficiently all-embracing concept of empire to cover all cases, let alone a 'theory' of imperialism that adequately accounts for their rise, development, and fall.

Two complications are particularly important. The first is that empire, as a derivation of the Latin *imperium*, originally and for much of the time afterwards meant primarily authority: sovereign and central authority. That meaning persisted through the Middle Ages, and can still be seen clearly, for example, in the famous pronouncement of the 1533 Act in Restraint of Appeals of Henry VIII that 'this realm of England is an empire, entire of itself'—meaning that there was no appeal—say to Rome—from the supreme and final authority of the English king (Armitage 2000: 35).

The meaning of empire as sovereignty can be quite independent of the second main meaning that also developed—though somewhat later—with the later Roman Republic and especially the Empire itself. The sheer size of Rome, its expansion to so many corners of the known world, and its rule over a multiplicity of peoples, led to the use of *imperium* to designate rule over a large space and many peoples. Here was conceived that principle of universality that is so common to empires: all aspire ultimately to be the only empire, the sole source of civilization and security, the empire *totius orbis*, of the whole world. Here too was accepted the principle of plurality that marks such large domains. Empires incorporate people of many kinds. They aim to civilize and enlighten them, through the agency of law and other common institutions, including language. They may, as the Romans eventually did, extend citizenship to all the subjects of empire. But they rarely aim at cultural homogenization; they are rarely exclusive in a racial or ethnic sense. To do so (as was practised by the Nazi Empire, for instance) is to invite a swift demise. Empires are multicultural and multinational almost by definition, in this second and, in the modern period, increasingly popular sense.

The distinction—in principle separable—between empire as sovereignty and empire as rule over diverse peoples is one of the things that complicates attempts at a unified concept or definition of empire. Another that became increasingly prominent with the development of modern empires is the distinction between formal and informal empire. It was noted, particularly with the growth of the British Empire in the nineteenth century, that formal possession of territories in the form of settlements and colonies was only one way in which empire expressed itself. Equally important were all the informal ways that states can put pressure, often of a determining kind, on the policies and practices of other nominally independent states and peoples. Thus the British did not formally rule Egypt at any time; but for much of the period from the 1880s to the 1950s no one doubted that it was British interests and British policies that determined the affairs, internal and external, of Egypt. Similarly, Britain never formally annexed Argentina; but, for much of the nineteenth and well into the twentieth centuries, Argentinian development, political and economic, was overwhelmingly dictated by British financial and commercial interests. Empire means rule; but it can also mean simply control. For many purposes, effective control is more efficient and economical than formal rule. In any case, say John Gallagher and Ronald Robinson in a highly influential account, to understand empire by focusing only on its formal elements is 'rather like judging the size and character of icebergs solely from the parts above the water-line' (Gallagher and Robinson 1953: 1).

These distinctions, and the differing forms and aspects of empire that they highlight, illustrate well the problems of achieving consensus on the meaning of empire. For some theorists the inclusion of informal empire, for instance, throws open the door intolerably and impossibly wide, making it almost impossible to study empires as specific political formations (e.g. Baumgart 1982). Others argue that to ignore informal aspects of empire would, as Gallagher and Robinson suggest, be to leave out some of the most important ways in which large states can control the politics of other states without taking them over—and thus to leave out a large part of the impact of imperialism (e.g. Fieldhouse 1973; see also Louis 1976). It looks as if we must remain content with some broad characterization that allows us to include most of the best-known varieties of empire without its being so comprehensive as to be useless.

A widely accepted definition of empire, in these terms, is that of the political scientist Michael Doyle: 'Empire . . . is a system of interaction between two political entities, one of which, the dominant metropole, exerts political control over the external and external policy—the effective sovereignty—of the other, the subordinate periphery' (Doyle 1986: 12). There are various helpful elements to this definition. The emphasis on 'two political entities' indicates the *foreignness* of imperial rule, the fact of imposition of rule by one polity (the metropole) over another (the periphery). Note that this allows us, in relevant cases, to speak of the creation of several well-known nation states as 'imperial', and the resulting creations as in effect empires in miniature, or 'mini-empires'. This might apply to Great Britain, Spain, the France of the 'hexagon', perhaps even united Italy and Germany. In all these cases what came to be thought of as nation states was the result of an internal process of conquest and colonization, akin in many cases to the construction of more conventionally regarded land empires such as the Ottoman, Russian, and Habsburg empires (Kumar 2009).

The focus on 'control' allows for the existence of both formal and informal systems of power and influence. It is this, for instance, that gives rise to the widespread discussion of 'the American empire', since, although America has conspicuously turned its face against the formal acquisition of overseas territories, to many commentators its global power is nothing if not imperial (e.g. Mann 2003). The controversies surrounding the 'American empire' (see Steinmetz 2005; Maier 2006) show well the problematic nature of the concept of informal empire. If America sometimes behaves in an imperial way, it has also often—consistent with its own anti-imperial foundation—supported the anti-imperial cause, even if sometimes in a self-interested way. A good example would be Franklin D. Roosevelt's well-known hostility to the British Empire, and the important role he played in forcing on the pace of British decolonization after the Second World War. It may in some ways be necessary to hold on to the idea of informal empire, but we need to be careful about how we apply it; it runs the risk of being too widely and indiscriminately used.

Doyle's definition of empire also points to the radical inequality of the relationship between metropole and colony, centre and periphery. This too, of course, can be replicated in the conventional nation state, many of which—such as Italy—have 'backward', less-developed regions that are sometimes considered—and that sometimes consider themselves—to be in the nature of internal 'colonies'. The United Kingdom has, for instance, been discussed in terms of 'internal colonialism', with the 'Celtic fringe' of Scotland, Wales, and Ireland being considered the colonial peripheries in relation to the English metropole (Hechter 1999). But, although these parallels can be illuminating, it is usually fairly clear how empires differ from nation states in this respect. It is not simply that great physical distance often separates the metropole from the colonies or peripheries, as is obvious in the case of overseas empires. There are also frequently great differences of race and culture, such that the interaction of metropole and colony has a very different character from that between the centre and periphery of even the most unequally divided nation state. There is an 'otherness' in empire that is generally one of its most striking features, greater even than the actual degrees of inequality, which can indeed often be approximated by nation states.

If this is empire, then naturally 'imperialism is simply the process or policy of establishing or maintaining an empire' (Doyle 1986: 45). But this simple statement conceals an important historical divide. It was only in the nineteenth century that people began to ask seriously why states became empires, what drove them to it, who benefited most from empire, and similar questions of ideology and interest. The empires of the past certainly had both apologists and critics—the great debates over the Spanish Empire in the sixteenth century are proof enough of this, as are the equally well-known controversies within the Roman Empire about its purpose and mission. But they had not been self-conscious about empire as such, and about imperialism as an explicit policy and goal. It was only when, in response to what seemed to them novel in its scope and intent, nineteenth-century thinkers began to reflect systematically on empire, that such thinking could be redirected to past empires, as instances (perhaps) of a common pattern. Then, too, attempts could be made to distinguish between 'modern' and 'ancient' imperialism, and other such questions relevant to the study of empire. But first of all empire had to become imperialism, the theory and practice of empire.

THEORIES OF IMPERIALISM

For some students of empire, empire represents an ever-present possibility, because imperialism is a drive that is inherent in the very nature of human society and politics. States will always strive to subdue and control other states, because it is in their manifest interest to do so. All that inhibits or prevents this is the like motivation of other states, leading to the characteristic pattern of the rise and fall of empires, as some states acquire empires only to lose them to other, rising, states. In this view, the only thing that prevents a powerful state from becoming an empire is the existence of other empires that, for the time being at least, populate and possess the world. Given the opportunity, all states wish to be empires (e.g. Baumgart 1982; Doyle 1986: 26–47; Münkler 2007: 28-46; Go 2008).

This realpolitk view of empire gets considerable support from the history of empire in the West, though it is somewhat problematic in other cases. China, for instance, was easily the wealthiest and most powerful state in the world in the early fifteenth century, sending great fleets across the oceans and clearly capable of establishing an overseas empire. Yet, for reasons much discussed, it chose not to do so. In the early Ming period it destroyed its fleets and turned in on itself (Abu-Lughod 1989). Whether or not China is itself to be considered an empire—another controversial matter (Purdue 2005)— there seems no doubt that it gave up the opportunity to become an even greater one. Imperialism perhaps needs a greater explanation than simply human propensity, or at least the universal propensity of states.

Such a view gained conviction in late nineteenth-century Europe. Commentators were, of course, aware of earlier empires, and freely made comparisons between them and modern empires—Rome being an especially popular point of comparison (e.g. Lucas 1912). But they also felt that there was something new about modern empires, and especially about the phase of empire-building that took place in the late nineteenth century—the phase sometimes called the 'new imperialism', and associated particularly with the 'scramble for Africa' among European powers. The intensity of the struggle, the rivalries it called forth, and the sense among the players that what was at stake was nothing less than their survival as great powers, lent to that period of imperialism a special character, and seemed to call for a special explanation (Mommsen 1982; Hobsbawm 1987: 56–60).

'Imperialism', as a term, came into the European political lexicon trailing clouds of suspicion and disapproval that it has never quite been able to dispel. It seems first to have been applied by the British to express their revulsion from the 'despotic' regime established by Louis Bonaparte and his Second Empire following the *coup d'état* of 1851. Imperialism—seen as an unfortunately persistent French trait—here recalled the First Empire of Napoleon; it connoted not simply popular authoritarianism and Caeserism but military adventurism and the search for glory through conquest. In this sense—which also harks back, though with disparaging overtones, to the original meaning of *imperium* as authority—it came to be employed in the 1870s by English critics of Benjamin Disraeli's imperialist policies, also seen as inimical to peace abroad and freedom at home. Imperialism thus moved from being a description, mostly unflattering, of a system of (French) domestic politics to a way of conceiving the policies—initially in a negative light—of the largest and most powerful empire of the time—the British Empire (Koebner and Schmidt 1964: chs 1–6).

But, in the hands of politicians such as Disraeli, Chamberlain, and Rosebery, and such great proconsular figures as Cromer, Curzon, and Milner, not to mention popular writers such as Rudyard Kipling and Rider Haggard, imperialism could also be presented positively, as the noble and necessary task of civilizing the world. Such a view was widely found across the political spectrum in France, Germany, and Italy as well as Britain in the late nineteenth and early twentieth centuries. It was perhaps precisely because imperialism became so popular, so taken for granted by a large section of public opinion, that there was so little attempt to *theorize* empire from the perspective of those who favoured it. There were indeed several important commentaries, by sympathetic travellers, publicists, and historians—Charles Dilke's *Greater Britain* (1868), John Seeley's *Expansion of England* (1883), and James Froude's *Oceana* (1886) being among the most influential in the British case—but little in the way of systematic theorizing about empire and imperialism by imperialists themselves (Koebner and Schmidt 1964: 166–95; Bell 2007).

What have come down to us as 'theories' of imperialism are almost wholly critical. This is largely because of the essentially Marxist character of most of them. Even non-Marxist theories, being largely reactions and responses to Marxists ones, retained the critical edge. They merely argued that economic explanations of imperialism were wrong or insufficient. Especially in the wake of the Russian Revolution of 1917, and in tandem with the gathering wave of anti-colonial nationalist movements of the twentieth century, accounts of imperialism generally accepted that imperialism was indefensible on moral grounds and, if necessary for the purposes of economic or political development, a regrettable necessity.

The most influential theory of modern imperialism was in fact penned not by a Marxist or even a socialist but by a self-professed English liberal, J. A. Hobson. Though not unsympathetic to the imperial idea—as expressed, for instance, in the

Roman case—Hobson considered that modern imperialism had irretrievably corrupted that idea by its collusion with capitalism. This to him was clear from both the Boer War (1899–1902) and the Spanish–American War (1898), which he regarded as imperialist wars. In his *Imperialism* (1902) Hobson argued that imperialism was the more or less inevitable product of 'underconsumption'—a lack of purchasing power due to the poor standard of living of the industrial working class—and the resulting need to find new outlets for 'surplus capital' that could not make profitable investments at home. The undeveloped areas of the world, in Asia and Africa especially, provided rich opportunities for such investment—hence the scramble to occupy as much of them as possible for one's own nation. Thus, while in the past it was the warlike aristocracy that had been the driving force of imperialism, now it was the capitalist class—the bankers and financiers especially—and its hangers-on (such as the press magnates who whipped up popular sentiments of jingoism) that were the principal agents. Compelling economic motives had taken over from power and glory as the mainsprings of imperialism.

Hobson's account of imperialism had curiously little impact, at least initially, in his home country, even on the Left. But on the European continent it had a spectacularly successful career. It was quickly taken up by Marxists and other socialists, ensuring that it became the single most important theory of imperialism in modern times. One of the reasons that the Left turned to Hobson rather than Marx was that Marx himself had so little to say on the question of imperialism (he uses the word only once in his writings, to describe the political system of Napoleon III in his *The Eighteenth Brumaire of Louis Bonaparte* (1852). Marx, like many other mid-Victorian writers in the era of free trade, believed that formal imperialism or colonialism was a feature mainly of early capitalism. He expected that the capitalist powers of his day would indeed divide the world up between them, but the imperialism this represented was what was later to be called the 'imperialism of free trade', not that of formal conquest and colonization. Late in the nineteenth century, however, shortly after Marx's death in 1883, the capitalist nations everywhere seemed hell-bent on just that struggle for empire that Marx thought should disappear with the further development of capitalism. How to account for that? Hobson provided a satisfying explanation, fitting nicely within orthodox Marxist theory, with his theory of imperialism through proletarian impoverishment and the resulting crisis of underconsumption.

Marxists could conveniently ignore the other parts of Hobson's argument—crucially the view that imperialism was not inherent in capitalism as such, but resulted from the plutocratic and radically unequal class structure of the most advanced European societies. Hence imperialism could be avoided, and capitalism preserved, by measures of radical social reform and by state policies designed to redistribute wealth (that is, something similar to what John Maynard Keynes would later urge with greater success). For Marxists, this view simply reflected Hobson's liberal-bourgeois class position; for them, eliminating imperialism would demand nothing less than socialist revolution. Nevertheless they always acknowledged the importance of Hobson's pioneering analysis of imperialism.

It was Lenin, in his *Imperialism: The Highest Stage of Capitalism* (1917), who did most to popularize Hobson's theory and, through the influence of the Bolshevik Revolution of 1917, to ensure that it remained central to debates about imperialism in the first half of the twentieth century. Together with Hobson, the other admitted influence on Lenin was Rudolf Hilferding's *Finance Capitalism* (1910), the subtitle of which—'the latest phase of capitalist development'—provided Lenin with his own. Hilferding also complemented Hobson in showing imperialism not simply to be an offshoot of capitalism—and hence one remediable by reform—but an intrinsic part of capitalism's development, one that corresponded to its monopoly phase, the phase of 'finance capital' with its massive concentrations in trusts and cartels, and its dominance by banks. Finance capital called for a strong state, protectionist measures, and the conquest of foreign markets, if need be by acquiring colonies. Lenin followed Hilferding in seeing this latest, or 'highest', monopoly stage of capitalism as leading more or less inevitably to war between the imperial powers—clearly demonstrated to Lenin by the First World War—and so to the collapse of capitalism. 'In the violent clash of hostile interests', said Hilferding, 'the dictatorship of capitalist magnates is turned into the dictatorship of the proletariat.' For Lenin, the year 1917 was to prove the confirmation of Hilferding's prediction, even if the world revolution of the proletariat that Lenin and the Bolsheviks expected did not materialize. Such a failure also attended the hoped-for outcome of an imperialist war as analysed in another powerful Marxist work of these years, Rosa Luxemburg's *The Accumulation of Capital* (1913), a rigorous extension of Hobson's basic argument that imperialism was the result of capitalism's need to look to overseas, non-capitalist regions, to make good the deficiencies of the home market and the lack of opportunities for profitable investment there.

The Leninist and more generally Marxist theory of imperialism has been endlessly and extensively debated (Kemp 1967; Kiernan 1974; Lichtheim 1974: 97–142; Etherington 1982; Mommsen 1982: 29–69; Semmel 1993: 131–76; Wolfe 1997). Much of it has been discarded, though the core remained to inspire a wave of Marxist 'dependency' theorists in the second half of the twentieth century. But, just two years after Lenin's pamphlet, there already appeared a vigorous counter-Marxist account of imperialism by the Austrian economist and sociologist Joseph Schumpeter. In his 'The Sociology of Imperialisms' (1919), Schumpeter argued that, far from imperialism's being a necessary product of capitalism, as the Marxists held, it was actually more evocative of pre-capitalist society. The 'new imperialism' was a continuation of the old imperialism, with the significant twist that it was now grafted onto a new society, a bourgeois capitalist society, which was still struggling to be born. Late-nineteenth-century imperialism, argued Schumpeter, was an 'atavistic' throwback to an earlier period of European history. Imperialism—'the objectless disposition on the part of a state to unlimited forcible expansion'—expressed the ethos and aspirations of the warrior aristocracy of feudal Europe, a class that had with a remarkable degree of success clung on to power in the industrializing societies of nineteenth-century Europe, and had indeed plunged the nations of Europe into world war. Sooner or later, though, the bourgeoisie would throw off the aristocratic encumbrance and with it the lust for empire and glory. Bourgeois society would develop according to its 'natural' principles, which were those of free trade and peaceful exchange.

Schumpeter's sparkling and provocative account was not entirely original. It borrowed much from the German sociologist Max Weber, with his stress on the prestige factor of empire and its link to old-fashioned 'predatory capitalism', as opposed to modern 'rational capitalism'. It also had in it something of an echo of Hobson. Like Hobson, Schumpeter saw imperialism as something unnatural, something anachronistic. The difference was that the anachronistic class in Hobson's case was the parasitic plutocracy, while for Schumpeter it was the old European aristocracy. But both—like Weber—denied the necessity of the link between capitalism and imperialism. Capitalism—sober, rational, calculatin—had little need of the violence and aggression of imperialism, to which indeed it was in principle resolutely opposed.

IMPERIALISM AFTER EMPIRE

Marxists theories of empire predominated in the interwar years of the 1920s and 1930s. They added little new to the fundamental contributions of Hobson, Hilferding, Luxemburg, and Lenin. Essentially they remained commentaries and, increasingly, calls to action, as in the Maoist version. Whether or not they were actually Communists, most writers were sympathetic to the Soviet Union and felt constrained to work within the basic Leninist paradigm.

On the Right, too, thinking turned increasingly to activism rather than analysis. Both Mussolini and Hitler, for instance, saw themselves as imperialists. Mussolini hoped to reinstitute the Roman Empire in the Mediterranean, and Hitler's 'thousand-year' Third Reich was a self-conscious revival of the Holy Roman Empire of the German Peoples. But neither in their writings nor those of their apologists does one find any fresh insights into the nature of empire and imperialism. The only novel thing perhaps was the adulation of empire, in an era in which the European empires were increasingly on the defensive. Later, in post-fascist analyses, the main development was to link fascism to earlier European imperialism, and to see the latter as a form of 'hyper-nationalism' and racialism that prepared the ground for fascism (e.g. Arendt 1958).

Right-wing imperialism was thoroughly discredited by the Fascist and Nazi experience. The Left's assaults continued into the post-war period, accompanied now by the worldwide movements against colonialism. In the decades from the late 1940s to the early 1970s, these culminated in a more or less complete process of decolonization. The great European empires of Britain, France, Belgium, the Netherlands, and Portugal broke up. To some observers there still remained two great empires, the American and the Soviet. But, if these were empires, they were empires of a peculiar kind, both founded explicitly on anti-imperialist premises and both promising, in the increasingly strident tones of the cold war, aid and assistance to anti-colonial 'national liberation' movements everywhere (though in the case of the United States such rhetoric was soon toned down, as it turned out that many of the new nations were of a distinctly socialist, if not communist, cast of mind).

But what could a theory of imperialism be in a world without formal empires? Here the concept of 'informal empire' proved highly serviceable. The tendency, in Marxist writing, to make capitalism and imperialism more or less synonymous became distinctly more pronounced in the 1960s and 1970s, as the colonial empires dissolved. For it appeared that the new nations of the 'Third World' were independent only in name. Economically and politically they remained highly dependent on the great northern powers, either of the capitalist West or the Communist East. Soviet imperialism had its critics, in the West and increasingly among dissidents in Eastern Europe. But it was the impact of an increasingly global capitalism on the less-developed nations that produced the most important attempts to rethink imperialism. Here one seemed to be in face of the 'imperialism of decolonization', the continuation of Western imperialism by other means (Louis and Robinson 1994).

Marxists had always, without necessarily naming the concept, operated with the idea of informal imperialism. It was implicit in their view that imperialism was simply an offshoot of the wider and more fundamental operations of capitalism, which sometimes made use of formal empire, and sometimes was content with more informal forms of control. But, just as the non-Marxist Hobson gave Marxists their lead, so too in the post-1945 period it was two non-Marxist historians of the British Empire, John Gallagher and Ronald Robinson, who most fully elaborated the concept of informal empire, in their influential article 'The Imperialism of Free Trade' (Gallagher and Robinson 1953). The British, they pointed out, had always been pragmatic about how far their interests were best served by formal empire and how far by less direct forms of influence and pressure. Informal 'control' was always an alternative, often cheaper and more effective, to formal 'rule'. In their work on the British Empire in Africa, they showed how the British government only reluctantly intervened in the activities of merchants and missionaries. It was in response to a spiralling series of local crises, fuelled by European rivalries, that it found itself forced to take over rule of particular territories (Robinson, Gallagher, and Denny 1961). As John Gallagher put it: 'people do not become imperialists as a matter of ideology; they do so as a matter of necessity' (Gallagher 1982: 141). One further consequence of the work of Gallagher and Robinson was to displace the emphasis on the metropolis, as the focus of study hitherto by both Marxists and non-Marxists, onto the colonial peripheries, as the source of many of the concerns that brought about European rule. Key among these were the interests and conflicts of local elites, whose collaboration with the imperial powers was seen as essential to European rule in nearly all the European empires (Robinson 1972, 1986; see also Fieldhouse 1973).

Informal imperialism, but with a strongly Marxist bent, was at the heart of the analysis of a powerful school of scholars that went under the label of 'dependency' theory (e.g. Frank 1967; Cardoso and Faletto 1979). Late-twentieth-century capitalism, they argued, no longer had need of formal empire; it instead proceeded by the informal means of 'neo-colonialism'—'the last stage of capitalism', as the Ghanaian leader

Kwame Nkrumah hopefully pronounced. Through the agency of the great multinational corporations, headquartered in the West, Western capitalism was able to exert effective control over the development—or rather 'underdevelopment'—of Third World societies. An important aspect of this control—similar to earlier formal imperialism, in the Robinson–Gallagher model—was the collaboration and collusion of local elites and 'puppet' regimes, which benefited from Western aid and the trading regime set up by the Western corporations, and which could count if necessary on Western force to maintain them in power and see off challenges from local radicals and revolutionaries.

A particularly powerful variety of dependency theory was the social–psychological approach of Frantz Fanon, who stressed the psychic damage to native populations wrought by imperialism (Fanon 1967). This entailed that a colonial mentality of low self-esteem and lack of confidence persisted in the nominally post-colonial society. Merely political independence brought no mental or cultural independence. Fanon deeply influenced a group of literary and cultural theorists of empire, notably Edward Said, whose books *Orientalism* (1979) and *Culture and Imperialism* (1993) became the bibles of 'post-colonial' scholars attempting to trace the deep psychological and cultural effects of empire. The 'age of imperialism' may be, as Wolfgang Mommsen says, 'dead and buried' (Mommsen 1982: 113), but to these thinkers, as to many others, imperialism has a long afterlife. It lives on in the hearts and minds of colonized and colonizers alike.

The danger of these approaches, as in the Marxist approach generally, is that imperialism becomes such an inflated concept that its usefulness is seriously endangered. It loses all specificity. It becomes no more than a synonym for capitalism, in whatever phase or condition the theorist chooses to find it—'financial', 'monopoly', 'late', 'global', and so on. Such a tendency reaches an extreme in such works as Michael Hardt and Antonio Negri's *Empire* (2000), in which empire is everywhere and nowhere, a kind of spectral presence, symbolizing global capitalism, that haunts the world and checks all efforts at liberation. Such a view may have its uses; but, for an understanding of empire and imperialism as they have actually operated in human history, we need finer and more precise tools. Empires have indeed been powerful and pervasive presences in world history; but they have not been the only kinds of political communities. We need to examine them in terms that suit their own forms and principles.

References

Abu-Lughod, Janet (1989). *Before European Hegemony: The World System AD 1250–1350*. New York: Oxford University Press.
Aldrich, Robert (2007) (ed.). *The Age of Empires*. London: Thames and Hudson.

ARENDT, HANNAH (1958). *The Origins of Modern Totalitarianism.* 2nd edn. New York: Meridian Books.

ARMITAGE, DAVID (2000). *The Ideological Origins of the British Empire.* Cambridge: Cambridge University Press.

BAUMGART, WINFRIED (1982). *Imperialism: The Idea and Reality of British and French Colonial Expansion, 1880–1914.* New York: Oxford University Press.

BELL, DUNCAN (2007). *The Idea of Greater Britain: Empire and the Future of World Order, 1860–1900.* Princeton: Princeton University Press.

CARDOSO, F., and FALETTO, E. (1979). *Dependency and Development in Latin America*, trans. M. M. Urquidi. Berkeley and Los Angeles: University of California Press.

DOYLE, MICHAEL W. (1986). *Empires.* Ithaca, NY: Cornell University Press.

ETHERINGTON, NORMAN (1982). 'Reconsidering Theories of Imperialism', *History and Theory*, 22/1: 1–36.

FANON, FRANTZ (1967). *The Wretched of the Earth*, trans. Constance Farrington. Harmondsworth: Penguin Books.

FIELDHOUSE, D. K. (1973). *Economics and Empire 1830–1914.* London: Weidenfeld and Nicolson.

FRANK, ANDRÉ GUNDER (1967). *Capitalism and Underdevelopment in Latin America.* New York: Monthly Review Press.

GALLAGHER, JOHN (1982). *The Decline, Revival and Fall of the British Empire: The Ford Lectures and Other Essays.* Cambridge: Cambridge University Press.

GALLAGHER, JOHN, and ROBINSON, RONALD (1953). 'The Imperialism of Free Trade', *Economic History Review*, 6/1: 1–15.

GO, JULIAN (2008). 'Global Fields and Imperial Forms: Field Theory and the British and American Empires', *Sociological Theory*, 26/3: 201–29.

HARDT, MICHAEL, and NEGRI, ANTONIO (2000). *Empire.* Cambridge, MA: Harvard University Press.

HECHTER, MICHAEL (1999). *Internal Colonialism: The Celtic Fringe in British National Development.* 2nd edn. New Brunswick, NJ: Transaction Publishers.

HETHERINGTON, NORMAN (1982). 'Reconsidering Theories of Imperialism', *History and Theory*, 21/1: 1–36.

HOBSBAWM, E. J. (1987). *The Age of Empire, 1875–1914.* London: Weidenfeld and Nicolson.

KEMP, TOM (1967). *Theories of Imperialism.* London: Dobson.

KIERNAN, V. G. (1974). *Marxism and Imperialism.* London: Edward Arnold.

KOEBNER, RICHARD (1961). *Empire.* Cambridge: Cambridge University Press.

KOEBNER, RICHARD, and SCHMIDT, HELMUT DAN (1964). *Imperialism: The Story and Significance of a Political Word, 1840–1960.* Cambridge: Cambridge University Press.

KUMAR, KRISHAN (2009). 'Empire and Nation: Convergence or Divergence?' in George Steinmetz (ed.), *Sociology and Empire.* Durham, NC: Duke University Press.

LICHTHEIM, GEORGE (1974). *Imperialism.* Harmondsworth: Penguin Books.

LOUIS, WM ROGER (1976) (ed.). *Imperialism: The Robinson and Gallagher Controversy.* New York: New Viewpoints.

LOUIS, WM ROGER, and ROBINSON, RONALD (1994). 'The Imperialism of Decolonization', *Journal of Imperial and Commonwealth History*, 22/3: 462–511.

LUCAS, C. P. (1912). *Greater Rome and Greater Britain.* Oxford: Clarendon Press.

MAIER, CHARLES S. (2006). *Among Empires: American Ascendancy and its Predecessors.* Cambridge, MA: Harvard University Press.

MANN, MICHAEL (2003). *Incoherent Empire*. London: Verso.

MOMMSEN, WOLFGANG J. (1982). *Theories of Imperialism*, trans. P. S. Falla. Chicago: University of Chicago Press.

MULDOON, JAMES (1999). *Empire and Order: The Concept of Empire, 800–1800*. Houndmills: Macmillan.

MÜNKLER, HERFRIED (2007). *Empires: The Logic of World Domination from Ancient Rome to the United States*, trans. Patrick Camiller. Cambridge: Polity.

PAGDEN, ANTHONY (1995). *Lords of All the World: Ideologies of Empire in Spain, Britain and France c.1500–c.1800*. New Haven: Yale University Press.

PURDUE, PETER C. (2005). *China Marches West: The Qing Conquest of Central Eurasia*. Cambridge, MA: Harvard University Press.

ROBINSON, RONALD (1972). 'Non-European Foundations of European Imperialism: Sketch for a Theory of Collaboration', in Roger Owen and Bob Sutcliffe (eds), *Studies in the Theory of Imperialism*. London: Longman, 117–42.

ROBINSON, RONALD (1986). 'The Excentric Idea of Imperialism, with or without Empire', in Wolfgang J. Mommsen and Jürgen Osterhammel (eds), *Imperialism and After: Continuities and Discontinuities*. London: Allen and Unwin, 267–89.

ROBINSON, RONALD, GALLAGHER, JOHN, with DENNY, ALICE (1961). *Africa and the Victorians: The Climax of Imperialism*. New York: Anchor Books.

SAID, EDWARD W. (1979). *Orientalism*. New York: Vintage Books.

SAID, EDWARD W. (1993). *Culture and Imperialism*. London: Vintage.

SCHUMPETER, JOSEPH (1974). *Imperialism* and *Social Classes: Two Essays by Joseph Schumpeter*, trans. Heinz Norden. New York: New American Library.

SEMMEL, BERNARD (1993). *The Liberal Ideal and the Demons of Empire: Theories of Imperialism from Adam Smith to Lenin*. Baltimore: Johns Hopkins University Press.

STEINMETZ, GEORGE (2005). 'Return to Empire: The New US Imperialism in Comparative Historical Perspective', *Sociological Theory*, 23/4: 339–67.

WOLFE, PATRICK (1997). 'History and Imperialism: A Century of Theory, from Marx to Postcolonialism', *American Historical Review*, 102/2: 388–420.

CHAPTER 40

....

THE IDEA OF THE
WELFARE STATE

....

DONALD MOON

POLITICAL philosophers have always been deeply concerned with human welfare, including its material components, and have long discussed issues bearing on what we now call the welfare state, issues such as poverty, taxation, property, the regulation of trade and production, and the provision of education and health care. But until the twentieth century no one had a concept of the "welfare state," though some of its elements can be detected in the work of earlier theorists. That is because the welfare state is conventionally understood to be, in Asa Briggs's well-known formulation,

> a state in which organized power is deliberately used ... to modify the play of market forces in at least three directions—first, by guaranteeing individuals and families a minimum income ... second, by narrowing the extent of insecurity by enabling individuals and families to meet certain "social contingencies" ... which lead otherwise to ... crises; and third, by ensuring that all citizens without distinction of status or class are offered the best standards available in relation to a certain agreed range of social services. (Briggs 1961: 228)

So defined, the welfare state presupposes a modern, market economy, one in which a person's well-being depends to a significant degree upon one's income, or the income of one's family, and in which most people's main source of income is employment. Because employment can be interrupted by contingencies to which all, or nearly all, are subject, such as job loss, sickness, disability, and old age, a large majority of the population has an interest in mitigating these conditions, and so in the guarantees provided by the welfare state. The welfare state also rests upon a commitment to equality, such that the provision of services, and the type and quality of services that are provided, are not differentiated by class or other markers of unequal status. As these presuppositions began to be realized in the late nineteenth and early twentieth centuries, or were anticipated by theorists, the practices and ideals of the welfare state began to develop and to be theorized.

Theorizing the welfare state, however, has not been a tidy business, even by the undemanding standards of political theory. Unlike socialism, liberalism, or fascism, there is nothing approaching a common frame of reference within which contending theories vied to present the most adequate account of a political ideal, where the criteria of adequacy make reference to core (if necessarily somewhat vague or at least open-ended) values such as equality and positive freedom, liberty, and individuality, or the unity of the nation and its struggle to realize itself in a world of conflicting peoples. Nor was the welfare state clearly articulated as the realization of a critical utopia by theorists widely recognized as seminal thinkers, in the way that Marx, for example, was seen by subsequent socialist thinkers—even when they criticized him. To a large extent, the "theory" of the welfare state emerged as the welfare state itself emerged, and, since it took quite different trajectories in different contexts, we find a plurality of theories, differentiated not only by national and regional histories, but also by their emergence from and engagement with different theoretical traditions.

In this chapter I will outline the history of welfare state theorizing, beginning with a discourse that is likely to be most familiar to Anglophone audiences, which view the welfare state as emerging from a critical, and largely internal, interrogation of liberalism, with its commitment to juridical equality, individualism, and liberty. This tradition of theorizing was especially important in English-speaking countries. In much of continental Europe, where liberal ideas were less established, the idea of a welfare state emerged from a critical, and again largely internal, interrogation of socialism—more particularly, Marxism—with its commitment to solidarity, science, and positive freedom. A third stream of theorizing giving rise to the ideal of the welfare state can be found in Christian—more specifically Catholic—discourses, but, even more than with liberalism and social democracy, this stream manifested itself in political programs and policies more than in theoretical reflection.[1] By the middle of the twentieth century—following the end of the Second World War—the idea of the welfare state as a distinctive social formation had emerged, and the separate traditions of theorizing were drawn into dialogue with each other, eroding their distinctiveness. Although discourse about the scope and structure of social policy continued to engage large issues of political philosophy, social scientists began to raise narrower and more technical questions about the effectiveness of the policies and programs of the welfare state, which fed into ongoing political debates, often leading to policy redesign or even retrenchment. There can be little doubt that the welfare state is a permanent feature of modern polities, but it continues to provoke new forms of controversy, even as the older issues and dilemmas remain unsettled.

---

[1] See Van Kersbergen (1995), especially ch. 10, "The Intellectual Origins of Christian Democracy and Social Capitalism." He traces a distinctively Catholic account of the welfare state to what he calls the "little tradition" of "social Catholicism" rather than the "'grand tradition' of official Vatican social teaching" (1995: 228).

LIBERALISM

Perhaps the most familiar story of the welfare state, at least in Anglophone countries, focuses on the rise of the "new liberalism" in the UK in the late nineteenth century. T. H. Green, Hobhouse, Hobson, and others developed a sustained critique of "classical" liberalism, particularly its individualism, its focus on negative liberty, and above all its endorsement of a relatively unfettered market economy. The core argument they advanced was that realizing basic liberal values such as freedom and individuality was possible at least in an industrial society only if people had access to basic resources and opportunities, and enjoyed protection against social contingencies such as sickness, unemployment, and old age, protections that were best provided by the community rather than being left to individual efforts.

There is much to this story, but it leaves out a great deal as well. Thomas Horne (1990) has argued that even in the seventeenth and eighteenth centuries many thinkers, drawing on Locke and similar accounts of private property, set out a case for the systematic provision of welfare services as a condition for the legitimacy of private property itself. And Thomas Paine famously called for the abolition of the poor law, advocating instead a system of grants or subsidies as a matter of right, which would enable poor families to educate their children, enjoy a minimal level of income, and provide pensions to elderly people who lack other resources. More significantly, as Asa Briggs (1961: 236 ff.) points out, it neglects the important role of Bentham and the utilitarians in forging both the intellectual grounds for government intervention and many of the mechanisms needed to equip the state to perform that role.[2] Bentham's core principle, that institutions, laws, and policies be tested by their tendency to promote the "greatest happiness of the greatest number," provides a framework conducive to the expansion of state provision of welfare services so long as the policies are effective in enhancing the experienced well-being of those affected. His commitment to utility, and his understanding of utility in terms of the pleasure and pain, put a premium on empirical investigation to determine the actual consequences of policies. It is no wonder that his followers played key roles in debating and studying the conditions of industry and the industrial working classes in nineteenth-century England, which led to the factory acts and other early forms of social legislation. Utilitarianism also rejects a host of ideal-regarding principles, such as ideals of individual responsibility giving rise to desert claims, which undermine the legitimacy of many social policies. Further, the utilitarian commitment to the self-conscious, rational construction of law, policy, and institutions fits well with the idea of the welfare state as deliberately intervening in society to realize specific ends.

---

[2] Briggs points out that these nineteenth-century British developments also had their origins in conservative thinking, which held that the state had the responsibility to ensure the well-being of every class in society, though, of course, the classes themselves were hierarchically structured. Unlike traditional views that the society or government is responsible for the poor, the welfare state is marked by its commitment to equal citizenship (see Marshall 1977 [1950]).

Still, the emphasis on the role of the new liberals is well taken, since they were the first to begin articulating the principles of the welfare state itself, specifically the idea of state provision as a matter of right, based on ideals of equality and democracy, rather than the traditional idea that society should relieve extreme poverty. T. H. Marshall, in his famous essay "Citizenship and Social Class" (1977 [1950]) outlines the history of the welfare state as the culmination of the extension of citizenship to include everyone, the first stage of which was the extension of full civil rights to all, the second stage being the extension of political rights, and the third stage the establishment of the social rights of citizenship, and the new liberals were the first to recognize and systematically put forward the ideas that gave rise to the social rights of citizenship. Although we can find important strands of such thinking in Mill, T. H. Green (1967 [1882]) might be said to have begun the reorientation of traditional or classical liberalism by posing the question of "the nature and extent of the individual's claim to be enabled positively to realize that capacity for freely contributing to social good" (1967 [1882]: 206), and to canvass the social conditions that undermine that capacity, concluding that "the state may remove obstacles to the realization of the capacity for beneficial exercise of rights" (1967 [1882]: 210). In the work of the next generation of thinkers, these hints are spelled out in a program that develops something approaching a full theory of the welfare state.

Hobhouse's *Liberalism* (1964 [1911]) can be taken as representative of this movement, offering a succinct restatement of the central claims of liberalism, building on and at the same time transforming the work of earlier theorists. Locating liberalism historically, Hobhouse depicts it as a movement against authoritarian rule, but whose positive vision was emerging clearly only in his own time, though he argues that it could be discerned in the classical texts if one looked closely. At the risk of oversimplifying his analysis, I would focus on two key moves. The first, and perhaps most familiar, was to insist that freedom and restraint were not opposed, but interconnected. Just as the "restraint of the aggressor is the freedom of the sufferer," so in general "liberty depends on and is measured by the completeness with which by law, custom, or their own feelings [people] are restrained from mutual injury" (1964 [1911]: 50–1). Law or regulation, then, far from being conceived as a restriction on liberty (as it was by, for example, Mill), and thus in need of justification, can be seen as an enlargement of liberty[3] when it makes freedom effective, by enabling people to make choices and exercise powers, and by equalizing those opportunities and powers among individuals within the community: "the struggle for liberty is also, when pushed through, a struggle for equality" (1964 [1911]: 21). This line of argument supplies a justification for an active state, promoting effective freedom by equalizing opportunity and limiting the power of the privileged to pursue their own advantage.

---

[3] Although Hobhouse does not cite Locke, this formulation is reminiscent of Locke's well-known view of law: "the end of law is not to abolish or restrain, but to preserve and enlarge freedom: for in all the states of created beings capable of laws, where there is no law, there is no freedom: for liberty is, to be free from restraint and violence from others; which cannot be, where there is no law" (Locke 1970 [1689]: 324).

A second key move was to push a traditional liberal ideal in a new direction. "Liberalism," he argued, holds that "a true community can be built" only on the "self-directing power of personality"—that is to say, on the duty of each person to treat the other "as a rational being" (1964 [1911]: 66). This notion, arguably, is implicit in the idea of a society based on a social contract of each with all the rest, concluded under conditions of equality, which implies that the basic principles on which the society is founded are principles that each person, as a rational agent, has good reasons to accept. Hobhouse argues that a universally acceptable, reasoned justification— including a justification for a system of individual rights—requires an appeal to the common good, for only the common good provides a grounding to which all citizens can rationally appeal to justify their claims. And he argues further that a common good can be posited because humans are social beings, so that, if a society is properly ordered, it will be characterized by a broad harmony of interests. Thus the role of the state is to "secure the conditions upon which mind and character may develop themselves" (1964 [1911]: 83), enabling all citizens to function as rational agents who support institutional structures that realize the common good and so bring about a harmony of interests. He thus calls for an activist state providing a range of social services through universal provision and social insurance—that is, in a form that is fully compatible with the equal dignity and standing of all citizens, and that provides the conditions necessary for citizens to realize their "self-directing power of personality." Hobhouse is quick to add that duty and right are reciprocal: just as the state owes citizens "the means of maintaining a civilized standard of life," so the citizen "owes the State the duty of industriously working for himself and his family." Under-lining his point that basic resources and services are rights, Hobhouse adds the duty of society "is not adequately discharged by leaving [each citizen] to secure such wages as he can in the higgling of the market" (1964 [1911]: 86).

As Freeden (2003) has argued, the new liberals offered "a paradigm shift in the conceptualisation of human nature and the consequent nexus of institutions, practices, responsibilities and goods these entailed" (2003: 43). The strong claims about the common good and the harmony of interests mentioned above are examples of that paradigm shift, and there are other sharp breaks with traditional liberal positions as well—such as Hobhouse's endorsement of a thoroughgoing paternalism, at least as a matter of principle (1964 [1911]: 76). In other ways, though, the new liberals worked very much within the conceptual resources they inherited. Against individualist theories, they insisted upon a panoply of social rights enabling workers to maintain "a civilized standard of life," but, when those rights were provided, someone failing to fulfill the duty of self-support "may fairly suffer the penalty of being treated as a pauper or even, in an extreme case, as a criminal" (1964 [1911]: 86). Hobhouse even holds out the possibility of the unemployed but able-bodied being sent to a "labor colony" (1964 [1911]: 179).

It should be stressed that the new liberalism did not argue for a welfare state. Indeed, the language of the time contrasted individualism and collectivism, and Hobhouse and his contemporaries tended to use terms like "liberal socialism" or "economic liberalism" to describe their ideals. And, like the individualist theories against which they argued, they saw the role of the state in perfectionist terms. Earlier liberals argued for a limited state that did not provide a significant range of social services, so that individuals would be free—but also required—to provide for themselves, and thus led to cultivate such virtues as self-reliance, independence, and self-restraint. The new liberals likewise sought to cultivate individual virtue and self-development, but argued that an activist state and a more equal distribution of resources were necessary for that end.

Social Democracy

In the UK and the USA the political theory of the welfare state can be usefully viewed as emerging from debates within broadly liberal traditions, but on the Continent we find a different range of voices. In particular, from the late nineteenth century Marxism was on important interlocutor, and in several countries including Germany it dominated discourse on the left of the political spectrum. Because of its commitment to the abolition of capitalism and revolutionary change, its adherents were often disposed against ameliorative measures, and critical of nascent welfare state ideas, fearing that palliatives might deflect the working class from its revolutionary mission. It is not surprising, then, that in Germany the earliest welfare state initiatives came from the right, including famously Bismark's push for old age and sickness pensions. Although Marx himself endorsed policies such as restrictions on child labor, he clearly saw such policies in strategic terms. By putting forward demands for minimum wages, restrictions on work hours, and various social protections, workers could perhaps be mobilized in support of the socialist movement, but he was unwavering in his insistence that their liberation was possible only through a revolutionary (though perhaps not necessarily violent) displacement of capitalism by collective or social ownership of productive resources. And the revolution would be possible only when (at least in the most advanced countries) the forces of production had developed to the point that capitalist property relations impeded their further progress. At this point, class polarization would have advanced to the point that the working class would constitute the overwhelming majority of society, and the bourgeoisie—the owners of the means of production—would no longer play a productive role in the economy, since large-scale firms would be managed by professional managers, and owners would be reduced to the status of rentiers.[4]

Przeworski has argued that the acceptance of this analysis of society, in conjunction with the steady extension of the suffrage, posed serious problems for the socialist movement. Socialists had little choice but to participate in electoral politics, soliciting

---

[4] This specific formulation might be said to owe more to Engels than to Marx, but it is very much in keeping with the view of leading socialists in the late nineteenth and early twentieth century. See Engels (1978 [1892]).

the votes of newly enfranchised workers, since these workers were being actively courted by other parties, appealing to other aspects of their identities, such as their religious, language, or national affiliations. But, to contest elections, socialists needed to put forward a platform, and, to contest them successfully, they could hardly confine their appeal to the working class, since nowhere did it constitute a majority of the electorate even after universal suffrage had been attained.

In this context, many activists were attracted to the ideas of those who were calling for a revision of Marx's theories, the most well known being Eduard Bernstein. Bernstein was deeply versed in Marxist theory, having known Marx and Engels when he was a young man, and being a close associate of Kautsky, Bebel, and other major figures in the movement. Nonetheless, he developed a powerful critique of key aspects of Marx's theories. Many of his arguments turned on the ways in which Marx's account of the dynamics of capitalist society were not borne out in the years after his death. Although the proletariat continued to grow, as Marx predicted, other social groups were not being absorbed into the proletariat, and the wages and living conditions of industrial workers were measurably improving over time. More importantly, Bernstein projected a vision of political action and social transformation in which political agency in the present was central. Contrary to Marx's vision of a revolutionary movement creating a socialist society when structural conditions had ripened, Bernstein pro-claimed what Sheri Berman has called the "primacy of politics," a commitment to a political program addressing specific problems or needs experienced by workers and other relatively disadvantaged groups in society through a vast extension of the scope of state action. Over time, Bernstein argued, the cumulative effects of these changes would bring about a transformation of society, as capitalism would give way to socialism, but the key for him was not the realization of socialism itself, but an evolutionary process through which organized workers and their allies in other social groupings would mobilize to achieve concrete changes, and gradually shape the conditions of their lives through their own actions and the efforts of the Social Democratic Party. In famously (or infamously) proclaiming that the goal of socialism was nothing, but the movement to socialism was everything, Bernstein was not devaluing the full socialism but affirming the political agency of workers and ordinary citizens, which he saw as the governing ideal of socialism itself.

Bernstein and "revisionism" prepared the ground for the welfare state, but they did not project a vision of the welfare state as a political ideal or, for that matter, as a distinctive political formation, one that carried with it its own standards and offered itself as what Rawls would call a "realistic utopia"—a vision of a good but also feasible political society. Rather, they envisioned an activist state gradually displacing capitalist forms of property and market relationships to the point that the society had become fully socialist. Again, theorizing would have to await practice, as the components of the welfare state were put into place at various times and combinations, depending upon the exigencies of different societies.

Heclo has argued that one key development necessary for the emergence of the welfare state was the emergence of Keynesian economics, or, more generally, a theoretical understanding and practical tools needed for the government to manage the economy. One of the reasons why the early twentieth-century movements, whether liberal or social democratic, presented themselves as socialist was that they accepted the prevailing understanding of market society, according to which markets were largely self-regulating, and governments—like firms and individuals—had to balance their budgets. Needless to say, this view sharply limited the ability of government to provide the social benefits that the new liberals and social democrats called for. Such benefits required relatively high levels of government expenditure, and, if governments had to balance their budgets during economic downturns, it would be difficult or impossible to sustain those expenditures, and so the benefits could not be provided as a matter of right. In the long run, then, a program of extending social rights would prove incompatible with market society, requiring a transition to a planned, socialist economy. A welfare state, committed to the modification of market forces rather than their displacement, did not appear to be feasible.

As a result of the new understanding of economics offered by Keynes and others during the 1930s, however, a new model of society emerged, one in which the basic structure of the economy was capitalist, but a form of capitalism in which the government both played a key role in economic management and provided an extensive range of social rights of citizenship, enabling citizens to maintain "a civilized standard of life." This was possible because the new understanding of economics allowed or even required the government to run deficits during economic downturns, thus sustaining the social programs of the welfare state, contrary to the prescriptions of classical economic theory. Thus, by mid-century, the possibility of the welfare state as a social and political ideal in its own right, and not simply as a way station on the road to socialism, had emerged.

POST-WAR THEORIZING

Social insurance schemes were first introduced in Europe in the late nineteenth century and in Canada and the USA in the early decades of the twentieth. Following the First World War they were gradually extended to include more and more people, and to cover a wider range of contingencies. Although the paths followed by different countries varied significantly, the average growth of social insurance coverage in Western Europe and North America was fairly constant from the end of the First World War through the 1960s.[5] Nonetheless, as a social ideal, the welfare state is often viewed as a post-Second World War phenomenon, inspired at least in the UK by the Beveridge Report of 1942, which called for an integrated range of social programs to cover all of the contingencies that could undermine one's ability to be a fully

---

[5] See, for example, the charts in Flora and Heidenheimer (1981: 55, 85).

participating member of society. The Beveridge Report set out a vision of social policy that was broadly consistent with a market economy, and thus set out a distinctive vision rejecting both socialism as traditionally understood and laissez-faire capitalism. Although many labor and social democratic parties did not fully break with their traditional commitments to nationalization of industry and socialist planning for some time, their actual policies soon reflected the goal of the welfare state to manage capitalism in such a way that class inequalities were ameliorated through the realization of the social rights of citizenship.

An important conceptual innovation in the political theorizing that accompanied the post-war consolidation of the welfare state was the emergence of a distinctive view of the value of equality. Rather than thinking about equality in terms of the distribution of social resources or advantage, however natural that interpretation is, theorists such as Marshall and Tawney argued that "equality of status is more important than equality of income" (Marshall 1977 [1950]: 113). Indeed, the welfare state itself contributes to inequality when, for example, its programs provide differential benefits to people based on their having contributed at different rates to a common program, thus maintaining or even reinforcing income differences in a society. Old age pensions are an obvious example, where higher income individuals receive higher pensions.[6] As Tawney puts it:

> What is repulsive is not that one man should earn more than others, for where community of environment, and a common education and habit of life, have bred a common tradition of respect and consideration, these details of the counting house are forgotten or ignored. It is that some classes should be excluded from the heritage of civilization which others enjoy, and that the fact of human fellowship, which is ultimate and profound, should be obscured by economic contrasts, which are trivial and superficial. What is important is not that all men should receive the same pecuniary income. It is that the surplus resources of society should be so husbanded and applied that it is a matter of minor significance whether they receive it or not. (1964 [1931]: 113)

Though few would argue that this ideal has been fully realized, it has figured prominently in debates about equality in political philosophy since 1971.[7]

Political theorizing has come to reflect the increasing institutionalization of the welfare state. The decades following the war saw what might be heyday of welfare state theorizing. A number of theorists, including Marshall and Titmuss in the early days, and more recently Plant, Harris, Goodin, and Rothstein, sought to lay out the ideal of the welfare state and project its future course, while more empirically minded social scientists studied its origins and structures, delineating various models of the

---

[6] Although it should be added that such programs typically reduce inequality relative to the baseline established by the labor market, because the "replacement rate" of income is inversely related to the amount of one's "contributions."

[7] See Wolff, Chapter 36, this volume.

welfare state characterized by different ideals and institutions.[8] The compatibility of the welfare state with market institutions came to be a major subject of investigation, as scholars rigorously examined the ways in which public provision could enhance efficiency by overcoming market failure.[9] Much, perhaps most, of this work draws on political theory and philosophy but also incorporates history, economics, and the other social sciences. More than most areas of political philosophy, welfare state theorizing is a site of interdisciplinarity.[10]

Inevitably, political theorists have not only explored the contours of the welfare state; they have also offered sustained critiques. Perhaps the most widely publicized are revivals and restatements of the arguments that attended the birth of welfare state theorizing. Thinkers such as Hayek and Friedman attacked the core values and practices of the welfare state, vigorously setting out the case for a limited state and market and social provision of welfare, though even they conceded the need for one of its core principles, that everyone ought to enjoy a minimum level of material well-being as a matter of right, provided through the state in a non-discretionary manner.[11] Both the UK and the USA saw "conservative" political movements that called for the containment, if not the dismantling, of the welfare state, and everywhere we have seen a reduction in the growth of social spending and moves to reduce or limit government's role in regulating the economy. Although often marked by strong, even extreme rhetoric (especially in the USA), much of this discourse at least in the political arena itself is continuous with the welfare state theorizing discussed above, focusing on the correct mix of policies rather than seriously challenging the core principles that constitute the welfare state.

Feminist scholarship and theory have articulated a second, and more original, line of criticism of the welfare state and traditional welfare state theorizing. Classical theories were developed to address what was known a century ago as the "social question," the problem posed by the emergence and mobilization of the industrial working classes in capitalist societies. Conservatives and classical liberals were anxious about the threat these groups posed to the social order, while radicals sought to enlist them in a revolutionary project to overthrow it. Many of the arguments canvassed above can be seen as efforts to integrate the working class into a stable democratic order by changing the economic structure in such a way as to satisfy their basic needs and interests.[12] Feminist criticism calls attention to the way in which this focus on class

---

[8] For three prominent examples of the latter, see Esping-Anderson (1990); Goodin et al. (1999); and Huber and Stephens (2001).

[9] For a brief survey of efficiency-based accounts, see Barr (1993).

[10] The literature in this area is extensive, and the sources mentioned here are only illustrative; it would be impossible in a short article to review even the most important works produced since the Second World War.

[11] It should be said, though, that they would not have put it in quite this way. For Friedman's defense of a floor under income in the form of a negative income tax, see (1962); for Hayek's see (1976).

[12] In the "Preface" to the second edition of his *Division of Labor* Durkheim explicitly set out a set of political and social reforms designed to stabilize capitalist society; although he did not speak of a welfare

obscures and presupposes a gendered configuration. Most famously, T. H. Marshall's historical sketch of the development of equal citizenship, mentioned above, ignores women in describing the extension of civil, political, and finally social rights in distinct phases since the sixteenth or seventeenth century, since only men won these rights during the periods Marshall delineated. More generally, theorists' call for the provision of social rights and their focus on providing security for wage earners and their families presupposed a traditional set of gender roles. They talked of the individual or the citizen, but they referred to men; they demanded that relations of dependency be abolished, but proposed institutions that reinforced the dependency of women within a family headed by a male breadwinner.

If one of the great promises of the welfare state is that it can deliver real freedom for all citizens because it attends to the needs they have in the real situations they face, feminist criticism suggests that realizing this promise not only for men but also for women poses a serious, even radical, challenge to the welfare state—especially one that is committed to respecting the plurality of religious and cultural traditions in a society, and the resulting differences in values and philosophical orientations among its citizenry. An obvious example is the provision of social insurance for disability and old age through paid employment, a classic mechanism of the welfare state in which worker contributions in the form of taxes earns a reciprocal benefit in the form of old age or disability pensions. For women to be treated equally with men under this model, they would have to take up paid employment at the same rate as men—what Fraser calls the "universal breadwinner" model. But that proposal fails to make adequate allowance for the social need for care-giving, and burdens those—mostly women—who "are unwilling or unable to shift [care-giving responsibilities] elsewhere" (Fraser 1997: 52). And it systematically burdens those cultural or religious groups that reject the idea that men and women have the same role and responsibility regarding paid employment. It is not possible to pursue these ongoing debates in the space available here, but it is clear that they pose significant challenges to the welfare state.

A third, related set of discussions also echoes earlier arguments for state provision of services on the grounds that access to certain opportunities and resources as a matter of right is necessary if citizens are to achieve the level of functioning necessary for their equal membership in society. I referred to Hobhouse's discussion of this issue above, and it has certainly not been settled. Some contemporary theorists have embraced a strong form of paternalism, calling on the government to design programs to inculcate the virtues of self-discipline and the capacity rationally to pursue their self-interests so that those who are marginalized by poverty and unemployment may assume the status of equal citizenship (Mead 1997). At the same time, leftist thinkers also worry about the effects of long-term or structural unemployment on social inclusion. Anthony Giddens (1998), for example, would replace the traditional welfare state with what he calls the

state, his proposals include many of the features of contemporary social-democratic welfare states, including the universal provision of critical social goods such as education and corporatist structures designed to limit and modify the play of market forces.

"social investment state," which would invest in "human capital" rather than providing services, with the aim of including as many as possible in the workforce. To achieve this end, he proposes that people who do unpaid work in the "social economy" receive monetary rewards for their efforts. As Rose argues, the contemporary "organization of freedom" views individuals as best able to "fulfil their political obligations in relation to the wealth, health, and happiness of the nation not when they are bound into relations of dependency and obligation, but when they seek to fulfil themselves as free individuals," which depends "upon the activation of the powers of the citizen" (Rose 1999: 166). But this "activation of the powers of the citizen" comes with new forms of social control, forms that may undercut the promise of effective freedom and equality that the welfare state itself holds out. Clearly, the theory of the welfare state is a work in progress, wrestling with the deepest issues of social and political theory today.

References

Barr, Nicholas (1993). *The Economics of the Welfare State*. 2nd edn. London: Weidenfeld and Nicolson.

Bentham, Jeremy (1948 [1823]). *An Introduction to the Principles of Morals and Legislation.* Oxford: Blackwell.

Berman, Sheri (2006). *The Primacy of Politics*. Cambridge: Cambridge University Press.

Bernstein, Eduard (1961 [1899]). *Evolutionary Socialism*, trans. E. Harvey. New York: Schocken Books.

Beveridge, William (1942). *Social Insurance and Allied Services*. Basingstoke: Macmillan.

Beveridge, William (1945). *Full Employment in a Free Society*. London: Allen and Unwin.

Briggs, Asa (1961). "The Welfare State in Historical Perspective," *European Journal of Sociology*, 2: 221–58.

Collini, Stefan (1979). *Liberalism and Sociology*. Cambridge: Cambridge University Press.

Durkheim, Emile (1984 [1902]). *The Division of Labor in Society*. 2nd edn. New York: Free Press.

Engels, Friedrich (1978 [1892]). "Socialism: Utopian and Scientific," in *The Marx–Engels Reader*, (ed.) Robert C. Tucker. New York: Norton.

Esping-Anderson, Gosta (1985). *Politics against Markets*. Princeton: Princeton University Press.

Esping-Anderson, Gosta (1990). *Three Worlds of Welfare Capitalism*. Princeton: Princeton University Press.

Flora, Peter, and Heidenheimer, Arnold J. (1981) (eds). *The Development of Welfare States in Europe and America*. New Brunswick, NJ: Transaction Books.

Fraser, Nancy (1997). *Justice Interruptus*. London: Routledge.

Freeden, Michael (1978). *The New Liberalism*. Oxford: Oxford University Press.

Freeden, Michael (2003). "The Coming of the Welfare State," in T. Ball and R. Bellamy (eds), *The Cambridge History of Twentieth-Century Political Thought*. Cambridge: Cambridge University Press.

Friedman, Milton (1962). *Capitalism and Freedom*. Chicago: University of Chicago Press.

GIDDENS, ANTHONY (1998). *The Third Way: The Renewal of Social Democracy*. Cambridge: Polity.

GOODIN, ROBERT, HEADEY, BRUCE, MUFFELS, RUUD, and DRIVEN, HENK-JAN (1999). *The Real Worlds of Welfare Capitalism*. Cambridge: Cambridge University Press.

GREEN, THOMAS HILL (1967 [1882]). *Lectures on the Principles of Political Obligation*. Ann Arbor: University of Michigan Press.

GUTMANN, AMY, and THOMPSON, DENNIS (1996). *Democracy and Disagreement*. Cambridge, MA: Harvard University Press.

HARRIS, DAVID (1987). *Justifying State Welfare*. Oxford: Blackwell.

HAYEK, FRIEDRICH (1976). *The Mirage of Social Justice*. Chicago: University of Chicago Press.

HECLO, HUGH (1974). *Modern Social Politics in Britain and Sweden*. New Haven: Yale University Press.

HOBHOUSE, LEONARD T. (1911). *Social Evolution and Political Theory*. New York: Columbia University Press.

HOBHOUSE, LEONARD T. (1964 [1911]). *Liberalism*. Oxford: Oxford University Press.

HORNE, THOMAS (1990). *Property Rights and Poverty*. Chapel Hill, NC: University of North Carolina Press.

HUBER, EVELYNE, and STEPHENS, JOHN D. (2001). *Development and Crisis of the Welfare State*. Chicago: University of Chicago Press.

LOCKE, JOHN (1970 [1689]). *Two Treatises of Government*. 2nd edn. Cambridge: Cambridge University Press.

MARSHALL, T. H. (1977 [1950]). "Citizenship and Social Class," in *Class, Citizenship, and Social Development*. Chicago: University of Chicago Press.

MEAD, LAWRENCE M. (1997) (ed.). *The New Paternalism*. Washignton: Brookings Institution.

MILL, JOHN STUART (1989 [1859]). *On Liberty and Other Writings*, (ed.) S. Collini. Cambridge: Cambridge University Press.

PAINE, THOMAS (2003 [1776]). *Common Sense and Other Writings*, (ed.) Gordon Wood. New York: Modern Library.

PATEMAN, CAROLE (1988). "The Patriarchal Welfare State," in A. Gutmann (ed.), *Democracy and the Welfare State*. Princeton: Princeton University Press.

PAUL, ELLEN (1997) (ed.). *The Welfare State*. Cambridge: Cambridge University Press.

PIERSON, PAUL (1994). *Dismantling the Welfare State*. Cambridge: Cambridge University Press.

PRZEWORSKI, ADAM (1985). *Capitalism and Social Democracy*. Cambridge: Cambridge University Press.

RAWLS, JOHN (2001). *Justice as Fairness: A Restatement*. Cambridge, MA: Harvard University Press.

ROSE, NIKOLAS (1999). *Powers of Freedom*. Cambridge: Cambridge University Press.

ROTHSTEIN, BO (1998). *Just Institutions Matter*. Cambridge: Cambridge University Press.

TAWNEY, R. H. (1964 [1931]). *Equality*. Barnes and Noble.

TITMUSS, RICHARD (1963). *Essays on the Welfare State*. 2nd edn. Boston: Beacon Press.

VAN KERSBERGEN, KEES (1995). *Social Capitalism*. London: Routledge.

WALDRON, JEREMY (1993). *Liberal Rights*. Cambridge: Cambridge University Press.

CHAPTER 41

....

LIBERTARIANISM

....

ERIC MACK

THIS brief history of libertarian political philosophy focuses on hard-core libertarian theorists. It begins with the explication of two core postulates, which all such libertarians share, and three disputes, which divide these theorists. (Softer core versions of libertarianism involve less stringent or less exceptionless versions of these postulates.) Since libertarianism as a well-defined body of doctrine emerges in the modern world as theorists defend and work out the implications of these core postulates in their opposition to the modern nation state, this chapter focuses on six nineteenth- or twentieth-century thinkers: Herbert Spencer (1820–1903); Lysander Spooner (1808–87); Gustav de Molinari (1819–1912); Ayn Rand (1905–82); Murray Rothbard (1926–95); and Robert Nozick (1938–2002).

CORE POSTULATES AND RECURRENT DISPUTES

....

The core *prescriptive* postulate of libertarianism is that individuals have strong moral claims to the peaceful enjoyment of their own persons and their own legitimate extra-personal possessions along with similarly strong claims to the fulfillment of their voluntary agreements with others. All (non-pacifist) libertarians take these moral claims to be so strong and salient that force and the threat of force may permissibly be employed to defend against and to rectify their infringement. On the other hand, only infringements of these core claims trigger the permissible use or threat of force. Other deployments of force or the threat of force are taken themselves to be violations of the moral claims asserted by the prescriptive postulate.

The core *descriptive* postulate is that general compliance with the claims of the moral postulate is the key condition of desirable and mutually beneficial social and economic coordination. A framework of security for persons, their possessions, and their con-tractual claims precludes individuals from advancing their particular purposes through plunder and fraud and, thereby, requires and enables them to advance their purposes through production, voluntary exchange and accommodation, and honest dealing. When such a framework obtains, individuals tend to converge upon increasingly beneficial cooperative interactions and relationships, which maximally draw upon the special knowledge, capacities, and preferences of those individuals and which in retrospect *appear* to be governed by a benevolent invisible hand.

> The natural effort of every individual to better his own condition, when suffered to exert itself with freedom and security, is so powerful a principle, that it is alone, and without any assistance, not only capable of carrying society to wealth and prosperity, but of surmounting a hundred impertinent obstructions with which the folly of human laws too often incumbers its operation. (Smith 1981 [1776]: bk IV, ch. v; ii. 42–3)

Economic and social order that is in tune with the diverse and distinct capacities, dispositions, and desires of individuals grows up from the ground of natural liberty. In the twentieth century, F. A. Hayek (1899–1992) was the most dedicated champion of the theme that desirable and rational economic and social order need not be a centrally planned and directed organization; instead, such economic and social orders are most apt to arise when there is general compliance with "rules of just conduct" that secure individuals in their lives, liberties, and estates. Hayek's lifelong project of investigating the fecundity of grown order itself grew out of the socialist calculation debate of the 1920s and 1930s in which Ludwig von Mises (1881–1973) and Hayek argued that central economic planners could not acquire the knowledge needed to make rational judgments about the efficient allocation of economic resources. A third common feature of hard-core libertarian theorists is a deep suspicion of political power and those who seek it, and an insistence that holders of political office are fully subject to the same restrictive norms that apply to ordinary honest individuals.

Despite being united by subscription to these postulates, libertarian theorists have been divided along (at least) three important dimensions. First, they are divided about the proper construal of the core prescriptive postulate. Almost all hard-core (and softer-core) libertarian theorists offer either a *natural-rights* justification or an *indirect-mutual-advantage* justification of the core prescriptive postulate. Advocates of the natural-rights justification maintain that certain fundamental truths about individuals—for example, their existence as equal and independent beings (Locke, the godfather of libertarianism), or their being agents who rightly seek their continued existence or happiness (Spooner, Rand), or their being persons whose separateness must be taken seriously (Nozick)—are the basis for ascribing to individuals *as rights* the claims affirmed in the core prescriptive postulate. Advocates of the indirect-mutual-advantage justification maintain that compliance with the prescriptive postulate or something close to it—for example, the law of equal freedom (Spencer), or the evolved rules of conduct that undergird freely coordinated interaction (Hayek)—is justified because such compliance is mutually advantageous.

Second, these theorists hold to a range of distinct views concerning the extent and stringency of individual property rights—especially property rights over land—that is, the raw material of the earth. Libertarian theorists have taken four stances within this dispute. From left to right, they are: (1) the earth itself originally is jointly owned by all mankind and must remain jointly owned; (2) all segments of the earth are subject to private ownership, but an acquired claim to some segment of the earth remains valid only so long as the claimant is occupying and using it; (3) all segments of the earth are subject to private ownership, but there is a proviso that requires that in some significant way no individual be disadvantaged by privatization of the earth or by the decisions that private owners make with their sanctified private holdings; and (4) all segments of the earth are subject to private ownership, period.

Third, libertarians are divided about whether even a minimal state is justifiable. Whilst minimal statists take the nightwatchman state (and nothing beyond it) to be justified, individualist (or free-market) anarchists hold that even the nightwatchman state employs force and the threat of force too extensively to be justified. While minimal statists take the nightwatchman state to be the obvious institutional device for the protection of the claims expressed in the prescriptive postulate, anarchist libertarians argue that any state must violate these strictures either by funding itself through coercive taxation or by forbidding competing protective agencies to function.

NINETEENTH-CENTURY LIBERTARIANISM

This short survey can go back no further than to the most prominent libertarian theorist of the nineteenth century, Herbert Spencer. Here I will focus on the early and radical Spencer—especially the Spencer of *Social Statics* (1850)—rather than the later, more conservative, and pessimistic Spencer of *The Man versus the State* (1884) and *The Principles of Ethics* (1897). Indeed, the most radically libertarian Spencer appears in his early series of letters *The Proper Sphere of Government* (1843). In these letters, much more than in any of his later works, Spencer seems to appeal to Lockean natural rights. Governments are created

> to defend the natural rights of man—to protect person and property—to prevent aggressions of the powerful upon the weak—in a word, to administer justice This is the natural, the original, office of government. It was not intended to do less; it ought not to be allowed to do more. (1981 [1843]: 187)

Nevertheless, even in this work these rights are cast as the basic norms that rational individuals would agree to in order to escape from a condition in which each may blamelessly prey upon others (1981 [1843]: 185). Since everyone is subject to predation, the recognition of rights that are protective of person and property serves everyone's interests. Spencer insists that a consistent recognition of these rights calls for free speech, free religion, and free trade.

Rational individuals will assign to government the role of enforcing these freedoms and *not* the role of exercising command and control of the social and economic order because

> they know, or they ought to know, that the laws of society are of such a character, that natural evils will rectify themselves; that there is in society, as in every other part of creation, that beautiful self-adjusting principle, which will keep all its elements in equilibrium . . . so the attempt to regulate all the actions of a community by legislation, will entail little else but misery and confusion. (1981 [1843]: 186–7)

The alternative to having the government enforce mutually advantageous norms of justice is to have government empowered to advance the "general good." However, this would effectively allow government to do whatever it chooses. For, "the expression "general good," is of such uncertain character, a thing so entirely a matter of opinion, that there is not an action that a government could perform, which might not be contended to be a fulfillment of its duties" (1981 [1843]: 187).

Along with many other nineteenth-century theorists, Spencer is deeply concerned about the "land question." He tells us that "Man *has* a claim to a subsistence derived from the soil" (1981 [1843]: 201). However, Spencer takes this to be a claim to the opportunity to engage in labor and *thereby* attain the fruits of that labor rather than an unconditional claim to the fruits of (someone's) labor. In effect, Spencer seems to affirm a type of Lockean proviso; private property arrangements may not be such as to deprive individuals of the opportunity to earn their subsistence. Presumably, no rational person would accept norms that sanctioned the denial of this opportunity. According to Spencer, "iniquitous laws" and "oppressive taxation" underlie the denial of this opportunity; hence, those laws must be destroyed (1981 [1843]: 202).

In his much better-known *Social Statics* (1850), Spencer embraces the greatest happiness principle as the ultimate normative standard and yet vociferously rejects any direct appeal to this standard in the assessment of actions, policies, or institutions. "It is one thing, however, to hold that greatest happiness is the creative purpose, and quite another thing to hold that greatest happiness should be the *immediate* aim of man" (1970 [1850]: 61) Happiness is "a gratified state of all the faculties." Since people have differing sets of faculties in differing degrees of development, different people have radically different conceptions of happiness, and there is no one sound formula for the attainment of everyone's happiness. Moreover, even if we could give determinate content to the idea of the greatest happiness, we are, in practice, incapable of identifying which concrete political policies, which trade-offs amongst persons' possible gratifications, would be genuinely expedient. Fortunately, however, certain deep and persistent facts about human beings and their interactions—certain "fundamental necessities of our position" (1970 [1850]: 62)—show that compliance with certain basic norms—in particular, the law of equal freedom and the requirement of negative justice that each is to enjoy or suffer the consequences of his own chosen actions—will most advance happiness in society. General happiness is best served by putting that end out of mind and adhering strictly to those basic norms. Thus, Spencer's ultimate stance seems to be a sort of indirect utilitarianism. However, it is actually a version of indirect mutual advantage doctrine. For Spencer's inquiry about what basic norms should be affirmed is guided by the idea that the greatest happiness requires the advancement of *everyone's* happiness. To identify the norms that promote the greatest happiness, we must identify the norms that promote each individual's happiness.

Since each man's pursuit of happiness accords with the "creative purpose" and each man's happiness requires that he be free to exercise his faculties, each man ought to be free to use his faculties; and this amounts to each man having a right to use his faculties "for the due satisfaction of every mental and bodily want."

> Man's happiness can only be produced by the exercise of his faculties. Then God wills that he should exercise his faculties. But to exercise his faculties he must have liberty to do all that his faculties naturally impel him to do. Then God intends he should have that liberty. Therefore he has *a right* to that liberty. (1970 [1850]: 69)

This case for a right to liberty was restated, without the theological coloration, in Spencer's 1884 essay "The Great Political Superstition."

> Those who hold that life is valuable, hold, by implication, that men ought not to be prevented from carrying on life-sustaining activities. In order words, if it is said to be "right" that they should carry them on, then, by permutation, we get the assertion that they "have a right" to carry them on. (1981 [1884]: 150)

Since this right to liberty is a right possessed by all, each man's rightful freedom must "be bounded by the similar freedom of all" (1970 [1850]: 69). The fundamental social norm is, then, "*Every man has freedom to do all that he wills, provided he infringes not the equal freedom of any other man*" (1970 [1850]: 95). Of course, given people as they actually are, the gratification that some people derive from the exercise of their faculties will preclude other people from attaining gratification through the exercise of their faculties. Nevertheless, as the ways in which individuals seek their gratification become more adapted to the "social state" (1970 [1850]: 62), individuals will more conform their conduct to this law of equal freedom.

In *Social Statics*, all further rights—including the rights of free speech and the rights of women and children—are advanced as implications of this law of equal freedom. Two of these rights are especially striking. Spencer now maintains that private ownership of the earth infringes upon the equal liberty of the non-owners. For, "if the landowners have a valid right to [the earth's] surface, all who are not landowners, have no right at all to its surface. Hence, such can exist on the earth by sufferance only" (1970 [1850]: 104). Hence, the surface of the earth is owned jointly by "the human race" (1970 [1850]: 112). Or in any case, within any society, "the lawful owner" of the land is "Society" (1970 [1850]: 107). Instead of there being private landlords, there should be only one landlord who will lease portions of the earth to individuals. As a consequence, "all men would be equally landlords; all men would be alike free to become tenants" (1970 [1850]: 111). Except for the rental payments due to Society, Spencer envisions Society's tenants having full private property rights over the fruits of their labor. However, it is not clear whether an individual tenant is supposed to have a private right to his "surplus produce" simply because it is the product of his permissible labor (1970 [1850]: 118) or because the tenant's lease contract gives him "the exclusive use of the remainder of that produce" (1970 [1850]: 116). In either case, one has to wonder how much "surplus produce" will be left for the tenant after he negotiates his lease with "the great corporate body— Society" (1970 [1850]: 111). In his later life, Spencer sought to blunt the cutting edge of the social ownership doctrine by maintaining that it was already incorporated in the commonplace recognition that "ultimate proprietorship . . . vests in the community" (1981 [1897]: 107) and that, if anything, the taxes paid by private landholders exceed what the cost to them would be of leasing that land from society (1981 [1897]: 459).

The second striking right asserted in *Social Statics* is the right to ignore the state— that is, "to drop connection with the state—to relinquish its protection, and to refuse paying toward its support." Those payments may be required only from those who have voluntarily subscribed to them. For government is "simply an agent employed in common by a number of individuals to secure to them certain advantages, the very nature of the connection implies that it is for each to say whether he will employ such an agent or not" (1970 [1850]: 185). The state that does not exceed its just limits is merely a "mutual-safety confederation" that individuals may hire or not hire as they see fit (1970 [1850]: 185). However, Spencer provides no positive discussion of what recourse is available to the individual who ignores the state when his liberty is threatened. The chapter on "The Right to Ignore the State" disappears from later editions of *Social Statics*, and nothing like this chapter appears in Spencer's final systematic statement, *The Principle of Ethics* (1897).

In the United States during the nineteenth century, hard-core libertarian thought was represented by the individualist anarchists who flourished from the 1830s into the 1890s.[1] The most philosophically engaging and forceful voice among them was Lysander Spooner, whose most characteristic theme was the Ciceronian invocation of unchanging and universal principles of natural justice against criminal state action. Spooner was trained as a lawyer, and he thought of the unchanging principles of natural justice as the true law. Moreover, the fundamental natural rights that consti- tute the true, universal, and unchanging natural law were readily known to human beings. Spooner proclaimed that "honesty, justice, natural law, is usually a very plain and simple matter, easily understood by common minds" (1971 [1882]: 8). Indeed, children

> very early understand that one child must not, without just cause, strike or otherwise hurt, another; that one child must not assume any arbitrary control or domination over another; that one child must not, either by force, deceit, or stealth, obtain the possession of anything that belongs to another, that if one child commits any of these wrongs against another, it is not only the right of the injured child to

[1] Martin (1970 [1953]) provides an excellent history of these individualist anarchists.

resist, and, if need be, punish the wrongdoer, and compel him to make reparation, but that it is also the right, and the moral duty, of all other children, and all other persons, to assist the injured party in defending his rights, and redressing his wrongs. (1971 [1882]: 9)

Spooner goes beyond appeals to moral intuition to provide arguments (i) for the existence of natural justice and (ii) for natural justice taking the form of natural rights of life, liberty, and property.

With regard to (i), "from time immemorial" men have spoken and written about justice; they have identified various acts as criminal and contrasted criminal with non-criminal acts. If people have not been totally deluded when they have been engaged in this practice and if men's claims that legitimate governments are those that act justly have not been "the mere gibberish of fools," it must be because there is such a thing as natural justice.

> If justice be not a natural principle, then there is no such thing as justice; and all the crimes of which the world has been the scene, have been no crimes at all; but only simple events, like the falling of the rain, or the setting of the sun; events of which the victims had no more reason to complain than they had to complain of the running of the streams, or the growth of vegetation. (1971 [1882]: 11)

If there are no such rights, no such truths of justice, then all of the moral vocabulary that men have used in their judgments and contentions "should be struck out of all human language as having no meanings" (1971 [1882]: 14).

With regard to (ii), if there are rights, they must mark each person's standing "as a being with will, judgment, and conscience of his own" and hence not "as a mere instrument" that may be disposed of "as if he were but a dog" (1971 [1886]: 32). They must secure for each person the conditions necessary for his attainment of his "highest happiness." Moreover, the right that is "indispensable to every man's highest happiness" is precisely the right to dispose as one chooses of one's own life, liberty, and legitimate possessions. For this right protects "every man's power of judging and determining for himself what will, and what will not, promote his happiness. Any restriction upon the exercise of this right is a restriction upon his rightful power of providing for, and accomplishing his own well-being" (1971 [1886]: 7). Moreover, if there are natural rights, they must be rights whose ascription to each man is "always consistent and harmonious with each and every other man's rights" (1971 [1886]: 22). This is also a feature of the right to dispose of one's person and property as one sees fit. This freedom to dispose of oneself and one's property as one chooses is both the least and the most that any man may reasonably demand of all others (1971 [1886]: 15).

Spooner advanced a Lockean labor-investment view of just initial acquisition—including just initial acquisition of land.

> He holds the land in order to hold the labor which he has put into it, or upon it. And the land is his, so long as the labor he has expended upon it remains in a condition to be valuable for uses for which it was expended; because it is not to be supposed

that a man has abandoned the fruits of his labor so long as they remain in a state to
be practically useful to him . . . (1971 [1855]: 22)

Thus, against his fellow individualist anarchists,[2] Spooner held that one did not need
to continue to occupy and personally use one's land in order to retain title to it. Thus,
rental income from land—along with all other property—was perfectly legitimate. Still,
Spooner held that, if the issuance of credit were not illicitly restricted by the state, credit
would be readily available for individuals who wanted to purchase land. Hence, there
would not be much rental of land. In addition, Spooner held that almost all large land
holdings are in fact the illegitimate results of criminal predation, not the legitimate
results of labor investment: "wherever any people have advanced beyond the savage
state, and have learned to increase their means of subsistence by the cultivation of soil,
a greater or lesser number of them have associated and organized themselves as
robbers, to plunder and enslave all others . . ." (1971 [1882]: 16). For the most part
the slave-owning robber class has emancipated its slaves only when it has discovered
that its interests are better yet served by giving its slaves "so much liberty as would
throw upon themselves . . . the responsibility of their own subsistence, and yet compel
to sell their labor to the land-holding class" while maintaining its near monopolies on
"all other means of creating wealth" (1971 [1882]: 19) These monopolies are sustained
through legislation—the point of which is always to contravene and overturn the
simple and easily perceived natural law.

Spooner considers and rejects two purported vindications for legislation. In *No
Treason, No. 6* (1870), he systematically criticizes attempts to found legislative or
constitutional authority on some species of consent. And, in *A Letter to Grover Cleveland* (1886), he argues that no coherent meaning can be given to the notion of the
common good and, hence, its invocation merely provides a smokescreen behind which
powerful interests advance their ends at the expense of others' interests and rights.
However, it does not follow that all "government" must be illegitimate. For individuals
do need to secure protection for their rights; and a "government" that was freely
established by individuals to serve this purpose would be perfectly legitimate. It
makes sense for each individual to subscribe to "some plan or system of judicial
proceedings, which, in the trial of causes, should secure caution, deliberation, thorough
investigation, and as far as possible, freedom from every influence but the simple desire
to do justice" (1971 [1882]: 7). Still, each individual must remain free to make his own
decision about what bargain, if any, he will strike for "outside protection"; and "other
persons have no occasion to thrust their protection upon him against his own will"
(1971 [1886]: 14).

Spooner's fellow Boston Anarchist Benjamin Tucker was more explicit than Spooner
in embracing a free market in protective services. According to Tucker, "defense is a
service like any other service . . . and therefore an economic commodity subject to the

---

[2] See "Property under Anarchism" in Tucker (1926). I am grateful to Roderick Long for correcting
my understanding of Spooner on rent.

law of supply and demand."[3] However, the proposal that the legitimate activity of government—namely, the production of security—be carried out by competing enterprises had been worked out earlier and in considerable detail by the Belgium economist Gustav de Molinari.[4] Molinari was the most radical member of an influential circle of strongly laissez-faire mid-nineteenth-century French economists whose best-known representative is Frederic Bastiat (1801–50). Although Bastiat endorsed the minimal state, his best known quip was "The state is the great fictitious entity by which everyone seeks to live at the expense of everyone else." (Bastiat 1964 [1848]: 144). In his 1849 essay "The Production of Security" and in the "Eleventh Lecture" of his 1849 book *Les Soirées de la rue Saint-Lazare*, Molinari maintains that the same considerations that show that a competitive market better supplies goods and services than socialism or protectionism also shows that the protection of persons' lives, liberties, and property would be best supplied by a competitive market. Moreover, just as no supplier of any standard good or service has the right to suppress competition or the right to require consumers to purchase from it, "no government should have the right to prevent another government from going into competition with it, or to require consumers of security to come exclusively to it for this commodity" (Molinari 1849*a*: 3). Molinari anticipates and responds to some of the standard objections to such a system of competing protective agencies. Since their potential customers will want the peaceful protection of their rights, protective agencies will cooperate with one another in the pursuit of criminals and in the resolution of disputes amongst their respective clients. They will also cooperate against any renegade agencies or foreign power that threatens the security of their clients—at least to the extent that their clients are willing to pay for such cooperation against aggression (Molinari 1849*b*).

However, toward the end of his life, Molinari recognized that individuals may not be willing to pay for security to a degree commensurate with their desire for security—precisely because of the public-goods character of its provision. If security is produced, it will be at least very difficult to exclude individuals who have not paid for it from enjoying it. Thus, individuals may so extensively seek to free ride on others' payment for the production of security that security will not be funded; and, hence, no one will enjoy its provision. On the basis of this concern, Molinari maintained that individuals could be required to pay into a fund for the provision of the collective good of security. Despite this acceptance of forced—albeit mutually beneficial—exchange, Molinari hoped that some benefits of free competition would still be realized within the domain of government by requiring governments to contract out the actual production of security and by requiring them to recognize robust rights of secession so that individuals would have some degree of choice concerning to which government they would be required to make payments.[5]

---

[3] Benjamin Tucker, "On the Picket Line," *Liberty*, July 30, 1887: 4.
[4] See Hart (1981–2).
[5] On this final phase of Molinari's thought, see Hart (1981–2: 5/4: 423–6).

Twentieth-Century Libertarianism

With the exception of the strongly classical liberal Austrian school of economics—which by the mid-1930s was dispersed from its home base in Austria—the first half of the twentieth century saw little in the way of theoretically interesting libertarian thought. Hayek's very tentative *The Road to Serfdom* (1944) and Milton Friedman's *Capitalism and Freedom* (1962) both sought to reintroduce at least soft-core libertarian themes by arguing that private property and free markets were crucial to the survival of personal (and political) liberties. Hayek's later *The Constitution of Liberty* (1960) was an important attempt to recast the sort of utilitarian defense of liberty offered by Mill in *On Liberty* (1978 [1859])—with greater emphasis on the importance of economic liberty and evolved moral and legal norms. The first volume of Hayek's *Law, Legislation, and Liberty* (1973) was the culmination of Hayek's strongly anti-statist—but not hard-core libertarian—investigation of the nature and virtues of spontaneous social order.

Most of the credit for the re-emergence of libertarian theorizing in the later part of the twentieth century has to be given to the novelist and non-academic philosopher, Ayn Rand. Rand has been the subject of more ill-informed intellectual abuse than any other libertarian thinker—albeit Rand herself rarely passed up a chance to argue *ad hominem*. Rand's rights-oriented endorsement of laissez-faire and radically limited government was grounded in her strongly secularist endorsement of the separate and ultimate value of each individual's life and happiness. Rand argued that a code for the guidance of human action is needed precisely because each individual's maintenance and enhancement of his life is conditional upon his discovery and engagement in the specific forms of conduct that sustain and enhance life and that, therefore, the function of a moral code is to point the way toward the attainment of those outcomes in the agent's life (1964: 16–18). Rand boldly embraced the label of "egoist." For she sought to confront head on the enshrinement of self-sacrifice that she saw at the core of religious morality and all forms of political collectivism. Rand was also a strong advocate of natural rights of the familiar Lockean sort (1964: 108–17), although she did not recognize the tension between two distinct strands of her thought about rights. On the one hand, the tone of much of her writing implies a strongly deontic conception of rights. No individual may be treated as a sacrificial animal. It is because others are moral ends-in-themselves that one must eschew conduct that subordinates them to oneself. On the other hand, Rand thinks that her egoism precludes acceptance of any reasons to constrain oneself in one's conduct toward others except reasons that are ultimately self-regarding. According to this strand of her thought, the case for strict compliance with a norm against imposing sacrifices on others rests on the proposition that—at least under anything like normal social circumstances—compliance with this norm fosters the well-being *of the complying agent*. Crucial to Rand's perception of the coherence of her joint advocacy of egoism and rights was her embrace of the descriptive postulate that general compliance with libertarian rights is the recipe for peaceful, non-predatory, and mutually advantageous social order.

Rand defended property rights as a necessary condition of people exercising their talents and energy to advance their own good in their own chosen ways, and also on the grounds of persons (often) deserving the fruits of their productivity and what they have gotten in exchange for those fruits. An important feature of Rand's position was her special celebration of capitalist acts of innovative economic productivity. A proper secular individualist code esteems the producer who transforms the material world in ways that promotes his own (and others') earthly well-being. Most of the heroes of Rand's immense novel *Atlas Shrugged* (1957) are such economic producers; and the ultimate vice of the semi-socialist, semi-fascist cultural and political order that exploits these individuals—and against which *they* go on strike—is that this order does not recognize the *virtue* of their productivity. Although Rand does not claim that all economic outcomes within a laissez-faire economy are deserved, she emphasizes the *desert* of the producers much more than, for example, Hayek or Nozick do.

Rand offered no particular view about initial acquisitions of portions of nature. Yet she clearly took nature itself to be originally unowned (and, by itself, economically worthless); and she almost certainly would have rejected any sort of Lockean proviso. Rand held that the minimal state is the appropriate mechanism for the protection of individual rights. Aside from the usual equation of anarchy with chaos, Rand argued that the norms articulated and enforced by the minimal state—but not those articulated and enforced by a network of competing agencies—would be "objective" law. In addition, she accuses the market anarchist of joining the socialist in failing to recognize that there is and ought to be a fundamental difference in character between political and economic institutions (1964: 131–2). Still, Rand rejected taxation and expressed the hope that a minimal state could fund itself through the sale of its services (1964: 135–40). She seems to have been unaware of the difficulties of assembling voluntary financing for the production of goods—like national-scale defense—to which non-contributors may have as much access as contributors.[6]

The economist Murray Rothbard played Molinari to Rand's Bastiat. Rothbard joined Rand in affirming natural rights. He argued that, if one rejects moral nihilism and thereby affirms that there must be *some* sound fundamental political principle, *and* one rejects utilitarianism as that principle, then there must be *some* sound ascription of fundamental natural rights. If fundamental rights must be universal rights and one rejects the ascription to everyone of an equal right over everyone, one is left with each individual's right over himself as the only plausible fundamental natural right. Thus, Lockean self-ownership is the prescriptive bedrock (Rothbard 1978 [1973]: 28–30); and Lockean investment of one's labor in segments of nature is the basis for property rights in extra-personal object (Rothbard 1978 [1973]: 31–7). Rights of self-ownership and

---

[6] If the minimal state can charge monopoly prices for those of its products—e.g. court services—from which it *can* exclude non-contributors, perhaps it can accumulate the funds needed to provide the services from which it *cannot* exclude non-contributors.

rights of property define the spheres of freedom of action that each individual may justly demand be recognized and that each individual may defend—or arrange for the defense of. Moreover, respect for people's freedom of action within their protected spheres is, in Smithian and Millian fashion, the condition under which individuals can pursue their own personal and economic ends in peace and to mutual advantage.

Against Randian minimal statism, Rothbard brings both the moral arguments that no protective agency has the right to suppress its competitors or the right to forbid potential clients from patronizing those competitors and the economic arguments that: (1) rights protection, like any valuable service, is best supplied when consumers can choose among competing suppliers, and (2) only market choices can properly deter-mine how many resources ought to be allocated to the production of which protective services. Rothbard takes the imposition of taxation to be so closely connected to the nature of the state that the only way to escape this core violation of rights is to escape from the monopoly state. Rothbard provides a more elaborate discussion than Molinari did of how competing protective agencies might cooperate so as to provide acceptable, reliable, and peaceful dispute resolution for their clients (Rothbard 1978 [1973]: 215–37). He envisions a libertarian "legal code" emerging from agreements amongst these agencies about what substantive and procedural norms will be followed by the police and courts that those agencies will singly or jointly operate. Like Spooner, Rothbard presumes a high degree of convergence amongst individuals about what constitutes natural justice; and this convergence guides the formation of that legal code. In contrast, in his *The Machinery of Freedom* (1989 [1973]), David Friedman envisions quasi-libertarian law emerging from a market for law simply because people are more willing to pay more to be let alone than to prevent other people from being let alone. Like Molinari, Rothbard was aware of the contention that attempts to attain voluntary financing for public goods—like national-scale defense—might fail. Unfortunately, Rothbard largely evaded serious discussion of this contention. He pointed out—as Spencer had in 1843—that there would be no problem for anyone about financing national-scale defense if *everyone* foreswore national-scale military operations. And he sought to deny conventional wisdom about the need for national-scale defense by maintaining that the USSR had not actually been a threat that required anything like the military expenditure that was undertaken by the US government out of fear of the USSR (Rothbard 1978 [1973]: 237–41).[7]

Robert Nozick's *Anarchy, State, and Utopia* (1974) made hard-core, rights-based, libertarian doctrine known to the academic world. In his preface, Nozick acknowledges that Rothbard's defense of free-market anarchism awakened him to the need to defend minimal statism against this anarchist view. Yet Nozick is interestingly silent on why he subscribed to the rights-based minimal state position to begin with. Nozick begins *Anarchy, State, and Utopia* with the bold proclamation that "individuals have rights, and there are things no person or group may do to them, without violating their rights"

---

[7] For more serious discussions of public goods, see Mack (1986) and Schmidtz (1991).

(1974: p. ix). These rights are so extensive and so robust that they throw into question whether *any* state can be justified. Unfortunately, Nozick's *defense* of the existence of these rights is much less extensive and robust. Nevertheless, Nozick does provide some defense, which consists largely of his adaptation of John Rawls's invocation of the "separateness of persons" against utilitarianism.

The core claim is that, summoning individuals to sacrifice their interests for the sake of the net social good, utilitarianism does not take seriously the separateness of persons. Even in Rawls, there is the strong suggestion that an appreciation of the significance of the separateness of persons does not merely undermine the case for utilitarianism; it also supports regulative social principles that express the moral inviolability of persons. Nozick modifies Rawls's argument in three important and related ways. First, much more persistently than Rawls, he takes the argument to be a critique of the call for individual sacrifice. Second, all conceptions of "an overall social good"—not just aggregative conceptions—are guilty of failing to take seriously the separateness of persons. Third, the suggested regulative rule that emerges from the insight that "there is no justified sacrifice of some of us for others" is the Randian-sounding principle that "no one is to be sacrificed for others" (1974: 33).[8]

The moral immunity against being so sacrificed is codified by the ascription to persons of natural rights; and Nozick proceeds to affirm Lockean rights of self-ownership (Nozick 1974: 172). But, rather than argue in standard Lockean fashion that property rights arise through one's investment of one's rightfully held labor in some extra-personal material, Nozick argues for the superiority of his historical entitlement theory of justice in holdings over any end-state or pattern theory. Part of that argument is that end-state and patterned theories turn on themselves by refusing to uphold the rights that people have been accorded by those theories (1974: 160–4). Nevertheless, Nozick's crucial argument is that end-state and pattern theories "institute (partial) ownership by others of [productive] people and their actions and time" (1974: 172). Why, though, does the seizure of that which an agent has produced count as instituting ownership in that *person* (or her actions or time)? It looks as though Nozick's answer has to revert to the Lockean claim that her person (or her actions, time, or labor) has been invested in that object; *that* is why any institution of end-state or pattern doctrines trespasses upon persons. Nozick also reintroduces advocacy of a Lockean proviso into libertarian theorizing—bringing back in questions about whether the systematic rise of private property or owners' deployment of that property might impermissibly constrain others' opportunities. Such a proviso can be seen as an attempt to insure that a regime of libertarian rights would in some significant sense not be to any (non-faulty) person's disadvantage.

Nozick's most protracted and difficult arguments are directed against the free-market anarchist contention that no protective agency has the right to suppress any

---

[8] Nozick's subscription to the libertarian descriptive postulate is manifest in his appeal to invisible hand explanations (1974: 18–22) and his discussion of the generation of utopias (1974: 297–334) via Smithian–Hayekian invisible hand processes.

competing, non-renegade, protective agency. Nozick seems to think that he will have met the anarchist's challenge if he can broaden the range of agencies that are subject to suppression by the "dominant protective agency." He seeks to do this by focusing on relatively unreliable agencies—including individual self-protectors—and invoking the principle that relatively unreliable agencies can be suppressed if they are compensated for disadvantages that arise from that suppression. The problem here for Nozick is that he never shows why the "dominant protective agency" itself might not be the sort of network of cooperating, but also competing, agencies envisioned by the anar-cho-capitalist. Moreover, Nozick slides past the utterly *non-political* character of the minimal state that he takes himself to have vindicated. For the Nozickean minimal state would be funded entirely through the sale of its services to voluntary purchasers; and which particular packages of rights-enforcement services it would offer (and at what prices) would be determined by that enterprise's profit-maximizing calculations. There will be nothing like electoral or legislative processes. For better or for worse, the Nozickian minimal state would simply be another market institution. (Perhaps *polit-ical/constitutional* features will be introduced to counteract the state's capacity to charge monopoly prices.)

Highlighting the Nozickian state's need to sell its services brings us back to what may be the common problem for anarchist and minimal state libertarians—namely, the public-goods character of large-scale protective services.[9] If this difficulty cannot be overcome without coercion, does the libertarian have to choose between forgoing the effective protection of rights and endorsing some degree of rights-violating tax-ation? Perhaps the same sort of principle that underlies Nozick's advocacy of a Lockean proviso—namely, that the structure of rights must be such that compliance with it is (in some suitably explicated sense) mutually advantageous—allows escape from this dilemma. For, according to this principle, *if* all members of the relevant "public" would be worse off vis-à-vis the protection of their rights were their property rights under-stood to exclude their being taxed to fund that protection, those rights ought *not* to be understood as excluding that taxation. Rather, those rights should be understood as allowing these takings if due compensation is paid—and that compensation would be paid in kind by the financed provision of rights-protecting services. Interestingly, Nozick's reaffirmation of a generally libertarian stance in his final work, *Invariances* (2001: 236–301), takes our fundamental norms to be those rules that facilitate cooper-ative and mutually advantageous interaction.

Libertarian theorizing neither began nor ended with Nozick's *Anarchism, State, and Utopia*. More recent sympathetic explorations of libertarian themes can be found in, for example, Loren Lomasky's *Persons, Rights, and the Moral Community* (1987), Jan Narveson's *The Libertarian Idea* (1989), Douglas Rasmussen and Douglas DenUyl's *Norms of Liberty* (2005), David Schmidtz's *Elements of Justice* (2006), and various essays by the present author (1986, 2009, 2010).

---

[9] The issue of the voluntary financing of public goods did not occur to Nozick in the course of writing *Anarchy, State, and Utopia* (personal conversation).

REFERENCES

BASTIAT, FREDERIC (1964 [1848]). "The State," in *Selected Essays on Political Economy*. Irvington-on-Hudson, NY: Foundation for Economic Education, 140–51.

FRIEDMAN, DAVID (1989 [1973]). *The Machinery of Freedom*. 2nd edn. Chicago: Open Court.

FRIEDMAN, MILTON (1962). *Capitalism and Freedom*. Chicago: University of Chicago Press.

HART, DAVID (1981–2)."Gustave de Molinari and the Anti-Statist Liberal Tradition," *Journal of Libertarian Studies*, 5/3: 263–90, 5/4: 399–434, 6/1: 83–104.

HAYEK, F. A. (1944). *The Road to Serfdom*. Chicago: University of Chicago Press.

HAYEK, F. A. (1948). *Individualism and Economic Order*. Chicago: University of Chicago Press.

HAYEK, F. A. (1960). *The Constitution of Liberty*. Chicago: University of Chicago Press.

HAYEK, F. A. (1973). *Law, Legislation, and Liberty*, i. Chicago: University of Chicago Press.

LOMASKY, LOREN (1987). *Persons, Rights, and the Moral Community*. Oxford: Oxford University Press.

MACK, ERIC (1986). "The Ethics of Taxation," in D. Lee (ed.), *Taxation and the Deficit Economy*. San Francisco: Pacific Research Institute, 487–514.

MACK, ERIC (2009). "Individualism and Libertarian Rights," in J. Christman and T. Cristiano (eds), *Contemporary Debates in Politcial Philosophy*. Oxford: Blackwell.

MACK, ERIC (2010). "The Natural Right of Property," *Social Philosophy and Policy*, 27/1 (Winter), 53–79.

MARTIN, JAMES (1970 [1953]). *Men against the State*. Colorado Springs: Ralph Myles Publishers.

MILL, J. S. (1978 [1859]). *On Liberty*, (ed.) E. Rapaport. Indianapolis: Hackett.

MOLINARI, GUSTAV DE (1849a). "The Production of Security." http://praxeology.net/MR-GM-PS-htm

MOLINARI, GUSTAV DE (1849b). "Eleventh Lecture," *Les Soirees de la rue Saint-Lazare*, trans. in Hart (1981–2).

MOLINARI, GUSTAV DE (1904 [1889]). *The Society of Tomorrow*. New York: G. P. Putnam's Sons.

NARVESON, JAN (1989). *The Libertarian Idea*. Philadelphia: Temple University Press.

NOZICK, ROBERT (1974). *Anarchy, State, and Utopia*. New York: Basic Books.

NOZICK, ROBERT (2001). *Invariances*. Cambridge, MA: Harvard University Press.

RAND, AYN (1957), *Atlas Shrugged*. New York: New American Liberty.

RAND, AYN (1964). *The Virtue of Selfishness*. New York: New American Library.

RAND, AYN (1967). *Capitalism: The Unknown Ideal*. New York: New American Liberty.

RASMUSSEN, DOUGLAS, and DENUYL, DOUGLAS (2005). *Norms of Liberty*. University Park, PA: Pennsylvania State Press.

ROTHBARD, MURRAY (1978 [1973]). *For a New Liberty*. Rev. edn. New York: MacMillan.

ROTHBARD, MURRAY (1982). *The Ethics of Liberty*. New York: Humanities Press.

SCHMIDTZ, DAVID (1991). *The Limits of Government*. Boulder, CO: Westview Press.

SCHMIDTZ, DAVID (2006). *Elements of Justice*. Cambridge: Cambridge University Press.

SMITH, ADAM (1981 [1776]). *The Wealth of Nations*, (ed.) E. Cannan. Indianapolis: Liberty Classics.

SPENCER, HERBERT (1970 [1850]). *Social Statics*. New York: Robert Schalkenbach Foundation.

SPENCER, HERBERT (1981 [1843]). *The Proper Sphere of Government, in The Man versus the State and Other Essays*, (ed.) E. Mack. Indianapolis: Liberty Classics.

SPENCER, HERBERT (1981 [1884]). *The Man versus the State, in The Man versus the State and Other Essays*, (ed.) E. Mack. Indianapolis: Liberty Classics.

SPENCER, HERBERT (1981 [1897]). *The Principles of Ethics*, (ed.) T. R. Machan. Liberty Classics.

SPOONER, LYSANDER (1971 [1855]). *The Law of Intellectual Property, in The Collected Works of Lysander Spooner*, (ed.) C. Shively. 6 vols. Weston, MA: M & S Press, iii.

SPOONER, LYSANDER (1971 [1870]). *No Treason, No. 6, in The Collected Works of Lysander Spooner*, (ed.) C. Shively. 6 vols. Weston, MA: M & S Press, i.

SPOONER, LYSANDER (1971 [1882]), *Natural Law, in i The Collected Works of Lysander Spooner*, (ed.) C. Shively. 6 vols. Weston, MA: M & S Press, i.

SPOONER, LYSANDER (1971 [1886]). *A Letter to Grover Cleveland, in The Collected Works of Lysander Spooner*, (ed.) C. Shively. 6 vols. Weston, MA: M & S Press, i.

TUCKER, BENJAMIN (1881–1908) (ed.). *Liberty*, Boston.

TUCKER, BENJAMIN (1926). *Individual Liberty*. New York: Vanguard.

VON MISES LUDWIG, (1981 [1922]). *Socialism: An Economic and Sociological Analysis*. Indianapolis: Liberty Classics, 1981.

CHAPTER 42

···

RELIGIOUS TOLERATION

···

PEREZ ZAGORIN

THE fullest development of the concept of religious toleration in the West occurred in Christian Europe between the sixteenth and eighteenth centuries, as the work of a line of Christian thinkers who were primarily occupied with the problem of toleration between differing Christian churches, sects, and individual believers and the relationship between the Christian state and religion.

Toleration, whether as a moral and intellectual attitude or as a practice, may extend to different domains and subjects, but in none has it been more significant and powerful than in religion. The emergence and establishment of religious pluralism in modern societies, and most notably in the Western world, has been very largely the result of the evolution and gradual victory of the principle of religious toleration on a variety of grounds. Historically, the importance of the development of religious toleration can hardly be overestimated not only in its effect upon religion but in its contribution to the formation of liberal polities and the achievement of freedom in realms other than religion such as freedom of thought in general.

The concept of religious toleration can be understood in two different but somewhat related ways. Some philosophers and political analysts prefer to conceive it restrictively to denote a policy of forbearance or indulgence according to which the adherents of a dominant or state religion permit, usually for reasons of political expediency, the existence of another and minority religion, despite their disapproval and rejection of the latter's teachings. From this point of view, toleration expresses a decision to coexist with and suffer the exercise of the faith that is tolerated. It is also implicit in such a situation that the regime or authority that grants the privilege of toleration to a dissident religious body has likewise the power to withdraw or cancel it. A second view of religious toleration identifies it more broadly with the gradual increase of freedom of religion in the direction of what has been called universal toleration—that is, the freedom of individuals to believe and worship in accord with their conscience without interference by the state. This freedom has often been characterized as liberty of conscience and has been considered by many people in recent times to be a natural or a human right. Today the concept of religious toleration is generally taken to mean religious freedom in its fullest sense rather than as a privilege granted under various limitations to a hitherto prohibited religious creed. It may be succinctly defined as the principle that society and the state should, as a matter of right, extend complete freedom of religious belief and expression to all their members and citizens irrespective of their faith, and should refrain from imposing any religious tests, doctrines, or form of worship or religious association upon them.

Among the world's great monotheistic religions, Christianity has been the most intolerant. Except for Christians and Jews, the peoples and nations of the Roman Empire were polytheistic. The religion of the Roman state required sacrifices to the Olympian gods and to the divine emperor, but, apart from these exceptions, Roman society adopted a policy of practical toleration that was hospitable to the existence of a variety of religious cults mainly of Eastern origin with large numbers of followers. Religious pluralism and toleration existed at a pragmatic level in the polytheistic Roman world and seem never to have been subjects of legal or philosophical debate. The intermittent outbreaks of persecution of Christians by the Roman government in the first three centuries of their existence were due principally to their refusal to participate in the idolatrous imperial cult and their rejection of Roman polytheism as a religion of demons. This persecution ceased following the embrace of Christianity by the Emperor Constantine in the early fourth century. Under the latter and his imperial successors, the Christian Church and Roman state became closely joined. The Christian Roman Emperors took a dominant part in the rule of the Church, and Christianity during this period became the sole legal religion of the Roman Empire. From being a persecuted faith, it turned into a persecuting religion itself, supported by the Roman imperial government.

Christian intolerance was endorsed by many of the foremost Catholic thinkers and spiritual leaders of the patristic era and the Middle Ages. Early Christianity was intolerant of Judaism, from which it had to separate itself, and of ancient paganism, whose suppression it demanded. Medieval Christendom has been called a persecuting society because of the repression and violence it directed against heretics, Jews, and other stigmatized groups. Later, during the Protestant Reformation, which gave birth to new churches and sects, the foremost Protestant leaders did not hesitate to advocate the use of force to maintain religious orthodoxy and to silence both Catholics and sectarian dissenters from Protestant state churches. The fact that for many centuries Catholic and Protestant Christians of high standing rejected religious toleration between Christians, despite Jesus's preaching of non-violence and love of one's fellows, would be inexplicable had there not come into being from an early time in Christian history a widely accepted rationale and structure of argument in favor of coercion to enforce religious orthodoxy, unity, and conformity. This rationale constituted a Christian theory of persecution that remained dominant for centuries. Its main element was the concept and fear of heresy, which first appeared in the New Testament.

Hairesis, the Greek term from which the word "heresy" derives, commonly meant a choice of opinions and also referred without any negative connotation to the differing tenets of philosophical schools and sects. In the New Testament, however, the word acquired a pejorative meaning in some of the letters of the apostles, where it referred to false opinions and theological errors propagated by wicked men who bred schism, disharmony, and division among Christians. Although the New Testament recognized heresy as a danger to religious truth and the Christian communities, it did not enjoin the forcible silencing or physical punishment of those who introduced heresies. Instead it recommended that such persons should be admonished and expelled from the religious community if they failed to heed these warnings.

Heresy entailed the existence of its opposite, orthodoxy, which meant right thinking and true belief. The theological differences and controversies that arose in the Christian Church between the second and fifth centuries gave rise to numerous doctrines that ecclesiastical authorities and general councils of the Church condemned as heretical. Orthodoxy was equated with scriptural and apostolic teaching, decrees of church councils, and official religious creeds that summarized orthodox belief. The foremost subject of dispute was the nature of Christ and the doctrine of the Trinity. The church council of Nicaea, summoned in 325 by the Christian Emperor Constantine and attended by more than 300 bishops, condemned and anathematized the influential Arian heresy denying the true divinity of Christ, and affirmed the orthodox Trinitarian doctrine that God was three persons in one substance, consisting of the Father, the coequal, coeternal divine Son, and the Holy Spirit.

Following the union of Christianity with the Roman state, imperial legislation proscribed heresy as a crime sometimes punishable by death. The church fathers wrote treatises describing and denouncing various heresies. It is impossible to exaggerate the significance of the emergence of the concept of heresy within the Christian religion as a means of thought control and the enforcement of orthodoxy. Heresy was a spiritual offense, and not simply an error but a false and sinful teaching that brought damnation upon those who embraced it. The Catholic Church taught that there was no salvation outside the Church; if detected and not recanted, heresy led to excommunication from the Church and hence to the loss of salvation and eternal punishment. The existence of heresy was seen as a danger to all Christians who might be contaminated by it. The heretic was defined as a person who obstinately refused correction and adhered to his error in willful opposition to the Church and religious truth as defined and declared by ecclesiastical authority. One of the greatest of Catholic thinkers, St Augustine (d. 430), made the most important contribution to the Christian theory of persecution by his justification of the use of force against heretics. Although at first opposed to coercion, he later reversed his position when dealing with the widespread Donatist heresy and its schismatic church in Roman Africa. While acknowledging that physical force was incapable of changing belief, he argued in a number of influential writings that threats and fear of punishment (the pedagogy of fear), plus coercive measures such as imprisonment and controlling what heretics were allowed to hear, read, and say, could make them receptive to a right way of thinking in which they would abandon their heresy and submit to the Catholic Church. Augustine considered the heretic a creature of pride and enemy of society, and explicitly distinguished between just and unjust persecution, the first being that which the church of Christ inflicts on the wicked, the second that which the wicked inflict on the church of Christ. He supported his view with two parables in the New Testament, the parable of the feast in the Gospel of Luke (Luke 14:21–3) and the parable of the tares or weeds in the Gospel of Matthew (Matthew 13:24–30), which he interpreted allegorically to justify religious persecution. Augustine never went so far as to propose the killing of heretics, but, while the parable of the tares seemed to teach that both good people and sinners should be left until the Last Judgment to receive their due, he took it to mean that the evil people should be uprooted when they are recognized and known. The two parables and the words "compel them to come in" (*compelle intrare*) in the parable of the feast, understood to mean the approval of compulsion against heretics, were to be frequently quoted and discussed in later centuries in arguments over toleration.

During the Middle Ages, the Catholic Church and secular governments created a large institutional machinery and body of legislation for the suppression of heresy. While some of the heresies that appeared in the medieval period were abstruse theological propositions, others, like the teachings of the Waldensians, Cathars, Lollards, and Hussites, led to the emergence of broad popular movements directly opposed to the Church's doctrines, wealth, and power. In the early thirteenth century Pope Innocent III proclaimed a crusade against the Cathars, a sect that existed in large numbers in the south of France. Later in the same period, Pope Gregory IX and his successors established the papal inquisition, which grew into a powerful heresy-hunting organization with its own officials, courts, and legal procedure. In the late fifteenth century, inquisitions under royal control were established in Spain and Portugal, and later extended to most of the other states of the Spanish empire in Europe and the Americas. The main object of inquisitional tribunals was to obtain a confession from the accused, and they permitted the use of torture on uncooperative defendants. The penalties they inflicted included public penances, loss of property, and imprisonment; in the gravest cases, unrepentant heretics were handed over to the secular power for execution. Control of printing and book censorship became part of the apparatus dealing with heresy.

The Christian theory of persecution rested on premises that were almost universally accepted as unquestionable truths during the Middle Ages. St Thomas Aquinas (d. 1274) was typical of many medieval thinkers in explaining that heretics deserved not only to be separated from the Church but to also be shut off from the world by death. The Christian theory of persecution was concerned primarily with belief as a condition of mind rather than simply with external conformity. Its chief aim was to move the conscience and bring about a change of mind. If the convicted heretic were not to suffer death, he had to confess his error, perform penances, and recant his belief.

The Protestant Reformation initiated by Martin Luther's revolt against Catholicism introduced an era of confessional hatreds and religious conflicts, massacres, and wars of religion within and between states. The Catholic Church failed to prevent the spread of Protestantism, but its combat against Protestant heresy took thousands of lives and forced large numbers of people to flee their homes and seek refuge elsewhere in Europe and later in America. The mainstream Protestant churches, Lutheran, Zwinglian,

Calvinist, and Anglican, that emerged in the sixteenth century were all intolerant and inclined to persecution. They hated Catholicism as a spiritual tyranny and idolatrous faith and were also intolerant toward one another. Protestant leaders and reformers generally accepted the Christian theory of persecution, and maintained that governments and the civil magistrate had an absolute duty to uphold religious orthodoxy against heretics and dissenters. Protestant authorities banned Catholic worship, abolished monasteries, killed priests and monks, and confiscated Catholic Church property. In his early days as a reformer, Luther (d. 1546) advocated mildness and persuasion in the treatment of heresy, but, after witnessing the religious and social disorders bred by the Reformation, he altered his view and demanded the forcible repression of religious rebels and heterodox beliefs. Calvin (d. 1564), the most eminent figure in Protestantism in the generation after Luther, was relentless in his hatred of heresy and opposition to those who disagreed with his teachings. Among European intellectuals, the Catholic humanist scholar, Erasmus (d. 1536), the most celebrated writer of the age, deplored the religious conflicts bred by the Reformation and favored moderation in the treatment of religious differences. His friend Sir Thomas More, on the other hand, whose famous pre-Reformation book *Utopia* (1516) had pictured an ideal society that allowed for religious pluralism, became a persecutor of Protestant heretics, whom he considered a deadly threat to Christian civilization. He died a Catholic martyr, executed in 1535 by Henry VIII for refusing to disavow the pope's supremacy over the English Church.

The sole exception to the approval of religious persecution in sixteenth-century Europe were a few Protestant fringe groups outside the mainstream Protestant churches, notably anabaptists, spiritualists, and Socinians or unitarians, who all belonged to what modern historians have called the Radical Reformation (see Michael Baylor, Chapter 14, this volume). These sects were voluntary religious societies with their own distinct beliefs, and all were victims of persecution, especially the anabaptists, hundreds of whom were put to death as heretics and religious rebels. Despite their conviction of their own rightness, however, they were all opposed to religious compulsion and to the union of religion and the state.

By its creation of new churches and sects, the Protestant Reformation compelled Western society and governments to address the novel and unwanted situation of lasting religious division and the challenge of confessional coexistence. By the same token, the question of religious toleration and freedom of conscience became for the first time in Western civilization an inescapable, hugely consequential problem affecting many thousands of human beings. The Protestant churches were nearly all state churches supported or ruled by royal, princely, or civic governments and to which all subjects were required to conform. Every Christian church claimed that it alone possessed the truth in religion, a condition that made the acceptance of religious coexistence and pluralism very difficult.

Between the later sixteenth-century and the eighteenth-century Age of Enlightenment, religious toleration was one of the dominant subjects of controversy in European thought and politics, producing a mass of writings by theologians, philosophers, clerical and lay authors, and political publicists in many countries. The main sites of this controversy in the seventeenth century were England, which in the mid-century experienced a revolution against the Anglican state church and Stuart monarchy, and the Dutch republic, which had emerged by 1600 as an independent Protestant state in consequence of the revolt of the Netherlands against Spanish rule and became in due course the most tolerant country in Europe. The authors on the side of toleration were nearly all unorthodox Protestants who believed that toleration and freedom of conscience were essential to the spiritual welfare of Christianity and the only road to religious peace. Some tended toward religious skepticism or a form of rational religion like deism or Socinianism. They frequently shared a common allegiance to a moralized or ethical Christianity that abhorred persecution, placed conduct above doctrine, and mandated toleration of differences. Amid the many notable writers who took part in the toleration controversy, I will briefly refer to a few of special importance whose arguments made a lasting contribution to the gradual shift in opinion that prepared the ground for the acceptance of religious coexistence and the attainment of freedom of religion at a later period.

Sebastian Castellio (d. 1563), a French Protestant humanist scholar, biblical translator, and professor of Greek in the Swiss university of Basle, was the first European thinker to mount a comprehensive attack against the Christian theory of persecution, directed in particular at the persecuting mentality of Calvin and Calvinism. In 1553 Calvin played a merciless central role in bringing about the trial and execution in Geneva of the unorthodox Spanish physician and theologian Michael Servetus, who was convicted of heresy as an antitrinitarian and anabaptist, and burned at the stake. In a subsequent book and other publications Calvin justified the killing of heretics, contending that heresy was an offense against God's honor and that civil authorities had an absolute duty to punish incorrigible heretics by death if necessary. Servetus's execution became a cause célèbre in European Protestantism. Castellio condemned it and religious persecution in a number of writings that became classics of tolerationist literature. The first and best known was his pseudonymous Latin work *Concerning Heretics and Whether they should be Persecuted* (1554). This book was structured in several parts, which mustered a range of arguments in favor of toleration and pronounced a severe and eloquent indictment of religious persecution as totally evil and contrary to the will of Christ, a merciful and loving savior. Castellio deplored "the license of judgment" that reigned in his day and wrongfully spilled the blood of those who were called heretics. Interrogating the meaning of heresy, he deconstructed the concept, reducing its significance to no more than a difference of opinion on controverted points of religion. Heretics, he therefore explained, were not persons of whose errors one could be certain, but simply people with whom one disagreed in religion, as was evident from the fact that almost all sects looked upon the rest as heretics. He introduced a strain of skepticism into all of his writings in pointing out that many things in the Bible were unclear and impossible to understand with any certainty; hence Christians showed their ignorance when they persecuted each other over obscure doctrines like baptism, free will, and communion, for, if the matters in dispute were as obvious as the proposition that there is only one God, Christians would all easily agree. He denied that secular rulers had any authority over spiritual offenses like heresy or infidelity, and, citing the parable of the tares, urged princes to beware of killing or burning anyone for faith and religion, "which above all else should be free." Rejecting all arguments for persecution based on the Bible, he pointed out that neither Christ nor the apostles ever used carnal or worldly weapons. He denied that force could change belief and criticized the burning of books and silencing of heretics. It was because religion was not left free, he maintained, that error and spiritual tyranny were able to establish their dominion. In *Concerning Heretics* and other works, he expressed a keen respect for the subjective religious conviction of the individual conscience, which ought to render it immune from any kind of coercion. A formidable controversialist and believer in intellectual freedom, he criticized on both rational and Christian grounds Calvin's intolerance of difference and refusal of free and equal debate in favor of the forcible repression and killing of those with whom he disagreed. One of Castellio's most memorable statements was his comment upon Calvin's claim to be a defender of true doctrine: "To kill a man is not to defend a doctrine, it is to kill a man. When the Genevans killed Servetus, they did not defend a doctrine, they killed a man." Among his final writings on behalf of religious toleration and freedom of conscience was *Advice to a Desolate France* (1562), addressed to his country then falling into a religious civil war. He found the basic cause of the war to lie in the forcing of conscience by Catholics and Protestants alike, and counseled all of the parties to cease persecution and allow everyone who accepted Christ to serve God in accord with their own beliefs. His last work, left unfinished, was a remarkable epistemological treatise, *The Art of Doubting*, a defense of both toleration and reason in religion, which validated doubt and discussed the question of when to doubt and when to believe. Castellio was one of the greatest and most courageous thinkers in the toleration controversy. His work was not forgotten and exerted a considerable influence upon a number of writers who argued for toleration in the century and a half following his death.

Another outstanding champion of religious toleration was Roger Williams (d. 1683), an English Puritan cleric dissatisfied with the Anglican Church who emigrated to Massachusetts in 1631 to become minister of the church in Boston. His religious radicalism and belief in autonomous separatist churches quickly made him a thorn in the side of the Puritan theocracy that governed the Massachusetts Bay colony. Expelled from the latter in 1635, he moved south to found Providence and the colony of Rhode Island as a home of religious freedom. A religious sectarian, he was especially sympathetic to the Baptists but was apparently never a member of a Baptist church. He was noted for his friendly and equitable relations with the native Indian tribes near whom he dwelt and whose language he learned.

In 1644, while on a mission to England on behalf of the Rhode Island colony, he published *The Bloudy Tenent of Persecution*, one of the major English works of the seventeenth century in favor of religious freedom. Written in the form of a dialogue between Truth and Peace and steeped in the Bible as its principal source, it was aimed particularly at the regime of intolerance in Massachusetts and its spokesman the Revd John Cotton, but its propositions pertained to religious freedom in general and derived from principles that Williams regarded as inviolable truths. His fundamental argument, based on an interpretation of Christian history, was that Christ's coming marked the end of the theocratic type of Jewish kingdom, which united civil and religious authority as described in the Old Testament, and opened a new epoch of complete separation between the political and the religious–spiritual domains, so that henceforth Christian magistrates and civil governments were prohibited by Christ from exercising any power over the Church and religion. From this thesis he drew a number of conclusions that removed religion from any connection or subordination to political authority and treated it as entirely a matter of personal belief dictated by conscience. Williams pronounced the union of the state and church a calamity for Christianity, commenting that "the unknowing zeal" of Constantine and other Christian Roman Emperors had done greater harm to Christ's crown and kingdom than "the raging fury of the most bloody Neroes." He condemned the doctrine of persecution, which he accused of always falling heaviest on the most godly people. The Church in his view was a voluntary private society of spiritual persons that governed itself and was separate from the world and the civil order. One of his most frequent metaphors, which he related to the Gospel's parable of the tares, was his comparison between the church as a garden and the world as a field. He complained of those who tried to extend the field of the world into the garden of the church, and was probably the first to speak of "the wall of separation" that must divide the two, a phrase later used frequently in American legal and constitutional discussion of the relationship between church and state. Williams was an advocate of universal toleration and freedom of religion for all denominations and faiths, including Islam, Judaism, and even Catholicism, the last of which, in the view of many Protestant writers, should be denied toleration because it was itself intolerant. The civil or political order existed only for secular ends, Williams held, and in light of Christ's ordinance it could have no power over "spiritual and Soul-causes." The peace of the city or state, he consistently argued, depended on a civil type of union, and could therefore remain safe and unbroken amidst religious diversity. Recognizing that Christians might differ about fundamentals and that there was no authoritative judge to decide these controversies, he insisted on the supremacy of the individual conscience in determining religious belief. He undermined the traditional meaning of heresy, pointing out that what one person took as heresy was conscientious conviction to another. Williams was one of the earliest of European thinkers to advance a systematic case chiefly on religious grounds for the complete separation of church and state in a Christian society. His primary reason for holding this position was the harm religious persecution did to religion and to the small number of true Christians, whose consciences should be left free from all compulsion. For him universal toleration was identical with religious freedom and the bloody tenet of persecution contrary to humanity and the law of Christ. He constantly insisted on the purely secular character of the civil order by denying it any authority over religion and conceived the Church as simply one type of voluntary association among many others in the same society. One of the main outcomes of his argument was to demonstrate that religious pluralism and differences were fully compatible with a common political citizenship and the political unity of the state.

Many other notable seventeenth-century thinkers could be discussed here. These include the Jewish philosopher Baruch or Benedict de Spinoza, whose *Theological-Political Treatise* (1670), a work of political theory and biblical criticism, advanced a powerful plea for the recognition by the state of both freedom of religion and freedom of thought in general. The Frenchman Pierre Bayle, and the Englishman John Locke, were profoundly affected by the reign of persecution in their own countries; in England the government and state church's persecution of Protestant dissenters in the reigns of Charles II and James II; in France the cruel mistreatment and forced conversion of Protestants by the Catholic monarch Louis XIV. This ruler's revocation in 1685 of the Edict of Nantes, which in 1598 for the maintenance of peace had granted freedom of worship under various restrictions to the French Calvinist Reformed churches, was an event of European significance that caused thousands of French Protestants to seek refuge in Protestant countries. At the time of the Revocation, Locke and Bayle were both exiles living in Holland and witnessed its grievous effects in the stream of Protestant refugees fleeing France. Bayle's main work on toleration was his *Philosophical Commentary on these Words of Jesus: Compel them to Come in* (1686), a condemnation of the use of force in religion, defense of the rights of conscience, and critique of St Augustine's recommendation of the coercion of heretics. No more acute analysis of the wrongfulness and unreason of persecution has ever been written. Locke's Latin *Letter on Toleration* (1689), anonymously published in the same year as his political work *Two Treatises on Government*, was in some respects a distillation and synthesis of many of the preceding arguments advanced in support of religious pluralism and freedom. Locke claimed that religious toleration was the chief mark of a true church, and running through his work was an ethical condemnation of persecution founded on the view that the essence of the Christian faith lay in love, charity, and goodwill. His basic approach to the problem of toleration, however, was the distinction he sought to clarify describing "the true bounds between the church and commonwealth," and the very different ends of religion and of civil government. He went on to explain that civil government was concerned solely with the goods of human life in this world, whereas religion concerned the future life and the care of the soul. The jurisdiction of the civil power was accordingly limited to securing subjects in such civil goods as life, liberty, and property, for which compulsion was a necessary means. Religion, on the other hand, pertained only to the individual, who was incapable of abandoning his personal interest in his salvation by adopting under compulsion the faith prescribed by the ruler or some other person. God, Locke held, had not given anyone authority to compel the faith of others, nor could mankind give such authority to the civil magistrate. Not only was it impossible to force people to believe, but the religious doctrines that were imposed by princes or a country's laws might not be the true religion. Locke thus placed the entire responsibility for the destiny of the soul on the personal religious faith of each individual. Mere external conformity without the full inward persuasion of faith was hypocrisy and contempt of God; hence every religious person must work out his faith for himself in all sincerity and as the nearest he could come to the truth. By emphasizing the primacy of subjective conscientious conviction in everything to do with religion, Locke took away the magistrate's power over religion. In keeping with this view, he defined the Church as a free and voluntary society of people who joined in worship in the way they believed was acceptable to God for their salvation. No church could have power over other churches, or depend on the government to enforce its teachings, or invoke any sanctions against its own members other than exhortations, appeals to conscience, and ultimately expulsion. Locke would have withheld toleration from doctrines harmful to society and good morals and likewise from Catholics, because they were intolerant themselves and owed allegiance to the pope, a foreign sovereign. He would also have denied toleration to atheists, on the weak ground that no promises or oaths could obligate persons who did not believe in God. It is quite clear that Locke equated toleration with religious freedom and regarded the latter as an inherent right of individuals and subjects, which Christian rulers and governments were obliged to respect. In analyzing the problem of toleration primarily in light of the difference between the purposes of religion and of government, he followed a line of argument that was to be of great significance in the ultimate establishment of religious freedom as a right of citizens in Western society.

During the eighteenth century, religious freedom was increasingly conceived as a natural right. Among its most effective advocates were the celebrated French writer and satirist Voltaire and, in America, Thomas Jefferson, author of the Virginia Statute of Religious Freedom of 1786. The last war of religion in Europe was the Thirty Years War, 1618–48, which, beginning in Germany as a conflict between Protestant and Catholic rulers, evolved into a secular conflict of European great and lesser powers whose alignment was not determined by their religion. The treaties of Westphalia that concluded this war recognized the coexistence of Catholic, Lutheran, and Calvinist states in Germany and the Holy Roman Empire, required subjects to conform to the religion of their prince, but permitted them to practice their faith in private if it differed from the state religion. In England, the Toleration Act of 1689, a legislative landmark passed after the Revolution of 1688 that deposed James II, ratified religious pluralism by permitting freedom of worship to Protestant dissenters from the Anglican Church, including notably Presbyterians, Congregationalists, and Baptists, while withholding it from Catholics and disbelievers in the Trinity. In the American colonies in the seventeenth and eighteenth centuries, Maryland, founded by Catholics, and Pennsylvania, founded by Quakers, ordained toleration for all Christians as part of their law. The French Revolution affirmed the natural right of freedom of religious opinion and granted equal citizenship to Jews. The first amendment in the bill of rights added in 1791 to the new United States Constitution prohibited the federal congress from establishing a state religion and proclaimed the right of free exercise of religion along with the rights of freedom of speech, the press, and assembly. The progress of the principle of toleration and religious freedom between the age of the Reformation and the late eighteenth century encountered many obstacles. This progress, although due to a variety of factors including the widespread recognition of the benefits of religious peace, could not have occurred without the arduous efforts of a large number of writers and thinkers to discredit the Christian theory of persecution and demonstrate the moral, spiritual, intellectual, political, and other advantages of religious coexistence and pluralism. It would be altogether mistaken, however, to suppose that the early advocates of religious freedom wished to reduce religion to a purely private and individual concern without any public role in society or politics. Nearly all of them took it for granted that the Christian faith was vital to public well-being and the regulation of morals and conduct, and that human life and government were subject to God's providence.

The modern era, following the revolutions of the eighteenth century, saw the gradual expansion of the principle of religious toleration in Western society as part of the emergence of liberal ideas and polities and the growth of parliamentary and representative government. In Britain the penal laws against Catholicism were repealed in 1829. In Europe as a whole, despite the persistence of anti-Semitism, the emancipation of the Jews from a ghetto existence to equal rights of citizenship occurred in a number of countries in the nineteenth century, although not in czarist Russia. The one great institution that continued to held out against religious toleration and freedom was the Roman Catholic Church. The first Vatican Council of 1870 pronounced a wholesale condemnation of liberalism and toleration. It was not until the second Vatican Council in 1965 that the Catholic Church finally embraced the doctrine of freedom of religion by its authoritative Declaration on Religious Freedom. Together with political freedom, freedom of religious choice and opinion, including atheism and the spurning of all religion, has become one of the most cherished freedoms in Western society. Following the Second World War, the United Nations Universal Declaration of Human Rights of 1948 named freedom of religion, conscience, and thought as basic human rights. We have good reason, moreover, to hope that the richness of the tradition of religious tolerance and freedom developed in the modern West since the sixteenth century contains the moral and intellectual resources that will enable the defeat of different forms of religious extremism, while assuring religious freedom to peaceable and tolerant people.

REFERENCES

Primary sources

BAYLE, P. (1987 [1686]). *Philosophical Commentary on these Words of Jesus: Compel them to Come in*, ed. and trans. A. Goldman. New York: Peter Lang.
CASTELLIO, S. (1965 [1554]). *Concerning Heretics and Whether they should be Persecuted*, ed. and trans. R. Bainton. New York: Octagon Books.
CASTELLIO, S. (1975 [1562]). *Advice to A Desolate France*, ed. M. Valkhoff, trans. W. Valkhoff. Shepherdstown, WV: Patmos Press.

Castellio, S. (1981 [1563]). *De arte dubitandi et confidendi ignorandi et sciendi* (*The Art of Doubting, Believing, Being Ignorant, and Knowing*), ed. E. F. Hirsch. Leiden: Brill.

Locke, J. (1968 [1689]). *Epistola de tolerantia. A Letter on Toleration*, ed. R. Klibansky, trans. J. Gough. Oxford: Oxford University Press.

More, T. (2002 [1516]). *Utopia*, eds G. Logan and R. Adams. 2nd edn. Cambridge: Cambridge University Press.

Spinoza, B. (2001 [1670]). *Theological-Political Treatise*, eds S. Shirley and S. Feldman. 2nd edn. Indianapolis: Hackett.

Williams, R. (1963 [1644]). *The Bloudy Tenent of Persecution*, in *The Complete Writings of Roger Williams*. 7 vols. New York: Russell and Russell.

Secondary sources

Garnsey, Peter (1984). "Religious Toleration in Classical Antiquity, in W. J. Sheils (ed.), *Persecution and Toleration*. Oxford: Blackwell.

Jordan, W. K. (1932–40). *The Development of Religious Toleration in England*, 4 vols. Cambridge, MA: Harvard University Press.

Lecler, J. (1960). *Toleration and the Reformation*. 2 vols. London: Longmans.

Marshall, John (2006). *John Locke, Toleration and Early Enlightenment Culture*. Cambridge: Cambridge University Press.

Mendus, Susan (1988) (ed.). *Justifying Toleration: Conceptual and Historical Perspectives* Cambridge: Cambridge University Press.

Moore, R. I. (1987). *The Formation of a Persecuting Society*. Oxford: Blackwell.

Nederman, Cary J., and Laursen, John Christian (1996) (eds). *Difference and Dissent: Theories of Toleration in Medieval and Early Modern Europe*. Lanham, MD: Rowman and Littlefield.

Zagorin, Perez (2003). *How The Idea of Religious Toleration Came to the West*. Princeton: Princeton University Press.

CHAPTER 43

....

REPUBLICANISM

....

RICHARD DAGGER

REPUBLICANISM is an ancient tradition of political thought that has enjoyed a remarkable revival in recent years. As with liberalism, conservatism, and other enduring political traditions, there is considerable disagreement as to exactly what republicanism is and who counts as a republican, whether in the ancient world or contemporary times. Scholars agree, however, that republicanism rests on the conviction that government is not the domain of some ruler or small set of rulers, but is instead a public matter—the *res publica*—to be directed by self-governing citizens.

This conviction historically has led republicans to be suspicious of or downright hostile to monarchy, to the point where opposition to monarchy is often taken to define republicanism. Hence the eminent historian of political thought Quentin Skinner refers to 'a republican (in the strict sense of being an opponent of monarchy)...' (Skinner 2008: 84). Dictionaries frequently add to this negative definition the positive feature that republicans advocate government by elected representatives. Both points are correct insofar as republicans have generally opposed monarchy and favored representative government, but there is also reason to be cautious here—and reason to look more closely at the definition of republicanism before turning to its history.

DEFINING REPUBLICANISM
....

Caution is necessary because important thinkers commonly linked to the republican tradition, such as Aristotle and Cicero, were neither unequivocally opposed to monarchy nor clearly committed to representative government. As they saw it, a form of government is good if it will promote the public good. The problem with monarchy is not that it cannot do this; in some circumstances, Aristotle says, monarchy is the form of government most likely to promote the public good. The problem is that monarchs are all too likely, when unchecked by others, to become tyrants. That is why Cicero and other classical republicans came to favor the *mixed constitution* (or *mixed government*) as a way of preserving *the rule of law*. A mixed constitution blends the rule of one with the rule of the few and of the many, so that the monarchical element will be limited rather than absolute, with the monarch under the law rather than above it. In this limited, constitutional sense of 'monarchy', republicans need not be opposed to monarchical governments. If, however, one means by 'monarchy' rule by one person who holds complete, unchecked authority, then a republican will necessarily be opposed to monarchy.

The connection between republicanism and representative government is similarly complicated. As the historical accounts of the development of political representation indicate, the terms 'republic' and 'republican' antedate the idea of government by elected representatives. Mixed constitutions require that the few and the many have a voice, but not that the members of either group elect those who speak for them. The rule of law cannot be effective where no one makes laws, or discerns them in nature or custom, but the legislator or legislators need not be elected. If the circumstances allow, in fact, republicans may even embrace a form of direct democracy in which the people as a whole are free to assemble, debate, and cast their votes for or against proposed laws. To be sure, modern and contemporary republicans are typically advocates of representative government, but that is because they do not think that circumstances are favorable to the exercise of direct democracy—not, at least, when the public business must be conducted on a scale as large as that of the modern state.

How, then, does a republic differ from a democracy? James Madison's famous answer in *Federalist 10* distinguished 'a pure democracy, by which I mean a society consisting of a small number of citizens, who assemble and administer the government in person' from a 'republic, by which I mean a government in which the scheme of representation takes place . . .' (Ball 2003: 43–4). Madison was surely right to think that no republican could countenance 'pure democracy', at least if it were understood to be a form of government in which the people 'assemble *and administer* the government in person' (emphasis added). Few self-professed democrats would disagree with republicans on this point, however. The important question is how a republic differs from a democracy when the latter term is taken in the sense commonly attached to it in current political discourse—that is, as *representative* democracy. To this there is no clear-cut answer. Contemporary republicans, as we shall see, are committed to both moral and political equality, so that they conceive of the republic as a kind of democracy, not as something distinct from or opposed to it. The difference is thus a matter of degree, not of kind. Republics and democracies are both forms of popular government, but the republican—always fearful of unrestrained power—will be less sanguine about the prospect of rule by the people than will the enthusiastic democrat. The people must be heard, the republican will say, for government is the public business of self-governing citizens; but government by the people should not be confused with doing whatever the majority of the people want whenever they happen to want it. A republic, according to the ancient formula, is the empire or government of laws, not of men. If a democracy maintains its respect for the rule of law, then it is a democratic republic; if not, it may be a populist, majoritarian, or plebiscitarian form of democracy, but it cannot be a republic. That is why republicans historically have preferred the mixed constitution to one that is wholly popular or democratic.

Most republicans have preferred the mixed constitution, I should say, for, in this respect, as in many others, those who have thought of themselves as republicans have not always agreed with one another. John Adams and Thomas Paine disagreed on this point, for example, with Adams staunchly defending mixed government and Paine rejecting it in favour of 'simple' forms: 'I draw my idea of the form of government from a principle in nature which no art can overturn, viz., that the more simple anything is, the less liable it is to be disordered and the easier repaired when disordered' (Paine 1953 [1776]: 7). Yet each considered himself a republican. In this and other respects Adams and Paine exemplify two tendencies within republicanism that another eighteenth-century thinker, Montesquieu, previously had identified as 'aristocratic' and 'democratic'.[1] Nor is this the only point on which the history of republicanism has been marked by disagreement and divergent tendencies.

REPUBLICANISM CONSIDERED HISTORICALLY

Whether Adams (1735–1826), Paine (1737–1809), Montesquieu (1689–1755), or any other modern thinker really was a classical republican, or even a republican at all, is not a settled matter. According to J. G. A. Pocock, 'Paine was no classical republican, only a hater of monarchy . . .' (2003 [1975]: 575). For Pocock, who traces the 'Atlantic republican tradition' of the seventeenth and eighteenth centuries back through Machiavelli to Polybius and Aristotle, Paine's approval of a national debt is reason enough to deny his republican credentials. Debt is a form of *dependence*, and therefore something that republicans want to avoid, not embrace; for a self-governing citizenry must be free from dependence on those whose money or power would enable them to control or corrupt the republic.

Pocock's emphasis on the continuity of the republican tradition puts him at odds with a prominent group of scholars who believe that 'classical republicanism' is a term that should be reserved for ancient philosophers and polities. As those in this group see it, Plato, Aristotle, Cicero, and the other *classical* republicans of the ancient world praised *civic virtue*—that is, the republican citizen's willingness to sacrifice personal interest for the public good—because this virtue protected and preserved the *polis* or *civitas* in which the highest virtues could be cultivated: 'Wherever the genuine classical republican tradition still lives, there is some kind of agreement as to the supreme value of the intellectual virtues, and of a life spent in leisured meditation on the nature of justice, the soul, and divinity' (Pangle 1988: 61). *Modern* republicans, by contrast, are

---

[1] 'In a republic when the people as a body have sovereign power, it is a *democracy*. When the sovereign power is in the hands of a part of the people, it is called an *aristocracy*' (Montesquieu 1989 [1748]: bk I, ch. 2, p. 10; emphasis in original).

more likely to value individual rights and liberties than civic duties or virtuous devotion to the public good. These modern or 'liberal' republicans—notably John Locke (1632–1704), Montesquieu, and the American founders—share enough in common with the classical thinkers to deserve to be called republicans, including devotion to self-government and the rule of law. Under the influence of Machiavelli, however, they depart from the classical tradition and embrace an aggressive or expansive republic in which representative government supplants direct participation and virtue is as likely to be the commercial virtue of the merchant as the civic virtue of the loyal citizen (Pangle 1988; Rahe 1992; Zuckert 1994; Sullivan 2004).

Still, Pocock is not the only scholar to trace a continuous line of development in republicanism from the ancient world to the modern. For some of them, however, the line reaches back not to Greece but to Rome. Those who join Pocock in tracing republicanism to Aristotle and Athens tend to emphasize the importance of active participation in public affairs—of ruling and being ruled in turn, as Aristotle said in *The Politics* (1283^b42–1284^a3). Those who see a closer link to Roman theory and practice are more likely to stress the republican commitment to the rule of law (Sellers 1998) and to freedom as the absence of arbitrary or dominating power—to 'neo-roman liberty', in Skinner's terms (1998). Scholars in both the Athenian and the Roman camps agree that a modern political thinker can be a classical republican, then, but disagree as to exactly what a classical republican is (Honohan 2002). Some even push the distinction to the point of arguing that the Athenian school of thought is really tracing the development of *civic humanism* rather than classical (or civic) republicanism. That is, civic humanism is 'a political philosophy centered on the idea of promoting a specific conception of the good life as consisting in active citizenship and healthy civic virtue on the one hand, while combating any sort of corruption that would undermine these values on the other' (Lovett 2006: §3.1). As such, it differs from the more modest philosophy of classical (or civic) republicanism, which takes political participation and civic virtue to be '*instrumentally* valuable for securing and preserving political liberty, understood as independence from arbitrary rule' (Lovett 2006: §3.2). From this point of view, a modern, civic, or neo-republican can be a classical republican, but only if classical republicanism is understood to be distinct from civic humanism.

For present purposes, it seems best to take an inclusive or expansive approach to republicanism, leaving the reader to decide what to make of these scholarly debates and distinctions. Such an approach will begin with the thinkers of classical Greece, at the latest. Indeed, some of the leading themes of republican thought are sounded in dramatic works, such as the exchanges between Oedipus and Creon in *Oedipus the King* (ll. 626–30) and between Creon and Haemon in *Antigone* (ll. 734–40)—exchanges in which Sophocles (496–406/5 BCE) implies that the city state (*polis*) is not the sole possession of the king, to be ruled simply as he sees fit, but a public trust. In his *Oresteia* trilogy, Aeschylus (525–456 BCE) makes another proto-republican point with regard to the rule of law, which the plays depict as superior to endless blood feuds and acts of private vengeance. Similar themes mark the work of Greek philosophers. In his *Republic*, for example, Plato (427–341 BCE) insists that the proper role of rulers is to protect the interests of the people, not to advance their own; and in the *Statesman* and *Laws* he argues for the importance of the rule of law as, among other things, a constraint on those who hold power.

Aristotle and Polybius, however, are the two Greek thinkers most often associated with republicanism. As previously noted, Pocock and others take Aristotle (384–322 BCE) to be a republican largely because of his praise of the active life of the citizen who rules and is ruled in turn. But his famous, if not entirely original, division of governments into six basic forms in Book III of *The Politics* (especially 1279ᵃ22–1279ᵇ10) also links him, in two further ways, to republicanism. First, Aristotle's criterion for distinguishing 'true' from 'perverted' forms of government is whether 'the one, or the few, or the many, govern with a view to the common interest . . . or with a view to the private interest . . .' of the ruler(s) (*Pol.* 1279A29–32). The 'true' form of rule by the many he calls 'polity' (*politeia*); the 'perverted' form, in which the many rule in their own interest as a class, is 'democracy'. Second, he subsequently refers to 'polity', in a different context and perhaps in a distinct sense of the word, as government by the middle class that mixes two of the perverted forms, oligarchy and democracy. As he says in Book IV, Chapter 11, moreover,

> it is manifest that the best political community is formed by citizens of the middle class, and that those states are likely to be well-administered in which the middle class is large, and stronger if possible than both the other classes [i.e. the rich and the poor], or at any rate than either singly, for the addition of the middle class turns the scale, and prevents either of the extremes from being dominant. Great then is the good fortune of a state in which the citizens have *a moderate and sufficient property*; for where some possess much, and the others nothing, there may arise an extreme democracy, or a pure oligarchy; or a tyranny may grow out of either extreme . . . but it is not so likely to arise out of the middle constitutions and those akin to them. (*Pol.* 1295B34–1296A21; emphasis added)

Like Aristotle, Polybius (*c.*200–*c.*118 BCE) believed that mixing two or more of the forms of government would check the tendencies of the ruling group—whether comprising one person, the few, or the many—to pursue its own interests, and thus would promote the common good. Polybius took the idea further than Aristotle, however, and he drew on Roman history and practice as much as Greek experience in developing the theory of the mixed constitution. As a Greek leader held hostage in Rome for seventeen years, Polybius had the opportunity to study what the Romans had long regarded as their *res publica*—that is, the 'public thing' that was their body politic. In his *Histories*, Polybius argued that each of the true or good forms of government suffers from a tendency to degenerate over time into its corresponding corrupt or perverted form: monarchy into tyranny; aristocracy into oligarchy; and rule by the many, which he called 'democracy', into mob rule. Yet Rome had found a way to stave off political decay and corruption by mixing or balancing rule by the one (the Roman consuls), the few (the Senate), and the many (the people through various powers, such as the power to elect tribunes and to reward and punish their leaders). Corruption might be inevitable, but for Polybius the republic, with its mixed constitution, offered the best chance for a stable and long-lasting government in the public interest.

Roman political practice was probably more important to the subsequent development of republicanism than Roman political philosophy, but Cicero (106–43 BCE) contributed in at least two ways to republican theory. First, he reinforced the claim that there are both true and perverted forms of rule by one, the few, and the many, and he agreed with Polybius when he insisted, in book I, §§54 and 69, of his *Republic*, that the surest way to prevent corruption is through 'an alloy' that is 'balanced and compounded from' these forms of rule (1999: 24, 31). Cicero's second contribution was his famous definition of the republic, or commonwealth, as 'not any group of men assembled in any way, but an assemblage of some size associated with one another through agreement on law and community of interest' (1999: 18). For Cicero, indeed, 'agreement on law' seems to be a large part of the 'community of interest' shared by the citizens of a republic. Like the historians Sallust (*c*.86–34 BCE) and Livy (59/ 64 BCE–17 CE), he took the republic to be an empire of laws, not of men (Wirszubski 1960: 9).

An empire of men, or Caesars, soon eclipsed the Roman republic, however, and republican theory declined along with republican institutions. The rise of Christianity, with its tendency to discount the value of politics, may also have played a part in this decline. Republican ideas survived in the Roman legal tradition, to be sure, and they did not disappear completely from the political theory of late antiquity and the Middle Ages. Thomas Aquinas (*c*.1225–74), for example, drew heavily on Aristotle in his natural-law theory, defining law in his *Summa theologiae* (I–II. 90, 4 *in c.*) as an 'ordinance of reason for the common good'; and later declaring (*ST* I–II. 95, 4 *in c.*) that 'a form of government which is a mixture of the other types...is the best' (Aquinas 2002 [1266–73]: 82–3, 136). But it was a Renaissance Italian Niccolò Machiavelli (1469–1527) who seems to have contributed most to the revival of republican thought.

This revival began in the late Middle Ages, perhaps as early as 1085, when one after another of the cities of northern Italy asserted its independence of the authority of the papacy and the Holy Roman Empire (Skinner 2002: ch. 2). The revival eventually included Machiavelli's Florence, where the republic was under continual threat from both internal and external opponents. Although he is best known for the apparently callous advice he offers in *The Prince*, Machiavelli stated his preference for republicanism in his *Discourses on the First Ten Books of Titus Livius*. In particular, he endorses mixed government in Book I, Chapter 2, of the *Discourses*, praising Lycurgus for establishing such a government in ancient Sparta and acknowledging Fortune for fostering, in Rome, a republic in which 'all of the three types of government had their shares', thereby producing 'a perfect state'. Friction played as much a part as Fortune, though, as Machiavelli maintains that the Roman Republic achieved 'this perfection...through the discord between the people and the Senate...' (Machiavelli 1965: 200).

Machiavelli had in mind the discord that emerges as the elements of a mixed constitution check and balance one another—that is, the healthy discord or friction that sustains the rule of law as it prevents any one element from dominating the others. But it was the discord of the religious and political upheavals of early modern Europe that spread the revival of republicanism. The early Protestants did not think of themselves as republicans, but they began to resort to republican ideas to justify the stances they took with regard to the secular authorities. Thus John Calvin (1509–64) found himself appealing, in his *Institutes of the Christian Religion* (1536: bk IV, ch. 20, §31) to the Spartan office of the *ephor* and the 'popular tribunes' of Rome when he suggested that Christians may justly disobey their rulers when 'any magistrates appointed for the protection of the people and the moderation of the power of kings' lend their authority to disobedience (Calvin 1956 [1536]: 81). Subsequently, in the English Civil War and Glorious Revolution of the seventeenth century, a number of writers pressed the 'neo-roman' conception of liberty, according to which freedom is the absence of dependence or domination (Skinner 1998). So conceived, freedom is not simply the absence of restraint or interference, but freedom under or through the law, with the law to be determined in some fashion by self-governing citizens.

The most notable of these neo-roman writers was probably James Harrington (1611–77), the author of *Oceana*. In the 'Preliminaries' chapter of *Oceana* Harrington distinguishes between two ways of defining 'government'. On one side of the divide are those who define 'government . . . *de jure* or according to ancient prudence' as 'the empire of laws and not of men'; on the other, those who define it '*de facto* or according unto modern prudence . . .' In the former group he places Aristotle, Livy, and 'Machiavel (whose books are neglected . . .)'; in the latter category are Thomas Hobbes (1588–1679) and others who regard government as 'the empire of men and not of laws' (Harrington 1992 [1656]: 8–9). Linking himself to the former group, Harrington goes on to endorse mixed government and two other schemes less commonly associated with republicanism. One is a *rota*, or a system of rotating public offices so as to avoid concentrations of political power; and the other is an agrarian law that would redistribute land in order to prevent concentrations of economic power—concentrations that would render some citizens dependent upon the will of others.

In the eighteenth century republican concerns were central to the revolutions in North America and France, with Harrington a writer much admired by the American revolutionaries. Perhaps the clearest evidence of their republican tendencies appears, however, in the new governments that emerged from these revolutions. In the United States, the Constitution ratified in 1788 guarantees every state of the union 'a Republican Form of Government' (art. IV, §4); and in the next decade the French revolutionaries—who attempted to replace the traditional *monsieur* and *madame* with *citoyen* and *citoyenne* (citizen)—declared the abolition of the monarchy and the formation of the French Republic. In the course of the ratification debates, moreover, the principal authors of *The Federalist*—Alexander Hamilton (1757–1804) and James Madison (1751–1836)—drew on Montesquieu's *Spirit of the Laws* to counter the claim that the new country would be too large to survive as a republic. It would not be too large, they argued, especially in Hamilton's *Federalist 9*, because the United States would be a 'compound' or 'confederate' republic—that is, a large republic composed of smaller republics.

What exactly should be the proper relationship between this large republic and its constituent republics became the subject of long and sometimes ferocious controversy in the United States. That the country should be a republic, however, was never in dispute. Agreement as to the desirability of republican government became increasingly widespread in Europe and Latin America, too, though not without resistance on the part of defenders of monarchy, theocracy, and, in the twentieth century, fascism and communism. By the twentieth century, however, republicanism was no longer a central concern of political philosophers. In part this was the result of the growing attention to democracy, and in part the result of the rise of liberalism, conservatism, and socialism—all of which bear the traces of republican concepts and principles.

CONTEMPORARY REPUBLICANISM

For much of the twentieth century, at least in the English-speaking world, republicanism seemed more a matter of historical than of philosophical interest (e.g. Fink 1962 [1945]; Robbins 1959; Pocock 2003 [1975]). Books such as Hannah Arendt's *On Revolution* (1965) and Sheldon Wolin's *Politics and Vision* (1960) powerfully stated republican themes, but neither Arendt nor Wolin advertised these books as contributions to republican theory. Interest in the possibilities of such a theory revived in the last decades of the century, however, and especially so with the publication of Philip Pettit's *Republicanism* (1997).[2] Pettit's book and subsequent essays are noteworthy for many reasons, but in particular for his claim that 'the supreme political value' of republicanism is freedom, with freedom understood to be freedom from domination (Pettit 1997: 80). Whether this is a uniquely republican or even an adequate conception of freedom is now the subject of considerable controversy, with Pettit and Skinner vigorously responding to their critics (e.g. Pettit 2008; Skinner 2008). Whether republicanism itself is an adequate or distinctive political philosophy is the subject of a broader controversy (e.g. Gey 1993; Goodin 2003; Brennan and Lomasky 2006). There is no doubt, though, that a republican revival is well underway, with various civic or neo-republicans working to demonstrate the merits of this ancient theory in the twenty-first century (e.g. Sandel 1996; Viroli 2002; Maynor 2003). These efforts include attempts to draw out the implications of republicanism for economic matters (e.g. Dagger 2006 and Pettit 2006, both responding to Gaus 2003), for criminal justice and the law more generally (e.g. Braithwaite and Pettit 1990; Besson and Marti 2009), for welfare policy (White 2003), and for the problems of culturally pluralistic societies

---

[2] See Dagger (2004) for a more complete account of these developments.

(Laborde 2008). These and similar efforts may or may not prove to be widely persuasive among political philosophers, but they testify nevertheless to the enduring conviction that animates republicanism—that is, the conviction that government is a public matter to be directed by self-governing citizens.

References

Primary Sources

AQUINAS, THOMAS (2002 [1266–73]). *Political Writings*, ed. and trans. R. W. Dyson. Cambridge: Cambridge University Press.

ARENDT, HANNAH (1965). *On Revolution*. New York: Viking.

ARISTOTLE (1988). *The Politics*, trans. J. Barnes, ed. S. Everson. Cambridge: Cambridge University Press.

BALL, TERENCE (2003) ed. *The Federalist, with Letters of Brutus*. Cambridge: Cambridge University Press.

BESSON, SAMANTHA, and MARTI, JOSE LUIS (2009) eds. *Legal Republicanism: National and International Perspectives*. Oxford: Oxford University Press.

BRAITHWAITE, JOHN, and PETTIT, PHILIP (1990). *Not Just Deserts: A Republican Theory of Criminal Justice*. Oxford: Oxford University Press.

BRENNAN, GEOFFREY, and LOMASKY, LOREN (2006). "Against Reviving Republicanism," *Politics, Philosophy and Economics*, 5: 221–52.

CALVIN, JOHN (1956 [1536]). *On God and Political Duty*, ed. J. T. McNeill. Indianapolis and New York: Bobbs-Merrill.

CICERO, MARCUS TULLIUS (1999). *On the Commonwealth; and, On the Laws*, ed. J. E. G. Zetzel. Cambridge: Cambridge University Press.

DAGGER, RICHARD (2006). "Neo-Republicanism and the Civic Economy," *Politics, Philosophy and Economics*, 5: 151–73.

GAUS, GERALD (2003). "Back to the Future: Neorepublicanism as a Postsocialist Critique of Market Society," *Social Philosophy and Policy*, 20: 59–91.

GEY, STEPHEN (1993). "The Unfortunate Revival of Civic Republicanism," *University of Pennsylvania Law Review*, 141: 801–98.

GOODIN, ROBERT (2003). "Folie républicaine," *Annual Review of Political Science*, 6: 55–76.

HARRINGTON, JAMES (1992 [1656]). *The Commonwealth of Oceana and A System of Politics*, ed. J. G. A. Pocock. Cambridge: Cambridge University Press.

LABORDE, CÉCILE (2008). *Critical Republicanism: The Hijab Controversy and Political Philosophy*. Oxford: Oxford University Press.

MACHIAVELLI, NICCOLÒ (1965). *The Chief Works and Others*, i, trans. A. Gilbert. Durham, NC: Duke University Press.

MAYNOR, JOHN (2003). *Republicanism in the Modern World*. Cambridge: Polity.

MONTESQUIEU, C. L.-S. (1989 [1748]). *The Spirit of the Laws*, trans. A. M. Cohler, B. M. Miller, and H. S. Stone. Cambridge: Cambridge University Press.

PAINE, THOMAS (1953 [1776]). *Common Sense and Other Political Writings*, ed. N. F. Adkins. Indianapolis: Bobbs-Merrill Co.

PANGLE, THOMAS (1988). *The Spirit of Modern Republicanism: The Moral Vision of the American Founders and the Philosophy of Locke*. Chicago: University of Chicago Press.

PETTIT, PHILIP (1997). *Republicanism: A Theory of Freedom and Government*. Oxford: Oxford University Press.

PETTIT, PHILIP (2006). "Freedom in the Market," *Politics, Philosophy and Economics*, 5: 131–49.

PETTIT, PHILIP (2008). "Republican Freedom: Three Axioms, Four Theorems," in Cécile Laborde and John Maynor, eds. *Republicanism and Political Theory*. Oxford: Blackwell.

POLYBIUS (1922–7). *The Histories*, trans. W. R. Paton. 6 vols. Cambridge, MA: Harvard University Press.

SANDEL, MICHAEL (1996). *Democracy's Discontent: America in Search of a Public Philosophy*. Cambridge, MA: Harvard University Press.

SKINNER, QUENTIN (2008). "Freedom as the Absence of Arbitrary Power," in Cécile Laborde and John Maynor eds. *Republicanism and Political Theory*. Oxford: Blackwell.

WHITE, STUART (2003). *The Civic Minimum: On the Rights and Obligations of Economic Citizenship*. Oxford: Oxford University Press.

WIRSZUBSKI, CHAIM (1960). *Libertas as a Political Idea at Rome during the Late Republic and Early Principate*. Cambridge: Cambridge University Press.

WOLIN, SHELDON (1960). *Politics and Vision: Continuity and Innovation in Western Political Thought*. Boston: Little, Brown.

Secondary Sources

DAGGER, RICHARD (2004). "Communitarianism and Republicanism," in Gerald Gaus and Chandran Kukathas (eds), *Handbook of Political Theory*. London: Sage.

FINK, ZERA (1962 [1945]). *The Classical Republicans: An Essay in the Recovery of a Pattern of Thought in Seventeenth-Century England*. Evanston, IL: Northwestern University Press.

HONOHAN, ISEULT (2002). *Civic Republicanism*. London: Routledge.

LABORDE, CÉCILE, and MAYNOR, JOHN (2008a). 'The Republican Contribution to Contemporary Political Theory', in Cécile Laborde and John Maynor (eds), *Republicanism and Political Theory*. Oxford: Blackwell.

LABORDE, CÉCILE, and MAYNOR, JOHN (2008b) (eds). *Republicanism and Political Theory*. Oxford: Blackwell.

LOVETT, FRANK (2006). 'Republicanism', *Stanford Encyclopedia of Philosophy*. http://plato.stanford.edu/entries/republicanism.

POCOCK, J. G. A. (2003 [1975]). *The Machiavellian Moment: Florentine Political Thought and the Atlantic Republican Tradition*. Princeton: Princeton University Press.

RAHE, PAUL (1992). *Republics Ancient and Modern: Classical Republicanism and the American Revolution*. Chapel Hill, NC: University of North Carolina Press.

ROBBINS, CAROLINE (1959). *The Eighteenth Century Commonwealthmen*. Cambridge, MA: Harvard University Press.

SELLERS, M. N. S. (1998). *The Sacred Fire of Liberty: Republicanism, Liberalism, and the Law*. London: Macmillan.

SKINNER, QUENTIN (1998). *Liberty before Liberalism*. Cambridge: Cambridge University Press.

SKINNER, QUENTIN (2002). *Visions of Politics*, i. Cambridge: Cambridge University Press.

Sullivan, Vickie B. (2004). *Machiavelli, Hobbes, and the Formation of a Liberal Republicanism in England*. Cambridge: Cambridge University Press.

Viroli, Maurizio (2002). *Republicanism*, trans. A. Shugaar. New York: Hill & Wang.

Zuckert, Michael (1994). *Natural Rights and the New Republicanism*. Princeton: Princeton University Press.

CHAPTER 44

....

POLITICAL OBLIGATION

....

GEORGE KLOSKO

THE CONCEPT

....

By political obligation, theorists generally mean a moral requirement to obey the law of one's state or one's country. Traditionally, this has been viewed as a requirement to obey the law *because it is the law*—that is, because of the authority of the legislator, as opposed to the content of particular laws. Thomas Hobbes viewed this feature as central to commands: "Command is where a man saith, *Doe this* or *Doe not this*, without expecting other reason than the Will of him that sayes it" (Leviathan, ch. 25; in Hobbes 1991: 176). As a rule, political obligation becomes a topic of interest only when requirements to obey are seriously questioned. As we will see, this was not the case for much of Western history, when it was generally assumed that laws—divine or human—should simply be obeyed. Political authority was generally viewed as the natural state of affair (Lewis 1974: i. 160).

In the liberal tradition, on which I will focus, liberty is a central value, and so the fact that some individuals should obey others must be explained. In the absence of a convincing account, people retain their liberty and are not obliged to obey. The liberal—or "modern"—view of political obligation, as I will refer to it, is classically expressed in John Locke's *Second Treatise of Government* and has become deeply rooted in popular consciousness. In accordance with such views, a satisfactory account should provide answers to a series of linked questions. Central to Locke and to liberal theorists more generally, political obligations hold only within definite bounds and so are capable of being dissolved by circumstances or overridden by conflicting requirements. Thus, in addition to providing moral reasons to obey the law, a developed view should explain their limits. In addition, according to Locke, political obligation must stem from an individual's own consent, and so must be self-assumed, based on a specific action or performance by each individual himself.

In tracing the history of political obligation, this chapter is in two (unequal) parts: historical developments that culminated in the liberal conception; and then subsequent developments that have called elements of that conception into question.

Early History

Amongst the ancient Greeks, the subject of political obligation received little attention. As classically expressed in Book I of Aristotle's *Politics*, the Greeks had an undeveloped concept of the individual. The person was viewed as a part of society, which was conceptually prior to him, and on which he depended to achieve the moral and intellectual development central to the good life. Against this backdrop, at least on a theoretical level, the need to obey the law was accepted almost without question. The subject of political obligation receives little or no attention in major works of Greek political theory: Plato's *Republic* and *Laws*, Aristotle's *Politics*, and others.

The main exceptions center on Socrates' trial and imprisonment, as recounted by Plato, especially Socrates' purported dialogue with the Laws of Athens in the *Crito*. Having been condemned to death and facing imminent execution, Socrates inquires into the rights and wrongs of escaping from prison. He puts into the Laws's mouth a series of arguments for obedience, based on claims that to disobey would harm the state and, strikingly, an argument from agreement. Because Socrates has stayed in Athens for so long when he had opportunities to go elsewhere, he has agreed (*hômologêkenai*) to obey the laws (51c–52e). This particular argument is well developed and more sophisticated than many subsequent accounts of political obligations resting on consent, especially on tacit consent. But Socrates' arguments raise important difficulties. For one, they establish too much, a requirement to obey the law "whatever it commands" (*ha en keleuê*) (51b), the authoritarianism of which does not rest well with Socrates' views in other dialogues. In the *Apology*, especially, Socrates clearly says that he will obey the command of the gods and continue his mission, more or less regardless of what the Athenian courts demand (*Ap.* 29d–30a). However, the strong conclusion of the *Crito* is required by immediate circumstances. Socrates has been wrongfully tried and convicted and faces execution. Nothing less than an extreme position would oblige him to remain in prison and accept punishment.

Christian Influences

Like the ancient Greeks, the early Christians appear not to have worked out a developed conception of political obligation. The basic position of the early Church is expressed in Chapter 13 of St Paul's Epistle to the Romans: "Let every person be subject to the governing authorities. For there is no authority except from God, and those that exist have been instituted by God" (Rom. 13:1). This categorical statement suited the Christians' political situation, as a small and suspect minority, threatened by Roman power. However, although Romans 13 entails that disobedience is a sin as well as a crime, the early Christians argued for an important limitation. In accordance with Jesus's commands to render unto Caesar what is Caesar's and to God what is God's (Matthew 22:21), and the injunction to obey God rather than man (Acts 5:29), they believed it was necessary not to obey commands that went directly against religious obligations. This condition was bound up with an important distinction, between non-obedience or passive resistance and active or forcible resistance. Although injunctions that went against God's word were not to be obeyed, the subject could not resist forcibly and so must accept the consequences, which often meant martyrdom. In the *Martyrdom of Polycarp*, the earliest extant account of a Christian martyrdom, Polycarp resists commands to acknowledge Caesar's divinity, claiming "we have been taught to render fit honor to rulers and authorities appointed by God in so far as it is not injurious to us" (*Martyrdom*, 10; in Sparks 1978: 143).

EMERGENCE OF THE MODERN CONCEPTION

The development of a recognizable modern conception of political obligation took place during a protracted period, from roughly the twelfth century until the the mid-seventeenth, culminating with the works of Hobbes, the Levellers, and Locke.[1] This process involved a large number of thinkers and doctrines—too many to be reviewed in detail here. Passages from numerous earlier works might appear to express modern views of political obligation, or at least important components of such views.[2] But, as a rule, even particular ideas that were sharply expressed were not clearly woven into the kind of worked-out network of ideas necessary to represent clear accounts of political obligation.

As with other components of liberal political theory, the modern view of political obligation emerged in the Church, and did so according to a distinctive dynamic. As important as the early Christians' strong requirement of obedience were limitations they recognized. As indicated above, the subject of political obligation receives serious attention only when requirements to obey are widely questioned. The need to articulate principles justifying non-obedience to particular commands forced theorists to work out reasons why subjects *should* obey and their limits, in order to demonstrate that those limits had been crossed. In subsequent centuries, as questions of non-obedience

---

[1] The account in this section is indebted to Tierney (1955, 1964, 1982, 1997), Figgis (1960), Skinner (1978), and, especially, Oakley (1962; 1999: ch. 4).

[2] See e.g., Henry of Ghent (1217–93) (McGrade, Kilcullen, and Kempshall 2001: 307–14); Godfrey of Fontaines (1250–1306) (McGrade, Kilcullen, and Kempshall 2001: 315–20).

became more pressing and non-obedience evolved into resistance, the liberal view of political obligation developed.

With the revival of European society in the eleventh and twelfth centuries, a series of developments converged on the fundamental idea that political power is limited. A recognizable social-contract view was expressed by Manegold of Lautenbach, a Saxon monk, in the late eleventh century, during the investiture controversy (Tierney 1964: 78–80). During this period, monarchs in different jurisdictions were either compelled to or found it advantageous to consult with the grandees of their realms. Limitations on royal authority were classically expressed in the Magna Carta (1215), while the initial meeting of the English model parliament was in 1295, and of the Estates-General in France in 1302. On a more theoretical level, as the Church began to infuse Roman law ideas into its administrative procedures, ground was laid for an interpretation of church structure according to which the community of believers was the source of papal authority, that this power was delegated to church officials, and on a conditional basis. Several centuries of commentaries on the canon law, initiated by Gratian's *Decretum* (*c.*1140), developed a corporate or "conciliarist" conception of the Church, providing theoretical resources for later use. Implications were developed by radical thinkers, notably Marsilius of Padua, who presented a sophisticated argument for the community as the source of authority in both the temporal and sacred realms, in his *Defensor pacis* (1324). According to Marsilius, the community was not only the only legitimate legislator and source of coercive authority but was able to depose rulers who transgressed their authority (esp. I. 12; I. 19).

Conciliar and related ideas assumed practical relevance when employed in political conflicts. Most important was the Great Schism of the Church, in the late fourteenth century, as two and later three competing popes denounced each other. The Council of Constance (1414–18), summoned to address the crisis, declared the authority of the Council over that of the pope, deposed the sitting popes, and elected a new one. Even though the conciliar position was decisively defeated in subsequent years by resurgent papal supremacy, the Council provided an important precedent for later thinkers, especially as interpreted by sophisticated theorists, including Jean Gerson and Pierre d'Ailly (Tierney 1955, 1982). Moreover, in accordance with basic medieval assumptions, its claims concerning the locus of authority were believed to be applicable to secular bodies as well. To use John Figgis's words, the Church was viewed as "one of a class of political societies," with similar principles applying to all (Figgis 1960: 56).

Along with their contention that the community is the source of authority, the conciliarists argued that this was placed in the ruler's hands to enable him to pursue the community's interests. This set of ideas was reinforced by rising popularity of the idea of consent. Practical as well as theoretical concerns, including increasingly prevalent consultative practices in political bodies, promoted the idea that legitimate authority must be accepted by the community—which generally meant by the leading figures in the community. But, as Francis Oakley notes, this does not amount to consent in the modern or Lockean sense (as discussed below), but rather acceptance of authoritative directives by the community (Oakley 1999: 111–12). Subsequent years would deepen the implications of this form of consent.

A similar role was played by resurgent ideas of natural law, which also placed limits on the legitimacy of law. According to standard natural-law doctrine, positive laws result from an application of natural law and are legitimate only as long as their content coincides with this source. Thus, according to St Thomas Aquinas, "every human law has just so much of the nature of law as it is derived from the law of nature. But if, in any point, it deflects from the law of nature, it is no longer a law but a perversion of law" (*ST* I–II. 95. 2; Aquinas 1988: 130). Although his ideas on this subject were not clearly developed, St Thomas authorized resistance to rulers who rule unjustly, though only by "public persons" (*On Kingship*, ch. 6; 1988: 267–71).

Ideas concerning limits on political power were sharpened by the Protestant Reformation and conflicts leading up to it. Under these conditions, doctrines of forcible resistance—as opposed to mere non-obedience—were widely expressed. Specific circumstances included conflict between the pope and the king of France at the beginning of the sixteenth century, between Catholic rulers and Protestant subjects in England and Scotland, and religious wars in France in the late sixteenth century. These events called forth major statements of the nature and limits of political legitimacy by Jacques Almain and John Major, John Ponet, George Buchanan, and other important theorists. But, in spite of their forcefulness, these and other sixteenth-century views fall short of a modern conception of political obligation in being oriented to the community rather than the individual. Central to the modern notion is consent of the autonomous individual, who has a real choice as to whether to accept the demands of political authority. Although thinkers—including Ponet and Buchanan—traced the origin of the community back to the individuals who founded it and spoke of consent, they did not envision individuals making such a choice. The consent they spoke of was generally acceptance of specific edicts or laws by the community (Oakley 1999: ch. 4). Focus on the community rather than the individual is clearly expressed in the late sixteenth-century resistance tract, the *Vindiciae contra tyrannos*, which advanced the standard, late medieval view that resistance was permissible only by public persons, who represent towns or regions, rather than by individuals: "We speak not here of private and particular persons considered one by one, and who in that manner are not held as parts of the entire body, as the planks, the nails, the pegs, are no part of the ship, neither the stones, the rafters, nor the rubbish, are any part of the house" (Q. 2; Mornay 1963: 100).

Reasons for the fundamental shift in orientation from the community to the individual are complex. One possibility is the first stirrings of the market society that would be central to the development of capitalism (Macpherson 1962). A more plausible factor is the individualistic orientation of various Protestant religious sects, especially those that formed congregations through individual consent (Oakley 1999: 132–7). In regard to the development of subsequent political theory, an enormously important factor was the emergence of a recognizable conception of natural rights—"subjective natural rights." Thirteenth- and fourteenth-century canonists first developed the concept in regard to individual rights to property and self-preservation. By the sixteenth century, sophisticated accounts were presented by a series of Spanish theorists, including Francisco Vitoria, Bartolomeo de Las Casas, and Francisco Suarez (Tierney 1997). Arguing according to a strong conception of natural law, these theorists viewed society as arising through the combination of individuals, originally in a natural state—referred to as the "state of nature" by Luis de Molina (Skinner 1978: ii. 156). Political power was ceded by the community to rulers, for the sake of pursuing the common good, with implications in regard to resisting unjust authority drawn especially by Suarez and Juan de Mariana. Whilst these theorists approximated a modern conception of political obligation in central respects, once again they fell short in not focusing on individuals choosing whether or not to accept authority. Implications of their sophisticated doctrines of natural rights were drawn by subsequent theorists.

In order to see how the ideas we have surveyed both approximate and fall short of the modern conception of political obligation, we will look briefly at Buchanan's *The Powers of the Crown in Scotland* (1579), one of the most radical and, in various ways, most modern sixteenth-century tracts. *Powers of the Crown* was written to justify the forced abdication of Mary Queen of Scots in 1567. Buchanan's account is largely secular, based on appeal to Roman and Greek texts and historical precedents, including conciliar claims concerning the locus of church authority. He argues from a rough state of nature. Men originally "lived in hovels or even caves, and wandered about as lawless vagabonds" (Buchanan 1949: 45). Driven into society by the law of nature implanted within them, they were led by disagreements to recognize the need for rulers. The latter, like physicians, are established in order to advance the interests of their charges, rather than their own. To make sure kings behave appropriately, they should be bound by law. At his coronation, the king takes an oath to "maintain the law in justice and goodness." The oath represents "a mutual compact between King and citizens" (1949: 142). If the king breaks this compact, the people have the right to withdraw their obedience. Should kings rule tyrannically, it is just to wage war against them. Buchanan's view on this point is radical: "it is not only right for the whole people to destroy an enemy, but for the individual to do so." (1949: 143). However, in the course of developing these ideas, Buchanan pays virtually no attention to subjects' obligations to obey, which are taken for granted. Concerned with the locus of political authority and its limits, Buchanan assumes without question that subjects should obey the law, as long as rulers behave appropriately. At time Buchanan appeals to the consent of the community. But this is in regard to whether the community regards the ruler as legitimate (see 1949: 54), and so is far removed from the consent of each individual to accept political authority.

Consent Theory

Although the genius of Hobbes and Locke cannot be reduced to the political circumstances to which they responded, these undoubtedly played a significant part. Faced with the crisis of the English Civil War, Hobbes presented a fully modern theory of political obligation. With Hobbes, the burden of argument shifts. Whereas, in the late medieval period, the default position favored obedience, Hobbes's starting point is individual freedom: "there being no Obligation on any man, which ariseth not from some Act of his own; for all men equally, are by Nature Free" (*Leviathan*, ch. 21; Hobbes 1991: 150). Hobbes, of course, paints the state of nature in the bleakest of terms. To escape this situation, people are willing to transfer their rights to a sovereign with virtually unlimited power. To avoid the limitations on royal authority discussed in the previous section, Hobbes devises a compact mechanism that is not a contract. Each individual authorizes the sovereign to act for him, but the sovereign is not party to this agreement, and so not limited by its terms. In response to the contention that, after transferring authority to a ruler, the community retains rights against him, Hobbes argues that there is no community (except in the person of the sovereign). Power is ceded separately by each individual (ch. 18; 1991: 122–3).

Although Hobbes's view of political obligation is based on consent, as with other features of his theory, his view of this notion is idiosyncratic. Alongside his elaborate compact of government, Hobbes argues for sovereignty "by acquisition"—that is, through conquest. According to Hobbes, the relationships between ruler and subjects are the same, regardless of how the ruler gains his power (ch. 20; 1991: 142). Whilst the view that conquest conveys political authority is common in the history of political thought, Hobbes is unusual in claiming that this rests on a form of consent, agreement by the subjugated to recognize the conqueror's authority, in return for being allowed to live: "It is not therefore the Victory that giveth the right of Dominion over the Vanquished, but his own Covenant" (ch. 20; 1991: 141). This is in keeping with Hobbes's expansive conception of consent, according to which coerced agreements are binding, even a forced agreement to surrender money to a thief (ch. 14; 1991: 141).

Additional features of Hobbes's theory are intended to remove limits on the power of the sovereign. This power cannot be divided between different branches of government. Hobbes goes to great lengths to argue that it cannot be limited by religious obligations, as the sovereign in effect interprets these, as it is also part of his role to govern his subjects' consciences. Nor can the sovereign be limited by natural law, since he determines the content of natural law, which he does by instituting positive laws. As a result, the "Law of Nature and the Civil Law contain each other and are of equal extent" (ch. 26; 1991: 185).

The one real limitation on the subject's obligation that Hobbes recognizes concerns subjects' need for protection. When the sovereign can no longer supply this, obligation ceases (ch. 21; 1991: 153–4). Similarly, subjects retain rights to self-defense. Because it is for the sake of preserving oneself that subjects authorize the sovereign, they are not required to obey orders that directly threaten this end (ch. 14; 1991: 93–4, 98–9). There is some gray area here, in that subjects cannot renounce "the means of so preserving life, as not to be weary of it" (1991: 93). But Hobbes clearly wishes to limit this exception.

It is important to realize that Hobbes was not alone in positing the free individual as his starting point, and so in presenting a modern view of political obligation. For instance, at roughly the time he was writing *The Elements of Law* (1640), the first version of the theory eventually presented in *Leviathan*, the Levellers, early English democrats, argued from similar premises concerning originally free individuals binding themselves to government through their own consent.[3]

As noted above, the *locus classicus* for political obligations based on consent and for the modern view more generally is Locke's *Second Treatise of Government* (1690). Like Hobbes, Locke envisions people as naturally free, although subject to the law of nature in the state of nature. Because there is no authority to enforce the natural law, Locke subscribes to the "strange Doctrine" (*Second Treatise*, sect. 13) that in the state of nature all men have the right to enforce it for themselves. Locke views the state of nature as relatively peaceful, but conflict arises from people's tendency to interpret both the circumstances of disagreements and the law of nature itself in self-interested ways. To avoid these conflicts, people are willing to surrender their rights of self-enforcement, which they do in two stages. First, they join with one another to establish a community, which then establishes a legislative power. In joining the community, individuals agree "to submit to the determination of the majority, and to be concluded by it" (*Second Treatise*, sect. 97), although the legislative authority is empowered to act only in regard to the areas in which it was granted power, and to make only laws that correspond to the law of nature (*Second Treatise*, sect. 135). These limitations on political authority are supported by strong rights of resistance, including a right for "any single man" to resist, whenever he believes "the Cause of sufficient moment" (*Second Treatise*, sect. 168). Locke hedges in regard to this provision, arguing that it is not likely to cause people frequently to revolt, as this right "will not easily engage them in a contest, wherein they are sure to perish" (*Second Treatise*, sects 208, 225).

Locke's doctrine of consent is at first sight strong. Authority may be created only by the individual's own consent. One may not be bound by the consent of one's father, or by the terms of an original contract made at the foundation of society (*Second Treatise*, sect. 116–18). However, although Locke recognizes that "express consent" establishes clear political bonds, he also realizes that few people consent in this way. And so he turns to what he calls "tacit consent," actions performed by most people that are capable of binding them:

> And to this I say that every Man, that hath any Possession, or Enjoyment of any part of the Dominions of any Government, doth thereby give his tacit Consent, and is as far forth obliged to Obedience to the Laws of that Government, during such Enjoyment, as any one under it; whether this his Possession be of Land, to him and his Heirs for ever, or a Lodging only for a Week; or whether it be barely traveling freely on the Highway; and in Effect, it reaches as far as the very being of any one within the Territories of that Government. (*Second Treatise*, sect. 119)

Although the actions Locke lists would account for the political obligations of virtually all inhabitants of the relevant territory, this raises a different problem. In providing means through which virtually all individuals more or less automatically

---

[3] See e.g., R. Overton, "An Arrow Against all Tyrants" (1646); repr. in Aylmer (1975: 68–70).

consent to government, Locke deprives consent of its moral significance. As one commentator says, "we are likely to feel cheated by Locke's argument...why go through the whole social contract argument if it turns out in the end that everyone is automatically obligated?" (Pitkin 1965: 995). In spite of this and other problems, Locke's view was enormously influential—for example, it was drawn upon in the preamble to the *Declaration of Independence*.

Locke's view of tacit consent was classically criticized by David Hume, in the latter's essay "Of the Original Contract" (1748). Hume agrees with what he views as Locke's fundamental claim concerning the limited nature of political power. But he rejects the existence of an actual historical contract into which people entered, as there is no record of one. Like Locke, he believes that most people have not consented expressly to government, since they have no recollection of doing so. But, in regard to tacit consent, Hume argues that, given the realities of his society, it cannot be viewed as performed voluntarily:

> Can we seriously say that a poor peasant or artizan has a free choice to leave his country, when he knows no foreign language or manners, and lives from day to day, by the small wages which he acquires? We may as well assert, that a man, by remaining in a vessel, freely consents to the dominion of the master, though he was carried on board while asleep, and must leap into the ocean, and perish, the moment he leaves her. (Hume 1985: 475)

Hume believes he is able to establish conclusions similar to Locke's on more reasonable principles. The basis of his argument is social utility. Government is necessary for the good of society and so should be obeyed as long as it promotes this end. If it ceases to be useful, it loses its *raison d'être* and so also its authority: "The cause ceases; the effect must cease also" (*Treatise*, III. ii. 9). However, given the enormous costs of changing governments, this is justifiable only if governments become egregiously tyrannical (*Treatise*, III. ii. 9). In substance, this conclusion resembles Locke's, but Hume believes that his account has the considerable advantage of doing without the fictions of an original state of nature, individual consent, and social contract. Hume's view also breaks with traditional notions of political obligation. According to his reasoning, one should obey the law because of the beneficial effects of doing so. The fact that an authority has commanded obedience plays little or no role in his account.

SUBSEQUENT DEVELOPMENTS

The seventeenth and eighteenth centuries were the high point for social-contract theory. Classical versions of the contract were employed by Rousseau and, later, Kant. Kant is responsible for a considerable theoretical advance in viewing the contract as purely hypothetical, rather than an actual historical occurrence. In his view, the fact that it is rational to consent suffices for obligations, rather than one's having actually to consent. Kant forbids resistance against government (1970: 81), but contends that the power of government is limited by required hypothetical consent. This obliges "every legislator to frame his laws in such a way that they could have been produced by the united will of a whole nation" (1970: 79; see Waldron 1987).

As confidence that political obligations derive from individual consent waned, the traditional view was undermined from a variety of directions. The utilitarian tradition, epitomized by Jeremy Bentham, bases requirements to obey on the benefits of obedience (Bentham 1988: ch. 1). This approach departs from the voluntarism of consent theory, as the subject is bound to obey the law in most cases, even though he has not consented to do so. In addition, as with Hume, requirements to obey particular laws depend on the moral circumstances; the fact that they are commanded is of little relevance. The main problem with a consequentialist account is that it is frequently undone by circumstances. In many cases, because the consequences of some individual's disobeying the law are undetectable while the individual receives tangible benefits from disobedience, consequentialism cannot ground general political obligations.

Contemporary debates about political obligation have been heavily influenced by the popularity of so-called philosophical anarchism. In *In Defense of Anarchism* (1970), Robert Paul Wolff argues for a fundamental incompatibility between political obligation and individual autonomy. Because we are obligated to preserve our autonomy, we cannot surrender this to requirements to obey the law. Unlike traditional anarchists such as Mikhail Bakunin, who declared himself an enemy of the state (Bakunin 1990: 178), philosophical anarchists support much that the state does, in spite of the absence of requirements to obey the law because it is the law. They believe there are moral reasons to obey many laws, to be decided on a case-by-case basis. In his influential *Moral Principles and Political Obligations* (1979), A. John Simmons presents sophisticated criticisms of different possible bases of political obligations—mainly consent, fairness, gratitude, and a natural duty of justice—and concludes that none of these bears scrutiny. But, like Wolff, he contends that, nevertheless, we have moral reasons to obey many laws, mainly so as not to harm or inconvenience other people. On this view, the consequences of an absence of traditional political obligations are less dire, and so less improbable, than with traditional anarchism.

In order to counter philosophical anarchism, scholars have pursued a number of different strategies. First and most obviously, they have attempted to counter the criticism of Simmons and other skeptics, and defend traditional views of political obligation. Recent years have witnessed reworkings of theories of political obligations based on all the principles that Simmons criticizes.[4] Other scholars have attempted to develop theories of political obligation on new grounds. Two notable approaches are theories based on principles of association or membership and a variant of the natural duty of justice, which was made prominent by John Rawls in *A Theory of Justice* (1971: sects 19, 51; see Wellman 2001). Arguments from association are notable because, in

---

[4] For consent, see Beran (1987); for fairness, see Arneson (1982); Klosko (1992); Dagger (1993); for gratitude, see Walker (1988); for natural duty, Waldron (1993).

basing requirements to obey the law on our belonging to or being members of society, to some extent they reverse the modern assumption that individuals are by nature free, and so that political obligations must be explained (Horton 1992).

Influential scholars have pursued a course that resembles those of consequentialists and philosophical anarchists, in discarding political obligations in the traditional sense.[5] These scholars distinguish between a state's having "legitimacy" and "authority." The former refers to the state's ability to take morally appropriate action, for instance, to aid people in need or to punish moral malefactors. Although in pursuing these tasks the state cannot claim rights to anyone's obedience merely because it is the state, people are morally required to comply with specific laws because of other reasons, such as those noted above. Authority adds to legitimacy the state's right to claim obedience because it commands this, without appeal to other moral principles. These scholars argue that authority is not necessary, that important state functions can be accomplished without political obligations in the traditional sense.

Scholars who pursue this approach not only reject the traditional view of political obligations, but they also break with philosophical anarchism. In contending that different considerations are able to ground general requirements to obey the law, these scholars deprive philosophical anarchism of much of its polemical force. In addition, skeptical scholars have generally approached the traditional theories from a particular perspective, criticizing them *seriatim*, one after another. The best-known practitioner of this approach is Simmons, but other scholars have taken similar tacks.[6] What this strategy overlooks is the possibility that general reasons to obey the law can be established by combining different principles, and so overcoming the weaknesses of a theory based on a single principle. (Klosko 2005: ch. 5). All these issues are debated in the contemporary literature. As scholars have moved away from traditional conceptions of political obligation, the future of the subject has opened to new possibilities.[7]

References

History: Primary Sources

AQUINAS, ST THOMAS (1988). *On Law, Morality, and Politics*, eds W. Baumgarth and R. Regan. Indianapolis: Hackett.

AYLMER, G. E. (1975) ed. *The Levellers in the English Revolution*. Ithaca, NY: Cornell University Press.

---

[5] Edmundson (1998); Copp (1999); A. Buchanan (2002).

[6] Smith (1973); Raz (1979: ch. 12); Simmons (1979); Green (1988).

[7] I am grateful to Julian Franklin and John Simmons for comments on previous versions of this chapter.

BAKUNIN, M. (1990). *Statism and Anarchy* [1873], ed. and trans. M. Shatz. Cambridge: Cambridge University Press.

BENTHAM. J. (1988). *A Fragment of Government* [1776], ed. R. Harrison. Cambridge: Cambridge University Press.

BUCHANAN, G. (1949). *The Powers of the Crown in Scotland* [1579], ed. and trans. C. F. Arrowood. Austin, TX: University of Texas Press.

BURNET, J. (1900–7) ed. *Platonis Opera*. 5 vols. Oxford: Oxford University Press.

HOBBES, THOMAS (1991). *Leviathan* [1651], ed. R. Tuck. Cambridge: Cambridge University Press.

HUME, D. (1969). *A Treatise of Human Nature* [1739], ed. E. Mossner. Harmondsworth: Penguin Books.

HUME, D. (1985). *Essays: Moral, Political and Literary* [1748], ed. E. Miller. Rev. edn. Indianapolis: Liberty Fund.

KANT, I. (1970). *Kant's Political Writings*. ed. H. Reiss, trans. H. Nisbet. Cambridge: Cambridge University Press.

LOCKE, J. (1988). *Two Treatises of Government* [1690], ed. P. Laslett. Cambridge: Cambridge University Press.

MARSILIUS OF PADUA (2005). *The Defender of Peace* [1324], ed. and trans. A. Brett. Cambridge: Cambridge University Press.

McGRADE, A., KILCULLEN, J., and KEMPSHALL, M. (2001) eds. *The Cambridge Translations of Medieval Philosophical Texts, ii. Ethics and Political Philosophy*. Cambridge: Cambridge University Press.

MORNAY, P. (1963). *A Defence of Liberty against Tyrants* [1579] [1924], ed. H. Laski. Gloucester, MA: Peter Smith.

PONET, J. (1942). *A Short Treatise of Politike Power* [1556], repr. in *John Ponet*, ed. W. Hudson. Chicago: University of Chicago Press.

SPARKS, J. (1978) ed. *The Apostolic Fathers*. Nashville: Thomas Nelson.

TIERNEY, B. (1964) ed. *The Crisis of Church and State 1050–1300*. Englewood Cliffs, NJ: Prentice Hall.

History: Secondary Sources

FIGGIS, J. N. (1960). *Political Thought from Gerson to Grotius: 1414–1625* [1916]. New York: Harper Bros.

LEWIS, E. (1974) (ed.). *Medieval Political Ideas* [1954]. 2 vols. New York: Cooper Square.

MACPHERSON, C. B. (1962). *The Political Theory of Possessive Individualism*. Oxford: Oxford University Press.

OAKLEY, F. (1962). "On the Road from Constance to 1688: The Political Thought of John Major and George Buchanan," *Journal of British Studies*, 1.

OAKLEY, F. (1999). *Politics and Eternity: Studies in the History of Medieval and Early Modern Political Thought*. Leiden: Brill.

PITKIN, H. (1965). "Obligation and Consent, I," *American Political Science Review*, 59: 990–9.

SKINNER, Q. (1978). *The Foundations of Modern Political Thought*. 2 vols. Cambridge: Cambridge University Press.

TIERNEY, B. (1955). *Foundations of the Conciliar Theory: The Contribution of the Medieval Canonists from Gratian to the Great Schism*. Cambridge: Cambridge University Press.

Tierney, B. (1982). *Religion, Law, and the Growth of Constitutional Thought: 1050–1650.* Cambridge: Cambridge University Press.

Tierney, B. (1997). *The Idea Of Natural Rights: Studies on Natural Rights, Natural Law, and Church Law, 1150–1625.* Atlanta: Scholars Press.

Contemporary Debates

Arneson, R. (1982). "The Principle of Fairness and Free-Rider Problems," *Ethics*, 92: 616–33.

Beran, H. (1987). *The Consent Theory of Political Obligation.* London: Croom Helm.

Buchanan, A. (2002). "Political Legitimacy and Democracy," *Ethics*, 112: 689–719.

Copp, D. (1999). "The Idea of a Legitimate State," *Philosophy and Public Affairs*, 28: 3–45.

Dagger, R. (1993). "Playing Fair with Punishmen," *Ethics*, 103: 473–88.

Edmundson, W. (1998). *Three Anarchical Fallacies.* Cambridge: Cambridge University Press.

Green, L. (1988). *The Authority of the State.* Oxford: Oxford University Press.

Horton, J. (1992). *Political Obligation.* London: Macmillan.

Klosko, G. (1992). *The Principle of Fairness and Political Obligation.* Savage, MD: Rowman and Littlefield.

Klosko, G (2005). *Political Obligations.* Oxford: Oxford University Press.

Rawls, J. (1971). *A Theory of Justice.* Cambridge, MA: Harvard University Press.

Raz, J. (1979). *The Authority of Law.* Oxford: Oxford University Press.

Simmons, A. J. (1979). *Moral Principles and Political Obligations.* Princeton: Princeton University Press.

Smith, M. B. E. (1973). "Is There a Prima Facie Obligation to Obey the Law?" *Yale Law Journal*, 82: 950–76.

Waldron, J. (1987). "Theoretical Foundations of Liberalism," *Philosophical Quarterly*, 37: 127–50.

Waldron, J. (1993). "Special Ties and Natural Duties," *Philosophy and Public Affairs*, 22: 3–30.

Walker, A. D. M. (1988). "Political Obligation and the Argument from Gratitude," *Philosophy and Public Affairs*, 17: 191–211.

Wellman, C. (2001). "Toward a Liberal Theory of Political Obligation," *Ethics*, 111: 735–59.

Wolff, R. P. (1970). *In Defense of Anarchism.* New York: Harper and Row.

CHAPTER 45

ANARCHISM

MARSHALL SHATZ

THE ANARCHIST IDEA

AT the beginning of the *Politics*, Aristotle declared that the state is a natural institution and that man is by nature a "political animal." By contrast, anarchism rejects the state as an inherently despotic institution that must be abolished in order for human nature to flower. This does not mean the absence of social order, however, for anarchism also contains a positive vision of the kind of community it expects to arise when political authority is eliminated. Although it shares liberalism's commitment to individual autonomy and Marxism's commitment to social equality, anarchism claims that it can implement those principles more fully and effectively without utilizing the mechanism of the state.[1]

Anarchism as a secular political philosophy originated as a product of the Enlightenment and the French Revolution, and anarchist thought was the cumulative product of a number of different individuals in different countries who elaborated its basic principles. This chapter traces the main continuities and changes in the evolution of anarchist ideology.

GODWIN

The first major theorist of anarchism, though the term itself had not yet come into use, was William Godwin (1756–1836). Born into a family of religious dissenters, he entered the ministry but left it to make a precarious living as a writer. In the 1790s

[1] The term "anarchism," designating a political ideology, must be differentiated from "anarchy," which in modern usage has come to mean chaos, or license. In much of the older literature, however, the term anarchy was often used to designate what today would be called anarchism, causing modern readers considerable confusion.

he belonged to a circle of English radicals who sympathized with the French Revolution in its initial phase.

Godwin's reputation as a political thinker rests on his one major work, *Political Justice*. He published it in 1793, but the revised edition of 1798 is considered the fullest expression of his views. Godwin's roots in the Enlightenment are readily apparent in *Political Justice*, where his rejection of government and his vision of a stateless society rest on his confidence in man's reason. Each individual must be free to exercise his independent judgment and owes obedience only to his own convictions and conscience—what has aptly been termed "moral self-direction" (Crowder 1991: 11). Government is inherently evil, Godwin argued, because it uses force, or the threat of force, to substitute its own judgment for that of the individual. As human knowledge increases and men perceive the truth about the institutions under which they live, the foundations of government will erode. The end result will be "the true euthanasia of government" (Godwin 1976: 247–8).

Godwin agreed with Rousseau that individuals owe obedience only to measures they themselves have consented to, but he rejected Rousseau's (and Locke's) concept of the social contract. He pointed out that no one has actually consented to the government and laws under which he currently lives. On the same grounds, he rejected—as would all later anarchists—representative government, however democratically elected, for here, too, someone else's reasoning is imposed on the individual. Furthermore, state laws are based on abstract generalizations, but every particular case is different and must be judged according to its own specific circumstances.

The form of social organization that Godwin envisaged to replace the state was a small, face-to-face community—districts, or parishes, as he called them. Within the parish a jury of peers would be selected to investigate internal conflicts or offenses against the community and arrive at reasoned decisions based on the circumstances of each case. However, they could only reason with the parties involved, not dictate to them or impose penalties on them. Eventually the need even for juries would diminish, and "the empire of reason" would prevail. In the event of external aggression, Godwin allowed for federative agreements among local parishes, but he regarded such instances as rare occurrences that did not require the maintenance of a standing army.

Much of the motivation for crime would be eliminated in the stateless society by the equalization of property. Anticipating some of the tenets of socialism, Godwin believed that every individual was entitled to the means of subsistence from the general stock of material goods, which were the product of the labor of the community as a whole. He considered the accumulation of wealth for its own sake to be unjust and abhorred useless luxury, but he did not want to abolish private property, regarding it as essential to individual liberty. Once it was equally distributed, however, the incentive to steal or murder would disappear. Half an hour of manual labor a day from each member of the community would suffice to supply the community's needs, and its members could then devote themselves to intellectual or cultural pursuits (Godwin 1976: 746–7). Godwin was certain that, once the justice and rationality of such a system became apparent, no one would wish to accumulate more property than he needed. If he did, he would be censured by the community as absurd and "uninitiated in the plainest sentiments of reason" (Godwin 1976: 739).

Godwin's unshakable belief in the persuasive power of reason prompted him to reject violent revolution as the path to a stateless society. In part he was reacting to the development of the French Revolution, which had turned from its initial moderation to the use of terror. "Revolution is engendered by an indignation against tyranny," he declared, "yet is itself ever more pregnant with tyranny" (Godwin 1976: 269). As a time of passions, violence, and revenge, it was hardly conducive to justice and benevolence. Social improvement must proceed gradually, through education, reasoned discussion, and the progress of knowledge and understanding, until men's minds were ripe for change and a peaceful transition could occur.

In both his denunciation of government and his vision of a society without one, Godwin foreshadowed almost the entire ideology of anarchism as it would subsequently develop. Oddly enough, there is no evidence that he influenced later anarchists or that they had even heard of him, until he was rediscovered at the end of the nineteenth century. Nevertheless, he anticipated their thinking to such a degree that he can be considered, if not the father of anarchism, then at least its godfather.

At the same time, Godwin's doctrines raised a crucial issue that would plague anarchism throughout its history. On the one hand, he was so thoroughgoing an individualist as to suggest that theatrical performances and concerts, which require collective effort, would disappear in an anarchist society (Godwin 1976: 760). However, the social order of the small community he envisaged rested ultimately on the power of public opinion. Behavior would be regulated by "the general inspection that is exercised by the members of a limited circle over the conduct of each other," a force as effective as "whips and chains." If an individual remained recalcitrant, the disapproval of his neighbors would make him so uncomfortable that he would voluntarily move to another community (Godwin 1976: 545, 554). Only by assuming that all men are amenable to the voice of reason, and that all men can agree on what the voice of reason tells them, was Godwin able to conceive of a society each of whose members would be free to act solely according to his own personal judgment without disturbing the peace and harmony of the community.

PROUDHON

If Godwin was the godfather of anarchism, the French theorist Pierre-Joseph Proudhon (1809–65) can justly be considered its father. Writing in 1840, he boldly declared: "I am an anarchist" (Proudhon 1969: 335). He was evidently the first to use this term, although he continued to use the word "anarchy" rather than anarchism. Proudhon was a rare bird among anarchist (or socialist) theorists, in that he was an actual worker. He came from a peasant and artisan background, and worked as a printer before becoming a writer and journalist. He was an inveterate radical who once wrote in a letter: "I dream of a society where I shall be guillotined as a conservative" (see Hoffman 1972: 119). Although his anarchist ideas are dispersed throughout his various works, the clearest expression of them can be found in his 1851 book *General Idea of the Revolution in the Nineteenth Century.*

The foundation of Proudhon's thought, like Godwin's, was his commitment to individual autonomy—so much so that some scholars have found his pronouncements on the subject comparable to those of John Stuart Mill (Vincent 1984: 214). His ideal was "the government of each man by himself" (Proudhon 1969: 103). Every individual must make his own decisions, based on reason, in all matters that concern him. Hence he rejected the authority not only of the state but of all abstract political and social entities that seek to subsume the individual, such as "society," "the general will," or even "the people." To Proudhon these were fictions with no existence of their own apart from the individuals composing them. Similarly, statutory law represented empty generalizations artificially imposed on large numbers of disparate cases. How, then, could the absolute freedom of the individual be reconciled with the social bonds that Proudhon believed human beings craved and required for their well-being?

Proudhon made his reputation as a radical thinker with a book he published in 1840 with the provocative title *What Is Property?* In the first paragraph he gave an equally provocative answer: property is theft. In fact, however, he did not condemn all property, only capitalist property, from which the owner derived income in the form of interest or rent without working. He regarded small property-holdings (which he termed "possession" rather than property) that were economically productive, such as an artisan's tools and workshop, or a peasant's land, as legitimate. While Godwin had advocated the equalization of property as a means of social harmony, Proudhon made the economic relations among these smallholders the very foundation of a new social system called "mutualism."

Under this system, individuals, or associations of individuals, would enter into contracts with each other for the exchange of goods and services, valued solely according to the labor expended on them and their costs. The parties would assume their obligations voluntarily and for their mutual benefit. Even large enterprises that required collective labor, such as mines or railroads, could be included in this system, but they must be run by the workers themselves and democratically organized as self-governing associations. All workers must receive equal pay for equal amounts of labor, for Proudhon believed that the production of a collective enterprise, and indeed all wealth, was a social product to which each individual made an essential contribution.

For larger needs, social groups and economic associations could form communes linked into voluntary federations. Each would make its own rules and laws depending on its circumstances and the consent of its members. Thus government would dissolve as society transformed itself into an intricate network of voluntary relationships serving a variety of economic and social functions. Towards the end of his life Proudhon extended this federative idea to entire nations and even international relations.

Like Godwin, Proudhon rejected the idea of forcible revolution as the means of implementing an anarchist society, convinced that such efforts led inexorably to dictatorship. He wanted to do away with capitalism, but he rejected the plans of some socialists to use the forces of the state to achieve social reform, for that would inevitably increase centralized state power. As an anarchist, he insisted that change must come from below, by the efforts of the people themselves, and not be imposed from above by political means. These views made him a lonely figure amongst the radicals of his day.

It also created a serious paradox in his thought, for, unlike most anarchists, he did not glorify the inborn rationalism or moral qualities of the laboring classes. He wrote, for instance, of the people's "ignorance, their primitive instincts, the violence of their needs, the impatience of their desires" (quoted in Hoffman 1972: 192). Yet, these were the same people from whom the transformation of society was to emanate. He seems to have believed that social progress and the moral growth of its bearers could be achieved simultaneously through the experience of mutualism. In the very process of being treated equally and justly in mutual economic and social relationships, individuals would recognize their own human dignity and that of others. Eventually, their example would spread through the entire society, leading to the growth of social solidarity. An indication of the educational process he had in mind was his attempt to create a People's Bank in 1849. The bank was to issue "exchange notes" that could circulate as currency, representing the goods and services produced by its members, and it would provide interest-free credit to producers and worker associations. The bank never got off the ground, but Proudhon believed it would have shown how a society could function on the basis of reciprocal economic exchange without the need for either government or capitalist finance.

Proudhon's anarchist ideology looked both backward and forward. On the one hand, it was rooted in the world of independent artisans and peasant smallholders from which Proudhon himself came, a world that was rapidly being eroded by the growth of industrialization. On the other hand, his idea of self-governing worker associations managing their own enterprises provided inspiration for the subsequent rise of anarcho-syndicalism. This variety of anarchism, which became particularly influential in France and Spain, rejected parliamentary activity and viewed trade unions both as the nuclei of a future stateless society and as the instrument for achieving it through industrial action. More generally, Proudhon elaborated and bequeathed to the anarchist movement of the later nineteenth century the basic principles of anarchism that Godwin had first articulated.

BAKUNIN

The June Days of 1849, when the forces of the newly formed Second French Republic shot down protesting workers in the streets of Paris, did a great deal to discredit liberalism in the eyes of the working class. Anarchism now moved closer to socialism— that is, to a more collectivist form of social and economic organization than Godwin or Proudhon had contemplated. At the same time, anarchism became not just an ideology but an international revolutionary force. This was largely the work of Michael Bakunin, a Russian nobleman who was the most colorful and charismatic figure in the history of anarchism. Born into a serf-owning family, Bakunin was destined for a military career, but in 1840 he left Russia to study philosophy in Berlin. There he was drawn into radical activities and in 1842, in a German journal and under a French pseudonym, he published an article whose radical message was camouflaged in murky philosophical language but concluded with the most famous sentence he ever wrote: "The passion for destruction is a creative passion, too" (Bakunin 1965: 406).

Like Proudhon's "property is theft," this statement, too, is somewhat misleading. Bakunin did not seek revolutionary upheaval for its own sake, as is often charged, but had a positive vision of the new world that was to spring from it. He did, however, devote most of his prodigious energies to fomenting rebellion. Arrested in Dresden, Saxony, in 1849 while participating in an insurrection, he was eventually extradited to Russia, where he was imprisoned under harsh conditions for eight years. He was then banished to Siberia for life but managed to escape across the Pacific and made his way back to Western Europe. Previously he had devoted himself to liberating the Slavic peoples from imperial rule, but in the 1860s he adopted anarchism.

He proceeded to form a series of small conspiratorial groups, most of them existing only on paper, that would sweep away the state and all the forms of hierarchical authority it supported. In a program that he drew up for one of these groups in 1868, he wrote: "we intend to destroy all States and all Churches, together with all their institutions and all their religious, judicial, financial, police and university, economic and social laws" (Bakunin 1973: 167). Suspicion has often arisen as to the role the conspirators would play after the Revolution, but Bakunin always maintained that the function of the intellectuals was not to dictate to the masses but merely to encourage and assist them in carrying out a social (as opposed to a political) revolution. Unlike Godwin and Proudhon, Bakunin had a romantic view of revolution as a purgative force that would instill the masses with the spirit and confidence to take charge of their lives. An irrepressible rebel himself, he believed that the masses hovered on the brink of revolution, which needed only a spark to ignite it.

For the mass base of the social revolution, Bakunin looked not to the industrial proletariat, which he regarded as too "bourgeoisified," especially in Germany, but to the most downtrodden and alienated social strata in the least developed parts of Europe: the peasants and urban poor, particularly in Italy, Spain, and the Slavic countries. Reprising his 1842 article, he declared that these groups "frequently evince a real passion for destruction" (Bakunin 1990: 28). In Russia he cited Razin and Pugachev, the leaders of the great Russian peasant rebellions of the seventeenth and eighteenth centuries, as models of revolt (Bakunin 1990: 203, 211). Thanks to his efforts, anarchist movements arose in Italy and Spain, as well as among the skilled watchmakers of the Swiss Jura region, where Proudhon had gained some influence.

Bakunin's vision of the anarchist society was somewhat more vague, in part because, like all anarchists, he believed that it would have to be created by the people themselves, out of their own social instincts. He conceived it largely in Proudhonist terms—he had met Proudhon in Paris in the 1840s and engaged in lengthy conversations with him—as a society built not "from above downward," as in a state, but "from below upward," composed of a network of voluntary associations of workers, peasants, and communes. He went a step further in the direction of socialism than Proudhon, however, believing that all the land, factories, and other means of production should be socially owned; they would be run by their workers, who would be paid according to the labor they contributed.

Bakunin's best-known work, which has been translated into many languages, is called *God and the State*, written in 1871 but published only in 1882.[2] It shows that, even though Bakunin advocated collectivization of the means of production, he shared the fundamental anarchist focus on the individual. Like Godwin and Proudhon, he was deeply suspicious of all abstract political and social categories and collective entities, and regarded them as instruments of potential tyranny. This included the concepts of "science," in the broad nineteenth-century sense that included the social sciences. By its very nature, science deals in categories and has no interest in individuals, only with people in general. "What does [science] care for the particular conditions and chance fate of Peter or James?" he asked. It regards them merely as material for its social theories—like rabbits, as he put it—and therefore its practitioners could not be allowed to govern Peter or James (Bakunin 1970: 58). A belief in the uniqueness of the individual and the irreducible diversity of human beings, and the inherent repressiveness of subsuming them under general laws or theories, lay at the very core of the anarchist outlook. More specifically, Bakunin's warning of the pretensions of intellectuals who claimed the authority of science was aimed at Marx and his followers in the First International.

Both Marx and Bakunin were prominent members of the International Working Men's Association, which had been founded in 1864 and sought to bring together the various currents of the socialist and labor movements. Both men were dominating personalities and vied for leadership of the organization. More important than any personal friction between them, however, were their ideological differences. These had been foreshadowed back in 1846, when Marx proposed to Proudhon, who was much better known in radical circles at the time, that they collaborate on the publication of a journal. Proudhon replied cordially, but in his letter he firmly rejected the goal of a *political* revolution that Marx had in mind (Woodcock 1962: 119–21).

This was the issue that now came to the fore. Marx, though anticipating the "withering away of the state," believed that the state could, and should, be utilized to effect the transition to a socialist society. Bakunin, as an anarchist, believed that the first task of the revolution must be the total destruction of the state. Moreover, political activity required some degree of centralization within the International and coordination of its sections. The anarchists believed that their organizations should serve as

---

[2] Bakunin's editors found the work in his papers after his death and published it under this title. It was unfinished and had been intended as part of a larger work, itself unfinished, as was frequently the case with Bakunin.

models of their social ideals and wanted merely a loose federation of autonomous local groups. In the end, at the Hague Congress of the International in 1872, Marx succeeded in having Bakunin expelled from the International and in relocating its headquarters to New York to keep it out of the hands of his adversaries. Removed from its European base, the International soon expired.

In the following year Bakunin wrote his last major work, *Statism and Anarchy*, in which he issued a dire warning of the consequences to be expected from the Marxists' program of political activity. Their objective was to seize control of the state, he wrote, but a state necessarily means "domination and consequently slavery." It would be ruled by a small number of socialists, popularly elected, perhaps, but constituting "a new and very small aristocracy of real or pretended scholars." They would govern the masses in a temporary "dictatorship of the proletariat," but, like any dictatorship, it would inevitably seek to perpetuate itself. He ended his attack with a famous passage that cleverly played on Marx's description in the *Communist Manifesto* of the measures that a "dictatorship of the proletariat" would introduce. In Bakunin's words, the leaders of the Communist Party—that is, "Marx and his friends"—would take over all of the society's economic resources. They would then divide the population into agricultural and industrial armies "under the direct command of state engineers, who will form a new scientific and political class" (Bakunin 1990: 177–81).

This passage has often been seen as a prophetic description of the Soviet Union under Stalin. In any case, the battle lines were now joined between anarchists, advocating immediate abolition of the state, and Marxists, seeking to take political power as a stepping stone to the same objective. The Marxist and anarchist wings of the anti-capitalist movement were henceforth irreconcilable enemies.

KROPOTKIN

Bakunin was succeeded as the most prominent spokesman of anarchism by another Russian nobleman of even more aristocratic lineage, Prince Peter Kropotkin (1842–1921). Like Bakunin, he was destined for a military career but was ultimately drawn into radical activities. Arrested and imprisoned, he made a daring escape from a prison hospital and eventually settled in England, where he remained until the Russian Revolution of 1917 enabled him to return to Russia. He became a respected, full-bearded Victorian patriarch who almost succeeded in putting a benign face on anarchism.

Before he became a revolutionary, Kropotkin had achieved scientific recognition as a geographer and explorer of Siberia, and he sought to give anarchism a foundation in the natural sciences. One of his most influential and enduring books was called *Mutual Aid*, in which he rejected the Darwinian concept of the struggle for survival as the driving force behind evolution and argued instead for the primary importance of social cooperation within species. He cited numerous examples of social solidarity and reciprocity, starting with the natural world, in species such as bees and ants, and extending to the human world. He focused particularly on the medieval town as a model of self-rule and mutual aid that had been ruined by the advent of the modern state. Thus he presented the social solidarity fundamental to anarchism as rooted in the very nature of human beings.

In *The Conquest of Bread* Kropotkin provided one of the most detailed—though highly idealized—descriptions in anarchist literature of the revolution that would bring about an anarchist society. He presented it as a spontaneous, virtually bloodless mass uprising against the state and capitalism, so overwhelming that the government would simply melt away. The people would then proceed to expropriate the "excess" dwellings, clothing, and food stocks of the rich and redistribute them to the poor. The decency and sense of justice of the masses would ensure that this was achieved equitably and with a minimum of violence. They would then proceed to rebuild society "from the bottom up" on the basis of free contracts between individuals and groups. Existing voluntary associations, ranging from lending libraries and learned societies to the Red Cross and the European railway network could serve as models for the provision of public services in the absence of government and laws.

In regard to the economic organization of the anarchist society, Kropotkin went beyond the collectivism that Bakunin had espoused and advocated what he called anarchist communism. Not only the means of production but the means of consumption would be socialized, and, in place of a wage system based on the amount of an individual's labor, society would supply everyone free of charge with the goods required for subsistence. The principle "to each according to his work" would be replaced by the principle "to each according to his needs." Kropotkin argued that modern science and technology—machinery, intensive methods of agriculture, new inventions—could increase economic productivity to such a degree that the resulting material abundance would easily meet the basic needs of the population. All members of the community would be required to perform some manual labor, but he calculated that a mere five hours of work per day would be enough to produce material well-being for everyone (Kropotkin 1995: 93). Godwin, it will be remembered, had made a similar calculation, estimating that half an hour of manual labor would suffice.

If anyone absolutely refused to do his share of the work, Kropotkin added, he would be isolated by his fellow citizens and perhaps find it best to leave the community and go elsewhere (Kropotkin 1995: 139). Godwin had made the same suggestion, and Bakunin had once advocated banishment as the proper method of dealing with recalcitrant individuals (Bakunin 1973: 69), though all three expressed assurance that these would be extraordinary cases. Given their distaste for laws, courts, and prisons, emigration or expulsion was the anarchists' solution to the tensions and passions that might arise in a small, self-governing community. It rested on the conviction that, once human beings were liberated from the coercive forces of the state, their innate rationality and social instincts would produce a harmonious consensus. While the anarchists' commitment to individual liberty brought them close to liberals like John Stuart Mill, they did not share the misgivings he expressed in *On Liberty* in regard to the pressure for social conformity that public opinion could exert even in the absence of political tyranny.

As Woodcock observes, "A stateless society . . . may be very far from a free society as far as the personal lives of its members are concerned" (1962: 216–17).

Terrorism

By the end of the nineteenth century, the theoretical foundations of anarchism were largely complete. In the absence of any concept of anarchist "orthodoxy" or means of enforcing it, however, anarchist ideology came in several different flavors. In addition to anarchist-communists and anarcho-syndicalists, there were individualist anarchists, who emphasized sovereignty of the individual over social obligation, and, more peripherally, the Christian anarchist-pacifist followers of Count Leo Tolstoy (1828–1910), yet another Russian nobleman (see Shatz 1971: 229–65). The main question the anarchists now faced was one of means rather than ends. Since a spontaneous mass insurrection showed little sign of breaking out, some anarchists turned to acts of terror, which they termed "propaganda by deed," as distinct from verbal or written propaganda. They carried out numerous assassinations of high officials or industrialists, bombings, and other individual actions in various countries from the 1880s and 1890s into the early years of the twentieth century. Their motives varied, from taking revenge for egregious instances of injustice, to sowing panic in political and capitalist circles, to arousing the masses by showing that their oppressors were vulnerable. Some, especially in Russia, engaged in indiscriminate terror, such as throwing bombs into cafés or first-class railway carriages, aiming not at particular individuals but at the well-to-do in general (Geifman 1993: 123–38). Belying the gentle image Kropotkin sought to create, anarchism now became firmly associated in the public mind with acts of violence, as reflected in the spate of novels at the time that depicted anarchist terrorists, such as Henry James's *The Princess Cassimassima*, Joseph Conrad's *The Secret Agent*, and G. K. Chesterton's *The Man Who Was Thursday*.

It should be kept in mind, however, that there was nothing in anarchist theory that mandated such deeds. Even Bakunin had always urged mass insurrection, not individual bombings or assassinations. Kropotkin, for all the mildness of his demeanor, was sympathetic to self-sacrificing acts of revolt against injustice, but he, too, favored collective social action, not mere acts of revenge (Cahm 1989: 92–151). In the end, many anarchists came to realize that such violence did little to stir up the masses but a great deal to incite police repression, while discrediting the seriousness of their movement.

Conclusion

The political upheavals of the first half of the twentieth century seemed to offer new opportunities to put anarchism into practice. During the Russian civil war that followed the Revolution of 1917, a peasant insurrection led by Nestor Makhno attempted to implement anarchist practices in parts of Ukraine (see Avrich 1967: 209–22); and in 1936, at the start of the Spanish Civil War, similar efforts were made in Catalonia and Andalusia (see Joll 1964: 253–74). Under the pressures of war and civil war, neither anarchist experiment was able to maintain itself for more than a few months. After the Spanish Civil War, the anarchist movement was reduced to little groups of intellectuals and students scattered in various countries. In renouncing the quest for political power, anarchism had remained true to its principles but relinquished the possibility of implementing them. With the collapse of the Soviet Union in 1991, those anarchists who remained at least had the satisfaction of seeing that the Marxist experiment ultimately fared no better.

As a political philosophy, however, anarchism remains of considerable interest. Historically, it served in a sense as a voice of conscience in the ear of liberalism and Marxian socialism, challenging them to live up to their ideals of individual liberty and social justice. Intellectually, instead of asking what is the best kind of state, a staple of political inquiry at least since the days of Plato and Aristotle, anarchism, as Nozick (1974: 9) points out, asks a more provocative and even more basic question: is the state really necessary at all? In doing so, it has made its own distinctive contribution to the history of political thought.

REFERENCES

Primary Sources

BAKUNIN, M. (1965). "The Reaction in Germany" [1842], trans. M. -B. Zeldin, in J. Edie et al. eds, *Russian Philosophy*. New York: Quadrangle Books, i. 385–406.

BAKUNIN, M. (1970). *God and the State* [1871]. New York: Dover Publications.

BAKUNIN, M. (1973). *Selected Writings*, ed. A. Lehning. London: Jonathan Cape.

BAKUNIN, M. (1990). *Statism and Anarchy* [1873], ed. and trans. M. Shatz. Cambridge: Cambridge University Press.

GODWIN, W. (1976). *Enquiry Concerning Political Justice* [1798], ed. I. Kramnick. Harmondsworth: Penguin Books.

KROPOTKIN, P. (1902). *Mutual Aid*. London: Heinemann.

KROPOTKIN, P. (1970). *Selected Writings on Anarchism and Revolution*, ed. M. Miller. Cambridge, MA: MIT Press.

KROPOTKIN, P. (1995). *The Conquest of Bread* [1892] *and Other Writings*, ed. M. Shatz. Cambridge: Cambridge University Press.

PROUDHON, P.-J. (1876). *What Is Property?* [1840], trans. B. Tucker. Princeton, MA: B. R. Tucker.

PROUDHON, P.-J. (1923). *General Idea of the Revolution in the Nineteenth Century* [1851], trans. J. Robinson. London: Freedom Press.

PROUDHON, P.-J. (1969). *Selected Writings*, ed. S. Edwards, trans. E. Fraser. London: Macmillan.

SHATZ, M. (1971) ed. *The Essential Works of Anarchism*. New York: Bantam Books.

Secondary Sources

Avrich, P. (1967). *The Russian Anarchists*. Princeton: Princeton University Press.

Cahm, C. (1989). *Kropotkin and the Rise of Revolutionary Anarchism, 1872–1886*. Cambridge: Cambridge University Press.

Crowder, G. (1991). *Classical Anarchism: The Political Thought of Godwin, Proudhon, Bakunin, and Kropotkin*. Oxford: Clarendon Press.

Geifman, A. (1993). *Thou Shalt Kill: Revolutionary Terrorism in Russia, 1894–1917*. Princeton: Princeton University Press.

Goyens, T. (2007). *Beer and Revolution: The German Anarchist Movement in New York City, 1880–1914*. Urbana, IL: University of Illinois Press.

Hoffman, R. (1972). *Revolutionary Justice: The Social and Political Theory of P.-J. Proudhon*. Urbana, IL: University of Illinois Press.

Joll, J. (1964). *The Anarchists*. London: Eyre & Spottiswoode.

Nozick, R. (1974). *Anarchy, State, and Utopia*. New York: Basic Books.

Pernicone, N. (1993). *Italian Anarchism, 1864–1892*. Princeton: Princeton University Press.

Vincent, K. (1984). *Pierre-Joseph Proudhon and the Rise of French Republican Socialism*. New York: Oxford University Press.

Woodcock, G. (1962). *Anarchism: A History of Libertarian Ideas and Movements*. Cleveland: World Publishing Company.

CHAPTER 46

·····································

FEMINISM

·····································

NANCY J. HIRSCHMANN

THE topic of feminism within the history of political philosophy and political theory might seem to be quite ambiguous. Indeed, at first glance, one might think that it is an oxymoronic relationship: for do not feminists urge us to abandon the study of "dead white males"? Susan Moller Okin's provocative opening inquiry in *Women in Western Political Thought*, "whether the existing tradition of political philosophy can sustain the inclusion of women in its subject matter, and if not, why not?" (Okin 1979: 4) could, arguably, lead to an indignant "no, because the history of political philosophy is fundamentally sexist!" The storm of controversy over "political correctness" pilloried by Allan Bloom in *The Closing of the American Mind* painted feminists as radical, if not hysterical, rejecters of the classic texts of the canon, not only in political philosophy but in literature as well. They allegedly urged the replacement of the key texts of the history of political philosophy and literature with *I, Rigoberta Menchu*, Judith Butler's *Gender Trouble*, and other more "relevant" contemporary texts that attended to issues of diversity. It might, then, seem that a chapter addressing "feminism" in a volume on the history of political philosophy would simply say: chuck it out.

But of course such stereotypes are just that. Indeed, the topic of "feminism" within the history of political philosophy is so vast, embodying so many different approaches and perspectives to the history of political philosophy, it is impossible to address this topic adequately in a single chapter. "Feminism" is at once a substantive analysis (what role do women and men play in this text?), an epistemological framework (what is the basis for the claims theorists make about women's and men's respective natures, characters, or functions?), a methodology (how does recognizing "women" as a category shape how we read the texts?), a political project (what are the power relations between men and women of various sexualities, classes, and races and how is such power expressed and enacted in the theory?), and an ethical project (what normative conclusions and recommendations do we wish to make based on our understanding of these power differentials?).

So, while there may have been some feminists and others on the left who advocated the complete abandonment of the canon, most feminist scholars, particularly those in philosophy and political theory, did not. Indeed, Okin's own query did not show that women were irrelevant to the canon any more than that the canon was irrelevant to women. Her argument demonstrated that women's inequality and subordination in the family were instrumental to political philosophers' abilities to develop their theories of political life, and that they thereby could not sustain their arguments without such tacit assumptions about women's place. Feminists interested in the history of political philosophy did not urge the abandonment of the canon at all, but were instead protesting the way in which political philosophy was studied: the questions that were asked, the answers that were developed, and the subjects that were deemed important and political. They thus advocated "opening up" the canon, rather than its abolishment.

There have been at least five ways in which this "opening" of the canon has been developed by feminists in the history of political philosophy: the treatment of women by male canonical thinkers; adding women philosophers to the canon; how gender changes the enterprise of political philosophy; how gender deepens our understanding of the major concepts that lie at the base of political philosophy; and the relevance of the history of political philosophy to contemporary political issues affecting women and gender. In this chapter, I will concentrate on the first three, with only brief recounting of the last two in my concluding section. But all five of these ways do not only demonstrate that the history of political philosophy is important to feminism; they also demonstrate that feminism is important to the history of political philosophy, and philosophers, historians, and political theorists all perform a serious intellectual disservice when they ignore feminism, gender, and women.

WOMEN IN WESTERN POLITICAL THOUGHT

The first of these ways of opening the canon was what has sometimes been called "women in Western political thought." It is arguably the case that this is how feminism got its start in political theory and political philosophy in the 1970s, when feminist theory declared itself a significant framework for engaging the canonical texts in political theory, and demanded acceptance by the relevant disciplines of political theory, philosophy, and intellectual history. Examining the history of political philosophy from ancient theorists such as Aristotle and Plato to liberal theorists such as John Locke and John Stuart Mill to nineteenth-century continental figures such as Hegel, Marx, and Nietzsche, feminists started to ask: where are the *women* in the history of political philosophy? They opened up an entirely new range of questions, approaches, and methods for political philosophers and theorists.

In this kind of feminist political philosophy, feminists first and foremost examine the literal place of women in these theorists' texts: how much the theorists attend to women and, indeed, whether they discuss them at all; what the theorists say about women as human beings, what their "nature" is taken to be; their role in the family and the state, their relationship to men, sex, and reproduction. In the process, feminists also bring out aspects of the theories that had previously not been thought "political" at all. Such aspects include the structure of the family, the relationship of reproduction to key elements of the state, such as citizenship and property, the (im)balance of power between men and women in the family and society, the relation of women to economics, and the ways in which gender was defined in terms of other analytic categories such as class and race.

Most central to these themes was the structure of the family, since, until the mid- to late twentieth century, women's place in the family virtually defined their existence. One of the first major works in this vein, Okin's *Women in Western Political Thought*—from which title the field subsequently derived its name—demonstrated that the family played a central role in the history of political philosophy. Okin argued that women were defined in the history of political thought by their "function," which for most philosophers revolved around the family. From ancient Greece's dependency on slaves and women to maintain the household, thereby enabling men to devote their time to political life, to the modern era's reliance on patriarchal monogamy to solidify institutions of property through inheritance, women's role in political theory was founded on a "functionalist" world view. That is, whereas men's "nature" dictated their roles in society as the citizens, the statesmen, and the rulers, women's roles in society—their functions as bearers and rearers of children, as managers of the household, and as caretakers, if not personal or sexual servants, of men—dictated that their natures were to be defined as irrational, unintelligent, dependent, inferior. The history of political philosophy, Okin argued, revealed that the family was essential to the state, and that women's subordination was essential to the family: their function was to serve men and raise children, and that function determined their nature as inferior, irrational, and powerless. Women, thus, were not left out of the history of political philosophy, they were instrumental to it; but only insofar at they were seen and treated as less important than men, perhaps even less human, and placed in a subordinate position.

Feminists since then have excavated a wide variety of issues pertaining to the family as central to understanding political philosophers' constructions of the state and conceptions of the political, from Plato's abolishment of the family and private property (O'Brien 1981; Spelman 1994), to Locke's stress on inheritance in a patrilineal system of property as central to political power (Brennan and Pateman 1979; Hirschmann 2008a), to Rousseau's explicit articulations of women's subordination to men in the private sphere (Morganstern 1996; Wingrove 2000), to Mill's ambiguous advocacy of women's equal participation in the market while simultaneously maintaining that most married women should not work outside the home (Annas 1977; Goldstein 1980; Shanley 1981). It would be impossible in a single chapter to trace all of the different modes of feminist engagement with the history of political philosophy that followed on Okin's heels, but feminists have taken a wide variety of thematic approaches to the history of political philosophy, including the wide-ranging studies of specific individual figures just mentioned, as well as studies of family configuration and power (Elshtain 1981; Di Stefano 1991; Botting 2006); gender identity and sexuality (Zerilli 1994; Marso

1999); women's relationship to property and economics (Clark 1977; Hartmann 1981; Hartsock 1984; Hirschmann 2008*b*), the gendered character of concepts as they have developed in the canon (Pateman 1988; Okin 1989; Hirschmann 1992, 2008*a*), and feminism's methodological impact on the history of political philosophy (Brown 1988; Wright 2004). And, although the list of books would be far too long to include in a parenthetical reference, the excellent *Rereading the Canon* series published by Pennsylvania State University Press—a collection of volumes each dedicated to "feminist interpretations of" a large number of historical figures, ranging from Plato to Quine, that is continually growing—illustrates the degree to which this subset of feminist theory, and of the history of political philosophy, has developed.[1]

All of these works fall under the rubric of "women in Western political thought," even if many of their authors would chafe at that denomination, particularly those who are uncomfortable with the breadth and lack of specificity found in the term "woman." I somewhat share that unease, an issue I will return to later in this chapter; furthermore, many of these works simultaneously illustrate other dimensions of feminist theory, also to be discussed in subsequent sections. But my point here in classifying these texts returns me to my central argument that feminism's contribution to the history of political philosophy has involved an "opening-up" of the canon. All of these works show us that women figure significantly in the history of political thought in a wide variety of ways, raising a vast range of themes that had not been articulated before—indeed, themes that were not *capable* of being articulated unless one considered women and gender relations.

In other words, these feminists, and those that followed, showed us that we must analyze the history of political philosophy *politically*, and not just historically or philosophically, to understand it fully and correctly. I say it is "political" because it relates to the ways in which knowledge is formed and established in the context of power relations; the knowledge that one gains is shaped to a large degree by the questions one asks, and the questions that are asked are shaped to a significant extent by who gets to ask them. Feminism, by putting women on the radar screen of political philosophical inquiry, has drastically shifted those questions, and thereby shifted our understanding of the power relations embedded in the history of political philosophy.

RECONSTITUTING THE CANON

In the process of critically reading the primary texts of the Western canon, unearthing the themes of gender inequality and subordination that had been previously unrecognized, and shifting our understanding of what counts as an "appropriate" set of topics for the history of political philosophy, feminists also showed us that the primary texts usually taught in university classrooms were not always the most revealing in regard to

---

[1] A list of the various volumes may be found at www.psupress.psu.edu/books/series/book_SeriesRe Reading.html

these issues. Most of the best-known canonical texts did not give a prominent place to gender, much less to women. Plato's remarkable proposal for "the community of women" among the "gold" people takes up only a small segment of his *Republic*. Aristotle's infamous remarks about women take up only a few pages of his chapter on the family in the *Politics*, with only brief discussions in a few other places. Hobbes's *Leviathan* makes scant mention of women, and yet makes the quite radical claim that mothers in the state of nature have dominion over children, and that men can gain dominion only through war—which they will not necessarily win. He then rather contradictorily defines the family without mentioning women at all. Discussions of the family and reproduction similarly take up a small proportion of the arguments of Locke's *Second Treatise*, and some of his most revealing comments were even made in an offhand way. Locke's rejection of patriarchy as the foundation of political authority, so key to his rejection of Robert Filmer's *Patriarcha* in his *First Treatise*, was complemented in his *Second Treatise* by remarks on women's and men's relative equality in marriage; though men, as the "abler and stronger," had to have the final word. Similarly, Mill's *On Liberty*, despite Mill's claim that Harriet Taylor was a profound influence on the argument, even a co-author, made hardly any mention of women. Rousseau, the great advocate of equality, made only a few passing references to women in *The Origin of Inequality* and *The Social Contract*.

Thus the project of feminist analysis required close reading of scattered and brief remarks that had to be pieced together to unlock the puzzle of women in Western political thought. But certain texts from a few of these "malestream" figures that did pay particular attention to gender in some of their writings not often attended to by political theorists and philosophers, such as Mill's *Subjection of Women*, Rousseau's *Emile* and *Julie*, Montesqieu's *Persian Letters*, and Locke's *Essay on the Poor Law*, were given new prominence by feminist philosophers and theorists. Such texts were not often seen as "major" texts of these authors in comparison to more overtly "political" texts previously mentioned. Feminists strove to establish their importance to the political philosophy canon precisely because they revealed the role of women in their political theories, and how their theories of state depended on their assumptions about the patriarchal family.

Thus, the project of "women in Western political thought" raised questions about what constituted "the canon" of the history of political philosophy, which texts were included, which ignored, and why. It seemed logically to follow from this undertaking that feminists would start considering the "forgotten" female figures in the history of political philosophy. In this second "opening" of the canon of the history political philosophy, writers and theorists such as Mary Wollstonecraft, Harriet Taylor, and Charlotte Perkins Gilman, whose names were known but whose texts were frequently ignored by political philosophers, were returned to with renewed interest. Figures who were quite known in other disciplines, such as Simone de Beauvoir, were reconsidered from the perspective of political philosophy and recognized for their contributions to our understanding of the political power of gender—and the gender of political power—in society (e.g. Simons 1995). Other figures that few had previously heard of before, such as Christine de Pizan (1994, 1999), Margaret Cavendish (1992*a, b*), and Mary Astell (1996), are being lifted from historical obscurity to become the object of new inquiry.

Many of these historical figures were contemporaries of, and in some cases knew quite well, various male figures who are standard bearers in the history of political philosophy canon. Margaret Cavendish, for instance, with her husband William Cavendish, the first Duke of Newcastle-upon-Tyne, had regular contact with Thomas Hobbes and René Descartes while exiled in France. Though she claimed that she did not partake in the discussions those gentlemen had, in keeping with conventions of the day, and that she was influenced only by her husband, brothers, and brother-in-law, she shared with Hobbes a concern with questions of how to secure order in an absolute monarchy; and, in her *Description of a New World, Called the Blazing World*, she offers advice to an empress whose success is due largely to a female advisor—namely, the Duchess of Newcastle (Cavendish 1992*b*; James 2003). Her *The Contract* took up the connections between the marriage contract and the social contract and, implicitly, the engagement controversy surrounding the question of whether prior obligations to Charles I made new obligations of allegiance to Cromwell's government null and void (Cavendish 1992*a*; Kahn 2004). Cavendish critiqued hierarchical power relations between husbands and wives, as well as the lack of educational opportunities for females (Smith 1982; Suzuki 2003), and offered trenchant insights on the English Civil War (Wright 2009). Mary Astell, a royalist contemporary of Locke, provided an interesting counterpoint to and critique of Locke, with her sardonic question in *Some Reflections on Marriage*: "If *all Men are born free*, how is it that all Women are born slaves?" (Astell 1996: 18). Astell, a single woman who supported herself by writing, similarly advocated women's education as the foundation for women's participation in the economic and political spheres, though, as a royalist, she did not take the liberal line that was to develop from Locke in favor of popular representative democracy (Springborg 2005). Mary Wollstonecraft, probably alone among the female figures not to have been largely forgotten, similarly advocated education for women as key to their freedom and equality. Her *Vindication of the Rights of Women* not only critiqued the "marriage market" in terms much harsher and more radical than those of Astell, but urged a national system of education for boys and girls of all classes together, benefiting from not only the development of reason but "the jostlings of equality" as well (Wollstonecraft 1999: ch. 12). However, while she briefly suggested that women needed to be economically independent, that they could participate in a number of professions, and that education was the key to such economic participation, her primary argument for women's equality and education was that this would make them better mothers, and that good mothering was the key to raising a new generation of good citizens. Whether this was a reactionary position, in reassuring her readers that educating women would not disrupt existing social relations, or a radical one in giving the act of childrearing a key political significance, is a matter of debate (Falco 1996).

Harriet Taylor, whose "The Enfranchisement of Women" has at times been credited by various authorities to John Stuart Mill, was acknowledged to be not only an important influence on Mill, but a significantly more radical one. For instance, in their companion essays on marriage and divorce, Taylor advocated the complete abolishment of marriage, whereas Mill merely urged people to marry later in life, permitting them to make wiser choices, and thereby reducing the likelihood of divorce, which he saw as necessary but nevertheless frowned upon (Mill 1970; Taylor 1970b). Indeed, it was arguably the case that Taylor's contributions largely explained the more radical strains of what scholars had long perceived as something of a split personality in Mill's writings—the "two Mills" that Gertrude Himmelfarb (1974) posited, though she disparaged Taylor's contributions. But J. Ellen Jacobs (2002) argues for Taylor's profound influence, and claimed that Mill was much more radical when writing with Taylor than when he wrote alone. This is particularly evident in Mill's *Political Economy*, where Taylor pushed him toward socialism and toward a recognition that women's working for wages was more important than he thought on his own. Indeed, the detailed notations that J. M. Robson has made to Mill's *Political Economy*, detailing the changes he made to the text with each successive edition, show that she had a definite influence, which was modified by more conservative changes Mill made to the text after she had died (Mill 1965; Hirschmann 2008a, b). But Mill, in the dedication to what is arguably his most famous, and most progressive, work, *On Liberty*, explicitly credited Taylor with a deep influence over its argument.

At the turn of the twentieth century, Charlotte Perkins Gilman's *Women and Economics* critiqued marriage as a "sexual–economic" relationship where women traded sex for economic support. She argued that women's separation from the world of production resulted in stunting their own personal growth and hindered the development of children. But the question that had always stopped previous feminists from such a radical position was the question of how women could combine mothering with work, given that primitive contraceptive techniques virtually guaranteed that any woman who had a sexual life would also be a mother? This was a question that predecessors such as Wollstonecraft and Taylor had avoided, tacitly through the presumed existence of a servant class. Gilman, by contrast, argued that the kitchen was the primary cause of domestic drudgery, and suggested an early feminist socialist utopia of collective housing with shared kitchens that relieved women of much of the burden of household labor for individual husbands and children, far beyond what Marx or Engels had been able to imagine (Gilman 1998).

There are many more figures that could be discussed here (see Waithe 1987, 1989, 1990, 1994; Atherton 1994; Smith, Suzuki, and Wiseman 2007). The apparent radicalism of some of these arguments should not obscure the fact that many of these theorists developed ideals of freedom, equality, and individuality that are central to the canon of modern political theory. They did not argue that these core liberal values were at odds with women's welfare, as some late-twentieth-century feminists were to contend, but rather that, under its patriarchal forms, liberalism was failing to live up to its own ideals. The provision of freedom, equality, and individuality required that these ideals be applied to all, particularly women.

Yet, despite the fact that these female theorists were responding to, took up, and further developed the arguments of the male canonical figures, relying on many of the same central ideals, these theorists continue to have an ambiguous relationship to the canon of historical political philosophy. None is included in the leading survey works of the field (Russell 1945; Wolin 1960; Sabine 1973; Strauss and Cropsey 1987). Few women are generally taught in college survey courses on the history of political thought, with perhaps one or two female figures, usually Wollstonecraft, briefly included as a tokenistic nod.[2] The justification for this is generally that their works were not the large and historically significant treatises written by figures such as Aristotle, Hobbes, Hume, or Hegel. But, since that was also arguably the case for many works that are considered standards of the canon, such as Locke's *Letter concerning Toleration*, Thomas Paine's *Common Sense*, and John Stuart Mill's *On Liberty*, that now strikes one as hardly a legitimate reason for their exclusion. Moreover, some figures, like Cavendish, did in fact write quite a lot (eleven volumes, according to Susan James 2003). Indeed, in the 1970s, historians of intellectual thought such as John Pocock (1975) and Quentin Skinner (1978) argued that one could not understand the history of political thought by simply examining the "major" figures but one had also to study the lesser figures "in between." Intellectual historians advocated a focus on political pamphlets written in the seventeenth and eighteenth centuries, with particular attention paid to lesser-known figures such as Hugo Grotius, Thomas Hutchinson, and Samuel Pufendorf. This approach substantially changed the undertaking of the history of political philosophy in ways that opened the door to include female writers in the body of work known as "the history of political philosophy."

GENDER AND METHOD

As intellectual historians, philosophers, and political theorists were pushed to rethink how they approached their subject matters, feminists were also taking up questions of method and approach that led to a renewed emphasis on the history of political philosophy. This constituted a third way in which feminism sought an "opening-up" of the canon of the history of political philosophy. As feminist political philosophy developed out of its early Marxist and radical strains in the late 1970s and early 1980s, questions of method started to gain prominence (Keller 1985; Harding 1986a, b). By the early 1990s, the idea of "feminist methodology" was being actively developed by philosophers and political theorists. Though much of this work left the history of political philosophy behind to focus on "the science question in feminism," late-twentieth-century configurations of sex and gender, and social phenomena like sexual

---

[2] A sample of anthologies of the history of political thought show no female figures in Morgan (1992), Wootton (1996), Hallowell and Porter (1997). Cohen and Fermon (1996) contains selections from six women out of forty-four representative figures.

assault, these studies led feminists back to the history of political philosophy, which, from a feminist perspective, needed to be reread in terms of the questions that we asked, the evidence that we assessed, the interpretations we legitimated. In this, "women in Western political thought" did not simply entail the attention to women or even to gender, much less the simple inclusion of female writers. It also included a different set of questions and approaches to the interrogation of texts (Hartsock 1984; Hekman 1990; Hirschmann 1992).

For instance, recognizing that patriarchy was not simply about masculine power, but about power instantiated in particular *forms of* masculinity, feminists attended to the fact that it was not just "men" whom canonical figures were writing about, but men of a specific race, class, sexuality, and social location. Similarly, they started to complicate the categories of the "women" that were referenced and excluded in these theories to understand the ways in which the meaning of gender was altered by terms of class location, racial identification, culture, and reproductive status (Brietenberg 1996; Carver 1996; Hirschmann and McClure 2007; Hirschmann 2008*a*).

It also involved a critical assessment of just what it was that we were studying. As the meaning of the term "woman" became an important topic in feminist philosophy and political theory in the 1980s and 1990s, particularly with the advent of "queer studies," lesbian and gay philosophy, and feminism of color, the question of who these "women" were in "Western political philosophy" began to be challenged. The notion of "intersectionality" gained particular currency: the recognition that nobody, male or female, occupies only one identity category (Crenshaw 1991). All women and men are not just "women" and "men" in the abstract, but also have a particular race, class, nationality, sexuality, and so forth. Yet, when dealing with the history of canonical political thought, it is extremely uncommon to find any of these various categories considered at all, much less in tandem with each other. Even feminist analysis of the canon often tends to deal with "women" as an undifferentiated category; while the importance of race, class, and sexuality is invoked in contemporary analysis, once we reach back before the late twentieth century, "women" are once again treated as a unitary category, tacitly white and upper to middle class.

The ostensible reason for this could be that the majority of women in canonical political thought *are* white and upper to middle class: the wives and daughters of the men who were the primary subjects of political theory. Thus, for instance, it is rare to find remarks about men of color, much less women of color, in the works of many Enlightenment theorists (but see Mills 1997). Kant made some brief references to Native American men and women in his *Anthropology*; Mill an oblique reference to African-American female slaves in his *On the Subjection of Women*—though only so that he could compare the situation of black slaves with the plight of white married women in England. Gender aside, Mill, on the one hand, excoriated American slavery and yet seemed to defend British colonial rule over "primitive" peoples in India (Mill 1984*a*, *b*, 1991*a*, *b*). Rousseau made passing recognition of "savages" in *The Origin of Inequality* and argued, following Montesquieu, that people from southern, warmer climates—who were also likely to be darker skinned—were less industrious, and therefore not appropriate subjects for democracy, any more than were women from any climate. References in Locke's work to Africans of either gender are extremely scarce, making his apparently inconsistent views on slavery vexingly difficult to discern (Farr 1986; Glausser 1990; Armitage 2004). Montesquieu's *Persian Letters* stand out as a rarity in taking up issues of racial difference, sexual difference, and even lesbianism and homosexuality (Montesquieu 1973; Mosher 1994).

However, what we now call "class" issues were considered at somewhat greater length by theorists such as Aristotle, Mill, Kant, and Locke, as a number of commentators have shown us, and this category may provide us with greater opportunities for complicating the notion of gender in the history of political philosophy. In the remainder of this section I will illustrate the difference that a feminist intersectional approach takes by considering Locke's *Essay on the Poor Law*, in which Locke maintains that poor women, including poor mothers, should be required to work for wages. A central theme in his *Second Treatise* is the connection Locke makes between industry and rationality; if property is produced by adding your labor to things in nature, it is rational to work. Hence the poor lack property because they are lazy, which is a function of their irrationality; and, by forcing such people to work, you will force them to develop their rational capacities (Locke 1997; Hirschmann 2002).

This was no less true of women than of men. Yet, what about women's responsibility for childrearing? Locke proposes that poor children over the age of 3 be placed in "working schools," which were basically wool factories. Though childrearing is generally burdensome enough to prevent women from working out of the home full time, Locke maintained, it does not completely fill their days: women have many "broken intervals in their time" during which they "earn nothing" and "their labour is wholly lost" (Locke 1997: 189). This position stands in stark contrast to what Locke says in the *Second Treatise*—namely, that the rigors of childbirth disable women from participation in the same activities as men. A human female is "capable of conceiving" almost immediately after giving birth, "and de facto is commonly with Child again, and Brings forth too a new Birth long before the former is out of a dependency." This is why men have obligations of fidelity to the family, to support their wives and children, being "under an Obligation to continue in Conjugal Society with the same Woman longer than other creatures" (Locke 1988: para. 80). By contrast, in *Poor Law* Locke argues that "more than two children at one time, under the age of 3 years, will seldom happen in one family," so women are not normally overly burdened by children (Locke 1997: 182). This divergence in views about reproduction reflects a class differential: the *Two Treatises*, with its central concern of property, refers explicitly to bourgeois women, for whom annual pregnancies were desired, in order to ensure male heirs (Wright 2007). By contrast, the *Poor Law*, fairly obviously, refers explicitly to the propertyless, for whom reproduction carries a different social function.

Understanding class distinctions among women provides valuable insights into one of the central issues over which feminists have argued concerning Locke—namely, whether women are rational. Feminists like Butler argue that Locke wanted girls to be fully educated alongside boys (M. Butler 1978: 148); others such as Clark (1977) and

Eisenstein (1981) maintained that Locke believed women were for the most part irrational. If we consider the ways in which women were divided by class, however, we get a more complicated understanding. Poor women are able to obtain no more than the most basic rationality, just like men: enough reason to be able to see that it is in their own self-interest to work industriously. Girls and boys alike put in "working schools" will not be given the elaborate disciplinary training, much less the lessons in Latin and mathematics, that are prescribed for wealthier boys in *Thoughts concerning Education*. Those boys' sisters, however, are another matter. In a letter to Mrs Edward Clark—Locke's *Education* originated in a series of letters to her husband, Edward Clark, concerning the education of their son—Locke said: "Since, therefore I acknowledge no difference of sex in your mind relating... to truth, virtue and obedience, I think well to have no thing altered in it from what I have writ" for the son to be applied to daughters (Locke 1927: 12). However, note that Locke's reference to females' "truth, virtue and obedience" does not include any reference to "reason"; and the entire first half of the book is dedicated not to formal education but to advice about physical upbringing so as to make children hardy and healthy: detailed advice about diet and exercise, proper modes of non-binding dress, and cultivating strict obedience in the child's character. The development of reason, by contrast, requires the learning of Latin and mathematics; and, though Locke clearly states that these subjects, particularly mathematics, are largely the province of the propertied classes—only "those who have the time and opportunity" should learn it (Locke 1996a: 178)—there is no evidence in Locke's writings that girls would learn the same academic material as boys. Indeed, considering that Locke's greatest concern for girls appeared to be protecting their complexions from sunburn, one wonders how unconventional his *Thoughts on Education* really are for females. "Where the Difference of Sex requires different Treatment," Locke notes in his letter to Mrs Clark, "'twill be no hard Matter to distinguish" (Locke 1927: 12). But, given contemporary norms about educating girls, this is hardly reassuring. Indeed, as Locke says in *The Reasonableness of Christianity*, laborers and "those of the other sex" can understand only "simple propositions" (Locke 1958: 76).

But such irrationality is not natural or essential. Locke says: "We are born to be, if we please, rational creatures, but it is use and exercise only that makes us so, and we are indeed so no farther than industry and application has carried us" (Locke 1996a: 178). Poor and women, then, are not innately incapable of reason; rather, the "constant drudgery to their backs and their bellies" (Locke 1996b: 181) means laborers have insufficient time and energy to develop it. But whereas poor women, just like poor men, will not develop reason because they lack the resources and the time to do so, wealthy girls and women have the resources in their very homes. Do they benefit from them?

That is unlikely. Locke says that it is "ridiculous... that a father should waste his own money and his son's time in setting him to learn the *Roman language*, when at the same time he designs him for a trade" (Locke 1996a: 121); it would likely be just as ridiculous to teach them to women. After all, women could not be members of the clergy or parliament; they could not even vote, since at the end of the seventeenth century—before Locke wrote his *Thoughts concerning Education*—parliament had expressly debarred women from voting, after a number of women had tried to do so in prior decades (Mendelson and Crawford 1998: ch. 7). Moreover, as Locke says, only "gentlemen" have the "time and leisure" to study Latin and mathematics, in contrast to busy tradesmen. Running a household in the upper classes in seventeenth-century England was a demanding job, including accounting skills and management, particularly considering that two households, a city house and country estate, were often maintained by wealthy families. Such tasks certainly require more reason than is needed by poor women, but it is not the "right reason," which Locke reserves for "gentlemen."

From the perspective of class analysis, laboring women, like laboring men, have sufficient reason to understand the importance of their work, but not enough to participate in lawmaking or voting. There is little difference between women and men. By that measure, bourgeois women should have reason equal to bourgeois men. That they do not suggests that Locke's notion of reason is decidedly a function of gender as well as of class. For it is only girls and women of the gentry who would *need* to have their natural capacity for reason less developed than their male peers. The link between labor, industry, and reason reveals why it was desirable that poor women to work but not wealthy women; for not only do poor women *need* the same basic level of reason that poor men need, but their developing it does not threaten Locke's linkage between property and politics, for neither poor men nor poor women would have sufficient reason to be political agents, only enough to see the wisdom in labor and obedience. By contrast, upper-class women were potentially in a position to challenge their second-class status, if they could only access the resources of education and the development of right reason that existed in their own home. In order to make sure that what they learn is obedience rather than "right reason," bourgeois women's education must be curtailed by comparison with males of the same class.

I have discussed the example that Locke provides at some length to show that class is an important feature for feminists to consider when they analyze the place of "women" in Western political thought. The link between gender and class is more than a mere parallel, however. For class not only affects how different women are situated within the theories as well; it also affects the meaning of gender itself: what it means to be a woman or man, differs considerably by class, with gender becoming more sharply differentiated the higher the class. By looking at other aspects of identity, such as race, sexuality, and class in particular, feminists engaged in the history of political philosophy must examine women's practical and legal relation to property, paid labor, reproduction, marriage, the family, and the law in specific countries in specific time periods.

In doing this, feminists, who have been so good at reminding political philosophers of the *political* part of their subject matter, need to re-emphasize its *historical* dimensions. Sticking with critical analysis of texts alone does not provide us with an adequate understanding of those texts, because the theorists were often unaware of their own attitudes: the subordination of women was such a normalized part of their societies that it did not seem worthy of notice by the canonical figures, much less of theoretical analysis. Certainly, this unconscious bias is an important part of the subtext that feminists have uncovered through their careful textual readings. But a deeper understanding of historical and social context enhances our understandings of gender in a different way, and women's social historians have conducted valuable research—even if they have been rather uninterested in women's intellectual history (Smith 2007; Wright 2009). For instance, Mendelson and Crawford's study of women's economic and social situation in sixteenth- and seventeenth-century England provides insights into women's participation in paid labor, their status in the family at various class levels, the tensions between law and social practice regarding women, the relationship of women to religion and the Church, medicine, and business, all of which form the context in which Filmer, Hobbes, Locke, Harrington, and Pufendorf, not to mention Cavendish and Astell, all wrote. Such historical data provide insights into the variability of the category of gender, and indeed how the meaning of gender changed by virtue of class.

Conclusion

In the various enterprises I have surveyed thus far, rather than simply being *about* the history political philosophy, feminism has become *part of* it. By this I mean not just the aforementioned rediscovery of women theorists, but a different way of understanding what the canonical project is about. This is particularly evident in the two remaining ways in which feminists have "opened" the canon of the history of political philosophy, which at this point will be only briefly recounted. The first is feminist interpretations of key political concepts such as "freedom" and "justice." Most of this work does not utilize the history of political philosophy *per se* (Okin 1989; Brown 1995; Cornell 1999), which is why it is being treated so briefly here. But some authors specifically took up canonical thinkers, particularly of the modern and early modern eras, exploring not just the ways in which women were excluded by laws and practices that prevented them from benefiting from the conceptual ideals that were being promoted by the theorists, but *the ways in which those ideals themselves were conceptualized, which were fundamentally gendered* as well. Carole Pateman's *The Sexual Contract* argued that the foundation for consent theories of obligation, the social contract, was a contract made explicitly by and between men, premised on a prior "sexual contract" that men made, not with women *per se*, but rather between themselves *over* women (Pateman 1988). My own *Rethinking Obligation* followed this with an argument that the notion of obligation itself as self-assumed, which this sexist conceptualization of contract produced, was "structurally sexist" in its very foundations. It was premised, not only on women's exclusion from the social contract, and thereby from the very idea of obligation as self-assumed, but on women's assignment to an entire range of duties and obligations about which women had little or no choice (Hirschmann 1992). I later took up the concept of freedom in the modern canon, arguing that a consideration of how the concept developed cannot be fully appreciated without an examination of gender. A two-tiered structure of freedom, with some conceptualizations of freedom designated for men and the wealthy, and other conceptualizations designated for laborers and women, demonstrated once again that class and gender were important dimensions to be explored when examining the history of political philosophy (Hirschmann 2008*a*).

A final way in which feminism has opened up the canon is its relevance to contemporary politics. Again, much of this work goes beyond the purview of what most political philosophers would consider the "*history* of political philosophy," because it deals with issues as they are being lived in the contemporary world. But it is important to recognize that feminist political philosophers are today *making* that history. In *The Use and Abuse of History*, the noted misogynist Friedrich Nietzche warned us of a fetishization of history that does not attend to the dynamic of the present and does not help us live our lives. Any approach to the history of political philosophy that does not recognize the important role that gender has played there must of necessity be based on a denial of the importance of the role that gender plays in our contemporary lives. Hence feminists are arguing that political philosophers need to rethink our relationship to the history of political philosophy; and work that considers the relevance of Kant to ecofeminism (Wilson 1997), Mill to domestic violence (Morales 2007), or Locke to twentieth-century welfare policies (Hirschmann 2002), can not only open up different angles of analysis of the historical texts, but can prove their continued relevance to the contemporary world. There is no greater contribution that can be made to the history of political thought, and feminists are on the leading edge.[3]

References

Primary Sources

Aristotle (1962). *Politics*, ed. Ernest Barker. New York: Oxford University Press.

Astell, M. (1996). "Some Reflections on Marriage, Occasioned by the Duke and Duchess of Mazarine's Case, Which is Also Considered" [1700], in M. Astell, *Political Writings*, ed. P. Springborg. New York: Cambridge University Press.

Cavendish, M. (1992*a*). *The Contract*, in *The Description of a New World, Called the Blazing World, and Other Writings*, ed. K. Lilley. New York: New York University Press.

Cavendish, M. (1992*b*). *The Description of a New World, Called the Blazing World* [1666], in *The Description of a New World, Called the Blazing World, and Other Writings*, ed. K. Lilley. New York: New York University Press.

de Pizan, C. (1994). *The Book of the Body Politic* [1406], ed. K. Forhan. Cambridge: Cambridge University Press.

---

[3] Thanks to George Klosko and Joanne Wright for their helpful suggestions on this chapter.

DE PIZAN, C. (1999). *The Book of the City of Ladies* [1405], trans. R. Brown-Grant. London: Penguin.

FILMER, ROBERT (1991). *Patriarcha Non Monarcha* [1680], in *Patriarcha and Other Writings*, ed. J. P. Sommmerville. New York: Cambridge University Press.

GILMAN, C. P. (1998). *Women and Economics: A Study of the Economic Relation between Men and Women as a Factor in Social Evolution* [1901]. Mineola, NY: Dover Publications.

HOBBES, T. (1968). *Leviathan* [1651], ed. C. B. Macpherson. New York: Penguin Books.

KANT, I. (1974). *Anthropology from a Pragmatic Point of View* [1798], trans. M. J. Gregor. The Hague: Martinus Nijhoff.

LOCKE, J. (1927). *The Correspondence of John Locke and Edward Clarke*, ed. B. Rand. Oxford: Oxford University Press.

LOCKE, J. (1958). *The Reasonableness of Christianity* [1695], ed. I. T. Ramsay. Palo Alto, CA: Stanford University Press.

LOCKE, J. (1988). *Two Treatises of Government* [1688], ed. Peter Laslett. New York: Cambridge University Press.

LOCKE, J. (1996a). *Some Thoughts Concerning Education* [1693], in *Some Thoughts Concerning Education and Of the Conduct of the Understanding*, eds R. Grant and N. Tarcov. Indianapolis: Hackett.

LOCKE, J. (1996b). *Of the Conduct of the Understanding* [1706], in *Some Thoughts Concerning Education and Of the Conduct of the Understanding*, eds R. Grant and N. Tarcov. Indianapolis: Hackett.

LOCKE, J. (1997). *An Essay on the Poor Law* [1697], in John Locke, *Political Essays*, ed. Mark Goldie. London: Cambridge University Press.

MENCHU, R. (1984). *I, Rigoberta Menchu: An Indian Woman in Guatemala*. New York and London: Verso.

MILL, J. S. (1965). *Principles of Political Economy: With Some of their Applications to Social Philosophy* [1871], ed. J. M. Robson, in *Collected Works of John Stuart Mill*, ii, iii. Toronto: University of Toronto Press.

MILL, J. S. (1970). "On Marriage and Divorce" [1832], in John Stuart Mill and Harriet Taylor Mill, *Essays on Sex Equality*, ed. Alice S. Rossi. Chicago: University of Chicago Press.

MILL, J. S. (1984a). "The Negro Question" [1850], ed. J. M. Robson, in *Collected Works*, xxi. *Essays on Equality, Law, and Education*. Toronto: University of Toronto Press.

MILL, J. S. (1984b). "The Slave Power" [1862], ed. J. M. Robson, in *Collected Works*, xxi. *Essays on Equality, Law, and Education*. Toronto: University of Toronto Press.

MILL, J. S. (1991a). *The Subjection of Women* [1869], in *On Liberty and Other Essays*, ed. J. Gray. New York: Oxford University Press.

MILL, J. S. (1991b). *Representative Government* [1861], in *On Liberty and Other Essays*, ed. J. Gray. New York: Oxford University Press.

MILL, J. S. (1991c). *On Liberty* [1859], in *On Liberty and Other Essays*, ed. J. Gray. New York: Oxford University Press.

MONTESQUIEU, CHARLES DE SECONDAT, BARON DE (1973). *Persian Letters* [1721], ed. C. J. Betts. New York: Penguin Books.

NIETZSCHE, F. W. (1957). *The Use and Abuse of History for Life* [1874]. New York, Liberal Arts Press.

PLATO (1991). *The Republic of Plato*, ed. Allan Bloom. New York: Basic Books.

ROUSSEAU, J.-J. (1973a). *The Origin of Inequality* [1755], in Rousseau, *The Social Contract and Discourses*, ed. G. D. H. Cole. London: Everyman.

ROUSSEAU, J.-J. (1973*b*). *The Social Contract* [1762], in Rousseau, *The Social Contract and Discourses*, ed. G. D. H. Cole. London: Everyman.

TAYLOR, H. (1970*a*). "The Enfranchisement of Women" [1851], in J. S. Mill and H. Taylor, *Essays on Sex Equality*, ed. A. Rossi. Chicago: University of Chicago Press.

TAYLOR, H. (1970*b*). "On Marriage" [1832], in J. S. Mill and H. Taylor, *Essays on Sex Equality*, ed. A. Rossi. Chicago: University of Chicago Press.

WOLLSTONECRAFT, M. (1999). *A Vindication of the Rights of Woman and A Vindication of the Rights of Men* [1792]. New York: Oxford University Press.

Secondary Sources

ANNAS, J. (1977). "Mill and the Subjection of Women," *Philosophy*, 52: 179–94.

ARMITAGE, D. (2004). "John Locke, Carolina, and 'The Two Treatises of Government,'" *Political Theory*, 32/5: 602–27.

ATHERTON, M. (1994). *Women Philosophers of the Early Modern Period.* Indianapolis: Hackett.

BLOOM, A. (1988). *The Closing of the American Mind.* New York: Simon and Schuster.

BOTTING, E. H. (2006). *Family Feuds: Wollstonecraft, Burke, and Rousseau on the Transformation of the Family.* Albany, NY: State University of New York Press.

BRENNAN, T., and PATEMAN, C. (1979). "Mere Auxiliaries to the Common-Wealth: Women and the Origins of Liberalism," *Political Studies*, 27: 183–200.

BRIETENBERG, M. (1996). *Anxious Masculinity in Early Modern England.* Cambridge: Cambridge University Press.

BROWN, W. (1988). *Manhood and Politics: A Feminist Reading in Political Theory.* Totowa, NJ: Rowman & Littlefield.

BROWN, W. (1995). *States of Injury: Power and Freedom in Late Modernity.* Princeton: Princeton University Press.

BUTLER, J. (1990). *Gender Trouble: Feminism and the Subversion of Identity.* London: Routledge.

BUTLER, M. (1978). "The Early Liberal Roots of Feminism: John Locke and the Attack on Patriarchy," *American Political Science Review*, 72/1: 135–50.

CARVER, T. (1996). *Gender is Not a Synonym for Women.* Boulder, CO: Lynne Rienner.

CLARK, L. M. G. (1977). "Women and John Locke: Or, Who Owns the Apples in the Garden of Eden?" *Canadian Journal of Philosophy*, 7/4: 699–724.

COHEN, M., and FERMON, N. (1996) (eds). *Princeton Readings in Political Thought.* Princeton: Princeton University Press.

CORNELL, D. (1999). *At the Heart of Freedom: Feminism, Sex, and Equality.* Princeton: Princeton University Press.

CRENSHAW, K. (1991). "Mapping the Margins: Intersectionality, Identity Politics, and Violence against Women of Color," *Stanford Law Review*, 43: 1241–99.

DI STEFANO, C. (1991). *Configurations of Masculinity: A Feminist Perspective on Modern Political Theory.* Ithaca, NY: Cornell University Press.

EISENSTEIN, Z. (1981). *The Radical Future of Liberal Feminism.* New York: Longman Publishers.

ELSHTAIN, J. B. (1981). *Public Man, Private Woman: Women in Social and Political Thought.* Princeton: Princeton University Press.

FALCO, M. J. (1996) (ed.). *Feminist Interpretations of Mary Wollstonecraft.* University Park, PA: Pennsylvania State University Press.

FARR, J. (1986). "So Vile and Miserable and Estate: The Problem of Slavery in Locke's Political Thought," *Political Theory*, 14: 263–89.

GLAUSSER, W. (1990). "Three Approaches to Locke and the Slave Trade," *Journal of the History of Ideas*, 51/2: 199–216.

GOLDSTEIN, L. (1980). "Mill, Mary, and Women's Liberation," *Journal of the History of Philosophy*, 28: 319–34.

HALLOWELL, J. H., and PORTER, J. M. (1997) (eds). *Political Philosophy: The Search for Humanity and Order*. Scarborough, Ontario: Prentice Hall Canada.

HARDING, S. (1986a). *The Science Question in Feminism*. Ithaca, NY: Cornell University Press.

HARDING, S. (1986b) (ed.). *Feminism and Methodology: Social Science Issues*. Bloomington, IN: Indiana University Press.

HARTMANN, HEIDI (1981). "The Unhappy Marriage of Marxism and Feminism," in L. Sargeant (ed.), *Women and Revolution*. Cambridge, MA: South End Press.

HARTSOCK, N. C. M. (1984). *Money, Sex, and Power: Toward a Feminist Historical Materialism*. Boston: Northeastern University Press.

HEKMAN, S. J. (1990). *Gender and Knowledge: Elements of a Postmodern Feminism*. Boston: Northeastern University Press.

HIMMELFARB, G. (1974). *On Liberty and Liberalism: The Case of John Stuart Mill*. New York: Alfred A. Knopf.

HIRSCHMANN, N. J. (1992). *Rethinking Obligation: A Feminist Method for Political Theory*. Ithaca, NY: Cornell University Press.

HIRSCHMANN, N. J. (2002). "Liberal-Conservativism Once and Again: Locke's *Essay on the Poor Law* and US Welfare Reform," *Constellations: An International Journal of Critical and Democratic Theory*, 9/3 (Sept.), 335–55.

HIRSCHMANN, N. J. (2008a). *Gender, Class, and Freedom in Modern Political Theory*. Princeton: Princeton University Press.

HIRSCHMANN, N. J. (2008b). "Mill, Political Economy, and Women's Work," *American Political Science Review*, 102/2: 199–213.

HIRSCHMANN, N. J., and McCLURE, K. M. (2007) (eds). *Feminist Interpretations of John Locke*. University Park, PA: Pennsylvania State University Press.

JACOBS, J. E. (2002). *The Voice of Harriet Taylor Mill*. Bloomington, IN: Indiana University Press.

JAMES, S. (2003). "Introduction," in M. Cavendish, *Political Writings*, ed. S. James. Cambridge: Cambridge University Press.

KAHN, V. (2004). *Wayward Contracts: The Crisis of Political Obligation in England, 1640–1674*. Princeton: Princeton University Press.

KELLER, E. F. (1985). *Reflections on Gender and Science*. New Haven: Yale University Press.

MARSO, L. J. (1999). *(Un)Manly Citizens: Jean-Jacques Rousseau's and Germaine de Stael's Subversive Women*. Baltimore: Johns Hopkins University Press.

MENDELSON, S., and CRAWFORD, P. (1998). *Women in Early Modern England, 1550–1720*. Oxford: Clarendon Press.

MILLS, C. (1997). *The Racial Contract*. Ithaca, NY: Cornell University Press.

MORALES, M. (2007). "Rational Freedom in John Stuart Mill's Feminism," in N. Urbinati and A. Zakaras (eds), *J. S. Mill's Political Thought: A Bicentennial Reassessment*. New York: Cambridge University Press.

MORGAN M. L. (1992) (ed.). *Classics of Moral and Political Theory*. Indianapolis: Hackett.

MORGENSTERN, M. (1996). *Rousseau and the Politics of Ambiguity*. University Park, PA: Pennsylvania State University Press.

MOSHER, M. A. (1994). "The Judgmental Gaze of European Women: Gender, Sexuality, and the Critique of Republican Rule," *Political Theory*, 22/1: 25–44.

O'BRIEN, M. (1981). *The Politics of Reproduction*. London: Routledge & Kegan Paul.

OKIN, S. M. (1979). *Women in Western Political Thought*. Princeton: Princeton University Press.

OKIN, S. M. (1989). *Justice, Gender and the Family*. New York: Basic Books.

PATEMAN, C. (1988). *The Sexual Contract*. Palo Alto, CA: Stanford University Press.

POCOCK, J. G. A. (1975). *The Machiavellian Moment: Florentine Political Thought and the Atlantic Republican Tradition*. Princeton: Princeton University Press.

RUSSELL, B. (1945). *A History of Western Philosophy*. New York: Simon and Schuster.

SABINE, G. H. (1973). *A History of Political Theory Fourth Edition*, rev. T. L. Thorson. Florence, KY: Thomson Learning.

SAXONHOUSE, A. (1976). "The Philosopher and the Female in the Political Thought of Plato," *Political Theory*, 4: 195–212.

SHANLEY, M. L. (1981). "Marital Slavery and Friendship: John Stuart Mill's The Subjection of Women," *Political Theory*, 9/2: 229–47.

SIMONS, M. A. (1995) (ed.). *Feminist Interpretations of Simone de Beauvoir*. University Park, PA: Pennsylvania State University Press.

SKINNER, Q. (1978). *The Foundations of Modern Political Thought*. Cambridge: Cambridge University Press.

SMITH, H. L. (1982). *Reason's Disciples: Seventeenth-Century English Feminists*. Urbana, IL: University of Illinois Press.

SMITH, H. L. (2007). "Women Intellectuals and Intellectual History: Their Paradigmatic Separation," *Women's History Review*, 16/3 (July), 353–68.

SMITH, H. L., SUZUKI, M., and WISEMAN, S. (2007) (eds). *Women's Political Writings, 1610-1725*. 4 vols. London: Pickering & Chatto Publishers.

SPELMAN, E. V. (1994). "Hairy Cobblers and Philosopher-Queens," in N. Tuana (ed.), *Feminist Interpretations of Plato*. University Park, PA: Pennsylvania State University Press.

SPRINGBORG, P. (2005). *Mary Astell, Theorist of Freedom from Domination*. Cambridge: Cambridge University Press.

STRAUSS, L., and CROPSEY, J. (1987) (eds). *History of Political Philosophy*. Chicago: University of Chicago Press.

SUZUKI, M. (2003). *Subordinate Subjects: Gender, the Political Nation, and Literary Form in England, 1588-1688*. Burlington, VT: Ashgate.

WAITHE, M. E. (1987). *A History of Women Philosophers*, i. *Ancient Women Philosophers, 600 BC–500 AD*. New York: Springer.

WAITHE, M. E. (1989). *A History of Women Philosophers*, ii. *Medieval, Renaissance, and Enlightenment Women Philosophers, 500-1600*. New York: Springer.

WAITHE, M. E. (1990). *A History of Women Philosophers*, iii. *Modern Women Philosophers, 1600-1900*. New York: Springer.

WAITHE, M. E. (1994). *A History of Women Philosophers*, iv. *Contemporary Women Philosophers, 1900-Today*. New York: Springer.

WILSON, H. (1997). "Rethinking Kant from the Perspective of Ecofeminism," in R. M. Schott (ed.), *Feminist Interpretations of Immanual Kant*. University Park, PA: Pennsylvania State University Press.

Wingrove, E. (2000). *Rousseau's Republican Romance*. Princeton: Princeton University Press.

Wolin, S. (1960). *Politics and Vision: Continuity and Innovation in Western Political Thought*. Princeton: Princeton University Press.

Wootton, D. (1996). *Modern Political Thought: Readings from Machiavelli to Nietzsche*. Indianapolis: Hackett.

Wright, J. (2004). *Origin Stories in Political Thought: Discourses on Gender, Power, and Citizenship*. Toronto: University of Toronto Press.

Wright, J. (2007). "Recovering Locke's Midwifery Notes," in *Feminist Interpretations of John Locke*. University Park, PA: Pennsylvania State University Press.

Wright, J. (2009). "Not Just Dutiful Wives and Besotted Ladies: Epistemic Agency in the War Writing of Brilliana Harley and Margaret Cavendish," *Early Modern Women: An Interdisciplinary Journal*, 4 (Fall), 1–26.

Zerilli, L. (1994). *Signifying Woman: Culture and Chaos in Rousseau, Burke, and Mill*. Ithaca, NY: Cornell University Press.

CHAPTER 47

ANIMAL RIGHTS AND
POLITICAL THEORY

JULIAN FRANKLIN

In the ancient world, the idea that killing animals for food is wrong arose mainly from belief in a deep continuity between the animal and human psyche. Animals, like humans, seem able to reason. The animal victimized may even be a human psyche incarnated in another form. The soul of an animal, or perhaps even of a vegetable, may share in a divine spirit. The cries and pain of animals, especially when they are being slaughtered, should awaken the human capacity for compassion. These forms of continuity do not exclude each other, and in the most sophisticated versions of the vegetarian idea they go together. The underlying thought is that the victimization of an animal is sinful and dehumanizing.

In India, intimations of this idea go back to the second millennium BCE, and a vegetarian diet gradually also becomes an essential of the Hindu route to Brahma. After 600 BCE non-violence (*ahmisa*) becomes a central principle of Buddhism and Jainism. A parallel among the Greeks, who were perhaps influenced by Eastern ideas via Egypt, appears soon after with Pythagoras and his school. Orphic ritual and mysticism mixed with philosophy prescribe a vegetarian diet as a condition of self-purification. Pythagorean vegetarianism is continued in Empedocles; Theophrastus, perhaps Aristotle's best-known student, argues for vegetarianism and against animal sacrifice on the ground that justice was due to animals as well as to humans. In the Roman Empire, vegetarianism, inspired by compassion as well as by a sense of justice, is poetically embraced by Ovid. Seneca makes justice to animals a duty, notwithstanding its all but universal denial by other Stoics. But the richest group of essays, often remarkably modern in their point of view, are the essays in Plutarch's *Moralia* supporting vegetarianism, condemning cruelty to animals, and demonstrating animal intelligence.

Perhaps the major extant work on vegetarianism dating from classical antiquity is *On Abstinence from Animal Flesh* by the neo-Platonist Porphyry, the student and biographer of Plotinus, himself a vegetarian. Writing late in the third century CE,

Porphyry argued against the Stoics that animals have reason, even if not as fully as do humans; that non-human animals communicate with each other and understand human speech; that the psyche of every animal reveals the presence of an ultimate divine principle; and that humans cannot attain assimilation to the divine, which is their proper goal, without giving justice to all sentient beings. But for Porphyry as for many of his predecessors these prescriptions are directed mainly to those who are capable of a contemplative life—that is, the philosophical elite.

Moral obligation to animals based on their kinship with humans is also deeply embedded in the Hebrew Bible, which is especially remarkable for laying down rules for the kind treatment of animals as they live and work. These rules, moreover, are meant to be binding law for an entire people, and their scope is constantly expanded in rabbinic commentaries and glosses. Genesis 1:26–9, indeed, is expressly vegetarian, in that God gives only the green plants as food not only for humans but for animals as well. Not until Genesis 9:2–4 is Noah (and humanity in general) given permission to eat flesh. Yet vegetarian longings do not disappear in Jewish law. Concern for the suffering of animals continues in the Mosaic rules of slaughtering and other elements of Kashruth.

Not only was Kashruth ended in the early Church, but the basic tradition of kindness in Judaism was largely submerged for many centuries as well. Paul was notoriously severe on the status of animals. Augustine took over the Stoic claim that vegetarianism made no sense. And St Thomas developed out of Aristotle the view that animals were made for human use (*Summa contra gentiles*). As part of his argument, St Thomas also denied that animals could be resurrected (*Summa theologiae*). Some of the later scholastics, and especially Ockham, even insisted that animals had no "mind" at all and were moved quasi-automatically by sense (Lagelund 2004). In more than one respect, the absurdities of the animal machine propagated by Descartes was a continuation of this view, and it served him as well as the Ockhamites as a guarantee against the presence of animals in heaven.

Such generally dismissive views of animals were not universal, and individual Christian writers continued to recommend vegetarianism. But the most serious challenge to the official doctrine, on this point as on many others, came from "heretical" movements. The Jewish Christians, or Ebionites, around the time of Paul had a gospel of their own in which Jesus declares for vegetarianism (Akers 2000). The Manicheans in Augustine's time, and the Manichean Bogomils and Cathars in the early and later Middle Ages respectively, were dualists who claimed sparks of the divine were present in the flesh of all sentient beings. Despite certain similarities to neo-Platonism, however, these movements were founded not on compassion but on the quest for ascetic self-purification. Abstention from animal flesh was considered absolutely essential to this goal, so much so that adherents of the Manichean movements would literally prefer to die rather than kill an animal or eat its flesh. The spread of Manicheanism among the poor in the Middle Ages provoked brutal reactions from the Church. Vast numbers of Cathari met death in the Albigensian crusade (Spencer 2000); and fear of them may help explain the harshness with respect to animals in St Thomas and other scholastics.

This stance remained dominant in official Catholicism well into the nineteenth century. Softer views reappear in Christianity with the Reformation, and by the seventeenth century far-reaching pleas for kindness were voiced by sectarians and pietists.

The Enlightenment did not extend ideas of rights to animals. Pufendorf and other natural lawyers in the seventeenth century, reasoning somewhat like the ancient Stoics, excluded animals from the protection of the law of nature because they could not make agreements. Even in the eighteenth century, where there is a new sensitivity to the feelings of animals as well as of humans, major writers such as Mandeville, Hutcheson, Hume, Rousseau, and Bentham, who insist on the commonality of feelings between animals and humans, condemn cruelty to animals but do not embrace vegetarianism. They stop just short of acknowledging that animals have rights.

This reluctance to go the whole way is also exhibited by enlightened exponents of Christianity. John Wesley offers an ingenious argument on the innocence of animals after Eden, but seems not to have publicly endorsed vegetarianism, even though he personally practiced it. And Humphry Primatt in his *Dissertation on the Duty of Mercy and the Sin of Cruelty to Brute Animals* (1776) incorporates most of the rabbinical and prophetic teachings of kindness into the Christian message, but is not prepared to endorse vegetarianism.

On a more popular level, vegetarianism, along with modern protests against cruelty, began in the seventeenth century and became an incipient movement in the century following. In the nineteenth century the anti-cruelty movements grew rapidly. The first anti-cruelty legislation in the United Kingdom was passed in 1822. The SPCA was formed in 1824 and its American counterpart, the ASPCA, in 1866. But of special interest for present purposes is the growth of vigorous vegetarian movements. Invocations of Porphyry and Pythagoras, which begin as early as the seventeenth century, are especially marked in Romantic and Transcendentalist ideas of the ultimate unity of the natural and spiritual worlds. With the French Revolution and its aftermath, the goal of a purely natural harmony is advanced by Joseph Ritson and Shelley. But the more immediate sources of inspiration for the present are writers like Wagner, Tolstoy, Shaw, Gandhi, and Schweitzer, whose message is less theological or philosophical than a broad appeal to the possibilities of the human spirit. A splendid example is *Animals' Rights* (1892) by Henry Salt, whose many works include a biography of Thoreau. "Man, to be truly man," says Salt, "must cease to abnegate his common fellowship with all living nature . . . and the coming realization of human rights will inevitably bring after it, the tardier but not less certain realization of the rights of the lower races" (1980: 131).

After a lull during and after the Second World War, the upsurge of egalitarian protest movements—for racial and gender equality and against imperialism—prepared the ground for a new era in animal rights. In 1975 Peter Singer's immensely popular book *Animal Liberation* argued that the interests of animals were entitled to equal respect with human interests, and it did so on strictly secular and rational grounds. Singer is a modern utilitarian who went back to Bentham's thought on animal pain. Bentham had said: "The question is not, Can they reason? nor, Can they talk? But, Can they suffer?" (Bentham 1948: 311 n.). Bentham stopped short of equality, but Singer drew the logical conclusion. The pain (or pleasure) of an animal differs from that of humans only in its quantity, and so, if the quantity of pain (or pleasure) for both is equal, the utility for the animal is the same as for a human. Singer, broadly reasoning this way, rightly concludes that animals are entitled to equality of respect with humans for all the interests relevant to their condition. Anything less is "speciesism," a term that Singer popularized.

Singer is thus able to rule out eating animals. He would permit medical and scientific experimentation on animals but only under stringent conditions. Experimentation could be done only if patently necessary and closely controlled. The testers, further-more, must be willing to use mentally defective humans for that purpose as well as animals.

Animal Liberation almost immediately generated a new movement for animal rights[1] as distinct from a program limited to animal welfare, animal protection, and prevention of cruelty. Organizations limited to the latter goals still predominate in the overall movement. The Humane Society of the United States (HSUS), the largest of these with over 10,000,000 members in 2004, is not committed either to vegetarianism or to abolishing animal testing. But People for the Ethical Treatment of Animals (PETA), the formation of which in 1980 was directly inspired by Singer's book, is completely committed to these goals. Its militancy and tactics of direct confrontation have alienated some adherents of the older organizations. But PETA had over 1,500,000 members in 2004, and there are at least a score of other organizations, not always as militant, that also work for animal rights. Indeed, the general public tends to use the term "animal rights," albeit vaguely, to characterize the movement as a whole. Overlapping memberships notwithstanding, the overall movement is now numerous enough to be a political force. The larger groups have lobbies on all levels of govern-ment, and political action committees have been formed as well.

Considered theoretically, Singer's argument betrays some weaknesses. One obvious lapse is his case for eating lower animals if it were possible to kill them painlessly. Humans and other higher animals may not be killed even painlessly, because, having ideas as to their future selves, they have a "preference for life," which, according to "preference utilitarianism," is to be counted as a plus. Chickens, like other lower animals, have no such preference; they wish only to avoid immediate pain and immediate threats. Hence nothing is lost if they are painlessly killed and replaced (Singer 1999: 126–7). But Singer fails to show why we cannot do the same to an unwanted human. Even conceding that normal humans have a "preference for life" in Singer's sense, we could imagine replacing one such preference with another of equal intensity without loss of "preference utility" as long as the death of the first, like the death of that chicken, is painless and unanticipated (Franklin 2007).

---

[1] Properly speaking there is no such thing as inherent rights for a utilitarian beyond equal consideration of all interests. But Singer (2002) does not object to the more general term for ordinary use.

This difficulty, of course, is tangential to Singer's main concerns and could readily be given up. The more fundamental problem is the weakness of utilitarianism as a moral principle. Most damaging here is the absence of a rule to determine how pains and pleasures should be distributed among members of a group. The sole aim of utilitarianism is to maximize utility as an aggregate, and it does not and cannot matter how that aggregate is distributed among individuals. If a group has ten members, each of which has the same utility index, then it makes no difference in principle whether all ten of the members are made equally but moderately happy, or whether one of the members or any other fraction of the whole is given a disproportionate share of happiness, as long as the aggregate of happiness of the group remains unchanged. Serious forms of this anomaly rarely occur in reality. But utilitarianism cannot in principle have a rule of right distribution. All that the individuals may claim is an equal right to have their interests counted equally. But they cannot protest any distribution of utilities within a group on grounds of justice. The distribution need only maximize the aggregate utility. Singer, unfortunately, glosses over this and other difficulties in *Animal Liberation*; his style is a semi-popular appeal to "common sense" (Franklin 2005: 5–10).

Tom Regan, on the other hand, has developed a theory of rights for animals as individuals entitled to equal protection of their interests in his *The Case for Animal Rights* (1983). His approach to ethical issues is to begin from a pre-reflective moral intuition, which becomes a "considered belief" when it passes the test of being impartial, rational, cool, and broad in scope. The denial that "animals may be treated in any way we please" and the idea that "legitimate moral constraints apply to our treatment of them" are such considered beliefs and are found in "all serious writers."[2] Regan's next step, which is decisive theoretically, is to find a general moral principle that sustains this considered belief The first to be considered is the idea of "indirect duty" to animals, which holds that mistreatment of animals is wrong because it will encourage mistreatment of one's fellow humans. Regan quite properly finds this inadequate, because it regards the mistreatment of animals as a wrong done not to them but to humans. The carry-over to humans is no more than the transfer of a psychological state rather than recognition of a common duty. And, after refuting several other versions of indirect duty, Regan quite properly concludes that none supports or can support his considered belief. He then turns to consider the class of "direct duties" to animals.

The lone existing member of this class is utilitarianism, and Regan restates the usual criticisms in a very suggestive form. The utilitarian treats individuals as so many receptacles of pleasure and pain and then aggregates the contents of all of them, which is to deny any unique value to the receptacle itself. For Regan it is just the opposite. The individual "receptacles" are *loci* of subjectivity, each of which has equal

---

[2] Regan (1983) is technically speaking only of mammals of a year or more in age, since only these are "subjects-of-a-life" which can go well or ill for them. But he then includes fowl (1983: 349) and then any animal that can feel pain (1983: 366), and this is how most animal rights adherents proceed.

"inherent value." Whether the individual be a saint or a villain, an animal or a human, each of them owns, feels, and values its own life, for which there is no substitute. Of these lives one cannot say that one is more valuable than another, for that implies a hierarchy of lives in some order of perfection, which would yield the idea of slaves by nature as well as animals as food by nature. If, therefore, "perfectionist" distinctions are ruled out, and yet the subjectivity of animals has inherent value, how can recognition of equal rights be withheld? This is not to say that all animals must be treated in exactly the same way as human animals, but only that their relevant interests must be respected. Nor does it deny that human beings have a right of self-defense against animal as well as human aggression, albeit in a different way and with different remedies.

Hence Regan's vegetarianism, unlike Singer's, is absolute. And he is also absolute in rejecting any form of painful or disabling animal testing. Beyond noting how danger-ously misleading these tests can be, he reassures people alarmed at the prospect of halting them by citing alternatives to animal testing such as computer simulation, statistical analysis, and various forms of non-invasive testing. He also anticipates that abolition of animal testing will motivate a quicker pace in developing such alternatives. But, since fully adequate alternatives are unlikely to be found in the near future, at least some sacrifice on our part seems to be implicit in this position.

In his comment on animal rights in the environment, Regan is relentlessly individu-alistic. Thus he will not countenance killing an individual member of an abundant species to save one of a scarce and threatened species, if the former has more to lose by death. He refers to the "holism" of Aldo Leopold and other proponents of the "land ethic" as "environmental fascism" because it subordinates the individual to the whole. Yet such questions on the preservation of species and the right of human intervention are not so easily dismissed. Humans and animals have been in conflict over the control and use of nature since time immemorial, and even now control of the "wilderness" is indispensable for both. The rightness or wrongness of any particular human interven-tion or expansion should depend on whether it is needed to sustain a population large enough and comfortable enough to live a comfortable and cultivated existence—by which standard, the earth is presently overpopulated by humans and their numbers should be shrunk. The imperative is, therefore, conservation, which also justifies human intervention to preserve threatened species (Franklin 2005).

Finally, in his lifeboat case, now famous among friends of animals, Regan argues that, where a lifeboat is overloaded and in danger of sinking, a large dog among the passengers should be thrown overboard rather than any of the humans. This is because the dog has less to lose by death, its inherent value notwithstanding. Singer charges Regan with thus invoking considerations of utility in the last analysis—a charge that Regan denies on two related grounds. He argues, first, that the comparison of loss by death is confined to a class of emergencies like the lifeboat case in which everyone will be destroyed unless one or a few are given up. And he argues, second, that he does not aggregate utilities but rather compares individuals one on one, on which basis he would throw a million dogs overboard rather than a single human—the loss by death for each dog being less than for each human. There are other questions concerning the lifeboat case and its solution, but on this issue Regan seems to win his point (Franklin 2005).

Indeed, whatever the problem here or with his views on the environment, Regan's fundamental argument on inherent value and the right of animals seems basically correct. The only important weakness seems to be his point of departure—a "considered belief" that animals "count." That principle can be denied and often has been—on which account I have tried to find its equivalent in Kant's categorical imperative. This is not to reject the main point of *The Case for Animal Rights*. Regan himself indicates a bias toward a Kantian sense of right. My purpose simply has been to find a more fundamental basis for his "considered belief."

The first and, according to Kant, the basic form of the categorical imperative, The Formula of Universal Law, bids one to "act such that the maxim of thy will may be taken as a universal law by every rational being." Amongst other things, this rules out deliberate harming of innocent human individuals. But Kant, although personally humane, did not include animals in the protection against deliberate harm, which might follow from this and the other forms of the categorical imperative. He did not deny that animals had feelings, but for him they were technically "things," and thus was he all too easily led to leave the larger implications of his own basic rule for testing maxims unexplored. A proper test requires a perfectly general statement of the maxim to be tested—a maxim that does not include any exception designed to favor a particular individual or group. Any such reservation, explicit or implicit, would negate the maxim's universality. Thus "I will respect religious freedom for Jews and Christians" is an illicit maxim in implicitly excluding other faiths. "I can harm any animal I choose" is similarly unacceptable as a maxim, because, as it is usually understood, it contains an implicit exception for human animals. Kant's formula of universal law (FUL), as a test of maxims, is thus relevant for animals, but not in the sense that *they* are bound to observe universal law. All humans both are beneficiaries of the rule of universal law and are also bound to will it as a test of their maxims. Animals, on the other hand, are its beneficiaries only.[3]

The second and more famous form of the categorical imperative is "to treat humanity in ourselves as well as others never as a means only but also at the same time as an end." Since humans are intellectual beings, they have an absolute value for Kant and cannot be used simply as a means. Animals, on the other hand, have only a relative value as means, "and they are called things" because their existence is purely "natural." But, since the formula of humanity (FH) is a corollary of FUL, its scope is just as wide. If, as has been argued, FUL bans mistreatment of any sentient being, then it bans exploitation also. Hence animals, no less than humans, should never be treated as a means only. The second form of the categorical imperative should thus be rephrased accordingly as FS not FH. "Treat sentience in yourself as well as every other sentient being never as a means only but also at the same time as an end."

---

[3] Fruitarians would extend this protection to living vegetables as well.

The third and final form of the categorical imperative is the formula of the kingdom, or realm, of ends (FKE). "A will," says Kant, "that legislates universal law in all its maxims" leads "to another very fruitful concept . . . that of a kingdom of ends," which he then describes as "a whole of all ends in systematic connection." This idea has been variously interpreted. But, in view of what has been said about the first two formulae, no interpretation of FKE can be valid that does not include animals as members. Since animals are not subjective sources of universal law, they cannot legislate, but, since they are nonetheless entitled to treatment as ends, they are members of the whole and are entitled to full respect insofar as their ends and needs are consistent with general community. Thus interpreted, the categorical imperative lays a solid foundation for animal rights.

Christine M. Korsgaard, who professes allegiance to the Kantian tradition, also argues for animal rights in *The Sources of Normativity* (1996) and in "Fellow Creatures: Kantian Ethics and our Duties to Animals" (2004). But she turns sharply, and avowedly, away from Kant in her reading of the categorical imperative. She denies that the formula of universal law (FUL) is to be taken as the principle of moral law. It is rather a requirement laid on every individual to choose some rule or "law" according to the individual's conception of its "practical identity." The categorical imperative on this interpretation is neither moral nor immoral, neither good nor bad. What Korsgaard calls "the moral law" is instead derived directly from the Kingdom of Ends, independently of the Formula of Universal Law. "The moral law," she holds, "tells us to act only on maxims that all rational beings could agree to act on together in a workable cooperative system" (Korsgaard 1996: 99). Although humans alone are the legislators in this system, animals (meaning non-rational sentient beings) will be included as "passive citizens" (Korsgaard 2004: 26). They, no less than humans, will be able to pursue their "natural goods" or life satisfactions, which Korsgaard understands in a loosely Aristotelian sense.

This move from the primacy of FUL to the primacy of FKE seems to remove any trace of obligation in Kant's moral theory. Building the "workable cooperative system" is not something we must or "ought" to do, Korsgaard's vague allusions left aside, but rather something that might make life better for most sentient beings if we agreed to construct it. Since Korsgaard defines no *summum bonum* as the inner and ultimate goal of all sentients, or even of humans only, there is no unifying final end that requires all sentients to seek the "kingdom." The categorical imperative, as she now interprets it, does not help here. Reduced to a principle for choosing a personal identity, it applies to the warlike as well as the peace-loving.

There are now a number of Judeo-Christian theologians who also move toward animal rights. But few of these commentators are able to overcome the formidable obstacle of the gift to Noah in Genesis 9:2–4, which specifically allows humanity to eat animal flesh. In *On God and Dogs* (1988), Stephen Webb argues that the love of a "cosmic Christ" introduces a new age of full respect. But two influential commentators, Karl Barth and Abraham Kook, see a "utopian danger" in attempts to realize in the present era God's promise of complete reconciliation of humans and animals in some final end. Most theologians admit consumption of animal flesh as a last resort;[4] they usually pass over experimentation on animals; they rarely mention biological engineering of animals to create better objects of research. To my knowledge, Andrew Linzey is the one great exception to this reticence on engineering in mainstream theology. But I am not sure that Linzey or any other Christian theologian, in moving toward vegetarianism, can get past the fact that Jesus is reported to eat fish in the Gospels and very likely tasted meat as well.

Finally, process theology, or metaphysics, as developed by Charles Hartshorne out of Whitehead, would endow all natural objects with feeling, and would understand God not as a person but as an endless series of ever more complex attempts to bring all of nature into organic harmony. Sentient beings, and humans especially, are and always remain free to resist as well as follow any organic design, which means that the process has no end. Humans have the largest latitude of choice between following and resisting, between vice and virtue. Yet human responsiveness to God's "lure" does not give salvation in any usual sense, but only deeper insight into one's fellow humans and one's fellow creatures (Dombrowski 1988).

There are two main divisions within the overall movement on behalf of animals. One, already mentioned, is the caution of old line organizations versus the militancy of some of the new ones like PETA. The other, overlapping, conflict is between welfarism with limited ends and complete abolition of the property status of animals; this latter position is held by a minority of theorists led by Gary L. Francione. Welfarists press for anti-cruelty legislation within the juridical status quo; abolitionists disdain and even decry that approach, contending that animal protective statutes are almost always loose, and that district attorneys, courts, and regulatory agencies will always interpret them in the light of the interest, not of the animals, but of their owners. Indeed, much anti-cruelty legislation is said to be not merely useless but counter-productive, because it leads decent people generally to believe that all is well. Thus the decision of McDonald's or of Whole Foods to impose humane standards of slaughter on those who supply their meat serves only to reassure the doubting carnivore—and even more so because moves like this have gained support from an impressive list of animal welfare organizations, including PETA. The anti-cruelty of these groups, wrote Francione, is *Rain without Thunder* so long as animals continue to be property. The most that he would endorse are measures that actually detract from the right of property, like prohibition of cages for hens and crates for calves (Francione 1996a).

By way of reply, Robert Garner concedes that abolition has the high ground philosophically, but argues that tolerance of cruelty is not directly generated by the property status of animals; rather it arises more fundamentally from the moral and cultural level of the society. The UK, where the institution of property is as strong as in the USA, is far ahead in effective animal protection, which, far from being

[4] There is also an ingenious rabbinical opinion that rules out the meat of all animals raised on factory farms. Such meat cannot be kosher, since a basic rule of kosher slaughtering is to minimize animal pain.

counter-productive, has generated ever increasing public support for animal protection. PETA claims that there are a million new vegetarians each year and that one-quarter of college students want access to vegan foods. There are signs of judicial support for animal interests as well. When McDonald's brought a libel suit in the UK against pamphleteers charging it with cruelty, the court found for the defendants, going beyond the standard deference to how farm animals are normally treated to investigate and condemn things that actually happen on farms. This "welfarist" decision in the "McLibel" case is big with possibilities, attempts to belittle it notwithstanding. And, even more recently, the high court of Israel has banned *pâté de foie gras*, expressly rejecting the claim that it was justified by traditional farming practice.

Although I am personally committed to abolition, I do not see why pursuit of that goal need be incompatible with measures against cruelty. Abolition of meat and of harmful testing can hardly be expected in a near future, and the right kind of welfarism can help shorten the wait. Campaigns to limit testing, to buy only free-range eggs, to eat no veal, to abolish the crating of pregnant sows, to permit civil suits to stop cruel practices—all such efforts not only bring a measure of blessed relief to animals in the present; they also serve to raise consciousness in the public of how animals are made to suffer, which may produce still further movement in the future. Nevertheless, abolition ought to be the final goal, and those who support reforms in the present should clearly state that abolition is their ultimate objective.

References

Extended Histories

Finsen, Lawrence, and Finsen, Susan (1994). *The Animal Rights Movement in America*. New York: Twayne.

Spencer, Colin (2000). *Vegetarianism: A History*. London: Grub Street.

Stuart, Tristram (2006). *The Bloodless Revolution*, New York: W. W. Norton.

Ancient World

Dombrowski, Daniel A. (1984). *The Philosophy of Vegetarianism*. Amherst, MA: University of Massachusetts Press.

Dombrowski, Daniel A. (1988). *Hartshorne and the Metaphysics of Animal Rights*. Albany, NY: State University of New York Press.

Newmyer, Stephen T. (2006). *Animals, Rights and Reason in Plutarch and Modern Ethics*. New York and London: Routledge.

Porphyry (2000). *On Abstinence from Killing Animals*, trans. Gillian Clark. Ithaca, NY: Cornell University Press.

Sorabji, Richard (1993). *Animal Minds and Human Morals*. Ithaca, NY: Cornell University Press.

Religious Traditions

AKERS, KEITH (2000). *The Lost Religion of Jesus*. New York: Lantern Books.

AQUINAS, ST THOMAS (1924). *The Summa contra Gentiles*, trans. English Dominican Fathers. London: Burns, Gates and Washburn.

AQUINAS, THOMAS (1975). *Summa Theologiae*, trans. R. J. Batten O. P. London: Blackfriars,

AUGUSTINE, ST (1966). "The Catholic and the Manichean Ways of Life," in *The Fathers of the Church*, trans. Donald A. Gallagher and Idella J. Gallagher, vol. 56. Washington: Catholic University Press.

BARTH, KARL (1961). *Church Dogmatics*, eds G. W. Bromley and T. E. Torrance. Edinburgh: T&T Clark.

KALECHOFSKY, ROBERTA (1992) ed. *Judaism and Animal Rights*. Marblehead, MA: Micah Publications.

KOOK, ABRAHAM (1978). *Abraham Isaac Kook*, trans. Ben Zion Bokser. New York: Paulist Press.

LAGELUND, HENRIK (2004). "John Buridan and the Problems of Dualism in the Early Fourteenth Century," *Journal of the History of Philosophy*, 42/4: 369–87.

LINZEY, ANDREW (1995). *Animal Theology*. Urbana, IL: University of Illinois Press.

PRIMATT, HUMPHRY (1776). *Dissertation on the Duty of Mercy and the Sin of Cruelty to Brute Animals*. London: T. Constable.

SCHWARTZ, RICHARD H. (2001). *Judaism and Vegetarianism*. New York: Lantern Books.

WEBB, STEPHEN (1988). *On God and Dogs*. Oxford: Oxford University Press.

WESLEY, JOHN (1990). "The General Deliverance," in Andrew Linzeyand Tom Regan eds, *Animals and Christianity*. New York: Crossroad.

Secular Modern Sources

BENTHAM, JEREMY (1948). *The Principles of Morals and Legislation*. New York: Hafner.

FRANCIONE, GARY L. (1996a). *Rain without Thunder*. Philadelphia: Temple University Press.

FRANCIONE, GARY L. (1996b). "Animal Rights and Animal Welfare," *Rutgers Law Review*, 48/2 (Winter), 397–469.

FRANKLIN, JULIAN H. (2005). *Animal Rights and Moral Philosophy*. New York: Columbia University Press.

FRANKLIN, JULIAN H. (2007). "Killing and Replacing Animals," *Journal of Animal Law and Ethics*, 2 (May), 77–89.

GARNER, ROBERT (2004). *Animals, Politics, and Morality*. Manchester: Manchester University Press, 2004.

KANT, IMMANUEL (1993). *Grounding for the Metaphysics of Morals*, trans. James W. Ellington. Indianapollis: Hackett.

KORSGAARD, CHRISTINE M. (1996). *The Sources of Normativity*. Cambridge: Cambridge University Press.

KORSGAARD, CHRISTINE M. (2004). "Fellow Creatures: Kantian Ethics and our Duties to Animals," Tanner Lecture.

PUFENDORF, SAMUEL (1991). *On the Duty of Man and Citizen*, trans. Michael Silverthorne. Cambridge: Cambridge University Press.

REGAN, TOM (1983). *The Case for Animal Rights*. Berkeley and Los Angeles: University of California Press.

SALT, HENRY S. (1980). *Animals' Rights*. Clarks Summit, PA: Society for Animal Rights.

SINGER, PETER (1999). *Practical Ethics* 2nd edn. Cambridge: Cambridge University Press.

SINGER, PETER (2002). *Animal Liberation*. New York: Ecco.

SULLIVAN, MARIANN, and WOLFSON, DAVID (2007). "What's Good for the Goose . . . The Israeli Supreme Court, Foie Gras, and the Future of Farmed Animals in the United States," *Law and Contemporary Problems*, 70 (Winter), 139–73.

PART IV

NON-WESTERN PERSPECTIVES

CHAPTER 48

CONFUCIAN POLITICAL PHILOSOPHY

DAVID WONG

CONFUCIANISM is above all an ethics, and as an ethics it is tied intimately with political philosophy. A. C. Graham (1989) describes the crucial period in the classical age as one of fundamental change and uncertainty, one in which the established social and political order was breaking down. Each philosophy responded by offering a diagnosis and a cure—a *dao* (way or path) out of the turmoil. Confucius (551–479 BCE), as Kongzi or Master Kong came to be known later in the West, diagnosed the problem as breakdown in the moral authority of rulers. According to the text that is the most reliable guide to the teachings of Confucius, the *Analects* (*Lunyu*), Confucius took the Mandate of Heaven (*tianming*) as a guide (*Analects* 2.4, 3.13, 16.8). The Mandate was formulated during the early period of the Zhou dynasty (the "Western" Zhou period, 1122–771 BCE) to justify the overthrow of the Shang dynasty and to legitimate the rule of the Zhou kings. The doctrine holds that the last Shang kings lost their authority to rule because of their corruption and wickedness, while the early Zhou kings gained authority through their virtue. The later Eastern Zhou period (770–221 BCE) saw rule by Zhou kings in name only and increasing conflict and intrigue within and between Chinese states. The Confucian diagnosis of China's troubles suggests that the way out of the turmoil required a moral transformation led by the top ranks of Chinese society, a *return* to the virtue of the early Zhou kings.

RULING THROUGH VIRTUE

In *Analects* 2.3 Confucius says that leading people through coercive regulations and punishment will only make them evasive, while leading them with virtue and keeping them in line with ritual will enable them to have a sense of shame, and they will rectify themselves (for translations, see Ames and Rosemont 1998: 76; Slingerland 2003: 8). The word translated here as "virtue"—*de*—has the connotations of "power" and "excellence." An informative gloss on the Chinese term is "moral charisma." *De* as moral excellence has the power to draw people toward it and to influence them in morally appropriate ways (*Analects* 2.1, 2.21, 12.17, 13.6, 13.13, 15.5). Moral charisma is associated with the ideal of the *junzi*, most frequently translated as "gentleman" (e.g. Lau 1979; Waley 1989; Slingerland 2003), but "exemplary person" (Ames and Rosemont 1998) may be less misleading, given contemporary sensibilities. Among the virtues connected to this ideal are filial piety, a respect for and dedication to the performance of traditional ritual forms of conduct, and the ability to judge the right thing to do in the given situation.

The *junzi* is equated with the person who is *ren*. The concept of *ren* originally referred to the strong and handsome appearance of an aristocrat. But in the *Analects* the concept is of a moral excellence, and it may have been Confucius' central creative achievement to make the central focus of an ethics a kind of moral nobility that is achievable by anyone regardless of bloodline. *Ren* often appears to have the meaning of complete or comprehensive moral excellence, lacking no particular virtue but having them all. I will here use "goodness" to refer to the comprehensive Confucian virtue. *Ren* in some places in the *Analects* is treated as one virtue among others such as wisdom or courage. In the narrower sense of being one virtue among others, it is explained in 12.22 in terms of caring for others, and accordingly I will here use "caring" to refer to *ren* as one virtue among others.

THE ROLE OF RITUAL IN THE CULTIVATION OF GOODNESS

One of the most distinctive marks of Confucian ethics is the centrality it accords to ritual performance in the ethical cultivation of virtuous character and especially of *ren* as goodness. In the *Analects*, *li* includes ceremonies of ancestor worship, the burial of parents, and the rules governing respectful and appropriate behavior between parents and children. Later the word came to cover a broad range of customs and practices that spelled out courteous and respectful behavior of many different kinds. On a Confucian view, any complete description of self-cultivation toward the ideal of the exemplary person must include the assiduous performance of ritual. By providing conventionally established, symbolic ways to express respect for others, ritual forms give participants ways to act on and therefore to strengthen their dispositions to have respect for others.

The conventional ritual forms are regarded as a necessary language for expressing respect. While there are non-conventional dimensions of what it is to show respect such as providing one's parents with food (*Analects* 2.7), the particular way one provides food to parents will be deeply influenced by customs that specify what is a respectful way of serving food. On the Confucian view, doing so in a graceful and whole-hearted fashion as spelled out by the customs of one's community is part of what it is to fulfill one's humanity. In the everyday processes of moral socialization, children learn what their behavior means to others, and what it should mean, by learning how to greet others, to make and answer requests, and to serve others, all in a respectful manner.

These reasons lying behind the emphasis on ritual in Confucianism—the import-ance of certain kinds of custom in cultivating moral attitudes and in providing a language for their expression, and the aesthetic value of graceful and emotionally resonant human interaction according to custom—help to explain why Confucianism is regarded by not a few to offer a significant alternative to Anglo-American moral and political philosophy as it is usually practiced these days (e.g. Fingarette 1972; Hall and Ames 1987; Rosemont 1991; Cua 2002). Confucian ethics provides an alternative to understanding the nature of the moral life that is different from an understanding that is based primarily on abstract principles, even abstract principles that require respect for each person. This is why there is significant resonance between Confucianism and communitarian philosophies such as those defended by Alasdair MacIntyre (1984, 1989) and Michael Walzer (1983). One of the distinctive marks of communitarianism is the theme that much of the substance of a morality is given, not in abstract principles of the sort typically defended in modern Western philosophy but in a society's specific customs and practices.

Some have objected to the importance Confucianism places on tradition, pointing out the problems of justifying any particular tradition in light of internal change within a tradition or given alternative traditions. Hansen (1992) has pointed out the pivotal role of Mozi and his followers in pressing this kind of criticism against Confucianism. Mozi (probably fifth century BCE) argued that tradition does not hold normative authority simply because it is tradition, since there was a time when it was not tradition but new (*Mozi*, ch. 39; see Watson 1967 for a translation). As an alternative to reliance on tradition, Mohism emphasizes the criterion of promoting benefit and avoiding harm as the standard for judging which traditions to keep and which to discard. For example, Mohists argued against elaborate and expensive burial rituals on the grounds that they amounted to burying resources that could be used to feed and clothe people (*Mozi*, chs 25, 32).

It is eminently arguable that the Confucianism represented by the *Analects* is fundamentally conservative in spirit. The Confucius of this text presents his ethical insights as derived from the early Zhou culture, and part of what makes it great, in his view, is that it built on the past traditions, taking what was best from the past (2.23, 3.9). However, this last point illustrates how a conservative orientation is compatible with a critical perspective toward one's tradition. One does not simply absorb one's tradition wholesale (see A. Chan 2000). Sometimes fundamental change is accomplished by reinterpretation of values such as the change in the meanings of *junzi* and *ren* that is reflected in the *Analects*. It is consistent with the conservative orientation of the *Analects* to apply Neurath's point about scientific language to the project of revising tradition: that we are like sailors who have to reconstruct their ship on the open sea but are never able to start afresh from the very beginning (Neurath 1959: 201). With all that said, however, critics of Confucian conservatism could still complain that reform in a conservative framework will not work if the ship is structurally unsound. The Mohists pressed this kind of criticism with respect to the arena of conflicts between loyalty to those with whom one has a special relationship and allegiance to impartial public justice and concern for all.

MOZI AND MENCIUS IN THE DEBATE OVER FILIAL LOYALTY VERSUS IMPARTIAL CONCERN

Along with the emphasis on *li*, the centrality of filial piety is one of the most distinctive characteristics of Confucian ethics. Filial piety requires that one serve and protect parents' interests. Upon being told of a son turning in his father to the authorities for stealing a sheep, Confucius responds that uprightness is found in sons and fathers covering up for each other (*Analects* 13.18). In this case, at least, loyalty to parents or to children takes precedence over loyalty to ruler or to public justice. This precedence is one implication of the Confucian doctrine of care with distinctions ("love with distinctions" is one translation, but perhaps "care with distinctions" is less misleading because it covers both the emotionally freighted attitude toward kin and a more distanced attitude toward strangers). Though all people are owed moral concern, some are owed more than others, according to the agent's relationship to them.

Mozi, as far we know, never commented on the sheep-stealing story, but he might well have taken it as an example of what was wrong with Chinese society. Mozi rejects partiality toward one's own (oneself, one's family, one's state) as the root of all destructive conflict (*Mozi*, ch. 16). To counter partiality, he advocates the doctrine of *jianai*—care for all. "Care for all" apparently means equal care, but practical discussions of how people are to behave in the *Mozi* seem to fall far short of requiring equal *treatment* of everyone, but rather to require that one interact with others in mutually beneficial ways and to be ready to contribute something to the basic material needs of those with whom one comes into contact, especially those with no family to care for them. One possible way to resolve this tension within the Mohist position is to require equal *care* as an ethical attitude but to recognize that equal *treatment* of everyone by each individual agent is practically impossible. On this construal, the normative bite of requiring equal care is not as a principle guiding the action of individual agents but as a principle requiring that social and political practices and institutions be structured so as to result in something like equal benefit for all. The ruler in particular may be charged with promoting this aim.

The substantial following that Mohism gained during the classical period forced a response from Confucians. They had to respond to two questions. First, what is required by way of concern for all people and how is such concern to be reconciled with the greater concern for one's own that the doctrine of care with distinctions requires? Second, what kinds of concern are motivationally possible for human beings? Mengzi, or, as he is known in the West under his Latinized name, Mencius (fourth century BCE), took up the defense of Confucianism against Mohism. In the text purporting to be a record of his teachings (see Lau 1970 for a translation), he explicitly sets himself to the task of defending Confucianism not only against Mohism but against the teachings of Yang Zhu (fifth to fourth centuries BCE). Mencius portrays Yang's teachings as sitting on the opposite end of the spectrum from Mohism (there is no surviving text purporting to articulate and defend Yangism). According to Mencius' characterization, Yang Zhu criticized both Mohism and Confucianism for asking people to sacrifice themselves for others. Yang Zhu on this view was an ethical egoist—that is, one who holds that it is always right to promote one's own welfare. Mencius positioned Confucianism as occupying the correct mean between the extremes of having concern only for oneself, on the one hand, and having an equal degree of concern for everyone.

Part of the Mencian argument rests on the idea that the sort of natural compassion that is the root of caring for strangers develops first and in its most compelling form in relation to family members. "Compelling" here means not only "psychologically compelling" but also involving the recognition that one has the most reason to care for one's family. Children owe their lives and nurture to parents, and parents are specially responsible for those they bring into the world. However, probably in response to Mohist criticism, the Mencius text does frequently recognize that we have and ought to feel compassion for people outside the family. Mencius famously declares that we all respond to a child about to fall into the well with alarm and distress, and it does not matter whose child it is (*Mencius* 1A6).

According to the Mencian theory of the original goodness of human nature, we are all born with the beginnings or sprouts (*duan*) of goodness, feelings and intuitive perceptions of actions as appropriately deferential or respectful, right, or shameful. We have a natural compassion that comes out in spontaneous responses such as the adults' alarm at the child about to fall into a well. The Mencian response to (what is characterized) as the Yangist position that it is against nature to extend ourselves on behalf of others is that it is in our nature to feel for and to judge the rightness of extending ourselves. The Mencian response to the Mohists (as their position is characterized by Mencius) is that, while care is owed to all, one does not owe equal care to everyone in *all* situations. In dialogue with a Mohist (3A5), Mencius asserts that the case of the child about to fall into the well has a special feature that makes it relevant to treat it as one would any child. That special feature seems to be innocence. The Mencian position is premised on the principle that it is right to treat all people alike only when the ways they are alike are the most ethically relevant features of the situation. Mencius believes that, in many instances, the presence or absence of a family relationship to a person is the most relevant feature (in deciding which children to give gifts, the fact that one child is one's elder brother's son and the other child is one's neighbor's child may be the most relevant feature).

Two issues arise from this response to Mohism. One issue is whether Mencius has sufficient warrant to trust the kinds of intuitive judgments he attributes to human nature. Mencius holds that Heaven implants in human beings the beginnings of morality, but, in the absence of such a metaphysical warrant, can these intuitive judgments be accepted, particularly the ones that underwrite care with distinctions? Doubt about the metaphysical warrant may not doom Mencius' response to Mohism, however, if one holds that all normative theories ultimately depend on intuitive judgments (even theories based on the idea of promoting benefits and avoiding harms) and if one has no good reason to be skeptical about these judgments. Thus one might hold that, whether or not there is a metaphysical warrant, there is a great deal of plausibility to the intuitive judgment about owing parents more concern because they are the source of one's life (in the case of biological parents) and nurturance. Of course, one might also hold, as Mencius appears to hold, that people are owed concern in virtue of their being human, and the possibility for conflict of duties arises from these different sources of concern.

The second issue is how the Mencian text deals with conflicts of the sort exemplified by the sheep-stealing case in the *Analects*. The text contains themes embodying the theme of filial loyalty, and, as in the *Analects*, such loyalty takes precedence over public justice. *Mencius* 7A35 tells a story about the sage-king Shun that illustrates this theme. Because Shun was renowned for his filial piety, Mencius is asked what Shun would have done if his father had killed a man. Mencius replies that Shun could not stop the judge from apprehending his father, because the judge had the legal authority to act. But then, Mencius says, Shun would have abdicated and fled with his father to the edge of the sea. *Mencius* 5A2 and 5A3 describe the way that Shun dealt with his half-brother Xiang's conspiring with his father and stepmother to kill him. He enfeoffed Xiang, because all he could do as a brother is to love him. At the same time, the fiefdom he awarded his brother was far away from the seat of the throne, and Shun appointed officials to administer the fief and to collect taxes and tributes, to protect the people of Youbi from Xiang's potentially abusive ruling. That is why some called Shun's act a banishment of Xiang. The Shun stories in the *Mencius* exhibit a complexity that differentiates them from the story of the sheep-stealing cover-up in the *Analects*. Though filial loyalty is clearly given a priority in each story, there is in Shun's actions an acknowledgment of the other value that comes into conflict with filial loyalty. Though Shun ultimately gives priority to filial loyalty in the case of his father, his first action acknowledges the value of public justice by declining to interfere with the judge while he is king. While Shun declines to punish his half-brother, he protects both himself and the people of Xiang's new fiefdom.

These Shun stories illustrate that an agent's response to a situation in which important values come into conflict need not be a strict choice between honoring one value and wholly denying the other. While some sort of priority might have to be set in the end, there are also ways to acknowledge the value that is subordinated, but how exactly that is to be done seems very much a matter of judgment in the particular situation at hand. The Shun stories are an expression of the Confucian theme that rightness cannot be judged on the basis of exceptionless general principles but is a matter of judgment in the particular situation.

FAMILY AS THE PARADIGM IN A RELATIONAL AND COMMUNAL CONCEPTION OF POLITICAL SOCIETY

In responding to Mozi's criticism that those who are partial to their own will take care only of their own, the Mencian text exemplifies an enduring theme in the Confucian tradition: the modeling of political society after the family. The ideal Confucian ruler will take care of the people because he is the "father and mother to the people" (*Mencius* 1A7). As parent to the people, he will ensure that they have means sufficient to support their own parents, wives, and children, that they will always have sufficient food in good years and in bad years enough to escape starvation. If they do not have such means, all their energy will be focused on survival, and they will have no time to spare for learning about ritual and what is morally appropriate. To fail to provide sufficient means but to punish the people when they run afoul of the law is to set a trap for them (1A7). The modeling of political society after the family defines the way that Confucian political philosophy is relational and communal in character. Members of that society are not conceived as having a moral status independent of their relationship to each other. They are not conceived as having a default status as independent, unencumbered agents whose political obligations must then be justified. Members of political society are conceived as belonging together as members of a family belong together: it is a matter of the natural and healthy course of human development. The idea that one belongs to oneself alone does not have a home in the Confucian tradition. One's body is a gift from one's parents, to be cared for as a debt of gratitude to them.

It is often said that the Confucian tradition subordinates the individual to the group and that it fails to recognize the value of individual autonomy, but this characterization overlooks important distinctions. The value of individual autonomy usually includes several different dimensions that do not necessarily accompany one another: (1) prioritizing individual interests over group or collective interests when these conflict; (2) giving moral permission to the individual to choose from a significantly wide range (within certain moral boundaries) of ways to live; and (3) emphasizing the importance of living according to one's own understanding of what is right and good even if others do not see it the same way.

Confucian ethics in significant part, though not in all parts, accepts autonomy in the sense of (3) (see Shun 2004). Confucius is often depicted in the *Analects* as emphasizing the importance of cultivating one's own character, even when others do not recognize or appreciate one's efforts (e.g. *Analects* 4.14) and of acting independently of what is conventionally approved or disapproved (e.g. 5.1). Mencius and Xunzi (fourth and third centuries BCE), the most pivotal thinkers in the classical Confucian tradition after Confucius, both articulate the necessity to speak up when one believes the ruler one is serving is on a wrong course of action (e.g. *Mencius* 1A3; *Xunzi* 29.2; see Knoblock 1988–94 for a translation of the *Xunzi*). On the other hand, none of these classical thinkers argues for the necessity of protecting a frank subordinate from a ruler who is made angry by criticism, and it could be argued that Confucianism does not fully endorse autonomy in sense (3) because it fails to endorse such protection for those who wish to engage in moral criticism of the powerful.

Most interpretations present Confucian ethics as rejecting (2). There is a way for human beings to live, a comprehensive human good to be realized, and there can be no choosing between significantly different ways of life that are equally acceptable from a moral perspective (for an important exception to this kind of interpretation, see Hall and Ames 1987, who construe Confucius' *dao* as a human invention, collective and individual). On the other hand, Confucian ethics de-emphasizes legal coercion as a method for guiding people along the way and instead emphasizes moral exhortation and inspiration by way of virtuous example. While Confucians might believe in a single correct way for human beings, they might endorse a significant degree of latitude for people to learn from their own mistakes and by way of example from others (see J. Chan 1999, 2000).

Confucian ethics does not accept (1), but not because it holds in the subordination of individual interests to group or collective interests (for criticism of the rather common view that Confucianism subordinates the individual to the group, see Hall and Ames 1998). Rather, there is a different conception of the relationship between individual and group interests. The best illustration of this different conception is a story to be found in the *Mencius* that concerns sage-king Shun. When Shun wanted to marry, he knew that his father, influenced by his stepmother, would not allow him to marry. In this difficult situation, Shun decided to marry without telling his father, even though he was renowned for his filial piety. Mencius in fact defends the filiality of Shun's act in *Mencius* 5A2. He observes that Shun knew that he would not have been allowed to marry if he told his father. This would have resulted in bitterness toward his parents, and that is why he did not tell them. The implication of this version of Shun's reason is that filiality means preserving an emotionally viable relationship with one's parents, and in the case at hand Shun judged that it would have been worse for the relationship to have asked permission to marry. The conception of the relation between individual and group interests embodied in this story is not one of subordination of one to the other but is rather about the mutual dependence between the individual and the group. Shun's welfare depends on his family and therefore he must make his family's interests part of his own (he resolves to do what is necessary to preserve his relationship to his parents), but his family's welfare depends on Shun, and therefore his interests do constitute part of its welfare (the family should recognize that it is damaging itself in requiring Shun to deny himself the most part important of human relationships).

Debate over the Goodness or Badness of Human Nature and its Relation to Morality

Xunzi explicitly opposes Mencius' position on the goodness of human nature. Rather than being originally good, human beings start out with a love of profit, and with feelings of envy and hatred. Recognizing the destructive conflict caused by the unrestrained pursuit of natural desires, the sage-kings invented ritual principles and precepts of moral duty to reform human nature and guide it in the proper channels so as to be consistent with the *dao*. Reshaping our nature through morality makes possible the kind of cooperation that produces an abundance of resources in favorable times for the satisfaction of reasonable desires and minimizes suffering and frustration in unfavorable times. Xunzi's theory of the relation between human nature and morality suggests a different response to the Mohist critique of Confucian traditionalism: rather than appealing to Mencian sprouts of morality imparted by Heaven and construing morality as part of Heaven's order, Xunzi asserts that the content of morality is *constructed* by especially wise human beings in response to the problems created by our own natures. Xunzi presents a functional conception of morality (not unlike the one Hobbes was to formulate considerably later), according to which it is invented to harmonize the interests of individuals and to constrain and transform the heedless pursuit of short-term gratification for the sake of promoting the long-term interests of the individual and the group. Ritual principles and moral precepts are invented to accomplish such a function, and human nature constrains which of the possible principles and precepts are better or worse for accomplishing that function.

Xunzi's functional theory of morality bears added interest for those exploring the possibilities of a naturalistic approach to morality. Xunzi rejects a conception of morality as part of the natural grain of things imparted by *tian*. His conception of *tian* is in some respects closer to nature—an order-giving force in the cosmos that seems neutral to whatever human beings have come to regard as right and good. Xunzi stresses that *tian* operates according to patterns that remain constant, no matter what human beings do or whether they appeal to it for good fortune (Xunzi, ch. 17). It is the proper task of human beings to understand what these patterns are in order to take advantage of them (for example, so that they may know to plow in the spring, weed in the summer, harvest in the fall, and store in the winter).

CONFUCIANISM PERFECTIONISM AND TWO MEANINGS OF HARMONY AS A CONFUCIAN VALUE

Because Confucian political philosophy is centered on a deeply relational conception of how to live, it qualifies as a perfectionist political philosophy: the life of fulfilling relationship is to be promoted for members of political society. On the face of it, the relational conception leaves little room for a Rawlsian "reasonable pluralism" in conceptions of the good life (Rawls 1971, 1996). However, the Confucian doctrine that coercive regulations and punishment will only make the people evasive and not confer on them a sense of shame prevents any automatic inference from Confucian perfectionism to coercive interventions into the lives of individuals and their families. It may be more consistent for Confucians to promote their conception of the good life through education and positive incentives designed to enable people to live according to that conception (J. Chan 1999, 2000).

Furthermore, while it is in the spirit of Confucianism to regarded disagreement over conceptions of the good life as undesirable and to be avoided if possible, realism about the inevitability of disagreement may prompt Confucians to urge reconciliation between disagreeing parties rather than eliminating disagreement altogether. Antonio Cua, in presenting his interpretation of the Confucian virtue of *ren*, suggests that the virtue involves an orientation toward human conflicts aimed at the reconciliation of the contending parties by repairing the rupture of human relationship rather than by deciding who is right and who is wrong, and accordingly attempts to shape the expectations of the contending parties along the line of mutual concern, to get them to appreciate one another as interacting members in a community (Cua 1989).

This leads to the important value of *he* or harmony. Harmony is the value that promotes reconciliation and congruence between the individual's interests, the interests of others, and the group's common projects (ends that members are striving to achieve qua members of that group). Consider *Analects* 13.23: "The exemplary person seeks harmony rather than agreement; the small person does the opposite." What does harmony mean if not agreement? In the *Zuo Commentary to the Spring and Autumn Annals*, harmony is compared to making porridge. The cook blends the various ingredients harmoniously to achieve the appropriate flavor. When it is too bland, the cook adds flavoring. When it is too concentrated, he dilutes it with water. In the relationship between ruler and minister, harmony requires analogous adjustments. When the ruler considers something right and yet there is something wrong about it, the minister should point out what is wrong as a way of achieving what is right. For a minister to say that whatever the ruler says is right is like seasoning water with water. This, it is said, is the inadequacy of "agreement" (Ames and Rosemont 1998: 254–5).

One implication of these passages is the necessity for an airing of divergent views so as to maximize chances for identifying the best, most well-founded view. The reference to the blending of ingredients and things accommodating each other on equal terms suggests something in addition to the need for debate and a diversity of views. Harmony requires the mutual willingness of the parties concerned to adjust their *interests* to those of the others. The story of sage-king Shun's marriage, told earlier, suggests not only that the interests of individuals and of their groups are interdependent, but also that the process of adjusting these interests to one another is a dynamic process accomplished in different ways. One may negotiate compromises between conflicting interests. One may need to assert one's interests and ask that others adjust, as Shun did in marrying without telling his parents, but at other times yield to others. Further, the history of who has asserted and who has yielded is relevant to the present decision.

Xia Yong (1992) expresses a related theme in differentiating between harmony and unity. Harmony, he says, is a proper balance between separation and connection. He believes that the West has overdeveloped separation in the form of competition and conflict, whereas China has erred in the direction of too much connection. To illustrate the kind of harmony that is compatible with the recognition and acceptance of a degree of separation, Stephen Angle (2002: 231–2) asks us to imagine a married couple, each partner with a career. What they need to do for success in their respective careers puts a strain on their family life. The ideal of unity might require something like the entire family placing a priority on either the husband's or the wife's career. When the husband gets a good job offer in another city, for example, there is no question as to what ought to be done. However, the ideal of harmony would rely less on the idea of there being a fixed priority upon which everyone agrees in advance, but rather on balancing, negotiation, tweaking, and cajoling. Suppose the wife gets an especially compelling offer, but, rather than simply deciding to move the family solely on the grounds of her career, the couple may work very hard at finding him a good opportunity in the new city, and decide to move only after they have found such an opportunity. Or another way of negotiating may be "taking turns."

This interpretation of the ideal of harmony fits with the Confucian theme that human beings are profoundly social beings. It means that our identities, our senses of who we are, are bound up with our social roles and our relationships with particular people, and it also means that our sense of what our legitimate interests are is bound up with our judgments about what is needed to sustain our most important relationships. The husband and wife in Angle's example have interests in their own respective careers, but they also have interests in the flourishing of each other's careers, and they have interests in their relationship and their family life that influence their senses of how far their career interests can go and still be legitimate. The "harmonization" of each partner's interest in a career would involve weaving it into the nexus of all the other interests that matter to the family members.

Alongside the interpretation of harmony that aims for the mutual accommodation of potentially conflicting interests possessed by different members of the community, there is another interpretation that stresses and aims at agreement on the *right* way to combine interests. In Xia Yong's terms, the tilt in this conception of harmony is toward unity. This emphasis on harmony as unity is often tied to the need for a government with absolute or near absolute power. For example, while Xunzi emphasized the need for moral autonomy on the part of ministers in their speaking truth to power, he did not endorse institutionalized protection for ministers who displeased their rulers by speaking truth. Neo-Confucians such as Zhu Xi (1130–1200 CE) sought to utilize private academies as an institutional mechanism outside state officialdom to promote social and political reform. But their strategy was to influence rulers and not to constitute the academies as a separate realm of action distinct from state action. It was morally imperative to work within the parameters of officially sanctioned ideology until this ideology clearly failed (Lee 1994). The worry is that, when it fails, that is the time when it is most likely that dissent and honest speech will get crushed.

A Confucian harmony that is kept separate from unity depends on fostering a sense of willingness to interpret and adjust one's interests in light of one's interests in relationships with others in political society. Ritual plays a key role in such fostering. In *Analects* 1:12, Master You said that, when practicing the ritual, what matters most is harmony. Yet harmony cannot be sought for its own sake, but must always be subordinated to the ritual. One reason why harmony cannot be sought for its own sake is that aiming directly at harmony lacks the power of summoning forth attitudes that may be shaped into mutual respect between the participants. At the same time that sacrifice to ancestors and the burial of parents train and focus attitudes of reverence, gratitude, and grief, they also foster a common bond between the living participants, a sense of community that is rooted in the past and stretches onward into the future (see Bell 2008 for an argument that rituals in East Asian societies continue to fulfill this function and may even help to reduce inequality in income and wealth by satisfying the need to differentiate oneself from others through the social status marked by hierarchical rituals rather than having more material possessions and wealth).

Another reason in support of harmony for its own sake is that ritual has a power to foster a sense of shared purpose and common fate that does not depend on agreement on a relatively specific set of values and normative doctrines. Ritual consists in not just spoken word but also stylized, emotionally resonant actions that represent some aspects of the participants' life together. The performance creates a common experience and a sense of what binds them together that are not reducible to any discursive explanation. The common experience is sufficiently open textured and ambiguous, so that participants can disagree about the specific content of their responsibilities to each other while affirming a shared understanding (see Madsen 1984 for a description of this function of ritual in a twentieth-century Chinese village). Participation in ritual understood in this way contributes to willingness to interpret and adjust one's individual interests in light of one's interests in relationship with others in political society. Modern Western political philosophy, preoccupied with theoretical issues of justification, has not much appreciated the crucial function of ritual in binding together those who will inevitably disagree. Democratic theorists might fruitfully consider the attractions of rituals adapted to a democratic society (Wong 2006: 266–72).

Democracy, Rights, Gender Equality, and Confucianism

The interpretation of harmony as requiring diversity of views and the mutual accommodation of potentially conflicting interests bears on the question of whether Confucianism can be hospitable to individual rights to dissent and criticism. It will not be hospitable if the only basis for the recognition of rights is a conception of what each individual, qua individual, is entitled to claim from other members. Underlying such a conception is the assumption that the individual has a substantial domain of morally legitimate personal interests that may conflict with the goal of promoting public or collective goods. Rights constitute constraintsor limits on the extent that individual personal interests may be sacrificed for the sake of public or collective goods. Let me call this kind of ground for the recognition of rights "the autonomy ground."

However, another possible ground for the recognition of rights is their necessity for promoting the common good (Wong 2004). The airing of divergent views helps to inform leadership of its errors and limitations in its information as to how its policies are affecting all segments of political society. It helps the process of the mutual adjustment of potentially conflicting interests, because the interests of some are liable to be ignored or automatically subordinated to those of the powerful. A good case can be made that it is necessary to recognize a duty for all, especially on the part of those in power, to honor a protected space for speech and dissent. As argued earlier, relying on the moral courage of subordinates to speak truth to power is insufficient protection for the kind of sustained discussion that might advance the common good. In the twentieth century, Chinese thinking about democracy entertained such a justification for civil rights. The influential political thinker, Liang Qichao saw rights as consisting of that which it is appropriate for the citizen to do (see Angle and Svensson 2001; Angle 2002). His thought was that political participation would unleash energies that would contribute to collective welfare. Some thinkers following Liang's lead argued that China's problem in modernizing stemmed from the systematic overconcentration of power, yet they did not put forward the autonomy ground for rights.

Rights grounded in community will not be precisely the same as rights grounded in autonomy. If one were to justify individual rights only by reference to the moral requirement of autonomy, one might justify a rather broad and virtually unrestricted right to freedom of expression. If, however, one allows the value of community independent weight as a factor in determining the scope of the right of freedom of expression, one might find that only a more restricted right of freedom of expression can be justified (Buchanan 1989). However, even if rights with a purely communal ground do not have the same scope as rights with a strong autonomy ground, the area of overlap will not be insignificant.

Some Confucians might hesitate at the thought of according rights a prominent role in a genuinely Confucian ethics, worrying that doing so might promote the sort of contentious attitude and assumptions that the interests of individuals inevitably conflict, and that all these are incompatible with the sort of mutual caring and trust they believe must underlie social harmony. Even with such concerns, Confucians might recognize a role for rights "backup" protections to be invoked when relationships break down and cannot be repaired through the restoration of mutual caring. In such cases, individuals' interests need protection (see J. Chan 1999).

For Confucianism, political authority and legitimacy do not, in the last analysis, rest on the consent of the people or on democratic institutions that make possible widespread participation in the election of leaders or in the formulation of policies and laws. Rather, they rest on the moral values of social harmony, *ren*, and more particular ideals of social relationship such as filial piety. Those who are the most qualified and can effectively promote these values have the authority to rule. However, for the reasons cited earlier, democratic institutions and the rights they embody might have instrumental value for the promotion of these values (J. Chan 2007). Contemporary thinkers who are deeply sympathetic to Confucian values, therefore, might hold that Confucian meritocracy could appropriately be combined with democratic institutions.

One possibility for such a combination is to have a two-house legislature, the members of one house selected on the basis of their qualifications for office (and assessing them might involve competitive examinations of the sort used in China for some two millennia and that served as the inspiration for the British and American civil service systems), and the members of the other house democratically elected in free and fair elections (Bell 2006). The idea is for the "meritocratic" house to contribute the kind of good judgment that is often compromised when one needs to think about getting elected or re-elected, and for the "democratic" house to deliver the kind of accountability that is the hoped-for effect of being elected to office. It is not really surprising that theorists should think of such combinations. Viable democracies in complex societies need some element of meritocracy (the judicial branch, as well as the civil service, of the US government may fulfill such a role). And, on the other side, truly meritocratic elites will often see the need to set up channels of communication with and some degree of accountability to those whose welfare they are charged with protecting and promoting.

There may be deeper reasons to be serious about such a combination, on both the democracy and Confucian sides. On the democracy side, there is a good case to be made that a society, even one that tends toward strongly liberal values of personal choice among a range of conceptions of the good life, must foster certain values that favor some conceptions and not others. It should foster a degree of mutual respect and concern among its citizens, if for no other reason than that it promotes a widespread concern for the rights of personal choice of all citizens, and not just oneself or one's own. With respect to the right to speech, this means that even liberal democracies might have to acknowledge some constraints on the right to speak for the sake of protecting bonds of mutual respect and concern. For example, liberal democracies fall on a spectrum with the United States at one end placing very few constraints for that reason and countries such as the United Kingdom, Canada, and Germany placing more stringent restrictions on hate speech and expressions of racism.

Furthermore, if it is right to be concerned about the ability of all to exercise such rights effectively, there will be concern for equality of opportunity and a minimum level of material security. Arguably, a willingness to take less and give more to a societal effort to protect and ensure the "worth" of individual rights for all will require a sense of community and shared fate that is one of the strengths of Confucianism. Feminists have argued forcefully for the need to consider the ways in which traditional family structures contribute to the diminution of women's autonomy and to their material disadvantage (especially when there is divorce and women face diminished job and salary prospects because of the time they have taken off from education and work to raise children). The stronger such arguments are, the more reason there is for reform and regulation of gender roles and power relations within the family. And this places more constraint on autonomy of choice between competing conceptions of the good life insofar as they contain ideals of gender ideals and family structure. The family is a sphere where the personal is becoming increasingly political, and Confucianism is a political philosophy that has very much recognized that from the beginning.

On the Confucian side, increasing pluralism in conceptions of the good life may be occurring as societies with a Confucian heritage enter the first world and experience the effects of globalizing culture. The reduction in the number of children that usually occurs with higher living standards and the entry of more women into the professions, occupations, and public offices that have previously been dominated by men will introduce changes into the family structure. The Confucian valuing of family will have to confront new forms of family. Within the Confucian tradition, it can be argued that the subordination of women unnecessarily restricts the ways in which women can make a contribution to the common moral ends of the community and deprives them of the dignity that would come from making such a contribution. Furthermore, it has been argued persuasively that foundational Confucian texts, the *Analects* of Confucius and the *Mencius*) provide no basis for the exclusion of women from aspiration to become exemplary persons (S. Y. Chan 2000) who could take their places in the leadership of their societies. Enduring moral traditions have the sort of internal complexity that allows for significant change that is at the same time in accordance with at least some of their core values. Chinese and Western traditions have this sort of complexity that allows for mutually beneficial interaction (see Tan 2004, for a discussion of correspondences between Confucianism and a Deweyan conception of democracy).

REFERENCES

Primary Sources

Analects (Lunyu)
Most translations are based on the "received" text assembled by He Yan, 190–249 CE, though fragments of the text have recently been discovered and dated as early as 55 BCE.
AMES, ROGER T., and ROSEMONT, HENRY JR. (1998) (trans.). *The Analects of Confucius: A Philosophical Translation*. New York: Ballantine Books.
LAU, D. C. (1979) (trans.). *Confucius: The Analects*. Harmondsworth: Penguin.
SLINGERLAND, EDWARD G. (2003) (trans.). *Confucius Analects: With Selections from Traditional Commentaries*. Indianapolis: Hackett.
WALEY, ARTHUR (1989) (trans.). *The Analects of Confucius*. New York: Vintage.

Book of Rites (Li Ji)
A text describing the court rituals and social forms of the Zhou dynasty, compiled during the Warring States period, 475–221 BCE.
LEGGE, JAMES. (1967) (trans.). *Li Chi: Book of Rites*. 2 vols. New York: University Books.

Mencius (Mengzi)
The version edited by Zhao Qi, second century CE, is the received version used in translations.
BLOOM, IRENE (2009) (trans.). *Mencius*. New York: Columbia University Press.
LAU, D. C. (1970) (trans.), *Mencius*. Harmondsworth: Penguin.

Mozi
A diverse collection of texts associated with Mozi and his school, ranging in their dating from the fifth century BCE to the third century BCE.
WATSON, BURTON, trans. (1967) (trans.). *Basic Writings of Mo Tzu, Hsün Tzu, and Han Fei Tzu*. New York: Columbia University Press.

Xunzi
Much of the text was composed during Xunzi's lifetime in the third century BCE, and the received version edited by Yang Liang dates from the ninth century CE.
KNOBLOCK, JOHN (1988–94). *Xunzi: A Translation and Study of the Complete Works*. 3 vols. Stanford, CA: Stanford University Press).

Zuo Commentary to the Spring and Autumn Annals (Zuo Zhuan)
The earliest work of Chinese narrative history covering the period from 722–468 BCE.
WATSON, BURTON (1989), *The Tso chuan: Selections from China's Oldest. Narrative History*. New York: Columbia University Press.

Secondary Sources

ANGLE, STEPHEN C. (2002). *Human Rights and Chinese Thought: A Cross-Cultural Inquiry*. Cambridge: Cambridge University Press.
ANGLE, STEPHEN C., and SVENSSON, MARINA (2001) (eds). *The Chinese Human Rights Reader: Documents and Commentary 1900–2000*. Armonk, NY: M. E. Sharpe.

BELL, DANIEL A. (2006). *Beyond Liberal Democracy: Political Thinking for an East Asian Context*. Princeton: Princeton University Press.

BELL, DANIEL A. (2008). *China's New Confucianism: Politics and Everyday Life in a Changing Society*. Princeton: Princeton University Press.

BUCHANAN, ALLEN E. (1989). "Assessing the Communitarian Critique of Liberalism," *Ethics*, 99: 852–82.

CHAN, ALAN (2000). "Confucian Ethics and the Critique of Ideology," *Asian Philosophy*, 10/3: 245–61.

CHAN, JOSEPH (1999). "A Confucian Perspective on Human Rights for Contemporary China," in Joanne R. Bauer and Daniel A. Bell (eds), *The East Asian Challenge for Human Rights*. Cambridge: Cambridge University Press.

CHAN, JOSEPH (2000). "Legitimacy, Unanimity, and Perfectionism," *Philosophy and Public Affairs*, 29: 5–42.

CHAN, JOSEPH (2007). "Democracy and Meritocracy: A Confucian Perspective," *Journal of Chinese Philosophy*, 34: 179–93.

CHAN, SIN YEE (2000). *"Gender and Relationship Roles in the Analects and the Mencius,"* *Asian Philosophy*, 10: 115–31.

CUA, ANTONIO (1989). "The Status of Principles in Confucian Ethics," *Journal of Chinese Philosophy*, 16: 273–96.

CUA, ANTONIO (2002). "The Ethical and Religious Dimensions of Li," *Review of Metaphysics*, 55: 471–519.

FINGARETTE, HERBERT (1972). *Confucius: The Secular as Sacred*. New York: Harper & Row.

GRAHAM, ANGUS. C. (1989). *Disputers of the Tao: Philosophical Argument in Ancient China*. Chicago: Open Court.

HALL, DAVID L., and AMES, ROGER T. (1987). *Thinking through Confucius*. New York: State University of New York Press.

HALL, DAVID L., and AMES, ROGER T. (1998). *Thinking from the Han: Self, Truth, and Transcendence in Chinese and Western Culture*. Albany, NY: State University of New York Press.

HANSEN, CHAD (1992). *A Daoist Theory of Chinese Thought*. Oxford: Oxford University Press.

IHARA, CRAIG K. (2004). "Are Individual Rights Necessary? A Confucian Perspective," in Kwong-loi Shun and David B. Wong (eds), *Confucian Ethics: A Comparative Study of Self, Autonomy, and Community*. Cambridge: Cambridge University Press, 11–30.

LEE, THOMAS H. C. (1994). "Academies: Official Sponsorship and Suppression," in Frederick P. Brandauer and Chun-Chieh Huang (eds), *Imperial Rulership and Cultural Change*. Washington: University of Washington Press.

LI, CHENYANG (2007). "Li as Cultural Grammar: On the Relation between Li and Ren, in Confucius' Analects," *Philosophy East & West*, 57: 311–29.

MACINTYRE, ALASDAIR (1984). *After Virtue: A Study in Moral Theory*. 2nd edn. Notre Dame, IN: University of Notre Dame Press.

MACINTYRE, ALASDAIR (1989). *Whose Justice? Which Rationality?* Notre Dame, IN: University of Notre Dame Press.

MADSEN, RICHARD (1984). *Morality and Power in a Chinese Village*. Berkeley and Los Angeles: University of California Press.

NEURATH, OTTO (1959). "Protocol Sentences," in A. J. Ayer (ed.), *Logical Positivism*. New York: Free Press, 199–208.

RAWLS, JOHN (1971). *A Theory of Justice*. Cambridge, MA: Belknap Press of Harvard University Press.

RAWLS, JOHN (1996). *Political Liberalism*. New York: Columbia University Press.

ROSEMONT, HENRY, JR (1991). *A Chinese Mirror: Moral Reflections on Political Economy and Society*. Chicago: Open Court.

ROSEMONT, HENRY, JR (2000). "State and Society in the Xunzi: A Philosophical Commentary," in T. C. Kline III and P. J. Ivanhoe (eds), *Virtue, Nature, and Moral Agency in the Xunzi*. Indianapolis: Hackett.

SHUN, KWONG-LOI (1993). "Ren and Li in the Analects," Philosophy East & West, 43: 457–79; modified version in Bryan Van Norden (ed.), *Confucius and the Analects: New Essays*. Oxford: Oxford University Press, 2002.

SHUN, KWONG-LOI (2004). "Conception of the Person in Early Confucian Thought," in Kwong-loi Shun and David B. Wong (eds), *Confucian Ethics: A Comparative Study of Self, Autonomy, and Community*. Cambridge: Cambridge University Press, 183–99.

TAN, SOR-HOON (2004). *Confucian Democracy: A Deweyan Reconstruction*. New York: State University of New York Press.

WALZER, MICHAEL (1983). *Spheres of Justice: A Defense of Pluralism and Equality*. New York: Basic Books.

WONG, DAVID B. (2004). 'Rights and Community in Confucianism', in Kwong-loi Shun and David B. Wong (eds), *Confucian Ethics: A Comparative Study of Self, Autonomy and Community*. Cambridge: Cambridge University Press.

WONG, DAVID B. (2006). *Natural Moralities: A Defense of Pluralistic Relativism*. Oxford: Oxford University Press.

XIA, YONG (1992). *Renquan gainian qiyuan [The Origin of the Concept of Human Rights: A Chinese Interpretation]* (Zhongguo zhengfa daxue chubanshe); an excerpt of the former is translated under the title "Human Rights and Chinese Tradition," in Stephen C. Angle and Marina Svensson (eds), *The Chinese Human Rights Reader: Documents and Commentary 1900–2000* Armonk, NY: M. E. Sharpe, 2001, 372–89.

CHAPTER 49

....

THE MUSLIM TRADITION
OF POLITICAL PHILOSOPHY

....

SHAHROUGH AKHAVI

PRELIMINARY CONSIDERATIONS

....

CONTEMPORARY Muslim political philosophy (or, preferably, political theory) covers a broad expanse that brings under its rubric at least two diverse tendencies: (1) an approach that stresses the integration of religion and politics, as often expressed by the phrase that "Islam is both religion and state" (al-Islam din wa dawla) or its alternative variant that "Islam is both religion and the world" (al-Islam din wa dunya); and (2) an approach that insists on their separation.

Advocates of the first approach seem united in their desire for the "Islamization of knowledge," meaning that the epistemological foundation of understanding and explanation in all areas of life, including all areas of political life, must be "Islamic."[1] Thus, one needs to speak of an "Islamic anthropology," an "Islamic sociology," an "Islamic political science," and so on. But there is also a distinction that one may make among advocates of this first approach. One can find (a) writers who insist that the political model that characterized the early Islamic community must be the model for contemporary Muslim society; but (b) also those who maintain, at least rhetorically, if not persuasively on the level of theory, that it is up to every generation to devise the political system that it believes is best suited to promote their interests—even though they maintain that the early period provides the indispensable foundation for later generations to draw upon.

Finally, one can say about many, perhaps most, advocates of the first approach that they feel an *urgency* to apply Islamic law (shari'a) throughout all arenas of society.

---

[1] This tendency began with a meeting of North American Muslim scholars at Illinois State University in 1971, led by a Pakistani professor of religion at Temple University, Ismail R. Faruqi. The movement has three sites in Kuala Lumpur, Cairo, and Herndon Virginia.

Consequently, they emphasize the importance of applying Islamic law in all legal domains: administrative law; civil law; constitutional law; commercial law; financial law; penal law; and personal-status law (relating to such matters as marriage, divorce, inheritance, and custody of children). As suggested, they wish this process to occur as soon as possible. A small minority of these people are willing to resort to violence, under a range of circumstances, to bring this about. Whether they are violence prone or not, the term often used to characterize these advocates is "Islamism."[2]

As for the approach stressing the separability of religion and politics, these thinkers reject the program of "Islamization of knowledge," maintaining that there are universal concepts that are available to scientists, although, to be sure, most accept varying degrees of cultural relativism arguments, especially when they feel that they are being lectured to by Western observers whom they feel seek to denigrate their traditions. They criticize the urgent desire to apply Islamic law across the board, attacking those who wish to do so for reifying *shari'a*. It is their view that no monolithic body of rules exists that constitutes Islamic law, because different schools of law exist, and different jurists even within the same school of law differ in their interpretations of what the law is and what the believer must do in relationship to the law. Given these variations, it begs the question to insist on the implementation of the holy law.

In other respects, separability advocates adhere to various models of political theory, but the dominant ones are some form of liberal pluralism or social democracy. In articulating these positions, separability advocates will seek, where they can, to find Islamic analogues for certain concepts, such as *shura* (a word that literally means "consultation") to gloss "public opinion." But in doing so, separability advocates note that "public opinion" is a broader concept, and they admonish that "consultation" may, in any given case, be interpreted very narrowly. Thus, they warn, a leader may consult with his advisors (and not with the broad masses), and, even then, he may ignore their advice. These advocates maintain, by contrast, that, although public opinion can be ignored by leaders, it inhabits a wider political field; accordingly, they feel, acknowledgment of its role in society may be considered as a requisite for any definition of democracy.

This is an important distinction. The stock in trade of the "religion and politics" advocates is to resurrect traditional Islamic expressions and substitute them in reified fashion as analogues for certain contemporary political concepts. With regard to *shura*, for example, these advocates typically maintain that it is the "Muslim" version of public opinion—nay, it *is* democracy. The separability advocates hold this attempt to equate the two as tendentious. Central to this difference in these two approaches is the

---

[2] The word is a neologism from the French *islamisme*. Note the difference between "Islamist" and "Islamic," the standard adjectival term used when one wants to convey the idea of pertaining to the Islamic religion. One may characterize Islamists as Islamic in their faith, but not all those who are Islamic by faith (that is, Muslims) are Islamists. A final point: one sometimes sees the expression "Political Islam" applied to Islamism. Although this proliferation of terms is not always in the best interests of clarity, such terms are now part of the discourse and cannot simply be ignored.

ahistoricism of the "religion and politics" writers and the demand for historicization on the part of the separability advocates.

POLITICAL THEORY AND THE HISTORICAL MUSLIM INTELLECTUAL EXPERIENCE

Political science did not have an autonomous existence as a field of study in the Islamic world until the nineteenth century. The classic and still utilized word for politics is *siyasa*, from a root referring to the training of horses. From this comes the idea of taming, regulating, and attending to—that is, administering. It is true that one may find attention to themes at the heart of the study of politics, such as the state or leadership, in the manuals of Muslim legists. However, the treatment of these subjects in these manuals was basically part of the more general discussion of the place of law in Islamic civilization. In other words, politics was not an independent subject of study. Thus, for example, one could expect to find a discussion of *jihad*[3] toward the end of monographs discussing the *shari*ʿa (Islamic law). Or, in the constitutional treatises of these jurists, one would encounter descriptions of the qualifications and functions of the caliph (successor of the Prophet). But it was the rare thinker—for example, ibn Khaldun (d. 1406)—who even considered asking about such matters as the relationship between the social bases of power and the structure of authority, or the connection between group solidarity and the rise and decline of political institutions and leaders.

It is true that political philosophy did enjoy a certain vogue among some circles for a brief period in the medieval era of Islam (from about 850 to 1200). These philosophers, especially al-Farabi (d. 950), ibn Sina (Avicenna) (d. 1037), and ibn Rushd (Averroes) (d. 1198), were pious believers who sought to create a synthesis out of Islamic law (*shari*ʿa) and the political philosophy of Plato and Aristotle. In their time, jurists were constructing a political philosophy whose core was the Islamic caliphate— the institution of rule in the Muslim community that they considered to be divinely ordained. As a consequence, the thought of these philosophers was constrained by the latitude that the holy law permitted to them. Because Greek philosophy ultimately rested on a greater concern with anthropocentric understandings of the human being's

---

[3] *Jihad* has often been presented in an oversimplified manner to mean "holy war," with the implication of justifying violence against unbelievers. Historically, jurists have been careful in their conceptualizations of this expression. It comes from a root meaning to exert oneself for the sake of God. Muslims are mandated to exert themselves in an effort of internal purification so as to be worthy of God's trust. However, if the community is perceived to be under attack, then the believers should engage in such exertion for the defense of the collective body. Even under those circumstances, though, it is up to the leader of the community to appoint the defenders, and not all individuals participate in the effort. This is a far cry from the vulgarizations of the term that one finds in the contemporary media or even in some "scholarly" works that, for whatever reason, adopt a stereotypical view toward Islam and Muslims as fanatical.

role in the world, the place they occupied in Muslim thought more generally was on the periphery. There were a number of reasons for their marginalization in both Muslim academic and governmental circles.

First of all, the political philosophers were judged to be too heavily influenced by Greek thought, with its emphasis upon the use of reason and empirical inquiry in the pursuit of truth. Such an emphasis was considered misplaced, since the revelation was the appropriate framework for such pursuit. In the second place, law and theology, which stressed the study of God's commands, followed at a distance by the study of God's attributes, were considered by Muslim scholars historically to be far more seemly, given the Islamic faith's stress on what God wants believers to do and how God should be construed in the eyes of the faithful. Third, rulers of Islamic states discouraged political philosophy on the whole because they believed that its supporters would inevitably become critics of their rule. (For a fuller discussion, see Charles Butterworth, Chapter 11, this volume.)

An exception to this generalization was the patronage extended by rulers to a stream of political philosophy in the Islamic world that may be called the "mirror for princes" tradition. Among the most well-known writers of this genre were Nizam al-Mulk (d. 1092), the powerful grand vizier (*wazir*) of the Saljuk Dynasty. This tradition essentially consisted of manuals of statecraft containing advice to leaders on a myriad of topics related to their taking and holding on to power. But these leaders ruled out of bounds political philosophy more broadly construed, including the study of such principles as justice, right, freedom, equality, obligation, community, the state, interests, and the like. As for the "mirror for princes" tradition itself, because of its overt concern with the ability of the ruler to exert his power, it inevitably became enmeshed in the vicissitudes of secular rule. With the Mongol destruction of the caliphate (epitomized by the fall of Baghdad in 1258), the manuals of statecraft stream of writings came to an end.

In sum, Muslim political philosophy and the advice genre of the mirrors for princes exercised little practical influence of a long-term nature. Even the towering figures of Muslim political philosophy and Muslim manuals of statecraft were suspect in the academies and were ironically better known in the West than in their own homelands.

One may link the minimal influence of Muslim political philosophy to the suppression of the rationalist movement known as the *Mu'tazila*, whose period of influence in Muslim theology, and then later in Muslim political philosophy, spanned several generations in the period from about 750 to 900. In sum, both imperial courts and seminaries saw philosophical rationalism as a threat to the prevailing political and religious orders.

EUROPEAN DOMINATION

As European great powers began to inflict military defeats upon Middle Eastern and Islamic systems of rule, such as the Ottoman (1312–1923), Mughal (1526–1858), and

Qajar (1785–1925) empires, political ideas began to infiltrate from Europe as well. Eventually, reformers emerged who tried to uphold the integrity of their own civilization while also seeking to utilize some of these ideas to defeat the foreigners' plans to dominate them. It is thus with the Young Ottomans of the Tanzimat reform movement in the Ottoman Empire (1839–76) that we begin to see the emergence of political science as a discipline in the Islamic world. These reform efforts also spread to places such as Tunisia, Egypt, and Iran. Alongside these intellectual efforts were also nativisitic activist movements that arose in North Africa, the Arabian peninsula, and the Sudan. Unlike the Tanzimat reformers and their associates in Tunisia, Egypt, and Iran, the ideas of these nativistic movements were not influenced by Western concepts, such as constitutionalism, but rather derived from Islamic thought. Such thought contained mechanisms of renewal that could be elicited against the dead hand of blind imitation of the past. The thrust of the nativistic efforts was to reject constant validation of one's actions by reference to the works of the founders of the legal schools that had been established in the period roughly from 725 to 850; and to replace the emulation of those legal schools by direct recourse to the putative model of the Prophet (d. 632). Ironically, in their effort to eliminate imitation of the legists, these nativistic efforts nonetheless advocated imitation of another kind: what they believed constituted the pattern established by the Prophet. Another aspect of the activities of the nativistic movements was their reliance on Sufi (mystical) leaders and organizational structures.

Despite the rise of these reformist and nativistic movements, European economic and political domination of Muslim lands persisted. In the Middle Eastern parts of the Islamic world, we can mark that domination from the 1770s until the 1950s. As noted earlier, conquering armies opened the doors to European influence, and European ideas passed through these open doors. A thorough analysis of the ideas that passed through these portals is not possible here because of considerations of space, so the remainder of this chapter will be organized around the following themes: (1) the individual and society; (2) the state; and (3) democracy. Owing to considerations of space, I will focus below on the theme of democracy.

THE INDIVIDUAL AND SOCIETY

Contemporary Muslim political theory takes essentially the same position on the relationship between the individual and society as in the classic, medieval, and early modern periods of Islam: society is prior to the individual, and its interests trump that of the individual. The two words in contemporary political discourse for the word "individual" are *fard* (pl. *afrad*) and *shakhs* (pl. *ashkhas*). The former term in early Islam in fact was utilized to refer to God as the "only," the "solitary," the "unique," and "the incomparable." The latter term was used in Muslim philosophy to connote individuation, and was applied as a neutral expression to provide the meaning of a person. In recent times, under the influence of Western legal traditions, the concept of "legal personality"—absent earlier—arose, with the implication or specification of political entitlements as against the state.

In any case, because the doctrine of salvation in Islam centers on the community of believers [*umma*], it is this unit's interests that are central. If one is not a member of the community, one has no chance of "walking pleasingly in the sight of God" and being rewarded in both this world and the afterlife. The ethos of collectivism is deeply embedded in the Islamic tradition, and it never occurred to jurists or philosophers or theologians to advance any claims on behalf of the individual apart from his or her membership in the community.

In the nineteenth and twentieth centuries, Muslim thinkers tried to accommodate the principles of their faith with "the rights of man and the citizen." These intellectuals read the social-contract theorists, especially Locke and Rousseau, and sought to harmonize natural-law doctrines—which were at the heart of contractarian thought—with divine law. They ultimately failed in this task on the theoretical level, but this did not prevent them from advancing *ad hoc* propositions that the Islamic tradition was not incompatible with a doctrine of individual rights. Both Turks and Iranians in the late nineteenth and early twentieth centuries sought to underpin such rights with concepts in Islamic law such as that of *hisba* (roughly a holding to account) and *al-amr bi al-maʿruf wa al-nahy ʿan al-munkar* (commanding the good and forbidding evil). Much more recently, many thinkers advance the proposition that in fact "Islam" is exemplary in its guarantee of individual rights, even as it equates the interests of the *umma*—of the group—with godliness.

Even the most ardent advocates of individual rights among contemporary Muslim thinkers are leery of pushing too strongly for them, because of traditional notions that one's prospects for welfare, happiness, and salvation itself lie in one's participation as a member of the community. Furthermore, individualism is so closely associated with the capitalist order and the political culture of the colonial states that exploited the Muslims during the long years of their rule over them that liberal thought is viewed warily at best and with hostility at worst.

This is why there has always been a stronger tradition in the Muslim world in the modern period for communitarian theories. For many Muslims, apparently, the problem lurking in liberalism is its potential perversion into a doctrine of "possessive individualism." Such possessive individualism would be very difficult for any Muslim thinker to adopt, as it treats the individual

> as essentially the proprietor of his own person or capacities, essentially owing nothing to society for them. The individual was seen neither as a moral whole, nor as part of a larger social whole, but rather as an owner of himself. The relation of ownership, having become for more and more men the critically important relationship determining their actual freedom and actual prospect of realizing their full potentialities, was read back into the nature of the individual. The individual, it was thought, was free inasmuch as he is proprietor of his person and capacities. The human essence is freedom from dependence on the wills of others, and freedom is a function of possession. Society becomes a lot of free equal individuals related to each other as proprietors of their own capacities and of what they have acquired

by their exercise. Society consists of relations of exchange between proprietors. Political society becomes a calculated device for the protection of this property and for the maintenance of an orderly relation of exchange. (MacPherson 1964: 3)

Yet, liberal thought has many variants. Utilitarianism, which insists on "the greatest good for the greatest numbers," is an advance upon "possessive individualism." However, its weakness is that it would still leave some members of society (those not fortunate enough to be counted in "the greatest numbers") disadvantaged. John Rawls's "justice as fairness," with its insistence upon not harming the interests of the least advantaged in society, ought to be more acceptable. But contemporary Muslim writers rarely parse liberal thought and so essentially treat it as monolithic.

THE STATE

Classically, the state was discussed in the legal manuals of Muslim jurists under the topic of the caliphate, the institution of rule that arose upon the death of the Prophet. However, the treatment of this topic was mainly limited to a descriptive account of the qualifications and the functions of the caliph, and not an analysis of the caliphate's institutional structure or the processes by which it operated. In other words, jurists tended to equate the state with the leader, rather than consider it as a sovereign political and legal structure, comprised of multiple structures, agencies, and jurisdictions, that, as Weber put it, "(successfully) claims the monopoly of the legitimate use of physical force within a given territory" (Weber 1958: 78). The consensus was that the caliphate should conform as closely as possible to the model of rule established by the Prophet during the decade before his death in the city of Medina. The jurists, with few exceptions, considered the caliphate as a divinely ordained entity.

In 1925, shortly after the abolition of the caliphate by the government of Turkey in 1924, the Egyptian jurist, ʿAli ʿAbd al-Raziq (d. 1966) argued in his book *Islam and the Foundations of Rule* that the historical caliphate was a man-made institution and hence is not mandated by Islam. Muslims, in his view, could create any model of state they wished, as long as it generally conformed to Islamic norms—"not prohibiting what God has permitted nor allowing what God has proscribed" (ʿAbd al-Raziq 1925: *passim*). The book immediately provoked controversy and was banned by the leadership of al-Azhar, Sunni Islam's most important seat of learning. It continues to draw the fire of conservative thinkers and Islamists but is praised by advocates of the separation of religion and politics.

The Shiʿi Iranian Islamist thinker and activist Ayatollah Ruhollah Khomeini (d. 1989) argued along different lines. Since Shiʿism was persecuted by the Sunni caliphs from 661 until 1924, Shiʿi jurists condemn the institution of the caliphate. They substitute for it the institution of the Imamate, specifically the institution of rule by the twelve Shiʿi Imams (who lived collectively from c.600 until 873/74, with the twelfth entering into hiding and expected to return as the Mahdi, or messiah, at the end of time). The Imams are considered the proofs of God's existence and are believed to be endowed with inerrancy, prescient knowledge, and exemplary justice. Doctrine holds that only they are entitled to rule, but, because of their persecution (only the first actually ruled), rank, and file Shiʿites were counseled not to advance this claim for an indefinite period of time. This left the door open for secular rulers to govern, but Khomeini argued innovatively in a series of lectures in early 1970 that the *clergy* should rule as the deputies of the hidden imam, given the historical tendency of secular rulers to behave in corrupt and autocratic manner.

Today, Islamists who theorize about the state adopt an apologetic tone and, instead of empirically analyzing the behavior of Muslim states over the course of historical time, focus on Islamic ideals. Even sophisticated conservatives and Islamists refuse to acknowledge that the long centuries of authoritarian rule by caliphs and other leaders have anything to do with Islam and insist that Islam should be judged not by this empirical record but by ideal norms (al-ʿAwwa 1989 [1975]: 133–4).

The radical Sunni Islamist writer Sayyid Qutb (d. 1966), whose thought has been lionized by various militant Islamist groups ever since the mid-1960s, has advanced the argument that all contemporary Muslim states were led by apostate leaders because of their violations of God's commands. Taking his cue from the Pakistani thinker Abu al-ʿAlaʾ Mawdudi (d. 1979), Qutb applied an innovative reading to certain Qurʾanic verses in the fifth and twelfth chapters of that scripture to contemporary rulers to find their rule to be hostile to God's commands. The three verses in Qurʾan 5: 44, 45, and 47 use the words "unbelievers, oppressors, and evil-doers" to refer to "those who do not judge according to God's revelation." But Mawdudi, Qutb, and their followers substitute the word "rule" for "judge," utilizing a secondary meaning of the word "judge" (imperfect form *yahkum*). Their target, of course, is contemporary rulers, whom they accuse of not ruling according to God's revelation. The two verses in Qurʾan 12: 47 and 60 state: "Truly, judgment [*hukm*] belongs to God alone." Again, Mawdudi, Qutb, and their followers use the secondary meaning of the Arabic word *hukm*, thus changing the operative noun from "judgment" to "rule." Accordingly, the total destruction of contemporary states and their replacement with "counter-states" whose leaders would apply God's laws has become the mantra of the radical Islamist cause.

DEMOCRACY

Democratic thought presupposes that people make their own decisions about matters affecting their political interests and the role of the state in this context. Originally, democratic thought arose in the small-scale community of ancient Athens, where direct decision-making in the Assembly by the relatively few enfranchised citizens was possible. The Greek model disappeared for various reasons that cannot be examined here. Suffice it to say that democratic thought and practice suffered eclipse in the long centuries of the Hellenistic era, the Roman Empire, its successor tribal states, and the Holy Roman Empire. Ideas about democracy reappeared in Europe at a time roughly coordinate with the Treaty of Westphalia (1648), when large territorial states had emerged at the center of the continent's politics. It was, therefore, no longer possible to think in terms of the ancient Greek notions of direct democracy. In order to conceptualize the possibilities of democracy under the new conditions of absolutist monarchies, seventeenth- and eighteenth-century thinkers—notably Hobbes, Locke, Rousseau, Kant, and Ferguson—concerned themselves with the process by which human beings could try to guarantee their rights. The upshot was a series of writings that came to be known as "social-contract theory." The central idea was that people should unite to entrust their rights in an arbiter (variously called the Leviathan, the Legislator, or other expression) and in the meanwhile have their interests indirectly represented. Should they feel that their entrusted rights were being abused, they would be entitled to reappropriate them and reassign them. The bedrock idea was, of course, continuing ability to surveil these rights and so to guarantee their ultimate control over the means by which they could promote their interests. (For a fuller discussion of democracy and social contract, see Warren, Chapter 29 and Sommerville, Chapter 33, this volume.)

Tanzimat reformers in the late Ottoman period, together with their counterparts in Egypt, became fascinated with such ideas in the context of dissatisfaction with the Ottoman sultanate and caliphate as custodians of the Muslim people's rights. Most of these reformers believed it was possible to adopt social-contract theory principles within the limits of the rule of the *shariʿa* (Hourani 1962; Mardin 1962). Eventually, the ideas of these reformers were broadened by twentieth-century thinkers such as Lutfi al-Sayyid (d. 1963) and Muhammad Husayn Haykal (d. 1956) as liberal and conservative advocates of democracy respectively. Both of these thinkers were well aware of the hypocrisy of British colonialists in moralizing about the superiority of English democracy and yet their refusing to allow Egyptians to apply democratic values. But this did not stop them from extolling the virtues of democracy, in their different ways: Lutfi from the perspective of separating religion and politics and stressing individual liberty values, and Haykal by apologetically "materializing" its principles, especially a tutelary form of democracy he believed was rooted in Islamic traditions of normative order (Ahmed 1960: 85–112; Smith 1983: *passim*).

In the 1960s and 1970s, writers on democracy from a "liberal" perspective included the Egyptian populist writer Muhammad ʿImara, and the Egyptian jurist and historian Tariq al-Bishri. But, more recently, both of them have turned increasingly in a conservative direction, with ʿImara currently associating himself with the Islamization of knowledge movement; for his part, Bishri seems to have turned away from his earlier leftist-inspired historical writings to carry the banner of national unity forged primarily through the ethos of Islamic belief (Binder 1988: 243 ff; Akhavi 2009).

Without defining democracy, ʿImara ahistorically asserts that democracy is an endemic Islamic concept, a point he attempts to demonstrate by reference to the aforementioned concept of *shura*. He claims that the Prophet established the principle, even though only indirect evidence exists that it acquired recognizable organizational form. He writes that the Qur'an contains two verses mandating consultation (3:159; 38:42). The Prophet sought the advice of his companions about battle tactics, he notes. And those companions consulted among one another in selecting the leader of the Islamic community after the Prophet's death. This proves, to 'Imara, that "Islam" is characterized by democracy. Note two things here. In the first place, he reifies Islam, whereas "Islam" does not act—rather, it is Muslims who act. Yet, 'Imara ignores the historical record of their action. In the second place, 'Imara is exporting his late-twentieth-century understanding of democracy back into the seventh century and finds this democracy full blown in Qur'anic verses and the practice of the Prophet. He does not define democracy, nor does he show the people freely disposing of their will in regard to political matters. There is no analysis of democracy in Islamic history—showing how it arose out of the give and take, and contention and cooperation of groups in historical times and places. He does not distinguish between elites making decisions and people actively participating in the determination of decisions. In fact, he acknowledges elsewhere that the historical record has been bereft of democracy in the Islamic world for 1,300 years ('Imara 1980: *passim*; 1989: 33; 1991: 14).

On the other side of this debate is, for example, the Egyptian philosopher Fu'ad Zakariya, who has urged Arab thinkers to stop reifying Islam, to underpin their analysis with empirical evidence, and to avoid apologetic argumentation, which by its very nature is forced to rely upon hypostatizations of concepts that are alleged to be purely "Islamic" and hence superior to any alternatives. Zakariya does this with telling effect in the following discussion about his reactions to an article written by Shaykh Khalid Muhammad Khalid[4] in the Egyptian main daily newspaper *al-Ahram* on June 24, 1985. In that article, Khalid discussed the concept of *shura* (consultation). As with so many "religion and politics" advocates, Khalid converts the consultation verses in the Qur'an into a theory of democracy.

Khalid merely asserts in his article that Islam's concept of democracy is exactly what one sees in other democratic countries: national sovereignty; the separation of powers; the people's right to elect their leaders and representatives; a loyal opposition; a multi-party system; and freedom of the press. "That, my brother, is the system of rule in Islam, without perversion or distortion."

To this litany, Zakariya objects that all Khalid has done here is present aspects of an ideal type of democracy. He stresses that the concept of *shura* is narrow in scope and is in no way tantamount to democracy. Muslim jurists never used *shura* so broadly as to vindicate a theory of democracy. He criticizes Khalid for trying to materialize democracy in "Islam" by suggesting that "Islam" in fact had anticipated the political principles at the heart of the thought of Locke, Montesquieu, Rousseau, and Jefferson. Although Zakariya is a strong critic of Western imperialism and its role in the Muslim world, he

---

[4] Khalid was originally a follower of 'Ali 'Abd al-Raziq, but in 1980 he underwent a change of heart. Subsequently, his writings took on an apologetic cast that featured the usual *Islam din wa dawla* formulation. He died in 1996.

insists that it is Khalid's reading of Western political theorists that has led him to excavate the Islamic heritage and to fabricate a theory of democracy in that heritage. To put it bluntly, could Khalid have explained *shura* in this manner had he himself not embraced democratic ideas through his own reading about the experiences of Western societies and their political systems? If Khalid's reply is "yes, the Islamic heritage alone has yielded up to him the theory of democracy," then Zakariya has a telling question for him: why have the principles of democracy never been adumbrated nor implemented throughout the entire history of Islam (Zakariya 1998: 166–8)?

CONCLUSIONS

Contemporary Muslim political theory faces a number of challenges. The best work has come either from expatriates or from indigenous scholars who have been willing to challenge traditional "sacred cows." The influence of the latter continues to be dominant, if not hegemonic. Muslim political theorists who advocate the "Islamization of knowledge" need to ask some hard questions. One can understand why they are skeptical of those who believe that knowledge is a matter of "scientific objectivity" and "value neutrality." After all, among other things, claims that all concepts are universal are simply not credible in the West itself, where postmodernist theories have been arguing that all claims to truth must be viewed skeptically. But neither is the claim compelling that all knowledge can and must be Islamized.

   In the period of the early ʿAbbasid caliphate in Baghdad (750–825) and also the Cordoba caliphate in Spain (930–1030), Westerners came to the Islamic court to learn about the advances in such fields as astronomy, mathematics, chemistry, and many others. One of the explanations for the richness of Muslim intellectual efforts was the willingness of thinkers also to borrow some ideas from outside their own civilizational orbit. If that was the case for the most fruitful periods in Islamic history, then why the current need to Islamize knowledge? This is not to deny, of course, that cultural relativism arguments should not be made when they clearly offer advantages. But to go to the extreme with such arguments seems like a prescription for stagnation and stultification of thought.

   What is to be done? Advocates of a revival of the methodology of the long-marginalized rationalist school known as the Muʿtazila will need to press their advocacy with greater clarity and persuasion. They must be willing, at the same time, to acknowledge the excesses of that school, such as scholasticism. At the same time, a major shortcoming of contemporary Muslim political theory is its ahistoricity. One of the most important facets of political theory in any civilization is its efforts to explain change. Thus, for contemporary Muslims to analyze and find solutions for the major problems facing their social and political systems today, they have to be able to understand how things have developed in the way they have and thus how things have reached the present pass. Ignoring the historical record, for example, will not permit them to understand the failure of political parties, or endemic succession crises, or the unaccountability of rulers, or the inability of civil society institutions to enforce transparency on regime policies (as opposed to their historic successes in keeping an intrusive state at bay). It remains to be seen whether breakthroughs of the nature suggested will occur, but, if they do not, contemporary Muslim political theory will continue to wander aimlessly for quite some time to come.

REFERENCES

Primary Sources

'ABD AL-RAZIQ, 'ALI (1925). *Al-Islam wa Usul al-Hukm* [Islam and the Foundations of Rule]. Cairo: Matba'a Misr.

ARKOUN, MOHAMED (1984). *Pour une critique de la raison islamique*. Paris: Maisonneuve et Larose.

AL-'AWWA, MUHAMMAD SALIM (1989 [1975]). *Fi al-Nizam al-Siyasi li al-Dawla al-Islamiyya* [On the Political System of the Islamic State]. 7th edn. Cairo: Dar al-Shuruq.

HANAFI, HASAN (1988). *Min al-'Aqida ila al-Thawra* [From Belief to Revolution]. 5 vols. Cairo: Madbuli.

'IMARA, MUHAMMAD (1980). *Al-Turath fi Daw' al-'Aql* [The Heritage in the Light of Reason]. Beirut: Dar al-Wahda.

'IMARA, MUHAMMAD (1989). *Al-Islam wa Huquq al-Insan* [Islam and Human Rights]. Cairo: Dar al-Shuruq.

'IMARA, MUHAMMAD (1991). *Ma'alim al-Manhaj al-Islami* [Benchmarks in the Islamic Method]. Cairo: Dar al-Shuruq.

KHOMEINI, RUHOLLAH (1971). *Hukumat-i Islami* [Islamic Government]. Qumm.

KHOMEINI, RUHOLLAH (1981). *Islam and Revolution: Writings and Declarations of Imam Khomeini*, trans. Hamid Algar. Berkeley: Mizan Press.

JABIRI, MUHAMMAD 'ABID (1984, 1986, 1990). *Naqd al-'Aql al-'Arabi* [Critique of the Arab Mind]. 3 vols. Beirut: Markaz Dirasat al-Wahda al-'Arabiyya.

LAROUI, ABDALLAH (1974). *La Crise des intellectuels arabes: Traditionalisme ou historicisme*. Paris: Maspero.

MAUDOODI, SYED ABUL ALA (1971). *First Principles of the Islamic State*. Lahore: Kazi Publications.

MAUDOODI, SYED ABUL 'ALA (2007 [1939]). *Jihad in Islam*. Lahore: Islamic Publications,

QUTB, SAYYID (1947). *Al-'Adala al-Ijtima'iyya fi al-Islam* [Social Justice in Islam]. Cairo.

QUTB, SAYYID (1964). *Ma'alim fi al-Tariq* [Milestones]. Cairo: n. p.

SHARI'ATI, 'ALI (1968). *Islamshinasi* [Knowing Islam]. Tehran. Husayniyah-yi Irshad.

SHUHRUR, MUHAMMAD (1990). *Al-Kitab wa al-Qur'an: Qira'a Mu'asira* [The Book and the Qur'an: A Contemporary Reading]. Damascus: al-Ahali li al-Taba'a wa al-Nashr wa al-Tawzi'.

SURUSH, 'ABD AL-KARIM (1999). *Pluralizm-i Dini* [Religious Pluralism]. Tehran: Ruznamah-yi Salam.

SURUSH, ʿABD AL-KARIM (2000). *Reason, Freedom and Democracy in Islam*. trans., ed., and intro. Mahmoud Sadri. New York: Oxford University Press.

ZAKARIYA, FUʾAD (1998). *Al-Haqiqah wa al-Wahm fi al-Harakah al-Islamiyah al-Muʿasirah* [Reality and Fantasy in the Contemporary Islamic Movement]. Cairo: Dar Qabaʾ li al-Tabaʿa wa al-Nashr.

Secondary Sources

ABU RABIʿ, MUHAMMAD (1996). *Intellectual Origins of Islamic Resurgence in the Arab World*. Albany: State University of New York Press.

AHMED, JAMAL MOHAMMED (1960). *The Intellectual Origins of Egyptian Nationalism*. New York: Oxford University Press.

AKHAVI, SHAHROUGH (2009). *The Middle East: The Politics of the Sacred and Secular*. London: Zed Books.

ARJOMAND, SAID (1984). *The Shadow of God and the Hidden Imam*. Chicago: University of Chicago Press.

BAYAT, ASEF (2007). *Making Islam Democratic: Social Movements and the Post-Islamist Turn*. Stanford: Stanford University Press.

BINDER, LEONARD (1988). *Islamic Liberalism: A Critique of Development Theories*. Chicago: University of Chicago Press.

BOROUJERDI, MEHRZAD (1996). *Iranian Intellectuals and the West: The Tormented Triumph of Nativism*. Syracuse, NY: Syracuse University Press.

BOULLATA, ISSA (1990). *Trends and Issues in Contemporary Arab Thought*. Albany, NY: State University of New York Press.

BROWERS, MICHAELLE (2006). *Democracy and Civil Society in Arab Political Thought: Transcultural Possibilities*. Syracuse, NY: Syracuse University Press.

CRONE, PATRICIA (2004a). *God's Rule*. New York: Columbia University Press.

CRONE, PATRICIA (2004b). *Medieval Islamic Political Thought*. Edinburgh: University of Edinburgh Press.

ENAYAT, HAMID (1980). *Modern Islamic Political Thought*. Austin, TX: University of Texas Press.

ESPOSITO, JOHN L. (1998). *Islam: The Straight Path*. 3rd edn. New York: Oxford University Press.

EUBEN, ROXANNE (1999). *Enemy in the Mirror: Islamic Fundamentalism and the Limits of Rationalism*. Princeton: Princeton University Press.

GERTH, HANS. H., and WRIGHT MILLS, C. (1958) (eds). *From Max Weber*. New York: Oxford University Press.

HOURANI, ALBERT (1962). *Arabic Thought in the Liberal Age*. London: Oxford University Press.

KEPEL, GILLES (2006). *Jihad: The Political Trail of Islam*. Cambridge, MA: Harvard University Press.

KERR, MALCOLM (1966). *Islamic Reform*. Berkeley and Los Angeles: University of California Press.

LAPIDUS, IRA (2002). *A History of Islamic Societies*. 2nd edn. New York: Cambridge University Press.

LEE, ROBERT D. (1997). *Overcoming Tradition and Modernity*. Boulder, CO: Westview Press.

MACPHERSON, C. B. (1964). *The Political Theory of Possessive Individualism: Hobbes to Locke*. New York: Oxford University Press.

MARDIN, SERIF (1962). *The Genesis of Young Ottoman Thought*. Princeton: Princeton University Press.

MARDIN, SERIF (1989). *Religion and Social Change in Modern Turkey*. Albany, NY: State University of New York Press.

MAYER, ANN E. (2007). *Islam and Human Rights*. 4th edn. Boulder, CO: Westview Press.

MOADDEL, MANSOOR (2005). *Islamic Modernism, Nationalism and Fundamentalism*. Chicago: University of Chicago Press.

MOTTAHEDEH, ROY P. (1985). *The Mantle of the Prophet: Religion and Politics in Iran*. New York: Simon and Schuster.

NASR, SAYYED VALI REZA (1996). *Mawdudi and the Making of Islamic Revivalism*. New York: Oxford University Press.

PISCATORI, JAMES (1986). *Islam in a World of Nation States*. New York: Cambridge University Press.

ROSENTHAL, E. I. J. (1958). *Political Thought in Medieval Islam: An Introductory Outline*. Cambridge: Cambridge University Press.

SALVATORE, ARMANDO (1999). *Islam and the Political Discourse of Modernity*. Reading: Ithaca Press.

SMITH, CHARLES D. (1983). *Islam and the Search for Social Order in Modern Egypt*. Albany, NY: State University of New York Press.

TIBI, BASSAM (2005). *Islam between Culture and Politics*. 2nd edn. Basingstoke: Palgrave Macmillan.

WEBER, MAX (1958). *From Max Weber: Essays in Sociology*, ed. Hans H. Gerth and C. Wright Mills. New York: Oxford University Press.

ZUBAIDA, SAMI. ISLAM (1993). *The People and the State*. 2nd edn. London: Zed Books.

CHAPTER 50

···

HINDU POLITICAL
PHILOSOPHY

···

DENNIS DALTON

THE long tradition of Hindu philosophy in India had several distinct peaks of system-atic thought. The apogee of its *political* theory developed during the nineteenth and twentieth centuries as a response to the British imperial authority, commonly known as the *Raj*. This chapter focuses on modern Hindu political philosophy's admixture of its classical tradition with contemporary Indian nationalism as it encountered British theories of freedom, equality, power, and social or political change. The result was an original and cogent system of ideas that at once responded to the British intellectual challenge and reconstituted key elements of the classical Indian philosophical tradition.

The leading formulators of this formidable project were four major Hindu theorists, each self-identifying himself as Hindu in thought and practice: Swami Vivekananda (1863–1902); Aurobindo Ghose (1872–1950); Rabindranath Tagore (1861–1941); and Mohandas Karamchand Gandhi (1869–1948). These four, however marked their differences, will be characterized here as a distinctive school of modern Hindu philosophy because they are intricately connected by a logical nexus of concepts derived from their common religion, their interpretative intellectual project of reforming Hinduism in the face of British colonialism, and their significant commitment to the cause of Indian independence.

Vivekananda was born Narendranath Datta into a high-caste, relatively affluent family of lawyers, and received a solid Western-style education. His birthplace of Calcutta seethed with dialogues among advocates of British and traditional philoso-phies, so he became conversant early in the ideas of Herbert Spencer, Thomas Huxley, Jeremy Bentham, John Stuart Mill, and Charles Darwin, among others. From the influence of his father, he seemed certain to enter the profession of law. But, at age 18, he met Sri Ramakrishna, a revered Hindu ascetic, who placed his hand on the young Anglophile and instantly tapped within him an undiscovered spring of trad-itional Hindu thought.

After Vivekananda had spent two years studying with his Master (as he never ceased calling Ramakrishna), he began a meteoric career as a Hindu missionary to the world, with an astonishing debut at the First World Parliament of Religions in Chicago. His extraordinary natural gift of oratory struck his audiences like a lightning bolt, and immediately propelled him into an unprecedented speaking tour throughout America and England.

Four years later, he returned to India as a hero, and soon established the Ramakrishna Mission, dedicated to social service and religious education with centers around the globe. His zeal to serve the poor, inspired by Ramakrishna, proved contagious to the Indian nationalist movement, especially to Gandhi's program of social reform. Vivekananda's message remained clear and emphatic, wherever he spoke. He demanded a total reformation of Hinduism in particular, and world religions in general, to teach that each person has a divine self and our common quest must be to discover and release this spirit, thereby uplifting India and the whole of humanity.

There is a direct line of influence from Vivekananda to Aurobindo Ghose (known to his devotees as Sri Aurobindo). Like Vivekananda, Aurobindo was born into a wealthy upper-caste and class Calcutta family. His father, a physician, sent him at an early age to attend the finest schools in England. By the time he turned 20, Aurobindo had graduated with first-class honors from Cambridge University, and seemed destined for a distinguished career in the elite British Indian Civil Service, the institutional steel frame of the Raj. But when he returned to India in 1893, Aurobindo, like Vivekananda, discovered his Hindu tradition. Consumed now with the passion of the nationalist movement, he quickly rose to leadership of the extremist faction of the Indian Congress, captivating his followers with an elegant style of writing that he had acquired at Cambridge. The Raj could not tolerate his use of Hindu symbolism to foment violent protest.

Eventually he was arrested and jailed, but in prison another transformation happened. Aurobindo heard the voice of Vivekananda, who had died eight years previously, calling him to pursue spiritual unity, truth, and non-violence. Immediately after his release, he found refuge in meditation, yoga, and philosophy by spending the rest of his long life in the small French colony of Pondicherry. There he wrote prolifically, establishing his system of political and moral philosophy. His main attempt was to show a philosophical correspondence between individual freedom as self-realization and universal human unity in which each recognizes one's spiritual identity with all. The result was the most sophisticated statement of these ideals to emerge from any of the four members of the school, yet Aurobindo never again returned to political activism.

Rabindranath Tagore, too, came from Calcutta, born and raised in one of the most highly cultured families to exist anywhere in the world. He was the fourteenth of the Hindu philosopher Debendranath Tagore's fifteen children, many of whom became accomplished musicians, artists, and writers. Rabindranath flourished in this environment and by the age of 20 had achieved distinction as a Bengali poet, no small achievement in such a culture. In 1912, Tagore published a collection of his poems entitled *Gitanjali* (*Song Offerings*) that earned the admiration of William Butler Yeats. In the following year, he received the Nobel Prize for Literature. The literary world was amazed, India awestruck, and Bengal in ecstasy.

Tagore matched his prolific writing with devotion to educational reform, and by 1921 he established his own Vishva-Bharati University at Shantiniketan in Bengal, dedicating it to the ideals of artistic and philosophical creativity and world peace. His political thought focused on the cult of nationalism as a dangerous threat to individual freedom, social tolerance, and universal harmony. Gandhi called him the "sentinel" or conscience of India's independence struggle because of Tagore's deep and abiding suspicion of politics. He directed his critiques mainly at the Raj but also at authoritarian excesses within the nationalist movement, and he repeatedly warned Gandhi of the corruption of power.

Mahatma ("Great Soul") Gandhi, the most famous Indian of the modern era, applied his theory to practice by leading perhaps the largest mass political movement in history. Unlike the three Bengalis, he was born in the western province (now state) of Gujarat, and into a lower-caste but no less devout Hindu family. He studied law in London and passed the bar there in 1891, but not before becoming deeply influenced by the teachings and example of Christ. He said that the Sermon on the Mount and Leo Tolstoy's version of Christianity in *The Kingdom of God is Within You* ranked second only to the *Bhagavad Gita* among the works that had shaped his thought.

Gandhi's synthesis blended these and many other ideas of East and West into a reconstruction of Advaita philosophy. Advaita (literally "non-dualism") is a school of Vedanta thought systematized by the eminent philosopher Shankara around AD 850. It is a theory of monism that provided Gandhi and each of the others with a vital underpinning for their ideal of spiritual unity. The idea found expression, too, in the *Bhagavad Gita*'s maxim that the enlightened sage is "one who sees the self in all creatures and all creatures in the self" (*Bhagavad Gita* 1986: 69). No single line is more illustrative of Hinduism and the philosophy of all four theorists.

Gandhi shared with the three others a youthful immersion in British culture and learning. While studying law in London, as he reflected ruefully later in his life, he struggled vainly to play the stereotypical role of the English gentleman, trying to imitate its mannerisms and style. As an anglicized barrister, he chose to practice law in South Africa, where he arrived in 1893 to represent members of the Indian minority.

By 1906, the harsh discrimination of apartheid forced him to fight, not in the courts, but through direct action, using the power of non-violent protest. This did incorporate Thoreau's theory of civil disobedience, but the method was a Gandhi original that he named *satyagraha* (literally "holding fast to the truth"). He emphasized the singular form of power released through self-sacrifice and strict adherence to a creed of non-violence.

The form of pacifism that he brought to India when he returned in 1915 was unlike any that the world had seen before, but it soon defined the methods of the school and the movement. Within four years, he would be at the helm of Indian National Congress, dominating it for decades in ways that Aurobindo or any other Indian leader never approached. More than Aurobindo or Tagore, Gandhi applied Vivekananda's maxim proclaimed by him in 1900, "If you want to speak of politics in India, you must speak through the language of religion" (Vivekananda 1955–62: viii. 77).

Gandhi's method of change contended that social progress could come only through a moral transformation of the self in society, involving an individual quest for liberation known as *swaraj* (an ancient Sanskrit word meaning "self-rule"). Gandhi enlarged and reinterpreted this word to connote a "pilgrimage" undertaken by the individual and society to freedom and autonomy. Gandhi's political philosophy rested, above all, on the essential connection that he developed between his constructions of power and freedom, *satyagraha* and *swaraj*.

This chapter will examine how the four Hindu theorists noted above constructed a political philosophy through the development of conceptual correspondences—that is, the relation of select concepts, usually derived from ancient Indian thought, to modern ideas, usually imported from the West. The purpose of these particular Indian thinkers was at once to preserve continuity with their own tradition and yet to reform it substantially: to reconstitute Hindu philosophy in credible ways demanded by a society in critical need of intellectual innovations.

"There is always a close connection," remarked John Plamenatz in his study of Western political philosophy, "between a philosopher's conception of what man is, what is peculiar to him, how he is placed in the world, and his doctrines about how man should behave, what he should strive for, and how society should be constituted" (Plamenatz 1963: i, p. xiv).

This analysis examines fundamental questions that have traditionally concerned Western political philosophy, as suggested in the passage quoted from Plamenatz above, as relevant to modern Hindu political theory:

What philosophically distinguishes human nature? If an absolute Truth or God exists, what are its form and its relevance to the sphere of politics? What is the right relation of the individual to society, and what constitutes an ideal social order? Finally, most important for Gandhi and the independence movement, what is the right method of social and political change?

These few questions do not exhaust all the issues examined by Western political philosophers; nor are the problems that they raise exclusively political in nature. They will be used, in this chapter, only because they pose questions of the Indian Hindu thinkers considered here that reveal the fundamental assumptions of their political and social thought, as well as their essential agreement on basic concepts. Vivekananda, Aurobindo, Tagore, and Gandhi all rested their political and social thought on certain characteristically Hindu beliefs concerning human nature and the divine. As Plamenatz's observation would imply, they were closely connected with their view of "how man should behave, what he should strive for, and how society should be constituted." For each of these Indian thinkers, a divine essence not only exists, but pervades all being. The highest aim of a person always remains the discovery of one's own nature; the attainment of this goal they called self-realization or spiritual freedom.

In order to achieve this, human conduct in society should conform with a prescribed Hindu code of ethics. This could be so individualistic in spirit that, as Gandhi often said, it may ultimately emanate from the "still small voice" within the individual's own conscience. Once each individual had discovered the essential divine truth of his being, the ideal society might be achieved, a Utopia in which the highest form of freedom was coincident with a perfect state of local harmony.

These are, in brief, the assumptions that underlie the thought of the Indians considered here, and they have profound implications for this school's entire political and social system of ideas. Since Vivekananda was the earliest of this group, he was in a position to exert a seminal influence on modern Hindu philosophy as India moved toward independence from British rule in 1947. Aurobindo, Gandhi, and Tagore each emphasize his direct influence on their thought as well as on the vital discourse that followed, termed "the Indian Renaissance" of political philosophy in the twentieth century.

The Western Impact and the Indian Response: "Preservation by Reconstruction"

> The suddenness with which we stepped out of one era into another with its new meaning and values! In our own home, in our neighbourhood and community, there was still no deep awareness of human rights, human dignity, class equality. (Tagore 1961: 347)

Tagore's candid characterization of late-nineteenth-century India is representative of his school. Among the attempts to revive Hinduism in the face of the Western impact, incredible claims were made for the Indian past. This school is noteworthy, both for the relative restraint it exercised toward its own past, and for the vigorous attacks it made on the orthodoxy of the present. "There are two great obstacles on our path in India," said Vivekananda, "the Scylla of old orthodoxy and the Charybdis of modern European civilization" (Vivekananda 1955–62: iii. 151).

Vivekananda definitely and defiantly saw "old orthodoxy" as an obstacle: his vehement tirades against caste and priestcraft make the proposed reforms of more Westernized Hindu leaders look pale in comparison. "I disagree with all those," he said, "who are giving their superstitions back to my people. My hope is to see again the strong points of ancient India, reinforced by the strong points of this age. The new stage of things must be a growth from within" (Vivekananda 1955–62: iii. 151; viii. 266).

India's growth required, in the minds of these four thinkers, an assimilation of positive aspects of the Western as well as of the Indian traditions. Negative outbursts occurred among them against the whole of Western civilization; but these were the exception. The main spirit of the school is indicated in these words that Vivekananda addressed to his countrymen:

> Several dangers are in the way, and one is that of the extreme conception that we are the people in the world. With all my love for India, and with all my patriotism, and veneration for the ancients, I cannot but think that we have to learn many things from other nations. We must be always ready to sit at the feet of all, for, mark you, everyone can teach us great lessons. (Vivekananda 1955–62: iii. 272)

If these thinkers shared relatively few illusions about their own tradition, they had even fewer about the prospects of India achieving its fruition in a Western form. They sought, above all, to create a new harmony out of what they saw as a present state of discord. Nothing troubled Vivekananda more than the "Europeanized Indians": "A mass of heterogeneous ideas picked up at random from every source and these ideas are unassimilated, undigested, unharmonized" (Vivekananda 1955–62: iii. 151).

This dissonance, they all believed, was perpetuated by problems that a foreign civilization had posed, but not solved. Tagore expressed the resultant state of mental turmoil in his eloquent condemnation of nationalism. He regarded it as a lethal virus contracted from Europe that pitted "the organized selfishness of nations" against "the spiritual life" and "higher ideals of humanity" (Tagore 1950: 51).

Tagore, however, did not feel overwhelmed by the Western impact; rather he regarded it as a challenging stimulus to innovation. "The dynamism of Europe," he said, "made a vigorous assault on our stagnant minds. It acted like the torrents of rain that strike into the dry underearth, to give it vital stirrings and bring forth new life" (Tagore 1961: 342–3). The opportunity he envisioned was to use India's past as a source of inspiration, a platform for reconstruction, on which a modern framework of ideas might be built, liberated by cosmopolitanism from the narrow, violent national-ism evident in the world war.

This theme of "universal man" was developed philosophically by Aurobindo Ghose. He perceived two opposing currents within modern Hindu political theory, the first a reactionary invocation of a imagined Indian tradition, "a vindication and reacceptance of everything Indian as it stood because it was Indian," and the other "a more subtle assimilation and fusing" that will "at once meet and satisfy the old mentality and the new, the traditional and the critical mind . . . a synthetical restatement" to "revivify" the "spirit of the ancient culture." He concluded that, "of this freer dealing with past and present, this preservation by reconstruction, Vivekananda was the leading exemplar and the most powerful exponent" (Ghose 1951: 39–40).

No phrase describes better the overriding intent of this school than Aurobindo's term "preservation by reconstruction," the development of "forms not contradictory of the truths of life which the old expressed, but rather expressive of those truths restated, cured of defect, completed" (Ghose 1951: 6).

One of the main purposes behind this reconstruction was the creation of a philoso-phy of social and political action. The basis for this philosophy was uncovered by Vivekananda in his interpretation of the *Bhagavad Gita*'s theory of karmayoga (path of

social action). Few examples illustrate better the nature of "preservation by reconstruction" than the approach that these thinkers assumed toward the Gita, the central sacred
text of Hinduism.

> What, however, I have done [said Gandhi] is to put a new but natural and logical
> interpretation upon the whole teaching of the Gita and the spirit of Hinduism.
> Hinduism, not to speak of other religions, is ever evolving. It has not one scripture
> like the Quran or the Bible. Its scriptures are also evolving and suffering addition.
> The Gita itself is an instance in point. It has breathed new life into Hinduism.
>
> The Gita is not an aphoristic work; it is a great religious poem. The deeper you
> dive into it, the richer the meanings you get. With every age, the important words
> will carry new and expanding meanings. But its central teaching will never vary.
> The seeker is at liberty to extract from this treasure any meaning he likes so as to
> enable to enforce in his life the central teaching. (Gandhi 1950: 157; 1956: 133)

"The seeker is at liberty to extract from this treasure any meaning he likes...":
Gandhi's words bear repetition, for they underline the nature of this school's approach.
These men went to their Hindu tradition with a purpose, to uncover ideas that would
meet the demands of a modern India. They were engaged in a consciously selective
effort; and no one was more aware than they of the extent of this selectivity.

The broad rationale behind this eclecticism rested on a distinction between
what they deemed as the "essential" and "non-essential" elements of Hinduism, the
difference between its "spirit and form." Gandhi's relentless attack on untouchability
as an unnatural accretion, which must be purged from the pure state of Hinduism,
is one outstanding example of this approach. But Gandhi's attempt was preceded,
a generation earlier, by Vivekananda's stern indictment of "don't touchism" on precisely the same grounds (Vivekananda 1955–62: iii. 167).

Tagore, again with an eye to the corruption of caste in Hinduism, made the point in
compelling terms:

> When the form becomes more important than the spirit, the sand in the riverbed
> becomes more pronounced than the water, the current ceases to flow, and a desert is
> the ultimate result. The spirit tells us to revere all good men irrespective of their
> caste, but the form enjoins respect for the Brahmin, however unworthy. In sum, the
> spirit of religion leads to freedom, its form to slavery. (Tagore 1961: 188–9)

MAN, GOD, AND FREEDOM

> The God of heaven [Vivekananda wrote] becomes the God in nature, and the God in
> nature becomes the God who is nature, and the God who is nature becomes the God
> within this temple of the body, and the God dwelling in the temple of the body at last
> becomes the temple itself, becomes the soul in man and there it reaches the last words
> it can teach. He whom the sages have been seeking in all these places is in our own

hearts; the voice that you heard was right, says the Vedanta, but the direction you gave to the voice was wrong.

That ideal of freedom that you perceived was correct, but you projected it outside yourself, and that was your mistake. Bring it nearer and nearer, until you find that it was all the time within you, it was the Self of your own self.

The only God to worship is the human soul in the human body . . . The moment I have realized God sitting in the temple of every human body, the moment I stand in reverence before every human being and see God in him that moment I am free from bondage, everything that binds vanishes, and I am free. The Impersonal Being, our highest generalization, is ill ourselves, and we are That "O Shvetaketu, thou art That." (Vivekananda 1955–62: ii. 128, 334)

The conceptual correspondences, evident in this passage, which are fundamental to Vivekananda's thought, were those drawn among his ideas of human nature, God, human equality, and the meaning of freedom. By alluding to a well-known verse from the *Chandogya Upanishad* (Hume 1962: 246–50), he links this series of correspondences with the Indian tradition.

The Upanishads do, in fact, make these correspondences among the three basic concepts of man, God, and freedom: Brahman, the Absolute, is seen as identical with the human soul, the Atman, the Self; and with self-realization came mukti, spiritual freedom, release from all bondage.

But Vivekananda is a modern Hindu philosopher with a mission, to advocate religious reconstruction. Spiritual freedom meant, for him, the ultimate expansion of the human Self, which brought realization of one's identity with the Absolute, and with all mankind. However, he put this conception of spiritual freedom to an unprecedented use in the development of his social and political thought. Classical Indian philosophers had never championed social or political equality and liberty in the sense of Locke, Rousseau, or Mill. Vivekananda, widely read in European thought, tried to bring to India a defense of the individual's right to free thought and action vis-à-vis society, the State, or the nation, to incorporate aspects of modern Western views of political and social liberty into the traditional Indian theory of spiritual freedom.

The crux of his development rested with his insistence that man's expansion or growth demands enjoyment of freedom at all levels of consciousness: physical and material, as well as political and social realms. All Indians, regardless of caste or class, should have freedom of opportunity to achieve liberation or *swaraj*. The deprivation of such freedom, at any stage of personal evolution, may prevent one's quest for self-realization. Thus, all forms of freedom become desirable, for each may contribute to individual growth. This idea of freedom with equality was again unprecedented in Indian thought.

Once this innovation was introduced, though, Vivekananda turned to the task of maintaining continuity with his tradition. Man may be free, he pointed out, in a physical or intellectual, social or political sense; yet, unless he directs his liberty, on these lower levels of consciousness, toward attainment of the highest goal, spiritual freedom, these lesser freedoms will prove meaningless.

"The Hindu," he asserted, "says that political and social independence are well and good, but the real thing is spiritual independence. This is our national purpose". And, then, in words that were often to be echoed by the later members of his school, Vivekananda said: "One may gain political and social independence, but if one is a slave to his passions and desires, one cannot feel the pure joy of real freedom" (Vivekananda 1955–62: v. 458, 419).

In one important sense, then, Vivekananda stands in agreement with the traditional view that spiritual freedom (*mukti* and *moksha* are used synonymously) represents man's highest goal. In another sense, though, he invests the Indian tradition with a value that was quite foreign. Social and political freedom were presented not only as desirable expectations, but as expectations made desirable by swamis like himself, clad in saintly garb, which symbolized, above all, spiritually free souls. These Hindu theorists never ceased to stress the supreme desideratum of spiritual freedom; and, if this insistence on the value of spiritual freedom directed their attitude toward political liberty, it pervaded, as well, their ideas of social justice, equality, and a vision of an ideal society.

The Individual and Society: Freedom, Harmony, and Equality

The ideal social order was set forth, in ancient India, in the theory of varnashrama-dharma. The system of four vamas or social orders ensured, in theory, the interrelationship of four social functions: that of the brahman (spiritual authority); kshatriya (temporal power); vaishya (wealth); and sudra (labour). The working of society depended upon the fulfillment, by each of these varnas, of its social role as prescribed by dharma, or the sacred law. The remaining element of this theory, that of ashrama, indicated the division of the individual's life into four ashramas or stages of existence: those of the student; the householder; the wandering solitary seeker; and the self-realized ascetic who returns to society as a saintly presence in a spirit of renunciation (*sannyasin* or *sadhu*).

This social order is seen in the Brihadarayanaka Upanishad as divinely created; and right performance of social duty, as set forth by dharma, ensured the harmony of society with the whole of the universe (Hume 1962: 84–5). Only within the framework of vamashramadharma could men attain their individual aims of artha (wealth), kama (pleasure), and dharma (righteousness). The main function of the king was to protect this order and preserve social harmony, "thereby giving the optimum chance of spiritual progress to as many individuals as possible" (Basham 1963: 13, 16).

For the highest aim of man was *moksha*, spiritual freedom; and the social harmony of the four vamas remained of value only as long as it contributed to individual spiritual advancement through the four ashramas.

Emphasis should be placed on Basham's observation that in ancient India thought

> The ultimate aim of all valid and worthy human activity is salvation, which cannot
> be achieved by corporate entities such as peoples, castes and families, but only by
> individual human beings. Government exists to serve society, and, on final analysis,
> society exists to serve the individual. This latter proposition is hardly to be found in
> implicit form, but it is a necessary corollary of the fundamental presuppositions on
> which all Hindu thought was based. (Basham 1963: 21–2)

It was in this manner that the theory of varnashramadharma sought to achieve an ideal
correspondence between social harmony and spiritual freedom.

Although traditional Indian thought never viewed government as a force hostile to
society, there was among ancient Indian thinkers "general agreement that government
is an unfortunate necessity in an age of universal decay" (Basham 1963: 12). Moreover,
in Basham's discussion of the question of whether a theory of the state existed in
ancient Indian thought, he argued:

> Many modern scholars, perhaps motivated by the idea that the concept of the state
> is a sine qua non of a civilized system of political thought, have tried to find
> evidence of such a concept in ancient Indian political writings. Though they have
> usually succeeded to their own satisfaction, it seems doubtful whether there was any
> clear idea of the state in pre-Muslim times.
>
> As used in the West the term seems to imply a corporate entity controlling a
> definite territory, which maintains its identity and continues to exist, irrespective of
> changes in the governing personnel. In the writings of the more doctrinaire
> theorists, the state seems to take on the character of a living entity, greater than
> the sum of its parts. In India, such political mysticism was discouraged by the
> doctrine of Dharma, which concerned society and not the state, and by the
> fundamental individualism of all the metaphysical systems. (Basham 1963: 21)

While, then, classical Hindu philosophy cannot be regarded as anti-political, it did
see government as an "unfortunate necessity"; and not only did it place the social
sphere above that of the political, it also insisted upon the primacy of the individual's
spiritual aims. A striking exception to this generalization is the *Arthasastra* by Kautilya,
a classical text that is sometimes compared to Machiavelli's *Prince*. From the perspective of the school of Hindu theorists discussed here, it is noteworthy that none of the
four derives his thought from Kautilya.

All four do claim to base their views of the right relation of the individual to society
and of the ideal social order on the theory of varnashramadharma. Society, and never
the state, serves for them as the framework within which the individual enjoys social
harmony and through which he may ultimately attain spiritual freedom.

Vivekananda, in describing the "fabric of Aryan civilization," wrote: "Its warp is
varnashramadharma, and its woof, the conquest of strife and competition in nature"
(Vivekananda 1955–62: v. 536). Tagore, moreover, extols the harmony of the four
ashramas as against the discord of "rampant individualism" (Tagore 1931: 202).
Gandhi elevates the value of social duty to a prominent position in his thought. The

ideal of varnashramadharma demanded that each individual contributing to the welfare of all by responsibly fulfilling his particular role in society. His most significant departure from this ideal is that each individual also, in conditions of unjust political rule, has a supreme duty to disobey the state.

The avoidance of competition and cultivation of cooperativeness and harmony through the disinterested performance of one's social duties: this is the ideal that the modern school envisioned; and they discovered its basis in ancient Hindu thought.

If these thinkers drew freely on the traditional Indian theory of society, they also introduced critical innovations, which had no precedent in the idea of varnashrama-dharma. Gandhi's famous doctrine of civil disobedience has been noted, but the school went further, to assert a fundamental view that was decidedly anti-political.

As noted above, traditional Indian thought had regarded government as an "unfor-tunate necessity"; but, undesirable as government may have appeared to the ancients, it still remained a necessity. In the Dharmasastra and especially the Arthasastra literature, the king is seen as an indispensable force for protection of society and maintenance of justice. Spiritual freedom and social harmony were thought attainable within the framework of varnashramadharma, and government became an essential part of this framework.

The modern Hindu thinkers, however, regarded state and government as alien to society; and, although one must use care in applying Western terms like "anarchism" to the Indian situation, the fact that both Aurobindo and Gandhi saw themselves as "philosophical anarchists" does indicate the severity of their indictment, as well as their intense distrust of political authority in general. Gandhi is representative of the school, in this respect, in that he regarded

> an increase in the power of the State with the greatest fear, because . . . it does the greatest harm by destroying individuality, which lies at the root of all progress. The State represents violence in a concentrated and organized form. The individual has a soul, but as the State is a soulless machine, it can never be weaned from violence to which it owes its very existence.

The ideal society would be one of "enlightened anarchy," where "everyone is his own ruler, and there is no political power because there is no State" (Gandhi 1961: 28–9). This age of enlightened anarchy was envisaged not as a sudden occurrence, but rather as a product of a gradual spiritual evolution. In a future ideal era, the moderns hoped, the essential spirit of varnashramadharma might be fulfilled as never before.

The manner in which Vivekananda incorporated the Western idea of political and social liberty into his theory of the individual and society has already been mentioned. In another like attempt at innovation, these theorists sought to assimilate the Western concept of social equality into the theory of varnashramadharma. Spiritual equality, in the sense that all men were thought part of the divine Absolute, was explicit throughout the traditional writings; perhaps it occurred most notably in the advaita school of Vedanta philosophy and the *Bhagavad Gita*. On this religious basis, the moderns tried to construct an idea of social and political equality. This attempt, once again, began with Vivekananda, but its implications for a program of social reform were most fully developed by Gandhi.

> In my opinion [said Gandhi] there is no such thing as inherited or acquired superiority. I believe in the rock bottom doctrine of advaita and my interpretation of advaita excludes totally any idea of superiority at any stage whatsoever. I believe implicitly that all men are born equal. All whether born in India or in England or America or in any circumstances whatsoever have the same soul as any other. And it is because I believe in this inherent equality of all men that I fight the doctrine of superiority, which many of our rulers arrogate to themselves. I have fought this doctrine of superiority in South Africa inch by inch, and it is because of that inherent belief, that I delight in calling myself a scavenger, a spinner, a weaver, a farmer and a labourer. And I have fought against the brahmanas themselves wherever they have claimed any superiority for themselves either by reason of their birth, or by reason of their subsequently acquired knowledge. I consider that it is unmanly for any person to claim superiority over fellow being. And there is the amplest warrant for the belief that I am enunciating in the Bhagavadgita.
> But in spite of all my beliefs that I have explained to you I still believe in Varnashrama Dharma. Varnashrama Dharma to my mind is a law which, however much you and I may deny, cannot be abrogated. (Gandhi 1935: 385)

This is precisely the nature of the attempt at reconstruction, which is representative of the school: first, the statement of a classical Hindu principle, in this case the advaita doctrine of the unity of all being; then, its application to the contemporary Indian social order, which usually involves criticism of the old orthodoxy; and, finally, an insistence that this reinterpretation is consistent with the spirit of the traditional teachings. No single attempt in modern Indian political thought to establish social equality is more significant than Gandhi's attack on caste. The social innovation that Gandhi hoped to achieve was immense; yet he continually couched his reforms in traditional language and themes. Consider his following appeal for dignity and equality ending in a characteristic reconciliation of ancient Hindu thought with the ideal of democracy:

> When we have come to our own, when we have cleansed ourselves, we may have the four varnas according to the way in which we can express the best in us. But varna then will invest no one with a superior status or right, it will invest one with higher responsibility and duties. Those who will impart knowledge in a spirit of service will be called brahmanas. They will assume no superior airs but will be true servants of society. When inequality of status or rights is ended, everyone of us will be equal. I do not know, however, when we shall be able to revive true Varna Dharma. Its real revival would mean true democracy. (Gandhi 1958–94: 62, 291)

In these few lines, Gandhi has managed to alternate the themes of continuity and innovation with values from India and the West. The discussion is of the four varnas, an ancient theory of Hinduism, but, with Gandhi, they become a framework for modern social equality. They no longer represent distinctions of social status, but rather opportunities for social service; and those who fulfill the ideals embodied in these transformed varnas become, not only upstanding nationalists or democrats, but also good brahmanas. Gandhi's concluding two sentences, which equate Varna Dharma with democracy, illustrate, as sharply as such few words are able, the admixture in his thought of continuity and innovation.

The Western impact reached its high water mark, in terms of political philosophy, with its introduction in nineteenth-century India of the ideals of freedom and equality. The thinking behind this Indian school's response, the reasoning with which it sought to answer the challenge posed by these two great ideals, are well expressed in an early speech of Aurobindo. The assumptions underlying this key statement are directly in line with those voiced earlier by Vivekananda; they were to be further developed, not only by Aurobindo, but by Gandhi and Tagore as well.

"Liberty and equality," Aurobindo began, are among the great ideals that have become the "watchwords of humanity," with "the power of remoulding nations and Governments." Then, he continues:

> These words cast forth into being from the great stir and movement of the eighteenth century continue to act on men because they point to the ultimate goal towards which human evolution ever moves. This liberty to which we progress is liberation out of a state of bondage. This is what our own religion teaches. This is what our own philosophy suggests as the goal towards which we move, mukti or moksha. We strive to shake off the bonds, we move forward and forward until we have achieved the ultimate emancipation, that utter freedom of the soul, of the body or the whole man that utter freedom from all bondage towards which humanity is always aspiring.
>
> We in India have found a mighty freedom within ourselves, our brothers in Europe have worked towards freedom without. We have been moving on parallel lines towards the same end. They have found out the way to external freedom. We have found out the way to internal freedom. We meet and give to each other what we have gained. We have learned from them to aspire after external as they will learn from us to aspire after internal freedom.
>
> Equality is a thing which mankind has never accomplished. From inequality and through inequality we move, but it is to equality. Our religion, our philosophy, see equality forward as the essential condition of emancipation. All religions send us this message in a different form but it is one message. Christianity says we are all brothers, children of one God. Mahomedanism says we are the subjects and servants of one Allah, we are all equal in the sight of God.
>
> Hinduism says there is One without a second. In the high and the low, in the Brahmin and the Sudra, in the saint and the sinner, there is one Narayana, one God and he is the soul of all men. Not until you have realized him, known Narayana in all, and the Brahmin and the Sudra, the high and the low, the saint and the sinner are equal in your eyes, then and not until then you have knowledge, you have freedom, until then you are bound and ignorant.
>
> The equality which Europe has got is external political equality. She is now trying to achieve social equality. Nowadays, their hard-earned political liberty is beginning to pall a little upon the people of Europe, because they have found it does not give perfect well-being or happiness and it is barren of the sweetness of brotherhood. There is no fraternity in this liberty. It is merely a political liberty. They have not

either the liberty within or the full equality or the fraternity. So they are turning a little from what they have and they say increasingly, "Let us have equality, let us have the second term of the gospels towards which we strive."

Therefore socialism is growing in Europe. Europe is now trying to achieve external equality as the second term of the gospel of mankind, the universal ideal. I have said that equality is an ideal even with us, but we have not tried to achieve it without. Still we have learned from them to strive after political equality and in return for what they have given us we shall lead them to the secret of the equality within. (Ghose 1952: 93–6)

Two observations may be made on this passage. First, Aurobindo's incorporation of the Western values of social and political freedom and equality into his theory of society is rooted in Vivekananda's earlier distinction between the "spiritual" or "internal" and sociopolitical or "external" forms of these values. The appropriation of the "internal" forms exclusively to the Hindu tradition is typical of this school.

Second, again following Vivekananda's lead, Aurobindo sees a necessary correspondence between freedom and equality: "Not until . . . the Brahmin and the Sudra, the high and the low, the saint and the sinner are equal in your eyes, then and not until then you have knowledge, you have freedom, until then you are bound and ignorant."

Thus, the Indian tradition is made to underwrite a theory of society that embodies not only the old goals of spiritual freedom, spiritual equality, and spiritual harmony, but also the necessary interrelationship of these values with social and political freedom and equality.

METHOD OF CHANGE

The tidal wave of Western civilization is now rushing over the length and breadth of the country. It won't do now simply to sit in meditation on mountaintops without realizing in the least its usefulness. Now is wanted, as said in the Gita by the Lord Krishna, the discipline of KarmaYoga, with unbounded courage and indomitable strength in the heart. Then only will the people of the country be roused. (Vivekananda 1955–62: vii. 185)

The final principle that unites the members of this school, and reflects their views on the themes of continuity and innovation, lies in their attempt to think out a way of social and political action. On the one hand, all of the thinkers considered here desired India's political independence, and each directed his efforts in some way toward that goal. On the other hand, all saw their task as primarily suprapolitical in nature: they insisted that, though their activities might influence the political sphere, and though their ideas might embrace political issues, their ultimate purpose went beyond politics to require individual self-realization.

Only in this way, they believed, could a radical transformation of society occur. The inspiration for a theory of action through which this transformation might be achieved came from Vivekananda. Much of his thought and energy became channeled into the task of awakening a spirit of service among the Indian people; but his plea was always based on the belief that, through service to society, the individual would further his own quest for self-realization.

> Look upon every man, woman, and everyone as God. You cannot help anyone, you can only serve. I should see God in the poor, and it is for my salvation that I go and worship them. The poor and the miserable are for our salvation. (Vivekananda 1955–62: iii. 246–7)

No Indian of this age carried this aspect of Vivekananda's thought further than Gandhi. Once, when Gandhi was asked by a Western visitor if his work in the villages was simply "humanitarian," he replied:

> I am here to serve no one else but myself, to find my own self-realization through the service of these village folk. Man's ultimate aim is the realization of God, and all his activities, political, social and religious, have to be guided by the ultimate aim of the vision of God. The immediate service of all human beings becomes a necessary part of the endeavour simply because the only way to find God is to see Him in His creation and be one with it. This can only be done by service of all. And this cannot be done except through one's country. I am a part and parcel of the whole, and I cannot find Him apart from the rest of humanity. My countrymen are my nearest neighbours. They have become so helpless, resourceless and inert that I must concentrate on serving them. If I could persuade myself that I should find Him in a Himalayan cave, I would proceed there immediately. But I know that I cannot find Him apart from humanity. (Gandhi quoted in Tendulkar 1960: iv. 88)

It is emphatically at this point that the school's views on human nature, God, freedom, and justice support a program of social action: the nature of man is divine; through service to mankind the individual may realize his divinity, and with that will come spiritual freedom and a sense of his unity with all being. The effect of this idea was to promote a program of social and political reform. But, at its base, the school's theory of the way of right action is motivated by an intensely individual quest for self-purification and self-realization. Only in this way might the primary aim of the spiritual transformation of the individual in society be achieved.

The end result of Vivekananda's emphasis upon social service was to reconcile an individualistic approach to self-realization with a program of social and political reform. In making this attempt at reconciliation, Vivekananda turned to a work that had achieved a similar reconciliation centuries before, the *Bhagavad Gita*. The problem of the *Gita*, however, was not Vivekananda's problem: the former sought a philosophical justification for the preservation of an ancient social order; the latter desired a dynamic method of modern social and political change. Yet the formula that the *Gita* had set forth met Vivekananda's needs. This appeared in the theory of karmayoga (the yoga of action), which taught that one path to self-realization was disinterested action for the welfare of society. The individual should act, but in a religious spirit; that is, in a spirit of renunciation and self-sacrifice, surrendering the fruits of his action to God and to mankind. Few concepts have emerged with more meaning for modern Hindu thought than that of karmayoga; and Vivekananda, in the concluding chapters of his book called *Karma Yoga*, indicates the meaning that this ideal had for him: "Give up all fruits of work; do good for its own sake; then alone will come perfect nonattachment. The bond of the heart will thus break, and we shall reap perfect freedom. This freedom is indeed the goal of Karma Yoga" (Vivekananda 1955–62: i. 107).

The demand for continuity and innovation in the formulation of a method of action was most fully met by Gandhi. Following the lead of Aurobindo, Gandhi stressed the need for political, as well as social, service in the individual's quest for freedom.

> I am impatient to realize myself [he said] to attain moksha in this very existence. My national service is part of my training for freeing my soul . . . For me the road to salvation lies through incessant toil in the service of my country. So my patriotism is for me a stage in my journey to the land of eternal freedom and peace. Thus it will be seen that for me there are no politics devoid of religion [repeatedly insisting] that those who say that religion has nothing to do with politics do not know what religion means. (Gandhi 1960: 504)

The marriage of politics and religion had been voiced by Aurobindo, an early leader of the Indian National Congress; it was consummated in the theory and practice of Gandhi, whose long reign over the Congress and the nationalist movement remains unprecedented. He, like Aurobindo, blessed the union with sacred symbols and beliefs; unlike Aurobindo, he pointed out the path that both partners should pursue toward their common goal of swaraj. Key traditional words, themes, and images, none more than karma yoga, blossomed forth in Gandhi's great innovation of satyagraha.

From its inception, when Gandhi was a young defender of the rights of his Indian community in South Africa (1893–1914), satyagraha meant that apartheid must be met with non-violent protest, requiring his followers "to conquer this hatred by love. We do not attempt to have individuals punished but, as a rule, patiently suffer wrongs at their hands." Gandhi soon came to dislike and reject the term "passive resistance," which was initially assigned to the civil disobedience. He replaced it with satyagraha, in order to avoid a foreign term that lacked the Hindu spirit that he sought. "When in a meeting of Europeans," he records in his *Autobiography*, "I found that the term 'passive resistance' could be characterized by hatred [as with the British suffragettes], and that it could finally manifest itself as violence, I had to demur to all these statements and explain the real nature of the Indian movement" (Gandhi 1960: 318).

Hatred and violence were incompatible with the method that Gandhi had developed, because his theory rested squarely on the principle of ahimsa (literally in Sanskrit "not violent"), which he variously translated as both non-violence and love. This idea of ahimsa he had taken from the Indian tradition, where it meant a strict observance of personal non-violent behavior, though not through participation in a political movement. Thus, he could conclude that his political philosophy dictated that "I am an uncompromising opponent of violent methods even to serve the noblest of causes" (Gandhi 1958–94: xxv. 423).

In his creation of satyagraha, Gandhi reinforced his Hindu affirmation of ahimsa with ideas that he found in Tolstoy and the Sermon on the Mount; the result was a method that evoked rich religious symbolism and contributed to a philosophy of action unique in Indian history.

Satyagraha may be seen as a commentary on the themes of continuity and innovation discussed in this chapter. The new interpretation of social action found in the theory of karma yoga and the application of traditional language and symbols to the modern Indian scene were Vivekananda's and Aurobindo's contributions to a distinctly Hindu philosophy of social and political change.

Yet it was left for Gandhi to carry the method to fruition through his experiments with satyagraha. The theory of satyagraha, however, was no more complete an embodiment of continuity and innovation than the satyagrahi, the Mahatma, behind it: a figure seen by some as a sannyasin, by others as a politician; a man who behaved like a karma yogin, yet spoke in these terms of his mission: "It is the whole of Hinduism that has to be purified and purged. What I am aiming at is the greatest reform of the age" (Gandhi 1958–94: i. 352).[1]

REFERENCES

Primary Sources

GANDHI, M. K. (1935). *Young India, 1927–1928*. Madras: S. Ganesan.

GANDHI, M. K. (1950). *Hindu Dharma*. Ahmedabad: Navajivan Press.

GANDHI, M. K. (1956). *The Gita According to Gandhi*, ed. and trans. Mahadev Desai. Ahmedabad: Navajivan.

GANDHI, M. K. (1958–94). *The Collected Works of Mahatma Gandhi*. 100 vols. Delhi: Publications Division, Government of India.

GANDHI, M. K. (1960). *An Autobiography, The Story of my Experiments with Truth*, trans. Mahadev Desai. Boston: Beacon Press.

GANDHI, M. K. (1961). *Democracy: Real and Deceptive*. Ahmedabad: Navajivan Press.

GHOSE, AUROBINDO (1951). *The Renaissance in India*. Pondicherry: Sri Aurobindo Ashram.

GHOSE, AUROBINDO (1952). *Speeches*. Pondicherry: Sri Aurobindo Ashram.

GHOSE, AUROBINDO (1962). *The Ideal of Human Unity, War and Self-Determination*. Pondicherry: Sri Aurobindo Ashram.

TAGORE, R. (1931). *The Religion of Man*. London: Allen and Unwin.

TAGORE, R. (1950). *Nationalism*. London: Macmillan Press.

TAGORE, R. (1961). *Towards Universal Man*. London: Asia Publishers.

VIVEKANANDA, SWAMI (1955–62). *The Complete Works of Swami Vivekananda*. 8 vols. Calcutta: Advaita Ashrama.

---

[1] Parts of this chapter are excerpted from my Ph.D. dissertation (University of London, 1965), published as *Indian Idea of Freedom* (1982), and online by IDEAINDIA.COM (2007).

Secondary Sources

BASHAM, A. L. (1954). *The Wonder That Was India.* New York: Grove Press.

BASHAM, A. L. (1963). "Some Fundamental Political Ideas of Ancient India," in C. H. Philips (ed.), *Politics and Society in India.* London: Allen and Unwin.

BHAGAVAD GITA (1986), trans. Barbara Miller. New York: Bantam Press.

BONDURANT, J. (1988). *Conquest of Violence.* Princeton: Princeton University Press.

BROWN, J. (1989). *Gandhi: A Prisoner of Hope.* New Haven: Yale University Press.

DALTON, D. (1982). *Indian Idea of Freedom.* Gurgaon: Academic Press; repr. as IDEAINDIA. COM. London: Cooperjal Limited, 2007.

DALTON, D. (2012). *Mahatma Gandhi. Nonviolent Power in Action.* New York: Columbia University Press.

GORDON, L. (1974). *Bengal: The Nationalist Movement, 1876–1940.* New York: Columbia University Press.

HUME, R. E. (1962). *The Thirteen Principal Upanishads*, trans. R. E. Hume. London: Oxford University Press.

IYER, R. N. (1973). *The Moral and Political Thought of Mahatma Gandhi.* New York: Oxford University Press.

PLAMENATZ, J. (1963). *Man and Society: A Critical Examination of Some Important Social and Political Theories from Machiavelli to Marx.* 2 vols. London: Oxford University Press.

RUDOLPH, S. (1983). *Gandhi.* Chicago, University of Chicago Press.

TENDULKAR, D. G. (1960). *Mahatma.* 8 vols. Delhi: Government of India Publications Division.

VARMA, V. P. (1960). *The Political Philosophy of Sri Aurobindo.* London: Asia Publishers.

ZAEHNER, R. C. (1962). *Hinduism.* London: Oxford University Press.

INDEX